THE
COLLECTED LETTERS
OF
W. B. YEATS

GENERAL EDITOR: JOHN KELLY

THE
COLLECTED LETTERS
OF
W. B. YEATS

General Editor · JOHN KELLY

———

VOLUME THREE

1901–1904

EDITED BY

JOHN KELLY

AND

RONALD SCHUCHARD

CLARENDON PRESS · OXFORD

OXFORD

UNIVERSITY PRESS

Great Clarendon Street, Oxford OX2 6DP

Oxford University Press is a department of the University of Oxford
It furthers the University's objective of excellence in research, scholarship,
and education by publishing worldwide in

Oxford New York

Athens Auckland Bangkok Bogotá Buenos Aires Calcutta
Cape Town Chennai Dar es Salaam Delhi Florence Hong Kong Istanbul
Karachi Kuala Lumpur Madrid Melbourne Mexico City Mumbai
Nairobi Paris São Paulo Singapore Taipei Tokyo Toronto Warsaw

and associated companies in Berlin Ibadan

Oxford is a registered trade mark of Oxford University Press
in the UK and in certain other countries

Published in the United States
by Oxford University Press Inc., New York

ISBN 0-19-812683-2

Printed in Great Britain
on acid-free paper by
Biddles Short Run Books
King's Lynn

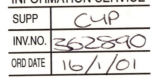

ACKNOWLEDGEMENTS

Our thanks are due first to Anne Yeats, and to Michael and Grania Yeats, without whose help and hospitality this edition would not have been possible. We also gratefully acknowledge the generosity of those who have allowed us to make copies of Yeats material in their possession: Joann M. Andrews, W. Barrington Baker, Stuart Bennett, Lord Bridges, the late Mary Ellmann, Stephen Fay, Neil Foggie, Alan Clodd, the late James Gilvarry, David Gould, Mrs Basil Gray, Richard Lancelyn Green, Terry Halliday, the late Richard M. Kain, Francis King, Michael Macalagan, Mary McGee, Douglas Sealy, the late John Sparrow, David Walker, Ann Weygandt, Anna White, the Hon. Gerald Yorke.

This volume has been greatly assisted by grants and other financial help from the British Academy, the Leverhulme Trust, the President and Fellows of St. John's College, Oxford, the Oxford English Faculty, Emory University Research Committee, and the President and Fellows of Wolfson College, Oxford.

We are also indebted for help and advice to Nathalie F. Anderson, Swarthmore College; Hugh Baker; Jerome Beaty, Emory University; Robert S. Becker; John Bell, Anne-Marie Bouché, Mills College Library; David C. Braasch, Morris Library, Southern Illinois University; Rand Brandes, Lenoir-Rhyne College; Bruce M. Brown, Colgate University Library; R. R. Cain, News International Library; Margaret Campbell, London; Aldo R. Cupo, Beinecke Library, Yale University; David J. DeLaura, University of Pennsylvania; Paul Delaney; Alan Denson; Denis Donoghue, New York University; the late Richard Ellmann; Julia Emmons; Catherine Fahy, National Library of Ireland; Catherine Farragher, Galway County Libraries; William J. Feeney, De Paul University; Joan P. S. Ferguson, Librarian, Royal College of Physicians, Edinburgh; Agnes Fisher, Macmillan Company, New York; Roy Foster, Oxford University; R. A. Gilbert, Bristol; David Gould, London; Warwick Gould, Royal Holloway and Bedford New College, London; R. A. Gekoski, London; George Harper, Florida State University; Sir Rupert Hart-Davis; Diana Haskell, the Newberry Library, Chicago; Edward Hathaway, Minneapolis Public Library; Narayan Hedge, Stony Brook, SUNY; the Historical Society of Pennsylvania; Diana Hobby, Rice University; Sara S. Hodson, Huntington Library; Brian Ll. James, University College Library, Cardiff; Mark Jeffreys, Emory University;

Klaus Peter Jochum, University of Bamberg; Jeri Johnson, Oxford University; Richard M. Kain; Glenn Kellum, Emory University; Kate Kelly, Bristol University; Elizabeth A. Kraft, University of Georgia; Sister M. Campion Kuhn, St Mary's Archives, Notre Dame; A. Walton Litz, Princeton University; Andrew Lockett, Sean Manning, Inverin, Co. Galway; Taffy Martin; Colin McDowell; Greta Matthews, Dolmetsch Concerts; Linda Matthews, Woodruff Library, Emory University; Bernard Meehan, Trinity College Library, Dublin; Lore Metzger, Emory University; Bruce Morris, Palo Alto; Maureen Murphy, Hofstra University; William M. Murphy, Union College, Schenectady; Beairthe O'Conaire, An Spidéal, Co. na Gaillimhe; Fr Liam O'Connell SJ, Conglowes Wood College, Co. Kildare; Bernard O'Donoghue, Magdalen College, Oxford; Leonard Orr, Washington State University; Stuart Ó Seanóir, Trinity College Library, Dublin, James Pethica, Wolfson College, Oxford; John Pitcher, Oxford University; Mrs R. M. Popham, Dorset County Library; Harry Rusche, Emory University; Judy Harvey Sahak, Scripps College Library; Carolyn Della Salla, Plainfield Public Library; Christa Sammons, Beinecke Library, Yale University; Helen Q. Schroyer, Purdue University Library; Dr. Richard Sharpe, Oxford University; S. M. Simpson, National Library of Scotland; Timothy A. Slavin, Archdiocese of Chicago Archives; Colin Smythe; Jon Stallworthy, Oxford University; Janet Wallwork, John Rylands Library, Manchester; George Watson, University of Aberdeen; Margaret Weare, Ellen Terry Memorial Museum; Robert Welch, University of Coleraine; Trevor West, Trinity College, Dublin: Ann Weygandt, Frances Whistler; Patrcia C. Willis, Beinecke Library, Yale University; Melanie Yolles, New York Public Library.

CONTENTS

THE LETTERS 1901–1904

LIST OF ILLUSTRATIONS

Between pages 362 and 363

CHRONOLOGY

1865   **13 June**   William Butler Yeats (WBY), eldest child of John Butler Yeats (JBY) and Susan Mary Yeats (née Pollexfen), born at Georgeville, Sandymount Avenue, Dublin.

1866   **Jan**   JBY called to the Irish Bar. **25 Aug**   Susan Mary (Lily) Yeats (SMY) born at Enniscrone, Co. Sligo.

1867   **Late Feb/early Mar**   JBY gives up the law and moves to London to enrol at Heatherley's Art School. **Late July**   Susan Yeats, WBY, SMY, and Isabella Pollexfen (aunt) join JBY at 23 Fitzroy Road, Regent's Park.

1868   **11 Mar**   Elizabeth Corbet (Lollie) Yeats (ECY) born in Fitzroy Road. **Summer**   Family holiday in Sligo.

1869   **Summer**   Family holiday in Sligo; children remain there until Dec.

1870   **27 Mar**   Robert Corbet (Bobbie) Yeats born in Fitzroy Road. **Apr**   WBY ill with scarlatina. **Summer**   Family holiday in Sligo.

1871   **29 Aug**   John Butler (Jack) Yeats born in Fitzroy Road. **Sept**   Short family holiday in Sligo.

1872   **23 July**   Yeatses leave London for Sligo where Susan Yeats and the children remain for more than two years, living at Merville.

1873   **3 Mar**   Bobbie Yeats dies suddenly in Sligo. **Oct–Dec**   JBY painting portraits at Muckross Abbey.

1874   **Winter–spring**   JBY painting portraits at Stradbally Hall; rejoins his family in Sligo in the summer. **Late Oct**   Yeatses move back to London, settling at 14 Edith Villas, North End (West Kensington).

1875   **29 Aug**   Jane Grace Yeats born at Edith Villas.

1876   **6 June**   Jane Grace Yeats dies of bronchial pneumonia; the same month, JBY's mother dies of cancer in Dublin. **Summer**   Yeatses holiday in Sligo. JBY returns alone to London and, having decided to abandon portrait painting for landscapes, spends extended periods at Burnham Beeches. **Autumn**   WBY joins his father at Burnham Beeches, lodging with the Earles in Farnham Royal.

1877 **Jan** Susan Yeats and the other children return to Edith Villas. **26 Jan** WBY enrolled at the Godolphin School, Iffley Road, Hammersmith.

1879 **Spring** Yeatses move to 8 Woodstock Road, Bedford Park. **Summer** Family holiday at Branscombe, Devon.

1881 **Easter** WBY leaves the Godolphin School. **Summer** JBY's chronic financial difficulties worsen; in the autumn he rents a Dublin studio. **Late autumn** JBY brings his family (except Jack, who is living permanently in Sligo with grandparents) to Ireland and they settle at Balscaddan Cottage in Howth. WBY enrolled at the Erasmus Smith High School, Harcourt Street, Dublin.

1882 **Spring** Yeatses move from Balscaddan Cottage to Island View, Harbour Road, Howth. **Autumn** WBY meets his distant cousin, Laura Armstrong, and is attracted to her.

1883 **20 Nov** Attends lecture by Oscar Wilde in Dublin. **Dec** Leaves the Erasmus Smith High School.

1884 **8 Jan** Begins play, *Vivien and Time*, for Laura Armstrong. **Early spring** Yeats family forced by financial considerations to leave Howth for 10 Ashfield Terrace, in the south Dublin suburb of Terenure. **May** WBY enrols as a student at Metropolitan School of Art, Dublin. **Sept** Laura Armstrong marries Henry Byrne.

1885 **19 Jan** John O'Leary returns from exile in Paris; WBY meets him later in the year. **Mar** WBY's first publications, 'Song of the Faeries' and 'Voices', in the *Dublin University Review* (*DUR*). **Apr–July** *The Island of Statues* published in *DUR*. **16 June** First meeting of Dublin Hermetic Society, WBY presiding. **Late June** C. H. Oldham introduces WBY to Katharine Tynan at her house in Clondalkin. **Aug** JBY's finances deteriorate after death of Mathew Yeats, his uncle and agent. **21 Nov** Contemporary Club founded by Oldham. **18 Dec** Attends meeting of Young Ireland Society.

1886 Poems, plays, and literary articles appearing regularly in *DUR*, *Irish Monthly*, and *Irish Fireside*. **Apr** Leaves the Metropolitan School of Art. **10, 11 Apr** Hears William Morris lecture in Dublin and meets him at the Contemporary Club. **Oct** *Mosada*, WBY's first publication in book form, privately printed in Dublin. Begins first part of 'The Wanderings of Oisin'. **11 Dec** Discussion of historical drama with Hyde at the Contemporary Club.

1887 **10 Jan** Accompanies Katharine Tynan to a meeting of the Protestant Home Rule Association. **3 Mar** JBY to London to arrange for family's return there. **Early Apr**   The family join JBY in England; WBY lodges at 6 Berkeley Road, Regent's Park, London, until the family house is ready. **Early May**   WBY joins the family at 58 Eardley Crescent, South Kensington. **May**   Meets Ernest Rhys. WBY out of sorts; works on reviews, articles, and poems at the Art Library, South Kensington Museum. First visit to Mme Blavatsky, lately arrived in London. **19 June**   Attends lecture at William Morris's house in Hammersmith; meets May Morris. Thereafter WBY regularly attends the Morris 'Sunday Nights'. **11 Aug**   Arrives in Sligo to stay with his uncle, George Pollexfen, at Rosses Point; working on 'Oisin'. **Late summer**   Susan Yeats has her first stroke. **Oct**   WBY moves into Sligo town to stay with his grandparents. **18 Nov**   Finishes 'Oisin'. **22 Nov**   To Dublin where he stays with Katharine Tynan; O'Leary begins to organize subscriptions for WBY's book of poems. **Dec**   Susan Yeats suffers another stroke and falls down a back stair.

1888   **Jan**   WBY experiences severe nervous disturbance at a Dublin seance. **26 Jan**   WBY returns to London. **Feb**   Commissioned by Rhys to edit a book of Irish folklore. **12 Feb**   Meets George Bernard Shaw at William Morris's house. **12 Mar**   Deposits MS of *The Wanderings of Oisin and Other Poems* with Kegan Paul. **21 Mar** First visit to the Southwark Irish Literary Club. **24 Mar**   Yeats family moves to 3 Blenheim Road, Bedford Park. Susan Yeats and SMY go there from Yorkshire on 13 Apr. **Apr**   WBY attending French lessons at the Morrises'. **Early May**   Publication of *Poems and Ballads of Young Ireland*. **13 June**   WBY lectures to the Southwark Irish Literary Club on 'Sligo Fairies'. **28 July**   Meets Lady Wilde and becomes a frequent guest at her Saturday afternoon 'at-homes'. **11 Aug**   In Oxford copying out Caxton's edition of Aesop's *Fables* at the Bodleian. **Late Sept**   *Fairy and Folk Tales of the Irish Peasantry* published. **Nov**   Attacked by 'lunar influences'. Joins Esoteric Section of the Theosophical Society. **1 Dec**   SMY begins work as embroidress at May Morris's. **Mid-Dec**   Composes 'The Lake Isle of Innisfree'. **25 Dec**   Spends Christmas Day with the Oscar Wildes.

1889   *c.* **10 Jan**   *Oisin* published. **22 Jan**   First reviews of *Oisin*. **Late Jan**   Yeats family financial problems particularly acute. **30 Jan** Maud Gonne (MG) visits Blenheim Road. **31 Jan**   WBY dines with MG in London. **Feb**   Begins *The Countess Kathleen*. **3 Mar** Spends night at the Ellises' probably to discuss a proposed edition of *The Works of William Blake*. **1 May**   In Oxford copying Blake's

The Book of Thel. **6 May**   Reads *The Countess Kathleen* to Florence Farr (FF). **29 May**   Lectures on Mangan to the Southwark Irish Literary Society. **6 Aug**   WBY in Oxford copying an Elizabethan book for Nutt. **23 Aug**   *Stories from Carleton.* **15 Oct**   Ellen O'Leary dies in Cork. **20–3 Oct**   WBY sees O'Leary in London. **Late Dec**   Ellis and WBY discover Linnell's MS of Blake's *Vala.* **20 Dec**   Meets with Annie Besant and other members of the Esoteric Section of the Theosophical Society to renew their pledges to Mme Blavatsky.

1890   **Early Jan**   Ill with Russian influenza. **11 Jan**   With Rhys, founds the Rhymers' Club. **7 Mar**   WBY initiated into the Hermetic Order of the Golden Dawn (GD) in Moina Bergson's studio, 17 Fitzroy Street. **16 Mar**   Dispatches MS of *Representative Irish Tales.* **5 May**   Attends performance of Todhunter's *A Sicilian Idyll* at the Club House in Bedford Park. **Aug**   Ellis signs contract with Quaritch for publication of *The Works of William Blake.* **11 Oct**   First number of the short-lived *Weekly Review* to which WBY and other Rhymers contribute. **Mid-Oct**   Asked to resign from the Esoteric Section of the Theosophical Society. **Autumn**   In state of semi-collapse; a slight heart ailment is diagnosed. **18 Nov**   Verdict in the O'Shea divorce case precipitates a political crisis in the Irish Party. **1–6 Dec**   Irish Party debate on the leadership crisis ends in a split between Parnellite and anti-Parnellite factions.

1891   **Mar**   *Representative Irish Tales.* **8 May**   Mme Blavatsky dies in London. *c.* **17 July**   WBY arrives in Dublin. **22 July**   Meets MG in Dublin; his love for her revives. **23 July**   Stays with Charles Johnston near Downpatrick. **Early Aug**   Returns to Dublin, to stay at various addresses while writing 'Rosy Cross Lyrics'. **31 Aug**   MG's son dies in Paris. **15 Sept**   Inaugural Meeting of the Young Ireland League, organized by WBY and O'Leary to unite various Irish literary societies. **7 Oct**   Charles Stewart Parnell dies in Brighton. Funeral in Dublin on 11 Oct. *c.* **21 Oct**   WBY returns to London. **Early Nov**   *John Sherman and Dhoya.* **28 Dec**   Meeting at Blenheim Road to plan an Irish Literary Society.

1892   **Jan**   WBY planning a new Library of Ireland. **13 Jan**   Present at meeting which formally decides to establish an Irish Literary Society in London. **17 Jan**   Lectures on 'Nationality and Literature' to the Clapham Branch of the Irish National League. **Feb**   *The Book of the Rhymers' Club.* **8 Feb**   Fisher Unwin takes over unsold stock of *Oisin* from Kegan Paul. **May**   *Irish Fairy Tales.* **6 May**   Copyright performance of *The Countess Kathleen* at the Athenaeum Theatre, Shepherd's Bush. **Mid-May** WBY arrives in Dublin to found a central Irish Literary Society. **9 June** Speaks at Public Steering Committee meeting of the National Literary Society held at the Rotunda. **14 June** WBY and MG appointed to the Libraries Sub-committee of the National Literary Society. **8 Aug** Public meeting at the Mansion House, Dublin, to discuss the revival of Irish literature, the foundation of a publishing company, and the circulation of books. **16 Aug** Inaugural Meeting of the National Literary Society with Gavan Duffy in the chair; address by Sigerson; WBY also speaks. **Late Aug** *The Countess Kathleen and Various Legends and Lyrics.* **Early Sept** Newspaper controversy over proposed New Irish Library. **22 Sept** WBY appointed secretary of the Library Committee of the National Literary Society. **Oct** In Sligo, where his grandmother, Elizabeth Pollexfen, dies on 2 Oct. **29 Oct** Rolleston and Gavan Duffy begin negotiations with Fisher Unwin for publication of the New Irish Library, thus angering WBY and O'Leary. **12 Nov** William Pollexfen dies in Sligo. **20 Nov** WBY returns to Dublin from Sligo. **25 Nov** Hyde inaugurates the first lecture session of the National Literary Society. **Mid-Dec** WBY goes to London to confer with the Committee of the Irish Literary Society, London, and Fisher Unwin about the rival schemes for the New Irish Library. **Late Dec** Preparing for the Portal examination of the GD.

1893 **20 Jan** Undergoes the Portal Ritual for entry to the Second Order of the GD; also takes the 1st Point part of the $5° = 6°$ grade, the lowest grade of the Second Order. **21 Jan** Takes 2nd and 3rd Points of $5° = 6°$ grade. **22 Jan** Arrives in Dublin. **23 Jan** Travels to Cork with Hyde to promote the National Literary Society at a public meeting. **Late Jan** Small-paper version of *The Works of William Blake* ready. Large-paper version appears in mid-Feb. **Mid-Feb** Brief visit to Sligo where he stays with George Pollexfen. **4 Mar** Delivers the address at the National Club, Dublin, on Robert Emmet. **21 Mar** Formal agreement for publication of the New Irish Library signed by Fisher Unwin and Gavan Duffy. **4 May** Katharine Tynan marries Henry Albert Hinkson. **19 May** WBY lectures on 'Nationality and Literature' to the National Literary Society. **Late May** Returns to London. **30 May** Attends a Council of Adepts at the Second Order of the GD, Clipstone Street, where he continues to pay regular visits throughout the summer. **31 July** Gaelic League founded in Dublin. **29 Aug** Begins small white notebook in which many of the poems to be published in *The Wind Among the Reeds* are drafted. **Mid-Sept** Returns to Dublin with Lionel Johnson, to plan an Irish literary magazine. **4 Oct** Present at Annual General Meeting of the National Literary Society. **21 Nov** Lectures to the Belfast Naturalists' Field Club. **Late Nov** *The Poems of William Blake*. **Dec** *The Celtic Twilight*. **Late Dec** Returns to London.

1894 **7 Feb** Stays with the Matherses in Paris. Sees MG and Verlaine but fails to meet Mallarmé. **26 Feb** Accompanies MG to a performance of Villiers de l'Isle Adam's *Axel* at the Théâtre de la Gaité. *c.* **27 Feb** Returns to London. **Mar** Begins writing *The Shadowy Waters*. **29 Mar** *The Land of Heart's Desire* produced at the Avenue Theatre, London, until 14 Apr. **Apr** Meets Olivia Shakespear (OS). *The Land of Heart's Desire* published, and on 21 Apr revived at the Avenue Theatre with Shaw's *Arms and the Man* until 12 May. **June** *The Second Book of the Rhymers' Club* published; meets Lady Augusta Gregory (AG) for the first time. **6 Aug** MG's daughter, Iseult, born. **23 Aug** Present at marriage of Jack Yeats to Mary Cottenham White. **10 Oct** Arrives in Dublin. **25 Oct** Goes to stay with George Pollexfen in Sligo. Spends much time revising poems and plays for collected edition, and writing *The Shadowy Waters*. **Mid-Nov** Stays at Lissadell and contemplates asking Eva Gore-Booth to marry him. Collects folklore and lectures on fairy tales.

1895 **Mid-Jan** Joins in a controversy with Edward Dowden over Irish literature. **27 Feb** Begins a controversy in the Dublin *Daily Express* over 'The Best 30 Irish Books'. **Late Feb** WBY and George Pollexfen ill with influenza. **Early Mar** *A Book of Irish Verse*. **27 Mar** Finishes revision of his poems for collected edition. **13 Apr** Leaves Sligo to visit Hyde at Frenchpark, Co. Roscommon. **16 Apr** Visits Castle Rock in Lough Key. Returns to Sligo on 1 May. **4 May** Leaves Sligo for Dublin *en route* to London. **19 May** Calls on Oscar Wilde to offer sympathy and support during his trial. **July–Oct** Four articles on Irish literature in the *Bookman*. **16 July** Visits Kent with OS. **13 Sept** Aunt Agnes Pollexfen Gorman arrives at Blenheim Road, having escaped from a mental home. **Early Oct** Leaves the family house and takes rooms with Arthur Symons in Fountain Court, the Temple. **Oct** Delivers the address at a Parnell Commemorative Meeting in London.

1896 **Late Feb** WBY moves from the Temple to rooms at 18 Woburn Buildings. Begins an affair with OS; starts work on *The Speckled*

Bird. **Summer** Visits Aran Islands. **Dec** To Paris, where on 21 Dec he meets Synge.

1897 **Mid-Jan** Returns to London. **Mar** Visits Robert Bridges. **Apr** *The Secret Rose*. **May** In Sligo. **June** *The Adoration of the Magi*. **June** Visits Edward Martyn at Tillyra Castle. **Late July** To Coole to stay with AG for two months; WBY collects folklore and they discuss the possibility of a 'Celtic Theatre'. **Nov–Dec** Returns to Dublin and thence back to London.

1898 Working at 'Celtic mysticism' with MG and members of GD. **Jan** Synge calls on him in London. **Early Mar** Short visit to Dublin. **1 Apr** Meets Wilfrid Blunt. **Late Apr–May** Visits Paris to discuss Celtic mysticism with Mathers and MG. Successfully lobbies MPs to change theatrical licensing laws in Dublin. **May** Sits to Rothenstein for portrait. **8 June** To Dublin, and thence to Coole on 20th. **Mid-Aug** In London and Dublin for '98 banquets and celebrations. Controversy with AE and John Eglinton over 'Literary Ideals in Ireland' in Dublin *Daily Express*. **Sept–Nov** Staying with George Pollexfen in Sligo. **Late Nov** To Dublin, where MG tells him she has long been in love with him but cannot marry him.

1899 **Late Jan** Returns to London. **Feb** Short visit to Paris, where he again proposes to MG. Returns to London to arrange rehearsals of Irish Literary Theatre plays with FF, George Moore, and Martyn. **Late Mar** Martyn worried by supposed heresy of *The Countess Cathleen*, but is reassured. **Apr** *The Wind Among the Reeds*. F. H. O'Donnell attacks *The Countess Cathleen* with support of Cardinal Logue. **8 May** *The Countess Cathleen* performed at the Antient Concert Rooms as first production of Irish Literary Theatre (ILT). **May** Revised edition of *Poems*. At Coole until Nov except for short trips to Dublin and Belfast. **Late Oct** Begins collaboration with Moore on *Diarmuid and Grania*. **17 Nov** Returns to London.

1900 **3 Jan** Susan Yeats dies. **19–24 Feb** Second season of the ILT. **Mar–Apr** Protests against Queen Victoria's visit to Dublin. **17–25 Apr** Mathers sends Aleister Crowley to seize the GD headquarters but WBY evicts him and guards the rooms against him. **June** Takes on A. P. Watt as his literary agent. **23 June** To Dublin and thence to Coole. **14 Oct** Returns to London. Disputes with Moore over writing of *Diarmuid and Grania*; play finished on 12 Dec.

1901 **Early Jan** Influenza and neuralgia; revising *The Countess Cathleen* and *Diarmuid and Grania*. **7 Jan** Negotiates with Mrs Pat

Campbell about her possible production of *Diarmuid and Grania*. **19 Jan** Arthur Symons marries Rhoda Bowser. **21 Jan** Tea with Sturge Moore. **22 Jan** Queen Victoria dies. **23 Jan** *Ideals in Ireland* published. Benson agrees to produce *Diarmuid and Grania* in Dublin. **Late Jan** Discussions with Moore over collaboration on *Diarmuid and Grania*. **1 Feb** Attends contentious Council Meeting of the GD. **4 Feb** Sturge Moore, Binyon, and Masefield to dinner. **5 Feb** Dines with George Moore and AG. **8–16 Feb** Working at the British Museum, where he sees a lot of AG. **9 Feb** With AG at Emery Walker's for tableaux, listens to AG's essay on folk ballads. *c.* **13 Feb** Accompanies AG to Benson's production of *Coriolanus*. **16 Feb** Lectures on the psaltery at the Fellowship of the Three Kings, with FF and Anna Mather chanting. **19 Feb** Tea with Sturge Moore and Gibson. **26 Feb** Attends General Meeting of the GD to discuss a new constitution. **27 Feb** WBY, AEFH, and Brodie-Innes resign their offices in the GD. **16 Mar** Resigns from committee of the Irish Literary Society (ILS) over blackballing of George Moore. AG gives up her London apartment. **17 Mar** Asks Pamela Colman Smith to perform *The Countess Cathleen* at the Fellowship of the Three Kings. Dines at the Shorters' with George Moore. **30 Mar** Impressed with stage scenery in Gordon Craig's production of Purcell's *Dido and Aeneas* and *The Masque of Love*. **1–5 Apr** Working on *The Speckled Bird*. **2 Apr** At Euston Station seeing off George Moore who is moving to Dublin. Frank Harris invites WBY to join staff of his new weekly, the *Candid Friend*. **7 Apr** Visits Masefield in Walthamstow. **8 Apr** Craig to dinner to discuss stage scenery. **10 Apr** Sees Sarah Purser. **11 Apr** Visits the Rhyses. **12 Apr** Dines with Arthur Symons and his new wife. **19 Apr** Dines with AG on her return from the Continent; she gives him a Montenegro lute. **20 Apr** Accompanies AG to Irving's production of *Coriolanus*. **23–8 Apr** At Stratford-upon-Avon to write about Shakespeare and Benson's productions for the *Spectator*. **29 Apr** Newbolt, Sturge Moore, and Christopher Wilson to dinner and to his 'Monday Evening'. **4 May** Lectures on 'Magic' to the Fellowship of the Three Kings. **6 May** *The Land of Heart's Desire* produced in New York prior to US tour. **7 May** WBY puts all his publishing affairs into A. P. Watt's hands. **9 May** Crosses to Dublin and stays with George Moore. **17 May** Meeting at George Moore's to discuss the Irish theatrical movement. **18 May** Unexpectedly meets Bullen in Dublin, and finds him astonished at hostility of Irish booksellers to WBY's works. **19 May** Dines with

Bullen, who gets drunk. **20 May** Leaves Dublin to stay with George Pollexfen in Sligo until 20 June, revising his book of Blake selections, collecting folklore, and writing *The Speckled Bird*. **20 June** To Dublin from Sligo to see MG. *c.* **21 June** Sees over Sandymount Castle, once home of his great-uncle Robert Corbet. **23 June** Goes with Sara Purser to enlist George Coffey's continuing support for the ILT. **July–early Oct** At Coole, working on 'Baile and Aileen', one of a planned series of poems on the Irish heroic age. **27 July** WBY and Hyde speak at Galway. **8 Aug** Meets Violet Martin (Martin Ross) who is staying at Coole with her mother. **9 Aug** Literary conversation with Violet Martin. **11 Aug** Finishes 'Baile and Aileen' and begins writing *On Baile's Strand*. **20–3 Aug** Attends Pan Celtic Congress in Dublin. **21 Aug** Speaks at Pan Celtic Congress on the revolutionary impact of the language movement. **22 Aug** Advocates Celtic evening dress at Pan Celtic Congress. **23 Aug** Attends Kuno Meyer's lecture at the Pan Celtic Congress and in the evening addresses the Congress's closing Ceilidh on 'Ireland and the Arts'. **27 Aug** Much excited by his first experience of the Fays' productions. **29 Aug** Travels from Dublin to the Galway Feis. **Sept** Jack and Cottie Yeats at Coole. **Mid–Oct** To Dublin from Coole to attend rehearsals of *Diarmuid and Grania*. **21 Oct** Makes curtain speech at first night of Benson's production of *Diarmuid and Grania* at the Gaiety Theatre. The play runs until 23 Oct. **23 Oct–3 Nov** Dublin exhibition of JBY's and Nathaniel Hone's pictures a success. **25 Oct** Jack Yeats exhibits sketches of life in the West of Ireland in Dublin. **1 Nov** WBY speaks at AG's 'at-home' to publicize Jack Yeats's pictures and the ILT. **Early Nov** The Fays put AE's *Deirdre* into rehearsal. **4 Nov** WBY and AG dine with the Hydes. *c.* **15 Nov** WBY returns to London from Dublin. **16 Nov** Attends FF's Egyptian plays at the Victoria Hall. **19 Nov** Sees Mrs Pat Campbell's production of Bjørnson's *Beyond Human Power*. **Late Nov** Working at *On Baile's Strand* at British Museum and sorting out his folklore for a book. Entertains possibility that Fays might produce *Cathleen ni Houlihan*. **26 Nov** Calls on Mrs Pat Campbell. **2 Dec** Binyon at WBY's 'Monday Evening'. **Early Dec** Working with Dolmetsch on chanting and is writing new essays for revised *Celtic Twilight*. **11 Dec** Visits the Shorters. **13 Dec** Attends a Johnson Club supper at the Cheshire Cheese as a guest of Unwin. **23 Dec** Sees MG off from Euston Station for Ireland. **28 Dec** WBY's first letter to John Quinn. **29–30 Dec** Working at *On Baile's Strand*. **31 Dec** Up until 5 a.m. working on mystical matters.

1902 **Early Jan** WBY in fairly good spirits after a gloomy time. **7 Jan** Dines with Bullen. **9 Jan** AG sends him £10 on account for Preface to *Cuchulain of Muirthemne*. **13 Jan** MG to tea on her way through London to Paris. **Mid-Jan** Working on new edition of *The Celtic Twilight* and on magic rites. **20 Jan** Masefield calls prior to moving to the country. **21 Jan** Sees FF's and OS's Egyptian plays and reviews them for the *Star*. **22 Jan** Visits to Watt, Bullen, British Museum, and attends a committee meeting of the Irish Literature Society. **22–6 Jan** Weekend guest of the Gibsons in Surrey. **26 Jan** Dines with AG who has returned to London. Decides finally to allow the Fays to produce *Cathleen ni Houlihan*. **27 Jan** Lunches with AG and she later attends his 'Monday Evening' to hear FF chant; Newbolt also present. **Late Jan** Occupied with his mystical work. **Mid-Feb** Reads *Mademoiselle Maupin*. **24 Feb** Lady Margaret Sackville, Violet Hunt, Stephen Gwynn, Standish James O'Grady, and H. W. Nevinson at WBY's 'Monday Evening'. **6 Mar** Goes over *Cathleen ni Houlihan* with MG. **14 Mar** Attends Omar Khayyám Club dinner at Frascati's Restaurant. **17 Mar** Attends Elizabethan Stage Society's production of *Everyman* in afternoon, and later goes to the Great Queen Street Theatre to introduce Symons to Craig. **22 Mar** Dines with FF and Nevinson. WBY thinking of going on the stage. **24 Mar** Dolmetsch praises the chanting at Woburn Buildings. *c.* **26 Mar** Crosses to Dublin. **2–4 Apr** Fays score a success with their production of AE's *Deirdre* and WBY's *Cathleen ni Houlihan*. **3 Apr** Dictates a version of new 2nd act of *Diarmuid and Grania* to George Moore, who is to work on it in Paris. Meets O'Grady in the morning, and in the evening Colum reads him an early version of *Broken Soil*. **5 Apr** Meeting at the Contemporary Club to discuss setting up a National Theatre; WBY, AE, Martyn, the Fays, and Cousins present. **8 Apr** Returns to London. **Mid-Apr** Dictating *The Speckled Bird* at the typists. **22 Apr** Sees FF's Egyptian plays once again. **25 Apr** Meets AG and Robert Gregory on their return from Italy. **26 Apr** Dines with AG and Blunt, and accompanies them to the ILS where he takes the chair at J. Campbell's lecture 'An Old Irish Rath'. **Mid-Apr** Plans *The Hour-Glass* and *The Pot of Broth*. **30 Apr** Dines with Dolmetsch and FF, and they arrange for six more psalteries. **May–June** Persistent eye trouble. *c.* **14 May** Lectures on 'The Theatre' to the Pioneer Club. **15 May** WBY and FF give a private Demonstration Lecture on the psaltery for critics. **16 May** Sturge Moore meets William Sharp at WBY's. **17 May** Goes to Oxford, stays with Eric Maclagan at Christ Church, and sees Robert Gregory. **18 May**   Lectures on 'The Theatre' to St John's College Essay Club. **19 May**   Lunches with Robert Gregory in Oxford before returning to London. **22 May**   Visits oculist, who prescribes new glasses. **25 May**   Meets Sydney Cockerell at Emery Walker's and discusses his sisters' plans for setting up a printing-press in Ireland. **28 May**   Attends Dolmetsch concert at which FF chants. **Late May**   Writing 'The Players Ask for a Blessing on the Psalteries and on Themselves'. **3 June**   Calls on Bullen. **Early June**   Quarrels with Althea Gyles. **10 June**   Gives public lecture on the psaltery. **14–16 June**   Weekend at Blunt's with Cockerell, Neville Lytton, Eddie Marsh, and Alfred Douglas and his wife. **16 June**   Maclagan discusses embroidery with SMY at WBY's 'Monday Evening'. **18 June**   Visits Dolmetsch and experiments with the psaltery. **19 June**   Attends a private performance of Lugnë Poe's production of Maeterlinck's *Monna Vanna*. **21 June**   Crosses to Dublin and stays with George Moore. **22 June**   Visits Tara with Moore and Hyde to investigate unauthorized excavations. **23 June**   Travels from Dublin to Coole. **24 June**   Attends celebrations at Coole for Robert Gregory's Coming of Age. **Late June–early July**   Finishing *Ideas of Good and Evil*. **Early Aug** The Irish National Theatre Society (INTS) founded. **8 Aug** INTS moves into the Camden Street Hall and begins rehearsals. **9 Aug**   INTS elects a committee and officers: WBY appointed President. **Aug**   Cornelius Weygandt at Coole to discuss Irish literature with WBY and AG; the American actress, Mabel Taliaferro, visits Coole and WBY persuades her to act *The Land of Heart's Desire* for him. **20 Aug**   Attends the Connacht Feis in Galway and sees Hyde's *An Pósadh*. **Late Aug**   John Quinn stays at Coole. **31 Aug**   WBY attends the Killeenen Feis with AG, John Quinn, Hyde, and Jack Yeats. **1 Sept**   Quinn suggests that WBY should undertake an American tour. **Sept**   Quinn sends WBY Nietzsche's *Thus Spake Zarathustra*. **Late Sept–early Oct**   Writing *Where There Is Nothing* in a hurry to forestall Moore. Helped by AG and Hyde. **3–7 Oct**   Goes to Dublin to watch rehearsals of INTS and to arrange for publication of *Where There Is Nothing* in the *United Irishman*. **4 Oct**   Death of Lionel Johnson. **5 Oct**   Attends MG's lecture on 'Emer'. **7 Oct**   Returns to Coole from Dublin. **8 Oct** Synge visits Coole until 13 Oct. **27 Oct**   FF in Dublin demonstrates chanting with explanations by WBY. **29 Oct–1 Nov**   WBY attends INTS productions, including *The Pot of Broth*, at the Antient Concert Rooms. **30 Oct**   *Where There Is Nothing* appears in the *United Irishman* (dated 1 Nov). **1 Nov** In the afternoon WBY and FF lecture on 'Speaking to Musical Notes', and attend INTS plays in the evening. **Early Nov** First meeting with James Joyce who tells him he is too old to help. **3 Nov** AG invites Joyce to dine with her, WBY, and JBY at the Nassau Hotel. *c.* **14 Nov** Returns to London from Dublin; begins rewriting *Where There Is Nothing.* **17 Nov** Pixie Smith, Annie Horniman (AEFH), Sturge Moore, and Duncombe-Jewell at WBY's. **18 Nov** Reads the revised *Where There Is Nothing* to Bullen. **19 Nov** Dines with the Rhyses at the Shorters'. **Late Nov** WBY having trouble with his eyes. **24 Nov** The Dun Emer printing-press arrives at Gurteen Dhas. **26 Nov** Reads revised *Where There Is Nothing* to Binyon, Sturge Moore, Rhys, and others. **Late Nov** Reading allegories at the British Museum in preparation for his selection from Spenser. **1 Dec** Pixie Smith shows WBY stage designs at his 'Monday Evening'. **2 Dec** Looks after Joyce who is passing through London on his way to Paris. **4 Dec** Visits A. P. Watt; later to Charlotte and George Bernard Shaw to discuss staging of *Where There Is Nothing.* **9 Dec** Visits Edith Craig to meet members of the Stage Society. **10 Dec** Calls on Cockerell at Clifford's Inn. **15 Dec** Reads *The Hour-Glass* and *The Pot of Broth* to Edith Craig, Pixie Smith, and others. **17 Dec** Sees Laurence Housman's *Bethlehem*, designed by Craig. Meets Ellen Terry and Edith Craig, who shows him the lighting secrets. **Mid-Dec** Reading Nietzsche; finds him a 'strong enchanter'. **29 Dec** Sees W. G. Fay in London and discusses future INTS programmes. **31 Dec** Calls with Masefield to see Cockerell.

1903 **Early Jan** Mme Troncy doing WBY's portrait. **5 Jan** FF gives 'her worst performance ever' on the psaltery at WBY's 'Monday Evening'. **7 Jan** WBY sees Watt and Bullen about publication of his Irish plays. **9 Jan** Consults Cockerell about the printing of *In the Seven Woods.* **12 Jan** Dines with Stephen Gwynn to discuss visit of the INTS to London. Synge, MG, AEFH, Sturge Moore, and others attend WBY's 'Monday Evening'. **17 Jan** Conference with Cockerell, Lady Margaret Sackville, and others about a new magazine, the *Celt.* **18–22 Jan** Joyce in London; WBY introduces him to various editors with a view to journalistic work. **19 Jan** Synge spends evening with WBY. **20 Jan** WBY hears Synge read *Riders to the Sea* at AG's. **21 Jan** Spends morning with Synge. **23 Jan** Calls on Cockerell to discuss the *Celt.* **26 Jan** Synge at WBY's in the evening. **1 Feb** INTS formally founded with WBY as President. **2 Feb**   Synge at WBY's reads *Riders to the Sea* to MG and Chesterton. **3 Feb**   WBY with Synge at FF's recital. **5 Feb**   Dines with Cockerell, Lady Margaret Sackville, and FF, and accompanies them to *Othello* at the Lyric Theatre. **7 Feb**   WBY lectures on 'The Future of Irish Drama' to the Na Geadhna Fiadaine at the Bijou Theatre. **9 Feb**   AG and WBY read *On Baile's Strand* to Synge, Masefield, Edith Craig, Jack Yeats, Binyon, and others. **10 Feb**   Synge dines with AG and WBY, and reads his play to Symons. **14 Feb**   Visits Lady Margaret Sackville in early evening. **17 Feb**   MG received into the Catholic Church. **19 Feb**   WBY lectures on 'The Irish Faery Kingdom' at the Cory Hall in Cardiff. **20 Feb**   Lectures to the Welsh Society at University College, Cardiff. **21 Feb**   MG marries Major John MacBride in Paris. **26 Feb**   The 'big wind' devastates Coole and the West of Ireland. **2 Mar**   Synge dines with WBY. **7 Mar**   WBY lectures in London. **12 Mar**   Crosses to Dublin. **14 Mar**   Lectures on 'The Reform of the Theatre' between performances of *The Hour-Glass* and *Twenty-Five* at the Molesworth Hall. *c.* **15 Mar**   Travels from Dublin to Coole. **17 Mar**   Announces the setting up of the Masquers Theatrical Society. **27 Mar**   Visits Dun Emer on short trip to Dublin. **31 Mar–11 Apr**   Dictates first draft of *The King's Threshold* to AG. **Apr**   Joins protests against Royal Visit to Ireland. *c.* **25 Apr**   Returns to Dublin from Coole; upbraids Joyce for bad behaviour towards London editors. **27 Apr**   WBY at the Contemporary Club until 4.00 a.m. talking of the theatrical movement. **28 Apr**   Leaves Dublin for London. **29 Apr**   Calls on Cockerell for advice about Dun Emer ecclesiastical banners. **30 Apr**   Sees the Craig–Terry production of Ibsen's *The Vikings of Helgeland*. **2 May**   INTS's first visit to London a resounding success. **4 May**   MG tells WBY that her marriage is unhappy. In evening WBY reads *The King's Threshold* and *The Travelling Man* to guests at his 'Monday Evening'. **5 May**   Dines at Sir Henry Lawrence's before going on to lecture with FF on 'Recording the Music of Speech' at Clifford's Inn Hall. **May**   *Ideas of Good and Evil* published. **12 May**   Lectures with FF on 'Heroic Folk Literature' at Clifford's Inn Hall. **13 May**   William Sharp calls on WBY. **15 May**   WBY lectures with FF and Mary Price Owen on 'What the Theatre Might Be' at the Caxton Hall. **16 May**   Lectures with FF on 'Chanting' at the ILS. **17 May**   Travels to Manchester with FF. **18 May**   Lectures with her on the psaltery at Owens College, Manchester. **19 May**   WBY and FF return to London. **23–5 May**   Weekend with Gilbert Murray. **25 May**

Calls on Cockerell in afternoon. **26 May**   Calls on Cockerell again. **29 May**   Lectures with FF on 'Poetry and the Living Voice' at Clifford's Inn Hall. **Late May**   *Where There Is Nothing* published as vol. I of 'Plays for an Irish Theatre'. **Early June**   WBY goes to Dublin. **3 June**   JBY sketches WBY. **3–4 June**   New York Irish Literary Society put on WBY's plays at the Carnegie Lyceum. **8–13 June**   WBY stays with Hyde at Frenchpark. **9 June**   Visits Cruachan and Rosnaree with Hyde and AG. **13–21 June**   Visits George Pollexfen at Rosses Point, Sligo. *c.* **21 June**   Goes from Rosses Point to Coole. **3 July**   Leaves Coole for London, seeing AE and the Fays on his way through Dublin. **6 July**   Attends business meeting of the Masquers Society in Clifford's Inn. **9 July** Returns to Coole from London. *c.* **19–21 July**   Stays at Ballydonelan Castle, Loughrea. **Aug**   *In the Seven Woods* published. **15 Aug**   Goes to Dublin from Coole to cast *The King's Threshold*. *c.* **16 Aug**   Returns to Coole. **Late Sept**   MG, Hyde, Digges, and Maire Quinn withdraw from the INTS in protest against *In the Shadow of the Glen*. **3 Oct**   WBY goes to Dublin from Coole. **8 Oct**   *The King's Threshold* and *In the Shadow of the Glen* at the Molesworth Hall. **19 Oct**   WBY crosses to London from Dublin. **20 Oct**   Tea at AG's with Robert Gregory, Cockerell, and Frank Fay. **24 Oct**   Speaks after a lecture on Daniel O'Connell at the ILS. **4 Nov**   Leaves from Liverpool for extended tour of USA. **11 Nov**   Arrives in New York. **12 Nov**   The Masquers Society dissolved. **15 Nov**   WBY moves from hotel to Quinn's apartment. **16 Nov**   First American lecture at Yale. **17 Nov**   Lecture at New Haven followed by a reception. **18 Nov** Lectures at Smith College and later at Amherst College. **19 Nov** Lectures at Mount Holyoke. **20 Nov**   Lectures at Trinity College, Hartford. **22 Nov**   Returns to New York. **23 Nov**   Travels to Philadelphia, and lectures at the University of Pennsylvania. **24 Nov**   Dines with Dr Furness. **25 Nov**   Returns to New York; meets Archbishop Ireland; lectures at the City College; supper with Irish-American writers and journalists. **26 Nov**   Sees Bryan about Irish anthology; interviewed by the *Critic*; meets Horatio Krans. **27 Nov**   Revises proofs of *The King's Threshold*; is photographed for newspapers; *c.* 9.00 p.m. leaves for Boston on overnight train. **28 Nov**   Lecture at Wellesley College, followed by reception. **30 Nov** Second lecture at Wellesley College. **1 Dec**   Lectures at Harvard and meets William James. **3 Dec**   Lectures at Bryn Mawr. **4 Dec** Lectures at Vassar College. **5 Dec**   Lecture in Brooklyn followed by reception at the Hamilton Club. **7 Dec**   Further lecture at Bryn

Mawr. **8 Dec** Lectures at Contemporary Club, Philadelphia, and stays with Joshua Lippincott. **8–20 Dec** Writes 'Old Memory'. **9 Dec** Returns to New York; lectures at Patterson. **10 Dec** Lectures at the Cosmopolitan Building, New York. **15 Dec** Returns to Philadelphia to lecture to the Science and Art Club. **17 Dec** Lectures at McGill University, Montreal. **19 Dec** Lectures to the Twentieth Century Club, Brooklyn. **20 Dec** Given a dinner in New York by the Sligo Men's Association. **22 Dec** Lectures in Plainfield, and stays overnight with the Hydes. **25–6 Dec** Spends Christmas with Judge M. J. Keogh. **26 Dec** Reception for WBY at Hamilton Club. **27 Dec** Travels to Washington. **28 Dec** Lunches with President Roosevelt at the White House. **29 Dec** Press Club reception and luncheon in New York. **30 Dec** INTS registered under the Friendly Societies Act. WBY lectures to the New York Arts Club. **31 Dec** Attends performance of *Parsifal*, followed by a reception at the Authors' Club, New York.

1904 **1 Jan** WBY working on his Carnegie Hall lecture. **2 Jan** Practises lecture at the Carnegie Hall; in evening lectures at the Brooklyn Institute. **3 Jan** Lectures on 'The Intellectual Revival in Ireland' at the Carnegie Hall; after lecture John Devoy brings a deputation from the Clan-na-Gael to meet him. **4 Jan** WBY leaves New York for St Louis. **5 Jan** Lectures to the St Louis Society of Pedagogy. **6 Jan** Lectures to the Wednesday Club of St Louis. **7 Jan** Sees representatives of the Irish concession at the St Louis World Fair. **8 Jan** Leaves St Louis for Indianapolis. **9 Jan** Lunches with James Whitcomb Riley in Indianapolis; in evening lectures at Butler University. **10 Jan** Given a banquet luncheon by the Emmet Club of Indianapolis. **11 Jan** Leaves Indianapolis for Lafayette; interviewed by the *New York Herald*. **12 Jan** Lectures at Purdue University. **13 Jan** Leaves Lafayette for Chicago where he lectures to the Twentieth Century Club at Harriet Pullman's house. **14 Jan** Lectures to the Chicago Women's Club, followed by lunch; in evening attends performance of *The Land of Heart's Desire* by the Chicago University Dramatic Club. **15 Jan** Lectures at Notre Dame and in evening at St Mary's College. **16 Jan** Lectures at St Mary's College; in afternoon sits in on a literary class at Notre Dame; in evening lectures on the Intellectual Revival and sits up talking with the priests. **17 Jan** Returns to Chicago from Notre Dame. **18 Jan** Leaves Chicago at 8.30 a.m. for lecture at Indiana University, Bloomington, returning to Chicago by overnight train. **20 Jan** Leaves Chicago for St Paul on overnight train. **21 Jan** Dines with Archbishop Ireland and Knights of Columbus before lecturing at the St Paul Seminary. **22 Jan** Sees James Carlton Young in Minneapolis before leaving for San Francisco. **26 Jan** Arrives in San Francisco; MG's son, Seán MacBride, born in Paris. **27 Jan** WBY lectures in afternoon at Berkeley; in evening lectures at the Alhambra Theatre; interviewed by *San Francisco Examiner* and dines with Phelan. **28 Jan** Drives to the ocean with Phelan and dines with his friends. **29 Jan** Lectures at Stanford in afternoon and at Santa Clara College in evening; tours printing-presses of the *Daily Mercury* and spends night in San Jose. **30 Jan** Lectures at the Alhambra Theatre, San Francisco. **1 Feb** Dines with Phelan and local literary people at the Bohemian Club. **2 Feb** Lectures at the Sacred Heart Convent, San Francisco, with Archbishop Montgomery in audience. **3 Feb** Lectures to the Thursday Club, Sacramento. **4 Feb** Leaves Sacramento for Chicago. **7 Feb** Arrives in Chicago from California. **8 Feb** Lectures at Hull House, Chicago. **9 Feb** Lectures at the University of Wisconsin. **10 Feb** Second lecture at the University of Wisconsin in afternoon; in evening lectures at Beloit College. **11 Feb** Lectures at Mrs Ward's in Chicago in morning; in afternoon leaves Chicago for Canada. **12 Feb** Lectures at Kingston, Ontario; leaves for Toronto by overnight train. **13 Feb** Lectures at the University of Toronto. **14 Feb** Returns to New York from Toronto. **15 Feb** Leaves New York for Baltimore, gives two lectures to the Women's Club. **17 Feb** Lectures to Arundel Club, Baltimore, and leaves for New York. **18 Feb** Lectures to the Fenelon Reading Circle, Brooklyn. **19 Feb** Lectures at Wells College. **21 Feb** Lectures at the Catholic University in Washington. **24 Feb** Lectures at Newark. **25 Feb** Lectures at Bridgeport, Connecticut. **28 Feb** Lectures on Emmet at the Musical Academy, New York. **2 Mar** Lectures to Women's Club, New York. **4 Mar** WBY meets Witter Bynner; lectures at the Pratt Institute, Brooklyn. **5 Mar** WBY given a dinner at Metropolitan Club. **6 Mar** Reception and lecture at Newark, New Jersey. **8 Mar** Lectures at Dobbs Ferry. **9 Mar** Quinn gives farewell dinner for WBY, who afterwards sails on the *Oceanic*. **9–16 Mar** Sketched by William Strang on the *Oceanic*. **16 Mar** Arrives in Liverpool. **17 Mar** Returns to London. **18 Mar** Discusses St Louis World Fair with Horace Plunkett at AG's; sees George Brett about publishing in USA. **22 Mar** Attends performance of *The Land of Heart's Desire* by the Chelsea Mummers. **26 Mar** INTS perform at the Royalty Theatre, London; WBY given a curtain call. **29 Mar** WBY leaves London for Coole. **6 Apr** P. J. Kelly expelled from the INTS. **8 Apr** WBY goes to Dublin to discuss purchase of Mechanics Institute with AEFH. **11 Apr** WBY, AEFH, and Holloway inspect the Mechanics Institute. **15 Apr** WBY conducts rehearsals of *The King's Threshold* at the Camden Street Theatre. **16 Apr** Delivers a petition for Abbey Theatre patent to Dublin solicitor; in evening leaves Dublin for London. **23 Apr** Introduces Synge to Ricketts and Shannon. **25 Apr** WBY crosses to Dublin for performances of *The King's Threshold* and *The Shadowy Waters*. **27 Apr** Returns to England from Dublin. **29 Apr** American productions of *The Land of Heart's Desire* and *The Hour-Glass*. **30 Apr** WBY and AG attend abridged version of Aeschylus' Oresteian Trilogy at Stratford. **10 May** Dines with AG, Robert Gregory, Gilbert Murray, and Blunt. **16 May** Dines with Shannon and Archie Russell. **20 May** Dines at Ricketts's and Shannon's with Rothenstein. **26 May** Attends Murray's version of *Hippolytus*. **28 May** Meets William Boyle at ILS to discuss revisions to *The Building Fund*. **1 June** George Moore refuses to meet WBY at Symons's house. **2 June** Lectures in Cambridge. **3 June** Lunches with James Phelan and afterwards accompanies AG to last performance of *Hippolytus*. **4 June** Speaks after Chelsea Mummers' performance of *The Land of Heart's Desire* and *The Poorhouse*. **6 June** Maclagan and Nevinson at WBY's 'Monday Evening'. *c.* **21 June** Attends meeting to discuss Lane's proposal for Dublin Exhibition. **26–9 June** Stage Society production of *Where There Is Nothing* at the Royal Court Theatre. **28 June** AG introduces WBY to the Countess of Cromartie. **29 June** Meets Queen Alexandra at Stafford House. **30 June** WBY at Walford Robertson's. **1 July** Accompanies FF to the Bernhardt–Campbell *Pelléas et Mélisande*; in evening WBY calls on Ricketts and Shannon. **5 July** WBY attends Violet Hunt's 'at-home'. **11 June** Goes to Coole from London. **12 June** Begins work on *Deirdre*. **Late July** Synge and AE join WBY at Coole. *c.* **2 Aug** WBY goes to Dublin in preparation for Abbey Theatre patent application. **3 Aug** Lunches with Plunkett. **4 Aug** WBY testifies at the Abbey Theatre patent hearing; afterwards inspects work on the Theatre. **5 Aug** Sees Fitzgerald. *c.* **9 Aug** Returns to Coole from Dublin. **17 Aug** Accompanies AG to the Great Connaught Feis in Galway. **20 Aug** AEFH staying at Coole. **31 Aug** WBY, AG, and Quinn attend first rehearsal at the Abbey Theatre. **Late Sept** Elinor Monsell and Frank Fay at Coole. *c.* **14 Oct** WBY goes to Dublin from Coole. **25 Oct** Calls on Quinn and takes him to JBY's studio, and then to lunch; reception and dinner for Quinn in evening. **26 Oct** Breakfasts with Quinn; they go on to JBY's studio; lunch with Quinn; reconstitutes the Reading Committee of the INTS; dinner with Quinn and AG, and afterwards to rehearsal. **27 Oct** Breakfast with Quinn; to JBY's studio; lunch with W. F. Bailey at the University Club; dinner with AG and Quinn. **28 Oct** Breakfast with Quinn at JBY's studio; tea at AG's with Quinn, the Hydes, and Martyn; evening at meeting of INTS. **29 Oct** Dinner with Quinn, AG, the Fays, and Stephen Gwynn. **30 Oct** Dinner with AG and Quinn; afterwards dictates part of 1904 *Samhain*. **1 Nov** Crosses to London from Dublin. **Early Nov** Sees Beerbohm Tree's production of *The Tempest*. **3 Nov** Appears before an Income Tax Enquiry. **4 Nov** Accompanies Quinn and Robert Gregory on visit to Ricketts and Shannon. *c.* **5 Nov** Sees *John Bull's Other Island*. **6 Nov** Takes Quinn to hear FF recite to the psaltery. **7 Nov** Entertains Quinn, FF, and O'Donovan to dinner. *c.* **8 Nov** Invites the Symonses to dinner to meet Quinn. *c.* **10 Nov** Stays with Quinn at the Carleton prior to Quinn's departure for New York; Jean de Reszke's mistress inadvertently calls to his room. **12 Nov** Sees Ricketts at AG's. *c.* **20 Nov** Travels from London to Dublin to attend rehearsals for the opening of the Abbey Theatre. **21 Nov** Inspects Con Markiewicz's painting. **26 Nov** At Contemporary Club to discuss Martin Harvey's production of *Hamlet*. **3 Dec** Ends his quarrel with George Moore. **8 Dec** Proposes vote of thanks at George Moore's lecture on modern painting. **14 Dec** Private view of the Abbey Theatre. **16 Dec** WBY at first dress rehearsal at the Abbey Theatre. **17 Dec** At dress rehearsal at the Abbey Theatre. **27 Dec** First productions at the Abbey Theatre.

1905 **Early Jan** Returns to London. Enlists support for Hugh Lane's proposed Dublin gallery of modern art. **9 Jan** Learns that MG is seeking a divorce. **May** Advises Roberts and Hone on establishing the Maunsel Press. **13 June** Friends give WBY a copy of the Kelmscott *Chaucer* for his 40th birthday. **8 July** Attends production of *The Shadowy Waters* at the Annual Congress of the Theosophical Society. *c.* **11 July** Leaves London for Coole and begins a radical rewriting of *The Shadowy Waters*. **9 Aug** MG granted a legal separation. **20 Sept** WBY and Synge travel to Dublin from Coole to reorganize the INTS into a limited liability company. **Late Nov** Abbey company on tour to Oxford, Cambridge, and London. **4 Dec** WBY returns to Dublin to find dissension in the new National Theatre Society.

1906 Theatre business; lecturing. **Aug** Quarrel with ECY over books for the Dun Emer Press. **Late Sept** *The Poems of Spenser.* Reading Jonson, Donne, and Jacobean dramatists. **Oct** *Poems 1899–1905.*

1907 **Late Jan** Riots over Synge's *Playboy of the Western World.* **16 Mar** Death of O'Leary. **May** WBY accompanies AG and her son Robert on a visit to Italy. **Dec** Difficulties with the Fays. *Discoveries* published. **21 Dec** JBY leaves for New York where he is to remain for the rest of his life.

1908 **13 Jan** Fays resign from the Abbey company. **Spring** Affair with Mabel Dickinson. **Late June** Visits MG in Paris. **Sept–Dec** *Collected Works* published in 8 vols. **Nov** Mrs Patrick Campbell plays *Deirdre* in Dublin and London. **Dec** WBY goes to Paris to work on *The Player Queen.*

1909 **1 Feb** AG's illness causes concern. **24 Mar** Synge dies. **Aug** Quarrel with John Quinn. Dispute with Dublin Castle over production of Shaw's *Blanco Posnet.* **Late autumn** Plans for buying out AEFH's interest in the Abbey.

1910 **May** Stays with MG in Normandy. **7 May** Abbey remains open on day after Edward VII's death, causing violent row with AEFH. **June** Jack Yeats moves from Devon to Ireland. **9 Aug** WBY granted a Civil List pension of £150 per annum. **Sept** George Pollexfen dies. **Autumn** Talk of WBY taking up Edward Dowden's TCD professorship. **Dec** *The Green Helmet and Other Poems.*

1911 **Late Jan** C. P. Scott offers to arbitrate in the dispute between AEFH and the Abbey directors. **Mar** WBY meets Winston Churchill. **Apr** Visits Paris, where Ezra Pound calls on him. **May** Scott finds in favour of the Abbey directors. **26 July** *Synge and the Ireland of His Time.* **13 Sept** Accompanies the Abbey Players to USA. **23 Oct** Returns to London. **Nov–Dec** Helps Nugent Monck with the Abbey School in Dublin.

1912 **Jan** Abbey Players arrested in Philadelphia. **May** Third Home Rule Bill introduced. **June** Meets Tagore. **Aug** Stays with MG in Normandy. **Sept** Solemn League and Covenant in Northern Ireland. **Oct** WBY staying with the Tuckers in Devon. **Nov** Severe nervous indigestion. **13 Nov** *The Cutting of an Agate.* **Dec** AG in USA with Abbey Players.

1913 **Jan** Home Rule Bill thrown out by House of Lords. **Spring** Visiting Mabel Beardsley in hospital. Active in getting support for

Lane's Dublin Art Gallery. **4 Apr** Dowden's death renews WBY's interest in Chair of English at TCD. **May** AG and Abbey Players return from USA. Ulster and National Volunteers organized. **Summer** Experiments in automatic writing with Elizabeth Radcliffe. **Oct** *Poems Written in Discouragement.* Rents Stone Cottage in Sussex with Pound as his secretary from Nov.

1914 **31 Jan** Leaves for American tour. **Mar** Resumes broken friendship with John Quinn. **Apr** Returns to London. **May** Investigates miracle at Mirabeau with MG and Everard Feilding. **25 May** *Responsibilities.* **July** Home Rule Bill passed but suspended because of European situation. **4 Aug** First World War begins. **Autumn** Begins his memoirs.

1915 **Jan–Feb** At Stone Cottage with Ezra and Dorothy Pound. Reading Wordsworth. **May** Hugh Lane drowned on the *Lusitania.* **Summer** WBY helps to obtain a grant for Joyce from the Royal Literary Fund. **Dec** Refuses a knighthood.

1916 **Jan–Mar** At Stone Cottage with the Pounds. **20 Mar** *Reveries over Childhood and Youth.* **Late Mar** Macmillans become his publishers. **4 Apr** *At the Hawk's Well*, first of WBY's Noh plays, produced at Lady Islington's. **24 Apr** Easter Rising in Dublin. **July–Aug** Stays with MG in Normandy and on 1 July asks her to marry him. Reads the modern French poets with Iseult Gonne and discusses marriage with her. **Oct–Dec** AG and WBY begin campaign to have the Lane pictures brought to Dublin.

1917 **Jan** Quarrel with D. S. MacColl over Lane biography. **Late Jan** Elected to the Savile Club. **Late Mar** Buys the Tower at Ballylee from the Congested Districts Board. **7 Aug** Arrives in Normandy to stay with MG; proposes to Iseult but is refused. **Late Aug** Lectures in Paris. *c.* **24 Sept** Proposes to George Hyde-Lees and is accepted. **Early Oct** Visits Coole. **20 Oct** Marries George Hyde-Lees at Harrow Road Registry Office. Honeymoon in Ashdown Forest, WBY ill. **27 Oct** George Yeats (GY) begins the automatic writing that is eventually to form the basis of *A Vision.* **8 Nov** Moves to Stone Cottage with GY. **17 Nov** *The Wild Swans at Coole.* **20 Dec** After a short stay in London, Yeatses move to Ashdown Cottage to escape Zeppelin raids.

1918 **Jan–early Mar** Move to Oxford. **18 Jan** *Per Amica Silentia Lunae.* **23 Jan** Robert Gregory killed in action. **Mar–early Apr** To Ireland, to stay at Glendalough and Glenmalure. **6 Apr** Visit to Coole. **May–Sept** At Ballinamantane House, near Coole, to supervise restoration of Thoor Ballylee. **Late Sept** Move into

Ballylee. In Dublin, WBY rents 73 Stephen's Green. **Nov** GY
seriously ill with pneumonia. **11 Nov**   First World War ends. **Late
Nov**   Quarrel with MG. **14 Dec**   General election, in which Sinn
Fein scores resounding success.

1919 **Jan** *Two Plays for Dancers.* **26 Feb**   Anne Yeats born. **9 May**
WBY returns to England. **25 May**   Stage Society produces *The
Player Queen.* **25 June**   Gives up 18 Woburn Buildings. **Summer**
At Ballylee. **July** Invitation to Japan. **Oct**   Move to 4 Broad
Street, Oxford. Guerrilla warfare in Ireland.

1920 **13 Jan** With GY, sails for USA on the *Carmania*; lectures in
America until 29 May. **Aug**   Invited to Ireland by MG to help
resolve Iseult's marital problems. GY has miscarriage. **Oct**
Gogarty removes WBY's tonsils. **Autumn**   Guerrilla War in
Ireland intensifies.

1921 **Feb** *Michael Robartes and the Dancer.* **17 Feb**   WBY denounces
British policy in Ireland at the Oxford Union. **Apr–June**   Oxford
house let; move to Minchin's Cottage, Shillingford. **May**   Lectures
for the Abbey Fund. **28 June**   Move to Cuttlebrook House,
Thame. **11 July**   Truce in Anglo-Irish war. **22 Aug**   Michael
Yeats born in Thame; has operation in Dublin in Sept. **7 Oct**
Return to Oxford. **28 Oct**   *Four Plays for Dancers.* **Late Oct**
Michael Yeats operated on in London. **Nov**   WBY lectures in
Scotland. **Dec**   *Four Years.* Anglo-Irish Treaty debated by the
Dáil.

1922 **7 Jan** Dáil ratifies the Treaty, leading to civil war in Ireland.
Mid-Jan   WBY and GY attend Irish Race Conference in Paris. **3
Feb**   JBY dies in New York. **20 Mar**   Move from Oxford to 82
Merrion Square, Dublin. **Mar–Sept**   At Ballylee; Civil War rag-
ing. **19 Aug**   Ballylee bridge blown up by Republicans. **20 Sept**
Return to Dublin. **Oct**   *The Trembling of the Veil.* **3 Dec**   Dines
with T. S. Eliot in London. **11 Dec**   Becomes a Senator. **20 Dec**
Honorary degree at TCD. **24 Dec**   Bullets fired into the Yeatses'
house.

1923 **Jan–Feb** In London campaigning for Dublin's right to the Lane
pictures. **12 Apr**   First production of O'Casey's *Shadow of a
Gunman* at Abbey. **July**   To London to arrange a nursing home for
SMY who is seriously ill with consumption. **Nov**   Awarded the
Nobel Prize. **27 Nov**   *Plays and Controversies.* **Dec**   In Stockholm
for Nobel Prize ceremony.

1924   **6 May** *Essays*. **June–July** Helps with the short-lived publication
Tomorrow. **11 July** Honorary degree at Aberdeen. **29 July** John
Quinn dies in New York. **Aug** WBY attends the celebrations connected with the Tailteann Games. **Autumn** Suffering from high
blood pressure.

1925   **Jan–Feb** Visit to Sicily and Rome. **11 June** Speech on divorce
in Senate causes controversy.

1926   **15 Jan** *A Vision*. **Feb** *The Plough and the Stars* causes controversy at the Abbey. **Early Apr** WBY has slight rupture and
measles. **19 May** Appointed chairman of the committee on
coinage design. **July** Reads Spengler's *Decline of the West*. **5 Nov**
Autobiographies. **Nov** In London seeing leading politicians and
public figures about Lane pictures.

1927   **Jan–Feb** Violent attack of arthritis followed by influenza. **10 July**
Assassination of Kevin O'Higgins. **Nov** Yeatses at Algeciras,
Seville, and Cannes; WBY seriously ill with congestion of the lungs.

1928   **Jan** At Cannes. **14 Feb** *The Tower*. **17 Feb** To Rapallo to look
for an apartment. **Early Apr** Return to Dublin. **Early June**
Controversy over rejection by the Abbey of O'Casey's *The Silver
Tassie*. **31 July** Sells 82 Merrion Square and moves to a flat at 42
Fitzwilliam Square. **Sept** Resigns from the Senate. **Nov** To
Rapallo flat for the winter.

1929   **Early Jan** Visit to Rome. **Mar** Meets Gerhart Hauptmann and
George Antheil. **Early May** Return to Dublin by way of London,
where he meets Wyndham Lewis. **Nov** Haemorrhage of lungs delays
departure for Rapallo. **Dec** Dangerously ill in Rapallo with Malta
fever; makes an emergency will witnessed by Pound and Basil Bunting.

1930   **Jan–Mar** Slow convalescence at Rapallo. Reads Swift. **3 July**
Leaves Italy by sea to arrive in Dublin, via London, on 17 July. **23
July–6 Aug** Portrait painted at Renvyle by Augustus John.
Sept–Oct At Coole. **Early Nov** Visits Oxford where on 5 Nov
Masefield organizes a recitation of his poems. Visits May Morris at
Kelmscott and meets Walter de la Mare and Virginia Woolf at
Garsington. **Nov–Feb 1931** Winter in Dublin.

1931   **Feb–May** Stays at South Hill, Killiney. **May** Cuala Industries
in financial difficulties and bailed out by WBY. **26 May** Honorary
D.Litt. at Oxford. **1 June** Delivers bulk of MS for proposed
'Edition de Luxe' to Macmillans. **July–Aug** Works on Berkeley
with Mario Rossi. AG in decline and WBY spends most of the
autumn and winter at Coole. **Sept** Broadcasts for BBC Belfast.

1932 **Winter and spring** At Coole. **Feb** Reads the autobiography of
Shri Purohit Swami in MS. **16 Feb** General election, after which
de Valera and Fianna Fáil form government. **Early Apr** In
London, WBY discusses setting up of an Irish Academy of Letters
with Shaw. Acts as unofficial go-between in Anglo-Irish controversy
over the oath of allegiance. **10 Apr** Broadcasts for BBC London.
22 May AG dies at Coole. **July** Moves to his last Irish home,
Riversdale, Rathfarnham, Dublin. **Sept** Foundation of Irish
Academy of Letters. **21 Oct** Sails from Southampton on last tour
of USA. **26 Oct–7 Nov** Lectures in New York and north-east.
Nov Midwest and Canada. **14 Nov** *Words for Music Perhaps*.
Dec Lectures in New York to raise funds for Irish Academy of
Letters.

1933 **22 Jan** Sails from New York. **Mar** Meets de Valera. **June** In
London, Oxford, and Cambridge. **July–Aug** Becomes involved in
the Blueshirt movement; their march in Dublin on 12 Aug banned.
19 Sept *The Winding Stair and Other Poems*. **Nov** *Collected Poems*.

1934 **Jan–Mar** In Dublin. **5 Apr** To London for Steinach operation.
June With GY to Rapallo to dispose of their flat. **Oct** Speaks on
'The Dramatic Theatre' at 4th Congress of the Alessandro Volta
Foundation in Rome. Begins friendship with Margot Collis. **Late
Oct** In London for discussions about the Group Theatre. **13 Nov**
Wheels and Butterflies. **30 Nov** *Collected Plays*. **7 Dec** To
London to arrange for committee meetings of Group Theatre;
preparing poems for *A Full Moon in March*. **Late Dec** Begins
friendship with Ethel Mannin.

1935 **11 Jan** Returns to Dublin. **Mid-Jan–early Mar** Renewed congestion of lungs causes collapse and confinement to bed. **Late Mar** In
London on Group Theatre business, suffers a further attack of congestion. **Late Apr** GY goes to London to look after him. **3–4 June**
Stays with Dorothy Wellesley in Sussex for the first time. **13 June**
Celebrations in Dublin for his 70th birthday, including a PEN dinner
on 27 June. **17 July** AE dies in Bournemouth; WBY attends his
funeral in Dublin on 20 July. **14–23 Aug** Visits Dorothy Wellesley
with Anne Yeats. **Early Sept** Clerical attacks on the Abbey. **16 Oct**
Operation to remove a lump on his tongue. **27 Oct** In London for
special 'birthday' production of *The Player Queen* at the Little Theatre.
22 Nov *A Full Moon in March*. **28 Nov** WBY sails from Liverpool
for Majorca, where he and Shri Purohit Swami are to collaborate on a
translation of the Upanishads. **9 Dec** *Dramatis Personae*. **From 12
Dec** In Majorca working on the Upanishads and *The Herne's Egg*.

1936 **Late Jan** Severe collapse with heart and kidney ailments; GY, summoned by the doctor, flies to Majorca on 2 Feb. **Feb–Apr** Slow recovery from illness. *c.* **14 May** Margot Collis arrives unexpectedly, suffering from a temporary fit of insanity. Yeatses go to Barcelona to help. On return to Majorca WBY sees Shri Purohit Swami off for India. **25 May** Leaves by steamer for London. **June** In London and Sussex. **Late Sept–early Nov** In London for BBC broadcast and to arrange distribution of *Broadsides*. **19 Nov** *Oxford Book of Modern Verse* causes controversy.

1937 **Feb** Broadcast of WBY's poems from Abbey stage by Radio Eireann not a technical success. **16 Feb** Elected a member of the Athenaeum. **Early Mar–24 Apr** In London. **Apr** BBC broadcast 'In the Poet's Pub'. Begins friendship with Edith Shackleton Heald. **18 Apr** *The Ten Principal Upanishads*. **22 Apr** BBC broadcast 'In the Poet's Parlour'. **26 May** Announces his retirement from public life. **8 June–21 July** BBC broadcast 'My Own Poetry'. **17 Aug** Irish Academy of Letters dinner for Patrick MacCartan and WBY's Irish-American benefactors. **9 Sept–1 Nov** In London, at Steyning and Penns in the Rocks. **7 Oct** Revised edition of *A Vision*. **29 Oct** BBC broadcast 'My Own Poetry Again'. **Nov–Dec** Planning *On the Boiler* and helping to reorganize the Cuala Press. **14 Dec** *Essays 1931 to 1936*.

1938 **8 Jan** Leaves Dublin for South of France, where GY joins him in Menton on 4 Feb. **23 Mar** Arrives in London; remains in England, visiting Steyning and Penns in the Rocks, until 13 May. **18 May** *New Poems*. **June** In Dublin to arrange affairs at the Cuala Press and the Abbey. **Early July–8 Aug** In England. **10 Aug** First production of *Purgatory* at the Abbey causes theological controversy. **3 Oct** OS dies. **Late Oct** WBY leaves Dublin for England. **26 Nov** With GY, leaves London for South of France.

1939 **28 Jan** Dies. Buried at Roquebrune. **10 July** *Last Poems and Two Plays*. **Sept** *On the Boiler*.

A NOTE ON
EDITORIAL PRINCIPLES

Our ambition in this volume, as in the edition as a whole, is to give as accurate and yet readable a text as possible. In the case of Yeats this modest aim presents more difficulties than one might wish. As he wrote to Katharine Tynan in March 1888 when seeking employment, 'Todhunter says my bad writing and worse spelling will be much against me . . .' (I. 56). These faults, together with lack of punctuation and a failure to date his letters, continued into later life and are also much against editors who wish to be at once true to what Yeats wrote and tactful to the reader. The poet himself was eager that his letters should be emended when they appeared in print. He instructed Katharine Tynan to show him any of his letters that she intended to publish in her memoirs so that she could correct them, and as late as 1938 asked his wife, when passing on a letter to his daughter, to 'put spelling right & make it legible'. But to correct and regularize as he would have wished would be to lose much of the immediacy and personality of his correspondence. Besides, we could even argue that in our editorial practices we are following his own lead, for in a letter to Edwin Ellis of February 1893, discussing the publication of Blake's poems, Yeats writes: 'I incline myself, to the irregular text on the ground that the "tincture" to quote the Lavatar Notes "has entered into the errors & made them physiognomic"' (I. 353).

We have, therefore, attempted to reproduce the physiognomy of his letters, orthographic warts and all, but endeavouring always to hold back from an officious pedantry that would involve the reader in unnecessary confusion. To have marked with '*sic*' every misspelling or solecism would have been wilfully tiresome, and so errors in spelling and punctuation are silently reproduced. Any editorial emendations appear within square brackets—as, for instance, where we have supplied letters or sometimes whole words omitted through carelessness, when such omission would be otherwise confusing or unprofitably irksome. Where Yeats has used a word obviously in error for another we have given, again in square brackets, the most likely intended reading—for example (p. 45), 'my [*?for* much]'. The poet's hand can be extremely difficult, and uncertain readings are preceded by a query in square brackets. Where proper names have been so grievously mangled as to be unrecognizable or misleading, we have supplied the correct form in square brackets. Careless repetitions and false starts are silently excised, as are directions (such as 'P.T.O.' or 'Second Page') no longer applicable to the form of the letter as printed. Significant cancelled passages, where they can be deciphered, are printed within angle brackets (⟨ ⟩). Words underlined once in the original are printed in italics, twice in small capitals, three times in full capitals. Yeats's use of superior letters— 'M^r', 'D^r', 'R^d'—has been adhered to throughout. Punctuation follows the original, except that full stops have been supplied where clearly intended, and where their omissions would cause confusion. Opening or closing brackets, and opening or closing inverted commas, have also been supplied where Yeats has forgotten them; and single and double inverted commas have been regularized where they are mismatched in the original.

The format of the letters has been slightly standardized in that addresses and dates, where present, are always placed at the top right regardless of where they occur in the MS, with vertical rules to indicate the original line-divisions. Printed and blind-stamped addresses are given in small capitals. Yeats's abbreviated complimentary closes—e.g. 'Sincly', 'Yrs trly'— have not been expanded, and no points are used in signatures. Postscripts are placed uniformly at the end of the letter (thus following the temporal sequence of composition), with a note in square brackets indicating their position in the original. Letters to newspapers and periodicals follow the original published form exactly except for the signature, which has been regularized.

Each letter is headed by a line giving the addressee, if known, and the date. Since Yeats rarely dated his letters in full, many of these dates, the most accurate we have been able to fix upon, are conjectural and appear within square brackets, often with a preceding query or 'c'. A line following each letter identifies the copy-text and describes it (ALS, TS, etc.; see List of Manuscript Sources for the abbreviations used), recording where possible the postmark and the address to which the letter was sent (this also reproduced as Yeats wrote it); gives its location; and lists the first and/or most significant instances of previous publication.

A feature of this volume is the appearance for the first time of dictated letters. These fall into two categories: those taken down in longhand by an amanuensis (usually Miss Horniman), and those dictated to a typist. We have edited the holograph letters on the same principles as those applying to letters in Yeats's own hand, with spelling errors and unconventional punctuation reproduced. We have tried in all cases to identify the amanuensis and this information is given at the foot of the letter concerned. Typed letters are also reproduced as written, with the exception that obvious and trivial typing mistakes ('typos') have been silently corrected.

Synge wrote that all art is collaboration, and we might add that this is also true of some of Yeats's letters. On occasion he and Lady Gregory would write what amount to joint letters (see, for example, pp. 243–5 and 635–9), and we have included all such letters, even when not actually signed by Yeats. We have also included those letters written under instruction from Yeats, even if not directly dictated by him, as for instance the letters John Quinn wrote on his behalf in November 1903 and January 1904 (see pp. 469–72 and 514–16). We have also tried to reconstruct, or at least cite, lost or untraced letters from other sources such as references in replies, memoirs, diaries, etc. (see, for example, p. 18). Necessarily, many of these recoveries must be conjectural both as to content and date, and by the nature of things we would not claim that our list is exhaustive. We consider such items, no matter how slight, worth including for the light they throw upon Yeats's biography, work, and range of interests. In some, but not all cases, lost items referred to in existing letters are also cited in this way.

This volume sees Yeats's role in public life expanding, especially as it related to theatrical affairs, and this resulted in a number of business documents, memoranda, draft proposals, etc. We have printed all the material of this kind that we have been able to trace. We also reproduce printed dedications to books when cast in an epistolary form (see, for example, p. 226–7).

In this period, as ever, Yeats was ready to plunge into public controversy, and he contributed letters and articles to the press with some frequency. On occasion his letters were sub-edited into the form of an article, and we have included any item for which there is internal or external evidence that this has occurred.

Yeats is an allusive correspondent, and so the footnotes attempt not only to identify individuals and to provide information on particular points or references but also to supply wider contextual material. Certain important correspondents, and other individuals and institutions which figure largely in this volume, are given fuller treatment in the Appendix at p. 693, unless they have already appeared in earlier volumes, in which case the relevant back-reference is provided. References to Yeats's works (see List of Abbreviations) are to the original editions or, where a collected edition is in question, to the best text available at the time of this volume's preparation; *Variorum Poems* and *Variorum Plays*, together with the two-volume *Uncollected Prose*, are cited where possible.

LIST OF MANUSCRIPT SOURCES

INSTITUTIONS

Arsenal	Bibliothèque de l'Arsenal, Paris IVe
Belfast	City of Belfast Public Libraries
Berg	The Henry W. and Albert A. Berg Collection, New York Public Library
BL	British Library
Bodleian	Department of Western MSS, Bodleian Library, Oxford
Brown	John Hay Library, Brown University Library, Providence, RI
Bucknell	Ellen Clarke Bertrand Library, Bucknell University, Lewisburg, Pa.
Buffalo	Lockwood Memorial Library, State University of New York at Buffalo
Cambridge	University Library, University of Cambridge
Catholic University	Catholic University of America, Washington
Claremont	Ella Strong Denison Library, Scripps College, Claremont, Calif.
Colgate	Colgate University Library, Hamilton, New York
Cornell	Cornell University Library, Ithaca, New York
Dolmetsch	Carl Dolmetsch Archives, Haslemere, Surrey
Emory	Robert W. Woodruff Library, Emory University, Atlanta, Ga.
Gainesville	University of Florida Libraries, Gainesville, Fla.
Glasgow	Glasgow University Library, Glasgow
Harvard	Houghton Library, Harvard University, Cambridge, Mass.
Higginson	Higginson Family Museum, Scarborough, Ont.
Huntington	Henry E. Huntington Library, San Marino, Calif.
Illinois	University Library, University of Illinois at Urbana—Champaign
Indiana	Lilly Library, Indiana University, Bloomington
Kansas	Kenneth Spencer Research Library, University of Kansas Libraries, Lawrence
Kenyon	Chalmers Memorial Library, Kenyon College, Gambier, Ohio

LC	Library of Congress, Washington, DC
Leeds	Brotherton Library, University of Leeds
McGill	McGill University Library, Montreal, Que.
Mills College	Mills College Library, Oakland, Calif.
N. Carolina	Southern Historical Collection, University of North Carolina, Chapel Hill, NC
NLI	National Library of Ireland
Newberry	The Newberry Library, Chicago
NYPL	New York Public Library
NYU	Fales Library, New York University, New York City
Penn State	Pattee Library, Pennsylvania State University, University Park, Pa.
Philadelphia	Philadelphia Historical Society, Philadelphia, Pa.
Pierpont Morgan	Pierpont Morgan Library, New York
Reading	University of Reading Library, Whiteknights, Reading
Routledge	Routledge & Kegan Paul, Ltd., London
San Francisco	Richard A. Gleeson Library, University of San Francisco, Calif.
Southern Illinois	Morris Library, Southern Illinois University at Carbondale
TCD	Trinity College Library, University of Dublin
Tenterden	Ellen Terry Memorial Museum, Tenterden, Kent
Texas	Harry Ransom Humanities Research Center, University of Texas at Austin
Toronto	University of Toronto Library, Toronto, Ont.
UCD	Archives, University College, Dublin
UCLA	William Andrews Clark Memorial Library, University of California at Los Angeles
Washington	University of Washington Libraries, Seattle
Wellesley	Wellesley College Library, Wellesley, Mass.
Widener	Widener Library, Harvard University, Cambridge, Mass.
Yale	Beinecke Rare Book and MS Library, Yale University Library, New Haven, Conn.

PRIVATE OWNERS

MBY   Mr Michael B. Yeats, Dublin

Other MSS designated 'Private' are in the hands of the following individuals:
Irene Dwen Andrews Collection, Yucatan, Mexico
Mr W. Barrington Baker, Oxford
Mr Stuart Bennett, Bath
Lord Bridges, London
The late Mrs Mary Ellmann, Oxford
Mr Stephen Fay, London
Mr Neil Foggie, Galashiels, Scotland
Mr Alan Clodd, London
The late Mr James Gilvarry, New York
Mr David Gould, London
Mrs Basil Gray, Abingdon
Mr Richard Lancelyn Green, London
Mr Terry Halladay, New Haven, Conn.
The late Professor Richard M. Kain, Louisville, Ky.
Mr Francis King, London
Mr Michael Maclagan, Oxford
Mrs Mary McGee, Leamington
Mr Douglas Sealy, Dublin
The late Mr John Sparrow, Oxford
Dr David Walker, University of New South Wales
Miss Ann Weygandt, Landenberg, Pa.
Mrs Anna White, Dublin
The late Gerald Yorke

LIST OF ABBREVIATIONS
AND SHORT FORMS

WBY = W. B. Yeats

ECY = Elizabeth Corbet Yeats (Lolly)

GD = Golden Dawn

GY = Mrs George Yeats

JBY = John Butler Yeats

SMY = Susan Mary Yeats (Lily)

FF = Florence Farr

AG = Lady Augusta Gregory

MG = Maud Gonne (later Madam MacBride)

AEFH = Annie Horniman

OS = Olivia Shakespear

ILS = Irish Literary Society

INTS = Irish National Theatre Society

ILT = Irish Literary Theatre

The following abbreviations are used in the description given with the provenance at the foot of each letter:

AD   autograph draft

ALS   autograph letter signed

ALCS   autograph lettercard signed

APS   autograph postcard signed

Dict   dictated

Frag   fragment

MS copy   handwritten copy in another hand

TLS   typed letter signed

TL   unsigned typed letter

TS copy   typewritten copy

TS memo   typed memorandum

Principal Sources Cited or Quoted
PUBLISHED

BY W. B. YEATS

Aut   *Autobiographies* (1955)

AV   *A Vision* (1937)

Bax   *Florence Farr, Bernard Shaw, W. B. Yeats Letters*, ed. Clifford Bax (1946)

Bridge   *W. B. Yeats and T. Sturge Moore: Their Correspondence, 1901–1937*, ed. Ursula Bridge (1953)

CP   *Collected Poems* (1933)

CW	*Collected Works*, 8 vols. (1908)
E&I	*Essays and Introductions* (1961)
Expl	*Explorations*, sel. Mrs W. B. Yeats (1962)
G-YL	*The Gonne–Yeats Letters 1893–1938* ed. Anna MacBride White and A. Norman Jeffares (1992)
IGE	*Ideas of Good and Evil* (1903)
Mem	*Memoirs*, ed. Denis Donoghue (1972)
Myth	*Mythologies* (1959)
OBMV	*The Oxford Book of Modern Verse*, ed. W. B. Yeats (1936)
Oisin	*The Wanderings of Oisin, and Other Poems* (1889)
PW	*Poetical Works*, 2 vols. (1906–7)
Saddlemyer	*Theatre Business*, ed. Ann Saddlemyer (1982)
Speckled Bird	*The Speckled Bird*, ed. William H. O'Donnell (Toronto, 1976)
UP	*Uncollected Prose*, ed. John P. Frayne, 2 vols. (1970–5)
VP	*The Variorum Edition of the Poems of W. B. Yeats*, ed. Peter Allt and Russell K. Alspach (1957)
VPl	*The Variorum Edition of the Plays of W. B. Yeats*, ed. Russell K. Alspach (1966)
Wade	*The Letters of W. B. Yeats*, ed. Allan Wade (1954)
YA	*Yeats Annual* nos. 1–10 (1982–93)
YL	Edward O'Shea, *A Descriptive Catalog of W. B. Yeats's Library* (New York, 1985)

OTHER WORKS

Abbey Theatre	*Joseph Holloway's Abbey Theatre*, ed. Robert Hogan and Michael J. O'Neill (Carbondale, 1967)
Bentley	*William Blake's Writings* II. ed. G. E. Bentley, Jr (Oxford, 1978)
Bibl	*A Bibliography of the Writings of W. B. Yeats*, ed. Allan Wade, rev. Russell K. Alspach, 3rd edn. (1968)
Blunt	Wilfrid Scawen Blunt, *My Diaries*, 2 vols. (1919, 1920)
BSCL	*Bernard Shaw Collected Letters*, ed. Dan H. Lawrence, 5 vols. (1972–90)
Campbell	Mrs Patrick Campbell, *My Life and Some Letters* (1922)
Cave	George Moore, *Hail and Farewell*, ed. Richard Cave (Gerrards Cross, 1976)
Craig	Edward Gordon Craig, *Index to the Story of My Days* (1957)

CRB
The Correspondence of Robert Bridges and W. B. Yeats, ed. Richard J. Finneran (1977)

Devoy
Devoy's Postbag, ed. William O'Brien and Desmond Ryan, 2 vols. (Dublin, 1953)

Denson
Letters from AE, ed. Alan Denson (1961)

Harper
George Mills Harper, *Yeats's Golden Dawn* (1974)

Hogan and Kilroy
The Modern Irish Drama, ed. Robert Hogan and James Kilroy, vols. I–III (Dublin, 1975–8)

Hone
J. M. Hone, *W. B. Yeats 1865–1939*, rev. edn. (1962)

Howe
Ellic Howe, *Magicians of the Golden Dawn* (1972)

James Joyce
Richard Ellmann, *James Joyce*, rev. edn. (Oxford, 1982)

JBYL
J. B. Yeats, *Letters to His Son W. B. Yeats and Others*, ed. Joseph Hone (1944)

JMSCL
The Collected Letters of John Millington Synge, ed. Ann Saddlemyer, 2 vols. (Oxford, 1983, 1984)

JMSCW
J. M. Synge Collected Works, 4 vols. (1962–8)

LGM
The Letters of George Meredith, ed. C. L. Cline, 3 vols. (Oxford, 1970)

LJJ
Letters of James Joyce, ed. Stuart Gilbert and Richard Ellmann, 3 vols. (1957, 1966)

LWBY
Letters to W. B. Yeats, ed. Richard J. Finneran, George Mills Harper, William M. Murphy, with Alan B. Himber, 2 vols. (1977)

McGurrin
James McGurrin, *Bourke Cockran* (New York, 1948)

Many Lines
Oliver St John Gogarty, *Many Lines to Thee: Letters to G. K. A. Bell*, ed. James F. Carens (Dublin, 1971)

MNY
B. L. Reid, *The Man from New York* (New York, 1968)

Murphy
William M. Murphy, *Prodigal Father: The Life of John Butler Yeats 1839–1922* (1978)

My Brother's Keeper
Stanislaus Joyce, *My Brother's Keeper* (1958)

Nic Shiubhlaigh
Maire Nic Shiubhlaigh, *The Splendid Years* (Dublin, 1955)

70 Years
Seventy Years: Being the Autobiography of Lady Gregory, ed. Colin Smythe (Gerrards Cross, 1974)

Sharp
Elizabeth A. Sharp, *William Sharp (Fiona Macleod), a memoir* (1910)

SP
Charles Ricketts, *Self-Portrait*, ed. T. Sturge Moore and Cecil Lewis (1939)

SQ	Maud Gonne MacBride, *A Servant of the Queen* (1938)
Taylor	*Frank Pearce Sturm: His Life, Letters, and Collected Work*, ed. Richard Taylor (Urbana, 1969)
Ulysses	*'Ulysses': A Critical and Synoptic Edition*, prepared by Hans Walter Gabler, 3 vols. (1984)
Young	Percy M. Young, *Elgar O. M.* (1955)

PERIODICALS

DUR	*Dublin University Review*
TLS	*Times Literary Supplement*

All other published sources are cited in full at the first mention. The place of publication is London unless otherwise indicated.

UNPUBLISHED

Belfast	City of Belfast Public Libraries
Berg	The Henry W. and Albert A. Berg Collection, New York Public Library
Cornell	Cornell University Library, Ithaca, New York
Emory	Robert W. Woodruff Library, Emory University, Atlanta, Ga.
Huntington	Henry E. Huntington Library, San Marino, Calif.
LC	Library of Congress
London	University of London Library, Senate House
MBY	Michael B. Yeats, Dublin
NLI	National Library of Ireland
NYPL	New York Public Library
Princeton	Princeton University Library, Princeton, NJ
Quaritch	Archives of Bernard Quaritch Ltd., London
Rylands	John Rylands Library, Manchester
Southern Illinois	Morris Library, Southern Illinois University at Carbondale, Ill.
TCD	Trinity College Library, University of Dublin
Texas	Humanities Research Center, University of Texas at Austin
UCD	Archive, University College, Dublin

Other MS material in private hands is designated 'Private' when cited or quoted in the notes.

INTRODUCTION

I

'Then in 1900', Yeats was to write in *The Oxford Book of Modern Verse*, 'everybody got down off his stilts'. The round figure '1900' is no doubt too tidy, but as the letters in this volume show, he himself certainly came down to earth between 1901 and 1904. All great artists are in a constant state of change, perpetually interrogating their art and its possibilities, but the rate of change and the intensity of the interrogation are rarely constant, and for Yeats the early years of the new century proved to be a period of unusual self-reflection and remaking. As the letters in this volume show, the causes of this reappraisal are many, and involve emotional, intellectual, social, and political, as well as aesthetic factors. Indeed, after reading a little in the correspondence that follows we may ask whether Yeats actually climbed down from his stilts in an act of voluntary aesthetic descent, or was knocked off them by the turbulence of personal disappointments, by the irritations and frustrations of running a theatre, and by the public and private attacks that seemed now to be mounted from every quarter.

Yeats himself was quickly aware of the fundamental shift in his aesthetic views. He recognized that his earlier poetry of transcendence and longing was incapable of rendering the new experience of love irrevocably lost and the day-to-day irritations of public disputation. As he was to write to AE in May 1903, the 'close of the last century was full of a strange desire to get out of form to get to some kind of disembodied beauty and now it seems to me the contrary impulse has come. I feel about me and in me an impulse to create form, to carry the realisation of beauty as far as possible.' In the 1890s his poetry had been grounded in a symbolist aesthetic and animated by a vision of larger cultural movements in which Irish literature would inspire a general imaginative awakening. Now it was increasingly borne in upon him that such an awakening was a vain dream, and, even worse, that Ireland, so far from leading the way to the new dispensation, seemed to be growing ever more intolerant and philistine. But if transcendence and symbolism were inappropriate to the expression of these new perceptions, it was by no means clear in 1901 what forms were appropriate. The following years were to prove that it was not in any case a matter of simple appropriation, but the laborious hammering out of a new style under the pressure of powerful private and public dynamics.

II

What were these pressures? The most anguished and obvious was the shock of Maud Gonne's marriage. In 1898 they seemed to have reached a new intimacy following her revelation of her affair with the French journalist, Lucien Millevoye, and Yeats even supposed that they had contracted a 'mystic marriage'. Now he found himself challenged by a potent but most unmystical rival. In 1901 she undertook an extended tour of the USA with Major John MacBride, whose pro-Boer exploits in South Africa had made him a nationalist hero. Yeats's suspicions were apparently not aroused, and he was to share an artistic and political triumph with her after her return, when she took the leading role in his *Cathleen ni Houlihan*. Then early in 1903 she suddenly announced her conversion to Catholicism and her imminent marriage. Yeats's devastated response is registered in the anguished letter he wrote (pp. 315–17), begging her to call the wedding off, and mixing grief at personal loss with desperation at the supposed surrender of her intellectual, social, and political position. That he knew by April of the same year that the marriage was a disaster merely increased his dejection and sense of waste. Poems of longing and hope, such as he had written to her in the 1890s, had become impossible.

Nor was the change in relationship wholly a matter of emotion. Maud Gonne, a leader of Inghinidhe na hEireann and an influential member of Cumann na nGaedheal, was deeply involved in publicizing the nationalist cause, and as it became evident that Yeats had no intention of allowing the theatre to become a vehicle for political propaganda, she began to add her voice to the swelling criticism of his artistic policies. In 1903 she resigned her Vice-Presidency of the Irish National Theatre Society, and followed this with public and private attacks on the theatre, stinging him into a sharp riposte early in 1904 (see pp. 526, 530).

III

Yeats's deepening interest in drama exerted another set of pressures that reshaped his art, causing changes in technique and new perceptions of his relationship with his audience. Writing for the theatre forced him to re-examine the texture of his verse, and to repudiate what was merely decorative or painterly for a style that was dramatic and aural. Moreover, the theatre brought him into closer contact with John Synge, whose exuberant plays, and uncompromising rejection of the shadowy and bloodless products of the Celtic Twilight in favour of embodiment, energy, and physical passion, made a deep impression on him.

Yeats had already begun to tire of the Celtic Twilight, and in one of the first letters in this volume praises Laurence Binyon for reviving 'the beauty of the heroic life', a beauty that he contrasts with the merely 'voluptuous beauty' of the modern sensibility, but which has hitherto come to him only as 'something far off that I reach for on unsteady feet'. Now he began to pursue the heroic, and by July 1901 was able to inform his father that he was 'writing narrative poems of the Irish heroic age', which would 'make a series I have intended to write ever since I was 20'. What now made these poems possible was a growing confidence in his ability with blank verse, and the new versions of the legends made available through Lady Gregory's translations. On 20 July 1901 he told Bridges that after finishing 'Baile and Aileen' he planned 'other stories of the same epoch', and that he had embarked on what he had always intended 'to be the chief work of my life—The giving life not to a single story but to a whole world of little stories, some not endeed very little, to a romantic region, a sort of enchanted wood.'

In fact, his involvement in drama was to redirect his ambition of writing long heroic poems, and his renderings of the Irish legends were not in the main into narrative verse but into poetic drama. He told Sturge Moore in August 1901 that he was 'starting a little heroical play about Cuchullin & am curious to see how my recent practical experience of the stage will effect my work'. He added that the play was 'part of a greater scheme', and at this time the scheme still involved 'a series of poems', but he was already making rapid strides in his knowledge of the drama. Not only was he learning the practical crafts of the theatre—engaging Frank Fay in a correspondence on acting and verse-speaking, and studying the effects of scenic design and lighting from Gordon Craig's productions—but also revising his own dramatic works in the light of his experience at rehearsals and performances. In November 1902 he warned a correspondent that his plays had been 'so much reconstructed on the stage, that I don't think you need, as yet, bother much about the printed versions'. This continual experimentation was at once the cause and product of fresh imaginative vigour. He told Lady Gregory in January 1903 that he was 'never so full of new thoughts for verse though all thoughts quite unlike the old ones. My work has got far more masculine. It has more salt in it.' Later in the same month he confided to Gilbert Murray that with 'a homogenious audience' and 'a little company who will do just what they are told out of sheer enthusiasm' it would be possible to build up 'the whole dramatic art entirely afresh from the foundations'.

The 'little company' he thought he had found in the Fays' troupe; the homogenous audience proved more problematic. Indeed, the theatre brought Yeats into direct contact—and conflict—with a live audience for the first time, and this experience was so bruising that it obliged him to radically rethink his position in the cultural life of Ireland. The first volume of the *Collected Letters* proved that Yeats was an engaged controversialist: this volume reveals that after the turn of the century the controversies became more bitter, their ultimate success more in doubt. He might have lost some of his earlier battles, but the outcome of the war—the war against materialism, abstraction, and philistinism—seemed assured, especially in Ireland. Even the more recent attacks on the Irish Literary Theatre did not disturb him unduly—were they not the inevitable, and even desirable, accompaniment to the birth of a new aesthetic? 'We cannot have too much discussion about ideas in Ireland', he wrote in the autumn of 1901, going on to insist that the 'discussion over the theology of "The Countess Cathleen", and over the politics of "The Bending of the Bough", and over the morality of "Diarmuid and Grania," set the public mind thinking of matters it seldom thinks of in Ireland, and I hope the Irish Literary Theatre will remain a wise disturber of the peace'. As the Irish Literary Theatre came to an end and was succeeded by the Irish National Theatre Society, the plays seemed to provoke more disturbance than wisdom. By 1903 it was apparent that Yeats's controversies were undertaken less to broaden public outlook and perceptions than in a desperate effort to cling on to what little tolerance already existed. As he confessed to Quinn in June that year, he found himself 'often driven to speak about things that I would keep silent on were it not that it is necessary in a country like Ireland to be continually asserting one's freedom if one is not to lose it altogether'.

In these years the Dublin press became almost universally hostile to him and his movement. D. P. Moran's weekly *Leader* had already by 1901 settled into a fixed adversarial position, censuring him on religious, moral, and social grounds. The *Irish Daily Independent*, under the proprietorship of Parnell's old enemy, William Martyn Murphy, launched similar attacks (pp. 444–5), while the editor of the influential *Freeman's Journal* refused a notice of his work because he was 'a dangerous man' (p. 342). Even Griffith's *United Irishman*, although at first friendly, began to snipe at him for refusing to write nationalist propaganda, and after his defence of Synge was to rival the *Leader* in vituperation. By the autumn of 1904 Yeats was so used to this incessant carping that he wryly proposed calibrating Irish papers with a 'thermometer of abuse'. As early as April 1903 he had instructed his publisher Bullen not to send his books to Dublin papers, since their reviews 'sell no copies & I don't see why I should give them the oppertunity of attacking me'. Bullen was already aware of this. On a visit to Ireland in 1901 he had been astonished at the antipathy to Yeats among both Catholic and Protestant booksellers (p. 71).

IV

As these attacks gathered force Yeats was obliged not merely to defend but to redefine his own position, and in this process of redefinition we find him turning to a new critical terminology. Imagination and passion are still the paramount qualities of art, but imagination and passion need focus and control. Hitherto the symbol had offered such a focus and discipline, but now he began to call on concepts such as 'conscience', 'tradition', 'will', and 'precision'.

The disputes in the Golden Dawn, the occult society to which Yeats had belonged since 1890, played their part in this reorientation. The rebellion against the autocratic leadership of MacGregor Mathers in 1900 had brought to light facts that called into question not merely the conduct, but the authenticity of the Society. Much of Yeats's symbolist aesthetic had been grounded in his magical studies and he related the poet's management of words and metres with the magician's casting of spells. Both depended upon the energies of symbols, but the revelation that the rituals of the Golden Dawn might be, if not spurious, at least a modern redaction, put into question the relationship between the mind, the imagination, and language that Yeats had thought secured by a proven tradition. Although he hedged the question, he could no longer rely upon symbols to carry the weight of signification he had taken for granted in the 1890s. The quest for transcendence, already qualified by the experience of writing for the theatre, redirects itself into an attempt at realization, embodiment, and dramatization.

By 1901 Mathers's control of the Society had been broken, but other problems, notably Florence Farr's encouragement of heterodox and potentially divisive 'Groups', led to a quarrel which, while ostensibly about the administrative minutiae of a private club, actually raised issues of freedom and authority, conscience and tradition, even good and evil, that were to be of increasing concern to Yeats. One of the more irritating of his opponents in this dispute was the obscure Robert Palmer Thomas who, like D. P. Moran, represented a class which 'flouts our traditions of courtesy'. Palmer had passed none of the Society's examinations, and even more shockingly had 'not even consecrated his implements', while the Resolution framed by his Group showed like disregard for exactitude and rule. It was 'all about freedom', yet its inattention to the niceties of procedure would, Yeats argued, soon result in an autocracy far worse than that they had just thrown off. As the inadequate expression of a dangerously ill-disciplined imagination it would produce 'illusionary suspicion, illusionary distrust more irremediable than if they had real cause', since 'whatever we build in

the imagination will accomplish itself in the circumstance of our lives'.
Adherence to the precision of ritual prevents the wayward and unruly
forces of the imagination loosening into mere anarchy, and into worse, into
evil, for in his final appeal to the Golden Dawn (pp. 42–5) he condemned
the Groups' turgid and vague Resolution for blithely ignoring the possibility of evil in a glib surrender of control. Tradition and precision were,
he argued, agencies of the will which could keep evil at bay, and later in
the same letter he associated the evil he had in mind directly with original
sin. In its sentimental verbosity, the Groups' Resolution emanated 'from
powers that seek ends that are not the ends of this Order, and that say to
their followers as the Evil Powers once said to theirs "Your eyes shall be
opened and ye shall be as Gods knowing Good and Evil"'.

   T. S. Eliot claimed that the rediscovery of original sin was a significant
element in Modernism and it is clear from his letters and other writings
that part of Yeats's descent from his stilts involved the perception that he
inhabited a fallen world. Much of his poetry and prose of the 1890s had
been preoccupied with edenic states that lay on the borders of consciousness and might be repossessed through the imagination. His new understanding that the earthly paradise is unobtainable, that we begin to live
when we conceive life as tragedy, is registered, as the very title suggests, in
a poem like 'Adam's Curse'.

V

The imagination is more important than the will, but the will now becomes
a more crucial factor in Yeats's aesthetic. In a magical society such as the
Golden Dawn, the will is realized in rituals that contain and focus; in art it
expresses itself in technique. As he pointed out to Horton in July 1901, in
'art as in the spiritual life the will is all but all in all & if you cannot force
yourself to get over the mechanical & tecnical difficulties of art you will in
all likelihood fail in the spiritual life as well'. Horton, AE, and the minor
poetasters who imitated the crepuscular indulgences of the Celtic Twilight,
provided examples of would-be visionary artists who let their visions over-
ride technique, whose imagination, undisciplined by the will, dissipated
itself in blurred imprecisions.

   Will and technique he associated with precision, a quality he was from
now on to prize highly. In a letter to Mrs Pat Campbell of November 1901
he described her acting as having 'the perfect precision and delicacy and
simplicity of every art at its best. . . . the very essence of genius, of whatever kind, is precision'. He made the same point to Fiona Macleod later
that month, contrasting her less convincing elaborate style with her precision when 'you forget everything but the myth', and explaining that, 'hav-

ing a very fierce nation to write for', he had 'to make everything very hard and clear. . . . to be precise and simple'. In October 1903 he suggested in the *United Irishman* that the great need in Irish national life was the discovery of 'more precise thought, of a more perfect sincerity', as opposed to a loose-lipped passion that would make the mob drunk.

But in what does the will reside and how are its prescriptions to be executed? It is to be noted that Yeats specifically refused to invoke the law against the dissident Groups in the Golden Dawn on the grounds that right conduct must be 'left to the individual conscience', and 'conscience' is a term he found himself using with increased frequency. He returned to the question of conscience later in the year, in a letter to the *Freeman's Journal* offering an alternative to the coercive rule of censorship: 'I believe that literature is the principal voice of the conscience, and that it is its duty age after age to affirm its morality against the special moralities of clergymen and churches, and of kings and parliaments and peoples. But I do not expect this opinion to be the opinion of the majority of any country for generations, and it may always be the opinion of a very small minority.'

VI

As he found his writings and ideas under attack it was perhaps natural that Yeats should turn increasingly to that sense of élitism that is implicit in Romantic theory: the poet as one of the few gifted with more powerful imagination and a finer conscience. The issue presented itself again when the Irish Literary Society insisted on blackballing the perverse but talented novelist, George Moore. This dispute indicated that while rules might be necessary, rules could be used by the timid and conventional to reduce everything to a mediocre common denominator. A society that became 'a Court of opinions and morals' would, Yeats argued, soon 'reject on one ground or another almost every man of vigorous personality. The weak and the tame would alone speak through it', for it 'would be of necessity governed by the average thought, the thought which exhibits itself in the newspapers, and it would not be able to do its proper work, which is to find occasions when thought that is too sincere, too personal, too original for general acceptance, can express itself courageously and candidly'.

The precision of rules was necessary, but it must be precision animated by passion, to focus energy, not to suppress it. 'Conscience' takes on special Yeatsian connotations; it does not express the opinions of the average but the insight of the imaginative few. As he wrote in the *United Irishman* of 7 December 1901, literature is 'the principal voice of the conscience', that the writer 'will not bemoralise his characters, but he will show, as no other can show, how they act and think and endure under the weight of that destiny which is divine justice. No lawgiver, however prudent, no preacher, however lofty, can devote to life so ample and so patient a treatment. It is for this reason that men of genius frequently have to combat against the moral codes of their time, and are yet pronounced right by history.' Literature is 'the voice of what metaphysicians call innate knowledge, that is to say, of conscience, for it expresses the relation of the soul to eternal beauty and truth as no other writing can express it'.

In postulating two aspects of conscience, as the voice of received ethics, and as the expression of 'the relation of the soul to eternal beauty and truth', Yeats inevitably moves to an élitist position. Although as a Romantic he had always supposed that the poet was more richly endowed with imaginative insight, in the 1890s he had hoped that the poet was in a fruitful reciprocation with his society. His experience at the hands of the press and theatre audiences showed that this relationship was far more problematic than he had wanted to believe, and he resigned himself to a more restricted audience. Taste, the manifestation of tradition and manners, and the preserve of a limited cognoscenti, joins conscience as a sanction of authority, and he now 'felt that my mission in Ireland is to serve taste rather than any definite propaganda'. He reaffirmed this position in the face of mounting hostility in June 1901, describing his 'business in Ireland' as 'not so much to appeal to enthusiasm as to try & lift peoples standards of taste in a few things'.

At this stage he cited Verhaeren, Santayana, and Shelley in support of these views, but the following year John Quinn was to press upon him the writings of Friedrich Nietzsche, who provided him with a language which articulated and amplified his new views.

VII

These categories, authority, tradition, heroism, taste, conscience, were useful but unstable and needed closer definition, and this Nietzsche provided. Yeats did not become a Nietzschean overnight and from the beginning he had important reservations about aspects of his thought, especially his exaggeration and violence, but at this time Nietzsche was a vital influence, for Nietzsche helped to clarify these issues and gave him an enabling terminology. In December 1902 Yeats apologized to Lady Gregory: 'I have written to you little and badly of late I am afraid, for the truth is you have a rival in Nietzsche, that strong enchanter'. Nietzsche, he went on to tell her, 'completes Blake and has the same roots'. It is not so much, then, that Nietzsche marks a new departure: rather he helps Yeats to define more precisely ideas which have already been present in his mind for some time. In particular, Nietzsche's distinction between the Apollonian, shaping impulse in art, and the Dionysian or instinctive aspect, seemed to fit precisely the distinction that Yeats now wanted to make about his old and new style—though in taking over the terms he gives them a peculiar Yeatsian complexion.

In the letter to Binyon of January 1901, Yeats distinguished between heroic and voluptuous beauty. Nietzsche helped him to define what he meant by 'heroic'. Finding in Nietzsche the celebration of a joy that became defiant in the face of fate and death also helped him to redefine attitudes that had long been in his mind. Early in the 1890s he admitted to Katharine Tynan that a number of his poems were escapist, but that he hoped one day to write poetry of insight and knowledge. However, the tone even in *The Wind Among the Reeds* (1899) is one of retreat, of hiding from the world under the mantle of his beloved's hair or sitting on a green knoll apart. His reading of Nietzsche now helps him to bring into his poetry qualities of self-sufficiency. We do not begin to live, he was to write, until we have recognized that life is a tragedy; but caught in the tragedy, man should meet the inevitable with a defiant gaiety. The world may be more full of weeping than we can understand, but tragic heroes do not break up their lines to weep. Admiration for the quality of tragic joy, which he first found in Nietzsche, remained with him for the rest of his life. It had been anticipated, as he pointed out to Quinn, in his play *Where There Is Nothing*, and is even more apparent in *The King's Threshold*.

The cultivation of tragic joy was enjoined upon his heroes by Nietzsche because Nietzsche was much concerned with the need for heroes in a world where orthodox religion and morality seemed to be outdated; Nietzsche looked for man's salvation through man himself, not God, or rather through a certain type of new man who would take to himself the sort of authority and power traditionally regarded as the prerogative of God. Such men, standing out against the kind of mentality that would blackball George Moore or denounce Synge's plays, needed a mask of sufficiency, in living up to which they would strengthen their own personality while at the same time protecting their private concerns from the hostile or insolent mob. For Yeats, intensely conscious of the divisions in his own nature and now increasingly uncomfortable in his public role as director of the Abbey and butt of newspaper attacks, Nietzsche's ideas on the need for a mask and the creation of a heroic personality were at once exciting and sustaining.

Nietzsche saw that his new men would need a new morality, an aristocratic code which took little cognizance of received Christian values. Yeats, distressed by what he saw as the encroaching philistinism of the Irish middle classes, went some of the way with Nietzsche on this, but stopped well short of his more extreme views. For Nietzsche thought that his supermen had obligations only to equals and how they treated others was a matter of indifference. For Yeats, as for Standish James O'Grady and Augusta Gregory, the idea of an aristocracy implied responsibilities and sacrifices. In a short while he would balance the influence of Nietzsche with that of Castiglione.

VIII

If Nietzsche's philosophy was liberating, so was Yeats's tour of America in 1903. The importance of this visit, arranged by Quinn, can hardly be exaggerated. Almost his last act before leaving Ireland was an appeal in the press for tolerance and freedom of thought (pp. 451–3). In America he found such toleration taken for granted and delighted in the priests of Notre Dame who welcomed him without any sectarian hesitations, and who boasted of their non-conformist and Jewish students. His lionization in America—packed audiences, lunch with President Roosevelt, special lectures to the Clann-na-Gael—did much to restore his faith in himself and his work after the undermining backbiting of Dublin, and he saw that success in America would oblige Dublin to take the movement more seriously.

Distance did not lend enchantment to the view of Ireland, but it did help him to put his own views into a new perspective. The unexpected and to some degree unwelcome invitation to deliver the Emmet lecture in New York revealed, rather to his surprise, 'how completely I have thought myself out of the whole stream of traditional Irish feeling on such subjects. I am just as strenuous a Nationalist as ever, but I have got to express these things all differently.' America also gave him the opportunity to think through his evolving aesthetic views, and his letter of late December 1903 to James Huneker, who had defended him against the criticism of Paul Elmer More, indicates the nature of this evolution. More, part of the new 'classicist' impulse that was to find various Modernist inflections in the writings of Hulme, Babbitt, and Eliot, touched Yeats on a raw nerve by accusing him of faults he had already left behind him, of failing to distinguish between exalted mysticism and loose reverie, of luxuriating in 'a sense of failure and decay, rather than of mastery and growth', and of espousing French decadence.

Although Huneker's wide-ranging article impressively refuted these charges, the criticisms they contained remained particularly disturbing to Yeats in that he regarded himself as developing in precisely the opposite direction, and over the next few years he was to elaborate his new views in a series of brief essays, 'Discoveries', in which he detected 'two ways before literature—upward into ever-growing subtlety . . . or downward, taking the soul with us until all is simplified and solidified again'. This descent from his stilts involved dramatization and self-dramatization, and this in its turn raised questions about poetic language. Yeats was to address this question in his final revision of *The Shadowy Waters* in the summer of 1905, and in an essay written shortly afterwards argued that in 'literature, partly from the lack of that spoken word which knits us to normal man, we have lost in personality, in our delight in the whole man'. A letter to Agnes Tobin, written shortly before he left America, indicates how far he had already moved towards this position. Poets, he told her, 'should dramatise our emotions. There is no other way of writing well, but we must always be certain that the emotion has in it ecstasy.'

IX

After America Yeats was a different man, more assured in political and aesthetic attitudes; in *Hail and Farewell*, George Moore expresses malicious astonishment at his astrakhan coat and aristocratic stance. He returned to find Miss Horniman's purchase of a Dublin theatre well under way. Only three years before he had wished to escape the chores of theatrical administration; now he found himself caught up in a movement more ambitious than he could have anticipated. A London trip in 1903 had given the INTS an international reputation, and he was back in time to attend an even more successful visit in 1904. The summer he spent organizing witnesses and briefs for the Patent application, and the autumn in overseeing the final refurbishing and decorating of the Mechanics Institute as it transformed into the Abbey Theatre.

The change in his aesthetic of these years is summed up in a letter to AE in 1904, following the publication of *New Songs*, an anthology which reproduced and exaggerated all those 'Celtic' attributes that he had now left behind him. He would probably underrate the poems, he confessed, 'because the dominant mood in many of them is one I have faught in my self & put down. In my "Land of Hearts Desire" & in some of my lyric verse of that time there is an exageration of sentiment & sentimental beauty which I have come to think unmanly. . . . it is sentament & sentimental sadness & a womanish interspection—my own early subjective verse at rare moments, & yours nearly always rises above sentiment to a union with a pure energy of the spirit but between this energy of the spirit, & the energy of the will out of which epic & dramatic poetry comes there is a region of brooding emotions full of fleshly waters & vapours which kill the spirit & the will, ecstasy & joy equally. . . . I cannot probably be quite just to any poetry that speaks to me with the sweet insinuating feminine voice of the dwellers in the country of shadows & hollow images. I have dwelt there too long not to dread all that comes out of it. We possess nothing but the will & we must never let the children of vague desire breath upon it nor the waters of sentiment rust the terrible mirror of its blade. . . . Let us have no emotions, however absurd, in which their is not an athletic joy.'

He put this into practice; in September he contrasted his play, *Deirdre*, with AE's earlier version, finding that his work (pp. 651–2) 'at any rate is not melancholy but full of a sort of tragic exultation'. His interest in the drama had not only curtailed his plans of writing narrative poems on heroic themes, it had also interfered with his lyrics. As he told the French critic, Henry Davray, in December 1904, he had 'been so long writing poetical dramas, for my little theatre here in Dublin, that I have only done two lyrics in the last year'. Of these, one had only been written because of a commission, and 'I have sent the other to somebody & for the life of me, I cannot recollect who.' Players and painted stage took all his love, and with a permanent theatre to rehearse his work he was able to revise and rewrite to his heart's content. Immediately after the inaugural productions at the Abbey he announced to Lady Gregory that he wanted to 'rewrite "Bailes Strand". I can make a great play out of it by rewriting a good deal . . .' But the theatre was more than a testbed for his dramatic ideas; it was already a cultural institution upon which he believed much of the future imaginative vigour of Ireland depended. Comparing the situation with that of Norway when Ibsen began to write, he told William Archer that in Ireland 'too we have all to fight against the plebeianising of life through party politics. Our Theatre flourishes like a blade of grass between big stones which have all high-sounding names.'

THE LETTERS
1901–1904

1901

To Lady Augusta Gregory,[1] [4–5 January 1901]

18 Woburn Buildings | Euston Road.[2]
⟨Friday.⟩ Friday and Saturday

My dear Lady Gregory: A good deal has happened since I wrote. We found it impossible to get a definite promise about Dublin out of M[rs] Patrick Campbell so Moore read play to Benson & Benson,[3] was delighted & offered at once to do it in Dublin. Nothing is definitely settled but the probabilates are that M[rs] Campbell will acquire the London rights alone & Benson the Dublin & provincial rights. I do not enjoy the thought of M[rs] Benson as Grania but Moore is convinced she will do very tolerably & gives me a variety of reasons including the fact that 'she plays her body';[4]

[1] Augusta, Lady Gregory (styled more familiarly throughout this edition Lady Augusta Gregory, or AG; 1852–1932; see Appendix), Irish folklorist and playwright, was WBY's closest friend, patron, and correspondent from 1897, when he began to spend his summers at her house, Coole Park, in Co. Galway.

[2] WBY had taken the upper floors of 18 Woburn Buildings in February 1896 and was to retain them until June 1919. In *So Long to Learn* (1952), 140–1, John Masefield, who had met him the previous November, gives an account of the rooms and of WBY's exotic local reputation at this time: 'I have been told that his neighbours called him "the toff what lives in the Buildings"; and said that he was the only man in the court for whom the postman ever brought letters. The general impression in the court was that he was a foreign nobleman in exile for political actions or opinions. The one particular impression about him that I myself gathered there was that he was a dangerous character in some secret society. My informant ended up with the remark that he wouldn't care to go down a dark lane at night with him.'

[3] Beatrice Stella (Mrs Patrick) Campbell, née Tanner, (1865–1940), the most celebrated English actress of her generation, had formed her own company in 1899, and moved in January 1900 to the Royalty Theatre from which she made occasional provincial and Irish tours. She had been in negotiation with WBY and Moore over the production of their three-act legendary play, *Diarmuid and Grania*, since at least December 1900 and had from the beginning envisaged a lavish production. George Moore (1852–1933), novelist and dramatist, had been collaborating with WBY for over a year in writing *Diarmuid and Grania*, produced by the Benson company on 21 Oct 1901 but not published until 1951. Francis Robert Benson (1858–1939), the English actor-manager, had established the Benson company in 1883.

[4] Constance Benson (1860–1946), who had earlier acted under the name of Featherstonhaugh, joined Benson's company in 1884 and became his wife and leading actress in 1886. WBY's fears were evidently justified: after the first performance Joseph Holloway complained (*Abbey Theatre*, 14) that the 'lackadaisical manner and eternal attitudinising of Mrs. Benson as the fickle "Grania,"

& the rest of the Benson company is excellent & the man who would do Conan the very best possible.[5] Mrs Pats difficulty about Dublin is that she insists that the play wants very elaborate scenery dresses etc that she could not have them ready in time or bring them over, without great expense, if she had. Benson will at any rate do it better than we could & the Dublin people like him. *Moore will try & dispose of the American rights he says for £500 as soon as these agreements are signed. Benson & York Powell[6] both say that the play is better than 'The Heroes of Helgoland' of Ibsen the great example of its kind of play. I had an anxious day or two last week. Moore carried out one of his usual peices of comedy. I was laid up with the influenza (mild but just turned to rheumatism) & had left the negociation altogeather to him. On Sunday night Moore came to tell me that he had withdrawn the play from Mrs Campbell because her acting manager had writen to invite him to call at the Theatre instead of himself calling at

---

* He has just been in & says he will wait till play is performed.

together with her almost uniform die-away inaudibleness nearly wrecked the play. Mr. T. O'Neill Russell summed her performance up as "d——d bad," and I am compelled to say "hear, hear!" to his verdict.'

Mrs Benson later wrote (*Mainly Players* [1926], 213) of her problems in trying to reconcile WBY's romanticism and Moore's realism: 'the difficulties lay in the fact that what Edmund [*sic*] Yeats liked, George Moore hated, and vice versa. It was impossible to please both dramatists, and I am sure we ended by pleasing neither.' She recalled that WBY was 'very boyish in those days, and had boyish enthusiasms. He was charmingly unsophisticated.' A presumably less charming example of his lack of sophistication occurred on the first night of the play when, still dissatisfied with the performances, he made a speech in front of the curtain and 'seized the opportunity to indulge in an invective against English actors, English companies and all their works. His eloquent periods were abruptly cut short by Mrs Benson grasping his coat-tails and dragging him back on to the stage. Three-parts Irish herself, she volubly protested that we were an English company, that at his invitation we had crossed the stormy St George's Channel, and had done our best . . . for his play.' Chastened, WBY reappeared to qualify his remarks and make honourable amends. (F. R. Benson, *My Memoirs* [1930], 311.)

[5] The part of Conan the Bald was played by Arthur Whitby (1869–1922), who had acted regularly with the Bensons since 1892. WBY had seen him in a number of Benson's Shakespearian productions at the Lyceum in 1900.

[6] Frederick York Powell (1850–1904), a close friend and neighbour of the Yeatses at Bedford Park since 1887, was president of the Irish Texts Society and had been Regius Professor of modern history at Oxford since 1894. He was an expert on the Nordic sagas and upon folklore generally. Henrik Ibsen's *Haermaendene paa Helgeland* (1858) was first published in English as *The Vikings at Helgeland* in vol. III of William Archer's 5-volume edition of *Ibsen's Prose Dramas* (1890–1). Drawing eclectically on the *Volsungasaga* and various Icelandic Family Sagas, it dramatizes dynastic struggles and mismatched marriage partners. WBY frequently compared the Scandinavian and Irish dramatic movements; in the first number of *Beltaine* (1899) he wrote (6) that the contemporary drama of Norway 'grew out of a national literary movement very similar to that now going on in Ireland', and reprinted C. H. Herford's article, 'The Scandinavian Dramatists', which argued (17) that '*The Warriors at Helgeland* . . . might worthily claim to embody the dramatic ideal of Norwegian art. One of the supreme tragic stories of all literature, the tale of the Volsungs, was here reproduced in terms of the more human and familiar world of the Sagas, and in their simple, nervous, and transparent prose. Danish critics . . . shrank in fastidious horror from what seemed to them the savage realism of Ibsen's manner.'

Victoria St.[7] He explained to me that he did this because should the negociations break down he would be able to say that he had with drawn the
play & get up a contraversy in the papers as to whether acting managers
should call on authors or authors on acting managers. I meanwhile, he said,
was to see Mrs Pat Campbell & tell her that no rudeness to her Etc was
intended. I said I rather objected to telling fibs wheron Moore insisted that
he was really very indignant. There being nothing else to be done I saw
Mrs Pat, & explained that Moore was an impulsive guileless childlike person. She forgave him & now we are all at peace again. Monday I see her
manager to arrange terms. I should have seen him before but for rheumatism Etc.

I am not rheumatic today & but for effect of lack of exercise would be
quite well. I have had a fairly bad time with influenza—it coming down on
me with periodical stupour—Grania too has been continually reto[u]ched.
The chief work I have done is a long new scene in 'The Countess Cathleen' which is finished but for some four or five lines. About four or five
days will get the new edition out of my hands.[8]

Watt has got a good offer for the American rights of 'Shadowy Waters'
which is being very well reviewed.[9] I send you 'Saturday' with article by
Symons.[10] 'Chronicle' had long eulogistic article.

Yrs always
W B Yeats

---

[7] See *Aut*, 441–2. WBY may refer to Ian Robertson (1858–1936), actor, producer, and Mrs
Campbell's stage manager, but probably means Arthur Bertram (1860–1937), her business manager from 1899–1902. George Moore lived at 92 Victoria Street, London SW.
[8] The experience of actually staging *The Countess Cathleen* in May 1899 had persuaded WBY
that he should make the play more dramatic, and he added a love scene between the Countess and
Aleel at the beginning of Act III (*VPl*, 81–93). The revised version appeared in the third edition of
Poems published in April 1901.
[9] Alexander Pollock Watt (1837–1914) was born in Edinburgh; after a period in his brother-
in-law's publishing firm, he began to act for the Scottish novelist, George MacDonald, and
quickly became the foremost British literary agent. He introduced the flat fee of 10% of royalties
that has become the standard agents' charge, and was skilled at placing books and articles for both
authors and publishers. WBY, whose publishing affairs were tangled and unsatisfactory, had
probably been recommended to seek his help by the clergyman and publisher, William Robertson
Nicholl (1851–1923), and he became WBY's exclusive agent in May 1901.
The English edition of *The Shadowy Waters* had been published by Hodder and Stoughton in
December 1900; the American edition, issued by Dodd, Mead & Co., appeared in April 1901.
[10] Arthur Symons (1865–1945), poet and critic, and friend of WBY's since the early 1890s, had
reviewed *The Shadowy Waters* anonymously in the *Saturday Review*, 29 Dec 1900 (824–5), finding
that 'Mr. Yeats, in his new play, more perhaps than in any of his former work, has realised, not
only that verse must be as simple and straightforward as prose, but that every line must be packed
with poetical substance, must be able to stand alone, as a fine line of verse, all the more because it
challenges at once the standards of prose and of poetry.' The notice in the *Daily Chronicle* on 3
Jan 1901 (3), entitled 'The Latter Oisin', was by Henry Woodd Nevinson (1856–1941), a journalist and man of letters who frequently reviewed WBY's works. After praising the 'delicate beauty'
of the highly symbolic play, he turned 'with some relief to the songs the poet gave us before the

I thought Rollestons reply to Moran suprizingly good.[11] He seems to have been really angry & that kept his wits alive.

ALS Berg, with envelope addressed to Coole, postmark 'LONDON JA 5 01'.

To Laurence Binyon,[1] [?5 *January 1901*]

18 Woburn Buildings | Euston Road.
⟨Monday.⟩ Saturday night.

My dear Binyon: I have not read all your book yet but I have just finished 'Tristram' & must write you what I think. It seems to me a great poem among the greatest for many years. I cannot criticize it. One criticizes the

fairies quite got him for their own'. Nevinson subsequently reprinted this, and other reviews of WBY's works, in *Books and Personalities* (1905). The only other review up to this date was an unfavourable notice in the *Glasgow Herald* of 27 Dec 1900.

[11] David Patrick Moran (1871–1936), Irish-Irelander and journalist, had founded the *Leader*, a pietistic nationalist weekly, in September 1900. The issue of 22 Dec 1900 (264) had condemned the recently published anthology, *A Treasury of Irish Poetry in the English Tongue*, edited by Rolleston and his father-in-law, the Revd Stopford Brooke, for its Anglo-Irish bias, asserting that '"Celtic" symbolists' such as WBY and men 'developed in Trinity College' could never reach the heart of Irish peasants and Catholics. In his spirited refutation of Moran on 5 Jan 1901, Rolleston insisted that he knew 'many Irish hearts that have been deeply moved by Mr. Yeats's poetry', named eleven Trinity men from Grattan to Douglas Hyde who had 'deeply influenced the history and touched the heart of Ireland', and asked in conclusion (296): 'Are Davis and Ferguson and Yeats and A.E. to be nothing to the Irish Catholic because he is a Catholic, and are De Vere and Griffin and Mangan to be nothing to me because I am a Protestant?'

  T. W. Rolleston (1857–1920; see I. 508–9), a civil servant and man of letters, had been a founding member of the Rhymers' Club and the first secretary of the ILS. Since 1899 he had been working for the newly created Irish Department of Agriculture as organizer of lectures. WBY was surprised by the effectiveness of Rolleston's reply because he thought gentility had sapped his powers of expression, but AG was to reveal in her undated answer to this letter (Berg) that AE (the poet, journalist and Co-operative Society organizer, George William Russell, 1867–1935; see I. 509–11) had 'urged Rolleston to write to the Leader, & he gave him all his points—this accounts for its unusual fire'.

[1] Robert Laurence Binyon (1869–1943), poet, dramatist, and art historian, was an assistant in the Department of Prints and Drawings at the British Museum, where he became Keeper of Oriental Paintings and Prints in 1913. Now best known as a poet for his 'For the Fallen', his first volume, *Lyric Poems*, had appeared in 1894. His eighth book of verse, *Odes*, was published in December 1900 and included 'The Death of Tristram', a three-part poem in which Iseult and the dying Tristram recall their first meeting and subsequent passion. WBY's admiration for the poem persisted: in 'Friends of My Youth', a lecture delivered in 1910, he commended it as 'a wonderfully live poem, a most exquisite and astonishing thing . . . very delicate in style and entirely vocal: all beautiful speech. In some of his works he is affected by the academic attitude, but in that one poem I think he has done a beautiful thing' (*Yeats and the Theatre* [1975], 41), and he included it in *OBMV* (1936), where he described it (xvi) as 'Binyon . . . at his best'.

imperfect but when the perfect comes one can but say 'How gladly I would have died such a death or lived such a life'. There is something in this poem & in Sturge Moores recent themes—though he lacks as yet the crowning perfection of a great style—that moves one with a strange personal emotion.[2] It is as though a new thing, long prophesied, but never seen, had come at last. It is the beauty of the heroic life. It has come to you & him in visable substance, lyric or dramatic, to me only as something far off that I reach for on unsteady feet, an invisible essense, a flying star, a wandering wind.[3] It is that beuty which Blake says 'changes least from youth to age' & one turns to it, as though it were the visable face of eternity appearing amid the 'voluptuous beauty', which he says is all the moderns know.[4] Swinburne[s] 'Tristram' has the 'voluptuous beauty' in its heart & Mathew Arnold's has but stray beautiful passages & nothing in its heart.[5] But in your poem is the whole shining substance & for generations & generations it will come to lovers not as literature, but as their own memories. There will never be a true lover, who shall read it without tears, I think. I do not know whether I can rightly judge, rightly measure it for it is to me like some religious voice, some ritual, heard in childhood & then heard again after many years among ⟨heathe⟩ barbarous peoples—it is the voice, the ritual of heroical beauty.

Yrs sny
W B Yeats

ALS Private.

[2] Thomas Sturge Moore (1870–1944), poet, dramatist, art critic, and designer, was the elder brother of the philosopher, G. E. Moore. He had recently been introduced to WBY by Binyon and was to become a lifelong friend and correspondent. WBY had been impressed with his recent volume, *The Vinedresser and Other Poems*, and by his play, *Aphrodite Against Artemis*, which Sturge Moore had read to him in manuscript and which was to be published in the summer of this year. As with Binyon, WBY approved of Sturge Moore's attempts to restore the heroic to poetry; in *OBMV* he described them both (xvi) as descended from Virgil.

[3] An early indication of WBY's growing discontent with his 'nineties' style, and of his wish to move towards embodiment and dramatization in his verse.

[4] A misquotation from Blake's *Descriptive Catalogue* (1809): 'The face and limbs that deviates or alters least, from infancy to old age, is the face and limbs of greatest Beauty and perfection'. The phrase 'voluptuous beauty' does not occur in Blake, although WBY was to use it again in the opening sentence of his story '"And Fair, Fierce Women"' (*Myth*, 57).

[5] Swinburne's *Tristram of Lyonesse* (1882), a nine-part version of the tale in rhymed couplets, begins with an extended apostrophe to Love, and revels in the voluptuous possibilities of the subsequent incidents. Arnold's three-part 'Tristram and Iseult' (1852), the first modern treatment of the legend in English, differs from Binyon's in being told largely through the narrative of a later Breton bard, while its only sustained excursion into drama, a *Liebestod* in rhymed trochaic lines, produces wooden formality rather than passionate intensity. WBY may recently have reread it, for he gave ECY a copy of Arnold's *Poems* for Christmas 1900.

To T. Sturge Moore, [5 January 1901]

18 Woburn Buildings | Euston Road.
Saturday

My dear Sturge Moore: Yes I shall come with pleasure Wednesday 9th.[1]
You do not say what hour. I shall assume that it is seven unless you write
to the contrary.

Excuse my delay in answering but I have had an influenza attack & have
had other exciting episodes.

Benson company accept for Irish production the legendary play I have
done with Moore & Mrs Pat Campbell accepts for London. Busines[s]
matters amount of royalties etc have yet to be settled. I see acting manager
on Monday to settle details about Mrs Pat Campbells production.

The play is prose so that it should find none of the difficulties verse has
to meet.

Yrs ev
W B Yeats

ALS Texas. Bridge, 2.

To Lady Augusta Gregory, [8 January 1901]

18 Woburn Buildings | Euston Road. | London
Tuesday,

My Dear Lady Gregory: I saw Mrs Pat Campbells manager yesterday, &
am waiting for his formal proposal of terms. He said that he could tell me
very little because Mrs Pat was so full of the play, when he saw her, that
she said nothing about its business side. He also told me that the reason
why the 'Independent' made that amazing attack on Maeterlinck was that
it was by big Manning, & big Manning had just lost a wager to some of
Mrs Pats company. They had bet they could produce among themselves a

[1] On 9 Jan Sturge Moore recorded in his diary (London) that he had asked 'Yeats to dine to
meet Effie', but that only Effie Cook came because 'Yeats ill'. Besides introducing him to 'Follies'
actress Effie Cook, Sturge Moore would also have wanted to discuss with WBY the 'Romantic
Theatre' they were planning with Charles Ricketts. This was formally established as the Literary
Theatre Club and inaugurated in July with the reading of Sturge Moore's *Aphrodite Against
Artemis* at the Dalton Theatre. On 27 Jan 1901 Ricketts recorded in his diary (BL) that he had
discussed with Sturge Moore 'the foundation of a Theatre society for Romantic Drama . . . which
would be managed by him, in which the scenery would be done on a new decorative, almost symbolic principle'.

taller man than Manning & they did—he beat Manning by $\frac{1}{2}$ an inch. Before that he had praised everything.[1]

My rheumatism has changed into a neuralgic headache which comes on in the after noons, but I am taking care of myself & going out little at night, & have laid in a supply of Phenacetin.[2]

A man called Dell or O Dell or some like name was—according to a letter I got from Weeks (a good time ago) the man who wanted to exclude Jacks drawings from Cornhill. A little later Weeks told me that O Dell was going to attack me, or the movement, in the 'Review of the Week'. I now hear that the article has appeared but I have not seen it. I hope Jack has not suffered for any unpopularity of mine.[3] I thought they had definitely

---

[1] On 25 Aug 1900, during a fortnight's engagement at the Theatre Royal, Dublin, Mrs Pat Campbell's company had produced Maurice Maeterlinck's *Pelléas and Mélisande*, a play which she and Forbes-Robertson had made famous in 1898. The *Irish Daily Independent* of 27 Aug marked the production with two swingeing attacks on Maeterlinck, one in a review of the play, the other in an editorial. The review (2) criticized the play for having 'nothing of that legendary glamour or of those aspirations for higher ideals which marks the dramas of the Celtic revival', and complained that there were 'many extravagancies of poetical expression, and the lovers are often lachrymose enough to put one in the blues'. The editorial (4) was even less complimentary, describing the piece as 'a whinge in five acts', and concluding that it was 'almost impossible to conceive' how Maeterlinck 'could have come to be treated seriously as a writer, much less have achieved a world-wide reputation. The play is hopeless in its ending, it is helpless in its development, it is silly in its mystery, and more silly still in its whining mournfulness. That a work of the kind should be regarded as one of the foremost dramas of the day is an alarming indication of the decay of moral fibre among those who pretend to regulate the standard of what is most excellent on the stage.' Mrs Campbell's indignation was apparently unassuaged by praise for the 'magnificent staging and superb acting' nor by the back-handed compliment that she had acted 'a part of meagre possibilities with the best effects that could be extracted from it'.

M. A. Manning (d. 1908), the very antithesis of the shadowy Maeterlinckian hero, being a 'genial giant', 6' 6" tall and—reputedly—26 stone, was a well-known journalist and story-teller who had come to Dublin from Waterford, where he had founded the Irish Dramatic Company and gained a reputation as an actor, singer, politician, and electioneering expert. A member of the IRB and an active member of the Gaelic League and the National Literary Society, Manning was formerly editor of the *Weekly Independent* and had recently become the town clerk of Kingstown (now Dun Laoghaire).

[2] Phenacetin, a coal-tar derivative, was introduced in the 1890s as an antipyretic and analgesic drug, taken as a 'mixture' for neuralgia, rheumatism, and headaches.

[3] Robert Edward Dell (1865–1940), journalist, art critic, and editor of the *Review of the Week*, was to become editor of the *Connoisseur* in September 1901 and of the *Burlington Magazine*, 1903–6. From 1907 to 1938 he was a well-known political journalist and foreign correspondent for the *Manchester Guardian*. He had evidently advised the *Cornhill Magazine* not to publish Jack Yeats's illustrations to AG's article 'The Felons Of Our Land' which had appeared there in May 1900. WBY was reminded of the incident not merely by Dell's review, but because the *Argosy* had just done the same thing over AG's article, 'The Poet Raftery'. As she explained in an undated reply to this letter (Berg): 'Nobody cd have behaved worse than the Argosy people—They wrote asking Jack for drawings, then wrote to say they liked them, & asking the price—He said 3 guineas each—He heard nothing more, they did not return them, but simply printed my article without them.'

Charles Alexandre Weekes (1867–1946), Irish poet, lawyer, journalist, and close friend of AE, had attended the Dublin High School with WBY, who included two of his poems in *A Book of Irish Verse* (1895). He had moved to London in 1896, and after a period as reader for the publisher George Allen, was now working as an editor and journalist.

accepted the drawings. The accepting of the drawing & the so getting you to accept low terms, & then leaving out the drawings is really a kind of fraud, I should think.

'The Leaders' first attack on the Anthology was, like the article on my Jug, undoubtedly Ryan[4] but the second attack was I feal very certain Moran. I would not call its passing allusion to my self exactly an attack—as Moran understands such things. The "even" ("even Mr Yeats has not" Etc) was meant for a kind of politeness ⟨as Moran understands politeness⟩; and from Morans point of view, the point of view of a man who only cares for the mob the sentence was true. Had he not given Hyde his promise there would doubtless have been no 'even'.[5] His reply to Rolleston was curiously week & irellevant, &, I almost thought, conscious of its folly. Ryan is a man who wanted to send Moore a play to read a while back, & though I urged Moore to write to him & though Moore promised & I think his letter was unanswered. It was a pity for Ryan has all his life lived

---

[4] William Patrick Ryan (1867–1942), Irish journalist and novelist, lived most of his working life in London, where he was a member of the ILS and Secretary of the Gaelic League. He had apparently written the first attack on the Brooke–Rolleston anthology which appeared in the *Leader* on 1 Dec 1900 (220–1), in which the book is made to bewail its discordant components: 'Having been put into form by human hands and minds I feel necessarily in a sense like man, but know when consideration comes that I am a motley if slightly interesting monster. . . . For the hair of my head Mr. Yeats is responsible. . . . My tongue is of Young Ireland all compact. And oh! good sir, I have a Trinity College liver!'

An article entitled 'Mr. Yeats's Jug', signed 'Seang Siuir' and published by the *Leader* on 3 Nov 1900, (155), mocked a pretentious interview with WBY in the London society paper *M.A.P.* of 20 Oct 1900. The interviewer had described (369) the 'many vicissitudes' of tea *chez* WBY 'in the way of the fire refusing to burn, the sugar being dropped into a tobacco jar instead of the cup, and, at the last moment, Mr. Yeats going out to purchase milk'. In his parody of 'this wonderful Society idyll' for the *Leader*, Ryan archly tried to visualize WBY's milk-jug: 'Was it of earth, or after-earth, or of Orchill's under-earth, manufacture, that Jug which, "with reverent hands", the poet bore out into the spellful night what time the blithe nymph was tea-thirsty?'

[5] In his review of 22 Dec 1900 (see p. 6, n. 11) Moran had lamented the absence of any Anglo-Irish poet who could speak to the heart of Ireland as Burns spoke to that of Scotland: 'Even Mr. Yeats does not understand us, and he has yet to write even one line that will strike a chord of the Irish heart. He dreams dreams. They may be very beautiful and "Celtic", but they are not ours.' Douglas Hyde (1860–1949; see I. 493–5) wrote mainly in Irish and was co-founder and president of the Gaelic League. As such he fulfilled Moran's ideal of an Irish man of letters and had some influence over him; in her letter of 7 Jan AG told WBY 'Moran had promised Hyde not to attack you'.

Moran's limp reply to Rolleston's letter (see p. 6) appeared immediately under it and read in part: 'Mr. Rolleston is in reality an educated Englishman who thinks that he is an Irishman, whilst we belong to the legion who have awakened to the fact that they ought to have been brought up Irish, but were educated West Britons. There is, therefore, a gulf between us and men like Mr. Rolleston, and in our several outlooks on many matters affecting Ireland, we must agree to differ. . . . We profess to be no oracle, and we ask no man, not even the humblest, to swallow our views, but rather to consider them and agree with or reject them as he may think fit.' He went on to defend his attack on the Trinity College representatives in the *Anthology* (32 out of 120 poets) on the disingenuous grounds that the other writers had appeared in previous anthologies whereas 'the Trinity College instalment . . . struck us as being the feature of the book that was new'.

under a sense of wrongs. He had a complicated quarrel with Duffy & the Irish Lit Society & will I have no doubt avenge himself on all his enemies from behind the wall [of] the Gaelic League. He had some unfriendly remarks about 'The Shadowy Waters' for being in 'an alien tongue' & for attempts to carry out theories in Symons symbolist book.[6] It is wonderful the skill with which these people play on subtle hints of heresey when they review A E or my self; & after all they are right from their point of view. It is as much their very respectable instinct for heresey, as rage against something they cannot understand, that keeps them ever harping on symbols, only they should be more open.

Watt has got good terms for the American rights of 'The Shadowy Waters'.

I have just heard an amusing saying of some English officer about the African War. He said that the English have as much chance of catching De Wett as a Lords Mayors Procession of catching a burglar in Hampstead. Gen Collville is a friend of friends of mine & I hear that he is in great spirits & thinks he is going to win but you will hear enough of the war everywhere.[7]

Yrs sinly

W B Yeats

[*On back of envelope*]
I hope you got the 'Saturday Review' I sent.[8]

ALS Berg, with envelope addressed to Coole, postmark 'LONDON N W JA 9 01'.

[6] Ryan's *The 'Wake' of the People/ 1847*, a tragedy set in Famine times, appeared in the Christmas number of the *Weekly Freeman* on 14 Dec 1901 (26). It was reprinted in *Plays for the People* (1904) but never produced. In his book *The Irish Literary Revival* (1894), Ryan had expressed reservations about the role of Sir Charles Gavan Duffy (1816–1903) as editor of the New Irish Library and President of the ILS (see I. 483–4), and this had led to controversy in *United Ireland*. In his dismissive review of *The Shadowy Waters* in the *Freeman's Journal* of 1 Jan 1901 (7), Ryan advised that there was 'not much . . . that calls for new discussion. . . . At times Mr. Yeats seems desirous of illustrating in poetry some of the things which Mr. Arthur Symons set so delicately and yet so unconvincingly in prose in "The Symbolist Movement in Literature". . . . We have become rather accustomed to neo-dreamers' fairy play in a foreign speech, with essentially clear and artistically sane things in a language and literature they do not understand.' Symons's influential study, *The Symbolist Movement in Literature* (1899), was dedicated to WBY.

[7] Christian Rudolph De Wet (1854–1922), 'the old grey fox', the Boer general who became commander-in-chief of the Free State forces in 1901. His daring exploits and tactics earned him an international reputation and he was still eluding capture when the war ended in June 1902. The English officer may have been Col. Maurice Moore (1854–1939), who was serving with the British Army in South Africa and supplying his brother, George Moore, with anti-War information. Major-General Sir Henry Edward Colvile (1852–1907) had commanded the 9th Division in South Africa until his delay in following Lord Roberts's orders led to the capture of the Imperial Yeomanry at Lindley in May 1900. Relieved of command, he later returned to service in Gibraltar, but when Roberts became commander-in-chief of the army he was recalled to England and on 19 Jan 1901 was to be ordered into retirement. Sir Henry ('Tenax Propositi') and Lady Zelie Isabelle Colvile ('Semper') were close friends of FF and fellow members of the Second order of the GD.   [8] See p. 5.

To T. Sturge Moore, [8 January 1901]

18 Woburn Buildings | Euston Road
Tuesday

My dear Sturge Moore: I am sorry to say that I am so full of rheumatism
& neurlalgia that I shall have to dissapoint you tomorrow. I should have
written before but I thought to be well by this. Yesterday however—as the
result of a walk home from a friends on Sunday I think—I developed bad
neuralgic headache & to day, after waking quite well, I have found it come
on again though less severely. I am very sorry, I have had to write to Benson, who had sent me a box to post pone that too until next week. I had
hoped to go to his theatre on Thursday.[1] He is I think taking our provincial rights in 'Grania'.

I hope you will let me dine with you as soon as I am well. This weather
has up set me in a way weather has never done before;[2] & rheumatic fever
is one of the things I have always to be stearing round (for I have had it
twice), & with that rock about I can spread but little sail.[3]

Yours alway sincely
W B Yeats

ALS Texas. Bridge, 3.

To T. Fisher Unwin,[1] [8] January 1901

18 Woburn Buildings | Euston Road. | London.
Tuesday,
Jan. 1901

My dear Mr Unwin: I did not write to you before because I have been at
work, under considerable difficulties, on the new edition of 'Poems.' Now

[1] The Benson Company, in the course of their Shakespearian season at the Comedy Theatre,
produced *The Taming of the Shrew* on 10 Jan, and *The Merchant of Venice* the following week.
[2] There had been a heavy fall of snow on 7 Jan and the 8th was a 'dull, gloomy' day, with temperatures well below freezing, easterly winds, and intermittent snow.
[3] JBY constantly alerted WBY to this danger. In an undated letter written in the autumn of
1899 (MBY) he had warned him 'to be careful as regards all Rheumatic symptoms. You yourself
when a boy had an attack of rheumatic fever.' In another undated letter (MBY) he expressed the
hope 'that you have no return of the Rheumatic symptoms—if I were you I should be careful
about them. They are always most serious things.'

[1] Thomas Fisher Unwin (1848–1935) had been WBY's main publisher since 1891 when he
issued *John Sherman and Dhoya*. He had founded his firm in 1882 and was to continue to publish
Poems until he was taken over by Ernest Benn in October 1926. In a copy of the 1929 edition of

however that it is almost done it is time for me to discuss with you the clause in the agreement about American rights. You will remember that I reserved this matter for further consideration. The draft agreement says 'that the proceeds of the sale of rights of translation & of advance rights to the United States of America shall be received by the said T Fisher Unwin & divided in the proportion of one half to the said T Fisher Unwin & one half to the said W B Yeats'. It seems to me that when you act as practically a literary agent you should—& I am sure you will see this at once when I point it out—receive no more than the 10 per cent usual in the case of a literary agent. I am quite ready to myself make all arrangements with America, should you prefer to take over the English rights alone, but if you wish for the Agency for the American rights I am ready to give you ten percent of the profits.

I think too that 7 years is a longer period than we agreed for last time— I have not my copy of old agreement immediately at hand. 5 is I think long enough, but you can have it for 6. As soon as we get these things settled I will give you full details of all my books, published & unpublished, which Lawrence & Bullen have rights over.[2] One 'The Shadowy Waters' has as I dare say you have seen passed into 'Hodder & Staughtons' hands.

Yrs snly
W B Yeats

ALS Texas.

To Lady Augusta Gregory, [9 January 1901]

18 Woburn Buildings | Euston Road.
Wed

My dear Lady Gregory: I find I wronged Dell or O'Dell or who ever he is. His article has just come. It is a quite good humoured mockery of my 'imitators' & is not only civil to me but civil to Hyde & his big book, which it

Poems WBY wrote (*Bibl*, 156–7): 'This book for about thirty years brought me twenty or thirty times as much money as any other book of mine—no twenty or thirty times as much as all my other books put together'.

[2] Arthur Henry Bullen (1857–1920), publisher and scholar, was the partner of Harold Lawrence from 1891 to 1900. Their firm published WBY's *The Celtic Twilight* (1893) and *The Secret Rose* (1897). Although sometimes exasperated by Bullen's inefficient business methods, and his heavy drinking, WBY retained an affection for him and in *Aut* (447) described him as an 'Elizabethan scholar, a handsome man with a great mass of curly grey hair'. Bullen published WBY's *Collected Works* in 1908, and WBY was to support his application for a Civil List Pension in 1912–13.

describes as having bewildered them by showing what the celt really is like.[1]

Do you remember M & Madam Horus who took in Macgregor.[2] A poor lady of no very great intelligence but of much benevolence came to me yesterday in distress. They & three friends had planted themselves upon her & were running up bills in her name & she was in too great terror to send them away. I am not going to act in the matter my self, but my mystics are off to hunt them.

This poor lady had been in some remote part of the world when the English reverses in Africa began. She explained to me yesterday with great naivety, that she asked her self "what could have caused them, how could the English be defeated unless by black Art". Then suddenly she thought "It is Macgregor. Macgregor is doing it" & she came to England to get some mystic to stop him. In England she met the Horuses', fresh from rooking the terrible Macgregor himself & all went well until they told her that she was the woman clothed with the sun[3] & that the world was not convex but concave with the sun in the middle—& then she doubted. She is a good soul & felt that the world might have what shape it

[1] In 'The Twilight of the Celts' in the *Review of the Week* of 4 Jan 1901, Dell praised (263) WBY's 'fine work' but poured scorn on the 'literary invertebrates' guilty of 'boundless inept imitation', who had in 'their *own* word . . . snatched the Celtic banner from the hand of Mr. Yeats, and drained it to the dregs'. While commending Hyde for dealing 'the Celtic movement a well-meaning, mortal blow', he found little to admire in the Gaelic tradition he had revealed: 'We approached his volumes of translations with awe, and closed them in disappointment. We had looked for splendour, and we found a civilisation far below the Homeric. . . . We found much that was charming and delightful, little that was great . . . and since that unfortunate rending of the veil which hid the unknown magnificent the Celtic movement has been slowly dying.'

[2] Samuel Liddell MacGregor Mathers (1854–1918; see I. 497–9), magician and occultist, had initiated WBY into the GD in 1890. In 1892 he and his wife moved to Paris where they set up the Ahathoor Temple, but in April 1900 he quarrelled with the London Temple and his friendship with WBY came to an end. Shortly before this, Frank and Edith Jackson, fraudulent American occultists posing as Theodore and Laura Horos, duped Mathers into believing that she was the German Adept Anna Sprengel, the Order's supposed source of authority, and made off to London with some GD rituals. After an unsuccessful attempt to set up as occultists in South Africa, they returned to England in October 1900 and tried to infiltrate the GD. WBY was shortly to warn Mathers that they were back in circulation, and he replied on 12 Jan (MBY) with an account of their treachery in Paris. The Horoses made twelve court appearances in 1901 for fraudulent conspiracy before being convicted in December of the rape of Daisy Adams, a 16-year-old girl, at a spurious GD initiation ceremony. The notoriety that the trial, held in December 1901, brought upon the Order led it in June 1902 to change its name to the Hermetic Society of the Morgenröthe. The Horoses cheated numerous people in London, Brighton, Birkenhead, and other English towns between November 1900 and their indictment on 26 Sept 1901, but the woman who visited WBY may have been Mrs Bell Lewis, a faith-healer who ran a boarding-house in Gower Street, to whom the Horoses owed money.

[3] See Revelation 12: 1.

liked, but that she could not beleive that St John had made all that fuss about her.

Yours since always
W B Yeats

ALS Berg, with envelope addressed to Coole, postmark 'LONDON JA 9 01'.

To T. Sturge Moore, [*10 January 1901*]

18 Woburn Buildings | Euston Road.
Thursday.

My dear Sturge Moore: I am much better, endeed had I known yesterday evening [I] was going to be I would have ventured to go to you after all, I think. Sunday unhappily I must stay in for the middle of the day for I have promised to go out in the evening if well enough, & so must keep midday for work. Let me go to you one evening shortly.[1]

Yours sinly
W B Yeats

ALS Texas.

To T. Fisher Unwin, [*11 January 1901*]

18 Woburn Buildings | Euston Road.
Friday.

My dear Mr Unwin: I have written to A P Watt to enquire about American arrangements & will let you know the moment I hear.

Now to answer your question about the changes I have made.

I describe them pretty fully in the preface, but roughly I may say I have written a critical preface. I have added a new love scene to 'The Countess Cathleen' as well as new passages elsewhere. I believe I have made it a much stronger play than it was. I have also written in several new passages

---

[1] WBY evidently dined with Sturge Moore on Friday, 25 Jan, for the latter recorded in his diary (London) on 21 Jan: 'Met Yeats at tea he walked with me to Miss Dickens [?]talking about his spiritual theory of Shelley & other poets, I trying to convince him that reason was the sole ground for my preferences. No success, though I think he understood my objection to Countess Kathleen. He said he would come on Friday.' They also met on 4 Feb, when the conversation was apparently more earthy: 'With Binyon out to have dinner with Yeats, felt quarrelsome and thought Masefield very dull. Yeats brother had seen an old man bite off the testicles of calves when a boy. He did one after another. It was his trade.'

to the "Land of Hearts Desire"; and made some slight revisions in other parts of the book.[1]

Yr snly

W B Yeats

ALS Texas.

To MacGregor Mathers, [c. *11 January 1901*]

Mention in letter from Mathers, 12 January 1901.

A letter Mathers indignantly described as 'couched in friendly terms', telling him of the Horoses activities in England, and asking for information about them.[1]

MBY.

---

[1] The 2nd revised edition of *Poems* had appeared in May 1899. The 3rd edition (see p. 12) had a new preface, dated January 1901, an enlarged note on *The Countess Cathleen*, and the textual revisions that WBY mentions on p. 13.

[1] See p. 14, n. 2. Mathers's reply began with a fierce attack on WBY for 'associating yourself with a set of rascally rebels to thieve by a dishonourable trick the result of my work and labour for years. . . . You have indeed begun well! and now it only remains for you to betray your country to the Saxons with whom you seem so proud to associate yourself!' Although entertaining the 'profoundest contempt' for WBY, Mathers 'condescended to notice your communication' because of its mention of the Horoses, and he went on to give an account of their nefarious conduct in Paris: 'With regard to these persons, viz:—Swami Vive Ananda, alias Marie Louise of the Commune, alias Mrs. Horos, alias Mrs. Dutton, alias perhaps Mrs. Johnson! Mr. Theo Horos, alias Mr. Dutton, [and] Dr. Rose Adams: these three persons came to us some time ago with an introduction from a well known person here the Countess de Maffroy.' Mrs. Horos introduced herself and her companions as members of the GD, exhibited impressive knowledge of its grades, and 'stated that they had come to help us with our Isis movement here. . . . They were present at one if not two meetings of the Ahathoor Temple . . . and borrowed some Rituals from me as well as other things and books which they have not yet returned. So far from giving me "hundreds of pounds" (for the Isis movement), it was I who helped them with what little I had, for I offered all three as much hospitality as I could when I saw that getting meals was an object to them. They had to leave Rue Lauriston as their trunks were seized for rent; but a few weeks later they came to Paris and paid enough to take them away. They also called on me several times but I would not receive them. For the woman; she is probably the most powerful medium living and her mediumship differs from the usual. At times she has been controlled by very great and high forces, but much more frequently by evil spirits. For she is frequently a shell without honour, truth, or morality . . . I believe her and her accomplices to be emissaries of a *very powerful* secret Occult Order who have been trying for years to break up other Orders and especially my work, and the G.D. as connected therewith.' He added that 'on more than one occasion I conversed face to face with the *real* "Sapiens dominabitur astris" [*i.e. Anna Sprengel, see p. 14, n. 2*] in this woman', but that 'on another occasion I detected a demoniac simulacrum of that transformation'.

To T. Fisher Unwin, [*14 January 1901*]

18 Woburn Buildings | Euston Road
Monday.

Dear Mr Unwin: I conclude that my book of poems will be a nett book as before. If it were not a nett book I would understand your counting 13 as 12. In the present case I do not understand.[1]

Had you offered me 16 per cent I should have refused as I could get 20 per cent else where. You offered me 17½ and I accepted as I wished to go on publishing with you, but the 13 as 12 would reduce the 17½ to practically 16 per cent. On these grounds I must continue to object to 13 counting as 12.

Yrs snly
W B Yeats

ALS Texas.

To the Editor of the Daily Express *(Dublin), 16 January 1901*

18 Woburn Buildings, | Euston road, | N.W.

DEAR SIR—Please contradict par. about Irish Literary Theatre.[1] Definite announcement will be made in a few days. I can only say at present that the performances of the Irish Literary Theatre will take place as usual, and

---

[1] The Net Book Agreement, passed at a General Meeting of the Publisher's Association on 24 Feb 1899, had been drawn up to end the steady erosion of profits by underselling; it stipulated that a book published at a net price should not be sold at a lower price except under carefully defined conditions. Existing books were to be converted into net books by taking off one-sixth of the current price. Unwin had accepted the agreement in time for the 2nd edition of *Poems* (see p. 16 n. 1) to be a net book.

[1] On 12 Jan 1901 (5) the Dublin *Daily Express* had reprinted a paragraph from the English weekly, *Literature*, which suggested that the ILT was 'on the eve of disintegration. The play by Mr. Yeats and Mr. Moore, based on an old Celtic tale, which was to have been produced this year in Dublin, has been bought, we are informed, by Mrs. Patrick Campbell, and will be produced by her instead of by the Irish Literary Theatre. Unless Mr. Martyn steps into the field and produces a play of his own besides the short piece in Irish promised by Dr. Douglas Hyde, it is difficult to see how there is to be the usual week's performance in Dublin next May.' WBY or Moore must also have written to *Literature* (where the paragraph had appeared on 12 Jan [23]), as the following week it published a correction and announced that *Diarmuid and Grania* was to be 'first performed by Mr. F. R. Benson's company in Dublin, which has undertaken the production on the lines of the Irish Literary Theatre. Mrs. Campbell will afterwards produce it in London.' This correction was duly reprinted by the *Daily Express* on 19 Jan.

that no play by Mr. Moore and myself will be performed in London before
it has been performed in Dublin under the auspices of the Irish Literary
Theatre. Our own country has the first claims.—Yours, etc.,

W B Yeats

Printed letter, *Daily Express* (Dublin), 16 January 1901 (5).

To Alfred Ernest Scanlan,[1] [c. 21 January 1901]

Mention in letter from Scanlan, 22 January 1901.
Asking whether one's own or others' membership of the GD need be mentioned in Anglican or Catholic Confession.

LWBY I. 79–80.

To Lady Augusta Gregory, [23 January 1901]

18 Woburn Buildings | Euston Road
Wedny

My dear Lady Gregory: 'Ideals' is out & should reach you before this. I
have wasted a couple of hours over it & certainly I think it a really powerful little book. I think I like Hydes verses the best of anything [in] it.[1]
There have come at last quite good orders from Irish shops. Eason takes a
hundred 'on sale or return' & writes hopefully of future orders. Combridge
will display it in his window etc etc.[2] I send you a letter I have had from

---

[1] Alfred Ernest Scanlan (1857–1930) was a medical doctor practising in Middlesborough, Yorkshire. He had joined the Horus Temple, No. 5 (Bradford) of the GD in 1893, and advanced to the
Second Order on attaining the grade of 5 = 6 on 25 April 1896. WBY was possibly enquiring on
behalf of MG's sister, Kathleen Pilcher, or her cousin, May Gonne, both of whom had joined the
Order on 13 July 1900. Scanlan replied that Anglican and Catholic authorities agreed that, if a
Society had good as its aim, one's own membership need not be mentioned in Confession, and
that the membership of others must not be confessed as 'the penitent may not try to implicate
others'.

[1] *Ideals in Ireland*, edited by AG, contained essays by WBY ('The Literary Movement in Ireland'), AE, D. P. Moran, George Moore, Douglas Hyde, and Standish O'Grady. Hyde also contributed an Irish prose poem, 'Filleadh na Feinne' ('The Return of the Fenians') with an English
translation, to which WBY refers. AG, who had been anxious for some weeks at the book's non-
appearance, did not receive her copies until Saturday, 2 Feb, but by then had 'lost interest in it by
the long wait, & the cover is a disappointment' (diary, Berg).

[2] Eason and Son, 85 Abbey St., and Combridge and Co., 18 Grafton St., were Dublin booksellers.

Mac Colium[3]—I [*for* he] asked me if you could do anything a while back
& I said I would speak to you, & asked him to write what was wanted
hence this letter of his, of which I keep a copy.

This is miserable paper but I have no note paper left. I cannot write a
decent letter on this paper. It has the wrong associations.[4] I must make up
by a proper letter in a day or two.

I think Moran is merely puzzled as so many self taught men are puzzled
at finding a mysterious heirarchy, governed by standards they cannot
understand. The first result of a man's thinking for himself, when he has
no cultivated tradition behind him, is that he values nothing but the obviously useful, the obviously interesting, the obviously forcible. Such men—
I have met a few—commonly judge all poetry by Burns because they can
see his effect on Scots men & because he is easy to understand, or by some
like poet, & all prose by some writer like Huxley, some man with a lucid
argumentative style. They feal about all the rest like a certain socialist
workman who shouted out in the middle of a lecture of Taylors 'Religion
& political economy, the enemies of the working man'. The rest is to them
a trap, a mystification invented by the priviledged classes to keep the poor
man out of his rights. When the self taught man adds to this inevitable
instinct a special doctrine of his own, whether socialism or the gaelic
league, he grows as lively as a Dancing Dervish.[5] Moore, who is back well

---

[3] Evidently Fionán MacColuim (1875–1966), an Irish folk-song collector whose first volume,
Bolg an tSolátair (*Miscellany*), appeared in 1904. He was a member, with WBY and AG, of the
Irish Texts Society. From 1898 to 1899 he was secretary of the Gaelic League in London, where
he promoted numerous Irish organizations until he returned to Ireland in 1902 to become organizer of the League in Munster.

[4] The letter was written on ruled paper, taken from an exercise book.

[5] His controversies with Moran were WBY's first sustained encounter with the attitudes of
what he saw as a newly emergent Irish Catholic middle class, an experience which was gradually
to alter his perception of Irish cultural life and his position in it. In a letter dated 'Sunday' [21 Jan
1901; Berg], to which this is a reply, AG had told him she was 'vexed by that new article of
Moran's—I wonder what has stirred him up—someone must have been talking or writing or making mischief, for Hyde said he seemed completely puzzled by you but not spiteful as he seems to
be now' (see also *70 Years*, 394). The article to which she and WBY refer, entitled 'Literary
Expression', had appeared in the latest number of the *Leader* on 19 Jan, and attacked (334–5) 'a
school of literary cant that threatens to do much damage to the revival of the Irish national Intellect. . . . It is plainly the business of a man who desires to say anything to any given class of
people, to say it in such a manner that it will be understood [*sic*] of such people. . . . When we
all think in symbols let our poets say their say to us through their medium; but as at present we
have not as a nation reached a very high state of educational development, as we are rough,
homely, and unaccustomed to habits of sustained thinking, what the country requires, if it is to be
moved by poetry and ballads, is an Anglo-Irish Burns, and not an Anglo-Irish mystic' . . . Effective literary men who desire to influence their time, take the people as they find them, and aim to
make themselves as interesting as possible, other literary men—who wonder that they are not
either successful or effective—abandon themselves to inordinate egoism, consider the world was
made in order to supply them with material for theory-waving. They never dream of attempting
anything so low as interesting the people, but unanimously vote humanity a low thing, because it
. . . will not stand still and do nothing but admire them. . . . Our symbolists irritate us because of

satisfied with his proposed Dublin house, but sad at the thought of moving, tells me he talked to Moran like a father.[6] He pointed out that 'The Leader' should draw to it everybody, who beleived in intellectual nationalism & that it was no use Moran's trying to change me by abusing me, for I wouldnt & couldnt change, but that he might keep me from writing for him, if he went on abusing me. Moran replied why did I not write like Burns etc etc. Moore replied 'could he change the shape of his nose by trying' which ought to have been conclusive.[7]

The Benson matter is settled—unless the Queens death which shuts all theatres for a couple of weeks breaks Benson—but the M[rs] Pat Campbell matter still waits a final settlement.[8] I wrote last Monday to hurry up her

their "superior" airs, and because we know the temper of our degenerate and anglicised generation is such that it will fall an easy prey to any new sham. They irritate us all the more because we think they are the weak victims of a senseless shibboleth, a literary catch cry. There are many men now wasting their time writing symbols who are quite capable of writing sense.' The *Leader* was to continue to attack WBY at frequent intervals, and on 19 Nov 1913 WBY described Moran (diary, MBY) as 'the most offensive of Irish clerical personalities, but an amiable fat man in presence'.

Thomas Henry Huxley (1825–95), Darwinian naturalist, determinist, and scientific positivist, had argued that man's certain knowledge does not extend beyond states of consciousness, and first coined the term 'agnosticism' to describe his philosophical and religious position. As such he stood for everything that WBY hated in Victorian thought and attitudes, and in *Aut* (157, 168) is lumped in with 'the Huxley, Tyndall, Carolus Duran, Bastien-Lepage rookery'. John F. Taylor (1850–1902), a Dublin barrister, journalist, and 'obscure great orator', whose defence of the Irish language is quoted both in *Aut* (96–7) and the Aeolus episodes in *Ulysses*, was a conservative nationalist who had little time for agrarian or proletarian agitation.

[6] George Moore had moved to London in 1869, and thereafter lived the life of an absentee Irish landlord. Now, outraged by Kitchener's brutalities in the Boer War, he had determined to shake the dust of England from his feet and return to Dublin. He made the move in early April of this year, taking a house at 4 Upper Ely Place. A notice in the *Academy* of 16 Mar 1901 announced (219) that he intended to contribute weekly articles to the *Leader* explaining 'why he found existence in England no longer bearable', but no such articles appeared.

[7] Moran had alluded to this conversation in his article of 19 Jan (see above, n. 5): 'Having expressed the view to a well-known Irish literary man that the writings of another Irish literary man were all stuff and nonsense, he demurred. "Do you understand that?" we demanded, pointing out a specimen of his work. "I don't," was the candid reply, "but I take it that it is my misfortune that I am unable to grasp his meaning." We recognise the certain amount of sense that is behind an attitude of that kind; but we see clearly, too, that in the present state of Ireland such an attitude . . . will work a great deal of harm.' The need for an Irish Burns, to which he had referred in his latest article, was a preoccupation of Moran's. In criticizing the remoteness of the '"Celtic" symbolists' in the *Leader* of 22 Dec 1900 (see p. 6, n. 11), he had asserted (264) that there was 'no Anglo-Irish poet . . . who can talk straight to the heart as Burns talked to the heart of Scotland', and he returned to this point, with specific reference to WBY, on 29 Dec. WBY was to address this challenge directly in his 1902 essay 'What is Popular Poetry', by arguing (*E & I*, 6) that Burns was not an authentically 'popular' poet, but articulated a modern, deracinated, middle-class sensibility: 'Despite his expressive speech which sets him above all other popular poets, he has the triviality of emotion, the poverty of ideas, the imperfect sense of beauty of a poetry whose most typical expression is in Longfellow'.

[8] The closing of the theatres as a mark of respect after Queen Victoria's death on 22 Jan did threaten to have serious consequences for *Diarmuid and Grania*, and on her return to London on 9 Feb AG recorded in her diary (Berg) that 'Benson has been nearly ruined by having to close his

business man, as I imagine we should make some kind of authoratative statement.

In the middle of Feb 'The Three Kings'[9] give a conversatione, at which I lecture on chanting & Mrs Emery & Miss Mathers chant.[10] Will you be over by then.

Yrs alway

W B Yeats

A thousand thanks for the pheasants. I kept one & brought one to Miss Horniman.[11]

ALS Berg, with envelope addressed to Coole, postmark, 'LONDON W.C. JA 25 01', and enclosing a cutting from the *United Irishman*.[12]

theatre for the Queen's death, & may break altogether, & Mrs. Pat is so cross at having lost thousands from the same cause that she won't make a definite offer'. Benson survived to produce the play, but Mrs Campbell finally declined it, largely because WBY and Moore insisted on a first production in Dublin.

[9] The Fellowship of the Three Kings was a society organized by WBY and others in January 1900. In February 1900 WBY lectured to it on Shelley's mystical ideas; in October 1900 he spoke on the Theatre; and in May 1901 he was to give his essay on 'Magic'. Members of the society included Algernon Blackwood, who also belonged to the GD, and John Watkins, the occult bookseller. Watkins's son told Virginia Moore (*The Unicorn*, [New York, 1954], 133) that the object of the Society was 'the study of Mysticism . . . not Occultism', but the membership, and the subjects of WBY's lectures, suggest that it was interested in both topics. It was also a literary society, and on 17 Mar 1901 Pamela Colman Smith wrote to Albert Biglow Paine (Huntington) that WBY had asked her to give a performance of *The Countess Cathleen* 'to the "Brotherhood of the Three Kings" a crazy Irish sort of literary society!' There is no record of this performance.

[10] Florence Farr Emery (FF; 1860–1917; see I. 485–6), actress, author, and member of the GD, had divorced her actor husband, Edward Emery, in 1894. WBY discovered her beautiful speaking voice in a production of John Todhunter's *A Sicilian Idyll* at Bedford Park in 1890. The two had demonstrated their theories on chanting to the ILS in December 1900, and were to continue experiments and demonstrations regularly over the coming decade. Anna Mather had played Oona to FF's Aleel in the first production of *The Countess Cathleen* in May 1899. She gave frequent verse-speaking recitals in London and was to assist intermittently in the chanting experiments until March 1909.

[11] In her letter of 21 Jan (see above, n. 5) AG had told WBY 'I sent you some pheasants yesterday just to show they are no longer like chickens!' Annie Elizabeth Fredericka Horniman (AEFH; 1860–1937; see Appendix) was WBY's friend, amanuensis, fellow member in the GD, and patron of his dramatic aspirations from 1894 to 1910.

[12] A cutting of an article, 'The Fate of the Clann Ui H-Eilighe', a satire in bardic style on the reunification of the Irish Parliamentary Party in which Ruadhmon (John Redmond) makes peace with the Clann Ui H-Eilighe (the Healys). It was written by William Stanton Pyper under his pseudonym 'Lugh', and had appeared in the *United Irishman* on 19 Jan 1901 (6–7).

To W. J. Stanton Pyper,[1] *[? 24 January 1901]*

18 Woburn Buildings | Euston Road | London
Thursday

My dear Pyper: I should have written to you days ago about a conversation
I have had with Watt, but I have been revising my poems for a new edition. I asked Watt about your book and he said, to my surprise, that war
books have not been doing well that the only book he knew that had—he
must have meant lately for there is always the great success of Fitzpatricks
book—was Conan Doyles; but that he was sending your book about.[2] This
is not very cheering but I thought it better to tell you. I expect that the
truth is that the British are sick of this business. They thought they were
going to get a little cheap glory & they find that they are in for a deal of
expensive ignominy. I should have thought however that you were certain
of a publisher.

No I did not see that note about Moore. I beleive I have missed a number on Tara which Miss Gonne asked me to look out for.[3] I wish you
would send me a copy.

[1] William Stanton Pyper, the son of a naval officer, was a journalist associated with the *United
Irishman,* for which he wrote under the name of 'Lugh' (see p. 21, n. 12). WBY was hoping to
get his book on the Boer War published through the agency of A. P. Watt, but it never appeared
(see *LWBY* I. 81). Pyper had first met WBY at Katharine Tynan's house in the late 1880s and
recalled him in the *Dublin Magazine* of January 1924 (522) as 'tall and lithe, with jet-black locks
and pale thoughtful face, few could mistake him for what he was, and yet, in spite of our admiration for him, we could not help feeling that he had already begun to act the part'. Recalling an
incident when a policeman ejected them from a Dublin museum because WBY was declaiming
his verse, Pyper took credit 'for having recognised in Yeats from the very first, something that set
him apart from the rest of us, and I subscribed to the first volume he ever published'. Pyper subsequently emigrated but returned to Ireland after the Great War. His translation of V. I.
Nemirovitch-Dantchenko's *With A Diploma* was published in 1915.

[2] J. P. Fitzpatrick's *The Transvaal from Within: A Private Record of Public Affairs* (1899) was an
apology for Uitlander action in the Transvaal during the period of the Jameson Raid in 1895–6.
The book had been written in August 1896, but was banned by President Kruger. It was privately
circulated in London in June 1899 and published in an enlarged version in September of the same
year, during the renewed tension that preceded the outbreak of the Boer War in November. Its
theme was the need for Britain to intervene in the Transvaal to ensure justice, and to put a stop
to the financial scandals, race-hatred, and corrupt government that Fitzpatrick alleged flourished
there. It was an immediate best-seller, and did much to swing popular opinion behind the declaration of war. J. 'Percy' Fitzpatrick (1862–1931) was born in South Africa, and after school in
England returned to the Transvaal in 1884, where he became a partner in a gold-mining company. He served as Secretary of the Reform Committee and was imprisoned after the Jameson
Raid. He was MP for Pretoria East in the Union Parliament from 1910 to 1920.

Arthur Conan Doyle's narrative account of the hostilities in South Africa, *The Boer War,* was
first published in the autumn of 1900, and went through 16 revised editions, culminating in a
final, post-war version late in 1903.

[3] On 5 Jan (4) the *United Irishman* had published a paragraph on the ILS's blackballing of
George Moore: 'A hundred years hence a member of the Irish Literary Society of London . . .
will be unveiling a memorial window or a monument to the rejected one, and everyone present

It was more or less inevitable that the "United Irishman" & "Leader" should fall out & if the "United Irishman" does not let criticism become more violent than precise, as our Irish way is, all will be as should be. "The Leaders" weakness is that it tries to convince people that a nation can drop a century & half out of its life, as if Irish history ceased to be Irish history when the men that made it spoke English. The "United Irishman" should stand for the whole nation and affirm that cause against the "Leaders" catholic gaelic sectarianism. "The Leaders" plan for an Irish Ireland in other things than politics was needed however.[4]

You will get, I mean the United Irishman will, a copy of 'Ideals in Ireland' a book of essays on the language movement chiefly, by some half dozen writers. Should you have anything to do with the reviewing of it, you should keep in mind that it was *refused unread* by two Dublin publishers, Sealey Bryers & Gill, & *accepted unread* by a London publisher. I dare say you know that 'The New Irish Library' was rejected by every Dublin publisher & yet people tell us we should publish in Ireland. O'Grady is the one hope in the matter.[5] Eglington's little book is very good in its queer

will weep in sympathy. What a red letter day it will be, and how proud the by-standers will feel and how they will despise the Philistines who boycotted George Moore when he was alive! It takes a century to make anyone "respectable". Burns, Shelley, Clarence Mangan, Byron, are all "respectable" now. So there is hope for poor Mr George Moore!' Members of the Society had objected to Moore because of anti-Catholic and anti-Irish sentiments in some of his early works, and WBY was waging a vigorous campaign on his behalf; see below pp. 49–51.

In the same issue (5) the *United Irishman* published an atmospheric piece on 'Tara of the Kings' by 'M. Q.' Evoking a Christmas visit to Tara, the ancient capital of Gaelic Ireland, the writer recalls that 'the Christian festival and the pagan ruins brought me strange sad thoughts'. A vision of 'shuddering misty forms, gazing curiously at me' resolved itself into the shape of 'one who was tall and fair, and very beautiful. . . . the guardian of the Sovreignty of Ireland. . . . in her grave blue eyes was the calm knowledge of Destiny'. When, later, the vision reappeared the air seemed filled with the words 'Tara, Tara of the Kings shall be free, but first the river of blood shall flow. Those who would serve me must accept the sacrifice.' The sex of the writer is not divulged, and 'M. Q.' may be a compositor's error for 'M. G.'; the style and allusions—the mixture of Christian and pagan associations, the seeing of visions in ancient places, references to the Lia Fail (the Stone of Destiny), and apocalyptic prophesies—are characteristic of Maud Gonne, who was in Ireland for Christmas 1900.

[4] The *United Irishman* had welcomed the first appearance of the *Leader* in September 1900, but the anti-clerical Griffith soon found Moran's pietism excessive, his Gaelic racialism bigoted, and his political ideas suspect. On 29 Dec 1900 (4) the paper attacked Moran for describing the call 'Ireland a nation' as a 'cry for the moon', and denounced 'the sham that bellows out that non-speaking Irishmen are not Irish, while it can't speak Irish itself'. On 12 Jan 1901 (4) it accused the *Leader* of harbouring 'sly pro-English sentiments', but, in line with WBY's views on non-violence, went on to explain that it did 'not desire to write at all harshly of our contemporary, but we advise it to take its own advice and discard sham'. Griffith thought this advice was disregarded and continued his criticism: on 13 Apr (4) he described the magazine as 'Whig Catholic', and on 17 Aug (2) denounced its bigotry. The fact that the *Leader* now had a larger circulation than the *United Irishman* may also have fuelled his hostility.

[5] Reviewing *Ideals in Ireland* in the *United Irishman* on 23 Feb 1901 (2), Pyper not merely kept WBY's facts in mind but, adding some melodramatic flourishes of his own, devoted nearly a third of his notice to the iniquities of Irish publishers. The *United Irishman* had already drawn attention

furtive way.[6] I will send your letter to Erskine as soon as I can find his address.[7]

Please do not forget to send me that copy of UI with Moore note & the Tara article.

Yours sny
W B Yeats

P.S. I asked my publisher to send "UI" a review copy of "The Shadowy Waters" not because I thought it the kind of book "UI" could or would or

to the shortcomings of Irish publishing in an article, 'Irish Authors and Irish Publishers', on 12 Jan 1901 (3) and continued the attack in a review, 'Two Books by Irishmen', on 2 Feb (6). The New Irish Library, established in 1892 to supply the long-felt want of enterprising Dublin publishers (see I. 500–1), had been taken over by the English firm of T. Fisher Unwin, after the Irish-born publisher Edmund Downey withdrew from the venture. Standish James O'Grady (1846–1928; see I. 501–3), an historian, novelist, and journalist, had recently set up a publishing firm in Kilkenny, and had just issued John Eglinton's collection of essays, *Pebbles from a Brook*, but was to produce very few further books. In his review of Eglinton's book in the *United Irishman* of 2 Feb, Pyper commented (6) that 'Ireland owes a debt of gratitude to Mr. Standish O'Grady for courageously coming forward at the present time and standing in the gap. But for him this country would have remained in the disgraceful position of not having a single publisher worthy of the name.' Pyper's vehemence was perhaps not wholly unrelated to his difficulties in getting his own book published (see above, n. 1).

[6] Both Pyper and WBY reviewed Eglinton's *Pebbles from a Brook* for the *United Irishman*. Pyper (see above, n. 5) detected 'a tinge of "preciousness" . . . here and there, and the influence of Goethe. . . . But these cannot weigh down the scale. "In spite of the Scylla and Charybdis of sensuality and *ennui*, the human soul is enamoured of the ideal." This is the keynote of the book, a book well worth reading.' WBY's notice did not appear until 9 Nov 1901 (*UP* II. 255–62), because, he confessed, he had been put off reading it 'for many months by certain petulances which are strange in so scrupulous a writer', but now, in spite of serious reservations and Eglinton's 'curious, furtive style', he found the central argument 'formidable': 'He thinks that States and every other institution of man begin by fostering men's lives, and then gradually perfect themselves at the expense of men's lives, becoming more and more separated from life . . . so that men, if they would keep alive . . . must fly from them . . .' While agreeing with Eglinton's criticism of modern civilization, WBY could not accept his remedies: 'that which has made John Eglinton turn from all National ideas and see the hope of the world in individual freedom . . . has made me see the hope of the world in re-arrangements of life and thought which make men feel that they are part of a social order, of a tradition, of a movement wiser than themselves.' John Eglinton was the pseudonym of the Dublin-born William Kirkpatrick Magee (1868–1961), who had known WBY since their days at the High School. After a distinguished career at Trinity College, Dublin, he became an assistant at the National Library, and at this time was much under the influence of Emerson, Thoreau, and Wordsworth. WBY had reviewed his first book, *Two Essays on the Remnant*, in the *Bookman* of May 1895, and their 1898 controversy in the Dublin *Daily Express*, over the nature of Irish drama, had subsequently appeared as *Literary Ideals in Ireland*. From 1904–5 Eglinton was to co-edit the rationalist monthly, *Dana*, but he moved to England after the establishment of the Irish Free State. His account of WBY appeared in *Irish Literary Portraits* (1935), and in a copy of *Some Essays and Passages*, inscribed for James Healy in July 1938 (Stanford), WBY wrote of him: 'Eglinton was the sceptic of our movement, always for the individual against the race. We lived in our better moments.'

[7] The Hon Joseph Stuart Ruaraidh Erskine (1869–1960), the second son of the 5th Baron Erskine, was a Scottish nationalist and Gaelic enthusiast. Pyper probably wished to communicate with him about his forthcoming monthly bilingual periodical, *An Bard*, the April publication of which was announced in the *United Irishman* on 9 Feb (4). At this time Erskine was living at Lonach, Strathdon, Aberdeenshire.

should review but because somebody in the office might like to have it. I hope it reached safely. It was addressed only "United Irishman" Dublin.[8]

Moran is certainly bewildering this last week. His reply to Rolleston, who points out an obvious contradiction in his argument, is a wonderful cloud of words, & his ar[g]ument in a different article that as the Irish people are "rude & rough & lacking in the power of sustained thinking" or some such words, all Irish writers should become as they are—for that is the upshot—shows an almost pathetic ignorance of the way literature is written.[9] Like so many Irishmen he cannot distinguish between journalism, which is written for a man's own day & literature which is written, however it may fail of its purpose, for all days.

WBY

T copy Private.

To Florence Farr, [*29 January 1901*].

18 Woburn Buildings | Euston Road
Tuesday.

Cara Soror S.S.D.D.,[1] I was amazed at what you told me last night about action in Council to legalize groups.[2] I agreed with you, as the representative

---

[8] The *United Irishman* did not review the 1900 edition of *The Shadowy Waters* because, as Griffith reported on 9 Feb (4), the copy sent by WBY had 'not yet reached us. We have had no direct legal opinion on the contents of "The Shadowy Waters", but so far as our own observation goes, it contains nothing which can be construed as in any way treasonable to the British Constitution. Further, we happen to know that divers copies of the book have been despatched through the post and have reached their destination. The book is offered for sale at various bookshops, and no copies have yet been seized. Now, we are loathe to believe that Post Office officials are in the habit of stealing books addressed to THE UNITED IRISHMAN. It may be a case of "inadvertence". Perhaps the Post Office can resolve our doubts.'

[9] In his article, 'Literary Expression', which appeared in the *Leader* on 19 Jan (see p. 19, n. 5), Moran had asserted that 'we are rough, homely, and unaccustomed to habits of sustained thinking'.

[1] The initials of FF's GD motto, Sapientia Sapienti Dona Data (Wisdom is Given to the Wise as a Gift).

[2] The expulsion of MacGregor Mathers from his dictatorial leadership of the GD in April 1900 (see p. 14, n. 2) had by no means ended the Order's internal dissensions, and this letter is the prelude to a crisis that was to alter irrevocably WBY's position in it. FF had taken charge of the London Temple, the Isis-Urania, in April 1897, and with Mathers's approval, weakened its structure by dispensing with examinations and permitting the formation of special 'groups' for the study of occult matters. Her 'Sphere' group, the largest with twelve members, was devoted to the study of Egyptian symbolism and rituals. Following Mathers's departure, WBY and the readmitted AEFH were eager to root out the irregularities that had been allowed to flourish, in particular the Sphere group, which they thought divisive, badly instructed, and dangerously heterodox. They had begun their attack in September 1900, accusing FF of unauthorized use of the Order's rooms, and

of your group, on a compromise. You were (1) to invite Theorici who were in sympathy to join your group—this you have done I am told, (2) you were to write an account of formulae for Theorici generally (I have your letter on this subject) (3) you were to admit no more Zelatores. We have several (2) times discussed the compromise and assumed it as the basis of action. I agreed to it under the belief that it would satisfy Soror *Fortiter*,[3] but when I found that it would not I honourably held to it, and when she decided not to stand again for office and to resign from the Twelve (as she felt unable to work under it) I made no serious attempt to prevent her as the great question was to prevent irritation. I now ask you as a woman of honour to carry it out on your side. It is your manifest duty to leave no stone unturned to prevent your group, or any member of it, from doing anything against this compromise, and, should you fail, it is your duty to oppose to your utmost on council any attempt of the kind & should the majority of your group go against you to resign any position you may hold in the group, to cease to be responsible for it in other words.

I shall await your reply with considerable anxiety as much will depend upon it. If you will keep faith with me—and I cannot suppose that you mean to do anything else—we can do much together. The G.D. is only part of a much greater work—work that may bring you greater opportunities (I am [*remainder of letter in WBY's hand*] ⟨unable to tell you all about the theatrical project, as it concerns the secret of others, but I tell you now, in strict confidence, that I have been approched by a group of writers & artists with a view to a theatre of art.⟩) We can make a great movement &

of withholding valuable occult information, but she and her followers, nettled by what they regarded as officious and bullying behaviour, counter-attacked. She and WBY had, however, recently reached a truce, whereby her group would be tolerated, although not legally sanctioned, provided that she stopped drawing unproficient members from the lower grades, and admitted only those who had become Theorici ($5 = 6$). In a long 'semi-official statement to the Theorici', written on 17 Jan, probably shortly after her 'compromise' with WBY, FF had set out her grievances and described her group's occult practices. She also posted a notice in the Order's headquarters announcing that any sympathetic members of the Order could join her group 'on their attainment of the grade of Theoricus'.

This compromise was jeopardized when on 25 Jan Marcus Blackden asked AEFH to place motions to legalize groups on the agenda for Executive Council meeting of 1 Feb. WBY discovered on 28 Jan that FF knew and approved of this initiative, and this letter is a desperate but vain attempt to dissuade her from supporting the motions.

[3] Fortiter Et Recte (Bravely and Justly) was the motto of AEFH, who had been expelled from the Order by Mathers in December 1896. After Mathers's own expulsion in 1900, WBY had invited her back as Scribe (Secretary). She was even more strongly opposed to FF's group than he, believing that it disseminated esoteric knowledge to those unqualified to understand it, and that its ill-drafted rituals left it open to dangerous lower occult powers—an opinion corroborated to her satisfaction when she felt herself bombarded with a hostile force by a statue in the British Museum. Although implacable in her disapproval of the groups, she had, at WBY's urging, agreed to 'show my fraternal feeling by helping to hush up the scandal'. The 'Twelve Seniors' were the twelve most advanced Adepts who nominated the Moderator, the Scribe, and the seven Adepti Litterati to the Executive Council.

in more than magical things but I assure you that if (through week vitality, through forgetfulness or through any other cause) you make it difficult for us to reley upon one another perfectly you make everything impossible.[4] ⟨It is not that I should wish to⟩ I know through long experience that practical work is an endless worry, an endless waste of time, unless every body carries out their promises, in serious matters, with the most scrupulous care for letter & spirit alike. Years ago Rolleston failed me in the negociations over the 'New Irish Library', & he has made all work in common impossible. We are very good friends but we have never sat on a committee togeather since & I do not think we ever will. We agreed upon a *modus vivendi*, between two contrary projects & he abandoned it, while I was in Ireland, under the influence of Gavan Duffy flatteries & promises.[5] In the arts, & in social life one can be tolerant, one can forgive, in public life one can seldom forgive without doing great mischief.

Yrs fratny
DEDI[6]

I am very sorry to have to write you a letter like this.

AD, partly dictated to AEFH, signed WBY; MBY.

To Lady Augusta Gregory, [*31 January 1901*]

My dear Lady Gregory—
    Yes Tuesday night. I am delighted that you are coming.
    The books should go to you to day. It was a note to Moores essay that caused delay.[1]

Yrs ev
W B Yeats

ALCS Berg, with envelope addressed to Coole, postmark 'LONDON W C JA 31 01'.

[4] A barely veiled threat that her heterodoxy in magical matters would jeopardize her participation in his secret plans with Sturge Moore and Ricketts for a literary theatre in London (see p. 8).
[5] See I. 329–36; 343–52. In 1892 Rolleston had told Sir Charles Gavan Duffy of WBY's plans to publish a series of Irish books through Unwin. The two had subsequently persuaded Unwin to adopt this scheme as the 'New Irish Library', and WBY, excluded from it, never forgot what he considered Rolleston's breach of trust, writing in *Aut* (228) that 'it would have surprised and shocked him if any man had told him that he was unforgiven'.
[6] WBY's motto was Demon Est Deus Inversus (The Devil is God Inverted), an occult expression of his enduring belief that polarity and opposition are constitutative of a final Unity. He had probably taken it from the chapter-title of Section IX, Part II, Book I, of Madame Blavatsky's *The Secret Doctrine* (1888).

[1] AG travelled to London on the night of 4 Feb, 'the worst crossing I ever remember, storm all the way, & my sickness never ceased' (diary, Berg). In his lecture, 'Literature and the Irish

To Mark Perugini,[1] [*1 February 1901*]

18 Woburn Buildings | Euston Road.
Friday.

Dear Sir: I am afraid I may have misled you about 'the Aldine.' I am ashamed that my memory for facts is so bad & it is so long since I did my Blake editing that I mixed up Pickering with the Aldine Pickering, which I asked for at 'The Museum' yesterday to verify my impression but found to be in use, is I conclude the little black covered book containing 'Long John Brown & Little Mary Bell.' If this be so it is Pickering who had access to a MSS source since seemingly lost—(Ellis knows more of these things than I & has a better memory) & gave some three or four poems from it. 'The Aldine' (W. M. Rossetti's book) used 'The MSS Book' & may have copyright to this small extent.[2] W M Rossetti adopted Dante Gabriel Rossetti's too copious emendation of Blake & made some new ones of his own.[3] Bell & Son may (though they have not hitherto, I think, claimed it) have copy right in these emendations & I conclude the publishers of Gillchrist's

---

Language', delivered on 22 Feb 1900 to supporters of the ILT and subsequently published in the *New Ireland Review*, Moore had announced that in 1901 they had 'decided to give a play in our own language—the language which to our great disgrace, we do not understand. Alas! there will be fewer in the theatre who will understand the Irish text than a Latin or Greek one; so the play will be performed for the sake of the example it will set.' When she republished the lecture in *Ideals in Ireland* (1901) AG added a note (45) saying that she did 'not agree with Mr. Moore in thinking there will be but few in the theatre who will understand an Irish play. He underrates the success of the Language Movement in Dublin.' At the last moment Moore had insisted that a red-ink slip should be pasted into the book, explaining that at the time of the lecture he 'did not know of the extraordinary revival of the Irish language in Dublin'.

[1] Mark Edward Perugini (1876–1948), London-born author, editor, and journalist, published *Selections from the Works of William Blake* in June 1901. WBY had a copy in his library (*YA4*, 280).

[2] WBY's mix-up is understandable. He had evidently confused an edition of Blake by William Pickering (1796–1854) with one by his son, Basil Montague Pickering (1835–78). Although William Pickering was the original publisher of the Aldine edition of the British poets (1830–53), his edition of *Songs of Innocence and Experience* (1839) was not part of this series. Nor was Basil Pickering's 'verbatim' edition of 1866, which published 'Long John Brown and Little Mary Bell' for the first time from Blake's 'Ballads Manuscript'. It was this Pickering edition, or its successor, *The Poems of William Blake* (1874), that WBY ordered in the British Museum Library. As copyright holder, and in protest against the editorial liberties taken by the Rossettis, Basil Pickering would not allow W. M. Rossetti to print the poem in his Aldine edition of *The Poetical Works of William Blake*, published later in 1874 by George Bell (who had acquired the rights to the series after the death of William Pickering).

Edwin John Ellis (1848–1916; see 1, 484–5) was a poet and painter, with whom WBY had edited *The Works of William Blake Poetic, Symbolic and Critical* (1893).

[3] Dante Gabriel Rossetti (1828–82) acquired Blake's notebook ('The Rossetti Manuscript') which he used in making copious editorial alterations and additions to Blake's poems in vol. II of Alexander Gilchrist's *The Life of William Blake*, published by Macmillan in 1863.

'Life' might claim copyrights in D. G. Rossetti's emendations, though they can hardly have ever claimed them as almost every editor has adopted them. I have given Blake's own text very carefully in the Muses Library & I cannot think anybody has any copyrights in it.[4] If Bullen does not write & make an appointment—I left my card on him some days ago—I will send him your first letter & let you know what he says.

Yrs ever

W B Yeats

ALS Private, with envelope addressed to 1 Brooklyn Road, Shepherds Bush, W., postmark 'LONDON W.C. FE 1 01'.

To the Twelve Seniors of the Golden Dawn,[1]
2 February 1901

18, Woburn Buildings, | Euston Road.

Feb. 2nd 1901.

To the Twelve Seniors.

Care et V H Fratres & Sorores[2]

I do not know whether it would be your wish to nominate me as a member of the Executive Council. But I think that it may save you trouble if I asked you not to do so, you will have no difficulty in understanding my

---

[4] In his Muses' Library edition of *The Poems of William Blake* (1893) WBY had followed the Pickering tradition of copying Blake's text unamended (see 1. 353). Neither he nor Perugini included 'Long John Brown and Little Mary Bell' in their editions, but Perugini did acknowledge the permission of the present copyright holders, including 'Lawrence & Bullen and Mr. W. B. Yeats . . . for permission to use their text of some of the poems' (xlii).

[1] WBY's appeal to FF (see pp. 25–7) had been unsuccessful; the Council Meeting of 1 Feb quickly developed into a confrontation in which WBY and AEFH, who wanted to restore the Order to its rules and hierarchical structure, were opposed by the rest (mostly members of the Sphere group), who found such structures constricting and tyrannical, and who had been offensive in expressing their views. This letter, written to the twelve senior members of the Second Order, who were responsible for nominating candidates for the Executive Council, shows WBY still smarting; however, a General Meeting had been called for 26 Feb to settle contentious matters once and for all, and prior to this WBY was to compose three more reasoned letters to all the Adepti of the Second Order in an attempt to persuade them to repudiate the policies of the Council and abide by the constitution of the Order.

[2] i.e. Dear and Truly Honoured Brothers & Sisters.

decision when I have brought to your attention a very remarkable scene which took place yesterday at a meeting of the Executive Council.[3]

Two resolutions were brought forward, one proposing that two extra Scribes be appointed by the Council to ensure that the Scribe appointed by the whole body of the Adepti should not juggle with the election papers; and one proposing for still greater security that the balloting papers of country members should be sent to 36, Blythe Road, and not to the Scribe, who alone is responsible for their safe keeping.

These resolutions were withdrawn as soon as the proposers discovered that her scheme, read to them at the opening of the meeting, gave her no opportunity of discovering which papers she might possibly disapprove of, but on the contrary insured the secrecy of the ballot. I need hardly point out that this made matters no better, but only made these amazing suspicions the plainer. It is my duty to add that only one of the Adepti and he not the most guilty has apologized.[4] I feel that it would ill become my dignity to continue longer than my duty towards the Order requires, an elected member of a Council where party feeling has run to such extravagance. I am ready to teach anything I may know of magical philosophy to any fratres and sorores who may desire; but I shall take no other part in the business of the Second Order until its moral health has been restored. I have sat on many committees in my own country and elsewhere, but I am proud to say that I have never met among the mechanics, farmers and shop-assistants with whom I have worked in Ireland, a stress of feeling so ignoble or resolutions so astonishing as those I had to listen to yesterday. I desire to keep my reverence for the august symbols of our Order, but I could not do so if I had to sit through more scenes of the kind before the

[3] WBY had been nominated to the Executive Council of the Second Order at the reforming General Meeting of 21 Apr 1900 which followed MacGregor Mathers's expulsion. New elections were due at the end of February 1901, and AEFH had been asked to draw up procedures for these but her plans were attacked at length at the Council Meeting of 1 Feb. Marcus Blackden (1864–1934), under his GD motto Ma Wahanu Thesi, opposed her suggestion that she should be responsible for sending out and counting the ballot papers, and urged that two more Scribes should be appointed and voting slips be in triplicate so that no 'errors' could occur. When AEFH explained the confusion this would cause, the proposal was dropped—whereupon WBY, as she reported, 'got very excited . . . he burst out with something like this,—"You let that proposal drop when you found that Fortiter could not burn the ballot-papers she objected to". That made a great scene of excitement, the "group" all calling for "order" as soon as a voice was raised in defence of the Scribe' (Harper, 228). Robert Palmer-Thomas ('Lucem Spero') then interrogated her as to where she intended to open the voting papers, and there were demands that this should be done at the Order's premises at 36 Blythe Road, rather than in the privacy of her apartment. Finally AEFH was reduced to exhibiting the actual ballot papers and envelopes, to show that there could be no tampering with them. The meeting, which also legalized the groups, brought home to WBY how deeply suspicious the other members were of AEFH, and to some extent of himself, and also showed him how powerful the Sphere group was on the Executive Council.

[4] AEFH reported (Harper, 233) that at the end of the meeting Blackden 'showed a sense of good behaviour by trying to assure me that he had meant no insult'.

very door of the Tomb of Christian Rosenkreuz in the very presence of the Cross of the Obligation.[5]

Vale Sub Umbram Alarum Tuarum.[6]

יהוה

D.E.D.I.

TLS Private. Harper, 235–6.

To T. Fisher Unwin, 2 February [*1901*]

⟨HI MONTAGU MANSIONS, | PORTMAN SQUARE. W.⟩
18 Woburn Buildings | Euston Road.
Feb 2

Dear Mr Unwin: I send you the MSS of my new edition of 'The Poems' & will send corrected agreement tomorrow.

Yr ever
W B Yeats

ALS Texas.

To the Adepti of R.R. et A.C., [c. *10 February 1901*]

A First Letter to the Adepti of R.R. et A.C. upon the Present Crisis.—[1]

Care et V. H. Fratres & Sorores,
I was among those who invited you some months ago to throw off an unendurable burden and to make this order worthy of its high purpose.

[5] According to tradition, Father Christian Rosenkreuz had founded the Rosicrucian Society in the 15th century. The Second Order initiate took the oath or obligation of secrecy and spiritual purification on the wooden Cross of Obligation, or Suffering, to which he or she was tied in a symbolical crucifixion, and subsequently entered the heptagonal Tomb of the Adepti, the symbolic burying place of Christian Rosenkreuz, where the magical instruments were consecrated. Spaces had been left in the typescript for the words 'Tomb of Christian Rosenkreuz' and 'Cross of the Obligation', which were later added in pen so that the typist should not be privy to these secret phrases.

[6] 'Farewell, Under The Shade Of Your Wings. Jehovah.' This was the form of valediction recommended as 'especially desirable' for members of the Order by William Wynn Westcott in his manual 'The History of the Rosicrucian Order', since its effect was 'to directly maintain the psychic link which has ever served to bind the Members of this Ancient and Honourable Order one to the other;—in this light it is something more than a mere form'. No doubt WBY thought it even more 'especially desirable' at such a time of dissension. The four Hebrew letters are those of the Tetragrammaton for Jehovah.

[1] This letter, addressed to all the members of the Second or Inner Order of the GD, also known as the Order of the Rose of Ruby and the Cross of Gold, sets out WBY's version of the dissensions in the Council, and is part of his attempt to muster wider support against FF and her group.

The complicated reorganisation made necessary by this change came about swiftly and quietly, and there is now more ardour of study and of labour among us, than at any time I can remember. One anomaly was however forgotten, and it is now causing the only trouble that has arisen among us. We have cast out the tyrannical rule of Frater S.R.M.D.,[2] and we must see to it, that a "group" which originated from that tyranny does not bring the Order into a new subjection, which would be none the less evil, because purely instinctive and unconscious, and because the mutual distrust and suspicion, it would spread among us, would have their foundation in good intentions.

About 1897 when through distrust of Frater S.R.M.D., the Order had lost much of its central fire, Soror S.S.D.D. in London and Frater Sub Spe[3] in Edinburgh formed private groups and bound them with some kind of understanding or promise of secrecy. When the change came the Edinburgh group abandoned its secrecy, but the London groups continued as before. Those of us who did not belong to them had forgotten their existence or had never heard of them, or we would have urged their immediate dissolution.

The scribe you appointed at the last General Meeting, was the first to give them serious thought, and she became convinced rightly or wrongly, that they were the cause of various irregularities in the working of the Order, that they led to unconcious favoritism and neglect of fratres and sorores who do not belong to them. She urged their dissolution in private, and drew attention to the irregularities before the Council. It was her duty to do both, but she found (as everybody has found, who has had to do with secret societies that busy themselves even unconsciously with matters outside their own borders) that if she complained of one member, all the members were indignant, that everything she said had as many echoes, and often very distorting echoes as there were members in the group. She discovered, too, that of the 11 members of the Council, 7 certainly belong to a group of twelve, which tries to keep its membership and its doctrine secret, one almost certainly to a smaller group, working under the same leadership and under the same conditions, and that one of the three remaining was married to a member of the larger group.[4]

---

[2] i.e. MacGregor Mathers, whose Order motto was 'S Rioghail Mo Dhream', Scottish Gaelic for 'Royal is My Tribe'.

[3] J. W. Brodie-Innes (1848–1923), Sub Spe (Under Hope) was Chief of the Amen-Ra Temple in Edinburgh, where he was a well-known lawyer. He contributed numerous articles to Scottish occult periodicals, and was the author of *Scottish Witchcraft Trials* (1891) and *The True Church of Christ, Exoteric and Esoteric* (1892).

[4] The Group comprised Marcus Blackden, Miss Harriet Butler, FF, Dr R. W. Felkin, E. A. Hunter, Dorothea Hunter, Florence Kennedy, Cecilia Macrea, Henrietta Paget, Helen Rand, Robert Palmer-Thomas, and Ada Waters. Of these Blackden, FF, the Hunters, Paget, Rand, and Thomas were on the Executive Council. Mrs Reena Fulham-Hughes ('Silentio') was probably a

She was powerless, and face to face with an ever-growing suspicion and ever-deepening irritation. She resolved not to seek re-election, and to leave the matter to mend itself, as the Order grew more interesting, and slowly gathered the fire into its own heart again.—Meanwhile I thought I had arranged a compromise, Soror S.S.D.D., the organiser of the groups, was to invite members of the Theorici degree, who were sympathetic, to join the larger group, and to make a statement of formulae to all Theorici, and as I thought to admit no more Zealators.[5] I hoped by this means that the "Group" would gradually be absorbed by the Theorici degree, where it would be a strength and not a weakness to the Order. The invitation was given, and the statement made though somewhat meagrely,* but suddenly the "Group" resolved to force itself upon the Order.[6] The Council was to invite you to declare it not only legal but admirable.—A Council meeting was summoned. It began with a strange event, which I can but describe to you by quoting a letter that I wrote to the Twelve Seniors in the first heat of my indignation. [*At this point WBY quotes the entire letter 'To the Twelve Seniors', printed on pp. 29–31*]

To such a wonderful state of suspicion[†] has a number of well bred and ⟨well intentioned⟩ friendly people been reduced by a secret society, in itself quite harmless, but moving within our Order, using its rooms and its formulae, or a modification of its formulae, but not responsible to our Order, and seeking ends that are not entirely its ends. The Frater who so insulted your Scribe, and you, in the person of your Scribe, is Frater Lucem Spero,[7] who has never past [*for* passed] an examination in the Second Order, who has not even consecrated his implements. A Hierarchy which is not ours has given him courage to flout our traditions of courtesy, and to deny the respect that we owe to the Heads of our Order. I have requested him to resign his position as Sub-Imperator of Isis-Urania till he has apologised to your Scribe, but no apology can make amends for such a scene.

* Your Scribe has only received it through the courtesy of Frater Sub Spe.
† Their suspicion was an outburst that they doubtless remember with astonishment. It was perhaps irritation masquerading as suspicion. They all knew in their hearts that our Scribe's sense of law is almost too great. Party feeling is a wonderful thing.

member of the smaller group, and Dr Felkin's wife, Mary, had been co-opted on to the Council in the course of the year.
5 Zelators belonged to the lowest but one grade (1 = .10) in the GD, and were not members of the Second Order.
6 See p. 25, n. 2.
7 Frater Lucem Spero was Robert Palmer-Thomas (1851–1918), a railway official, and prominent member of the GD, who on 1 Feb had insinuated that AEFH wished to violate the secrecy of the ballot (see p. 30, n. 3). He had joined the Outer Order of the GD in 1896, but did not progress into the Second Order until 21 Apr 1898, after FF had relaxed the rules, and had consequently not taken the appropriate examinations. He did, however, claim that he had consecrated his magical implements (Harper, 254). He had evidently been Sub-Imperator of the Temple since April 1900.

After this scene, whose object is obscure, if indeed it had any object which I doubt a resolution was past [*for* passed], pledging the Council to invite you to declare all "Groups" of whatsoever kind legal and admirable. A General Meeting is to be summoned for the purpose. The Majority consisted of members of the "Groups," and the Minority of the Scribe and of one Frater, who like the Scribe does not belong to any. A Soror, who is only married to a member of a "Group" did not vote, but got an offensive word removed from the Resolution.—I cannot quote the Resolution, for no copy was given to the Scribe, an irregularity she is accustomed to, but I have given its sense with accuracy. Its oratory, which was all about freedom, if I remember rightly, I cannot give.[8]

When this resolution is brought before you at the General Meeting, I shall propose the following amendment—"That this Order, while anxious to encourage among its members, friendly associations which are informal and without artificial mystery, cannot encourage associations or "Groups" that have a formal constitution, a formal obligation, a distinct magical personality which are not ⟨of⟩ the Constitution, the Obligation, or the Personality of this Order." Furthermore I shall ask you to call upon S.S.D.D. to invite two members of the larger "Group" to add their signatures to the statement of formulae issued to the Theorici ⟨in addition to herself⟩. This is necessary, because we are making a precedent and because we are told that the formulae of this "Group" varies among its members. One person must be liable to give undue importance to his or her own practice. I shall ask you also, and this is the most important point of all, to call upon Soror S.S.D.D. to admit no more Zelators into any formal Group.[9]

Should you desire to go further, and to call upon her to dissolve her "Groups", I shall sympathise with you, but shall think that you are asking, it may be, too much of human nature.

> *Vale Sub Umbram Alarum Taurum*
> Demon est Deus Inversus,—
> Imperator of Isis-Urania Temple.

TLS Private. Harper, 237–40.

[8] In her account of the meeting, AEFH records (Harper, 233): 'The motion was now put;— "groups" were to be legalised, no one of any seniority or grade is to be allowed to make any enquiries or to see after the working of members in any way. "Groups" are to be encouraged and the Order merely used as a screen. Per Aspera ad Astra [*i.e. Mrs Mary Felkin*], who did not vote at all, showed good feeling by insisting that "and prying" should be removed from the motion. Six voted for it and the Demon and I against it. We were beaten and the "group" triumphed on the Council.'

[9] The motion on 'groups', passed by the Executive Council, was put to the General Meeting, which postponed a final vote until the Constitution and Rules of the Order were revised and formally adopted. In the interim WBY explained his position in two privately printed pamphlets, *Is the Order of R.R. & A.C. to Remain a Magical Order?* and *A Postscript*, which appeared in April and May.

To Dora Sigerson Shorter,[1] [*15 February 1901*]

18 Woburn Buildings | Euston Road.
Friday

My dear Mrs Shorter: I cannot get to you on Sunday I am sorry to say.

I am lecturing on 'New Methods of Speaking Verse' or in other words on 'chanting' tomorrow (Friday)[2] at 8.15 at Cliffords Inn. Mrs Farr & Miss Mather will give examples.

Should you care to come the enclosed will admit you.

Yrs ever
W B Yeats

ALS BL.

To Violet Hunt,[1] [*15 February 1901*]

18 Woburn Buildings | Euston Road
Friday.

My dear Miss Hunt: I send you a card for an experiment that may perhaps interest you. It is an attempt to recover the rhythmic speach, half speach half song of the first poets.

Yrs snly
W B Yeats

ALS Berg.

[1] Dora Sigerson (1866–1918), Irish poetess and daughter of the Dublin physician and man of letters, George Sigerson, married the journalist, Clement Shorter, in 1896 and moved to London. WBY, who was a frequent dinner guest at the Shorters, gave her advice about her poetry, and Masefield recalls him (*Some Memories of W. B. Yeats* [Dublin, 1940], 12–13) taking up a book 'saying that there was a magnificent poem in it, which he wanted to read. He then read aloud Dora Sigerson's poem *Cean Duv Deelish* (*Dear Black Head*). . . . He stressed the rhythm till it almost became a chant . . .'. Introducing her in the Brooke–Rolleston anthology, Douglas Hyde wrote (439) that her 'very absence from Ireland has made her . . . more Irish than if she had never left it . . .'.

[2] An error for 'Saturday', 16 Feb 1901, when WBY gave his first public demonstration lecture on speaking to musical notes to the Fellowship of the Three Kings; see p. 21.

[1] Isobel Violet Hunt (1862–1942), novelist and biographer, was the daughter of Alfred William Hunt (1830–96), the Pre-Raphaelite water-colourist, and the novelist Margaret Raine Hunt (1831–1912). She had first met WBY in the 1880s at Mrs Anna Bryce's, and had re-met him on 23 Dec 1900 at the Shorters, where he put her into a trance. She described him in her diary (Cornell) as 'A wild dark-skinned strong featured red lipped youth. . . . His collar wanted new silk facing. . . . He was very mad at supper; wouldn't drink the Queen's health which Shorter wanted

To the Adepti of R.R. et A.C., [mid-February 1901]

A Second Letter to the Adepti of R.R. et A.C. on the Present Crisis.

Care et V. H. Fratres & Sorores

I have delayed this letter day after day in the hope that the fratres and sorores who were anxious to have "groups" declared not only legal but admirable would make a reply to my letter which would be as public as my letter. I am sorry to say they have confined themselves to private letters which I cannot answer fully as only faint rumours of their contents have come to me. I am sure that had they considered the matter they would have seen that it would have been fairer to have answered my letter openly. Even the most careful of us do not always remember these things in controversy. The chief of the faint rumours is that they re-affirm the harmlessness of their "groups" and blame your Scribe for suspiciousness and for a passion for red tape. I must therefore go into certain details, which I would prefer to pass over in silence and make certain criticisms upon the business capacity of the organiser of the "groups",[1] which I hope you will receive in the spirit in which I make them. Were I to speak of her in any other capacity than that of an official of this Order I would have no occasion for anything but praise.

During the proceedings that led to the disposition and expulsion of Frater S.R.M.D. I found that her inexperience in the procedure of Societies was so great that she could not hope to carry this Order safely through the necessarily unsettled period that would elapse before the new Constitution had become a habit. Though I would sooner not do so I must give a couple of examples for the decision you will have to make on Feb. 26th is too important to be made in ignorance. On one occasion during the crisis she told me that a certain decision had been come to by a certain committee of seven. I knew that the committee, of which I was a member, had not met and asked for an explanation. She told me that she had con-

---

him to do to tease him and told the most awful stories about the Theosophists Madame Blavatsky and Mr Moheeny . . . they were very funny and quite unpoetical. . . . Yeats looked rather like a gipsy's baby. He has a very queer nose—something about the shape of the bridge? . . . From the front it looks broad; about an inch wide—yet profile-wise one would call it sharp and Greek in outline. It looks carved out of wood anyway. He has a solemn naïve expression especially when he laughs.' She had already moved into South Lodge, 80 Campden Hill Road, Kensington, which she made a meeting-place for writers and artists, and where from 1910 to 1915 she was to live notoriously unmarried to Ford Madox Hueffer (1873–1939) after his unsuccessful attempts to divorce his first wife. In 1901 she was known as a socialite as well as a novelist, and Stephen Gwynn recalled in *Experiences of a Literary Man* (1926), 149, that 'People accused her of a dangerous tongue; I never knew it to be more than pleasantly malicious: but how quick!'

[1] i.e. FF, Moderator of the Order. The irregularities in procedure had occurred in late April 1900.

sulted three of the members, who accepted her proposal, and that this was legal as three members constituted a quorum. A little later this committee was empowered to draw up a constitution for the Order. Two meetings, at which the Moderator was present, discussed a certain clause, which was perhaps the most important of all, and at the second meeting the clause was written out by the Moderator in the form that had been unanimously decided upon. I need hardly point out to you that it is usual for the members of a committee to sustain before a General Meeting the decisions they have come to in committee. This custom is necessary to prevent a General Meeting from pushing too far its right to upset after a few moments of careless discussion, decisions, which have been come to after long and anxious thought. At the General Meeting the Moderator proposed that all the clauses of the constitution be taken "en bloc". I objected as I thought that the Meeting should have full opportunity for discussion. When I moved the adoption of the clause, which I held in the hand-writing of the Moderator, she rose and moved its rejection on the ground that she had never given it any consideration or understood it before. Her influence, which depended largely, though I did not know this at the time, upon the existence of secret "groups" was sufficient to secure the rejection of the clause with very little discussion. If I had not known that Soror Fortiter et Recte was ready to return to the Order I would have despaired of the future of an Order where the only person who had the leisure to devote herself to its affairs and the influence to make her devotion effective, was so unfitted by nature to consider the little wearisome details on which its stability depended. With the unanimous consent of all the working members, though with much regret, as I knew that it would look like bad taste to invite the return of a member he had expelled, almost in the hour of S.R.M.D.'s own expulsion, I invited Soror Fortiter et Recte to return to the Order and to become its Scribe. We had all perfect confidence in her business capacity. Before I went to Ireland[2] I remember saying to her something like this. "You will have a hard task, you will have to see that laws and precedents are observed, that everything is recorded." And I remember adding that in every society or movement that succeeds there is some person that is built into it, as in old times a sacrificial victim was built alive into the foundations of a bridge. I knew that for most of us the Order was one of several things we cared for, but that for the new Scribe it would be the chief thing in life and that she had the leisure to devote herself to its welfare. When I returned[3] I found that she no longer considered it possible to carry out her duties successfully. I heard that attempts had been made to evade laws and precedents and that the effort to get everything recorded

---

[2] i.e. before 23 June 1900.   [3] i.e. after 14 Oct 1900.

thing recorded had been wearisome in the extreme, and that she laid the blame upon the action, the doubtless unconscious action of certain secret "groups". On her first coming into office she noticed great irregularities in the list of members and in the book of Admissions and Examinations, the most important record that we possess; and only after considerable difficulty got the information necessary to put this right, but her chief complaint was that the Moderator tried continually, not I think because of any deliberate desire, but because of unusual inexperience, and a constitutional carelessness in all such matters, to act without consulting the Council. I will summarise certain of these irregularities but only summarise as full details will be placed in the hands of the Chairman of the General Meeting. I am very sorry that it is necessary to go into the matter at all. The Scribe prevented an addition being made to the Corpus Christi Ceremony without the consent of the Council and the Twelve Seniors, she remade the diagram of the Minutum Mundum, the central diagram of our system on finding that it had been altered avowedly for the greater convenience of the "groups".[4] She prevented the set of lectures which are known as the Portal Lectures being withdrawn without consulting the Council and the Twelve Seniors. She was unable to prevent an altered form of the Portal Ceremony being performed without the consent of the Council and the Twelve Seniors, and most important of all she had to oppose vigorously a perfectly serious and decided proposal to admit a candidate "privately" with "a modified o = o" ceremony without the consent of the Council.[5] I need not remind you that the admission of a candidate is among the most important business that can come before an Order such as ours. These irregularities are little worse than I have heard of in connection with Catholic Religious Houses, which have begun to occupy themselves with business affairs, but none the less they would have made a series of prece-

---

[4] The Corpus Christi Ceremony in early June was the most important festival in the GD calendar. The Chief Adept, in a black robe of mourning and with the chain of humility around his neck, was bound to the Cross of Suffering (see p. 31, n. 5) and pledged himself 'for the due performance and fulfilment . . . of the Oath taken by each member . . . at his admission to the grade of Adeptus Minor'. In his pamphlet *Is the Order of R.R. & A.C. to remain a Magical Order?*, written in March 1901, WBY reminded the members that this was done 'in the name of the Third Order, which thereby takes upon itself the sins of all the Fratres and Sorores, as wisdom takes upon itself the sins of the world', and argued that it was 'indeed necessary, for by it the stream of the lightning is awakened in the Order, and the Adepti of the Third Order and of the Higher Degrees of the Second Order summoned to our help'. The Minutum Mundum was the first section of the *Liber Hodos Chameleonis*, and explained the significance of the Minutum Mundum diagram which represented the Cabbalistic Sephiroth.

[5] On 12 Aug 1900 FF had written to AEFH (Howe, 236) with proposals to initiate Princess Aribert of Anhalt, a 28-year-old granddaughter of Queen Victoria. FF wanted the initiation to be private because her social position made it impossible for the Princess to go to Mark Masons' Hall, and suggested a modified Neophyte Ceremony at the Colviles' (see p. 11) country house. AEFH clearly quashed the proposal at once, and there is no evidence that Princess Aribert ever joined the GD.

an autocracy like that we have thrown off with so much difficulty. Under ordinary circumstances they could have been quietly pointed out and quietly corrected and no discomfort would have followed, but the existence of "groups" bound to the Moderator by a bond formed in the super-conscious life, the closest of all bonds in the nature of things, made every correction, no matter how quietly made, raise a general irritation. The Scribe found herself alone on a hostile or indifferent Council fighting for the Order against a carelessness that threatened its constitution. The Council voted always honourably, when their attention was drawn to irregularities, but only the Scribe felt free as it seems to point them out. She was soon in a very invidious position and I confess that when I returned from Ireland I thought that one who had raised so much irritation against herself could hardly be in the right. It is only now when I have gone through all her papers carefully that I understand the difficulties of her position; a position that became impossible instead of merely difficult when the irritation against her broke out into the strange scene of February 1st. But for her the inexperience and carelessness of the Moderator, supported artificially by her secret "groups" would have modified beyond recognition the Constitution, that we formed with so much difficulty.

In addition to the faint rumours of the replies made by the "group" to my first letter, I have been sent one whole sentence. "Our group is bound by no oaths nor ruled by any Constitution."[6] I never said that the "groups" were bound by oaths, though they certainly have an understanding or an obligation to keep secret their membership and their doctrines; but I have said or implied that they have a formal constitution. The members of the chief "group" have certainly formed themselves into a magical personality made, by a very formal meditation and a very formal numerical system. Unless magic is an illusion, this magical personality could not help, the moment it came into contact with the larger personality of the Order, from creating precisely the situation it has created. It was a formal evocation of disruption, a formal evocation of a barrier between its own members and the other members of the Order, a formal intrusion of an alien being into the conscious and what is of greater importance into the super-conscious being of our Order, an obsession of the magical sphere that has descended to us, as most of us believe, from the Frater Christian Rosencreuz by a sphere created at a time of weariness and disappointment. Such a personality, such a sphere, such an evocation, such an obsession even if it had not supported the real disorders I have described, would have created, so perfectly do the barriers of the conscious life copy the barriers of the

[6] The note was probably from FF; she had made the same claim in her January statement to the Theorici (see p. 25, n. 2). WBY had described them as held together by 'some kind of understanding or promise' (see p. 32).

super-conscious, illusionary suspicion, illusionary distrust more irremediable than if they had real cause. We who are seeking to sustain this great
Order must never forget that whatever we build in the imagination will
accomplish itself in the circumstance of our lives.

Nobody proposes to pass a law condemning even the most formal
"groups" and I would oppose any such law, for all such matters must be
left to the individual conscience, but I have a right to believe that you will
not pass a law giving your sanction, and the sanction of this Order to this
"group" or to any "group" of the kind. I shall therefore propose the
amendment, which I again repeat. "That this Order whilst anxious to
encourage among its members friendly associations, which are informal
and without artificial mystery, cannot encourage associations or "groups"
that have a formal constitution, a formal obligation, a distinct magical personality, which are not the constitution, the obligation or the personality of
this Order."

Vale, s.u.a.t.

יהוה

D.E.D.I.

P.S. As I have not received Frater Lucem Spero's resignation I have suspended him from his office as Sub-Imperator of the I.U.T.[7] till he has
made such apology as may be acceptable to the Scribe and to the General
Meeting for his principal share in the scene of February 1st.

TLS Private. Harper, 241–5.

To Lady Augusta Gregory, [21 February 1901]

18 Woburn Buildings | Euston Road
Thursday.

My dear Lady Gregory: Is your cold better. Are you back at the Museum.[1]
I have not been there to day as I have some kind of slight liver or
rheumatic attack. I have stayed indoors & corrected proofs. If I am well I

---

[7] i.e. Isis-Urania Temple; see p. 25.

[1] AG had applied for a reader's ticket at the British Museum on 8 Feb to begin research for
Cuchulain of Muirthemne, which was to be published in April 1902. On 1 Apr she was to recall
(diary, Berg) 'a very busy time in London—almost every day working at my "Cuchulain" at the
British Museum—very pleasant work, & then wd have lunch or tea with Yeats & talk over what
we were doing'. She also remembered that 'a week of feverish cold kept me in'.

will go to Museum tomorrow if not I shall go on with proofs. Mystical affairs too mixed to describe.

Yrs ever
W B Yeats

ALS Berg, with envelope addressed to Queen Anne Mansions, postmark 'LONDON FE 23 01'.

To Violet Hunt, [21 February 1901]

18 Woburn Buildings | Euston Road.
Thursday.

My dear Miss Hunt: I got a letter to day, which sets me to a dull peice of writing[1] which will I fear make it impossible for me to get to the theatre to night. I hope you will give me another chance of meeting your friend.

I wish you had heard our chanting on Saturday. It roused the indignation of ⟨all⟩ a large part of an audience consisting almost wholly of teachers of elocution for far as I could make out, & woke a real enthusiasm in some few.[2] To me it was the first quite musical speach of any verse in our time,

---

[1] The latest letter to the Adepti of the Second Order; see next letter. The friend was probably Lady Margaret Sackville, who was eager to meet WBY.

[2] The lecture had attracted numerous poets and drama critics. A sceptical AG reported (diary, Berg) that it was 'amusing enough—but only a "fad". Mrs Emery's voice is better in ordinary reciting, and Miss Mathers hadn't much voice at all. Yeats didn't give a regular lecture but warmed up after criticism by Todhunter & [Herman] Vezin [*b. 1829, and a famous Shakespearian actor*], & said . . . that all lyrics were sad, & that all the finest poetry was the fruit of an [*indecipherable*] sadness.' J. F. Runciman wrote in the *Saturday Review* of 23 Feb (236–7) that WBY, having 'superfluously stated that he knew nothing of music . . . proceeded to reveal his new musical art. . . . Perhaps it may be effective in the theatre . . . but at Clifford's Inn it sounded neither like good, or even bad, singing nor good recitation.' Among those in whom WBY 'woke a real enthusiasm' was H. W. Nevinson, whose review in the *Daily Chronicle*, 18 Feb 1901 (5), was appreciative of the chanting and faithful to WBY's intent: 'For the poet's purpose is really to revive the old chanting of ballads and lyrics as it was done by the bards of Ireland and most European countries—certainly by the Homeric rhapsodists of Greece, where Mr. Yeats maintains even the drama was chanted or intoned. Admirable examples of the poet's meaning were given by Miss Florence Farr (Mrs. Emery) and Miss Anna Mather, with the accompaniment of a harp and even so familiar an instrument as the piano, where one felt the lyre, the tympan, and the Pan-pipe alone would have been in place. The effect . . . was peculiarly beautiful, but the idea of introducing such methods on the stage stirred the wrath of Mr. Herman Vezin and other critics, whose feeling was not prehistoric enough for the sort of thing the Three Kings enjoyed.'

with the exception of our Irish experiments.[3] I am going on to elaborate the thing much more highly. It is the rudiments of music—music as it was in early Greece.

Yrs sny
W B Yeats

ALS Berg.

To the Adepti of R.R. et A.C., 21–2 February 1901

A Final Letter to the Adepti of R.R. et A.C. on the Present Crisis.

Care Fratres et Sorores,

I have just received from the Chairman of the General Meeting a copy of the Resolution that is to declare all "groups" of whatsoever kind not only legal but admirable. It is long, the longest Resolution I have ever seen made out of such light material, and yet it contains but a single sentence. This sentence winds hither and thither with so much luxuriance, that I am convinced it requires a closer study than you could give it at the General Meeting. I therefore send it to you—it is as follows:

"If the liberty and progress of individual members—and of this Order as a whole—is to be maintained—for progress without liberty is impossible— it is absolutely necessary that all members of the 2nd Order shall have the undisputed right to study and work at their mystical progress in whatsoever manner seems to them right according to their individual needs and conscience—and further it is absolutely necessary that they shall be at perfect liberty to combine, like minded with like minded, in groups or circles formed for the purpose of that study and progress, in such manner as seems to them right and fitting and according to their consciences, and that—without the risk of suffering from interference by any member of any grade whatever, or of any seniority whatever,—and furthermore that this is in perfect accord with the spirit and tradition of our Order which is always to allow the largest liberty for the expansion of the individual, and has always discountenanced the interference of any and every member with private affairs, whether mystical or otherwise of any other member."

After some difficulty I have discovered amid this luxuriance certain distinct ideas (1) that all fratres and sorores shall be free to do anything they like so long as it is something mystical, (2) that they shall be free to form

---

[3] WBY and FF had experimented in chanting some of Aleel's lines for the first production of *The Countess Cathleen* in May 1899. A prompt copy of the play, with musical directions in her hand, is at Kansas.

any kind of groups they like so long as they are mystical, (3) that to do so is true not only to the spirit but to the letter of the Father Christian Rosencreuz,[1] (4) that nobody, no not the highest or the oldest of our Adepti, shall "interfere" with them in any way.

That is to say, that this Order is to surrender the right it has always possessed to "interfere" with fratres and sorores who flagrantly misuse their magical knowledge, and that these fratres and sorores have only to organize themselves into secret groups to be free to misuse that knowledge in the Rooms of the Order itself. They may even evoke the genius of another, a forbidden thing even when done without evil intention; they may cast about that genius an enchantment of sensual passion; they may evoke the spirits of disease to destroy some enemy—and a member of this Order who is now expelled once boasted that he had done no less[2]—they may hold any kind of Witches Sabbath they like before the door of the Tomb, and thereby send out among the fratres and sorores from that symbolic Tipharath, that symbolic Heart,[3] a current of evil magic and merely because they call themselves a group, no officer of this Order, "of any grade whatever, or of any seniority whatever" shall have even the poor right of knowing what they do. They may be the youngest members of the Second Order, and he the oldest, but he cannot even be present, much less object.

You, the Adepti of R.R. et A.C. are responsible before the Laws of this Land, and before far subtler Laws, for all that happens in the rooms of your Order, but you must not "interfere" and you have no right even to be curious. You have recently expelled certain fratres whose "consciences"

---

[1] This name, together with certain other esoteric terms (i.e. 'magical', 'evoke the genius', 'genius', 'evoke the spirits', 'magic', and 'Vale s. u. a. t.') have been added later in pen that the typist might not know them.

[2] In 1897 'Respiro' reported in a pamphlet, *The Man, the Seer, the Avatar, or T. L. Harris, the Inspired Messenger of the Cycle*, that following an attempt by an occultist to injure him magically, socially, and professionally he had 'invoked the aid of arch-natural powers, and was informed that within 12 months the guilty would be punished. . . . just within the predicted time the avenging force of the reverse current culminated and the enemy was occultly crushed; this being followed in a few weeks by a great disaster on the material plane.' 'Respiro' was Dr Edmund William Berridge (d. 1920), whose usual motto was 'Resurgam'. He had quarrelled with AEFH and was a follower of Thomas Lake Harris (1823–1906), founder of 'The Brotherhood of the New Life', who promulgated a new religion made up of Swedenborgianism, Spiritualism, belief in a bisexual God, and the sexual doctrine of 'counterparts'. In a copy of the pamphlet sent to the GD member H. C. Morris (Cavendo Tutus) he had written a squib on the appropriate page: 'Oh! F.E.R. [*i.e. AEFH*], you should not let / Your angry passions rise. / Your feline claws were never meant / To scratch a Frater's eyes.' Edmund Berridge was suspended from the GD for three months in May 1897, and was banished altogether in April 1900, when he came out in support of Mathers. He revenged himself by writing anonymously to AEFH's father, telling him that his daughter belonged to a Secret Order that practised witchcraft.

[3] Tiphereth [not 'Tipharath'], the highest of the Sephiroth on the Cabbalistic Tree of Life, represented Beauty.

and whose expression of what "seems to them right" were not to your minds, and I have heard even members of the "groups", and in Open Temple too, accuse some of these expelled fratres of the worst of evil magic[4] but from next Tuesday onward for ever you are to trust everybody. You are to believe no longer in the ancient magical tradition that bids even the highest look lest he fall, and you are to trust to your clairvoyants and introducers so profoundly that you are to believe no unfit person shall ever again enter this Order. The medium, the mesmerist, the harmless blunderer or the man who seeks a forbidden pleasure by symbols that are now better known than they were, may form his secret "group" from the moment he has passed the ceremony of $5 = 6$, and gather his secret "group" about him in the rooms of your Order.

I ask you to examine this Resolution carefully, and to ask yourselves whether it has come from the Powers who represent the Personality of this Order, its Constitution, its Tradition and its future, or whether it has come from powers that could see, with indifference, the dissolution of this Order, its Constitution, its Tradition and its future. All that we do with intensity has an origin in the hidden world, and is the symbol, the expression of its powers, and even the smallest detail, in a professedly magical dispute may have significance. This Resolution is not a small detail. It is the chosen weapon of the members of the council who belong to the secret "groups". I do not say that it has come from evil powers, but it seems to me that it has come from powers that seek ends that are not the ends of this Order, and that say to their followers as the Evil Powers once said to theirs "Your eyes shall be opened and ye shall be as Gods knowing Good and Evil."

Sometimes the sphere of an individual man is broken, and a form comes into the broken place and offers him knowledge and power if he will but give it of his life. If he give it of his life it will form a swirl there and draw other forms about it, and his sphere will be broken more and more, and his will subdued by alien wills. It seems to me that such a swirl has been formed in the sphere of this Order, by powers, that though not evil in themselves are evil in relation to this Order.

Vale s.u.a.t.

יהוה

D.E.D.I.

February 21.

P.S. I gather from a letter received this morning, that the private replies to my first open letter say that only a "group" can decide whether it has a "formal constitution" or not, and that therefore no group must be con-

---

[4] i.e. Mathers, Berridge, and company; see p. 14, n. 2.

demned. This is an example of the confusion of mind that hangs over this dispute. *It is the members of "groups" and not we who have proposed legislation.* We know from the statements of its founder and of others that the largest of the existing groups has what we consider a "formal constitution", but in most cases nobody could know; and this is one of the reasons why I have stated that I would oppose any legislation against groups, as such. At the same time this must not be understood as surrendering the right that the Order already possesses to "interfere" with any collective or individual practice of a distinctly mystical kind, which is a dangerous breach of our obligation or its right to any supervision over its rooms it may think necessary.

D.E.D.I.

February 22.

TLS Private. Harper, 246–9.

To Lady Augusta Gregory, [*22 February 1901*]

18 Woburn Buildings | Euston Road.
Friday.

My dear Lady Gregory: I got your note just after writing. I shall dine with you to-morrow night with pleasure. My rheumatism my [?*for* much] better.

Yrs snly
W B Yeats

ALS Berg.

To the Adepti of R.R. et A.C., *27 February 1901*

London,
Feb. 27th 1901.

Care et V. H. Fratres et Sorores,

At the meeting to consider Ma Wahanu Thesi's Resolution[1] which was held last night Frater Sub Spe proposed the following amendment—

"That before any other matter can be considered it is necessary that the Constitution and Rules of the Order shall be revised and formally adopted and that a small Committee be forthwith appointed to draft and submit to the Order a scheme for this purpose. And that in the meantime there shall

---

[1] See p. 34.

be no interference with any group which does not transgress the laws of the Order, and that no group shall interfere with or alter the working of the Order." A state of things which Sub Spe speaking to his amendment described in the language of Mediaeval politics as a "Truce of God".

This amendment was negatived apparently by a mechanical majority, who failed to comprehend its effect, for the same proposals were afterwards affirmed by the same majority. Frater D.E.D.I. then proposed his amendment in the following modified form—

"That this Order while anxious to encourage among its members associations which are informal and without artificial mystery neither desires to encourage nor condemn associations, or "groups" that have a formal constitution, a formal obligation, a distinct magical personality which are not the Constitution, the Obligation or the Personality of this Order. That the resolution proposed by Frater Ma Wahanu Thesi and this amendment be submitted in writing to all the Adepti of the Second Order and that this Meeting adjourn until the votes have been received, those who cannot attend personally to be permitted to vote through the post." This amendment was negatived.

The principle of non-interference of "groups" who did not transgress the laws of the Order was the substratum of Ma Wahanu Thesi's vague resolution as he explained it to the Meeting. And on his explaining that he did not ask for a vote of confidence in any "group" or for any positive action being taken, Frater Sub Spe said that this was identical with the last sentence of his amendment and he accordingly voted for the motion. Soror Fortiter et Recte and Frater D.E.D.I. did not vote with him in this.

Frater Sub Spe affirms that—

The Meeting not only did not express its confidence in any "group" but that it did not and could not give them any legal status. Nothing that has happened has any force either to reduce the primary authority of the Obligation nor the right and responsibility of the Order which it derives from the Obligation itself to enforce it.

The expediency of a revision of the Rules was unanimously acknowledged, but we must also state that this revision is a legal necessity. Two of the signatories were unaware of the legal aspect of the matter until the last few days. There are at present no rules that are binding on the Order except the Obligation.[2] The body of Adepti should understand that at present the power heretofore possessed by D.D.C.F.[3] resides in them as a whole. There is no power to take any single step even by a majority of the Adepti until a unanimous vote of the whole body has given such power, either to a majority of the whole or to a committee, when this is done a

---

[2] See p. 38, n. 4.
[3] i.e. MacGregor Mathers, whose alternative GD motto was Deo Duce Comite Ferro.

committee can draft a constitution and revise rules. These must then have the assent of the whole body or of such majority as the whole body shall determine. The necessity for such rules was abundantly proved and acknowledged at the Meeting and only as above pointed out can they be made binding on the whole Order. The long experience of Fortiter et Recte in the business of the Order has taught her that fixed rules and a just enforcement of them would give the members that peace which is necessary for occult study.

After the discussion on the Rules, the case of Lucem Spero came up for consideration; he was voted back into his place by a large majority. Frater D.E.D.I.'s action was declared illegal and unjust. (A certain number of members did not vote at all considering that there can be neither legality nor illegality where there are as yet no laws.) Frater D.E.D.I. has resigned his position as Imperator of Isis-Urania Temple, but not because of this vote; having considered the legal aspects he cannot acknowledge the tribunal which considered the matter. He resigns because he does not wish to be a cause of dissension in the Order; he hopes that the Order when the new Rules have been formed will return to its normal state.

Vale s.u.a.t.
Fortiter et Recte T.A.M.[4] Late Scribe.
Sub Spe T.A.M. Late Imperator of Amen Raa.
Demon est Deus Inversus. Late Imperator of Isis-Urania.

P.S. In the statement of the majority of the Council various accusations have been made against me, all of which I hereby categorically deny. F.E.R.

P.S. I do not think the letter of 'the majority of the Council' calls for any comment from me. Nobody untroubled by party feeling will believe that I removed Frater Lucem Spero from his office because of a difference of opinion at a meeting of the Council, and the other statements in so far as they concern myself are unimportant. D.E.D.I.

TLS Private. Harper, 256–8.

---

[4] i.e. Theoricus Adeptus Minor, the 5 = 6 GD grade. WBY had passed four parts of the examinations for this in June 1895, but did not take the last (on 'Magic') until 10 July 1912.

To Clement Shorter,[1] [*? 14 March 1901*]

18 Woburn Buildings | Euston Road.
Thursday

My dear Shorter: Please forgive me for not having explained about Sunday before. I got your telegram while I was expecting one from Moore in reply to one of mine, inviting myself to his place to discuss business about the play.[2] I did not hear from Moore however until it was to[o] late to let you know. Many apologies.

Yrs snly
W B Yeats

ALS Berg.

To Clement Shorter, [*? 15 March 1901*]

18 Woburn Buildings | Euston Road.
Friday

My dear Shorter: Moore has just embarrased me very much. He asked me what I was doing Sunday evening. I said dining with you & then [he] said "Well I'll go with you. Ask Shorter if I may. I want to meet M[rs] Shorter before I go to Ireland". He has taken a Dublin house as you know & goes there in a couple of weeks. Now what am I to do. I am afraid you dont care about Moore but embarrased as I am I shall be four times as embarrased if I may not bring him.[1] Send me a note tomorrow & tell me what to do.

Yr ev
W B Yeats

ALS BL. Wade, 348.

[1] Clement King Shorter (1857–1926), editor, journalist (see p. 35, n. 1), and husband of Dora Sigerson, was the biographer of the Brontës, Mrs Gaskell, and others. Editor of the *Illustrated London News* from 1891 to 1900, he was the founder editor of the *Sphere* (1900) and the *Tatler* (1903). WBY was a frequent dinner guest.
[2] *Diarmuid and Grania*; see pp. 3–4.

[1] George Moore was to move to 4 Ely Place, Dublin, at the beginning of April (see p. 20, n. 6), and was busy seeing people in London before he left. His request was, however, more embarrassing than WBY realized: as Ernest Rhys recalled in an account of another dinner party (*Wales England Wed* [1940], 185–6), Mrs Shorter 'had a temperamental and incurable hatred for George Moore. It was easily to be seen during the dinner, for she openly flouted him, even to the point of giving him the drumstick of the bird she was carving, and the rest of us felt the atmosphere somewhat strained.' Later, when the men had gone upstairs, she told Mrs Rhys: 'Ye know, Grace, I hate George Moore. Ye know those big white slugs ye find in the back garden. Well, they're just like George Moore's nose!'

To Hugh Law,[1] *16 March 1901*

18, Woburn Buildings, | Euston Road, N.W.
March 16th, 1901.

Dear Mr. Law,

Will you please read what I am about to say to the Committee of the Irish Literary Society. Last Spring Mr. George Moore was asked to let his name go up for election as a member of the Society by the Honorary Treasurer who wrote in his official capacity. Finding that Mr. Moore's name had not come up for election I brought it forward. To my great surprise Mr. Barry O'Brien declared that he would do his best to get Mr. George Moore blackballed. I let the matter drop for nearly two months and brought it up again at the last meeting of the Committee, when you heard Mr. Barry O'Brien declare that he would resign if Mr. George Moore was elected. I am well aware of all that Mr. Barry O'Brien has done for the Society. It certainly owes him more than it does to any other member, and I can well understand that I have put the Committee in a serious difficulty. On the one hand they have to weigh Mr. Barry O'Brien's services and on the other they have to weigh the principle of tolerance and courtesy. I cannot persuade myself to continue to force this choice upon them, nor can I persuade myself to carry on a personal contest with Mr. Barry O'Brien after so many years of work in common. I therefore withdraw Mr. Moore's nomination[2] but as I believe that my duty to my own Order as a man of letters makes it impossible for me to share the most indirect responsibility for what I consider an act of

---

[1] Hugh Alexander Law (1872–1943), barrister and Irish MP for West Donegal, was Assistant Secretary of the ILS. He was a cousin of Grace Rhys.

[2] See p. 22, n. 3. Moore's attempts to join the ILS had been thwarted by the threat of resignation by R. Barry O'Brien (1847–1918), barrister, journalist, editor, and author, a founding member and current Chairman of the Society. Moore had inadvertently been invited to apply for membership by Charles Russell, the Society's Treasurer, who, not realizing what he had done, subsequently insisted that the Committee should blackball him. Much of the opposition to Moore stemmed from his treatment of sexual themes, and from the contemptuous attacks he had made on Ireland and Catholicism in a number of his early works: Russell objected to an anti-Catholic passage in *A Drama in Muslin* (1886); O'Brien—who had described him in *Truth* on 11 Aug 1887 (246) as 'a night-soil novelist'—to his offensive 1887 pamphlet, *Parnell and His Island* (which Moore had subsequently withdrawn). WBY recalled the incident in *Aut* (433): 'I got rid of Charles Russell by producing his letter of invitation, but Barry O'Brien remained, and after a long fight I withdrew Moore's name and resigned rather than force his resignation'. The ILS was not the only Irish society to object to Moore. Shortly after his move to Dublin later this year, George Roberts proposed him for membership of his branch of the Gaelic League, supposing that they would be delighted to enlist so distinguished a writer, but, as he reported in the *Irish Times* of 19 July 1955 (5), the 'teacher, a middle-aged buxom woman who hailed from the Aran Islands, threw up her arms in horror at the idea of George Moore so much as entering the sacred premises and associating with the young vestal virgins who were her pupils. "Do you want to turn the branch into a bad house?" she shrieked.'

intolerance I resign my position on the Committee and ask that this letter be placed upon the Minutes. I shall not seek re-election so long as the principle of tolerance I have defended is unable to govern the actions of the Society. A Literary society which ⟨finds it impossible or undesirable⟩ refuses to elect a man of letters of Mr. George Moore's eminence, because of an objection to his opinion makes itself an example of intolerance which only ceases from being mischevious by becoming ridiculous. The authorities of Oxford made themselves ridiculous when they expelled Shelley for his atheistical opinions and Shelley was an unknown undergraduate and held those opinions at the time of his expulsion. The Committee of the Society has been invited to make itself many times more ridiculous. It has been invited to blackball Mr. George Moore, whom it had itself through its Treasurer invited to stand for election, because of a book written ⟨nearly twenty⟩ fifteen years ago and since withdrawn ⟨and [?]repudiated⟩. Mr. Moore has done his best for the last two ⟨or three⟩ years to serve the cause of the Irish language and other Irish causes both as an essayist and a playwright. He has given up his London house because he thinks it his duty to live in Ireland, but all this is to count as nothing because he once held certain opinions which were never so offensive to Ireland as opinions about Ireland and about the Catholic religion expressed with far greater vehemence by Swift. The Irish Literary Society has never, so far as I can remember, blackballed anybody and it has elected among its Vice-presidents men like Mr. Carson,[3] who has poured insult on much that the majority of its members respect, and it has invited men like Mr. Frank Hugh O'Donnell[4] to speak at its meetings but none the less ⟨is it invited⟩ has it been asked to blackball one of the most eminent of Irish men of letters.

If the Society were to become a Court of opinions and morals it would soon find that it would have to reject on one ground or another almost every man of vigorous personality. The weak and the tame would alone speak through it and history would alone remember it for its follies. A Society that was a Court of opinions and morals would be of necessity gov-

[3] Sir Edward Henry Carson (1854–1935), the Dublin-born lawyer who had appeared for the prosecution in the Wilde case, was now the outspoken leader of Irish Unionism. He had been knighted in 1900 for his service as Solicitor-General in the Conservative government. In 1912 he was to organize resistance to the Home Rule Bill, and helped to found and arm the Ulster Volunteers.

[4] Frank Hugh O'Donnell (1848–1916), author and politician, dubbed by *United Ireland* in the 1880s as 'Crank Hugh O'Donnell', had been expelled from the Irish Parliamentary Party by Parnell, and fallen out with WBY over their activities in the '98 Centennial Commitee, when he had libelled Michael Davitt and MG. Reprimanded by WBY and John O'Leary, he had taken his revenge by attacking WBY and *The Countess Cathleen* in his pamphlet, *Souls for Gold! Pseudo-Celtic Drama in Dublin* (1899), which he circulated widely in Dublin and which prompted Cardinal Logue's condemnation of the play. He was suspected of being in the pay of the Austrian and perhaps the English governments. He regularly attended ILS meetings and often spoke to papers and lectures there.

erned by the average thought, the thought which exhibits itself in the newspapers, and it would not be able to do its proper work, which is to find occasions when thought that is too sincere, too personal, too original for general acceptance, can express itself courageously and candidly. The only worthy spirit for Societies or for individual men and women to consider the work of men of letters in, is to remember whatever of good and forget, as time forgets, whatever of evil they have written. Good writers are in their work, and often in their lives, discoverers and experimentalists and for this a large freedom is essential.

In conclusion I urge the Committee to consider my resignation and this letter as sufficient defence of the principle and to thereby retain the invaluable services of Mr. Barry O'Brien.

Yours sincerely

W B Yeats

TS copy MBY.

To the Editor of the Saturday Review, [*16 March 1901*]

Sir,—Two or three weeks ago Mr. Runciman said that I called a method of speaking verse, of which I approve, "Cantilation."[1] Now that a morning paper has announced that an "epidemic of Cantilation" has reached New York and that a New York clergyman has lectured about the "glorious future" that lies before America in "developing Cantilation,"[2] you will perhaps permit me to say that Mr. Runciman invented the word. I never used it, and I don't mean to, and I don't like it, and I don't think it means anything.—[3]

Yours sincerely

W B Yeats

Printed letter, *Saturday Review*, 16 March 1901 (336). Wade, 348.

[1] See p. 41, n. 2. In his notice of 23 Feb 1901 John F. 'Runcy' Runciman (1866–1916), the *Saturday Review*'s music critic, had attacked WBY's lecture (236), as 'a display of what he called cantilating'.

[2] An article from a New York correspondent, entitled 'What Does Mr. W. B. Yeats Say?', had appeared in the *Morning Leader* on 7 Mar 1901, reporting (5) that a Revd Dr Peters had recently 'delivered a panegyric on America's glorious future in cantilation', and that the New York *Evening Sun*, which had traced the craze to London, 'protests against it as a reversion to the barbarous system of our remote ancestors'.

[3] In a note printed immediately under this letter Runciman alleged that 'Mr. Yeats himself gave me the word some months ago. I have never heard it used by anyone save Mr. Yeats.'

To the Secretary of the Purcell Society, [*28 March 1901*]

18 Woburn Buildings | Euston Road.
Thursday.

Dear Sir: I would very much like to see 'Dido & Aeneas'.[1]
Could you let me have a seat for Saturdays Afternoon performance?
If not I shall have to buy one & hawk should not peck out hawk's eyne.[2]
Yours sincly
W B Yeats

ALS Texas.

To Nora Dryhurst,[1] *2 April* [*1901*]

18 Woburn Buildings | Euston Road.
April 2.

Dear Mrs Dryhurst: I think you know Gordon Craig.[2] I want you to send him the enclosed. It is about his wonderful scenery at Purcell Society, the

[1] The Purcell Operatic Society produced *Dido and Aeneas* (1689) and *The Masque of Love* from 25 to 30 Mar 1901 at the Coronet Theatre, Notting Hill Gate, with a matinée performance on Saturday 30 March. The Society had been founded in 1899 by Martin Fallas Shaw (1875–1958), composer and director of music, with the purpose, as a note in the current programme explained, 'of bringing forward on the stage dramatic works, whether by Purcell or other composers, that have been undeservedly forgotten by the English public at large'. The Secretary of the Society was Nora Dryhurst (see below).

[2] An English proverb first cited in James Sanford's *The Garden of Pleasure* (1573), but WBY had probably come across it in chap. 30 of Sir Walter Scott's *Rob Roy*: 'hawks winna pike out hawks' een'.

[1] Mrs Nora Florence Dryhurst (*c.* 1856–1930), a journalist and suffragette, was Secretary of the Purcell Operatic Society, which Martin Shaw had founded at her suggestion. She was married to A. R. Dryhurst, Assistant Secretary of the British Museum, and her daughter, Sylvia (1888–1952), was to marry the Irish novelist, Robert Lynd. She wrote occasional articles on Irish history and literature for the *Daily Chronicle* and Irish papers, and her Hampstead house was the centre for a large circle of artists and writers. She and her daughter were members of an amateur dramatic club, the Chelsea Mummers, and were to appear in WBY's *The Land of Heart's Desire* in June 1904. In *Changes and Chances* (1923), H. W. Nevinson describes her (193) as 'always bringing with her the wit of Ireland, the kindling inspiration, the flaming wrath, and a sarcasm like the lick of a lioness's tongue'. In *Some I Knew Well* (1951) Clifford Bax (98) gives as an example of WBY's absent-mindedness that 'having talked to a lady for an hour, he politely peered forward and asked, "Am I speaking to Mrs Podmore or Mrs Dryhurst?"'

[2] Edward Gordon Craig (1872–1966; see Appendix), illegitimate son of the architect Edward William Godwin and the actress Ellen Terry (after her marriage to the painter G. F. Watts), was an actor, producer, author, editor, and stage designer whose symbolic scenes and lighting effects were greatly to influence WBY's dramaturgy. Until he was 20 he had been known as Edward Henry Gordon Wardwell (the surname that of his mother's second husband, who acted as 'Charles Kelly') but on 24 Feb 1893 he announced in *The Times* that henceforth he would take the name Edward Gordon Craig.

only good scenery I ever saw. I have asked him to let me have a talk with him as I want to write a little essay on his scenery. I have therefore asked him to come dine with me & the enclosed is the invitation. I want to make my little essay a eulogy of that wonderful purple that was like the edge of eternity,[3] & endeed of all the rest of his arrangements. I have asked Frank Harris if he will take it for his new paper.

Yrs sny
W B Yeats

ALS Texas.

To Gordon Craig, 2 April [*1901*]

18 Woburn Buildings, | Euston Road
April 2

Dear Mr. Craig: I thought your scenery to 'Aeneas and Dido' the only good scenery I ever saw. You have created a new art. I have written to Frank Harris to ask him to let me do an article on the subject in his new paper "The Saturday Review".[1]

I would like to talk the thing over with you. Could you dine with me here Monday next if you do not mind a not very excellent dinner? Seven o'clock and of course not dress. I am just behind New Street, St. Pancras Church. Ring the top bell.

If you are not free on Monday I would like some other opportunity of talking things over.

Yours sincerely
W B Yeats

Text from Craig, 239.

[3] WBY's enthusiasm was not universally shared: in *Up to Now* (1929) Martin Shaw, recalling the 'great backcloth of purple-blue', relates (29) that after the curtain one critic 'rushed into the bar and collapsed on the counter, murmuring "Flossie, for God's sake give me a drink! I've got purple on the brain".' A more sober but enthusiastic view was taken by Nevinson, who wrote in *Changes and Chances* (299) of the 'Great beauty of the purples and greys and greens in the "Dido" against the vast background of purple eternity. . . . Daring colours and arrangements, white figures and greys and greens, with but rare touches of red, the more brilliant for their rarity.'

[1] James Thomas 'Frank' Harris (1856–1931) had been editor of the *Saturday Review* (to which WBY mistakenly refers) from 1886 to 1898, but now, recently returned from an unsuccessful attempt to run luxury hotels on the French Riviera, was planning a new weekly, the *Candid Friend*. This was to appear on 1 May 1901 but its promise 'to add to the amusement of our readers by drawing attention to the virtues and failings of public men and public institutions', soon reduced it to a mere retailer of gossip and it was discontinued in August 1902. WBY never contributed to it, but he found occasion to praise 'Mr. Gordon Craig's purple back-cloth that made Dido and Aeneas seem wandering on the edge of eternity' in his next published essay, 'At Stratford-on-Avon', in the *Speaker* of 11 May (*E & I*, 101).

To Ernest Rhys,[1] *2 April* [*1901*]

18 Woburn Buildings | Euston Road.
⟨March⟩ April 2.

My dear Rhys: Yes Thursday with pleasure.
Sunday was out of the question as I am going to Walthamstow that day.[2]

Yours ever
W B Yeats

ALS Kansas.

To Lady Augusta Gregory, 3 April [*1901*]

18 Woburn Buildings | Euston Road.
April 3.

My dear Lady Gregory: You will be glad to hear that I am at "Michael" &
he is going well, 'flying strong' as I heard a sailor say of a crow that he had
seen, or at any rate sworn he had seen, 300 miles from any land.[1] Frank
Harris has written & asked me to go on the staff of his new paper 'The
Candid Friend', which will fill up the gap made by 'The Dome'[2] & I have
offered him an article on 'Gordon Craigs' scenery at an Opera of Purcells
that I saw last week. It was the only good scenery I have ever seen, a perfect

---

[1] Ernest Rhys (1859–1946; see I. 506–7) poet and editor of Welsh extraction, had met WBY in
1887, introduced him to literary London, and arranged the publication of *Fairy and Folk Tales of
the Irish Peasantry* (1888). In 1890 he had helped WBY found the Rhymers' Club and the two
remained friends for life.

[2] WBY was presumably visiting John Masefield (1878–1967), the young poet, who was in
lodgings in Walthamstow, a suburb in the north-east of London. WBY had met him the previous
autumn in circumstances which he later described to Willard Connely, who recalled them in
Adventures in Biography (1956), 48: 'John Masefield was at that time a bank clerk in London. He
wrote me a letter asking whether he could come and see me. He came, told me how he had always
wanted to write, and said, "What shall I write about?" I said, "Your life. Then you will find out
about yourself." Upon this Masefield acted, and brought to the poet a chapter a week, and read it
to him.'

[1] Michael Hearne is the hero of WBY's unfinished novel, *The Speckled Bird*, commissioned in
1896 but abandoned in typescript in 1907 and not published until 1974. An unidentified press
cutting, dated by AG 6 June 1901, announced, presumably upon information provided directly by
WBY, that 'Mr. W. B. Yeats . . . intends to break new ground before long with a novel. The book
is already well under way. Its title, "The Speckled Bird", hints at the nature of the story. The
hero, with whose soul-history the plot is principally concerned, is an Ishmael among men, and
treated by them as a speckled bird is treated by its plain-coated bretheren. The story is mystic in
tone, and decidedly original in treatment. It remains to be seen whether Mr. Yeats will do what
no poet before him has done—succeed in a lengthy work of prose fiction.'

[2] The *Dome*, the illustrated monthly to which WBY frequently contributed, had been discontinued in July 1900. The *Candid Friend* (see p. 53, n. 1) listed him as a contributor from May to
September 1901, but he never published there.

fulfillment of the ideal I have always had. He got wonderful effects by purple robed figures against a purple back cloth. It was like watching people wavering on the edge of infinity, somewhere at the Worlds End. Moore came here yesterday after noon on his way to Ireland. He goes first to Wales for a few days, & as I said good by to him at the Euston Hotel, where I had gone with him to let Mrs Old cook less, I heard a waiter say "somebody for you in drawing room sir". Part of his farewell to London ⟨I suppose⟩ ⟨I wonder⟩, or another student of the language movement in Wales?[3] He has got no quite definite statement from Benson yet but is cheerful about the matter. Mrs Benson, he says is quite bent on playing Grania so she & Benson will do their best to get the play done. The difficulty now is the play in Irish which Benson thinks will offend his Shakespeare people.[4] Moore has pointed out how bad it would be for Benson if it got out & "such things always get out" that he had refused to do the Irish play. He gave him a moving description of the indignation of the Pitt & Gallery. Benson poor man is now between the Gaelic League & Alexandra College[5] wondering how he is to please both. I am to try & see him tomorrow.

I hear 'Coriolanus' comes out at the Lyceum on the 15th[6] & as I shall hardly get in the first night you will find me here still.

Synge's address is or was

90 Rue d'Assas,
Paris.[7]

---

[3] George Moore had long taken pains to ensure that his philandering was notorious, and so WBY perhaps supposed that the Welsh trip had a sexual motive. Mrs Sarah Martha Old (1855–1939) was WBY's cook and housekeeper, inherited from Arthur Symons. In *Some Memories of W. B. Yeats* (Dublin, 1940), Masefield described her (14) as 'a tall, strong country-woman', who at their last meeting, in 1928, told him 'I shall never forget the blessed days with Mr. Yeats at Woburn Buildings, for, oh, they were blessed days'. She died in the same month as WBY.

[4] WBY and Moore, a recent but vociferous convert to the Irish language movement, were trying to persuade Benson to let them produce Douglas Hyde's one-act Gaelic play, *Casadh an tSugain* ('The Twisting of the Rope'), in a double bill with *Diarmuid and Grania*. In this they finally succeeded and the play was performed to an enthusiastic audience by Irish-speaking amateurs from the Keating Branch of the Gaelic League.

[5] Alexandra College had been founded in Dublin in 1866 to provide higher education for women. Associated with Trinity College, it was, in contrast to the Gaelic League, Unionist in outlook and Anglo-Irish in aspiration. The Benson Company appealed to such sentiments; as AG remarked in her diary on 14 Jan 1901, 'he is so very respectable, Merrion Sq & Trinity College could hardly boycott him'. The Benson Company played *King Lear* from 24 to 26 Oct 1901, immediately after *Diarmuid and Grania*.

[6] The Lyceum's unsuccessful production of *Coriolanus*, with Henry Irving in the title role and Ellen Terry as Volumnia, was to run for only 37 performances from 15 Apr to 25 May. WBY and AG had seen Benson's production of the same play in February.

[7] John Millington Synge (1871–1909; see Appendix), playwright and poet, had graduated from Trinity College, Dublin, in 1892 and had been studying at the Sorbonne since 1895. WBY had met him in Paris on 21 Dec 1896 when he had discussed his writing and advised him to go for themes to the West of Ireland and the Aran Islands. Synge had taken a room at 90 rue d'Assas, in the VIe *arrondissement*, in November 1898, and was to retain it until March 1903.

I send "the wind among the reeds" which I forgot to send with Robert.[8] If it is too late, as I rather expect, it cannot be helped. It is my fault & you can give the copy to somebody & so not have the trouble to bring it home in its dull clothes as it went out.[9]

Yours ever
W B Yeats

ALS Berg, with envelope, addressed to Ca' Capello, S. Polo, Venezia, Italy, postmark 'LONDON W.C. AP 4 01'.

To Clement Shorter, [*? 7 April 1901*]

18 Woburn Buildings | Euston Road.
Sunday

My dear Shorter: I got in last night after twelve & found your telegram.[1] I intended to reply to day but I am sorry to say it went out of my head. I hope it did not inconvenience you not hearing. I was dining out to night & could not go to you. I am sorry.

Yours ever
W B Yeats

ALS Berg.

To Lady Augusta Gregory, *11 April* [*1901*]

18 Woburn Buildings | Euston Road.
April 11

My dear Lady Gregory: I hope this will find you before you set out for Paris.

---

[8] William Robert Gregory (1881–1918), Lady Gregory's only child, was currently a second-year undergraduate reading Classics at New College, Oxford. He subsequently became an artist and designed scenery for a number of Abbey plays; WBY celebrated him in three elegies after he was shot down and killed over Italy in January 1918.

[9] Evidently the alternative binding of the 3rd English edition of *The Wind Among the Reeds* (1900), issued in blue-grey boards and with Althea Gyles's full-cover design of interlaced reeds stamped in black (rather than gold on dark blue cloth). No doubt AG was hoping to have the volume rebound in vellum by her Venetian bookbinder, who rebound several WBY's books for her.

[1] Shorter's telegram had seemingly invited WBY to dinner on Sunday, 7 Apr, but he was dining with Masefield in Walthamstow (see p. 54).

I have suddenly remembered that I once heard that there is a translation of the Tain Bo in MS at the Royal Irish Academy, that it was this O Grady used for his Cuchullain epic.[1] Perhaps you might care to ask him &, if I am right, see it on your way to Coole. I remember, I think, hearing that it is sufficient perhaps for literary purposes but not scientific enough for the Academy to publish it. It is I have no doubt bad enough in style. It was done I think about 30 or 40 years ago perhaps by O Donovan.[2]

Sarah Pursur is passing through London. The new church at Lough Rea has been put into the hands of Hughes, herself & others to decorate & she is now looking for a stained-glass expert to teach them.[3] I brought her yesterday to Selweyn Image for his advice. 10,000 is to be spent I think, & she is on the look out for Irish art students of talent. The matter is it seems half private yet I suppose she means in its details, for the main outline is public already. It may give us a Dublin School of Art work. The chief work will be stained-glass, & sculpture & such work as making of holy-water basins & the like.[4]

---

[1] The *Táin Bó Cúailnge* (*The Cattle Raid of Cualnge*), the central story of the Ulster cycle of heroic tales, recounts Cuchulain's deeds in the war between Ulster and the rest of Ireland over the Brown Bull of Cualnge. WBY's discovery was crucial to AG's work, as she noted in her diary (*70 Years*, 398): 'Yeats has been to the Royal Irish Academy and seen the manuscript translation of the *Tain* I had heard of. . . . A great relief, for I was beginning to feel the want of the great central tale to work at, and if I could not have got the *Tain* all my work would have had to lie by.'
   Standish James O'Grady's versions of the heroic tales had been an inspiration to the Irish literary revival. Cuchulain's exploits largely take up his 2-volume *History of Ireland: Heroic Period* (1878–80), condensed as *Cuculain: An Epic* in 1882.
[2] John O'Donovan (1809–61), Gaelic scholar and translator, was best known for his edition of *The Annals of the Four Masters* (1848–51). The Royal Irish Academy's *Catalogue of Irish Manuscripts* indicates that O'Donovan contributed notes to the MS, but the translator and scribe was John O'Daly (1800–78), who finished it in 1857.
[3] Aided by the Dublin painter, Sarah Purser, Edward Martyn (1859–1923), a Galway landlord, playwright, Gaelic Leaguer, and later president of Sinn Fein, who had long been a critic of the quality of Irish ecclesiastical art, had persuaded T. P. Gill, Secretary of the Department of Agriculture, to establish classes in stained glass at the School of Art in Dublin (which had recently come under the Department's jurisdiction). They consulted the English designer, Christopher Whall, who promised them his best pupil, A. E. Child, as instructor, provided that the project was put on a sound footing. Purser immediately set about founding a stained-glass co-operative, An Túr Gloine (Tower of Glass), which opened at 24 Upper Pembroke Street in January 1903. The commission for St Brendan's Cathedral, Loughrea, occupied the early years of the firm, but it also executed windows for the Abbey Theatre. John Hughes (1865–1941), sculptor and instructor at the Metropolitan School of Art in Dublin since 1894, gave up teaching in 1901 to work on his *Man of Sorrows* and *Madonna and Child* for Loughrea Cathedral, although completion of the latter was delayed until 1908–9 because in 1903 Hughes won a commission for a memorial statue of Queen Victoria.
[4] Selwyn Image (1849–1930), poet and artist, had designed stained glass for the Century Guild, St Luke's, Camberwell, and Morthoe Church, Devon. In 1900 he was elected Master of the Art Worker's Guild and appointed Slade Professor of Art at Oxford from 1910 to 1916.

I have several odds & ends of news about other things that I must reserve until I see you. I expect I shall go to Sligo in a couple of weeks.

Yours alway
W B Yeats

ALS Berg, with envelope addressed to Ca' Capello, S. Polo, Venezia, Italy, postmark 'LONDON N.W. AP 11 01'.

To T. Fisher Unwin, 11 April [*1901*]

18 Woburn Buildings | Euston Road.
April 11

Dear Mr Unwin: I enclose that 'errata' slip. It goes between pages 184 & 185.[1]

Yours snry
W B Yeats

PS. let me have proof of slip

ALS Texas.

To Lady Augusta Gregory, [*13 April 1901*]

18 Woburn Buildings | Euston Road.
Saturday night

My dear Lady Gregory: Your letter has just come. Yes I will dine with you on the 19th with pleasure & I will take stalls for the 20th for Coriolanus which I am longing to see.[1] I am very glad you are coming so soon for I have practically made up my mind to go to Stratford on Avon for Bensons 'festival'.[2] 'Speaker' will give me my expenses & it is a chance that may

---

[1] WBY made holograph alterations to five lines of *The Land of Heart's Desire* in AG's advance presentation copy (Emory) of *Poems* (1901), and an errata slip listing these changes (see *VPl*, 207–8, ll. 406a, 407, 411, 418, 423) was subsequently inserted in the edition. These emendations were not made in the two subsequent printings of the play (*PW*, II [1907] and *CW* III [1908]), but were incorporated into Unwin's separate editions and thereafter became part of the canon.

[1] AG, on her way back with Robert from Venice and Trieste, would have found this letter when she arrived in Paris in mid-April to stay with Count Florimond de Basterot at 10 Place de la Borde. Henry Irving's long-delayed but disastrous production of *Coriolanus* (see p. 55) was to open at the Lyceum on 15 Apr. Recalling this visit to the theatre in her diary (Berg) on 12 May 1901, AG reported that 'poor Irving's voice is quite gone, & sounds as if coming from a phonograph'. The following year the Lyceum company went into liquidation.

[2] Benson's company first performed at the Shakespeare Memorial Theatre, Stratford-upon-Avon, in 1886, and for the next 33 years provided the plays for the annual spring festival, producing in that period all Shakespeare's plays except *Titus Andronicus* and *Troilus and Cressida*.

never come again to see 'King John' & all the plays of the Wars of the Roses acted right through in consecutive order. I was hesitating & chiefly that I did not like to miss you. I want to talk over several things. Perhaps you might care to go to Stratford on Avon on your way to Ireland. Benson will give you seats. I find that my return ticket will be only 16/-, & I am trying to find out about lodgings. I have a lot of things to say about Shakespear & this seems the time to say them. It will go into the book of essays[3] rather well. I dare say I can say some things I want to say about the theatre generally when talking about Shakespear. I have only asked the 'The Speaker' £4 (which I calculate will pay expenses even if I do not find a cheap lodging) unless I do them more than one article, in which case they will of course pay me more. They want two articles.[4] I am delighted about the one stringed lute. One string should do much to restrain the irrelevant activities of the musician.[5]

I dined with Symons yesterday. I think he is a little anxious about his expenses. He pays £80 a year rent for his flat, & his wife looks no housekeeper. I told Mrs Old that I wanted to ask them to diner & she said 'I dont mind Lady Gregory or Miss Symons but cooking for her!'—she then became inarticulate. Mrs Symons was beautifully dressed when I dined there.[6]

Yrs snry
W B Yeats

---

[3] The collection of 19 essays published as *Ideas of Good and Evil* in May 1903.

[4] The *Speaker*, edited at this time by J. L. Hammond, commissioned Yeats to write 'At Stratford-on-Avon', published in two parts in the issues for 11 and 18 May; see p. 53, n. 1.

[5] AG, who was currently touring Dalmatia and Montenegro, had evidently written to tell WBY of her purchase in Cattaro of a one-stringed Montenegrin lute to accompany the chanting. According to William Rothenstein (*The Arrow* [1939], 16), it became a feature at WBY's 'Monday Evenings': 'When Yeats came down, candle in hand, to guide one up the long flight of stairs to his rooms, one never knew what company one would find there. There were ladies who sat on the floor and chanted stories, or crooned poems to the accompaniment of a one-stringed instrument.' See also 'The Statesman's Holiday' (*VP*, 627): 'Here's a Montenegrin lute / And its old sole string / Makes me sweet music / And I delight to sing. . . .'

[6] Symons had married Rhoda Bowser (1874–1936), daughter of a Newcastle shipbuilder, on 19 Jan 1901. They had met in 1898 when she came to London to study at the Royal Academy of Music, and after the marriage they took up residence at 134 Lauderdale Mansions, Maida Vale. His wife was not generally liked; after a dinner party on 21 June 1903, Nevinson recorded (Bodleian) meeting 'Arthur Symons—pallid, heavy-eyed, unwholesome & soft, with conspicuous little wife—pale, thin, bright brown eyes, viper mouth, very cruel & full of lust'. On 10 May 1900, even before their marriage, she had warned Symons that she was 'horribly extravagant— *never* out of debt', and although she had inherited a very large sum on the death of her father in January of this year, she and her husband looked upon this as her private fortune. Symons's continuing financial problems obliged him to overwork during the coming years, and were a major cause of the severe breakdown he was to suffer in 1908. His elder sister was Anna Martyn Symons (1864–1933), who, after the death of their father in 1898 had joined the Sisters of the Poor of the West London Mission.

Do not forget to tell me your London address. You have not told it me. Do you return to Queen Annes Mansions.[7]

W B Y

ALS Berg, with envelope addressed to 10 Place de Laborde, Paris, postmark 'LONDON AP 13 01'.

To H. A. Hinkson,[1] [*16 April 1901*]

18 Woburn Buildings | Euston Road.
Tuesday

Dear M[r] Hinkson: I am ashamed of my self for not having answered your invitation long before. I was uncertain about whether or not I should be able to be free on the 20th. A friend, who was I knew to pass through London about then & a possibility of my being in Ireland kept me undecided. Alas it is, as I thought, I cannot get to you on the 20th. I would like however to go out to see you one day before I go back to Ireland, if I can manage it. I am I think going to Stratford on Avon for a few days but shall be back here afterwards for a week I think.

Please tell your wife that I have met lately a M[r] Ranking, who is a brother of a M[r] Ranking, a poet, she used to know years ago. He wants to meet her & has asked me to manage it.[2]

Yrs sny
W B Yeats

ALS Harvard, with envelope addressed to Wrentham, Longfield Road, Ealing W., postmark 'LONDON W.C. AP 15 01'.

[7] AG had given up her rooms in Queen Anne's Mansions before leaving for Italy on 17 Mar, and during her stop-over in London from 19 to 21 Apr stayed with her old friend Sir Arthur Birch (1837–1914) and his daughter, Una, at 3 Savile Row. Although at this time she did not intend to set up in London again, she leased new rooms in Queen Anne's Mansions at the beginning of 1902.

[1] Henry Albert Hinkson (1865–1919), a lawyer and an author of historical romances, had married Katharine Tynan (1859–1931; see I. 516–18), poet, novelist, and friend of WBY, in 1893. At this time they were living in Ealing in West London.

[2] Boyd Montgomerie Ranking (1841–88) was a poet, editor, and journalist who frequently reviewed for the London *Graphic*. He had met Katharine Tynan in 1885 and thereafter wrote numerous enthusiastic notices of her poetry. His younger brother, Lieutenant-Colonel George Speirs Alexander Ranking (1852–1934), entered the Indian Medical Service in 1875 and became a distinguished Arabic and Persian linguist. He was to be University Lecturer in Persian at Oxford from 1905 to 1920.

To Violet Hunt, [23 April 1901]

18 Woburn Buildings | Euston Road.

Dear Miss Hunt: I am sorry to say I am just off to Stratford on Avon for the 'Shakespeare Cycle'. Benson is to do King John, Richard II Henry IV (part II) Henry VI (Part II) & Richard III & I see an opportunity of doing an essay on Shakespeare I have long wanted to do.

Yrs sny
W B Yeats

ALS Private, with envelope addressed to Campden Hill, Kensington, postmark 'STRAT-FORD ON AVON, 23 AP 01'.

To Lady Augusta Gregory, [25 April 1901]

Shakespeare Hotel, | Stratford on Avon.
Thursday.

My dear Lady Gregory: I saw Mrs Benson yesterday. They are quite decided about 'Grania' & we can make our announcements when we like. Will you write to the papers, or shall I & Moore draw up some letter when I am passing through Dublin? She had the play on her table & is evidently full of it.

This is a beautiful place. I am working very hard, reading all the chief criticisms of the plays & I think my essay will be one of the best things I have done. The more I read the worse does the Shakespeare criticism become. And Dowden is about the climax of it.[1] I[t] came out [of] the mid-dle class movement & I feal it my legitimate enemy.

The Benson Company are playing wonderfully & realy speaking their verse finely. Mrs Benson was a realy admirable 'Doll Tear Sheet' last night in Henry IV. It is delightful seeing the plays in an atmosphere of enthusi-asm & in this beautiful place. The theatre is a charming gothic red brick building in a garden with a river flowing by its walls. It is thronged every night—endeed they had to get me a kitchen chair to sit on the night I came. I see a good deal of the Company & would see more but I am very

[1] Edward Dowden (1843–1913; see I. 482–3), Professor of English Literature at Trinity Col-lege, Dublin, established his reputation with *Shakspere: A Critical Study of His Mind & Art* (1875) and consolidated it with further Shakespearian studies and his biography of Shelley. To WBY, Dowden's criticism epitomized the Victorian middle-class assumptions by which, his essay alleges (*E & I*, 103, 106), 'Shakespearian criticism became a vulgar worshipper of success'. He repeated his argument that Shakespeare 'meditated as Solomon, not as Bentham meditated' in *Aut* (235), where he says Dowden 'turned Shakespeare into a British Benthamite'.

busy. One young man keeps coming to me here to invite [me] up the river in a boat—but I am too busy. I am working in the library of the Shakespeare Institute which is attached to the theatre & the library [*for* librarian] has given up to me his private room. But for a half hour or so for lunch I am here all day, from 10 to six when I dine & dress for the theatre. I feal that I am getting deeper into Shakespeare'[s] mystery than ever before & shall be perfectly happy until I have to begin to write & that will be, as always misery. The boy has just brought me a translation of Jervinus 'Commentaries' & I must to work again.[2] I do not even stop for Afternoon tea.

Yrs ev

W B Yeats

ALS Berg, with envelope addressed to Coole, postmark 'STRATFORD ON AVON 25 AP 01'. Partly in Wade, 349.

To Henry Newbolt,[1] [c. 25 April 1901]

Shakespeare Festival Club | Stratford-on-Avon

Dear Mr Newbolt,

Can you come & see me on Monday evening? I shall be back at 18 Woburn Buildings, Upper Woburn Place. I am asking Sturge Moore.

I have come here for the Shakespeare Cycle.[2] I have brought your book

---

[2] Georg Gottfried Gervinus's *Shakespeare* (1849–50) was translated from the German by F. E. Bunnett as *Shakespeare Commentaries* (1862). WBY blamed German criticism for initiating the Victorian utilitarian attitude towards Shakespeare, and lumped Gervinus with Dowden in his essay (*E & I*, 104, 106).

[1] Henry John Newbolt (1862–1938), poet and editor of the *Monthly Review*, had published two volumes of poetry, *Admirals All* (1897) and *The Island Race* (1898), containing the patriotic naval poems and ballads that led Walter de la Mare to dub him the 'nautical Kipling'. Quoting this letter in *The Later Life and Letters of Sir Henry Newbolt* (1942), Newbolt wrote (5–6): 'I went accordingly, asked for a contribution, and got it . . . I enjoyed every moment I spent in his company, whether I went to meet poets like Sturge Moore or Secret Agents like Madame [Olga] de Novikoff. As a host he was unconventional and amusing: as a talker he was miraculous—almost too miraculous, for he would recount experiences of his own which, though told with convincing sincerity, left the hearer in a desperate plight—faced with the impossible necessity of reconciling the world of science with a strongly contrasted world of magic.' Newbolt published WBY's essay, 'Magic', in the *Monthly Review* of September 1901. He was knighted in 1915.

[2] The second week of the Stratford Festival in 1901, 22–7 Apr, became known as the 'Week of Kings'. In 'At Stratford-on-Avon' WBY wrote (*E & I*, 96–7): 'I have seen this week *King John*, *Richard II*, the second part of *Henry IV*, *Henry V*, the second part of *Henry VI*, and *Richard III* played in their right order, with all the links that bind play to play unbroken; and partly because of a spirit in the place, and partly because of the way play supports play, the theatre has moved me as it has never done before. That strange procession of kings and queens, of warring nobles, of insurgent crowds, of courtiers, and of people of the gutter, has been to me almost too visible, too audible, too full of an unearthly energy.'

with me, & read it at intervals in my work. You have set many wise & true & beautiful things to rhyme. Yours is patriotism of the fine sort—patriotism that lays burdens upon a man, & not the patriotism that takes burdens off. The British Press just now, as I think, only understands the other sort, the sort that makes a man say 'I need not trouble to get wisdom for I am English, & my vices have made me great.'[3]

Any time Monday after 8.

Yrs snly
W B Yeats

MS copy Private. Wade, 366.

To Constance Benson, [26 April 1901]

THE SHAKESPEARE HOTEL, | STRATFORD ON AVON.
Friday.

My dear Mrs Benson: I send you the book of my poems I promised you.[1] It contains 'The Countess Cathleen' the play we acted in Dublin our first year of 'The Irish Literary Theatre'.

I would like to see Mr Benson again to day or to morrow. I want to propose to him a method of subscribing the cheaper seats for 'Dairmuid and Grania'. If he thinks well of the plan I could see Mr Harold Large[2] in London next week & take the needful steps to carry out the plan on my way through Dublin the week after. I want to see to the matter now as I shall be in the west of Ireland all summer & may have no other chance.

Yrs sny
W B Yeats

ALS Private.

[3] WBY owned the 2nd edition (1899) of *The Island Race* (*YA4*, 286), which included 'Drake's Drum', the best known of Newbolt's poems and the only one that WBY printed in *OBMV*. In April 1937 WBY read the poem during his BBC broadcast, 'In the Poet's Pub', describing it as 'one of the few great patriotic poems in English'. The British press of this time was strident with Boer War jingoism.

[1] Presumably on 24 Apr; see p. 61.

[2] Harold Large, a New Zealand sportsman and would-be actor, joined the Benson company in the late 1880s and helped Frank Benson start a Folk Drama Association in Stratford-upon-Avon. As manager of Benson's various theatre schemes his enthusiasm tended to outrun his administrative skills, and the National Drama Company which the two had founded in 1900 was about to fail, largely owing to his mismanagement.

To Henry Newbolt, [? 28 April 1901]

18 Woburn Buildings | Euston Road.
Sunday

My dear Newbolt: Can you come & dine with me here to morrow at 7? ⟨wire wire telegraph⟩ I wrote to you from Stratford on Avon, where I had not got your address. I wrote c/o Elkin Matthews, & I am not sure it has reached you.[1]

I expect after dinner a man, who has set one of your poems. He is Bensons musical man.[2] I also expect Sturge Moore.

Yrs sny
W B Yeats

ALS Emory.

To William Stevens,[1] [c. 1 May 1901]

18 Woburn Buildings | Euston Road.
Wednesday.

Dear m^r Stenvens: I send you a copy of the American edition of my last poem. It is much nicer than the English edition. I would have sent it before but my copies have only just reached me.[2]

---

[1] Charles Elkin Mathews (1851–1921) had published WBY's *The Wind Among the Reeds* (1899), as well as Newbolt's first two volumes of poetry.

[2] Christopher ('Chris') Wilson (1874–1919), English composer and conductor, became Benson's Music Master in 1900, and subsequently wrote the incidental music for several Shakespearian productions. In 1932 Benson commemorated Wilson and other 'Old Bensonians' in a memorial window in Stratford's Picture Gallery and Museum. Wilson, who composed one of his finest songs, 'Come away, Death', in 1901, did not publish his setting of Newbolt's poem.

[1] William Stevens (d. 1908), editor of the *Leisure Hour*, 1887–1900, *A Girl's Own Paper*, and *Sunday at Home* was also a proprietor of the Tract Society. In these posts he had put work the Yeatses' way, publishing prose and verse by WBY, a story of Jack Yeats's, and numerous illustrations by JBY. On 20 Dec 1900 (MBY) JBY had asked WBY to send a copy of *The Shadowy Waters* to Stevens '& put your *inscription* in it, he is really so broadminded & loves ideas more than anybody I ever met. There is also plenty of strength and concentration in the old fellow, & he is as receptive as York Powell.'

[2] Included with this letter was a copy of the first American edition of *The Shadowy Waters*, inscribed 'W. Stevens | from W B Yeats | with all good wishes. 1901'. The edition, in grey boards with a white label, was published by Dodd, Mead and Co. and two copies were received at the Library of Congress on 25 Apr 1901.

You were I think the first editor in England who ever published verse or prose of mine.[3]

Yrs sinly
W B Yeats

ALS Private.

To the Editor of the Irish Daily Independent, [2 May 1901]

Sir—I have just sent the following letter to the editor of the "Daily Mail":—[1]

"Sir—I have been sent a cutting from the 'Daily Mail' of April 26th beginning—'A representative of the "Daily Mail" had a short conversation yesterday with Mr. W. B. Yeats, the poet, who, with Mr. George Moore and Mr. Robert Martin,[2] is practically responsible for the Irish Literary Movement.' It is no part of my purpose to correct the inaccuracies in this sentence, or in the report of my opinions which follows it, but I think it my duty to state that your representative did not ask permission to publish my opinions. It is obvious that the practice of quoting in the Press private conversations, however unimportant in themselves, if generally adopted,

---

[3] Stevens had published 'King Goll', WBY's first contribution to an English periodical, in the *Leisure Hour* of September 1887.

[1] Thomas Marlowe (1868–1935) was editor of the *Daily Mail*, the first mass-circulation British daily paper, which maintained its popularity partly by its frequent invasions of privacy. In the interview, 'The New Irish Literary Movement', WBY reportedly stated (5) that Ireland would be bilingual in fifty years and speaking Gaelic in a century, that the Irish were 'not so degraded in their taste as the majority of the English', and that the language movement would detach Ireland from English cultural influence by eventually bringing her 'closer to the Latin races'. Although WBY sent this letter to the *Daily Mail* it was not published there, and, anticipating this, he took the precaution of sending copies to the *Irish Daily Independent and Nation*, to the *Academy*, where it appeared on 4 May 1901 (see *UP* II. 246–71), and probably to other Irish and British newspapers.

[2] An error for Edward Martyn (see p. 57, n. 3). The mistake would have been particularly offensive to Martyn and WBY since Robert Martin (1846–1905), eldest brother of the novelist Violet Martin ('Martin Ross'), was a journalist and comic song-writer in the stage-Irish tradition; his 'Killaloe' and 'Ballyhooley' were particularly popular, and he wrote numerous pieces for burlesques at the Gaiety Theatre. His *Bits of Blarney* had appeared in 1899 under the pseudonym 'Ballyhooley'.

would make it impossible to receive a representative of the Press as the
equal of men of breeding.' "

Yours sincerely
W B Yeats

Printed letter, *Irish Daily Independent*, 2 May 1901 (6).

To T. Fisher Unwin, 2 May 1901

18 Woburn Buildings, | Euston Road. | W.C.
May 2nd,/01

Dear Mr Unwin,

I am dictating this letter to a friend because I am tired out, when I am
tired out my writing is even more illegible than usual. I found "Colloquies
in Criticism" on my arrival from Stratford-on-Avon, I have read a little of
it and will read more.[1] I think the poet who is called Beranger in the Colloquies is not intended for me as I think you supposed, but for Arthur
Symonds. I am criticised in the book but I am not, so far as I can yet see,
one of the characters. The curious things about the book is that while its
criticism is hopelessly Philistine, the verses which it puts into the mouth of
Beranger and which seem to me an imitation of Arthur Symons' verse, are
once or twice really beautiful. The writer is perhaps somebody who has
been taught by a false theory of life, (the theory that the soul and therefore
the imagination exists for society for the order of the World and not that
all things exist for it's sake) who has been taught by a false theory of life to
distrust the sense of beauty. His praise of the Laureate means I suppose
that he has been reading Max Nordau.[2]

I am sorry to say that I am unable to accept your invitation to dinner, as
I go to Ireland early next week. I should have written to you before about

[1] The anonymous author of *Colloquies of Criticism: or, Literature and Democratic Patronage*
(1901), thought literature should concern itself (178) 'with interests and problems external to
itself, and . . . problems arising out of the practical movement of affairs and the changing conditions of society and social intercourse.' He consequently criticized the symbolists, empitomized by
the poet 'Beranger', for 'their passivity and self-abandonment'. While some of Beranger's verse
uses Yeatsean images, WBY is compared favourably to him, and even described as 'a most genuine poet in his way', although too apt to 'escape into a visionary past that has no meaning for the
present'. The Poet Laureate, Alfred Austin (1835–1913), is held up as the model (129) because
his poetry takes 'as its material all life's great activities—not only passion but intellect, political
ambition, religion and philosophy'.

[2] Max Simon Nordau (1849–1923), Hungarian-born author and physician residing in Paris,
made a famous attack on the values of decadent writers and artists in *Entartung* (1892), translated
as *Degeneration* in 1895 (see I. 477).

this but I found a lot of things to do when I arrived here & so procrastinated. I did not realise until I got your letter how many days had passed.

Yours sinrly
W B Yeats

Dict AEFH, signed WBY; Texas.

To Lady Augusta Gregory, [7 May 1901]

18 Woburn Buildings | Euston Road.
Tuesday

My dear Lady Gregory: I cross over to Dublin Thursday night. You will
be sorry to hear that I have let Oldmeadow pay me about half what was
really due—the truth is I wanted money & saw no chance of getting full
payment out of him. Runciman asked Oldmeadow & myself to go & have a
drink with him afterwards as the barmaid was a palmist & he wanted her to
tell my hand. Then came a very funny scene. She said a lot of complimentary things to me—she did not know our names—and this excited Oldmeadow to ask to have his hand told. She looked at it very graveley, & said
with evident ⟨sense of the importance⟩ sincerity 'very fond of women'—&
then emphatically 'you look after your own interests before any body elses'.
By this time Oldmeadow was looking depressed especially as a considerable
audience had gathered. She went on 'as you get older you will be subject to
deep fits of meloncholy'. Oldmeadow cheered up for this sounded romantic & asked what they would be caused by. She considered a long time &
then said 'I dont know. I cannot be sure, but yes I am almost sure the
cause will be—drink'.[1]

I have arranged with Watt that henceforth he will take full responsibility
as to who I publish with.[2] I am to say 'I have handed over all my affairs to
him' & so escape the difficulty ⟨of⟩ caused by ones personal relations with
publishers. I certainly mean also to deal with Oldmeadow through him,
which will an[n]oy Oldmeadow.

---

[1] Ernest James Oldmeadow (1867–1949), was an author, former editor of the *Dome*, and publisher of *Beltaine* (1899–1900). WBY was seeking payment for his essay, 'The Philosophy of Shelley's Poetry'. The first part had appeared in July 1900, but the second part was not published, as
the *Dome* folded. Oldmeadow, who had been a Nonconformist minister in his twenties and was
now preparing for conversion into the Catholic Church, was, with his well-known interest in good
wines, an excellent butt for the barmaid's reading. He tempered the augury by serving as editor of
the *Tablet*, a Catholic weekly, from 1923–36, but gave it some legitimacy by also becoming a Soho
wine merchant under the name of 'Francis Downman'. For Runciman see p. 51, n. 1.
[2] A. P. Watt the literary agent; see p. 5.

About 600 copies of 'Ideals' have been sold, which seems to me very good endeed.

The old mystic I told you of is still declaring I am a jesuit. Somebody said to him they did not beleive it, last Sunday & he answered '& are you going to set your opinion up against mine on a subject I have studied for 65 years'.[3]

Dolmestch is interesting himself in the 'chanting' & has taught Mrs Emery to write out the notes she speaks to.[4] Mrs Emery is trying to get engagements to 'chant' at parties.

Yrs always
W B Yeats

I have just noticed that there ⟨are 3 lines⟩ is something missing in the poem that begins 'with a womans name'. I suppose that what you have sent is a copy. Would you mind looking at what you have copied from & see what ⟨are the lines [?]that come after 'sail upon the wind'⟩ line comes after 'long lived ones'? It out [*for* ought] to rhyme with 'heart'.[5]

ALS Berg, with envelope addressed to Coole, postmark 'LONDON W.C. MY 7 01'.

To D. J. O'Donoghue,[1] [*17 May 1901*]

⟨FEIS CEOIL, | CENTRAL OFFICE: | 37 MOLESWORTH STREET, | DUBLIN.⟩
4 Upper Ely Place | Dublin.

My dear O'Donahue: I am staying at the above address with George Moore. He expects a few people to night & has asked me to ask you

[3] The Revd W. A. Ayton (see p. 149, n. 9), who had a life-long aversion to the Jesuits.

[4] Arnold Dolmetsch (1858–1940) was born in France of a Swiss father, and studied at the Brussels Conservatoire before moving to the Royal College of Music. In the 1890s he led the revival of early English music by performing it on the instruments for which it was written. He played for the Rhymers' Club, was championed by Shaw, and wrote music for William Poel's Elizabethan Stage Society. Sympathetic to restoring the alliance of poetry and music, he began to work with WBY and FF after they attended one of his concerts on 26 Feb 1901. George Moore used him as the model for the musician, Mr Innes, in his novel *Evelyn Innes* (1897).

[5] 'Under the Moon', written at Coole on 3 Sept 1900, which WBY wanted to send to the *Speaker* (see p. 77). The 'woman's name' is 'Brycelinde', and the missing line as first printed was: 'Land of the Tower, when Aengus has thrown the gates apart'. In a letter of 24 May (Berg) AG wrote: 'I enclose the copy of the poem I have—corrected by you, but evidently a line missing. I don't think there was an MS copy, I remember your dictating it from fragments of paper in your different pockets.'

[1] David James O'Donoghue (1866–1917) born in London of Cork parents, was a leading light in the Southwark Irish Club in the 1880s, and helped WBY found the ILS, London, in 1892. He had moved to Dublin in 1896 and set up as a bookseller. A self-educated man, he devoted himself to Irish literature and history, publishing the compendious *Poets of Ireland* in 1892, and biographies of William Carleton (1896), Mangan (1897), and Robert Emmet (Dublin, 1902).

to come. Any time after 8.30. We want to discuss the Theatre & the like.[2]

Yrs snry
W B Yeats

ALS Gainesville.

To W. A. Henderson,[1] *[17 May 1901]*

⟨FEIS CEOIL, | CENTRAL OFFICE: | 37 MOLESWORTH STREET, | DUBLIN.⟩

4 Upper Ely Place, | Dublin.
Friday

Dear Henderson: Can you come & see George Moore & myself this evening? We expect Russell, Macgrath[2] & some others. Any time after 8.30.

Yrs sinly
W B Yeats

ALS NLI.

To Lady Augusta Gregory, [18 May 1901]

⟨18 Woburn Buildings⟩
4 Upper Ely Place | Dublin.
Saturday.

My dear Lady Gregory: I have been to the Royal Irish Academy & seen O'Daly translation. It is, so far as I can see, *a full translation*. It is nearly 400 MSS pages & is about the same length as the original. The librarian

---

[2] George Moore had moved permanently to Dublin at the beginning of April (see pp. 19–20), and WBY was eager to introduce him to literary figures; see p. 48. The present meeting was to discuss the possibility of organizing a travelling stock company under William Fay's management to tour with plays in Irish and English.

[1] W. A. Henderson (1863–1927) had been Secretary of the National Literary Society from 1898. WBY knew him to be a keen student of the theatre and had spoken to his paper 'The Stage Literature of Ireland', delivered to the National Literary Society on 8 Mar 1897, and published in the *New Ireland Review* in May of the same year. Henderson was to become business manager of the Abbey Theatre 1906–7, and was reappointed in February 1908. His volumes of scrapbooks about the theatre, now in NLI, are an invaluable source for the history of the Irish dramatic movement.

[2] John McGrath (1864–1956; see I. 262) was a Dublin journalist. As assistant editor of *United Ireland* in 1892 he had given WBY valuable support in setting up the National Literary Society.

says he has always understood that it is a full translation.[1] There is also a
lythograph copy of the original, which you can buy from the Academy for
£2 should you wish to try & compare translation & original & be unable to
do all the work at the Academy. The librarian thinks the translation good
enough for ordinary purposes.

I have done my Shakespeare essay. It goes to two numbers of 'The
Speaker' and is I think good. The second part is out to day. Moore is
delighted with it. I have also worked over some emendations, which are
great improvements, to Act Second of 'Grania' & have introduced Moore
to a number of people so I have been busy. I go to Sligo on Monday—my
address will be C/o George Pollexfen, Sligo.

Moore is boisterously enduring the sixth cook.[2]

Yours alway
W B Yeats

ALS Berg, with envelope addressed to Coole, postmark 'DUBLIN MY 19 01'.

To Lady Augusta Gregory, [*21 May 1901*]

C/o George Pollexfen, | Sligo
⟨18 Woburn Buildings | Euston Road.⟩
Tuesday.

My dear Lady Gregory: I got here last night.

I had written this sentence when your letter came. I will send off the
card. I was endeed this moment looking in vain for copies which I thought
I had brought to send you.[1] The essay runs to two numbers, & has
delighted Moore. I think I really tell for the first time the truth about the
school of Shakespear critics of whom Dowden is much the best.

Last Saturday & to my great surprize I met Bullen in Dublin. He has
not as I had hoped handed my books over to Hodder & Staughton—the

---

[1] See p. 57. In a letter of 24 Apr (Berg) AG said she thought the Royal Irish Academy *Táin*
MS 'promising', but wanted most to know 'whether it is a complete translation or only of
episodes—you may be able to look at it passing through'. John O'Daly (1800–73) was a bookseller,
teacher, and translator of Irish literature. In her notes to *Cuchulain of Muirthemne*, AG acknowledges her use of the MS.

[2] Since George Moore's palate was notoriously undiscriminating, his attempts to pose as a
gourmet were a standing joke among his acquaintances (see *Aut*, 443–4), and this tale of his
unhappy reintroduction to Irish cooking quickly spread through Dublin. Susan Mitchell gleefully
recounts the story of his seven cooks in her *George Moore* (1916), 110.

[1] In a letter of 'Monday' [20 May 1901; Berg] AG had told WBY that she could not 'make out
if yr Shakespear article is in print—I will put in a card, which please fill & post'. This was evidently an order for the relevant issues of the *Speaker*, which reached her on 28 May.

negociation may however come off—& has been trying to sell copies in
Dublin. He told me that he was amazed to find the hostility to me of the
booksellers. Gill,[2] he declared, seemed to hardly like to speak my name. I
am looked upon as hetredox it seems. 'The Secret Rose' was strange to say
particularly dissaproved of, but they spoke with hostility of even 'The
Shadowy Waters'. Russell told me before I saw Bullen that clerical influence was he beleived working against me because of my mysticism. He
accuses Father Finlay & his jesuits of working behind Moran.[3] Memory of
'The Countess Cathleen' dispute accounts for a good deal. Bullen found
the protestant booksellers little better & asked me if TCD disliked me.
Magee,[4] the College publisher said 'What is he doing here. Why doesnt he
go away & leave us in peace.' He seems to have suspected me of some deep
revolutionary design. As Bullen, was rather drunk when he told me these
things, I asked his traveller, whom I saw on Monday & got the same
account. He had tried to sell a book of Carletons too, & said that Carleton
and myself were received with the same suspicion. This was of course
because of his early stories.[5]

I imagine that as I withdraw from politics my friends among the nationalists will grow less, at first at any rate, & my foes more numerous. What I
hear from Bullen only confirms the idea that I had at the time of 'the
Countess Cathleen' row that it would make a very serious difference in my
position out side the small cultivated class. Which reminds me that I met
Grace in Dublin. He had it seems written to me asking permission to play
The Countess Cathleen at Burr where ever that is, but the letter had gone
astray.[6] It was very daring of him & I would rather like to have seen him
try the experiment.

[2] Henry Joseph Gill (1836–1903) was head of the Dublin publishing firm of M. H. Gill & Son,
50 Sackville St., founded by his father, Michael Henry Gill (1794–1879).
[3] The Revd Thomas A. Finlay, SJ (1848–1940), former rector of Belvedere College (1882–7),
was editor of the *New Ireland Review* and Lecturer in Mental & Moral Philosophy at the Royal
University of Ireland. He was a leading member of the Irish Agriculture Organisation Society,
and a friend of D. P. Moran. On 2 June AG told WBY (Berg) that when questioned by AE,
Moran had admitted that he attacked WBY 'on religious grounds'.
[4] William Magee, a Dublin bookseller and publisher with the Dublin University Press, not to
be confused with the essayist and librarian William Kirkpatrick Magee (see p. 24, n. 6), who
wrote under the pseudonym of 'John Eglinton'.
[5] Although of peasant and Catholic background, the Irish novelist William Carleton
(1794–1869) had been converted to Protestantism as a young aspiring writer, and was taken up by
the rabidly anti-Catholic editor, the Revd Caesar Otway, for whose publication, the *Christian
Examiner and Church of Ireland Magazine* (1825–69), he wrote a number of anti-Catholic stories.
He later revised his work to tone down its religious bias, but continued to be regarded with great
suspicion by Irish critics, as WBY discovered when he edited *Stories from Carleton* in 1889 (see I.
174, 205–7). Bullen had republished his novel *The Black Prophet*, illustrated by JBY, in 1899.
[6] Valentine Grace (1877–1945) had played Shemus Rua in the first production of *The Countess
Cathleen* in May 1899. He ran travelling stock companies and evidently planned to take the play
to the small town of Birr in King's County (now Offaly), but, as P. L. Dickinson testifies in *The*

'Beltaine' ought to come out quite early this year—Moore & Old-meadow both think it should.[7] I am very much inclined to ask A P Watt to try & arrange for it somewhere ⟨at Hodder & Staughton for instance⟩ on a Royalty basis. This partly for the pleasure of referring Oldmeadow to Watt—I have handed all my books to Watt except the book Unwin has. I think I should hand that over too although he can do nothing for me there at present, & will of course take ten percent. It seems to me that it will be better worth his while to look after my affairs if he has all, & that I should be able to say 'He does everything' & so not have to make an invidious selection. What do you think? I feal I ought to hand it over before arrang-ing about 'Beltaine'. I have as you know given Watt complete discretion about the other books. 'Beltaine', should be a Gaelic propaganda paper this time & might really sell very well.

I brought a man to Moore, to propose a Gaelic dramatic touring com-pany.[8] Moore is excited about the scheme, & will try & get money for it. It was in part a sheme of poor Rooneys, whose death has plunged everybody into gloom. Griffith has had to go to hospital for a week so much did it effect him.[9]

My Uncle, who is High Sherrif this year has had a hint from people here, that I must not go near the Constitutional Club, where I have no desire to go.[10] This because of my letter about the late queen. Between my

Dublin of Yesterday (1929), although he had 'served an apprenticeship with Tree and . . . was a really fine actor in dramatic parts', the other members of his company were theatrically and socially less accomplished, so that he 'confined himself, rather wisely, to plays that he knew were popular in Dublin and the Irish provinces, and never took the risk of bringing out new or original productions. . . . There was a tale told of an Irish gentleman in one play who had occasion to drink a glass of champagne, beginning by blowing the froth off it, while he remarked, "This is a lovely wine".' (95–6).

[7] There were in fact no further numbers of *Beltaine*; it was superseded in October 1901 by *Samhain* which had a similar format and was also an occasional review given over to theatre mat-ters.

[8] William Fay (see p. 69, n. 1); nothing came of the plan.

[9] William Rooney (1873–1901), poet and nationalist, died suddenly on 6 May. He had been a member of the Dublin Celtic Society with Arthur Griffith and became his chief assistant on the *United Irishman*. Eulogies appeared in the paper for months after his death, and the tone was set by Griffith's obituary of 11 May 1901 (4): 'The Davis of the National revival is dead—dead in the spring of life—a martyr to his passionate love of our unhappy country. Ireland has lost the son she could least have spared, and we have lost our leader, our comrade, and our life-long friend.' In 1902 he edited Rooney's *Poems and Ballads*, where he described him (p. x) as 'the greatest Irishman whom I have known or whom I can ever expect to know', and WBY dedicated the 1st edition of *Cathleen ni Houlihan* (1902) to his memory.

[10] George J. Pollexfen (1839–1910), a maternal uncle with whom WBY often stayed in Sligo. A leading freemason, and dedicated astrologer, he had joined the GD ('Festina Lente') in 1893. As High Sheriff of County Sligo, it was his duty to preside at county elections, to attend on judges of assize, and to see that writs and sentences were properly executed. The membership of the Constitutional Club, which had premises in Stephen Street, Sligo, was overwhelmingly Unionist and Protestant, and would thus have been offended by WBY's letter in the *Freeman's Journal* of 20 Mar 1900 protesting against Queen Victoria's visit to Ireland.

politics & my mysticism I shall hardly have my head turned with popularity.

Moore dismissed his sixth cook the day I left—six in three weeks. One brought in a policeman, Moore made so much noise. Moore brought the policeman into the dining room & said 'Is there a law in this country to compell me to eat that abominable omlette?'

Yours snly
W B Yeats

ALS Berg, with envelope addressed to Coole, postmark 'SLIGO MY 21 01'. Wade, 349–51.

To Gordon Craig, [c. *21 May 1901*]

C/o George Pollexfen | Sligo. | Ireland.

Dear Mr Craig:

Just a word to say that you will find some remarks of mine on your scenery in 'The Speaker' of May 11.[1] I shall return to the subject.

Yrs sny
W B Yeats

ALS Arsenal.

To Mrs Nora Dryhurst,[1] [*24*] *May* [*1901*]

C/o George Pollexfen | Sligo.
May 25

Dear Mrs Dryhurst: I was in Ireland when the day of your picknics came round. I ment to write to you the night I left but I forgot until it was too late to get a postage stamp, & procrastinated when I got here until this moment. I hope you will excuse me. I was very sorry endeed to miss your walk in the woods.

Yrs snly
W B Yeats

ALS BL, with envelope addressed to 11 Downshire Hill, Hampstead, London, postmark, 'SLIGO MY 24 01'.

[1] See p. 53, n. 1. In 'At Stratford-on-Avon', published in the *Speaker* on 11 May, WBY wrote that Craig's scenery for the Purcell Society performance 'was the first beautiful scenery our stage has seen. He created an ideal country where everything was possible, even speaking in verse, or speaking to music, or the expression of the whole of life in a dance, and I would like to see Stratford-on-Avon decorate its Shakespeare with like scenery' (*E & I*, 100–1).

[1] See p. 52.

To Lady Augusta Gregory, [25 May 1901]

C/o George Pollexfen | Thorn Hill | Sligo.
Saturd

My dear Lady Gregory: yes we should offer Beltaine to Dublin publishers, but insist on its being done as well as possible—I certainly like the wood cut idea—and then if the publishers refuse send it to Watt & write a note in Beltaine on those publishers. I dont know which would do most good, publication in Dublin or the note on publishers. I certainly agree to give profits to Gaelic League.[1] The only thing I really care about is the get up of the thing. I have always felt that my mission in Ireland is to serve taste rather than any definite propoganda.

It is of course possible that Bullen and his traveller may have had too great expectation of the success they would have with my books & so have exaggerated the significance of the opposition. Gill was I understand especially emphatic. It is of course impossible to know to what extent the feeling against me is more than a vague distrust, a vague fealing that I am hetredox.

My father is delighted with my second article on Shakespeare. He has just written to say that it is 'the best article' he 'ever read'. He has sent off four copies. The truth is that Dowden has always been one of his 'intimate enemies' & chiefly because of Dowden's Shakespeare opinions.[2]

I am in a hurry to catch the post.

Yr snly
W B Yeats

PS. I fear I wrote in rather a depressed state of mind the other day, but the truth is I have been in rather low spirits about my Irish work lately &

---

[1] *Beltaine* was superseded by *Samhain*; see p. 72, n. 7. In a letter dated 'Friday' [24 May 1901; Berg] AG had written 'As to Beltaine, I am very strongly of opinion it should be printed and published in Ireland. We must take advantage of every wind that blows, and the home industry people would be put in good humour. . . . And we want all the aids to popularity we can get for the theatre, having your enemies and Moore's enemies and the Castle in general against us. . . . Sealy Bryers might be afraid to take the risk, but I don't think there could be much risk, and it could probably be managed. If there is a profit, do you think it might go to the Gaelic League? Of course it should be well brought out, as an example—We could do woodcuts for it if we liked.' The Irish artist Alice Kinkead had taught AG how to do woodcuts during her visit to London in February, and she was evidently eager to put her new skill to use. In the event, *Samhain* contained no woodcuts, but the profits from the October 1901 number were given to the Gaelic League.

[2] JBY's letter is now lost. As William Murphy has shown (*Prodigal Father* [Ithaca, 1978], 97–100) WBY's views on Shakespeare, and especially on *Richard II*, are almost identical with those his father had advanced in an argument with Dowden in 1874.

quite apart from anything Bullen said. I am in an ebb tide & must wait the flood.

ALS Berg, with envelope addressed to 20 Lower Baggot St, Dublin, postmark 'SLIGO MY 25 01'. Wade, 351–2.

To Lady Augusta Gregory, [28 May 1901]

⟨18 Woburn Buildings⟩
C/o George Pollexfen | Rosses Point | Sligo.
Tuesday

My dear Lady Gregory: please advise me what I should do about the enclosed letter. I suppose he wants a copy of the book. He is the man who used to write to me on my birth day &, if I remember rightly he sent a birth day ode.[1] He once wrote to Jack for his Autograph. Let me have the letter back that I may answer it.

My uncles old servant heard a wailing cry—presumably the banshee the other day and next day he got word of the death of a friend.[2] My uncle has developed a new characteristic which does not enliven our walks. He declares that the roads are so hard & his feet so tender that he can only walk at a crawling pace.

We will have to get an English publisher also for Beltaine I expect, as there are a good many English readers. If (say) Sealy Bryers took it in Ireland & Hodder & Staughton in England this might result in Hodder & Staughton advertizing in it. A P Watt might draw up both agreements. I am rather anxious to let some publisher who has books of mine have some share in it as I have a vague idea of turning it some day into a kind of Irish *Fors Clavigera* in which I could comment on what ever Irish matter I

---

[1] Thomas Hutchinson (1856–1938), headmaster of Pegswood Voluntary Board School, Northumberland, for more than 40 years published a number of volumes of light verse and essays. He made a habit of writing to literary and artistic figures and in June 1894 had sent WBY an ode in celebration of his twenty-ninth birthday (see I. 390). On this occasion Hutchinson had composed a sonnet on *The Countess Cathleen*, and evidently mentioned a difficulty in obtaining a copy of *Poems* (1901).

[2] Mary Battle, George Pollexfen's second-sighted servant, frequently had supernatural visions and dreams, which WBY discusses in *Aut* (70–4; 258–9). Her mind, he explained (70–1), answered his uncle's gloom with merriment and 'was rammed with every sort of old history and strange belief'. In AG's *Visions and Beliefs in the West of Ireland* (1920) he recalled (I. 293) that she 'used to say that dreams were no longer true "when the sap began to rise" and when I asked her how she knew that, she said; "What is the use of having an intellect unless you know a thing like that"'.

liked.³ In any case I think A P Watt should do the busines[s] part. This
will keep the Irish publisher up to the mark. We could of course go to the
publisher & say will you bring out this magazine? If you will A P Watt will
write to you. As I may have to go to Dublin before I go to you I may be
able to see Bryers.⁴ The only complication is that ⟨I have told A P⟩ A P
Watt might think Bryers terms too bad & want to go elsewhere. You might
ask Hyde to let you have a corrected copy of his play so that we could put
the magazine togeather the moment I got to Coole.⁵

Yrs alwy
W B Yeats

ALS Berg, with envelope addressed to 20 Lower Baggot St, Dublin, postmark 'SLIGO MY 29
01'.

To George Russell (AE), [late May 1901]

Mention in letter from AE, 'Saturday' [? 1 June 1901].
Asking about the purchase of white pastels in Dublin; saying that he thinks
conflict with the clerical party in Ireland is inevitable; and apparently asking about the grounds for Moran's attacks on non-Catholic things and
thinkers.

LWBY I. 70–1, where it is dated '[autumn 1900]'.

---

³ *Samhain, Beltaine's* successor, was published in Dublin by Sealy Bryers & Walker and in
London by T. Fisher Unwin. John Ruskin used *Fors Clavigera*, an irregular monthly publication
which ran from 1871 to 1884, to preach his views on social, political, economic, and ethical topics
to working men, its purpose being 'to explain the power of Chance, or Fortune (Fors), as she
offers to men the conditions of prosperity; and as these conditions are accepted or refused, nails
down and fastens their fate for ever, being thus "Clavigera",—"nail-bearing."' *Samhain* was too
closely tied to the Irish dramatic movement to have the range that WBY envisages here, but he
took up the idea again at the end of his life with his periodical *On the Boiler* (1939), telling
Dorothy Wellesley on 17 Dec 1937 (Wade, 902), 'I am writing my *Fors Clavigera*; for the first
time in my life I am saying what are my political beliefs'. In September 1900 WBY had hoped
that Standish James O'Grady would make his *All Ireland Review* 'a kind of Irish "Fors Clavigera"' (*UP* II. 242–3), but, although he continued to regard O'Grady as the 'Irish Ruskin' (see
p. 168, n. 6), he had evidently decided to take on this task himself
⁴ George Bryers (1854–1908) was chairman of Sealy Bryers & Walker, which had published
WBY's first book, *Mosada*, in 1886. Earlier he had been a director of the Dublin Steam Printing
Works and was associated with both the Irish Protestant Home Rule Association and the Imperial
Home Rule Association.
⁵ Hyde's *The Twisting of the Rope* (*Casadh an tSugain*) was published in Gaelic and in Lady
Gregory's English translation in the first issue of *Samhain*. It was produced on 21 Oct 1901 by the
Keating branch of the Gaelic League on the same bill as *Diarmuid and Grania*; see p. 55.

To Lady Augusta Gregory, [*1 June 1901*]

C/o George Pollexfen | Rosses Point | Sligo.
⟨June 1⟩ Saturday

Dear Lady Gregory: Bullen is getting out a new edition of my little Blake anthology. You would greatly help me if you could get me from Mudies a copy of Vol 1 of Gilchrists Life of William Blake. I have to correct some slips in my preface, and for the facts I want to look up Gilchrist is the Authority. If you could get Mudie to send me the book at once I would be greatly obliged.[1]

I hope Bryers or who ever takes 'Beltaine' will get it up uniform with the other numbers. It must be well printed even though the[y] have to make it a penny or two dearer. I always feal that my business in Ireland is not so much to appeal to enthusiasm as to try & lift peoples standards of taste in a few things. I will write to Edward as you suggest. It will be very pleasant putting Beltaine togeather at Coole & the wood cuts will be a great amusement if we can manage them.[2] ⟨I am afraid though they may be⟩ I have sent the poem to 'The Speaker' which should have it in next week.[3]

Yrs alway
W B Yeats

ALS Berg, with envelope addressed to 20 Lower Baggot St, Dublin, postmark 'SLIGO JU [?] 01'.

[1] Bullen's plans for a new edition of *The Poems of William Blake* (1893) did not materialize, and in 1904 the Muses' Library was transferred to George Routledge & Sons who brought out the new edition in June 1905. WBY drew little on Gilchrist in making his few alterations for this edition, and the most substantial change is his identification of Dr Carter Blake (see I. 152, 164 n. 4) as the source for his account of Blake's Irish genealogy. He also corrected Blake's address on p. xxii and made minor verbal emendations on pp. xviii, xix, and xxiv. Mudies was a major circulating library that flourished 1842–94 and lasted into the 1930s.

[2] *Samhain*, which was uniform with *Beltaine*, sold for sixpence, except for the 1904 number, enlarged to mark the opening of the Abbey, which cost one shilling. In her letter of 24 May (see p. 74, n. 1) AG had suggested that 'we should get something from Edward to keep the Church quiet', and followed this up on 'Thursday' [30 May 1901; Berg] by urging WBY to 'ask Edward for an article on some special side of the question . . . it would be stupid to have him just attacking London theatres again'. Although his letter is now lost, WBY evidently did write for Martyn contributed 'A Plea for a National Theatre in Ireland' to the magazine, in which he outlined (14–15) the artistic and economic benefits of a national theatre, and advocated the setting up of a stock company and an acting school. However, *Samhain* contained no woodcuts, apparently because of Moore's opposition, since on 4 June (Berg) AG reported that she had 'told Seely about woodcuts and he assented, but Moore is very suspicious of them!'

[3] 'Under the Moon' (*VP*, 209–10) appeared in the *Speaker* on 15 June 1901. See p. 68.

To Edward Martyn, [c. *1 June 1901*]

Mention in previous letter.
Asking Martyn to contribute an article to the forthcoming *Samhain*.

To Maud Gonne,[1] [? *early June 1901*]

Mention in letter from MG, Monday [? 9 June 1901].
Asking about her trip to America; hoping to see her for occult work; and
telling her of his new work on the rites for the Castle of Heroes.[2]

G–YL, 141

To Mabel Taliaferro,[1] [*early June 1901*]

Mention in the *Evening Telegram* (New York), 5 Feb 1908, p. 5.
A 'perfectly illegible' letter saying that he wanted to see her.

---

[1] Maud Gonne MacBride (MG; 1866–1953; see I. 488–92) met WBY in 1889 and immediately
became the inspiration of much of his poetry. Her beauty and intensity made her an effective
speaker for the nationalist cause, although she had made her home in Paris. She and Major John
MacBride, whom she was to marry in 1903, had returned *c.* 24 May 1901 from a four-month tour
of America to raise money for the Irish cause. In her reply to this letter (*G–YL*, 141) she told
WBY that she had 'succeeded very well in America but will tell you all about this when we meet'.

[2] WBY was at work on rites for the Castle of Heroes, a plan he shared with MG of establishing a mystical Order, 'an Irish Eleusis or Samothrace', at Castle Rock, Lough Key. He had first
had the idea while visiting Douglas Hyde in April 1895, and in *Aut* he recalls (254) that 'for ten
years. . . . my most impassioned thought was a vain attempt to find philosophy and to create ritual for that Order'. The rituals were based on GD practice adapted to Irish use by the incorporation of traditional Gaelic talismans and the Celtic pantheon. In her reply to this letter MG said
that she would like to 'do a little occult work' with him: 'I have not done much, but on the boat I
did a little, writing down some of my visions which may possibly be of use in the rite. I quite
agree with your divisions of the ceremonies.'

[1] Mabel Taliaferro (b. 1889) played the Faery Child in the American production of *The Land
of Heart's Desire* (see below, pp. 86–7), and WBY was beginning to receive newspaper notices
praising her performance. She did meet WBY: in the summer of 1902 her father took her to Ireland where she was introduced to him at a Galway castle rented by wealthy Irish-Americans. As
she recalled in the New York *Evening Telegram* of 5 Feb 1908, WBY 'proved to be the most
eccentric of men. He wore homespun, a flannel shirt and a flowing tie. In the middle of our first
conversation, he rose abruptly and left the room. I wondered if I had offended him in some way,
but six hours later we met again at dinner, as if nothing had happened. . . . After dinner, at his
request, I acted out the play for him that he might see how we had done it in America. It was the
greatest ordeal I had ever been through. Only our hosts and the poet were present. After it was
over, there was a tense moment of silence. Then Mr. Yeats leaned over and said slowly:—"That
is just as I should like to have it done". It was a great relief.' Later in the same trip she stayed at
Coole and performed the play in Gort with members of the INTS.

To Lady Augusta Gregory, [*6 June 1901*]

c/o George Pollexfen | Rosses Point | Sligo.
Thursday

My dear Lady Gregory: I want you to send me the correct form of the phrase which I have quoted incorrectly as 'lose thy life to save it' on page XXIII of the introduction in my little Blake book. I have no bible & could not find the text if I had.[1] Could you also send me either a copy of your article in Cornhill on Arran ballads—it has appeared I think—or if not a copy of your translation of that ballad which has the verse 'you have taken the sun from me you have taken the moon from me etc'. I want to quote a few lines in an essay on popular poetry as contrasted with that of the middle class, which I have ready all but the quotations. I want to send it to the 'Speaker' that I may have some money when I get to Dublin.[2]

My uncle has rheumatism & the way he is going groaning & sighing about the house has me beside myself with supressed rage. Mary Battle who is always praising him always ends up her praise by saying 'It is such a pity he never thinks of any body but himself'. She says this I think, in part, because when ever she is ill he takes no notice, as he is convinced it is bad for her to encourage her to speak of her illness. He himself has scarcely an other subject. I have at last come to the conclusion that he is not a little of a miser. He used to tell me how poor he was but this year he has changed the theme. He now laments that he cannot see anything on which he would like to spend his money. I have suggested that he make this house a little more comfortable—his own room is the only comfortable one in it—but he says they might raise his rent if he did. They would think that he valued the house so much that he would stick to it at all cost if he put in more furniture, or put out the wind. He sighed deeply the other day as he looked over at Jacks drawing & said 'I bought that drawing but I did not want it'.

[1] In *The Poems of William Blake* (1893) WBY had written (p. xxiii) that the change in Blake from 'pure artist' to 'visionary' after *Edward III* (*c.* 1778) 'made him a greater poet and greater artist; for the commandment "lose thy life to save it" is not less true of the intellectual than of the moral life'. He was quoting Luke 9: 24 inaccurately, and in the revised 1905 edition this was corrected (p. xix) to: 'He that findeth his life shall lose it, and he that loseth his life for My sake shall find it.'

[2] AG's article, 'West Irish Folk Ballads', was not published until October 1902, when it appeared in the *Monthly Review*; it was reprinted the following year in *Poets and Dreamers*. She sent WBY an MS version of the poem, 'The Grief of a Girl's Heart', almost immediately and he quoted it in full towards the end of his essay 'What Is "Popular Poetry"?' (*E & I*, 3–12), which appeared not in the *Speaker* but the *Cornhill Magazine* of March 1902. The poem ends: 'You have taken the east from me; you have taken the west from me; you have taken what is before me and what is behind me; you have taken the moon, you have taken the sun from me; and my fear is great you have taken God from me!'

While the weather is fine this is a pleasant place enough however & I am getting on slowly with Michael.[3]

The Life of Blake came to day. Many thanks

Yr ever
W B Yeats

ALS Berg, with envelope addressed to Coole, postmark 'SLIGO JU 6 01'.

To J. B. Yeats,[1] 8 June [1901]

Rosses Point | Sligo. | Ireland.
Jun 8

My dear Father: I enclose £3 which I think is the amount I borrowed from you a while since. I am sorry to have delayed so long about it. I have just been paid for my two 'Speaker' articles.

I have been on the point of writing to Jack to ask to see the play, & hope to do so in a day or so.[2]

We have plans of sending out a travelling company here in Ireland to go through the little towns & play in Irish and English, but the plays this company will play will have to be rough propagandist things with I fear little literary merit. I am rather inclined to think that the movement here is going to pass into a phase of this kind generally—for a time.

I saw Bullen in Dublin to my surprise. I found him at the Contemporary[3] & he came on to Moores where he got more or less drunk. I dined

---

[3] In a letter dated 'Sunday ev' [2 June 1901; Berg] AG told him: 'I dreamed last night that I saw you, & you said you had not been working at Michael. I hope this was but a dream!'

[1] John Butler Yeats (JBY; 1839–1922; see I. 518–20) was in 1901 struggling with debts, somewhat relieved later in the year when a successful exhibition of his work in Dublin led to a commission to paint the portraits of famous Irishmen.

[2] Jack Butler Yeats (1871–1957), painter, author, and younger brother of WBY, had recently completed *James Flaunty or the Terror of the Western Seas*, a short play 'for the Miniature Stage' published by Elkin Mathews in 1901. In an undated letter (MBY), to which this is the reply, JBY had commended it to WBY as 'the prettiest & most poetical little play I ever read. . . . You read it in five minutes & it is only when you read the last line that the tenderness & beauty of the whole idea flashes upon you—The play is done with the most wonderful stage craft. You & Moore & Pinero & Alfred [*sic*] Jones had better take lessons from Jack. I assure you the play haunts me. He must have a real gift for *construction*.' His enthusiasm was not reciprocated and he later reported himself (MBY) 'greatly disappointed to hear . . . that you did not seem to care much for Jack's "Flaunty". I do think you are quite wrong—I do want you to encourage Jack as much as possible to go on writing these little plays, which are something quite fresh & original.'

[3] The Contemporary Club (see I. 481–2), founded in 1885 by C. H. Oldham to provide a forum for all shades of Irish opinion on political, literary, and social questions of the day, had premises at Lincoln Place, Dublin. Its members, who needed to have nothing in common other than being alive at the same time, included JBY, John O'Leary, J. F. Taylor, and George Sigerson.

with him on Sunday night, when he got still more drunk. He asked Moore & myself to dine with him that evening to meet Easons man, which more indignantly refused to do. Eason[4] is going to refuse Moores book & Moore objected on other grounds also. He said to me "why should I dine with Bullen & a tradesman who want to get solidly drunk". The more I think of it the less I apreciate poor Bullen as busines[s] man. He has treated me very well however, & I have told him to do as he likes about my books. He knows that I have given A P Watt absolute control over all my business affairs but he knows also that I wont resent it iff he refuses Watts offers. I shall interfeare in such things no more. Watt can send my things to any publisher he likes.

I do not remember the evening with Todhunter at Moores so cannot tell what his manner signified.[5] When I left Moore in Dublin he was just going to dismiss his seventh cook.[6] I think he was well contented to be in Dublin.

Yours affectely
W B Yeats

ALS MBY.

To Lady Augusta Gregory, [*13 June 1901*][1]

C/o George Pollexfen | Rosses Point | Sligo.
Thursday.

My dear Lady Gregory: Miss Gonne goes to Dublin in a week & goes to Paris before July 5th.[2] I would prefer to go to Dublin in a week & stay there three or four days & then go to you, or better still to go to you so soon as you are ready for me & then to Dublin about the 28th, but I think I must stay with my uncle as long as I can. I dont like to seem to take the

[4] Eason and Son had been founded in 1886 and was now the largest firm of newsagents and booksellers in Dublin. It had evidently given notice of its refusal to stock Moore's *Sister Teresa*, published by T. Fisher Unwin in July 1901 as the sequel to *Evelyn Innes*.

[5] John Todhunter (1839–1916; see I. 515–16), physician turned poet, dramatist, and essayist, was a neighbour of the Yeatses. His plays had impressed WBY as a young man and his *Comedy of Sighs* had been produced on a double bill with *The Land of Heart's Desire* in London in 1894. On his return from his recent trip to Dublin JBY had asked him about an evening with WBY at George Moore's and was answered (*JBYL*, 65–6) in 'a very surly manner—significant of God knows what'.

[6] See p. 70.

[1] WBY's thirty-sixth birthday.

[2] On her return from America in late May (see p. 78), MG had gone back to France, but had written to tell WBY (*G–YL*, 141) that she was now in London nursing her sister, Kathleen, who had been taken seriously ill.

first excuse to get away—though indeed that I am afraid is what I would like to do. I think therefore that I had best stay with him another fortnight & go to Dublin then. What do you think?[3] I have just refused to take any walks with him until the weather improves. I have been driven to this by a series of colds in the head, which were gradually getting worse. He has the idea that if he does more than creep he gets too hot as well as hurts his feet. Hence forth I shall walk alone & go quick enough to keep warm.

Michael goes on slowly enough but he goes on somehow; & I have some more faery tales. I have one about the devil who came blowing down the road in the shape of "the Irish Times".[4]

I have looked up the Stars for Oct 21—the date of 'Grania'; & I expect another row. I have sent the positions to an astrologer for advice about details but row of some kind there will be. The stars are however much better than they were for the first night of 'The Countess Cathleen' (by the by you might let me know by looking up 'Beltaine' if I am right in thinking that night was May 15).[5] For days before & days after that night the "transits" as they are called, that is to say the relation of the stars to their places when I was born were so bad that it is a marvel we had any measure of success at all.

If you would send me again the time of Roberts birth I will get my uncle to cast the horoscope.[6] He is very good at it.

A great many thanks for the ballad. It is a beautiful thing.[7]

Yrs alway
W B Yeats

ALS Berg, with envelope addressed to Coole, postmark 'SLIGO JU 14 01'.

---

[3] In a letter dated 'Saturday' [15 June 1901; Berg] AG replied that, although she was ready for him, and looking forward to his visit 'I would not like you to offend or hurt yr uncle, so perhaps it will be best for you to go to Dublin this next weekend, on Miss Gonne's arrival—& then here—He is used to yr slipping off to Dublin, & won't be offended at that.'

[4] WBY was preparing an enlarged edition of *The Celtic Twilight*, published in July 1902. In 'The Devil', one of the new stories, a young woman was 'out on the road late at night waiting for her young man, when something came flapping and rolling along the road up to her feet. It had the likeness of a newspaper, and presently it flapped up into her face, and she knew by the size of it that it was the *Irish Times*' (*Myth*, 41).

[5] As AG reminded him in her answering letter (see n. 3), the first night of the play was 8 May 1899. She also reported that 'Hyde is strongly of opinion there will be rows if Moore can't be induced to take out his singing of the breasts & 3 or 4 other "fleshy" sentences. . . . Moore having a bad name, everyone will be looking out for passages of this kind'. In the event, the 'fleshy' sentences were retained, including Grania's reminiscence that the 'world was singing and the singing came into my breasts' (*VPl*, 1176), but there was no row at the performance.

[6] In her answering letter AG recalled that 'Robert was born May 20, 1881, 9.00 p. m. in London'.

[7] 'The Grief of a Girl's Heart'; see p. 79. WBY recited the poem frequently in his various lectures on the Irish Revival.

To Thomas Wentworth Higginson,[1] [? *13 June 1901*]

C/o George Pollexfen, Esq, | Rosses Point, | Sligo.
Thursday.

Dear Sir: your letter has been forwarded to me here & I can only regret very greatly that I shall not be in London for some months, unless some unforseen chance compells me. Will you be in London in early Autumn? I shall be there then. I should have much liked to meet my critic.

Yrs v snly
W B Yeats

To Col Thomas Wentworth Higginson
If you can send me a postcard with Miss Guiney's address I should be much obliged.[2]

ALS Higginson.

---

[1] Thomas Wentworth Higginson (1823–1911), American reformer, soldier, author, and critic, was the first to encourage Emily Dickinson to write, and edited two volumes of her verse. He wrote all the poetry reviews for the *Nation* (NY) from 1877 to 1904, and his love of local colour led him to commend the Celtic scenes in WBY's early verse. He had sent WBY a presentation copy of his *Tales of the Enchanted Islands of the Atlantic* (1899; *YA4*, 284), and in his most recent review, of *The Wind Among the Reeds* on 22 June 1899 (479), he had even praised the prose notes as 'so impregnated with Celtic visions that is is really hard to tell where the verse ends and the prose begins'. Higginson made his third and final trip to Europe in 1901, evidently writing to WBY from Italy before arriving in England in July. They were eventually to meet and dine together with several members of the Boston Author's Club at Wellesley College after WBY's lecture there on 30 Nov 1903, and WBY subsequently sent him a copy of Quinn's private edition of *The King's Threshold* inscribed 'To Col. Thomas Wentworth Higginson with kind regards from W B Yeats July 1904'.

[2] Louise Imogen Guiney (1861–1920), poet and author, was the daughter of a Boston lawyer from Tipperary. She had resigned her post at the Boston Public Library on 27 Dec 1900 and settled in England in March of this year. After some weeks in Devon she had moved to Oxford, where she was to spend the remainder of her life. WBY had met her in 1890 (see I. 222) and she had reviewed a number of his books, as well as helping him to place poems in American papers. He had evidently heard that she had now moved to England but did not know her English address. Higginson was a friend of hers from Boston.

To Lady Augusta Gregory, [*22 June 1901*]

Am just starting for Dublin where my address will be
                              73 Lower Mount St.[1]
I have sent off the book to Mudie's,[2] & have also sent my bag to Coole, as
you suggested.[3]

Yrs truly
W B Yeats

ALCS Berg, addressed to Coole, postmarked 'SLIGO JU 22 01'.

To Susan Mary Yeats,[1] *28 June* [*1901*]

73 Lower Mount St. | Dublin.
June 28

My dear Lilly: I sent you some roses from an old rose bush in Sandymount Castle garden. I went out to see the house last week & was shown
over by M^r and Mrs Greer who have it at present. It is again a single
house—it has been 3 houses—& is a boys school. The oak room was burnt
down last year but has been rebuilt in the old form. It has a largish house
attached—a new house. The rest is unchanged. One can recognize in the
remnant of the garden—now the school playing grounds—an old avenue of
trees which is in the photographs & I think other trees & bushes. The
house is manifestly a really old house, very quaint & twisted within. The
young man who brought me there & introduced me to the Greers is a
teacher in the school & engaged to a neice of Greers. On the way out the[y]
showed me a house where he said the neighbours said I had been born.

It was Mrs Greer who gave me the roses. She is full of curiosity about
the photographs which I told her about. Should Lolly be coming over for

---

[1] 73 Lower Mount St. was the address of the Derrybawn Hotel, run by an IRB man, T. Murty
O'Beirne, and his wife. MG had been asked by Mrs O'Beirne, a member of Inghinide na hEireann, to recommend the Hotel to her friends, and in October 1900 told WBY (*G–YL*, 136): 'I
think you would be comfortable here, the prices I know are moderate—' MG had recently
informed him (*G–YL*, 141) that she would be staying there when in Dublin.

[2] Presumably he was returning vol. I of Gilchrist's *Life of William Blake* (see p. 77), which had
arrived on 6 June.

[3] In her letter of 15 June (see p. 82, n. 3) AG suggested that, since he was going first to
Dublin, he had 'better send yr heavy luggage straight here from Sligo'.

[1] Susan Mary ('Lily') Yeats (SMY; 1866–1949), the elder of JBY's two surviving daughters,
and particularly close to the poet. She was still living in the Yeats family home at 3 Blenheim
Road, Bedford Park, with her father and sister, but they were to move back to Dublin in October
1902.

the Literary Theatre in October & care to see the Castle she would get a great welcome if she brought the photographs for them to see, but you might not like to trust them upon a journey.[2]

George Moore is getting on very well here. He is trying to moderate [h]is dislike of Proff Mahaffey so far as to get it into an article which a newspaper will print. When I saw him at work on it he was labouring a comparison between Mahaffey and 'a long pink pig'. He says he is writing on Mahaffey as "the type of the Irish sychophant".[3]

Yours affecly

W B Yeats

ALS MBY.

[2] WBY was born in a semi-detached house, 1 George's Ville, 3 (later 5) Sandymount Avenue, and his first outings as an infant were in the gardens of Sandymount Castle, an 18th-century, subsequently Gothicized, country house owned by JBY's uncle by marriage, Robert Corbet (1795–1872). After his bankruptcy and suicide it was turned into a boy's school, Sandymount Academical Institute, now being run by William A. Greer. The young man who brought WBY to the house may have been James Cousins, a minor poet and later playwright, who had been engaged since 1900 to William Greer's niece by marriage, Margaret 'Gretta' Gillespie (1878–1954). She had been teaching at the school since 1898, and although there is no evidence that Cousins taught there, he was later a master at the Dublin High School and may have been filling in from time to time. Following this visit WBY sent a copy of his *A Book of Irish Verse* to the school, inscribed (Indiana): 'To Sandymount Castle School Library from W. B. Yeats, July 1901'.

In her reply, dated 1 July 1901 (MBY), SMY thanked WBY for the roses and this letter which had 'set Papa thinking & talking of "the time that was". I may be over in October & will show the photographs with pleasure, sad to think of the oak room being burnt down, after all the merry breakfasts that used to be there.' The house exerted a powerful and lasting influence on WBY; on 11 Sept 1930 he recorded in his diary (*Expl*, 318–19) 'a dream which I dream several times a year—a great house which I recognise as partly Coole and partly Sandymount Castle. . . . In all these dreams Sandymount gives the tragic element. . . . I never think of Sandymount Castle and would not have seen it except from the road had I not been shown over it by the headmaster of the school that had what remained—the garden disappeared long ago. The impression on my subconscious was made in childhood, when my uncle Corbet's bankruptcy and death was a recent tragedy, the book with Sandymount Castle printed on the cover open upon my knees. I vividly recall those photographs of ornamental waters, of a little rustic bridge, of the Oak room where celebrated men had sat down to breakfast, of garden paths . . .'

Elizabeth Corbet ('Lolly') Yeats (ECY; 1868–1940), WBY's younger sister, was teaching art in a Froebel school in London, and had published four textbooks on brushwork, the latest being *Elementary Brushwork Studies* (1900).

[3] The Revd John Pentland Mahaffy (1839–1919), at this time a Senior Fellow of Trinity College, Dublin, was a classical scholar of international reputation, a Protestant clergyman, a Unionist, and a critic of attempts to revive the Irish language. He became the centre of controversy in February 1899 when, in evidence to the Commission on Intermediate Education, he asserted that all Irish-language textbooks were either silly or indecent, and that it was 'almost impossible to get hold of a text in Irish which is not religious, or does not suffer from one or other of the objections referred to'. He returned to the attack in the *Nineteenth Century* of August 1899 with an article entitled 'The Recent Fuss About the Irish Language', in which he deplored (222) the 'attempt to resuscitate an artificial Irish language by means of teaching children to smatter it from bad grammars and bad text-books'. Since he himself knew no Irish, these remarks caused great anger in the Gaelic League, as did his reported comment: 'If they must learn Irish, teach them that beautiful

To John Butler Yeats, 12 July [*1901*]

COOLE PARK, | GORT, | CO. GALWAY.

12 July.

My dear Father: I have just got a letter from the American Theatrical manager who produced 'Land of Hearts Desire', enclosing press-cutting. He produced it to geather with Brownings 'In a Balcony'. I thought you might like to hear the result.[1] He went to all the chief towns and seems to have had a very great success, with both plays. Allmost all the notices are enthusiastic, all I think outside Washington & New York, where a certain number of papers liked neither play. In Chicago there was it seems a great success & countless notices & so too in all the other towns. Many of the notices speak of the actors being called again & again before the curtain. One notice says that after the fall of the curtain on 'The Land of Hearts Desire' the actors were called four times.[2] The Wife & the Child, who

---

pre-Gaelic speech of which only three words remain. Anyone with a little aptitude can learn them in a week.' He had subsequently been appointed a Commissioner for Intermediate Education, and as such continued to oppose all efforts to have the Irish language placed on the curriculum for secondary schools. His views were diametrically opposed to Moore's recent but flamboyant conversion to the Irish-Ireland movement, and he attacked Mahaffy in a long and vituperative article, 'The Culture Hero In Dublin Myth', which appeared in the *Leader* of 20 July 1901 (329–31), and which, in the guise of folklore, retold many of the anecdotes about Mahaffy current in Dublin. He portrayed Mahaffy as a social-climbing squireen, lackying obsequiously to rank and title, but stopped short of comparing him directly to 'a long pink pig', contenting himself with the description of 'a man in full health, of large size, with rosy cheeks, and fair faded hair spread thinly over a heavy round crown'.

[1] JBY did. In a letter of 27 July 1901 (MBY) he wrote: 'I am so long about answering yr letter that you must think I have not fully realized the *significance* of such an event as the success of yr play in America—however I do fully realize it, & have thought a great deal about it.'

[2] WBY would have received clippings from Otis Skinner (1858–1942), the American actor-manager, whose company produced *The Land of Heart's Desire* and *In a Balcony* at the Knicker-bocker Theatre in New York on 6 May 1901, and subsequently took the plays on a tour that included Baltimore, Boston, Chicago, Indianapolis, Ithaca (NY), Lancaster (Pa.), Louisville, Milwaukee, Philadelphia, Pittsburg, Providence, Richmond (Va.), St Louis, and Washington, DC. The Washington papers were the least enthusiastic. The *Washington Evening Star* of 17 May tartly observed (16) that WBY's play 'proved sufficiently mystical to content the most profound cultist. Possibly it was the contrast with this labored allegory that made Browning seem so lucid', while the *Washington Post* of 17 May thought (2) it had 'less reason than the Browning drama for stage presentation'. Chicago made up for this disparagement: the three performances at the Grand Opera House on 27–8 May drew the largest audiences of the season, and on 28 May the *Chicago Journal*, regretting that the plays could not run 'until every man and woman in Chicago has seen them', praised (5) the production as 'entirely opposed to the sordid commercialism of which the modern theater is continually accused . . . the entertainment last night was managed with amazing shrewdness to appeal in every possible manner to the refined sensibilities of the esthetic and intellectual man'. There were similarly enthusiastic reviews in the Chicago *Daily News*, *Inter-Ocean*, and in the *Dial* of 16 June.

Though none of the notices traced specifies four curtain calls, on 15 May the *Philadelphia Press* reported (8) that 'the curtain was raised several times in response to the applause', and on 4 June

seems to have made a big effect with the crusufix scene, were the chief success.[3] The notices seem to me the expression of a genuine enthusiasm, & not of any desire to encourage a merely curious experement. One notice says that the same audience that welcomed 'The Casino Girl' one night welcomed Brownings play & my play the next night. America is certainly an astonishment.[4] I have unfortunately no American rights in my play, as it would have made some money for me. It seems to ha[ve] been beautifully acted & staged, with music especially written for it.[5]

I am writing narrative poems of the Irish heroic age,[6] the first things of the kind I have done since I wrote 'The Wanderings of Usheen'. They will make a series I have intended to write ever since I was 20. I have shrunk from begging [*for* beginning] them until my blank verse seemed sufficiently varied. I have also plans for a new play with Moore, a religeous Don Quixote, which may or may not be carried out.[7]

Yr affectly son
W B Yeats

ALS MBY, with envelope addressed to 3 Blenheim Road, Bedford Park, London. W., postmark 'GORT JY 14 01'.

---

the *Pittsburg Leader* wrote (9) that 'those who were there refused to leave until the actors had responded to a call. In an artistic and literary way the matinee takes rank of any theatrical production given in Pittsburg for a number of years.'

[3] The part of Shaun Bruin's wife, Maire, was played by Nora O'Brien, a recent graduate of the Sargent School, and that of the Faery Child by Mabel Taliaferro (see p. 78). The Chicago *Daily News* of 28 May reported (3) that she made 'an instantaneous hit as the fairy child, which elfin sprite she played with exquisite feeling and intelligence and wonderful variation of humor and grace. Nora O'Brien was adorable, too, as Shawn's bride . . .'.

[4] Skinner's Company had opening-night competition not only from Harry Bache Smith's *The Casino Girl* (1900), a three-act musical comedy titillatingly billed at the Illinois Theatre as 'the Great Girly Drollery', but also from Frank Pixley's musical comedy *King Dodo* at the Studebaker, and W. A. Brady's revival of *Uncle Tom's Cabin* at the Auditorium. As the *Inter-Ocean* wrote, a 'theatrical night of infinite variety in the matter of opening attractions found the poetic lines of Robert Browning competing with the doggerel nonsense of the up-to-date librettists of musical comedy, the idealism of Yeats conflicting with the realism of conventional melodrama'.

[5] The music for the production, composed by Julian Edwards, was described on 16 May by the *Baltimore News* (11) as 'a strain of Irish music—sombre, wailing, enigmatical, with occasional piercing high notes which sank into dark laments', and the *Baltimore Morning Herald* praised (6) the discreet use of 'a weird, Irish folk tone; a sort of leit motif that betokens the presence of the evil fairy'.

[6] WBY's narrative poem, 'Baile and Aillinn' (*VP*, 188–97), was first published in the *Monthly Review* of July 1902.

[7] The first mention of WBY's proposed collaboration with George Moore on *Where There Is Nothing* (1902), which was to cause a breach in their friendship.

To Maud Gonne, [c. *12 July 1901*]

Mention in letter from MG, [July 1901].
Asking about her plans for visiting Dublin, and enquiring about places to stay there.[1] Also sending her the scenario of a play he had made for Douglas Hyde.[2]

G–YL, 142.

To Arthur Griffith,[1] *16 July* [*1901*]

c/o Lady Gregory | COOLE PARK, | GORT, | CO. GALWAY.
July 16

My dear Griffith: my little play 'The Land of Hearts Desire' has had so far as I can make out a real success in America. Lady Gregory a few days ago got the idea that you might perhaps write a paragraph on it if she sent you materials. She has copied out as you will see by the enclosed a great many press notices, in which you may find something to quote. She thinks it will help our Theatre as it will make people take me more seriously as a dramatist. However that may be I would like some little record in some Irish paper & in your paper by preference. I always write for my own people though I am content perforce to let my work come to them slowly. I am just starting a little play about Cuchullin & Concobar partly I dare say encouraged by this American success.[2] The seeming impossibility of getting my work sufficiently well performed to escape mere absurdity had rather discouraged me.

I thought your comment on Moores letter entirely admirable. It was

---

[1] MG advised him (*G–YL*, 142) not to stay at Mrs O'Beirne's (see p. 84, n. 1) as her hotel would be overcrowded during Horse Show week.

[2] Perhaps the scenario for *An Naomh ar Iarraid* (*The Lost Saint*), based on WBY's story 'Where There Is Nothing, There Is God', but not dramatized by Hyde until August 1902. Hyde had written his first play, *Casadh an tSugain* (*The Twisting of the Rope*) in August 1900 from another scenario by WBY.

[1] Arthur Griffith (1872–1922; see Appendix) was founder and editor of the *United Irishman*, a nationalist weekly which put politics before art and which was to become increasingly critical of WBY and J. M. Synge. Griffith passed the cuttings (with this letter) to his drama critic, F. J. Fay, who used them as the basis of an article on 27 July.

[2] *On Baile's Strand*, first published in *In The Seven Woods* (1903).

vigerous just & courteous.[3] I hear he has just finished his attack on Mahaffey which is certain to be amusing, & by no means courteous.[4] I hope he does not make a martyr of Mahaffey though.

Yrs snly
W B Yeats

ALS Private. Wade, 352–3.

To Douglas Hyde, [mid-July 1901]

Mention in letter from Hyde, [July 1901].
Discussing plans for the Pan Celtic Congress; asking who is to attend; questioning Hyde about the Gaelic League's attitude towards it; and suggesting a Conversazione to which the delegates could be invited as guests rather than official representatives.[1]

MBY.

---

[3] In a letter to the *Irish Daily Independent* on 1 July 1901 (6), Moore had argued at length that England would gain greater sympathy for her own interests if she undertook to restore Gaelic as the language of Ireland. In the *United Irishman* of 6 July 1901 (4) Griffith criticized Moore for thinking 'that the remedy for our lack of loyalty is the facilitating by the Government of England of our efforts to revive our language. . . . Mr. Moore labours under a delusion if he thinks that Irish Nationalists would barter their belief in the necessity for separation from England, even for such a tempting bribe as official facilities for teaching Irish. As for Mr. Moore's hint to the Government that England should grant our desires because she wants soldiers . . . we fancy England will look in vain for any but the worst class of Irishmen for her army.'
[4] See p. 85, n. 3.
[1] The Pan Celtic movement, a loose alliance of cultural associations established in 'Celtic' countries, had organized a Congress in Dublin from 19 to 23 Aug. The Irish Committee of the movement had been established in Dublin on 2 Dec 1898, with Lord Castletown as Chairman, E. E. Fournier as Secretary, and WBY on the committee. It had planned to hold a Congress in Dublin in 1900, but this was postponed owing to the outbreak of the Boer War. From the beginning, the Gaelic League was divided in its attitude to the Pan Celtic movement. Hyde, Eoin MacNeill, and Patrick Pearse were generally sympathetic, but other influential members, particularly P. J. Keawell, Nora Borthwick, Margaret O'Reilly and Fr. Peter O'Leary, were implacably opposed to it, partly on ideological grounds—they thought it was federationalist rather than Home Rule in politics, and would diffuse Irish energies—and partly because of intense personal animosity towards Castletown, who was not only a peer but had been an influential opponent of the Land League in the 1880s. An invitation to Hyde from the Irish Committee of the Congress had been turned down by the League's Executive Committee without a vote, because as Hyde explained to AG in December 1898 (diary, Berg) they were 'afraid of its taking money from the G. L. & the Feis people are afraid it will take money from the Feis'. Hyde's and Pearse's attendance at the Welsh National Eisteddfod in 1899 as Gaelic League delegates was bitterly attacked in *Claidheamh Soluis*, and in August that year the League formulated its official policy towards the Pan Celts in a six-point statement which advocated peaceful coexistence: no League branches were to affiliate with the movement, but nor should they show overt hostility. This compromise did not satisfy the anti-Pan Celtic faction, and with the help of D. P. Moran they began to intrigue against Hyde's leadership of the League. An article, 'Wanted—A Man', published in the

To Robert Bridges,[1] *20 July* [*1901*]

c/o Lady Gregory | COOLE PARK, | GORT, | CO. GALWAY.

July 20

My dear Mr Bridges: Certainly Mrs Waterhouse may include 'The Lake Isle of Innisfree' and 'The Sorrow of Love' in her book.[2] I confess I grow not a little jealous of the 'Lake Isle' which has put the noses of all my other children out of joint; & I am not very proud of 'The Sorrow of Love'—I wonder does she know my book 'The Wind among the Reeds'—but as she will.

I shall be away all summer for I shall not leave Ireland until after the performances by 'The Irish Literary Theatre' which begin on Oct 21. I shall hardly be back until early November. Might I not run down to you for a winter day or two.[3] The country is always beautiful whatever the season.

I take up your letter again & notice to my distress that it is dated June 18 but the reason of the delay is that I have been moving about & so have only just opened the box of books & letters, which my housekeeper in London sent on to me here.

I am writing a half lyrical half narrative poem on two old Irish lovers, Baile, Honey Mouth & one Alyinn—to write the names as they are spoken.

Leader on 1 June 1901, sniped at him and insinuated the need for a clerical successor, and Fr O'Leary was to attack the Pan Celtic Congress violently in the same periodical on 27 July. WBY's questions about Hyde's attitude to the Pan Celtic Congress came therefore at a particularly sensitive time. In his reply Hyde said that he did not 'exactly know who is coming' nor whether the attitude of the League had changed: 'The position is awkward to say the least of it. If we take any official notice we will run the risk of raising a row.' He added that WBY's 'idea seems the best, to give a Conversatione & invite the delegates to it as guests', and he promised to enquire about the feasibility of this.

[1] Robert Seymour Bridges (1844–1930), poet, dramatist, essayist, and Poet Laureate from 1913 to 1930. He had first written to WBY in 1896, praising *Poems* (1895), and the two had met in 1897.

[2] On 8 July 1901 (*CRB*, 19) Bridges had written to WBY on behalf of his mother-in-law, Mrs Elizabeth Waterhouse (1834–1918), who wanted to include these two poems in an anthology she was editing. They duly appeared in *A Little Book of Life and Death*, which she published in June 1902 as part of Methuen's Little Library series. WBY had a copy in his library (*YA4*, 289).

[3] WBY had first visited Bridges at his country home at Yattendon, near Newbury, Berkshire, in late March 1897 but the two had lost contact of late and on 18 June 1901 (*CRB*, 18–19) Bridges had written to say that he was 'sorry never to have a chance of meeting you. . . . Is it *possible* that you will honour us by another visit this summer? . . . Please come if you can.' He repeated the invitation in his letter of 8 July (see above, n. 2). WBY may have already been feeling guilty over the matter, for in an undated letter (MBY), written in the summer of 1899, JBY had reported that 'York Powell asked me to get you to write to the poet Bridges explaining that you were too busy &c. to go down to see him. It seems he is rather hurt that you never accepted his invitations to come & see him . . .'. Since both Bridges' father-in-law and wife were seriously ill over the winter, it is unlikely that WBY paid his visit.

I then go on to other stories of the same epoch. I have in fact begun what I have always ment to be the chief work of my life—The giving life not to a single story but to a whole world of little stories, some not endeed very little, to a romantic region, a sort of enchanted wood. The old Irish poets wove life into life thereby giving to the wildest & strangest romance, the solidity & vitality [of] the *Comedie Humaine* & all this romance was knitted into the scenery of the country. 'Here at this very sport [*for* spot] the faery woman gave so & so the cup of magic meed. Not there by the hillock but here by the Rock' & so on. This work has not been possible to me hitherto, partly because my verse was not plastic enough & partly for lack of a good translation. But now my friend Lady Gregory has made the most lovely translation putting the old prose & verse not into the pedantic 'hedge school master' style of her predecessors, but into a musical caressing English, which never goes very far from the idioms of the country people she knows so well. Her book, which she is about two thirds through, will I think take its place between the *Morte D'Arthur* & The *Mabinogion*.

I have a notion of getting one of these stories, in which there are dialogues in verse spoken by a reciter who will chant the dialogues in verse to a psaltery. Dolmetsch has interested himself in the chanting—about which you ask me—and has made a psaltery for Miss Farr. It has 12 strings, one for each note in her voice. She will speak to it, speaking an octave lower than she sings. In our experiments in London we found your verse the most suited of all verse to this method.[4] She recites, your 'Nightingales' your 'Muse & poet'[5] and a third poem of yours whose name I forget. You should hear but had better wait until she has got used to the Psaltry & has perfected the method with Dolmetsch a little more. We found that the moment a poem was chanted one saw it in a quite new light—so much verse that read well spoke very ill. Miss Farr has found your verse & mine ⟨&⟩ a little modern lyric verse to be vocal, but that when one gets back a few generations lyric verse ceases to be vocal until it gets vocal as song not as speech is, as one approaches the Elizabethans. We had great difficulty even with Keats & though we got a passage which is splendidly vocal we had to transpose a line because of a construction, which could only be clear to the eye which can see several words at once.[6]

[4] Arnold Dolmetsch continued to experiment with the psaltery, and it was not until 6 Oct that he could announce to FF (London): 'It has gone through many tribulations; but it is now perfectly satisfactory, and, I think, very pleasant to see.' The final lyre-shaped instrument, made of satinwood, had 26 alternating strings of fine steel and twisted brass arranged an octave apart so that the octave could be played with one finger. This original psaltery survives and is in the possession of Michael Yeats.

[5] 'The Nightingales' was published in *Shorter Poems, Book V* (1893), and 'Muse and Poet', WBY's title for 'Will love again awake', in *Poems* (1879). WBY included both poems in *OBMV* (1936).

[6] Anna Mather had chanted Keats's 'Bacchic Ode' at the February lecture (see pp. 21, 35), and WBY was to chant it during a dinner at 'Michael Field's' in June 1902.

I shall be altogether content if we can perfect this art for I have never felt that reading was better than an error, a part of the fall into the flesh, a mouthful of the apple.

Yours sinly
W B Yeats

ALS Private. Wade, 353.

To W. T. Horton,[1] *20 July* [*1901*]

C/o Lady Gregory | COOLE PARK, | GORT, | CO. GALWAY.
July 20

My dear Horton: I cannot say any good thing about the verses. I am sorry not to be able to praise them even a little. You are not a poet, & I cannot think that you can ever become one—you have not the instrument. You are an artist—in these very verses you are trying to make pictures as an artist makes them. Take up your drawing again & no matter how irksome it is force yourself to work hard at it. Listen to no voice even though it seem that of an angel of light that tells you to turn poet.[2] In art as in the spiritual life the will is all but all in all & if you cannot force yourself to get over the mechanical & tecnical difficulties of art you will in all likelihood fail in the spiritual life as well. Remember that in the astral light lives the prince of the air & that one of his temptations is a false spirituality, which offers the soul ease. I think you would be wise to turn from the visions for a while for after all one's craft what ever it be, has been sent to one to harden the will & the soul, as a sword is tempered by the smith.

I thought your book of child's pictures excellent. Why not go on with that kind of work.[3] I know that to almost every artist & poet too, perhaps to almost every craftsman, there comes a time when he grows weary of his own craft & longs for some thing else. Then come the deceiving voices & he is lost if he obey them.

Yrs sny
W B Yeats

ALS Texas.

[1] William Thomas Horton (1864–1919), visionary, artist, and illustrator, probably first met WBY in the winter of 1895–6, and their friendship lasted until Horton's death. WBY wrote an introduction for his *A Book of Images* (1898), and in 'All Soul's Night' (*VP*, 471) recalled him as one 'who loved strange thought / And knew that sweet extremity of pride / That's called platonic love . . .'. Despite WBY's advice, Horton did publish his poetry, and some of the poems he had shown WBY on this occasion were probably among the 48 which appeared in *The Way of the Soul: A Legend in Line and Verse* (1910), all of which exhibit the characteristics described in this letter.

[2] See 2 Cor., 11:14, 'for Satan himself is transformed into an angel of light'.

[3] Horton did 12 colour illustrations for *The Grig's Book* (1900), a shilling collection of ten

To T. Mullett Ellis,[1] *20 July* [*1901*]

COOLE PARK, | GORT, | CO. GALWAY.
July 20.

Dear Sir: on looking over a mass of letters, which I have not had time to deal with hither to, I find one from you dated July 8th. asking for a poem for 'The Thrush'. I am sorry to say that I have no finished poem by me— I write very little & very slowly. In any case all my my affairs are in the hands of an agent, who settles all such questions. I write so little, that I have to ask rather high prices.

Yours sinly
W B Yeats

APS Private.

To F. J. Fay,[1] [c. *22 July 1901*]

Mention in letter from Fay, 23 July 1901.
Discussing the history of verse speaking in the theatre.[2]

Private.

nursery rhymes. He dedicated the book 'To Andrew Lang, friend of All Children from One of Them—THE ARTIST'. WBY had an inscribed copy in his library (*YL*, 919).

[1] T. Mullett Ellis (1850–1919) poet and novelist, had given up his architect's practice for literature, and helped found the *Evening News*, the first halfpenny Conservative newspaper. On 'the first day of the new century' he had started the *Thrush* as a monthly 'Periodical for the Publication of Original Poetry', which was 'intended to bring thoughts of beauty and the consolation of exalted ideas into the hearts of the people', and, as he explained in the August number, was 'continuing to make every effort to get the best available work of the most eminent living Poets to place before our readers'. In this he was only moderately successful: WBY, Thomas Hardy, and A. E. Housman declined to publish with him and, although he printed some work by. Arthur Symons, Gilbert Murray, Victor Plarr, and Richard Le Gallienne, the magazine was dismissed in the *Academy* on 21 Dec 1901 as 'devoted mainly to the effusions of the amateur poet'. It did not long survive this attack, folding after its 14th number in February 1902.

[1] Francis John 'Frank' Fay (1870–1931; see Appendix), actor and drama critic, was writing theatre reviews for Arthur Griffith in the *United Irishman*. He and his brother, William G. Fay, were the leaders of an amateur dramatic group, the Ormond Dramatic Society, which was to become the Irish National Theatre Society (INTS) in 1902.

[2] This was probably the first letter of an extensive correspondence between Frank Fay and WBY on methods of speaking dramatic verse. WBY had evidently asked Fay for information about the way verse was spoken at different periods, and particularly whether it was chanted. Fay obliged with a detailed account of the French stage from the age of Molière and Racine, and the English stage from the time of Betterton and Garrick, explaining that 'I just write these particulars for you in order to place the position before you, because you have probably had neither the time nor the inclination to read up theatrical history'.

To Elizabeth Corbet Yeats, 25 July [*1901*]

COOLE PARK, | GORT, | CO. GALWAY.
July 25

My dear Lolly: Please tell me who the A L Lilley spoken of in the enclosed may be, & return me the letter. I had rather not have taken the chair on the whole, as he may want to criticize my own work & my presence may embarrass him, but tell me who he is in any case. The committee probably think I know. I do not & would like to before I answer.[1]

I am getting towards the end of a longish poem—longish for me, 60 or 70 lines on an Irish legendary subject. After that I do another of about 40 or 50 lines & then start on a little play about Cuchullin, as long as 'The Shadowy Waters'. I expect to have a new book of verse ready by next spring, & one much more likely to please Irish people than any I have done. Lady Gregory is completing a wonderful book of translations from the Irish, the best translations from the Irish any body has ever done, a really great book & her work makes possible for the first time a number of poems I have been waiting to do since I was twenty.

I suppose you read Moore on Mahaffey. When Moore got to Dublin he went to the Gaelic League & asked what he could do for the cause. They said 'attack Mahaffey, he is being mischiefous on the Intermediate Board'. Moore said "I will. I have come over to be use ful. You say he is doing mischief that is all I want to know. I saw him once." He then wrote in a relegous spirit of impartial hate & I think the League is a little bewildered & surprized. Now he wants more work, like the spirit who rose, when the wizards servant opened his masters book.[2]

[1] The Revd Canon Alfred Leslie Lilley (1860–1948), Vicar of St Mary's, Paddington, from 1900 to 1912, was born in Co. Armagh and educated at Trinity College, Dublin, where he was a medallist in modern literature. His *Modernism: A Record and Review* appeared in 1908. In his lecture, 'Recent Irish Poetry', not delivered to the ILS until 31 May 1902, with Sidney Colvin, rather than WBY, in the chair, he said (*Freeman's Journal*, 5 June 1902, p. 6) that WBY, though young, 'might be classed in the very front rank of modern poets. . . . Mr. Yeats had all the traits of that Celtic imagination which is never happy except in hunting some dim shadowy phantom. Throughout the poetry of Mr. Yeats there was always present the love for nature, the sympathy with sorrows of all earth born things, and an intense passionate outcry against the wrongs done on the weak—characteristic indeed of all Irish poetry.' ECY had been elected to the Committee of the ILS in March 1900 and, as SMY reported on 1 July 1901 (see p. 85, n. 2), spent 'many hours a week at I.L.S. Committees'. The *Irish Literary Society Gazette* of March 1901 reported (2) that she had attended 15 of the 22 committee meetings that year.

[2] See p. 85 n. 3. Moore lived to regret his intemperance and the consequent loss of Mahaffy's intellectual companionship, writing in *Salve* (Cave, 95) that 'if it had not been for a ferocious article published at the time, attacking him for his lack of sympathy for the Gaelic Movement, we might have spent many pleasant hours together'. WBY had probably found 'the spirit who rose', a version of 'The Sorcerer's Apprentice' folk-motif, in 'The Master and his Pupil', published in Joseph Jacobs' *English Fairy Stories* (1890).

I have been very much bored by a young lady who has insisted on painting my portrait & has made me look like the manager of a creamery.[3]

Yr ev
W B Yeats

ALS MBY.

To George Moore, [c. *26 July 1901*]

Mention in letter from Moore, 27 July 1901.
Discussing *Diarmuid and Grania*; suggesting that Finn and Grania should
speak the funeral oration, not King Cormac; pointing out the inconsistency
that Grania lays Diarmuid's spear, Broad Edge, on his litter, although it
had been left in the house;[1] and asking Moore to write an article for the
forthcoming *Beltaine.*[2]

LWBY I. 85–6.

To F. J. Fay, [c. *28 July 1901*]

Mention in letter from Fay, 29 July 1901.
A letter Fay described as 'full of interest', telling him that WBY has found
a theatre manager interested in the recitation of verse;[1] discussing possible
indications by Shakespeare of how his verse should be spoken;[2] evidently

---

[3] Alice (Annie) S. Kinkead (1871–1926), portrait and landscape painter (see p. 74, n. 1), was
born in Tuam, a daughter of Dr Richard Kinkead (d. 1928), Professor of Obstetrics at University
College, Galway. She held her first show in 1897 and subsequently exhibited at the Royal Hibernian Academy, the Royal Society of Portrait Painters, and the Society of Women Artists. Miss
Kinkead was a guest at Coole during the summer, and her portrait of WBY was exhibited at the
Royal Hibernian Academy in 1904. She had recently moved to London where she lived for the
rest of her life.

[1] In the published version of the play all three characters speak briefly over Diarmuid's body,
and the authors surmount this technical difficulty by use of the future tense. At the end of Act II
Diarmuid refuses to take his heavy spear, 'Broad Edge', on his fatal boar-hunt lest men accuse
him of hunting 'with his battle gear upon him', and in the final scene Grania declines to place
Diarmuid's lighter spear on his litter, promising that she 'will lay beside him the Broad Edge that
I bade him take instead of this spear I warned him not to take' (*VPl*, 1221).
[3] Moore contributed 'The Irish Literary Theatre' to *Samhain* 1901, a short article which
sketched the trials and tribulations of the ILT during its three-year existence.

[1] In his reply Fay expressed surprise 'that you have found a theatrical manager who took an
interest in it. Who was he—Jalland? And certainly, I should not, from their delivery, imagine that
any of the younger Bensonites took an interest in anything lower than athletics.'
[2] See below, p. 98, n. 4.

asking about the delivery of verse on the Restoration stage;[3] describing FF's plans for recitation;[4] and recalling 'Miss Frazer's' performance as Maire Bruin.[5]

Private.

To W. Barrington Baker,[1] [*31 July 1901*]

COOLE PARK, | GORT, | CO. GALWAY.

Dear Mr Baker:

I shall do my best to go the the *Ceilidh*. I am going to Dublin for Miss Milligans plays in the Ancient Concert Rooms, at any rate. They begin on the 26 I beleive. So if the *Ceilidh* is near that date I shall go to it, of a certainty.[2]

Yrs sny
W B Yeats

ALS Private, with envelope addressed to Bank House, 40 Capel St, Dublin, postmark 'GORT JY 31 01'.

[3] Fay told WBY that 'there is reason to believe that, by the actors of the Restoration, considerable attention was paid to the declamation of verse', and he promised to show WBY 'a passage in Colley Cibber's *Apology* which will lead you to that conclusion'.

[4] Fay replied that WBY's 'description of what Miss Farr is to do has raised my expectations to a high pitch'.

[5] Winifred Fraser, née Exton (b. 1872) had, as Fay recalled in his article on the play's reception in America, acted the part of Maire Bruin in the original production of *The Land of Heart's Desire* at the Avenue Theatre in 1894. WBY had evidently commented upon the article and praised her acting, for Fay replied: 'Yes, although she has not an Irish voice, Miss Frazer must have played Maire Bruin beautifully. She made her name in Ibsen however. But an Irish voice is *essential* in an Irish play. I don't refer to accent but to quality.'

[1] William Barrington Baker (1875–1957), who, like WBY, had attended the Dublin High School, served as Librarian and Assistant Secretary of the National Literary Society from 1896 to 1902. An employee of the Provincial Bank, he was posted to the North of Ireland in 1916, and settled there for the rest of his life.

[2] Alice Milligan (1866–1953), pseudonym 'Iris Olkryn', was a poet, novelist, editor, and dramatist whose one-act play, *The Last Feast of the Fianna*, had been staged by the ILT in 1900 and published in *Beltaine*. Her new plays, *The Deliverance of Red Hugh* and *The Harp that Once*, were produced by the Fays for Inghinidhe na hEireann (The Daughters of Erin), a nationalist politico-cultural society of young women founded by MG, and performed on alternate days during the week of 26–30 Aug at the Antient Concert Rooms. The National Literary Society had acted upon WBY's suggestion, and arranged a ceilidh, an evening of traditional Irish dancing and music, and a conversazione on 23 Aug in honour of the delegates to the Pan Celtic Congress (see p. 89, n. 1).

To Douglas Hyde, [c. *31 July 1901*]

Mention in letter from Hyde, 1 August 1901.
Discussing the danger of a split in the Gaelic League over the Pan Celtic Congress and the growth of sectarianism in the League, but noting that it has the extreme Nationalist party behind it. Also telling him that he thinks very highly of AG's work on Cuchulain; that he has done a scenario for Hyde; and that *The Land of Heart's Desire* has been a success in America.[1]

LWBY I. 87–9.

To F. J. Fay, 1 August [*1901*]

at | COOLE PARK, | GORT, | CO. GALWAY.
August 1.

Dear Mr Fay: I was altogeather pleased with your article on 'The Land of Heart's Desire' in the 'U.I'.[1] I am very glad too that you are going to say something about the Gaiety Theatre's dread of naming either Moore or

---

[1] WBY's suggestion that a conversazione might offer neutral ground upon which Gaelic Leaguers and delegates to the Pan Celtic Congress could meet (see p. 89) had not found favour with the League's Executive Committee, as Hyde had written to inform him on 24 July (MBY), complaining that the 'whole Pan-Celtic business has been a thorn in our sides from the first. It lost us some of our very best workers, and has produced more friction than anything else inside the League. It will be a great pity if the distinguished foreigners go home with the idea there is no movement here or that Ld Castletown *is* the movement, but it would be worse to dislocate the League by trying to make it alter its determination.' Although he still toyed with the idea of going to Dublin 'to see the foreign visitors & explain matters', he doubted if he 'could prudently take part in any processions or the like, or any banqueting'. But by the time of his reply to this letter, on 1 Aug, the crisis in the League was so grave that he could not even entertain the prospect of attending the conversazione for fear that he 'would rouse furious animosity' among those 'who would say their President was betraying them & appearing in a semi-official position' and he concluded that he would 'be doing best for the League . . . by keeping away altogether from the Nat^l Lit^y Soc^y's Conversazione'. He added that he was 'delighted beyond measure' that WBY thought so highly of AG's work, and offered to translate portions of it into Irish as a Gaelic League book. He said he was also 'very curious about your scenario of a new play', and that he'd 'do my best on it' (see p. 88, n. 2).

[1] This, based on the American press cuttings WBY had sent Griffith on 16 July (see p. 88), had appeared on 27 July, and in his letter of 29 July 1901 (see p. 95) Fay hoped that it had not put him 'in a false light': 'I love that little play and tried to show it in what I said but know how inadequate I am to deal with your work.' In the article Fay had called for a Dublin production of the play, 'but knowing Mr. Yeats's fastidiousness with regard to the delivery of his verse, one must, I suppose, be content with reading *The Land of Heart's Desire*, and be thankful one has it to read'. This thought led Fay, who had formed his amateur Ormond Dramatic Society in 1891, to drop WBY a broad hint about their future collaboration by suggesting that 'if Yeats's gifts as a dramatist are to be of use to his countrymen his plays must be acted and acted by Irish actors. Cannot he get together a company of amateurs and train them in the way he wants them to go?'

myself. I am more surprised at Hylands stupidity than at his fear, for he can hardly expect us not to say what 'the play by an Irish author' is. He has been very nervous from the start & even feared that doing an Irish play by us might keep people away from Bensons Shakespeare performances. The ordinary theatre going person in Dublin, of the wealthier classes dislikes our movement so much that Hyland has something to say for himself. An esteemed relative of my own told me, a while back, that Douglas Hyde had said "in a speech that he hoped to wade through Protestant blood", & would hardly beleive me when I denied it. They look on us all in much the same way—'Literary Theatre' 'Gaelic League' are all one to them.[2]

I think Jalland probably was the stage manager I ment but I am not sure.[3]

I dont beleive in those 'under scorings' in the folio but I certainly thought it a good sign to meet an actor that did.[4]

I wish very much that my work were for the Irish Language for many reasons. I hope to collaborate with Hyde in a little play in it shortly.[5]

[2] In his letter Fay had drawn attention to the baldness of the advance announcement of *Diarmuid and Grania* in the Dublin papers ('Mr Benson is to produce an original Irish play by a Dublin author'), adding that he hoped 'to say a word on the matter in the *UI*. I suppose they are afraid to mention W. B. Yeats and George Moore. There is nothing gained by hiding the matter because everyone who takes an interest in such things knows what the play is and who are the authors.' Charles Hyland was general manager and secretary of the Gaiety Theatre, and in charge of publicity. WBY's 'esteemed relative' was his uncle, George Pollexfen.

[3] i.e. the stage manager interested in the recitation of verse; see p. 95, n. 1. Henry Jalland (1861–1928), an original member of the Benson company, became a business manager when Benson opened at the Globe Theatre in 1889. Thereafter he was periodically associated with Benson, and in 1900 he was manager at the Lyceum.

[4] In his letter WBY had evidently mentioned a discussion with an actor (probably from Benson's Company) about underlinings in Shakespeare's First Folio, and Fay commented that it was 'most interesting to know that Shakespeare has left any hint, however slight, of the way he would like his lines delivered; but it is amazing to find *actors* taking notice of such a thing. The average actor to whom I have spoken looks on anyone who attempts to take him seriously as an ass, and I am not so sure that he is not quite right.' For Shakespeare to have underscored the Folio would indeed have been 'most interesting' since he had been dead for seven years by the time of its publication in 1623.

[5] At this time Fay was an enthusiastic member of the Gaelic League, and in his letter of 29 July had confessed that his 'only regret is that your work is not for the *Irish* language, which was *made* for dramatic utterance'. In his article, too, he had wished 'to see Irish only used in plays dealing with Ireland; but this will not be possible for some years, and in Mr. Yeats's case I suppose that will never come to pass'. Douglas Hyde had already taken one of WBY's stories, 'The Twisting of the Rope', as the scenario for *Casadh an tSugain*, which was to be produced with *Diarmuid and Grania* in October of this year (see p. 55), and WBY had suggested further collaboration (see pp. 88, 97). Hyde was to help WBY write *Where There Is Nothing* in the early autumn of 1902, and was to use a number of AG's plots and stories as the basis for his plays in Irish.

I shall be in Dublin for your performances in 'The Ancient Concert Rooms'. I see by the paper that they begin on the 26th.

Yr sny
W B Yeats

ALS Private, with envelope [NLI] addressed to 12 Ormond Road, Rathmines, postmark 'Gort AU 1 01'. Wade, 355.

To the Editor of the Daily Express *(Dublin), 2 August* [*1901*]

August 2

Sir,

I find in your issue of July 19, which I have but just seen, a paragraph copied from an English paper. The paragraph makes me say, on the evidence of a supposed interview in a paper called the "Free Lance," that "I hope to see Irish becoming the language of the artistic and intellectual world of Anglo-Saxondom," and that, "of course, it will take centuries."[1]

It then comments—"Mr. Yeats is anxious to beat Methusaleh's record." As the Irish opposition to movements of enthusiasm and of intellect has always found anonymous anecdotes among the chief of its weapons, I will take the trouble to contradict this one. The interview in the "Free Lance"

---

[1] The *Free Lance*, 'A Popular Society and Critical Journal', was edited from its founding in 1901 by Clement Scott (1841–1904), previously a well-known drama critic. In the course of a lengthy interview, published on 20 July (363) WBY was quoted as saying that he had 'had few opportunities of learning Irish, and until lately my knowledge of my own language was very scanty. . . . However, I am acquiring my native tongue by degrees . . . and I hope I may live to see Irish becoming the language of the artistic and intellectual world in Anglo-Saxondom. Of course, it will take centuries, but I have no doubt as to the ultimate result.' The *Daily Express* quoted this part of the interview with the comment that WBY was 'anxious to beat Methusaleh's record', but this letter, attempting to put the record straight, led to further recriminations (see below, pp. 113–14). The *Free Lance* 'interview' continued: 'It is always the minorities that tell in the long run, whether in language or in any other department of mental activity. The few intelligent people will always rule the many unintelligent. Now I think the average Irishman is infinitely more intelligent than the average Englishman; and it follows that, if Irishmen will only insist upon using their own language, and developing their own literature in their own language, the best thinkers will be compelled to turn to Ireland and to learn the Irish language, in order not to be hopelessly behind the age. It is not numbers that count; it is the few best heads that impose their language and thoughts and methods on the "general".' WBY had complained in May of an 'interview' in the *Daily Mail* (see pp. 65–6), similar in sentiment to this one.

never took place. It is not the first time this year I have had to complain of a spurious interview in an English paper.[2]

Yours truly

W B Yeats

Printed letter, *Daily Express* (Dublin), 5 August 1901 (4). *UP* II. 253.

To Cornelius Weygandt,[1] 3 August [1901]

at | COOLE PARK, | GORT, | CO. GALWAY.

August 3

Dear Sir: 'The Irish Literary Theatre' performances take place this year in Dublin, on October 26th, when the Benson company will produce under our auspices 'Dairmuid & Grania' by George Moore & myself & *Casad an T Sugan* a play in Irish by D[r] Duglas Hyde.[2] The performances will take place in 'The Gaety', & the actors of D[r] Hyde's play will be him self & some members of the Gaelic League. 'Beltaine' has not come to an end. A substantial number, containing a translation of the play in Irish, will be issued in September but whether by its old publishers or not I cannot say.[3]

Yr snry

W B Yeats

APS Private, with envelope addressed to College Hall, University of Pennsylvania, The College, Philadelphia, postmark 'GORT AU 3 01'.

[2] In an ALS draft of this letter, dated 2 Aug (Berg) the last two sentences read: 'The interview in "The Free Lance" is spurious. I have given no interview to any English paper recently.'

[1] Cornelius Weygandt (1871–1957), a professor of English at the University of Pennsylvania, wrote to WBY periodically from 1897 to gather information on the intellectual movement in Ireland. His *Irish Plays and Playwrights* (1913) and *The Time of Yeats* (1937) grew out of his correspondence and meetings with WBY and other Anglo-Irish writers. WBY and Weygandt first met at Coole in August 1902.

[2] The plays were in fact first produced on 21 Oct, but WBY may have deliberately given the date as the 26th, since he announced in *Samhain* that Hyde's play 'may be played by anyone after October 26th as he does not reserve acting rights'.

[3] See p. 75. As he explained in the first issue, WBY changed the magazine's name to *Samhain*, 'the old name for the beginning of winter, because our plays this year are in October, and because our Theatre is coming to an end in its present shape'.

To T. Fisher Unwin, 3 August [*1901*]

C/o Lady Gregory | COOLE PARK, | GORT, | CO. GALWAY.
August 3

Dear Mr Unwin: I am so worried by people asking for photographs, & my photographs are so bad, that it has occured to me that you may have some extra prints of the frontispeice to my book of poems.[1] If this is so & you could let me have half a dozen I would be greatly obliged. The success of my little play 'The Land of Hearts Desire' in America has just brought me one or two new applications.

Yr sny
W B Yeats

ALS Texas.

To Lafcadio Hearn, [*August 1901*]

Mention in letter from Hearn, 24 September 1901.
Sending an autograph version of 'Baile and Aillinn', and replying to Hearn's protests about the revision of his earlier poems.[1] WBY promised a partial restoration of 'The Folk of the Air' and discussed his alterations to it: '[I] doubt if the [*suppressed*] stanza is wanted at all . . . [I] like to close so short a poem with a single unbroken mood. . . . Surely the [*suppressed*] stanza merely tells, without rhythmical charm, what is *implied* by the other

---

[1] The frontispiece portrait for the 1899 and 1901 editions of *Poems* was a pencil sketch by JBY.

[1] On 22 June 1901 Lafcadio Hearn, a lecturer in English literature at the Imperial University of Tokyo, had sent WBY a letter of 'violent protest' over the revisions to 'The Host of the Air' (*VP*, 143–5) in *The Wind Among the Reeds*: 'You have mangled it, maimed it, deformed it, extenuated it—destroyed it totally. . . . you have really sinned a great sin! *Do* try to be sorry for it!—reprint the original version,—tell critics to go to perdition, if they don't like it,—and, above all things, *n'y touchez plus!*' Lafcadio Hearn (1850–1904), born of a Greek mother and Irish father, was a literary critic and orientalist. In this lost answering letter WBY sent Hearn an MS version of his latest poem, 'Baile and Aillinn', and promised to restore parts of 'The Host of the Air' to their original form. WBY evidently knew Hearn's work, for Reginald Hine reports that in December 1908 he observed *a propos* of Gavin Douglas's *Palice of Honour*: 'If ever you want a definition of poetry, there has been none, not in this last four hundred years, as short and to the point as his "pleasance and half wonder," though sometimes I prefer the full wonder of Lafcadio Hearn's "There is something ghostly in all great art"' (*Confessions of an Un-Common Attorney* [1945], 152).

stanzas.' WBY also suggests that the phrase 'blacken with dread' had become rhetorical and threadbare.[2]

MBY.

To Thomas Hutchinson,[1] *August* [*1901*]

at | COOLE PARK, | GORT, | CO. GALWAY.
August

Dear Mr Hutchinson: I have just opened a great bundle of letters which I have hitherto been unable to attend to and I am sorry to find one of yours, which has I am ashamed to say been weeks without an answer. I am heartily glad that you have not got my last edition of 'Poems' for I have had a number of letters from friends & strangers—the last from the professor of English literature in the University of Japan—complaining of my corrections. I have come to the conclusion, that even when one certainly improves ones work, as when one disengages a half hidden meaning or gets rid of a needless inversion, no body who liked the old will like the new. One changes for the sake of new readers, not for the sake of old ones. When the old ones come on the changes they do not send one kind sonnets like that you sent me on 'The Countess Cathleen' but indignant letters.

Yrs sny
W B Yeats

ALS Kansas.

[2] 'The Host of the Air' had originally appeared in the *Bookman* in November 1893, and been republished in *The Second Book of the Rhymers' Club* (1894) and, in a revised form, in *The Wind Among the Reeds*. In this latest printing WBY had omitted the penultimate stanza: 'He knew now the folk of the air, / And his heart was blackened by dread, / And he ran to the door of his house; / Old women were keening the dead;' (*VP*, 145). Despite his promise to Hearn he never restored the poem to its original form.

[1] For Thomas Hutchinson see p. 75. In this reply WBY was following the advice given by AG on 30 May (Berg): 'you had better write an answer in the half humbugging tone the letter is written in, & say you are glad on the whole he has not seen the new edition, as another old reader of yours (Russell) is just now loudly lamenting the changes you have made, & he might probably do the same . . .'.

To Charles Elkin Mathews, [c. 3 August 1901]

at | COOLE PARK, | GORT, | CO. GALWAY.

My dear Matthews: you told me that you were getting the block deepenned of the cover of 'The Wind among the Reeds'. If you have any copies printed from the new block I would like to have one, which you can put down to my account.

If you are printing a new edition any time, remember what we talked over about the covers. They were to be black on grey I think for the ordinary copies & there were to be certain more expensive copies printed in gold on parchment. I would like to see specemen covers when the time comes.[1]

Yrs snly
W B Yeats

ALS Reading, dated 'Aug 4 1901' in another hand.

To George Russell (AE), [c. 9 August 1901]

COOLE PARK, | GORT, | CO. GALWAY.

My dear Russell: I send you the letter I got from Fay a while back. I dare say you have seen him but I send you the letter in case you have not. The objection is I imagine to working with any one not in full political sympathy.[1] Griffith is I think strong on this point & influences the others. He

[1] See p. 64, n. 1. Mathews issued the next (1903) edition in light mottled blue paper boards with buff linen spine, lettered in black on the front cover, with a label, printed in black, pasted on the spine.

[1] WBY had discussed with Moore, AE, and Fay the possibility of organizing a Gaelic theatrical touring company (see p. 72) and AE, as he reported in an undated letter to WBY, written shortly before this one (MBY), had mentioned the plan to Valentine Grace (see p. 71) who 'jumped at it. He said he would *put money* into it. He had himself taken a company round the Green Isle and knew the business. He has also in his possession properties including the scenery of the Countess Cathleen, which he bought, and these might lessen the starting expenses of Fay's company. I suggest your talking to Fay about him, and, if Fay approves, I will write to Grace, who is in the country, and arrange a meeting in Dublin, at which they might discuss matters. . . . though Grace does not know Gaelic, he might be useful in the English dramatic sketches.' At this time the Fays were radical nationalists and Grace, in so far as politics concerned him, was a Unionist and the heir to a baronetcy. In his reply to this letter (*LWBY* I. 97; dated 1902) AE told WBY: 'I saw Fay yesterday. The objections to Grace are political.' The Fays were not to persist in their political views; on 30 Jan 1903 W. G. Fay told WBY (NLI) that 'a Theatre is no more a Political Party than its a Temperance platform. . . . For pity sake let Art at least be free.'

objects to the Feis Coal & dreads its example, rightly or wrongly.[2] I dont know what Grace thinks politically but I dare say you may. Of course artistic matters should be outside politics, but on the other hand these fierce people who are so valuable need politics, it may be to keep them in spirit even in artistic matters.

I have written a large part of a longish poem on Baile, the sweet spoken, & Aillin.

Yours ev
W B Yeats

ALS Indiana.

To T. Sturge Moore, 11 August [*1901*]

at | COOLE PARK, | GORT, | CO. GALWAY.
August 11.

My dear Moore: now that I have your play in print I think even better of it than I did when you read it. I am much more satisfied with your verse, & your theory of verse, than I was. You certainly get vivid effects out of your modern words & I do not now find any of the verse too intricate in its thought though I do sometimes regret an inverted phrase.[1] The play should act admirably, & one regrets vivid as they are the few little things that do not come within the limits of the stage. If they were not there you would have an admirable chance of being pirated in America at once. They have just pirated my 'Land of Hearts Desire' & played it with great success, to judge by the press cuttings, through all the chief towns. They did it with 'In a Balcony' by Browning & seem to have had very much more than *a succes d'esteme*. Quite ordinary papers were enthusiastic & wrote under such headings as 'the triumph of the literary drama'. In Chicago, at any rate they played not only to a full house but to increased prices.

---

[2] The Feis Ceoil Association was formed in 1897 to promote the study and cultivation of Irish music, to hold an annual festival, or Feis Ceoil, and to collect and publish the old airs of Ireland. Griffith objected to it because he considered it West British in tendency and because it did not require Irish bands to learn Irish music.

[1] *Aphrodite against Artemis* (see p. 8, n. 1), a one-act play based on the Phaedra–Hippolytus legend, was published by The Unicorn Press in August 1901. Although predominantly in blank verse, the characters move into free verse at moments of emotional intensity. WBY did not retain his good opinion of the play. Writing to AG on 4 Apr 1906 (Berg) he described its first production (on 1 Apr 1906) as 'a failure': 'It had imaginative moments, but was made intolerable by a whole series of mistakes. I saw it with the greatest sympathy, for there were gathered together all the mistakes I had ever committed myself. I read the thing years ago, and evidently knew nothing about the business when I did read it, for I thought it was going to succeed.'

All seems to me to show that if one writes actable little plays now, without too many characters they will find there way on to some stage. I think you have done the best play of the kind there is. I hope you will soon publish your 'Herod' also.[2]

I am starting a little heroical play about Cuchullin[3] & am curious to see how my recent practical experience of the stage will effect my work. I have a strong plot, with some ironical humour. The play is part of a greater scheme. I am doing all the chief stories of the first heroic age in Ireland in a series of poems. I have just finished a half narrative half lyrical poem of about 200 lines, which is I think good.

Theseus, himself, is I think about the finest, but all the characterization in your play is good—perhaps 'the maidens' do not seem of very 'good family' but they are all the more vivid.[4]

Yr sny
W B Yeats

ALS Texas. Bridge, 1–2.

To W. T. Horton, 11 August [1901]

at | COOLE PARK, | GORT, | CO. GALWAY.
August 11.

My dear Horton: I should have written to thank you for the drawing long ago.[1] It is like all you do characteristic, full of your personal colour as it were. You ought to succeed because of this personal quality but like most visionary & imaginative artists your difficulty is to force yourself to study not the visionary truth but the forms & methods by which it has to be expressed in this world. I liked your 'Grigs Book'[2] because I thought the tecnical qualities were nearly quite adequate. You had got mastery over a medium over that exact form of colour & line, & the general fantasy & pretty grotesqueness made any errors in drawing unimportant. What you

---

[2] Sturge Moore's play about Herod was *Mariamne*, not published until 1911.

[3] i.e. *On Baile's Strand*; see p. 88.

[4] A Chorus of 'maidens of good family' attending on Phaedra provide comic relief by fluttering at the indifferent Hippolytus, and by singing a coyly indecorous song at a tragic juncture in the play.

[1] Pasted into AG's copy of Horton's *A Book of Images* (Emory) is an original ink drawing by Horton, possibly of WBY, dated 27 July 1901 and inscribed 'William T. Horton to W. B. Yeats in affection and deep gratitude'. The drawing, entitled 'Aspiratus', is reproduced overleaf.

[2] See p. 92.

William T. Horton to W. B. Yeats in affection and deep gratitude. 13/7/01

'Aspiratus', Horton's drawing, possibly of WBY.

should do I am certain is struggle for such mastery. Keeping to subjects, which have a certain sweetness & composure, or at most a satirical grotesqueness & struggling to draw as well as possible. Your success or failure will depend on your drawing not on the visitings or passings away of the spiritual imagination. That will never go far from you. It is quite certain to me that you should force yourself to study from the life & from nature in every form but this I fear you will not do.

Again thanking you for the drawing.

Yrs sinly

W B Yeats

ALS Texas, with envelope addressed to 42 Stanford Road, Brighton, postmark 'GORT AU 12 01'.

To the President of the National Literary Society,[1] [*mid–August 1901*]

COOLE PARK, | GORT, | CO. GALWAY.

Mr W B Yeats presents his compliments to the President & Council of the National Literary Society & has pleasure in accepting their kind invitation for Friday 23rd.[2]

ALS Private.

[1] The President of the National Literary Society from 1893 to his death was George Sigerson (1839–1925), physician, scholar, and man of letters; (see I. 25). He published poems, essays, and books on Irish politics, history and society, as well as editing a number of anthologies, the best known being *Bards of the Gael and Gall* (1897).

[2] The invitation was to speak at the National Literary Society's ceilidh and conversazione arranged at the Leinster Lecture Hall, Molesworth Street, for the delegates to the Pan Celtic Congress (see p. 89). WBY gave a version of his essay 'Ireland and the Arts', which was to be published in the *United Irishman* on 31 Aug 1901 (2), and used the occasion to argue that the Celtic revivalists 'were not fighting for provincialism, but against the source of all vulgarity, tepid emotions, and half-beliefs. They were trying to create an art which would be founded upon the songs of the people.' (*Irish Daily Independent*, 24 Aug 1901, p. 6.)

To the Revd J. K. Fielding,[1] *[mid–August 1901]*

COOLE PARK, Gort, Co. Galway, Ireland.

Chairman Committee of Arrangements:

Dear Sir.—Will you be good enough to give my thanks to the Gaelic League of America for inviting me to their National Convention.

I very much regret that it is impossible for me to be present this year, though it is possible I may be able to attend at some future time, as I look forward to some day visiting America.

The work before the Gaelic League of America and the Gaelic League of Ireland is perhaps the most important that is before the Irish people to-day. The nationality of Ireland is in her songs and in her stories, and in her chronicles and in her traditions, and this nationality can be ever present with the exile as with those at home, but it can only be perfectly present with those who understand the language of Ireland.

Very sincerely,
W B Yeats

To the Rev. J. K. Fielding.

Printed letter, the *Gael* (NY), October 1901 (303).

To the Editor of Nationality,[1] *18 August* [*1901*]

at | COOLE PARK, | GORT, | CO. GALWAY.
August 18.

Dear Sir: I have found your jurnal 'Nationality' full of thoughts that are wholesome to all men just now. The time when a nation surrenders the

---

[1] The Kilkenny-born Revd James K. Fielding (1870–1940), assistant priest of St Thomas's Church in Chicago, was national chaplain of the Gaelic League in America, which held its fourth annual convention in Chicago 25–6 Aug 1901. In October of the following year he was transferred in disgrace to another church after making himself, as the *Gael* (NY) reported in Dec 1902 (398), 'unpleasantly conspicuous' at the 1902 Gaelic League convention 'by claiming to represent the state of Illinois in opposition to his own pastor, whose name had been *forged* to a document published without his knowledge in Father Yorke's personal "organ", the Leader, for which no apology has yet been offered'.

[1] *Nationality* (*Nationalist* after the first issue), a quarterly founded in October 1900, was published at the price of 3d from 30 Furnival Street, Holborn, London. It was edited by John Basil Barnhill, author of *Gounod's 'Faust': a plea for the lyric drama* (Belfast, 1894), and dedicated to 'Advocating the Interests of the Smaller Nationalities of the World'. It did not survive long, producing only three issues, and closing with the October 1902 number, in which WBY's letter appeared. The only file so far traced is in the Berg. The editor corrected 'jurnal' to 'journal'.

right to ⟨admire⟩ applaud Thermopylae and Salamis[2] cannot be other than a time of peril for all generous ideas. The conquest of Ireland was begun long ago[3] & even the best men ⟨cannot always escape get & find it hard⟩ often lack the hardihood to escape out of the entanglements of old wrong, but in this South African business[4] England has deliberately & newly gone into the net.[5] You & others who are telling her of those thoughts of her greatest men, of her Shelleys & Byrons, that she is putting from her, are doing all that we men of ideas can do.[6] ⟨I think that⟩ The hands, which shall some day amend her ways, but whether from within or without nobody can foretell, will be rougher hands than ours.

Yours sny
W B Yeats

ALS Berg. Published in *Nationalist*, October 1901 (1).

To Lady Augusta Gregory, [*23 August 1901*]

Derrybawn Hotel | 73 Lower Mount St, | Dublin.
Friday

My dear Lady Gregory: I wish you could have come. The Congress is really a very considerable success. There are a great many delegates with interesting things to say & the Concerts with their display of national

---

[2] WBY was to offer the battle of Salamis, the decisive naval battle of 480 B.C. in which the Athenians defeated the Persian forces under Xerxes, as an example to the Irish quest for national identity in his poem 'The Statues' (*VP*, 610), and also mentions it in *Expl* (451), and *Aut* (290). He cited the battle of Thermopylae, in which Leonidas and his force held up the Persian advance, also in 480 B.C., in a review in the *Gael* (Dublin) of 1887.

[3] The English conquest of Ireland began with the landing of Robert fitz Stephen's Norman forces at Bannow Bay, Co. Wexford, in May 1169.

[4] *Nationality* was strongly pro-Boer, and a manifesto, printed on the first page of its first issue, declared: 'The extermination with which the British Imperial Cabinet threatens the Boer Republics of South Africa is a Presage of the Fate which, according to the programme of the Great Powers, awaits all the Smaller Nationalities of the World'. The editor had evidently written to many anti-Imperialists on the issue of the South African War, and WBY's reply was printed with others. The War was now in its guerrilla phase, and on 7 Aug 1901 Joseph Chamberlain had offered the Boer 'bitter-enders' the option of surrendering by 15 Sept, or losing their right to remain in South Africa. As printed the letter reads 'the South African business', not 'this South African business'.

[5] Compare 'the nets of wrong and right' in 'Into the Twilight' (*VP*, 147).

[6] The first issue of *Nationality* had printed passages from Byron in defence of political liberty.

costumes of all kinds, & the robed Gorsed with its picturesque ceremonial & traditional chanting are crowded.[1]

I have just come from the last meeting of the congress. It was discussing the inclusion or exclusion of Cornwall among celtic countries. The executive was trying to postpone the question & a Cornish miner was pleading vehemently for its inclusion & putting Lord Castletown out very much by continually straying to the South African War. 'Did not the Cornish miners side with the boers. Did not that prove them Celts' Etc.[2]

I cannot get away until Wednesday for Miss Milligans' more important play comes on Tuesday.[3] Shall I go direct to the Galway Feis or will you be there on the second day (Thursday)?[4] I have persuaded several of the delegates to go to it. Old Carmichael (author of *Carmina Gadaelica*) and his daughter a very charming person who is herself a scholour in both Irish & Scottish gaelic will be there.[5] They go first to Doneraile & then there. So will Stuart Glennie & Stuart Erskine I think.[6]

[1] The first Pan Celtic Congress, held in Dublin from 19 to 23 Aug 1901 under the auspices of the Celtic Association, attracted delegates from Wales, Scotland, Ireland, Brittany, and the Isle of Man. Its purpose was to devise and introduce national costumes, preserve Celtic games and customs, foster national languages and encourage bilingual education in all Celtic countries. WBY contributed vigorously to the day-to-day proceedings and a full report of his interventions, and the Congress's deliberations, appeared in *Celtia* on 1 Sept 1901 (129–148). The second Congress was held in Caernarvon in 1904, and another in Edinburgh in 1907.

The Congress opened with a *Gorsedd* (Convocation of Bards), a ceremony described in the *Gael* (NY), October 1901 (316): 'The delegates met in Mansion House on the first morning of the Congress, and there on the lawn, their costumes shining in the brilliant sunlight, they went through the long and impressive ceremonies of the Welsh Gorsedd. The Arch-Druid, Rev. Mr. [Rowland] Williams in the world of every-day (in Celtia Hufa-Mow), a most regal figure in flowing white robes and crowned with oak-leaves, chanted strange verses, conferred bardic degrees, and declared peace among the nations by clashing into its scabbard the great Welsh sword, held up by his bardic followers, while all assembled shouted an echoing "peace" that resounded into the streets beyond.'

[2] Lord Bernard Edward Castletown (1849–1937), head of the New Unionist Party, chaired the Congress as president of the Celtic Association. He had succeeded to the barony in 1883 and, after his marriage in 1874, made his home in Doneraile, Co. Cork, which several delegates visited after the Congress. Although Castletown had been vice-president of the Irish Loyal Patriotic Union in the 1880s, he temporarily emerged as a leader of Irish opinion during the controversy with Britain over financial relations in 1896–7), but subsequently equivocated and Jasper Dean, the backsliding hero of George Moore's *The Bending of the Bough*, is partly modelled on him. The Cornish support for the Boers would have been particularly embarrassing for him since he had just returned from serving with the Household Cavalry in South Africa.

[3] The Fays' production of Alice Milligan's *The Deliverance of Red Hugh* on Tuesday, 27 Aug, at the Antient Concert Rooms had a profound effect on WBY who recalled (*Aut*, 449) that he 'came away with my head on fire. I wanted to hear my own unfinished *On Baile's Strand*, to hear Greek tragedy, spoken with a Dublin accent.'

[4] The first Connacht Feis, organized as a Gaelic festival for the whole province, was held 28–9 Aug 1901 at St Patrick's Temperance Hall, Galway. WBY was recorded by the *Freeman's Journal* of 30 Aug (5) as being present on the second day only.

[5] Alexander Carmichael (1832–1912), a Scots scholar and a leader of the Celtic Association, had published his 2-volume *Carmina Gadelica*, a collection of Highland hymns and incantations, in 1900. Elizabeth Catherine Carmichael, afterwards Watson (d. 1928), became editor of the *Celtic*

I saw Bryers & I think put things all right.[7]

I left a one pound note in the pocket in the lid of the leather despatch box—or what ever it is?—you gave me to keep money in. Please send it me. I also brought your rug away by chance but remembered it in time to leave it at the station at Gort for you.

Kuno Meyer told me yesterday that 'spit' is right in that passage & Miss Carmichael told me that there is Cuchullain folk lore in Campbells 'Tales of the West Highlands' & old Carmichael has given me a name of a scholour who knows all about it.[8]

Yours snly
W B Yeats

[*On back of envelope*]
I am at this hotel after all. They assured me they would have no lack of room.

ALS Berg, with envelope addressed to Coole, postmark 'DUBLIN AU 24 01'.

Review in 1904, and lectured to the National Literary Society on 'Celtic Folklore' in December of the same year. Her beauty and demeanour had much impressed Nevinson, when he met her on 13 Oct 1900, and he described her fulsomely in his diary (Bodleian) as 'a beautiful Highland girl . . . daughter of Carmina Gadelica, strong, full-grown with shapely arms & copious breast, all white or cream, fine full head with masses of loose dark hair hanging low, decisive nose & mouth, dark eyes with eyebrows almost meeting, bright cheeks, & pleasant voice, a most wholesome & refreshing sight among the worn townspeople. Talked quite simply of her islands & the poems which she read or recited in Gaelic.'

[6] J. S. Stuart-Glennie (d. 1909), a Scots delegate, read a paper on 'The Land and Language Problem in the Highlands'. WBY had discussed his 'new theory of the origin of civilization' in a review of *New Folklore Researches: Greek Folk Poesy* (*UP* I. 409–12) which appeared in the *Bookman* in October 1896. The Hon. Joseph Stuart Ruaraidh Erskine (see p. 24), said in his short address (Dublin *Daily Express*, 21 Aug 1901, p. 2) that the Highlanders 'regarded this movement in Scotland as indissolubly bound up with the prosperity of their race. Many races were included in the population of Scotland, but the Celtic was the dominant one; and the Celtic spirit prevailed there widely (applause).'

[7] See pp. 74, 75. WBY was probably making final arrangements for the publication of *Samhain*, and had perhaps broached the possibility of Sealy and Bryers publishing AG's *Cuchulain of Muirthemne*.

[8] Kuno Meyer (1858–1919) the distinguished German-born Celtic scholar, was Professor of Teutonic Languages at University College, Liverpool, but was often in Dublin, where he was to found the School of Irish Learning in 1903. He delivered one of the most important papers of the Congress, 'The Present State of Celtic Studies'. WBY had reviewed his translations of *The Vision of MacConglinne* (1892) and *The Voyage of Bran* (1895) in the *Bookman* (*UP* I. 261–3; *UP* II. 118–21). In Chap 5 of *Cuchulain of Muirthemne*, Findabair describes Cuchulain's eyebrows as being 'as black as the blackness of a spit'.

John Francis Campbell (1822–85; see I. 186), a scholar and folklorist, published his *Popular Tales of the West Highlands* in 1860–2, but this included only a few scattered stories about Cuchulain, as WBY was soon to discover. Although AG made some use of Campbell in *Gods and Fighting Men* (1904), she took nothing from him for *Cuchulain of Muirthemne*. The 'scholour' was probably Donald Mackinnon (d. 1914), Professor of Celtic Languages at Edinburgh University since 1882, and Miss Carmichael's consulting editor for the *Celtic Review*.

To George Moore, [c. *25 August 1901*]

Mention in letter from Moore, 'Tuesday' [27 August 1901].
Two or more letters with small corrections to *Diarmuid and Grania*;[1] also
telling him about Irish-speaking actors.

MBY.

To Douglas Hyde, [c. *27 August 1901*]

Mention in following letter.
Hoping that the presence of Pan Celtic delegates at the Connacht Feis
would not drive all Gaelic Leaguers out of the town of Galway.

To Lady Augusta Gregory, [*27 August 1901*]

73 Lower Mount St, | Dublin.
Tuesday.

My dear Lady Gregory: Yes I shall not go to Galway until Thursday. I
shall go down, of course, by the early train, & O Donovan[1] will be with
me. I want you to look out for the Carmichaels & be nice to them. I feal
that Zimmer & Kuno Meyer are the Gaelic League's business & if it
chooses to be rude that is its business too[2] but Old Carmichael has done
beautiful literary work & is our business. I have written to Hyde to say that

[1] Moore was in Paris on his way back from Bayreuth and in his reply assured WBY that he
would 'send the slight correction to Benson—I sent him my text for I despaired not hearing from
you. I did not send the bit to replace "the gods are in the room". I left that as I did not hear from
you.'

[1] Father Jeremiah 'Jerry' O'Donovan (1871–1942), administrator of Loughrea parish, was an
active member of the Gaelic League and the Irish Agriculture Organisation Society. Deeply committed to the revival of Irish crafts, he had lectured on 'Native or Foreign Art' to the National
Literary Society on 25 Mar 1901, and put his ideas into practice by commissioning Irish artists,
including Sarah Purser and Jack Yeats, in the construction and decoration of St Brendan's Cathedral, Loughrea, one of the architectural achievements of the Irish Revival. In 1904 he left
Loughrea and the priesthood, and moved to London where he married, took up a literary career,
and later became the lover of Rose Macaulay. He was a friend of George Moore, who based the
priests in his short story, 'Fugitives', and novel, *The Lake*, on him.

[2] Zimmer and Meyer (see p. 111, n. 8) were the two most distinguished Continental scholars
attending the Pan Celtic Congress. Henrich Zimmer (1851–1910), an active participant in the
proceedings, was Professor of Sanscrit and Celtic Languages at the University of Greifswald and
best known for *The Irish Element in Medieval Literature* (1891). AG drew upon his scholarship in
writing *Cuchulain of Muirthemne*. Normally the Gaelic League would have fêted such celebrated
visitors, but its uneasy relationship with the Pan Celticists had led to its boycotting the whole
Congress (see p. 97).

I hope the presence of the delegates will not drive all Gaelic Leaguers out of the town of Galway. Even Mac Neill fled from Dublin.[3] I have found out that Father O'Leary is a great tyrant in his own parish.[4]

Russell has arranged for Jacks show at 9 Merrion Row.[5]

You need not mind about Campbells 'Highland Tales'.

Yours alway
W B Yeats

ALS Berg, with envelope addressed to Coole, postmark 'DUBLIN AU 27 01'.

To Maud Gonne, [*early September 1901*]

Mention in letter from MG, [September 1901].
Sending her his article, 'Magic',[1] and telling her that he is in good health, contented, and working well.

G–YL, 143–5.

To the Editor of the Free Lance, *6 September* [*1901*]

Coole Park, Gort, Co. Galway.
September 6

"Dear Sir,—Your letter of August 15 has only just reached me, as I have been moving about. My letter to 'Express' (sic) did not attribute to your paper (sic), but to the comment in 'Express' paragraph the remark about

---

[3] Eoin (John) MacNeill (1867–1945), one of the founders and most influential members of the Gaelic League, was editor of its bilingual weekly, *An Claidheamh Soluis*, where, in July, WBY had published his essay, 'By the Roadside'. MacNeill became Professor of Early Irish History at University College, Dublin, in 1908, and was later a leader of the Irish Volunteers. A scholarly, moderate, and courteous man, he might have been expected to take a more conciliatory attitude towards the Congress, especially since he had originally been sympathetic to the Pan Celtic Movement (see p. 89, n. 1).

[4] Father Peter O'Leary (1839–1920), parish priest at Castlelyons, Cork, was a Gaelic playwright, translator, and avid supporter of the Gaelic League and opponent of the Pan Celts. He became well-known for his folk-novel, *Séadna* (1904), which traces the adventures of a country cobbler in conflict with the Devil. A man of definite opinions, O'Leary brooked little opposition, and his outspokenness, evident in his recent article in the *Leader* (see p. 89, n. 1), caused him to be frequently passed over for promotion. His autobiography, *Mo Sgeal Fein*, appeared in 1915.

[5] Jack Yeats's exhibition, 'Sketches of Life in the West of Ireland', ran at the gallery, 9 Merrion Row, from 23 Oct to 3 Nov, and was reviewed by AG in the *Leader* on 2 Nov (158–9).

[1] Published in the September number of the *Monthly Review* (see p. 62, n. 1).

Methusaleh.[1] This matter is unimportant, as my objection was to an interview, which never took place. I have no doubt that some person sent you a careless report of some private conversation of mine, but a private conversation is not an 'interview,' even when accurately quoted. You are probably as much a victim as I am in these matters. London journalism has sunk into such a state of degradation that I can well understand that an editor must find it almost impossible to keep his pages clean of offence. Even had I wished to ignore the matter I could not, as the silly extravagance your correspondent attributed to me was certain to be used, as it has been (the last time in last week's 'Spectator'),[2] against the cause I represent.—[3]

Yours, &c.,
"W B Yeats"

Printed letter, *Free Lance*, 21 September 1901 (578–9). *UP* II. 253–4.

To Ernest James Oldmeadow, [c. 7 September 1901]

Mention in letter from Moore, 'Monday' [? 9 September 1901].
Evidently telling Oldmeadow that he was arranging for *Samhain* to be distributed through T. Fisher Unwin, not the Unicorn Press.

MBY.

[1] See WBY's letter of 2 Aug 1901 to the *Daily Express*, p. 99. A paragraph immediately before the present letter reported: 'Mr. W. B. Yeats, the well-known Irish poet and organiser of the Pan-Celtic movement, if I mistake not (writes a correspondent), sends me the following letter. . . . I hope you, Mr. Editor, will give it due space verbatim et literatim.' The author of the 'interview' in the *Free Lance* on 20 July had evidently seen WBY's remonstration in the Dublin *Daily Express* of 5 Aug and had written privately to him on 15 Aug insisting that the interview was accurate and that WBY was wrong in attributing the comparison with Methuselah to the *Free Lance*.
[2] A correspondent in the *Spectator* of 31 Aug 1901 (280) alluded to WBY's interview at the end of a letter on the Pan Celtic Congress: '*A propos* of this extreme Celtomania among us, there is a story to the effect that one of the leaders of the Celtic movement recently declared that since the language of the cleverer race tended to oust that of the less gifted (sic?), he confidently expected that Irish would be the language of culture in the erstwhile English-speaking world. But perhaps the great man had his tongue in his cheek.'
[3] In a paragraph immediately following this letter, the *Free Lance* correspondent stuck to his guns: 'May I be allowed to say a few words in reply (continues my correspondent)? I don't know why Mr. Yeats beats about the bush. . . . His letter is very ingenious, though, unfortunately, not ingenuous. It is a poor soul that cannot admit the truth. Contrary to Mr. Yeats' expectation, I know the difference between a private conversation and an interview. I saw him manifestly, and, as I told him, for the purpose of interview. To assert the opposite is to say the thing which is not. As for "the pages clean of offence" of London journalism and the "silly extravagance," I imagine there will be more pages clean of offence and less silly extravagance when Mr. Yeats stops writing for the ill-used Press.'

To George Moore, [c. *7 September 1901*]

Mention in letter from Moore, 'Monday' [? 9 September 1901].
Telling Moore he had written to Oldmeadow;[1] and apparently asking
about the proofs of *Samhain*.

MBY.

To Richard Best,[1] *28 September* [*1901*]

at Coole Park, | Gort, Co Galway.
28th Sept

Dear Mr Best,

It is considered that on account of the low price of gallery tickets in
Dublin, which I was unaware of till I met your committee in Dublin,[2] it
would not be worth while making an effort to raise funds for the purpose
of admitting the artizan classes, more especially as we are assured by everybody that there will be no difficulty in filling the cheaper parts of the
house. We are therefore laying aside the project for the present.

I agree with you that Mr Large's[3] proposal about tickets sold beforehand
is altogether inadequate. When I saw him he was particularly anxious to
have the tickets sold beforehand, and looked upon this as a most necessary
condition of success. I may add that the *Inghean na h-Eirean* organization[4]
is persuaded I am told that they made a very great mistake in not selling
tickets beforehand for their last performances. Even though but few tickets
are sold in this way, the value to the theatre from the advertisement is
immense.

When I got your sub-committee together I looked upon this sale of tickets however, important as it is, more as the ostensible than as the more
important business of the committee. I had hoped that the committee

---

[1] Suspicious of Oldmeadow's business methods and efficiency (see p. 67), WBY and AG had
decided to find a new English publisher for *Samhain*, and had evidently written to enlist Moore's
help. He obliged, and on 10 Sept wrote to T. Fisher Unwin urging him 'to publish this interesting "brochure" in London. The Dublin firm will supply you with copies at 3d each, half price.
Will these terms satisfy you? I hope so for there is no time for bargaining; the matter must be settled at once' (*George Moore in Transition*, ed. Helmut Gerber [Detroit, 1968], 218–9).

[1] Richard Irvine Best (1872–1959), a Celtic scholar, had played the part of Ainle in the amateur production of AE's *Deirdre* in January. He was Assistant Director of the NLI from 1904 to
1924, and subsequently succeeded Thomas Lyster as Director. Joyce portrayed him as a dilettante
and aesthete in the Scylla and Charybdis and Circe episodes of *Ulysses*.

[2] This was a short-lived committee to plan the future of the ILT. In *We Two Together* (1950)
James Cousins recalled (62) that he attended its 'one and only meeting' on 23 Sept 1901.

[3] See p. 63.   [4] See p. 96, n. 2.

would find work for itself in forming public opinion upon the question of a National Theatre. This would come into the terms of their 'reference' which included such matters as safeguarding the interests of the Theatre in the Press. I enclose certain of the proof sheets of *Samhain*, this years publication of the Theatre committee. In these proof sheets Mr Edward Martyn and myself explain the project of a National Theatre. If we are to get such a Theatre we must get it now, when the work of the Literary Theatre is in people's minds.[5] Should the Committee wish to take up this matter of forming public opinion, they who are on the spot will be the best judges of how it is to be done. A little while ago, some two weeks ago, Mr George Moore asked me to write to the Freeman in order to stir up a controversy or discussion on the subject, I was unable to do so, but if your Committee had then been meeting it might have organised that discussion far better than I. I hope they will see their way to doing something of the kind.

The proof sheets I sent you are private, and must not go beyond the sub Committee.

As to the meeting at the Mansion House,[6] Mr Benson is I have no doubt quite willing to have it, and to explain there his views as to how a National Theatre could be formed, but it is possible that there should be first some expression of Irish opinion and some attempt to stimulate that opinion. [*Remainder of letter in WBY's hand*]

I write in my personal capacity as I have had no chance of consulting the other members of the committee of the Theatre.

> Yours sincely
> W B Yeats

I enclose rather more proofs than are wanted for your purpose, as they may interest you, but I have marked the parts that especially concern Committee.

TLS NLI.

---

[5] With the completion of the ILT's three-year programme, *Samhain* concerned itself with possible ways of continuing the dramatic movement. WBY reviewed the arguments for and against an Irish national theatre, but refused to commit himself: 'I am not going to say what I think. I have spent much of my time and more of my thought these last ten years on Irish organisation, and now that the Irish Literary Theatre has completed the plan I had in my head ten years ago, I want to go down again to primary ideas' (*Expl*, 77–8). Martyn, in a more positive article. 'A Plea for a National Theatre in Ireland' (see p. 77, n. 2), used financial arguments in support of a national theatre, arguing that it would help prevent 'the scandalous outpouring of Irish money into the pockets of Englishmen and other foreigners' who were 'Anglicising and corrupting the taste of the Irish people'.

[6] Since the Committee met only once (see n. 2), the Mansion House meeting presumably never took place.

To George Bernard Shaw,[1] *[early] October 1901*

at | COOLE PARK, | GORT, | CO. GALWAY.

Oct 1901

My dear Shaw: I write to urge you to come over & see our 'Theatre' this year. You will find all that is stirring in Dublin gathered to geather—& Dublin is full of stir just now—& we will get you to speak, if you will be so good. Come over & help us to stir things up still further. Both Lady Gregory—with whom I am staying—& myself are regretting that we did not try & get 'The Devils Diciple' from you for our Theatre. It was the very play for this country—as indeed you said to me—but I did not understand.

Some of the young men of the Extreme National party are reading you just now with great satisfaction. 'The United Irishman' had a long quotation from your "Napolean" about English character a few weeks ago.[2] They would welcome you over with enthusiasm.

Yr ev
W B Yeats

ALS BL.

To Lady Augusta Gregory, [mid-October 1901]

Yesterday we were rehersing at the Gaety. The kid Benson is to carry in his arms,[1] was wandering in & out among the artificial ivy. I was saying to myself 'Here are we a lot of intelligent people, who might have been doing some sort of intelligent work that leads to some fun, yet here we are going through all sorts of trouble & annoyance for ⟨a *[indecipherable]* ⟩ body of

[1] George Bernard Shaw (1856–1950), the Dublin-born playwright and social reformer, had left Ireland in 1876, but WBY was eager to involve him in the Irish dramatic movement. The two first met at William Morris's house in February 1888 (see I. 50), and in 1894 had shared the stage when FF produced *Arms and the Man* and *The Land of Heart's Desire* at the Avenue Theatre. Shaw's *The Devil's Disciple*, first produced at the Princess of Wales Theatre, Kensington, in September 1899, and set in the period of the American Revolution, culminates in the success of the New England rebels over the British army of General Burgoyne, who is asked in the final act whether he has 'realized that though you may occupy towns and win battles, you cannot conquer a nation?' Shaw did not attend the ILT productions in 1901, but in March 1900 had proposed writing a play for the ILT.

[2] In the *United Irishman* of 14 Sept 1901 (2), 'Cuguan' (Arthur Griffith) described Shaw as 'the most brilliant writer we have' and quoted Napoleon's lengthy satirical description of the English as 'a race apart' from *The Man of Destiny* (1896).

[1] In Act II of *Diarmuid and Grania* Diarmuid and a shepherd enter 'carrying fleeces'; in planning the production, Benson, against George Moore's advice, wanted to carry a sheep on stage for shearing, but by rehearsal time had been persuaded to substitute a goat.

ignoramuses who prefer Boucicault[2] an audience a mob that prefers Boucicault to us, & the Freemans Journal to [?]Ruskin⟩ a mob that knows neither literature nor art. I might have been away in the country, in Italy
perhaps writing poems for my equals & my betters.[3] That kid is the only
sensible creature on this stage. He knows his business & keeps to it.' At
that very moment one of the actors called out 'Look at the goat eating the
property ivy.'

A frag Berg, Wade, 355–6.

To the Editor of the Freeman's Journal, *14 November* [*1901*]

November 14.

Dear Sir—A phrase in a letter which you publish to-day makes it desirable
that I should define the attitude of the Irish Literary Theatre and my own
attitude towards the proposed censorship. Mr. Moore makes his proposal
on his own authority.[1] The Irish Literary Theatre gives no opinion. When
Mr. Moore told me his plan I said that I had no belief in its practicability,
but would gladly see it discussed. We cannot have too much discussion
about ideas in Ireland. The discussion over the theology of "The Countess
Cathleen", and over the politics of "The Bending of the Bough", and over
the morality of "Diarmuid and Grania," set the public mind thinking of
matters it seldom thinks of in Ireland, and I hope the Irish Literary Theatre will remain a wise disturber of the peace. But if any literary association
I belong to asked for a clerical censorship I would certainly cease to belong

---

[2] Dion Boucicault (?1820–90), the Dublin-born dramatist and actor-manager, was perhaps the
most successful man of the 19th-century theatre in Ireland, England, and the USA. He is best
known for his numerous melodramas, and especially for those set in Ireland, *The Colleen Bawn*
(1860), *Arrah-na-Pogue* (1865), and *The Shaugraun* (1875). WBY always despised Boucicault's
plays, but his ear for vivid Irish idiom, and exploitation of theatrical effects, influenced Shaw,
Synge, and O'Casey.

[3] See 'The People', ll. 1–21; *VP*, 351–2.

[1] In an interview, published in the *Freeman's Journal* on 13 Nov 1901 (5), George Moore had
advocated ecclesiastical censorship of the theatre in Ireland: 'I do not know what the Committee
of the Literary Theatre think about it, but I am convinced that a censorship is necessary. . . . The
intelligent censorship of the Church will free the stage from the unintelligent and ignorant censorship of the public. . . . It is from that censorship that I wish to rid the stage . . .' He returned
to the subject in a letter to the editor on the following day, arguing that the 'Church has always
been considered sufficient guide in matters of faith and morals. I am willing to accept the censorship of the Archbishop.' WBY, with the memory of Archbishop Logue's 'guidance' over *The
Countess Cathleen* still fresh in his mind, hastened to dissociate himself from the proposal.

to it. I believe that literature is the principal voice of the conscience, and that it is its duty age after age to affirm its morality against the special moralities of clergymen and churches, and of kings and parliaments and peoples. But I do not expect this opinion to be the opinion of the majority of any country for generations, and it may always be the opinion of a very small minority. If Mr. Moore should establish a national theatre with an ecclesiastic for a censor, and ask me to join the management I shall refuse, but I shall watch the adventure with the most friendly eyes. I have no doubt that a wise ecclesiastic, if his courage equalled his wisdom, would be a better censor than the mob, but I think it better to fight the mob alone than to seek for a support one could only get by what would seem to me a compromise of principle.

A word now upon another matter. You suggest in your review of Mr. Martyn's plays that certain changes made by Mr. George Moore in his adaption of "The Tale of a Town," for the Irish Literary Theatre, were made for political reasons. This is not the case. Every change made was made for literary and dramatic reasons alone.[2]

W B Yeats

Printed letter, *Freeman's Journal*, 15 November 1901 (4). Wade, 356–7.

To Lady Augusta Gregory, [*19 November 1901*]

18 Woburn Buildings | Euston Road, | London
Tuesday.

My dear Lady Gregory: That is good news about my father. I should think that he had better get some kind of agent—there must be such people—to arrange the matter in America, if he knows nothing of Quinn. There must

---

[2] Both WBY and Moore had been disappointed with the construction and characterization of Edward Martyn's political satire, *The Tale of a Town*, and persuaded him to rewrite it with Moore's help. This collaboration soon broke down and Moore's more accomplished version was the one produced by the ILT in February 1900, under the title *The Bending of the Bough*. Martyn published his version as *The Tale of a Town* in November 1901 and, reviewing it on 14 Nov 1901 (3), the *Freeman's Journal* suggested that those who remembered the ILT's production of *The Bending of the Bough* would 'on reading the play now published, experience . . . a devouring curiosity as to the reason for the change. Possibly last year the idea that the Unionists who pretended to support the Financial Relations movement might support the Irish Literary Theatre was not quite dead, and care for their susceptibilities was too great to admit of letting Mr. Martyn's satire loose upon them unmuzzled.' Since WBY had given Moore a great deal of help in rewriting the play, he was all the more eager to refute this insinuation.

be some way of doing this sort of thing—Osbourne should know. I need
hardly say that he is quite welcome to sell the portrait I have.[1]

How Moore lives in the present.[2] If the National Theatre is ever started
what he is & what I am will be weighed & very little what we have said or
done. A phrase more or less matters little. When he has got more experience
of public life he will know how little these things matter—yet I suppose we
would both be more popular if I could keep from saying what I think & he
from saying what he does not think. You may tell him that the wisest of men
does not know what is expedient, but that we can all get a very good idea as
to what is our particular truth. The more we keep to that the better. Cajol-
ery never lighted the fire. If he knows Harold Large's address get him to
send it to me—if you meet him. No you need not ask him—I shall write to
him myself as I have to ask him about other things. I have a book of highland Fianna material, which I can let you have when ever you like—'The
Fians' by J G Campbell. Grania in this book is the wife of Fion before she
runs away with Dairmuid & is described as not very particular in the choice
of her lovers. Finn in one version has her buried alive. I am half inclined to
write for the printed text of the play a preface describing the various versions of the tale—& so dispose of Irish criticism once for all.[3]

I saw Bjornsons 'Beyond Human Power' to day.[4] It is manifestly an

---

[1] On 16 Nov 1901 AG wrote (Berg) to tell WBY that she had just seen JBY who was 'in great
spirits, having had a letter from some man called Quinn, writing from Broadway, New York, who
has read the accounts of his pictures, and apparently wants to buy them all, King Goll, John
O'Leary's portrait, and a portrait of you'. The Irish-American lawyer and patron of the arts, John
Quinn (1870–1924; see Appendix), had heard of JBY's successful exhibition with Nathaniel Hone,
which ran in Dublin from 21 Oct to 3 Nov 1901. In his reply to Quinn, written on 19 Nov
(MBY), JBY offered his 1900 portrait of WBY for £20: 'It is a life size head & considered very
like by my son & his friends—Since it was painted two years ago it has hung in my sons sitting
room.' Walter Frederick Osborne (1859–1903) was a popular Dublin painter who occupied JBY's
old studio at 7 St Stephens Green until his sudden death in 1903.

[2] In her letter of 16 Nov (see n. 1) AG wrote: 'After I began this letter Moore came in, rather
cross, says your letter [*i.e.* to Freeman's Journal; *see pp. 118–19*] is injudicious (his usual diplo-
macy) and that you have thrown everything into Edward's hands. But, in detail, this only means
that if a National Theatre were to be started just now, Edward would be appointed manager, and
this does not seem a pressing danger. . . . He is taken up with the idea of Fay now, and would do
him a peasant one act play if we will give him a subject, couldn't you think of one out of your
over abundant stock of ideas?'

[3] WBY admired the work of John Gregorson Campbell (1836–91), Scots Highlander, clergyman, and folklorist, who had published *The Fians* in 1891. He was particularly eager to find versions of the Fenian tales at this time because *Diarmuid and Grania* had been censured in a number
of Irish journals, particularly the *Leader*, as immoral and inauthentic. He also hoped that AG
would follow up her collection of the Cuchulain tales with a book of Fenian folklore.

[4] Mrs Patrick Campbell produced Bjørnstjerne Bjørnson's *Beyond Human Power* (*Over Evne*,
1883) at the Royalty Theatre for a series of nine matinées from 7 to 21 Nov 1901. Its theme, the
relationship between miracle and faith, is focused through Pastor Sang, who describes himself as
'all emotion', and who finds himself gifted with miraculous powers in a life of perpetual self-
sacrifice and love. He apparently cures his sceptical wife of chronic illness by prayer, but she rises
from her bed only to expire in his arms, and he dies immediately afterwards questioning the

unbeleivers account of beleif. The hero, a parson who works miracles, or what seem miracles through his faith is made talk like any common zealous, gushing preacher. One feals that Bjornson does not take the religeous genius seriously, though he wants to. He cannot understand that the religeous genius like every other kind of genius differs from mere zeal because it is perfectly precise. His parson would have occupied himself with nothing transcendental, but probably with the housing of the working classes or the like. He is even not a little vulgar; he is astonishingly like Tom Lyter [*for* Lyster] of the 'national library'[5] & one is not happy until he is gone from the stage. Apart from this it is a really absorbing play & Mrs Pat Campbell plays it beautifully.

I have not yet been to see A P Watt but may go to morrow.

I have written to Dolmetsch to talk about the chanting with him; & have proposed a lecture with illustrations to pay him for the Psaltery. I saw Mrs Emery last night. She had arranged to give Dolmetsch £4 for Psaltery, & he forgot all about this & spent £10 on it. I shall do an article & get it into one of the Reviews & then give the lecture, & so get Mrs Emery out of the difficulty.[6] She paid part of the money by performance of a very amateurish Egyptian play rather nicely on Saturday.[7]

Yours snly
W B Yeats

ALS Berg, with envelope addressed to 21 Lower Baggot St, Dublin, postmark 'LONDON N.W. NO 20 01'. Partly in Wade, 359.

meaning of the miracle. Although described by his wife as a man whose religious temperament matches the elemental qualities of the Norwegian landscape, he is off stage for the greater part of the play, and during his appearances exhibits a fussy if kindly tolerance. Mrs Campbell took the part of Mrs Sang in a translation by Jessie Muir. WBY had William Wilson's 1893 version of the play (under the title *Pastor Sang*) in his library (*YL*, 197).

[5] Thomas William Lyster (1855–1922), Head Librarian at the NLI 1895–1920—he appears as the 'Quaker Librarian' in Joyce's *Ulysses*—was one of the first to encourage WBY to write. WBY described him as 'the most zealous man I know' (*UP* II. 305), and in 1926 chaired the Lyster Memorial Committee. Lyster's well-meaning fussiness and self-effacement were a standing joke in Dublin, and in an undated letter, probably written on 20 May 1902 (MBY), JBY described to WBY 'a speech by Tom Lister—a characteristic speech—he did so apologize for himself, he was well received, & well cheered—his apologies seemed to excite a sort of affectionate laughter—he sat down & got up apologizing'.

[6] WBY published 'Speaking to the Psaltery' in the *Monthly Review* of May 1902, prior to lecturing on 'Speaking to Musical Notes', illustrated by FF, on 10 June 1902. See p. 194.

[7] The first performance of *The Beloved of Hathor* took place at the Victoria Hall, Archer Street, on 16 Nov 1901 in celebration of the inaugural meeting of the Egypt Society, whose President, Marcus Blackden of the Egyptian Archaeological Survey, was also a member of the GD and a member of FF's Egyptian orientated Sphere group (see pp. 25–7). Nevinson, noting the presence of WBY and Shaw, wrote in his diary (Bodleian): 'Mrs. Emery's introduction very good, play delightful to watch & listen to, but the end unsatisfactory. Mrs. Emery's voice superb.' The play, written by FF and OS, was revived with another of their Egyptian pieces, *The Shrine of the Golden Hawk*, on 20–1 Jan 1902 at Victoria Hall, and reviewed by WBY in the *Star* on 23 Jan (*UP* II. 265–7). They were produced again in the same hall from 20 to 21 April 1902.

To Mrs Patrick Campbell, [c. *19 November 1901*]

18, Woburn Buildings.

Dear Mrs. Patrick Campbell,

. . . Will you permit me to thank you by letter for the performance? Your acting seemed to me to have the perfect precision and delicacy and simplicity of every art at its best. It made me feel the unity of the arts in a new way. I said to myself, that is exactly what I am trying to do in writing, to express myself without waste, without emphasis. To be impassioned and yet to have a perfect self-possession, to have a precision so absolute that the slightest inflection of voice, the slightest rhythm of sound or emotion plucks the heart-strings. But do you know that you acted too well; you made me understand a defect in Björnson's play which I had felt but had not understood when I read it. Björnson's hero could only have done those seen or real miracles by having a religious genius. Now the very essence of genius, of whatever kind, is precision, and that hero of his has no precision. He is a mere zealous man with a vague sentimental mind—the kind of man who is anxious about the Housing of the Working Classes, but not the kind of man who sees what Blake called 'The Divine Vision and Fruition.'[1] I happened to have in my pocket 'The Revelation of Divine Love,' by the Lady Julian, an old mystical book;[2] my hand strayed to it all unconsciously. There was no essential difference between that work and your acting; both were full of fine distinction, of delicate logic, of that life where passion and thought are one. Both were utterly unlike Björnson's hero.

The actor played him to the life;[3] but I was miserable until he was off the stage. He was an unbeliever's dream of a believer, an atheist's Christian. . . .

. . .

W B Yeats

Text from Campbell, 162. The original of this letter was sold to an untraced buyer at Sotheby's on 3 Feb 1943. Wade, 360.

[1] In 'Night the Third' of *Vala or the Four Zoas* (1797), Ahania tells the Prince that by listening to the voice of Luvah

thou art compell'd
To forge the curbs of iron & brass, to build the iron mangers,
To feed them with intoxication from the wine presses of Luvah
Till the Divine Vision & Fruition is quite obliterated.

[2] The *Revelations of Divine Love*, a meditation upon her mystical experiences by Dame Julian, or Juliana, of Norwich (1342–after 1416), is distinguished by its freshness, economy, and precision. Completed shortly before 1400, it was first printed in a modern text in 1670; WBY probably had the new edition published in July 1901, the first since 1872, which refers to 'the lady Julian' rather than to 'the mother Juliana' as in earlier editions.

[3] Pastor Sang, played by George S. Titheradge (1848–1916), was, according to the *Pall Mall Gazette* of 8 Nov 1901 (2), 'safe in the hands of so earnest and unaffected an actor'.

To Mrs Patrick Campbell, [c. *21 November 1901*]

18, Woburn Buildings.

. . . Yes, I agree with you that Björnson's play is a fine thing—living, passionate, touching issues of life and death. In London the subjects which people think suitable for drama get fewer every day. Shelley said that when a social order was in decay, the arts attached themselves to the last things people were interested in—imaginatively interested in. Here people look on the world with more and more prosaic eyes, as Shelley said they did in dying Greece. There, as here, nothing kept its beauty but irregular love-making. He called the poetry that had irregular love for subject and was called immoral, 'The Footsteps of Astrea departing from the world'.[1]

. . .

W B Yeats

Text from Campbell, 162–3. The original of this letter was sold to an untraced buyer at Sotheby's on 3 Feb 1943. Wade, 360–1.

To Fiona Macleod,[1] [c. *23 November 1901*]

18 Woburn Buildings, London,
Saturday.

My dear Miss Macleod,

I have been a long while about thanking you for your book of poems,[2] but I have been shifting from Dublin to London and very busy about various things—too busy for any quiet reading. I have been running hither and thither seeing people about one thing and another. But now I am back in

[1] In 'A Defence of Poetry' (1821) Shelley writes that social corruption 'begins at the imagination and the intellect as at the core, and distributes itself thence as a paralysing venom, through the affections into the very appetites until all become a torpid mass in which hardly sense survives. At the approach of such a period, poetry ever addresses itself to those faculties which are the last to be destroyed, and its voice is heard, like the footsteps of Astraea, departing from the world.'

[1] 'Fiona Macleod' was the pseudonym from 1894 of William Sharp (1855–1905), author of romances, stories, novels, poems, and biographies. Sharp, continuing to write under his own name, kept his identity with Fiona, who wrote Celtic tales and mystical prose and verse, a secret until his death, although WBY and AG had already guessed the situation.

[2] On 31 Oct 1901 'Fiona Macleod' had sent WBY a copy of what she described in an accompanying letter (*LWBY* I. 92) as 'the much changed, cancelled, augmented, and revised American edition' of *From the Hills of Dream,* originally published in 1896, and recently reissued by Thomas B. Mosher of Portland, Maine. The section entitled 'Foam of the Past', containing poems written between 1896 and 1900, opens with a lengthy dedication to WBY.

my rooms and have got things straight enough to settle down at last to my usual routine. Yesterday I began arranging under their various heads some hitherto unsorted folk-stories on which I am about to work, and today I have been busy over your book. I never like your poetry as well as your prose, but here and always you are a wonderful writer of myths. They seem your natural method of expressions. They are to you what mere words are to others. I think this is partly why I like you better in your prose, though now and then a bit of verse comes well, rising up out of the prose, in your simplest prose the most, the myths stand out clearly, as something objective, as something well born and independent. In your more elaborate prose they seem subjective, an inner way of looking at things assumed by a single mind. They have little independent life and seem unique; your words bind them to you. If Balzac had written with a very personal, very highly coloured style, he would have always drowned his inventions with himself. You seem to feel this, for when you use elaborate words you invent with less conviction with less precision, with less delicacy than when you forget everything but the myth.[3] I will take as example, a prose tale.

That beautiful story in which the child finds the Twelve Apostles eating porridge in a cottage,[4] is quite perfect in all the first part, for then you think of nothing but the myth, but it seems to me to fade to nothing in the latter part. For in the latter part the words rise up between you and the myth. You yourself begin to speak and we forget the apostles, and the child and the plate and the porridge. Or rather the more mortal part of you begins to speak, the mere person, not the god. You, as I think, should seek the delights of style in utter simplicity, in a self-effacing rhythm and language; in an expression that is like a tumbler of water rather than like a cup of wine. I think that the power of your work in the future will depend on your choosing this destiny. Certainly I am looking forward to "The Laughter of the Queen".[5] I thought your last prose, that pilgrimage of the soul

[3] WBY, in preparing the new edition of *The Celtic Twilight*, was rereading Macleod's collection of Celtic folk-tales, *The Washer of the Ford* (1896).

[4] 'The Last Supper', a story from *The Washer of the Ford* (1896), describes the dream of a lost child who is carried by 'the Fisher of Men', Iosa, into the Shadowy Glen where he meets the Twelve Weavers gathered for porridge at the last supper. All weave immortal shapes on the shuttles of Beauty, Wonder, and Mystery, except Judas, who weaves Fear on the shuttles of Mystery, Despair, and the Grave. Restored to his mother by Iosa, the child looks back but sees only the Weaver of Hope singing a song learned from the Weaver of Joy.

[5] 'The Laughter of the Queen' appeared in *Barbaric Tales* (1897), reviewed by WBY in the *Sketch* on 28 Apr 1897 (*UP* II. 42–5). It tells how Scathach, the Amazonian Queen of Skye, runs mad through unrequited love for Cuchulain and has twenty Vikings strung up by their hair in oak trees 'like drooping fruit. . . . Then Scathach the Queen laughed loud and long . . . for then the madness was upon her' (59–60). WBY had evidently seen the dedicatory poem in Mosher's edition and had forgotten that he had already reviewed the tale from which it came.

and mind and body to the Hills of Dream promised this simple style.[6] It had it indeed more than anything you have done.

To some extent I have an advantage over you in having a very fierce nation to write for. I have to make everything very hard and clear, as it were. It is like riding a wild horse. If one's hands fumble or one's knees loosen one is thrown. You have in the proper sense far more imagination than I have and that makes your work correspondingly more difficult. It is fairly easy for me, who do so much of my work by the critical, rather than the imaginative faculty, to be precise and simple, but it is hard for you in whose mind images form themselves without ceasing and are gone as quickly perhaps.

But I am sure that I am right. When you speak with the obviously personal voice in your verse, or in your essays you are not that Fiona who has invented a new thing, a new literary method. You are that Fiona when the great myths speak through you. . . .

Yours
W B Yeats

I like your verses on Murias and like them the better perhaps because of the curious coincidence that I did in summer verses about lovers wandering 'in long forgotten Murias'.[7]

Text from Sharp, 334–6. Wade, 357–8.

---

[6] *The Divine Adventure: Iona: By Sundown Shores* (1900) is a collection of symbolic and legendary tales in which the narrator explores the spiritual history of the self, the island of Iona, and the Highlands. In 'The Divine Adventure' the Body, the Will, and the Soul discover their relation to each other on their pilgrimage to 'the dim blue hills in the west, the Hills of Dream, as we called them'.

[7] 'Murias', one of the five poems that make up her sequence 'The Dirge of the Four Cities', had been published in the October *Fortnightly Review* under the title 'Requiem'. Macleod had directed WBY to the poem in her letter of 31 Oct (see above, n. 2). It was not to be included in the new Mosher edition, and first appeared in book form in the English edition of *From the Hills of Dream* (1907). In WBY's 'Baile and Aillinn' (*VP*, 196) two swans are said to 'know all the wonders, for they pass / The towery gates of Gorias, / And Findrias and Falias, / And long-forgotten Murias'. When this poem was published in the *Monthly Review* in July 1902 WBY added a note (*VP*, 188), explaining that 'Findrias and Falias and Gorias and Murias were the four mysterious cities whence the Tuatha De Danaan, the divine race, came to Ireland, cities of learning out of sight of the world, where they found their four talismans, the spear, the stone, the cauldron, and the sword'. In *From the Hills of Dream* (105) Murias is described as 'the sunken city', one of the four cities 'that no mortal eye has seen but that the soul knows'.

To Lady Augusta Gregory, [*26 November 1901*]

18 Woburn Buildings | Euston Road. | London.
Tuesday

My dear Lady Gregory: I am working on Cuchullain at the British Museum; but go to call on M[rs] Pat Campbell in about an hour. She has asked to see 'Grania' again but I doubt if anything will come of it.[1] I am glad Moore is fierce if it will get him to write for the U I to which I have just sent a note on 'literature & the conscience'.[2] Martyns idea is a good one. I think we should get Fay to arrange for the acting of both the Irish play & 'The Poor Old Woman' & make a point of our second night being the first attempt at a permament Irish company. He might even try Cuchullain, though I should prefer he did not, 'The Shadowy Waters' would be beyond him—unless M[rs] Emery came over & worked with him. Digges could play the hero quite adequately. Martyn will certainly not think Cuchullain confused now. It will be a better acting play than 'The Shadowy Waters' but will need a good actor for Cuchullain's part. On the whole Fay had better keep to the Irish play & "the poor old Woman" perhaps. If he undertook both these, & to find a few dummies for 'Cuchullain', it would save money which Martyn might consider enough to get me

---

[1] See pp. 3, n. 3; 20, n. 8. Mrs Campbell was now toying with the idea of performing the play on her forthcoming tour of the USA.

[2] In a letter dated 'Sunday ev' [? 24 Nov 1901; Berg] AG had reported: 'G. Moore here yesterday, very cross with Moran, & wanting to attack either him or anybody else'. On 2 Nov 1901 D. P. Moran's *Leader* had published two separate articles attacking most aspects of *Diarmuid and Grania*, but picking out for particular censure its moral perversity. The theatre critic accused WBY and Moore (155) of altering the 'real story' so as to turn it into 'a degenerate and unwholesome "sex" problem', while in the second article 'Mac an Cuill' denounced (158) the 'insult to our mind and heart, and to our whole nature, by their misrepresentation of the story in its moral aspect'. The following week Moore replied (174–5) with a reasoned defence of the play, and of the right of dramatists to choose their own reading of a given legend. This merely roused Mac an Cuill to greater fury and on 16 Nov he asserted (188–9) that Moore's reading was 'false to the very core': 'I thought . . . that it might be unconsciously false, but Mr. Moore's explanation shows only too plainly that its falseness was determined upon at the very beginning. . . . Mr. Moore's apologia is therefore worse than his original offence. He has added insult to insult, and injury to injury. But he has unconsciously done us one great service. He has shown us, as with an electric searchlight, the gulf between the English mind and the Irish mind. "It passes my understanding", he says . . . "to divine the critic's meaning when he says that such a story is un-Irish". Of course it passes Mr. Moore's understanding. . . . The English mind does not understand the Irish, and never will.' To be told that he was irredeemably English was particularly galling to the Irish-born Moore, who had returned to Dublin full of fervour for things Irish (see pp. 20, 85).

Although the *United Irishman* had also criticized *Diarmuid and Grania* for not keeping to the original legend, it found the *Leader*'s excessive piety absurd and on 2 Nov 1901 had published two ironic letters on the subject. WBY's article, 'Literature and the Conscience', arguing that literature was the principal voice of conscience (see pp. 118–19), appeared there on 7 Dec.

a really good actor for that play if he thinks it simple enough.[3] I have been
working on Cuchullain & sorting out my folk lore to finish that folklore
book but have hardly recovered my uprooting yet. I am improving daily
however & like to be quite industrious soon. I have been looking up Keeting & Whitely Stokes in Encyclopedia about the Fians.[4] I find that Keeting
agrees with the folk tales in making 'Grania' Finns wife before she met
Dairmiud—so much for the 'Leader'.[5] I find from Stokes that the Fenians
were all servile tribes, who had presumably revolted & that Ulster alone
had no Fenians.[6] The Fenian tales are therefore in a sense the reply of the
four provinces to the Cuchullain stories. Is not that interesting. One might
make a defeated man of the four provinces fortell the coming greatness of
Finn, in a day when Ulster would have no heroes. Ferdead was of the
Tribe which afterwards became the Clanna Morna.

Yrs ev
W B Yeats

[3] In her letter of 'Sunday ev' (see above, n. 2), AG told WBY that she had discussed plans for
next year's plays with Edward Martyn, who had just arrived in Dublin. If his new play, *An
Enchanted Sea*, was not ready in time, Martyn thought that he might produce *The Tale of a Town*,
but he was adamant that all work must be new and Irish, and he excluded Shaw: 'He suggested as
a possible solution, The Poor Old Woman [*i.e. Cathleen ni Houlihan*], The Shadowy Waters, & an
Irish play, on the same night. . . . I spoke of Cuchulain, but he says the plot you told him seemed
confused—However I suppose it won't be so when you have done it on the new lines. . . . Edward
also spoke of Russell's Deirdre. I wish it was a little better, it would be better than Tale of a
Town anyhow—'. The Fays, whose Ormond Dramatic Company had greatly impressed WBY in
Alice Milligan's plays and helped produce Hyde's *Casadh an tSugain* (see pp. 110; 76, n. 6), had
recently put AE's *Deirdre* into rehearsal and were eager to secure a play by WBY to go with it. It
was finally decided that they should perform *Cathleen ni Houlihan* and AE's *Deirdre* in April 1902,
productions which led to the formation of the Irish National Dramatic Company. Although no
Irish-language play was produced on that occasion, they presented P. T. MacGinley's *Eilís agus
an Bhean Déirce* (*Lizzie and the Beggarwoman*) in December 1902.

[4] Geoffrey Keating (*c.* 1570–*c.* 1645), priest, poet, and one of the most influential Irish histori-
ans, wrote his seminal *Foras Feasa ar Eirinn* (History of Ireland) between 1629 and 1631; he
devotes several pages to the Fenians, and tries to disengage the historical facts from the 'poetical
fables'. Whitley Stokes (1830–1909), a noted philologist and Celtic scholar, had published an
article on the Fenians in the 9th edition (1879) of the *Encyclopaedia Britannica* (vol. IX). Whether
he would have approved of WBY's use of it is doubtful, since his biographer (Richard I. Best,
Whitley Stokes, [1951], 13) reports an admiration well this side of idolatry: 'that minstrel's work I
cannot enjoy. His verses seem to me as emasculated as Burne Jones' knights, whom I always long
to kick.'

[5] Among the many criticisms levelled at *Diarmuid and Grania* (see above, n. 2), the *Leader* on
16 Nov picked out particularly the failure 'to mention that Grainne had already seen Diarmuid
and had fallen in love with him' before she married Finn.

[6] Stokes had written (see n. 4) that the Leinster and Meath Fenians were of 'subjugated tribes'
and that the 'Connaught Fenians, the *Clanna Morna*, so called from a stemfather *Morn*, were also
a servile tribe, the *Tuath Domnann*, settled in Erris in the west of Mayo. *Ferdiad* son of *Daman*,
whose combat with *Cúchulaind* forms the finest episode of the *Táin Bo Cuailnge*, was of this tribe.
. . . It is worthy of note that Ulster, whose warriors of the *Craebh Ruaid* or Red Branch are the
most prominent figures in the Heroic period, had no Fenians.'

PS.

Martyn [?]can do a fine stroke of business if he got Gordon Craig to do his scenery. It would attract a lot of attention being the first time the ordinary theatre has adventured anything in the new direction, & might be no more expensive than other scenery & Gordon Craig has his name to make & would work cheap.

ALS Berg, with envelope addressed to 21 Lower Baggot St, Dublin, postmark 'LONDON W.C. NO 26 01'.

To T. Fisher Unwin, [? 26 November 1901]

18 Woburn Buildings | Euston Road.
Tuesday

Dear Mr Unwin: I shall be round to you shortly to talk over the publication of 'Dairmuid & Grania'—perhaps this week. Arrangements about acting may cause a delay but I think not.[1] I enclose the slip of paper you sent me, which you can answer as you like.

Yr snly
W B Yeats

ALS Texas.

To Lady Augusta Gregory, [27 November 1901]

18 Woburn Buildings | Euston Road.
Wednesday

My dear Lady Gregory: The little sketch for Hyde I had forgotten.[1] ⟨You⟩ Hyde can make ⟨a play out of it either way. Raftery as ghos⟩ a good little

---

[1] It had not been possible to publish the play before production because of disagreements with Moore over style and structure, but now that it had been staged WBY was eager to see it in print (see p. 135). He was slightly hesitant because of Mrs Pat Campbell's renewed interest (see previous letter), although, as he foresaw, this came to nothing. In fact, he and Moore continued to tinker with the text and probably this, and their later falling-out over *Where There Is Nothing*, persuaded him to abandon the idea of publication. The play finally appeared, posthumously, in the *Dublin Magazine* of April 1951.

[1] On 21 Nov 1901 AG had sent a scenario to WBY (Berg), asking whether it would suit Hyde: 'it is founded on one of Raftery's poems, and on the carts and provisions that used to come to Biddy Early's house. But I am not sure if it should be real Raftery, or his heaven-sent ghost. Write out any suggestions or criticisms.' Hyde used it as the basis of his one-act play, *An Pósadh* (*The Marriage*), first produced on 20 Aug 1902 at the Connacht Feis, Galway, and AG included

play out of it, but let the people who come in be very few, or their going out will be too artificial. Two or three car or cart loads of people would be enough. When I read it first I did not notice that they were *driving* from the market. I think when he opens the door, ⟨they should hear the sound of the⟩ & the little boys come in Raftery should point out through the door & show them the cars coming down the hill from the market. Do not let the newly married couple offer Raftery a nights lodging—it is unnecessary & unlikely under the circumstances. They give him what food they have & a seat by the fire. When they call to the passer by at the end—if Hyde decide[s] for the supernatural turn to the story—they might say there ⟨is one of the little boys who was holding the horses for the people. It should not be a mere voice one does not know whose that answers & one rather wants to know where the little boys had gone too. The boy might ⟩ ⟨somebody passes by⟩ is somebody else coming down the hill, he will know where Rafter[y] has gone or the like—not to have the answer a mere voice. I cannot however make up my mind whether the supernatural end is good or bad. I think the story might seem more convincing as an actual chapter out of Rafterys life—it is is it not? I am very uncertain though. Let Hyde decide. The supernatural has the advantage of explaining the fright of the horses, & the ease with which the people are got rid of. The person who announces the restlessness of the horses might be one of the little boys. I suppose the little boys were left holding them.

I send the 'scenario' back to you & think Hyde might make a fine thing out of it. He gets great praise in the 'St James' I see for 'The Twisting of the Rope'. They say there is no one act English play it would not make seem unreal. The same article, which is perhaps by Gwyn, praises the 'Enchanted Sea' but says the rewriting of 'The Tale of the Town' by Moore was quite necessary as it had no human-nature & so on.[2] I have

her English version of the play in *Poets and Dreamers* (1903). In the final version a blind fiddler, given hospitality at the meagre wedding feast of a young impoverished couple, reveals himself as the poet Raftery, and tells them to invite their neighbours to hear him play. The neighbours, returning from a fair and excited by Raftery's fame, crowd in and he exacts a wedding present for the couple and money for himself from each of them. When all is collected, he gives his money to the newly-weds and slips away while they are counting it. A newly arrived guest, asked if he has seen Raftery, tells them he attended his funeral three days before. In this version, four boys are the first to be attracted by Raftery's playing, and he sends them out to bring in those returning from the fair. While opting for the 'supernatural' ending, AG and Hyde (who wrote the play on 6 and 7 Feb 1902) toned it down and there are no frightened horses.

[2] The anonymous review of *Samhain* and Edward Martyn's *The Tale of a Town* and *An Enchanted Sea*, probably by Stephen Gwynn, appeared not in the *St. James* but the *Pall Mall Gazette* of 26 Nov 1901 (9). Describing Hyde's play as 'a gem', the reviewer found it difficult 'to recall any English one-act piece that deserves to be mentioned in the same breath with it. . . . And it would be extremely likely to knock the bottom out of any play that was put up behind it.' He thought *An Enchanted Sea* 'a weird and gruesomely effective blend of fairies and Fenians' which, although 'too queer to be a tragedy', contained a striking and memorable heroine. He was less impressed by *The Tale of a Town*, considering that the 'characters are less vividly drawn, and

heard from Gwyn. I rather gather from his letter that he has greatly praised the Theatre as a whole but did not much like 'Grania' on which I am much at ease for I am very certain of 'Grania's' measure of power.³

I forgot to tell you that when I got back here I found that O'Brien Butler⁴ had been enquiring about the floor under me. You will remember his desire to go & live near you & Martyn. I have told Mʳˢ Old that I wont have him in this house. To do him justice he said that he would have to ask my leave.

Yr sny
W B Yeats

ALS Berg.

To John Millington Synge, [*1 December 1901*]

18 Woburn Buildings | Euston Road.
Sunday Nov 31

My dear Singe: I have no excuse for not having written except first pro-crastination & then forgetfullness. You will find me in at above address any Monday. If you come next Monday you will meet Binyon & a few others.¹ I did think one or two passages towards the end too personal. We can discuss them when you come.²

Yrs ev
W B Yeats

ALS TCD. Saddlemyer, 32.

show a mobility of principle that is almost Gilbertian and quite destroys any sense of stress. A consciousness of these shortcomings may have been the reason why Mr. George Moore was called in to revise it for presentation in Dublin, which he did, changing its title to "The Bending of the Bough".' WBY welcomed these remarks as refuting the implication in the *Freeman's Journal* (see p. 119) that the rewriting had been prompted by political considerations.

³ Gwynn's letter has not survived, but evidently mentioned his article, 'The Irish Literary Theatre and Its Affinities', which appeared in the December number of the *Fortnightly Review*. Although judiciously well-disposed towards the ILT, Gwynn did 'not think *Diarmuid and Grania* an admirable production', particularly in its 'unedifying' portrayal of Grania, and he spent some time (1055–8) contrasting it unfavourably with its legendary sources.

⁴ 'T. O'Brien Butler' was the pseudonym of the Irish composer Thomas Whitwell-Buller (1861–1915). WBY had introduced him to AG on 3 May 1900. At this time he was collaborating with Nora Chesson on *Muirgheis* (*The Sea Swan*) an 'Irish Legendary Grand Opera'.

¹ WBY hoped to meet Synge in London on his way back to Paris from Dublin, but in fact he had made only a brief stop-over, and was already back in Paris by 27 Nov.

² WBY had read the MS of *The Aran Islands*, to be published jointly by Maunsel and Elkin Mathews in 1907. There is no evidence that Synge revised his text in the light of discussions with WBY.

To Clement Shorter, [*? early December 1901*]

18 Woburn Buildings | Euston Road.

My dear Shorter,

Yes I shall go to you Wednesday with great pleasure.[1]

Yr sny

W B Yeats

ALS Berg.

To the Editor of the Academy,[1] [*7 December 1901*]

Binyons 'Odes' because of the poem in it about Tristram & Iseult, which seems to me perhaps the most noble & pathetic love poem on an old theme written in my time; & Sturge Moore's 'Artemis ⟨& Ap⟩ against Aphrodite'[2] which is powerful with a beautiful constrained passion. I have read only one other book published during the year, but cannot think from what I hear that had I read many I would have thought otherwise.

W B Yeats

ALCS NLI. Printed in the *Academy,* 7 December 1901 (568). *UP* II. 264–5.

To the Editor of the United Irishman, [*7 December 1901*]

A phrase in my letter to the *Freeman's Journal* about the proposed clerical censorship of the National Theatre has caused a good deal of misunderstanding. "Irial," for instance, objects to my description of literature as "the principal voice of the conscience," and himself defines literature as

[1] The Shorters' dinner parties were usually held on Sundays, but WBY dined there on Wednesday 11 Dec 1901 and wrote out 'The Lake Isle of Innisfree' in Dora Sigerson's visitors' book (*Gazette of the Grolier Club,* n. s. 2, October 1966, p. 9).

[1] The *Academy,* as was its annual custom, had asked a number of well-known men and women to choose their two favourite books of the year on a card printed: 'The two new Books which have pleased and interested me most in 1901 are:—'. Laurence Binyon also named Sturge Moore's play, and both Arthur Symons and Stephen Gwynn chose WBY's *The Shadowy Waters.* For Binyon's *Tristram* see pp. 6–7, and for Sturge Moore's *Aphrodite against Artemis* pp. 104–5.

[2] The *Academy* corrected this to *Aphrodite Against Artemis.*

"any piece of writing which in point of form is likely to secure permanence."[1] If "Irial" will recall the names of a few masterpieces he is much too intelligent not to see that his description is inadequate. Let him recall to mind "Don Quixote," or "Hamlet," or "Faust," or Tolstoi's "War and Peace" and "Anna Karenina," or almost any novel by Balzac or Flaubert, or any play by Ibsen, his "Enemy of the People" let us say. If he will do so, he will understand why literature seems to me, as indeed it seems to most critics of literature, to be the principal voice of the conscience. A great writer will devote perhaps years, perhaps the greater part of a lifetime, to the study of the moral issues raised by a single event, by a single group of characters. He will not bemoralise his characters, but he will show, as no other can show, how they act and think and endure under the weight of that destiny which is divine justice. No lawgiver, however prudent, no preacher, however lofty, can devote to life so ample and so patient a treatment. It is for this reason that men of genius frequently have to combat against the moral codes of their time, and are yet pronounced right by history. "Irial" will recall many examples, of which the most recent is Ibsen.[2] A play or a novel necessarily describes people in their relation to one another, and is, therefore, frequently concerned with the conscience in the ordinary sense of that word, but even lyric poetry is the voice of what metaphysicians call innate knowledge, that is to say, of conscience, for it expresses the relation of the soul to eternal beauty and truth as no other writing can express it. That apparently misleading sentence of mine was,

[1] 'Irial' was the pseudonym of Frederick Ryan (1874–1913), rationalist, socialist, agnostic, and journalist. Although at this time an ally of Arthur Griffith, he was later to reject Griffith's concept of nationalism as too narrow. He co-edited the independent Dublin periodical, *Dana*, (1904–5) and in 1907 founded the *National Democrat*. His friendship with Wilfrid Blunt led to his becoming assistant editor of the *Egyptian Standard* in Cairo, and he returned to London as editor of *Egypt* shortly before his death. His article, 'Censorship and Independence', published in the *United Irishman* on 23 Nov 1901 (3), praised WBY's letter to the *Freeman's Journal* (see pp. 118–19) for refusing to countenance censorship of the ILT but argued that 'Mr. Yeats rather maladroitly bases his claim to independence on the wrong grounds' by declaring that literature was 'the principal voice of conscience'. In offering the definition of literature which WBY quotes here, Ryan insisted that it was 'curious to speak of literature as though it had any special moral characteristic', since 'fine writing is not by any means always on the side of the true and the just'. He went on to assert that independence should be claimed 'as a right and not as a concession, and we must claim it boldly on the ground of policy that the free play of public opinion, unhampered by checks and authorities, is the best in the long run. . . . if a people be degraded so that they prefer impurity, it is not by censorships they can be redeemed, but only by education—an education which will lead them spontaneously to prefer the best.' As a radical and free-thinker, Ryan opposed censorship throughout his life, and this exchange continues a debate begun during the controversy over *The Countess Cathleen*, when he had argued (*United Irishman*, 20 May 1899, p. 4) that WBY should not have sought clerical approval of the play since this implied that the attacks upon it would have been valid without such approval. His last attack on censorship appeared in the *Irish Review* in January 1912.

[2] WBY's repeated use of Ibsen as an example was probably prompted in part by his knowledge that Ryan was a keen Ibsenite.

indeed, but an echo of a sentence of Verhaeren's, the famous Belgian poet. He says that a masterpiece is a portion of the conscience of the world.[3] An essay on poetry by Shelley and certain essays by Schopenhauer are probably the best things that have been written on the subject by modern writers, but Mr. George Santayana has written a book called "The Sense of Beauty," which deals profoundly with the whole philosophy of aesthetics.[4] "Irial" should read it. He can buy it for half-a-crown if he is lucky.

Now, another matter. I am doing an historical note on the various versions of the Diarmuid and Grainne legend, of which there are many. The critics who have objected to Mr. Moore's treatment and mine only seem to know one version and that a late literary form of the story, and this version they misunderstand. They have not even consulted so obvious a source as J. G. Campbells' book, "The Fians," which gives several Highland folklore versions of the legend which are also current in Ireland. I may send my note to you when I have time to finish it, but in any case, if Mr. Moore consents, as I have no doubt he will, it shall go with the printed text of the play.[5]

W B Yeats

[3] WBY, who did not read French, had been introduced to the work of Émile Verhaeren (1855–1916) by the teacher and critic Osman Edwards (1864–1936), and refers to his conception of poetry in his 1898 article 'John Eglinton and Spiritual Art' (*UP* II. 131), and in 'The Celtic Element in Literature' (*E & I*, 187). Edwards, a frequent visitor at WBY's Monday Evenings in the 1890s, was a close friend and translator of Verhaeren, and his essay 'Emile Verhaeren' had appeared in the *Savoy* of November 1898, immediately before WBY's 'The Tables of the Law'.

[4] Shelley's essay was 'A Defence of Poetry' (see p. 123, n. 1), which asserted not only that the 'great instrument of moral good is the imagination; and poetry administers to the effect by acting upon the cause' but that 'the greatest poets have been men of the most spotless virtue'. Arthur Schopenhauer (1788–1860), the German idealist philosopher who exerted a significant influence on the Symbolist Movement, maintained that art vouchsafes knowledge superior to that of science in that it communicates the permanent and essential forms of the world. WBY may have been thinking in particular of his 'Ideas Concerning the Intellect', in which he deplores those artists who are infected by the 'consciousness of the times', and argues that it is 'only the absolutely genuine poet or thinker who rises superior to all such influences', citing as an example Shakespeare, who 'wished to show in the mirror of poetry *men*, not moral caricatures; and so everyone recognizes them in the mirror and his works live today and for all time' (*Parerga and Paralipomena* [Oxford, 1974], II. 66–7). In *The Sense of Beauty* (1896) the Spanish-born American philosopher George Santayana (1863–1952) had set out to formulate a complete aesthetic theory that would (6) 'reveal the roots of conscience and taste in human nature and enable us to distinguish transitory preferences and ideals, which rest on peculiar conditions, from those which, springing from those elements of mind which all men share, are comparatively permanent and universal'. All three thinkers, like WBY, owed much to Plato.

[5] WBY was eager to take this opportunity of refuting the critics who had accused him and Moore of using a false version of the Diarmuid and Grania legend. Although the *Leader* had been most vituperative on this topic (see p. 126 n. 2), the *United Irishman* had made a similar objection to the play in its review on 2 Nov 1901. WBY did not send a fuller note to the paper, and the play was not published in his lifetime.

P.S.—I must add a sentence or two to what I have said about the conscience. It is made sensitive and powerful by religion, but its dealings with
the complexity of life are regulated by literature. "Irial" spoke of a book
which discusses problems of the hour and yet seems to him at once literature and iniquitous. He is certainly mistaken. Literature, when it is really
literature, does not deal with problems of the hour, but with problems of
the soul and the character.[6]

Printed letter, *United Irishman*, 7 December 1901 (3). *UP* II. 263-4.

To T. Werner Laurie,[1] *[10 December 1901]*

18 Woburn Buildings | Euston Road.
Tuesday

Dear Mr Laurie: I find I have made rather a mess of things. Lady Grego-
rys old publisher was Murray.[2] She therefore sent her book to him first.
She ⟨got it into her head⟩ thought that he had refused it and wrote so to
me. I thought I was free (as she had sent me the MSS) to offer it to M^r
Unwin. When I got back to day I found a telegram from her saying that
Murray had accepted it. I dont quite know what is [*for* has] happened, but

[6] In illustrating his argument that fine writing need not be on the side of 'the true and the just'
(see n. 1), Ryan cited a recent 'book on the South African War by an Englishman, very nicely
written, admirably phrased, the work of a scholar, and yet it was all arguing a lie'. In replying to
the present letter in the *United Irishman* of 14 Dec 1901 (5), he maintained that there was 'no
hall-mark by which we can unmistakably determine what book is "literature". . . . Even the test of
permanence is arbitrary', and therefore returned to his 'main contention that the claim to independence for art did not involve such delicate and disputable propositions. . . . it is sufficient to
fall back on the argument for all independence and for all democracy. . . . When we can only keep
a people pure by censorships we are in the last stages of corruption.'

[1] T. Werner Laurie (1866-1944), publisher, was at this time Unwin's manager, but in 1904 he
set up under his own imprint and was to publish WBY's *The Trembling of the Veil* (1922) and *A
Vision* (1925). Unwin's trade manager, A. D. Marks, later told Stanley Unwin (*The Truth About a
Publisher* [1960], 84) that Laurie was 'a combination of rake and religion. . . . He and George
Moore wrote risky [*sic*] stories for a racing journal called *The Hawk*, and as a sideline Laurie him-
self wrote sermons and sold them to parsons at 7*s* 6*d* each.'

[2] Sir John Murray (1851-1928), publisher, had taken over his father's publishing house in
1892. Although he had, in fact, published only one of AG's books to date, *Sir William Gregory:
An Autobiography* (1894), AG had submitted *Cuchulain of Muirthemne* to him and, as she recalled
in her diary (Berg) on 6 Jan 1902, the mix-up occurred because she thought he had turned it
down: 'After an ineffectual attempt to deal with Bryers (who has not yet sent me a definite
answer!) I sent it to Murray who kept it a month—then sent it back with a rather disparaging & I
must say silly letter from some wise man he had consulted—the point of which was that I shd
write it down to English comprehension, that is to the level of Jacob's fairy tales—& also prefix to
it a history of Ireland & especially of Ulster at that time!!—I indignantly refused this suggestion &
sent the M.S. to Yeats to dispose of—Then Murray wrote that he didn't mean to refuse the M.S.
& was willing to publish it at his own risk—so, Yeats having retrieved it from Fisher Unwin, it
has so been arranged, & I am already revising proofs.'

I know that she will want to give it Murray who is not only the publisher of her other books—except one which she published at her own expense[3]—but a personal friend. Could you let me have the MSS back under the circumstances. I am very sorry as I have certainly got things into a mess.

I shall be bringing you 'Grania' by Moore & myself next week I think.

Yours snly
W B Yeats

ALS Texas.

To Mrs Patrick Campbell, [? *11 December 1901*]

Mention in letter from Mrs Campbell, 11 December 1901.
A telegram asking if he could attend her rehearsals,[1] and apparently suggesting that she should take *Diarmuid and Grania* on her forthcoming American tour.[2]

MBY.

To Lady Augusta Gregory, *13 December 1901*

| Handed }
in at } | Of Last evening
West Central Dist at 6.25 PM | Received }
here at } | 8.40 PM |

TO {Lady Gregory Gort Co Galway Ireland

Seen Murray all right about books

Yeates

Telegram Berg, stamped 'GORT AM 6 DE 14 01'.

[3] *Mr Gregory's Letter-Box 1813–35*, published in 1898 by Smith Elder & Co. after it had been turned down by Murrays and Longmans.

[1] See p. 126, n. 1. Mrs Campbell had ended her season at the Royalty Theatre on 16 Nov, and was now rehearsing her repertory for her imminent American tour. WBY evidently still hoped that she would take *Diarmuid and Grania* with her and had asked if he could attend its rehearsal if so. She replied that she did not mind who attended her rehearsals 'as long as I get my own way'.

[2] Mrs Campbell and her Company embarked at Liverpool for her first American tour on 14 Dec. The tour, undertaken because she was almost bankrupt, opened in Chicago on 30 Dec, and was a resounding triumph. An aggressive publicity campaign kept her in the headlines, and by the time she left for home on 22 May 1902 she had wiped out over half her debts. Her repertory, based on her well-tried London successes, included Pinero's *The Second Mrs Tanqueray* and *The Notorious Mrs Ebbsmith*, Maeterlinck's *Pelléas and Mélisande* (see pp. 8–9), Sudermann's *Magda*, and Bjørnson's *Beyond Human Power* (see pp. 120, n. 4; 122–3), but not *Diarmuid and Grania*, although in her reply she assured WBY that it 'would be delightful to me to do "Grania" in America but I am not sure that I will have the opportunity—I am taking it with me—& should the opportunity arise I would cable for you! & I hope you or both of you would come & help—'.

To Lady Augusta Gregory, [14 December 1901]

18 Woburn Buildings | Euston Road
Saturday.

My dear Lady Gregory: I had brought the book to Unwin when I got your wire about Murray. I wrote to Unwin—I enclose his answer[1]—& the moment the MSS reached me—it took a couple of days for some reason or other—I went to Murray. He is writing terms to you. He approves of my preface. I am to explain the dialect you have written in Etc. I think he will push on the book at once.[2] There is no hurry about preface he says as that will be printed last. I can have all the proofs before me when I write it—I dare say you will be in London then which will be a great advantage.[3] I have got the references to Dierdres three children. You should work them in. Mananan took care of them & one of them married one of the Kings of faery Cuchullain faught against for Labraid. This will greatly humanize those defeated kings[4]—I saw Newbolt at Murrays. He has my 'Baile & Aillin' poem & I think means to use it. He says my 'magic' was "brilliantly successful" & he wants other work.[5] Courtney has taken the "Morris" at £3 a 1000 words. I asked Watt to get a definite promise as to date of publication but do not know whether he has done so.[6] I am doing & have done

---

[1] See p. 134. Unwin had acknowledged WBY's letter on 11 Dec 1901 (MBY) saying 'Of course we returned the manuscript without delay. Naturally I should have been proud to be connected with its publication, but I am content for John Murray to take the venture.'

[2] As AG reported to WBY on 17 Dec 1901 (Berg), Murray had written to give his account of this meeting: 'Mr Yeats called here yesterday and I had a most agreeable and interesting conversation with him. He most politely—but most uncompromisingly rejected every one of my critics and my own suggestions, and I daresay he is quite right. I still adhere to my opinion that the colloquial vernacular of today is now and then adopted in a somewhat excessive form, but provided that this is fully explained in the preface I have nothing more to say.' She went on to say that she had offered 'to modify some of the "colloquialisms"' where this could be done 'without departing from the Irish idiom', and that she had 'accepted his terms, and am very glad to get them'. *Cuchulain of Muirthemne* was published in April 1902.

[3] In a PS to a letter of 7 Dec (Berg) AG had asked WBY if he would do a preface for the book on strictly business terms: 'I feel sure it would be a great help. . . . I think some explanation of what the book aims to be will be necessary, and also I think a preface by you would help to balance the grotesque element in the earlier stories . . .'

[4] WBY had found this reference in the Dublin learned journal *Atlantis* (see pp. 144–5), where two, not three, children are mentioned. In her reply (see above) AG asked WBY to send her 'the bit about Deirdre's children', but was 'doubtful about using it, it may add too many years to Cuchulain's age'. In the end she did make a passing reference to Aebgreine, the daughter of Deirdre and Naoise (*Cuchulain of Muirthemne*, 219).

[5] Newbolt had published WBY's essay on 'Magic' in the September number of the *Monthly Review* (see p. 62, n. 1); 'Baile and Aillinn' appeared in the same magazine in July 1902.

[6] William Leonard Courtney (1850–1928) was editor of the *Fortnightly Review* from 1894, and drama critic and literary editor of the *Daily Telegraph* from 1895. WBY's essay on William Morris, 'The Happiest of the Poets', which he included in *IGE*, did not appear in the *Fortnightly Review* until March 1903.

new little essays for "Celtic Twilight" which "the Speaker" will I have no doubt take.[7] I am working every week with Dolmetsch at the chanting.

The day I got your MSS I read 'Conary' & the 'luring' out & Emer's & Dierdre's laments to a couple of friends whom I came on by chance. They listened enchanted. If you meet any old countryman, who knows about the Fians, ask about "Grania" for me.

Yr always
W B Yeats

PS. I went to that Club with Unwin, a dreadful, sordid Fleet Street air about it all—successions of dull improprieties & meaningless historical gossip.[8]

PS Murray thought your title page inadequate & we made out another which I dont much like. How would this do.

> Cuchullain of Murthemne
> Being traditional stories
> of the Champions of
> the Red Branch;
> rearranged & put into English
> by Lady Gregory.

'Partly Retranslated' was an inadequate word as you put all into your own English. The preface, yours or mine will explain what you have done. 'Partly Retranslated' makes one expect a mixture of styles—yours & other peoples. Or you might write 'put into the English of the Galway country people'.[9]

ALS Berg, with enclosure, and envelope addressed to Coole, postmark 'LONDON DE 16 01'.

---

[7] The *Speaker* published twelve stories by WBY between 18 Jan and 26 Apr 1902 under the running heading 'New Chapters in the Celtic Twilight'. They were all incorporated in the 1902 edition of the book.

[8] Unwin had invited WBY to attend a meeting of the Johnson Club at the Cheshire Cheese on 21 Dec. In a conversation with John Sparrow on 27 May 1931 (Private), WBY recalled that 'Many years ago I dined with the Johnson Club in London and I found that the only man I agreed with was a man who deplored the passing of the Reform Bill of 1832. We spent the whole evening agreeing. I was then an extreme Irish revolutionary.' By 1901 the Club, which Unwin had founded in 1884, largely consisted of minor literati, 18th-century scholars, and lawyers.

[9] In her reply (see above) AG wrote that she liked 'your title page' and had sent it on to Murray. The subtitle as printed reads: 'The Story of the Men of the Red Branch of Ulster Arranged and Put into English by Lady Gregory.'

To Lady Augusta Gregory, [22 December 1901]

18 Woburn Buildings | Euston Road.
Sunday night.

My dear Lady Gregory: that dedication of yours is quite beautiful. It tells the essential things also.[1] Here is another suggested inscription for the title "Cuchullain of Murthemne: being stories of the men of the Red Branch arranged and put into the English of the Connaught Country people by Lady Gregory". I think "arranged" is better than "re arranged" & "men of the Red Branch" better than "Champions of the Red Branch". Or you might say "put into the English of the men of Connaught" instead of what I have written down. "Men of Connaught" would echo "men of the Red Branch" but no "Connaught Country people" is better. You need not wright [*for* write] about Cuchullain aged so far as the story of Deirdres children is concerned. If need be you can say when you come to that defeated King "It was he who was afterwards married to ———— the daughter of Naisi & Deirdre." I feal that it will greatly help to humanaize the faery part of "the Only Jealousy" as well as bring the Deirdre story more into the general structure. Manannans care of the children will help to explain Deirdres allusion to him.[2] I have written a new lyric—quite a good one—& also a little essay about old Farrell & the woods of Coole which is less good & some 'Celtic Twilight' odds & ends.[3] Bullen comes in to morrow night. A P Watt has strongly advised my accepting Bullen's offer to take the book of essays instead of the novel as £50 on account is more than one can ordinary get for essays.[4] Bullen was to have seen A P Watt on Friday about it. He was to arrange terms for new 'Celtic Twilight' also, also I think for new edition of 'Secret Rose' (this in two volumes one to contain "Hanrahan" re written as we planned & the other the other stories[5]—3/6 a

---

[1] AG dedicated *Cuchulain of Muirthemne* to 'the People of Kiltartan' in an open letter addressed to 'My Dear Friends', and dated March 1902 in the final version.

[2] See pp. 136, 144.

[3] The new lyric was 'The Folly of Being Comforted' (*VP*, 199–200), published in the *Speaker* on 11 Jan 1902, and the essay was 'Enchanted Woods', which appeared in the *Speaker* on 18 Jan (*Myth*, 60–4). The latter tells the folklore associated with Inchy Wood at Coole, much of it collected from John Farrell, AG's woodman. AG gives an account of Farrell in *Coole* (Dublin, 1931), 31–2.

[4] In December 1896, when he began *The Speckled Bird* for Lawrence & Bullen, WBY had been promised an advance of £105 against royalties, of which he received the first half in 25 weekly instalments of £2. 4s. 0d. Bullen, despairing after five years of ever seeing the book, now offered to take *IGE* instead and to pay WBY £50 of the remaining £55. Although WBY was to continue tinkering with the novel for a few more months, he accepted this offer.

[5] There was no new 2-volume edition of *The Secret Rose*, but the tales, rewritten with AG's help, were published as *Stories of Red Hanrahan* by the Dun Emer Press in 1905. After the publication of *CW* in 1908, Bullen eventually brought out a single volume, *Stories of Red Hanra-*

volume). I told A P Watt & Bullen both that I would do just as A P Watt advised. If Bullen gets these books I have all but persuaded him to turn Irish publisher (he is Irish) that is to say to have a Dublin office of some sort & to think seriously about Irish writers & printers. I have also got him gently excited about the idea of publishing a series of Irish Catholic religious pictures by Jack & other people. He has been greatly tickled by the idea of Jacks crusafixian with the impenitant thief as principle character— he kept chuckling over it for a long time.[6] When A P Watt rather advised Bullen & not only for the 'Celtic Twilight' etc but for the new books I told him that Bullen was anything but steady. A P Watt merely muttered something like "the better they are the more they drink" or "the better the man the more he drinks" or something equally surprizing coming from such a whitehaired father Xmas. You will remember "Mosada" a bad early play of mine—which is in the Usheen book—& which was printed in a shilling pamphlet long ago in Dublin. Well a shabby relation of mine (father of "the bold bad one") has prosicuted a borrower of books & got £5 instead of Mosada which the borrower had lost. I wrote a letter for the prosacuted man, who called on me, saying it was worth so far as I knew nothing (I said I thought there was no demand). However my miserable relation got Elkin Matthews to sware it was worth £10. I heard nothing of the case until the borrower came to me on the morning of the trial.[7]

Yrs always
W B Yeats

I suppose you will be hear in January some time—before I do my preface at any rate.

Dolmetsch says 'the chanting' is now quite perfect in theory & only requires a little practice. He says it is 'a new art'. We can now make a perfect record of everything.

ALS Berg, with envelope addressed to Coole, postmark '[PAD]DINGTON. W. DE 23 01'. Partly in Wade, 361–2.

han: The Secret Rose: Rosa Alchemica (1913), and Macmillan published *Stories of Red Hanrahan and The Secret Rose* in 1927.

[6] 'The Crucifixion', included in the October exhibition, emphasises the thieves rather than Christ. When selling the picture to John Quinn in 1903, Jack Yeats remarked (NYPL) 'I don't think anyone before has made so much of the thieves when painting a Crucifixion'. In spite of his mirth, Bullen never took up WBY's proposal.

[7] *Mosada*, published separately as a reprint from *DUR* in 1886, was included in *The Wanderings of Oisin* (1889). The 1886 edition is now among the rarest of WBY's works. WBY's 'shabby relation' was probably George Pollexfen's improvident younger brother, Frederick (1852–1929), who fathered nine children after his marriage in 1882. His extravagances led to his exclusion from the Pollexfen family company and to his wife divorcing him in 1901. His daughter Ruth (at this time 'the bold bad one') went to live in JBY's household in January 1900, and the Yeatses later looked after another daughter, Hilda.

To John Quinn, [28] December [1901]

18 Woburn Buildings | Euston Road | London.

Sat Dec.

Dear Sir: I hope you will excuse my long delay in answering your letter.[1] I have been busy over so many things since I got back from Ireland. I am particularly glad to have 'Human Mortality' for I have long been curious about Prof James opinions. I remember reading in some essays of Fredrick Myrers [*for* Myers] that Prof James, alone among writers of the modern school beleived in the heredity of ideas which seemed to me so like that memory of nature, I spoke of in my essay on Magic, that I spent a day going through Prof James writings in the British Museum in a vain hunt for anything on the subject. Now I shall master at least one bit of his writing & that may help me with the rest.[2]

Again thanking you I remain

Yrs snly
W B Yeats

ALS NYPL, with envelope addressed to 120 Broadway, New York, postmark 'LONDON W.C. DE 28 01'.

To Lady Augusta Gregory, [28 December 1901]

18 Woburn Buildings | Euston Road. | London.

Sat.

Dear Lady Gregory: A great many thanks for the wine & the other things—all things I am very glad of. I am eating one of the biskets, now

[1] See p. 119. Quinn had evidently written to WBY shortly after approaching JBY about the purchase of pictures. This, WBY's reply, marks the beginning of a correspondence and friendship that, with one interruption from 1909 to 1914, lasted to Quinn's death. After Quinn's death WBY was to recall (MBY) that he 'was at first one of those vague persons one thinks so seldom about, and often with annoyance, who writes for an autograph, or a manuscript, or to discover some fact. Then I met him at the Galway *feis* in honour of the poet Raftery, where I was one of the speakers. Next day he proposed a lecture tour that gave me my first substantial sum of money.'

[2] William James (1842–1910), brother of the novelist and Professor of Philosophy at Harvard, had published *Human Immortality* in 1898, and Quinn had probably sent WBY the 2nd (1899) edition, which remained in his library throughout his life (*YL*, 1008). James took an active interest in supernatural phenomena and supported the founding of the Society for Psychical Research in London in 1882, serving both as vice-president and, from 1894 to 1896, as president. The notion of the 'Anima Mundi' is central to WBY's essay on 'Magic' (see p. 113), although his concept differs from James's 'heredity of ideas', to which WBY would have been directed in Myers's *Science and a Future Life* (1893). Frederic W. H. Myers (1843–1901), philosopher, essayist, poet, and founder-member of the Society for Psychical Research, was a close friend of James, who was to review his posthumous *Human Personality and Its Survival of Bodily Death* (1903), a book that WBY was to cite with approval in 'A General Introduction for My Work' (*E & I*, 514).

while I am writing, eating it with my coffey. I send you a new press cutting—which belongs I suppose to the theatre book.[1] I cannot find the slip
of paper on which I wrote Sharps referance for Deirdre Children so I have
asked him to give me the referance again. I will then look it up & send you
what I find. I had a days research into 'Grania' character lately. I find that
she so hated Finn, when he was her husband & before she ran away with
Dairmiud that she said her hate of him made "a clot of blood form under
her heart" & "the sinews of her body swell". The text on which 'The
Leader' based its criticism only exists in MSS later than about 1720, and is
manifestly a very modern idealization. I am greatly excited about your
Finn book, the doing of which will be I should think a very great joy.[2]
Your idea of Finn only getting his wisdom by a kind of stroke of hazard &
not by any right of nature is I think very admirable.

My suggestion to my uncle about helping his brothers children has I am
sorry to say born unexpected fruit, if indeed it was my suggestion that had
the effect. Instead of doing something for the children, he replied to an
appeal from their father for £200 to pay his clerks, & rent, by sending the
£200. The £200 was spent in a few days in speculations.[3] I should feal
even more regret than I do if I did not think that my uncle George even in
this amazing fit of generosity (which I certainly never thought him capable
of) avoided trouble. It was like Elkin Matthews & Althea Gyles. He found
it too much trouble to make her a small allowance (seeing the work done
for it every week) & so gave her £10 in a lump for the loss of which he
blamed me for years.[4]

I have not yet heard what arrangement, if any has been made between A
P Watt & Bullen about my books. It will be a great thing if he does really
turn Irish publisher. He spoke of it quite definitely the other day & said he
would ask me to get him some good Irish work. The drawback is that my

---

[1] Lady Gregory's collection of press clippings on the Irish Theatre is in NLI.

[2] This is the first mention of *Gods and Fighting Men*, published in 1904 with a preface by
WBY. In an appendix to 'The Legendary and Mythological Foundation of the Plays and Poems',
printed in *The Poetical Works* (1907), WBY wrote (*VP*, 843): 'Almost every story I have used or
person I have spoken of is in one or other of Lady Gregory's "Gods and Fighting Men" and
"Cuchulain of Muirthemne"'. AG had started collecting material on Finn McCoole in November
and on 21 Nov (Berg) reported that she was puzzled about Finn: 'Who was he? What did he
mean? Why was he given the knowledge from the sacred trees if he was a mere militia captain?'
Her holograph MS (Berg) is dated 30 Dec 1901–25 May 1903.

3 Following his uncle Frederick's embarrassing behaviour over *Mosada* (see p. 139, n. 7), WBY
had evidently written to George Pollexfen for assistance in putting his finances on a surer footing.
JBY was irritated by the Pollexfens' refusal to do anything for Frederick's children, but in 1904
George agreed to pay for Ruth's education.

[4] This had happened in 1898, when Althea Gyles was designing the cover of *The Wind Among
the Reeds*.

sister says he has very little money. Certainly his London office is not imposing. It is almost opposite Oldmeadows.[5]

I suppose you will be in London at the end of January, & have proofs sometime before that.

I have been working to day & yester day on "Cuchullain" once again.

This is a very scrappy letter—A good Xmass to you & Robert & all

Yrs ever
W B Yeats

ALS Berg, with envelope addressed to Coole, postmark 'LONDON W DE 30 01'.

[5] Bullen's office was across from Oldmeadow's Unicorn Press in Cecil Court, St Martin's Lane, but was shortly to move to 47 Great Russell St., where it remained until his partnership with Frank Sidgwick ended in 1907.

1902

To Clement Shorter, [*? 2 January 1902*]

18 Woburn Buildings | Euston Road.
Thursday.

My dear Shorter: I owe you many apologies about last night. I was up to
five o clock the night before, not seeing the New Year in but doing some
very exaustive work for some of my mystics.[1] When I got your note it was
morning & I was fresh but when I sent my second wire I was fit for nothing. I was very anxious to meet Watson[2] whom I have not met for years, as
well as you all.

Yrs snly
W B Yeats

ALS Berg.

---

[1] See p. 147.
[2] The poet William Watson (1858–1935) had come to notice with his *Wordsworth's Grave*
(1890), reviewed by WBY in the *Providence Sunday Journal* on 15 June 1890 (*Letters to the New
Island* [1934], 210), and his elegy on Tennyson, *Lachrymae Musarum* (1892). His anti-Imperialist
poems, and in particular his pro-Boer stance, had lost him favour, and probably cost him the poet
laureateship, although his measured, Virgilian *Ode on the Day of the Coronation of King Edward
VII*, published in April of this year, set him on the road to rehabilitation, and he was knighted in
1917. In *OBMV* (xi–xiii) WBY, recalling the 1890s, wrote: 'Victorianism had been defeated,
though two writers dominated the moment who had never heard of that defeat or did not believe
in it; Rudyard Kipling and William Watson. . . . "Wring the neck of rhetoric" Verlaine had said,
and the public soon turned against William Watson, forgetting that at his best he had not rhetoric
but noble eloquence. As I turn his pages I find verse after verse read long ago and still unforget-
table . . .' Watson, who had first met WBY at Edward Dowden's house in the later 1880s, was less
generous: in a review of 1892 he had found *The Countess Cathleen* lacking in technical accomplishment (see 1. 218), and Gogarty identifies WBY as the target of his epigram: 'I met a poet
lately, one of those / To whom his life was one continual pose. / A wise man this, for, take the
pose away, / What else were left 'twould pose the gods to say' (*William Butler Yeats: A Memoir*
[Dublin, 1963], 21).

To Maud Gonne, [c. *5 January 1902*]

Mention in letter from MG, 6 January [1902].
Inviting her to call on him on her way through London.[1]

G–YL, 147.

To Lady Augusta Gregory, [6] *January* [*1902*]

18 Woburn Buildings | Euston Road
⟨Feb⟩ Jan.

Dear Lady Gregory: I have looked up the Children of Deirdre & feal certain they should be incorporated in your book. I send extract from Atlantis Vol 3, Page 421 & neighbouring pages. The children will improve the tale of Deirdre by giving one a better & fuller fealing of her married life in Scotland & they will also link Mananan more into the tale as well as humanize the supernatural part of the Sick Bed. It also seems to me that Deirdre was the kind of woman who should have children just as Grania is the kind of woman who should not. I shall bring both children into my Deirdre play. They are an integral part of the myth. Deirdre is the normal, compassionate, wise house wife lifted into imortality by beauty & tragedy. Her fealing for her lover is the fealing of the house wife for the man of the house. She would have been less beautiful, considering her type if she had not been fruitful. I should say nothing about the war with Concobar made by Mananan & Gaer. I should merely speak of the birth of the two children & of their being given to Mananan to foster when Deirdre & the sons of Usna return to Ireland. I should then in "the Sick bed" when I came to Rinn & his father say something like this "this he it was who had married Aebgreeni, daughter of Deirdre. Manana[n] had brought them togeather in the Land of Promise" or "the Land of Youth" or some such phrase. Or I should say 'He it was who after wards married' Etc. Or if only Echaidh Iuel comes into the tale (& I think Rinn is in it) I should say 'He it was who was father to that Rinn who married' Etc. A considerable part of the charm & value of your book is that it does just this patching togeather, that it brings togeather long scattered things, long forgotten beads.[1]

---

[1] MG had been in Dublin since 23 Dec 1901. In her reply she told him she would 'be in London on the 13th & will have tea with you at 4 o'clock if you will have me'.

[1] See p. 136. WBY's notes survive in Berg. Eugene O'Curry's 'The Exile of the Children of Uisnech', published in *Atlantis*, 3 (1862), 377–422, discusses the various versions of the legend

I do not know what length my preface to your book will be. It may be quite short. I shall have to read the proofs before I know what length. It may be fairly long. I am as you can imagine short enough of money.[2] I have just scraped on by various expedients. 'The Celtic Twilight' new chapters are coming in 'The Speaker' at a low price though & I have got a friend to advance me the price of them as I have written each one, but for this I should have collapsed.[3] In a few days I hope the Agreements for 'The Celtic Twilight' new edition will be signed & then I shall get a few pounds in advance & that will keep me going till I am paid for some of the things A P Watt has placed. I may wire to you for £3 or £4 for preface but I shall wait until I see if this Agreement gets signed all right. I dine with Bullen tomorrow. If I am absolutely on my beams ends I shall simply wire the words "Shall I do preface now" & you will understand. I will probably not finish the preface any way until you are over if that will do. It will hardly be wanted just yet as it will be the last thing printed. After a rather gloomy time I seem to have emerged into fairly good spirits—the best for a very long time. Masefield has got a post in the country whither he goes in about 8 days.[4] When he is gone I shall I expect be gloomy enough until you are over but just now I am so well content, & I cannot tell why that I feal as if I had no nerves, as if I were a mere wooden image, a philistine that is. I "evoked" myself into this state on New Year night.

and prints the oldest text, that of 1391, from the Yellow Book of Lecan. This makes no reference to Deirdre's children, but at the end of the article, O'Curry presents two fragments which tell how Mananan, King of the Isles of Man and Hebrides, reared Deirdre's son, Gaiar, and daughter, Aibgréni (sometimes Aebgreiné), and invaded Ulster with Gaiar to avenge the deaths of Naoisi and his brothers. The second fragment adds (422) that '*Aebgreiné* now, the daughter, she married *Rinn*, the son of *Echaidh Iuil*, of the Land of Promise'. In 'The Sick Bed of Cuchulain' Cuchulain wounds Echaidh Iuil, and in her version of this tale, entitled 'The Only Jealousy of Emer', AG notes (*Cuchulain of Muirthemne*, 219) that it 'was to the son, now, of this Eochaid Juil of the Land of Promise, that Aebgreine, the daughter of Naoise and Deirdre was given afterwards in marriage by Manannan'. WBY's distinction between Deirdre and Grania mirrors that he draws between Morris's and Rossetti's heroines in his essay of this year, 'The Happiest of the Poets' (*E & I*, 56–9). He did not introduce the children into his play *Deirdre*, although the heroine's characterization is as described here.

[2] In a letter dated 31 Dec [1901] (Berg), AG had asked whether WBY would 'like to be paid for the preface in advance? How long do you suppose it will be?'

[3] The five articles, 'New Chapters in the Celtic Twilight', appeared at roughly monthly intervals in the *Speaker* from 18 Jan to 26 Apr 1902 (see p. 82). The friend who advanced him money was probably AEFH.

[4] John Masefield (see p. 54, n. 2) had resigned his job in the bank in the summer of 1901 and was about to take up a one-year post as exhibition secretary in the art gallery of the Wolverhampton Arts and Industrial Exhibition, May–October 1902. While he was away, in November 1902, Grant Richards published his *Salt-Water Ballads*, in which he dedicated 'A Wanderer's Song' to WBY.

I met M^r & Mrs Strong yester day.[5] They asked about you & are going to ask me to dinner for Mr Strong wants to talk about my "wonderful essay on Magic". He thinks he has identified the magician & doctor in the vision but is not sure. He says it was a wonderful historical picture & must be a picture of some definite man.[6]

Yrs alway
W B Yeats

ALS Berg, with envelope addressed to Coole, postmark 'LONDON JA 6 02'. Partly in Wade, 362–3.

To Lady Augusta Gregory, [13 January 1902]

18 Woburn Buildings | Euston Road. | London.
Monday night.

My dear Lady Gregory: that £10 is very much too much. I really do not know what I can find to say which will be worth that but I will do my best. Let me have a copy of the complete proofs & I may do something not as inadequate as I fear.[1] I am still envolved in the new edition of the Celtic Twilight. The mere writing out of what I have already done takes a surpizing time, but the book will be much better than it was. I am using a good deal of my Sligo information. I should be done this week of a certainty &

[5] Sandford Arthur Strong (1863–1904), librarian to the Duke of Devonshire and the House of Lords, art editor, and Professor of Arabic at University College, London, married Eugénie Sellers (d. 1943), archaeologist and art historian, in 1897. AG first met them in 1898, when he confided (diary, 3 Oct, Berg) that the Library 'was in great disorder & the Lords don't read much'. Sturge Moore, who was introduced to them at the Binyons in July 1902, reported that he 'was a great friend of Renan's and is reckoned a first rate scholar . . . and is supposed to be very influential and a terrible enemy if you offend him' (Sylvia Legge, *Affectionate Cousins* [1980], 203). Mrs Strong later wrote *Apotheosis and After Life* (1915), essays on art and religion in the Roman empire, which WBY consulted (*YL*, 2015) in his search for cyclical patterns of history, and from which he probably drew his symbol of the dolphin, described (215) as 'a mystic escort of the dead to the Islands of the Blest'.

[6] In his essay, 'Magic' (*E & I*, 31–3), WBY described a magical experiment in which an 'evoker of spirits' (i.e. Mathers) had summoned up a 16th-century Flemish doctor who, with the aid of a human effigy, was 'trying to make flesh by chemical means, and though he had not succeeded, his brooding had drawn so many evil spirits about him that the image was partly alive'. The doctor, made mortally ill by these spirits, was saved by a man in a conical hat who drove the magical life out of the effigy. Mathers told WBY that the doctor 'would in part recover, but he would never be well. . . . He was accursed. He was a magician.'

[1] See p. 145, n. 2; AG had sent him £10 in advance for the Preface to *Cuchulain of Muirthemne*. In a letter of 9 Jan (Berg) she had written: 'Don't bother about the preface till I come over. The proofs though they are coming quicker now, are only as far as Conaire. Whatever you write will be beautiful, but I don't think you need write much, the chief thing is to show that you, representing the literary movement, accept the book, & that it is not rubbishy amateur work, as critics might be prepared to think. Perhaps you may have to do a note on Cuchulain symbolism . . .'

then I shall get back to Cuchullain & I hope finish him out of hand, finish him enough at any rate for Martyn to judge of it. I have my 'chanting' essay to do also[2]—it will be a considerable addition to the book of essays but is in any case a necessity that I may launch Mʳˢ Emery.

I have done a great deal of work at my Magical Rites, sketched them all out in their entirety.[3] I have gone through some black spir[i]ts too but have emerged at last into a cheerful mood, which really seems as if it were going to last for a while.

Yrs alway
W B Yeats

ALS Berg, with envelope addressed to Coole, postmark 'LONDON N. W. JA 14 02'. Wade, 363–4.

To Lady Augusta Gregory, [19–20 January 1902]

18 Woburn Buildings | Euston Road.

My dear Lady Gregory: I have just received through A P Watt an account of the sales of 'Samhain'. They printed 2000 & have sold 1628 & sent about 100 out to review so they have only about 300 (rather less) unsold. Royalties amount to £5. 14. 3. which I shall ask A P Watt to send (minus his 10 percent) to the Sec of Gaelic League Dublin. Do you think I should specify the purpose? Say an *Auructas* prize. I merely said in *Samhain* that the proceeds should be given to the Gaelic League. If we asked them to give (say) £5.5 ⟨(They might squander the 14.3 as they liked)⟩ (A P Watts royalty will swallow 10/-) for the best Irish song to an Irish air & did it in the name of 'the Irish Literary Theatre' that song would advertize us for ever. Is not that a subtle device. Will you ask ⟨Hyde &⟩ Martyn ⟨consent & Moore if they approved⟩ if he approves? Is it necessary to ask Hyde? The money is my own & so I need not drag in the Theatre & can give it from the editor of 'Samhain' if I like but the theatre would get an advertisement.[1]

Edward Martyn is being called a pagan at last. I send you the Catholic

---

[2] Martyn had thought WBY's proposed plot for *On Baile's Strand* 'seemed confused' (see p. 127, n. 3). The 'chanting essay' was 'Speaking to the Psaltery' (see p. 121).

[3] See p. 143.

---

[1] The Oireachtas, the Gaelic League's annual cultural festival, was modelled on the Welsh Eisteddfod and the Highland Mod, 'to reflect as far as possible the growth in the artistic side of the language movement'. The sixth Oireachtas, held from 19 to 23 May in the Rotunda, Dublin, offered a variety of Irish prizes for music, drama, literature, and dancing, but none of the prizes was associated with the ILT or *Samhain*, although the money was sent to the Gaelic League.

Register with the only letter in the contraversy that I have seen.[2] I shall get the other copies. I am afraid the bad reception that Edwards plays seem to be getting wont improve the hopes of the Literary Theatre. To night before I go to bed I shall take out my MS of Cuchullain & do a few lines for I have just finished 'Celtic Twilight'. It is nearly twice as big as it was & will have beside my fathers drawing of 'The Last Gleeman' Jacks 'Memory Harbour' in colour & perhaps Russells drawing of 'Knocknarea'. It will be the same size as 'The Secret Rose' & but be plainly got up but for some little emblem in the corner.[3] My other books will be issued in the same form so as to make a uniform edition. I have had a letter from an Edinbough publisher asking me to edit a book of selections from 'Spenser' for £35. It is good pay & I am writing to ask when it will be wanted. I may do it if I have not to do it at once. I have a good deal to say about Spenser but tremble at the thought of reading his six books.[4]

12.30. Masefield—who is off to the country to be sec to a picture gallery—has been in, so I shall not begin Cuchullain to night.

⟨Perhaps after [. . .] could be taken [. . .] for the Irish Literary Society night or Gaelic League⟩ The little bit about Maeve that you sent me has come very well into 'The Celtic Twilight'.[5] Russells 'Deirdre' rather embarrases me. I do not beleive in it at all. If it is offered to us I shall have to vote against it & if I do I shall seem to be doing so perhaps in the interest of my

---

[2] In a review of Martyn's *The Tale of a Town* and *An Enchanted Sea* on 27 Dec 1901, Wilfrid Meynell's Catholic London paper, the *Weekly Register*, asserted (805) that his work displayed a 'morbid and misty spiritualism, with a possible residuum of a kind of knowledge expressly and repeatedly condemned by the Church. The chief work of the Irish Literary Theatre . . . is, in its essence, pagan.' Martyn replied on 10 Jan 1902 (51–2), denying 'as a Catholic' the charge that he accepted legend as dogma and refuting the allegation of paganism. The controversy continued on 17 Jan when the reviewer brought WBY into the discussion, claiming (82–3) that his mysticism attempted 'to establish relations with unseen powers, real or supposed, which are distinctly forbidden to Catholics'.

[3] The enlarged edition of *The Celtic Twilight* did not include any of these drawings. Jack B. Yeats's 'Memory Harbour', a favourite of WBY's among his brother's paintings and hung over his mantelpiece, was eventually used as an illustration to *Reveries Over Childhood and Youth* (1915). Uniform with *The Secret Rose*, *The Celtic Twilight* was bound in dark blue cloth with the lettering and Althea Gyles's design stamped in gold on the front cover and spine. Bullen used this format twice again, but with the design on the spine only, for *Poems, 1899–1905* (1906) and *Poems: Second Series* (1909).

[4] T. C. and E. C. Jack, Edinburgh publishers, asked WBY to prepare and introduce a selection of Spenser's poems, but, although he completed his essay later in 1902, *Poems of Spenser* did not appear until October 1906. The introduction was included as 'Edmund Spenser' in *The Cutting of an Agate* (1912).

[5] In *70 Years* AG recalls (398) writing to WBY of an 'old woman in Galway Workhouse' who told her that 'Queen Maeve was very handsome and she used the hazel rod which her enemies could not stand against. But after that she grew very disagreeable, "It's best not to be talking about her. How do we know it is true? Best leave it between the book and the readers". She had evidently some scandal about Fergus in her mind.' WBY used this material with some modifications at the end of his essay 'And Fair, Fierce Women', published in the *Speaker* on 19 Apr, and in the revised edition of *The Celtic Twilight* published later this year.

own 'Cuchullain'. Maud Gonne saw two acts of it played at the Coffeys & I must say liked them very much.[6] She is anxious by the by to play Kathleen Ny Hoolihan for us. She will certainly be a draw if she does. Fay could easily find all the rest of the company.[7] It will be a great pity if Martyn withdraws. Hydes new play, with Hyde in it & Maud Gonne in my play would really draw a fine house.[8]—& Cuchullain will really be very good to[o].

When do you come over? Soon now I suppose.

Let me know at once what you think about the proposed Gaelic League prize.

Yr alwy
W B Yeats

my Alchemist is very anxious to have a look at that Magic book of Roberts. He says it is really valuable. Could you bring it when you come? He has just made what he hopes is the Elexer of Life. If the rabbits on whom he is trying it survive we are all to drink a noggin full—at least all of us whose longevity he feals he could honestly encourage.[9]

ALS Berg, with envelope addressed to Coole, postmark 'LONDON JA 20 02'. Wade, 364–5.

[6] With her letter of 9 Jan (see p. 146, n. 1) AG had sent on one from AE, evidently about his play, *Deirdre*, adding 'I wish I cd think Deirdre will be good enough to give, but my hopes are much more on Cuchulain'. AE's *Deirdre* was written in reaction to what he considered the 'unheroic' portrayal of bardic characters in *Diarmuid and Grania*. Its first production, by amateur actors, had been mounted on 2 and 3 Jan 1902 in George Coffey's house at 5 Harcourt Terrace, Dublin. James Cousins recalled (*We Two Together* [Madras 1950], 69–70) that it 'took two eminent men to work the curtain between the dining-room-stage and the drawing-room-auditorium, to wit, T. W. Rolleston . . . and E. E. Fournier. . . . Miss Gonne supervised the custuming [*sic*]. George Moore pervaded the outskirts of the proceedings.' Despite WBY's continuing doubts about the play, he did not vote against it, and it was put on with his *Cathleen ni Houlihan* in April.

[7] MG had had tea with WBY on 13 Jan on her way through London to Paris. On 6 Jan she had written from Dublin (*G–YL*, 147) that 'Russell's Deirdre is very good. He & Miss Young acted it at Mrs Coffey's last week—Miss Young is a *very* good actress quite exceptionally good.' She also told him that she thought Fay would be able to manage *Cathleen ni Houlihan*, and that they would 'talk more over all this when we meet'. It was evidently at this meeting that she offered to play Cathleen, since hitherto she had thought of Elizabeth Young for the part.

[8] Hyde's new play, *The Fairy and the Tinker* (*An Tincéir agus an tSidheóg*), was not produced by the ILT, but privately performed in George Moore's garden on 19 May 1902 for delegates to the Oireachtas. The play was published in the *New Ireland Review* in May 1902. In *Samhain* (1902) WBY wrote (6) that it 'is a very good play, but is, I think, the least interesting of his plays as literature'.

[9] WBY's 'alchemist', the Revd William Alexander Ayton (1816–1909), formerly Vicar of Chacombe, had been a member of the GD since 1888 and was the clergyman who married MacGregor and Mina Mathers in 1890. In *Aut* (184) WBY describes meeting with Mathers, 'an old white-haired Oxfordshire clergyman, the most panic-stricken person I have ever known, though Mathers' introduction had been, "He unites us to the great adepts of antiquity"'. Ayton kept his alchemical laboratory in a cellar where the Bishop could not see it and told WBY that he 'once made the elixir of life. . . . but the first effect of the elixir is that your nails fall out and your hair falls off. I was afraid that I might have made a mistake and that nothing else might happen, so I put it away on a shelf. I meant to drink it when I was an old man, but when I got it down the other day it had all dried up.' Robert Gregory's 'magic book' is untraced.

To Lady Augusta Gregory, [*22 January 1902*]

18 Woburn Buildings
Wednesday

Dear Lady Gregory: It is a great pleasure to think that you are coming over.[1] I am not free Sunday I am sorry to say. I am to go down to the Gibsons from Saturday to Monday morning with my sister; & if I should change my plans it might upset hers.[2] Can I lunch with you on Monday? Monday night I have to be at my rooms as usual for Mʳˢ Emery is to chant in the new Dolmetsch way to Newbolt & others. Will not you come too? But in any case let me come to lunch.

I have just re-read your letter & it occurs to me that if you like I can come up from the Gibsons Sunday after noon so as to get to you for dinner. Monday lunch will be best but if you are full up Monday & prefer Sunday let me know.

I have been running about all day. A P Watt—Bullen—typewriter—museum—Irish Lit committee[3] & so on. Bullen gave me a book on Carden that he published. I have been dipping into it. Carden describes himself as having 'a cold heart & a hot head'. Does not that describe a certain type of man very wonderfully. A certain kind of intemperate intellect.[4]

I must write about the Spenser at last & so must end for the time.

Yrs ev
W B Yeats

ALS Berg, with envelope addressed to Coole, postmark 'LONDON JA 23 02'.

[1] Although AG had given up her rooms in Queen Anne's Mansions—as she thought permanently—in March 1901 (see p. 60, n. 7), she had now decided to take another apartment in the same building, recording in her diary for 26 Jan 1902 (Berg): 'London, Q mansion, a new flat, same as the old, but 7th floor—Yeats to dine & I dined with him next day to hear Mrs Emery chant on the new instrument, with moderate success—'. She had left Coole for London on 25 Jan.

[2] WBY was a guest at Moorehouse, Holmwood, the Surrey home of the Hon. William Gibson (1868–1942), Secretary of the ILS, London, and High Sheriff of Dublin in 1901. Gibson, whose father, Lord Ashbourne, had been Lord Chancellor of Ireland since 1895, was an enthusiastic member of the Gaelic League and was described by W. P. Ryan in *The Pope's Green Island* (1912) as 'easily the most picturesque, the most social, and yet in some respects the most elusive individuality. In his Gaelic garb he goes everywhere. He is the Happy Traveller and philosophic enthusiast of Gaeldom' (213). The Gibsons had visited Coole the previous summer.

[3] WBY had evidently been persuaded to rejoin the Committee of the ILS; see pp. 49–51.

[4] Bullen had published W. G. Waters's *Jerome Cardan: A Biographical Study* in 1898 (*YA4*, 289). In a lengthy self-description (44) Cardan confesses that he is 'timid, with a cold heart and a hot brain, given to reflection and the consideration of things many and mighty, and even of things which can never come to pass'. Girolamo Cardano (1501–76), a Milanese physician and mathematician, was the author of numerous treatises and commentaries, and a volume of memoirs, *De Vita Propria* (1654). An ardent student of the occult, his writings were laced with discourses on demons, apparitions, spirits, and evocations. Although his work passed the ecclesiastical censor in 1562, he was eventually imprisoned in 1570–1 for publishing a horoscope of Christ.

To George Russell (AE), [*26 January 1902*]

⟨COOLE PARK, | GORT, | CO. GALWAY.⟩
18 Woburn Buildings | Euston Road.
Sunday

My dear Russell: I could not write to you about my play until I had seen Lady Gregory as she had been anxious that it should be first done by the Irish Lit Theatre. After talking things over with her, I agree to Fay doing it with Dierdre & will send you a copy in a couple of days.[1]

Yr ev
W B Yeats

ALS Indiana.

Charles Elkin Mathews to A. P. Watt, *27 January 1902*

Vigo Street | London W
Jany 27th 1902

Private
Messrs. A. P. Watt & Son.

Dear Sirs,

"Wind Among the Reeds"

This book—together with "The Shadowy Waters" was promised to me in 1894 (shortly after M[r] John Lane left me) and I included both in my Autumn Catalogue of that year as "In preparation", and they continued to be announced in this way until 1899 in the Spring of which year I published "The Wind Among the Reeds" having agreed to give up "The Shadowy Waters".

At this later date (1899) an Agreement was drawn up and approved by M[r] Yeats and it was posted him for his signature, however, he wrote to say that he had lost or mislaid it.

---

[1] Martyn's prevarication over the funding of the ILT (see p. 149) was putting the future of the Irish dramatic movement in doubt, and WBY and AG had evidently decided that nothing would be lost by acceding to AE's request that they allow the Fays to produce *Cathleen ni Houlihan* with his *Deirdre*. As it fell out, much was gained. The huge success of the productions, from 2 to 5 April, led to the INTS and a new departure for the movement as a whole. AE replied on 28 Jan (MBY), 'I am very glad you are giving the Fays your play. The Fay people are developing an enthusiasm which will carry them far.' On 17 Feb Frank Fay wrote (*LWBY* I. 93) to tell WBY that the play had 'reached us safely through Mr Russell, and it is now in rehearsal'.

I only retained notes in my possession, briefly as follows:—
  £12 in advance
  Royalty 12½ per centum
  American rights, half profits
  The Agreement to hold for 5 years from date of publication
These were the terms agreed upon in the original instance (1894) and further endorsed by the Author when I published "The Wind Among the Reeds" in 1899.

There are more than two years of the term to run at the end of it I might be willing to increase the royalty.

Also, I should be glad to have the offer of any new book by M^r W B Yeats.

I am, Yours very Truly
Elkin Mathews

[*In WBY's hand at top of first page*]
Send Lane a copy
          Yeats[1]

ANS Private.

To Maud Gonne, [c. 28 January 1902]

Mention in letter from MG, Sunday [2 February 1902].
Telling her that he has given *Cathleen ni Houlihan* to the Fays; evidently asking which date would suit her for the performances; and disclosing that Edward Martyn had given up the ILT.

G–YL, 147–8.

---

[1] Watt stamped this letter as received on 28 Jan 1902, and presumably sent it on immediately to WBY, whose note was probably appended c. 29 Jan. WBY had probably asked Watt to sort out the tangled contractual arrangements over the book during his visit to him on 22 Jan (see above, p. 150). The matter was complicated not merely by WBY's carelessness in mislaying the contract, but also because the American edition was in the hands of John Lane, and because both the American and English editions were printed by him in New York. Since the contract with Lane did not stipulate that it was for five years only, WBY was to have great difficulty in retrieving the American rights.

To Lady Augusta Gregory, [*29 January 1902*]

18 Woburn Buildings | Euston Road | London
Wednesday

Dear Lady Gregory: I find I cannot get to you either tomorrow or Thursday as I shall be occupied with my mystics both evenings. Can I come to you Friday? Or failing that Sunday? I shall bring back the Folk lore book.[1]

Yrs alway
W B Yeats

ALS Berg, with envelope addressed to Queen Anne Mansion, postmark 'LONDON N.W. JA 29 02'.

To Henry Newbolt, [*2 February 1902*]

18 Woburn Buildings | Euston Road.
Sunday

Dear Mr Newbolt: Is there any chance of your being able to use my essay on 'Speaking to Musical Notes' in your March number if I write it an [*for* at] once? I want to arrange it for a lecture as soon as I can.[1]

Yrs ev
W B Yeats

ALS Emory. With note at top of page in Newbolt's hand: 'doing best to pub. quickly—4–2–2'.

To A. P. Watt, 8 February [*? 1902*]

18 Woburn Buildings | Euston Road.
Feb 8.

Dear Mr Watt: you have certainly done much for me, in the short time I have been with you, especially in America. American publishers ⟨are to me at any rate most unintelligible and mysterious⟩ & copyright laws are not in

---

[1] Presumably the notebook in which AG recorded the folklore she heard in the Gort workhouse and surrounding country. She had probably loaned it to WBY to provide him with new material for the revised *Celtic Twilight*; besides 'the little bit about Maeve' (see p. 148, n. 5), she also gave him the substance of his story 'Dreams that have no Moral' (*Myth*, 125–37).

[1] See p. 147. Newbolt, who had attended WBY's Monday Evening on 27 Jan (see p. 150), published WBY's 'Speaking to the Psaltery' in the *Monthly Review* of May 1902, and it was reprinted in *IGE*. The lecture was held on 10 June 1902 in Clifford's Inn.

my world.[1] Apart from all else it is a pleasure to know that my agreements have ⟨at last⟩ now some chance of not being lost.[2]

Yours sincerely
W B Yeats

ALS Private.

To Maud Gonne, [c. 15 February 1902]

Mention in letter from MG, Sunday [? 16 February 1902].
Telling her that he has been ill, but that AG is in London and taking care of him.

G–YL, 148–9.

To Violet Hunt, [? 18 February 1902]

18 Woburn Buildings | Euston Road.
Tuesday

Dear Miss Hunt: I have been laid up with some kind of influenza attack, which has dislocated all my correspondence & my arrangements. I should so much have liked to have gone to you on the 15th. I hope you will excuse me under the circumstance. Till the last few days I have been laid up with good friends giving me bread & milk.

Will you come to me some Monday? Miss Farr is to speak to musical notes for me next Monday. If you can come come any time after eight. I hope in any case you will let me go to see you.

Yrs ever
W B Yeats

ALS Berg.

---

[1] From time to time A. P. Watt published private volumes of testimonials from his celebrated and satisfied clients. The first had appeared in 1893, followed by others in 1894 and 1898. He had probably elicited this letter for a projected new edition, which does not seem to have appeared. WBY contributed later letters to such collections in 1905, 1924 and 1929.
[2] Unlike that of *The Wind Among the Reeds* (see p. 151).

To Violet Hunt, [*20 February 1902*]

18 Woburn Buildings | Euston Road.
Thursday.

Dear Miss Hunt: The 'chanting' is at my rooms on Monday. I hope presently to give a lecture in Cliffords Inn or some such place. As yet we are rather experimental—trying one thing & another.

Of course if you can bring Lady Margaret Sackville I shall be delighted.[1]

I have been reading 'Madamoisel De Maupin'. Why is it that the more a writer describes his heroes fealings the less do we see him as a distinct character? Tell a little & he is Hamlet tell all & he is nothing. Nothing has life except the incomplete.[2]

Yr ev
W B Yeats

ALS Private.

[1] Lady Margaret Sackville (1881–1963), daughter of the 7th Earl De La Warr, was a poet and dramatist whose first volume, *Poems*, had been published in 1901. Encouraged by Wilfrid Blunt and WBY, in 1903 she edited the *Celt*, a short-lived magazine 'Devoted to Irish Interests'. In 1909, influenced by WBY's theories of verse speaking, she founded the Poetry Recital Society. Her portrait appeared in the *Tatler* on 4 Sept 1901. In *Experiences of a Literary Man* (1926) Stephen Gwynn reveals (149–50) that Violet Hunt asked him to escort them to this meeting with WBY and that Lady Margaret's family insisted on sending her, 'then a very slender delicate and picturesque young woman', in their brougham: 'The elderly coachman looked a good deal puzzled when I told him to drive to Woburn Buildings. . . . After some difficulty we found the entrance, got out, knocked at the cobbler's shop and were admitted into the big dark room. Several people were there, and among them I think, Florence Farr. . . . as usual, Yeats talked extremely well of the things that interested him: but about eleven, there came a knock at the door and the cobbler's wife with a frightened face entered saying there was a man below wanting to know what had happened to Lady Margaret Sackville. I was asked to go down . . . and I found in the alley the cockaded footman standing sentry at the door, but like a martyr at the stake: for about him swarmed all the brats and urchins from the surrounding tenements who had never seen the like of him before and were determined to make the most of their opportunity. I reported to this effect: but that fragile young lady had a stony heart and left him there in purgatory for another hour while she and the major poet discussed matters pertaining to their art.'

[2] Théophile Gautier's novel, *Mademoiselle de Maupin* (1835), was written partly to advance his theories of *l'art pour l'art* and partly to 'épater les bourgeois' through the behaviour of Mademoiselle de Maupin, disguised as the hero, Théodore. An English translation of the novel was published by Vizetelley & Co. in 1887.

To Stephen Gwynn, [? 21 February 1902]

18 Woburn Buildings | Euston Road.
Friday,

My dear Gwynn:
Yes come by all means. I shall be delighted to see you all.[1]

Yr ev
W B Yeats

ALS Berg.

To John Butler Yeats, [c. 21 February 1902]

Mention in letter from JBY, 22 February 1902.
A 'most interesting letter' discussing Joseph Nunan.

MBY.

[1] See previous letter. Having been asked to escort two important ladies, Gwynn was apparently making sure that WBY would have room for him.

[1] On 9 Feb (MBY) JBY wrote that he had met Nunan, 'a T.C.D. man member of the Historical Society where he heard with marked appreciation your speech [*i.e. on 30 May 1899*]. . . . He is an exceedingly good Irishman & I urged him to call upon you some Monday Evening'. Nunan evidently did call, probably on Monday, 17 Feb, and WBY wrote to tell JBY of their meeting in this lost letter, for JBY replied on 22 Feb: 'Nunan expects very shortly to be made governor of British sphere in Central Africa—he has his career marked out, he looks a steadfast fellow, & will always remain a good Irishman'. Joseph Nunan (1873–1934) had a distinguished academic career at both University College and Trinity College, Dublin, where he read Law. Called to the Irish Bar in 1898, he subsequently served as Chief Judicial Officer and Vice-Consul in British Central Africa from 1900 to 1902, and was appointed Presiding Judge of the High Court from 1902 to 1906. In 1906 he became Acting Attorney General in British Guiana, and held a number of senior judicial and administrative posts there until 1925, when he retired to practice at the English Bar. He was knighted in 1924.

To William Rothenstein,[1] 25 February [1902]

18 Woburn Buildings | Euston Road.
Feb 25

My dear Rothenstein: I owe you a great many apologies. I have been very stupid. I have just this moment met some body at the British Museum, who has just reminded me that I am engaged next Thursday to a number of my fellow mystics, whom I am to lecture to.[2] I had absolutely forgotten it, & as they are scattered about & out of reach (I have not even their addresses) I cannot put them off. Could you arrange for me to meet Stirling some day next week—I have no engagement for any day but Monday I am certain.[3] Please tell Mrs Rothenstein[4] how sorry I am.

Yr ever
W B Yeats

ALS Harvard.

To the Editor of the Saturday Review, 5 March 1902

London, N.W., 5 March, 1902.

SIR,—J.F.R. in last week's SATURDAY REVIEW condemned the Purcell Society and practically told his readers that the performances, which are to be

---

[1] William Rothenstein (1872–1945), artist and friend of WBY, was born in Yorkshire of German immigrant parents and educated at the Slade School and Julian's Académie in Paris. He became a friend of WBY while drawing him in 1898, finding, as he explains in *Men and Memories* (1931), I. 282, that although 'he had an artificial manner, and when he was surrounded by female admirers his sublimity came near to the ridiculous . . . he was a true poet, and behind the solemn mask of the mystic there was a rare imagination and, what was less often suspected, shrewd wisdom. Yeats, like Shaw, was a man of great courage, who championed losing causes and men who were unfairly assailed.' In 1912 he enlisted WBY's help in translating and publishing the work of Rabindranath Tagore, and in 1937 arranged for WBY to be elected to the Athenaeum Club.
[2] Probably at 'The Three Kings' (see p. 21, n. 9).
[3] WBY evidently succeeded in meeting William Stirling (1861–1902), who was to commit suicide on 24 Apr of this year by cutting his throat. A Scots book-collector, and lecturer on architecture at University College, London, he had presented his theories on the symbolic groundplans of early churches in *The Canon* (1897), 'An Exposition of the Pagan Mystery Perpetuated in the Cabala as the Rule of All the Arts', and Elkin Mathews was to advertise this, with excerpts from reviews, in his 1904 edition of WBY's *The Tables of the Law*.
[4] Rothenstein had married Alice Mary Knewstub (1870–1958) in June 1899 and they were living at 1 Pembroke Cottages, Edwardes Square, Kensington. The daughter of Walter John Knewstub, the only pupil of D. G. Rossetti, Mrs Rothenstein had acted under the name of Alice Kingsley.

given in Great Queen Street next week, will not be worth going to.[1] I
know nothing of music. I do not even know one note from another. I am
afraid I even dislike music and yet I venture to contradict him. Last year I
saw "Dido and Æneas" and "The Masque of Love", which is to be given
again this year, and they gave me more perfect pleasure than I have met
with in any theatre this ten years. I saw the only admirable stage scenery of
our time, for Mr. Gordon Craig has discovered how to decorate a play
with severe, beautiful, simple, effects of colour, that leave the imagination
free to follow all the suggestions of the play. Realistic scenery takes the
imagination captive and is at best but bad landscape painting, but Mr.
Gordon Craig's scenery is a new and distinct art. It is something that can
only exist in the theatre. It cannot even be separated from the figures that
move before it. The staging of "Dido and Æneas" and of "The Masque of
Love" will some day, I am persuaded, be remembered among the important events of our time.[2]

Yours truly
W B Yeats

Printed letter, *Saturday Review*, 8 March 1902 (299). Wade, 365–6.

To an unidentified correspondent,[1] [? *5 March 1902*]

18 Woburn Buildings | Euston Road.
Wednesday.

Dear Sir: I owe you many apologies about that photograph. The evening
before I got your last note I suddenly remembered I had not answered the
other & looked for my photographs. I found I had not got one, but they are
realy horrid things—I photograph very badly. Could you not use the por-

---

[1] J. F. Runciman's review, 'Musical Dilettantes', in the issue of 22 Feb, contended (233) that
Purcell's music had been distorted in being re-scored for the piano rather than the harpsichord,
and that consequently 'the Purcell Operatic Society should not be supported: that is all that can
be said about it'. He did not discuss the scenery.

[2] WBY had been greatly impressed in March 1901 by Craig's scenery for Purcell's *Dido and
Aeneas* and *The Masque of Love* (see pp. 52–3). The latter was revived with Handel's *Acis and
Galatea* for eight matinée performances at the Great Queen Street Theatre from 10 to 17 March.
Some 'vague idea of the weird effect of Mr. Craig's stage management' could be gained, accord-
ing to the *Tatler*, from his photographic studies of *Acis and Galatea* which appeared in that mag-
azine on 12 Mar 1902 (469): 'The purple monochrome backcloth which he invented for *Dido and
Aeneas* at the Coronet last year was a revelation in its effectiveness, while the crowd in *The
Masque of Love* was extraordinarily vivid.'

[1] This letter may have been written to the editor of *Great Thoughts* which published an appreciative article on WBY in its April 1902 number, illustrated with an early photograph of him.

trait in the frontispi[e]ce of my poems. I can send you a copy of that if you like. Last summer I ⟨practically⟩ decided to give people no more photographs & arranged with Unwin that I could get copies of that instead.[2]

I have a pencil sxetch which has never been produced. You can produce it if you like,[3] but it is not so good a like ness as the one in the poems. If you let me know I will send it you at once. You will of course return it to me in safety.

Yrs sny
W B Yeats

ALS Private.

To Gordon Craig, [*13 March 1902*]

Dear Craig: I have been trying to find time to write to you. I was delighted with 'The Masque of Love' in all its details, as delighted as ever, and with certain scenes of the 'Acis and Galatea'. Surely that second Polyphemus scene, the scene where he kills Acis, belongs to an art which has lain hid under the roots of the Pyramids for ten thousand years, so solemn it is. . . .[1]

Text from Craig, 242, where it is misdated '13 March 1903'.

To Gordon Craig, [*17 March 1902*]

18 Woburn Buildings | Euston Road.
Monday.

My dear Craig: I am very sorry endeed to hear of your ill luck. I wish I knew some rich person who could come to your help, but I do not.[1] However you will have made your name any way. Symons is here & has been

---

[2] See p. 101.
[3] The pencil sketch by JBY; see p. 101.

[1] In the final scene of Handel's opera, Polyphemus, spurned by Galatea, takes his revenge by crushing her protector and lover, Acis, with a boulder. To assuage her grief, Galatea turns Acis into a river-god, while the Chorus comfort her and celebrate his immortality in words by John Gay: 'Hail thy gentle murmuring stream / Shepherd's pleasure, muses' theme; / Through the plain still joy to rove / Murmuring still thy gentle love.'

[1] Craig's productions were withdrawn after 17 Mar 1902 because he could not meet expenses and had accumulated debts of £200. WBY schemed unsuccessfully to drum up alternative funding, and urged Edward Martyn to employ him (*Aut*, 446), but Craig finally abandoned hopes of further performances in the spring of 1903 when his circular, offering to stage the plays in private drawing-rooms, met with no response.

reading me a longish article on your scenery, which he purposes to send to 'The Monthly Review'.[2] He wants to see you though. Could you come rather earlier to the theatre to night than I suppose you usually do? Could you be there at 5.30? He & I will call at the theatre (we will go on from 'Every man' at St Georges Hall) but if you are busy do not mind about it or trouble to answer.[3]

Symons wants to talk over your methods & to get you to explain things personally

Yrs ev
W B Yeats

ALS Arsenal.

To H. W. Nevinson, [c. *18 March*[1] *1902*]

18 Woburn Buildings | Euston Road.

Dear M[r] Nevinson: I will come with pleasure. I would have written before, but I heard from Craig about his misfortunes & waited to see if he was going on. M[rs] Emery tells me however that she has seen you & your invitation is not dependent on Craig going on.[2] Please forgive my not having written.

[2] Symons had attended the first night of the productions, having written to WBY on 'Tuesday' [4 Mar 1902; MBY] that 'Gordon Craig is doing Purcell's "Masque of Love" on *Monday* at the Great Queen Street Theatre. Are you going? If alone, could you ask Craig (whom I do not know) for a seat for me, beside you, in order that I might do an article in the *Academy*?' Excited by what he saw, Symons wrote reviews for both the *Academy* and the *Star*, and now wanted to discuss Craig's experiments at greater length. His essay, 'A New Art of the Stage', appeared in the *Monthly Review* for June 1902 (157–62) and was reprinted in *Studies in Seven Arts* (1906). Symons saw in Craig's experiments 'the suggestion of a new art of the stage, an art no longer realistic but conventional, no longer imitative but symbolical', and suggested that WBY's *The Countess Cathleen* needed 'as a background, the vast purple cloths which Mr. Craig used last year in his setting of Purcell's *Dido and Aeneas*, and, for costumes, the shadowy purple draperies which melted into that background; it wants this dim lighting from the roof, this atmosphere in which dreams can move freely, as if at home there. Here then, in Mr. Craig, is the stage-manager for Mr. Yeats; and here, in Mr. Yeats, a playwright waiting to be staged by Mr. Craig.'
[3] The Elizabethan Stage Society's production of *Everyman* ran at St George's Hall, Langham Place, from 17 to 26 Mar 1902. WBY attended the opening matinée and then went on to the Great Queen Street Theatre to introduce Symons to Craig.
[1] On the evening of 19 Mar Nevinson recorded in his diary (Bodleian) that he had received a 'Charming little note from Yeats', and quoted the penultimate sentence of this letter.
[2] Nevinson, a guarantor of the Purcell Society, had been unable to stay for *The Masque of Love* on the opening night, 10 Mar, and had invited WBY and FF to accompany him to the performance on Saturday, 22 Mar, and to dinner afterwards. In fact, the production had closed by then, but the three met for dinner at the Comedy Restaurant, Panton Street, Haymarket, where, as Nevinson recalled in his journal, the conversation turned upon 'Schemes for a Purcell concert & Yeats' marriage [*presumably the 'mystical marriage' contracted with MG in 1898*] which seems to me

I am reading your book with great delight—but of that presently. Many thanks for it.[3]

Yrs ev
W B Yeats

ALS Private.

To Lady Augusta Gregory, [22 March 1902]

18 Woburn Buildings | Euston Road.
Saturday

Dear Lady Gregory: you will have heard from Hallam Murray about the printers mistake.[1] He sent me a proof & you the MSS. I corrected what I could but could not correct the spelling of some of the names or any of the phonetic spellings. I hope therefore that you have sent your own corrected proof. It will not delay book it seems as the matter comes at the end.

I am going to surprize you by an idea that has been in my head lately. I never until yesterday spoke of it to anybody. I have an idea of going on the stage in small parts next autumn for a few months that I may master the stage for purposes of poetical drama. I find I could get on quite easily, & that with the exception of rehersal times it would only take my evenings. Does the idea seem to you very wild? I should make about £2 a week, & learn my business, or at any rate never have to blame myself for not having tried to learn it. I would not of course go on in my own name & I would tell people exactly why I did the thing at all. I beleive that I construct all right—with wild confusions which I get out of—but I have a very little sense of acting. I dont see my people as actors though I see them very clearly as men. Moore sees them always as actors.[2]

atrocious. . . . Yeats singularly humane & clear-visioned, talked with wonderful insight on ordinary things—politics, Ireland, drama, & even gossip. Told some stories of a fine old sailor grandfather in Sligo . . .' A longer account of this evening appears in *Changes and Chances* (301–2).

[3] Nevinson's collection of stories, *The Plea of Pan*, was published by John Murray in April 1901. Nevinson sent a copy to WBY in 1902 after bumping into him near Woburn Buildings on the night of 20 Dec 1901: 'Did not know me but remembered my name later & knew I had been in S[outh] A[frica] & had heard of Pan' (Bodleian).

[1] Hallam Murray (1854–1938) was the younger brother of AG's publisher, John Murray (1851–1928), and worked in the family firm. The printer's mistake evidently involved the spellings of the list of place names which appear at the back of *Cuchulain of Muirthemne*.

[2] AG was lukewarm about this idea. Her immediate response, in a letter of 25 Mar (Berg), was that 'it would be an amusing experiment, but wd soon bore you I think. Anyhow you have to turn yr mind to narrative poems in the summer,' and in a further letter of 27 Mar she implored him not to make the plan public as it would be thought that 'you were trying to emulate S. Phillips. I don't believe your stage idea will last . . .' She was right, for nothing came of the plan.

Moore writes to me, by the by, that 'the acting of Russells play is the silliest he ever saw'—Miss Quinn I suppose, is the sinner.[3] He wants *Kathleen Ny Holihan* not to sit down by fire & croon but to walk up & down in front of the stage, so as to dominate the stage. He thinks she should be excited as the French are going to land. I have replied that she looks far ahead & far back-ward & cannot be excited in that sense, or rather she will be a less poetical personage if she is. However I have told Miss Gonne, to whom I have sent Moores letter to do as she likes.[4] One must judge of these things on the stage. I shall go over & see for myself on Wednesday or Thursday. I shall stay at 8 Cavendish Row.[5]

Yrs ever
W B Yeats

ALS Berg, with envelope addressed to Hotel de Russie, Florence, Italy, postmark 'LONDON W.C. MR 22 02'. Partly in Wade, 367.

To Maud Gonne, [c. 22 March 1902]

Mention in letter from MG, Monday [? 24 March 1902].
Enquiring anxiously about the rehearsals of *Cathleen ni Houlihan* and AE's *Deirdre*, and complaining about Maire Quinn's acting.[1]

G–YL, 152.

[3] Maire T. Quinn (d. 1947), an original member of the Fay company and Secretary of Inghinidhe na hEireann (The Daughters of Ireland), played the role of Deirdre in AE's play. She left the company in 1903 following a dispute over Synge's *In the Shadow of the Glen*.

[4] MG, in a letter which probably crossed with WBY's (*G–YL*, 151), complained that Moore wanted Cathleen 'to be wandering round the cottage all the time & make the most of her remarks from the front of the stage instead of from the corner of the fire—I dont agree with Moore at all about this, for I think one must keep up the idea of the poor old weary woman who would certainly sit down & rock herself over the fire & not get up & walk about until the idea of meeting her friends comes to her.' On receiving this and Moore's letter she replied (*G–YL*, 152) 'we have kept your stage direction exactly . . . George Moore doesn't the least understand the piece & would spoil it if we listened to him.'

[5] 8 Cavendish Row, at Rutland Place, off Parnell Square, was the address of the Cavendish Hotel, under the proprietorship of Ellen Hehir. MG had been staying there since early March.

[1] This letter was provoked by George Moore's complaint about the acting of *Cathleen ni Houlihan* (see above, n. 4). MG replied reassuringly that the play was 'going *splendidly*, last night we had a dress rehearsal. Russell & several others were present, they all thought it very good, & begged us not to alter anything.' She added that the first act of AE's *Deirdre* dragged a little 'because Miss Quinn's acting is not, as you say, inspiring but she is much *improved*'. Both WBY and MG had doubts about Maire Quinn's histrionic ability, and on 6 Jan 1902 MG had told him (p. 149, n. 7) 'Fays' company is working hard but Miss Quinn is very bad'.

To Edward Elgar, 23 March [*1902*]

18 Woburn Buildings, Euston Road.
Monday, March 23

Dear Sir:
Yes certainly. With great pleasure. I must give myself the pleasure of letting you [know how] wonderful, in its heroic melancholy, I thought your Grania music. I wish you could set other words of mine and better work than those verses, written in twenty minutes but you are welcome to them.[1]

Yrs sincerely
W B Yeats

Excuse this scrawl I am very busy as I am off to Dublin to look after the rehearsal of a play of mine.

Text from Young, 97, where it is misdated '1903'.

To Lady Augusta Gregory, [*24 March 1902*]

Dear Lady Gregory: I have just noticed with some alarm the bit of boudlerizing (how do you spell that word) on page 20.[1] I know you told me

[1] At the request of George Moore, Edward Elgar (1857–1934) had composed the music for the production of *Diarmuid and Grania*, including a horn motif, some incidental music, a Funeral March, and a setting of 'Spinning Song' (*VP*, 770), written by WBY the previous summer (Care, 316). This last Elgar was now seeking permission to publish, and it appeared later in the year. It had recently received its first concert performance, in London, at a Queen's Hall Symphony Concert on 18 Jan 1902, where, according to the *Stage* of 23 Jan (18) it 'was well received by the large audience assembled'. The text of the song had appeared in *A Broad Sheet* in January 1902, but was omitted when the play was first published in 1951. Elgar's music stayed with WBY and by 1935 all that he could recall of the play (*Aut*, 443) were 'Benson's athletic dignity in one scene and the notes of the horn in Elgar's dirge over the dead Diarmuid'.

The commission of an English composer had offended certain Irish critics, and Moore felt obliged to explain (the *Leader*, 28 Sept 1901, p. 79) that he had tried both Stanford (whom he found 'anti-Irish') and Augusta Holmes (who was too busy) before turning to Elgar.

[1] A well-known incident in the *Táin Bó Cúailnge* tells how as a boy Cuchulain fell into such a violent rage that the warriors of Emain Macha were in danger from him. To avert their destruction, 'three fifties' of the townswomen were sent out naked to meet him; he hid his face in modest shame at this sight, was captured, and soused in vats of cold water to cool his fury. In bowdlerizing this story, AG described (20) the women coming to meet him with 'their breasts uncovered'. In a tetchy reply of 27 Mar (Berg), AG acknowledged WBY's 'agitated letter' 'but I declare I can't make head or tail of it. In one part you mention page 150, in another, page 20. I have not the proofs, having given them to be bound. If it is page 20 you allude to. . . . It was to shock Cuchulain's modesty it was done, as we know by his hiding his face, & the partial undressing was enough for that. Priests might legitimately say the other called up an indecent picture. I

about it but I did not take it in. I beg of you to insert in your notes something like the sentence I send you. The original incident is so well known & has so many folk lore ramifications that people will notice its absence & suspect your text everwhere else. They will not understand your reasons & will resent your having done, what both you & I say you have not done— add something of your own. I am sure I am right. If you send your note at once it cannot be too late. I go to Ireland (8 Cavendish Row) tomorrow night for a week or so.

Yours in great hurry & some alarm
W B Yeats

If too late I would even be inclined to insert a slip of paper like an errata slip in the part for notes.

[*Enclosure*]

To follow the words 'A Swift messenger' at end of first paragraph of notes.

⟨In one⟩
⟨I have also modified⟩
In one case I have endeed ⟨intended to modify⟩ altered an incident. Cuchullains reception ⟨at Emain⟩ by the Three times Fifty Queens on page 150 is not quite as it is in the MS. My justification is that ⟨I wish my book to be re I hope that these stories⟩ I did not wish for the sake of one sentence, ⟨to create an arbitary to make it difficult to get the book into the hands set up a possible⟩ to perhaps prevent the book from getting into the hands of the country people in Ireland, & I have written always with ⟨them in⟩ the country people in my mind.

ALS, with enclosure, Berg, with envelope addressed to Hotel de Russie, Florence, Italy, postmark 'LONDON W. C. MAR 24 02'.

say in my dedication, "I have left out many things that for one reason or another you would not like"—I think that is sufficient explanation, & I give the sources of every story, & I doubt that anyone who takes the trouble of looking will regret any of my slight Bowdlerizing.' Although she did not alter the proofs for the first edition, or insert the explanatory note that WBY urges, in the second edition (1902) she changed the description so that the women meet Cuchulain generally 'uncovered', and by the third edition (1907) they are described as 'red-naked'.

To Lady Augusta Gregory, [*25 March 1902*]

18 Woburn Buildings | Euston Road | London
Tuesday

Dear Lady Gregory: I got your note to day & went at once to Queen Anne Mansions. No proofs—they had seemingly been sent on & no letter from O Grady.[1] Two letters were there I thought might be his but they were only emmense essays from your old Clergyman.[2] I have no doubt that you will have despatched proofs by this time. Should they reach me unless you wire the single word 'no' which will cost you 2/- (address & all) I shall add a sentence about the peice of "bowdlerizing" which still disturbs me as much as ever.[3] I think it really serious, especially as you will have quoted against you with some justice the old saying that a nude statue if you put a stocking on it would become 'improper' at once. I have heard a woman art student say that a quite nude model always seems perfectly natural & right but a partly dressed model always seems 'improper'. I merely quote these to show you that there is a perfectly understood doctrine on the subject which will set the reviewer mocking, & make him suspicious if he does not know your valid defence. This would be quite enough "I have endeed ⟨altered⟩ regretfully modified one incident, at the end of the Boy Deeds, as

---

[1] In a letter of 22 Mar 1902 (Berg) AG complained that Murrays were still sending proofs of *Cuchulain of Muirthemne* to her London address, although she was in Italy: 'I am afraid you must go there & ask the porter for any letters not forwarded, & try and find them. You might also try if there is a letter from S. Hayes O'Grady sending back list of place-names. An upright hand, something like the other Standish.' In fact, the proofs had already been sent on from Queen Anne's Mansions, as she told WBY in a letter of 25 Mar which crossed with this one. Standish Hayes O'Grady (1832–1915), civil engineer and antiquarian, was the cousin of Standish James O'Grady (see p. 23, n. 5). He was introduced to Old Irish studies by Eugene O'Curry and John O'Donovan, and after a period as an engineer in the USA, moved to London and spent the rest of his life working on the *Catalogue of Irish MSS. in the British Museum.* His best known work is *Silva Gadelica* (2 vols, 1892), a collection of Irish tales, with an English translation, loosely arranged under the headings of hagiography, legend, Ossianic lore and fiction. AG later recalled (*70 Years,* 318) that O'Grady 'had refused . . . to join the Irish Literary Society or the Gaelic League, declaring them both Fenian organizations. But yet he was so little English that he boasted to me near his life's end, that though he had lived forty years in England, he had never made an English friend.'

[2] Probably the Revd William Dodge (1845–1930), Vicar from 1884 to 1909 of St Stephens, Southwark, the parish for which AG had been making subscription appeals since 1888 in a series of pamphlets entitled *Over the River.*

[3] In her reply to this letter of 28 Mar (Berg), AG told him that she was going to wire 'No': 'It wd be absurd to put such a note as you propose saying I had modified "one incident". I have modified others. . . . I look on this change . . . as a translation of an idea of that time into an idea of today. . . . I feel sure it wd be a mistake & an insincerity to apologise now. . . . I don't "regret"—I was particularly careful about the Boy Deeds, thinking it might be made a school reading book—& I didn't put stockings on the women, I only stopped them from taking their stockings off.'

I am anxious that an objection to a single sentence might not prevent this book coming into the hands of those for whom I intended it".

⟨On consideration I shall⟩

Yours alway

W B Yeats

I go to Ireland to morrow night. Dolmetsch was here last night & was enthusiastic over 'the chanting'. He kept saying "beautiful, beautiful".

ALS Berg, with envelope addressed to Hotel de Russia, Florence, Italy, postmark 'LONDON MR 25 02'.

To Lady Augusta Gregory, 3 April [1902]

8 Cavendish Row | Dublin.

⟨NATIONAL LIBRARY OF IRELAND, | KILDARE STREET, | DUBLIN.⟩

April 3.

My dear Lady Gregory: I have sent back proofs but Murray has been guilty of another folly. He sent me your proofs & asked me to copy on them my corrections; but did not send me my own proofs, which I gave him long ago. I have therefore simply returned proofs as they came from you & told him to find mine & see that my corrections of my preface & note are made. I thought it better to do this than to make a few now, which would not be complete, & would enable him to get confused between the old & new proof sheets. He has really been as absurd as if he had been a Dublin publisher, & I am feeling rather cross. I have made no note (such as you suggest)[1] about that incident in the boy deeds (though Tom Lyster thought it would be better to make the note) & chiefly because it might land Murray in some new folly. If any reputable paper objects to the bowdlerizing I can write & explain, & I shall hope to get you to change the incident in a new edition. I have been reading out the book to Miss Gonne & it seems to me more wonderful every page I read.

The plays came off last night & both wery [*for* were] really very great successes. They took to Dierdre from the first. The hall was crowded & great numbers could not get in. I hated Dierdre. In fact I did not remain in the Theatre because I was so nervous about it. I still hate it, but I suppose

---

[1] In her letter of 28 Mar (see p. 165, n. 3), AG had told WBY that if 'there is time, & yr mind wd be easier, I don't object to yr putting a note at the end of yr Emer note, saying I have modified this & *some other* incidents, and either blaming me or justifying me, as pleases you best'.

Moore is the only person who shares my opinion. When I saw it in rehersal I thought it superficial & sentimental, as I thought it when it came out in the All Ireland Review. Kathleen Ny Hoolihan was also most enthusiasly received. Its one defect was that the mild humour of the part before Kathleen came in kept the house in such delighted laughter, that it took them some little while to realize the tragic meaning of Kathleen's part, though Maud Gonne played it magnificently, & with wierd power. I expect that I should have struck a tragic note at the start—I have an idea ⸍of revising it before I put it in a book & of making Kathleen pass the door at the start. They can call her over & ask her some question & she can say she is going to old 'so & sos', & pass on (they might ask her to come in & she might not have time). When she came in the second time she might say that old so & so was shearing his sheep or the like & would not attend to her.[2] You will be sorry to hear that I have just dictated a rough draft of a new 'Grania' second act to Moore's type writèr. He is to work on it in Paris. He gave me a few ideas & I worked over them & I think got the most poetical & beautiful material that we have put into the play as yet. He is delighted & will write the act ⟨in Paris⟩ & then send it to me for revision.[3]

April 5.

The plays are over. Crowds have been turned away from the doors every night & last night was the most successful of all the performances. The audience now understands 'Kathleen ny Hoolihan' & there is no difficulty in getting from humour to tragedy. There is continual applause. And strange to say I like Deirdre. It is thin & faint but it has the effect of wall decoration. The absense of character is like the absense of individual expression in wall decoration. It was acted with great simplicity. The actors kept very quiet, often merely posing & speaking. The result was curiously dreamlike & gentle. Russell is planning a play on the Children of Turren[4] & will I imagine do quite a number of plays. The costumes &

---

[2] AE's *Deirdre* and WBY's *Cathleen ni Houlihan*, with MG in the title role, were produced by the Fays' Irish National Dramatic Company at St Teresa's Hall, Dublin, 2–5 Apr 1902 (see p. 151, n. 1). *Deirdre* had been published serially in the *All Ireland Review* from 6 July 1901 to 15 Feb 1902; it was partly reprinted in the *Celtic Christmas* for December 1902, and in *Imaginations and Reveries* (1915). In a letter of 10 April (Berg) AG, who had co-authored *Cathleen ni Houlihan*, urged WBY not to alter it, but in the final version Cathleen is seen passing the door at the beginning of the play on her way to where 'Maurteen and his sons are shearing sheep' and she is immediately identified with 'the strange woman that goes through the country whatever time there's war or trouble coming' (*VPl*, 216). The laughter had been in part caused because W. G. Fay, who played Peter Gillane, was known as a comic actor, and the audience had therefore supposed that the play would be a comedy.

[3] This may have been the version of the second act which Moore went to Paris to write in French (Cave, 250–4), although in *Ave* Moore places this in 1900. The revisions appear not to have been included in the published version.

[4] In 'The Tragic Death of the Children of Tuireann', Lugh enjoins a series of tasks (the last of which proves fatal) on Brian, Iuchair, and Iucharba, the sons of Tuirell Bicreo, in compensation for their killing of his father. In his article, 'The Dramatic Treatment of Heroic Literature' (see

scenery designed by him were really beautiful[5]—there was a gauze veil in front. It was really a wonderful sight to see crowds of people standing up at the back of the hall where they could hardly ever see because of the people in front—I heard this from one of them—& yet patient & enthusiastic.

I imagine that the De Freyne estate agitation is breaking down. Miss Gonne has had a number of letters from the tenants this week begging her to go down & arrange a settlement. All the tenants they say would agree to take ⟨much less than the⟩ quite a small concession. She wont interfear however as the United Irish League is in possession.[6]

I met O Grady this morning & found him groaning under the weight of his commercial responsibility.[7]

Cuchullain, which I have gone over with Moore is still in want of a little simplification which I am trying to get into it. I think I shall get it simple enough for Fay in the end.

Yrs ever

W B Yeats

ALS Berg, with envelope addressed to Hotel de Russia, Florence, redirected to Hotel Royal, Sienna, Italy; postmark 'DUBLIN AP 5 02'. Partly in Wade, 367–9.

p. 228, n. 1) AE prophesied that, treated by modern Irish writers, the 'children of Turann will start afresh still eager to take up and renew their cyclical labours . . .'. The tale, described by WBY as 'an old Grail Quest' (*E&I*, 186), is essentially undramatic.

[5] On 28 Jan 1902 AE had told WBY (MBY) 'I am designing my own scenery. I wanted to do it on visionary lines but have to modify it somewhat to meet possibilities.' Marie Walker recalled that the play 'was presented under a gauze upon which Fay played a green arc, giving the stage a ghostly, mist-like appearance. Costumes, made from designs by A.E., blended perfectly with the sombre background. The characters had the appearance of figures rising out of a mist' (Nic Shiubhlaigh, 19). Photographs of scenes from both plays appeared in the *Tatler* of 16 Apr 1902. Although, following the success of *Deirdre*, AE planned to write plays on the Children of Lir, on Cuchulain, and a sequel to Deirdre, little came of it: he published prose episodes based on 'The Children of Lir' in the *United Irishman* on 8 and 15 Mar 1902, but in August 1902 wrote to WBY (Denson, 43) that he had 'escaped from my brief folly of play writing'.

[6] Lord Arthur French De Freyne's estates in Roscommon had been a focal point of land agitation since 1888 and the long-running dispute intensified at Fairymount on 26 Dec 1901 when summonses were issued for unlawful assembly and intimidation against the protesting tenants and their supporters from the agrarian organization, the United Irish League. MG had taken an active interest in the dispute for many years.

[7] As well as the proprietorship of the financially precarious weekly *All Ireland Review* (1900–6), O'Grady had recently launched out as a publisher with Edward Martyn's *The Tale of a Town* and *The Enchanted Sea*, which he issued jointly with Fisher Unwin (see p. 148). Nevinson had met O'Grady at WBY's Monday Evening on 24 Feb 1902, describing him in his diary (Bodleian) as 'modestly exuberant, grey haired, ruddy, very Irish, "the Irish Ruskin" Yeats calls him because he takes extravagant little points and preaches truth from them . . .'.

To Henry Newbolt, 5 April [1902]

8 Cavendish Row | Dublin.
(after Wednesday next 18
Woburn Buildings, Euston Road)
April 5.

Dear Newbolt: I enclose the article of 'Speaking to the Psaltery' (or 'to musical notes' if you prefer that) & I would be greatly obliged if you put it in the May number. If it is not out then I shall not be able to give my lecture until Autumn.[1]

Our plays have been a great success—both 'AE's' Deirdre & my 'Kathleen Ny Hoolihan'. Crowds have been turned away at the doors & great numbers stood about the walls with patient enthusiasm. They had to stand through all the intervals too, for they were packed too close to move. It was only a hall not a theatre but we could have filled quite a big place, I think. Our actors were amateurs—but amateurs who are trying to act with wonderful simplicity & naivety. Their method is better than their performance but their method is the first right one I have seen. In 'Deirdre' a dim dreamlike play they acted without "business" of any kind. They simply stood still in decorative attitudes & spoke. AE had designed all the scenes & costumes & they were excellent. The night before last one of the actors, who a little while ago was an agricultural labourer, came round to read me a play which he has written about the United Irish league in the style of the only dramatist he has ever read—Ibsen.[2] It had real substance but little execution. Something I think must come out [of] all this energy & delight in high things.

Yrs snly
W B Yeats

PS. I suppose the bit of music I send will have to be photographed & reproduced in that way; as I imagine the marks are not all to be got in ordinary musical type. It is the work of Dolmetsch. Would you like to give a picture of the Psaltery.[3]

---

[1] See p. 121.

[2] The background of Padraic Colum (1881–1972; see Appendix), who became a poet, playwright, novelist, and man of letters, was less ruggedly picturesque than WBY suggests. His father had been the master of a workhouse in Co. Longford, and was now station-master at the Dublin suburb of Sandycove, while he was a clerk in the Irish Railway Clearing House. Colum played Buinne in *Deirdre*, and had read WBY an early version of *Broken Soil*, produced by the INTS on 3 Dec 1903, and published in a revised version as *The Fiddler's House* (1907).

[3] Dolmetsch's holograph notation of 'Impetuous Heart', a lyric from *The Countess Cathleen*, was reproduced in 'Speaking to the Psaltery', but there was no picture of the psaltery.

[*The cancelled opening of a letter to Oliver St. J. Gogarty is written on the last page*]

⟨18 Woburn Buildings | Euston Road.
Saturday

Dear Mr Gogarty: would it do as well if I went⟩[1]

ALS Emory. Partly in Wade, 369–7.

To John Millington Synge, 9 April [1902]

18 Woburn Buildings | Euston Road | London.
April 9

Dear Synge: I send you a book which the editor of 'The Speaker' sent me for review. I have asked him to take a review from you instead.[1] You might follow it up with other things.

Bullen is reading your book & I will let you know if he will take it in a short time now.[2]

Yrs ev
W B Yeats

ALS, with enclosure,[3] TCD. Saddlemyer, 34.

To John Butler Yeats, [c. 9 April 1902]

Mention in letter from JBY, 10 April 1902.
Sending back the MS of a story of JBY's which he has amended.[1]

MBY.

---

[1] Oliver St John Gogarty (1878–1957), surgeon, poet, essayist and wit, was at this time enjoying a leisurely career as a medical student. He had recently met WBY at a play-reading in the Nassau Hotel.

[1] The book was Seumas MacManus's *Donegal Fairy Stories*, which Synge reviewed in the *Speaker* of 21 June. He had previously reviewed *The Poems of Geoffrey Keating* in the issue of 8 Dec 1900.

[2] Synge's book, *The Aran Islands*, was rejected by Grant Richards, A. H. Bullen, Alfred Nutt, T. Fisher Unwin, R. Brimley Johnson, and Elkin Mathews before it was finally issued jointly by Maunsel & Co., Dublin, and Elkin Mathews in 1907.

[3] Enclosed with this letter is a note from the editor of the *Speaker*, dated 14 Mar 1902, asking WBY 'for a short review of. . . . Donegal Fairy Stories (MacManus) at his leisure.'

[1] Probably 'The Luck of the O'Beirnes', a tale of a pro-nationalist landlord in 1798, which appeared in the Christmas number of the *Irish Homestead* in December 1902. In his reply on 10 Apr JBY thanked WBY for all the trouble he had taken, and said that his corrections were 'many of them *most important* and I have adopted nearly all'. He also told WBY that he had another story in his head, which he intended to call 'An Irish Penelope'.

To the Editor of the United Irishman, *12 April 1902*

The acting of "Deirdre" delighted me by its simplicity. It was often a little crude, it showed many signs of inexperience, but it was grave and simple. I heard somebody say "they have got rid of all the nonsense," the accumulated follies of the modern stage. An amateur actor, as a rule, delights even more than a professional actor, in what is called "business," in gesture and action of all kinds that are not set down in the text. He moves restlessly about, he talks in dumb show with his neighbours, and so on. He wishes to copy at every moment the surface of life, to copy life as he thinks the eye sees it, instead of being content with the simple and noble forms the heart sees. The result is that he, like the professional actor, can act modern comedy, but he cannot act any kind of drama that would waken beautiful emotions. Beautiful art is always simpler and graver and quieter than daily life, and, despite many defects, the acting of "Deirdre" has left to me a memory of simplicity and gravity and quietness. The actors moved about very little, they often did no more than pose in some statuesque way and speak; and there were moments when it seemed as if some painting upon a wall, some rhythmic procession along the walls of a temple had begun to move before me with a dim, magical life. Perhaps I was stirred so deeply because my imagination ignored, half-unconsciously, errors of execution, and saw this art of decorative acting as it will be when long experience may have changed a method into a tradition, and made Mr. Fay's company, in very truth, a National company, a chief expression of Irish imagination. The Norwegian drama, the most important in modern Europe, began at a semi-amateur theatre in Bergen, and I cannot see any reason in the nature of things why Mr. Fay's company should not do for Ireland what the little theatre at Bergen did for Europe. His actors, now that he has set them in the right way, need nothing but continuous experience, and it should be the business of our patriotic societies to give them this experience. The audience is there, for an audience that could be moved by the subtleties of thought and sentiment of a play like "A.E.'s" "Deirdre," that could take pleasure in a beauty that was often as imponderable as the odour of violets, cannot be less imaginative than the men of the Rennaissance. Victor Hugo said somewhere: "It is in the Theatre that the mob becomes a people,"[1] and

---

[1] WBY is probably thinking of Chap. 6 of Book IV of Victor Hugo's *William Shakespeare* (trans. Melville B. Anderson, 1887), where Hugo urges poet and playwright to write for the mob since the 'mob is the human race in misery. The mob is the mournful beginning of the people.' WBY had quoted from the book in a review of William Watson in 1890 (*Letters to the New Island*, ed. Horace Reynolds [1934] pp. 204–5), and in December 1934 cited it in a note to 'Three Songs to the Same Tune' (*VP*, 836): 'A nation should be like an audience in some great theatre—"In the theatre," said Victor Hugo, "the mob becomes a people"—watching the sacred drama of its own history . . .'

it is certain that nothing but a victory on the battlefield could so uplift and enlarge the imagination of Ireland, could so strengthen the National spirit, or make Ireland so famous throughout the world, as the creation of a Theatre where beautiful emotion and profound thought, now fading from the Theatres of the world, might have their three hours' traffic once again.

W B Yeats

P.S.—I have said nothing of the acting of "Kathleen Ni Houlihan," for though altogether excellent of its kind, it was not of a new kind. The play tried to give the illusion of daily life, and the actors therefore acted it in the usual way, and quite rightly. That they did so well in two so different plays is a good promise for the future.

Printed letter, *United Irishman*, 12 April 1902 (3). *UP* II. 285–6.

To F. J. Fay, [*12 April 1902*]

Saturday

I have no criticism to make on you & Miss Walker and the young man who played Naisi, & very little on your Deirdre except she had a general lack of intensity. Naisi could hardly have been better, & your Concobar quite satisfied me.[1] Miss Walker would have been I think quite equal to a much stronger part. When I spoke of crudities & inexperiences, I had nothing more mysterious in my mind than the crude playing of the two brothers and the inexperienced playing of the Sons of Fergus who may both I should think make good actors in the end.[2] I would have preferred to give you unqualified praise but if I had done so, people who remember their extrinsic and accidental faults would have said I was insincere and have paid no attention to my words. I shall however return to the subject of your company again and again until I have got people to look to you and

[1] See previous letter. Frank Fay, who had seen an advance copy of WBY's letter to the *United Irishman*, wrote to thank him on 11 Apr (Private) and 'to ask you to point out . . . what you consider our defects and errors of execution which you refer to. . . . it is very necessary that now that we are, in your opinion, on the right way, we should at once begin to correct our defects. So I hope you will let me know what they are and do not hesitate to let me know.' Frank Fay took the part of Concobar, J. Dudley Digges (1879–1947) that of Naisi, and Maire Walker (d. 1958), who acted under the Irish form of her name, Maire Nic Shiubhlaigh, played Lavarcam; Maire Quinn (see p. 162, n. 3) was Deirdre. Maire Walker describes the production in Nic Shiublaigh, 16–20.

[2] Ardan and Ainle, Concobar's brothers, played by Fred Ryan and 'H. Sproule' (James Cousins), and Buinne and Illaun, the sons of Fergus, played by Padraic Colum and C. Caulfield, who also took the part of Patrick Gillan in *Cathleen ni Houlihan*. Of the four, only Colum acted in a subsequent production.

your company for the next dramatic development in Ireland at any rate. I find that by doing this, I get things taken up at last: I believe that the [?]carrying[3] slight, but manifestly sincere appreciation of a thing incline people far more towards it than enthusiastic and lengthy outbursts by their very emphasis. I think that what your company wants, is simply a few people capable of taking the quite small parts, and such practice in speaking as will teach those who are adequate, but no more, the sons and Fergus let us say. They speak their words not only musically, but significantly and speak them not like something learned but like something that was a part of themselves. Even a great orator only learns this by experience. A young Irishman here, called French has done a Folk Lore play in prose which I am told is good.[4] If it is I shall send it over that you may have a look at it. I see no serious difficulty before you but the getting of good plays in sufficient quantity at the start. In the autumn I had better write a new Samhain. You had better start formally with a proper blast of trumpets.

Your ev
W B Yeats

MS copy in W. A. Henderson's hand, NLI.

To Lady Augusta Gregory, [18 April 1902]

18 Woburn Buildings | Euston Road.
Friday

My Dear Lady Gregory: It has just occured to me that Wilfred Blunt having his essay "ready by the 15th" must mean that it is to appear on the first of May or rather a little earlier.[1] I think, if this is so you should write & tell Murray at once, or wire to me to tell him as that will save time, (wire 'Murray' & I will understand). Otherwise one review will come out before

---

[3] Possibly Henderson's mistranscription of WBY's 'apparently'.
[4] Cecil French's play was not produced or published.

[1] In a letter of 10 Apr (Berg), AG had told WBY that 'W. Blunt wrote yesterday, in a hurry to have some questions answered about Cuchulain, as he is doing an article on it to be ready 15th, & I told him to try and see you, if you were in town'. Wilfrid Scawen Blunt (1840–1922), poet, horseman, and traveller, was a flamboyant anti-Imperialist and a champion of nationalism in Ireland, Egypt, and India. From December 1882 to July 1883 he had been AG's lover, a relationship which inspired her sequence, 'A Woman's Sonnets'. In 1888 Blunt had served two months in Galway gaol for resisting the police during the suppression of a Land League meeting at Woodford, Co. Galway, during agrarian agitation on Lord Clanricarde's estate, and on 28 Jan 1888, while he was serving his sentence, WBY had reviewed his poetry and prose in *United Ireland* (*UP* I. 122–30). The two met through AG on 1 Apr 1898 when WBY tried an unsuccessful magical experiment on him. Blunt published his review of *Cuchulain of Muirthemne*, 'The Great Irish Epic', in the *Nineteenth Century* of May 1902.

the book does, perhaps, & the newspapers will be cross. Murray's man told me that they dislike giving advance copies for fear of this taking place. I had asked for a copy for Best that he may do it for 'Independent' in time to forestall some fool or farmyard bird.[2] He will give the copy. I asked him when the book will be out but he did not know (this was on Tuesday) but said it would be soon. Russell will do you in the U.I.[3] I wanted him to do it in 'Freeman'. I did not see Blunt as I only got your letter on 14th & did not realize the date until the 15th, & thought I should be rather at the heel of the hunt. Martyn has rather irritated me. I got him to write to U I about the plays & he has written rather abusing the actors, whom one wants to encourage. He is going to bring English actors over for his play & is 'laying pipe'.[4] I forgot this & poor Fay & his company did wonders. There is an announcement in this weeks U I of the Autumn 'Samhain' dramatic festival they are preparing.[5] I have a plan for a little religeous play in one act with quite as striking a plot as 'Kathleen'—It cannot offend anybody & may propitiate Holy Church. I have also a plot for a little comedy in one act.[6] Cousins Fay says has sent him the best one act play he has seen for years.[7] So all is going well. I am working at my novel—dictating to a type

[2] See p. 115. Richard Best had played the part of Ainle in the amateur production of *Deirdre* in January. He contributed an anonymous notice to the *Irish Daily Independent* on 12 May, and his signed review, 'Cuchulain and the Men of the Red Branch', appeared in the *New Ireland Review* of July 1902.

[3] AE's review of *Cuchulain of Muirthemne* appeared in the *United Irishman* on 24 May 1902, and was subsequently reprinted in *Imaginations and Reveries* (1915). He valued the book (2) as shaping the imagination of the rising generation and hoped it would restore the Irish to their archetypal heroic ideals, for in losing the bardic vision 'we have lost the vision of that life into the likeness of which it is the true labour of the spirit to transform this life'.

[4] Edward Martyn regarded Irish country people and country speech as vulgar, and was consequently out of sympathy with the Fays' use of Irish accents and emphasis. In the *United Irishman* of 19 Apr (1) he wrote that in *Deirdre* 'the movement and many dramatic situations would have been more manifest under conditions of a more competent acting and stage management', and, in a disparaging allusion to W. G. Fay's performance as Peter Gillane in WBY's play, maintained that only MG 'saved the disaster which otherwise must have come to destroy the high poetic significance of the play by reason of the low comedy-man air adopted by another actor'. AG reported on 17 May 1902 (Berg) that he was 'in treaty' with Geneviève Ward (1838–1922), the American-born actress, who had become a tragedienne in England with Irving and Benson. At this time she was primarily a drama teacher, although she was about to play the Marquise de St Maur in T. W. Robertson's *Caste* at the Haymarket Theatre. Martyn may have been drawn to her because of her admiration for Ibsen, but nothing came of their planned collaboration.

[5] The *United Irishman* of 19 Apr 1902 (1) announced that the Cumann na nGaedheal, a radical political and cultural organization founded in 1900 and the precurser of the Sinn Fein Party, had decided to institute an annual 'Samhain' gathering, to be held on the last Monday in October, at which plays in Irish and English would be performed.

[6] This is the first mention, respectively, of *The Hour-Glass*, first produced in March 1903, and the one-act farce, *The Pot of Broth*, produced in December 1902.

[7] In a letter of 15 Apr 1902 (Private) Frank Fay told WBY that 'we have got an exquisite little one act piece which Mr Cousins has given us. . . . I have fifteen years experience as a playgoer and I have never seen a one act play that could touch this; it is a bit of life.' This was *The Racing Lug*, a short melodrama in which the heroine loses her father directly and her mother indirectly

writer. I dictated 2000 words in an hour & ten minutes yesterday—& go on again to morrow. This dictation is really a discovery.

Certainly I shall keep the 25th free. I take chair at Irish Lit on the 26th.[8] The 'Quarterly' has an essay on 'Gaelic Revival' quoting your translation from Hyde & praising & quoting verses of mine. It is clearly Gwynns work.[9]

Yrs snry

W B Yeats

ALS Berg, with envelope addressed to Hotel de Russie, Florence, Italy, postmark 'LONDON W.C. AP 18 02'. Partly in Wade, 370.

To F. J. Fay, 21 April 1902

18 Woburn Buildings | Euston Road

April 21st,/02.

Dear Mr. Fay,

I have written a long reply to Edward Martin in which I have renewed my praise of your and your brother's company.[1] I want to make people understand the importance of the St. Teresa's Hall experiment, and to prepare them for future work. You might join in if you see a chance. When Edward Martin said to me that your brother over-acted his part I was not quite sure at first that there was not some truth in it. I was trying to find out the cause of the laughter, and as you know was planning alterations in

through the sinking of a fishing boat, but gains her true love. Cousins had written it in a week at the suggestion of the Fays, who produced the play on 31 Oct 1902.

[8] In her letter of 10 Apr (see above, n. 1) AG had written that she and Robert hoped 'to be in London Friday 25th only for a couple of days: so if you have no great temptation, you might keep that evening free'. On the evening of 26 Apr WBY took the chair at the ILS for a lecture on 'An Old Irish Rath' by John Campbell (b. 1870), Irish party MP for Armagh 1900–6. Blunt (II. 22) recorded his attendance at this meeting 'where the Cuchulain Saga was discussed. I spoke on it. . . . Yeats also spoke well. He is a pleasant talker on his own subjects, and in appearance is of that most interesting dark Irish type with pale face and lank hair.'

[9] Gwynn's unsigned omnibus review, 'The Gaelic Revival in Literature', appeared in the *Quarterly Review* for April 1902 (423–49), and included *Samhain* (1901), which contained AG's translation of *The Twisting of the Rope*, and WBY's *Poems* (1901) among the 14 books noticed. Gwynn did not comment on the quality of AG's translation, or name her as translator, but compared Hyde's play with WBY's story of the same name. He described WBY as 'the first of living poets' and noted (446) that 'if the characters of his poems tend to move more and more in dreamland, that is perhaps, in some measure, because Mr Yeats is a Celt, but more because he is himself'.

[1] See above, n. 4 and the following letter. In his *United Irishman* notice of 19 Apr 1902 (1) Martyn regretted 'that for the want of a little care some beautiful details of Mr. Yeats's play were lost on the audience. At the same time, the faults of the players were chiefly the faults of inexperience; and I do not doubt that with practice, Mr. Fay's company will improve and be able to grapple with the more advanced forms of modern drama.'

the play, blaming myself in chief. Friday night convinced me, however, that none of the blame was your brother's and very little of it mine. I did not criticise the acting in my letter to you not because I hesitated to tell you what I thought but because I really did not feel competent.[2] In two or three years I shall understand the subject but I don't yet. I know that all the acting of verse that I have seen up to this has been wrong, and I can see that you and your brother have struck out a method which would be right for verse, but, till I have seen that method applied by many different people, I will only be able to criticise acting very vaguely. George Moore has precise ideas because he likes the "natural school," and has therefore many examples to judge by. Two years ago I was in the same state about scenery that I now am in about acting. I knew the right principles but I did not know the right practice because I had never seen it. I have now however learnt a great deal from Gordon Craig. Now as to the future of the National Theatre Company. I read your letters to a wealthy friend, who said something like this "Work on as best you can for a year, let us say, you should be able to persuade people during that time that you are something of a dramatist and Mr. Fay should be able to have got a little practice for his company. At the year's end do what Wagner did and write 'a Letter to my Friends' asking for the capital to carry out your idea." Now I could not get from this friend of mine whether he himself would give any large sum, but I imagine that he would do something.[3] I think we must work in some such way, getting all the good plays we can from Cousins and Russell and anybody else, but carrying out our theories of the stage as rigorously as possible. The friend I have quoted is interested in me but Russell has his own following, and I think it likely that we will ultimately get a certain amount of money. I will do my best to do a good deal of strong dramatic work in the immediate future. I should not talk about what my friend said to me. It is all too vague, but I quote it to you to show how the wind may blow.

Yours sincerely
W B Yeats

[2] In his letter of 15 Apr (see p. 174, n. 7) Frank Fay hinted that WBY had pulled his punches on 12 Apr (see pp. 171–2): 'I had hoped that you might have been able to point out our sins without hesitation in a private letter.'

[3] On 15 Apr Fay had confessed that he entertained 'no great hopes for the future because we are trying to do what the majority don't like and don't want, and as I have shown you the halls available in Dublin are in the hands of people who do not consider us safe. Of course that applies everywhere but in places like London and Paris there are hundreds of halls where here, there are not above five possible ones, and all are in the hands of Unionists or the class of people who call themselves nationalists of the respectable type.' Although WBY carefully uses a masculine pronoun to preserve her anonymity, the friend and possible benefactor was AEFH, an avid Wagnerian, who was to lease the Abbey Theatre in 1904 and subsidize it until 1910. Richard Wagner's 'Communication to my Friends' (1852) set out his plans for a German National Theatre.

[*In WBY's hand*]

The Egyptian plays were chiefly interesting for being in something like your method & for adopting decorative scenery. The scenery which was supposed to represent Egyptian temple walls was made by simply turning ordinary scenery wrong way front. Against this grey mass very charmingly dressed people posed looking really very like Egyptian wall painting.[4] The acting except for Miss Farr herself was much behind the acting in Dublin. Miss Young & Miss Farr are playing in the better of the two plays tomorrow & I am going to see Miss Young.[5] The plays are fairly well written.

TLS Private.

To the Editor of the United Irishman, c. *21 April 1902*

I

I partly agree with you that the "laughter" that Mr. Martin says "greeted every word however serious that fell from Peter Gillane's lips" was due on the night of the first production to the relaxation of tension to which the audience had been brought by "Deirdre," but there were other causes.[1] Many phrases that have a tragic meaning in Connacht have no meaning or even a comic meaning in Dublin. "He looks like somebody that has got the touch" is, for instance, tragic in Connacht. In Dublin it means somebody that is not right in his head. The stroke of the fairy wand and the touch of a fairy hand are only remembered where folk tradition lingers, though we still talk everywhere of "a stroke of paralysis" and of being "touched." Another reason for the laughter was that Mr. Fay has so long

---

[4] See p. 121. In his letter of 15 Apr Fay asked WBY if he could tell him anything of *The Shrine of the Golden Hawk* and *The Beloved of Hathor* since 'I am like you interested in plays which try to reproduce novel atmosphere in the theatre'. Fay's interest had, perhaps, been excited by a notice in the *Academy* of 5 Apr, which announced (354) that 'the pictures presented are decorative in treatment, and the emotions treated are those of an interior world, little touched by the historical facts surrounding it'. In his review for the *Star* of 23 Jan 1902 (*UP* II. 265–7) WBY had praised the originality of 'the rigorously decorative arrangements of the stage, which imitated the severe forms of Egyptian mural painting' and suggested that the unearthly effect the plays achieved came 'more from the scenic arrangements, which did not grossen the imagination with realism, and from the symbolic costumes and from the half-chanting recitation of phrases of ritual, than from anything especially dramatic'. He preferred *The Shrine of the Golden Hawk* to *The Beloved of Hathor*, which 'irritated . . . by its chaos of motives and of motiveless incidents'. Gordon Craig published the two plays privately in an undated edition.

[5] Evidently Elizabeth Young ('Violet Mervyn'), who had played the heroine in the January performance of *Deirdre* (see p. 149, n. 6). She had subsequently moved to London and embarked on an acting career.

[1] In an editorial note to Martyn's letter, Griffith had defended Fay's acting and, noting that the audience did not laugh on the following evening, attributed the cause to WBY's play having released the tensions created in the opening night audience by the solemnity of *Deirdre*.

delighted Dublin audiences with excellent humorous acting that they are ready to laugh even before he speaks, as they did on the first night. I do not write to you, however, to argue with Mr. Martyn, but to say that if he had been in the theatre on Friday he would have seen Mr. Fay again and again rob himself of the laughter and applause that is the legitimate reward of the actor lest the play as a whole might suffer. Instead of trying to make points, he tried with admirable self-sacrifice to make his effect as subdued as possible.

I need hardly say that I do not agree with Mr. Martin as to the acting of "Deirdre." I think the difference between us comes from the difference of our arts. Mr. Martyn likes a form of drama that is essentially modern, that needs for its production actors of what is called the "natural school," the dominant school of the modern stage. The more experience an actor has had of that stage the better he is for Mr. Martyn's purpose, and almost of a certainty the worse for mine. English actors or Irish actors trained in England, for years to come, must serve his turn far better than Irish-trained Irish actors who are likely to be extravagant romantic, oratorical, and traditional, like Irish poetry and legend themselves. I can only repeat that I was delighted with the acting of Mr. Fay's company, that I cannot see any reason in the nature of things why it should not be the foundation for a National Drama. I have plans for a somewhat elaborate essay on the Theatre, and am also lecturing on the subject at Oxford next month, and I shall probably speak of that acting in both lecture and essay as the first example of right method that I have come upon. Its defects were the defects of inexperience and of all new things. A poet, or painter, or actor who is trying to make his art afresh is always more imperfect than one whose art is founded upon the current art of his time. One sees it in the imperfect drawing of the imaginative painters of a time when painting, like acting, has come to be founded upon observation rather than upon imagination. Until the stream of the world has begun to flow in a different direction, a Rossetti will always draw worse than a Millais.

II

When Mr. Fay's company have the time and money, and it will need little of either, I hope that they will apply the same principles that they have applied to acting to the scenery and the stage itself. The scenery of a play as remote from real life as "Deirdre" should, I think, be decorative rather than naturalistic. A wood, for instance, should be little more than a pattern made with painted boughs. It should not try to make one believe that the actors are in a real wood, for the imagination will do that far better, but it should decorate the stage. It should be a mass of deep colour, in harmony with the colours in the costumes of the players. I was, I think, the first to commend this kind of scenery,[2] and now Mr. Gordon Craig has used it to make certain old English operas the most beautiful sight that has been seen upon the modern stage. I do not think that he was influenced by me; but the reaction against the scientific age is setting decorative art in the stead of naturalistic art everywhere, and it was bound to come upon the stage.

I would try and make a theatre where realism would be impossible. I am not at all certain, but I think I would bring the floor out in front of the proscenium, as it was in the old theatres before the "natural school" drove out poetry. All the great poetical dramatists of the world wrote for a theatre that was half platform, half stage, and for actors that were, at least, as much orators as actors. William Morris once said to me of an eminent dramatist of our time, "He will never understand any art because he does not understand that all art is founded upon convention." It has been our pride, hitherto, to destroy the conventions of the Stage, and until we have restored them we will never have a dramatic art which the Englishman of the time of Shakespeare and the Greek of the time of Sophocles and the Spaniard of the time of Calderon and the Indian of the time of Kaladasa[3] would have recognised as akin to their own great art.

W B Yeats

Printed letter, *United Irishman*, 26 April 1902 (3). *UP* II. 291–3.

To Lady Augusta Gregory, [24 April 1902]

18 Woburn Buildings
Thursday.

My dear Lady Gregory: excuse this scrap of paper but I am writing in the British Museum.[1] I have got places in the Balcony (5/- each) for

---

[2] WBY had constantly stressed that scenery should be subordinate to words in the theatre, and that realistic scenery broke the conventions upon which poetic drama depended. Writing in *Beltaine* in 1899 he had insisted (23) that the 'theatre of Art' must 'discover grave and decorative gestures . . . and grave and decorative scenery, that will be forgotten the moment an actor has said "It is dawn" . . .' He delighted in the scenic art of Gordon Craig because it was decorative rather than realistic.

[3] The most famous of the three plays of Kālidāsa, the 5th-century Hindu poet and dramatist, is *Sakuntalā*. On 6 July 1899 the play was performed in a translation by Laurence Binyon, with lyrics by Arthur Symons and incidental music by Arnold Dolmetsch, in a tropical hothouse at the Botanical Gardens. WBY had earlier grouped Kālidāsa with Shakespeare, Sophocles, and Goethe in his review of Villiers de l'Isle Adam's *Axël* in the *Bookman*, April 1894 (*UP* I. 322).

[1] The letter is written perpendicular to the rule on paper torn from a copy book.

tomorrow: & you will see me about 7.[2] I shall have a good many things to talk over so I hope you are not off to Ireland in the morning.

I was at Murrays to day. Your book is to be out on Monday or Tuesday.[3]

Yours ever
W B Yeats

ALS Berg, with envelope addressed to Queen Anne Mansions, postmark 'LONDON N.W. AP 24 02'.

To Jenny Jones,[1] 27 April 1902

18 Woburn Buildings | Euston Road
April 27, 1902

Dear Madam—
The works you would, I think, find most useful for your purpose are
1 Anthology of Irish Poetry edited by Stopford Brooke & T. W. Rolleston—
2—A Book of Irish Verse ed W. B. Yeats—
3—Love Songs of Connaught. ed Douglas Hyde—
4—Homeward Songs by the Way—by A.E. (published in America by Moscher, but I think under another title.)[2]
I think this list will be enough for you to begin with, as you will find references to earlier poets in Mr. Brookes & Mr Rollestons Anthology—
You ask me only about Irish poetry, but you can hardly understand recent Irish poetry unless you know something of the legendary cycles which have had so much influence upon it—I would recommend you to read 'Finn & his Companions' by Standish J. O'Grady[3]—& above all

---

[2] The theatre tickets were perhaps for the penultimate performance of H. M. Paull's *The New Clown* at the Comedy Theatre. WBY and AG may have wanted to see the acting of James Welch (1865–1917), who took the leading part, and who had played in the first production of *The Land of Heart's Desire* in April 1894. Dion Boucicault's daughter, Nina, was also acting in Paull's play.

[3] *Cuchulain of Muirthemne* probably appeared on Monday, 28 Apr 1902. On 27 Apr AG had been acting as WBY's amanuensis, and in *70 Years* (400) she recalled that 'I left London for Coole on the very day *Cuchulain* was published'.

[1] Probably Jenny M. A. Jones who was to organize WBY's lecture at the Society of Pedagogy of St. Louis on 5 Jan 1904.

[2] Both the Brooke–Rolleston anthology, *A Treasury of Irish Poetry in the English Tongue*, and the revised edition of WBY's *A Book of Irish Verse*, had appeared in 1900, and Hyde's influential anthology, *Love Songs of Connacht*, in 1893. The pirated American edition of AE's *Homeward Songs by the Way* was issued by T. B. Mosher of Portland, Maine, and contained additional poems. WBY had reviewed it and the 2nd English edition in the *Bookman* in May 1895 (*UP* I. 356–8).

[3] *Finn and His Companions*, a retelling of some of the Finn legends for a juvenile audience, had been published in 1892 in Unwin's Children's Library.

"Cuchulain of Muirthemne" by Lady Gregory, just published by John Murray—

The greater amount of Irish poetry is however in the Irish language, & I think some of the time you mean to spend in study will be well spent in learning that language if you do not already know it—

Yrs snly
W B Yeats

Dict SMY, signed WBY; Southern Illinois.

To Lady Augusta Gregory, [*1 May 1902*]

18 Woburn Buildings | Euston Road.
Thursd.

My dear Lady Gregory: the enclosed came yesterday. I opened it by mistake. My eyes are bad from a cold so I cannot write a letter—Dolmetsch & Mrs Emery dined with me last night. More Psalteryes are to be made & quite cheap.[1]

Yr ev
W B Yeats

PS. I saw Nutt. I think he understands things. He wrote to society to complain about the lecture.[2]

ALS Berg, with envelope addressed to Coole, postmark 'LONDON W. MY 1 02'. No enclosure.

[1] Dolmetsch made six less elaborate psalteries for WBY's 'troubadours' at a cost of £2.10s.0d apiece. In March 1920 he bought three of them back from AEFH, at a cost of £1.10s.0d each, for use in teaching music to children at Bedales School, Petersfield.

[2] Alfred T. Nutt (1856–1910), the distinguished Celtic scholar, folklorist, and publisher, had written *Cuchulainn, the Irish Achilles* in 1900, and was probably complaining about Campbell's lecture at the ILS on 26 Apr, which WBY had chaired (see p. 175), and which no doubt fell short of his own high standards of erudition and exactitude. In September of this year he was to complain in *Folk-Lore* (33–5) of the inadequacies and inaccuracies in AG's *Cuchulain of Muirthemne*.

To Stephen MacKenna,[1] *3 May 1902*

18 Woburn Buildings, | Euston Road, | London.
May 3rd,/02.

My dear MacKenna,

Of course I shall be most delighted to see you & the fair Neo-platonist also. I am always in upon Monday evenings after eight. Most men find, I think, that when they marry, that the quieter life of the soul begins, for after all real freedom is only to be found within the limitations of settled habits and settled duties. We bachelors get up at the most irregular hours & are generally the most unsatisfactory of people. I asked John Murray to send you a copy of Lady Gregory's book & I hope that you will do for it whatever you can. I don't know any contemporary book that has a style that equals it in simplicity & naïve charm. You will have seen from the prefaces how great a book I think it is & it is only one of several into which she hopes to put the heroic literature of Ireland.

I am dictating this because I have a cold in my eyes & cannot write without considerable discomfort.

Yours sincly
W B Yeats

Dict AEFH, signed WBY; Southern Illinois.

To Violet Hunt, 13 May 1902

18, Woburn Buildings | Euston Road
May 13th 1902.

My dear Miss Hunt,

You introduced me I think to Lady Arabella Romney[1] (Was not that the name?) She asked me to go and see her, and I lost her address. Would

---

[1] Stephen MacKenna (1872–1934), journalist, classical scholar, and one of Synge's closest friends, was a special correspondent for the *New York World*. He married 'the fair Neo-platonist', Marie Bray (1878–1923), an American pianist, in London on 11 June 1902. MacKenna had supported WBY during the early quarrels in the National Literary Society (see *Aut*, 230), and in August 1899 had defended his 'weird' habits and lack of Gaelic in 'The Personality of W. B. Yeats', published in the *Gael* (NY). His interest in neoplatonists continued after his marriage and WBY was later to delight in his translation of Plotinus (1917–30). No review of *Cuchulain of Muirthemne* by MacKenna has been traced.

[1] Lady Arabella Charlotte Romilly (*c.* 1851–1907), the eldest daughter of James Carnegie, the 9th Earl of Southesk, had married in 1878 Samuel Henry Romilly (1849–1940), a barrister, of Huntington Park, Hereford. Their town house was 56 Eccleston Square, Westminster. Her posthumous volume of verse, *The Coming Dawn*, was edited by her husband in 1907.

you mind sending it to me, as I owe her somewhat copious ⟨excuses⟩ apologies.

Yrs sncly
W B Yeats

TLS Berg.

To Cornelius Weygandt, 15 May 1902

18 Woburn Buildings, | Euston Road. | London.
May 15th,/02.

Dear Sir,

"Dermot and Grania" has not yet been published, I suppose it will be sooner or later, but I cannot say who the publisher will be. "Kathleen Ny Hoolihan" will shortly be published by M*r* A. Bullen, he will in the first instance will issue a limited edition printed at a private press, at what price I don't know. The play however is quite short. It may possibly appear in your American-Irish magazine called "The Gael" & if so probably in the next number.[1] The Daily Express changed hands some time ago; it was under the control of M*r* Horace Plunket when it supported the intellectual movement in Ireland, now it is in the hands of its new proprietor Lord Ardilaun and of the extreme Tory party.[2] The Leader generally notices all intellectual activities but often in a somewhat narrow spirit.[3] The United Irishman alone gives full and sympathetic accounts of all intellectual activities of a literary kind in Ireland. Its offices are at 17 Fownes Street, Dublin.

[1] *Cathleen ni Houlihan*, first published in *Samhain* (1902), was issued in a limited edition for Bullen at H. G. Webb's Caradoc Press in October. WBY was, however, displeased with this hand-printed edition because of the amateurish, unattractive binding, and the book was transferred to Elkin Mathews in 1903. The play did not appear in the *Gael* (New York), although WBY published three poems and *The Pot of Broth* there in 1903.

[2] From 1898 to 1899 the otherwise staunchly Conservative Dublin *Daily Express* had come under the proprietorship of Horace Plunkett (1854–1932) and the editorship of T. P. Gill, who made it an organ of the Irish Agricultural Organization and the Irish Literary Revival. This literary and intellectual interlude came to an end in October 1899, when its owner, Edward Dalziel, sold it to a Unionist group, headed by Lord Ardilaun (1840–1915), grandson of the founder of the Guinness brewery. Although no longer open to literary articles, the paper, as Stephen Gwynn noted, continued to review WBY's work with 'intellectual acuity'.

[3] Under D. P. Moran, the *Leader*'s stance was narrowly nationalist and pietistically Catholic; see p. 6, n. 11.

I forgot to say that A Bullen's address [is] Cecil Court, S*t* Martin's Lane London.

Yours snrly
W B Yeats

Dict AEFH, signed WBY; Private.

To Lady Augusta Gregory, 23 May 1902

18, Woburn Buildings | Euston Road | W.C—
May 23rd 1902

My dear Lady Gregory

I am dictating this to Lily who has been so good as to come in to write letters for me, she & I went yesterday to the oculist, he has given me new glasses for distant objects, but I am to use the old ones for reading, the present trouble in my eyes is muscular & is doubtless dependent on my general health. He says that when my eyes are at all painful I should dictate as much as possible, & that I should generally rather economise my eye sight. Apart from weakness of the muscles which he attributes to my being older as well as to my general health, the eye itself is rather better, the bad eye remains however the same. One has to be careful because when one has conical cornea in one eye there is a slight danger of it going to the other. I shall go on dictating for the present for my good eye is getting better with the rest.

I return the letters. The truth is that if one has any kind of unorthodox philosophy people will always be suspicious they are much less suspicious of flat atheism they forgave Byron at once but it was three generations before they forgave Shelley.[1]

---

[1] In his Preface to *Cuchulain of Muirthemne* WBY had written that if 'we but tell these stories to our children the Land will begin again to be a Holy Land, as it was before men gave their hearts to Greece and Rome and Judea'. The reviews by Best in the *Irish Daily Independent* (see p. 174) and Robert Donovan in the *Freeman's Journal* of 2 May complained that this smacked of neo-Paganism (see following letter), and AG also received letters protesting the same point from Wilbraham Fitz-John Trench (1873–1939), Professor of English at Queen's College, Galway (who was in 1913 to be appointed to Dowden's Chair at Trinity College, Dublin, in preference to WBY) and a Miss Redmond (probably Johanna Redmond, a minor dramatist and daughter of John Redmond, leader of the Irish Party). Trench had written to AG on 15 May (Berg) to complain that WBY 'regrets the giving of the heart to "Judea" & the setting of Christ before the soul instead of faery-men. That Mr Yeats has his eyes closed to the eternal Truth & dreams of shadows instead is the greater pity for him. But to many of us—even if we appreciate Cuchulain or Homer—this neo-paganism is a hateful thing, and Christ & his doctrine are as dear as life. . . . I have just cut the stupid Preface out of my copy & without it the book is perfect. If I give away some copies the Preface shall come out of them too.' AG sent WBY both letters on 20 May with the comment (Berg), 'The case certainly looks bad against you! I never thought of it being read in that way.'

I send you a draft of a letter to 'United Irishman' I need hardly tell you how sorry I am about that unfortunate sentence.[2]

Kathleen ni Hoolahan is in the press, I wish you would let me know as soon as you can exact[ly] how to spell the name, is it Houlan or Hoolan is it Ni or Ny—should it be small n or capital N? Capital I suppose in a title.[3]

I think I shall give Arthur Symons my extra copy of 'Cuchulain' he hasn't been able to get an answer from the Atheneum who promised him the book. I am a little afraid that the Atheneum may have taken offence at the book & Blunts review coming out together.[4]

I got a note from Mrs. Dryhurst about something else which wound up 'doing Cuchulain for The Chronicle, beautiful beautiful!'.[5]

I had what was considered a very good audience for my lecture at Oxford, some thirty or forty students in some Don's room, I don't think I was very good, I need a somewhat larger audience. I was certainly a great deal better at the Pioneer, I am afraid I was rather dogmatic too, but a number of persons of mature years, whom I afterwards discovered to be Dons, asked me a number of commonplace questions, I think my answers were pretty good much better than my opening.[6] I stayed with Maclachan who is I think very clever a really fine temperament, he has done some beautiful pieces of missal painting.[7]

---

[2] On 17 May AG had written (Berg) 'I don't think it worth writing to the Independent or Freeman, it will only give them an opening for more silliness. I daresay you might as well write to U. I.—just to have your explanation on record. . . . If you write for U.I. I think you had better let me see it first.'

[3] In a letter dated 'Sunday' [25 May 1902; Berg] AG replied that 'Kathleen ni Houlihan is the best spelling—but are you wise in the name? I think 'the Daughter of Houlihan' better—The other will always be mixed up with the Countess Cathleen by people of fuzzy minds . . .'.

[4] Symons did not review the book, but in the *Academy* of 6 Dec 1902 described it as 'the most important book published during 1902'. It was noticed in the *Athenaeum* on 2 Aug 1902, evidently by Arthur Quiller-Couch (1863–1944), novelist and man of letters, who was at this time one of WBY's critical allies.

[5] In her unsigned review in the *Daily Chronicle* on 7 June (3), Nora Dryhurst quoted generously from the stories of Emer, Maeve, Findabair, and Deirdre, emphasizing that ancient Celtic writers gave especially strong characterization to their heroines and concluding that 'few countries have held within their volcanic-ringed plains more poetry and passion than these old legends disclose'.

[6] WBY had spent the previous weekend in Oxford and on Sunday evening, 18 May, had lectured on 'The Theatre' to St John's College Essay Society. The meeting, which was an open one, attracted many visitors and discussion lasted until 10.50 p.m. On Friday, 16 May, Sturge Moore wrote in his diary (London): 'Yeats is going on Saturday to lecture there on Sunday taking his toy theatre with my scene with him'. The Pioneer Club, 5 Grafton St. London, was a ladies' social club founded in 1892 'with the idea of bringing the professional woman and the real worker into contact with the woman of leisure, for their mutual assistance and the advancement of woman's interests'. It had 650 members and its current chairman was Lady Hamilton.

[7] Eric R. D. Maclagan (1879–1951), who was in his final year reading classics at Christ Church, Oxford, had recently published a book of verse, *Leaves in the Road*. He subsequently became an expert in ecclesiastical embroidery and in 1905 joined the Victoria and Albert Museum as an assistant in the department of textiles, eventually becoming Director of the Museum. He remained a friend of WBY and through him advised SMY on appropriate designs for her embroidery at Dun Emer Industries.

I lunched with Robert on the Monday & would have gone to him earlier but Maclachan & Roberts[8] had mapped out my time for me. I saw a good deal of him however both on Saturday & Sunday if I remember rightly, though not at his own rooms, he is I think in a clever set.[9]

My father writes to say that the play in Moores garden was a great success & better even than 'The twisting of the rope'. Hyde acted splendidly & so too did the girl who played the fairy.[10]

Yrs snly

W B Yeats

[*Typewritten on a separate sheet*]

P.S. I have had the draft letter to the United Irishman typed. I enclose it, I think it rather good. It is a little lacking in finish but the fact that I have dictated it has given it a kind of journalistic vigour. I think it will give O'Donovan, for I imagine that Freeman man was O'Donovan, a lesson.[11] Read it through and if there is nothing you object to, please post it to Arthur Griffith, United Irishman Office 17, Fownes Street, Dublin, and please do this at once as I happen to know that it is very important for it to reach the United Irishman immediately if it is to go in, I will explain some other time.[12]

Dict SMY, signed WBY; Berg.

[8] Hugh Aleth Roberts (b. 1882) was an undergraduate at Christ Church from 1901 to 1904 and subsequently went into the timber trade in Burma.

[9] See above, n. 5. Robert Gregory had written to AG (Emory) on 20 May from New College: 'Yeats has been up here; his visit and lecture were I think a great success, though a large part of the audience at the latter were rather unappreciative, and the Dons who asked questions were terrors.'

[10] In a letter (MBY) dated 'Thursday', presumably 22 May 1902, JBY told WBY that 'Hyde's Play acted in G Moores Garden was a great success—the wind blowing about the Fairy's long hair helped greatly. The Fairy was *very* pretty & acted extremely well, & as if she had a real talent. Moore had been in a great stew, lest it rained, but tho' it rained a little all went well—no one there from T.C.D. except Tyrrell whose feelings were not hurt by Moores article on Mahaffy. Hyde of course acted splendidly. It was better than the Twisting of the Rope.' The actress who played the Fairy in Hyde's *The Fairy and the Tinker* on 19 May was Sinéad Ni Fhlanagáin (1878–1975), who in 1910 became the wife of Eamon de Valera (1882–1975), President of Ireland 1959–73. When she asked George Moore's advice about making the stage her career he replied, 'Height, five feet four; hair, red; name, Flanagan; no, my dear.'

[11] Robert Donovan (1862–1934), journalist and critic, wrote leaders and literary articles for the *Freeman's Journal* from 1891 to 1923. This was not the first time he had attacked WBY: in a *Nation* review of 25 May 1889 (3), he had found little 'promise of better things' in *The Wanderings of Oisin* and asserted that WBY's 'imagination will never be brighter or more active in the future'; while later in the same year he criticized WBY for printing an anti-Catholic tale in his *Stories from Carleton* (see I. 205–7). WBY was to describe him as 'a bigoted Voteen' in the *Irish Packet* of 27 Apr 1908, but the following year Donovan got the chair of English literature at University College, Dublin, instead of WBY.

[12] AG did object, and the letter was not published in the *United Irishman*; see next letter, and below, p. 191, n. 1.

To the Editor of the United Irishman,[1] *[23 May 1902]*

⟨May 23rd, 1902⟩

Dear Sir,

A writer in "The Freeman's Journal" and another in "The Independent," which did not always follow "The Freeman" with such docility,[2] have quoted a sentence from my Introduction to Lady Gregory's book to accuse me, the one of "neo-paganism", the other of trying to substitute Cuchullin for Christ.[3] I do not as a rule argue with writers in a newspaper. It is not amusing to argue with a writer who thinks, like the Freeman reviewer, that "neo-paganism" was invented by the French decadents, who were all Catholics, proud of their orthodoxy; and that I have learnt a pagan "esotericism" from William Blake, who was so fervent a Christian that his death-bed was described by an old servant as the death-bed of a great saint.[4] If I had replied in "the Freeman" or in "the Independent" I should have been answered by new inaccuracies, and new misunderstandings.[5] I would ignore this last folly, as I have ignored so many others ⟨follies of Irish criticism⟩ did not the sentence they have founded their accusation upon occur in my preface to a friend's book. I do not wish a misunderstanding to keep a book which is, I am convinced, one of the great books of our time, from coming into the hands of those for whom it was written.

[1] This letter was not published. AG wrote from Galway on 'Sunday' [25 May 1902; Berg]: 'I haven't sent yr letter on to the UI. It is good enough for it, but not good enough for you, the attack on reviewers leaves an impression of fretfulness. I will keep it. I think, if there is another edition of Cuchulain within a reasonable time, & you change that sentence, I will in my own name send a letter to Freeman etc—quoting from yours—But anything we write must show kindly dignity, not vexation—They are only untaught children—'.

[2] The *Irish Daily Independent* had been founded as a Parnellite rival to the *Freeman's Journal* after the latter's defection to the anti-Parnellites in 1891. After its purchase by William Martin Murphy in 1900 it had, however, amalgamated with the anti-Parnellite *Daily Nation* and now supported Parnell's arch-enemy, Tim Healy.

[3] See p. 184, n. 1. On 2 May Donovan had accused WBY in the *Freeman's Journal* (5) of 'literary blaspheming' and an 'affectation of neo-Paganism. The blend is anything but Irish. It is a corruption of the French decadent school, from which the virility of France has already succeeded in rescuing French literature. . . . Mr. Yeats, who sees all things through a pair of esoteric spectacles, borrowed from the Englishman Blake, has rather seriously injured the Irish revival by these attempts at a foreign grafture.' Richard Best admonished in the *Irish Daily Independent* of 12 May (2) that the 'stories must not be told with the purpose of putting Cuchulain in the place which Christ holds in the minds of the people; and we feel certain that it was not with any purpose of this kind Lady Gregory undertook her task'.

[4] In the first volume of *The Life of William Blake* Gilchrist describes (361) Blake's death on 12 Aug 1827, 'the exact moment almost unperceived by his wife, who sat by his side. A humble female neighbour, her only other companion, said afterwards: "I have been at the death, not of a man, but of a blessed angel".' WBY had also misquoted this account in his preface to *The Poems of William Blake* (li): '"The death of a saint", said a poor woman who had come in to help Mrs Blake.'

[5] See AG's comment, p. 185, n. 2.

Writers who write for a very small circle of highly cultivated readers like
A. E. and myself, can whistle at the newspapers, for our readers are not
influenced by them, but unfortunately a book of the National Stories of
Ireland, a book meant for everybody the Iliad of a people, can for a little
time be kept ⟨out of the immense popularity which has always awaited all
such books⟩ from doing its great service to the nation. I wrote "If we but
tell these stories to our children, the land will begin again to be a Holy
Land, as it was before men gave their hearts to Greece and Rome and
Judea," I no more attacked Christianity than I attacked classical learning.
Christianity is Christ and not Judea, and those who believe with John
Eglington that every country should find its own Old Testament in the
stories of its heroes,[6] or that the old woman who is filled with devout
thoughts by her prayer at the Holy Well or by some tale of Christ walking
through the streets of her own village, is less a Christian than the good
bible-reading, but nationless Protestants I was brought up among. I do not
think it anti-Christian to believe with A. E. "That though we cannot compare Cuchullin the most complete ideal of Gaelic Chivalry, with that
supreme figure whose coming to the world was the effacement of whole
Pantheons of divinities," one may yet think "that since the thoughts of
men were turned from the old ideals our literature has been filled with a
less noble life."[7] I even think that Christianity itself will lose ⟨its power⟩
something of noble life if it cannot begin again to make the hills and fields
where men work and live mysterious and holy. I would restore the spirit of
the eleventh and of the twelfth centuries which were also the centuries of
perfect faith.

　　Two English Catholic papers have reviewed Lady Gregory's book and
my preface and neither paper has misunderstood me.[8] In English papers of

[6] AG used this and óther sentences from this paragraph in a reply to Trench (Berg) vindicat-
ing WBY's Prefacé (see p. 184, n. 1). In *Pebbles from a Brook* (see p. 24, n. 6) Eglinton had
explored the relationship between heroic literature and moral progress, observing (25) that 'it is
not the least significant event of our time, this coming into the hand of each nationality of its own
Old Testament or ancient scriptures, even where as in the case of Ireland, no Moses has appeared
to dominate them with his spirit, nor Homer resolved them into epic unity. This ancient race did
not achieve morality, and perished in the wilderness; so that the higher conquests are not embodied in its literature, but still remain open to the present inhabitants of the country, to whom a
breath of its valour is transmitted in its tales and legends, as well as in the poems of Ferguson,
Yeats and others.'

[7] These words are a direct and accurate quotation from what was evidently an advance copy of
AE's review of *Cuchulain of Muirthemne* (see p. 174, n. 3), which was to appear in the *United
Irishman* on 24 May. In her letter of 17 May (see p. 184, n. 2) AG had wished 'one cd venture to
say how much dearer & more sacred Christ wd become to us if the whole fabric of the Churches
cd be swept away, leaving only the Gospel, & the unwritten traditions of the people. But we shd
be burned for that.'

[8] These were the *Tablet* and the *Catholic Times*. The notice in the *Tablet*, 3 May (697), con-
curred enthusiastically with Wilfrid Blunt's review (see p. 173) that the book was suitable 'for
"home consumption" in all senses, evading in the love passages of ruder times all that in which

any importance, all books of any note are reviewed by men who have made some study of literature, who have given some proof of good taste. In Ireland no book is too important to escape the common hacks of the newspapers. These men never have the confidence of their opinions unless they feel themselves upheld by popular prejudice and so the finest work, work as fine as Lady Gregory's great translation must be helped to its Irish readers by English enthusiasm. Irish reviewers have other things to do, they have to gather up everything that can be said against Irish books, and if possible to find some stray sentence which can be taken from its context and ⟨cried out in⟩ whispered into the ear of the bigot and the hasty thinker. Too craven to praise but in conventional & meaningless sentences, they come into their courage when ignorance cries them on.

Yours sinly,
W B Yeats

TLS Berg. [*At the top of first page in WBY's hand*] 'The Freemans Journal' 'The Independent' & Lady Gregorys book.

To Maud Gonne, [c. 23 May 1902]

Mention in letter from MG, 24 May [1902].
Sending her political details and suggesting they enlist Tynan's help;[1] informing her that Arthur Symons and his wife have invited them to dinner when she is in London; complaining about the state of his eyes and telling her that he is to visit an oculist.

G–YL, 155.

"even the sensitive Irish soul" can find cause of offence, so that we may well doubt, with Mr. Blunt, if, for general reading, there will ever be a rendering "more acceptable, more brilliant, and more popular than Lady Gregory's".' The *Catholic Times* on 9 May (3) supported WBY's 'remarkable' opinion of the book's importance as 'scarcely too strong' and praised AG for catching 'the spirit of a great legend'. Both reviews were quoted in an advertisement for the book in *Samhain* (1902).

[1] This evidently relates to some dispute within the advanced nationalist factions. Tynan is perhaps P. J. P. Tynan, a leader of the Invincibles. In her reply from Dublin MG wrote: 'Things over here don't look very bright but somehow or other they must be made to mend. I don't think Tynan would be any use. I have seen Mr O'Leary.'

To George Russell (AE), c. 23 May 1902

Mention in letter from AE, 24 May 1902.
Asking AE to pass on a letter to MG; mentioning Miss Carmichael who is on a visit to Dublin;[1] and enquiring about AE's experiments with the psaltery.[2]

MBY.

To the Editor of the Times Literary Supplement, [*before* 27 May 1902]

Sir,—Mr. Churton Collins[1] has for many years commended accurate learning and the University teaching of literature as the only certain guides to good taste. It is, therefore, interesting to know that he himself, the accuracy of whose learning is notorious, thinks Blake's lines ending "Did He who made the lamb make thee?" not only "falsetto" but, when taken from their context, "nonsense pure and absolute." When I was a boy my father was accustomed to read to me passages of verse that seemed to him and to his friends great poetry, and this very stanza was among them; and now that I have edited Blake, and thought much over every line that he wrote, I

[1] AE replied that he had passed WBY's letter (see previous letter) on to MG 'whose house is next door', and that he had met Miss Carmichael (see p. 110) at the Hermetic Society as well as entertaining her in his own home.
[2] AE said that he could not 'get the notations of chants done so that I can recognise any likeness and I don't think I would care to send them over otherwise. The whole feeling is in the semitones and if these are left out there is nothing to care about, no spirit or charm.'

[1] Arthur Symons contributed three hostile but anonymous reviews of Stephen Phillips's poems and plays to the *Athenaeum*, the *Saturday Review*, and the *Quarterly Review*, in the last of which (April 1902, 498) he asserted that 'this work is neither original as poetry nor genuine as drama'. Defending the then highly-regarded Phillips (1864–1915) against these charges in the *TLS* of 9 May (132), J. Churton Collins criticized Symons for citing lines from William Blake's 'The Tiger' as a touchstone of great poetry, and for the cloyingly hyperbolic terms in which he did so. Symons, still writing anonymously, replied on 16 May (139–40) that Collins's rejection of his Blakean touchstone revealed a 'lack of that sense by which poetry is apprehended', so provoking Collins's rejoinder on 23 May (148–9) that in their context 'Blake's verses are intelligible and excusable as the extravagant and hysterical expression of rapt enthusiasm', but that out of context 'they are mere fanfarado—nonsense pure and absolute; and the Reviewer's commentary on them is . . . as false as it is ridiculous'.
John Churton Collins (1848–1908), journalist, editor, and, from 1904, Professor of English at Birmingham, was a champion of English studies at the universities. He had made his reputation as an exacting critic in 1885 with a devastating attack on the inaccuracies in Edmund Gosse's *From Shakespeare to Pope*, but when WBY met him in Oxford in the summer of 1888, he found him (I. 92) 'a most cheerful mild pink and white little man full of the freshest unreasonablest enthusiasms'.

cannot think that cry "Did He who made the lamb make thee?" less than a cry out of the heart of all wisdom. A recent article of Mr. Churton Collins about the importance of learning as a guide to taste almost converted me to his opinion,[2] but now I return to my own opinion that many a cultivated woman without learning is more right about these matters than all the professors.

I am, Sir, your obedient servant.

W B Yeats

Printed letter, *TLS*, 30 May 1902 (157). *UP* II. 293–4.

To Lady Augusta Gregory, 27 May 1902

18. Woburn Buildings | Euston Road | W.C— May 27th 1902—

My dear Lady Gregory

I dictate this to Lily as you see, my eyes are a good deal better, but I have no glasses I am to have new glasses for distance (pince nez) & my old ones are being turned into spectacles.

What do you think of "They shall be remembered for ever" as a title for the play?

My objection to the daughter of Hoolihaun is that it is not colloquial as the whole play is written in the living speech. I feel doubtful about a literary title I am not quite certain even that the old woman herself should say "some call me the daughter of Hoolihaun" I might call the play "Hoolihauns daughter".[1]

I have no doubt you are quite right about my letter to U.I. I allowed myself to show vexation with the thought that I might do so effectively it being anothers book.[2]

I saw Symons today he came to read me a letter which he is sending to

[2] In *Ephemera Critica* (1901), a collection of essays and reviews, Collins attacked (211) 'slovenly and perfunctory work . . . plausible charlatanry and pretentious incompetence which it has so often been our unwelcome duty to expose', and urged (156) that it was 'high time that some stand should be made, some protest entered against writings which cannot fail to corrupt popular taste and to degrade the standard of popular literature'.

[1] See p. 185, n. 3. WBY was preparing *Cathleen ni Houlihan* for publication but had still not settled on the title. 'They shall be remembered for ever' is the first line of a song sung by the Poor Old Woman at the close of the play (*VPl*, 229). In her reply of 29 May, AG told him that '"The daughter of Hoolihan" is quite as colloquial as "They shall be remembered for ever", and indeed as "Hoolihan's daughter"—the natural phrase wd be "a woman of the Hoolihans" but that wd not be in the tradition. "The Poor Old Woman" in inverted commas would really be best, but you said the publishers objected.'

[2] See pp. 186, 187–9.

the Saturday Review about the Philips controversy, there has been correspondence both in the 'Saturday' & in the 'Times' about his article in the
'Quarterly'. Sydney Colville [*for* Colvin] & Churton Collins respectively
started it.[3]

I have written a short letter to the 'Times' not about Philips but about a
certain poem of Blakes which was brought in on a side wind. Symons now
thinks that the reason why the 'Atheneum' did not give him your book is
that they made up their minds to give it to a Gaelic specialist. I made
Symons promise to do an article on the book somewhere if the chance
arose—& then send [*for* sent] him my extra copy, when he came this
morning he had only had time to dip into the book, but he said 'I could see
that it is extraordinarily beautiful'.

I met Cockrell on Sunday at a house where he had just given a copy to
the hostess, someone said Wyndham 'has been talking to him about it'.[4]
Whether the book has or has not a popular success I can see that it is
already coming into a great esortoric reputation.

I am very glad to hear that Robert thought my lecture a success I was
not particularly pleased with myself. I wish I had been as good as I was at
the Pioneer club three or four days before.[5]

I am trying to block in the rough a good many things to be worked over
in the smooth while I am with you, I am a little in dread of all the reading
for Spencer, but my eyes which are already so much better but [?*for* will] I
have no doubt come all right.

Your aly
W B Yeats

Dict SMY, signed WBY; Berg, with envelope addressed to Coole, redirected to 22 Dominick
Street, Galway; postmark 'LONDON MY 28 02'.

[3] See previous letter. Since his reviews of Phillips had been published anonymously, Symons
tried to pretend that what he had written in the *Quarterly Review* notice gave independent support to his comments in the *Saturday Review*. On 10 May, however, Sidney Colvin (1845–1927),
Keeper of Prints and Drawings at the British Museum, wrote to the *Saturday Review* to expose
this duplicity since the similarity in the two reviews proved that they were by the same hand.
In his final letter to the *Saturday Review* on 31 May, Symons acknowledged his authorship, defended himself against Colvin, and called for a policy of signed reviews to prevent misunderstandings.

[4] Sydney Carlyle Cockerell (1867–1962), former secretary to William Morris and to the Kelmscott Press, was from 1900 to 1904 a partner of Emery Walker (1851–1933) in a process-engraving
firm in Clifford's Inn. Cockerell wrote in his diary for Sunday, 25 May (BL): 'Went to lunch at
Walkers to meet W B Yeats who wanted to discuss a scheme that his sisters have for setting up a
printing press in Ireland'.

Sir George Wyndham (1863–1913), Irish Chief Secretary from 1900 to 1905, was later instrumental in securing a patent for the Abbey Theatre. His attitude towards AG's books was not
always unambiguous: in March 1904 WBY recorded in Quinn's copy of *Ideals in Ireland* that a
'national school teacher & his children in Donegal presented this book to Wyndham once & he
said "they must not expect him to sympathize with that"'.   [5] See p. 188, n. 8.

To Ernest Rhys, 28 May 1902

18 Woburn Buildings, | Euston Road,
May 28th/02.

My dear Rhys,

I am dictating because my eyes are bad. Come in and see me one Monday evening, I shall be off to Ireland in two or three weeks probably. Lady Gregory's book is out & I hope that you will manage to get it to review somewhere.[1] Yorke Powell has written to her "that it is a book he has been waiting for, for years" & "an abiding joy".[2]

Yrs sny
W B Yeats

Dict AEFH, signed WBY; Kansas.

To A. H. Bullen, 3 June 1902

18 Woburn Buildings, | Euston Road.
June 3rd/02.

My dear Bullen,

Now that I think of it, I send you the name of a Breton writer (I enclose his card) to whom I want you to send a copy of the "Celtic Twilight".[1] He is a charming person & he once made some headway with a French translation of the "Countess Kathleen". He gave it up because of the difficulty of finding French equivilants for my folk phrases & mythologies.

I read some document or other which you sent to A. P. Watt and found in it something about the Celtic Twilight being out by June 1st at latest. I was in a confiding mood & said to all urgent persons, "I shall be prosperous on June 1st". I am not. And that glue has still to dry! Do you think,—

---

[1] No review of *Cuchulain of Muirthemne* by Rhys has been traced.

[2] York Powell had written fulsomely from Oxford on receipt of the book (*70 Years*, 401–2): 'It is masterly. It is really a beautiful piece of English as well as a beautiful story and subject. You have the gratitude of everybody who cares for poetry of the highest kind, and the noblest tradition of Epic story. . . . Your *Cuchulain* is an abiding joy. . . . It opened up a great world of beautiful legend, which, though accounting myself an Irishman I had never known at all.'

[1] François Jaffrennou (b. 1879), pseudonym Taldir ab Herninn, a Breton poet, playwright, and historian. He was the delegate from Brittany to the Pan Celtic Congress, where he delivered an address in Breton. The revised *Celtic Twilight* was not published until July 1902.

through A. P. Watt of course,—need I say more. I have told my amanuen-sis how you burst out to-day against the Organ-grinder, or whatever he was. That happens to be a subject which interests her, indeed she has con-siderably reduced the incomes of quite a number of organ-grinders. She asks me to say that she is getting a Society for the Prevention of Street Noises to send you circulars.

Yours sincely
W B Yeats

Dict AEFH, signed WBY, with enclosure; Texas.

To Arnold Dolmetsch, 3 June 1902

18 Woburn Buildings, | Euston Road.
June 3rd,/02.

Dear Mr Dolmetsch,

I shall have to get a chairman for my lecture on June 10th & I would sooner have you than anybody else.[1] You are the only one, I suppose, in the World now, who knows anything about the old music that was half speech, and I need hardly say, that neither Miss Farr nor myself, could have done anything in this matter of speaking to notes, without your help. Please let me know, as if you cannot be my chair-man, I shall have to look round for some irrevelant man of letters. And besides, I suppose I had bet-ter send round a paragraph.[2] I have written a reply to Symonds' note in the Academy, my reply should appear next Saturday. I hear too that some singing-teacher is writing a rejoinder from the point of view of the modern musician to my essay in the "Monthly Review".[3] I am writing a "Prayer to the Seven Archangels to bless the Seven Notes". This prayer is to be

---

[1] WBY's well-attended lecture on 'Speaking to Musical Notes' at Clifford's Inn was illustrated by FF's first public performance with the Dolmetsch psaltery. The circular announced that the 'lecture will be given in order to start a fund for the making of Psalteries for these purposes'. Dol-metsch was in the chair and provided musical explanations.

[2] A copy of the handbill advertising this lecture, which WBY had printed and widely circu-lated to the press, is preserved in AG's press-cutting album (NLI).

[3] After attending a private demonstration for critics on 15 May, Symons expressed his reserva-tions about WBY's 'mechanical method' in his article, 'The Speaking of Verse', published in the *Academy* on 31 May and reprinted in *Plays, Acting and Music* (1903). WBY's reply appeared on 7 June (see pp. 196–7), but there was no rejoinder to his essay, 'Speaking to the Psaltery', which had appeared in the May issue of the *Monthly Review* (see p. 153).

spoken first by two voices and then by one voice, then the other voice, & then two voices again.[4]

Yours sincly
W B Yeats

Dict AEFH, signed WBY; Dolmetsch. Wade, 372–3.

To Eric Maclagan, 3 June 1902

Dictated.   18 Woburn Buildings, | Euston Road,
June 3rd / 02

My dear Maclagan,

I have been for some time meaning to write and tell you how much I enjoyed my visit to Oxford,[1] and now I have another reason for writing also. I think you said you would be up in London somewhere about the 15th and I shall not be going away until about the 17th at earliest. Could you come to me on Monday the 16th, I want you to have a talk with my sister; she used to do embroidery for William Morris and wants to try her hand at some altar-cloths for Irish chapels. I told her you might be able to tell her something about ecclesiastical symbolism.[2]

I think Bullen would be ready to throw himself into that project about the 'Prophetic Books'.[3] He is an agreeable person, and a man of letters, but I daresay you might find a better publisher. A. P. Watt however has been advising me to put my books in Bullen's hands.

Yours sincerely
W B Yeats

TS copy Indiana.

---

[4] This was the working title for 'The Players ask for a Blessing on the Psalteries and on Themselves' (*VP*, 212–13), a new poem composed for the lecture-recital. A few days earlier WBY read a version of the poem to 'Michael Field', and Katharine Bradley wrote in her diary: 'Yeats reads a little prayer to the Psaltery—a most charming poem. All the Archangels appear in it with shoes of the seven metals.' See Michael Field, *Works and Days* (1933), 263.

[1] See p. 185.

[2] SMY had learned the art of embroidery from May Morris (see I. 111, 123), and was to take charge of the embroidery department of the new Dun Emer Industries, founded in 1903 by Evelyn Gleeson in the village of Dundrum, near Dublin (see p. 185, n. 7). Her first major commission was a set of banners representing Irish saints for Loughrea Cathedral.

[3] Maclagan and A. G. B. Russell jointly edited *Jerusalem* (1904) and *Milton* (1907) for *The Prophetic Books of William Blake*, published by Bullen. WBY had inscribed presentation copies in his library (*YL*, 214–15).

To John Butler Yeats, [c. *3 June 1902*]

Mention in letter from JBY, 4 June 1902.
Saying that he will be passing through Dublin; evidently discussing the
end of the Boer War;[1] and giving an account of his lecture in Oxford.[2]

MBY.

To the Editor of the Academy, [*7 June 1902*]

SIR,—Mr. Arthur Symons has said, in his friendly account of my theories
about the speaking of poetry to musical notes,[1] that the fixing of the pitch
by a notation makes "any personal interpretation good or bad impossible."
The notation of a song is much more elaborate than any notation for
speech made by Mr. Dolmetsch or Miss Farr, and yet the singer finds
room enough for "personal interpretation." Indeed, I am persuaded that
the fixing of the pitch gives more delicacy and beauty to the "personal
interpretation," for it leaves the speaker free to preoccupy himself with the
subtlest modulations. Before we recorded pitch we made many experiments in rhythmical speech, and I found that Miss Farr would speak a
poem with admirable expression and then speak it quite ineffectively time
after time. She found it impossible to recall her moment of inspiration; but
now, though she varies, she does so within a far narrower range. Her best
inspirations are at least as good as they were, while her failures never sink
into disorder.

If Mr. Symons will borrow one of my psalteries and speak one of his
own poems to a notation of his own, he will find—for I think his ear is
good enough to speak to the notes without giving them too much attention—that he will light on all kinds of beautiful or dramatic modulations
which would never have occurred to him had not the cruder effects been
fixed by the notation. He will discover, too, that the right changes of pitch
can seldom be got at once, and that once got they will seem so important
that even the best recitation without fixed notes will generally show itself
for mere disorder. Everything in any art that can be recorded and taught

---

[1] The Boer War had ended on 31 May 1902 on terms which put an end to the independence of
the Boer Republics, but which left them with significant real and potential control over their own
affairs. JBY wrote that the 'peace is a great satisfaction. It is not merely that England has been
humiliated, but the cause of nationality has been served all over the world—& moreover, a great
people *the Boers have been born*—but for England they would never have discovered themselves.'
[2] In his letter of 4 June (MBY) JBY asked WBY if he had noticed 'when at Oxford the look of
the undergraduates there, how did they compare with ours?'

[1] See p. 194, n. 3.

should be recorded and taught, for by doing so we take a burden from the imagination, which climbs higher in light armour than in heavy. If Mr. Symons will then make an extremely simple tune, like the very simplest folk-music, and record it and speak his poem to this tune, he will find, I think, that this new art is also an extremely old one, and that it is probable that we should sometimes speak an old folk song instead of singing it, as we understand singing. I have heard Irish country-women, whose singing is called "traditional Irish singing," speak their little songs precisely as Miss Farr does some of hers, only with rather less drama. The tune must be very simple, for if there are more than a few notes the one tune will not adopt itself to the emotions of different verses. Is it not possible that we have been mistaken in considering this kind of little tunes merely as undeveloped music? It might have been wiser to have sometimes thought of them as the art of regulated speech, already perhaps near its decadence. I imagine men spoke their verses first to a regulated pitch without a tune, and then, eager for variety, spoke to tunes which gradually became themselves the chief preoccupation until speech died out in music.

From time to time indeed musicians have tried to give speech some importance, but music has always been their chief preoccupation and their "recitative" has got its variety from the accompaniment and not from the rhythm of the verse. If the speaker to musical notes will attend to the subtleties of rhythm as carefully as a singer attends to the musical inventions of the composer, his speech will not "drift" into "intoning." It was said that "the song of Rachel" degenerated into "sing song" with the rest of her company, but that did not prove that her method of speaking verse was wrong.[2] But after all, if I am right in claiming antiquity for this art of speaking to musical notes, discussion of its merits is idle. No art can pass away for ever, till the human nature it once delighted has passed away, and that can hardly be until Michael's trumpet.

Yours truly
W B Yeats

Printed letter, *Academy*, 7 June 1902 (590–1). Wade 373–4.

---

[2] Mademoiselle Rachel, stage name of Elisa Félix (1820–58), a statuesque tragedienne famous for her acting in French classical drama, particularly Racine's *Phèdre*. She was known for the penetrating quality of her melodious voice, described by Théophile Gautier (*Works* III [1901], 333): 'Her grave, deep, vibrating voice, so seldom rising loud or breaking into cries, well suited her self-contained, sovereignly calm acting.' Charlotte Brontë bears witness to the power of her acting in *Villette*, and her death is the theme of Matthew Arnold's 'Rachel' (1867): 'In her, like us, there clash'd contending powers, / Germany, France, Christ, Moses, Athens, Rome. / The strife, the mixture in her soul, are ours; / Her genius and her glory are her own.' Frank Fay had told WBY on 23 July 1901 (Private) that 'Rachel, until she became careless, seems to have been very careful to preserve the music of verse'.

To Lady Augusta Gregory, 9 June 1902

18 Woburn Buildings, | Euston Road. | W. C.
June 9ᵗʰ,/02.

My dear Lady Gregory,

You see I am dictating this. My eyes have not been quite as well during the last couple of days owing I think to a cold & I want to write to you at once about Althea Gyles. The M*rs* Kennedy who wrote to you is the lady that the notice speaks of; she has been paying £3 a week for Althea Gyles during the last year, I suppose as well as paying her debts. Althea Gyles has now left the Hydropathic having been the occasion of a "row" of some sort, she is evidently highly hysterical but her lungs have at any rate for the time being been cured. I must say that she fills me with despair, she hardly seems to me sane. She all but turned me out three times, the last time I was round, because I would not take up her quarrel about the Hydropathic.[1]

I believe that a friend of hers will take charge of her in July & that after that she can go to Conn Gore Booth (that was)[2] who may possibly bring

---

[1] On 6 June 1902 AG had written (Berg) to ask WBY if he knew anything of a communication she had received evidently asking for money for Althea Gyles (see p. 141), and 'if Althea is really in want, or what has happened? I could not give much, but would give a little if really needed.' Althea Gyles (1867–1949) came from a long-established family in Kilmurry, Co. Waterford, and was related to the Greys of Northumberland, who had paid her expenses at the Slade Art School. She had been in declining health for the past two years, and was possibly suffering from consumption, but her family, outraged by her Bohemian life-style, were reluctant to help her financially. Mrs Florence Kennedy, née Laing, a genre painter and Cecil French's aunt, was one of several patrons whom Miss Gyles was passed among, including Arthur Symons, who wrote to WBY on 5 Aug 1902 (MBY) that he had just seen 'Althea Gyles . . . she was irate with you, quite fat, with romantic tales of her night escape from a terrible sanatorium. Next day I met the lady *from whom* she had escaped. . . . She fixed me with a stern eye & said "I hope you are not taken in by Miss Gyles?"' Althea Gyles' 'Hydropathic' was the Bournemouth Hydropathic Establishment, in Durley Gardens on the West Cliff of the south coast resort of Bournemouth, which offered 'the water cure', treating diseases internally and externally with copious amounts of water, including Turkish, Electric, Hot Sea-Water, Russian, and other baths, at an inclusive weekly charge of 45*s*. The Resident Physician was W. Johnson Smyth, MD. Despite her irritation with WBY, Miss Gyles wrote him a cheerful letter (MBY) from a sanitorium at Stoke-by-Nayland in Suffolk: 'You will be surprised to hear from me. . . . I have got into quite comfortable quarters at last a Consumptive Sanatorium. The stuffing of food is beyond words but I have met with one or two nice creatures, quite different to Bournemouth.'

[2] Constance Gore-Booth (1868–1927), now the Countess Markiewicz, artist, suffragette, nationalist, and politician, was the daughter of Sir Henry Gore-Booth of Lissadell, Sligo (see 1. 418–9), and an old friend of Althea Gyles, with whom she had studied art at the Slade School in the early 1890s. In 1897 she went to Julian's Académie in Paris, to study under Jean-Paul Laurens, and met a Polish artist, Casimir Dunin, Count de Markiewicz (1874–1932), whom she married as his second wife in September 1900. They had recently settled in Dublin, where they were to play a vigorous part in artistic and theatrical circles. She became involved in Sinn Fein politics, was sentenced to death for her part in the Easter Rising of 1916, but reprieved—events recorded in WBY's poem, 'On a Political Prisoner' (*VP*, 397)—and was later a member of the first Dáil

her to Ireland where one can only hope she will somehow drift into the hands of her family who seem loath to do their duty in the matter. I doubt since I have seen Althea, if she will be able to work, at least to work enough to ever make her living. Her mind seems to me too unbalanced. She is absorbed in a feeling of indignation against everybody & everything. I could do nothing on Friday but repeat to her what Hume said about Rousseau "If Jean Jacques were in the right, too many people would be in the wrong."[3] (I think at this point she practically did turn me out.) I [shall] probably be with you about the 20.th as I think that you said that date would do. I am bringing a psaltery with me to Ireland & may stay a couple of days in Dublin to make some experiments with it with Russell. Every ticket is sold for my lecture to-morrow night and Archer has a long and laudatory article on the whole thing in the "Leader".[4] Dolmetsch is doing some little lilts for one or two of my poems, (lilts like that M*rs* Emery does the "Hymn of Pan" to.)[5] I am putting my essays together for Bullen.

Yours always
W B Yeats

P.S.
I have left the circular[6] at home—M*rs* Kennedy's address is—

    9 Cresswell Gardens,
        South Kensington.

Dict AEFH, signed WBY; Berg, with envelope addressed to Coole, postmark 'LONDON JU 9 02'.

Éireann and a cabinet minister. WBY's elegy for her and her sister, Eva Gore-Booth, 'In Memory of Eva Gore-Booth and Con Markiewicz' (*VP*, 475–6), was written shortly after her death.
    [3] Although this remark is not recorded in the letters, autobiography, or biographies of the Scottish philosopher David Hume (1711–76), he might well have made it. He befriended Jean-Jacques Rousseau (1712–78) in 1765, brought him to England in 1766, and went to considerable trouble to arrange a suitable residence and a royal pension for him. Rousseau's response was to accuse Hume of conspiring against him, and in June 1766 he sent him a long paranoid letter, denouncing his supposed duplicity. Flabbergasted, Hume wrote to a friend that Rousseau was 'very mad or very wicked or . . . both', and published a pamphlet in Paris and London giving his side of the quarrel.
    [4] Archer's detailed account of the private demonstration, 'Sing-Songing and Song-Singing', published in the *Morning Leader*, 7 June 1902 (4), had concluded that 'in this system of "lilting" Miss Farr, or Mr. Yeats, has hit on something very like a new art'.
    [5] The notation for FF's lilting of Shelley's 'Hymn of Pan' is printed in her *The Music of Speech* (1909), p. 23.
    [6] The circular on behalf of Althea Gyles (see above, n. 1). Mrs Florence Kennedy, a member ('Volo') of the GD, was the widow of Edward Sherard Kennedy, who had also been a genre painter. She exhibited from 1880 to 1893, and had shown four works at the Royal Academy, including 'Thinking it Over' and 'Love Me, Love My Dog'.

To Allan Wade,[1] *12 June 1902*

18 Woburn Buildings, | Euston Road.
June 12<u>th</u>,/02.

Dear Mr Wade,
I am very sorry that you missed my lecture which I think was successful. I am going to Ireland immediately, but I hope to repeat the lecture when I return as many people were unable to get in.

Yrs sincerely
W B Yeats

Dict AEFH, signed WBY; Indiana.

To Lady Augusta Gregory, 13 June 1902[1]

18, Woburn Buildings,
June 13th, 1902

My dear Lady Gregory
I propose to leave London on the evening of the 19th. I am waiting to see Maeterlinck's play "Monna Vanna" which is to be done by his French company. I am less anxious to see the play than to see the method of the performance.[2] My lecture was a great success. People were standing up and many could not get in. We sold £22 worth of tickets and if we had had the courage to take a big hall could have sold many more. We have spent the money on new psalteries[3] and on charming dresses for our troubadours to speak in. Dolmetsch is now making little tunes for my Wandering Aengus and some of my other things to be spoken to. I am taking two psalteries

---

[1] Allan Wade (1881–1955), editor and bibliographer, had even at this early date begun 'putting into an old note-book a list of all the writings of Mr. Yeats that I knew, and adding others from time to time, as chance led me to find them in newspapers or periodicals' (*CW*, VIII. 198). His first bibliography of WBY's works was published in 1908, and his compendious and well-organized *A Bibliography of the Writings of W. B. Yeats* in 1951. His edition of *The Letters of W. B. Yeats* appeared in 1954.

[1] WBY's thirty-seventh birthday.

[2] Maeterlinck's *Monna Vanna* (1902), which had been refused a licence by the Lord Chamberlain, was brought to the Victoria Hall, London, by Lugné Poë's company for private performances under the auspices of the Stage Society from 19 to 21 June. After seeing the performance on 21 June, Charles Ricketts wrote in his diary (*SP*, 78) of his 'painful surprise' that 'the hall was only half full, and filled by undistinguished people, among whom were many foreigners'.

[3] See p. 181.

to Dublin and think of leaving one with Russell. I am also bringing my model theatre[4] and have a plan of giving two lectures in the autumn. One on a simpler theatre, and one on the speaking of verse to notes. Perhaps I might get Mrs. Emery to come over for this lecture.[5] I have been trying to let my rooms and will know to-day whether I have succeeded. I am letting them for very little to Sturge Moore's sister. Merely for my rent, and for enough over to pay wear and tear.[6] She will be better pleased if she gets them till the end of November so I think of remaining on after the play which will be the last week of October and of giving these two lectures to fill up the time. I have almost finished a first draft of that little play I told you of "The Fool and the Wise Man".[7] And I hope they will do it with "Kathleen ny Hoolihan" in October. Gordon Craig is greatly delighted with the Scenario which I read him he wants to show the play to Irving but my belief in the commercial theatre liking such a thing is but slight. What is more to the point is that he is very anxious to stage some of my things himself, and so far as I can make out there is a possibility of his mother[8] taking part in the venture. But for divination I should believe that something will come of it. I shall stay a couple of days in Dublin and then would like to go on to Galway.

---

[4] See p. 185, n. 6. Gordon Craig had built WBY a miniature stage, for which Sturge Moore designed additional symbolic scenes.

[5] FF was to go over for Samhain week, 27 Oct–1 Nov 1902. On 27 Oct she and WBY were part of an opening night programme in the Antient Concert Rooms which included Irish music, dance, and recitation, and at which she chanted three lyrics after a brief introduction by WBY. On the afternoon of 1 Nov they gave their full-length lecture, 'Speaking to Musical Notes'. WBY apparently did not make use of Craig's model theatre in Dublin until his lecture, 'The Reform of the Theatre', on 14 Mar 1903.

[6] It was AG who had suggested on 30 May 1902 (Berg) that he should let his rooms now that they were 'more comfortable . . . . it would make a great deal of difference if instead of having the drain of Mrs Old going on, you were free of it & had a little in hand at the end, for of course you would charge more than you pay, as you have furnished the rooms.' Sturge Moore wanted temporary accommodation for his younger sister, Helen ('Nellie') Moore (1874–1919), a doctor, who had recently returned to London from a job in Newcastle Infirmary, and who in 1905 was to become a medical missionary in India. She moved into Woburn Buildings later in the month with her friend, a Miss Roberts. As Sylvia Legge recounts (*Affectionate Cousins*, 204), their tenancy was not entirely comfortable for 'Miss Roberts was at once bitten by a bed bug. Mrs Old . . . was most indignant and insisted that Miss Roberts must have brought it with her "but she thoroughly searched the room and parafinned the bed and used Keatings with a lavish hand and Miss Roberts had a quiet night, though Nellie was not sure whether she had been bitten".' Mrs Old had almost certainly calumnied Miss Roberts since WBY told Sturge Moore that he had caught a bed bug in his room and kept it under a wine glass for Mrs Old to see before she could be persuaded to take action.

[7] *The Hour-Glass*; see p. 174.

[8] Craig's famous mother, Ellen Alice Terry (1847–1928), first appeared on the stage at the age of nine, and made her name from 1878 as Henry Irving's leading lady at the Lyceum Theatre, a partnership which had only recently come to an end. She did subsequently form a company with her son, staging Ibsen's *The Vikings* at the Imperial Theatre in April 1903 and *Much Ado* in May. Both productions lost money and the association foundered.

[Remainder of letter in WBY's hand]
    I am sorry to say I am desperately hard up. I have paid my rent & everything up to date except type writing, but unless Elkin Matthews to whom I have written owes me something I shall get away with difficulty.

Yrs snry
W B Yeats

TLS Berg, with envelope addressed to Coole, postmark 'LONDON', date indecipherable. Wade, 375–6.

To George Russell (AE), [c. *13 June 1902*]

Mention in letter from AE, 16 June 1902.
Telling AE that he would be in Dublin on 19 June; enquiring about a place to stay there; and discussing chanting and the psaltery.

MBY.

To Lady Augusta Gregory, 16 June [*1902*]

18, Woburn Buildings | Euston Road
June 16th

My dear Lady Gregory,
    Many thanks. I am just up from Wilford Blount's where I was from Saturday to Monday. It was a very pleasant party. The younger Lytton and his wife, Alfred Douglas and his wife and Cockerell, whom I have got to like very much.[1] He is full of enthusiasm about you and your book, but these things can wait. Blount is quite bent on the Cuchullin play and proposes to take "the only jealousy of Emer" for his subject, which would fit into our plan very well. I shall have to find out in Dublin however whether

---

[1] Blunt held a 'Poets' Party' at his home in Sussex, apparently to celebrate WBY's thirty-seventh birthday. Neville Stephen Lytton (1879–1951), an artist, was the grandson of the novelist Edward George Bulwer-Lytton (1803–73) and the son of Edward Robert Bulwer Lytton (1831–91), Viceroy of India. Lytton had married Blunt's daughter, Judith Anne, in 1899. Lord Alfred Bruce 'Bosie' Douglas (1870–1945), poet, editor, and former friend of Oscar Wilde, had recently eloped with a poetess, Olive Eleanor Custance (1874–1944). They were joined at the party by Edward Marsh (1872–1953). On 15 June Cockerell wrote in his diary (BL): 'Yeats, Alfred Douglas and I sat on again till midnight discussing poetry and philosophy. A very memorable day.'

the young men will let an Englishman write for them. I did not tell Blount that I had any doubt on the matter but told him that I would write precise dates etc. in a couple of weeks.[2] I enclose a copy of verses. They are a prayer for blessings upon the Psaltery, and were spoken at my lecture the other night. I don't think the last two or three lines are quite right yet. C/o George Russell will be my best address in Dublin,[3] I shall have several little matters to look into. I have been suggested as one of three directors for the "U.I." under new management. I have refused (all this is private) as I considered I could not make myself responsible for their attitude towards the Irish members.[4] To my surprise my name was put forward as one that would be satisfactory to the extreme element. They would have found me anything but satisfactory but I am pleased at the compliment. As I am seeing you so shortly this letter is a mere piece of idleness.

Yours snly
W B Yeats

P.S. I enclose a letter from a man of the University of Pennsylvania. It has just come. Keep it for me, as I have not yet answered it. I wish the good man would stay at home and not follow my tracks in that way. He sends me a copy of the College Magazine with an essay by him on De Vere. I can just recall having had letters from him before but cannot in the least remember what they were about or how many of them I answered. He may be one of the people who wrote for lists of Irish writers, but I am not certain.[5]

TLS Berg, with envelope addressed to Coole, postmark indecipherable. Partly in Wade, 376.

[2] In his diary entry for 15 June, during WBY's visit to Newbuildings, Blunt wrote (28) that he was 'trying to dramatize one of the Cuchulain episodes for Yeats to bring out next year in his Cuchulain cycle of plays at Dublin'. Blunt's play, *Fand*, based on the same legend as WBY's *Only Jealousy of Emer*, was not produced until 20 Apr 1907, but this was because of Blunt's delay, not Dublin opposition. In her 17 June reply to this letter (Berg) AG admonished WBY: 'Don't let those Dublin youngsters be silly about Blunt's play. They can make rule that only Englishmen who have been in prison for Ireland are eligible to write.'

[3] Russell lived at 35 Coulson Avenue, Rathgar, a suburb in south Dublin, but in fact WBY stayed with George Moore.

[4] This reorganization did not take place until 31 Aug of the following year when a 'United Irishman' Publishing Company was formed, with six unpaid directors: Griffith, John O'Leary, MG, Thomas Kelly, Henry Dixon, and Seumas Macmanus. The major restructuring was to take place in 1906 when the paper was retitled *Sinn Féin* to make clearer its association with the Sinn Fein Party. The *United Irishman* was contemptuous of the Irish Parliamentary Party and lost no opportunity of accusing its members of self-seeking, veniality, and incompetence.

[5] Though WBY is evidently thinking of Cornelius Weygandt at the University of Pennsylvania (see p. 100), the article on 'Aubrey de Vere' in *The Alumni Register* for May 1902 was actually by Walter George Smith (1854–1924), Catholic philanthropist and trustee of the University. Weygandt probably wrote the appended editorial note, which quotes WBY's comments on de Vere.

To William Archer,[1] *18 June 1902*

18 Woburn Buildings, | Euston Road.
June 18th,/02.

Dear M*r* Archer,

I have been meaning for some few days to write and thank you for your most understanding article about "Speaking to Musical Notes". In the article itself you suggested my writing to the Morning Leader but really I had nothing to correct except what you said about my desire to apply the method to Shakespearean verse. I would have written to say that I had not thought of this but it hardly seemed worth writing for so little reason, and owing to the state of my eyes I have to wait for an amenuensis before I write. I failed to find one on Saturday. Your article has had quite a number of little echoes and has given us a great lift. I have been round at Dolmetsch's this evening and have found to my very great surprise that I have made the poems of mine which have most "folk" feeling, to actual little tunes, much like those A. E. writes to. What is most astonishing of all my little tune, "The Song of the Old Mother" is in the Irish gaped scale.[2]

Yours sncy
W B Yeats

Dict AEFH, signed WBY; BL.

---

[1] William Archer (1856–1924), the influential drama critic and translator of Ibsen, had contributed an informed article on WBY's theories of speaking verse to the *Morning Leader* on 7 June (see p. 199, n. 4). While sympathetic to WBY's ideas, he thought them inappropriate to blank verse: 'His system of ultra-rhythmical recitation (to describe it in the most general terms possible) seems to me wholly unadapted to blank verse drama. For the choruses of Greek tragedies, and lyric passages in the dialogue, it is exactly fitted; but for Shakespearean drama—no! True, I would far rather hear Shakespeare's verse chanted than have it (as is so often the case) reduced to clumsy and jerky prose. But the true art of Shakespearean delivery is to bring out the verse without for a moment trespassing upon the domain of song.' WBY did not take up the suggestion that he should write to the *Morning Leader*.

[2] Dolmetsch's notation of WBY's reading of 'The Song of the Old Mother' and 'The Song of Wandering Aengus', together with his notation of A. H. Bullen's reading of 'The Host of the Air', were printed in *CW*, III, and appended to 'Speaking to the Psaltery' in *Essays* (1924) and subsequent reprintings. The Irish 'gapped scale' was a pentatonic structure usually containing two intervals greater than a whole tone; those used to the heptatonic (seven-note) scale erroneously supposed that two notes were missing, and invented the misleading term 'gapped scale' to describe this mode.

To A. H. Bullen, 19 June 1902

18 Woburn Buildings, | Euston Road.
June 19th,/02.

My dear Bullen,

Please send presentation copies of the "Celtic Twilight" to—

Monsieur Jaffrennou[1]

71^e Regiment d'Infantrie,

8^e Compagnie

Saint-Brieuc

Bretagne

France.

and to　Mrs Clay[2]

28 Hyde Park Gate,

S. W.

I will send you more manuscript for the book of essays from Lady Gregorys where I shall be after next Monday. My address will be

Coole Park,

Gort,

Co. Galway

Ireland.

Please send my copies of the Celtic Twilight there.

Yrs sny
W B Yeats

Dict AEFH, signed WBY; Texas.

---

[1] See p. 193.

[2] Mrs May Gonne Bertie-Clay (1863–1928), a cousin of MG, had married N. S. Bertie-Clay, an English civil servant in the Indian Service, on 29 May of this year. She trained as a nurse and frequently cared for MG when she was ill, became guardian of Iseult when MG married John MacBride, and later shared MG's house near Calvados in Normandy. In early August 1902 MG wrote to WBY (*G–YL*, 157) that Mrs Clay 'got Celtic Twilight & wondered if it was for her or for me. She was afraid to write to thank you as she thought perhaps the book was *not* for her.'

To W. T. Horton, 19 June 1902

18 Woburn Buildings, | Euston Road,
June 19ᵗʰ,/02.

Dear Horton,

Here are two of the "Lights" which you lent me. I am afraid I have bundled out of sight for the moment the pamphlet,[1] but I will let you have it when I return. You see that Miss Horniman is letting me dictate some letters to her as my eyes are still very much out of sorts.

Yours sny
W B Yeats

Dict AEFH, signed WBY; Texas.

To William Angus Knight,[1] 19 June 1902

18 Woburn Buildings, | Euston Road.
June 19ᵗʰ/02.

Dear Sir,

I have found a letter of yours among a pile of my papers, I fear that it was never answered. I have done little but dramatic work lately & have therefore nothing by me that would suit your book. But considering that I am nothing of an Imperialist & very much of an Irish "extremist" I am afraid that in any case I could not take part in your venture.[2] I will neither

---

[1] WBY had probably asked Horton, a subscriber and contributor in 1902, for the back issues of *Light* (1881–1936), 'A Journal of Psychical, Occult, and Mystical Research', containing correspondence from MacGregor Mathers and other members of the GD about the Horos case (see p. 14, n. 2), which had come to trial in December 1901. On 11 Jan 1902 the paper published Mathers's account of their fraud, and on 18 Jan 'Resurgam' (i.e. Dr Edward Berridge; see p. 43, n. 2) wrote (36) that they had been punished by occult means, the Chiefs of the Order having sent out paralysing currents against Mrs Horus. He was answered on 1 Feb by 'Verité Sans Peur', who deplored his flaunting of occult powers. On 22 Feb 'Resurgam' replied (95) that occult power was not malignant or cruel, and discussed the organization of the GD. The pamphlet to which WBY refers was probably on an occult topic and also borrowed from Horton, but may have been *Is the Order of R.R. & A.C. to Remain a Magical Order?* (1901), which Horton would have been interested to see, although he had been a member of the Order for only a few months in 1896.

[1] William Angus Knight (1836–1916), Professor of Moral Philosophy at the University of St Andrews from 1876 to 1902, published extensively on literature and ethics, and was a renowned expert on Wordsworth. He had been one of Edward Dowden's rivals for the chair of English at Glasgow University in July 1889, a contest that WBY had viewed with some relish (see I. 175).

[2] Knight had evidently asked WBY to contribute to his anthology of 19th-century British and American poets, *Pro Patria et Regina* (Glasgow), which had been published in October 1901, and which was dedicated to Queen Alexandra. Knight explained in his Preface (p. vii) that the idea for the book came to him after 'reading the remarkable letter of her Royal Highness the Princess of Wales, now Queen of England,—written on the first day of January, 1901, and appealing for fresh

mix myself up with English royalties nor "English Soldiers & Sailors" with whom the Princess as you say, "is so much interested."

Yrs snly
W B Yeats

Dict AEFH, signed WBY; Pierpont Morgan.

To the Editor of The Times, *20 June 1902*

Sir,

Three matinées of Maurice Maeterlinck's new play, "Monna Vanna", first produced on the 17th. May at the Nouveau Théâtre, Paris, and since played at the Théâtre de la Monnaie, Brussels, have been announced to be given, in French, at the Great Queen Street Theatre, by the original company of the Théâtre de l'Œuvre. The play having been submitted in the usual way to the Lord Chamberlain, the King's Reader of Plays has announced his "irrevocable" decision not to recommend it for license. The play has been published by the Librairie Charpentier, and is now on sale in London. The name of Maurice Maeterlinck, and the singular nobility of his attitude towards moral questions and questions of conduct, are too well known to need more than mention. We, the undersigned, are of opinion that some protest should be made against a decision of the Censorship by which the representation, in French, of a play by a distinguished French writer, of the highest moral reputation, has been forbidden in England.[1]

We are, Sir, Your obedient Servants,

Arthur Symons
W B Yeats

TLS Yale. Published with slight changes in *The Times*, 20 June 1902 (7), where it was also signed by William Archer, Pearl Mary Teresa Craigie (John Oliver Hobbes), Richard Garnett, Thomas Hardy, Frederic Harrison, Mary St. Leger Harrison (Lucas Malet), Maurice Hewlett, Henry Arthur Jones, George Meredith, Algernon Charles Swinburne, and Laurence Alma-Tadema.[2]

contributions in aid of her Soldiers' and Sailors' Fund'. He was particularly pleased by the contributions from the American writers, which showed (p. ix) 'that in this, as in much larger matters, the two great branches of the Anglo-Saxon race have shewn a common interest in what is "true, and beautiful, and good".'

[1] Symons, who actually drafted this letter, told Edward Martyn on 21 June (Princeton): 'I wrote the letter and Miss Alma Tadema and I sent it round, and we got Swinburne, Meredith, Hardy, etc. to sign a protest. It is the most crazy thing the Censor has yet done.' The play explores the relationship of love to conventions of duty and honour through a plot which requires a wife to save Pisa by spending the night with the commander of a besieging Florentine army. He turns out to be a man of magnanimity, who has adored her from childhood and who respects her honour. They return to the relieved Pisa, but confronted with the suspicions and jealousies of her

To Lady Augusta Gregory, 20 June [1902]

18, Woburn Buildings
June 20th.

My dear Lady Gregory,
  I start for Ireland to-morrow morning, and will stay at George Moore's.
I shall go down to you by the 9.15 train on Monday.

Yours snry
W B Yeats

TLS Berg, with envelope addressed to Coole, postmark 'LONDON JU 20 02'.

To the Editor of The Times, 24 June 1902

Dublin, June 24.

Sir,—We have just returned from a visit to the Hill of Tara, where we
found that the work of destruction, abandoned a year or two ago, has
begun again.[1] Labourers are employed to dig through the mounds and

husband, she realizes the superiority of her admirer's love, and arranges to share it with him. In
'The Question of Censorship', published in the *Academy* of 28 June 1902, Symons continued the
protest, asking (22) whether it was 'merely Mr. Redford who is made ridiculous by this ridiculous
episode, or is it not, after all, England, which has given us the liberty of the press and withheld
from us the liberty of the stage?' George Alexander Redford (d. 1916), a former bank manager,
had been appointed Examiner of Plays in 1875, and was to remain censor until 1911. *The Times*
observed that 'any tinge of literary merit seems at once to excite his worst suspicions', and the
drama critic of the *Tatler* suggested (2 July 1902, p. 25) that the new king should celebrate his
coronation by abolishing the censor, since Redford's 'veto on Maeterlinck's *Monna Vanna* shows
the preposterousness of censorship. When I recall the crapulous farces which I have sat out and
think of Maeterlinck's drama, which is as the driven snow in comparison, I am simply lost in
wonder that an anachronism like the dramatic censorship should be allowed at the beginning of
the twentieth century.' Nevertheless, stage censorship was not abolished in Britain until 1968,
although *Monna Vanna* was finally granted a licence in July 1914.
  [2] For William Archer and Arthur Symons see pp. 204, 5. Pearl Mary Teresa Craigie
(1867–1906) was born in Boston, and wrote novels and plays under the name 'John Oliver
Hobbes'; Richard Garnett (1835–1906), poet and man of letters, was Keeper of Printed
Books at the British Museum from 1890 to 1899, and was the father of WBY's friend, Edward
Garnett; Thomas Hardy (1840–1928), the novelist and poet; Frederic Harrison (1831–1923), the
positivist philosopher, jurist, historian, and literary critic; Mary St Leger Harrison (1852–1931),
the daughter of Charles Kingsley, wrote novels under the name 'Lucas Malet'; Maurice Henry
Hewlett (1861–1923), novelist, essayist, and poet; Henry Arthur Jones (1851–1929), the popular
dramatist; George Meredith (1828–1909), the novelist; Algernon Charles Swinburne (1837–1909),
the poet; Laurence Alma-Tadema (1864–1940), who helped Symons organize this protest (see n.
1), the daughter of the painter Sir Lawrence Alma-Tadema, wrote novels, poems, and plays, and
had published translations of Maeterlinck's *Pelléas and Mélisande* and *Les Aveugles* in 1895.
  [1] In May 1899 an Englishman named Groome persuaded Gustavus V. Briscoe, the owner of

ditches that mark the site of the ancient Royal duns and houses. We saw them digging and shovelling without any supervision, hopelessly mixing the different layers of earth and altering the contour of the hill.

This is not being done through any antiquarian zeal, but, apparently, that the sect which believes the English to be descended from the Ten Tribes may find the Ark of the Covenant.

We are assured that the Commissioners of Public Works in Ireland can do nothing in this case, for by the Ancient Monuments Protection Act of 1882 they can only interfere when the "owner" has himself "constituted" them "the guardians of such monument."

All we can do under the circumstances is to draw the attention of the public to this desecration. Tara is, because of its associations, probably the most consecrated spot in Ireland, and its destruction will leave many bitter memories behind it.

We are, Sir, yours truly
Douglas Hyde, LL.D.
George Moore
W B Yeats

Printed letter, *The Times*, 27 June 1902 (11). *UP* II. 294–5.

To F. J. Fay, [25 June 1902]

COOLE PARK, | GORT, | CO. GALWAY.
Wednesday

My Dear Fay,
   I have only just arrived here, and am very anxious to apologise to you

---

the land on which Tara was sited, to let him make a search for the Ark of the Covenant. As the Revd John Healy explained in 'The Excavations at Tara' in the Dublin *Daily Express* of 21 Aug 1899: 'It has been generally assumed that he was an adherent of the Anglo-Israelite theory, which professes to have found in the inhabitants of these islands the lost tribes of Israel. . . . Such, however, is not the case. The only thing that Mr. Groom [*sic*] has in common with the Anglo-Israelites is that [he] believes that the Ark of the Covenant is concealed somewhere on the historic hill. How he arrived at this conclusion, it is hard for ordinary mortals to understand, but the data on which he worked are certainly not the same as those which have led the Anglo-Israelites to the same conclusion. . . . An extraordinary coincidence now occurred. A gentleman living in Scotland—an Anglo-Israelite—being quite ignorant of what was going on, dreamt that the Ark was actually found; and on the strength of that dream journeyed all the way to Tara, and arrived in time to find the excavations in progress.' The Board of Public Works banned the excavations, but Briscoe appealed under the Ancient Monuments Protection Act, had the ban lifted, and proceeded to make the diggings wider and deeper. The work was abandoned temporarily in 1900, but resumed in June 1902. The desecration is mentioned in WBY's poem, 'In the Seven Woods', written at Coole in August 1902: 'I have forgot awhile / Tara uprooted' (*VP*, 198). Tara was the seat of the Irish High Kings from *c.*200 to 565.

for having failed to keep my appointment with you either for Monday or Tuesday evening. Griffith will have explained to you about Monday. Though the Teampair business would as it turned out have kept me in Dublin in any case,[1] I did actually arrange the thing on purpose to go to your rehearsal.[2] I was both vexed & disappointed to find that Mr Moore had arranged a dinner party at which he expected me to be present. And being his guest I could not insist on going to you instead as I should have much preferred doing. I should have especially liked to know how you were getting on with the Psaltery.[3] I think you would do better to begin with "regulated declamation" rather than with the lilts. I am dictating this to save my eyes.

Yours sinly
W B Yeats

Dict. AG, signed WBY; Private, with envelope [NLI] addressed to 12 Ormond Road, Rathmines, postmark 'ORANMORE 27 JU 02'.

To A. H. Bullen, 27 June [*1902*]

COOLE PARK, | GORT, | CO. GALWAY.
June 27

Dear Bullen

I send you a lot more of the book of essays, everything indeed except two essays that are not yet finished—& the essay on 'The Happiest of the Poets'—& the Editor of the Fortnightly will I have no doubt lend you my M.S. of this, for I am sorry to say I have not a copy—[1]

I have written to 'The Speaker' to send you the copy containing 'The Way of Wisdom' a short essay.[2] I daresay it will reach you at the same time

---

[1] i.e. the dispute over the diggings at Tara. Tara was known as 'Teamair', the Irish for a conspicuous hill or acropolis.

[2] Fay's Company was rehearsing Cousin's *The Racing Lug* (see p. 174, n. 7), and his *Sleep of the King*.

[3] Frank Fay evidently continued experiments with the psaltery through the autumn, but remained unconvinced of its value. On 8 Nov of this year he was to publish a polite but non-committal review of WBY's and FF's lecture on the subject in the *United Irishman* and he told WBY in a letter of 15 Dec 1902 (NLI) that although he was experimenting with quarter tones and using the psaltery, he was dubious about it.

[1] The essay did not appear in the *Fortnightly Review* until March 1903, just prior to the publication of *IGE*.

[2] 'The Way of Wisdom', first published in the *Speaker* on 14 Apr 1900, was excluded from the collection. An account of the effect on WBY of Mohini Chatterji's 1885 visit to Dublin, it was later revised, retitled 'The Pathway', and included in *CW*, VIII.

with the copy I send. There are a few misprints which I will correct in proof—

I have had to borrow a copy of Hortons book, & of 'Beltaine', (2 numbers) from Lady Gregory containing essays, these I must beg you to return to her as soon as possible—[3]

I gave you the Shelley essays I believe—[4]

Please send my copies of The Celtic Twilight here, I am very impatient to see them—And will you send one copy with label I enclose—You might send a review copy to Arthur Symons,[5]

    134 Lauderdale Mansions
      Lauderdale Road
        Maida Vale—

As some of the longest essays in the book are about Blakes illustrations to Dante what do you think of giving his Francesca & Paolo as a frontispiece. You could photograph my copy.[6]

Yrs snly
W B Yeats

Dict AG, signed WBY; Harvard. Wade, 376–7.

To A. H. Bullen, 3 July [1902]

COOLE PARK, | GORT, | CO. GALWAY.
July 3

Dear Bullen—

I send you "the Way of Wisdom"—

The "Speaker" had not got a copy—so I am sending you the one from my own book of cuttings—I must beg you to take the great[est] possible

---

[3] The first two sections of WBY's 'Introduction' to Horton's *A Book of Images* (1898) were included in *IGE* as 'Symbolism in Painting'. The two essays in *Beltaine*, 'The Theatre' (May 1899) and 'The Irish Literary Theatre' (February 1900), were combined and printed with some deletions as 'The Theatre'; both had originally appeared in the *Dome*, in April 1899 and January 1900.

[4] Part one of 'The Philosophy of Shelley's Poetry' originally appeared in the *Dome* in July 1900. See p. 67, n. 1.

[5] Although Symons apparently did not review the book, he wrote on 5 Aug (MBY) to thank WBY for the new edition: 'I was glad to get it, and found many excellent new things in it. It seems to me a pity that you did not revise the old part, as I wanted you to do.'

[6] 'Francesca and Paolo' had long been one of WBY's favourite Blake engravings; in the Introduction to *The Poems of William Blake* (1) he said it 'must always haunt the memory with a beauty at once tender and august', and in *E & I* (126–7) described it as showing 'in its perfection Blake's mastery over elemental things'. In spite of this, Bullen did not use it as a frontispiece for the volume.

care of it & to return it to me, for there are things in the back of it I want—[1]

I also send P.S. to follow essays called "The Theatre".[2]

Do please let me know if Celtic Twilight is out—& if not when it will be out—

Yours sincly

W B Yeats

Dict AG, signed WBY; Texas.

To Wilfrid Scawen Blunt, 4 July [*1902*]

COOLE PARK, | GORT,

July 4.

My dear Mr Blunt,

I promised to write to you about your play on Cuchulain.[1] When I was in Dublin I told the manager of the theatrical Company about it, and he was of course very much pleased. 'A.E'. (George Russell) is writing a play on the death of Cuchulain,[2] and as I have done one about his killing his son, and have planned out another on the fight for the Championship, and as the Theatrical Company has already got A.E's Deirdre, we shall very shortly have the whole life of Cuchulain in dramatic form. I hear of other plays being written, but nobody has taken your subject. Of course our plans are as yet a little vague, and there may be some delay, but if we have good work it will sooner or later be performed. But we will try for next spring.

Would you care for us to look over your scenario? I find it a help to get mine looked through by those who have had practical experience of the stage. The tendency of the writer is to be carried away by detail. My own

---

[1] See p. 211, n. 2. On the verso side of the page on which the bulk of this article appears is a long notice of Benson's 1900 production of *The Tempest* by 'P. C.' This was presumably Philip Carr (1874–1957), later founder of the Mermaid Repertory Theatre, whose attempts to revive Elizabethan and Jacobean plays in authentic productions was greatly to impress WBY. While praising the acting of Benson's Company, 'P. C.' lamented that many scenes were over-elaborate in their execution and costuming, thus endorsing WBY's views on the distracting extravagance of scenery and decor in the commercial theatre. He also thought the music too much 'in the manner of concert pieces', and advocated 'subduing the musical side of the play to the right position of illusion and mystery', a suggestion to which WBY would have readily assented.

[2] See p. 211, n. 3. The postscript, probably taken from *Samhain* (1901), was not included in *IGE*.

[1] See p. 203, n. 2.

[2] On 24 May 1902 AE wrote to tell WBY (MBY): 'I am trying to think out a play on Cuchulain's death but cannot get the last scene clear in my mind as drama'. He subsequently abjured playwrighting altogether; see p. 168, n. 4.

way of working is to first of all write a scenario, and having talked this over with somebody who knows the stage, to write the whole play out in prose, and when I am quite sure the construction is right, to put the play into verse. This method of writing is far the quickest in the end. Of course the prose version is only roughly written. Dont make your scenery more elaborate than you can help.

I found when I got to Dublin that the Tara desecrators were not protected by police as one of our newspapers had said. I went down with Douglas Hyde, George Moore, and the Editor of the United Irishman. We found the landlord sitting on the hillside with a gun and a glass of whisky, two bailiffs and a number of dogs. He began by bullying and shouting out about the rights of property; then took to wheedling and then to bullying again. Hyde and myself saw the tenant, and he promised to go down on Sunday with a witness chosen by us and to order the landlord off the ground, which apparently he could do by his lease. The only thing he asked us to do was to threaten him, and to accuse him of being bought by English money, which we accordingly did by letter. 'If you write to me and say "You have been bought by English gold" the landlord will know I could not help myself' he said. Then Hyde chose Rolleston, in whom he has an incurable belief, for witness, and got the Gaelic League to arrange for special trains, and call a mass meeting on the hill to protest. Rolleston went down with the tenant, and instead of carrying out our plan took the landlord's assurance that he would give up digging, if the Royal Society of Antiquaries would take his place. Rolleston respects all dignitories, even drunken landlords. Neither Hyde nor the Gaelic League nor I myself feel any confidence on the Antiquaries doing this. They have probably neither the money nor the spirit. The Tara question will therefore in all probability come up again in a little while. The digging has meanwhile stopped for the present.[3]

[3] See p. 209. In the *United Irishman* of 15 Nov 1902 Griffith described (6) how they had found 'Mr. Groome engaged in directing several labourers who, with crowbar, pick and shovel, were demolishing the Rath of the Synods, and they found Mr. G. V. Briscoe seated with his back against the churchyard-wall looking on, a glass of whiskey clutched in his right hand, and a bottle of the same liquor on the ground beside him. With Mr. Briscoe were two retainers, one of them armed with a rifle. Mr. Briscoe challenged the right of Messrs. Hyde, Yeats, Moore, and Griffith to walk on Tara, and a lively conversation ensued, the visitors claiming that a public right over the hill existed. In the course of the conversation the Editor of THE UNITED IRISHMAN expressed with candour his opinion of Mr. Briscoe, and Mr. Briscoe vociferously reiterated that he was a gentleman. . . . Eventually, Mr. Briscoe stated that he would have the greatest pleasure in permitting Dr. Hyde and Messrs. Yeats and Moore to wander over Tara, but that as the Editor of THE UNITED IRISHMAN had denied his right and declined the hand he proffered in friendship, he would be compelled to oppose by force any attempt on that gentlemen's part to cross the hill. Accordingly, the man with the rifle was ordered up to the block the way. Rightly or wrongly it seemed to the Editor of this journal that the moment had come to definitely assert the right of the Irish people to stand on the site of the city of their kings, and accordingly he asserted it practi-

I found that the farming people of the neighbourhood were very indignant over the whole thing, and I think lacked nothing but a little oratory to make them break the peace. They are very scornful at the idea that the desecrators are looking for the ark of the Covenant. They believe them to be looking for the Golden Plough and the Golden Harrow which are fabled to lie buried there.[4] Lady Gregory, who is typing this, has been very busy over Roberts coming of age. All went off well, Robert made a very good speech, very simple very sincere, and effective merely as a speech.[5]

Yours snly

W B Yeats

TLS Private.

To George Russell (AE), [c. 5 July 1902]

Mention in letter from AE, 7 July 1902.
Sending AE scores of music for the psaltery for use at a musical gathering on Sunday, 6 July.[1]

MBY.

---

cally. The man with the rifle did not shoot—he grounded his gun and stood aside, and the visitors crossed Tara Hill without further opposition . . .' T. W. Rolleston announced in the Dublin *Daily Express* of 30 June (4) that he had 'just returned from a visit to Tara and its proprietor, Mr. J. V. Briscoe [*sic*]; a visit undertaken in company with Mr. Boylan, the present lessee of the lands on which the traces of the ancient site are to be found', and reported that no further destruction would take place since, after 'a prolonged discussion Mr. Briscoe voluntarily offered to place the further investigation of the site in the hands of the Royal Society of Antiquarians of Ireland'. WBY's misgivings were, however, justified, for in a letter to the Dublin press in November 1902 Rolleston confessed that his attempt had failed since the Royal Society of Antiquaries had 'just written to me to say that they cannot entertain the proposals which I was empowered to make to them' (*United Irishman*, 15 Nov 1902, p. 6). Despite this, public opinion was so opposed to the diggings that no further unauthorized excavation occurred.

    [4] WBY was to refer to the legend in his poem 'In Tara's Halls' (*VP*, 609): 'Thereon the man / Went to the Sacred House and stood between / The golden plough and harrow'. He also cited it in *The Unicorn From The Stars*, where (*VPl*, 706) a character is suspected of going 'to some secret cleft . . . to get knowledge of . . . the Plough that was hidden in the old times, the Golden Plough'.

    [5] Robert Gregory had come of age on 20 May 1902, but, since he and AG were in London for Edward VII's Coronation (subsequently postponed because of the King's ill-health), the tenants' celebrations did not take place until his return to Coole on 24 June. Reviewing the main events of 1902 in her diary on 4 Jan 1903 (Berg), AG recalled 'Robert's coming of age homecoming—bonfires—torches—dinner & dance—presentations—Thank God he is so well received & on such good terms with his people & has so good a name'. The celebration was reported in *Hearth and Home* on 24 July 1902 (570): 'The tenantry assembled at the gates of the Coole Park domain, and presented an address and some valuable gifts of plate, &c. The household also presented some handsome silver, which Mr. Gregory suitably acknowledged; the road from Gort Station being gay with bunting, the flags of all nations being included.'

    [1] AE had asked for these on 4 July, as he was getting 'one or two musical folk to try their hand

To Alfred Nutt, [c. 6 July 1902]

Mention in next letter.
Asking Nutt to keep the MS of *The Aran Islands* on the chance of seeing Synge.

To John Millington Synge, 6 July [1902]

COOLE PARK, | GORT, | CO. GALWAY.
(Dictated.)   July 6.

My dear Synge—

I send you a letter I have re^{cd} from Alfred Nutt about your book—I am disappointed that he has not taken it as it stands—You will see that he would like to talk to you about it, & I think you ought to see him on your way through London.[1] If you can get him to accept it by making any changes it would be well worth doing so as this is your first book. I daresay you & I might prefer the book as it stands, but the great thing is to get it published. I am writing to Nutt asking him to keep the M.S. on the chance of seeing you—

I thought your review of Lady Gregorys book in the Speaker most excellent.[2] Why not write to them & ask them to send you George Moores book of Irish stories ᴀn ᴄ-up 5ορᴄ—Sealy Bryers & Walker, Dublin.[3] There should be a good opening now for a critic of Irish books, & you

---

at it this evening'. He expressed doubt about Dolmetsch's system of notation and this was reinforced by his experiments, which, as he reported on 7 July, had not been successful since 'nearly everyone begins to sing when they see notes instead of speaking musically'. This experience proved that, in spite of what Dolmetsch said, quarter tones were 'absolutely necessary if the speaking is at all to be a rendering of the original chant or speech, and nobody should be allowed to vary at their own sweet will.'

[1] Alfred Nutt (see p. 181) had written to WBY on 30 June 1902 (TCD) rejecting Synge's *The Aran Islands*. Although impressed by its realism he thought it 'too shapeless, too without beginning or end, too much hung in the air', and in a letter to Synge on 13 Nov 1902 doubted its appealing to a large enough readership.

[2] Synge's enthusiastic but judicious review of *Cuchulain of Muirthemne* in the *Speaker* of 7 June 1902 (*JMSCW* II. 367–70) praised AG's 'wonderfully simple and powerful language that resembles a good deal the peasant dialect of the west of Ireland', commended the 'tact and success' with which she had arranged her material, and claimed that the book would 'go far to make a new period in the intellectual life of Ireland'. Like WBY (see p. 163 ff.) he regretted that she had 'omitted certain barbarous features' so that 'her versions have a much less archaic aspect than the original texts'.

[3] Moore's collection of short stories, *The Untilled Field*, was translated into Irish by Padraic O'Sullivan and published by Sealy Bryers & Walker as *An T-ur-Gort* in 1902. An enlarged version was published in English by T. Fisher Unwin in 1903. Moore described the book as 'my

ought to step in. You might also do them a "Middle" on plays in Irish. Articles in the 'Speaker' might probably lead to your doing work in the Daily News or Chronicle. It would be a great advantage to you to have a few good articles to show—

Lady Gregory sends her regards, & hopes you will come for a few days on yr way to Aran—[4]

Yours always
W B Yeats

Dict AG, signed WBY; TCD. Saddlemyer, 36–7.

To Cornelius Weygandt, 9 July [1902]

at | COOLE PARK, | GORT, | CO. GALWAY.
July 9

Dear Mr. Weygandt—

I must apologise for not having answered your letter—the truth is, I mislaid it, and I have been moving about, and have only today found it again—

I hope this may reach you before you leave Philadelphia—I shall not be in London for some months to come—or in Sligo—I am staying with friends here—

Lady Gregory & her son, with whom I am staying—desire me to say it would give them great pleasure to see you here for a few days if you should be coming to the neighbourhood & if you will write a few days beforehand as at some times the visits of other guests would interfere.[1]

---

portrait of Ireland' and in the Preface to the 1914 edition suggested (p. x) it was 'the source of Synge's inspiration. *The Untilled Field* was a landmark in Anglo-Irish literature, a new departure, and Synge could not have passed it by without looking into it.' Synge did not review the book, and Moore's claim is characteristically exaggerated.

[4] Synge was in Co. Wicklow, but visited Coole from 8 to 13 Oct on his way to the Aran Islands.

[1] See p. 203, n. 5. Weygandt spent a day with WBY at Coole in August 1902 and published an account of this visit, 'With Mr. W. B. Yeats in the Woods of Coole', in *Lippincott's Magazine* in April 1904, reprinted in his *Tuesdays at Ten* (1928). In the morning they discussed the revival of Irish heroic literature and 'always the talk turned again to the many phases of the movement that is striving to give Ireland a national life—to the Celtic art in Loughrea Cathedral; to Irish painting; to Irish music and to Mr. Yeats's own theories of the chanting of verse to the psaltery; and to "The Irish Literary Theatre" . . .'. During an afternoon walk WBY told him that he 'had never himself seen "The Other People" in the Woods of Coole . . . but many of the neighboring peasants had . . . . and he could not believe that some visions they spoke of were imaginings. . . . Strange visions had come to him, he said, after walking in these woods, visions of "immortal,

Yes, I shall have a good deal to tell you about the movement in Ireland—

Sincerely yours
W B Yeats

Dict AG, signed WBY; Private; with envelope addressed to the University of Pennsylvania,
postmark 'ORANMORE', date indecipherable.

To John Butler Yeats, [c. *10 July 1902*]

Mention in letter from JBY, 11 July 1902.
Sending JBY the new edition of *The Celtic Twilight*;[1] telling him that he is
working well, but complaining about his eyes.

MBY.

To John Butler Yeats, [c. *19 July 1902*]

Mention in letter from JBY, [? 21 July 1902].
Sending JBY a £2 loan.[1]

MBY.

To F. J. Fay, [c. *23 July 1902*]

Mention in letter from Fay, 25 July 1902.
A letter which Fay has passed on to his brother.[1]

Private.

mild, proud shadows", but always as dreams, and not as objective realities. At times, however, he
had seen visions in waking dreams, and he felt the border of the unseen so near that no man
should say that no man had crossed it' (*Lippincott's Magazine*, 487).

[1] In his reply JBY declared that *The Celtic Twilight* was 'an immortal book a convincing book.
Years ago L. C. Purser called it to me a wonderful book, but then on the other hand, I fear Judge
Madden thinks it rank nonsense. . . . This is well called "Celtic Twilight" & is only intended for
people who live in the twilight.'

[1] On 18 July JBY had asked WBY if he could 'lend me two or even one pound'. WBY obliged
immediately, and on 20 July JBY thanked him (MBY) for the loan, which he promised to repay
'as soon as possible'. This turned out to be on 5 Sept.

[1] This evidently gave an account of *The Hour-Glass* and *The Pot of Broth*, both of which WBY
had just finished writing.

To F. J. Fay, [c. *24 July 1902*]

Mention in letter from Fay, 25 July 1902.
Sending him the MSS of *The Hour-Glass* and *The Pot of Broth;*[1] suggesting the casts and that Fay should play the part of the Fool in the former;[2] disparaging James Cousins's *The Racing Lug*[3] and a play by Edward Martyn;[4] warning Fay that Douglas Hyde was worried about joining the theatre movement because of its political associations, and discussing the formation of an Irish National Theatre.

LWBY I. 99–102.

To Maud Gonne, [*early August 1902*]

Mention in letter from MG, Tuesday [August 1902].
Enquiring if she has received the copy of the new edition of *The Celtic Twilight* he had asked to be sent to her; drawing attention to one of the poems in it;[1] complaining that his eyes are still troubling him; and discussing the diggings at Tara.[2]

G–YL, 156–7.

[1] Acknowledging the arrival of the plays on 25 July, Fay reported that he had 'read them with much interest': '*The Hour-Glass* will be compared with the *Everyman* but your play has the advantage that the story is an Irish folk tale. . . . I think *The Hour-Glass* very fine though I do not like the holding of an unbeliever up to the scorn so to speak of this pretentiously pious country.'

[2] Frank Fay thought that WBY had 'cast the piece well' but doubted if he 'could act the Fool. It is hardly my line. Of course if you insist I will try . . .' He suggested that his brother should take the part.

[3] WBY had evidently criticized Cousins's play for its faulty construction and conventionality, but in his reply Fay dismissed both these objections: 'I don't know nor do I care about what is called construction; but the play will act. . . . *The Racing Lug* is founded on an incident that actually happened; if it doesn't tell anything new about human nature (and the plays that do are I should think rare), it is a very human story.'

[4] *The Placehunters,* published in the *Leader* on 26 July (but in the Dublin newsagents some days earlier), which was never produced.

[1] WBY published three poems in *The Celtic Twilight,* but probably refers here to 'Into the Twilight' (*VP,* 147–8).

[2] See p. 209. MG had led a 'Children's Excursion' to Tara where, 'in honor of an Independent Ireland', they set fire to a bonfire Briscoe had prepared to celebrate Edward VII's coronation. But she was apprehensive about the future: 'I don't think Groom & Brisco are really beaten at all. In a few weeks I expect they will be digging away as merrily as ever.'

To Frederick Ryan, [c. *11 August 1902*]

Mention in letter from Ryan, 14 August 1902.
Accepting the Presidency of the National Dramatic Society;[1] asking about the new Society's relationship to the Patent Laws and the commercial Dublin theatres;[2] and agreeing to give a lecture for the Society later in the autumn.

NLI.

To F. J. Fay, 13 August [*1902*]

COOLE PARK | GORT,
August 13.

My dear Fay,

I dont think there is any special book that will give you an understanding of the fool.[1] The fool, in the sense in which I use him is continually cropping up in folk-lore. There is something about him in an essay called 'The Queen and the Fool' in my new 'Celtic Twilight' which Russell has a copy of. But there is nothing there or anywhere else, that I can think of, which would help you much. If you play the part as incarnate fantasy, the fantasy of Richard the Second and Hamlet you will get the meaning well

---

[1] The 'National Dramatic Society' was now being put on a firmer footing. On 8 Aug it had moved into more permanent premises at the Camden Street Hall, and the following day the members had appointed a committee with officers: WBY as President; AE, MG, and Hyde as Vice-Presidents; and Frederick Ryan as Secretary. In this capacity, Ryan wrote on 10 Aug to tell WBY of his election, and of the hire of the Hall, and asked him to '"send us off" with a lecture, if at all convenient, in which we could explain our objects, hopes, ambitions &c and set out what are our plans & prospects'.

[2] WBY had had trouble with the Patent Laws in setting up the ILT in 1898, and was aware of the hostility of the Dublin commercial theatres to rival companies, but in a reply of 14 Aug (NLI) Ryan was able to reassure him that there would be no trouble from patent theatres since the Fays' Company had been playing for years at St Teresa's Hall. He also suggested that WBY might give his lecture just before the performances of the Cumann na nGaedheal plays at Antient Concert Rooms in October, and stressed that the Company's great need was for Irish plays.

[1] In a letter of the previous day (NLI) Fay had told WBY that the 'Hour Glass has been cast as you suggested [*see p. 218*]. Would you tell me where I could get some of the folk-tales . . . in which a fool similar to yours occurs.' In WBY's essay, first published as 'The Fool of Faery' in the *Kensington* of June 1901, the *Amadán-na-Breena* is the fool of the forth [*i.e. fairy 'fort' or dwelling*], 'maybe the wisest of all'. Fay played the Fool in *The Hour-Glass*, produced on 14 Mar 1903 at the Molesworth Hall, Dublin, and J. Dudley Digges (see p. 172)—evidently at WBY's original suggestion—took the part of the Wise Man. For the wild ass see Job 39: 5–8, where God, asserting His omnipotence, asks Job, 'Who hath sent out the wild ass free? or who hath loosed the bands of the wild ass? . . . He scorneth the multitude of the city, neither regardeth he the crying of the driver. The range of the mountains *is* his pasture, and he searcheth after every green thing.'

enough. The fool, as I understand him, is the fool merely because his imagination is too busy with its own over abundant life to turn to useful occupations. It is the wild ass of the bible, which refuses burdens. It is the untamed and untamable mind of the world.

I am not at all sure if I were in Dublin that I would not make you wise man, and Digges fool. It is impossible to cast a play from a distance, and I only meant to throw out suggestions. You people on the spot must make the final arrangements.

As to costume.[2] I have a piece of stuff to be made into a robe for the angel, and I have a halo, a pair of sandals and a gilded girdle.

I am trying to get two deer skins for the fool. And my brother is going to make me sketches for the other costumes, and also for the peasant interior you asked for. Will you please send me by return dimensions of stage, that we may not overcrowd the sketch.[3]

I shall write today to Bullen for my MS of Cathleen ny Houlihan, or for complete proofs if they are ready.[4] I have made some slight modifications which I am anxious you should rehearse when the time comes.

Yours sincerely

W B Yeats

TLS Private.

[2] In his letter of 12 Aug Fay had asked for 'sketches of the dresses. They would want to be put in hands soon, as seven or eight will have to be made.'

[3] The main purpose of Fay's 12 Aug letter had been to announce that he had found a hall which might serve as a permanent home for the company: 'It is not large and would perhaps seat 200; the Theatre Libre started in a hall that seated 300. . . . The hall is in Camden Street close to Harrington Street, and is No. 34. The trams pass the door, but it is so far from the street that there is no annoyance from tram bells. The stage is as deep as Clarendon Street but not so wide and we will have to resort to the simplest of scenery so as to have room to dress and store props during the shows.' The hall was rented for 12 months and the company moved in on 8 Aug, but only used it for one set of performances, from 4 to 6 Dec 1902, although it continued to serve as a scenery dock and workshop. The stage was less than nine feet deep and, since there were no dressing-rooms, actors had to change costume at the side of the stage. The auditorium, described by W. A. Henderson as 'a draughty ill-lighted hall and without fire', was approached down a long dark passage. In 1903 the company hired the more satisfactory and commodious Molesworth Hall before taking up residence at the Abbey Theatre.

[4] In his letter of 12 Aug Fay had asked to borrow a copy of *Cathleen ni Houlihan* since he had 'mislaid my copy and we cannot commence rehearsals without a book. You said something about it being about to be printed. Perhaps you could get me a rough proof. I want it at the earliest possible moment.' WBY had amended the acting drafts after the first performance (see p. 167), and sent his final version to Bullen as copy for publication by the Caradoc Press in October 1902. The play was also printed in *Samhain* in the same month.

To Cecil French,[1] *[20 August 1902]*

COOLE PARK, | GORT, | CO. GALWAY.

My dear French: I enclose part of a letter which explains itself. You might send it on to Miss Gyles. I have been for some time on the point of writing to you but letter writing is very difficult owing to the state of my eyes. I have read the little play once & had it read out to me once. I think it now moves perfectly up to the entrance of the man in white but the conversation after this has no sufficient construction. It is not a real living dialogue between a man & a woman. They do not catch fire from one another. There is one very beautiful sentance, that about "the graveyard dust" but the conversation as a whole would have to be remade from the foundation. I think you should put the little play aside for a time; & if you want to write plays go to the theatre all you can & read all the plays you can & try & think out what are their dramatic elements.

I have just got back from Galway Town where Hyde's new play 'The Wedding', has been played with great success.[2] Hyde played the chief part and was wonderful as he always is.

Yrs ev
W B Yeats

TS copy Private.

---

[1] Cecil French (1878–1953) an Irish poet, artist, and stage designer, first met WBY in 1899. He contributed regularly to the *Green Sheaf* (1903–4), although his first volume of poems and woodcuts, *Between Sun and Moon*, comprising work completed before World War I, was not published until 1923. He dedicated the volume 'To W. B. Yeats | In token of what he has given to the world'. His pencil drawing, 'The Rose of Dream', depicting a woman holding a rose between her lips, hung in WBY's sitting-room. French was also a friend and patron of Althea Gyles (see p. 198). WBY had mentioned his play to Frank Fay in April (see p. 173).

[2] For Hyde's *An Pósadh* (*The Marriage*), 'founded on the story of Raftery at the poor wedding at Cappaghtagle', and subsequently included in AG's *Poets and Dreamers*, see pp. 128–9. It was first performed at the Connacht Feis in Galway on 20 and 21 Aug. The *Freeman's Journal* of 21 Aug reported (5) that its 'appearance on the stage follows hot pace . . . upon the writing of it, for the parts were read from manuscript. . . . the function tonight was little more than a very early rehearsal in costume. . . . and as most of the players were, naturally, young people, more than the ordinary difficulties in the path of amateurs have to be allowed for. . . . Dr. Hyde's acting was very good.' In *Samhain* (1902) WBY described Hyde's acting (5) as a 'most important Irish dramatic event. . . . Through an accident it had been very badly rehearsed, but his own acting made amends. One could hardly have had a play that grew more out of the life of the people who saw it.' The production of a play about the Gaelic poet Anthony Raftery (*c*. 1784–1835) was opportune, for on 31 Aug WBY, AG, Hyde, Jack Yeats and John Quinn were to attend another Feis at Killeenan, Co. Galway, to unveil a memorial to his memory.

To George Russell (AE), [c. *24 August 1902*]

Mention in letter from AE, Monday [? 25 August 1902].
Asking what the Fays are doing; suggesting that plays submitted to the
INTS should be vetted by a Reading Committee;[1] enquiring about a com-
edy;[2] and telling him that he is writing a poem about Maeve.[3]

Denson, 43.

To F. J. Fay, [c. *27 August 1902*]

Mention in letter from Fay, 28 August 1902.
Sending him the MS of *Cathleen ni Houlihan*; and advising him that the
recitation of dedicatory verses at the Society's inaugural performances
would give an amateur air to the project.

Private.

To F. J. Fay, 7 September [*1902*]

COOLE PARK, | GORT.
Sept 7.

My dear Fay,
    I want to alter the title of 'The Beggarman'. Please change it to 'A pot of
broth' in any public announcement. I have a sufficient reason for this,
which I have not time to explain now.[1]

[1] This is probably the letter WBY refers to in writing to AE on 21 Feb 1903 (see p. 319) about
the constitution of the INTS: 'Why do you say that I asked for a veto? I wrote to you from Galway proposing precisely that arrangement which is now embodied in the rules for the submitting
of plays to the Presidents & Vice-Presidents. I have still the letter in which you replied saying
that you approved of my proposal & would submit it to the Fays.' AE replied that he did not
know what the Fays were doing 'except that they are rehearsing very energetically', but that he
'hoped to see W. Fay in a day or so and will talk to him about the matters referred to in your letter with which I agree'.
[2] WBY had evidently heard that the Fays were thinking of producing a comedy written under
the pseudonym 'Mise', and, fearing their bad taste in the choice of plays, had asked AE for more
information. He replied that he had 'heard nothing about the comedy by "Mise" before. I think
however it stands no chance of being acted at present as I know they will hardly be able to get
through the programme already fixed.'
[3] 'The Old Age of Queen Maeve' (*VP*, 180–7), a long narrative poem in blank verse, and a
companion to the recently published 'Baile and Aillinn', first appeared in the *Fortnightly Review*
in April 1903.

[1] WBY may have been worried about a possible confusion between this title and that of P. T.
MacGinley's play, *Eilis agus an Bhean Déirce*, usually translated as *Lizzie and the Beggarwoman*,
especially since the two plays were to be produced on successive days in late October.

You have not sent back my MS. of Kathleen ny Houlihan, and I find it difficult without it to judge of some of the points you raise. One is obviously a misprint. 'I dont know is it here she's coming' is of course right. No doubt too there is a confusion between the names Peter and Patrick in the other passage you speak of. Certainly you may add the word 'tomorrow' to the word 'married' in that speech of Delia's. I have no doubt it dropped out of the typing.[2]

Lady Gregory is trying to get the air of 'There's broth in the pot'. Your brother must get some common air for 'The Spouse of Naoise', and sing it as much as possible as traditional singing. I adapted the words from 'Ben-Eirinn i' in Walsh's 'popular Songs'.[3]

I will send sketches of costume for 'The Hour Glass' and will have the skins in time.[4] And we will get a few bits of crockery for cottage scenes.

I think it would be a mistake to have verses for the opening of the Theatre. Such things are never done well & give the air of a penny reading entertainment.[5]

[2] See p. 220. In a letter of 28 Aug 1902 (NLI) Fay reported that 'the script of "Kathleen ni Houlihan" arrived safely; but in the meantime my own copy had turned up', and that he would return WBY's 'in a day or so'. He added that he had 'made some of the alterations; but some of the additions at the very end were not clear. In the script there is a slip . . . Patrick has been talking about the old woman, but the words in your script are to the effect that *Peter* has been talking about the old woman. There is another alteration . . . but it does not seem to me so good as the way the speech originally ran. Patrick used to say "There's an old woman coming up the path. I don't know is it here she's coming." A very common provincial Irish idiom. It is altered thus, "There's an old woman coming up the path I don't know. Is it here she's coming?". . . . Then Delia's speech at the close runs something like this. "You won't leave me Michael and we going to be *married*." It seems to me that the way we gave it before is truer and consequently more touching. "You won't leave me Michael and we going to be married *tomorrow*".'

[3] In his 28 Aug letter Fay said that his brother wanted 'to know the *air* of "There's broth in the pot" and of "The spouse of Naosi"', and asked that they be sent 'at an early date'. In a note to *The Pot of Broth*, WBY wrote (*VPl*, 254): 'The words and the air of "There's Broth in the Pot" were taken down from an old woman known as Cracked Mary, who wanders about the plain of Aidhne, and who sometimes sees unearthly riders on white horses coming through stony fields to her hovel door in the night time.' The music for the air was printed when the play was published in 1904. AG and Hyde had taken down the words from Cracked Mary at Coole on 11 Jan 1899 (diary, Berg).

Towards the end of early versions of the play the Tramp, as part of his blarney, sings Sibby a song (*VPl*, 247) which he pretends was composed by her disappointed suitors on hearing of her marriage; in fact, it is an adaptation of the second verse of a traditional song, 'Ben-Eirinn I', printed by Edward Walsh in his *Irish Popular Songs* (1847) as

> The spouse of Naisi, Erin's woe—
> The dame that laid proud Ilium low,
> Their charms would fade, their fame would flee,
> Match'd with my fair, 'ben-Eirenn i.

After 1911 WBY replaced this song with 'Paistin Finn'.

[4] In his letter Fay said he would 'be glad of sketches of costume for The Hour-Glass, or shall I ask Mr Russell for suggestions. We have a tremendous number of things to get right between this & our starting & I wish to have nothing left *over*.'

[5] To mark the new home and new status of the INTS (see pp. 219–20) Fay had suggested that WBY should write some dedicatory verses to be recited, or chanted, at the opening of the next season.

I send you some Latin words which will do for the wise man's prayer. These are the Latin words, broken for the actor:—"Confiteor Deo omnipotenti—how does it go on?—Omnipotenti beatae Mariae—I cannot remember."[6]

Digges should not make up too old. The wise man is a man in the full vigour of life. I hear from Mr Quinn that he read the part very finely and you yourself I hear played very excellently, Quinn was very much struck.[7] I should like however to hear how 'The Pot of Broth' goes.

Let the fool's wig, if you can, be red and matted.[8]

Hyde has done several new plays, including a most beautiful Nativity play,[9] and will I think throw himself heartily into your work.

Yours sincerely
W B Yeats

TLS Private. Wade, 377–8.

[6] In his letter of 28 Aug Fay had asked for the text of the Latin prayer in *The Hour-Glass* 'or where we can get what will do', and added that Digges 'would like to have your ideas about the Wise Man'. In early printings of the play WBY substituted the Latin opening of Psalm 68, 'Salvum me fac, Deus', for 'The Confiteor' (a prayer from the first part of the Ordinary of the Mass) he is trying to recall here. In 1908, however, he restored the Latin of the Confiteor, which was retained in all subsequent printings of the prose version of the play.

[7] Quinn had visited Dublin for the first time in August 1902 and attended the Fays' rehearsals; two sketches of him at the Camden Street Hall by Jack Yeats are reproduced in plates 2 and 4.

[8] 'What sort of wig do you *see* the Fool wearing', Fay had asked in his letter of 28 Aug, adding that he had 'got nearly all the wigs we want & I want to get any more that may be necessary before the season commences when they rise in price. When I ask what *sort* I mean as to color because I assume the wigs will be "flow" wigs similar to what we used in "Deirdre".'

[9] Hyde and his wife stayed at Coole, following the Galway Feis, and remained there after the Raftery celebrations at Killeenan. It proved to be a productive time for him. Beside *Teach na mBocht* (later translated by AG as *The Poorhouse*), he also, on 25 Aug, wrote *An Naomh ar Iarraid* (translated by AG as *The Lost Saint*) based on an incident in the life of Aengus Céile Dé (see I. 148), and in early September turned to *Dráma Breite Críosta* (translated by AG as *The Nativity*). Although the Fays produced *The Poorhouse* in April 1907, *The Nativity* was not performed at the Abbey until January 1911. A proposed performance in Kilkenny was banned by the priests there in December 1904, and it was first played by the Loretto Convent School, Sligo, in early February 1905. That Hyde was now enthusiastic about the dramatic movement was a relief since, as WBY had warned the Fays in July (see p. 218), he had been concerned lest his association with the Society, which drew many members from Cumann na nGaedheal and Inghinidhe na hEireann, might compromise the 'no politics' rule he had set himself as President of the Gaelic League, and in his letter of 28 Aug Fay revealed that he had only assented to become a Vice-President of the National Drama Society 'subject to knowing exactly our programme on which he will be written to'.

To F. J. Fay, 15 September [1902]

Coole Park | Gort,
Sept 15.

My dear Fay,

As to costumes, I enclose a rough sketch of a student costume. I want to know how much material, in stuff 63 inches wide, the tunic and trews would take. They are much the same as Mr Fourniers, he could tell how much his take.[1] And the cloak I would like a separate calculation for. I think only two of the students should wear cloaks. Let me know how many students you will put on the stage. I am keeping the finished sketches for the present, as Lady Gregory is looking for materials in the right colours, and will give some pieces, which will be a help. We are trying to make the staging of the Hour Glass as artistic as possible, although quite simple and inexpensive.

Lady Gregory has picked up some pieces of crockery, and is getting more, so you need not do anything about furnishing dresser at present.[2]

We had, as you say, some verses at the opening of the Literary Theatre, but they did not seem to me to produce any effect.[3] I think they gave rather an amateur air. Such things are troublesome to write and for the most part rhetoric when done.

Tell Digges that the astrological allusions are out of the Paradiso of Dante.[4] He attributes the seven sciences to the seven planets and for the

---

[1] The sketches of the costumes for *The Hour-Glass* which WBY had promised on 7 Sept (see p. 223); in a letter of *c.* 8 Sept (Private), Fay had told him they were urgently required. Edmund Edward Fournier d'Albe (1868–1933), was born in London of Franco-Irish parents and was at this time living in Dalkey, where he had thrown himself into the Celtic movement. An enthusiastic proponent of Celtic national costume, he frequently appeared in garments which he supposed corresponded to this. As Secretary of the Celtic Association, he organized the Pan Celtic Congress (see p. 110, n. 1), as well as editing the Association's periodical, *Celtia*. He was also a physicist and inventor, and was to become Secretary of the Dublin Society for Psychical Research.

[2] In his letter of *c.* 8 Sept Fay revealed that the 'reason I am anxious to get the crockery is that I suppose down where you are, they use what in town would be very old fashioned things which could not be easily got here'.

[3] In an attempt to persuade WBY to change his mind about not having dedicatory verses (see p. 222), Fay had reminded him that 'Lionel Johnson wrote some verses for the opening performance of the I.L.T. Why should we be superior to them. But perhaps you are right.' Johnson's prologue for the opening of the ILT had been published in the first number of *Beltaine* in May 1899.

[4] In his letter Fay told WBY that 'Digges will not make up old, but in the way you suggest [*see previous letter*]. He would like an explanation of the astrological terms used in the long speech. Shall we pronounce the few Latin words as they are pronounced by priests or after the English fashion, I mean giving "i" the sound it has in "wide".' In *The Hour-Glass* the Wise Man alludes frequently to the seven stars and the seven sciences they govern. In the *Paradiso* Beatrice conducts Dante in an ascent through the seven planets of the ptolemaic system, each having its particular quality and influence. As WBY says, Saturn, the highest planet, is designated by Dante as the residence of those souls whose mortal lives were spent in holy retirement and contemplation.

most part for reasons that are obvious to an astrological student but would take too long to explain. For instance Saturn who presides over the birth of contemplative natures has philosophy attributed to him and so on. Pronounce the Latin words as they are pronounced by priests.

I have written to Hyde, who has left, about the motto.[5]

Do as you like about the wigs.[6]

I enclose the last page of Kathleen as you ask.[7]

Yrs snly
W B Yeats

TLS UCD.

To Maud Gonne, [*? 19 September 1902*]

Mention in letter from MG, Saturday [? 20 September 1902].
Sending her a copy of *Cathleen ni Houlihan*.[1]

G–YL, 158–9.

To Lady Augusta Gregory, *19 September 1902*

September 19, 1902.

To Lady Gregory:

I offer you a book which is in part your own.[1] Some months ago, when our Irish dramatic movement took its present form, I saw that somebody must write a number of plays in prose if it was to have a good start. I did

[5] In his letter Fay said that 'Dr Hyde wrote us a very nice letter and Mr Ryan sent him a note explaining our position. We have not since heard from him and I personally would like to have a letter from him that our explanation is satisfactory, so that we may get some notepaper printed. Is he staying at Coole Park. Perhaps you would say this to him if he is and ask him whether he could give us a motto in Irish with which to head our notepaper.'

[6] Fay was still preoccupied with the problem of wigs for *The Hour-Glass* (see p. 224, n. 8) and in his letter of *c.* 8 Sept asked if WBY knew 'how the hair was worn here during the period in which you have written *The Hourglass*? I suppose *flow* wigs (those used in *Deirdre*) will do.'

[7] Having returned WBY's copy (see p. 223, n. 2), Fay had discovered that he had neglected to collate fully his own version, and in his letter asked WBY to send 'the last page of *Kathleen* as altered in your copy. I am not altogether certain as to how it runs. Could you write or type that page and send it to me.'

[1] In her reply MG thanked him for 'that lovely little copy of Cathleen'. This was an advance copy of the Caradoc Press edition of *Cathleen ni Houlihan*, published in October. WBY was far from thinking it 'lovely' (see below, p. 236).

[1] This dedicatory letter was published in both versions of the 1902 New York edition of *Where There Is Nothing*. The large paper version has slight variations in wording and punctuation.

not know what to do, although I had my dramatic fables ready and a pretty full sketch of one play, for my eyes were troubling me, and I thought I could do nothing but verse, which one can carry about in one's head for a long time, and write down, as De Musset put it, with a burnt match.[2] You said I might dictate to you, and we worked in the mornings at Coole, and I never did anything that went so easily and quickly, for when I hesitated, you had the right thought ready, and it was always[3] you who gave the right turn to the phrase and gave it the ring of daily life. We finished several plays, of which this is the longest, in so few weeks, that if I were to say how few, I do not think anybody would believe me. I have spent a year at a play of no great length, and yet I do not think I could better these plays by taking time over them. We have the pleasure of knowing that our little Irish Theatre has found our work useful.

W B Yeats

Text from *Where There Is Nothing* (New York, 1902).

To Charles Elkin Mathews, 20 September [*1902*]

at | COOLE PARK, | GORT, | CO. GALWAY.
Sept 20

Dear Elkin Matthews: I see by account sent me from A P Watt that you had only 98 copies of 'The Wind Among the Reeds' last march. You must therefore have about exhausted the edition. I think it will be better in future to put the design in gold on a few vellumn copies & to bind the ordinary copies in plain boards with a paper label. People will be all the more glad to buy the vellumn copies if the design is not made common by printing it on all copies in some poorer way.[1]

Yours sinly
W B Yeats

ALS Private, with envelope addressed to Vigo St, Regents St, London, postmark 'ORAN-MORE SE 20 02'. Wade, 378.

[2] Alfred de Musset (1810–57), French poet and dramatist. His remark appears in his *Confession d'un enfant du siècle.*
[3] The large paper edition reads 'was almost always'.

[1] WBY was looking forward to the 4th English edition published early in 1903. On 9 Feb 1903 Robert Gregory wrote from Oxford (Emory) to tell AG that the 'new *Wind Among the Reeds* has come from Elkin Mathews. The gold leaf has not been put on very carefully in some places.' A certain number of copies in vellum were published with each of the editions. Quinn owned a 4th edition bound thus and inscribed by WBY 'the binding of this book pleases me well'.

To George Russell (AE), [c. 21 September 1902]

Mention in letter from AE, Monday [? 22 September 1902].
Asking AE for an article for *Samhain*;[1] and telling him that he is writing
Where There Is Nothing in spite of George Moore's objections.[2]

MBY.

To F. J. Fay, 21 September 1902

Mention in letter from Fay, 25 September 1902.
Fay wrote: 'In your letter of 21st you say "If you have no immediate inten-
tion of going to the country places, I might say that amateur societies out-
side Dublin are at liberty to produce either Lady Gregory's play or
Hyde's".'[1] WBY also said that he had written a new passage for *The Hour-
Glass*, discussed the withdrawal of the play from the Cumann na nGaed-

---

[1] At AE's suggestion, WBY partially reprinted his article, 'The Dramatic Treatment of Heroic
Literature' in the 1902 *Samhain*. The article, a reply to Standish James O'Grady's objection to
the dramatic portrayal of mythological heroes, had first appeared in the *United Irishman* on 3 May
1902, and was republished in *Some Irish Essays* (Dublin, 1906).

[2] The always uncomfortable friendship of WBY and George Moore was finally foundering on
a dispute over their collaboration on a play of mystical nihilism. On 3 July 1901 (NLI) Moore had
sent WBY a five-part scenario which sketched the Bohemian career of a university student after
his meeting with a tinker, culminating in his death at the hands of a mob in a ruined monastery.
When WBY subsequently withdrew from the venture (on the pretext that Moore was no longer a
member of the INTS), Moore announced that he was writing a novel based on the plot, and
would get an injunction if WBY used it. Hearing from AE that Moore had actually begun not a
novel but a play, WBY went to Coole and dictated his own version to AG and Hyde in a fortnight. He secretly arranged for the publication of this, now entitled *Where There Is Nothing*, as a
supplement to the *United Irishman* of 1 Nov 1902, later explaining to Allan Wade (*Bibl*, 60) that
'he knew Moore would not dare to issue an injunction against a Nationalist newspaper for fear of
getting his windows broken'. Moore took no legal action, and though Quinn tried to reconcile
them, WBY wrote (*Aut*, 454): 'we were never cordial again; on my side distrust remained, on his
disgust. I look back with some remorse. . . . Had I abandoned my plot and made him write the
novel, he might have put beside *Muslin* and *The Lake* a third masterpiece, but I was young, vain,
self-righteous, and bent on proving myself a man of action.'
    In his reply to this letter AE said he did not think Moore 'could do anything by an injunction'
but thought it would be 'delightfully funny to have your play brought into court and contrasted
with say The Mummer's Wife or the Drama in Muslin or any other ideal works of the author,
and ask the judge to decide where there were literary evidences of the mind of George Moore'.

[1] Ever since the formation of the National Literary Society in 1892 WBY had been eager to
bring drama to the Irish country people. He wanted to give permission to country drama societies
to perform his plays, as well as those by AG and Hyde, but not if this would damage possible
tours by the National Drama Society. In his reply Fay said there was 'no immediate intention of
going to the provinces. If the opportunity arise, we might perhaps do so but it would be difficult
for all our people to get off from business at the one time.'

heal Samhain festival;[2] asked when they intended to open the Camden Street Hall; about the method of choosing plays;[3] the performance of plays in Irish;[4] and the amount of material needed for costumes.

Private.

To F. J. Fay, 24 September 1902

Mention in letter from Fay, 25 September 1902.
Fay wrote: 'In your letter of yesterday you say that if we purpose producing these plays "I prefer to say that" (i.e. in *Samhain*)'.[1]

Private.

[2] In her letter of 'Saturday' (see p. 226) MG reported that Maire Quinn was 'most indignant over the withdrawal of the Hour Glass which was going splendidly & is far the best play they have. Fay has withdrawn it because he wants to keep it for the opening of their hall'. She had heard that Fay was 'most anxious not to be thought too strongly political', but asked WBY 'to write & urge Fay to go on with the *Hour Glass* & say that I told you I heard that the real reason of its withdrawal was to keep it for the opening of the National Theatre. . . . It was only after it was withdrawn & some of the Co protested loudly that it was *said* to have been withdrawn through want of time.' Fay had already confessed the real reason for holding the play back in a letter to WBY of 16 Sept (NLI): 'We discussed last night the importance of having at least one new play with which to open our hall and the unanimous opinion was that we should *not* act *The Hour Glass* for Samhain. My brother thinks it would be best try it on a small audience first, and moreover it will want more careful rehearsal than, with the number of pieces now being rehearsed, we can give it. My brother has an idea that it requires a special kind of acting, which it will take time to develop. He wants to avoid anything like realism in the expression. Besides we have our rent to make and we must have at least one novelty: the programme will be unique as it is.' However, in his reply to this letter, he maintained that they were 'not putting the *Hour Glass* by for lack of plays but because we do not feel in the stress of rehearsals for Samhain and the preparation necessary that such an important piece could get the amount of attention it requires'. And he asked WBY to send him the new passage for insertion in the prompt book.
[3] Fay replied that they did not know when the Hall would be open, but that he would be glad to chat about the choice of plays when WBY was next in Dublin, although he warned him that 'I have no special influence over our people and it would be far better for you as our president to ask that a meeting be called for the purpose of talking over things'. In February 1903 Fay recalled (NLI) 'a long discussion' with WBY at this time 'about a literary veto by individuals and I pointed out the fact that we could not run a voluntary society with an individual veto'.
[4] Fay, as he explained in his reply, had lost his former enthusiasm for plays in Irish. While welcoming them, and hoping the Society would do them, he took 'no interest in them as plays because they seem . . . to be copies of what one avoids in the regular theatre. . . . The plays which we are acting in English have thoroughly turned me from the theatre and it is this new class of play that I myself am interested [in].'
[1] WBY was still discussing the acting rights to the plays, and the possibility of their production by country drama groups (see above, n. 1). In his reply Fay said he doubted whether an announcement in *Samhain* would be sufficient to reserve the acting rights to their Company, and added that he did not think 'any of our plays suitable to country audiences and I certainly do not think they would be improved by being acted by absolute novices. Dr Hyde's plays would doubtless be suited to them as they are like all the other plays in Irish modelled on the sort of thing one

To Clement Shorter, 28 [September 1902]

COOLE PARK, | GORT, | CO. GALWAY.
28th

My dear Shorter

I enclose a paragraph about a spirited action of Captain Shawe Taylors[1] & w[d]. be very much obliged if you could put it into one of your sees in the theatre and do not say anything which might shock the unco'guid of which we have such large numbers in Ireland.' In the 1902 *Samhain* WBY did not specify which new plays the Company were to produce, but proclaimed (9–10) that the dramatic movement was 'a return to the people' and that they should 'busy ourselves with poetry and the countryman'.

[1] The rapid growth of the United Irish League, founded in 1898 as a successor to the Land League, had led to a long-familiar cycle of agrarian unrest and government repression. By the late summer of this year over half of Ireland had been proclaimed, and there was wide-spread imprisonment of Nationalist MPs and local politicians. In an attempt to break this dreary stalemate Captain John Shawe-Taylor (1866–1911), AG's nephew and a Co. Galway magistrate, had written to the Dublin papers on 2 Sept 1902 proposing a Conference to settle the Irish Land Question once and for all. Acting on his belief that there was not 'an Irishman, whatever his political faith, creed, or position, who does not yearn to see a true settlement of the present chaotic, disastrous, and ruinous struggle', he publicly invited representative politicians of various persuasions to meet tenants' representatives in Dublin. Among those invited were the Duke of Abercorn, a Unionist and owner of extensive estates in Donegal; Lord Barrymore, vice-president of the Irish Landowners Convention; Col. Saunderson, leader of the Unionists; John Redmond, leader of the nationalist party; the Lord Mayor of Dublin; The O'Connor Don, a landowner and descendant of the last high-king of Ireland; William O'Brien, a long-time member of the nationalist party and an agrarian activist; and T. W. Russell, a Unionist in process of converting to Home Rule, who had supported the Land Acts Commission in 1894 and who had become secretary of the Local Government Board in 1895.

Although greeted initially with scepticism, Shawe-Taylor's proposal began to gain influential support, including that of George Wyndham, the Chief Secretary, and the Nationalist leaders, but appeared to have been squashed when the three acknowledged leaders of the landlords, Abercorn and Barrymore on 20 Sept, and Saunderson a day later, refused to attend on the grounds that they had not been formally invited, and because it was a Conference 'called by a wholly irresponsible gentleman, and for which neither tenants, nor landlords . . . have expressed any wish or approval' (*The Times*, 22 Sept 1902 p. 8). Fortunately many landlords did approve. On 22 Sept a meeting of the Queen's County Deputy Lieutenants passed a resolution in favour of a Land Conference, other landlords wrote to the press voicing their support, and the places of the dissenting trio were eventually taken by the Earl of Dunraven, the Earl of Mayo, Col. W. H. Hutcheson-Poe, and Col. Nugent Everard. Dunraven chaired the two-week Conference in December 1902, and its recommendations were successfully incorporated into the Wyndham Land Act of 1903, which effectively solved the land question.

In his obituary of Shawe-Taylor in the *Observer* of 2 July 1911, WBY recalled this initiative and added 'I do not think I have known another man whose motives were so entirely pure, so entirely unmixed with any personal calculation, whether of ambition, of prudence or of vanity' (*E & I*, 344). William O'Brien (1852–1928), who had devoted his life to land reform and was the founder and leader of the United Irish League, wrote in the *Nineteenth Century* of July 1907: 'It is one of the most bizarre of history's little ironies, that a retired Army captain, unknown outside his Country Club the day before he wrote a certain newspaper letter of September, 1902, should have succeeded where the genius of Gladstone failed. Captain Shawe-Taylor, I believe, had no authority from any party, organisation or individual other than himself for writing his letter to the newspaper inviting four persons named from the landlord side, and four persons named from the tenants' side, to come together . . . to settle the Irish Land Question.'

papers[2]—I think it explains itself—It is taken from the Freeman—It would take me a long time to tell you of the extraordinary official intriguing that has gone on here—The Irish official hates all movements of enthusiasm for all enthusiasm tends to be national—The papers have had paragraphs written in Dublin, & then sent them to Buda-Pesth as evidence of spontaneous popular [?]indignation—its a queer story that I'll tell you when I get to London—

Yr sny
W B Yeats

Dict AG, signed WBY; BL.

To Charles Elkin Mathews, 29 September [1902]

Coole Park, | Gort,
Sept 29.

My dear Matthews,

I heard some time ago from Archie Russell.[1] He said that he proposed to you an edition of 25 vellum bound copies of "the Wind among the Reeds" with design in gold. He offered I understand to get purchasers for twenty. He did not mean a limited edition, for he added that 'Matthews will be able to use the same block for all future editions'. Doesn't this settle the question of the £6 block? If it does, then go ahead with the new edition, binding the ordinary copies in plain grey boards with a label possibly. You can bind the vellum copies as they are wanted, beginning with Archie Russell's edition of twenty five if you dont want to risk more. Dont print too large an ordinary edition I suggest. [*Remainder of letter in WBY's hand*] I

[2] WBY was probably sending Shorter, whose father-in-law, George Sigerson, had published an important book on land tenure in 1871, the long editorial from the *Freeman's Journal* of 25 Sept (4) under the heading 'The Landlords Learning Sense'. This welcomed the landlords' revolt 'against the dull petulant refusal of the landlord triumvirate. . . . It is hardly conceivable that Lord Barrymore and the Duke of Abercorn refused to attend the Conference because they were not pleased with the form of the invitation in which their attendance was requested. That they should be willing to wreck a hopeful movement for the settlement of the Irish Land Question on a mere point of etiquette would indicate an almost incredible silliness. If there is ever to be a real Conference, it was Captain Shawe-Taylor's bold proposal that made it possible. His proposal for a Conference was simple, practical, and prompt. He invited the admitted representatives of both interests to confer. The Tenants' representatives accepted; the Landlords' representatives declined. So the matter stands at present.' No notice of these events appeared in the *Sphere* or *Tatler*, both edited by Shorter, presumably because the initiative was attracting wide coverage elsewhere in the British press.

[1] See p. 195, n. 3. Archibald George Blomefield Russell (1879–1955) published editions of William Blake's letters and engravings.

may want to revise. Those notes have always anoyed me. I wont touch them now, unless youd like to leave them out.²

Yrs snly
W B Yeats

TLS Texas, with envelope addressed to Vigo St, Regent St, London, postmark 'ORANMORE SP 29 02'.

To Lady Augusta Gregory, [4 October 1902]

Nassau Hotel | South Fredrick St. | Dublin.
Saturday

My dear Lady Gregory: all is arranged with the United Irishman & Moore has no suspicion.¹ I have not told Russell my plan but have told him about things generally. He has seen Moore. Moore blustered & then Russell said 'Yeats will not lack money to fight it. His friends will give him any amount' on which 'Moore got plaintive' & after a little seemed inclined to give way. Russell sees him again to night. There is too much to write. Moore has several quite new & circumstantial lies. He says for instance that when he consented to my writing play he had an understanding that his name was to be to it also. 'Second, only second—second on the title page'. This was half way to half profits. Miss Gonne was emphatic about our not telling Russell the plan about play.

I saw rehersals last night. All very good. Ryans play is excellent.² It is a really very astonishing peice of satire. Am very busy.

Yours alway
W B Yeats

ALS Berg, with envelope addressed to Coole, postmark, 'DUBLIN OC 4 02'. Wade, 380–1.

² Well over a third of the 1st edition of *The Wind Among the Reeds* was taken up by WBY's notes. In *CW* he pruned them severely, and recalled (*VP*, 800) that 'Being troubled at what was thought a reckless obscurity, I tried to explain myself in lengthy notes, into which I put all the little learning I had, and more wilful phantasy than I now think admirable, though what is most mystical still seems to me the most true.'

¹ See p. 228, n. 2.
² Fred Ryan's Ibsenite play, *The Laying of the Foundations*, on the theme of municipal corruption in building contracts, was produced by the Cumann na nGaedheal at the Antient Concert Rooms on 29 Oct, and by the National Theatre Society at the Camden Street Hall in December. Ryan (see p. 132, n. 1) had recently become Secretary of the Irish National Theatre Society (see p. 219).

To Lady Augusta Gregory, [6 October 1902]

Nassau Hotel.
⟨Tuesda⟩ Monday

My dear Lady Gregory: I shall go down tomorrow if all goes well. Moore who seemed inclined to give way became obstinate again when Russell saw him on Sunday. Russell told him what he thought of his conduct & said he would see him no more. Moores last words were that he would consult Gill.[1] Moore went to Fay a couple of weeks ago & told them he would get out an injunction if they produced the play. Fay said 'you will', 'are you quite sure you will. You wont forget it will you.' Moore said 'no endeed I wont. I ll make it hot for you.' Fay replied 'Then I m a made man. I ll never have to advertize if you ll only take out that injunction'.

When Russell told Moore who was blustering a great deal that I would have money to fight, Moore got plaintive & said I was bulleying him. Russell proposed as a compromise that we should each use the story as we liked, & that what ever public statement was to be made about it should be written by him. Moore rejected this. I have insisted on Moore retracting if he wants to be on friendly terms with me. My father says he is jealous of Kathleen Ny Hoolihan.

Martyn has written a wonderful letter to the Fays. He offered £10 at the end of a year if they played an Irish play at every performance & performed three times a week. He also told them that they must get the accent & the manners of good society before they could do anything. They understood this to mean get English accents. Moore & Martyn are wonderful.[2]

It was only F Fay who played the fool over the plays. The rest like both your play & Hydes plays greatly & will play them.[3] W. Fay keeps saying

---

[1] Thomas Patrick Gill (1858–1931), a politician, agriculturalist, and widely experienced editor, whose house in Dalkey Moore frequently visited. From 1898 to 1899 Gill had been editor of the Dublin *Daily Express*, then under the control of Horace Plunkett (see p. 183, n. 2), who subsequently appointed him to the staff of the Irish Agricultural Organisation Society.

[2] Martyn's letter is now lost. He disliked Irish brogue (see p. 174, n. 4), and favoured Ibsenite drama. WBY was later to glance at the eccentricities of Martyn and Moore in his play *The Cat and the Moon* (see especially *VPl*, 797).

[3] AG's one-act play, *Twenty-five*, published in the *Gael* (NY) in December 1902 as *A Losing Game*, was first produced on 14 Mar 1903. Its plot, in which an emigrant returns from America as a rich man to marry his sweetheart but, discovering that she is now the wife of an impoverished farmer, deliberately loses to him at cards to save his farm, offended the more radical nationalists by its implication that emigration brought wealth not available in Ireland. In an Abbey programme of 23 Feb 1907 AG wrote: 'Before I belonged to the Irish National Theatre Society I sent in a little play, "Twenty-Five", and it was refused, one of the grounds being that some of the members "did not approve of money being won at cards"'. In a letter of 25 Sept (see p. 229, n. 1) Frank Fay had written: 'In my brother's opinion *Twenty Five* would not suit us. He thinks the dialogue excellent, but doesn't think an Irish peasant however hard up, would play a stranger for

that your dialogue is wonderful. They are however a little sad over the emigration difficulty. They want to get a play about a returned American who did not make any money at all there. Miss Gonne lectured last night on Emer, in the place of Miss Doyle & quoted your book all through. She described Emer as the type 'of heroic love & of dignity'.[4]

All our young people seem to know and admire your book. They are going to get up Tableaux out of it.[5]

Yrs ever
W B Yeats

ALS Berg, with envelope addressed to Coole, postmark 'DUBLIN OC 6 02'.

To George Bryers, [after 7 October 1902]

COOLE PARK, | GORT, | CO. GALWAY.

Dear Mr Bryers: I return proofs.[1] Can I have a final proof of all set up in pages.

Yours snly
W B Yeats

ALS Berg.

his money like old Michael does, and even assuming the possibility of that, my brother thinks the card playing scene too long. Again he doesn't approve of card playing as a means of getting money and he thinks the play in country districts might incite to emigration on account of the glowing terms in which America is spoken of. I may say for myself that I quite agree with this verdict.'

In addition to *The Marriage* and the nativity play (see p. 224, n. 9), Hyde had recently completed *An Naomh ar Iarraid* (*The Lost Saint*), translated by AG and published in *Samhain* in 1902. Frank Fay, having been a keen supporter of the Gaelic League, was now more dubious about putting on plays in Irish (see p. 229, n. 4).

[4] At the beginning of her talk, 'Emer', presented to the Inghinidhe na hEireann, and published in the *United Irishman* on 1 Nov 1902 (3), MG announced that she had 'taken almost all the material for this paper from Lady Gregory's book, "Cuchulain of Muirthemne"'. The lecture sketched the mythological accounts of Cuchulain's long-suffering wife, and concluded that her 'life was a glow of beauty and triumph; she would not outlive her dream, and her name stands in Ireland for faithful and heroic love and dignity'. MG was standing in for Christine M. Doyle (d. 1945), an enthusiastic member of the Gaelic League and author of *Women in Ancient and Modern Ireland* (1917), who had apparently intended to speak on Irish-manufactured dress-material.

[5] The children of the Inghinidhe na hEireann gave a number of tableaux vivants, but there is no record of their performing scenes from *Cuchulain of Muirthemne*. They were to produce Hyde's *The Lost Saint* in January 1903, and this was perhaps absorbing all their energies.

[1] For *Samhain*, published jointly by Bryers and Unwin in October 1902. In a letter of 28 Sept (*LWBY* i. 109) AE told WBY that he had 'returned proof to Sealys'.

To George Bryers, [c. *15 October 1902*]

COOLE PARK, | GORT, | CO. GALWAY.

Dear Mr Bryers: I return proof marked for 'press'. As Unwin wrote to me that he had arranged to have his name on I have added it to cover & tittle [*for* title] page. If some hitch has arisen, you can cross out my correction.

Yrs snly
W B Yeats

'Samhain' should be out at end of weak. This is important. Send to same papers as last year.[1]

ALS Berg.

To William Rothenstein, 17 October [*1902*]

COOLE PARK, | GORT, | CO. GALWAY.
Oct 17

My dear Rothenstein

Your letter has only just been sent on by my housekeeper—

I would like very much to see Stirlings manuscript when I get back to London in November—

My eyes are too bad to read M.S. but I will get one of my little mystical community to read it out to me—

Stirlings death was a terrible thing[1]—Sooner or later he was certain to do good work—He showed me a quantity of designs for some sort of a heathen temple which seemed very imaginative—I couldn't follow his

---

[1] *Samhain* (1902) was reviewed by William Archer in the *Morning Leader* on 22 Nov, by the *Academy* on 29 Nov, by Quiller-Couch in the *Daily News* on 22 Dec, and by the *Morning Post* on 26 Dec.

[1] See p. 157. Stirling had committed suicide on 24 Apr of this year under conditions recalled by Wyndham Lewis in *Rude Assignment* (1950): 'He supported out of his slender reserves an aged mother and sister . . . and lived in a small dark flat in the Adelphi. For two or three weeks no one saw him around. At last they broke in: he was lying just inside the front door with his throat cut. The rats, infesting the London sewers, had chewed away some of his flesh' (116). Rothenstein, who had been named literary executor in a will found by the body, evidently wished to consult WBY about the possibility of publishing his literary remains, but nothing came of this. At their meeting earlier in the year Stirling had expounded to WBY his latest ideas on symbolic geometry and architecture.

numerical speculations & indeed had no great trust in them, but he lit on all sorts of interesting things by the way—

Yours sincly
W B Yeats

ALS Harvard. Rothenstein, *Men and Memories* (1932), II. 20.

To Sydney Cockerell, 17 October [*1902*]

Coole Park
Oct 17

My dear Cockerell, I have been a scandalously long time about writing to you, but my housekeeper in London didn't send your letter on for a couple of weeks. And when it came to me, I was caught in a strange sort of spider's web of George Moore's spinning, which I will explain to you when we meet. My plans were changing every day, and I found it impossible to say what I should publish next. I am not quite out of that web yet, but I know at any rate that I shall have a book to consult you about when I get to London.

Bullen has published a little play of mine, *Kathleen ni Hoolihan*, at the Caradoc Press—and though it is better than mechanical printing it is bad enough.[1] I am sorry I agreed to it. It is not worth the price and I am ashamed to hear of anybody buying it. I shall get to London early in November. Many thanks for your letter and your promise of advice, which I am badly in need of.

Yours sincerely
W B Yeats

Text from Wade, 381.

---

[1] *Cathleen ni Houlihan*, issued in cream paper boards lettered in brown, at 5*s.*, was decorated, engraved, printed, and bound in pigskin by Hesba Dora Webb (1869–1930), a poetess, and Henry George Webb (1876–1914), painter, etcher, and book decorator, at their Caradoc Press, Bedford Park, Chiswick, in an edition of 300 (see p. 183). They also produced an edition of eight copies printed on Japanese vellum, but WBY did not see any of these until his visit to Quinn in 1903. Cockerell was in partnership with Emery Walker in a firm of engravers and designers (see p. 192, n. 4), and WBY was eager to consult him about the design of his own books, and for advice about the Dun Emer Press, about to be established by ECY.

To George Russell (AE), 18 October [1902]

COOLE PARK, | GORT, | CO. GALWAY.
Oct 18

My dear Russell: Many thanks for note about Moore. Of course I ⟨am going on with play⟩ will publish play. Tell Moore to write his story & be hanged.[1]

Yrs snly
W B Yeats

ALS Indiana, with envelope addressed to 25 Coulson Avenue, Rathgar, Dublin, and postmark 'Gort OC 18 02'. Wade, 381.

To A. H. Bullen, [c. 19 October 1902]

COOLE PARK, | GORT, | CO. GALWAY.

My dear Bullen: I enclose *Kathleen Ny Hoolihan* which goes second in the book; so that if you approve of the book & do not think Moore too much of a risk you can go to press at once.[1] I will get Watt to arrange terms, but dont wait for that or anything before going to press. We will arrange for a series of years as usual. I am getting on with a book of verse.[2]

Yr ever
W B Yeats

APS Buffalo.

[1] See p. 228. WBY had evidently just received AE's note, telling him that Moore had said WBY 'might write the play and be hanged' (see below, p. 238). Although Moore did not sue WBY, he evidently remembered this incident when he began to draft his play, *The Apostle* in 1911. He went immediately to see George Roberts, then a director of the Maunsel Press, and, as Roberts recalled in the *Irish Times* of 19 July 1955 (5), 'seemed somewhat perturbed, and hastened to tell me what was worrying him. "I have written the scenario for a play," he said, "and you know what a whispering gallery Dublin is. I am afraid that someone will collar my idea and anticipate my publication. So I want you to publish the scenario, so as to queer their pitch". I thought the danger was rather remote and told him so, but he would not be persuaded. "No," said he, "it's a great idea, and I cannot run the risk of some damned incompetent amateur annexing and spoiling it".'

[1] WBY was eager to bring out *Plays for an Irish Theatre* as soon as possible, and at this stage intended to publish four plays in the first volume. In fact, the first volume contained only *Where There Is Nothing*, and *Cathleen ni Houlihan* appeared as the first play in the second volume.

[2] *In the Seven Woods*, published by the Dun Emer Press in August 1903.

To the Editor of the United Irishman, *22 October 1902*

Mention in next letter.
Telegram telling the *United Irishman* that it could announce the publication of *Where There Is Nothing* for 30 Oct.

To John Quinn, 22 October [*1902*]

COOLE PARK, GORT.
OCT 22.

My dear Quinn,
  Your telegram came today, and I can only say how very greatly I am obliged to you for taking so much trouble about my affairs.[1] I have been waiting to write to you until I knew something more definite about Moore's attitude. Lady Gregory has told you about the arrangement with "the United Irishman." When I left Dublin, Moore still declared that he was going on with his injunction. Russell had however told him what he thought of his conduct, and refused to have any more to do with him. I then came back here, having made all necessary arrangements. A few days ago I got a note from Russell, saying that Moore had been round to see him and to say that I 'might write the play and be hanged'. I sent him back a message that he might 'write his story and be hanged'. So I suppose I am all right now, as I have Russell's letter written by his request. I cant say I think Moore gave way to any friendly impulse as Russell told me that Moore was very blustering until he told him that I was not only ready but able to fight. Whereon he got plaintive, and even said I was trying to bully him. Russell says that he kept from laughing with difficulty, but solemnly pointed out to him that under the circumstances a trial might run him into considerable expense. Russell left him faltering as he thought, but a few days after he grew blustery again. My own conviction is that he had never thought it possible that I could fight him in a court of law. I am of course delighted not to have a public row, which would have been very injurious to the movement. On receipt of your wire today I wired United Irishman

---

[1] Quinn's telegram of 21 Oct suggested that he should arrange for the publication of a paper-covered version of *Where There Is Nothing*. He subsequently offered the play to Dodd, Mead & Co, and to Scribners, but both rejected it, and he finally had it printed at his own expense by John Lane in New York to secure the American copyright. The edition, based on WBY's unrevised first draft, was entered for copyright at the Library of Congress on 24 Oct 1902, and filed there on 30 Oct. This paved the way for the 'Irish edition', issued as a supplement to the *United Ireland* on 1 Nov (see p. 228, n. 2). WBY continued to revise the play, which was performed by the Stage Society in June 1904, but it was never produced by the Irish National Theatre Society and was omitted from *Collected Plays*.

that they might announce the play for Oct 30. It is a great matter that owing to your kindness and energy I shall have secured the American copyright.

I need hardly say I will send you a copy of the Irish edition of the play as soon as it comes out. I have enlarged and enriched it in the last couple of weeks. And I will probably make a few more alterations before it comes out in its final form here. It was written in a fortnight and a day, and I will not know what it is really like till I have talked it over with my friends. At any rate it will serve one good purpose, it will give our little theatrical company in Dublin the long play they are beginning to feel a necessity. I shall be very curious to see the American edition. I was prepared to give up my copyright, not believing it possible to run it through so quickly, but Lady Gregory expressed a confidence in you, which has fully been justified.

I have also to thank you for the book.[2] I have long desired to have it. I bought a pamphlet with that name upon it in London but found it only contained about three chapters. Before I knew why you had sent it, I read out one or two bits to Lady Gregory, and said it sounded to me like Paul's talk. I thank you also for the North American Review, which otherwise I would probably not have seen.[3] I am going to call my book of plays 'Plays for an Irish Theatre'. I remember you did not like the idea of 'Plays for a Barn'. It will contain four plays in prose.[4] And I will shortly issue a play in

---

[2] In September Quinn had sent WBY his copy of Nietzsche's *Thus Spake Zarathustra*, translated by Alexander Tille in 1899. On 27 Sept 1902 he wrote (*LWBY* I. 106): 'I don't know whether you are acquainted with Nietzsche's writings or not. While his so-called philosophy is utterly abhorrent to me—the philosophy of the "blond beast", of the exaltation of brutality . . . nevertheless he has a wonderful epigrammatic style, and in recalling some of the dialogue of your play I was reminded of certain passages in *Zarathustra*. But since I sent the book to you I have received Lady Gregory's letter telling me that the play is finished so that you probably will not want to bother with the book at all.' WBY's pamphlet was Thomas Common's 1900 translation, containing only 'Zarathustra's Prefatory Discourse' and the Discourses 'Of the Three Metamorphoses' and 'Of the Bestowing Virtue'. During his American tour of 1903–4 WBY was to borrow and carry with him Quinn's copy of Common's *Nietzsche as Critic, Philosopher, Poet and Prophet* (1901).

[3] The *North American Review* of October 1902 published an article (473–85) on 'The Later Work of Mr. W. B. Yeats' by Fiona Macleod, who described WBY as a symbolist poet of genius, 'assuredly of that small band of poets and dreamers who write from no other impulse than because they see and dream in a reality so vivid that it is called imagination. With him the imagination is in truth the second-sight of the mind. Thus it is that he lives with symbols, as unimaginative natures live with facts.'

[4] See p. 237, n. 1. *Where There Is Nothing*, published by Bullen in 1903, was the first of a 3-volume series, Plays for an Irish Theatre. The three plays in the second volume (1904), *The Hour-Glass, Cathleen ni Houlihan*, and *The Pot of Broth*, were initially intended for inclusion in the first volume. WBY's original title for the series may have been suggested by Stendhal's recollection that his greatest theatrical pleasure had been a performance given by Italian strolling players in a barn, but Quinn was opposed to it, writing on 27 Sept 1902 (*LWBY* I. 108): 'you can find a much more fitting name for the book than "Plays for a Barn". That title does not *sound* like Yeats. It conveys no definite meaning and would, I fear, be misunderstood—at any rate in this country . . .'

verse[5] which naturally pleases me more than prose. Just lately I have been doing a somewhat elaborate essay on Spenser. The first draft of it is finished, but this morning has come a long letter from Yorke Powell putting me on the track of old allegorical poems which I shall have to look up in London.[6]

[*In WBY's hand*]
Again thanking you for all this trouble

Yours sincerely
W B Yeats

[*Vertically across top of letter in AG's hand*]
A great many thanks for yr letter, & for N. A. Review, & for all you are doing—You cannot think what a gt help it has been having a friend in the new world—

Yrs sinl
A Gregory

TLS NYPL.

To Frederick York Powell, [c. 22 October 1902]

Mention in letter from Powell, 23 October 1902.
Telling Powell that he is feeling better; that he is making good progress with his dictation; discussing his edition of Spenser and the allegorical tradition;[1] and mentioning that he intends to write in memory of Lionel Johnson.[2]

MBY.

[5] Evidently *On Baile's Strand*, first published in *In the Seven Woods* (1903).

[6] Powell's letter is now lost, but writing on 23 Oct 1902 (MBY) he said he would 'try to find a paper of Moulton's on *Faery Queen* whc. will, I think, interest you. It deals with the *allegorical* side of it, and does it rather well. O. Elton knows a lot about Spenser. The best text is Macmillan's, edited by Hales, the Globe Edition whc. is very good indeed.' In his introduction to *Poems of Spenser* (1906) WBY mentioned Dante, Bunyan, and Langland, but admitted (*E & I*, 382) that he was 'for the most part bored by allegory, which is made, as Blake says, "by the daughters of memory", and coldly, with no wizard frenzy'. For his selection, WBY chose only 'a few allegorical processions' which were sufficiently visionary, or passionate, 'to make one forget or forgive their allegory', and in 1937 recalled (*E & I*, p. vii) that in his youth he thought allegory had 'spoiled Edmund Spenser'.

[1] This was a reply to Powell's 'long letter' on allegorical poems (see above, n. 6). In his reply of 23 Oct Powell said he quite agreed 'with you as to the way of dealing with Spenser. One can only give one's own impression honestly but one wants to know exactly what he is driving at as well as his technique & that is the only use in reading his predecessors and models.' He also agreed with WBY in liking the 'solid actuality' of the poems.

[2] WBY's friend of the early 1890s, the poet and literary journalist Lionel Pigot Johnson

To Frederick York Powell, [*30 October 1902*]

Mention in letter from Powell, 31 October 1902.
Sending Powell a copy of the *United Irishman* containing *Where There Is Nothing.*[1]

MBY.

To John Lane,[1] *1 November* [*1902*]

Nassau Hotel | Dublin—
Nov 1

Dear Mr. Lane—
   You will have heard from Mr. Quinn about the play 'Where there is Nothing'—I send you the copy as printed in the United Irishman, which contains several modifications of the text as sent to New York—There is no longer anything to fear from Moore—he sent me a message about ten days ago that I might "publish my play & be hanged"—(to which I replied that he might publish his story "& be hanged"). The play has been out 3 days now, & I hear he feels himself beaten & says he will not read it—He did not find a single person here to back him up—I hope to be in London very soon & will talk things over with you—What I want to know for the moment is, if the plates of the American edition are stereotyped, because if not, I will make some [?]considerable additions. I do not know how far this is possible if it has been stereoed—It is important, in view of the English edition, which I want to be perfect—Will you kindly let me have an answer

(1867–1902; see I. 496–7), had died on 4 Oct. Powell had evidently referred to this in his lost letter of 22 Oct, and now replied that it was 'good that you mean to write on Johnson for I think as I told you a bit of prose or (still more) verse if you felt it that way would certainly have pleased him'. WBY did not write in memory of Johnson at this time, but in 1904 he edited a collection of his poems for the Dun Emer Press, subsequently wrote about him extensively in *Autobiographies*, and recalled him in 'In Memory of Major Robert Gregory' (*VP*, 324).

[1] In thanking WBY for the play, Powell said it was 'impressive and keeps up its key wonderfully I think. I don't think I quite understand it, but as a piece of poetic drama I admire it & am glad to have it'.

[1] John Lane (1854–1925), antiquarian and publisher, set up the Bodley Head with Elkin Mathews in 1887 and published the two Rhymers' Club anthologies and many of WBY's contemporaries. After the partnership broke up in 1894 he kept the Bodley Head imprimatur, and published and eventually edited *The Yellow Book* (1894–7). He opened a New York office in 1896, which published the American edition of *The Wind Among the Reeds* in April 1899, but, although he issued Quinn's private copyright edition (see p. 238) he published no further editions of *Where There Is Nothing.*

at once, by wire if possible, as to the possibility of alterations, as I want to know before writing to Quinn—

My two little plays performed here have just been very successful—[2]

Yours sincly
W B Yeats

Dict AG, signed WBY; Texas.

To James Joyce,[1] *[2 November 1902]*

Nassau Hotel | South Fredrick St | Dublin

Dear Mr Joyce: Lady Gregory begs me to ask you to come & dine with her at the Nassau Hotel tomorrow (Monday) at 6.45. to meet my father.[2]

Yrs sny
W B Yeats

ALCS Yale, addressed to 7 S. Peter's Place, Cabra, postmark indecipherable. *LJJ* II. 14.

[2] *Cathleen ni Houlihan* and *The Pot of Broth*, produced during the Samhain season, 27 Oct to 1 Nov 1902, at the Antient Concert Rooms. These productions received less attention than those in April and at first audiences were thin, but, as James Cousins recalled (*We Two Together*, [Madras, 1950], 77), things picked up on the last night: 'The audiences all through the inaugural performances of the Irish National Dramatic Company had been small, but we prided ourselves that they had been very select. On the last night of the season, Saturday, the public of Dublin discovered that interesting plays were being performed, that the very authors themselves could be seen walking about quite tame, and that the actors were actually Dublin people that may be some of them knew. The hall was packed. "A Pot of Broth" went down with gusto; and Yeats awoke to find himself a popular laughter-maker.' Griffith's review of the play in the *United Irishman* on 8 Nov (3) corroborates this, for he reported that the play 'convulsed its audiences with laughter. It is the first Irish piece which is not a caricature, but a kindly-Irish bit of humour, and which has genius as well as humour in it. We require many more pieces like it, for we had almost forgotten how to laugh in this country except to the Cockney note.'

[1] This is WBY's first surviving letter to James Joyce (1882–1941; see Appendix), Irish novelist, poet, and dramatist, who had applauded vigorously at the opening performance of the ILT in May 1899, and refused to sign a letter by his fellow students denouncing it. He had subsequently attacked the folk and mythological policy of the ILT in his pamphlet, *The Day of the Rabblement* (1901), but was now making an effort to introduce himself to Dublin writers. AE had written to WBY in August (Denson, 43) that he 'would find this youth of 21 with his assurance and self-confidence rather interesting', and on WBY's arrival in Dublin in October warned him that the 'first spectre of the new generation has appeared. His name is Joyce. I have suffered from him and I would like you to suffer.' Their first encounter occurred shortly after this and WBY later wryly recorded (*James Joyce*, 100–3) the nettling effect of Joyce's self-assured scorn for his literary preferences and endeavours.

[2] No account of this dinner exists but there is no reason to suppose that it did not take place. Joyce and Gogarty later met JBY briefly in Northumberland Road, when, as Gogarty records in *It Isn't That Time of Year At All!* (1954), Joyce urged him to ask the old man for two shillings: 'Savagely the old man eyed me and my companion. He looked from one to the other. At last he broke out: "Certainly not", he said. "In the first place I have no money; and if I had it and lent it to

To John Quinn, 8 November [*1902*]

Nassau Hotel | Dublin
Nov 8

Dear Mr Quinn,

I begin a letter to you feeling quite overwhelmed with the thought of all I have to thank you for, both in Mr Yeats name and my own.[1] What can one say? you have worked as some work for money and some for love, but none, as far as I have known up to this, for pure kindliness towards new friends. I can only say 'thank you' and he says 'thank you', but you will know that these unsatisfactory words that one uses for every small occasion, mean very deep and lasting gratitude, and a hope that some day or other we may be able in some part to make you know how truly we feel it.

As to the money part, it is only a part of your kindness to have thought of sharing the cost, but I cannot allow you to deprive me of the pleasure of taking that on myself.[2] It is no great load in any case, and I feel quite sure the play will pay it back some day, and if it should not, I owe so much already to Mr Yeats, even in that way, for without him there would be no Cuchulain, & no Finn, that I am only too glad to have a chance of repaying him a little on account.

Now to business, and now Mr Yeats is dictating or at least approving.

We could not write to you by last mail, for we had nothing definite from Lane. Since then Lane has written to say that he is ready to accept the book on the condition he gets Mr Yeats next book of verse. This is impossible, as it is already promised to his sisters, who are starting a private press. Mr Yeats will be in London in a day or two, and will show all the correspondence to A. P. Watt, his agent, and consult him about the whole matter. There was no time to consult him before. But now the copyrights are secured one can go about the matter deliberately. One difficulty is, he has

---

you, you and your friends would spend it on drink." He snorted. Joyce advanced and spoke gravely. "We cannot speak about that which is not." But old Yeats had gone off rapidly. "You see", said Joyce, still in a philosophical mood, "the razor of Occam forbids the introduction of superfluous arguments. When he said that he had no money that was enough. He had no right to discuss the possible use of the non-existent"' (69–70).

[1] Although typed by AG, this letter was written jointly with WBY, and is a response to a letter from Quinn of 25 Oct (NYPL) telling her of his arrangements for the copyright publication of *Where There Is Nothing* (see p. 238, n. 1). Quinn explained that he had arranged with Lane's New York manager, Paget, 'that if Lane does not take over the book upon terms as to royalty, etc. that are satisfactory to both sides, the property in the plates become mine . . . and in that event I can have the five hundred copies printed and arrange at my leisure with some other publisher here . . .'

[2] Quinn's letter concluded: 'If there should be any liability whatever I trust that, in order that "honors may be even" in this respect, you will accord me the privilege of dividing equally the liability and responsibility with yourself.'

been working over the play, and has made a good many changes, writing an entirely new beginning to the fourth act, which greatly increases its strength. We thought from your letter the book had been stereod, but Mr Lane writes 'I find the book has not been plated, so you will be in time to incorporate your corrections.' The United Irishman is also keeping its type set up till he has seen Watt. Lane wired to New York for information, so I suppose he is right about there being no plates as yet. Mr Yeats will write to you next week, directly he has seen Watt and Lane.

We have had a busy fortnight here in Dublin. The little dramatic company has made a good start. A play by one of the young men, The Laying of the foundations, has been very successful, and Kathleen ni Houlihan and Pot of Broth. These are the three favourites, and the acting was wonderfully good, especially the acting of W. Fay in the pot of Broth. They are throwing off the conventions of English acting, and may develop an art of their own. Except on Saturday when the hall was crowded, the audience was small, the 'respectable' classes being afraid of dangerous novelties, but a small profit, about £10 was made so it doesnt much matter. The 'respectable' classes are very funny here. A clergyman living in Merrion Square said to old Mr Yeats 'I shall be able to go and see the plays in the Antient Concert Rooms, of course one could not go to St Theresa's Hall'. Mr Yeats answered 'After all Christianity did not begin in Merrion Square'.

Stephen Gwynn was sent over by the Fortnightly to do an article on the plays, I will send it to you when it comes out.[3]

The secret of 'Where there is nothing' was well kept, and Moore had no suspicion. Only a few days before its appearance he had said to the Hydes 'Yeats will be a year at that play, he cant write more than five lines a month'. He was at the first night of the plays, in a back seat and did not come near any of us, but he never appeared in public after the play appeared, he must feel that he is beaten. He professes not to have read it, but said to Russell, 'Does the hero change clothes?' 'Yes' 'Has he a brother?' 'Yes' 'O then its exactly the same thing, absolutely mine!' He also says he feels towards Yeats as towards a man who dined with him and stole his spoons! But this does not matter now the play is out, Yeats ideas and the absence of Moore's ideas are too clearly manifest. Needless to say there is no talk of an injunction.

The play has startled people a good deal, and has already been denounced by a Jesuit.[4] However the number of the U. I. containing the

---

[3] Gwynn's article, 'An Uncommercial Theatre', appeared in the *Fortnightly Review* of December 1902 and reviewed the activities of the Irish theatre since the production of *Diarmuid and Grania*.

[4] Probably Fr. Peter Finlay SJ, who was particularly concerned at the morals of the Dublin stage. On 24 Oct 1903 the *Leader* quoted him (133) on the need 'to purify, if possible, the stage— the metropolitan stage particularly, which . . . is sinking, mainly through the connivance of Catholics, to the moral level of London and Paris'.

play had a very large sale, and it has had an increase of circulation this week. Someone has written it a letter which I am sorry is not to be published, saying that Mr Yeats has recommended to the Irish people 'drunkeness sensuality and the English game of cockfighting, and more blackguardly than all, finished by gloryfying the priesthood.'

Russell is delighted with it, and Magee, and Yeats father, and Jack, and Bulfin,[5] who made his bed shake under him with laughter while he read it. Mrs Emery who copyrighted it in London,[6] and had a caste of 17 says it went splendidly, and is a very fine stage play. She is going to send it to Forbes Robinson.[7] Yeats will send you the play in its perfect form in a day or two, we are still at it. He is making Paul a more lovable character, and lightening any part that seemed heavy with his fantasy.

I should like to go on writing many more little bits of gossip to you, but it is my last day for practical purposes as I go back to Coole on Monday, and I must go out now.

With many many thanks again,

Always many thanks
Augusta Gregory

[*On verso of last sheet in WBY's hand*]
I can only say that I thank you for all you have done. I am grateful to you. I entirely owe to you & to Lady Gregory the copyrighting of the play. I had given it up as impossible. I will write when I get to London.

Yours gratefully
W B Yeats

TLS Berg, with envelope addressed to 120 Broadway, New York, postmark 'DUBLIN NOV 8 1902'.

---

[5] William Bulfin (1862–1910) was born in Offaly but emigrated to Argentina in his teens and became the proprietor of the *Southern Cross* in Buenos Aires. He returned to tour Ireland in 1902 and published an account of his experiences in *Rambles in Eirinn* (Dublin 1907).

[6] *Where There Is Nothing* was read for copyrighting in London on 20 Oct 1902, an occasion recorded in Nevinson's diary (Bodleian): 'Early train to Uxbridge Rd & so to Victoria Hall & found Mrs. Emery. A number of men came. Sturge Moore the only one of importance, & he not of great importance but all friendly & cleverish. E[dith] W[heeler] read Sabrina admirably & I had to take the chief part of Paul . . . then "The Wise Man & the Fool". I had to take the wise man by Mrs. Emery's order & I saw Sturge Moore turn suddenly green—very absurd!'

[8] Johnston Forbes-Robertson (see p. 5, n. 7) was a leading London actor-manager.

To Thomas MacDonagh,[1] *9 November* [*1902*]

Nassau Hotel | Dublin
Nov 9

Dear Mr. McDonough—

I am returning your book with many thanks[2]—First of all, for the practical questions you ask me—A thousand is far too large an edition for a first book of verse—In England where there is a larger public for new verse than in this country, 500 or even 300 is a usual edition. I have very little practical knowledge of the expense of printing—but Seelys estimate for a thousand in paper cover does not seem to me exorbitant—but I would strongly urge you to consult a practical printer—What I w^d. advise you to do is print a very small edition, if you have definitely decided to publish, but to see that the paper is fairly good—You might also bind a very small number of copies in plain grey boards, as a paper pamphlet is likely to be ignored by reviewers, & see that these copies are sent to the papers—You will have to look after the printing, as no Irish printer can be trusted to make a page in which there will be no sign of inartistic antiquated method—I advise you to take some book of recent verse by a good writer & make the printer copy it—a book say published by Elkin Mathews or John Lane—

Now about the verses themselves—They show that you have a thoughtful and imaginative mind—but you have not yet got a precise musical & personal language—Whether you have poetical poems or not I could not really say—but I can say that you have not yet found yourself as a poet—If

---

[1] Thomas MacDonagh (1878–1916), poet, playwright, and a leader of the Easter Rising, was at this time teaching at St Kiernan's College, Kilkenny, and had recently joined the Gaelic League. His first book of poems, *Through the Ivory Gate*, appeared early in 1903, and his second, *April and May*, later in the same year. From 1903 he taught in Fermoy, but in 1908 took up an appointment in St Enda's, Padraic Pearse's Gaelic school in Dublin, and in October of that year his play, *When the Dawn Is Come*, was produced by the Abbey. After taking an MA at University College, Dublin, he joined the staff of the English Department there. Further volumes of poems appeared in 1906, 1910, and 1913, the year in which he published *Thomas Campion and the Art of English Poetry*. He co-founded the *Irish Review* (1911–15), and became a friend of WBY, whom he satirized as Earl Winton-Winton de Winton in his play *Metempsychosis* (1912). In 'Easter 1916' WBY celebrated him (*VP*, 392–3) as one who 'might have won fame in the end, / So sensitive his nature seemed, / So daring and sweet his thought'. His study of Gaelic and Anglo-Irish poetry, *Literature in Ireland*, appeared shortly after his execution in 1916.

[2] MacDonagh had evidently sent WBY the MS of *Through the Ivory Gate* with a request for criticism and advice about publication. The book, whose major theme is his religious crisis over a failed vocation, was published by Sealy Bryers & Walker early in 1903 and was dedicated to WBY. In sending him a copy in January 1903, MacDonagh confessed (Texas) that he had not followed all his advice: 'finding that the difference of cost between five hundred and a thousand copies was very small comparatively, I had the latter number printed: for the rest I will follow it, it will keep me from publishing more for a long time . . .'. MacDonagh was to give his own views on Irish publishing in the *United Irishman* on 23 Apr 1904.

you are young, & if you feel you have something you must give expression to, I strongly advise you not to publish for the present but (1ˢᵗ) to read the great old masters of English, Spenser, Ben Jonson, Sir Thomas Brown, perhaps Chaucer—until you have got our feebler modern English out of your head—When we read old writers we imitate nothing but their virtues—for their faults, which were of their time & not of ours have no charm for us—If we read modern writers we are likely to imitate their faults for we share their illusions—

(2ⁿᵈ) I will advise you to translate a great deal from the Irish—to translate literally, preserving as much of the idiom as possible. I dont mean that you will stop at this kind of writing, but it will help you to get rid of the conventionality of language from which we all suffer today—I am sorry not to be able to praise yr verses more—but your letters have interested me very much & I hope you will do good work yet—

If after this, you still care to dedicate the book to me, you are certainly welcome to do so—

Yours sinly
W B Yeats

Dict AG, signed WBY; Texas.

To John Quinn, 11 November [1902]

Nassau Hotel | Dublin.
Nov 11.

My dear Quinn,

I hoped to send you today but it is impossible, a copy of the play in what is I think its final form. I had persuaded myself it was finished when we went to Press, I am always persuading myself that my things are finished. However I think it is really done now.[1] You will find the opening of the first act lighter and livelier, and the tinkers better individualised and altogether more poetical people. Paul too is more loveable, and that fourth act which was a little sketchy is now the strongest in the play.

The American edition which has just come is very well printed, and has a nice cover.[2] But it fills me with shame at the thought of all the trouble you have been put to, getting it printed, and correcting it, and all the rest.

---

[1] In the event, WBY went on revising *Where There Is Nothing* into the new year, and did not send it to Quinn until 6 Feb 1903. By this time he had altered it throughout, although the main changes occur in Acts I, IV, and V (see *VPl*, 1064–165, especially pp. 1064–86; 1121–65).

[2] A copy of the American private copyright edition, arranged by Quinn and issued in grey paper covers; see p. 238, n. 1. In April 1903 Quinn published 30 further copies, printed on large paper and with errors corrected.

I can see how very carefully you went through, I had expected to be in London before this, but go there tomorrow, and will see A. P. Watt and probably Lane, I will write at once to you as soon as I have anything definite to say.

This is merely a line to thank you very much for the copies received and again, for all you have done. The printing is so much better than that of the United Irishman that I will do my best to have the English edition printed from it.

Yours very sincely
W B Yeats

[*In WBY's hand*]
Lady Gregory sends many kind regards.

TLS NYPL, with envelope addressed to 120 Broadway, New York, postmark 'DUBLIN NO 11 02'.

To Clement Shorter, [? 12 November 1902]

18 Woburn Buildings | Euston Road, | London.
Wednesday.

My Dear Shorter:

I am working at a theatrical project with Sturge Moore & some others, & he has just been round to ask me to go with him into the country on Sunday to see somebody in connection with the project.[1] I told him of my engagement to you & asked if any other Sunday would do. He found there was none other until after Xmas. Will you therefore let me come to you some other day instead of next Sunday? I am sorry.

Yrs sny
W B Yeats

ALS BL.

[1] In late 1900 Sturge Moore and Binyon had started an amateur Literary Theatre Club (see Appendix, pp. 722–3), and WBY soon encouraged them to join him in establishing a Romantic Theatre in London. He was probably being taken to Limpsfield to meet W. A. Pye, a wine merchant whose daughters, Sybil and Ethel, were members of the Club, and in whose drawing-room they rehearsed dramatic scenes. The Club dissolved in 1903 before any plays were performed, but FF revived it in December 1905 as the Literary Theatre Society, Ltd. WBY subsequently dined at the Shorters' on 19 Nov.

To John Lane, 15 November 1902

18 Woburn Buildings, | Euston Road, | W.C.
Nov. 15th.,/02.

Dear Mr Lane,

Please don't judge the merits of that play of mine from the proof you received from America which I am sorry to say was little more than a hasty sketch. I have expanded it & enriched it since then & I hope, got rid of the dull patches. I saw Mr A. P. Watt, who arranges my affairs, to-day. I hope to let him have by Monday a properly revised copy. I daresay you will hear from him.[1]

I am sending him all the correspondence about the play and I leave everything in his hands.

Yrs sinly
W B Yeats

Dict AEFH, signed WBY; Texas.

To James Joyce, [c. *15 November 1902*]

but I cannot say more than this. Remember what Dr Johnson said about somebody "let us wait until we find out whether he is a fountain or a cistern."[1] The work which you have actually done is very remarkable for a man of your age who has lived away from the vital intellectual centres. Your technique in verse is very much better than the technique of any young Dublin man I have met during my time.[2] It might have been the work of a young man who had lived in an Oxford literary set.[3] However men have started with as good promise as yours and have failed & men

---

[1] See p. 241.

[1] Hester Lynch Piozzi recalled (*Johnsonian Miscellanies* I [Oxford, 1897], 280) that, hearing her speak favourably of a visitor's character, Johnson replied: 'you cannot know it yet, nor I neither: the pump works well, to be sure! but how, I wonder, are we to decide in so very short an acquaintance, whether it is supplied by a spring or a reservoir?' WBY has added to this anecdote an echo of Blake's proverb from Plate 8 of *The Marriage of Heaven and Hell*: 'The cistern contains; the fountain overflows'. WBY's advice in this letter seems to be influenced by his first impression of Joyce as a dogmatic and possibly inflexible young man.

[2] At their first meeting (see p. 242, n. 1) Joyce read WBY his Epiphanies, 'a beautiful though immature and eccentric harmony of little prose descriptions and meditations', and had evidently sent WBY some of his poems, later published as *Chamber Music* (1907). A MS of *Chamber Music* sold with the Gilvarry Collection on 7 Feb 1986 was reputedly the one 'specially prepared for the occasion' from which 'in 1902 the youthful James Joyce read aloud his poems to W. B. Yeats'.

[3] 'You know, Dedalus, you have the real Oxford manner.' *Ulysses* I. 5.

have started with less and have succeeded. The qualities that make a man succeed do not shew in his work, often for quite a long time. They are much less qualities of talent than qualities of character—faith (of this you have probably enough), patience, adaptability, (without this one learns nothing),[4] and a gift for growing by experience & this is perhaps rarest of all.

I will do anything for you I can but I am afraid that it will not be a great deal. The chief use I can be, though probably you will not believe this, will be by introducing you to some other writers who are starting like yourself, one always learns one's business from one's fellow-workers, especially from those who are near enough to one's own age to understand one's own difficulties.[5]

Yrs snly
W B Yeats

Frag dict AEFH, signed WBY; Yale. *LJJ* II. 13–14.

To Thomas Hutchinson, [*? November 1902*]

. . . It should never have been advertised or sent for review. It is printed at a hand press & intended for certain very foolish people who are called collectors.[1] Jack B Yeats is my brother . . . 'Samhain' and 'Beltaine' are the old names for Hallow-Eve and May Day . . .

Printed extract from *The Library of John Quinn*, Anderson Galleries Catalogues (New York, 1924), V. 1139.

---

[4] Although WBY makes no open reference to it, this is a rejoinder to Joyce's high-handed repudiation of 'Mr. Yeats's treacherous instinct of adaptability' in his essay 'The Day of the Rabblement' (*The Critical Writings of James Joyce*, ed. Ellsworth Mason and Richard Ellmann [1959], 71).

[5] Perhaps a rueful echo of Joyce's parting shot at their first meeting (*James Joyce*, 103): 'Presently he got up to go, and, as he was going out, he said, "I am twenty. How old are you?" I told him, but I am afraid I said I was a year younger than I am. He said with a sigh, "I thought as much. I have met you too late. You are too old."'

[1] The indefatigable Hutchinson (see p. 75, n. 1) had evidently been enquiring about the Caradoc Press edition of *Cathleen ni Houlihan*.

To Lady Augusta Gregory, 18 November 1902

18, Woburn Buildings, | Euston Road,
November 18th 1902

My dear Lady Gregory.

I enclose two letters, one from the young man whose verses we looked through, the other a very touching letter which I have just received from a midshipman in Hongkong.[1] I want you to advise me how to answer him. I suppose he is discouraged and homesick. I suppose he has some faint hope that I may advise him to come home and take to literature, and possibly suggest some employment. The only thing I can think of is to urge him to work on where he is for some few years and see if things go better with him. And to advise him a little about his reading. I thought of advising him to make a record of what he sees and thinks, filling it with meditations. I might possibly send him a book of mine as a sign of good-will. I do not know whether the starry influences are bringing me this sort of thing now, but I had a still more difficult thing of the same kind last night. Pixie Smith[2] and Sturge Moore and Miss Horniman were round with me— Duncomb Jewell[3] came in looking very ill. He led the conversation round

---

[1] One of the letters was evidently from Thomas MacDonagh, probably in reply to WBY's of 9 Nov (see p. 246). The other was from Henry G. O'Brien (1883–1971), an Irish midshipman serving on HMS *Argonaut* in Hong Kong. O'Brien explained (*LWBY* I. 109–11) that he had failed his sub-lieutenant examinations and was, with some cause, regarded as one of the slackest officers on the ship. He explained that he lacked nautical zeal because he was constantly daydreaming about Ireland, and that he wished to be an Irish farmer and write books like WBY's. He left the navy in 1903, but became a priest rather than a farmer, and was for many years the parish priest of Kingsbridge, Devon.

[2] Pamela Colman ('Pixie') Smith (1878–*c.* 1955), an American artist, stage designer, book illustrator, and folklorist, moved to London from Jamaica in 1899, and met WBY. She was currently editing *A Broad Sheet* with Jack Yeats, and making plans to edit the *Green Sheaf* (1903–4). Her interest in WBY's methods of chanting poetry led her to join FF's 'psaltery people'; she helped illustrate one of his lectures at Clifford's Inn in May 1903, and, as a member of the 'Chelsea Mummers', played the Faery Child in a production of *The Land of Heart's Desire* on 22 Mar and 4 June 1904, reciting the part 'after the manner of an Irish lilt'. She later impressed small New York audiences by chanting WBY's poetry in the Farr manner. Her portrait appeared in the *Critic* of January 1899, and in the same year JBY gave WBY a vivid but affectionate description of her and her father (MBY; printed with some inaccuracies in *JBYL*, 61) as 'the funniest looking people. The most primitive Americans possible. . . . Her dressing is not a decorative success. The bluest of blue dresses . . . the hat is straw, with great black cock feathers sticking up out of it. She looks exactly like a Japaneze. . . . You at first think her rather elderly, you are surprised to find out that she is very young. . . . She has the simplicity & naïveté of an old dry as dust savant—a savant with a *child's heart.*' Masefield later recalled her (*Some Memories of W. B. Yeats* [Dublin, 1940], 16) as 'Blithe Pixie, singing Yeats's songs or telling / West Indian tales with her bright painted dolls'. In later life she took to drink, and embarrassed her friends over a series of unpaid loans.

[3] Ludovick Charles Richard Duncombe-Jewell (1866–1947) was to resume his surname, Cameron, by deed poll in 1904. A soldier, special war correspondent of *The Times* and *Morning Post*, sportsman, and sometime poet, he was a champion of the Cornish language, founded the

to divination and kept it there nearly all the evening. When Sturge Moore went away he asked Miss Horniman to divine for him as to what he should do in a certain matter which he could not describe in any way. She got out her tarot cards and spread them out. Her voice changed as it does under such circumstances she began advising, and in what I must say seemed to be very general terms but which [were] evidently very significant to him. He stayed on and when everybody had gone said [*in WBY's hand*] "I came back from Ireland on Wednesday. I have not slept since then, with the exception of a few hours today. I have been in great trouble. My conscience has been going here & there like a weather cock. I could not find out what I had to do—I wanted to do right. She has held my conscience still. I know now where it is pointing. But there may be no miracle play now. This may be social extinxion for me." I asked no questions but told him not to think clairvoyance infallible.

[*Typing recommences*]

I have found out what is wrong with the little play.[4] The inner thought does not quite correspond with the picture which the play raises before the mind. The travelling man meets a woman on the road, who is full of anxiety, who fears to knock at any door lest she should be refused admission. He sends her to a house where she is well received and becomes prosperous. Then, when he comes into the cottage himself he upsets things that he may help a child in its play. One can't get away from the fact that to do these things is not to be the supreme disturber we have thought him. We have tried to impose a meaning on the play instead of finding a meaning in it. Now it seems to me that the travelling man goes about seeking to persuade people [to] live in some near and innocent happiness, putting away anxieties and worldly things. He is only a disturber because they put between themselves and this innocent happiness idols of various kinds which are symbolized by the plates on the dresser, and perhaps by the woman's fear of what people would think of her. He is much the same as various spiritual beings in Blake's prophetic books, who bid man's mind not to look before and after. He is in truth almost God Pan who was I think in the Renaissance some-

Celtic-Cornish Society, edited *Armorial Cornwall*, and at the Pan Celtic Congress of 1901 had made a spirited plea for recognition of Cornwall as a Celtic nation. His poem, 'The Mermaid of Zennor', subtitled 'Written for the Psaltery, 10 Mîs Merh, 1903', was published in the 6th number of Pixie Smith's *Green Sheaf* (1903). He never wrote a miracle play. The details of the scandal Duncombe-Jewell feared are untraced, but WBY was careful not to divulge his name to the typist, adding it later, with the other sensitive passages, in his own hand.

[4] WBY was collaborating with AG on a one-act play, *The Travelling Man*, but was shortly to turn it over entirely to her. In the final of many versions a penniless girl, unfairly turned out of service, is befriended by Christ in the guise of a tramp, and brought to a house where she finds a husband and a comfortable life. When the tramp later returns and untidies the house in playing with her son, she throws him out, only realizing who he is after he has gone. AG subsequently rewrote the piece and included it in her *Seven Short Plays* (1909); it was produced at the Abbey Theatre on 2 Mar 1910.

times identified with Christ. I am afraid this means a good deal of re-writing of Christs part, but I will send you a sketch as soon as I can and get you to work over it for me. Now that I have persuaded myself that this is the true meaning of the fable, I have begun to fall in love with the little play. I have had a letter from A. P. Watt to-day saying that he has read through the Moore correspondence and that Moore seems to him to have no case. I read the amended "Where there is nothing" to Arthur Symons on Sunday. He was very enthusiastic about it. To-night I read it to Bullen. I shall try and arrange to read it to a number of people next week.

[*Remainder of letter in WBY's hand*]

Poor Mrs Emery is out of favour with all my psaltery people. Dolmetsch I hear is angry because she takes money for lessens as he taught her for nothing. Sturge Moore is angry because she wont work & doesnt keep tune & he says his own pupils are better & Pixie Smith says I hear that Mrs Emery gossiped scandal about Mrs Dolmetsch. She said to Miss Horniman 'I didnt know what to do, so the moment I came back I went down to Windsor to the Dolmetsches. I stayed with them & did my best to set Mrs Dolmetsch against Mrs Emery. Of course I didnt tell her why.'[5] I need hardly tell you that all this makes Miss Horniman grateful & happy. She is ordering six new psalteries. I hear that Dolmetsch talks of making some changes in the construction of the instrument.[6] I am to hear Miss Owen, whom Dolmetsh prefers to Mrs Emery on Friday.[7] I dont expect very much as she is so accomplished a ⟨musician⟩ singer that her elocution wiil probably be bad. I cant see how any body is likely to speak well who has been a bagpipes for years.

Yours always
W B Yeats

I am writing in a reusteraint & have no more paper. I am in the best of good spirits. Last year I began the winter in black gloom.

TLS Berg, with envelope addressed to Coole, postmark 'LONDON. N.W. 19 NOV 02'.

[5] Dolmetsch would have been particularly aggrieved by FF's mercenary behaviour since he had gone bankrupt in August 1901, and had been forced to quit his Charlotte Street studio and auction his instruments and music library. A wealthy pupil of his wife provided them with cottages at Boveney, near Windsor, while they restored their finances. He had married his divorced sister-in-law, the accomplished harpsichordist, Elodie, née Desirée, as his second wife in 1899, but was to divorce her after returning from their American tour of early 1903 on grounds of incompatibility. On 23 Sept 1903, four days after the decree was made absolute, Dolmetsch married his devoted pupil, Mabel Johnston (d. 1963), whose presence on the American tour had led to a difficult *ménage-à-trois*. This marriage lasted until Dolmetsch's death in 1940.

[6] In his diary for December 1902 (Private) Dolmetsch noted that he had received £7. 10s. 0d. on account from W. Yeats for six psalteries at £2. 10s. 0d. each. No changes were made in the construction of the instrument after October 1901.

[7] Mary Price Owen was a singer, actress, and friend of AEFH. In 1903 she was living at 33 Markham Square, Chelsea. She took acting roles with touring companies from time to time.

To F. J. Fay, [c. *18 November 1902*]

Mention in letter from Fay, [c. 19 November 1902].
A postcard asking about changes in the cast of *The Hour-Glass*;[1] enquiring about the first performances at the Camden Street Hall; and evidently mentioning the possibility of the Company performing in London.[2]

Private.

To A. P. Watt, [*mid-November 1902*]

Mention in next letter.
Letter sending on a communication from John Lane about the publication of *Where There Is Nothing*.

To John Quinn, 19 November 1902

18 Woburn Buildings, | Euston Road. | London. | W.C.
Nov.19th,/02.

Dear Mr Quinn,
    I hope to send you in a few days, a final copy of the play; but I am anxious to read it to one or two people more before putting the last word to it. I read it to Arthur Symons on Sunday & he was very enthusiastic about it. And last night to Bullen who now takes back some objections he had to it in its old form & likes it as much as I could desire. I keep hearing about it from various Irish people. My sister tells me in a letter that came this morning how a brick-layer who was mending her hearth made a big hole and said, "That would do for Mr Yeat's play 'Where there is nothing'."

---

[1] Fay replied that the 'only change in the cast of *The Hour-Glass* is the substitution of Miss Laird for Miss Quinn for the wife at Miss Quinn's request'. Maire Quinn was evidently still piqued by the Fays' refusal to produce the play for Cumann na nGaedheal (see p. 229), but when the play was finally produced on 14 Mar 1903, she did in fact take the part of the Wise Man's Wife, Bridget.
[2] WBY had apparently told Fay that Stephen Gwynn had suggested the Company should stage performances in London under the auspices of the ILS, and in his reply Fay asked when 'would it be safe to write to Stephen Gwynn?' But he sounded a note of caution, and hoped that WBY would 'not say anything about us to your London friends that will lead them to think that if we are able to go there they are going to see anything extraordinary. It would be better to talk about the plays, the fact that Irishmen are beginning to dramatise their own country.'

My sister said that, new from England as she was, it startled her to hear a brick-layer talk of such things.[1] I have also had a letter from a man in Ballyhaunnis who tried to get up an Amateur Company to play it there.[2] On the other hand, it has, I must say, shocked a good many people. I have handed over your copy of the Copy-right Act, the Moore letters etc. to A. P. Watt the agent and he will arrange the business details. I have sent him a letter which I got from Lane. However the really troublesome work, was the work that you did for me & I can never thank you enough. I hear that our little theatrical company is to play the "Hourglass" in Loughrea before it plays it in Dublin. They begin their Winter's work there in the first week of December.[3] They will probably start, judging by my talk with them in Dublin, with "The Foundations" & either my little farce "A Pot of Broth" or "Cathleen-ni-Houlahan". I don't think I sent you a copy of it, except in the "Samhain": Bullen has had a limited edition, 320 I think, printed at the Caradoc Press, a private press.[4] I am afraid that the printing is not really good, but the type is pleasant & the page well arranged. My sisters, who are printing my next book of verse, will do much better.

Yours sincely
W B Yeats

[*In WBY's hand*]

As you see by this letter my eyes are still troublesome. However it has been altogeather a blessing as it has taught me to dictate, which has taken away the labour of writing almost wholly. I do twice or thrice as much work as I used to do.

Dict AEFH, signed WBY; NYPL, with envelope addressed to 120 Broadway, New York, postmark 'LONDON W NO 19 02', and stamped in New York 'DUE 10 CENTS'.

---

[1] SMY and ECY had moved to Dublin from London by 1 Oct 1902, taking up residence at 'Gurteen Dhas', Churchtown, near Dundrum, with JBY, their cousin, Ruth Pollexfen, and two servants.

[2] Ballyhaunis is a country town in east Mayo and WBY must have felt that his work was at last getting down to the grass roots. There is, however, no evidence that *Where There Is Nothing* was performed there, and the enterprising would-be producer is untraced.

[3] The National Theatre Society delayed their visit to Loughrea until Easter week 1903, when they played AE's *Deirdre* and WBY's *The Pot of Broth* to a packed house in aid of the building fund for St Brendan's Cathedral; Maire Nic Shiubhlaigh gives a colourful description of the trip (Nic Shiubhlaigh, 35–6). From 4 to 6 Dec the Society gave its first performances in the Camden Street Hall to small but appreciative audiences, reviving Ryan's *The Laying of the Foundations*, WBY's *The Pot of Broth*, McGinley's *Eilis agus an Bhean Déirce*, and Cousins's *The Racing Lug*.

[4] Quinn already knew of this and had written to WBY on 27 Sept 1902 (*LWBY* I. 108) that Mathews had sent him one of the vellum copies (see p. 183): 'It makes a very fine little book and I am glad to have it'. *In the Seven Woods*, the first book published by the Dun Emer Press, appeared in August 1903. In March 1904 WBY wrote in Quinn's copy that it was 'the first book of mine that is a pleasure to look at—a pleasure whether open or shut'.

To Frank Pearce Sturm,[1] [c. *19 November 1902*]

Mention in letter from Sturm, 23 November 1902, and partly quoted in *Bon–Accord*, 4 June 1903 (5).
Offering a sympathetic criticism of Sturm's writings; advising him that his thought was 'shadowy'; evincing interest in Sturm's articles and poems; complaining of eye trouble; warning him against MacGregor Mathers; and asking him not to show his letter to anyone for whom it was not intended. In a review of John Watson's poems in *Bon–Accord* on 4 June 1903, Sturm quotes (5) from what is evidently this letter, revealing that WBY 'in a criticism he once made of some of my poems, advised me "to wait a little, because," he wrote, "your sense of music will gradually take to itself, in all likelihood, more passion and more thought"'.

LWBY I. III–13.

To Lady Augusta Gregory, 20 November [*1902*]

18, Woburn Buildings | Euston Road.
Nov. 20th

My dear Lady Gregory,
I forgot in my letter to tell you that I went to Fisher Unwin on Monday about your book. He took both your address and the address of Hodges and Figgis, and will I understand write to either you or Hodges. He seemed anxious for the book but wants I imagine to get proofs from Hodges before deciding.[1] All my Moore papers and also Quinn's letters about John Lane copyrights, etc. are now with A. P. Watt. He will keep

---

[1] This letter, which arrived on 'Thursday morning' [*i.e.* 20 Nov], was apparently the first that WBY wrote to Frank Pearce Sturm (1879–1942), surgeon, mystic, and minor poet, and initiated a correspondence and friendship that were to last intermittently for the rest of WBY's life. Sturm had been born in Manchester, and after a short apprenticeship to a chemist, entered Manchester University. In 1901, following the collapse of his father's business, he transferred to the University of Aberdeen to read medicine. Already interested in mysticism and the occult, he began to supplement his income through journalism, and in articles and reviews spoke warmly of WBY's works, describing him in *Bon–Accord* of 4 June 1903 (5) as 'the subtlest poet and most impeccable artist of our time', and on 2 July 1903 (8) as 'the greatest of all modern writers and the most profound'. He had sent WBY some of his early poems, and a volume of these, *An Hour of Reverie*, appeared in 1905, followed a year later by a translation of *The Poems of Charles Baudelaire*. Sturm was to check the facts and correct the Latin of WBY's occult works, particularly *A Vision*, and WBY described him to OS on 4 Mar 1926 as 'a very learned doctor in the North of England'. In June 1936 Sturm recorded in his diary that 'Yeats is one of the greatest poets who wrote in English. In my opinion perhaps the greatest of all.' (Taylor, 119).

[1] Although Fisher Unwin had been interested in handling AG's *Cuchulain of Muirthemne* (see p. 136), her *Poets and Dreamers* (1903) was published solely by Hodges and Figges in Dublin.

them with my other papers. I dined with the Shorters last night. Shorter had got that Chancellor photograph of me. It was really very good, the first good photograph. He will put it in the Sphere when my next book comes out.[2] Rhys and Mrs Rhys were there and Shorter tells me they are now beginning to prosper. Mrs. Rhys' last book was a considerable success.[3] The Pall Mall Magazine has taken my poem about the old men and the Monthly Review has sent me a proof sheet of Adam's Curse, so that is probably taken too. Courtenay is going to use the article on William Morris in January. The book of Essays is to be kept back until then.[4] I am going to add the Essays I had sketched out in the rough and one or two new little essays. I have come to the conclusion thinking over Bullen's objection to the sermon in "where there is nothing", that it is too impersonal for Paul as we have now made him. I can easily make this change and the change will make the sermon more convincing and also give it a meaning for the individual soul. The extinguishing of every candle will as I think now associate itself with some precise principle of thought. Bullen complained that I had not written Paul's part in verse. He said an Elizabethan would have done so.[5]

Yrs sny
W B Yeats

[*On back of envelope*]
Will write in a couple of days. Typed this in a hurry.
WBY.

TLS Berg, with envelope addressed to Coole, postmark 'LONDON W. NO 20 02'. Wade, 382.

[2] The cabinet photograph of WBY by Chancellor of Dublin was printed in the *Sphere* on 6 June 1903 (220), to accompany a review of *IGE*; it is reprinted in *YA3*.

[3] Grace Rhys, née Little (1865–1929), an editor of children's tales and a popular novelist (see p. 48), had her greatest success with *The Wooing of Sheila*, published in July 1901, in which an orphaned peasant girl, Sheila M'Bride, is wooed and won by Michael Power, a wealthy young farmer, but leaves him on their wedding day when she discovers that he has accidentally killed an enemy in a fight. Michael atones by a pilgrimage to a holy well and, after a second wooing, he leads her back to the nuptial home. Shorter had himself given an early boost to the book, foretelling in the *Tatler* of 18 Sept 1901 (595) that 'the most brilliant future will accrue to . . . Mrs Ernest Rhys', basing his prophecy on 'the real and genuine talent displayed in this novel'. It quickly went into a 2nd edition.

[4] 'The Old Men Admiring Themselves in the Water' (*VP*, 208) appeared in the *Pall Mall Magazine* of January 1903, 'Adam's Curse' (*VP*, 204–6) in the *Monthly Review* of December 1902. William Courtney (1850–1928) was editor of the *Fortnightly Review*, where WBY's article on Morris, 'The Happiest of the Poets', was not published until March 1903, so delaying the appearance of *IGE* until May.

[5] Paul delivers his sermon in Act v, ll. 272–358 (*VPl*, 1135–40), preaching the destruction of 'everything that has Law and Number, for where there is nothing, there is God', and extinguishing the candles in the chapel one by one. WBY did not revise the sermon as radically as he proposes here, but he did orchestrate it so as to build up more compellingly to Paul's final revelation. Bullen was an enthusiastic Elizabethan scholar (see p. 13, n. 2).

To Gordon Craig, 20 November 1902

18, Woburn Buildings | Euston Road
Nov. 20th, 1902

My dear Craig,

I am back as you see and have brought a long prose play with me,[1] which is at any rate unlike any other play. I am going to read it to a few friends next Wednesday evening. Will you come and be one? Come about eight. Our plays this year went very well in Dublin. Our little company has invitations coming in from various parts of the country, and should I think do very well. Of course we have begun on a very small scale but we are already playing verse very much better than it is played here. Our movement too is a real movement of the people. We don't play for the merely curious or for people who want to digest their dinners in peace, but for zealous bricklayers and clerks and an odd corner boy or two.[2] That is to say we have a thorough-going unruly Elizabethan audience. The poor parts of the house are always full. The Miracle play I sent you some time ago had to be postponed as the man who was going to play the hero was arrested under the Coercion Act. I see by the paper this morning that he has got three months.[3] Our little company is going down to Loch Reay however to play it some time during the winter.

Yours sny
W B Yeats

TLS Arsenal.

---

[1] i.e. *Where There Is Nothing.* Craig has written on this letter: 'Send me play. London theatre *soon*'. WBY evidently sent him a copy, for on 29 Jan 1903 (MBY) Craig asked him for 'another copy of "Where There Is Nothing", new version or old version', adding that he would like to produce it 'especially if the Stage Society is willing. You see, I shall have a theatre but say nothing about this to anyone.'

[2] Craig has underlined the words from 'who want to digest their dinners' to 'an odd corner boy or two' and added archly at the bottom of the page 'does the bricklayer go in for indigestion?'

[3] On 20 Nov the *Freeman's Journal* (2) reported that Timothy M'Carthy and Thomas O'Dwyer had been sentenced under the Coercion Act to two months hard labour, and Stephen Holland for one day, for publishing anti-eviction articles in the *Irish People* between July and September 1902. Which of the former two was to be the hero of *The Hour-Glass* (a version of which WBY had shown to Craig in June; see p. 201) is unknown: since neither had any connection with the Fays' company, it may be that WBY had mistaken the name, or was trying to impress Craig with an exaggerated account of the unruly energies of Irish theatrical life. It had been arranged since August that Digges and Frank Fay were to take the main parts in *The Hour-Glass*, and although the play was postponed, this was due to production policy (see p. 229, n. 2). It is possible, but very unlikely, that WBY had given permission for another company to stage the play before its production by Fay.

To an unidentified correspondent, 22 November 1902

18 Woburn Buildings, | Euston Road, | London.
Nov. 22nd,/02.

Dear Sir,

I hope you have succeeded in getting your copies of "Beltaine", because there was a mis-print which I have only just discovered. "S*t* Martin's Lane" is mis-printed "St Mark's Lane".[1] Russell's "Deirdre" is I understand to be published in the Xmas No. of "The Homestead" the organ of the Plunkett organisation. The office is at 22 Lincoln Place, Dublin. You might mention in writing why you want "The Homestead" as it is possible they may have changed their plans.[2] A play of mine appeared in the "United Irishman" a while back, Special "Samhain" Number. I have no doubt they have copies, but I strongly recommend you to wait until you can get it in book form, as it has been practically re-written.[3] The other plays have been for the most part so much reconstructed on the stage, that I don't think you need, as yet, bother much about the printed versions. It will be different when we have all got more experience.

Yrs snly
W B Yeats

Dict AEFH, signed WBY; Private.

To Wilfrid Scawen Blunt, 24 November 1902

18 Woburn Buildings, | Euston Road. | W. C.
Nov. 24th,/02.

Dear M*r* Blunt,

You see my eyes are still bad and I have to dictate. A great many thanks for the peasants, they come in good time to entertain a musician and a

---

[1] No such misprint occurs in the separate issues of *Beltaine*, nor in the one volume re-issue of all three numbers (*Bibl*, 247). The mistake was probably made in a publicity flyer for the bound volume which WBY had passed on to his correspondent.

[2] AE's *Deirdre* had first appeared serially in O'Grady's *All Ireland Review* (see p. 167, n. 2), and was to be reprinted on 6 Dec 1902 in the *Celtic Christmas* issue of the *Irish Homestead*, the weekly journal of Horace Plunkett's Irish Agricultural Organisation Society.

[3] i.e. *Where There Is Nothing*; see pp. 228, 238.

troubadour, but alas you do not like my troubadours.[1] One [?*for* Our] week of plays in Dublin was very successful, and they have now got a little miracle play of mine in rehearsal.

Yrs sny
W B Yeats

Dict AEFH, signed WBY; Private.

To Gordon Bottomley,[1] *24 November 1902*

18 Woburn Buildings, | Euston Road.
Nov. 24th,/02.

Dear Sir,

Your book has come to me from Ireland where I left it behind me & I have been looking through it. Unfortunately I have had a trouble in the eyes which has made reading very difficult for some time, I can see however that you have hit on a story with considerable dramatic possibilities. I doubt however if your verse is sufficiently speech. Too much of it seems to be descriptive verse. A great difficulty in writing a play is to make the people talk to each other, and not to describe each other or themselves. Then too, one has to get something of the sound of actual speech without breaking the form of verse or lowering the emotion. I remember sending a message to Michael Field[2] many years ago suggesting that they should try to master dramatic form in prose. I am now trying to do the same thing and I find it a fine discipline which helps me very much when I write in

---

[1] After hearing WBY lecture on chanting at Clifford's Inn on 10 June, Blunt wrote (ii. 28) that WBY 'was far from convincing me that the method was either new or good as a way of reading poetry, indeed it reduced the verse to the position it holds in an opera libretto'. Several days later, during his 'Poets' Party' (see p. 202), he recorded that 'all agreed that Yeats' theories of recitation were wrong, useful only for concealing indifferent verse'.

[1] Gordon Bottomley (1874–1948), poet and playwright, had sent WBY a copy of his one-act verse play, *The Crier by Night* (1902), in which a reincarnated Irish queen seeks eternal union with the married man she loves by bartering both their lives to Death (the 'Crier by Night'), only to find that at the moment of death he calls his wife's name. Although much inferior, the play has some affinities in theme with WBY's *The Only Jealousy of Emer* (1919). Bottomley modelled himself as a playwright on WBY, and his later verse dramas were particularly influenced by WBY's theories of poetic drama and verse-speaking. WBY included his 'To Iron-Founders and Others' in *OBMV*.

[2] See p. 384, n. 1. WBY had probably written to them in 1885 after reading their collection of plays, *The Father's Tragedy, William Rufus, Loyalty or Love*. In a draft review of the book (MBY) he complained that 'through all these plays the execution is to[o] complex and the conception to[o] simple', and accused 'Michael Field' of being 'over busy with trying the ring of your verse'.

verse. I can see that you have begun to think about construction, that is half the business. ⟨I doubt if your audience would feel the supernatural nature however of that old man while his presence⟩ You have not mastered clear simple dramatic speech. The subject however is poetical and you have got a good deal of atmosphere into it and you have packed a good deal of passion into it.

Yrs snly
W B Yeats

Dict AEFH, signed WBY; Private.

To James Joyce, [*? 25 November 1902*]

18 Woburn Buildings | Euston Road.
Tuesday

My dear Joyce. I have just heard from Lady Gregory about your plan of going to Paris to study.[1] ⟨She tells me⟩ It seems that you leave Dublin Monday night, & cross to Paris Tuesday night. If I am right I hope you will breakfast with me on Tuesday morning. I shall set my alarm clock & be ready for you as soon as the train gets in. You can lie down on my sofa after wards & sleap off the fatigue of the journey. You can dine with me & catch your Paris train after wards. I hope you will come to me as I should like a good talk. I think you should let me give you one or two literary introductions here in London as you will find it much easier to get on in Paris (where perhaps a great many people do not want to learn English) if you do some writing, book reviews, poems etc for the papers here. This

---

[1] AG had sent WBY a typed copy of an undated letter from Joyce (*LJJ* I. 53–4) asking for help because he was leaving Dublin on the night of 1 Dec 'to study medicine at the University of Paris supporting myself there by teaching English'. In a covering letter, AG suggested (*LJJ* II. 16) that WBY 'should write and ask him to breakfast with you on the morning he arrives, if you can get up early enough, and feed him and take care of him and give him dinner at Victoria before he goes and help him on his way'. Joyce spent Tuesday with WBY, and proceeded to Paris by way of Newhaven and Dieppe that evening. According to Gogarty (*Mourning Became Mrs. Spendlove*, [New York, 1948], 50), Joyce later composed a limerick on AG's charity:

> There was an old lady called 'Gregory'
> Said, 'Come to me, poets in beggary';
> But found her imprudence
> When thousands of students
> Cried, 'All, we are in that category!'

kind of work never did any body any harm. Your poems would bring you something at once, I should think.

Yours snly
W B Yeats

PS. I could get 'The Speaker' I have little doubt to take verse from you & to give you a chance of doing some reviewing. I brought them a young man a while back, whom they look upon as one of their best writers & I have no doubt they will be quite ready to expect as good from you.[2] But we can talk over these things.

ALS Cornell. *LJJ* II. 17.

To Lady Augusta Gregory, 27 November 1902

18, Woburn Buildings | Euston Square
November 27th, 1902.

My dear Lady Gregory.

I have had a message from the Stage Society they want to play "Where there is nothing" in January.[1] I am going down to A. P. Watt now to consult with him. I am inclined to think I ought to consent. Performance by the Stage Society is a slight drawback from the point of view of the ordinary Manager who likes to produce a play himself for the first time. On the other hand I have to decide at once about the State [*for* Stage] Society and if I consent it will be a very considerable advertisement. Shaw's plays were in the first instance performed either by the Stage Society or by the Independent Theatre or some similar body.[2] One at any rate has been taken up

---

[2] Although WBY went to some efforts to get Joyce work on the *Speaker*, only one of his reviews appeared there, a notice of a French translation of Ibsen's *Catilina* on 21 Mar 1903. The 'young man' to whom WBY refers could have been J. M. Synge (see p. 55, n. 7), whom Joyce was to meet in Paris in March 1903, or John Masefield.

[1] The Stage Society had been founded on 19 July 1899 'to promote and encourage Dramatic Art', to 'serve as an Experimental Theatre', and 'to provide for the establishment of a Repertory Theatre in London' (see Appendix, p. 722). Its first production, on 26 Nov 1899, was Shaw's *You Never Can Tell*, and by late 1902 it had 480 subscribers, of whom about thirty were actors, but no permanent theatre. It made its reputation in performances of Ibsen, but had produced plays by thirteen different dramatists, including Maeterlinck, Hauptmann, and Hardy. The Society's production of WBY's play was delayed until June 1904.

[2] J. T. Grein's Independent Theatre produced Shaw's first play, *Widowers' Houses*, on 9 Dec 1892 at the Royalty Theatre. Apart from *You Never Can Tell* (see above, n. 1), the Stage Society (of which Shaw was a member) had also given a private performance of the publicly banned *Mrs Warren's Profession* on 5 Jan 1902.

by an ordinary theatrical management after a performance by the Stage Society, though not in London. However I shall be guided by A. P. Watts. It was Edith Craig, Ellen Terry's daughter who introduced the play to them,[3] she says it is the only play for the last fifteen years she has cared about. She wants to play Sabina Silva. Harry Irving who is I understand good will play Paul and possibly Welsh who is a most accomplished comedian Charlie Ward. I hear there is a strange idea, doubtless started by Pixie Smith of getting Jack to play Paddy Cockfight.[4] If they do it I shall be requested to change the Franciscans into some order with black habits as they can make black habits much more effective on the stage. I hear that there was a good deal of disputing at the Society about the play but Miss Craig wrote to Dublin and got twelve copies which she distributed. The opposition then came over to her side. I read the amended version last night to Binyon, Sturge Moore, Rhys and a lot of ladies. Everyone considered it greatly improved and the only hostile criticism was that the act in the Monastery was in a different key from the others. This is certainly the case, but whether it is a defect or not I don't quite know. I have after all practically left the sermon unchanged. The only difference is that the last candles put out symbolise hope memory thought and the world and that man is bid do this when drunk with the wine which comes from pitchers that are in Heaven.[5] At the same time I will probably do a quite new sermon at my leisure but this one can remain for the present.

I am sorry that you are putting that voice back at the end of the Raftery play. It is I am certain quite wrong. One of the impossible things. If you feel that it is necessary to make the fact of Raftery being a ghost quite unmistakeable I think you had better discover some other means. Why should not the young man go to the door to see what has happened to

---

[3] Edith Geraldine Ailsa Craig (1869–1947), sister of Gordon Craig (see p. 52, n. 2), had become a regular member of Irving's Lyceum Theatre in 1890, playing small parts for ten years, during which she also acted for the Independent Theatre. In 1899 Irving employed her to make costumes for his production of *Robespierre*, and this led to her going into business as a stage dressmaker, although she continued to play in Stage Society performances. She and Pamela Colman Smith designed the Stage Society's production of *Where There Is Nothing*.

[4] H. B. 'Harry' Irving (1870–1919), son of the great Victorian actor, Henry Irving, was described by the *Tatler* on 19 Nov as 'The Stage Hero of the Moment' for his celebrated performances at the Duke of York Theatre. James Welch (see p. 180, n. 2), a versatile actor who distinguished himself in comic roles, had played Maurteen Bruin in WBY's *The Land of Heart's Desire*, and Petkoff in Shaw's *Arms and the Man* at the Avenue Theatre in April 1894. In the event, none of the three actors took part in the 1904 production of the play, when E. Lyall Swete played Paul Rutledge, Blake Adams played Charlie Ward, and the part of Paddy Cockfight was taken by Trent Adams, not Jack Yeats. Thyrza Norman, not Edith Craig, was Sabina Silva.

[5] See p. 257. The passage appears at Act v, ll. 346–53 (*VPl*, 1139): 'Give me wine out of thy pitchers; oh, God, how splendid is my cup of drunkeness. We must become blind, and deaf, and dizzy. We must get rid of everything that is not measureless eternal life. We must put out hope as I put out this candle. [*Puts out a candle.*] And memory as I put out this candle. [*As before.*] And thought, the waster of Life, as I put out this candle. [*As before.*]'

Raftery and see him vanish before his eyes. Perhaps into a little cloud of mist, or into a whirl of straw or shavings. After all those entrances and voices, another spoils the picture and the play. It takes away the complete-ness of the action in some way.[6]

I do not think the Ride to Paradise changes the motive of the little Christ Play from what I suggested. Paradise is happiness, the abundance of the earth, the natural life, everyman's desire, or some such thing.[7] Miss Owen spoke to the Psaltery for me last week, but one felt always that she was a singer. She had learnt what I believe they call voice production, which seems to upset everybody's power of speaking in an impressive way. You felt that she had learnt to take words as musical notes, and not as things having a meaning. However she did very much better when I tried her with the lilt. There is a Mrs. Elliott who is working at it.[8] She has a fine musical ear but has never learnt voice production, and she does it almost as well as Mrs. Emery. She makes her own little lilts and is extraor-dinarily impressive and poetical. She is a really beautiful person too and that helps things.

[Remainder of letter in WBY's hand]

I have just failed to see Watt. He was out but on the way I have thought

[6] In a letter of 22 Nov 1902 (Berg) AG had told WBY that Hyde was unhappy with the super-natural element in *An Pósadh* (*The Marriage*), which had been produced in Galway on 20 and 21 Aug (see p. 221), and which they were now revising for publication in *Poets and Dreamers*: 'He is not quite satisfied with Raftery "I don't think Maire's uncertainty if it be a ghost or not is effec-tive on the stage. I wd rather have the ghost out & out as early as possible & make it clear to the audience!" I rather agree with him, & think I will restore the voice at the door in my published version.' In the play, the ghost of the poet Raftery provides a feast and presents for a penniless newly-wed couple (see pp. 128–9), but in the published version the villagers only realize that they have been entertained by a ghost at the very end, when a late-comer tells them that he stood by Raftery's grave 'three days ago'.

[7] Demurring from WBY's view (see p. 252) that the Christ-figure in *The Travelling Man* was not 'the supreme disturber we have thought him' but the proponent of 'some near and innocent happiness', AG had given her interpretation of the theme in her letter of 22 Nov: 'I am not sure about your idea for the play. If the stranger wanted the child to be content with the things near him, why did he make the image of the garden of Paradise & ride to it? I am more inclined to think the idea is the soul having once seen the Christ, the Divine Essence, must always turn back to it again. One feels sure the Child will, through all its life—and the mother with all her com-forts, has never been quite satisfied, because she wants to see the Christ again. But the earthly side of her has built up the dresser, & the child will build up other earthly veils—yet never be quite satisfied. What do you think?' In the course of the play, the Travelling Man tells the Child that they can ride to Paradise; when the Child complains that they have no horse, the Travelling Man sits astride a bench with him and sings what WBY here calls 'the Ride to Paradise', with the refrain: 'Come ride and ride to the garden, / Come ride and ride with a will: / For the flower comes with the fruit there / Beyond a hill and a hill'. In a note to the play in her *Seven Short Plays* (1909), AG wrote: 'I owe the Rider's song, and some of the rest, to W. B. Yeats'.

[8] H. W. Nevinson, sitting next to the 'very sweet and charming' Eleanor Blanche Elliot at a Yeats–Farr lecture, reported in his Journal on 30 Jan 1903 (Bodleian) that she had so practised chanting WBY's lyrics that her husband cried out in his sleep 'Impetuous heart, be still, be still'. Both Mrs Elliot, née Bruce (1864–1947), and her husband, John Hugh Armstrong Elliot, were members of the GD.

of a very fantastic opening—a comedy opening for Act 4 which will bring
it into key with the rest. It is very wild.

I am reading at the allegorists in the Museum every day, for Spenser. It
is very interesting but there is so much to learn.[9]

Yrs always
W B Yeats

I send 5/- worth of stamps received from Mrs Coffey—one gurrantor but
who she does not say.[10]

TLS Berg, with envelope addressed to Coole, postmark 'LONDON', date indecipherable.
Wade, 382–5.

To W. G. Fay, 28 November 1902

Mention in following letter, also in letter from F. J. Fay, 11 December
1902, (NLI).
Frank Fay wrote: 'I was glad to see from a letter which you wrote recently
to my brother that you agree with me in thinking Oscar Wilde and GBS
[*i.e. George Bernard Shaw*] the only Dramatists of the nineteenth century
whose plays are worth going to *hear*'. Also evidently enquiring about the
dress rehearsal of *The Hour-Glass*.

To Lady Augusta Gregory, 28 November [1902]

18, Woburn Buildings | Euston Square,
Nov. 28th

My dear Lady Gregory,

I enclose a letter to Fay, which you can send on if you think well of it.[1]
I also send you a poem in Irish which Deeny has sent me.[2] Keep it among
your papers and read it to me when we meet. I find that I wrote you a

---

[9] See p. 240.
[10] Jane Sophia Coffey, née L'Estrange (*c.* 1847–1921), the wife of the antiquarian and archaeologist, George Coffey, was the first secretary of the ILT, of which both she and her husband were
guarantors.

[1] The letter to W. G. Fay is untraced, but was evidently sent on by AG; see above.
[2] Domhnall O'Duibhne (Deeney) was a national schoolmaster in Spiddal, Co. Galway, who
collected folklore for AG. WBY had reviewed his *Peasant Lore from Gaelic Ireland* in July 1900
(see UP II. 216–18). The Irish poem is unidentified.

letter the other day which I forgot to post. I dont remember what was in it but think I told you all the news. I have had some pheasants from Wilfred Blount who has I hear just started for Egypt.[3]

Yours alway
W B Yeats

ALS Berg, with envelope addressed to Coole, postmark indecipherable.

To F. J. Fay, [*late November 1902*]

Mention in letter from Fay, 11 December 1902.
Encouraging Fay to experiment with recitation to the psaltery.[1]

NLI.

To Lady Augusta Gregory, 4 December 1902

18, Woburn Buildings,
Dec. 4th, 1902.

My dear Lady Gregory,
    I have had a letter from W. Fay. He makes no mention of the Dress Rehersal, but speaks of starting with the Play in the middle of January. It seems that they want my Lecture by then and that their present performances are merely to keep the subscribers in good humour and themselves in practice. I have concluded therefore that he ⟨won't⟩ cannot get up that Dress Rehersal. I am very sorry but under the circumstances I suppose I must give up that Dublin journey.[1] I have just been with A. P. Watt who

---

[3] Blunt had a house outside Cairo to which he returned most winters, and where he wore Arab dress and collected material for his *The Secret History of the English Occupation of Egypt* (1907). He left London on or about 28 Nov and arrived in Alexandria, by way of France, on 4 Dec.

[1] A reply to Fay's letter of *c.* 19 Nov (see p. 254) in which he had asked what FF charged 'for copies of the lilts of your poems and are they *absolutely accurate*. I am giving a night in January at the Celtic Literary Society called "Readings from Irish Poets and Prose Writers" and I would like to do one or two pieces to the psaltery.' In replying to this letter Fay acknowledged WBY's 'former note about the lilts and shall be glad to study any you send me'. On 18 Dec (Private) he reported that the lilt for 'The Hosting of the Sidhe' had reached him, and that he was also working on 'Impetuous Heart'.

[1] The first production of *The Hour-Glass* had originally been planned for October (see p. 201), but did not finally take place until 14 Mar 1903, when it was followed by WBY's lecture on 'The Reform of the Theatre', part of which appeared in the *United Irishman* on 4 Apr 1903, before being reprinted with additions in *Samhain* (1903). AG was not pleased by the postponement, writing sternly the following day (Berg): 'I am afraid those excuses from Dublin are not enough for my conscience, which I suppose means time & money used for ones own pleasure'.

has read "Where there is Nothing". He is now of opinion that I should give it to the Stage Society. He praises the play very much but to use his own phrase "thinks that it deals with too high things for the English theatre under existing circumstances". He said he would show it to Forbes Robertson if I liked, but spoke of the difficulty of getting an immediate answer from so busy a man.[2] Delay might lose the chance of getting it performed at all. The performance by the Stage Society will not prevent it being taken up by somebody else. I have also been to see Bernard Shaw and found his wife[3] who was on the Committee of the theatre very anxious for the Play. In one matter I imagine little Pamela Smith went a little further in her enthusiasm than the facts quite warranted. She spoke of the Committee to me as unanimous. Mrs. Shaw, however, says there is a minority who are afraid of the expense of a Play with so many scenes and think that it will be injured by not being played by Irish actors. I doubt if the matter has been definitely decided by vote yet. I think, however, that it is practically decided. Shaw asked me if our Irish Company could be got to come over and play it. However I imagine that this is impossible. Last Monday evening Pamela Smith brought round a big sketch book full of designs for scenery for the Play made by herself and Edith Craig. They were particularly pleased because they know Gordon Craig's little stage dodges and are using them rather to his annoyance. He is rather disgusted at the chief part being offered to Harry Irving instead of himself.[4] I thought the design for the Monastery scene extremely impressive. The design for Act 1 was a little humdrum. To some extent that was my own fault for that Croquet lawn and garden path has been the opening of so many Plays. Suddenly while I was looking at it it occurred to me that it could all be made fantastic by there being a number of bushes shaped Dutch fashion into cocks and hens, ducks, peacocks &c. Pamela began sketching them at once. It can be supposed that these fowl have been the occupation of Paul Routledge's ironical leisure for years past I never did know before what he had being [*for* been] doing all that time.[5] The changes I am thinking of, the opening of the Monastery scene in no way touched the vitals of the Scene. They are all before the entrance of the Superior. I think that some comedy there will help the balance of the Play.

---

[2] On 1 Dec 1902 AG had suggested (Berg) that WBY should send a copy of *Where There Is Nothing* to the actor-manager Forbes Robertson (see p. 5, n. 7), adding that 'you ought to send it him & H. Irving and anyone else possible independently of Watt to save his percentage'.

[3] Shaw married the Irish-born and independently wealthy Charlotte Frances Payne-Townshend (1857–1943) in July 1898, whereupon she became his devoted companion in a childless and passionless marriage. At this time they were living at 10 Adelphi Terrace, London WC.

[4] In the event, E. Lyall Swete played Paul Ruttledge in the Stage Society's production of the play (see p. 263, n. 4).

[5] WBY retained the topiary in his stage directions for Act 1 in the 1903 edition.

Every other Act of the Play has comedy. I wouldn't mind if one of the early acts was quite serious. They would balance then.[6]

Yes, I have written to Quinn[7] and I have had Joyce with me for a day. He was unexpectedly amiable and did not knock at the gate with his old Ibsenite fury. I am trying to get him work on the Academy and Speaker and I have brought him to Arthur Symons. I have been twice to the Speaker about his affairs and have otherwise wasted a great deal of time.[8] These last few days I have been working particularly hard on the history of Allegory. I had no sooner began reading at the British Museum after my return when it flashed upon me that the Coming of Allegory coincided with the rise of the Middle Class. That it was the first effect on literature of the earnest spirit which afterwards created Puritanism. I have been hunting through all sorts of books to verify this and am now certain of it. I at last feel able to copy out and finish the Spenser Essay.[9] But my work at the Museum has made my eyes very feverish again and I don't quite know what to do for the moment.

Bernard Shaw talks again of writing a play for us. Certainly it would be a great thing for our Company if he will do us an Irish play.[10] I had the

[6] This idea did not meet with AG's approval and in an undated letter [5 Dec 1902; Berg] she described her dismay: 'I cannot believe it wd be an improvement. It is splendid as it is, & it is not true it is out of key. It only touches a deeper note. . . . What frightens me is your joy of creation, you are like Puppy after a chicken, when you see a new idea cross the path, tho' it may but end in a mouth full of feathers after all—'.

[7] In her letter of 1 Dec 1902 (see n. 2) AG had said: 'I opened & read Quinn's letter [*now lost*]—very kind—I suppose you have written to him? & that is a good idea to publish *Hour Glass* & *Pot of Broth* there'.

[8] Joyce had spent a busy day with WBY during his stop-over in London on 2 Dec, and he described WBY's efforts on his behalf in a letter to his family on 6 Dec (*LJJ* II. 19): 'Mr Yeats went to see the editor of "The Speaker" in London but he was ill and I expect a letter every day: he is also to go to the editor of the "Academy". He wrote to Miss Gonne, a letter of whose I enclose. He also introduced me to Arthur Symons and wants me to review for the Speaker a book of Symons's—a translation of *Francesca da Rimini*. I breakfasted, lunched and dined with him and he paid all the hansoms and busses.' Stanislaus Joyce recounts (*My Brother's Keeper*, 197–8) that when WBY and Joyce called on Symons 'he was hospitable and sympathetic. He offered to submit some of my brother's poems to various editors, and said that as soon as my brother had a volume of poems ready, he would try to find a publisher for it. . . . It was Symons who, in the end, persuaded Elkin Mathews to publish *Chamber Music* . . .' For the reference to 'knock at the gate' see the first act of Ibsen's *The Master Builder*, and the last sentence of Joyce's article, 'The Day of the Rabblement' (*The Critical Writings of James Joyce*, 72).

[9] This is the theme of Part III of WBY's essay on Spenser (*E & I*, 364–7). He had perhaps first come across the idea in Andrew Lang's review of *The Celtic Twilight* in the *Illustrated London News* of 23 Dec 1893 (see I. 409–10).

[10] See p. 117. Shaw did not get round to writing his contribution to the Irish dramatic movement, *John Bull's Other Island*, until 1904. As he explained in the Preface (1907, p. v), it was written 'at the request of Mr. William Butler Yeats, as a patriotic contribution to the repertory of the Irish Literary Theatre. . . . It was uncongenial to the whole spirit of the neo-Gaelic movement, which is bent on creating a new Ireland after its own ideal, whereas my play is a very uncompromising presentment of the real old Ireland.' WBY did not permit its performance in 1904, giving as his reason that it was beyond the company's resources, and the first production was at the

first proof sheets of my sister's print of the Poems, they look very well indeed. I think I have arranged that they follow them up with a very witty and unknown story of Bernard Shaw's.[11] He offers to correct the proofs entirely for the purpose of making the print look nice. He says Morris never revised for any other reason.

Yours always
W B Yeats

TLS Berg, with envelope addressed to Coole, postmark 'LONDON W.C. DE 3 02'. Wade, 385–7.

To the Editor of the Academy,[1] [6 December 1902]

But for a few ⟨promising⟩ books sent me by young authors I should have read no book published this year, so far as I can recollect, except Lady Gregory's 'Cuchullain of Muirthemne'. I am entirely certain of the immortality of that book, & doubt if such noble & simple English has been written since the death of Morris.

W B Yeats

ALCS Brown. Printed in the *Academy*, 6 December 1902 (633).

To F. J. Fay, 9 December 1902

Mention in following letter, also in letter from Fay, 11 December 1902 (NLI).
Sending him an edition of Oscar Wilde's Fairy Tales;[1] telling him that

Royal Court Theatre, London, from 1 to 11 Nov 1904. It was finally staged at the Abbey Theatre on 25 Sept 1916.
[11] Shaw's 'The Miraculous Revenge', originally published in *Time* in March 1885, was announced by the Dun Emer Press (which was currently printing WBY's *In The Seven Woods*) but never appeared. It was subsequently republished in the first number of the *Shanachie* in spring 1906.

[1] WBY had once again been asked to contribute to the *Academy*'s annual selection of favourite books; see p. 131.

[1] In his letter of *c.* 18 Nov (see p. 266, n. 1) Fay had asked WBY to enquire whether 'Nutt, the publisher, had copies of Oscar Wilde's Happy Prince at 3/- or 3/6 each'. David Nutt had published the 1st edition of *The Happy Prince and Other Tales*, illustrated by Walter Crane and George Percy Jacomb-Hood, in 1888, and the firm had just issued a 3rd edition at the original price of 3/6. WBY made a present of the book, and on 11 Dec Fay thanked him 'very much for the beautiful gift you have sent me', going on to explain that he was an 'intense admirer' of Wilde, and had read or seen much of his work: 'The *Fairy Tales* I have long desired and now, thanks to you they are here'.

Shaw had offered to write a play for their Company;[2] and asking for patterns of the purple designs for *The Hour-Glass.*[3]

To Lady Augusta Gregory, 9 December 1902

18, Woburn Buildings,
December 9th, 1902.

My dear Lady Gregory,

I am on my way down to Edie Craig's to see some of the Stage Society people. I have been writing hard at Spenser and think it will be done in a few days. I am only using what I dictated to you as what Moore calls a smoky ceiling. It is full of suggestion and has fine passages I think but it is too incoherent. I am basing the whole thing on my conviction, that England up to the time of the Parliamentary Wars was the Anglo-French nation and that the hitherto conquered Saxon elements rose into power with Cromwell. This idea certainly makes my essay very striking, it enables me to say all kinds of interesting things about that time. Sturge Moore has done me some designs for "the hour glass" working out Robert's sketch into practical detail. He is emphatic, however, about the great difficulty of getting a green that will go well with purple and wants me to have the curtains made of some undyed material I have written to Fay for patterns of the purple and to ask if there was to be any green in the costumes. I think the Moore design looks very impressive.[1] I have just been down to the Academy office to get them to take work from Joyce which they are ready to do. They showed me quite a long article there which some woman has

---

[2] Fay replied that it 'would be great if we could get a play by GBS but his pieces so far are dreadfully difficult and I doubt whether he could write anything about Ireland with which he has been so long out of touch: moreover he has no sympathy with our independence. However his conversion, if you can bring it about, would be a great victory.'

[3] Fay did not answer the question about the purple cloth, since he and his brother were still waiting for WBY to send them Sturge Moore's design.

[1] Sturge Moore's stage setting for *The Hour-Glass*, after a sketch by Robert Gregory, is reproduced with written instructions in Liam Miller's *The Noble Drama of W. B. Yeats* (Dublin, 1977), 80–2. In an accompanying letter Sturge Moore suggested that 'a raw undyed material would be best for the walls and ceiling', and WBY later noted in *CW* IV. 238–9: 'We always play it in front of an olive-green curtain, and dress the Wise Man and his Pupils in various shades of purple. Because in all these decorative schemes one needs . . . a third colour subordinate to the other two, we have partly dressed the Fool in red-brown, which is repeated in the furniture. There is some green in his dress and in that of the Wife of the Wise Man who is dressed mainly in purple.'

sent about "Where there is Nothing".[2] Walkley's comment on Bottomley's vague little play amused me very much. The insolence towards the present state of the stage which he found in poor Bottomley's stage direction is our wicked defiance and I am quite certain that it was Father Dineen's hare which has convinced him that all our stage directions are equally insolent.[3] I sent him a copy of "Samhain". I send you an Academy though no doubt you will see it with Symond's letter and mine about the best book of the year.[4] This is a very scatter-brained letter, but I have been running about doing a lot of things and am in a great hurry to get down to Edie Craig's. If the Stage Society does the Play it will be at the end of February. I had almost forgotten to tell you that Pamela Smith is bringing out a Magazine to be called the "Hour-Glass" after my play. I am to write the preface in order to define the policy which I have got them to take up. The Magazine is to be consecrated to what I called to their delight, the Art of Happy Desire.[5] It is to be quite unlike gloomy magazines like the Yellow Book and the Savoy. People are to draw pictures of places they would have liked to have lived in and to write stories and poems about a life they would have liked to have lived. Nothing is to be let in unless it tells of something that seems beautiful or charming or in some other way desirable. They are not to touch the accursed Norwegian cloud in any way, even though they

[2] The *Academy* published no contributions by Joyce. The unsigned article, 'Where There Is Nothing', appeared on 13 Dec, discussed the play at length, and concluded (662) that WBY, 'a poet first and last, a true poet', would teach men 'not with the weapons of a reformer, but with the wand of a poet—not as a practical leader of men, but as he himself says, as a revealer of "the things that never can be accomplished in time", by the music that lives in men's hearts, which concerns itself little with good governments or bad, but which is eternally alive in the joy of their souls, alive, and new, and fresh, though the world may grow old.'

[3] Arthur Bingham Walkley (1855–1926), the influential *Times* drama critic, reviewed Bottomley's *The Crier By Night* (see p. 260) in the *TLS* on 5 Dec. Censuring the stage directions as being 'couched in a language which declares an attitude of completely stupid insolence towards the playhouse and its audience', he declared that Bottomley had 'too diligently imitated Mr. Yeats and those foolish friends of his who by flattery are spoiling gifts which needed but chastening to make Mr. Yeats a real dramatist'.

Fr. Patrick S. Dinneen (1860–1934), a former Jesuit who had left the order in 1900, was a playwright, a Celtic scholar, and a prominent member of the Gaelic League. Describing his Irish-language play *Tobar Draoidheachta* (*The Enchanted Well*) in *Samhain* (1902), WBY recalled (*Expl*, 91) how he 'sent the rival lovers of his play, when he wanted them off the scene for a moment, to catch a hare that has crossed the stage. When they return the good lover is carrying it by the heels, and modestly compares it to a lame jackass. One rather likes this bit of nonsense when one comes to it, for in that world of folk-imagination one thing seems as possible as another.'

[4] See p. 269. Symons also chose *Cuchulain of Muirthemne*, describing it (633) as 'the most important book published during 1902'; see p. 185, n. 4.

[5] Pamela Smith dropped WBY's title in favour of the *Green Sheaf*, an enlarged and elaborated version of *A Broad Sheet*. It appeared irregularly in 1903 (eight numbers) and 1904 (five numbers), but although WBY became a contributor, he did not write a preface. 'The Art of Happy Desire' is a phrase from AG's translation of Raftery's poem, 'The Hill of Heart's Desire', which was published in the first number.

may be all good Ibsenites, and they are not to traffic in Gorky.[6] There is a fine mixture of metaphor. I tell you about it because I know they are going to ask you for some little stories out of your Finn book. Ricketts and Shannon are going to do them pictures and I think they will make quite a stir in the world for a little time at any rate.[7] I will write again to morrow if I can.

Yours always
W B Yeats

TLS Berg, with envelope addressed to Coole, redirected to 22 Dominick St, Galway; postmark 'LONDON W.C. DE 9 02'. Wade, 387–9.

To James Joyce, 9 December 1902

18, Woburn Buildings, | Euston Road
December 9th, 1902.

My dear Joyce,

I have been three times to the Speaker Office, but the Editor is still away. At last, however, I have got hold of the Editor of the Academy.[1] I think I interested him in your work. I send you a number of the Academy which he told me to give you. There are some signed "Middles", as they are called, by a man called—but no, I find they are not signed. They are headed "the Author and himself". He asked me to point them out to you as a kind of thing they are always glad to have. He says you should send him moments of your own spiritual life but you should make them *apropos* by hanging them on some peg—A book or current event. Lady Gregory sent me a quotation from a letter of yours to her, a passage beginning "I shall try myself against the Powers of the world, all things are inconstant

[6] Maxim Gorky (1868–1936), the Russian revolutionist, novelist, playwright, and short-story writer, was a social realist who had come to fame with *Sketches and Stories* (1898). Despite his dismissiveness here, WBY had 'never read a word' by Gorky, a fact he confessed in a letter of 28 Oct 1907 (Berg) to Clement Shorter. William Rothenstein, writing in *The Arrow* (1939), claims (17) that WBY came to his aid in America when 'it was discovered that the lady who accompanied Gorki was not his legal wife. No hotel would take them in. Yeats, indignant that no voice was heard in Gorki's defence, himself protested in the American Press, though he knew he was risking a popularity upon which, while in the States, he depended.' Since WBY was not in America at the time of Gorky's visit from April to October 1906, and since no protest by him has come to light, it is probable that Rothenstein is confusing him with H. G. Wells.

[7] Nothing by Ricketts or Shannon appeared in the *Green Sheaf* but it published both AG's 'The Hill of Heart's Desire' (see above, n. 5) and, in No. 5, her 'Cael and Credhe', reprinted with slight revisions in *Gods and Fighting Men*.

[1] Since 1899 the editor of the *Speaker*, a Liberal weekly, had been the journalist and social historian J. L. Hammond (1872–1949), but he was evidently still indisposed (see p. 268, n. 8). Charles Lewis Hind (1862–1927) had edited the *Pall Mall Budget* before moving to the *Academy* in 1896.

except the Faith and the Soul, that changes all things and fills their incon-
stancy with light".[2] He became enthusiastic at once and said "Ah! that is
what we want, why didn't he make an ode or a song out of that". I asked
him if he would like poems from you and he said they don't publish much
verse but would be glad to have anything that is really good. He suggested
that you should send me your poems and let me pick out something for
him. Do as you like about that. I imagine that the Speaker is more anxious
for poetry than the Academy. I suggested that the Academy should give
you a book of D'Annunzio's for review.[3] He said "No, we can't do that, we
couldn't trust a man we don't know with d'Annunzio, we have taken a certain line about him for years. We think him a great artist but detest his
morals." I imagine that the Academy has a somewhat more popular audience than the Speaker and it has to be a little careful about moral questions.

Yrs sny
W B Yeats

TLS Cornell.

To an unidentified correspondent,[1] [c. *10 December 1902*]

18 Woburn Buildings. | Euston Road

Dear Sir: Please excuse this paper but I have no note paper.[2] I mislaid
your letter & so could not answer before but got your address from some

[2] Joyce's letter to AG of November 1902 (see p. 261, n. 1). The letter continued: 'And though
I seem to have been driven out of my country here as a misbeliever I have found no man yet with
a faith like mine'. WBY had evidently told Hind of the 'Epiphanies', the 'sudden spiritual manifestation, whether in the vulgarity of speech or of gesture or in a memorable phase of the mind
itself . . . the most delicate and evanescent of moments' (*Stephen Hero*, [1944], 188), which Joyce
had read to him on their first meeting (see p. 249).

[3] WBY wanted Joyce to review Symons's translation of *Francesca da Rimini* (1901) by Gabriele
D'Annunzio (1863–1938), the Italian poet, dramatist, and novelist, which had been published in
London in December 1902 (see p. 268, n. 8). At this time WBY's own 'line' on D'Annunzio was
uncertain, as he was to reveal in the *San Francisco Examiner* on 31 Jan 1904, where he admitted he
could not 'make out' the *The Dead City*: 'His "Francsca da Rimini" I can follow easily enough, for
that is a flight of fancy. But as drama—Well, in the first act there is an admirable scene
with the jester—which has nothing to do with the play. And later there are an astrologer and a ped-
dler—and, as I remember, nothing to do with the play. But at present . . . I do not like to say that
I do not like D'Annunzio's plays. . . . I do see most lovely passages in his work, but it will take me
perhaps a long time to understand him as an artist that has influenced the whole of Europe.'

[1] The correspondent was probably Aubrey Smith (1863–1948), Secretary of the Stage Society
until 1904, who had evidently doubted the Society's ability to perform a play needing an Irish
ambiance and Irish accents (see p. 267).

[2] This letter is written on heavily lined paper, evidently torn from an exercise book.

one. I have talked over the whole matter of play with Miss Craig who will tell you what I think. Surely the stage society is well trained in "foreign atmospheres" by this time. That should not be a difficulty. The words if spoken naturally & without attempt at brogue will make their own atmosphere.

Yrs sinly
W B Yeats

ALS Buffalo.

To Lady Augusta Gregory, 12 December 1902

18, Woburn Buildings,
Dec. 12th, 1902.

My dear Lady Gregory,

I have made the changes in "Where there is Nothing". The new opening to Act IV. came quite easily. I have done a new opening to Act III. also as the Act was rather short and I thought rather hurried at the outset. I have also done a new version of the Sermon and some slight changes at the outset of Act V. I find I manage the dialect pretty well, but will get you to go over it. It is possible that I shall be reading the revised play to Harry Irving on Sunday evening. He is rather hesitating over the Part, I am sorry to say. He has begun to feel that it will be a very big undertaking. I am to read the "Hour-Glass" and "a Pot of Broth" to Edie Craig, Pamela and some other people on Monday night. I have had an enthusiastic letter from Maclagan about "Where there is Nothing" and a note from Grant Richards wanting to publish it.[1] No! I don't like that Sycamore poem I think it perfectly detestable and always did and am going to write to Russell to say that the Homestead mustn't do this kind of thing any more. I was furious last year when they revived some rambling old verses of mine but forgot about it. I wouldn't so much mind if they said they were early verses but they print them as if they were new work.[2] [*Remainder of letter in WBY's hand*] Fay

[1] Grant Richards (1872–1948) started his own firm in 1897 and built his reputation by publishing the early books of subsequently famous authors, though he did not publish any of WBY's works.

[2] WBY's 'She Who Dwelt among the Sycamores' (*VP*, 715–16) was published in *A Celtic Christmas*, the 1902 Christmas number of the *Irish Homestead*, the organ of Horace Plunkett's Irish Agricultural Organisation Society of which AE was Assistant Secretary. The poem had first appeared in the *Irish Monthly* of March 1887. 'The Fairy Pedant', published in the same issue of the *Irish Monthly*, had been reprinted as 'The Solitary Fairy' in the *Celtic Christmas* for 1901. The editor was Harry Felix Norman (1868–1947), AE's theosophist friend, and a founder-member of the INTS.

writes to say that they had thin audiences in Dublin last week but that the profits were excellent.[3] Brimley Johnson, who is becoming quite a large publisher,[4] (I mean a publisher of a lot of books,) writes to me 'what a lovely book Lady Gregory has given us. You did not say a word too much for it.'

Have you read Gwynn in Fortnightly on our Theatre.[5]

Yours alway
W B Yeats

PS. I will shortly send you a new version of 'The Travelling Man' to go over for me. If I only had the plays done I might get some money out of Bullen for them.[6] "The Travelling Man" will be wanted as "Kathleen" is not to go in I am sorry to say.

Could you send me that little bit about Finn killing the man of the children of Danu who burnt Tara to the sound of music. I want it for Spenser.[7]

TLS Berg, with envelope addressed to Coole, postmark 'LONDON W.C. DE 13 02'. Wade, 389–90.

To William Rothenstein, 13 December 1902

18 Woburn Buildings, | Euston Road.
Dec. 13ᵗʰ.,/02.

My dear Rothenstein,

I am back here now & have got through the first rush of odds & ends & could look at poor Sterling's M.S.[1] if you have a mind to send it or bring it, for I am still in on Monday evenings.

Yours sinly
W B Yeats

Dict AEFH, signed WBY; Harvard.

[3] Frank Fays' letter (see p. 269) is dated 11 Dec 1902.
[4] Reginald Brimley Johnson (1867–1932) founded his small publishing firm in 1900 and issued works by G. K. Chesterton and G. Lowes Dickinson. An editor and prolific scholar-critic, he praised AG's *Cuchulain of Muirthemne* at length in his annual 'letter' from England in the *Atlantic Monthly* of January 1903.
[5] 'An Uncommercial Theatre' appeared in the *Fortnightly Review* of December 1902; see p. 244, n. 3.
[6] See p. 252. *The Travelling Man* was not published by Bullen and WBY speeded up the publication of *Plays for an Irish Theatre* by printing *Where There Is Nothing* as the first volume.
[7] Aillen, chief of the Sidhe of Beinn Boirche, burned Tara on nine occasions after putting its defenders under the spell of his 'sorrowful music'. With the help of a magic spear Finn slew him and for this exploit was appointed head of the Fianna. WBY did not use the story in his Spenser essay, but AG retold it in *Gods and Fighting Men*.

[1] See pp. 157, 235.

To James Joyce, [*? 13 December 1902*]

18 Woburn Buildings | Euston Road.
Saturday.

My dear Joyce: I have been unable to see about your business until to day. I have been very busy & as several policemen in my neighbourhood told me that they did not know where Grenville St was (one said it was some where near) & as I had no time to search I left the matter over until to day. Now I find that I cannot get the money as you forgot to tell me the name of the sender. I enclose the order which you had better send to Dublin & get made payable to you in Paris. This will be quicker than sending it to me. I should have to get another order payable in Paris.[1]

Yours sny
W B Yeats

ALS Yale.

To George Russell (AE), [c. *13 December 1902*]

Mention in letter from AE, 22 December 1902.
An angry letter, complaining about the republication of his early poem, 'She who dwelt among the Sycamores' in the Christmas number of the *Irish Homestead* without his permission.[1]

MBY.

[1] This perhaps refers to the money order in payment for Joyce's first Dublin *Daily Express* review on 11 Dec 1902, which had evidently been made out to a London office, and which he was unable to cash in Paris. The Postal Telegraph Office at 16–17 Grenville Street, near Russell Square in west central London, was one of the closest post offices to Woburn Buildings. Joyce's experience of Parisian post offices was apparently no happier, and in the Proteus episode of *Ulysses* (I. 85) Stephen Dedalus recalls 'With mother's money order, eight shillings, the banging door of the post office slammed in your face by the usher. Hunger toothache. *Encore deux minutes.* Look clock. Must get. *Fermé.* Hired dog! Shoot him to bloody bits with a bang shotgun, bits man spattered walls all brass buttons.'

[1] See p. 274, n. 2. In his reply AE explained that the 'Editor just before the paper was going to printers regretted that he had nothing of yours, and it was I who was the culprit for I remembered this little poem which I read years ago. . . . I regret having done so and will see that you are always asked about your work in the future. . . . Personally I think "She who dwelt among the sycamores" a most beautiful poem. . . . I love your early work and think this poem a wonderful little portion of soul.'

To F. J. Fay, [c. *14 December 1902*]

Mention in letter from Fay, 15 December 1902.
Enquiring about the nature of James Cousins's new play, *Sold*;[1] commenting upon a review of the Company's latest performances in the *Evening Mail* (Dublin);[2] mentioning his quarrel with George Moore; telling Fay that he is planning a primer about speaking to the psaltery;[3] and asking whether French actors and he use quarter notes in recitation.[4]

NLI.

---

[1] On 29 Nov Fay had written (Private) that they had 'got a promising two act comedy from Cousins which we are starting to rehearse'. WBY, who had considerable reservations about Cousins' talents, had written to ask for more details, and in his reply to this letter Fay advised him to write 'to my brother about Cousins' play. It will I think be printed in UI. Personally I don't think that anything will be gained by criticizing plays. We must get plays that will act and we have got one in "Sold", the name of this play.'

[2] Fay had been particularly pleased with an article by 'R.M.' on the performances at the Camden Street Hall which had appeared in the *Evening Mail* on 5 Dec 1902 (2), and, describing it as 'excellently written, good humoured banter but appreciative and without ill-feeling', had sent WBY a copy of it with his letter of 11 Dec. WBY had evidently commented favourably on it, and on 15 Dec (NLI) Fay responded: 'I think the "Mail" article splendid. Jules Lemaitre described his journey to the first performance of the Theatre Libre somewhere [*see Germaine Durrière*, Jules Lemaître et le théâtre (*Paris, 1934), 100–1*]; I don't know whether he described its first performance; but this man has done that for us and I read his article over and over with pleasure.' The article made merry over the cold and primitive conditions at the hall, and advised that 'if the Irish Theatre Society wishes to make proselytes amongst the playgoers it must meet them at least halfway. . . . Spartan fare is only meet for Spartans . . .'. Recalling that Antoine had founded the Théâtre Libre with a company of amateurs in a hall that only held three hundred people, 'R.M.' noted that the INTS had 'taken up the work of the Irish Literary Theatre in a hall that holds little more than half as many, and it played last night to less than fifty people'. Turning to *The Laying of the Foundations*, he conceded that it 'would be unfair to apply the ordinary canons of criticism and comparison to either the play or the players. The difficulties against which the latter strove were great. Their scenery, such as it was, was poor, and their stage so small that one could not swing a cat on it—at least, not a very long cat, as Mark Twain would say. Yet, in spite of all drawbacks, there was much earnestness and some very creditable acting, notably by Mr F. J. Fay and Mr. Digges.' He found the play itself trivial and local, 'a drama of drain pipes after the Ibsen model', and suggested that when next performed 'the City Council should go there in state. It is really intended for their benefit, and might do them some little good.' *The Pot of Broth* he thought 'a delightful little bit of quiet drollery. . . . There was one really clever little study in this piece— Mr. W. Y. [*sic*] Fay's Beggerman, a tatterdemalion who brought a benign smile to the face of Mr. George Moore who came in when the play was half over. A piece in Irish followed, for which I did not wait, and I noticed that I was not the only deserter . . .'. The review concluded: 'If the Irish Theatre Society would keep free from fantastic dreams and insane ideals, if it would desert Scandinavia and evacuate Camden street, if it would leave Henrik Ibsen alone, and get away from mortar hods and concrete foundations, if it would rally its friends and stage topics of national— not merely Nationalistic—interest, creditably and with due regard for public comfort, it should not find it difficult to catch a public in Dublin and in Ireland.'

[3] Fay replied that he was 'glad to hear of the primer', and advised WBY to talk to some of the actors of the Comédie Française since it was 'a master of speech whose aid you need not a master of music however eminent. The French school of declamation goes right back to the time of Racine and should have something that would be useful to you.' Although WBY had written an

To Lady Augusta Gregory, [16 December 1902]

18 Woburn Buildings, | Euston Road.
Tuesday

Dear Friend: Fay writes that they think of putting your play[1] in rehersal at once. They have also a three act comedy by Cousins.[2] I have come to the conclusion that it will be better to publish 'Where there is nothing' by its self as Vol 1 of plays for an Irish Theatre. Bullen does not want Kathleen reprinted for the present. Without it I thought the other two little plays would be overweighted and if I waited to put in "the travelling man" I should have to wait until you came here before going to press. It would also keep me from getting them taken by a review in all likelihood. I can do another little play I have in my head & bring out all the little plays (including "Kathleen") later on as vol 2. Verse plays can follow. Another reason for this plan is that I can get some money at once out of Bullen on it as Paul is now ready (I have added a good deal here & there). What do you think of this plan? Yes I like that new ending for the Raftery very well on thinking over it.[3] I think it will make the play a good deal stronger. Do not

article on 'Speaking to the Psaltery' (see p. 121), it was FF, not he, who published the 'primer', *The Music of Speech*, in 1909.

    [4] Fay replied: 'With regard to the actors of the Comedie practising on the note or on quarter tones I can only tell you that in an article on 'The Making of an Actor', which appeared in *Time* for 1879 . . . M. Got, then a professor at the Conservatoire, is described as impressing his pupils with the fact that they were reciting very fine French verse but warning them not to sing it. And Coquelin in his book on the delivery of Monologues [i.e. *L'Art de dire le monologue* (Paris, 1884)], says that he holds that, so long as an author has not given you an air to which to sing his verses, one should use one's voice to speak verse and not to chant it. Of course, despite these directions, we are met with the invariable English description of French declamation as chanting.' He added that he himself used 'quarter and other vague tones. I am trying the psaltery and find that at worst it would be an excellent voice producer. In your letter you seem to care little about the poet's own song being reproduced. . . . If you are going to let each improvise why not let things go on as they are. There is no getting over the fact that the quarter tones are the distinction between the speaking and the singing voice, and that if you systematically suppress them you are chanting, as they do in churches which you object to. . . . I am unconvinced but thoroughly interested and will go on making my experiments.'

    [1] *Twenty-Five*; see p. 233.
    [2] James Cousins's *Sold*, 'A Comedy of Real Life in 2 Acts', was described by Arthur Griffith as 'the first real comedy of Irish life' when he printed it in the *United Irishman* for the week ending 27 Dec, but WBY, who thought it vulgar, succeeded in suppressing its production and detaching Cousins from the INTS. The play was eventually produced by the Cork National Theatre Society on 27 Dec 1906, and revived on 18 Mar 1907 at the Queen's Theatre, Dublin.
    [3] In a letter dated 'Monday' [?15 Dec 1902; Berg] AG said that she had rethought 'the Raftery play' (see p. 264, n. 6) and wondered 'if this end would do—After the Miser goes out, Raftery stands up, says "I won't be the only one in the house to give no present to the woman of the house" & hands her the purse of money, telling them to count it. While they are all gathered round counting it, he slips quietly from the door. As he goes out, wheels & horse steps are heard, & a farmer comes in, says, "What is going on". . . . They say it is a wedding party called in by

forget to make the marriage guests show plenty of amazement at the dead man come to life. I have very near finished Spenser—it is quite a new essay though it contains many passages of the old. An hours work will finish the critical part & then I have a days work to do on the life. After that comes "Cuchullain" & that must be amended at once for my sister,[4] & then the wind up the [?book] of which I have dictated some new little essays. I am getting along pretty well with my eyes except that I can no longer work at night at all, & have to spare them a good deal always. How are your eyes? Have they got over their weariness. I need not tell you that I am always wishing for the time to pass swiftly until we are togeather again.

Yrs alwy
WB Yeats

ALS Berg, with envelope addressed to Coole, postmark 'LONDON W.C. DE 16 02'. Wade, 390–1.

To Maud Gonne, [mid-December 1902]

Mention in letter from MG, 28 December [1902].
Complaining that his eyes are still bad; sending her an article from the *Fortnightly Review*;[1] and discussing the Irish theatre.

G–YL, 160.

To F. J. Fay, [c. 17 December 1902]

Mention in letter from Fay, 18 December 1902.
Complaining of troublesome eyes; evidently reporting on a conversation with Shaw about French verse-speaking;[1] discussing regulated

Raftery—but where is Raftery? Is he gone? They ask the farmer if he met with him outside—the poet Raftery—& he says "I did not, but I stood by his grave at Killeenin yesterday".' She went on to ask whether WBY thought 'that is better? It gets rid of the good-byes & the storm, & I don't think any amount of hints convey the ghostly idea strongly enough. Let me know at once . . .'. This ending was very close to the one finally adopted.
[4] *Cuchullain* was retitled *On Baile's Strand* and published in *In the Seven Woods* by ECY at the Dun Emer Press in August 1903. WBY was dictating and revising essays for *IGE*.

[1] i.e. Stephen Gwynn's 'An Uncommercial Theatre'; see p. 244, n. 3.

[1] Fay commented that 'Shaw was of course quite absurd in accusing Bernhardt of intoning, and besides he forgot that the intonation of the French tongue is not that of the English tongue; but I think you ought to talk to him about the quarter tone question'.

declamation;[2] telling him of a proposed volume of 'Plays for an Irish Theatre'; and mentioning a proposed production of *The Countess Cathleen* in
London.[3]

Private.

To Edith Craig, 18 December 1902

18 Woburn Buildings, | Euston Road.
Dec. 18.th/02.

Dear Miss Craig,

I am dictating this to a friend as my eyes make it unadvisable for me to
write much. I thought some of your brother's work last night most beautiful & solemn. That first abyssmal scene for instance & moments throughout. I think however that he is beginning to use his lights too much; they
begin to take away from the importance of the figures and the grouping &
throw strange colours upon the faces, sometimes when the natural colour is
what the story wants. Is not lighting, like brandy or like the supernatural
element in stories, a thing that grows upon the artist, until the man is
gone? I still think your brother's most beautiful work to have been the
"Masque of Love" which never seemed to me like the theatre at all, but
always like some strange real existence, when [?*for* which] I had come upon
unobserved, and by chance. I did not like the way the people spoke last
night. They spoke their verse as if it were prose & as you know, I feel savage upon that subject. I thought the little play rather thin, rather lacking in
passion & drama & I daresay your brother found that it bored him & so did
not take trouble.[1] [*Remainder of letter in WBY's hand*] I hope your mother

---

[2] Fay replied that he would 'be glad to have a specimen of what you call regulated declamation.
You will see that although I put forward objections I am quite interested in the matter. But I
could wish you had less to do with musicians. . . . Try how they may, music is more to them than
Speech.' And he added that regulated declamation seemed 'more feasible than the lilts which contain too many notes'.

[3] This production, planned by the Literary Theatre Club, did not occur (see below, p. 297, n. 4).

[1] Laurence Housman (1865–1959), dramatist, poet, novelist, and book illustrator, had
employed Gordon Craig to design and privately produce his two-act nativity play, *Bethlehem*,
which had been refused a licence by the Lord Chamberlain. The play was produced, as Shorter
explained in the *Tatler* of 13 Aug 1902 (290), 'by subscription so as to free it from the unintelligent direction of our Censor of Plays, and £1 1s will secure a bound volume of words and either
one front seat, two second, or three back seats at a single performance'. Five performances of the
play were given at the Imperial Institute from 17 to 20 Dec. A photograph of the first scene of
this production is reproduced in Craig's *The Art of the Theatre* (Edinburgh, 1905), as an example
of a stage illuminated by means other than footlights. In the first scene the Angel Gabriel appears
to a group of shepherds who speak an improbable Mummersetshire dialect in rhyming couplets.
The literary faults were evidently mitigated by Craig's setting, described by the *Morning Post* of

did not mind my foolish little story about her meeting me at Mrs Stan-
nards.[2] I seldom get credit for an absurd amount of timidity and shyness,
which has a way, when I meet any body for the first time or practically for
the first time, of hiding embarrasment under a brazen manner. The follies
I commit under these circumstances are the only sins I ever feal remosefull
for. Ones real sins one generally rejoices in remembering—one keeps the
thought of them for the solace of old age.

Yrs sny
W B Yeats

Dict AEFH and ALS; Tenterden.

To James Joyce, 18 December 1902

H1 Montagu Mansions, | Portman Square, | London.
Dec 18th.,/02.

My dear Joyce,
    The last time I went to the "Speaker" & I think I have been twice since
I wrote, I succeeded in finding somebody in. But when I spoke of my business, the man asked me to see the Editor, as he alone could act in such a
matter & told me that the Editor would not be in town till after Xmas. I
am sorry, but for the present you can send some prose to the Academy if
you feel an impulse to write. You had better mention my name so as to
remind the Editor of what I told him. I won't give him your little poem,[1]
for I gathered from his conversation that he does not like publishing verse,
unless it has an obvious look of importance. He told me for instance that
he would prefer two columns of verse if it were good, to a little lyric. If I

this very day (8) as 'one of the most beautiful we remember. For sky we had, we believe, nothing
but a draping with holes for stars; the shepherds were simply clad in clay-coloured garments of no
particular cut, and the sheep with which they rested in a circle of modern wooden hurdles were
represented by stuffed sacks. But the illusion was wonderful. Never before have we felt in the
theatre a vastness so illimitable, a loneliness so complete, or a silence so profound.'

[2] The *Morning Post* (see above) noted that Ellen Terry was among the 'intellectual and fashionable audience assembled' to see Housman's play, and that 'Mr. W. B. Yeats was only one of a
host of minor poets' present. Henriette Eliza Vaughan Stannard, née Palmer (1856–1911), wife of
Arthur Stannard, a civil engineer, wrote under the pseudonym 'John Strange Winter' a prolific
number of stories and novels, mainly on army life. WBY had probably met Ellen Terry at her
reception of 2 Mar 1889 when, as ECY recorded in her diary (MBY), he 'met some interesting
people . . . & stayed to supper not coming home till twelve'.

[1] In *LJJ* II. 23, Richard Ellmann identifies the poem as 'All day I hear the noise of waters', a
copy of which Joyce had sent to J. F. Byrne on 15 Dec. Stanislaus Joyce, however, suggests (*My
Brother's Keeper*, 209) that it was 'either "O Sweetheart, hear you" or "I would in that sweet
bosom be", probably the former. In both the thought is "thin", and both were subsequently
printed in the *Speaker*.' See, respectively, Joyce's *Chamber Music*, XXXV, XVIII, VI.

had had all your M.S. I might have picked a little bundle of lyrics, but I think you had really better keep such things for the "Speaker" which makes rather a practise of publishing quite short scraps of verse. I think the poem that you have sent me has a charming rhythm in the second stanza, but I think it is not one of the best of your lyrics as a whole. I think that the thought is a little thin. Perhaps I will make you angry when I say that it is the poetry of a young man, of a young man who is practising his instrument, taking pleasure in the mere handling of the stops. It went very nicely in its place with the others, getting a certain richness from the general impression of all taken together & from your own beautiful reading. Taken apart by itself it would please a reader who had got to know your work, but it would not in itself draw attention to that work. It has distinction and delicacy but I can remember that several of the other poems had more subject, more magical phrases, more passion. I would strongly recommend you to write some little essays. Impressions of books, or better still, of artistic events about you in Paris, bringing your own point of view in as much as possible, but taking your text from some existing interest or current event. You could send some of these at once to the Academy & others later on to the "Speaker". It is always a little troublesome getting ones first start in literature; but after the first start, one can make a pittance if one is industrious, without a great deal of trouble.

Yours sincly
W B Yeats

[*In WBY's hand*]
I am keeping the little poem as I have no doubt you have a copy.

Dict AEFH, signed WBY; Yale. *LJJ* II. 23–4.

To an unidentified correspondent, 20 December 1902

18 Woburn Buildings, | Euston Road.
Dec. 20th.,/02.

Dear Madam,
    I have been a long time about replying to your letter, but I have to dictate all my letters & have not always an amanuensis at hand. I should like very well to lecture to the Pharos Club but am not yet quite certain

whether I can do so, as I may find myself very busy.[1] I will let you know later on.

Yrs sincly
W B Yeats

Dict AEFH, signed WBY; Southern Illinois.

To John Millington Synge, 21 December 1902

18 Woburn Buildings, | Euston Road. | London.
Dec. 21st,/02.

My dear Synge,

Fay's company is going to produce a play of mine at the end of January. I shall go to Dublin for that.[1] However we will meet here, as you say & I will get you to shew me your play.[2] I thought the subject impressive and certainly it would be a fine thing for Fay if you got the play right. He is in danger of getting work which is quite articulate but also quite empty.[3] Meanwhile young Colum, who writes bye the bye rather like you, is full of matters but not yet quite articulate. I wonder if you have heard anything from Nutt about your book.[4]

Yours sincly
W B Yeats

Dict AEFH, signed WBY; TCD. Saddlemyer, 38.

[1] The Pharos Club, a 'Socialistic and Radical' dining and lecture society, met at 3 Henrietta St., Covent Garden, until it disbanded in 1905. George Palmer (1851–1913), Liberal MP for Reading, was the Secretary, but WBY's name may have been suggested by Conal O'Riordan, an active member of the committee in 1902, who had arranged debates and lectures by Chesterton, Belloc, Frank Russell, and others. Nevinson, who was to lecture there on 5 May 1903, recorded his impressions of it in his diary (Bodleian): 'a rather confused Bohemian sort of club, with a good deal of intellect and much sexual charm in rather faded blouses. One expected the women to put their feet on the table, but they did not. They only smoked and played Bridge. Large audience, very attentive . . .' There is no evidence that WBY ever spoke there.

[1] i.e. *The Hour-Glass*, which had controversially been put off, ostensibly so that the Fays could experiment with the Society's new hall in Camden Street, and which was eventually postponed until March (see p. 229, and p. 266, n. 1).

[2] Synge was in London from 10 Jan to 18 Mar 1903, and read *Riders to the Sea* to WBY, MG, and Chesterton at WBY's 'Monday Evening' on 2 Feb. He had drafted both it and *In the Shadow of the Glen* in the summer of 1902. WBY was later to contrast his work with Colum's.

[3] Synge was present when the Fays revived the Samhain plays at the Camden Street hall on 4 Dec, an event which helped him decide to join the theatre movement and to return to Dublin from Paris.

[4] See p. 215. Nutt had written to Synge on 13 Nov 1902 (TCD), rejecting *The Aran Islands* on the grounds that it would not appeal to a sufficiently large audience.

To Frank Pearce Sturm, [c. *24 December 1902*]

Mention in letter from Sturm, 26 December 1902.
A letter offering criticism of Sturm's writings; advising him to 'dramatize' himself, catching the moods as they come and go, instead of building up futile words; and arguing that modern poets needed a Movement 'that shall urge them to go to nature alone for what they want'.

LWBY I. 113–14.

To W. G. Fay, [c. *26 December 1902*]

Mention in following letter.
A 'very severe' letter, telling him that *Sold* is 'rubbish & vulgar rubbish', and that he might show the letter to whom he pleases. WBY suggests that they should play foreign masterpieces, and recommends the last act of [Marlowe's] *Doctor Faustus*.

To Lady Augusta Gregory, 26 December 1902

18 Woburn Buildings | Euston Road.

Dear Friend: I have written to you little and badly of late I am afraid for the truth is you have had a rival in Nietzsche, that strong enchanter. I have read him so much that I have made my eyes bad again. They were getting well it had seemed. Nietzsche completes Blake & has the same roots—I have not read anything with so much excitement, since I got to love Morris's stories which have the same curious astringent joy.[1]

Paul is at last finished, sermon & all & is going to press. I have written in a good deal here & there. Sermon gave me most trouble but it is right now. It is as simple as it was & no longer an impersonal but altogeather a personal dream & it has a latin text. Eddy Craig is as enthusiastic as ever & will I think stage it finely doing great things with the monastry scene which is the most admired scene. There is to be a stone wall, a Galway

---

[1] See p. 239. Describing his visit to Ireland in August 1902, Quinn later recalled (the *Outlook* [New York], 16 Dec 1911, p. 917) 'how interested [WBY] became in a volume of Nietzsche that I had with me, and how in reading out from it he quickly pointed out the resemblance of some of Nietzsche's ideas to Blake'. His memory, after nine years, may have been playing him false, for on 27 Sept 1902 he had written (see p. 239, n. 2): 'I don't know if you are acquainted with Nietzsche's writings or not'.

wall in every out door scene as a kind of repeated *motive*. Craig thinks ⟨I⟩ it
out [*for* ought] to have given it to him & I may have played the fool in not
doing so for I hear he is going into management with his mother. However
he gave me no details & one does not take vague promises from a man of
his kind. They are going to start with Ibsens "Heroes of Heligoland".[2]

I have written Fay a very severe letter about Cousins play "Sold" in
UI.[3] They talk of doing it at once. I have made no objection to their doing
it but I have told him that it is "rubbish & vulgar rubbish". I have wound
up by saying that I did not mark the letter "private". He might show it if
he liked. Cousins is evidently hopeless & the sooner I have him as an
enemy the better. I think Fay will see from my letter that, although I do
not interfear with their freedom to produce what they like, too much
Cousins would make work in common out of the question. I have suggested that they play foreign masterpieces. I find I can get through Miss
Horniman a translation of a fine play of the heroic age of Sudermans.[4] I
have not spoken of this yet but have suggested the last act of Faustus to F
Fay. I have learned a great deal about the staging of plays from "the Nativity"[5] endeed I have learned more than Craig likes. His sister has helped
me, bringing me to where I could see the way the lights were worked. He
was indignant—there was quite an amusing scene. I have seen all the costumes too, & hope to get patterns. He costumed the whole play—30 or 40
people I should say—for £25.

My indignation over the Cousins play has not been lightened by the fact
that it has been published with the statement that it was to be done before
I had received a copy. I have endeed had a letter from W Fay saying that
he was waiting to get proofs to send them. He may be away but I would
like to know if Hyde has received a copy. I do not think from his letter that
W Fay is to blame, but Cousins is one of Russells Hermetists. I am not
going to let the matter pass but am doubting as to whether to make my
protest now or when I see W Fay—this I think better. I wont decide until
I get his answer to my letter.

---

[2] The Craig–Terry production of Ibsen's *The Vikings of Helgeland* (see p. 4, n. 6) opened on 15
Apr 1903 at the Imperial Theatre, and WBY saw it on 30 Apr.

[3] See p. 278. WBY had just read *Sold* for the first time in the *United Irishman*, which, although
dated 27 Dec 1902, had actually been published on 24 Dec. He had told Frank Fay of his doubts
about the play, which was put into rehearsal on 28 Nov, even before reading it (see p. 277), and
now found his worst fears confirmed. He was further incensed by an announcement in the *United
Irishman* (1) that it was to 'be produced during the coming year by the Irish National Theatre
Society'.

[4] Hermann Sudermann (1857–1928), German playwright and novelist, published *Teja*, a
heroic play about the king of the Goths, in *Morituri* (1897). AG's later translation of the play was
produced at the Abbey Theatre on 19 Mar 1908. The entry of Synge, AG, and Colum into the
dramatic movement made the need for foreign plays less urgent, and no part of Christopher Marlowe's *Doctor Faustus* was produced by the INTS.

[5] i.e. Housman's *Bethlehem*; see p. 280.

I have got £5 from Bullen & I have two coming for a poem from the Pall Mall[6] so I am fairly well off for the moment. I have about an hours work still to do on Spenser & then to dictate it to a type writer—or some of it.

I shall see you soon now. I shall have so much to say & to hear, & to plan.

Yours in all affection,
W B Yeats

ALS Berg, with envelope addressed to Coole, postmark 'LONDON [?DEC] 26 02'. Partly in Wade, 379–80.

To [*? John Rogers Rees*],[1] *28 December 1902*

18 Woburn Buildings, | Euston Road, | London.
Dec. 28*th*,/02.

My dear Sir,

I have left your letter unanswered for a few days for I have a trouble of the eye-sight at present & must do my writing through an amanuensis, and I have not always one at hand. Of course I shall have great pleasure in accepting your kind invitation whenever my lecture comes off.

I have not yet heard the date of the lecture.

Yours sinly
W B Yeats

Dict AEFH, signed WBY; Private.

[6] 'The Old Men Admiring Themselves in the Water'; see p. 257, n. 4.

[1] This was probably to John Rogers Rees (d. 1923) of Avondale, Llandaff, with whom WBY was to stay when he lectured in Cardiff on 19 Feb 1903. Rees, a bank manager with literary leanings, was the author of *The Pleasures of a Bookworm* (1886), *The Brotherhood of Letters* (1889), and *In the Study and the Fields* (1890). A student of Celtic myth and folklore, he contributed 'The Norse Element in Celtic Myth' to *Archaeological Cambrensis* in 1898.

To F. J. Fay, [c. 28 December 1902]

Mention in letter from Fay, 29 December 1902.
Asking about French methods of declamation and intonation on the stage;[1] and telling Fay that he has arranged to discuss these matters with Mme Dudlay.[2]

Private.

To Padraic Colum, [c. 29 December 1902]

Mention in letter from Colum, 30 December 1902.
Commenting on criticism of Colum's prose-poem *Eoghan's Wife* in the *United Irishman*; suggesting that its language breaks up the unity of conception here and there;[1] offering to send him Ibsen's *Lady Inger* so that he

---

[1] In his reply Fay confessed that, although he was 'greatly interested in French declamation, my knowledge of the language is hardly sufficient to put questions concerning the principles of French diction, which of course has its root in the French language'. He recommended Raymond Solly's *Acting and the Art of Speech at the Paris Conservatoire*, Talma's *The Actor's Art*, and sent him his own copy of Coquelin's *L'Art de dire le monologue*, marking the pages that dealt with the delivery of verse. He added that his reading on French intonation suggested that the professors at the Conservatoire 'seem to direct their pupils to consider how a phrase would be said in colloquial speech and then transfer the tone to the words to be spoken. That is the English practice too. But I imagine the French practice to go deeper and to say "Consider how the *type* of man or woman you are representing would say so and so." That is certainly the basis on which Coquelin works and to my thinking is the only sound one in acting, as by it as little as possible of the actor's personality gets into the part.'

[2] Mme Dudlay was a Belgian actress, who had been educated at the Brussels Conservatoire, and became one of the leading tragediennes of the Comédie Française in the late 19th century. In his reply Fay suggested that WBY should ask her 'whether it is the custom of the actors of the Comedie to practise on pure notes and on quarter tones', whether 'there are any books of declamation by French actors and where they can be got', 'where one can get Delsarte's work on gesture', and whether 'the French actor *always monotones* verse or whether, while paying all attention to the laws of French verse, he tries to speak it in the tone used to express emotion in *real* life'.

[1] Colum's *Eoghan's Wife*, a prose dramatic monologue in which a bored wife reflects upon the murder of her husband by her would-be lover, appeared in the *United Irishman* of 20 Dec 1902, and was criticized on 27 Dec by 'AON' who urged him to aim for simplicity, to avoid the 'literary picturesque' and 'psychological analysis', and to 'write of the life he intimately knows or the passions he has intimately studied'. In his reply to this letter Colum said that AE and he had concocted a reply to his critic, but agreed with WBY 'that the language used breaks up the unity of my conception here and there. This is because I never quite made up my mind as to whether *Eoghan's Wife* would be a dramatic sketch or a prose poem'.

could study its construction;[2] and asking about progress on his play, *Broken Soil.*[3]

Hogan and Kilroy II. 43.

To Maud Gonne, [late December 1902]

Mention in letter from MG, 2 January [1903].
Complaining about the acceptance of Cousins's play, *Sold*, by the INTS, and arguing for the desirability of the INTS playing foreign masterpieces.[1]

G–YL, 161.

To Wilfrid Scawan Blunt, [late December 1902]

Mention in letter from Blunt, 4 January 1903.
Asking about progress on Blunt's play, *Fand.*[1]

LWBY I. 114–15.

To George Bernard Shaw, 31 December 1902

Mention in following letter.
Asking Shaw to allow Fay's company to produce *The Man of Destiny.*

---

[2] Although WBY disliked Ibsen's social realism, he approved of the early legendary dramas, but *Lady Inger of Östrat* (1857) may have been the suggestion of AEFH, who was acting as WBY's amanuensis at this time, and who was to tell 'George Birmingham' (J. O. Hannay) that there was 'a good deal to be learned from old fashioned machinemade plays like . . . Ibsen's *Lady Inger*, where the plot is like clockwork' (NLI). In his reply Colum told WBY he had read the play 'a long time ago', but that he had not paid much attention to its construction then.

[3] See below, p. 290, n. 5.

[1] See p. 277. WBY had probably voiced his disquiet about *Sold* in his letter of mid-December (see p. 279) and renewed this more vigorously when he read the play. MG replied from Paris on 2 Jan 1903 (*G–YL*, 161) agreeing that it was 'a horror—vulgar & full of bad jokes', and promising to write to Arthur Griffith about it since 'as he is great friends with the Fays, it will certainly come to them'. However, she disagreed that the Fays should play non-Irish drama, arguing that they had 'quite enough at present without foreign drama', and that they would 'have much more success if they keep to plays by Irish authors'.

[1] See p. 202. Blunt replied from Egypt (see p. 266, n. 3) that he had been 'rather dilatory', for, having finished the first act of the play to his satisfaction, he had 'dawdled over the rest'. Nevertheless, he hoped to have it finished and in type soon.

To Lady Augusta Gregory, 31 December 1902

18, Woburn Buildings | Euston Road
Dec. 31st, 1902.

Dear Friend

I saw Fay on Monday, and I think things will be all right I find that he himself has no liking for Cousins's work. He had "passed" it, as he says, because of the great trouble it was to have to play so many plays in one evening. He says he did no more than notice that Cousins's play was of the right length. I am not quite sure that we are out of the wood yet as when a play is once passed it has to be accepted by the company, and this play has been accepted. They had actually intended to play it with the "Hourglass". Against that I protested of course. In order to crowd it out I proposed that they should play Shaw's "Napoleon", and I have just written for his leave which I have no doubt we shall get.[1] Fay says he could put it in rehearsal at once. I am afraid that your play will not be done with the "Hourglass". The difficulty is to get three new plays of sufficient length and they do not want to put on one of the old plays again just yet. Fay now thinks of making the "Lost Saint" one of the three plays[2] but the worst of it is that unless they put on another play of some length like the "Napoleon" they will hardly get an evening's bill. I also proposed that they begin playing masterpieces of foreign lands and I am getting a friend of Miss Horniman's to translate a short little known costume play of Sudermann's[3] but Fay wants to get along with purely Irish work until Easter. He has a difficulty I imagine for one thing with the more orthodox members of his company who are likely to be affronted perpetually the moment they begin playing good literature, of European fame. He says that he is about to try and enlarge the company in order to have substitutes for the very pious. Miss

---

[1] Napoleon is the central character in Shaw's *The Man of Destiny* (1897); see p. 117. Shaw declined permission in favour of other of his plays, perhaps because he was currently discussing a possible London production in German with his translator, Siegfried Trebitsch.

[2] WBY had provided the scenario for Hyde's *The Lost Saint* (*An Naomh ar Iarraid*; see p. 224), and it had been published in Gaelic and in AG's English translation in this October's *Samhain*. Based on the same legend as WBY's story 'Where There Is Nothing, There Is God', it dramatizes the recognition of St Aongus Ceile Dé by a schoolmaster and pupils after his intercession turns a dunce into a scholar. Fay soon dropped the play from consideration and it was performed by children from the Inghinidhe na hEireann drama classes on 28 and 29 Jan at the Workmen's Total Abstinence Club in York Street. AG included the play in *Poets and Dreamers*, and Quinn gave her account of its composition in the *Outlook* of 16 Dec 1911 (see p. 284, n. 1); 'one morning she went for a long drive to the sea, leaving Hyde with a bundle of blank paper before him. When she returned in the evening, Dr. Hyde had finished the play and was out shooting wild duck. . .'

[3] See p. 285. AEFH's friend was Alice Spencer, who lived in Sussex. AEFH sent her translation to WBY at Coole, but it was lost, and *Teja* was eventually translated by AG.

Quinn has been giving so much trouble that he is afraid she will drop out altogether.[4] I did not say anything to him about his having passed Cousins before he had let me read it and for no better reason than that I forgot. However if I can bring off the Bernard Shaw arrangement and also get a promise of an original play from him I shall return to the point. I begin to think that presently it will be necessary to have some more definite ⟨spoken or written⟩ arrangement about the selection of plays. W. Fay struck me as being quite frank. He finds it hard work managing Cousins and his ⟨following⟩ like. He says that Cousins's vanity is so great that he alone out of all the writers refuses to listen to any criticism. I have had a nice letter from Collum to whom I wrote. He says he has got that play he showed us quite simple now but has made a new scheme of it in three short acts.[5] I am going to send him one or two books of plays. The material for the background in "The Hourglass" is to be made of sacking. The sacking is now being dyed green. Fay told me that some of the Gaelic Leaguers threatened "to make him" do plays in Irish and nothing else, but he defied them. He says he is not afraid of them as none of them pay more than 6d to go into any theatre and he has no sixpenny seats. I have finished the essay on Spenser. I had to rewrite it all though of course I found great masses of what I dictated in Ireland quite fit to go in. The general thread of the argument is weak. I am now redictating it from my manuscript to my present typewriter, and hope to be done in a couple of days. "Where there is nothing" has gone to Watt, in what I thought its final shape but other little changes or rather additions keep occurring to me. Quilter Couch in a cutting that was sent me the other day spoke of your book as having delighted hundreds of English readers, so we may consider that he makes amends for that old letter.[6]

---

[4] See pp. 162; 229, n. 2; 254, n. 1.

[5] Colum's first three-act play, *Broken Soil* (see p. 169), was produced on 3 Dec 1903; it was later revised and published as *The Fiddler's House* (1907). In his letter of 30 Dec (see above, p. 287) Colum wrote: 'I have left the Fiddler play over since I read it to you. But I have reconstructed the whole thing. The plot is quite simple now. I have cut out all literary matter and am going to avoid the "literary picturesque," it will be in three very short acts. I commenced the second act to-day.'

[6] The Quiller-Couch cutting was his 'Monday Causerie' in the London *Daily News* of 22 Dec 1902 (8) which he had devoted to a sympathetic review of *Samhain* (1902). In the course of this he praised 'an exquisite little Irish play by Dr. Douglas Hyde, exquisitely translated, under the title of "The Lost Saint" by Lady Gregory, whose own "Cuchulain of Muirthemne" . . . has in a short while brought delight to hundreds of English readers . . .'. In an unsigned notice of the book in the *Athenaeum* of 2 Aug 1902 (147) he had acknowledged its 'distinct merits', but suggested that 'those who know the subject at first hand will scarcely be prepared to endorse all the laudation which Mr. Yeats here bestows. His praise is at times so excessive that there is danger of its exciting in the reader expectations which may not be realized. What he calls "a speech beautiful as that of Morris . . ." proves to be no more than a specimen of suitable English style coloured by a few Irish idioms, some of which tend to become tedious by frequent repetition.'

[Remainder of letter in WBY's hand]

I urged Fay to do your play with mine as I said it would be a nuisance for you to go to Dublin later. He said it would need very careful rehersal as that card scene would need so many people that it would bring in the less experienced people of the cast.[7]

Yrs alway
W B Yeats

Just dictated last word of Spenser.[8]

TLS Berg, with envelope addressed to Coole, postmark 'LONDON DE 31 02'.

---

[7] AG's *Twenty-Five* (see p. 233, n. 3) and WBY's *The Hour-Glass* were, in fact, produced together on 14 Mar 1903 at the Molesworth Hall, Dublin.

[8] The essay is consistently dated October 1902 in its published form.

1903

To Padraic Colum, 2 January 1903

18 Woburn Buildings, | Euston Road, | London.
Jan. 2ⁿᵈ,/03.

My dear Collumb,

I send you "Lady Inger". You should read "The Pretenders" too, it is a very fine play, but it is not so fine a piece of dramatic writing as "Lady Inger".[1] If I can come across anything of Hauptmann's or Sudermann's I will send it to you. But I want you to make a real study of "Lady Inger". I thought your reply to your critic most convincing and eloquent.[2] I like the little poem you send, though not as well as that poem about the poor scholar[3]—that was a real achievement & I wish I was bringing out a new edition of my anthology, a "Book of Irish Verse" that I might ask your leave to put it in. I have made some corrections in metre in "Destiny" & suggested one emendation of the sense to get rid of an obscurity.[4] This is

[1] See p. 287. This letter is tipped into the front cover of vol. III of William Archer's *Ibsen's Prose Dramas*, containing *Lady Inger of Östrat*, *The Vikings of Helgeland*, and *The Pretenders*, and inscribed 'P. J. Columb from W. B. Yeats, Xmas 1902'. It is in answer to the letter of 30 Dec 1902 in which Colum said he wanted to reread *Lady Inger* and asked about translations of Hauptmann's and Sudermann's plays.

[2] With AE's help, Colum replied to 'AON's criticism of *Eoghan's Wife* (see p. 287) in the *United Irishman* of 3 Jan 1903 (6), arguing that simplicity had to take account of the heart's complexity, that sincerity should not shackle the creative imagination, and that most literature was unrealistic and 'literary': 'What the imaginative mind sees, or the heart in its wonder may feel—all this is the province of literature to express. . . . It is the art of the writer to find words for those who are voiceless, and who could never utter the life that is in them, and not to copy all the bad grammar and futilities that make up the speech of nearly all of us, even in our most tragic moments'.

[3] 'A Portrait', subtitled 'A poor scholar in the 'Forties', published in the *United Irishman* on 1 Nov 1902, is a short monologue in which the scholar, a man of contemplation, meditates upon the thanklessness of teaching the Classical languages in the West of Ireland at a time of political agitation. The second and final edition of *A Book of Irish Verse* had appeared in 1900, but the poem was anthologized in AE's *New Songs* (1904).

[4] Colum enclosed his latest poem, 'Destiny', with his letter of 30 Dec 1902, telling WBY that he had 'decided to submit to discipline and am working away at my verses till I get them quite regular'. The four-stanza poem in rhyming iambic tetrameters describes a son's sense of 'destiny' that he should fulfil his father's thwarted ambitions by emigrating in search of riches. It subsequently appeared in the *United Irishman* of 24 Jan 1903, p. 2, but was not republished thereafter.

not so important however, but the emendations of metre are really necessary.

Yrs sny
W B Yeats

Dict AEFH, signed WBY; NLI.

To W. T. Horton, 2 January 1903

18 Woburn Buildings | Euston Road | London.
Jan. 2ⁿᵈ,/03.

My dear Horton,

I am back as you see & my eye-sight no better. I have been back some
little while & I have been several times on the point of writing to you, but
when I had paper I had not your address. Look in on me some morning.
And please don't forget that you promised me an introduction to a spiritu-
alist. I shall have a little time this Winter & want to begin really serious
investigation.[1] You will find me in as usual any morning before 12 o'clock.

Yours sincerely
W B Yeats

Dict AEFH, signed WBY; Texas.

To Lady Augusta Gregory, [3 January 1903]

18 Woburn Buildings | Euston Road.

Dear Friend: Yesterday I sent off the Spenser essay to the publisher. It is a
great releif to have got it done. I think you will find it very good. It is
much saner than it was & yet quite as original. It is all founded now on a
single idea—the contrast between Anglo-French England & Anglo Saxon
England. I hope in a couple more days to have got 'Cuchullain' finally
right & sent to my sisters. Then (I am afraid you will be sorry to hear) I
propose to put certain parts of "The Hour Glass" into verse—only the part

---

[1] Following the disputes in the GD, and WBY's growing disillusionment with it, he was turning to spiritualism to find corroboration for the beliefs hé and AG had discovered in Irish folklore: 'I had noticed many analogies in modern spiritism and began a more careful comparison,
going a good deal to séances for the first time . . . in Soho or Holloway. . . . I did not go there for
evidence of the kind the Society for Psychical Research would value. . . . I was comparing one
form of belief with another, and . . . I was discovering a philosophy' (*Expl*, 30–1). He had avoided
seances in the 1890s (with the possible exception of a sitting with Charles Williams in 1899), following a disturbing experience at one in January 1888 (see I. 45).

with the Angel & the soliloques. I have got to think this necessary to lift the "wise mans" part out of a slight element of platitude. The play will then go to enlarge my sisters book.[1] I shall have a sub title printed in red before the two plays "Plays for an Irish Theatre" & have same sub title to "Where there is nothing" & the other plays when they come. It is rather difficult to manage the issue of the little plays at the same time with the long one. Kathleen is a difficulty that I could get over but if I put 'The Hour Glass' with the poems that is a worse difficulty. When you come we can do the little Christ play & that other one about the lawyer & make Bullen put Kathleen, Pot of Broth, Christ play & the new one togeather.[2] I am planning a performance here of 'The Hour Glass'. The finding of a wonderful "angel"[3] has moved me to it.

I want you to write & ask Kuno Meyer (or send me his address that I may) to return the faery lore articles of mine that he borrowed a year ago. I want them now. I am going to lecture in Cardiff on Feb 19 on 'The Irish Faery Kingdom'.[4] I am to be put up & to get £10. I am also going to lecture here on something or other & get £5. It looks as if lecturing was going to become profitable. Dolmetsch recommends it to me strongly.

I have just heard a ring & gone down to find that Mrs Old has stollen a march on me. For some time I have talked vaguely of getting a gass oven in my inner room. It would cook my breakfast & warm the room while I was eating it. At present I catch colds constantly—especially if the fire refuses to light. It seems that Mrs Old who wants the gass oven for her cooking went to the gass company without being told. It will cost me about £2.10 at the start. The gass man has just been & gone. Do you recommend me to have gass for lighting purposes or to keep it for cooking only. It will be a great comfort. I have a dressing gown (—a Xmas present but by that

---

[1] *The Hour-Glass* was not finally included with *On Baile's Strand* ('Cuchullain') in *In the Seven Woods* (1903).

[2] In her diary entry of 4 Jan 1903 (Berg) AG recalled that at the end of the summer of 1902 she and WBY began work on 'the little Christ play, the "Travelling Man"—'. They had also collaborated on *Heads or Harps*, a one-act satire on a lawyer who tries to switch political allegiance for professional and social advancement. AG later wrote (*Collected Plays*, IV. p. xi) that 'WBY and I made up this—but never put it on. It was chiefly his.' Bullen published *The Hour-Glass, Cathleen ni Houlihan*, and *The Pot of Broth* as vol. II of 'Plays for an Irish Theatre' in March 1904.

[3] Perhaps Mary Price Owen (see p. 253), with whom he was to present selections from the play as a duologue in his Westminster lecture of 15 May 1903.

[4] WBY had evidently loaned Kuno Meyer (see p. 111) some or all of his six articles on folklore which had appeared in the *Nineteenth Century*, *Fortnightly Review*, and *Contemporary Review* from January 1898 to April 1902. His draft of the lecture (Wellesley) and accounts in the Cardiff press show that he made full use of the articles: the *Western Mail* of 20 Feb (6) reported that he 'kept his audience deeply interested for nearly two hours with a description of the legends and folklore of Ireland, as gleaned by him from the lips of the peasantry'. He spoke in particular of the size and nature of fairies (see *UP* II. 65), fairy battles (*UP* II. 87), the relationship of Welsh and Irish mythology (*UP* II. 282), and the continuity of mythology and folklore as evidence for an *anima mundi* (*UP* II. 107–8).

hangs a tale—) & I can slip down and light it & have the room warm for breakfast, which can be always set out in the inner room.

I have just heard from Shaw he is afraid of our doing his 'Napoleon' which has never been well acted enough yet.

A Madame Troncey[5] is doing my portrait. She is a friend of Miss Horniman & is really a fine artist. It is the best yet. She is to give it me after sending it to the Salon. It is in black chalk. She is also to do a profile in colour which I am to have at once.

You have not told me anything about your essays. Are they being printed yet & when are they to be published?[6]

Yes it has been a good year with me too—a very good year.

Yours alway
W B Yeats

ALS Berg, with envelope addressed to Coole, postmark 'LONDON JA 3 03'. Wade, 391–3.

To Florence Farr, [early January 1903]

Mention in following letter.
Asking her for a copy of his poem, 'The Players ask for a Blessing on the Psaltery and on Themselves'.

To Lady Augusta Gregory, 6 January [1903]

18, Woburn Buildings | Euston Road,
Jan. 6th, 190⟨2⟩3.

My dear Friend

A great many thanks. I was just wondering what I was to do. After sending you that letter about the play I recollected how stupid I was. There was no reason in the world why including it in my sister's book should exclude it from the book of plays. However I will not include it in my sister's book if you still greatly object.[1] My reasons for wishing to do so are these. They

[5] The Parisian Madame Troncy was probably the wife of the French painter and illustrator, Emile Troncy, an officer of the Académie who exhibited at the Salon des Artistes Français. Her portrait of WBY was hung in the Green Room of the Abbey Theatre but WBY grew to dislike it. It ws removed in November 1906, and apparently returned to the artist in 1908.

[6] Essays that were to appear in AG's *Poets and Dreamers*, published in April 1903.

[1] In a letter of 4 Jan (Berg) AG had begged him not to include *The Hour Glass* in *In the Seven Woods* (see previous letter, n. 1): 'I feel so sure the *Hour Glass* would, with or without verse, weaken one book & strengthen the other—& I want every one of your books to be as strong as fine & as plentiful as possible.'

are going to charge ten shillings for the book and as an artistic press like theirs is forbidden to adopt the usual methods of padding out the poems, the Cuchullain play and all will come to about forty or fifty pages. This may be long enough. It will depend to some extent on the general look of the book. I do not agree with you that the Hourglass when I have put the verse into it would be out of tune with the rest. It repeats practically the Fool and Blind Man of the Hourglass[2] and would have something the same proportion of verse and prose. I am rather glad on the whole that you have ·protested so strongly against the exclusion of any of the plays from the little book. Armed with this new reason I shall press my opinion on Bullen. I have not done so hitherto because although he always acknowledges my right to do what I like with Cathleen I have not liked to make his loss over that foolish little book greater than necessary. Through a very needless piece of good nature he seems to have greatly overpaid the printer. The result is that though I think I got too little I do not think he has got anything at all. It must be a lesson to me in the matter of vague agreements. Now however that you object to its exclusion I shall go to Bullen and say "It's no use our wasting time while you are hoping to get back that lost money. We will both do very much better by bringing out the new plays soon, while the effect of the Stage Society performance of 'Where there is Nothing' lasts.[3] What is the soonest date at which you would agree to bring them out." I am not quite certain that it will be wise to publish them simultaneously with "Where there is Nothing", as the publication a little later will mean double the amount of reviewing and double the amount of advertising therefore for both books. I am also inclined to think that if we published them together we should have to call them volume one and two and charge for them both together a sum much smaller than we would have to charge for them if they were published separately. However I will go and see Watt tomorrow about it. I have begun to have the greatest possible contempt for my dear Bullen's business capacity.

Sturge Moore was round with me last night and he made to Gordon Craig (through a friend of Craig's that was there) an offer on Ricketts behalf.[4] He proposed that Ricketts should raise nearly £600 which should

---

[2] A dictation error: the Fool and the Blind Man are characters in *On Baile's Strand*; the Fool and the Wise Man in *The Hour-Glass*.

[3] See pp. 262–3. The Stage Society production of *Where There Is Nothing*, originally intended for January 1903, was delayed several times, and did not finally take place until June 1904.

[4] Charles de Sousy Ricketts (1866–1931), painter, sculptor, engraver, publisher, stage designer, and art critic, had proposed to use the projected receipts from his Vale Press edition of Marlowe's *Faustus* to finance the Literary Theatre Club's production of *The Countess Cathleen*, but the edition brought only £150 and plans were subsequently cancelled. WBY recalled (*Aut*, 169) that he had 'probably' been introduced to Ricketts and his lifelong companion, Charles Shannon, by Lionel Johnson in the 1890s, when Ricketts was editing the *Dial* (1889–97) and founding the Vale Press (1896–1904), but their intellectual friendship stems from early 1901, when Ricketts, fired by his

be used by Craig and Ricketts to stage my Countess Cathleen. All the
speaking of verse to be left entirely in the hands of Sturge Moore and of
course the author. I need hardly say that this performance which is evidently going to be a much bigger thing than I had foreseen will enormously strengthen my position. It makes me a little anxious about the
performance of "Where there is Nothing". I have left the securing of the
caste entirely to Miss Craig, and I have no way of judging whether she will
be able to get good performers.

I have arranged for another lecture (or did I tell you about it?) which I am
to give in London on March the 7th.[5] I am to get £5. I believe that Mrs.
Emery and myself are to get £20 between us for our lecture on the Psaltery
in Manchester on Ash Wednesday.[6] Mrs. Emery made me extremely cross
last night. I had some people there whom I had a particular reason (they
were friends of Craig's and Ellen Terry's) for wanting to hear her at her best
and out of sheer laziness she gave the worst performance on the Psaltery I
have ever heard. There are times when she makes me despair of the whole
thing. However Miss Owen is beginning to be a comfort. She has nothing
like Mrs. Emery's gift but she is immensely painstaking.

If you still feel that the Hourglass will be out of place in my sister's book
please write and tell me why you think so. Of course I shall not include it
in the ordinary edition of the poems. My sister's book is merely a specially
beautiful and expensive first edition of certain of my best things. I have
been thinking of putting a note at the end explaining why I have called the

growing interest in symbolic stage design, joined WBY and Sturge Moore in the Literary Theatre
Club (see p. 248, n. 1). WBY kept Ricketts in mind as a stage designer for several years, but it
was not until 1914–15 that he provided costumes and scenery for productions of *The King's
Threshold* and *On Baile's Strand*. His cover design for WBY's *Later Poems* (1922) adorned several
subsequent editions. An inveterate diary-keeper, his posthumous *Self-Portrait* (1939) contains a
number of entries on WBY. WBY described Ricketts as one of his 'chief instructors' in artistic
matters (*Aut*, 169), and as 'one of the greatest connoisseurs of any age, an artist whose woodcuts
prolonged the inspiration of Rossetti, whose paintings mirrored the rich colouring of Delacroix.
When we studied his art we studied our double' (*E & I*, 495).

[5] Probably an error for 7 Feb, when WBY lectured at the Bijou Theatre, Bedford Street, on
'The Future of Irish Drama' to Na Geadhna Fiadhaine ('The Wild Geese'), a society established
in June 1902 'to encourage and promote the study of Irish questions, historical, political, economic, and literary'. With P. T. MacGinley in the chair, and AG present, WBY 'advocated his
favourite theories of musical notation for dramatic speaking, and of the banishment of scenery as
far as practicable from the stage, and urged that the dramatist should depend alone upon the
excellence of his art. . . . The theatre in England was the theatre of the rich . . . but in Ireland
they should endeavour to establish a theatre of the people' (*Freeman's Journal*, 9 Feb 1903 p. 4). It
was probably just before this lecture that WBY received MG's letter telling him of her imminent
marriage to Major John MacBride, for she announced her engagement and conversion to Catholicism in the French press on 7 Feb. According to Richard Ellmann (*Yeats: The Man and the
Masks*, [1949], 163) 'For a moment . . . Yeats did not know what to do. Then he went through
with his lecture, and afterwards members of the audience congratulated him on its excellence, but
he could never remember a word of what he had said.'

[6] The illustrated lecture on 'Speaking to the Psaltery' by WBY and FF took place in the Whitworth Hall of Owens College, Manchester, on 18 May.

book by the name of one of the shortest poems "In the Seven Woods".[7]
Have you a copy of that poem which I wrote for three speakers—The one
calling for a blessing on the Psalteries.[8] I wrote to Mrs. Emery for a copy
and she sent me what I am afraid is her only one and I am afraid I have
lost it. I want to include it with the lyrics in my sister's book. I shall put
the Cathleen na Hoolihan poem also amongst them. If you have the poem
for the three voices please send it me at once.

Yours sinly

W B Yeats

TLS Berg, with envelope addressed to Coole, postmark 'LONDON JA 6 03'. Wade, 393–5.

To Florence Farr, [c. *6 January 1903*]

Mention in following letter.
Initiating an 'angry correspondence' with FF over her poor performance
on the psaltery on 5 Jan.

To Lady Augusta Gregory, [*8 January 1903*]

18 Woburn Building

Dear Friend: I went to Bullen and arranged that the plays come out in two
3/6 volumes making vol 1 & vol 2 of "plays for an Irish Theatre". Kathleen & Hour Glass both will be in vol 2. 3/6 a volume will enable Dublin
people to buy them.[1] I am in a great hurry as I have to get to Sturge
Moores. I am having an angry correspondence with Mrs Emery about
Mondays performance.

Yrs ev

W B Yeats

ALS Berg, with envelope addressed to Coole, postmark 'LONDON JA 8 03'. Wade, 395.

[7] The note, which separates the lyrics from *On Baile's Strand*, begins (*VP*, 814): 'I made some
of these poems walking about among the Seven Woods, before the big wind of nineteen hundred
and three blew down so many trees, & troubled the wild creatures, & changed the look of things;
and I thought out there a good part of the play which follows.'

[8] 'The Players ask for a Blessing on the Psalteries and on Themselves' (*VP*, 212–13), first published in *In the Seven Woods*. The 'Cathleen na Hoolihan poem' was 'The Song of Red Hanrahan'
(*VP*, 206–8), the revised version of an untitled poem in the story, 'Kathleen-ny-Houlihan', first
published in 1894, later entitled 'Kathleen the Daughter of Hoolihan and Hanrahan the Red' in
The Secret Rose (1897). The revised poem appeared in Jack Yeats's *A Broad Sheet* for April 1903
and in *In the Seven Woods*.

[1] A paper-covered edition was published in Dublin by Maunsel and Co. in 1905 for sale in
Ireland only.

To an unidentified correspondent, 9 January 1903

18 Woburn Buildings, | Euston Road, | London.
Jan. 9ᵗʰ.,/03.

My dear Sir,

I am just correcting the proof sheets of a book of poems to be called "In the Seven Woods". The first edition will be printed at my sister's private press (Emer Press, Dun Emer, Dundrum, Co. Dublin). It will be about 10/- but a cheaper edition will come out immediately after, published by A. H. Bullen, Great Russell Street, London. There is a cabinet photograph of me which can I believe be got from Chancellor, Dublin.[1]

I enclose a copy that I have made for you from one of my poems.

Yrs sny
W B Yeats

[*In WBY's hand*]

From 'Countess Cathleen'
Act 1.

Impetuous heart be still, be still,
Your sorrowful love can never be told:
Cover it up with a lovely tune.
He who could bend all things to his will
Has covered the door of the infinite fold
With the pale stars & the wandering moon.[2]
W B Yeats

Dict AEFH, signed WBY; Texas.

To A. E. Waite,[1] [c. 9 January 1903]

The Frater Demon est Deus Inversus, otherwise Frater Diabolus and yet otherwise Brother Devil, well known poet, also polytheist, idolater, vision-monger and theurgist, of the Brotherhood of the House of the Hidden

---

[1] Bullen did not publish an edition of the volume.
[2] These lines, one of Joyce's favourite Yeatsian quotations, are sung by Aleel at the end of Scene iv of *The Countess Cathleen* (*VPl*, 129).

[1] Arthur Edward Waite (1857–1942), mystic, author, editor, and translator of occult works, had joined the GD in January 1891 with the motto 'Sacramentum Regis' but resigned in 1893 to found the short-lived *Unknown World*. He was readmitted to the GD in 1896 but did not progress to the Second Order until 1899. In May 1903 he challenged the authority of the Chiefs, and in the following months was to split the Isis-Urania Temple by his insistence that the rituals should be

Stairs,[2] writes me under the hand of the impossible Soror Fortiter et Recte asking whether I will join him in petitioning the unspeakable triad[3] to reappoint the Ritual Sub-Committee, more especially as regards the 2 = 9 Ritual on which he and I worked together, but owing to throes, convulsions and revolutions the revision was suspended and our labours threatened to be wasted.[4]

Extract from A. E. Waite's 1903 Diary (Private), published in R. A. Gilbert's *A. E. Waite: Magician of Many Parts* (1987), p. 114.

To William Sharp, c. *13 January 1903*

Mention in following letter.
Asking on behalf of AG about Fiona Macleod's next book.

---

more sacramental and mystical, and by his discouragement of magic, so that by the end of the year WBY and others had seceded to set up the Stella Matutina temple.
  [2] Waite's nickname for the GD.
  [3] The three Chiefs who had assumed leadership of the GD in June 1902: Dr Robert W. Felkin (Finem Respice; d. 1922), Percy W. Bullock (Levavi Oculos; 1867–1940), and Brodie-Innes (see p. 32, n. 3).
  [4] The Ritual Sub-Committee had been set up after the expulsion of Mathers from the Order in 1900 and had as one of its remits the re-establishment of the grade ceremonies and the purging from them of the illicit practices that had grown up during FF's period as Praemonstratrix (see pp. 25–7). This was a task close to WBY's and AEFH's hearts, but the new Chiefs were less enthusiastic; the Sub-Committee was suspended, and AEFH after futile attempts to restore it, was to resign from the Order in February of this year. The 2 = 9 Ritual was the Ceremony of Advancement through which the Zelator progressed to the Grade of Theoricus. The first part consisted of the Ceremony of Admission to the path of Tau, the 32nd Path, for which the Zelator, dressed in a black tunic, carried a cubical Greek Cross. For the second part the Caduceus of Hermes was carried.

  Waite records in his diary that he wrote WBY 'an amicable reply, for until such time as a competent architect gets out the schedule of the House's dilapidations, our very joining in anything for it means & can come to nothing'. As the year progressed he began to see himself as the 'competent architect' (see above, n. 1).

To Lady Augusta Gregory, 13 January [*1903*]

18, Woburn Buildings | Euston Road,
Jan 13th

Dear Friend.

Let me know as soon as you can when I am to expect you. I hear that "Sold" has been given up, and that they are rehearsing Colomb's "Saxon Shilling".[1] I am very glad of this as it will encourage him and be nothing against our dignity. Maud Gonne also wrote and protested against "Sold". Bernard Shaw has given them leave to play either "Arms and the Man" "Widowers' Houses" or "The Devil's Disciple". Stephen Gwynne was dining with me last night and was full of the project of their coming to play in London. However I a little shrink in spite of my curiosity from seeing "Cathleen na Hoolihan" with either Miss Quinn or Miss Walker as the principal character.[2] I have written to William Sharpe asking your question about Fiona Macleod's book.[3] At the same time I doubt if any book of hers will interfere with either you or me. She is quite certain to turn it all into her own sort of wild romance while both you and I give the foundations themselves. Neither does it follow that her book is really on the edge of publication for she has been announcing books for years which have never come out. I should not wonder at all if her plans were to completely change before my question reaches her. I have heard from the Scottish publishers to whom I have sent the Spenser. They thank me for "a particularly interesting essay and selection", and send me £20 on account. At the same time they say that owing to the delay of several authors about the sending in of MSS. they have had "to reconsider" the series or the publication I forget which and that they cannot publish for some time. This makes me wonder whether the project may not be practically abandoned. I

---

[1] *The Saxon Shilling*, a one-act melodrama in which an Irish volunteer in the British army is shot by his sergeant when he tries to protect his family against eviction, was intended for production with *The Hour-Glass* on 14 Mar, but Fay tried to persuade Colum to alter the ending. MG, suspecting that Fay was attempting to curry favour with the British authorities protested fiercely, but the play was dropped from rehearsal in late January. It was subsequently produced by the Inghinidhe na hEireann at the Grocers Assistants' Hall (sometimes known as the Banba Hall) on 15 May 1903. For MG's protest against *Sold* see p. 288, n. 1.

[2] All three plays were eventually produced by the INTS, but not until October 1916 (*Widowers' Houses* and *Arms and the Man*) and February 1920 (*The Devil's Disciple*). Stephen Gwynn had written in praise of the Irish dramatic movement in the *Fortnightly Review* in December 1902 (see p. 275), and was now arranging through the ILS what turned out to be triumphant London productions in the coming May. MG had recently given Maire T. Quinn (whose acting WBY disliked) permission to play Cathleen ni Houlihan.

[3] Fiona Macleod's book of essays on Gaelic literature and legend, *The Winged Destiny*, was delayed by illness and did not appear until the summer of 1904. AG was presumably afraid that it might pre-empt her own *Poets and Dreamers* (1903).

imagine therefore that I shall write and make an enquiry or two of them before accepting the cheque. Will you be able to find room for my Shrine when you come?[4] You can leave the picture which is at the Nassau until we go over for the play as you would find it rather a trouble.

Yrs alway
W B Yeats

TLS Berg, with envelope addressed to Coole, postmark 'LONDON W.C. JA 13 03'. Wade, 395–6.

To Lady Augusta Gregory, [*14 January 1903*]

18 Woburn Buildings | Euston Road.

Dear Friend: I return the essay.[1] It is admirable. I have pencelled one or two things which explain themselves. They are chiefly in one sentence that was not quite vocal. I am very glad that you have done it. I am very pleased to think that both you & I will have some books out togeather which will be fairly cheap & altogeather for Irish readers. I am thinking of your essays & of my plays. I doubt if I could get "the [?]bard"[2] done, even if I could give it all my time, ready for my sisters when they got to that part of the book. I find that 'Cuchullain' wants new passages here & there. You need not be troubled about my poetical faculty. I was never so full of new thoughts for verse though all thoughts quite unlike the old ones. My work has got far more masculine. It has more salt in it. I have several poems in my head.

I beleive that my gass stove is to be put to rights to morrow. It will make a very substantial change for the better in my comfort.

I have heard from the Scottish publisher thanking me for a 'particularly

---

[4] WBY had a small shrine, which he usually kept at Woburn Buildings, but which could be folded for travelling, and which he had taken on his latest visit to Coole. It can be glimpsed just behind his right elbow in plate 10. Replying to this letter on 'Saturday' [14 Jan 1903; Berg], AG told him that even before 'yr little note came I had discovered the picture—& given it to the manager & asked him to take care of it for you. Perhaps yr sister wd. have it packed & sent on? Worse still, on undoing my own hold all, I found that wretched Shrine which I had brought up for you—& which is now landed here again!'

[1] Probably a draft of 'Irish Jacobite Songs' which was to appear in the *Speaker* on 24 Jan, and which was subsequently published in the delayed *Poets and Dreamers*.

[2] A working title for *The King's Threshold*, a draft of which WBY was to dictate to AG in late March and early April of this year.

interesting essay' & enclosing £20 on account but adding that the series is postponed & that my book will not come out for some time.

Yours alway
W B Yeats

ALS Berg, with envelope addressed to Coole, redirected to Queen Anne Mansions, postmark 'LONDON JA 14 03'. Wade, 396–7.

To Lady Augusta Gregory, [15 January 1903]

Dear Friend: Mrs Old has been urgent for me to remind you to bring over my bag. There are some night-gowns in bag which she has set her heart on my wearing I dont know why. I write to satisfy her. My gass stove is now in working order. I have cooked some very bad toast upon it—Toast like this

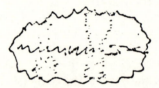

Black places are burnt parts over flame. The rest was white. I have been putting some passages into Cuchullain & am now about to correct proofs of essays.

Courtney offers £12 for 'Old Age of Queen Maeve'. I have asked when he can publish it & given him 3 months.[1]

Yr ev
W B Yeats

ALS Berg, with envelope addressed to Coole, redirected to Queen Anne Mansions, postmark 'LONDON.W. JA 15 03'.

[1] W. L. Courtney, who had dragged his feet over the publication of WBY's essay, 'The Happiest of the Poets' (see pp. 136, 257), was less cavalier with this poem, which appeared in the *Fortnightly Review* in April 1903. It was included in *In the Seven Woods*.

To W. G. Fay, [c. *16 January 1903*]

Mention in letter from Fay, 19 January 1903.
Telling Fay that Maire Quinn has applied through MG to play the part of Cathleen ni Houlihan;[1] reporting that Charles Ricketts is to fund the production of WBY's plays in London; and evidently enquiring if Fay had arranged with Stephen Gwynn the INTS's programme for their forthcoming productions in London.[2]

NLI.

To James Joyce, [c. *18 January 1903*]

18 Woburn Buildings | Euston Road

My dear Joyce.
  Come about 11 on Wednesday morning & I will send you straight to the manager of a big new Weekly who may be able to help you to your new ambition.[1] I cannot ask you to come before 11 as I shall be up late on Tuesday night & must sleep late.

Yrs sny
W B Yeats

ALS Yale.

---

[1] On 3 Jan MG had written to WBY (*G–YL*, 161) enquiring if Maire Quinn could understudy and play Cathleen ni Houlihan, since MG herself would be unable to act the part often in future, and WBY had passed on the request to Fay. Fay, detecting in this an undermining of his authority, responded angrily: 'About Miss Quinn's idea of playing Kathleen I must confess I am entirely at a loss to understand why in the first place she wrote Miss Gonne & in the second place asked her to speak to you. That Miss Gonne played Kathleen was your wish & her own, to which I offered no objections though at the time I stated here that I did not think it advisable for a Lady of Miss Gonne [*sic*] position to act in our little company and after results bore me out. But this is outside the present question. Miss Quinn is a member of my company whom my brother & self have taught what ever she knows of acting and it seems rather humourous [*sic*] to me that she should begin to think that she is the best judge of how parts should be given out in my company. I bitterly dislike underhand dealing of any sort and as far as I can prevent it, it wont find room in my company. As long as I stage manage my crowd I will give parts to the persons who seem to me the most fitted for them . . .' Nevertheless, Maire Quinn took the part until her resignation from the INTS later this year.
[2] Fay replied that he had 'written to Gwynn about the show I suggested Deirdre as a showier piece than the Foundations which is a style of acting Londoners have seen heaps of and better than ours and the piece is very limp in places'.

[1] Joyce stopped in London on his return to Paris from 21 to 22 Jan. The new weekly was *Men and Women*, 'A Popular Journal for Everyone', edited by George R. Sims (1847–1922), which ran from 14 Feb to 26 Dec 1903. According to Richard Ellmann, D. N. Dunlop (1868–1935), who

To Richard Ashe King,[1] *20* [*January 1903*]

18 Woburn Buildings | Euston Road
Tuesday 20th

My dear Ashe King
　I did not write to you last week because I had no amanuensis at hand, &
my eyes have been troubling me for some time.
　I shall always recollect a certain lecture of yours on Irish Oratory that
was almost the best lecture I ever heard[2]—You will remember that I had a
scheme in those days of getting lecturers to go to the small country towns
in Ireland to spread the intellectual movement—You were my great hope
& I am glad that you have made lecturing so much a business. Of course if
you care to refer anyone to me, I will say exactly what I have said to you in
this letter—

Yours sinly
W B Yeats

Dict AG, signed WBY; Private.

To Dora Sigerson Shorter, [*?* c. *21 January 1903*]

18 Woburn Building | Euston Road.

My dear Mrs Shorter: I found that Gordon Craig expected me last night,
that was what kept me from going to you.[1] I wonder if you & Shorter

had edited the *Irish Theosophist* from 1892 to 1897, and who had moved to London in 1899, told
Joyce (*LJJ* II. 25) that the magazine would be 'something between the "Spectator" and the
"Tatler"', but Joyce did not contribute to it.
　[1] Richard Ashe King (1839–1932), for 38 years the literary editor of the London weekly magazine, *Truth*. A retired Anglican curate, he published several popular novels under his own name
and under the pseudonym 'Basil'. He had moved from Dublin to London in the mid-1890s and
was now lecturing regularly to literary societies and social groups.
　[2] In a lecture entitled 'The Celt: The Silenced Sister' given to the National Literary Society,
Dublin, on 8 Dec 1893, King had denounced the stultifying effect of rhetoric and political oratory
on Irish literature and genius. A letter by Alice Milligan critical of the speech provoked WBY
into writing two letters on partisan politics and Irish oratory (see I. 369–73). The controversy left
a lasting impression on WBY, who, in dedicating his *Early Poems and Stories* (1925) to King,
recalled his lecture (*VP*, 854) as 'a denunciation of rhetoric, and of Irish rhetoric most of all; and
that it was a most vigorous and merry lecture and roused the anger of the newspapers'.

　[1] Ricketts and Sturge Moore had suggested that Gordon Craig should produce *The Countess
Cathleen* (see pp. 297–8), and he himself was interested in mounting a lavish performance of
Where There Is Nothing (see below, p. 312), so he and WBY had much to discuss at this time.

would come & dine with me on Saturday at 7.30. I would ask Lady Gregory to come & meet you. I go to see a Stage Society play on Sunday—²

Yr sny
W B Yeats

ALS Berg.

To C. Lewis Hind,¹ [c. *21 January 1903*]

18 Woburn Building | Euston Road.

Dear Mʳ Hind: This is the young Irishman I told you about.² He wants to see you to find out what he should send you with best change [*for* chance] of its being taken. He had an essay in the 'Fortnightly' 3 years ago when he was eighteen³ & so should be worth helping.

Yours sincerely
W B Yeats

ALS San Francisco.

² WBY attended the Incorporated Stage Society's performance of Ibsen's *When We Dead Awaken* at the Imperial Theatre on Sunday, 25 Jan. Besides its interest as Ibsen's last play, WBY was probably eager to see one of the Society's productions at a time when its staging of *Where There Is Nothing* was under discussion.

¹ Charles Lewis Hind (1862–1927), journalist, author, and former editor of the *Pall Mall Budget*, had become editor of the *Academy* in 1896 but was to resign later this year, writing 'An Editor's Retrospect' in the *Book Monthly* for December. In *Authors and I* (1921) he recalls (318–21) meeting WBY 'half a hundred times. . . . He always looks exactly the same: he always wears a blue serge suit, with a flowing black tie, and he always, at stated intervals, tosses his long straight hair away from his eyes.' At one of their meetings WBY 'intoned' *The Countess Cathleen* to him and another poet, reading 'on and on . . . indifferent to us: he did not see that the other poet had fallen fast asleep.' Hind roused his companion 'somewhere in the small hours', and both made their escape while WBY returned to his book, 'for as we creaked down to the streetdoor I heard him declaiming fine verse to our empty chairs'.

² WBY was introducing Hind to James Joyce, who wrote to his brother on 21 Jan (*LJJ* II. 25) that he had 'seen the editor of the "Academy" too and have left my article with him and he is to tell me whether he thinks I will suit his paper'. Joyce did not suit: Ellmann records (*James Joyce*, 119) that he was curtly dismissive in the trial book review Hind had asked him to submit, and when Hind remonstrated stuck doggedly by what he had written:

Hind was annoyed and said, 'Oh well, Mr. Joyce, if that is your attitude, I can't help you. I have only to lift the window and put my head out, and I can get a hundred critics to review it.'
'Review what, your head?' asked Joyce, ending the interview.

³ 'Ibsen's New Drama', Joyce's article on Ibsen's last play, *When We Dead Awaken*, had appeared in the *Fortnightly Review* on 1 Apr 1900.

To Clifford Bax,[1] *22 January 1903*

18 Woburn Building, | Euston Road.
Jan. 22nd./03.

Dear Mr Bax,

I don't think that I have a copy of the first edition of my poems. My sister had a few copies but I think that they were all handed over to Elkin Mathews. I don't know whether he has any now but I daresay he has.

Yrs snly
W B Yeats

Dict AEFH, signed WBY; Texas.

To Gilbert Murray,[1] *22 January 1903*

18 Woburn Buildings, | Euston Road. | London.
Jan. 22nd.,/03.

Dear Sir,

I should have thanked you for your letter days ago but I put it off thinking to get your "Andromache" but a bad cold kept me idling & now I can-

---

[1] Clifford Bax (1886–1962), poet, playwright, and critic, had been introduced to WBY by Ernest Rhys and records his memories of WBY in *Some I Knew Well* (1951). He was a member of the Blavatsky Lodge of the Theosophical Society and from 1907 to 1911 edited its transactions and journal, *Orpheus*. His first wife, the actress Gwendolen Bishop (d. 1926), was a close friend of FF, who left her correspondence with WBY and G. B. Shaw in Bax's care when she departed for Ceylon in 1912. Bax published the letters with the Cuala Press in 1941. In a letter of 30 June 1936 to Dorothy Wellesley (Private) WBY recalled Bax at this period as a 'thin pale youth who was always fetched home from my rooms by a man-servant who wrapped him up in a blanket. One day a Mrs Bishop, a handsome woman ten years or so his senior carried him off without any blanket & in six months he was so vigerous, that he ran away from her with a younger & more lively woman.'

[1] Gilbert Murray (1866–1957), classical scholar and translator, had been on the committee of J. T. Grein's Independent Theatre. In 1899 he resigned his chair of Greek at Glasgow and moved to Surrey, where he wrote poetic drama, joined the committee of the Stage Society, and renewed his efforts to help William Archer found an English National Theatre. His verse translations of Euripides began to appear in 1902 and led to a revival of Attic drama at the Court Theatre in 1904. He was appointed Regius Professor of Greek at Oxford in 1908. He had met WBY briefly at Edmund Gosse's house in 1896.

not wait any longer without writing to you.[2] Your letter was particularly welcome because you picked out those two plays for praise. For the most part people tell me that they want my lyrics & not my plays, while I myself can never get it out of my mind that our modern passion for the lyric is a little effeminate. I am going to bring out some prose plays & I would be very much obliged if you would exchange your "Andromache" for a book of them. We have founded a little company lately in Ireland & I have written these plays for it. I wonder if you yourself are going on writing plays & if you are, whether you have thought of carrying out any plan like ours?[3] To me to [*for* it] seems as if one must get a homogenious audience somewhere, even if it is only some thirty of one's friends & then get a little company who will do just what they are told out of sheer enthusiasm. When one has got that one can begin the business which is the building up of the whole dramatic art entirely afresh from the foundations.[4]

[*In WBY's hand*]

I have had to dictate this for my eyes are much out of sorts.

Your snly

W B Yeats

Dict AEFH, signed WBY; Bodleian.

[2] On 10 Jan 1903 Murray wrote to WBY (*LWBY* I. 115) to thank him 'for the extraordinary pleasure' which the plays had given him: 'I only came across them last week, & have been so living in the thrill of them ever since that I cannot resist the desire to write to you.' On the same day he told William Archer: 'I had read many poems of his before, and liked them, but the Countess Cathleen and the Land of Heart's Desire quite took my breath away' (C. Archer, *William Archer* [1931], 271). However, on 20 Jan he again wrote to Archer to announce that 'the extreme edge of my enthusiasm for a certain WBY is indeed wore off'.

The Stage Society had produced *Andromache*, a modern attempt at Greek drama, at the Strand Theatre on 24 Feb 1901. It was Murray's last play before he immersed himself in his translations. In his reply to this letter on 24 Jan (MBY), he wrote: 'I should like exceedingly to read your prose plays, and will tell Heinemann to send you copies of my two'. He also sent a couple of lyrics he had translated from Euripides and which he thought similar in sentiment to Old Irish poetry. The prose plays WBY sent were *The Hour-Glass* and *Where There Is Nothing*.

[3] In his reply (see n. 2) Murray confessed that he did 'not quite know what your Dublin plan is, in essentials' but that his 'personal experience of the English theatre has been rather excruciating' in that its 'system and atmosphere . . . seems somehow to kill out any poetry that there may be in a play' and that he imagined 'our general feeling on the subject was much the same'.

[4] In March of this year WBY was to persuade Murray to serve on the committee of the Masquers Society, founded to put these ideas into practice (see below, pp. 329, 344–5).

To W. G. Fay, 29 January 1903

Mention in letter from Fay, 30 January 1903.
Saying that MG had written to him complaining that Fay has suppressed
Colum's play, *The Saxon Shilling*, on political grounds.[1]

LWBY I. 117–19.

To F. J. Fay, [c. 29 January 1903]

Mention in letter from Fay, 30 January 1903.
Discussing a book by Delsarte on gesture,[1] and saying that he would like to
put *The Countess Cathleen* into rehearsal.[2]

Private.

To [John Rogers Rees], 5 February [1903]

18 Woburn Buildings | Euston Road | London
Feb 5

Dear Sir—
    I find it somewhat difficult to describe the nature of my lecture for pur-
poses of advertisement[1]—I have a great mass of material which I shall have
to go through next week & pick out what will be most suitable—However

---

[1] MG had written WBY a long letter on 'Monday' [26 Jan] threatening to resign her vice-
presidency of the INTS over Fay's interference with *The Saxon Shilling* (see p. 302, n. 1)
and giving her account of this. She alleged that Fay had imposed an absurd ending on the play,
probably because he thought the original one too nationalistic, and that she had upbraided him
for this. In his reply on 30 Jan, Fay gave his side of the dispute, asserting that he had altered the
ending on theatrical not political grounds, and pointing out that the play was in any case 'puny
enough from the political point of view'.

[1] François Delsarte (1811–71), a French professor of movement, formulated a teaching method
based on the nine laws of gesture by which the soul expressed itself. WBY had first heard of him
from the American aesthete Edmund Russell in September 1888 (see I. 96), and in his letter of 29
Dec 1902 (see p. 287) Fay had asked him to enquire 'where one can get Delsarte's work on gesture'. In fact, Delsarte wrote no books, but his ideas were disseminated in his disciples' publications. In his reply to this letter Fay said that he had 'a book published in America on Delsartean
physical culture' which also advertised 'a book on Delsartean Gesture', but he did not know
whether it would be useful.
[2] See p. 298. In his reply Fay said that he also would like to rehearse the play 'but not yet'.

[1] This letter is probably addressed to John Rogers Rees (see p. 286), who was evidently looking
after the arrangements for WBY's lecture in Cardiff (see p. 295, n. 4), and who was to put him up
during his visit to the city.

as that might be too late I may as well say now that I shall describe the
Fairy Belief of Galway & of the West of Ireland generally, & show how
much alive it still is—I will also try to prove that a very noble conception
of life which has all but died out elsewhere exists side by side with this
belief, & draws much of its life therefrom—I shall then argue that the Arts
must go back to the living legends of the people if they are to recover the
old heroic vision of the world—²

Yrs sny
W B Yeats

Dict AG, signed WBY; Wellesley.

To F. J. Fay, [early February 1903]

Mention in letter from Fay, 9 February 1903.
Discussing the staging of his play *The Shadowy Waters*,¹ and urging the
production of *The Land of Heart's Desire*.²

Private.

² This description of the lecture was incorporated directly into its announcement in the *Western Mail* on 17 Feb, with the addition that 'Mr. Yeats is an authority on all Irish dreams, fairies and ghosts'.

¹ On 21 Jan Fay told WBY that he had just read *The Shadowy Waters*, which AE had lent him, and, since he was tired of putting on peasant plays, wondered if he and his brother could produce it 'as a Costume Recital'. In an enthusiastic letter of 30 Jan he reported that the Company were going to read the play, regretted that it was so largely duologue, enquired how the names were to be pronounced, discussed the difficulty of arranging the harp, suggested Maire Walker as Dectora and himself as Forgael, and asked for a rough plan of the ship. In his reply to this letter, he went further into details of the staging.

² In his reply Fay warned that there would be religious opposition to the play, led by Digges: 'Both my brother and I wish as much as you do to act *The Land of Heart's Desire*, but Digges doesn't at all like the idea and for all I know there may be others of his way of thinking. The people to whom it would make no difference to play in it are not strong at acting, they are Ryan, Cousins, Starkey, Koehler Roberts and Miss Laird. I quite agree with the expression 'tortured thing' and think it would be a pity to remove it; but when the young blood of the Catholic University, who may be supposed to represent something of the progress Ireland has made, objected to the *Countess Cathleen* it is hardly likely they would swallow that "insult" to their religion! . . . . The principal reason that has prevented us from doing the play has been a desire not to lose Digges. I am inclined to think that even though he did not play in it himself he would smell hell if he associated with us.'

To John Quinn, 6 February [*1903*]

18 Woburn Buildings. | Euston Road.
Feb 6.

My dear Quinn,

I have been on the point of writing to you for the last three months, but the play always seemed on the point of being finished and I wanted to send you a completed copy. However as I might have foreseen it did not get itself finished until Lady Gregory came to London and helped me to re-shape what had been the meagre last act. I think when you read it you will find that we have made a new man of Paul. In the old version he did rather ram his ideas down people's throats and was not I think a very lovable person. Your suggestions were I could see intended to put this right, and I think it was a suggestion of yours that suggested to me the proposal one of the friars makes to him in the last act, to gather the tinkers and outcasts and march upon the world. I was afraid however to give him any new opinions, but I was anxious to get him for a little while away from opinions that I might make him more emotional, more merely passionate. I think you will be struck with the fourth act as it now stands, it is I think the most changed of all. In it and indeed throughout, I have tried to show Paul's magnetic quality, his power of making people love him and of carrying them away. I dont think he himself would have been in the ordinary sense sympathetic. I think he was a man like William Morris who was too absorbed and busy to give much of himself to persons. Edmond Gosse told me that he once got a letter from Burne Jones which began by saying that Morris was the noblest man he had ever known but said also that Burne Jones felt that if he were to die it would not make much difference to Morris. But he added that Morris's death would kill him.[1] People love Paul because they find in him a certain strength, a certain abundance. This abundance comes from him in the first three acts with a kind of hard passion, but his five years in the monastery as I understand him fills him with dreams and reverie, and detaches him from the things about which men are passionate.

Nobody here has as yet seen the new version, but the old one which I now hate, has had quite a success. Miss Edith Craig, Ellen Terry's daughter got hold of a copy by chance and persuaded the Stage Society to undertake its production. And now Gordon Craig her brother wants to produce it with elaborate scenery instead of the Maeterlinck which they has [*for* had] asked him to do. He is the great innovator here in the matter of

---

[1] See p. 247, n. 1. Burne Jones's letter to Gosse has apparently not survived.

scenery, and has begun experiments which may perhaps revolutionise the whole art.

I dont know how I can thank you too much for the three volumes of Nietzsche.[2] I had never read him before, but find that I had come to the same conclusions on several cardinal matters. He is exaggerated and violent but has helped me very greatly to build up in my mind an imagination of the heroic life. His books have come to me at exactly the right moment, for I have planned out a series of plays which are all intended to be an expression of that life which seem[s] to me a kind of proud hard gift giving joyousness. In some ways he completes or rather modernises the doctrine that I learned from Blake, and I dont find him apart from certain stray petulances incompatable with the kind of socialism I learned from William Morris.[3] He is vitally opposed to State Socialis[m] but for the matter of that [so] was Morris.

I am very busy just at present, correcting proofs of my book of essays which should be out in March,[4] and for my new book of poems which is being printed at my sister's private press. I am also about to put part of the 'Hour Glass' into verse.[5] I hope when I have got rid of these things to do some poems.

Yours always
W B Yeats

TLS NYPL, with envelope addressed to 120 Broadway, New York, postmark 'LONDON S.W. FE 7 03'. New York postmark 'FEB 15 1903'.

[2] Evidently the three volumes of *The Works of Friedrich Nietzsche*, edited by Alexander Tille in 1899, and companions to his translation of *Thus Spake Zarathustra*, which Quinn had sent WBY in September 1902 (see p. 239, n. 2). In revising his essay, 'William Blake and His Illustrations to the Divine Comedy' (1896), for inclusion in *IGE*, WBY replaced a reference to 'French mystics' whom Blake seemed to foreshadow and wrote instead (*I & E*, 130) that one was reminded 'still more of Nietzsche, whose thought flows always, though with an even more violent current, in the bed Blake's thought has worn'. WBY had probably first come across reference to Nietzsche's work in Havelock Ellis's article, 'Friedrich Nietzsche', parts of which were published in the *Savoy* simultaneously with his 'Rosa Alchemica' (April 1896) and his essay on Blake's illustrations (July and August 1896), and sometime between 1900 and 1902 he had acquired Thomas Common's pamphlet of selections.

[3] See I. 23, 26–7.

[4] *IGE*; see p. 59. WBY wrote in Quinn's copy of the first American edition: 'I got the title of this book out of one of Blake's MSS works if I remember rightly. He made the title-page with these words on it but I do not think—no, I know—he never printed the sections' (Wade, 63). Evidently it was not only Nietzsche who completed what Blake had begun.

[5] See pp. 294–5. WBY did not finish his poetic version of *The Hour-Glass* until 1913 when it was published in the April number of Gordon Craig's magazine the *Mask*; it was included in *Responsibilities* the following year. Both versions were printed in *Plays in Prose and Verse* (1922), but only the poetic version appeared in the standard *Collected Plays* of 1934.

To Maud Gonne, [c. *7 February 1903*]

Mention in letter from MG, Sunday [10 February 1903].
Protesting against her conversion to Catholicism,[1] and begging her not to marry Major John MacBride.[2]

G–YL, 166–7.

To Maud Gonne, [c. *8 February 1903*]

Mention in letter from MG, Sunday [10 February 1903].
A second letter protesting against her conversion to Catholicism, and begging her not to marry Major John MacBride.

G–YL, 166–7.

To Maud Gonne, [c. *9 February 1903*]

Mention in letter from MG, Sunday [10 February 1903].
A third letter protesting against her conversion to Catholicism, and begging her not to marry Major John MacBride.

G–YL, 166–7.

---

[1] MG was received into the Catholic Church on 17 Feb 1903, partly through the persuasion of her husband-to-be, although she had been contemplating the step for some time and had already apparently discussed it with WBY. He anticipated her conversion in a dream which he later recounted to St John Ervine (*Some Impressions Of My Elders* [1923], 274): 'A friend of his, he said, was contemplating submission to the Catholic Church. He had tried to dissuade her from this, but she went away to another country in a state of irresolution. One night, he dreamt that he saw her entering a room full of beautiful people. She walked around the room, looking at these beautiful people who smiled and smiled, but said nothing. "And suddenly, in my dream", he said, "I realized that they were all dead!" "I woke up", he proceeded, "and I said to myself, 'She has joined the Catholic Church', and she had."'

[2] Despite this and other pleas, MG married Major John MacBride in Paris on 21 Feb of this year. MacBride (1868–1916), a native of Westport, Co. Mayo, had worked for a wholesale grocers in Dublin before emigrating to South Africa, where he became an assayer in a gold mine. He had joined the Irish Republican Brotherhood while in Dublin, and on the outbreak of the Boer War formed and led the Irish Brigade, for which he was commissioned a major by President Kruger. After the Brigade was disbanded in 1900 he went to live in Paris, where he met MG, whom he accompanied on an American tour in 1901 (see p. 78). Their marriage was unhappy and MG secured a legal separation in 1905. Shortly afterwards MacBride was allowed to return to Ireland, where his continuing commitment to the separatist cause culminated in his participation in the 1916 Rising. He was captured, sentenced to death, and executed on 5 May 1916.

To Maud Gonne, [c. *10 February 1903*]

Dear Friend: ⟨I appeal to you in the name of 14 years of friendship to read this letter & [*indecipherable*]. It is perhaps the last thing I shall ever ask you.⟩[1] I thought over things last night. this thought came to me "you are not writing to her quite fully what you think. You fear to make her angry, to spoil her memory of you. Write all ⟨as long as you so long as you write nothing of ?her⟩ that you would have her know. Not to do so is mere self-ishness. It is too late now to think of anything but the truth. If you do not speak no one will." Then I thought that you had given me the ⟨write⟩ right to speak. I remembered this passage in one of the diaries in which I have written all that was of moment in ⟨my⟩ our dealings with spiritual things. (I have left out some expressions of fealing that might give you pain). Here is the passage it is dated december 12 1898. "I will write out what has hap-pened that I may read of it in coming years & ⟨remember it⟩ remember all the rest. ⟨I have dreamed of my friend many times but only once when her spirit came to me at Coole & bent over me did her lips meet.⟩ On the morning of Dec 7 I woke after a sleap less broken than my sleap is com-monly & knew that our lips had met in dreams. I went to see her & she said 'what dreams had you last night?' I told her what had happened & she said 'I was with you last night but do not remember much,' but in the evening she said some such words as these. 'I will tell you what happened last night. I went out of my body. I saw my body from outside it & I was brought away by Lug & my hand ⟨outside it & I was brought⟩ was put in yours & I was told that we were married. All became dark. I think we went away togeather to do some work.' There are other entries ⟨similar⟩ con-cerning this of earlier visions of mine.[2] Now I claim that this gives me the

---

[1] This is a draft of the fourth letter that WBY wrote to MG on hearing of her forthcoming marriage to John MacBride. The first three (see above) were written before 10 Feb, but the refer-ence to 'the last thing I shall ever ask you', the implication that he had written earlier, more circumspect letters, and the tone of MG's reply on 24 Feb, all point to this as his last and des-perate attempt to change her mind. The marriage was announced in the Dublin daily press on 9 Feb, and by the *United Irishman* on 14 Feb.

[2] On 11 July 1898 WBY had begun a private diary in which he recorded his dreams and visions. The entry for 12 Dec 1898, which he was evidently copying directly into this letter, read in full:

I awoke after a sleep less broken than my sleep is commonly & knew that our lips had met in dreams. I went to see her & she said 'what dream had you last night'. I said 'I have dreamed for the first time that I have kissed your lips. I have often dreamed that [?I have] kissed your hands & once you came while I was in a trance & bent over me & kissed me' or some such words. She said 'I was with you last night but do not remember much' but in the evening she said some such words as these 'I will tell you what happened last night. I went out of my body—I saw my body from outside it—& I was brought away by Lug & my hand was put in yours & I was told we were married. Then I kissed you & all became dark. I think we went away togeather to do

right to speak. Your hands were put in mine & we were told to do a certain great work together. ⟨That work⟩ For all who undertake such tasks there comes a moment of extreme peril. I know now that you have come to your moment of peril. If you carry out your purpose you will fall into a lower order & do great injury to the religeon of ⟨pure⟩ free souls that is growing up in Ireland, it may be to enlighten the whole world. A man said to me last night having seen the announcements in the papers 'The priests will ⟨re triumph over for gen⟩ exult over us ⟨her for generations⟩ us all for generations because of this'. There are people (& these are the greater number) who need the priest ⟨&⟩ or some other master but [there] are a few & you are of these for whom ⟨surr⟩ surrender to any leadership but that of their own souls is the great betrayal, the denial of God. It was our work to teach a few strong aristocratic ⟨[*indecipherable*]⟩ spirits that to beleive the soul was immortal & that one prospered hereafter *if one laid upon oneself* an heroic discipline in living & to send them to uplight the nation.³ You & I were chosen to begin this work & ⟨just⟩ just when ⟨you⟩ I ⟨come⟩ come to understand it fully you go from me & seek to thrust the people ⟨down⟩ further in to weakness further from self ⟨reliz⟩ reliance. Now on a matter on which I must ⟨say all⟩ speak if I am to say & beleive ⟨that it is not my⟩ that some that are more than man have bid me write this letter. You possess your influence in Ireland very largely because you come to the people from above. You represent a superior class, a class where people are more independent, have a more beautiful life, a more refined life. Every man almost of the people who has spoken to me of you has shown that you influence him very largely because of this. ⟨You are⟩ Maud Gonne is surrounded with romance. She puts ⟨away⟩ from her what seems an easy & splendid life that she may devote herself to the people. I have heard you called 'our great lady'. But Maud Gonne is about to pass away. ⟨You are going to do⟩ something which the people ⟨did⟩ never forgave James Stephens for doing, though he was a man for whom it matters far less, you are going to marry one of the people.⁴ ⟨you are⟩ This weakness which ⟨has⟩ has thrust down

some work.' The next night she came to me for a moment. She thought of herself as in a white dress but I saw her in a dress with red bodice.

Other entries describe his seeing MG in vision at the same time as she was thinking of writing to him; of foreseeing a dinner party with her and a man in highland dress; and, in September 1898, a dream of MG 'in some other life or state'. A moment of trance in July 1899 gave him a premonition that MG 'was about to separate herself from me in a way I have sometimes feared—a way, a needless sacrifice of herself, a way that may yet come'.

³ WBY's reading of Nietzsche is evident here.

⁴ James Stephens (1824–1901), founder and leader of the Irish Republican Brotherhood (IRB), was born in Kilkenny and trained as an engineer. He was wounded in the Young Ireland uprising of 1848 but escaped to Paris. He returned to Ireland in 1856 and two years later established the IRB (better known subsequently as the Fenians), becoming its Head Centre. He married Jane Hopper (1843–1895) in November 1863, with John O'Leary acting as best man, and the alliance

your soul to a lower order of faith is thrusting you down socially, is thrusting you down to the people. ⟨you will have no longer any thing to give.
Only those who are above them can ?but you ?If rob & there by robbing
you yo you⟩ They will never forgive it—they most aristocratic ⟨mind of⟩
minded ⟨of people & peasa⟩ the most thirsting for what is above them &
beyond them, of living peoples.[5] You have tried so much now I appeal, I
whose hands were placed in yours by eternal hands, to come back to your
self. To take up again the proud solitary haughty life which made [you]
seem like one of the golden gods. Do not, you ⟨whom⟩ seemed the most
strong the most inspired be the first to betray us, to betray the truth.
Become again as ⟨the⟩ one of the gods. Is it the priest, when the day of the
great hazard has come who will lead the people. no no. He will palter with
the government is [*for* as] he did at the act of union ⟨as he did when he
denounced the fenians⟩ He will say 'be quiet, be good cristians, do not ship
[?*for* shed] blood!' It is not the priest who has soften[ed] the will of our
young men—who has broken their pride. You have said all these [things]
to me & not so long ago for it is not only the truth & your friends but your
own soul that you are about to betray.[6]

[*unsigned*]

AD White. *G–YL*, 164–6.

caused much adverse comment among his friends and followers. WBY had probably heard of this
from O'Leary, who recalled in *Recollections of Fenians and Fenianism* 1. 245 (1896) that the marriage 'was anything but popular with the mass of "The Captain's" followers. . . . it was not so
much the fact that he was marrying that annoyed them as the fact that he was marrying, as they
chose to consider, beneath him—Miss Hopper being the daughter of a tailor in a small way of
business. Most of the men were furious democrats in theory, but not without a certain leaven of
that aristocratic feeling which . . . lies deep in the breasts of most Irishmen.' Although Mrs
Stephens was also blamed for distracting her husband from his political work, it was Stephen's
megalomania, dictatorial behaviour, and inability to manage the American Fenians, not his marriage, which led to his deposition as Head Centre in December 1866. After his overthrow he lived
in Paris and later Switzerland, before returning in 1891 to a sequestered retirement in Dublin.
   [5] See *Aut* (231): 'no country could have a more natural distaste for equality'.
   [6] MG had replied to WBY's first three letters on 10 Feb, telling him (*G–YL*, 166–7) that their
friendship need not suffer because of her marriage and that she knew she was fulfilling a destiny.
She defended her conversion to Catholicism on the grounds that, like him, she believed in one
great universal truth: 'I believe that each religion is a different *prism* through which one looks at
truth. None can see *the whole* of truth. . . . In the meantime ⟨my⟩ our nation looks at God or truth
through one prism, The Catholic Religion. . . . It seems to me of small importance if one calls the
great spirit forces the Sidhe, the Gods & the Arch Angels, the great symbols of all religions are
the same. . . . You say I leave the few to mix myself with the crowd while Willie I have always
told you I am the voice, the soul of the *crowd*.' In her reply to this letter, on 24 Feb, she told him
he was 'quite right to write frankly to me—We are surely sufficiently old & strong friends to be
able to be quite frank & open with one another.'

To Cecil French, 17 February 1903

18 Woburn Buildings | Euston Road
Feb 17 / '03

My dear French
I enclose a letter from Russell (A.E) about Miss Gyles' affairs. What should we do about it? I cannot go as I think she would turn me out.

Yours sincerely
W B Yeats

TS copy Private.

To George Russell (AE), 21 February 1903

18, Woburn Buildings, | Euston Road, | London.
Feb. 21st.,/03.

My dear Russell,
I send you a letter of Cyril French's which I have just received. I think that you might without doing any mischief, tell the Coffeys & Sarah Purser or any of that set you meet about Althea Gyles' sister sending the Charity Organisation Agent.[1] I found that the Coffeys' and Sarah Purser some time ago, had a tendency, probably from no other reason than a certain philistine dislike of an enthusiast, to side with Althea Gyles' relations. M*rs* Coffey, & I think Sarah Purser, knew one or both of the sisters. So far as I can see, the bigger the scandal the better, for it may bring these genteel Gyleses to their senses. They have behaved disgracefully to Althea Gyles for years & this offer of 8/- a week was only got after prolonged efforts on the

---

[1] Althea Gyles's financial problems and her family's indifference, which had first come to WBY's attention in June 1902 (see p. 198), were continuing. Sarah Henrietta Purser (1848–1943), the portrait painter and well-known Dublin wit, was a friend of the Yeatses, although less close to WBY who described her (*Mem*, 43–4) as 'so clever a woman that people found it impossible to believe that she was a bad painter . . . . though kind and considerate when her heart was touched, [she] gave currency to a small genuine wit by fastening to it, like a pair of wings, brutality'. She had helped change the course of JBY's career by organizing his Dublin exhibition of 1901 (see p. 120, n. 1), and later this year, with the help of Edward Martyn, she was to found an Irish stained-glass industry, An Túr Gloine (The Tower of Glass). For Mrs Coffey and Mrs Kennedy see pp. 198 and 265.

part of M*rs* Kennedy, (Cyril French's aunt) and others. I will let you know shortly about the lecture. I am just back from delivering it, or one something like it, in Cardiff where I had rather a good time. I was entertained by the Mayor and I addressed the University students.[2] I found however that the telling of stories in my lecture stopped the flow of my thoughts a good deal and I want to think out some new arrangement of the subject before deciding to lecture to the Hermetists in Dublin.[3] Of course I have no objection to a regular constitution being drawn up for the theatre. It was you who objected. I foretold when I saw you last Autumn that you would have disputes of precisely this nature, if you had not a regular constitution and rules. I remember saying to you, that I would prefer a committee of selection & when you objected to this, saying—that if the whole company were to choose the plays, I should like that fact embodied in a definite constitution. Both you & Miss Gonne said that things were going on so nicely that I ought to leave them alone. Why do you ṣay that I asked for a veto? I wrote to you from Galway proposing precisely that arrangement which is now embodied in the rules for the submitting of plays to the Presidents & Vice-Presidents. I have still the letter in which you replied saying that you approved of my proposal & would submit it to the Fays. When I got to Dublin I found that you & some others thought that I had asked for a veto. I contradicted this at the time & have been contradicting it ever since. I cannot think how the idea arose. I certainly disapprove of a democracy in artistic matters, but a veto is certainly not the form of government I would propose. I said to you once that the absence of all arrangements for the selection of plays might force upon me an informal veto; in the sense that I should have to make the dropping of very bad plays a necessity—or go. But this was certainly not proposing a veto.[4]

---

[2] The Mayor of Cardiff, Councillor Edward Thomas, who wrote under the name of 'Cochfarf' ('Redbeard'), presided at the lecture at the Cory Hall on 19 Feb. A report of WBY's pugilistic delivery appeared in the Cardiff *Evening Express and Evening Mail* (2) on the following day: 'He challenged a hand-to-hand combat with anybody who disagreed with his conclusions. . . . Mr Yeats is indefatigable in his self-imposed labour of gathering the fairy lore of Ireland . . . he has in his possession a mass of lore such as few others possess in any land.' The next night WBY became 'carried away' at a reception given in his honour by the Welsh Society of University College, Cardiff: 'He had only intended to deliver a brief address, but when his friends, who knew of his original intention, saw by their watches that the hour had passed before the speaker began his peroration, and that he was pouring out his heart on his favourite theme of having a literature-loving democracy, they knew he had been inoculated with what he is very anxious to witness, viz., the Welsh "hwyl."' (*Evening Express*, 21 Feb 1903, p. 2; see also p. 295 n. 4). WBY's unusual pugnacity and febrile energy may have owed something to the recollection of MG's impending marriage to Major John MacBride on 21 Feb.

[3] AE had asked WBY to give his lecture on the Irish Faery Kingdom to the Hermetic Society in Dublin, but there is no evidence that this took place.

[4] See p. 222. The disputes over the withdrawal from rehearsal of *Sold* and *The Saxon Shilling* (see pp. 284, 310) had underlined the need for firm rules governing the selection of plays to be

Synge has done an extremely fine play of Arran life; Symonds is enthusiastic about it & sending it to the Fortnightly. As soon as I can get a copy of this play, I will send it to the company.[5]

Yrs sny
W B Yeats

Dict AEFH, signed WBY; Indiana.

To Lady Augusta Gregory, February 1903

Feb. 1903

MY DEAR LADY GREGORY, I dedicate to you two volumes of plays, that are in part your own.[1]

When I was a boy I used to wander about at Rosses Point and Ballisodare listening to old songs and stories. I wrote down what I heard and made poems out of the stories or put them into the little chapters of the

produced. AE had written to WBY earlier in the month (*LWBY* I. 119–20) to explain that the Society had been in danger of splitting over the issue: 'There was a rebellion going on which was natural among voluntary workers at the way in which plays were accepted or rejected without their consent so I drew up and got them to pass the only rules which were possible under the circumstances. I think you got a copy of them. I knew you would not like them but if they were not passed I do not think there would be a theatre society. All the company contribute equally to the finances and neither Fay nor Miss Gonne nor you nor myself would be allowed to veto or accept any play or to do more than give an opinion which naturally has weight. . . . Now you will get copies of plays & can write your opinion before the company learn parts, and you will find it will work much better.' On 1 Feb Fred Ryan had sent WBY a draft set of rules (see Appendix), which had been discussed by a General Meeting of the INTS the previous evening, and these were formally adopted at a Meeting on 15 Feb. The rules setting up a Reading Committee, read:

IV. A Reading Committee of five members shall be elected who shall first consider all plays proposed for performance by the Society. No play shall be performed until it has been recommended by this Committee. Final acceptance or rejection of any play thus recommended shall rest with the members of the Society, to whom such plays shall be read at meetings summoned for the purpose when a three quarters majority of those present shall decide.

The author shall not be allowed to be present when the vote is taken.

V. No official of the Society shall have power to accept a play or to reject one which shall have been accepted and passed in accordance with the foregoing rules. The Stage Manager and Author shall have the sole right to decide on questions as to how a scene be acted and the choice of actors shall be left to the decision of the Stage Manager upon consultation with the author.

The friction that led to the formulation of these rules was evidence of the strain between those who saw the dramatic movement as artistic in aim, and those who regarded its primary function as political, a strain which was to cause secessions later in the year.

[5] Synge wrote to AG on 26 March that *Riders to the Sea* had been rejected by the *Fortnightly Review* as 'not suitable for their purposes'. It was published in *Samhain* for October 1903, but not produced until 25 Feb 1904.

[1] This letter, a dedication of vols 1 and 2 of 'Plays for an Irish Theatre', appeared in the May 1903 edition of *Where There is Nothing*, pp. vii–x.

first edition of 'The Celtic Twilight,' and that is how I began to write in the Irish way.

Then I went to London to make my living, and though I spent a part of every year in Ireland and tried to keep the old life in my memory by reading every country tale I could find in books or old newspapers, I began to forget the true countenance of country life. The old tales were still alive for me indeed, but with a new, strange, half unreal life, as if in a wizard's glass, until at last, when I had finished 'The Secret Rose,' and was halfway through 'The Wind Among the Reeds,' a wise woman in her trance told me that my inspiration was from the moon, and that I should always live close to water, for my work was getting too full of those little jewelled thoughts that come from the sun and have no nation.[2] I had no need to turn to my books of astrology to know that the common people are under the moon, or to Porphyry to remember the image-making power of the waters.[3] Nor did I doubt the entire truth of what she said to me, for my head was full of fables that I had no longer the knowledge and emotion to write. Then you brought me with you to see your friends in the cottages, and to talk to old wise men on Slieve Echtge, and we gathered together, or you gathered for me, a great number of stories and traditional beliefs. You taught me to understand again, and much more perfectly than before, the true countenance of country life.[4]

One night I had a dream almost as distinct as a vision, of a cottage where there was well-being and firelight and talk of a marriage, and into the

[2] In *Aut* (371) WBY recalls that in the spring of 1896 he 'went to consult a friend [i.e. Olivia Shakespear] who, under the influence of my cabbalistic symbols, could pass into a condition between meditation and trance. A certain symbolic personality who called herself . . . Megarithma, said that I must "live near water and avoid woods because they concentrate the solar ray". I believed this enigmatic sentence came from my own Daimon, my own buried self speaking through my friend's mind. "Solar" . . . meant elaborate, full of artifice, rich, all that resembles the work of a goldsmith, whereas "water" meant "lunar", and "lunar" all that is simple, popular, traditional, emotional.' When, the following year, he first visited AG at Coole and 'saw her great woods on the edge of a lake, I remembered the saying about avoiding woods and living near the water. Had this new friend come because of my invocation, or had the saying been but prevision and my invocation no act of will, but prevision also?' (*Aut*, 376).

[3] In *Myth* (80) WBY wrote: 'Did not the wise Porphyry think that all souls come to be born because of water, and that "even the generation of images in the mind is from water"? See also 'Coole Park and Ballylee, 1931': 'What's water but the generated soul?' (*VP*, 490). Porphyry (233–304) had put forward this idea in his *De Antro Nympharum* (*On the Cave of the Nymphs*), which WBY had read in an 1895 reprint of Thomas Taylor's 1823 translation. See also *E&I*, 82–6 and *AVB*, 220.

[4] On 30 Nov 1897 AG recalled in her diary (Berg) that during WBY's first extended stay at Coole in August and September of that year they 'searched for folk lore—I gave him over all I had collected & took him about looking for more—And whoever came to the door, fishwoman or beggar or farmer, I would get on the subject, & if I found the stories worth having wd call him down that he might have them first hand. We found startling beliefs & came to the conclusion that Ireland is Pagan, not Xtian.' WBY first visited Slieve Echtge (now Aughty), a range of mountains between Loughrea and Lough Derg, in July 1899.

midst of that cottage there came an old woman in a long cloak. She was Ireland herself, that Cathleen ni Houlihan for whom so many songs have been sung and about whom so many stories have been told and for whose sake so many have gone to their death. I thought if I could write this out as a little play I could make others see my dream as I had seen it, but I could not get down out of that high window of dramatic verse, and in spite of all you had done for me I had not the country speech. One has to live among the people, like you, of whom an old man said in my hearing, 'She has been a serving-maid among us,' before one can think the thoughts of the people and speak with their tongue. We turned my dream into the little play, 'Cathleen ni Hoolihan,' and when we gave it to the little theatre in Dublin and found that the working people liked it, you helped me to put my other dramatic fables into speech. Some of these have already been acted, but some may not be acted for a long time, but all seem to me, though they were but a part of a summer's work, to have more of that countenance of country life than anything I have done since I was a boy.

W B Yeats

Text from *VPl*, 232.

To the Editor of the Chicago Daily News, [*late February 1903*]

18 Woburn Buildings | Euston Road—

Dear Sir: I enclose the letter for you[r] St Patricks day number that you asked for.[1]

Yrs sny
W B Yeats

Editor 'Chicago Daily News'

ALS Newberry.

[1] See below, p. 327.

To an unidentified correspondent, 28 February 1903

18 Woburn Buildings, | Euston Road, | London.
Feb. 28th.,/03.

Dear Sir,

I should very much like to go to Cambridge but I cannot give the time at this moment. I have waited before replying to see if I could manage it.

Could I go down to you during the Summer Term?[1]

I would not read a paper, but I would speak which I suppose would be quite as good.

Yrs snly
W B Yeats

Dict AEFH, signed WBY; UCD.

To Edith Craig, 11 [March 1903]

18 Woburn Buildings
Wednesday 11

Dear Miss Craig

I did not know there was so much hurry about the poem[1]—Pixie Smith did not tell me when it had to be done—I will send it to you tomorrow by Express Messenger to the theatre—I could not do it today as I was very busy—I go to Ireland tomorrow night—

Yrs snly
W B Yeats

Dict AG, signed WBY; Tenterden.

[1] WBY's first visit to Cambridge took place in June 1904.

[1] Edith Craig (see p. 263) had asked WBY to provide verses for a lament in her brother's production of *The Vikings at Helgeland* which ran at the Imperial Theatre from 15 Apr to 14 May.

To John Lane, 11 March [*1903*]

18 Woburn Buildings | Euston Road
March 11

Dear Mr. Lane—

I shall be much obliged if you can let me have at once the two copies of "Where there is Nothing" which were forwarded to you from America—[1]

I have no other copies, except the manuscript—

Yrs sny
W B Yeats

Dict AG, signed WBY; Texas.

To A. E. Waite, [c. *11 March 1903*]

Mention in following letter.
Asking Waite to return Stirling's MS to William Rothenstein.

To W. Rothenstein, 11 March [*1903*]

18 Woburn Buildings
March 11

Dear Rothenstein

the delay has been partly my fault—When I got the M.S. I got Waite[1] to come here & dine to discuss it with me—

Instead of letting him take it away I said I would send it to him, & then I found that I had lost his address—Two or three weeks passed before he

---

[1] Of the seven known copies of John Lane's American copyright edition of *Where There Is Nothing* (see p. 238, n. 1), two are in the Library of Congress, one is in the Lilly Library at Indiana University, one at MBY, two in private hands, and one, WBY's presentation copy to AG, is in the Woodruff Library at Emory University.

[1] See pp. 300–1. Waite had dined with WBY on 19 Jan to hear about William Stirling (see p. 235), an occasion he described at some length in his diary (see *YA3*, 7–8). He received the MS from WBY on 10 Feb, and observed in his diary (*YA3*, 9) that it would not be 'a serious loss to the world' if it remained unpublished, remarking of Stirling's *The Canon* that if 'there ever was in the past . . . a canon which covered and ruled all the arts, then the most desirable thing that could happen is that it should have been lost . . . and the last thing that need be wished for is its recovery except as a matter of curiosity'.

got it—I have written to him now & I have no doubt you will hear from him direct in a few days—His address is

A. E. Waite
Sidmouth Lodge
S. Ealing—
W—

I am off to Ireland tomorrow for about a month—

Yrs snly
W B Yeats

I dont quite understand what your German friend[2] wishes for—the 2nd edition of the Celtic Twilight is the fullest one, he would not care for the other—I heard nothing from Matthews but met him by chance today—I can do nothing now till I return from Ireland—

Dict AG, signed WBY; Harvard.

To A. H. Bullen, 12 March 1903

18 Woburn Buildings, | Euston Road,
March 12th.,/03.

My dear Bullen,
I was at the Chiswick Press yesterday & they asked me to remind you that they are waiting both for the paper & the order to print. ⟨Please send them the order to print as soon as possible.⟩ I have arranged with them to give me three copies on "pull paper",[1] they will send these to you & you will send them to me at once. This is important. I shall be at Nassau Hotel, South Frederic Street Dublin until next Monday & after that at Coole Park, Gort, Co. Galway, Ireland. The three copies will only cost 5/- or 6/- & will be charged to you. You can put them down to me.

Yrs sny
W B Yeats

Dict AEFH, signed WBY; Texas.

[2] Probably Harry, Count Kessler (1868–1937), a patron of art and literature, who had an Irish mother, and was often in London. Rothenstein described him (*Men and Memories* II [1932], 17) as 'a generous friend to poets and painters, who knew everyone worth knowing, and who missed nothing that was either new, curious or vital in the literary, artistic and theatrical world'.

[1] WBY was eager to get copies of *Where There Is Nothing*, currently being printed at the Chiswick Press, to use as corrected copy for a new American edition. 'Pull paper' is paper of inferior quality used for proofs and test printing runs.

To Edith Craig, [*12 March 1903*]

Dear Miss Craig.

I send you the poem.[1] I have followed the version you sent as to the kind of verse, which is no dou[b]t the same as that in Ibsen. I have made one slight change in it, which hardly changes it to another measure, to express a change of emotion at the end. It is a fine thing & I did not like to alter it or to shorten it. Besides I dont like modern musicians & I dont want to help your man a bit, if he wants it shortened to make room for his notes. It is a mournful speach not a song & you should get the actor to speak it in a chanting voice, almost like an Irish keen. The musician should then write down the notes he uses & if he like compose a very simple acompaniment. But the great ob[j]ect should be to make Ibsens words, full as they are of the wandering of sorrow & of ancient wildness, as effective as possible. You should send a man to the top gallery & say to your musician now you must make the words get to that man who has never heard them before. If the man does not hear them without trouble you should make your musician try other notes until he does. If the accompaniment is anything like as loud as the voice, if it is too loud even to be forgotten he will never do this. If he wont do it dance on him & get another. Dolmetsch could do what you want or should want.

Yrs sny
W B Yeats

Do not what ever you do permit your actor to speak through music in the ordinary way.[2] The ancients knew nothing of that barbarity.

ALS Tenterden.

---

[1] See p. 323. WBY wrote verses for Örnulf's Act IV funeral chant over his seven dead sons. In Archer's translation the lament concludes: 'Hail, my stout sons seven! / Hail, as homeward ride ye! / Songcraft's glorious god-gift / Staunchest woe and wailing.' Despite his detailed instructions, WBY's verses were not in fact used. As Martin Shaw (see p. 52, n. 1), who wrote the incidental music, confessed in a letter to Allan Wade of 20 Feb 1951 (Indiana): 'In Craig's production of The Vikings he used Archer's translation & Yeats' verse seemed un-Ibsenish so, I almost blush to say, I set Archer's version instead—which should make all decent people shun me, I know, but there you are'. WBY's verse is untraced.

[2] Instructed by Dolmetsch, WBY was quick to divorce his method of verse-speaking from the art of melodeclamation, or dramatic reading to musical scores. Melodeclamation reached its heyday in the late 19th century, when it flourished in European drawing-rooms and recitals, before its gradual decline into the pit of the silent cinema. On 7 June 1902, following WBY's demonstration-recital for the press (see p. 194, n. 3), Archer reported in the *Morning Leader* (4) that Dolmetsch had emphasized 'that the system of "speaking through music" (known in Germany as melodrame) led to horrible dissonances and was wholly inartistic'.

To Edith Craig, [*13 March 1903*]

Nassau Hotel | Dublin.

Dear Miss Craig: I sent you the Ibsen verses on Thursday & hope you got them. I am a little anxious lest the 'Express Messinger' may have not known how to get into the Theatre[1] to deliver them. A Theatre looks so very shut during the day time—To night I have a dress rehearsal of 'the Hour Glass'. The performance is to morrow. I hear we will have a good audience.[2]

Yr ev
W B Yeats

ALS Tenterden.

To the Editor of the Chicago Daily News,[1] *16 March 1903*

I think the question you asked me was: "What is the greatest need of Ireland just now?" The greatest need is more love for thoughts for their own sake. We want a vigorous movement of ideas. We have now plenty of propaganda and I would not see less. For now the agrarian movement seems coming to a close the national movement must learn to found itself, like the national movement of Norway, upon language and history. But if we are to have an able nation, a nation that will be able to take up to itself the best thought of the world, we must have more love of beauty merely because it is beauty, of truth merely because it is truth. At present if a man make us a song, or tell us a story, or give us a thought, we do not ask, "Is

[1] See p. 323. Ellen Terry had recently become manageress of the Imperial Theatre, located in Tothill St., Westminster, and originally part of the grand design of the Royal Aquarium. It survived the demolition of the Aquarium in 1903, but in 1907 it too was pulled down to provide a site for the Central Hall, Westminster.
[2] The INTS productions of WBY's *The Hour-Glass* and AG's *Twenty-Five* at the Molesworth Hall on 14 Mar were a great success, and Holloway recorded (*Abbey Theatre*, 21) that the 'hall was thronged with an audience who listened enthralled to the clearly spoken and simply set representation of *The Hour Glass*'.

[1] See p. 322. WBY was among seven leaders of Irish opinion asked by the London bureau of the *Chicago Daily News* 'to address the American people on "What Ireland Needs" on St Patrick's Day'. The other respondents were William O'Brien, AG, R. Barry O'Brien, Douglas Hyde, Horace Plunkett, and Michael Davitt.

it a good song, or a good story, or a true thought?" but "Will it help this or that propaganda?"

W B Yeats[2]

Printed letter, *Chicago Daily News*, 16 March 1903 (3).

To Charles Elkin Mathews and Others, 17 March 1903

March 17th, 1903.

Dear Sir or Madam,

We, the undersigned, propose to hold a meeting to consider the formation of a society for the production of plays. masques. ballets and ceremonies, which convey a sentiment of beauty.[1]

The meeting will be held at 13, Henrietta Street Covent Garden, (Top floor)[2] on Saturday, March 28th, at 5 o'clock.

W.B YEATS.
ARTHUR SYMONS.
T. STURGE MOORE.
H. ELLIOTT.
EDITH CRAIG.
ETHEL WHEELER.
PAMELA COLMAN-SMITH.
LINA MARSTON.[3]

TL Reading.

[2] The replies were followed by facsimile signatures of the authors, but WBY's signature is in AG's hand.

[1] WBY wanted to call the society, which aimed to establish a theatre for romantic drama in London, 'The Theatre of Beauty'. When this was rejected, he suggested 'The Order of the Rose', but the committee adopted Walter Crane's suggestion that they call themselves 'The Masquers Society' (see Appendix, p. 723).

[2] This was the address of Edith Craig's new costumery.

[3] The signatories, with the addition of Walter Crane and Gilbert Murray, became the Managing Committee of the Masquers Society. John Hugh Armstrong Elliot (1861–1948), the husband of Eleanor Elliot (see p. 264), was managing director of Heinemann's medical books; as the Hon. Treasurer of the Society he received subscriptions at 26 Cheyne Row, Chelsea. He was a member ('Nobis Est Victoria') of the GD and joined the Stella Matutina temple after the schism of 1903. He also belonged to the Societas Rosicruciana in Anglia, a Masonic Rosicrucian Society, and owned the publishing house of Rebman & Co.

Ethel Rolt Wheeler (1869–1958), poet and critic, had acted in the Stage Society production of Gilbert Murray's *Andromache* (see p. 309, n. 2). On the staff of the *Academy* and a prolific journalist in the 1890s, she mentioned WBY in 'The Symbolism of the Unsightly', a short article on the symbolic handling of violence, published in *Literature* on 15 July 1899. She was a member of the ILS, became a contributor to the *Journal of the Irish Folk-Song Society*, 1904–5, and published

To Gilbert Murray, 17 March [1903]

COOLE PARK, | GORT, | CO. GALWAY.
March 17

Dear Mr. Murray

I have been commissioned to ask you to join a new sort of Stage Society—The Committee, which is being formed, & to which we ask leave to elect you, includes Arthur Symons, Sturge Moore, Edith Craig, myself, & others who agree in wanting plays that have some beauty, staging which shall be of the simplest, & acting that shall be simple too—It has been proposed that we call our society the Theatre of Beauty,[1] & we have drawn up a list of plays for possible production—Among these are Marlowe's Faustus, your translation of the Hippolytus, a translation of Edipus Tyrannus, a play of Congreves, & contemporary work of Robert Bridges (his 'Return of Ulysses') & myself—We have a notion too of doing some old masques & ballets.

Our cons[t]itution will be much the same as that of the Stage Society, but our work will, as you see, be altogether unlike theirs—We shall have little dealing with the problem plays & shall try to bring back beauty and beautiful speech—

We are all most anxious to have you upon our Committee, & are indeed awaiting your answer before sending out our prospectus.

I shall be back in London in about a month—I came over to see certain performances of our Irish National Theatre Society—They played a one-act morality play of mine last week to a crowded house & had a great success—They are to repeat it in Galway & Loughrea—[2]

It was staged in the simple way that our new society will adopt—There were two predominant colours, purple dresses against a green backcloth, & every body commended the result—But I am afraid it will take us a long

---

Ireland's Veil and Other Poems (1913). Lina Marston, Hon. Secretary of the Masquers, used the rooms which she shared with Edith Craig at 7 Smith Square, Westminster, as the office of the Society.

[1] See previous letter. Murray, who was at this time in Naples, reacted decisively against the proposed name, writing to his wife: 'A preposterous name. Even an offensive name. I shall decline to be on the Committee.' In fact, the name was not adopted (see next letter), and he was put on the committee in his absence.

[2] The INTS made its first tour to the West of Ireland during the Easter holidays, playing at the Court Theatre, Galway, and the Town Hall, Loughrea. The repertoire included WBY's *Cathleen ni Houlihan* and *The Pot of Broth*, AE's *Deirdre*, and *Eilis agus an Bhean Déirce*, a play in Gaelic by P. T. MacGinley.

time to get in London acting in so simple a method as the acting of our
little company—

Yours sincly
W B Yeats

Dict AG, signed WBY; Bodleian.

To T. Sturge Moore, [after 17 March 1903]

COOLE PARK, | GORT, | CO. GALWAY.

My dear Sturge Moore:

I am going to ask you to undertake a rather troublesome matter. I am
going to send you a bundle of plays to get copyrighted.[1] Mrs Emery, who
would have done this for me is away & for certain reasons these plays have
to be done at once. Miss Horniman who knows I think about stage matters
will I have no doubt help. You will be able to do the whole thing in an
afternoon. The plays after they have been sent to the censor will have to be
gabbled through on a properly licensed stage—say the Victoria Hall. Two
people must know their parts but the smallest parts will do. There must be
a bill out side—the smallest—& one person must pay for admission—
money handed back after wards. Your little company will just have a reading on a stage instead of at your rooms.[2] You will have to pay something
for the hall—I got one for 10/- last time; & for printing a bill. Will you
send plays to censor or if not will you send me his address. It might be as
well for you to send them. I will of course send you a cheque for the cost.
The censor[3] will have to get £1 an act (the worthless creature). I can send
you the plays in all likelihood next weak. I am sorry to give you this trouble but if I did not I should probably have to go to London myself, as these
plays must be licensed at once. On second thoughts you will have to send

---

[1] In March 1903 Sturge Moore wrote to Alfred Hugh Fisher (London) inviting him to the
readings of WBY's *On Baile's Strand* and AG's *Twenty-Five* on 'Thursday' [presumably 26 Mar],
at the Victoria Hall, Archer St., Bayswater. The two plays were entered in the Lord Chamberlain's register on 27 Mar. WBY was eager to license the plays so that they could be performed
during the INTS's forthcoming London visit, although in the event *On Baile's Strand* was not
produced then.
[2] This was the Literary Theatre Club, founded by Binyon and Sturge Moore in 1901, and
including among its members Ricketts, FF, and Sybil and Ethel Pye (see p. 248, n. 1). So far it
had only undertaken dramatic scenes and copyright performances, but Sturge Moore hoped to
produce WBY's *The Countess Cathleen* and *The Shadowy Waters*.
[3] George Alexander Redford; see p. 208, n. 1.

plays to censor as you will have to tell him date of performance. Miss Hornimans address is

H1 Montague Mansions
    Portman square.

I am sure she will get you any information you cannot get.

Yours always
W B Yeats

I shall be very glad of your criticism of plays.

ALS Texas. Bridge, 3–4.

To Sydney Cockerell, 18 March [1903]

Coole Park
March 18

My dear Cockerell, I have two letters to thank you for. I am glad you like the Morris article, which I think is one of the best things of the sort I have done.[1] It is a part of my new book *Ideas of Good and Evil.*

By the bye, I want your advice about the binding of this book. I find that Bullen is rather petulant and I don't think always listens very carefully to one's directions—so I want to write him directions that cannot possibly be misunderstood.

I should like to have it bound in boards, grey or blue, a white back, bound round with real cords, like one of the examples you showed me.[2]

Can you give me three or four sentences which Bullen can send to the binders? I don't know for instance how to describe the cords. I am telling him to bind the prose play in grey boards with unglazed holland back with a label on it. I suppose this is all right.[3]

I had a play performed in Dublin last week, a morality play. It was played with simplicity and beauty. It was a great success.

Yours sincerely
W B Yeats

Text from Wade, 397.

[1] i.e. 'The Happiest of the Poets', see p. 257.
[2] Cords, sewn to the back of the gatherings for added strength, were not used in the inexpensive binding of *IGE*, which was bound with green paper boards, a dark-green cloth spine, and a white label printed in black. Cockerell's brother, Douglas (1870–1945), a student of master-binder T. J. Cobdon-Sanderson, was the author of *Bookbinding, and the Care of Books* (1901), which illustrates the binding described to WBY.
[3] *Where There Is Nothing* was bound in grey boards, with a glazed holland (linen) spine and a white label printed in black.

To Florence Farr, 18 March [1903]

COOLE PARK, | GORT, | CO. GALWAY.
March 18

My dear M^rs. Emery

Could you come to Dublin for a lecture on April 27—to do some chanting?[1]

Please answer at once—How much could you come for. The Nat. Literary Society asked me to lecture on the Psaltery, & bring you over—I do not want to lecture on it again in Dublin & they have accepted my offer to lecture on the following subject "The ideal of manhood in heroic & folk literature"—You would chant the Emer lamentation—perhaps the Morte d Arthur lament—one or two joyful bits of heroic poetry which I will send you—the Douglas Hyde poems—that 'Holy Land' poem from the Oxford Anthology & it may be a bit of Nietzsche for the sake of the shock it will be to the pious—These are mere suggestions, I suppose you w^d. have to do 7 or 8 things anyway.[2] M^rs. Coffey w^d. put you up—Isn't this civil & humble on the part of the Nat Lit. Society?

Now as to the three London recitals[3]—[*an unknown number of pages are missing*] the kind seen outside Paris—The company are set on doing Shadowy Waters next—[4]

Yours ever
W B Yeats

Dict AG, signed WBY; Penn State. Marked in FF's hand 'The Tradition of the Power of Speech'.[5]

---

[1] WBY and FF had given an illustrated lecture on 'Speaking to Musical Notes' in Dublin on 1 Nov 1902; see p. 203, n. 5. The proposed lecture to the National Literary Society on 27 Apr was cancelled, and in WBY's place D. J. O'Donoghue lectured on 'The Writings of James Clarence Mangan'.

[2] FF's repertoire included 'Queen Emer's Lament for Cuchulain' from Lady Gregory's *Cuchulain of Muirthemne*, Sir Ector's 'doleful complayntes' over the dead Launcelot from Book XXI of Sir Thomas Malory's *Le Morte Darthur*, Ernest Rhys's 'Sir Dinadan and La Belle Isoud', Douglas Hyde's 'Will you be as hard, Colleen', and two translations from *Love Songs of Connacht*—'She casts a spell, O casts a spell', and 'For thee I shall not die'. Arthur Quiller-Couch had published the anonymous 16th century poem, 'As ye came from the Holy Land', in his anthology *The Oxford Book of English Verse* (1900): 'As ye came from the holy land / Of Walsinghame, / Met you not with my true love . . .' FF's own translations of passages from *Thus Spake Zarathustra* included 'A Dance Song' ('Pray you unlearn the hornblowing of affliction') from 'On the Higher Man'.

[3] WBY gave one of a current series of 'Westminster Lectures' on 15 May. He also delivered three lectures at Clifford's Inn, illustrated by FF and others, on 5 May ('Recording the Music of Speech'), 12 May ('Folk and Heroic Literature'), and 29 May ('Poetry and the Living Voice').

[4] See p. 311, n. 1. The INTS first performed *The Shadowy Waters* from 14 to 16 January 1904, while WBY was in America.

[5] Possibly an early title for one of the Clifford's Inn lectures, or else a book title suggested to

To John Quinn, 20 March [1903]

Coole Park | Gort
March 20

My dear Quinn—

I send you a set of proofs of 'Where there is Nothing'—I have told Bullen to delay publication until date of publication in America. When this is fixed, please ask Macmillan to wire to Bullen[1]—I have practically finished the second volume "Shorter Plays—Being Vol II of Plays for an Irish Theatre." It wants nothing indeed except a little lyric for one of the plays—I thought however that it would be best to let 'Where there is Nothing' have the start of it, for if they came out together, the reviewers would probably ignore the little plays—

The little plays are 'Kathleen ny Houlihan' 'The Pot of Broth' 'The Hour Glass' & 'The Travelling Man'[2]—Three of these are now stock plays with our little company—

The Hour Glass was played very successfully last week—It proved itself indeed as I always foresaw the strongest of the little plays—It is the first play in the production of which my ideas were carried out completely. The actors were dressed in ⟨a predominant⟩ purple with little bits of green here & there, & the back ground was made of green sacking. The effect was even more telling than I had expected. Everything seemed remote, naïve spiritual, & the attention, liberated from irrelevant distractions, was occupied as it cannot be on an ordinary stage with what was said & done.[3]

FF by WBY, who was urging her to write a primer on speaking to musical notes. She eventually wrote *The Music of Speech* (1909), which includes musical notations for several poems spoken to the psaltery.

[1] The American edition of *Where There Is Nothing* was copyrighted by Macmillans on 13 May, and published a few days later. Quinn had sent it to them on 17 Feb; one reader reported (NYPL) that while 'not so attractive as other dramas by the same hand', it was 'full of poetry', and the other that, being unstageable, 'it is interesting only as a literary piece of closet drama. I do not believe that it would have any sale worth mentioning here, and I do not see why it should be reprinted in this country, but . . . Mr. Yeats seems to be much talked of on the other side, and to be often mentioned here. It will do you good, therefore, to have his name associated with that of the house in a piece of work that will be carefully considered by the critics, even though not by the public.'

[2] *The Travelling Man*, later rewritten by AG, was omitted from the volume.

[3] Maire Nic Shiubhlaigh, who acted The Angel in the play, recalled this scenery: 'The scenery, such as it was, was calculated to centre the onlookers' attention principally on the dialogue and action. A background of dark-green tapestries; a rough desk, bearing a heavy book, open to show an illuminated text; a tasselled bell-pull and a wrought-iron bracket holding the hour-glass; these were the only properties employed. Costumes merged into the background, only those of two of the ten characters having tints of warmth in them. The dark austerity of the colour-scheme heightened the effect of the piece as nothing else could have done. It was an outstanding example of that classic simplicity of decor which is so often sought on a stage but seldom achieved. It was undoubtedly one of the most satisfactory settings for which Fay was responsible

There was a crowded audience, & a more distinguished one than we have had hitherto. This was partly owing to Lady Gregorys 'Twenty-Five' which followed it—Her play was well received, but will not produce its full effect until it is much better played—Fay had tried one of our younger actors in the chief part, & he made a very poor hand of it. We hope that Fay himself will take the part next time[4]—I do not however expect that any of our peasant plays will be at their best until we have been able to discover some method of putting a peasant cottage on the stage which will represent reality, but represent it as it is seen through the eye of an artist. The emotion of paint & ⟨pasteboard⟩ canvas, the pasteboard air, which we get from the stage under present circumstances, seems to me to destroy all noble effect. I see what is to be done with plays like 'The Hour Glass' but I cannot yet see clearly what is to be done with plays that come nearer to common life—I shall probably put an introduction to the book of shorter plays, dealing with the subject[5]—The plays will be done at Loughrea at Easter, & I think at Galway also—

The company took the Molesworth Hall, which holds 4 or 500 for this performance, as their own little hall turns out to be too small & too out of the way, & there are no dressing rooms—They hope some day to have a hall of their own, & if they go on doing such good work they will deserve it—For the present moment they will go on as best they can, & Fay says if he can get him £50 a year for 2 or 3 years he will be able to hold on till he has made his company a permanent one—I imagine that he will hire the Molesworth Hall three times a week—Hitherto every performance has made a small profit, but this has been put into the general fund, & no actor has been given anything—

The Company is at present rehearsing Shadowy Waters, rather against my wish, as I cant think it will be popular, but I did not like to refuse as they were so anxious to do it & I am busy now arranging the scene, a background of greens & blues, with figures dressed chiefly in dull ⟨red flame colour⟩ orange—After that I think they will do my new play "On Baile's Strand" in verse & prose—And they have just received two wonderful prose peasant plays from Synge,[6] who lives between Paris & the isles of Aran—Arthur Symons has the greatest admiration for these plays—

---

during his association with the theatre, and was probably never surpassed, although several attempts were made to improve on it through the years.' (Nic Shiubhlaigh, 33–4.)

[4] P. J. Kelly, who played Christie Henderson, the returned emigrant (see p. 233, n. 3). W. G. Fay took the part of the middle-aged farmer, Michael Ford, the heroine's husband.

[5] No introduction was included in the volume.

[6] *Riders to the Sea* and *In the Shadow of the Glen.*

Many thanks for 'The Dawn of Day'[7]—Nietzche remains to me as stirring as ever, though I do not go all the journey with him—He has been of particularly great service to me just now, because I am setting out to try & re-create an heroical ideal in manhood—in plays of old Irish life—

⟨I am thinking of sending either the Pot of Broth or the Hour Glass to the Gael, with a request that they will copyright it for me there, I can't publish these here⟩ (No, it would complicate things too much)—

Yrs sncly
W B Yeats

Best regards from *amanuensis*—
Many thanks for the telegram—

Dict AG, signed WBY; NYPL.

To Sydney Cockerell, 22 March [1903]

Coole Park
March 22

My dear Cockerell—I return proof of colophon, for which many thanks. It is charming, but I rather agree with you that it would be better somewhat larger. I don't quite know to what extent my sisters are in a hurry but Mr. Walker[1] probably knows this. I only saw them amid a whirl of people in Dublin and shall not be able to go into details with them for another week or more when I shall be in Dublin again.

---

[7] Quinn, who had sent him the first three volumes of the Unwin edition (see p. 313), now sent him *Morgenröte* (1881), translated into English as *The Dawn of Day* by Johanna Volz and published in 1903 by T. Fisher Unwin as vol. IV of *The Works of Friederick Nietzsche*. The copy in WBY's library was in fact inscribed to him from AG (*YL*, 1445).

[1] Emery Walker (see p. 192, n. 4), process engraver and typographical expert, whom WBY had first met at William Morris's, advised the Kelmscott, Doves, and Dun Emer Presses in book production. He became Master of the Art-Workers' Guild in 1904 and was knighted in 1930. A block made from Walker's design, and paid for in May, was used not as a colophon but as 'The Lady and the Tree' press mark, which appeared as a frontispiece in numerous Dun Emer and Cuala books, starting with *Twenty-One Poems by Katharine Tynan* in 1907. As WBY explained in 1932, in an inscription in William Maxwell's privately printed bibliography of the Dun Emer and Cuala Presses (Texas): 'I got Mrs Darwin [*i.e. Elinor Monsell*] to make this little design, but it owes its character to Emery Walker, who took great trouble with it. Mrs Darwin talked it over with him and I think redrew it more than once, that it might match the type. It represents Emer, Cuchulain's wife.' The first prospectus of the Dun Emer Press appeared in the summer of 1903, and an alternative colophon, printed in red at the end, established the inverted-delta format for *In the Seven Woods* and subsequent books.

The book is a long way yet from the level of the printing but Mr. Walker will know perhaps when they mean to bring out a prospectus and whether the colophon is to be a part of it.

Many thanks for your information about the binding. I left the little lecture behind me unfortunately, but I remember the look of it. I will write at once and tell Bullen to bind in your hand-made paper with the glazed holland back and to send you a dummy.[2]

Yours sincerely
W B Yeats

Text from Wade, 397-8.

To F. J. Fay, [c. 22 March 1903]

Mention in letter from Fay, 23 March 1903.
Telling Fay that the latest productions have pleased people; commenting favourably on W. G. Fay's acting; and suggesting that he would do well in serious as well as comic parts.

LWBY I. 120-2.

To the Committee of 'The Masquers' [c. 26 March 1903]

Mention in next letter.

To T. Sturge Moore, [c. 26 March 1903]

COOLE PARK, | GORT, | CO. GALWAY.

My dear Moore: I dont like the colour scheme at all.[1] I know the effect of gauze very well & it will not pull this scheme togeather. The white sail will throw the hounds into such distinctness that they will become an irrita-

---

[2] See p. 331. Dun Emer and Cuala books were also generally issued with glazed holland backs.

[1] See p. 311. On 23 Mar 1903 Frank Fay had written (*LWBY* I. 121-2) to confirm that the INTS would produce *The Shadowy Waters* in May, and to seek WBY's guidance on the music, costumes, and staging. WBY had evidently lost no time in asking Sturge Moore, who had helped design *The Hour-Glass*, for detailed advice, but in the end the play was postponed until January 1904.

tion.[2] I found that the brown back of a chair during the performance of 'The Hour Glass' enoyed me beyond words. Further the black, brown & white effect is just one of those effects which we like in London because we have begun to grow weary with the more obvious & beautiful effects. But [it] is precisely these obvious & beautiful effects that we want here. The fault is very largely mine for you had, as you thought, to bring in the red, black, & white hounds. Now that I have had to think things out I have come to the conclusion that the hounds must be all in some one colour & be almost lost in the main colour of the sail. Your scheme would upset all my criticism here. I have been ⟨insisting⟩ explaining on these principles.

(1) A back ground which does not insist on itself & which is so homogenius in colour that it is always a good back ground for an actor where ever he stand. Your back ground is the contrary of all this.

(2) Two pree-dominant colours in remote fanciful plays. One colour pree-dominant in actors, one in back cloth. This principle for the present at any rate until we have got our people to understand simplicity. 'The Hour Glass' as you remember was staged in this way & it delighted everybody.

Now what do you mean by back cloth to be continued. The wings of a theatre are ordinar[il]y about this proportion to whole stage.

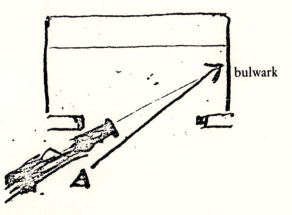

bulwark

If we continue your bulwark or sail in a straight line a man at A will see into the machinery. If we arrange our stage with emmense wings we will not fit into some of the halls we may have to play in. We shall have to bring the scene round like this

---

[2] The setting for *The Shadowy Waters* is the deck of a galley, and the stage directions (*VP*, 747) call for 'a great square sail. . . . Three rows of hounds, the first dark, the second red, and the third white with red ears, make a conventional pattern upon the sail.'

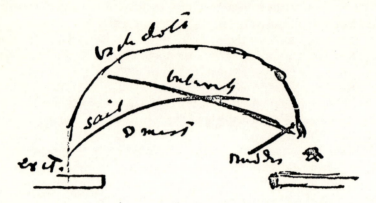

I have been working this out on a model & it has been rather a trouble-some thing. The sail had better slope like this when seen from front, as that

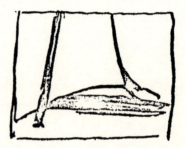

will hide the view into wings best & enable sailors at end to fight half hid-den by the sail as they are meant to. I have written to Fay for the exact measure of his stage, which is now a little la[r]ger than it used to be, the size of wings, etc.

Now as to colour scheme. The play is dreamy & dim & the colour should be the same—(say) a blue green sail, againtst an indigo blue back-cloth, & the mast & bulwark indigo blue. The persons in blue & green with some copper orniments. By making one colour predominate only slightly in backcloth & one only slightly in persons the whole will be kept dim & mysterious & like the waters themselves. What do you think? Now as to costumes. Nothing later than [*illegible*]th century—Wagners period more or less though a more medieval touch no harm. We want to keep to a vague period that our costumes may be combined & re-combined in various plays. Have I worried you too much over the thing? I can carry it out my

self but I would far sooner that you did. If you were over here five minutes
conversation would put all right & you could work as many hours a day as
you like with your Shakespear.[3] If I have not disgusted you & put you out
of patience I can send you the exact measurements after I have got all right
on my model & in consultation with Fay.

I hope all goes well at the meeting on Saturday.[4] I have written a letter
to be read out. Nothing yet from Gilbert Murray. I had not got his address
so wrote C/o Lord Carlisle—[5]

Yrs ev
W B Yeats

ALS Texas. Bridge, 5–7.

To R. Brimley Johnson, 28 March [*1903*]

COOLE PARK, | GORT, | CO. GALWAY.
March 28

My dear Johnson

I hear that you are still weighing the merits of Synges book on the Aran
Islands[1]—I think it is a fine book, that indeed it has in some ways more of
the country life in it than any book of the kind ever done in this country—
Would it make any difference in its prospects, or in the prospect of your
taking it, if I were to do a preface for it? I dont think Synge would object.
If you are to publish the book I shall be glad to write something praising it.
I think he will come to something as a writer, I have a strong admiration

---

[3] Sturge Moore was seeing through the press the 39 volumes of the *Vale Shakespeare* (1900–3),
designed and published by Charles Ricketts. He had already edited for the Vale Press *The Passionate Pilgrim* and *The Songs in Shakespeare's Plays* (1896), and *Shakespeare's Sonnets* (1899).

[4] A pilot meeting of the Masquers Society was held at 13 Henrietta Street, Covent Garden, on
Saturday, 28 Mar, with Walter Crane in the chair.

[5] Murray lived at Barford, Churt, Farnham, Surrey, but was at this time in Naples (see
p. 329). The 9th Earl of Carlisle, Charles James Stanley Howard (1843–1912), a landscape
painter, was the father of Gilbert Murray's wife, Lady Margaret Howard (1864–1956). His town
residence was 1 Palace Green, Kensington, and his country seat Castle Howard, York.

[1] See p. 170, n. 2. Synge had given the MS of *The Aran Islands* to Johnson at WBY's Monday
Evening on 9 Feb 1903, but on 26 Mar he wrote to AG (Saddlemyer, 41): 'I dont think that
Brimley Johnson intends to bring out the Aran book. I saw him on my way home, but he seemed
hopelessly undecided, saying at one minute that he liked it very much, and that it might be a
great success, and that he wanted to be in touch with the Irish movement, and then going off in
the other direction and fearing that it might fall perfectly flat! Finally he asked me to let him consider it a little longer.' In the end Johnson did not publish the book, which was eventually issued
jointly by Maunsel and Unwin in 1907.

for his plays especially, & expect one of them will soon be played by our little National Theatre Company.

Yours snly
W B Yeats

Dict AG, signed WBY; TCD, with unstamped envelope addressed to John S. Synge Esq, 31 Crossthwaite, Kingstown.

To F. J. Fay, [c. *29 March 1903*]

Mention in letter from Fay, 30 March 1903.
Sending him a book;[1] enclosing musical scores for *The Shadowy Waters*;[2] and reminding him that 'the Elizabethan dramatists had to fight popular opinion'.[3]

Private.

To William Archer, 4 April [*1903*]

at | COOLE PARK, | GORT, | CO. GALWAY.
April 4

Dear Mr Archer: I have asked Lady Gregory to send you her 'Poets & Dreamers', because of the translations of Hydes Gaelic plays.[1] I saw a sentence of yours in 'The Chronicle' about our Gaelic companies so I know you are interested.[2] Hyde's plays are the best dramatic work in Gaelic. They are immensely popular. They are better built than either Father

---

[1] Probably the book on Delsartean gesture Fay had enquired about *c*. 29 Jan; see p. 310.

[2] Fay thought the music 'just what we want. It is so simple that it ought to convince. We do not want the music to be uppermost.'

[3] On 20 Mar Fay had complained to WBY about the carping of the Dublin drama critics, commenting 'even if you gave these folk Elizabethan drama, they would not like it either'.

[1] AG's translations of Hyde's *The Marriage, The Twisting of The Rope, The Lost Saint,* and *The Nativity* were included in her *Poets and Dreamers*.

[2] A brief unsigned report in the *Daily Chronicle* of 16 Mar 1903 (6) reported that the new plays of the INTS (*The Hour-Glass* and *Twenty-Five*) had been 'enthusiastically received by a large and sympathetic audience'. WBY may, however, have been confusing the *Chronicle* with the *Morning Leader* in which, on 22 Nov 1902 (4), Archer had affirmed that 'So far as my neglected education will carry me, I love to follow the sayings and doings of the Irish Literary Party', and gone on to mention Hyde's and Fr. Peter O'Leary's plays in Irish.

Dineens or Father Peter O Learys[3] (who has built a little theatre in his parish at Macroom County Cork where he does his own plays I understand). Our English speaking company is going to do a lot of plays for 'The Irish Literary Society' in London on May 2nd—afternoon & evening—one socialistic nationalistic play by a man called Ryan, three of mine & one of Lady Gregorys, if all goes well.[4] All these plays have been played in Dublin, some of them a good many times, & some of them in country places. The company plays in Loughrea & Galway at easter. It is made up of clerks, shop boys & the like who work hard all day at their work, & who give all their evening to an endeavour to do for Ireland what Antoine[5] did in Paris. I mean they are really ambitious & take their art seriously.

Yrs ev
W B Yeats

ALS BL.

To A. H. Bullen, [5 April 1903]

Coole Park | Gort | Co Galway

My dear Bullen: I write to remind you of our rule to send no copies of my books to Dublin papers. You did not send 'Celtic Twilight' & it is still more desirable not to send 'Ideas of Good & Evil'. Reviews in Dublin papers sell no copies & I don't see why I should give them the oppertunity

---

[3] As well as his lexicographical work (see below, p. 350, n. 11), Dinneen also wrote plays (see p. 271, n. 3), including *Creideamh agus Gorta* (*Faith and Famine*), which WBY described in 1901 (*Expl*, 79) as the 'best Gaelic play' after Hyde's *Casadh an tSugáin*, and *An Tobar Draoidheachta* (*The Magic Well*), which WBY thought (*Expl*, 90) 'probably the best' Gaelic play of 1902 after Hyde's *An Pósadh*. In the 1901 and 1902 numbers of *Samhain* WBY had criticized O'Leary (see p. 113, n. 4) for excessive changes of scene, and asserted (*Expl*, 91) that his plays were unlikely 'to have any long life on our country stages'. However, during his 1903–4 American tour WBY consistently presented O'Leary's work as a testament to the imaginative vitality and enthusiasm of the Irish intellectual revival. Two of his plays, *An Sprid* (*The Ghost*) and *Tadhg Saor*, were especially popular in Munster.

[4] For their historic first visit to London on 2 May the INTS produced Fred Ryan's *The Laying of the Foundations*; WBY's *The Hour-Glass*, *Cathleen ni Houlihan*, and *The Pot of Broth*; and AG's *Twenty-Five*.

[5] André Antoine (1858–1943), French actor, producer and manager, founded the Théâtre Libre in Montmartre in 1887 with little experience or capital. Dedicated to the production of modern realist plays, the theatre was the model for J. T. Grein's Independent Theatre in London, of which the Stage Society was the direct heir. Although he did not sympathize with Antoine's realistic orientation, WBY frequently referred to his genius in creating a modern literary theatre.

of attacking me.[1] "The Freeman" reporter wrote a column the other day on my miracle play & the editor[2] crossed it out with the remark that I was "a dangerous man". I will sell better & not worse in Dublin from not inviting misunderstandings. I will ask you to send a copy to the editor of one friendly paper[3] but to him personally.

Yours ever

W B Yeats

ALCS Texas, addressed to Great Russell St., London, Irish postmark illegible, but postmarked on back of envelope 'LONDON AP 6 03'.

---

[1] On 20 May 1902, following attacks on WBY's Introduction to *Cuchulain of Muirthemne* (see pp. 184–6, 187–9), AG had written to him (Berg): 'you ought not to send yr own books for review to Irish papers in future. They have evidently an idea they shd be a sort of truffle dog where you are concerned, to scent out heresy however concealed.' A review of *IGE* appeared in the *Irish Times* on 22 May (7), but only one other Irish notice has been traced (see below, n. 3). The *Irish Times* notice fulfilled WBY's gloomy prophecy: 'Mr. Yeats is not at his happiest in this small volume of essays. The essay is not a congenial form of expression for writers of his calibre. Mr. Yeats is a dreamer, a mystic, a poet, and such an one is unlikely . . . to bring to discussion or debate that dispassionate analysis and serene judgment which crystallise into the essay proper. . . . Mr. Yeats' defects are more noticeable in his prose than in his verse. Indeed, one cannot get rid of the impression that prose is repugnant to him. . . . Moreover his persistent affectation is obtrusively present. In this lies, we believe, the great weakness of his work. In all that he says, in all that he affirms or denies, there is much beauty of idea and expression, but it is marred by the lurking suspicion engendered in the reader's mind of a want of sincerity on the part of the writer. If we could be only quite sure that Mr. Yeats really believes what he is preaching, our delight in his fine craftsmanship would be enhanced tenfold. But over and over again the conviction of a *pose* forces itself upon our minds.'

[2] The editor of the *Freeman's Journal* from 1892 to 1916 was William Henry Brayden (1865–1933), described in *Ulysses* I. 241 as 'a stately figure . . . steered by an umbrella, a solemn beardframed face. . . . Welts of flesh behind on him. Fat folds of neck . . .'

[3] i.e. Arthur Griffith: John Eglinton's review, 'The Philosophy of the Celtic Movement', appeared in the *United Irishman* on 27 June 1903 (3) and was reprinted under the same title in his *Anglo-Irish Essays* (1917). As a humanist and rationalist Eglinton questioned WBY's primitivism, and deplored his 'abandonment of the ordinary man, so to say, to his fate, and the contemptuous repudiation of all humanitarian ideals', concluding that 'in the tone adopted by Mr. Yeats towards the "middle class", which is simply the mass of mankind, we can gain some idea of how dangerous it would be for mankind that any section of it should achieve transcendental power or knowledge, and how wise are those Powers who so obstinately withold their secrets from men until they have graduated in faith, hope and charity.'

To John Quinn, 6 April [*1903*]

COOLE PARK, | GORT, | CO. GALWAY.
April 6[1]

My dear Quinn—

A great many thanks for the agreement & for all the trouble you have taken. The agreement will be all right if you can get Macmillan[2] to insert a clause making it terminable by either party after a term of years, 5 or 6, say—This is a clause that I have always put into all my agreements—I return the agreement to you signed, as I am sure there will be no difficulty about this—10 p c is a small percentage, but one's American pcs are never so good as one's English ones, & its a great thing to get Macmillan to publish for one, & to keep one's books in the same hands—I am sorry to hear about the misprints in Where There is Nothing—for it was a final proof I sent.[3] I had indeed found one error which I corrected in your proof in ink—& got put right in London—I would be very much obliged if you will ask to be shown the errors, & correct them, to save time—Title page (I thought I had sent you one) should be *Where There Is Nothing being vol 1 of Plays for an Irish Theatre*—(We have dropped 'Literary')—I imagine that the edition in London will be bound up in a day or two—but it will not be published till the American edition is ready—As to the shorter plays, I thank you very much for your offer to look for house room for them in America[4]—I am more anxious about their stage rights than their book rights, & more anxious about the stage rights of the Pot of Broth than of the others—I enclose you these two—& I will send next week the third play, which is almost ready—There is a good lyric in the third play so it may be more marketable than the others, but it is not so good a stage play. I would be perfectly satisfied if the Gael w^d. put them in—The great point

---

[1] Since this letter takes up a number of points raised in a letter from Quinn of 3 Apr (NYPL), which could not have reached Coole before *c.* 13 Apr, this date may be a slip for 'April 16'. However, there had been a vigorous three-sided correspondence between Quinn, WBY and AG on these matters for some weeks, and this letter may be answering queries in letters now lost. The proofs to which WBY refers had reached Quinn on 31 Mar.

[2] See p. 333. Quinn had arranged for *Where There Is Nothing* to be published by Macmillans in America, and had handed the copy text to George Brett, a Macmillan editor, on 4 Apr.

[3] In his letter of 3 Apr Quinn pointed out a number of misprints and inconsistencies in the proofs of the English edition of *Where There Is Nothing*, which was to be used as copy-text for the American edition, and had enclosed a separate slip of queries and suggestions for WBY's comments.

[4] In his letter of 3 Apr, Quinn promised to speak to Brett 'about the magazine publication in America of *A Pot of Broth* or *The Hour-Glass* in order to secure the copyright, and will let you know what he says about it'. In the event, Quinn placed *The Pot of Broth* in the *Gael* (NY), and *The Hour-Glass* in the *North American Review*, both in September 1903. Both plays were reprinted with *Cathleen ni Houlihan* in vol. II of 'Plays for an Irish Theatre' (1904).

is to get the Stage Copyright of 'Hour Glass' & 'Pot of Broth'[5]—I am writing this in a hurry, for mail, but will write again soon, in answer to yr very interesting letter—

Yours sinly
W B Yeats

Dear Mr Quinn—I am now writing for myself, to thank you for your letter of last week & your kind words abt 'Poets & Dreamers'—I wrote yr suggestion as to an American edition to Hodges & Figgis, & they like the idea, & ask if they shall write to Putnams—or if I prefer leaving it to you—I am telling them to try & arrange with Putnams—but that I will ask you, drawing as usual on yr kindness, to speak a good word for the book which may help—I enclose Figgis' letter—& also the Presidents letter which ought to help me on yr side![6]

Always yours from
A Gregory

[*At top of first page, also in AG's hand*]
There being nothing about dramatic rights in the agreement I suppose it is understood that they remain in my hands—[7]

Dict AG, signed WBY; NYPL.

To Gilbert Murray, 7 April [*1903*]

COOLE PARK, | GORT, | CO. GALWAY.
April 7

Dear Mr. Murray—
　Many thanks for your letter but it was the Committee I wanted you to go on—Your name & occasional advice w^d. be of great value to us. We all

---

[5] WBY was evidently still thinking of including *The Travelling Man* in the volume; see pp. 295, 333, n. 2. It included the 'Riding to Paradise' lyric (see p. 264, n. 7).
　[6] Hodges, Figgis & Co. were the Irish publishers of *Poets and Dreamers*, which had appeared in March of this year. In *70 Years* (402) AG records that John Shawe Taylor had shown her a newspaper report of a letter by President Theodore Roosevelt 'in which he said: "I have just been reading Lady Gregory's translation or paraphrase of the old Erse epic *Cuchulain of Murmethne* (Heaven forgive me if my spelling is wrong)—and I am delighted with it." He himself afterwards wrote to me that after he had read it, he had sent for all the books on Irish literature he could get hold of, to take upon a journey to the west.' *Poets and Dreamers* did not find an American publisher.
　[7] When Quinn sent WBY's contract for *Where There Is Nothing* back to Macmillans on 13 May 1903 he stipulated (NYPL) 'that the right of translation and right of dramatizations or dramatic representations are expressly reserved in the author, W. B. Yeats. I shall be glad if you will send me a line confirming this understanding.'

quite understand that living as you do out of town you will not often be able to attend.[1] I think that you yourself might find it an advantage should you desire to write plays. We will all be a good deal behind the scenes, or can be there if we have a mind to, & one certainly writes the better for getting some actual stage into one's head. It helps one to see the imaginary person of one's play, & the actor who is to express him, side by side—It is for this reason that I myself am working at the society. I dont believe it will create ideal conditions for the performers of plays. It begins at the wrong end. It will have to accept actors trained by the existing theatre, & the right way is to get a little company as Antoine did, & to train them in one's own way from the beginning. Experience however one must have oneself. The name of the society has been changed to 'The Masquers' which is at any rate harmless. I did not propose the title you object to,[2] but I welcomed it when it was proposed & precisely because I thought it would raise opposition—I think it is very good for most men, especially for intellectual men to fight a little. That is a form of discipline from which we have got great benefit in this country—I am quite confident that a good fight would be the making of Arthur Symons, who will I suppose be our critical voice—Now I suppose he will sink into comfortable ease—

Our little Irish Theatre which is being trained in the right way from the beginning will bring to London some of the plays it has been acting here & play them for the Irish Literary Society on May 2nd. If you are back I hope you will try & see them—You can get particulars from Irish Literary Society 20 Hanover Square—[3]

Yours sincly
W B Yeats

Dict AG, signed WBY; Bodleian.

---

[1] Murray was reluctant to serve on the committee of the Masquers (see p. 329, n. 1), and had evidently given his distance from London as an excuse. In fact, he became one of its most energetic and conscientious members.

[2] i.e. 'The Theatre of Beauty'; see p. 329, n. 1.

[3] In November 1901 the ILS had transferred from 8 Adelphi Terrace to larger rooms at St Ermin's Hotel, Caxton St., but in December 1902 it moved to Hanover Square.

To the Editor of the Freeman's Journal,[1] *9 April 1903*

Dear Sir—Like Mr. Edward Martyn I see nothing good in this Royal visit.[2] If the King is well received in this country, his reception will be used by the English Unionist papers as an argument against the Irish Nationalist movement. I remember that the "Times" and the "Spectator" used our supposed enthusiastic reception of the late Queen in this way,[3] and yet I have no doubt that they will join with the other papers in telling us that the King is above politics. But it matters very little to us what the English papers say. What does matter is that Royal visits, with their pageantry, their false rumours of concessions,[4] their appeal to all that is superficial and trivial in society, are part of the hypnotic illusion[5] by which England seeks to take captive the imagination of this country,[6] and it does this not by argument nor[7] by any appeal to the intellect, but by an appeal to what are chiefly money interests.[8] The shopkeeper must hang out a flag, not because he wants to, but because he will lose rich customers if he does not; the workman must pretend loyalty or he will be dismissed by his rich employer; the children of the poor must stand in troops and cheer under supervision, because their schools are afraid to offend rich patrons. A Royal visit has always been both a threat and a bribe, and even the Nationalist who considers what is called the "link of the Crown"

---

[1] A MS draft of this letter is in the Berg.

[2] The draft version omits this first sentence. Martyn's letter appeared in the *Freeman's Journal* on 4 Apr, and was reprinted in the London *Times* on 6 Apr. Hearing that British newspapers were declaring that the Irish people would receive the King 'as a welcome compensation for their deprivation of Home Rule', Martyn urged nationalist Ireland to 'tell the government with one voice that if they bring the King here under any other guise than as a restorer of our stolen Constitution they will regret their rashness'. On 10 Apr (8) *The Times*'s Irish correspondent cited both Martyn's and WBY's letters in deploring 'the considerations which the leading Irish literary movement commends to the nation at a moment of industrial awakening and political reconciliation. They explain the inability of this coterie to make any definite impression on the intellectual life of the country. Sincere admirers of Mr. Yeats's poetry will regret that he seems unable to realize the very narrow limitations of his considerable genius, one of them, which he shares with many of his followers, is the want of even an elementary sense of humour.'

[3] The draft reads: 'Punch & the Spectator put this very explicitly, & yet I have no doubt . . .'.

[4] The draft reads: 'their rumours of false promises'.

[5] The draft reads 'illusions'.

[6] The draft adds: 'This country is endeavouring to live according to its own lights, according to its own table of values & that endeavour is called the Irish Ireland movement. A Royal visit on the other hand appeals (appeals to enflames all that is English in this country, & appeals seeks to bribe us to accept) to this country to accept the lights and the tables of values of another country, & to do this not by argument . . .'.

[7] The draft reads 'not'.

[8] The draft reads: 'an appeal to the lowest interests'.

inevitable, should offer but the welcome that a man gives to a threat or a bribe.[9]

W B Yeats

Printed letter, *Freeman's Journal*, 9 April 1903 (5).

To Mrs Margaret Rogers Rees,[1] *16 April* [*1903*]

COOLE PARK, | GORT, | CO. GALWAY.
April 16

Dear Mrs. Rees—

Please forgive me for not having written to thank you for sending the collar—I hope your husband got his book 'Silver drops' all right,[2] I posted it before I left London—

Yrs snly
W B Yeats

Dict AG, signed WBY; Wellesley, with envelope addressed to Avondale, Llandaff, postmark 'GORT AP 16 03'.

To Lady Augusta Gregory, [*26 April 1903*]

Nassau Hotel.

My dear Friend: I send you a letter of Quinns. You should read it before writing to him. Perhaps to[o] you would tell him about the money. You will see he offers £20 a year for Fay for 2 or 3 years. Who should he send

---

[9] The draft reads: 'A Royal visit is always with a threat & a bribe, & even the nationalist who has no objections to what is called the link of the crown should offer but the welcome that a man of honour gives to a threat or a bribe.'

[1] Margaret Rees was the wife of John Rogers Rees (see p. 286), who had arranged WBY's lecture on 19 Feb, when WBY had stayed with the Reeses at 75 Cardiff Road, Llandaff, Cardiff.

[2] *Silver Drops, Or Serious Things* (?1670) by William Blake (*fl.* 1650–70), housekeeper to the Ladies Charity School of Highgate. WBY had probably borrowed the undated book out of curiosity about the author's possible connection with the poet William Blake (1757–1827). Prefaced by Blake's appeal to the 'Many Noble, Well-Disposed' lady subscribers, the book presents for their 'pious Thoughts' and 'Lilly Hands' four epistolary sermons, his 'Silver Drops', on Charity, Truth, Religion, and Virtue to persuade them to support the charity school in Highgate which caters for 'some 30 or near 40 poor and fatherless Boys'.

it too? I think you yourself. I will write about it if you prefer. Of course I will write about Nietzsche in any case.[1]

I was at Contemporary Club last night. I got a photograph of my fathers drawing of Taylor for you.[2] I stayed at Contemporary till 4 this morning, talking of theatre & all kinds of things. I dont think Cousins play was a success by what I hear.[3] Even Coffey did not seem to have liked it. I have not seen Russell yet. I missed him last night. He had gone to my fathers thinking to find me there. I followed him only to find he had gone back to Coulison Avenue looking for me again. Father O Donovan has ordered 10 banners from my sister, "as a beginning".[4] I go out to the works on Monday & will talk over the designs.

I hear that Stephen Gwyn is in difficulties about getting two children to play in 'The Hour Glass' as mothers object to their children saying they only beleive in what they can see & touch. He has now written to Mrs Gwynn who is away to know if his own children may take the parts.[5]

---

[1] On 12 Apr Quinn had written to WBY (NYPL) that he would 'be very glad to pledge £20 a year for the theatre if you will let me. If you or Lady Gregory will let me know that I may do it when next you or she writes I will send my check for this year (£20) at once.' He went on to say that he hoped to persuade Thomas Kelly (see p. 464, n. 8) to put up another £20 per annum, '& perhaps between us we can get a third person to add the remaining ten' to make it up to the £50 W. G. Fay thought necessary to the continuation of the theatre company (see p. 334). The last page or pages of Quinn's letter are missing, and so the reference to Nietzsche is unclear, but probably Quinn was taking up WBY's comments of 6 Feb 1903 (see p. 313). AG wrote to Quinn on 30 Apr (Berg).

[2] JBY's pencil drawing of John F. Taylor (1850–1902), barrister, journalist, and 'obscure great orator' (*Aut*, 96), at the Contemporary Club in 1885 is now at the National Gallery of Ireland and is reproduced in Plate 19.

[3] Cousins's three-act play, *The Sword of Dermot*, based on the tragic love affair between Una Dermot and Proud Costello that had also provided the theme for WBY's story 'Costello the Proud, Oona MacDermot and the Bitter Tongue' (1896), was produced on 20 Apr 1903 for the National Literary Society and published in the *United Irishman* on 2 May, with the note, 'not the author's final version'. Most reviewers found the play wordy and straining for literary effect. It differs significantly from WBY's treatment of the story.

[4] The Revd Jeremiah O'Donovan (see p. 112) was administrator of St Brendan's Cathedral, now under construction in Loughrea. WBY had dined with him in Loughrea on 13 Apr during the INTS performances there (see p. 329, n. 2), an occasion recalled in *E & I*, pp. 261–4. WBY was to seek advice on the designs from Eric Maclagan and Sydney Cockerell, who noted in his diary on 29 Apr (BL) that 'Yeats called, just back from Ireland and wanted to ask advice about designs for banners'. In the end the banners, which depicted Irish saints, were designed by Jack Yeats, his wife, Mary Cottenham ('Cottie') Yeats (1863–1947), Pamela Colman Smith, and AE, while SMY embroidered the main figures, beginning with the banner of St Ita in the summer of 1903. The Cathedral was completed in 1905 at a cost of £30,000.

[5] Stephen Gwynn recalls in *Experiences of a Literary Man* (206–7) that, although the parents on the ILS's committee had at first been eager for their children to take the parts, when they read the play they had misgivings, voiced by Barry O'Brien:

Here is my boy, and here is what he will have to say when the wise man questions him. 'Is there a heaven? is there a hell? is there a purgatory?' 'Oh no, father. There is nothing we can-

Moore I hear is discouraged about Ireland.[6] My father is replying to Leader & very politely. Edward Martyn surprized him very much by trying to persuade him to be 'rude & personal'.[7] By the by Martyn appears to have had another Kings visit letter in Freeman & to have been both 'rude & personal' but I have not seen it.[8]

I am sad to be away from Coole.

O but I forgot to say we talked of 'Cuchullain' last night & I thought from Bests tone that 'hedging' has begun.[9] I hear too that your friend

not see, there is nothing we cannot touch. Foolish people used to think there was, but you are very wise: you have taught us better.'

'Now,' said Barry O'Brien, 'this is to be the first time my boy will speak in public from any platform and I do not want these to be the first words that he will utter publicly.'

Gwynn therefore arranged for Geoffrey Dearmer, 9-year-old son of his friends Percy and Mabel Dearmer, and Sighle ni Guinn, his 7-year-old daughter, to play the children: 'It went well, the only trouble being that noises from behind disturbed the performance: Sheila [Sighle] and Geoffrey were playing football with Fay's bowler hat. They were both too young to have any nerves and got through their impieties admirably: both had a candour of aspect that was perfect for the occasion.'

[6] George Moore's discouragement had begun by September 1902 when he confessed to Dujardin (*Letters from George Moore to Ed. Dujardin*, ed. John Eglinton [1929], 44) that he had 'had enough of the Gaelic League and of Ireland'.

[7] JBY's letter 'A Plea for the Painter', appeared in the *Leader* on 9 May 1903. It was his final rejoinder in a two-month controversy with the art critic Robert Elliott (1863–1910), who had attacked his art and aesthetics. Elliott was particularly contemptuous of what he described as JBY's 'artistic hermetics'—the view that great artists should lose themselves in their subjects—and insisted that since painting is a matter of depicting appearances the artist should be an objective technician. On 18 Apr (121) he had denounced JBY's latest portraits as showing degeneration: 'His goal is uncertain, and he seems to have lost himself, indeed. . . . He is now softly shuffling over self-created difficulties, instead of manfully bearing them and overcoming them by force of that individuality which is the varied heritage of both artist and Philistine. . . . artists like Mr. Yeats gradually become involved in a kind of maze, where the unending walls are shadowy portraits of the painters they admire, and where the thought is distracted by the genealogies and idiosyncrasies of the sitters.' In his emollient reply of 9 May (173–4) JBY ignored Elliott's *ad hominem* animus, and reformulated his views on the relationship of personality and technique: 'an artist is a good deal more than a painter of appearances, with verisimilitude as his object. . . . One who looks on the world with only the eyes of observation is merely a student and a slave; he becomes an artist when he learns to use the eyes of desire, and he paints great pictures when he can make appearances so plastic to his hand that . . . he can create a world of desire, and do it in such good faith that, convinced himself, he convinces others.' Martyn's bellicosity was surprising because he was a friend of Elliott's and had contributed an admiring Preface to his *Art and Ireland* (1902).

[8] Martyn's letter, in the *Freeman's Journal* on 23 Apr 1903 (6), was a response to a report in the issue of 21 Apr (5) that the Baltinglass Board of Guardians had passed a resolution urging 'a cordial reception' of the King since the visit was 'another instance of the great interest he has taken in the affairs of this country, and having regard to the movement which is at present being made towards the settlement of the land question, and the adjustment of the differences between classes in this country . . .'. Martyn described the resolution as 'one of those deplorable exhibitions of incompetence by which Irishmen every now and then make themselves contemptible to foreign peoples'. He continued: 'If the Irish people could only realise how these dogs of English, especially their upper classes, talk of us Irish—how they sneer at Irish religion, priests, ideals of Nationality, language, literature, and art it might put more spirit into us Irish to resist the coming of those English now . . .'.

[9] See p. 184, n. 1. Best and other critics had evidently tempered their view that *Cuchulain of Muirthemne* had pagan tendencies.

Macdonell has been to the Royal Irish Academy & told them that if they did not rise to the level of a Continental Academy they must expect a revision of their status—or some such words. Their neglect of the Irish MSS is supposed to have been the cause of his words—that & the delay over the dictionary.[10]

The Limerick way to Dublin is comfortable enough. I had to change carriages at Ennis, getting into a through carriage that was hooked on. That was the only change & the ticket is a couple of shillings cheaper. I think however that the journey must be a little longer.

Yrs always
W B Yeats

ALS Berg, with envelope addressed to Coole, postmark 'DUBLIN AP 28 03'.

To Maud Gonne, [*late April 1903*]

Mention in letter from MG, Wednesday [April 1903].
Restoring communication after her marriage, and inviting her to tea on her next visit to London.

G–YL, 169.

---

[10] Sir Anthony Patrick MacDonnell (1844–1925), a Liberal statesman and a Catholic, had been appointed Under-Secretary for Ireland in 1902 by the Conservative Chief Secretary, George Wyndham, 'rather as a colleague than as a mere Under-Secretary to register my will', and gave him valuable service in preparing the Land Act of 1903. He retained office under Walter Long and, on the return of the Liberals, under James Bryce and Augustine Birrell, resigning in 1908. The Royal Irish Academy had been founded in 1786 by the 1st Earl of Charlemont and received its royal charter the following year. Its library contained 2,500 Irish manuscripts but, although some valuable editorial work had been done during the 19th century, the Academy was now thought to be too leisurely and exclusive in its procedures. Its cataloguing and storage of manuscripts gave cause for concern, as did its delay in producing the Irish–English dictionary it had undertaken over fifty years before. This project had originally been suggested at a meeting of the Irish Archaeological Society in November 1852 and its first editors were Eugene O'Curry and John O'Donovan. After their deaths work went extremely slowly, and had not accelerated under the direction of the current editor, Robert Atkinson (1839–1908), Professor of Sanskrit and Romance Languages at TCD. MacDonnell's threats evidently had little effect, for the first fasciculus (covering part of the letter 'D') did not appear until August 1913, and the second only followed in 1932. The work, under the title *Dictionary of the Irish Language*, was finally completed in 1976. In the mean time the Irish Texts Society was to publish a useful but far less ambitious Irish–English dictionary under the editorship of Fr. Patrick Dinneen in 1904.

To Lady Augusta Gregory, [*1 May 1903*]

18 Woburn Buildings

Dear Lady Gregory: There is going to be a fine audience on Saturday. Some days ago they had sold £150 worth of tickets. People seem greatly interested.[1] 'Shadowy Waters' & Columbs play have, I am sorry to say been put off for the present.[2] The Company had been over worked & wanted a holiday, or some of them did. They had rehersed everything endlessly & Digges & Miss Quinn & some others had played in Collumbs[3] play & Digges in 'The Dolls House'. They were all tired & excitable & flying at each other every moment. Miss Quinn threatened to resign & had said that this would mean Digges & Miss Gonnes resignation. Ryan came round to see me, & gave an alarming account of things. He thought Miss Quinn & Digges might try & form a company without the Fays who are rather rough with the actors. His sympathy seemed to be with Digges. A general meeting is summoned for first week in June to decide on future of company, programme for Autumn Etc. Fay counts on everybody having quieted down after a rest. I think though that he himself would like to abolish the democrasy in June. I think things will come right—the only anxiety is the possible loss of Digges. I think Fay would not mind this, but I should for we have nobody else capable of playing 'Sencan'. I think in spite of there being no 'Shadowy Waters' you had better come to Dublin in June as you will help to keep them quiet. I am afraid the Fays dictatorial ways are the chief support of the democratic arrangements & our chief difficulty. It is all important that Quinn should let us have

---

[1] Stephen Gwynn, as Secretary of the ILS, arranged for the INTS's visit to London, and guaranteed £50 for expenses. On 2 May the Society produced five plays at a matinée and an evening performance at the Queen's Gate Hall, South Kensington.

[2] Frank Fay had written to WBY on 23 Mar (see p. 336) to tell him that the INTS were putting *The Shadowy Waters* and Colum's *Broken Soil* into rehearsal for production in the third week of May. *Broken Soil* was eventually staged in Dublin on 3 Dec 1903 and *The Shadowy Waters* on 14 Jan 1904.

[3] Probably an error for 'Cousins's', whose *The Sword of Dermot* was produced at the National Literary Society on 20 Apr with Maire Quinn, Kelly, and Digges taking leading parts. Digges had also taken the part of Dr Rank in Flora MacDonald's Dublin production of *A Doll's House* in mid-April, and on 16 Apr Holloway recorded in his diary (NLI) that in 'manner, voice, & gesture he completely realized the part. It was a wonderful study in its way & very painful to behold.' The frequency with which Digges, Quinn, and Kelly were taking parts with other dramatic societies had led the INTS to adopt a new rule on 26 Apr 1903 that all such performances must be approved in advance by the Committee.

control of the money.[4] I hear that 'The Stage Society' talk of doing Paul next season.

I enclose a note of Masefields which explains itself. Miss Commelin (whom you met here—she came with Miss Fry the woman with the queer look in the eyes) is not in all ways the wife for him but she will look after him now when he most wants it—he is looking very delicate.[5] She has some money apparently & he him self has begun to do pretty well. He is doing sub-editing on 'The Speaker' for one thing. He was bound to marry some kind woman, with a confident will, for I have noticed that every woman who sets eyes on him wants to see that he gets regular meals.

'Paul' is bound now & I will get a copy sent you to day. I wonder when it will be possible to publish it. The essays are to be published on May 7th & bound copies should be ready to-day or to morrow.

I saw Vikings last night. I liked Ellen Terry in it & liked moments of the play altogeather & it all interested me. Craigs scenery is amazing but rather distracts ones thoughts from the words. The poor verses I made for them are spoken with great energy but are quite inaudible.[6] There is a kind of

[4] See p. 348, n. 1. Quinn was content to fall in with WBY's management of the money, and had asked him in his letter of 12 Apr to let 'me know when you write to whom I shall send the cheque'. In her reply of Saturday [2 May 1903; Berg], AG said that she had written to Quinn telling him 'it was important money sh^d be sent through you—but that it c^d. be lodged with me'.

[5] Masefield had written on 27 Apr 1903 (*LWBY* I. 122–3) to tell him 'that I am engaged to be married to Miss Crommelin, and that I am very happy and full of sky. It is goodbye to all my plans of travelling with the tinkers (you must tell Lady Gregory this) as if things go well we may be married in July.' Constance Crommelin (1867–1960), a daughter of Nicholas Crommelin of Cushendun, Co. Antrim, was over eleven years older than Masefield, and a teacher and former Senior Optime in the Cambridge Mathematical Tripos. She married Masefield in July and WBY gave him an inscribed vellum presentation copy of *IGE* as a wedding present. WBY's reservations about Miss Crommelin increased after the marriage, and he came to feel that her opinionated views and overbearing manner impaired Masefield's creativity, writing to Jack Yeats in 1912 (Anne Yeats) 'I find him surrounded with such a crew of female political economists & emotional journalists—forced on him by his wife I suppose. His friends are no longer the people who know & have taste—& I think few men who live with their inferiors keep their critical capacity.' In her reply AG said she felt 'as if Masefield were being sold into captivity, but I daresay he ought to have someone to look after him—You will be lonely without him, or rather without what he was.'

Isabel Fry (1869–1958), a younger sister of the art critic Roger Fry, had been a devoted friend of Constance Crommelin since 1891, and in 1897 they founded and ran a private school in London, which continued until 1912. In the summer of 1902 Miss Fry had participated in chanting experiments at Sturge Moore's rooms.

[6] See p. 4. The Craig–Terry production of Ibsen's *The Vikings at Helgeland* played at the Imperial Theatre from 15 Apr to 14 May. Others found the *mise-en-scène* the notable feature of the evening: James Huneker devoted several pages (31–44) to it in his *Iconoclasts* (1905), and *Men and Women* on 25 Apr (253) described the 'dull grey atmosphere, a mass of rugged rocks, the swish of the sea, the sting of the winter morning, a crowd of large, rough men, clothed in their fighting gear—like themselves, rough and gleaming dull. . . . Then a pause, and to the horde of wrangling men enters a queenly woman, helmeted and armed, with a bright yellow fur thrown round her—a woman with a wonderful face, crowned with ruddy hair. She stands at the top of the rocks with the Vikings crowded on each side, and the sullen sea beyond. It was a wonderful

lyre to which he is supposed to speak & out of that amazing lyre comes the whole orchestra wind instruments and all & every one of them makes the most of its naturrally loud voice. I suggested that the fortunes of the theatre might be restored (house was half empty) by their imitating 'the Times' & having a prize competition.[7] So many hundreds for any body who could hear three lines togeather & £5 a piece for words heard anywhere. This amused Miss Craig who had tried to get the verses properly spoken. The play is not I think a really very great play. One constantly finds when one pierces beneath the stage tumult that the passions, or rather the motives are conventional. There is a touch of melodrama in the characterization. These heroes alternate between impulses of very obvious christian Charity, & more barbaric energies in the suddenest way. I felt that Ibsen had not really grasped & unified the old life.[8] He had no clear thought or emotion about it. Of course however the play is better worth seeing than anything else that has been here this long while & for that reason it is failing. Ellen Terry whom I saw for a moment after it was over said 'Well it is a fine play to have made a failure with'. She added that everybody there had got a good living wage out of it & so it did not matter—everybody but she herself who would get nothing. She impresses me a good deal by her vitality & a kind of joyousness.

I saw Joyce in Dublin he said that his mother was still alive & it was uncertain whether she would die or not. He added 'but these things really dont matter'. I spoke to him about his behaviour at 'Academy' office & other things of the kind rather sternly. He took it unexpectedly well.[9]

Yr ever
W B Yeats

---

picture, and the rest of the play will pass from my memory long before I forget it . . .' It was little wonder that WBY could not distinguish the words of his Prologue, since Martin Shaw had set Archer's version; see p. 326, n. 1. Craig recalled that the play was 'a great success, but was taken off owing to the incapacity of the business manager, I forget his name, who failed utterly over the publicity! It could have been made into a roaring success' (Craig, 244).

[7] On 10 Apr *The Times* had announced (11) a competition with 93 prizes for those correctly answering a series of questions. The first prize was a scholarship of £1200 for a three-year course at Oxford or Cambridge.

[8] The alternations occur partly because Ibsen has drawn his material both from the heroic *Volsungasaga* and the Icelandic Family Sagas, where, as he says in the preface to the first German edition (1876), conditions and events are 'reduced to more human dimensions' (see p. 4, n. 6); and partly because the action of the play revolves around a double mismatch by which the heroic and ambitious Sigurd has married the home-loving and gentle Dagny, while his blood-brother, the gentle and home-loving Gunnar, is married to the ambitious and heroic Hjördis.

[9] For Joyce's behaviour at the *Academy* office see p. 307, n. 2. His mother, Mary Jane (May) Joyce, née Murray (1859–1903), was seriously ill with cancer of the liver and he had been summoned home by telegram from Paris, arriving in Dublin on 12 Apr. 'These things' mattered far more than he pretended, and Mrs Joyce's death, which occurred on 13 Aug of this year, became a haunting theme in *Ulysses*.

[*On back of envelope*]
In one of Quinns letters he spoke of misprints in 'Paul'.[10] Please send me a list of misprints if you can find letter. I would want it at once.

WBY.

ALS Berg, with envelope addressed to Coole, postmark 'LONDON MY 1 03'. Partly in Wade, 398–9.

To Lady Augusta Gregory, [*4 May 1903*]

My dear Friend: Forgive this absurd paper. I have no other.[1] The plays were a great success. I never saw a more enthusiastic audience. I send you some papers, all that I have found notices in. When I remember the notices I have seen of literary adventures on the stage I think them better than we could have hoped. 'The Daily News' one is by Phillip Carr I think. The Leader, is I imagine by Archer.[2] I have noticed that the young men, the men of my own generation or younger are the people who like us. It was a very distinguished audience. Blunt was there, but went after your play as he was just recovering from the influenza & seemed to be really ill.[3] I thought your play went very well. Fay was charming as Cristie. The game of cards is still the weak place, but with all defects the little play has a real charm. If we could amend the cards it would be a strong play too. Lady Aberdeen, Henry James, Michael Field, who has written me an enthusias-

---

[10] See p. 343.

[1] The letter is written on lined paper, evidently taken from an exercise book.

[2] Philip Carr (1874–1957), drama critic and producer, wrote in the *Daily News* of 4 May (12) that the Irish literary movement had 'brought to the theatre in Ireland what our English theatre can scarcely be said to possess at all to-day. It has brought the drama of imagination, the drama of ideas. With these productions of the Irish theatre we feel that in Dublin the theatre is beginning to be what it has not been for hundreds of years in England—the expression of the aspirations, the emotions, the essential spirit and movement of the people . . . the idealism and the poetry of the national sentiment.'
   William Archer, drama critic of the *Morning Leader*, said on 4 May (5) that in 'this so-called Celtic movement we so-called Saxons may find much which appears forced and affected. We incline to belittle a national sorrow which can find refuge and relief in art. . . . But the grief is real, and at last even John Bull is beginning to heed it. Good heavens, if Ireland becomes a nation again, and all the Irish return there, what a dull place England will become!'

[3] Blunt was ill, but it was evidently WBY's play as much as the virus which caused him pain: on his return home he complained in his diary (II. 54–5) that *The Hour-Glass* was 'a terrible infliction . . . a stupid imitation of that dull old morality, "Everyman," which bored me so much last year. What Yeats can mean by putting such thin stuff on the stage I can't imagine.' He was 'determined, however, to hear Lady Gregory's piece, "Twenty-five," and was rewarded, for it is quite the most perfect little work of art and the most touching play I have ever seen acted. Only it made me weep in my weak state. I could not stay on for the final piece, "Kathleen na Houlihan".'

tic letter about the acting, Lord Aberdeen, Mrs Wyndham, chief secretary
mother, Lord Montegale, Mrs Thackery Ritchie,[4] & I dont know how
many other notables were there & all I think were moved. Lady Aberdeen
has asked the Fay Company to go to the St Louis exhibition to play their
for six months. She wants them to give another performance in London
before the committee in summer & then if the committee like them all
capital would be found. The Company are so excited with their success that
they are inclined to go. They may be more sober next week. I conclude
they would have to give up their situations & become a regular company. It
would be a year hence. Fay is very anxious for it, as he thinks it would
start them with prestige & experience. My American tour would help them
I dare say. The evening audience was the more Irish of the two & 'Cathleen' & 'The Pot of Broth' got a great reception. 'The Pot of Broth' was
not gagged this time. Miss Laird[5] is now the mother in 'Cathleen' & is certainly much better than Miss Quinn was—endeed she seems to me as near
perfect as possible. 'The Foundations' went well, endeed everything went
well.

Yrs always
W B Yeats

ALS Berg, with envelope addressed to Coole, postmark indecipherable. Wade, 399–400.

[4] Ishbel Maria Marjoribanks, Lady Aberdeen (1857–1939), a Liberal, humanitarian, and leader
of the International Council of Women, was the wife of John Campbell Gordon, Lord Aberdeen
(1847–1934), Lord Lieutenant of Ireland in 1886 and again from 1905 to 1915. She was helping to
plan the Irish pavilion at the 1904 St Louis Exhibition, and although the Fays did not take their
company, a breakaway group composed of Kelly, Digges, and Maire Quinn did perform there.
   Henry James (1843–1916), the American novelist, had settled in England in 1876 and in the
early 1890s had unsuccessfully tried to establish himself as a dramatist. He was a friend of AG's,
but her attempt to introduce him to WBY in 1897 failed. He was to publish *The Ambassadors* later
this year.
   Sir George Wyndham's influential mother, Madeline (d. 1920), was a granddaughter of Lord
Edward Fitzgerald (1763–98), who fought for Irish independence with the United Irishmen.
   Thomas Spring Rice, Lord Monteagle of Brandon (1849–1926), one of the Irish theatre's
staunchest supporters, had arranged on 24 Jan 1903 for the INTS to perform *The Pot of Broth* at
his home in Foynes, Co. Limerick, where the Social Improvement Society was giving an entertainment.
   Lady Anne Isabella Ritchie, née Thackeray (1837–1919), authoress, biographer, editor, and
critic, was the eldest daughter of William Makepeace Thackeray and the aunt of Virginia Woolf,
who wrote after her death that she would be 'the unacknowledged source of much that remains in
men's minds about the Victorian age'.
[5] Helen S. Laird (1874–1957) was a member of Fay's original company, acting under the name
of 'Honor Lavelle'. She played Maurya in the first production of Synge's *Riders to the Sea* in February 1904, but seceded from the Abbey late in 1905 and joined the Theatre of Ireland. She
became a teacher at Alexandra College in 1904, and the following year she married Constantine
Curran (1874–1957), the friend of James Joyce.

To Robert Gregory, [c. 4 May 1903]

Mention in undated frag from AG, [c. 6 May 1903].
AG wrote: 'Robert told me to thank you for your letter "which was very
interesting and inspiring".'[1]

Berg.

To Lady Augusta Gregory, [5 May 1903]

18 Woburn Buildings

My Dear Lady Gregory: I send you press notices please keep them for the
Theatre book.[1] I got a note from Walkely saying that he will speak of
the performance in next "Times Supplement" & congratulating us all on
the excellence of our work.[2] Indeed the success of the whole thing has been
wonderful.

Poor Maud Gonne was here yesterday for two hours. I am afraid she has
been more foolish than any of us imagined possible. She is looking worn
out. This is the tale she told me. Though there has been nothing between
her & Milvouye[3] for years people in Paris do not know this & lately he
made her position impossible by advertising himself every where with an
actress. Maud Gonne said 'I dont know whether I felt it or not but I was
very angry & when I found that he had brought her to see Iseult, one day
when I was away, I resolved to get some one to keep him out & to make a
final breach. I married in a sudden impulse of anger'. I asked her if she was
unhappy. She said 'I have always told you that since a certain dreadful year

---

[1] WBY had evidently written to commend and encourage Robert in his recent decision to go to
Art School after graduating at Oxford. His letter would have been especially welcome since, as
AG revealed in the same fragment, it had 'not been broken to Mr Waithman [*i.e. her brother-in-
law*] yet that Robert is going to study art, and my sister is sad about it, thinks the profession over-
stocked, and has been reading a report of the Artists Benevolent Society, telling how many artists
leave wives and children unprovided for'. She also asked WBY if he could 'ask anyone likely to
know, about an artist, Roger Fry, who Mr Lytton thinks might give R some teaching'. Robert
Gregory enrolled at the Slade School in October 1903.

[1] AG's albums of press cuttings about the theatre movement (1897–1909) are now at NLI.

[2] In a lengthy and detailed review in the *TLS* on 8 May (146) A. B. Walkley (see p. 271, n. 3)
set out 'to record the keen pleasure which an afternoon with the Irish National Theatre has
afforded us, and to do our best to analyse that pleasure'. WBY published a shortened version of
the review in *Samhain*, in September 1903, and Walkley reprinted it in his *Drama and Life* (1907).

[3] Lucien Millevoye (1850–1918), French Boulangist deputy, political journalist, and editor of
La Patrie. MG had been his mistress from 1888 and bore him two children, a boy, Georges
(1890–1), and Iseult Gonne (1895–1954). WBY had known about the situation since December
1898, and had told AG at least some of the details.

I have been dead—capable of neither happiness nor unhappiness'. I told her what Miss Young said about her being happy & she laughed & said she had written nothing of the kind to any body.[4] I asked her about her catholocism & she said that the Catholic party in France was the anti-English party, & so on. She said I have often longed to denounce the priests & could not because I was a protestant but now I can.[5] I thought that her mind had gone back some years to a hardness & aridness she had been getting out of a little. She gave me a fealing of hopelessness. The 'U I' is I am afraid going to come to an end. Griffith has rejected contributions sent in by the Americans who have paid for it & they are angry. She has given it this year already £75 of her own & cannot give any more.[6]

I read out 'Sencan' last night. I think it was received with real enthusiasm. Granville Barker an actor thought it much the best of my things. He liked the little 'wild Hosse' too.[7] Miss Horniman was enthusiastic too & I think she liked it if anything better than the other.

[4] MG's marriage to John MacBride (see pp. 314 ff.) had begun to founder from the start. The honeymoon in Spain ended abruptly owing to her disgust at MacBride's drinking, and there were to be frequent quarrels about this and his sexual behaviour before a permanent separation in 1905. WBY wrote numerous dejected poems in the months and years following the marriage, including one in his 1909 diary (*Mem*, 145): 'My dear is angry that of late / I cry all base blood down / As though she had not taught me hate / By ⟨kindness⟩ kisses to a clown'. The 'dreadful year' was probably 1891, for that August her infant son died of meningitis (see above, n. 3). WBY's poem 'On a Child's Death', initialled and dated 5 Sept 1893 (*YA3*, Plate 16) was probably written in response to this event. For Ella Young see p. 381.

[5] MG had been received into the Catholic Church on 17 Feb 1903 (see p. 314). In a letter of 7 May, justifying the views she had expressed during their meeting, she explained (*G–YL*, 169–71) that she had joined the Catholic Church 'to become more completely united to one of my people. . . . it seemed to me it was better to be frank with each other. You think I acted insincerely in changing my religion. I do not think I did, I know I did what I felt to be right both as to that & as to my marriage, but I never analyse or reason out personal things very deeply or at least not consciously.' WBY did not conceal his continuing disappointment at her conversion and marriage from his friends. On 2 Mar Nevinson called on FF (Bodleian) and 'heard of Yeats's grief about Maud Gonne, who had not even told him about the engagement till the day before it became public as she hates marriage and all sex. They had a sort of understanding to be together in old age. Now he contemplates an onslaught on the Church.'

[6] The *United Irishman* had been in financial difficulties from its beginning on 4 Mar 1899, and in 1901 MG had helped keep it afloat with money she collected in America. Financial disaster was avoided when the paper was turned into a public company later this year, and it managed to run without interruption until 14 Apr 1906, when Griffith changed its name to *Sinn Fein* to make it more obviously the organ of the radical nationalist party that he helped to found.

[7] 'Sencan' was later entitled *The King's Threshold*; see p. 303, n. 2. The actor and playwright Harley Granville-Barker (1877–1946) was director of the Stage Society. His adventurous management of the Court Theatre with J. E. Vedrenne (1868–1930) was a focus of the dramatic revival in London from 1904 to 1907. Barker signed his name with a hyphen until 1918.

The 'wild Hosse' was another name for the protean *Travelling Man* (see pp. 252, n. 4; 264, n. 7). In *Our Irish Theatre* (64) AG recalled that the play 'was first my idea and then we wrote it together. Then Mr. Yeats wrote a variant of it as a pagan play, *The Black Horse.*' In an undated draft (entitled *The Country of the Young*) the travelling man rides a 'wild horse', a 'black horse, he is very wild' (MBY). On 4 May 1903 AG had written to WBY (Berg), 'I hope you are reading Wild Horse & Senchan tonight at your gathering'.

I enclose a letter of Cockerells about the plays.[8]

Yr awy
W B Yeats

I cannot find 'the Star' quite the best of the notices but I will send it when I get a copy.[9]

ALS Berg.

To Lady Augusta Gregory, [6 May 1903]

Dear Friend: I am sorry about your head ache & about Mrs Maxwells stupidity. Who would have thought that a man hung in 1820 could be so disturbing in 1903. Is it ill feeling among the country people she means, for who else is there who knows who 'M^r X' really was? Does she suppose they buy six shilling books?[1] I imagine that she is bitter against you on quite other grounds. If one is doing anything one always rouses anger somewhere or somehow among the people who are not. If for no other reason than that every movement of life is a movement against platitude & platitude is their breath of life. I dined with the Lawrences (Indian

[8] Sydney Cockerell wrote on 4 May (*LWBY* I. 123) to 'congratulate you & your friends most heartily on the unqualified success of Saturdays performances'. He praised the acting and staging, but found 'a touch of insincerity' in *The Hour-Glass* and thought the intonation in *Cathleen ni Houlihan* 'a little overdone'.

[9] The reviewer of the *Star* on 4 May (1) envied the Society's claim to be the 'Irish National Theatre' with its implication 'that a dozen unimportant people, acting a parochial drama and a drama of the soil with such talent as they have gathered from their surroundings do to some extent dramatically represent Ireland to a greater extent than any fashionable drama being acted to-day within our sacred half-mile radius of Charing-Cross can possibly be said to represent England'.

[1] In a letter of 4 May (Berg), AG told WBY that she had received 'a violent letter from Mrs Maxwell, granddaughter of "Mr X" who Anthony Daly was hanged for firing at. She attacks me for waking up ill-feeling, & says it was she herself who told me the story, which she certainly never did. I never thought the landlord who was fired at was blamed, but only the informers of Daly's own class.' Mrs Anne Celestine Maxwell (d. 1914), widow of the Revd Charlton Maxwell (d. 1895), and sister of the Australian explorer Robert O'Hara Burke (1821–61), lived at St Clerans, Craughwell, Co. Galway. Her grandfather had been the target of an assassination attempt in the 1820s, obliquely mentioned in AG's 'West Irish Ballads' (1901), recently republished in *Poets and Dreamers*. Mrs Maxwell had taken offence at AG's discussion of the origins of 'Fair-haired Donough' (4): 'It is likely the people of his own place know still to what family he belonged; but I have not heard it sung, and only know that he was "some Connachtman that was hanged in Galway". And it is clear it was for some political crime he was hanged.'

Lawrences)[2] last night, & [it] seemed to me that our Irish movement has for a chief privilege that it has all the platitudes against it. Somebody said 'what does Ireland want. Why does she not tell us what we are to do. She cries out & yet though we are anxious to do what ever is right she does not tell us.' I said 'nothing simpler, clear out'. The conversation languished after that for a little until somebody began saying how bad politics were for a country & so on. Then somebody spoke of the poverty of the Irish people being caused by their large payments to the priest. I said that the land laws & over taxation had something to do with it but the speaker, who was Lady Lawrence stuck to the priest because she had once known a butler who came in for £300 & she concluded he gave it to the priest "because nobody ever found out what he did with it". I behaved well but would not have been able to do so much longer. I was fortunately going on to Cliffords inn where I lectured to a fair audience on the Psaltery.[3]

I am very glad the interview with Maud Gonne is over. ⟨She seems to be further off from me than ever before⟩ I feal somehow that the Maud Gonne I have known so long has passed away. I had the fealing that a time of bitterness & perhaps of self distrust & of fading life has begun for her.

Tell me what you are doing now at Fion.[4]

I will attend to Quinns letter.

Yr ev

W B Yeats

ALS Berg, with envelope addressed to Coole, redirected to 22 Dominick St, Galway; postmark 'LONDON W. MY 6 03'.

[2] Sir Henry Waldemar Lawrence (1845–1908), younger son of Sir Henry Montgomery Lawrence who fell at the siege of Lucknow during the Indian Mutiny, had become 3rd Bt. Lawrence of Lucknow in 1898. He and his wife, Lady Emily Mary Lawrence, née L'Estrange (1845–1925), lived at Alenho, Ridgway, Wimbledon. WBY had first met them in the late 1880s through the Coffeys; Lady Lawrence was the sister of Mrs Coffey and had been brought up in Ireland.

[3] The illustrated lecture by WBY and FF, 'Recording the Music of Speech', was the first of the Clifford's Inn lectures (see p. 332, n. 3), delivered by WBY in May. It was widely reviewed in the press, notably in the *Manchester Guardian* on 9 May (8), where C. H. Herford (1853–1931), Professor of English at Manchester University, praised the experiment and prepared his Mancunian readers for WBY's forthcoming visit: 'It is thought that, apart from the larger public which might be attracted by a musical recitation of this somewhat novel kind, the numerous teachers in the neighbourhood who have to struggle unaided with the problem of how poetry ought to be "said" will welcome this opportunity of gathering at least some stimulus and suggestion.'

[4] See p. 141. As a sequel to *Cuchulain of Muirthemne*, AG had begun work on her *Gods and Fighting Men*, a retelling of the Fianna legends, for which WBY wrote a Preface. It was published in February 1904.

To John Quinn, [6 May 1903]

London

Satisfactory; wait corrections; Yeats.[1]

TS copy NYPL.

To John Quinn, 6 May 1903

18, Woburn Buildings,
May 6th, 1903.

My dear Quinn,

I have just wired you about book, and am now sending you a corrected copy of the English edition. You will find that I have adopted all your corrections and corrected a bad mistake which you had not noticed on page 81. I do not know why I did not do this long ago,[1] I imagine it went out of

---

[1] On 9 May 1903 (NYPL), after receipt of this telegram, Quinn told Brett that he had written to WBY 'in reply to his suggestions that the contract be terminable and as to the reservation of the dramatic rights and put it up to him to decide. I told him that if the terms were satisfactory he should cable me the word "Satisfactory".' Quinn's letter had been delayed because it was addressed to Coole, and on 1 May (NYPL) he had sent WBY a reminder: 'I hope to receive a cable from you the early part of next week in regard to *Where There Is Nothing*. Unless the Macmillans are advised by me to the contrary, the play will be published here on the 13th.' In his letter to Brett of 9 May, Quinn continued: 'He is undoubtedly making the corrections in the English edition because the page proof which I sent to you is the first proof of the English printers which he probably has changed to conform with the corrections which he cables me to wait for. . . . I am sorry that Yeats did not get my letter before but evidently they cannot publish in England by the 13th and hence we will have to delay and in delaying we want to make the thing right.' Brett copyrighted the book on 13 May, but wrote the same day to Quinn (NYPL) that he would not publish it 'until I know what the corrections are that Mr. Yeats desires made in it, but I hope that it may be possible to put these into my hands in time so that the book may come out on the 20th and that the English publisher will understand that he is free to issue the book at any time after the 13th, i.e. the day of copyright here'. Quinn cabled this information to WBY on 15 May.

[1] See pp. 343, 354. In a letter to Brett of 18 May Quinn reported that WBY had 'adopted all the corrections that I made in your Edition so that the only corrections you will need to make are those indicated on pages eighty and eighty-one'. The correction on p. 80 was to read 'himself' for 'itself' in the sentence 'He says that if a man can only keep his mind on the one high thought he gets out of time into eternity, and learns the truth for itself' (*VPl*, 1127). There were two emendations on p. 81: the deletion of the Second Friar's lines, 'What are they going to do now; are they going to dance?', and, in the following line, 'Third Friar' is changed to 'Second Friar' (*VPl*, 1128). These three changes reached Macmillan's too late, and they do not appear in the published text. A mistake on p. 81 that neither Quinn nor WBY spotted is the First Friar's statement that the Dancers 'are singing the twenty-second Psalm' when in fact the lines are from the twenty-third Psalm—an error which also remained uncorrected in subsequent editions.

my head. I have been very busy at rather exciting kind of work for the last couple of months. I have been doing a couple of new plays for the Irish theatre. I suggested a term of years, not because I had any idea of leaving MacMillan but because I felt in my ignorance of the amounts of royalties given in America that I would like to be able to get terms reconsidered, if necessary should my books become popular in the States. However it is a great point to get one publisher and that publisher Macmillan to take the work in America. I think this English edition which I send you is a good book to look at except in one thing. I prefer my books to be bound in any other colour than green because if one binds an Irish book in green one is thought to have done so on patriotic grounds. I did not see this book before I got the bound copy.[2] Bullen will see Brett[3] I understand here in London in a few days and can arrange with him about the English edition of the poems and of the second volume of plays. I have a fourth little play to add to this volume[4] but I cannot send it to you just yet for I cannot judge it yet. I can hardly send it to you until June. I dictated it to Lady Gregory during two days when I was very tired and I have not got yet to an impartial frame of mind about it. It suggests to me nothing but weariness and yet the few people who have seen it like it very much. My impression is that I shall like it too when I have been able to correct it a little.

I have been meaning to write to you and thank you for your most kind offer in the matter of the Irish theatre.[5] I got Lady Gregory to write for me as well as herself. The theatre has been here in London and has had an astonishing success. They played the "Hourglass", Lady Gregory's "Twenty-five", "Cathleen ni Hoolihan", Ryan's "Foundations" and "A Pot of Broth". The Daily News and the Chronicle the Morning Post the Star the Westminster Gazette and the Pall Mall all were enthusiastic. The Times has not yet noticed it but I had a note from Walkley on Sunday night saying that he was delighted and hoped that they would come over

---

[2] Quinn had in fact just issued 30 copies of a limited edition of the play in light-green boards. The English edition had a dark green spine with grey paper boards, but, on Quinn's instructions that green was not to be used, Macmillan's American edition appeared in dark blue cloth lettered in gold.

[3] See p. 343, n. 2. George Platt Brett (1859–1936), London-born publisher who had become the president of Macmillan in America, established a permanent publishing relationship between WBY and Macmillan New York when he issued *Where There Is Nothing* there. The firm later published *In the Seven Woods* (1904), *The Hour-Glass and Other Plays* (1904), and a 2-volume edition of *The Poetical Works of William Butler Yeats* (1906). Quinn had suggested that since the Dun Emer edition of *In the Seven Woods* was limited, WBY should arrange with Macmillans to sell the American plates for a general English edition.

[4] See pp. 343–4.

[5] Quinn's offer of financial assistance; see pp. 347–8.

again and come often.[6] Everybody was struck by the simplicity and naturalness of the acting. Granville Barker who runs the Stage Society told somebody that there was nobody upon the English stage except Welch[7] who was William Fay's equal in refined low comedy. Indeed we have been all amazed by our success. Lady Aberdeen has asked the company to come over to London in the summer and play before the Committee of the St. Louis Exhibition. She wants to get them engaged to play in the Exhibition in connection with the Irish industry section. I can see that the Company are taken with the idea but whether in a month's time they will be as ready to risk their livelihood I do not know. It would mean their becoming a professional company and returning to tour the Irish towns and to play in Dublin as a National Company in the real sense of the word. I am doing them a rather big poetical drama, big I mean in that it will require fine acting and is very long for my usual one act form.[8] They are enthusiastic and expect to make their biggest success in it. I return to Ireland the first week in June and will go to Sligo and perhaps to Roscommon before I go back to Galway where I hope to finish my poetical drama.

You might wire to Bullen the new date of publication as I imagine that a delay for correction will keep it considerably beyond the 14th, or rather you might get Macmillan to wire.[9]

Yrs sny
W B Yeats

TLS NYPL, with envelope addressed to 120 Broadway, New York, postmark 'LONDON N.W. MY 8 03', with American stamp 'COLLECT 8 CENTS POSTAGE'.

[6] For reviews by the *Daily News*, the *Star*, and *TLS* see pp. 354, 358, 356. Notices of the plays had also appeared on 4 May in the *Daily Chronicle*, which said (7) that 'the acting, though by amateurs, was of a very high standard'; the *Morning Post*, which declared (8) that 'If there is one thing clearer than that we have no national drama it is that the Irish have, and a drama that for sincerity of feeling and simple eloquence of expression can rarely, if ever, have been surpassed'; and the *Westminster Gazette*, which (3) looked forward to 'important results from these humble beginnings'. The reviewer for the *Pall Mall Gazette* of 5 May (11) hoped that the Society would 'before returning to Dublin, give us some more performances. Of their success we do not think there could be a doubt.'

[7] For James Welch see p. 180, n. 2, and p. 263, n. 4.

[8] i.e. *The King's Threshold*.

[9] See p. 360, n. 1. On 15 May Quinn wired WBY (Texas): 'Copyright thirteenth. Publication deferred awaiting corrections. Bullen liberty publish immediately.'

1. W. B. Yeats in 1903 by William Strang.

Rehearsing Willie Wigman
FAYS LITTLE THEATRE

2. A rehearsal of *The Hour-Glass* at the Camden Street Hall in 1902, by Jack B. Yeats.

3. The auditorium of the Abbey Theatre in December 1904.

4. John Quinn and George Russell at the Camden Street Hall rehearsals in 1902 by Jack B. Yeats.

5. The Abbey Theatre in December 1904.

6. Miss A. E. F. Horniman by John Butler Yeats.

7. Lady Augusta Gregory in 1905.

8. Florence Farr playing the psaltery.

9. Arnold Dolmetsch.

10. W. B. Yeats at 18 Woburn Buildings in 1904. See p. 560.

11. Maud Gonne MacBride, Sean MacBride, and John MacBride, published in *The Tatler* in February 1904 as 'Three Irish Irreconcilables in Paris'.

12. *Cathleen ni Houlihan*, St Teresa's Hall, April 1902. See p. 167: 'Maud Gonne played it magnificently, and with wierd power'.

W. B. Yeats by Elliott and Fry.
See p. 487.

W. B. Yeats in 1901 by Pamela Colman
Smith. See p. 387.

W. B. Yeats on his arrival in New York,
November 1903. See p. 466.

16. William Fay by John Butler Yeats.

17. Frank Fay by John Butler Yeats.

19. John Butler Yeats's sketch of John Tay
See p. 348.

18. George Russell (AE) by John Butler Yea

To Maud Gonne, [c. 6 May 1903]

Mention in letter from MG, Friday Evening [? 8 May 1903].
Offering to write her a letter on behalf of the *United Irishman* for American
benefactors,[1] and suggesting a protest about the production of vulgar English plays in Dublin theatres.

G–YL, 153–4, where it is dated '[?March/April 1902]'.

To Lady Augusta Gregory, [8 May 1903]

Dear Friend: I lecture on Tuesday on heroic & Folk poetry, Mrs Emery to
illustrate it on Psaltery. Could you send me that story about the favourite
music of the Fianna, & about Finn liking best 'what happens'.[1] I would
take great care of it & send it back safely. It would be a great help. I suppose if it went Sunday or first post on Monday I would get it by Tuesday
morning. The success of the plays here will help the chanting & all the
more practical sides of my work emmensely. What a beautiful notice
Walkeley has given us, in the Times Supplement.[2] The only unhappy
thing about the performances is that it was not 'the Irish Literary Society'
people but a general fashionable & artistic audience that filled the Hall. In
the evening there were a good many Irish people at the back but on the
whole our own people did not support us (at least Gwynn says they did
not). Those that were there however certainly made up for this by their
enthusiasm.

  I wish I was back in Ireland & at work again there, & with you near
me—London is worse than it was I think.

Yr ev
W B Yeats

---

[1] MG had told WBY of the *United Irishman*'s difficulties when he saw her in London (see
p. 357), and this notion of helping had perhaps just come to him. Since the paper endured
chronic financial problems, the letter may possibly refer to another crisis.

[1] WBY gave the second Clifford's Inn lecture (see p. 332, n. 3), 'Folk and Heroic Literature',
illustrated by FF and Pamela Colman Smith, on 12 May. The passage WBY asks for was eventually published in AG's *Gods and Fighting Men* (1904), p. 312: 'And one time Finn was holding a
feast at Almhuin, and he asked the chief men of the Fianna that were there what was the music
they thought the best. . . . And then Osgar was asked, and he said: "The best music is the
striking of swords in a battle". And it is likely he took after Finn in that, for in spite of all the
sweet sounds he gave an account of the time he was at Conan's house, at Ceann Slieve, it used to
be said by the Fianna that the music that was best with Finn was what happened.' AG evidently
got the extract to him in time, for he used it in the lecture, and retained it in the revised version,
'Heroic Literature of Ireland', which he delivered frequently on his American tour later this year.

[2] See p. 356.

[*On back of first page*]³

⟨(2)⟩
⟨all words must be expressive as words.
simplicity of music necessary.
music of verse the chief end.
fixed notes liberate voice for sub[t]le effects.
Effect of repeated lilt-notes.
　　　　　lilt
Movement against the external.
Future of Art.
Unnaturalness of print.
Poetry will recover power.
All but few too busy to read⟩

ALS Berg, with envelope addressed to Coole, redirected to 22 Dominick St, Galway; postmark 'LONDON MY 9 03'. Wade, 400–1.

To Mary Price Owen,¹ 9 May 1903

18 Woburn Buildings, | Euston Road,
May 9ᵗʰ.,/03.

My dear Miss Owen,
　I am lecturing at Westminster on Friday next on "The Theatre". I shall have to touch lightly on "Chanting in relation to the Stage".² Would you

---

³ These are evidently notes for one of WBY's chanting lectures.

¹ See p. 253.

² WBY's Westminster lecture, 'What the Theatre Might Be', was delivered on 15 May at Caxton Hall, assisted by FF and Miss Owen; see p. 332, n. 3. An advance announcement in the *Daily News* on 13 May (8) reported that the lecture was to be illustrated by Gordon Craig's model theatre, and would address 'the possibility of reverting to the original simplicity of the theatre, in scenery, acting, and elocution'. The notes printed in Hone (190) are probably for this lecture: 'We in Dublin are trying to do our part, and I want to talk to you about a theatre which some of us are trying to build up there. I have made a little model here of a stage where I have every reason to believe realism would be impossible (describe shape of theatre, reason of projecting platform, steps down towards audience, shallow stage, deep wings etc., speak also of lighting). I then go on to describe the secularisation of the theatre caused by the fading of the sanctity of the legends it had once founded itself upon and from the daily life of man. These are two of the marks, shafts of death. The theatre becoming secular was on the high-road to become vulgar, to become merely amusing, to merely tickle the eye. Describe how in Ireland we have the remnants of the old sanctity of the land itself and so are seeing in the ordinary energies of life supernatural energies, are seeking to restore the ancient stage.'

come & do the Angel's part for me out of the "Hour Glass"?[3] I will read the Wise Man's part, I mean that we will do just that one scene. I am going to get M*rs* Emery to do a ballad out of another play of mine. If you will come you will be the greatest possible help to me. I don't yet know where the lecture is to be, but I will let you know as soon as I know myself & I will get a ticket sent to you.

Yours sny
W B Yeats

[*Typed on separate sheets, with instructions in FF's hand*]

The Song of the Wandering Aengus.

Lilted.

> I went out to the hazel-wood
> C   D   B
> Because a fire was in my head,
> B A   C   B   D
> And cut and peeled a hazel-wand,
>   D C   D   B
> And hooked a berry to a thread.
> B   A   C B   D

Spoken

> And when white moths were on the wing
>   D
> And moth-like stars were flickering out,
>   D

Lilted

> I dropped the berry in a stream
> C   D   B A   C
> And caught a little silver trout.
> C   D   B   A   C

---

[3] WBY wrote in *Samhain* (1903) that certain 'passages of lyrical feeling, or where one wishes, as in the Angel's part in *The Hour-Glass*, to make a voice sound like the voice of an Immortal, may be spoken upon pure notes which are carefully recorded and learned as if they were the notes of a song' (*Expl*, 108–9). In his note on 'The Music For Use In The Performance Of These Plays' (*CW* III. 223) WBY wrote: 'I have rehearsed the part of the Angel in the *Hour-Glass* with recorded notes throughout, and believe this is the right way; but in practice, owing to the difficulty of find-ing a player who did not sing too much the moment the notes were written down, have left it to the player's own unrecorded inspiration, except at the "exit", where it is well for the player to go nearer to ordinary song.'

Lilted

When I had laid it on the floor,
　　C　　　　　　D　　B

I went to blow the fire aflame,
B　A　　C　　B　D

But something rustled on the floor
　D　　C　　　　D　　　B

And someone called me by my name.
　B　　A　　C　　B　　　D

Spoken

It had become a glimmering girl
With apple-blossoms in her hair,
Who called me by my name and ran
And faded through the brightening air.

Spoken

Though I am old with wandering
　　　Bb　　　　　　　　　　B♯

Through hollow lands and hilly lands,
　B♯

I will find out where she has gone
　C

And kiss her lips and take her hands;
　Db

Spoken

And walk among long dappled grass,
　　Bb

And pluck till time and times are done
　B♯

Lilted

The silver apples of the moon,
　　Db　　EbDbC Bb　　Db

The golden apples of the sun.
　　Db　　Eb Db C Bb　Db

Dict AEFH, signed WBY; Yale.

To Maud Gonne, [? 9 May 1903]

Mention in letter from MG, Monday [? 11 May 1903].
Sending her the letter on behalf of the *United Irishman*.

G–YL, 154, where it is dated '[March/April 1902]'.

To Florence Farr, 14 May 1903

18 Woburn Buildings, | W.C.
May 14th. 1903

My dear Mrs. Emery,

I hope that your illness is no worse than a day's discomfort and that you will be able to come after all to-morrow. Of course if you are ill there is no more to be said, but if you can come it will be of importance for it is much more important for that lecture to go well than for the Irish Literary Society evening to go well.[1] I shall be quite content if you do one single poem tomorrow. I have had a letter from the editor of the "Daily News" asking permission to interview me on the Theatre and the New Art.[2] Now to-morrow's lecture is got up by people connected with the "Speaker" and the "Daily News." If the lecture goes well it will help towards other lectures. I have an invitation for instance, from Edinburgh and if only we can get a little credit for this double performance of ours it may enable me to get the Edinburgh people to invite us both.[3] In some ways the Theatre is a more taking subject than the New Art itself. I have much more to say

[1] As well as lecturing on 'What the Theatre Might Be' on 15 May (see previous letter), WBY and FF were to lecture on 'Chanting' to the ILS on 16 May.

[2] FF made a timely recovery and G. K. Chesterton praised her performance in the *Daily News* on 16 May (8): 'Miss Florence Farr has developed a beautiful manner of so intoning some selections on a weird-looking instrument as to illustrate Mr. Yeats's meaning almost to perfection. And it is Mr. Yeats's theory that the remedy—at least the only feasible remedy at present, for this reign of vulgarity and cynical inattention which now, as he said in a fine phrase, "has made all the arts outlawed"—is to draw yet closer the circle of culture and to go on performing as specialities the things which were once universal habits of men, singing, telling stories, and celebrating festivals.'
Although the drama critic of the *Daily News*, E. A. Baughan, was attentive to WBY's work and favourably reviewed his London performances, no interview appeared in the paper, probably because it was already saturated with articles about him: on 7 and 13 May there were reviews of 'The Speaking of Verse' (8) and 'What the Theatre Might Be' (8), followed on 16 May by Chesterton's essay, 'Mr. Yeats and Popularity' (see above); WBY was the subject of Quiller-Couch's 'A Monday Causerie' on 18 May (8), and *IGE* was reviewed on 19 May (8).

[3] WBY's lecture in Edinburgh was delayed until 10 Jan 1906 when he travelled alone to speak on 'Irish Heroic Poetry' to members of the Celtic Union. FF subsequently joined him for a joint lecture-tour of several English cities in March 1906.

about it and can group all our activities under this one title. A rich subject like this will enable me to tax you much less. You will always be able to speak to the Psaltery much or little as

[*The rest of this letter is missing*]

Text from Bax, 38. Wade, 401.

To Lady Augusta Gregory, 14 May 1903

18, Woburn Buildings | Euston Road, W.C.
May 14th, 1903.

My dear Lady Gregory

  William Sharpe was in with me last night, and seems to have lived through as many dramatic events as usual. You were concerned in one of them. He met a Mrs. Newton at the Duchess of Sutherland's and the conversation turned on you.[1] She said that she was from your neighbourhood and used to know you long ago and that lately she had thought of calling but had heard that there were three people there "the sort of people that one never hears of and yet hears of, you know, in another way" she did not want to meet these three people who seemed to her very dreadful. Sharpe asked who they were and she replied, not recognising him, "Oh, a Dr. Douglas Hyde, and a Mr. Yeats, and a Mr. William Sharpe". She also added that whenever any royal event came round in Ireland you always hung out a black flag made of crape and that once Miss Maud Gonne and myself had gone out through the country with two red flags, but having failed to get up a demonstration returned to your house. I do not know whether t[h]is is one of Sharpe's fables or not but it is certainly the sort of thing I would expect to be true. Unionist Ireland has always had a gift for fabulous stories about Nationalists. However "The interior of the Duchess of Sutherland's drawing room" arouses my suspicion as a stage direction. Then, too, it was only one of many moving events that he narrated. However I must say that I have occasionally known him tell the same story in quite the same way after a considerable lapse of time so I suppose it is not all a development of that mytho-poic faculty which the Germans have found lately in certain stories he tells me.

  I lecture tomorrow at three thirty on the Theatre and speak on Saturday

---

[1] Probably Alice Newton with whom AG was on visiting terms in Galway and London. Lady Millicent Fanny Leveson-Gower, Duchess of Sutherland (1867–1955), was an author, humanitarian, and friend of AG. WBY was to frequent her salon—one of the most fashionable in London—over the coming years. WBY believed that because of Sharp's susceptibility to symbolic influence 'he never told one anything that was true' (see *Aut*, 339–41).

night on Chanting to the Irish Literary Society. On Sunday I go down to Manchester.

Yrs away
W B Yeats

TLS Berg, with envelope addressed to Coole, postmark 'LONDON MY 14 03'.

To George Russell (AE), *14 May 1903*

18, Woburn Buildings, | W.C.
May 14th, 1903.

My dear Russell,

I send you "Ideas of Good and Evil" a book which will I think have an interest. The only review that has been as yet is as enthusiastic as one could have wished.[1] The book is only one half of the orange for I only got a grip on the other half very lately. I am no longer in much sympathy with an essay like the Autumn of the Body, not that I think that essay untrue. But I think I mistook for a permanent phase of the world what was only a preparation. The close of the last century was full of a strange desire to get out of form to get to some kind of disembodied beauty and now it seems to me the contrary impulse has come. I feel about me and in me an impulse to create form, to carry the realisation of beauty as far as possible. The Greeks said that the Dionysisic enthusiasm preceeded the Apollonic and that the Dionysisic was sad and desirious, but that the Apollonic was joyful and self sufficient.[2] Long ago I used to define to myself these two influences as

---

[1] A review of *IGE* in that morning's *British Weekly* (117) had described it as 'full of profound thought and searching criticism, expressed in a style wonderfully simple and translucent when the novelty and difficulty of the subjects is considered. . . . This book cannot be what is called popular, but to many of us it will seem the most important book of criticism that has been published for a long time, worth a wilderness of clever books.'

[2] 'The Autumn of the Body' (*E & I*, 189–94), first published as 'The Autumn of the Flesh' in the Dublin *Daily Express* on 3 Dec 1898 and already reprinted in *Literary Ideals in Ireland* (1899), is one of WBY's most extravagant expressions of his then held belief in an imminent counter-revolution in the arts, and prophesies a turning away from realism and 'externality': 'We are, it may be, at a crowning crisis of the world. . . . The arts are, I believe, about to take upon their shoulders the burdens that have fallen from the shoulders of the priests, and to lead us back upon our journey by filling our thoughts with the essences of things, and not with things.' WBY was finding Nietzsche's Dionysian and Apollonian categories (or his understanding of them) extremely fruitful in redefining his earlier aesthetic. In his lecture two nights previously (see p. 363), as Nevinson reported in the *Daily Chronicle* of 13 May 1903 (7), he had 'followed out the distinction which Nietzsche drew between the Dionysic and Apollonic moods of poetry, which went to make up the perfection of the Greek drama. The folk poetry, corresponding to some extent to the Greek chorus, is the extravagant cry, the utterance of the greatest emotions possible, the heartfelt lyric of an ancient people's soul. With the heroic poetry comes the sense of form, the dramatic or epic portion of the work of art, the heroic–discipline, which, of course, has no relation to morality

the transfiguration on the mountain and the incarnation, only the Transfiguration comes before the Incarnation in the natural order. I would like to
know what you think of the book, and if you could make your Hermitists
read it I have a notion that it would do them a world of good. I have not
yet been through your poems for the truth is I had to ransack all my books
to find your two published volumes, and now that I have got one at any
rate and I think the two I am up to my ears in the preparation of lectures.
I shall have leisure however after next Tuesday, when I return from Manchester and will let you know at once then.[3]

Yrs sny
W B Yeats

TLS Indiana. Wade, 402.

To Douglas Hyde, *15 May 1903*

Mention in following letter.
Asking Hyde to read the poems of the Gaelic-speaker, O'Ceide, and to
look after him on his visit to the Dublin Oireachtas.

To Lady Augusta Gregory, *15 May 1903*

18, Woburn Buildings | Euston Road,
May 15th, 1903.

My dear Lady Gregory,
    I write in a great hurry as I am getting ready for my lecture which is to
be delivered in a couple of hours or so. I enclose a poem which I have
received from Deeny at Spiddal who took it down from that old man

---

as generally understood or to service to the State and mankind. In romance Mr. Yeats saw the
beautiful beginning of decline from the true heroic age, as we find it in the epics of Finn to whom
the sweetest music was "the thing that happened".'
    [3] As literary adviser to the Dun Emer Press, WBY was making a selection of AE's poems for
The Nuts of Knowledge, published in December 1903 as the Press's second book. Of the thirty-two
poems in the volume, ten each were taken from *Homeward Songs By The Way* (1894) and *The
Earth Breath* (1897), which AE had dedicated to him.

Ready[1] who recited me so many poems at the Feis. Deeny is very anxious that Hyde should hear the old man's poems and especially this poem, the end of which he is not certain that he got'down correctly. I have written to Hyde but as I do not know where he is staying in Dublin and had to write to the Gaelic League Office I did not enclose the poem. I have a recollection of letters written to me at an Irish Newspaper Office which awaited me three months and were then lost. I want you to read the poem yourself and send it on to Hyde. The old man knows no English and gets to Dublin on a Tuesday I suppose next Tuesday. Deeny evidently thought I would be in Dublin and look after him. The old man borrowed £2 to take him to Dublin that he might compete ⟨at the⟩ in some of the competitions. I have sent him 4/- towards his expenses. A few more notices of the plays still continue to come in and all are enthusiastic. I will send you William Archer's notice tomorrow.[2] My uncle is here but I am sorry to say is in Hospital having had an operation performed.[3] Please do not tell this to anybody for I am the only friend or relative who knows that he is there. I go to see him every day and have told him that I will go down and see him in June. The only date I have here, after the twenty-ninth, is a business meeting of the Masquers which I shall get called for as early as possible. I must attend it as they had a very disastrous time last meeting for lack of some articulate person.[4]

Yr ev

W B Yeats

TLS Berg, with envelope addressed to Coole, postmark indecipherable.

[1] Apparently a mishearing by the typist for 'Ceide'. Tomas O'Ceide, a shanachie from Spiddal, Co. Galway, did get to the Feis and went on to win the story-telling competition there. AG had probably first met him in the autumn of 1897 while staying in the district at the house of her friend Lord Morris. It may have been O'Ceide whom WBY met again at the Galway Feis in August of this year, and turned to symbolic account on his American tour, describing to an audience at the University of Pennsylvania on 23 Nov 1903 'an old Gaelic poet said to be one hundred and four years old who had just been rescued from the workhouse, singing one of his old poems. It was a curious sight to watch him, with his shrill, high voice of age, singing to the great audience, honoured again in his own village, where he had for so long been a pauper and an outcast. Many of us felt it was so too with the traditions of Ireland herself; like the pauper and the outcast, they had come back, to be honored again' (*The Alumni Register*, December 1903, p. 100). Deeney (Domhnall O'Duibhne) was the local Spiddal schoolmaster who helped AG in collecting folklore (see p. 265).

[2] Archer's second review of the London performances appeared in the *World* on 12 May, where he observed (784) that WBY was 'not only a poet of the truest and rarest quality, but a man of genuine dramatic talent', and that he had 'the fundamental gift of the dramatist in great perfection—that of throwing himself into the souls of his characters and giving each of them a clear and consistent individuality'.

[3] Although a notable hypochondriac, George Pollexfen was, it seems, genuinely ill on this occasion. He had suffered with neuritis the previous May.

[4] The Masquers Society met on 6 July in Clifford's Inn for their first business meeting, chaired by H. W. Nevinson, who noted in his diary (Bodleian): 'Much difficulty in getting the rules through and amended. . . . Yeats alone spoke with any real light and definite intention.'

To John Quinn, 15 May [1903]

• 18, Woburn Buildings | Euston Road,
May 15th,

My dear Quinn,

A great many thanks for your letter which Lady Gregory has sent on to me. I sent you a corrected copy of "Where there is Nothing" that you might revise the American book.[1] Tomorrow I shall send you my new book "Ideas of Good and Evil". I think you will like it, for it is certainly thoughtful. I feel that much of it is out of my present mood. That it is true but no longer true for me. I have been in a good deal better health lately and that and certain other things has made me look upon the world I think with somewhat more defiant eyes. The book is, I think, too lyrical, too full of aspirations after remote things, too full of desires. Whatever I do from this out will, I think, be more creative. I will express myself so far as I express myself in criticism at all, by that sort of thought that leads straight to action, straight to some sort of craft. I have always felt that the soul has two movements primarily, one to transcend forms, and the other to create forms. Nietsche, to whom you have been the first to introduce me, calls these the Dionysic and the Apollonic respectively. I think I have to some extent got weary of that wild God Dionysius, and I am hoping that the Far-Darter will come in his place.

I am delighted with your New York Irish Literary Society and think it should do great service. Your proposed President Charles Johnson was a school-fellow of mine as I daresay he has told you.[2] He is a clever man, and why he has not done much more with his cleverness I do not know. I dare say he has some great work hidden away. I have not seen him for a good many years and so do not know what he is doing. I think you had better choose for your actors "Cathleen ni Hoolihan" and the "Pot of Broth". They are in prose and that makes them easier. I do not know what to think about "The Land of Heart's Desire" as a play till we have done it in

---

[1] The corrections to *Where There Is Nothing* reached Quinn by 18 May; see p. 360, n. 1.

[2] In his letter of 1 May (see p. 360, n. 1) Quinn had sent WBY 'a notice of the first meeting for the organization of the Irish Literary Society of New York to be held this evening. I had a long talk with Charles Johnston who is doing magazine and newspaper work on this side. . . . all things considered I think that Johnston would make a good President and I am going to do the best I can to elect him.' Charles Johnston (1867–1931), author, translator, and journalist, had attended the Dublin High School with WBY and helped him found the Dublin Hermetic Society. He married Madame Blavatsky's niece in 1888 and, after a short period in the Indian Civil service, eventually settled in New York where he became a free-lance journalist and a prominent member of the Theosophical Society. Quinn succeeded in getting him elected President of the New York Irish Literary Society, and he gave its inaugural lecture on 30 May at the Carnegie Lyceum, speaking on 'The Recent Irish Literary Revival'.

Dublin. It was played in London successfully enough about seven years ago but certainly not well played or played with any right method. I wish I had seen the American performance of it.[3] However you had better stick to the prose for the present, more especially as there will be new verse plays of mine out shortly. These new plays written with so much more knowledge of the stage should act well. Besides they will give you a larger range of selection and so make it easier for you to pick what suits your players. I have not sent you the last play for the little book of short plays because I cannot make up my mind about it. I started it on one plan and re-wrote it on quite a different one and I have got so confused about it that I shall not be able to judge it for a few weeks more I suspect. Should I suddenly change my mind I will send it to you at once. I think it wants a few touches and that I had better forget it a little before I make them. There is a good lyric in it which Mrs. Emery speaks to the psaltery with great success.[4] It reminds me that I must send you the musical setting for the verses in "Cathleen" and in the "Pot of Broth".[5] I have left your letter at home and am dictating this at a typewriting office so please excuse me if I have left any of your questions unanswered. I will write again presently if I have. I must finish now as I am off to St. James' Park where I have to give a lecture on the Theatre. Mrs. Emery and another speaker to notes are to illustrate it.

Yours ever
W B Yeats

TLS NYPL, with envelope addressed to 120 Broadway, New York, postmark 'LONDON N.W. MY 18 03', with American stamp 'COLLECT POSTAGE 8 CENTS'. Wade, 402–4.

[3] In his 1 May letter Quinn told WBY that he hoped the new Society would produce some of his plays, suggesting '*Cathleen ni Hoolihan* and either *The Pot of Broth* or *The Land of Heart's Desire*'. WBY had not seen a performance of the last since the Avenue Theatre productions in the spring of 1894, although the play had been on tour in America in 1901 (see pp. 86–7, 88). In fact, the New York Society staged all three plays on 3 and 4 June at the Carnegie Lyceum.

[4] WBY was still struggling with *The Travelling Man* (see p. 252), and the 'good lyric' was 'The Happy Townland' (*VP*, 213–16), originally entitled 'A Rider from the North', and dated (Emory) 25 March 1903. The poem was published as 'The Happy Townland' in the *Weekly Critical Review* on 4 June 1903, and printed in *CW* III. 237, with FF's notations.

[5] The musical settings for the verses in the two plays were first printed in vol. II of 'Plays for an Irish Theatre'. As WBY explained in 'Note on the Music' (*VPl*, 234, 254), 'The little song in "Cathleen ni Houlihan" beginning, "I will come and cry with you, woman", is sung by our players to an old Irish air, and the lines beginning, "Do not make a great keening" and "They shall be remembered for ever" to an air heard in a dream by one of the players' (i.e. by MG; see pp. 482–3). For the music in *The Pot of Broth* see p. 223, n. 3.

To the Editor of the Academy, [*16 May 1903*]

SIR,—Your sympathetic notice of our Irish plays and players has it that they were produced under my direction. They were produced under the direction of Mr. W. Fay our stage manager, and Mr. F. Fay our teacher of speech, and by the committee of our dramatic society. Mr. W. Fay is the founder of the society, and from the outset he and I were so agreed about first principles that no written or spoken word of mine is likely to have influenced him much. I, on the other hand, have learned much from him and from his brother, who knows more than any man I have ever known about the history of speech upon the stage.[1]

Yours, &c.,
W B Yeats

Printed letter, *Academy*, 16 May 1903 (495). *UP* II. 303–4.

To Sydney Cockerell, 16 May 1903

18 Woburn Buildings
May 16th, 1903

My dear Cockerell, I have behaved very badly in not writing to you, but I have expected each morning to get down to Clifford's Inn. However I have been heavy with a cold and working hard preparing for a lecture which came off yesterday afternoon, and so have not got down to you after all. I am very sorry that I cannot go to you tomorrow, but I am going down to Manchester with Mrs. Emery to give a lecture on Speaking to the Psaltery.[1] We are getting £20 for it so the New Art is beginning to march.

[1] In reviewing the INTS's London productions and WBY's psaltery lecture of 9 May, the *Academy*'s drama critic, E. K. Chambers, had mistakenly described the performances (465) as being 'under the direction of Mr. Yeats. . . . It was an interesting experiment. The best hope for the future of the drama lies in its seeming to writers like Mr. Yeats a possible means of expression for the truth that is in them.'

[1] Henry Nevinson, who took WBY and FF to the train, wrote in his journal that evening (Bodleian): 'Went between violent storms to see Yeats and Mrs. Emery off to Manchester in a 2nd class dining saloon—a good caravan for strolling minstrels. Envied them very much that freedom and absolute devotion to art.' The illustrated lecture in the Whitworth Hall of Owens College, Manchester, on 18 May received a long notice from the *Manchester Guardian*'s music critic, who wrote the following day (7) that 'Mr. Yeats may be on the track of an important discovery' since any restoration of the harmony between music and poetry would 'almost certainly be by some such way as Mr. Yeats's—that is to say, by consulting the poet, who has hitherto not been allowed to exercise the slightest influence over the musician, except in the very rare cases where poet and musician have been identical, as with Wagner and Cornelius'.

I think the proof of the colophon very delightful. When can my sister have the block to experiment with? I know she is anxious for it.[2] I shall get back from Manchester on Tuesday, and Wednesday in all likelihood I shall look in on you and Walker. I want my sisters to bring out a Primer on the New Art. Dolmetsch is ready to write an Essay and to go through Mrs. Emery's notations.[3] To touch them up here and there and pick the best. I have been discussing with Dolmetsch the problem of music printing. As far as I can make out it will be impossible for my sisters to do this part of the work. What I want to know is, would it be out of the question to have the letter press printed by my sisters and the musical notations printed by the Chiswick Press (they have a charming musical type) and these notations made up into a little music book and put into a pocket made in the cover of the Primer? If this would be all wrong I must get Bullen to publish the Primer and to print the whole thing at the Chiswick Press.[4]

Please tell Lady Margaret and her cousin that I am very sorry not to have been able to meet them at your place tomorrow.[5]

Yours ever
W B Yeats

Text from Wade, 404–5.

[2] i.e. of the 'Lady and the Tree' press mark; see p. 335.

[3] A plan that WBY had discussed with Frank Fay the previous winter; see p. 277. The first prospectus of the Dun Emer Press announced a book on 'Speaking to the Psaltery', but it never appeared. Dolmetsch did in fact begin to draft the essay at the back of a notebook inscribed 'Workshop Material' (Dolmetsch), but he stopped in mid-sentence at the beginning of the fifth paragraph.

[4] A number of publishers used the services of the Chiswick Press, which had been founded in 1790 and had built up a reputation for fine printing and design. Bullen's friend, Charles T. Jacobi, was its managing partner and was to become adviser to the Shakespeare Head Press from 1904 to 1907. He had published *Some Notes on Books and Printing* (1892), was examiner in typography to the City and Guilds Institute, and in the *Egoist* of 1 Nov 1914 Ezra Pound was to list him as instructor in printing at his proposed College of Arts.

[5] Lady Margaret Sackville (see p. 155) had become a friend of Cockerell in 1900, when he described her (BL) as 'a lady of 19, who has already written some remarkable verse and from whom I hope for great things in the future'. Her cousin was Margaret Cicely Drummond (*b.* 1880), daughter of 11th Viscount Strathallan. As Cockerell records in his diary, WBY had lately been seeing a good deal of Lady Margaret: on 17 Jan 1903 there had been a conference of WBY, Lady Margaret, Katharine Horner, Emery Walker, and Cockerell 'about the proposed "Celt" which Lady Margaret is to edit'; on 23 Jan 1903 'Yeats called to talk about the "Celt" and Emer Press'; and on 5 Feb 1903 WBY had dined with Lady Margaret, Miss Horner, FF and Cockerell, and afterwards accompanied them to *Othello* at the Lyric Theatre.

To an unidentified musician, 16 May [? 1903]

Mention in following letter.
Telling her that as far as he is concerned she can set his work to music but that his publisher, Mathews, may be entitled to a fee.

To Charles Elkin Mathews, 16 May [? 1903][1]

18, Woburn Buildings | Euston Road
May 16th.

Dear Mr. Elkin Matthews,

I am always getting letters from people asking leave to include verses of mine in Anthologies, or to set them to music. I am not perfectly clear as to what the law is on the matter, whether it is you or I who should give this permission. Till lately Mr. Unwin has always left the matter to me so far as the book of mine that he published is concerned. Lately, however, he has insisted that it is his business and not mine and has begun charging anthologists, against whom he has an old grudge, he charged one £2 a poem the other day,[2] and now I have told him that I shall send all such letters both those from anthologists and musicians to him to answer. I want to be clear as to what you wish to be done, I cannot charge people and will not, and would like to hear definitely from you whether you claim your right or not in the matter. I have just replied to a musician[3] that she has full leave so far as I am concerned but that I believe you have some right, for whatever period of time our agreement runs to. If you do not care to exercise your right I shall give everybody free permission, for I have got tired of finding out the merits of the musicians and discriminating if there were no other reason, and if you do charge I suppose we should share the spoil. People will forgive a publisher for having an eye to business but they certainly will not forgive a poet. I have no pity for musicians who drown my words with complicated modern sentimentality, but I am full of sympathy for the anthologists having been one myself.

Yrs sny
W B Yeats

TLS Reading.

[1] From WBY's letter to Bridges of 20 July 1901 it is evident that he could give permission to anthologists without reference to his publishers, but by April 1905 he had to apply to Unwin to release G. K. A. Bell from charges.

[2] This may have been for 'The Island of Sleep', a passage from 'The Wanderings of Oisin', which was published in *Pearson's Irish Reciter and Reader* in September of this year.

[3] Perhaps Rebecca Clarke, who set 'Aedh Wishes For the Cloths of Heaven', taken from *The Wind Among the Reeds*, of which Mathews had the British rights at this time.

To the Committee of the National Council, [c. *16 May 1903*]

Mention in the *Freeman's Journal* of 18 May 1903 (6).
Requesting that his name be added to the committee of the National Council.

To the Editor of the United Irishman, *20 May 1903*

THE NATIONAL COUNCIL,[1] | 196 GREAT BRUNSWICK STREET | DUBLIN,
20th May, 1903.

DEAR MADAM, OR SIR—In view of the gravity of the situation caused by the report of the visit of the King of England to Ireland, it is imperative that Nationalists should take counsel to ensure that the National opinion of the country shall not be misrepresented, and also to protect the people from being coerced into a makebelieve acquiescence in reception displays, and to protect the children of the people from being used for a similar purpose.

It is clear to every Nationalist that no Irishwoman or Irishman who values National dignity or honour, who realises the condition to which our country has been reduced—a shrunken and still shrinking population—a destroyed trade—a plundered and still overtaxed people—an impoverished country—a Nation with rights stolen and still unrestored—can participate

---

[1] The National Council, originally known as the People's Protection Committee, was formed on 17 May by Edward Martyn, MG, Arthur Griffith, and others. WBY had suggested the idea for it to MG at their meeting of 4 May (see pp. 356–7), and she had written to Martyn about it on 7 May. Its purpose, as reported in the *Freeman's Journal* of 18 May 1903 (6), was to prevent a repetition during the coming royal visit 'of the undue pressure which was brought to bear on the working classes, particularly in Dublin, on the occasion of the visit of Queen Victoria to compel them to participate and to allow their children to participate in festivities and demonstrations of which they disapproved'. A letter from WBY (see above), requesting that his name be added to the committee, had been read out at the meeting. The committee sent a deputation to a nationalist meeting in aid of the Irish Parliamentary Fund at the Rotunda on 18 May 1903, to protest against the possibility of a loyal address being presented to the King, and a fracas occurred, described by AE (Denson, 47) as 'the most gorgeous row Dublin has had since Jubilee time. The Rotunda meeting was a free fight and two M.Ps are incapacitated.' The *Freeman's Journal* on 19 May reported (5) that the deputation, led by MG and including Edward Martyn, interrupted the meeting and that Martyn tried to hide behind MG during her heated exchanges with the Lord Mayor (Timothy Harrington): 'Then someone in the audience threw a chair on to the platform, and some injudicious person on the platform threw one back, and immediately the scene became most turbulent. The deputation and Mr. Martyn made a rapid retreat from the platform, Mrs. MacBride acting as an effective rere-guard. . . . the audience fought in small knots, the Lord Mayor jumped clean off the platform, seized several of the protagonists and separated them.' Partly owing to these demonstrations the Dublin Corporation decided against presenting a loyal address to Edward VII. The National Council was to remain in being after the King's visit, and in September 1908 joined the Sinn Fein movement.

in any address of welcome to the King of England, who can come only as the existing representative of the power responsible for all our evils.

We write from a National point of view, regardless of the different religious opinions of Nationalists. If we wrote from a Catholic point of view, we might ask—Can any Catholic welcome the King who, scarce two years ago, took an oath grossly insulting to their religion?[2]

It must not be forgotten that upon the occasion of the visit of the late Queen of England workers were, against their wills, locked out from their work, in order that the country should be misrepresented as participating in a National Holiday.

Neither should it be forgotten that, not only were the Schools under the control of the Government closed, but that attempts were made to coerce children to participate in loyal displays, and that every effort was made to induce each representative body of the country to vote addresses, while the very workhouse children were pressed into demonstrations, all with the object of misrepresenting the real National feeling of the country.

There can be little doubt but that the same tactics will be adopted to induce or compel the elected Boards, the Unions, and the Schools of the country to a like debasement of the National character.

In order that National self-respect shall be upheld, and that false representations of Irish opinion shall not be made, and that this undue interference with the liberty of the individual shall be prevented, it is essential that a Council, composed of representative Irishwomen and Irishmen, should be established.

We shall be glad to know if you are prepared to join this Council. If so, kindly forward the enclosed Assent.

Yours very truly,
Edward Martyn, Chairman
followed by thirty-seven additional signatures,
including W B Yeats

Printed letter, *United Irishman*, 6 June 1903 (5).

[2] The third part of the Coronation Oath asked 'Will you to the utmost of your Power maintain the laws of God, the true profession of the Gospel, and the Protestant Reformed Religion established by Law? And will you maintain and preserve inviolably the settlement of the Church of England, and the Doctrine, Worship, Discipline, and Government thereof, as by law established in England? And will you preserve unto the Bishops and Clergy of England, and the Churches there committed to their charge, all such rights and privileges, as by Law do or shall appertain to them, or any of them?' This oath was amended in 1937 for the Coronation of George VI.

To Gordon Bottomley, 20 May 1903

18 Woburn Buildings, | Euston Road. | London.
May 20.ᵗʰ.,/03.

Dear Mr Bottomley,

I am lecturing again on "Speaking to Musical Notes" on the afternoon of the 29.ᵗʰ at 5 O'clock. Mrs Emery, 67 The Grove, Hammersmith will supply tickets & information.[1] The National Theatre Co. went back to Dublin immediately after the performances & is not likely to be playing here for some time. If I remember rightly I got a letter from you some time ago to which I did not reply. You had misunderstood something I said about your play.[2] When I said that dramatic verse should be vocal, should have the accent of speech, I did not necessarily mean that it should be conversational. Oratory & song are also speech, I merely meant that it should be really written with that feeling for the natural order of the words & for the cadence of speech that makes easy speaking & easy hearing.

Yrs snly
W B Yeats

ALS Private.

To Lady Augusta Gregory, [22 May 1903]

18 Woburn Buildings | Euston Road.

My dear Lady Gregory: Please wire your permission for me to collect in your name the money due on 'Irish Ideals'; & send me all correspondence between you & Oldmeadow on the subject of royalty etc. A few days ago Oldmeadow demanded £10 from me because I took 'Symbolism in Painting' from 'A Book of Images'. He has been paid the £10 by Bullen who

---

[1] WBY's lecture on 'Poetry and the Living Voice' at Clifford's Inn was illustrated by FF, Pamela Colman Smith, and Mrs Eleanor Elliot, all of whom chanted to the psaltery. Bottomley was in the audience (a ticket survives among his papers), and, as he recalled in *The Arrow* (Summer 1939), p. 11, the experience had a lasting effect on him: 'since I heard that music of words in 1903 (and his words were the most musical of all) I have been increasingly concerned in the re-exploration of the nature and possibilities of spoken poetry which he initiated then'. Sydney Cockerell, who also attended this lecture, as well as one earlier in the day by Shaw on 'The Confessions of a Municipal Councillor', described the lecturers (BL) as 'two of the most gifted Irishmen of the day, and a great contrast between them. Yeats has more wisdom, Shaw of course more cleverness.'

[2] See pp. 260–1. Bottomley had evidently replied to WBY's letter of 24 Nov 1902, commenting on his play, *The Crier By Night*.

will of course pay himself out of my royalties. I had simply forgotten that publication in 'A Book of Images' being publication in a book was not like magazine publication. At the same time £10 much more than I got for essay is exhorbitant, especially as 'A Book of Images' has long ceased to sell.[1] Now Bullen is furious with Oldmeadow because of the tone of his letters & if you give me the right to collect that money Bullen will get a solicitor & amuse himself by getting it out of Oldmeadow. We can then hand it over to the Gaelic League. This new fact will keep him from anoying us on a still pending question—the insertion of an acknowledgement in the book.[2]

I am in a hurry for post.

Yr ev
W B Yeats

ALS Berg, with envelope addressed to Coole, postmark 'NORTH-WEST P.O. MY 22 03'.

To Allan Wade, 22 May 1903

18 Woburn Buildings, | Euston Road, | London.
May 22nd./03.

Dear Mr Wade,

I shall publish in about a week the first volume of "Plays for an Irish Theatre"; it contains a long play which we have not yet performed but which I daresay we will.[1] It will be followed by a book of three or four short plays, but when I don't quite know, anyhow some time this year.[2] One of the short plays—"Kathleen-ni-Houlihan" has been published. You

---

[1] See p. 67. Oldmeadow had published *Ideals in Ireland*, edited by AG in 1901, and also Horton's *A Book of Images* (1898) for which WBY had written an Introduction, part of which he had just republished in *IGE* as 'Symbolism in Painting', evidently without first getting Oldmeadow's permission. In her reply, dated 'Saturday' [23 May 1903; Berg], AG enquired 'Was there ever such a villain as Oldmeadow? I enclose all I have, his agreement. As well as I remember we talked it over, you and I and he, and he said he would write it—And when this arrived, I wrote agreeing to it. The rest of the correspondence consisted of letters from me asking for account, which had no answers, and letters asking for copies, which did not procure any—until you got me some this winter. I hope Bullen will be able to worry him. It makes one ill thinking of his getting that £10— he must feel so proud of himself.' In fact, Bullen had to pay Oldmeadow ten guineas.
[2] An acknowledgement was inserted in the 2nd edition of *IGE*.

[1] i.e. *Where There Is Nothing*. First produced by the Stage Society in June 1904, the play was not staged by the INTS but it was rewritten with AG's assistance as *The Unicorn from the Stars* and put on at the Abbey Theatre on 21 Nov 1907.
[2] The English edition of 'Plays For an Irish Theatre' (*The Hour-Glass, Cathleen ni Houlihan*, and *The Pot of Broth*), did not appear until March 1904.

can get it by sending 6d to Fisher Unwin for a copy of "Samhain", a little periodical which contains it.[3]

Yrs siny
W B Yeats

Dict AEFH, signed WBY; Indiana.

To Ella Young,[1] 22 May 1903

18 Woburn Buildings, | Euston Road, | London.
May 22nd.,/03.

My dear Miss Young,

Thank you many times for your stories. Both are interesting & the one about the fight for the harvest is really of great importance. It completes a link in my argument.[2] These are the "Seven Sanctuaries" are the "Seven Lights" of Celtic Religion—1st. Custom—2nd. Myth—3rd. Dancing—4th. Modes of Obeisance—5th. The Hidden Meaning of vegetable things—6th. "The Meaning of [?]Genus"—7th. The "Dim Shapes of the Blue Wood".[3] I think this is the right order but I am not sure if Custom came first or Myth. I have a memorandum of the thing somewhere but cannot find it at this moment. If anything occurs to you about the "Seven Lights" I shall be glad to hear it. I am afraid that I have been rather a long time about

---

[3] See p. 183, n. 1. *Cathleen ni Houlihan* had been printed by Unwin in the October 1902 issue of *Samhain*, which sold for sixpence. The Caradoc Press edition also appeared in October 1902, but WBY disapproved of it.

[1] Ella Young (1865–1951), poet and writer of children's stories, was the sister of the actress Elizabeth Young. She had been born in Co. Antrim but moved to Dublin, where she took a BA in Law and Political Science. She joined the Dublin Theosophical Society, and AE encouraged her to collect fairy folklore, and included her in his anthology *New Songs*. She cast horoscopes with WBY, but came to epitomize for him the complaisant and spiritualized sentimentality that he despised in the AE circle. A friend of MG's, Miss Young espoused the nationalist cause and supported the Republicans in the Civil War. In 1925 she emigrated to America and lectured on Celtic mythology at the University of California.

[2] WBY had long been interested in fairy battles; in the March 1899 number of *Folk-Lore* he reported (*UP* II. 146) that he was 'collecting material about fairy battles, and am trying to find out when they coincide with May Day, or November Day, or thereabouts, or else with death'. He had spoken of them lately in his Cardiff lecture (see p. 295, n. 4). Miss Young had been in Achill in 1902 and 1903 collecting folklore and conducting visionary experiments with Standish James O'Grady's wife, Margaret. Although she published a number of collections based on mythology and folk-tales, she appears not to have published the story about the fight for the harvest.

[3] In an 1898 note to 'The Poet pleads with the Elemental Powers' (*VP*, 174) WBY wrote: 'The Seven Lights are the seven stars of the Great Bear . . . and these, in certain old mythologies, encircle the Tree of Life . . .'.

replying to you, but my eyesight is bad, so I had to wait to get some one to
read your stories to me & to write this letter.

Yrs sny
W B Yeats

Dict AEFH, signed WBY; LC.

To Lady Augusta Gregory, [c. 24 May 1903]

Dear Lady Gregory: Bullen says you should send a letter like enclose[d] to
Oldmeadow, & also write a letter to me giving me authority—a letter I can
show 'that Meadow'.

I write in great haste.

Yr ev
W B Yeats

ALS Berg. No enclosure.

To Violet Hunt, 26 May 1903

18, Woburn Buildings, | Euston Road,
May 26th, 1903.

Dear Miss Hunt,

I should have very much liked to go to your at home at the Writers
Club,[1] but I am afraid it is impossible as I am lecturing at five o'clock.

Yrs sny
W B Yeats

TLS Berg.

[1] The Writers Club, established in 1892 for women engaged in literary or journalistic work,
had a membership of 300 and met at 10 Norfolk Street, Strand. The invitation conflicted with
WBY's lecture at Clifford's Inn on 29 May.

To Maud Gonne, [*late May 1903*]

Mention in letter from MG, [early September 1903].[1]
Asking about her position in the INTS.

G–YL, 173–4.

To Norah Holland,[1] [*early June 1903*]

Nassau Hotel, | South Fredrick St, | Dublin.

Dear Miss Holland: I got your letter the day before I left London. I would have wired to you & made an appointment but unhappily I mixed you up with somebody else, a woman who was coming up to London for a lecture of mine. I even at the lecture asked in a loud voice for Miss Holland. It was only next day that I suddenly ⟨remembered all about your arrival⟩ hit on the truth. I had not thought you would be in London this year, & that is why you did not come to mind. I am convinced that if one met ones own father in, let us say, Bagdad one would cut him dead. One would only recollect who he was days afterwards.

I am going West on Monday but will be in London again for a few days

---

[1] MG mislaid her reply to this letter, written to her while she was still in Dublin just before her return to France, and did not post it on until early September. Although this reply is now untraced, a covering letter makes it clear that it told WBY of her determination to resign her vice-presidency of the INTS, for the covering letter (*G–YL*, 173–4) re-affirms this intention.

[1] Norah Holland (1876–1925), WBY's Canadian cousin and granddaughter of Matthew Yeats (1819–85), had saved for five years to take a walking tour of England and Ireland. She did make her way to Gurteen Dhas, where she was an immediate success, as JBY reported in an undated letter (MBY), evidently written later this month: 'The cousin Nora Holland has turned up. She is extremely nice—Lilly & Lolly are delighted with her—she has been three months in England going every where on foot. . . . She has written lots of poems on you, & knows everything you have written . . . notwithstanding which depressing facts, she is not in the very least a bore, or aggressive—she looks 18—or 16. . . . She is really a sort of child, kept infantine by imagination & genius. She would be perfect in your Hearts Desire play as the fairy, she has no pose or affectation of any kind, is absolutely truthful.' She later achieved some reputation as a poet, and a selection of her verse, with a reproduction of a JBY sketch of her, was included in *Canadian Poets*, ed. John W. Garvin (1926). AG was a friend of the Francis Hollands, and WBY probably supposed that Norah Holland was related to them.

sometime at end of June or begg[inn]ing of July. If you come to Ireland you will I have no doubt look up my sisters at

Gurteen Dhas,

Dundrum,

Co Dublin.

I hope we may meet later on.

Yr ever

W B Yeats

ALS Southern Illinois.

To Michael Field, 11 June [1903]

RATRA | FRENCHPARK | CO. ROSCOMMON.

June 11

Dear Michael Field: I have been asked by the committee of the "Irish National Theatre Society" to ask you to let us see your "Dierdre".[1] I forget whether you have quite finished it but perhaps you would let us see what you have done. I am confident that we could give a good performance of the play should it prove as I am sure it will adaptable to our methods. I hope you will consent to let us read it at any rate. You had better right [*for* write] to me C/o Lady Gregory, Coole Park, Gort, Co Galway. I shall be there sooner or later; I am at present with Hyde.

Yr Sy

W B Yeats

ALS Private.

[1] 'Michael Field' was the joint pseudonym of Katherine Harris ('Michael') Bradley (1846–1914) and her niece, Edith ('Henry') Cooper (1862–1913). They received this letter on 13 June and, as recorded in their diary (BL), it gave them great delight: 'Nothing could have given me quite such pleasure. To be acted first by that little company, afire with national life, that little company of heads full of a great dream wd. be so much more to my mind than to be acted by Masquers. I want the talking & the faces.' They replied to WBY on 16 June:

It would give me very great pleasure for the Irish National Theatre Society to perform my Deirdre.

It has been laid aside not quite finished. I will have Acts I. II. IV typed as quickly as may be for you to read—with scenario of the incomplete parts.

I care very much for the theme, very much for Deirdre. I should be proud indeed if her own people would chaunt my sorrow of her story-telling.

They began sorting the drafts, dated 1898–1900, at once, and sent the complete play to WBY on 17 July.

To Wilfrid Scawen Blunt, [*12 June 1903*]

RATRA | FRENCHPARK | CO. ROSCOMMON.

Dear Mr Blunt: I wish I could accept your invitation but I am in Ireland staying with Douglas Hyde. I am looking forward very much to reading your Cuchullain.[1] We are getting ready for our Autumn work which will be the most ambitious our theatre has yet attempted. They begin with a poetical play of mine.[2]

Yrs sinly
W B Yeats

ALS Private.

To John Butler Yeats, [c. *14 June 1903*]

Mention in letter from JBY, [? 15 June 1903].
Praising an article by JBY.[1]

MBY.

To George Russell (AE), [*17 June 1903*]

My dear Russell: you can read enclosed to committee but I think on consideration, that the committee had better sim[p]ly refuse 'Sold' & give no reasons.[1] As I am writing privately to you I may as well say that its acceptance would at any time have ended my connection with the theatre. I have not said this to anybody as I do not care for making threats.

I cannot let Lane have the American rights of 'Seven Woods' for I have made certain arrangements there with the Macmillans. There is no reason however why he should not take copies of your book if he proposes a

[1] See p. 202. Blunt had invited WBY to Newbuildings from 13 to 15 June for a weekend party with Margaret Sackville, Katharine Horner, Alfred Austin the Poet Laureate, and Wilfrid Meynell. WBY stayed with Douglas Hyde from 8 to 13 June 1903.
[2] *The King's Threshold.*

[1] This may have been the plea for stronger support for the Royal Hibernian Academy (Murphy, 252), for in his reply JBY said 'I am very glad you like my article—I never see pictures here, except those by the R.H.A. which are not very exciting'.

[1] The INTS had set up a Reading Committee on 2 June to vet plays for production (see pp. 319–20) and Cousins or his friends had evidently seized this opportunity to resubmit his play, *Sold* (see pp. 284, 285, 288–9). It was, however, not produced by the Society.

proper price. There are only a few poems from your new book & considering the price of my sisters book it will not interfear with the new book in
any way.[2]

Yr ev

W B Yeats

I wish you would let me know how your health is. I had meant to ask you
about it on Sunday evening but you did not come.[3]

ALS Indiana, with envelope addressed to 25 Coulson Avenue, Rathgar, Dublin, postmark
'SLIGO JU 17 03'.

To George Russell (AE), [c. 20 *June 1903*]

Rosses Point | Sligo.

My dear Russell: I cannot bring my self to criticise 'Sold' in detail. You
will remember at the time that it was condemned by your self, by Mrs Mac
Bride (who wrote to Griffith saying that she could not understand how he
could publish such a thing) & by myself. I do not under the circumstances
feal inclined to re-read it. I would gladly take great trouble over a play that
was worth it but this is not. A few obvious things occur to me. Act 1 & 2
are quite seperate actions & a play can have only one subject. The first act,
if the husband had put his head through the door from time to time, like
the woman in MacGinlys farce, might have been made an amusing farce of
a rather unintellectual sort. There was no reason why the country woman
might not turn out the beggar woman at any moment, but there is a reason
why the husband in "Sold" should keep out of sight. I do not think however that Cousins could treat this situation for his unfamiliarity with the
writing of farce has made him deal with the love making in a spirit of
winking vulgarity.[1] He would not have done this if conventional stage situ-

---

[2] John Lane had published AE's first two volumes of verse but did not take the American
rights for his new book, *The Divine Vision*; it was published in January 1904 by Macmillans, to
whom AE transferred in the autumn of 1903. Eleven of the poems were to appear in *The Nuts of
Knowledge*, published by the Dun Emer Press at 10/- in an edition of 200 copies in December
1903.

[3] AE had suffered a severe attack of influenza in the late spring.

[1] See p. 288. The play is an ill-constructed two-act farce in which a bankrupt farmer, William
Mawhinney, avoids being sold up by making over his farm to a drunken pedlar and pretending to
be dead. His chief creditor, suspecting that he has been murdered, offers a reward for evidence,
and through a series of improbable machinations his 'widow' obtains the reward, pays off the
debt, and is reunited with her husband. The first act takes place in the Mawhinney's kitchen, and
has as its theme his supposed death and the signing over of the farm to the pedlar. The second
act, set in a Belfast solicitor's office, introduces a number of new characters and involves the

ations had not destroyed his own sense of what befits a writer. The seeming sale of the wife is so described that it would make the audience uncomfortable. Cousins has no originality as a writer—so far as I can judge. His
material is always old, his sentiment always conventional, & I see nothing
for our committee but firmness from the first. Every encouragement we
give him as a writer will only bring trouble on us in the future.

Yr alway
W B Yeats

ALS Indiana.

To Isabel Moore,[1] [c. *23 June 1903*]

C/o George Pollexfen | Rosses Point | Sligo

Dear Mrs Moore: Please excuse half sheet, but I am out of reach of stationery
shops & have no paper. Of course you may use the sxetch of me by Pixie
Smith & welcome. I quite forget it but I have no doubt it is good. Many
thanks for Charles Johnstons article which is well written & intelligent.[2] I

search for Mawhinney's supposed murderers. In the course of the first act both the pedlar and
one of the bailiffs turn out to have been former beaux of Mrs Mawhinney and both attempt to
woo her, causing her husband on one occasion to break cover and threaten the pedlar with violence. The pedlar makes it plain that he considers Mrs Mawhinney to be part of the transaction.

In P. T. McGinley's short farce in Irish, *Eilis agus an Bhean Déirce* (*Lizzie and the Beggarwoman*), a miserly countrywoman, Eilis, fakes death to avoid giving alms to a beggar woman.
While she hides in another room, however, her son decides to teach her a lesson by loading the
beggar with gifts; she puts her head round the door in frequent attempts to stop him but is finally
obliged to reveal herself. The play had been first produced on 27 Aug 1901 by the Fays' Ormond
Dramatic Society for the Inghinidhe na hEireann at the Antient Concert Rooms.

[1] Isabel Kellogg Moore (b. 1872) was a staff-writer on the *Reader* (NY). She wanted Pamela
Colman Smith's sketch, dated October 1901 (see Plate 14), for the August 1903 number (217)
which contained AE's article, 'The Poetry of William Butler Yeats', and her own poem, 'The
Celting Celt', inspired by WBY's work. An enthusiastic admirer of WBY, she described him as
'the high priest of accomplishment' in the *Reader* in February 1903.

[2] Miss Moore had probably sent Charles Johnston's anonymous article, 'The Irish Literary
Revival', which appeared in *Harper's Weekly* on 6 June 1903 (958). In the article, presumably
based on his inaugural lecture to the Irish Literary Society of New York (see p. 372, n. 2), Johnston described the Irish literary revival as 'one of the strongest and most vital forces in the literature of our common language' and defined its characteristics as 'enthusiasm for pure beauty, a
sense of the invisible, the spiritual significance of life, and a keen feeling for the life revealed
through nature, as an intimation of divinity'. Picking out WBY as the head of the movement and
'a born musician in words', he looked forward to the production of his plays by the New York
Irish Literary Society (see pp. 372–3). Johnston's laudatory review of the performances appeared
anonymously in *Harper's Weekly* on 20 June 1903.

had not seen it, though Quinn has sent me most of the papers that spoke of the plays.

Yrs sy
W B Yeats

ALS Yale.

To George E. Morrison,[1] *26 June* [*1903*]

c/o Lady Gregory | Coole Park, | Gort, Co Galway.
June 26

Dear Mr Morrison,

I am very much obliged for the trouble you have taken about the plays. Please tell Mr Fromann that I should be very glad to consider any proposal from him, and I have no doubt Lady Gregory would do so also.

Cathleen ny Houlihan and the Pot of Broth and the Land of Heart's Desire were played successfully in New York the other day under the auspices of the Irish Literary Society of New York.

I have only just got your letter which has been following me about Ireland.

Yrs siny
W B Yeats

TLS Texas.

To John Quinn, 28 June [*1903*]

Coole Park, | Gort, Co Galway.
June 28.

My dear Quinn,

I should have written long ago to thank you for all you have done but my eyes have been much worse than usual and I was moving about. I dont

---

[1] George E. Morrison (1860–1930), journalist and playwright, was drama critic of the *Pall Mall Gazette* (1900–7) and of the *Morning Post* (1907–24). He had praised the recent INTS productions in London, and had probably mentioned them to Frohman. Morrison's first play, *Sixteen Not Out*, was produced in 1892 and Benson staged his *Don Quixote* in 1907. His pamphlet, 'On the Reconstruction of the Theatre', appeared in 1919. Charles Frohman (1860–1915), the American theatrical manager and impresario, included many top companies in the USA and Britain in his theatrical empire. His interest in the Irish drama persisted, and in the spring of 1906 he travelled to Dublin to see productions at the Abbey with a view to an American tour.

know how to thank you enough for all you have done. You must have had endless work, for I know what the production of a play is. The success of the plays has been a great pleasure and encouragement. I remember very well that when I first began to write plays I had hoped for just such an audience. One wants to write for ones own people, who come to the play-house with a knowledge of ones subjects and with hearts ready to be moved. Almost the greatest difficulty before good work in the ordinary theatres is that the audience has no binding interest, no great passion or bias that the dramatist can awake. I suppose it was some thought of this kind that made Keats's lines telling how Homer left great verses to a little clan seemed to my imagination when I was a boy a description of the happiest fate that could come to a poet.[1] My work is I am afraid too full of a very personal comment on life, too full of the thoughts of the small sect you and I and all other cultivated people belong to ever to have any great popularity. But certainly if Finvara, that ancient god, now king of faery, whose sacred hill I passed the other day in the railway train,[2] were to come into the room with all his hosts of the Sidhe behind him, and offer me some gift, I know right well the gift I should ask. I would say 'Let my plays be acted, sometimes by professional actors if you will, but certainly a great many times by Irish societies in Ireland and through out the world. Let the exiles when they gather together to remember the country where they were born, sometimes have a play of mine acted to give wings to their thought'. I would say 'I do not ask even a fiftieth part of the popularity Burns has for his own people, but I would like enough to help the imagination[s] that were most keen and subtle to think of Ireland as a sacred land'.

Edward Martyn, excited I suppose by our success, has taken up another amateur company, and is getting them to play his plays. He took a big theatre for them last week, and I believe paid them. George Moore did the stage management, and the company played the Heather Field and the

---

[1] See 'Fragments of an Ode to Maia' (1818), ll. 7–8, where Keats speaks of Grecian 'bards who died content on pleasant sward, / Leaving great verse unto a little clan . . .'. It was one of WBY's favourite quotations; in *Aut* (120) he recalls that from the age of 17 he had 'constantly tested my own ambition with Keats's praise of him who left "great verse unto a little clan" . . .'. See also *The Poems of William Blake* (1893), p. xxx.

[2] Finvara, who appears as one of the Masters of the Elements in 'The Poet pleads with the Elemental Powers' (*VP*, 174), and as King of the Sidhe in 'The Cradles of Gold' (*UP* I. 413–18), reputedly dwelt in Cruachmaa or Knockma, a hill near Tuam in Co. Galway which WBY would have passed on his recent journey from Sligo. In *The Speckled Bird* (10–11) Peter Bruin points out Cruachmaa 'and fell to talking in a faint and fearful voice of Finvarra who kept his court there and of the great hogshead of some strange liquor that stood by his door that his people might dip their fingers in and touch their foreheads and become invisible, and the fair that people saw there sometimes on a May Day, and of the invisible horseman that came out of the hill and rode hither and thither through all Ireland.'

Dolls House.[3] I wasn't able to get to Dublin to see it, but Martyn seems satisfied with its success. I daresay this company may attract away a few of our actors, but I am not afraid of its rivalry and think it a good thing there should be two companies. Neither Martyn nor Moore would ever have been satisfied with our methods, and they have their own distinct work in training a company for the performance of the drama of social life. Our people have neither the accents or the knowledge nor the desire to play typical modern drama. We will always be best in poetical drama or in extravagant comedy or in peasant plays. Lady Gregory has done us a new play which I think very good, and Bernard Shaw has just written to me to say he will do us an Irish play as soon as he has finished a book he has now on hands.[4]

I am accepting no engagements to lecture in London this autumn or winter, on the chance that I may be going to America to lecture. We will talk that matter over when I see you.

[*In WBY's hand*]:

Many thanks for the new press cuttings which have just come,[5] addressed to Lady Gregory, she sends best regards & many thanks.

Yrs sny

W B Yeats

TLS NYPL, with envelope addressed to 120 Broadway, New York, postmark 'ORANMORE JU 28 03'. Partly in Wade, 406–7.

[3] Martyn and Moore left the ILT in 1902 (see pp. 151, 152) because they wanted productions of realist, not poetic drama. Martyn had in fact been a member of the Players' Club, which mounted occasional performances of plays by Ibsen and other realist dramatists, since the late 1890s, and it had produced *The Heather Field* and *A Doll's House* at the Queen's Theatre from 22 to 26 June 1903.

[4] AG's play was *The Rising of the Moon*, published in the *Gael* (NY) in November 1903, but not produced until 1907. Shaw was writing *The Common Sense of Municipal Trading* (1904), based upon six years' experience as vestryman and councillor for St Pancras. Enthusiastically advocating municipal participation in the development and management of public utilities, he described the tract as 'the best and most important book I have ever written'. Both WBY and the Fays had long been eager that he should write a play for the Society (see pp. 268, 270) and, although he was not to begin *John Bull's Other Island* until June 1904, WBY (no doubt basing his remarks on Shaw's now lost letter) permitted himself to speculate upon its qualities in the 1903 *Samhain*: 'His play will, I imagine, unlike the plays we write for ourselves, be long enough to fill an evening, and it will, I know, deal with Irish public life and character. Mr. Shaw, more than anybody else, has the love of mischief that is so near the core of Irish intellect, and should have an immense popularity among us' (*Expl*, 103).

[5] Quinn had sent WBY reviews of the New York Irish Literary Society's productions which had appeared on 4 June in the New York *American, Evening Sun, Sun, World, Times, Telegram, Herald, Mail,* and *Express.*

To A. B. Walkley, 28 June [1903]

Coole Park, | Gort, | Co Galway,
June 28

Dear Mr Walkley,

I agree with you that 'Where there is Nothing'[1] is very loosely constructed; too loosely constructed I think; I have a plan for pulling it a little more together before it is acted. However it is not quite as ramshackle as you think it. Those children were not Paul's but his brothers, in fact the fools that he begot. If you look again at page 7 and page 16 you will find that the children are a part of the situation. I have tried to suggest without saying it straight out that Paul finds himself unnecessary in his own house, and therefore the more inclined to take to the roads. I think too that I could arrange the acting so that the end of Act I would not be an anti-climax. I see the perambulator on the middle of the stage, or rather I cannot see it, for everybody is standing round it, stooping over it with their backs to me. Is it not the conqueror of all the idealists? And are not all those magistrates but its courtiers and its servants?

I am writing these prose plays knowing well that they are rather a departure from my own proper work, which is plays in verse. I am doing them because prose plays are necessary to our little theatre, and also because one likes to try experiments. I am trying to learn my business and am very grateful for any criticism such as yours. I tried deliberately in 'Where there is Nothing' to see how loose I could make construction without losing the actable quality. Perhaps I have lost it, but whenever I tried at the outset to construct more tightly I found Paul losing his freedom and spontaneity. Other people's souls began to lay their burden upon him. I thought I would try if a play would keep its unity upon the stage with no other device than one always dominant person about whom the world was always drifting away. I am writing a play now in verse but it is in one act, and I

---

[1] Walkley reviewed the published text of *Where There Is Nothing* in the *TLS* of 26 June 1903 (201–2). While acknowledging that the play offered 'something new', he also pointed to its lack of form: 'It is amorphous. Apparently Mr. Yeats disregards form on principle. The five acts are rather arbitrary divisions than really separate elements of an organic whole.' As an example of this arbitrariness he cited the end of Act I, where a potentially dramatic exit is spoilt by the arrival of a group of children, one in a perambulator: 'Mark that we have not seen these children before, and shall not see them again. Nothing is going to be made of the influence on their fate of their father's conduct. The . . . dialogue, people, and incident are all without an atom of dramatic significance. And sometimes, when Mr. Yeats does aim at the dramatically significant, he only achieves the ludicrous. At the close of Act III., after the hero has been arraigning society as represented by his county neighbours, he reserves a Parthian shaft for his brother. "You have begotten fools", he cries. This, if you please, is the sole reference in the play to the fact that his brother has any children at all, and we know nothing of them.'

am more confident in one act.[2] I am dictating this letter, for I have to keep all my eyesight for my play.

Yrs sny
W B Yeats

TLS Kansas, with envelope addressed in AG's hand to 'Times Office', Printing House Square, London, postmark 'ORANMORE JU 28 03'. Wade, 405–6.

To F. J. Fay, [c. *30 June 1903*]

COOLE PARK, | GORT, | CO. GALWAY.

Dear Fay,
  I pass through Dublin on Friday.[1] Can you & your brother come & see me at the Nassau Hotel at 5 oc & have tea with me. Please bring my keys there, or I wont be able to get into my rooms in London. Or if you cant come to see me, leave them in care of Manager at the Nassau.

Yr sny
W B Yeats

ALS Private.

To George Russell (AE), [*2 July 1903*]

at | COOLE PARK, | GORT, | CO. GALWAY.
Thursday

Dear Russell: I go to London to morrow for a few days. Can you come & see me at about six (The Fays come at 5 I think). We can dine togeather & I can catch the train at 7.40.

Yr ev
W B Yeats

ALS Indiana, with envelope addressed to 25 Coulson Avenue, Rathgar, Dublin, postmark 'ORANMORE JY 2 03'.

[2] WBY had dictated the first draft of his one-act verse play, *The King's Threshold*, to AG at Coole from 31 Mar to 11 Apr 1903 (see p. 303, n. 2), and was now evidently making his final copy. The play was first produced in October 1903.

[1] WBY was to return to London for the business meeting of the Masquers Society on 6 July. He had given Fay the use of 18 Woburn Buildings for a trip to London the previous weekend, but in the event Fay could only get off work for 26–27 June.

To Frances Ball,[1] *8 July 1903*

18 Woburn Buildings, | Euston Road.
July 8th.,/03.

Dear Mrs Ball,

Your invitation for June 29th has only just reached me. I have been away & found it on my table when I returned. I am very sorry that I was not in London to have gone to your "at home".

Yr sny
W B Yeats

Dict AEFH, signed WBY; Emory.

To Mary MacMahon,[1] *8 July 1903*

18 Woburn Buildings, | Euston Road. | London.
July 8th.,/03.

Dear Miss Macmahon,

There is a matter which I wish to bring before our "Parliamentary Sub-Committee". It is very important & should be acted upon immediately. I

[1] Possibly Frances Elizabeth Ball, daughter of W. E. Steele, Director of the Science and Art Museum, Dublin. In 1868 she married Robert Stawell Ball (1840–1913), Astronomer Royal of Ireland 1874–92, who was Director of the Cambridge Observatory and Professor of Astronomy from 1892 to his death. He was a Vice-President of the ILS, London, and had been knighted in 1886. His sister had been the first wife of WBY's Bedford Park neighbour, John Todhunter. Mrs Ball's 'At Home' may have been in celebration of her husband's 63rd birthday on 1 July, and may have been held at the ILS, for, as the *Irish Literary Society Gazette* of October 1899 (1–2) explained, '"At Homes" are given by lady members, and the "House Dinners" are organised by gentlemen members of the Society. . . . the hostess of an "At Home" issues special invitations to private friends, but welcomes any fellow member of the Society.'

[1] Mary Catherine MacMahon (1866–1938) was born in Tralee, Co. Kerry. In 1898, after some years as a governess to a French family, she became Assistant Secretary of the Irish Texts Society, of which WBY was a member. In 1900 she became the first paid secretary to the ILS, London, and held this post until 1906 when some injudicious remarks about members of the Society made to a journalist but not intended for publication, appeared in the *Daily News* and she was obliged to resign. In 1908 she went to Canada, where she taught the piano in Toronto, but returned to London in 1916 to help bring up the family of her widower brother.

don't know who is now Secretary to that Sub-Committee & I would be
very much obliged if you would forward the enclosed letter.[2]

Yours sny
W B Yeats

Dict AEFH, signed WBY; Belfast.

To an unidentified correspondent, 8 July 1903

18 Woburn Buildings, | Euston Road.
July 8th.,/03.

Dear Sir,

I found your letter awaiting me on my return a few days ago. I have
written no book called "The Hidden Beauty" & so cannot tell you where it
is to be got.

I wonder if your customer was thinking of a book of mine called "The
Secret Rose", published by A. H. Bullen.[1]

Yrs sny
W B Yeats

Dict AEFH, signed WBY; Private.

To Violet Hunt, [*9 July 1903*]

18 Woburn Buildings | Euston Road.
Thursday.

Dear Miss Hunt: I wish I could go to tea with you in the Dukes Kitchen
garden, which sounds delightful. Is it full of strawberries & are the walks

---

[2] The ILS's Parliamentary Sub-Committee had been formed in 1901 to bring pressure on Irish
MPs to seek government aid for Irish cultural enterprises. WBY was almost certainly asking it to
support the Irish Texts Society, of which he was a member, in its second attempt to raise funds
for the proposed Irish–English dictionary (see p. 350). The matter was of some urgency since
Archbishop Walsh (see p. 412, n. 3) had offered £20 if nineteen others would guarantee a similar
sum before the end of the present month. So far the response had been woefully inadequate, and
Eleanor Hull (1860–1935), Irish historian, folklorist, and co-founder of the Irish Texts Society,
had launched a desperate second appeal. The 'enclosed letter' (now lost), was probably from her.

[1] *The Secret Rose* had been published by Lawrence and Bullen in 1897; the correspondent's
customer was perhaps confusing it with Richard Kerr's *Hidden Beauties of Nature* (1895), a
natural history book, intended for younger readers.

lined with very old high thick box? But most unhappily I am off to Ireland to night.

Yrs sny
W B Yeats

ALS Private, with envelope addressed to Campden Hill, Kensington, postmark 'LONDON JY 9 03'.

To Margaret Cunningham,[1] [*? c. 10 July 1903*]

at | Coole Park | Gort | Co Galway

Dear Madame: I return to you the book you were so good as to lend me— It should have gone back long ago but you cannot think how hard it is for my clumsy fingers to make up a parcel & I have only just got at a friendly bookseller in Dublin. The book is beautiful with a kind of ritual beauty— as of things that have by very energy of fealing passed out of life, as though precious stones were made by the desire of flowers for a too great perfection. All such art delights one, as if it were part of some religeous service speaking to the whole soul, the passions not less than the moral nature uniting it to an unchanging order. Of course one can see influences but there is an origonal nature using all, a nature more delicate & sensitive but less cold [?bold] & logical than Beard[s]leys—whom I knew—How strange that these lyrical & decorative natures shoul[d] so often be short lived— Beardsly Keats, Shelley & lesser men that one has known, though the world has not.

Again thank you.
I remain yr sy
W B Yeats

I am really in Dublin but go to-morrow to the address I have given.

ALS Private.

[1] Margaret Cunningham was a member of a group of aesthetes in Dundee who embroidered designs made by the gifted young Scottish artist, George Dutch Davidson (1879–1901). Davidson had intended to become an engineer, but a severe illness at the age of sixteen left him a semi-invalid and he turned to art. He was much influenced by the Pre-Raphaelites, by Persian decoration, and by the Celtic Movement. One of his pictures was inspired by Fiona Macleod's poem 'From the Hills of Dream', and a drawing by WBY's 'A Dream of a Blessed Spirit' (later retitled 'The Countess Cathleen in Paradise'; *VP*, 124–5). Davidson died at the age of 21, shortly after a European tour, and in 1902 his colleagues on the Graphic Arts Association of Dundee published a memorial volume, *George Dutch Davidson 1879–1901*. Miss Cunningham, correctly surmising that WBY would be interested in the design inspired by his poem, lent him a copy of the book.

To the Editor of the Freeman's Journal,[1] *13 July 1903*

Dear Sir—I have noticed that somebody has said, in most of the discussion about the King's visit, that the King has given us the Land Bill.[2] I have even read that he is going to give us Home Rule. When George the IV. came to Ireland he got a great reception, because it was believed that he was about to give Catholic emancipation. A friend of mine has lately been through all the private correspondence of George the IV. about his visit to Ireland and found there much about the dinners he was to eat and the cooks that were to cook them, but nothing about Catholic emancipation.[3] Whenever Royalty has come to Ireland rumours of this kind have been spread and spread with an object. The Land Bill has not been given to us by English Royalty but won by the long labours of our own people.

Yours, etc.,
W B Yeats

Printed letter, *Freeman's Journal*, 13 July 1903 (6). *UP* II. 304.

[1] This, the latest in the series of WBY's letters protesting against Edward VII's impending Irish visit of 21 July to 1 Aug 1903, was perhaps inspired by MG's address to the Dublin Workmen's Club on 9 July which had been extensively reported in the *Freeman's Journal* (5) on the following morning. Reviewing all the 19th-century royal visits (including that of George IV in 1821), she maintained that they had all been prompted by political expediency and that, despite promises to the contrary, they had done nothing to improve the lot of the Irish people. For other comments on the visit see James Joyce's story 'Ivy Day in the Committee Room'.

[2] The 1903 Land Bill (the Wyndham Land Act) was receiving its 3rd reading and passed the House of Commons on 21 July. After minor modifications by the House of Lords it became law in mid-August. A consequence of John Shawe-Taylor's initiative (see p. 230), the Act offered Irish landlords a bonus as an incentive to sell their estates, which were then offered to the tenants at fixed prices, the initial capital being advanced by the state to be paid back over 68½ years by annuities at 3¼%. Although opposed by John Dillon, Michael Davitt, and the *Freeman's Journal*, the Act did more than any previous measure to solve the Irish land question, and by 1920 nearly 11,000,000 acres had either changed hands or were in the process of being sold. Some nationalists feared that social and economic amelioration of this kind might weaken the people's desire for independence, and this accounts in part for the opposition to the King's visit.

[3] The friend was AG, although 'lately' is an exaggeration, for she had gone through the correspondence in preparing *Mr. Gregory's Letter-Box* in 1898. Writing of George IV's visit to Ireland in the summer of 1821, she notes (151–2) that the 'hopes of the Catholics were raised to their climax in 1821, when George the Fourth came over, it was supposed with the desired gift of Emancipation in his hand. . . . I see no sign in the glimpse we get of the King's counsels in these letters that such a point was even considered amongst his arrangements. His cooks were to be sent, and his horses. . . . But the great question as to whether the promise given by England twenty-one years before was now to be considered as come of age, and kept no longer in abeyance, was, so far as we can see, not even seriously considered.' Catholic Emancipation was not granted until 1829.

To George P. Brett, 13 July [*1903*]

c/o Lady Gregory. | Coole Park, | Gort, Co Galway.
July 13

Dear Sir,

I send you the copy of my book of poems.[1] The pages I send are spoiled pages from my sister's edition. I believe I was to send the book to Mr Quinn, but I imagine he is on his way to Europe at present.

I have not your letter of terms at hand, but I think you were to give me 15 per cent. As my sister's book is ready for the binder, I hope you will let me know the date of publication as soon as possible, in order that I may publish on the same day here. It is most important that the play 'On Baile's Strand' shall be copyrighted in America as a play. I know if Mr Quinn is in New York he will do this for me, but if not, will you kindly see to it, and charge the registration fee to me.[2]

Yrs sinly
W B Yeats

[*In WBY's hand*]
I enclose the portraits you asked for. I dislike my photographs & so do not send any.[3]

TLS NYPL. No enclosures.

To John Quinn, 14 July [*1903*]

Coole Park, | Gort.
July 14

My dear Quinn,

I am sending by this mail the copy for the book of poems direct to Macmillan.[1] I think you asked me to send it to you, but I heard a few days ago in Dublin that you were leaving for Europe on the 10th. I think on the

---

[1] i.e. *In the Seven Woods*, published by Macmillans of New York on 25 Aug 1903. The Dun Emer edition was finished on 16 July and published simultaneously with the American edition. In Quinn's copy of the Macmillan edition WBY wrote (*Bibl*, 68): 'The printer followed my sister's edition in this book without consulting me, & spoilt in copying'.

[2] Quinn had delayed his departure for Europe and was therefore able to copyright *On Baile's Strand*.

[3] No portraits or photographs were published in the Macmillan edition of *In the Seven Woods*.

[1] *In the Seven Woods*, which contained *On Baile's Strand*.

whole it is a good book, though it will suffer to most readers from too much of it being in dramatic form. I am a very slow writer however of everything except dramatic verse, and if I were to wait to have a full book of lyrical narrative poetry I should have to wait years. My next poetical book I suppose will be Senchan,[2] a poetical drama which Fay's company is about to produce.

It is very good of you to send so much money to the company.[3] It is a great deal for one man to give, and we will have to work hard to deserve it. The first object I will keep in mind in the spending of it is to get regular performances all the winter. We couldn't do that as long as we had to look to this body or that other body to guarantee the expenses. We have made a few pounds during the winter, and with that money and your money we will be able not only to have regular performances but to have a proper proscenium and better lighting arrangements and a cottage scene for our peasant plays which will be a true Irish cottage.[4] I think all is going well in the company. We had some troubles last winter but they seem to be passing away.

I am not disappointed by not getting money from the three plays, for I above all people know how many are the expenses, and how few are the profits in an enterprise of the kind.[5] You have helped me enormously in America by performing the plays, of that I am certain.

I wonder why the Archbishop resigned. Was it 'where there is Nothing' or the old Countes Cathleen row? I have never attacked the Church as far as I know, but one must be able to express oneself freely, and that is precisely what no party of Irishmen Nationalist or Unionist, Protestant or Catholic, is anxious to permit one.[6] Lecky left the Irish Literary Theatre and a certain Judge another Society because of things I wrote or said.[7] I am

[2] Quinn had 100 copies of *The King's Threshold* printed for copyright and private circulation in March 1904, prior to A. H. Bullen's first English edition in the same month.

[3] See p. 348, n. 1. On 15 May 1903 (Texas) Quinn had told WBY 'I am sending Lady Gregory a check for twenty-five pounds and am telling her that you can assure the Society that a similar check will be forthcoming a second and a third year. I have also told her that I am sure I can get the other twenty-five pounds from Kelly but if I can't I will be glad to send it myself.'

[4] On 20 Mar WBY had identified this as essential if the peasant plays were to be seen at their best (see p. 334).

[5] Quinn had planned to send WBY a royalty of up to 50% of the proceeds from the New York productions of his plays (see pp. 372–3), but there were no profits from the $500 receipts.

[6] John Murphy Farley (1842–1918), the Irish-born Archbishop of New York, withdrew as an honorary vice-president of the New York Irish Literary Society, when he heard that WBY had also been elected, apparently because he believed WBY to be anti-clerical. Quinn was unable to muster sufficient liberal support to counter clerical hostility, and the Society soon withered away.

[7] William Edward Hartpole Lecky (1838–1903), historian, and Unionist MP for Dublin University, was one of the first guarantors of the ILT and in 1898 had been instrumental in changing the Theatre Patent law on its behalf. Although a close friend of AG's, he had withdrawn his support from the ILT on 3 Apr 1900 in protest at the 'discreditable language' used by WBY and George Moore in their agitation against the Irish visit of Queen Victoria. WBY's political activi-

often driven to speak about things that I would keep silent on were it not that it is necessary in a country like Ireland to be continually asserting one's freedom if one is not to lose it altogether.

I am looking forward to seeing you very soon here in Ireland, so need say no more.

Yours always
W B Yeats

TLS NYPL, with envelope addressed to 120 Broadway, New York, postmark 'ORANMORE JY 14 03'.

To the Secretary of the Irish Literary Society, New York, *14 July* [*1903*]

at | COOLE PARK, | GORT, | CO. GALWAY.
July 14

Dear Sirs: I have great pleasure in accepting the honour you have done me in making me one of the vice presidents of your society.[1] Your society has been a great encouragement to us all & it is certain of doing great service to the movement.

Yours snly
W B Yeats

ALS NYPL, with envelope addressed to the Irish Literary Society, 120 Broadway, New York, postmark 'ORANMORE JY 14 03'.

ties had also offended Sir Richard Henn Collins (1842–1911), Lord Justice of Appeal, as well as Sir Charles Stanford (1852–1924), who told A. P. Graves on 19 Nov 1900 (NLI) that he had resigned from the ILS 'after consultation with Lord Justice Henn Collins; & he has also resigned. They can't have this Yeats on the Committee if they wish to be considered non combative and nonpolitical.'

[1] Quinn had asked WBY to acknowledge his election as an honorary vice-president of the New York Irish Literary Society. The nomination had proved highly contentious because WBY was thought to be anti-clerical (see previous letter), but Quinn had finally managed to push it through, explaining to AE on 3 July (NYPL) that the 'Society is a literary Society and not a theological school. . . . Yeats's election as Vice-President stands.' The election was announced in Quinn's privately printed pamphlet (Harvard), *The Irish Literary Society of New York: Constitution and Officers* (1903).

To W. T. Horton, 17 July [1903]

Coole Park, | Gort, Co Galway.
July 17.

My dear Horton,

I am very sorry about my long delay in answering your letter, but my eyes are very bad these times, and I can only write letters when I have somebody to dictate to. The result is that my letters accumulate, and get quite out of hand. I have a whole bag full of unanswered letters at present. I certainly did not leave your name out with any intention of slighting you.[1] I had a footnote stating where the essay was from but took it out of the last proof. I took it out so far as I can recollect because I had not acknowledged the sources of any of the essays. To do so always seems to weaken the unity of a book. And I have had to pay Mr Oldmeadow £10 for this forgetfulness. When I wrote the essays originally I wrote it so that I could detach the general statement from the rest. In the same way I separated the statement of general principles as far as possible from the description of particular drawings, when reprinting my Blake essays. I did not include your name in a short general list of symbolists because interesting and beautiful as your work often is, I could not name it with mature and elaborate talents like Mr Whistler's[2] and Mr Ricketts', except in an actual introduction to your pictures. I think you are always upon the edge of some memorable expression of yourself and I am always hoping that some chance, the illustration let us say of some book perfectly suited to your temperament, may enable you to find that expression. I hope you will come and see me when I get back to London in the autumn, and bring your horoscope about which I feel very curious.

Yrs sncely
W B Yeats

TLS Harvard, with envelope addressed to 42 Stanford Road, Brighton, postmark 'ORANMORE JY 18 03'.

[1] WBY's essay, 'Symbolism in Painting', which had recently appeared in *IGE*, was based upon the 'Introduction' he had written for Horton's *A Book of Images* (1898), published by E. J. Oldmeadow at the Unicorn Press (see p. 380, n. 1). In revising the essay, WBY had omitted the entire third section dealing with Horton's work, and had deleted references to him elsewhere. Despite WBY's explanation, Horton remained obsessed by the omission. On 30 Mar 1917 he told WBY (G. M. Harper, *W. B. Yeats and W. T. Horton* [1980], 132) that he 'never really got over' the 'blow', which caused him to lose 'all initiative' in his work, and that 'from 1904 silently but ceaselessly a poison has been working'. He revealed that Oldmeadow had urged him to prosecute WBY, but he refused out of friendship, and that he 'never obtained a single farthing' of the £10 paid to Oldmeadow.

[2] James Abbott McNeill Whistler (1834–1903), the celebrated American artist who had settled in London in 1859, and who died on this very day. WBY had admired his 'pictures with patterns and rhythms of colour' (*UP* II. 134) since seeing them in a Dublin exhibition.

To an unidentified correspondent,[1] *17 July* [? *1903*]

at | Coole Park | Gort | Co Galway | Ireland
July 17

Dear Sir

Very many thanks for your note on my work.

I am afraid I cannot promise you a poem. I have just sent to press a new volume[2] so I have nothing unpublished and I am working on a volume of plays which [will] not be any use.[3]

Yr ever
W B Yeats

ALS Private.

To Susan Mary Yeats, [c. *19 July 1903*]

BALLYDONELAN CASTLE,[1] | LOUGHREA.

My dear Lilly: I saw Father O Donovan yesterday in passing through Loughrea. He does not like the S Patrick banner.[2] He does not think it reverent. He was satisfied with the others, but you should not go on with what he calls 'the hurler'. He said he liked it at first but not at all on second thoughts. I had a talk about your banners with Whall, & am trying to find out if there are any eccliastical traditions on the subject that will help you. I will write in a few days when I get answers to certain letters.

Yr ev
W B Yeats

I return to Coole Tuesday.

ALS MBY.

---

[1] The correspondent, and his note on WBY's work, are unidentified, but his request for a poem suggests that he was the editor of a magazine, and the fact that WBY includes 'Ireland' in his address that he was probably an American.

[2] i.e. *In the Seven Woods* which had been finished by the Dun Emer press the day before. WBY had sent Quinn the copy for the American edition three days previously (see p. 397).

[3] WBY was preparing *Plays for an Irish Theatre*, which was to be published in New York and London in March 1904.

[1] Ballydonelan Castle was the home of George K. Mahon (b. 1851), a landowner.

[2] See p. 348. In a letter to O'Donovan of 1 July 1935 (Private) WBY recalled that during his visit at Easter this year (see p. 329, n. 2) he had 'moralised over the broken pane of glass in the fan-light. I think you told me it had been made by a drunken woman who had some distaste for the Bishop. I remember saying it was the only sign of secular activity in the town.'

To Gilbert Murray, 21 July [*1903*]

COOLE PARK, | GORT, | CO. GALWAY.
July 21

My dear Murray—

I am very much amused at what you say about Sturge Moore. I am responsible for putting him on the committee.[1] He is occasionally both a fine poet & a fine dramatist but through some lack in the sympathetic part of the intellect, is hopelessly impracticable. The worst of it is that so far as I can see, his friend Ricketts has our only possible treasure chest—If we are to go on, somebody will have to see Ricketts, I imagine. He raised £150 by publishing Marlowes Faustus at his press, & put aside this £150 for a dramatic experiment—The proposal was, to stage my Countess Cathleen, which I am not at present very anxious to have staged,[2] & Sturge Moore was to train people to speak verse. I have seen for some time that he would never train them if left to himself. He has actually been teaching a number of young ladies, & I dont think with very good results, for he has none of the feelings of an actor. He cant find men to work with him. Now if Ricketts, who could also raise more money, could be put to stage the Hippolitus[3] (he would have no overwhelming objection to throw over Sturge Moore) we would get a beautiful series of dresses & stage pictures & might if we were lucky get tolerable speech. With Ricketts behind us I have not the smallest doubt that we could get a good many subscribers. My great difficulty is, that I dont know how things are done in London, & am necessarily dependent on Miss Craig & the others. I have I confess an instinctive feeling against our method of organization but that instinct may be ignorance—I would have organized the company first—My difficulty is increased by the fact that I am away a great deal—that I may even be in America during the coming Autumn—The only thing I see quite clear in the business is that that £150 ought not to be allowed to go adrift. Can you suggest any method of hooking that money, & Ricketts? After some years of realistic Theatre Libre, the romantic The-

---

[1] The Managing Committee of the Masquers Society; see p. 328, n. 3.

[2] The Vale Press, through which Ricketts raised £150 of an expected £600 from an edition of Marlowe's *Faustus*. The money was earmarked for the Literary Theatre Club's proposed production of *The Countess Cathleen*, but this never took place (see p. 298).

[3] WBY planned to open the Masquers Society with productions of *The King's Threshold* and Murray's translation of Euripides' *Hippolytus*. When these plans fell through, Murray gave the play to William Archer's New Century Theatre, for whom Granville-Barker produced it at the Lyric Theatre from 26 May to 3 June 1904. It was revived in October 1904 as the opening production of the Vedrenne–Barker matinées at the Court Theatre.

atre de l'Oeuvre arose.[4] Now it is just possible that the Theatre de l'Oeuvre might have worked in this way. It might have said to the T. Libre 'Here I am, with a great decorative artist & £150 & a beautiful translation from the Greek, & certain little private ambitions. Are you weary of realism? What do you offer? Conversion is pleasant, & may sometimes be merely partial'—On the other hand, things seldom happen that way—

To be quite serious—I dont think the Masquers should go on unless you & Miss Craig & ⟨the few practical ones⟩ Symons see your way perfectly clearly. I wanted to put Ricketts on the Committee, but Miss Craig objected on the I think quite mistaken ground that he would be extravagant—She had no objection however to getting him to stage a play—I didn't press the point as I knew he could be put on later. Dont think I am trying to shirk my responsibilities. I left all my work here, & went to London merely to attend that meeting—I recognise that I brought you & Symons into this business. I confess I was under the impression that the Stage Society was not only financially in low water, but also wedded to realistic plays which I still think probable[5]—I had been told about their being in low water quite definitely. If I were living in London I should not have the slightest doubt about making the Masquers a success, but I feel I cannot urge anybody to go on with what seems to be a very troublesome business of which I may not for some little time be able to take my share—I really have not set out on this with any thought of having my own plays done, which I can produce in Dublin. I think it would clear up many things if you could have a private talk with Miss Craig & with Symons—

My amanuensis, having got so far says 'Mr. Murray must feel as if he had been given a baby to hold for a minute, & then seen its mother vanish in the crowd—(to America!)'.

Yrs sincely
W B Yeats

[*In WBY's hand*]
This letter is private—not for committee.

---

[4] The Théâtre de l'Œuvre was founded in 1892 by Aurélien-François Lugné-Poë (1869–1940), the French actor and manager, who had started his career at Antoine's Théâtre Libre and Paul Fort's Théâtre d'Art. He directed the Théâtre de l'Œuvre until 1929, staging plays by Ibsen, Bjørnson, Strindberg, Hauptmann, D'Annunzio, and Wilde. WBY had seen his London production of Maeterlinck's *Monna Vanna* in June 1902 (see p. 200).

[5] The Masquers' intended to produce mainly poetic drama. Besides *The King's Threshold* and *Hippolytus*, they planned productions of Marlowe, Congreve, Ford, Sophocles, de Musset, Villiers de l'Isle Adam, Maeterlinck, and Bridges, as well as masques by Purcell, D'Annunzio and Gordon Craig.

[*In AG's hand*]

I have not yet had your [?]Geste[6] read to me—I will in the next day or two, & write—

I have asked Lady Gregory to send you her 'Cuchulain'[7] in hopes it might suggest to you a subject for a play for us over here—

Dict AG, signed WBY; Bodleian.

To the Committee of the Masquers Society, [c. *21 July 1903*]

Mention in following letter.

To Edith Craig, [c. *21 July 1903*]

PRIVATE.

Dear Miss Craig,

You can read the enclosed letter to the Committee if you like, but not this one. I gather from a letter I have had from Gilbert Murray that Sturge Moore has been more or less impracticable about something or other. Murray says 'any course of action that would lead to success would revolt his whole being'. Now I dont know what they have fallen out over, but if it is Ricketts and the Hippolitus, I can make a suggestion. Not a word of ⟨my having made⟩ it to any living soul, but I think Sturge Moore likes to keep at his own girdle the key that opens the Sybil's cave, where Ricketts murmurs prophecies into Shannon's ear. Now you will find it very much more practical dealing with Ricketts than with Sturge Moore. I suggest therefore that you send a deputation to Ricketts and ask him to stage something. A deputation is a compliment, and Ricketts has £150 we want. There is my suggestion, and in the name of everything holy, do not give me away. Of course I make it in ignorance as to what your difficulties are. I am thinking of writing a masque, a sort of mystic astrological marriage, but it is all

---

[6] Perhaps WBY's misreading for *Gobi*, an unpublished play which Murray had apparently adapted from his 1889 novel *Gobi or Shamo*, in which a party of English travellers discover an ancient Greek utopia in the middle of the Gobi desert.

[7] i.e. *Cuchulain of Muirthemne*.

vague in my imagination as yet, and I have a good deal to do before I get to it.[1]

Yr sy
W B Yeats

TLS Tenterden.

To *Wilfrid Scawen Blunt, 26 July* [*1903*]

at | COOLE PARK, | GORT, | CO. GALWAY.
July 26

Dear Mr Blunt: I missed my train & so did not get to you for lunch that day. I had left my card of invitation in Ireland & so did not know that another train would have got me in time. I need hardly say that I was sorry.[1]

When are we to see your play? The company is now rehersing 'The Shadowy Waters' a poetical play of mine, which they have insisted on doing though I certainly expect failure, for it; & are about to start on one which I think the best I have yet done. Lady Gregory has finished a beautiful little play 'at the Rising of the Moon'. It is much better than '25', more simple, more energetic, more buoyant & much more to act in it.[2] May we not see your play before our Autumn plans are finished & all rehersals started.

Yr sincly
W B Yeats

ALS Texas.

[1] WBY continued to work on this unpublished masque into September; see below, p. 409.

[1] Blunt had sent WBY an invitation to lunch at Crabbet Park, his stud-farm in Sussex, where he held his annual public sale of Arab horses on 4 July. Blunt recorded (II. 64) his disappointment that 'most of the fine ladies from London failed to come, only 300 persons sitting down to luncheon in the tent'.

[2] In AG's *The Rising of the Moon* (see p. 390, n. 4) a police sergeant, reminded of his nationalist past, allows a Fenian suspect to escape, despite a £100 reward. Blunt's play was *Fand* (see p. 202).

To Eric Maclagan, 26 July [*1903*]

Coole Park, | Gort, Co Galway.
July 26.

My dear Maclagan,

My sister, who worked for Morris, has started a school of embroidery near Dublin, and has been given an order for nearly sixty banners for Loughrea Cathedral. Every banner is to be different and they are to be all of Irish saints. The few that have been finished have been designed by A. E. or by my brother and my brother's wife. The money given is not sufficient to pay professional designers.

I feel that this may be the first of many large orders, and I am getting anxious about the designs. Quite upon my own responsibility I am trying to collect information, and it occurs to me you may be able to give me some. I have found out from a Catholic Dictionary that banners were in use in processions from the time of Constantine. There must be old drawings of such banners, or some definite tradition as to their shape and as to the nature of the designs. Can you tell me anything about them, or do you know of any book on the subject?[1] Only four of my sister's banners are processional banners. The rest are to be hung at the ends of the pews, in which the members of the sodalities sit on certain occasions. The form she has adopted so far is at any rate simple. The banner is square, and the saint who has generally some emblem associated with him, is worked in colour on a ground of gold coloured silk. Some of the designs seem to me striking, but some do not seem to me sufficiently traditional. That is why I am stirring myself in the matter.[2]

I am afraid I may be giving you trouble, but I dont know who else to turn to for information.

I am looking forward to your edition of the Jerusalem. Bullen showed

---

[1] See pp. 348, 401. SMY had worked as an embroideress for May Morris from 1888 to 1894; see p. 195. Maclagan, who was to publish *A Guide to English Ecclesiastical Embroideries* in 1907, was already gaining a reputation as an expert on the subject, and was shortly to join the department of textiles at the Victoria and Albert Museum. He replied on 29 July 1903 (*LWBY* 1. 126–8), confirming that banners had been used in Byzantium under Constantine and in France under Gregory of Tours. He added that, from the few Byzantine banners that he had seen, 'they tended to be rather like the Roman standards, i.e. elaborate poles with quite a small square cloth at the top'.

[2] In his letter Maclagan assured WBY that 'the only correct traditional shape is square or oblong; the banners with peaked and scalloped ends are a device of ecclesiastical milliners only. Such banners generally bore the figure of a saint with an emblem, as you describe the ones that A. E. and your brother have designed: from motives of economy they were often only of painted cloth.'

me a specimen page in London and I thought it looked very well.[3] I am just finishing a poetical drama which we are going to play in Dublin in the winter.

I remember your reading me one or two very beautiful translations of Irish hymns. Would you mind telling me if they were from the Latin or from the Irish, and where did you get them?[4]

Yrs snly
W B Yeats

TLS Private.

To Michael Field, 27 July [1903]

Coole Park, | Gort, Co Galway.
July 27.

My dear Michael Field,

I have read "Deirdre",[1] and I am afraid it would need a far bigger stage than we are likely to command for a long time to come. The company has just given up the idea of acting a play of Sudermann's for the same reason.[2] I am inclined therefore with your consent not to offer them the play.

To speak quite frankly I do not like it as well as your other work, and I should not like it to be the first of yours to be offered to them. Did you

---

[3] Maclagan and A. G. B. Russell's edition of Blake's *Jerusalem* was published by Bullen in December 1903. The Preface, dated July 1903, acknowledges the editors' indebtedness 'to the patient and sympathetic labours of Messrs. Ellis and Yeats, and our personal obligation to the latter for his ready help and kindness'.

[4] In his reply (see above, n. 1) Maclagan reminded WBY that all the hymns were in the *Irish Liber Hymnorum* published in two volumes by the Bradshaw Society in 1897: 'All the Irish hymns in that book have got English prose translations; but many of the hymns are Latin. I'm sending you two translations of the latter, very fine in the original; but I think the Irish hymns interested you most, and these are very hard (to me) to put into rhyme; I can only get one little one into shape at all, and that I'm sending with the others.'

[1] The five-act play had been sent to WBY on 17 July (see p. 384, n. 1). It is based on the earliest version of the legend, and follows Deirdre's fate from birth to her life and death with Conchubar after the murder of Naoise. Although unbiased commentators might find the play dogged in its construction and over-long, the authors (BL) thought the verse 'very cloudy & soft, the figure of Deirdre very tender', and were consoled in their disappointment by their friends Charles Ricketts and Charles Shannon, who praised the plot, and assured them that 'the fourth Act could be done for twopence by Gordon Craig'. Under the guidance of Ricketts they replied to WBY: 'I quite agree *Deirdre* wd be much too elaborate for your stage. I shall be glad therefore if you will kindly return it to me as [*for* at] once registered.' The play was never produced, but published posthumously by the Poetry Bookshop in 1918.

[2] i.e. *Teja* (see pp. 285, 289), which was eventually produced at the Abbey on 19 Mar 1908.

ever try your hand in a one act play? They are far easier to construct than a long play. I have myself as you know been writing one act plays in prose lately.[3] I have done this chiefly as a discipline, because logic (and stage success is entirely a matter of logic) works itself out most obviously and simply in a short action with no change of scene. If anything goes wrong one discovers it at once and either puts it right or starts on a new theme, and no bones are broken. But I suppose every playwriter finds out the methods that suit him best.

Yours sinly
W B Yeats

TLS Private. Wade, 407–8.

To Edith Craig, 28 July [1903]

Coole Park, | Gort, Co Galway.
July 28.

Dear Miss Craig,

I did get an agenda of last meeting, but it came too late to send back with notes. Your note dated 26th reaches me this morning, and my answer will only reach you in time for the committee if I can manage to send a special messenger to the Post Office, three miles off. This however will not so much matter as I have heard nothing of your arrangements, except that you are to begin in November, and that you would like to have 'Senchan'. I have heard nothing from Sturge Moore and so am not certain what you mean by 'opening ceremony'. Probably you mean an old project we had, a sort of dedicatory ceremony for the Theatre. I had hoped that Sturge Moore would have tried his hand at this, or Symons who would do it very charmingly and easily. I would suggest that whether it be Sturge Moore or Symons or another who undertake it it should be done in consultation with yourself. A thing of the kind must get its effect very largely from measured movement and contrasted costume, and should be worked out in close connection with these things, which are the materials of its expression, just as an embroideress works out her design from the suggestions of the wool and silk she is working in. It is just possible that I might be able to find the time for such a ceremony, but I would have to take that time in all likelihood from work that may be more valuable to you. In any case I could not

---

[3] This was not the first time WBY had suggested they should try prose drama; see p. 260.

definitely promise to do it.[1] The play about 'the starving man' will be finished in another week, and as my Irish players will produce it in October you may have it for November with pleasure.[2]

Gilbert Murray and Symons have both suggested I think that the Irish players should be invited over to perform it. Supposing they could find a day, which is probable, I foresee a difficulty. The caste is fairly large, and the expense of their railway fares &c would be rather heavy for merely one play. I think the Irish Literary Society gave them £50, but Stephen Gwynn would know this exactly. It paid the Irish Literary Society very well, but then there were six plays given and two performances.

I do not know what you have arranged for your second performance, but have heard something about Ricketts staging the Hippolitus.[3] I hope something of the kind can be arranged as I think that Rickett's name and work would be the greatest possible help to us. I find it difficult to say however whether the Hippolitus is or is not a good choice as I left Gilbert Murray's book in a linendraper's (who purloined it) before I had done more than started on it. I should think however from the beautiful translations in the

---

[1] WBY did in fact write an 'Opening Ceremony for the Masquers', originally entitled 'The Marriage of Sun and Moon', in early September 1903. The surviving draft (Berg) reads:

A man comes to one of the galleries of Theatre and blows a horn. The curtains part and a veiled figure comes out.

She asks who seeks her, speaking in rhymed verse. He answers that many people have come from afar to see her face and that they are there gathered together. She replies that she can only unveil her face to her servants and they have wandered away from her, she does not know where they are gone. He replies that they are straying here and there, because they have been blindfolded by her enemies. But now some have been sent for them, who are two [*sic*] young to have been blindfolded by the world, and they are bringing them to her.

In her presence innocence will be able to take the bandages from their eyes, for in her presence no enchantment can endure.

She asks have they their mirrors with them; he says yes, they have kept their mirrors through all their wanderings.

He says I will call them in. He blows the horn again. Many blindfolded people come in, carrying mirrors and led by children. If performed in a hall with a passage down the centre they should come down through the hall, and go up on to the stage by steps. If in an ordinary theatre they will have to come in by the wings.

They express their joy at hearing beauty's voice again, and wish that they could see her. She bids the children to take the hoodwinks off, for in her presence the enchantment is ended. The children take off the hoodwinks. The servants cry out at that alas she is veiled, they want to see her face. She says there are many there who can only see her face in the mirror of her servants the artists, but that her servants can see it. She kneels to God who has made her beautiful. She kneels down with her back to the audience. They say let us hold our mirrors that all who are worthy may see her face in the mirror.

They hold their mirrors so that the reflection can be seen by the audience. The children stand at the two sides of the stage singing the praises of beauty.

[2] i.e. *The King's Threshold*. The Masquers Society disbanded before it could be produced.

[3] A disingenuous attempt by WBY to give wider currency to his own suggestion—see p. 402.

other part of the book, which I read very carefully that we could not have a better choice.

Yours sny
W B Yeats

[*In AG's hand*]
I forgot to send the enclosed notes of Murrays to Walter Crane. Please do so, unless they are ancient history.

TLS Tenterden. No enclosure.

To Eric Maclagan, 31 July [*1903*]

Coole Park, | Gort, Co Galway.
July 31.

My dear Maclagan,

A great many thanks for your information about banners.

It is precisely the kind of thing I want to know. The banners my sisters made up to this are oblong, so that is all right. Their general form is evidently right but I am much more doubtful as to their designs.[1]

My brother's saints strike me as vigorous and simple, but I doubt if they are sufficiently traditional. The trouble is that my sisters are getting only three pounds a banner (or rather their school is for they have nothing to do with the commercial side), and cannot give more than 10/ of this for a design. The result is that they have had to pick, not the best possible designers, but those who will do designs for so small a sum or for the love of God. However now Mrs Traquaire, who has seen their present designs and work has offered to do one.[2] I wish you would try your hand at one. If you would, I would send you list of what saints they have already done. They must be all Irish. It is only at the beginning of what may be a great movement, the fortunes of which may depend on our making the

---

[1] See p. 406, n. 2. The banners have been preserved, and are still used at Loughrea Cathedral on the first and second Sundays of each month.

[2] Mrs Phoebe Anna Moss Traquair (1852–1936) Dublin-born wife of Ramsay Heatley Traquair (1840–1912), Keeper of the Natural History Collection at the Royal Scottish Museum, Edinburgh, was an artist and illustrator of Dante and Rossetti, and became a key figure in Patrick Geddes's Social Union. Besides painting, she also worked in enamels, metal, embroidery, and bindings. After seeing her paintings on 13 June 1906 WBY wrote to AG (MBY): 'I have come from her work, overwhelmed, astonished, as I used to come long ago from Blake, and from him alone. She differs from all other modern devout painters but him in this supreme thing. The nearer she approaches the divine the more passionate become the lines—the more expressive the faces, the more vehement is every movement. To the others the world is full and the spirit empty.'

Loughrea decorations beautiful. Very likely however you are too busy. I need hardly say that if you come across that description of S. Cuthbert's banner I should like to know what it was. Your letter is the first thing that has shed some light on the subject.[3]

Thank you very much for the hymns which I will read during the course of the day. Robert Gregory has got hold of an artist, and is busy drawing old men at the workhouse.

Only four of my sisters banners are for processions, the rest are to be hung on the ends of pews when the sodalities are there.

Yrs ever
W B Yeats

TLS Private.

To the Editor of the United Irishman, [*1 August 1903*]

SIR—I read in the English *Times* of July 25th this description of the room prepared for the King's reception at Maynooth: "The King's room afforded a very pleasant instance of the thoughtful courtesy of his hosts; for, by a happy inspiration hardly to have been expected in such a quarter, the walls were draped in His Majesty's racing colours, and carried two admirable engravings of Ambush II. and Diamond Jubilee.[1] When the King and Queen had taken their places in the refectory, Mgr. Molloy[2] read the following address," &c.

Even a heretic like myself can admire this loyalty, so perfect that it becomes an enthusiasm, not only for the King in his public capacity, but for his private tastes. I can well imagine that the narrow interests of the theological students needed enlarging, and I am glad to think that parishes

---

[3] Maclagan told WBY (*LWBY* I. 127) that there was 'an elaborate description of the Banner of St. Cuthbert at Durham, in a mediaeval account of the rites of that church printed by the Surtees Society'. This was *A Description . . . of All the Ancient Monuments, Rites, and Customs . . . within the Monastical Church of Durham before the Suppression* (1842); the description of the banner, an elaborate working of silver, red velvet, and gold and green silk, made to celebrate the victorious Battle of Durham over the Scots in 1346, occurs on pp. 22–3.

[1] St Patrick's College, Maynooth, was founded by the Irish Parliament in 1795 for the education of Irish priests. In 1910 it became a college of the National University of Ireland. King Edward and Queen Alexandra visited it on 24 July 1903. The King's racing colours were purple and scarlet. His horse, Ambush II, an Irish-bred steeplechaser, had won a number of classic races, including the 1900 Grand National. Diamond Jubilee, another of his horses, had been as successful on the flat, winning the 'Triple Crown' (the Derby, the Two Thousand Guineas, and the St Leger) in 1900.

[2] The Rt. Revd Monsignor Gerald Molloy (1834–1906), former Professor of Theology at Maynooth, was Rector of the Catholic University of Ireland and the author of *The Irish Difficulty, Shall and Will* (1897) and numerous scientific and literary essays.

in which race meetings are held will in future be the ones most desired. Hitherto the priest has been almost the only man in Ireland who did not bet, but that is to be changed, so powerful are the smiles of Royalty. I expect to read in the sporting column of the *Irish Times* that Cardinal Logue has "something on" Sceptre and Archbishop Walsh has "a little bit of allright" for the Chester Cup.—[3]

Yours sincerely
W B Yeats

Printed letter, *United Irishman*, 1 August 1903 (6–7). Wade, 408.

To John Butler Yeats, [c. 6 August 1903]

Mention in letter from JBY, 7 August 1903.
Commenting favourably on an article of JBY's.[1]

MBY.

To T. Sturge Moore, 8 August 1903

Mention in following letter.
Asking Moore to return Frank Fay's letters on acting.

[3] This occasion had given WBY an opportunity to strike back at the two most powerful members of the Irish Catholic hierarchy who were also his most formidable clerical opponents. Cardinal Michael Logue (1840–1924), Primate of All-Ireland since 1887, described by WBY as 'a dull, pious old man' (*Mem*, 120), had denounced Parnell in 1891 and, under the influence of Frank Hugh O'Donnell's *Souls for Gold!*, attacked *The Countess Cathleen* without bothering to read it. Archbishop William J. Walsh (1841–1921) had been educated at the Catholic University under Cardinal Newman, and at Maynooth, of which he had been President before his appointment as Archbishop of Dublin in 1885. WBY blamed him for thwarting his attempts to establish a vigorous New Irish Library (see I. 345, n. 3).

Sceptre, owned by R. S. Sievier, was the outstanding horse of his age: as a 3-year-old stallion in 1902 he had won six races, including four of the five classics—a feat equalled only once before—and he came first in five races in 1903. However, he failed to win the Gold Cup in 1904, to the chagrin of Blazes Boylan and Molly Bloom (see *Ulysses* III. 1659). Walsh was too late to wager on the Chester Cup, run over 2¼ miles on 6 May but, had he been in time, and his 'little bit' indeed 'all right', he would have augmented his archiepiscopal stipend at odds of 10 to 1 when Vendale galloped home by a length, so beating Throwaway (unbacked presumably by Leopold Bloom).

[1] Evidently an article (which may not have been published) attacking the admiration of things English. In his reply JBY said: 'I am glad you like my article. I feel the keenest desire to start a movement against England *socially*—admiration for English character is the greatest possible mistake—its source is largely a hankering after the *flesh pots* of their beastly civilization.'

To F. J. Fay, 8 August [1903]

Coole Park | Gort.
August 8.

My dear Fay,

I send back to you all but one of the articles which you lent me. I am keeping that one for a little time, as I think it may be useful to me in getting Samhain together. You mentioned having one on Antoine's theatre. I would very much like to see it if you could spare it for a little. I have written to Sturge Moore to send me back those letters of yours on the history of acting for possible use in Samhain also.[1]

I am sending your brother Seanchan to-day. (If you are reading it, pronounce 'Shanahan.') If I can get them done I shall send at the same time the maps of the more important positions. I think it will play about an hour and a half. It is quite a long elaborate play, and is constructed rather like a Greek play.[2] I think it the best thing I have ever done, and with the beautiful costumes that are being made for it[3] it should make something of a stir. I am afraid you will have an exhausting part in Seanchan, but you will find plenty to act and the best dramatic verse I have written to speak.[4] Your brother told me that he meant to cast you as Seanchan, and I am very glad of it. I have long wanted to see you with some part which would give you the highest opportunities. Your playing of the Fool in the Hourglass was beautiful, wise and subtle, but such a part can never express anyone's whole nature. It has to be created more or less from without. Your performance of Seanchan will I believe establish all our fames.

I wish very much you could send me the right measurements for a curtain, such a curtain as we can use when our fortunes have improved and our stage grown bigger. I want to get it embroidered if I can. I look upon it as part of the staging of Seanchan, for there is to be a prologue spoken by Mr Russell in the Wise Man's dress.[5] I want the dark dress and the dark

---

[1] None of this critical and historical material was included in the 1903 *Samhain*.

[2] Gilbert Murray's recent translation of Greek plays may have influenced WBY's ideas on dramatic structure. In an appendix to *CW* III. WBY explained (*VPl*, 1284) that *The King's Threshold* was 'founded upon a middle-Irish story of the demands of the poets at the Court of King Guaire of Gort, but I have twisted it about and revised its moral that the poet might have the best of it. It owes something to a play on the same subject by my old friend Edwin Ellis, who heard the story from me and wrote of it long ago.'

[3] AEFH designed and made the costumes for the play at her own expense, but opinions were to differ as to their beauty.

[4] WBY subsequently dedicated the play to Fay for 'his beautiful speaking in the character of Seanchan' (*VPl*, 256).

[5] At the end of August WBY rewrote the Prologue for Fay and published it in the *United Irishman* on 9 Sept 1903; it was not, however, used in the production since 'owing to the smallness of the company, nobody could be spared to speak it' (*VPl*, 314).

curtain to fix themselves on the minds of the audience before the almost white stage is disclosed. If I cannot get the measurements by Monday it may be too late, as the designer who is now here is going away.[6]

Russell hears there were 'brilliant rows' last Monday, but he doesn't know what they were about. I suppose there is no secret; if not I should like to know. All theatrical companies make rows but ours seems to have more than the usual gift that way.[7]

Yrs ev
W B Yeats

TLS Private, with envelope [NLI] addressed to 12 Ormond Road, and postmark 'GORT AU 9 03'. Wade, 409–10.

To Eric Maclagan, 12 August [1903]

Coole Park, | Gort, | Co Galway.
August 12.

My dear Maclagan,

Many thanks for your letter. I have waited to write until I could give size of banner. They are nineteen inches by thirty four inches. It will be very good of you if you will design a banner for my sisters. I am sure anything you do will be done with artistic feeling and in a right tradition. I am not quite satisfied with any design they have got as yet, and am anxious for a really good one.

The Saints there are already designs for are S. Columbanus, Attracta, Kevin, Berach, Dioclui(?)[1] Torlath, Laurance O'Toole, Ciaran, Ita,

---

[6] Presumably Robert Gregory, who was to help design a number of Abbey plays, or his unnamed artist friend, mentioned on 31 July (see p. 411).

[7] Friction was a constant threat at rehearsals, both because of the clash of temperaments and because the Fays' insistence on professional standards seemed mere bullying to the less committed members of the Company. James Cousins recalled (NLI) how when 'the word went round, "Frank is very nosey tonight" . . . we girt up our loins to resist our own tempers', and Padraic Colum remembered AE, present at a row during a rehearsal of his *Deirdre*, saying 'I foresee that the National Theatre Society will go down in a sea of fists' (*Dublin Magazine*, Oct–Dec 1949, p. 16).

[1] The query is WBY's. He was evidently dictating the names of the saints to AG from a handwritten list which he had difficulty in reading.

Brigit, Drecla, Columkill, Patrick, Colman, Asicus, and a sister of S Patricks.[2]

The figure[s] are worked on a gold coloured ground. Saint Brendan has also been engaged, and the saint must be an Irish one. I write in haste to catch early post.

Yrs sny

W B Yeats

TLS Private, with envelope addressed to Bishopsthorp, York, postmark 'GORT AU 12 03'.

To Edith Craig, 14 August [*1903*]

Coole Park, | Gort, Co Galway.

August 14

Dear Miss Craig,

I have heard from Gilbert Murray of Mrs Pat Campbell's proposal which he says he has also communicated to you. I think it should be

---

[2] St Columbanus (*c.* 543–615) was born in Leinster and had a controversial life as a missionary monk in Europe. St Attracta was a native of Sligo, and founded the convent of Killaraght (WBY borrowed her name for the heroine of *The Herne's Egg*). St Kevin (d. *c.* 618) was founder and Abbot of Glendalough. St Berach was the Abbot of Cluain Choirpthe in Connacht. St Dioclui was St Deicola or Deicolus (d. *c.* 625) an Irish disciple of Columbanus, who founded the Abbey of Lure. St Torlath, a misreading for Torbach (d. 808), Abbot of Armagh. St Laurence O'Toole (Lorcan Ua Tuathail; 1128–80), Abbot of Glendalough and Archbishop of Dublin from 1162 to his death, acted as peacemaker between Strongbow and the Irish chieftains after the English invasion of 1170. St Ciaran (*c.* 512–*c.* 542) was founder and Abbot of Clonmacnoise. St Ita (d. *c.* 570), founded the convent of Killeedy in Limerick where she led an ascetic life and was said to have educated a number of Irish saints, including St Brendan, the patron saint of Loughrea Cathedral. St Brigid (d. *c.* 525) the founder and Abbess of Kildare, was the subject of numerous stories and legends and widely venerated; she is the patron of blacksmiths and healers. St Drecla may be a misreading for St Declan, a pre-Patrician missionary, born in Co. Waterford. St Columba (Colum Cille) of Iona (*c.* 521–97) was born in Donegal and founded the monasteries of Derry, Durrow and Iona (in 563), from where he exerted an important missionary influence on Scotland and the north of England. St Patrick (*c.* 390–? 461) the Patron Saint of Ireland, was born in Britain and enslaved in Ireland; he escaped, but returned in 432 and helped to convert the nation to Christianity from his see in Armagh. There are about 300 St Colmans, but this was Colman of Lindisfarne (d. 676), an Irish monk of Iona, who became Bishop of Lindisfarne, the most important Irish monastery in Northumbria, but resigned in 664 after the Synod of Whitby where the king of Northumbria decided that in his kingdom the date of Easter should be calculated by the Roman rather than the Irish method; Colman subsequently founded monasteries on Inishboffin and in Mayo. St Asicus, a coppersmith, was one of the earliest disciples of St Patrick and the first Bishop of Elphin. St Patrick had two sisters, Assicus and Lupait, both holy women, although according to some accounts he ordered the death of Lupait for the sin of lust (see below p. 447, n. 2).

accepted, if the details can be arranged.[1] The point of course is the using
of our audiences for 'trying plays in their possession'. But I suppose they
are not likely to be so anxious for literary experiment as to swamp us. If we
accept however we should I think keep very close to the definitions in our
prospectus. If they can only perform for us plays which have a sentiment
of beauty we should do well. I think by what I know of Mrs Pat that she
would not object to this limitation. Her proposal is something like one that
you yourself made at the beginning. You proposed if I remember rightly
that certain people should be appointed as sort of honorary members.
They were to be called advisers I think and Miss Terry was to be one. I am
the more ready for the acceptance of this proposal because I have always
thought that the Masquers would not be able to experiment in new stage
methods to any great extent. They will use existing actors for the most part
and must accept their methods. I think experiment must be carried out by
some company of performers like that of Antoine or our National Theatre
Society. I say this because I think that Sturge Moore is like myself chiefly
interested in changing the stage methods. It may perhaps influence him to
accept Mrs Campbell's proposal if I suggest that this change of methods
must be made by some small company which would be invited to perform
by the Masquers. Our present business must be to organize talent and not
to create it, and above all to organize an audience. This new proposal
might make our fortunes as organizers. I have no fear that our authority as
founders of the society would be seriously interfered with by the bringing
in of these distinguished persons who will be much too busy to meddle
unduly. I think the whole business is so important that it should not be
rejected by a small meeting of committee. The arguments for and against it
might be formulated in writing, and absent members asked for an opinion.
At the same time this is always an imperfect method as it is hard to discuss
things by post. You can read this letter to the committee, if you like. Of
course I am so far away that I dont know details of your work, how many
subscribers you have and so forth.[2] Circumstances change so rapidly that
an opinion sent through the post is likely to make one look unpractical.

I am going to Dublin tomorrow for a couple of days to cast "Seanchan"
which is just finished, and which is to be performed in Dublin on Sept 24,

---

[1] Murray had approached Mrs Campbell in July about playing his *Hippolytus* for the Masquers
Society, but on 3 Aug she wrote (Bodleian) that she must decline his offer. It seems that she had
subsequently offered to co-operate with the Society if it would mount experimental productions
of plays she wished to stage commercially, but nothing came of this.

[2] Edith Craig had estimated that 300 members' subscriptions would be needed to pay for a
half-season, but they were slow in coming in, and by 7 July only 40 had been received. On 23 July
Symons had written more hopefully to Murray (Bodleian): 'Subscriptions and promises are coming in, & £68 is actually in hand'.

25, 26.[3] Miss Quinn, our leading actress, is envied by her fellows for having hit a policeman on the head with a soda water bottle in defending a
black flag during the King's visit.[4] Perhaps you had better not read this
sentence to the Committee.

Yours sincely
W B Yeats

TLS Tenterden.

To F. J. Fay, [*14 August 1903*]

Coole Park
Friday.

My dear Fay,

I shall be at the Nassau Hotel before 30c tomorrow, and hope to find a
note saying when I can see you.

I send the new scene between Seanchan and his pupils.[1] I think you will
find it enriches the play greatly. I want the whole opening of the play done
in a grave statuesque way as if it were a Greek play. I would like to read it
through to all the actors, and to discuss all the details. I shall bring the
other additions which are very few tomorrow.

Yrs sny
W B Yeats

TLS Private.

[3] In the event, *The King's Threshold* was not produced until 8–10 Oct.

[4] This incident occurred on 20 July, the day before the beginning of the royal visit. MG had
outraged her Unionist neighbours in Coulson Road by hanging out a black flag, and the police
were called in to keep the peace. When one of the loyalist neighbours climbed on to her roof to
capture the flag, Maire Quinn, who was lunching with her, hurled a bottle and knocked him
down. The anonymous Unionist was transformed into a policeman in the retelling, and this is
how MG recalled the story in a much later radio interview. The incident quickly became part of
WBY's mythology of the wild Irish: on 26 Mar 1904 he told Nevinson (Bodleian) 'of the Irish
contemplative societies & their joy when they had cracked a policeman's head with a soda-water
bottle'.

[1] WBY had evidently rewritten the scene (*VPl*, 262–8) in which, at King Guaire's instigation,
his pupils urge Seanchan to abandon his hunger strike for the restoration of the poets' ancient
rights, but are so impressed by his defence of poetry that they return to the King to plead on his
behalf.

To Gilbert Murray, 14 August [1903]

Coole Park, | Gort, Co Galway.
August 14

My dear Murray,

I have written to Miss Craig to say I think Mrs Campbell's offer should be accepted. I dont think it will injure our artistic aim if we keep our influence which should be easy, and it will certainly save us a great deal of trouble. I dont care so long as we have the arrangement of a few performances, and so long as the plays performed keep fairly within the definitions of our prospectus.

"Seanchan" will not be finished until this afternoon. I go to Dublin tomorrow to cast it, and will let you have a copy as soon as I can. It is to be played in Dublin on Sept 24, 25, 26 th. I wish you could manage to come over and see it.

Of course I agree with you about the beauty of the Deirdre story,[1] but I think the end of Lady Gregory's book, the luring out of Cuchulain and the lamentations of Emer for instance, even more beautiful. I may be influenced though by the fact that Deirdre is getting a little hackneyed here. Everybody writes plays and poems about it and none of them good. As the story has touched you, I wish you would write a play on it, it might have an immense popularity here, and rescue the story from its betrayers. Lady Gregory ordered the book for you long ago, and asks me to enclose Murray's[2] note. She says if you dont want two copies you might give one to Lord Carlisle.[3]

Yrs snry
W B Yeats

TLS Bodleian.

---

[1] Murray had perhaps written to remonstrate with WBY for turning down Michael Field's *Deirdre*. See also p. 404.

[2] i.e. John Murray, AG's publisher.

[3] Murray's father-in-law; see p. 339. AG had known him during her years in London and dined with him. A gifted landscape painter, Rothenstein described him (*Men and Memories* [1932], II. 67) as 'a link between the Impressionists and the Pre-Raphaelites. . . . he had an accurate eye and a charming mind, and the figures he put into his landscapes always had distinction'.

To Edith Craig, [late August 1903]

at | COOLE PARK, | GORT, | CO. GALWAY.

My dear Miss Craig:
I will send a sketch of that opening ceremony[1] to Sturge Moore in a couple of days & send a copy of 'Sencan' to yourself. I am very busy. I have to supply the "National Theatre Society" with a whole winters work in comedy. I mean I have to get or write a number of plays. I have done scenarios for friends who are new to the work & am getting new work of Hydes translated & writing a good deal myself. Sencan comes out on Sept 24 25 & 26 if all goes well. I shall be in London soon after. I go to America about first week in November I think.

Yr ev
W B Yeats

I am writing a quaint prologue for 'Sencan' in Dublin. It is to be spoken by an old man in a red dressing gown & night cap.[2]

APS Tenterden.

To Eric Maclagan, 24 August [1903]

Coole Park, | Gort, Co Galway.
August 24.

My dear Maclagan,
    If the King Aengus that he comes of was Irish, do St Fillan by all means. If not, either of the others that you name.[1]
    I shouldn't do a border to the banner as none of the others have it. Simply a figure or figures on a gold coloured ground. I think I sent to you the measurements of the banner. I should have written before but I had to go to Dublin to attend the first rehearsals of my play 'The King's Threshold' which will be played if all goes well at the end of September. Thank you

---

[1] See p. 409, n. 1.   [2] See p. 413.

[1] Maclagan had taken up WBY's suggestion that he should do a banner for Loughrea Cathedral, and had chosen the early 8th-century St Fillan, associated with Wexford and Ross-shire. WBY sent Maclagan's letter to SMY, who wrote on 28 Aug 1903 (Private) that it was 'very good of you to say you will design a banner for me' and to give him specifications, adding that she had 'as yet only one design St Brendan', and that he should do 'any Saint you like as long as he or she is Irish.' She wrote again on 3 Oct with 'many thanks for the Saint he is very fine & quite workable except for your charming interlacing which I am afraid I may find impossible to do . . .'.

very much for the description and sketch of S. Cuthbert's banner,[2] both very interesting, and for your offer of the loan of the missal, I think if you would let me see it some time when I am in London it would be useful to me in making suggestions to my sisters. We have got a very good design for a banner of S. Brendan the voyager, I like it the best we have yet. I look forward very much to seeing yours, which I suspect will be in the best tradition.

Yrs snly

W B Yeats

TLS Private.

To W. G. Fay, 31 August [1903]

Coole Park | Gort,
August 31

My dear Fay,

I have changed my mind about the prologue, and have written one for you to speak instead of one for Russell.[1] You will have to put on a long red dressing gown which you can wear over the Kinvara man's[2] dress if necessary. I hope you wont mind being your own uncle. I have an uncle but I cannot sacrifice him, as he is my only wealthy relation, and may be in the theatre besides, nor is he so unlike my old man that he mightn't find himself in it.[3] I think the Dublin audience will really be started by this glimpse

---

[2] See p. 411, n. 3. The sketch was Maclagan's own, for the Surtees Society volume contains no illustrations.

[1] See p. 413. The prologue (*VPl*, 313–14) is spoken by the supposed aged uncle of one of the actors in the play. Its function is to explain that WBY has altered the sources so as to 'put the poet in the right', and that in his version Seanchan does not die at the end because otherwise 'the ending would not have been true and joyful enough . . . and poetry would have been badly served'. It also tells that after his successful vindication of the poets' rights Seanchan abandoned the Court and sequestered himself among the poor people of the hills. WBY was to alter this ending during the fatal hunger-strike of Terence MacSwiney, the Lord Mayor of Cork, in 1920, and in all versions of that play thereafter Seanchan dies.

[2] William Fay took the part of the philistine Mayor of Kinvara in the first production of the play.

[3] George Pollexfen (see p. 72), who, like the prologue-speaking uncle, was constantly worrying about his health.

of a family jar.[4] I am longing to know what you think of the prologue. Dont let them arrange any more of the programme for a few days, there are some plays on the way to you.

Yours ever
W B Yeats

TLS Harvard.

To the Duchess of Sutherland, [late August 1903]

at | COOLE PARK, | GORT, | CO. GALWAY.

Dear Duchess of Sutherland: your letter was sent on to me here after some delay. I am very sorry not to have been able to send you anything for your book. I was busy every moment of my time over a play in verse for my little Irish company & now that it is in rehersal other work in connection with the company has arisen. It is just the time of the year when I am most busy. Your project is an interesting one & I am sorry not to have been able to help it.[1]

Yr sny
W B Yeats

ALS UCLA.

To the Duchess of Sutherland, [early September 1903]

at | COOLE PARK, | GORT, | CO. GALWAY.
Sept 1903

Dear Duchess of Sutherland: I have had a letter from Masefield as well as from yourself about my contribution to your book.[1] I did not think it could

---

[4] At the end of the prologue the old man bemoans his aches and pains, and complains that 'it would be better for me, that nephew of mine to be thinking less of his play–acting, and to have remembered to boil down the knapweed with a bit of threepenny sugar, for me to be wetting my throat with now and again through the night, and drinking a sup to ease the pains in my bones.'

[1] The Duchess of Sutherland (see p. 368) was President of the Potteries and Newcastle Cripples' Guild, instituted in the china and earthenware producing towns of North Staffordshire to give employment to crippled children. For the Guild's benefit she was putting together an anthology of poems by living poets, *Wayfarer's Love*, which was published in October 1904, and to which WBY eventually contributed 'Old Memory' (*VP*, 201). The 44 contributors included many leading poets of the period, and the cover was designed by Walter Crane.

[1] Masefield contributed 'Being Her Friend' to *Wayfarer's Love*.

much matter to you, but as it seems that it does I will do my best to send you something but I am afraid it will be prose. I have written only one lyric this summer & that went long since to some editor.[2] I am the slowest writer of rhyme I know of & cannot do it at all unless I have great quiet and very soon I shall be in Dublin or London amid a whirl of things. I think I could do you a little essay called perhaps "the black centaur" & of a kind that would not be irrelevant to your purposes.[3] Masefield has suggested that I send you a page or two out of a play but I cannot think that any part of one of my rather carefully constructed little plays could be turn [*for* torn] from its context & keep much meaning. Let me know however if prose will not do.

Yours snly
W B Yeats

ALS UCLA.

To Florence Farr, [*early September 1903*]

Mention in following letter.

To Edith Craig, [*early September 1903*]

at | COOLE PARK, | GORT, | CO. GALWAY.

Dear Miss Craig: I have sent 'Sencan' or 'The Kings Threshold' as I call it [to] Mrs Emery to be copyrighted & have asked her to let you have copy the moment she is done with it, which should be in a few days.[1]

Yr ev
W B Yeats

[*At top of card*]
I have sent sketch of ceremony to Sturge Moore.

APS Tenterden.

---

[2] 'The Happy Townland'; see p. 373, n. 4.

[3] Although WBY published no essay with this title, the image continued to fascinate him and in 1922 he wrote a poem, 'Suggested by a Picture of a Black Centaur', first printed in *Seven Poems and a Fragment* and subsequently revised and retitled 'On a Picture of a Black Centaur by Edmund Dulac' (*VP*, 442).

[1] FF copyrighted *The King's Threshold* with *Heads or Harps*, *The Rising of the Moon*, *In the Shadow of the Glen*, and *Riders to the Sea* in late September, for they were entered in the Lord Chamberlain's register on 5 Oct 1903.

To Maud Gonne, [c. 8 September 1903]

Mention in letter from MG, 9 September [1903].
Sending her *In the Seven Woods*; discussing her attitude to the INTS, and the performing rights of *Cathleen ni Houlihan*;[1] enquiring whether she would be in Dublin for the autumn productions; telling her that he has a cold; that his eyes are still troubling him; that he is writing 'a National play with Lady Gregory', but does not intend to put his name to it;[2] and asking her for introductions in America where he may be going to lecture.

G–YL, 174–5.

To Stephen Gwynn, 13 September [1903]

Coole Park, | Gort, | Co Galway.
Sept 13

My dear Gwynn,
It is not yet settled whether I am going to America, but if I do go I shall leave London early in November.
I have left unanswered a letter from Barry O'Brien, asking what plays the National Theatre Society should perform.[1] I think the programme should be arranged later, when we have had time to try our new plays. We have several plays that I think will be popular. I have no doubt you are right about Christmas being the best time for the plays, but I shall probably miss them if I go to America. On the 24th 25th & 26th of this month we are opening the season with 'The King's Threshold', a long one act verse play of mine; 'In the Shadow of the Glen' a comedy by Synge, and 'Cathleen ny Houlihan.' I wish very much you could manage to come over. We have got new scenes and costumes for everything, and in any case 'The King's Threshold' is the most ambitious thing we have attempted.

[1] In her reply MG said that the INTS had been 'a great disappointment to me & to all the nationalists interested in it', and went on to repeat allegations that Willie Fay was considered antinational, and that he had spoken slightingly of nationalist societies and drove hard bargains when playing for them. She also pointed out that since *Cathleen ni Houlihan* had been published it was out of copyright and that WBY had in any case given it to her 'for the use of any of the National Societies & particularly said it might be played by any of them & was not to be considered Fay's particular property'.
[2] i.e. *Heads or Harps* (see p. 295, n. 2). MG thought it a pity not to sign a nationalist play as 'it would do away with some of the misunderstandings that Fay's ridiculous talk has caused'.

[1] Following the success of the first foray (see pp. 354–6, 361–2), Stephen Gwynn and Barry O'Brien of the ILS were eager to arrange the INTS's second visit to London, although this did not finally take place until 26 Mar 1904.

I think it is the best thing I have ever done in dramatic verse.

I am correcting today the proofs of *Samhain*, it will have a new play of Dr Hyde's with translation by Lady Gregory and a new play by Synge.[2]

Yr snly

W B Yeats

[*In AG's hand*]
Remembrances from me
           A.G.

TLS Belfast. Wade, 410.

To James Sullivan Starkey,[1] [*15 September 1903*]

COOLE PARK, | GORT, | CO. GALWAY.

Tuesday

My dear Starkie—

You offer me the alternatives of Tuesday 22nd. & Thursday 24th. Is not 24th the first night of the theatre? If some change in the date has been made, please send me a wire, as it must be given correctly in *Samhain* & I am now revising the proofs—I have come to the conclusion that I would sooner give my lecture after the plays,[2] we will be all too busy beforehand

---

[2] Hyde's *Teach na mBocht* (*The Poorhouse*), written in collaboration with AG, was published in Irish and English in *Samhain* (1903). It was not produced at the Abbey Theatre until 3 Apr 1907: AG subsequently rewrote it as *The Workhouse Ward*, and it was performed under this title on 20 Apr 1908. Synge's *Riders to the Sea* was first produced at the Molesworth Hall on 25 Feb 1904.

[1] James Sullivan Starkey (1879–1958), actor, poet, and essayist, wrote under the pseudonym of Seumas O'Sullivan. His first volume of verse, *The Twilight People*, was published in 1905. He later founded and edited the *Dublin Magazine* (1923–58) and published two collections of literary and biographical essays, *Essays and Recollections* (1944) and *The Rose and Bottle* (1946).

[2] Starkey, who was a founding member of the INTS, had asked WBY to lecture on the Theatre during the week of the performances, which were postponed until early October (see pp. 409, 427). No evidence of a formal lecture by WBY has come to light, and it is probable that he agreed with Starkey that it should take the form of a curtain speech after the opening performances on 8 Oct. This he gave, and with very important consequences, for it was a major factor in persuading AEFH to make the INTS the offer of the Abbey Theatre. A substantial report of what he said appeared in the *Freeman's Journal* on 9 Oct, and he printed a fuller version in *Samhain* (1904) under the title 'The Play, the Player, and the Scene'. He called for non-realistic plays, performed by actors who had been trained to speak musically, against a background of non-realistic scenery, and he also said that the INTS should stage foreign masterpieces as well as Irish drama. The speech was not to everyone's taste. It was attacked in the *Irish Independent* on 13 Oct (see below, p. 444, n. 3), and Joseph Holloway complained (*Abbey Theatre*, 27) that 'Mr. W. B. Yeats was called after both his plays, and held forth at the end of *Cathleen ni Houlihan* in his usual thumpty-thigh, monotonous, affected, preachy style. . . . He generally makes a mess of it when he orates. Kind friends ought to advise him to hold his tongue.'

& the performances may lead to criticisms which I should like to answer—
Do as you like about the Audience—whether it is big or little I shall be
content—We can discuss the matter when I get to Dublin—

Yrs sny

W B Yeats

Dict AG, signed WBY; TCD; with envelope addressed to 80 Rathmines Road, Dublin, postmark 'ORANMORE SE 15 03'.

To A. E. F. Horniman, [*16 September 1903*]

Mention in following letter.

To F. J. Fay, [*16 September 1903*]

at Coole Park | Gort | Co Galway.

My dear Fay: No I have not heard from your brother about the new development. I think it is very probable that Peter White[1] did think that we
were going to produce the plays. You know how vague people are about
such things. I think that a political theatre will help us greatly in the end
by making it easier for us to keep a pure artistic ideal. It will satisfy the
propagandist feeling & at the same time make plain the great effectiveness
of our work. All progress is by opposition, & by polarization. The pity is
we will I suppose lose Digges. I cannot change the name of 'Samhain'
now[2] (it was I that gave the name to the *Cumman-naGael* festival when I
suggested it to M^rs McBride) for it is my own title & it will be easy to

---

[1] The suspicion with which William Fay was regarded by various nationalist clubs, initiated by
his refusal of Colum's *The Saxon Shilling* (see p. 310), had been aggravated by accounts of the
anti-national nature of Synge's *In the Shadow of the Glen*, now in rehearsal, and MG, Dudley
Digges, and Maire Quinn had decided to set up a rival company, the short-lived Cumann na
nGaedheal Theatre Company, which took responsibility for the production of five plays at the
Molesworth Hall during the annual Samhain festival, 31 Oct to 3 Nov 1903. Peter White, an amateur actor, was secretary of Cumann na nGaedheal and president of the Celtic Literary Society,
Dublin, both of which were to support the new Company, but he had evidently not yet heard of
the split, and supposed that Fay would be responsible for the Samhain productions, as he had
been in 1902. White had played the Governor of Dublin Castle in the Fays' production of Alice
Milligan's *The Deliverance of Red Hugh* on 27 Aug 1901 (see p. 96).

[2] Fay had evidently asked WBY to change the name of the INTS periodical, *Samhain*, to avoid
confusion with the new Company. In the 1903 *Samhain* WBY anticipated 'a more or less permanent company of political players, for the revolutionary clubs will begin to think plays as necessary as the Gaelic League is already thinking them. Nobody can find the same patriotic songs and
recitations sung and spoken by the same people, year in year out, anything but mouldy bread. It
is possible that the players who are to produce plays in October for the Samhain festival of
Cumann na n-Gaedheal, may grow into such a company' (*Expl*, 100).

explain things if any confussion rises. I think we should all welcome this new theatre in every way we can, & keep it from causing bad feeling.

I have written to Miss Horniman to say that if Silver paint will do for the harps to wire or write to your brother not to send them when she gets my letter.

Hyde has been asked by our rivals for leave to play his 'Nativity' & the 'T.C.D. Play'. He has refused leave for 'The Nativity' but gives leave for the other.[3] I think we should certainly do 'the Nativity', & I have already been thinking out the stage, but Hyde thinks we should get some convent to do it first if possible—Hyde thinks this might be managed—or could we do it for some religious society or the like. However we can talk over this later. You will get some new plays in a few days, & then we can consider all these matters.

I will return cast filled in either with this or in a day or two. Who is to play 2nd cripple? I see no name set down.[4]

'Samhain' has been sent to the publishers, so it is beyond the reach of change. It will contain a lot of notes & a new play by Hyde & Singes 'Riders to the Sea'.

Yrs always
W B Yeats

ALS Private, with envelope [NLI] addressed to 12 Ormond Road, and postmark 'GORT SE [1]6 03'.

To A. H. Bullen, [mid-September 1903]

at | COOLE PARK, | GORT, | CO. GALWAY.

My dear Bullen: send me the copies of new edition of Ideas here.[1] I have sent your note to my sister. I must have forgotten to give your name.

I will see you shortly in London about poems Etc. I propose to keep back the narrative & lyrical part of my sisters book till I have finished a Masque I am working at[2] & then to re-publish it with the new poems. This will make 3 volumes to be arranged for

[3] AG provided the scenario for Hyde's *Pleusgadh na Bulgóide* (*The Bursting of the Bubble*), a satirical skit on Mahaffy, Atkinson, and other anti-Gaelic dons at Trinity College, Dublin, who had opposed the teaching of Irish as an Intermediate subject in Irish schools (see p. 85, n. 3). WBY's new 'rivals' produced the play at the Molesworth Hall on 2 Nov; it had been published in the *New Ireland Review* in May 1903. AG also gave Hyde the scenario and English translation for his *Dráma Breite Críosta* (*The Nativity*; see p. 224), first published in the Christmas Number of the *Weekly Freeman* on 13 Dec 1902 (11), and subsequently in *Poets and Dreamers*. It was put on in Sligo Convent in December of this year.

[4] The Second Cripple gave E. Davis his first and last appearance in an INTS performance.

[1] The second edition of *IGE* comprised 1,090 copies.   [2] See pp. 408–9.

A book of poems (containing contents of seven woods up to page 25 (will space out a good deal) and new poems).[3]

The Hour Glass Etc being volume II of plays for Irish Theatre (This contains 3 prose plays)

The Kings Threshold (Etc) being vol III of same. (This contains new play in verse now rehearsing in Dublin & 'On Bailles Strand' from my sisters book).[4]

These last two books are practically ready.

My play here has been postponed to Oct 8th 9th & 10th.

Yrs ev
W B Yeats

ALS Buffalo. Wade, 411.

To W. G. Fay, [*mid-September 1903*]

Mention in undated letter from W. G. Fay, [mid-September 1903].
Two letters suggesting that the forthcoming INTS productions should be well advertised in the Dublin press; enquiring particularly about the attitude of the *United Irishman;*[1] asking about Digges' position in the Company;[2] and evidently discussing arrangements for the next INTS trip to London.[3]

NLI.

---

[3] This proposed volume became *Poems, 1899–1905*, published in October 1906. Up to p. 25 *In the Seven Woods* contains poems; the rest of the book is taken up with *On Baile's Strand.*

[4] A volume entitled *The Hour-Glass, Cathleen ni Houlihan, The Pot of Broth,* and another entitled *The King's Threshold: And On Baile's Strand,* were both published by Bullen in March 1904. The galley proofs of *The King's Threshold* (Private) are dated 31 Oct–7 Nov 1903.

[1] Fay agreed about the need for extensive advertising, but was 'not at all convinced of the deadly importance of the UI for I see they have be[en] giving the puff preliminary to the other show and I am quite sure that the show theyll back up will be the one which will do the bidding of their people'.

[2] In his reply, Fay told WBY he had no intention of having Digges 'hanging around sucking up information to carry it elsewhere & if he wants to come to us he can but I'm not going to bother about parts for people who are ready to run off at anybodys asking. . . . I know my Digges after 5 years where theres the most honor there will be the Digges. He think [*sic*] Cousins crowd are going up & we going down. If things reverse he will toddle back quite gaily to us and I am prepared to wait.'

[3] Fay reported that Stephen Gwynn wanted the Company 'to go to London for Boxing night & following nights with Shenahan [*i.e.* The King's Threshold] Hourglass Synge etc'. In the event the INTS's second visit to London was postponed until 26 Mar 1904.

To Frank Pearce Sturm, [c. 21 September 1903]

Mention in letter from Sturm, 22 September 1903.

Giving Sturm the 'formula of the "egg of light"' to use on a woman who sees an elemental bear,[1] and discussing the relationship of 'hysteria and mania' to occult experiences; accusing Sturm of 'playing with thaumaturgy' in his experiments with a silver pentagram, and apparently advising him to cast it into the sea;[2] and enquiring if Sturm reads contemporary poetry.[3]

LWBY I. 128–30.

To Maud Gonne, [c. 23 September 1903]

Mention in letter from MG, Friday [25 September 1903].

Discussing the Irish theatre; defending the Fays against her 'hear-say' charges;[1] disputing her account of the origin of the INTS;[2] and challeng-

---

[1] This formula is a method of ending trances without mishap, and on 11 Dec 1898 WBY had managed to bring Hester Sigerson out of an apparently unbreakable trance by putting her into the 'egg of light'. Egg symbolism, associated with the Egg of Brahma, the Auric Egg, and the Orphic Egg, plays an important part in Theosophy, the rituals of the GD, and William Blake's thought. In his and Ellis's edition of *The Works of William Blake* I. 317 (1893), WBY associates Blake's Mundane Egg with 'a certain symbol associated with Akasa', and the GD taught that Akasa represented the ideal condition, its oval geometric emblem inducing mind-enhancing trances. Sturm agreed to use the formula, but did not hold out much hope of success since the 'woman who sees this elemental bear is very easily thrown into an hypnotic trance. . . . When I tell her about the "egg of light" she will think I am trying to put her under the influence of "suggestion," and that will cause her to "auto-suggest" a contrary influence.'

[2] Sturm replied that his pentagram might 'be the death of me yet, but the results I get with it are so interesting that I can not find it in my heart to cast it into the Sea just yet awhile. I am not exactly "playing with thaumaturgy," as you suppose. All my experiments are planned with care and precision, and they are working towards a definite end.'

[3] Sturm answered that he did 'certainly read much contemporary poetry, especially Shelley and Rossetti' but not much poetry that was contemporary in a strict sense. He said that he liked the poems of Robert Bridges best, with the exception of WBY's own. 'You yourself have influenced me more than any writer living or dead, except, perhaps, Poe. When I am writing verse I find it difficult to escape from echoing you.' He added that he also read a great deal of French Symbolist verse.

[1] WBY had evidently protested about MG's allegations of Willie Fay's anti-nationalism, and her charge that the INTS would not have existed had it not been for the nationalist societies (see p. 423). MG repeated her criticism in her reply, adding that it 'was not "hear say" reports I sent you, to *me* Fay said that he didn't care a D— about the Nationalist Societies & other rude remarks. He made more of these remarks before the members of the N.T. Co. many of whom being Nationalists naturally resented them.'

[2] In her reply MG insisted that 'the existence of the National Theatre Society was originally due to Inginide na hEireann & Cumann na Gaedhal. If these Societies had not taken Fay up he would still be contentedly playing vulgar English farces in the Union Jack Coffee Palace. It was

ing her claim that the Inghinide and Cumann na nGeadheal had performing rights to *Cathleen ni Houlihan*.³ Also suggesting a form of words for
her letter of resignation from vice presidency of the INTS.⁴

G–YL, 176–8.

after Inginide na hEireann passed a resolution forbidding any of their members to act for Fay in
his English farces & for the Coffee Palace that he came to me & said he would rather act for
Nationalists if he could get National pieces & we introduced him to Russell who gave him or
rather gave us his 'Deirdre' to act. Have you forgotten how both Russell & I urged you to let us
have your 'Kathleen' how you said Lady Gregory thought you should not—& how at last to make
things smooth I consented to act Kathleen. It was Inginide na hEireann & Cumann na Gaedhal
who financed each of Fay's first attempts at National performances. On each occasion we not only
gave him the dresses & scenery we had paid for, but also gave him more than the fair share of
profits & even when there was a loss made up something for Fay, not for himself naturally but
with the idea of helping the formation of a National Theatre Co—Members of Cumann na Gaedhal personally gave money & collected money for the Company & all this because we wanted a
NATIONAL Theatre Co to help us combat the influence of the low English theatres & music
halls.'
³ In her reply MG accused WBY of forgetting 'repeatedly that in Dublin before members of
Inginide & Cumann na Gaedhal you stated you had given me for them the acting rights of that
play, & I hear it has repeatedly been acted in Ireland since. You remember you quite agreed with
me formerly that a play like 'Kathleen' which would do national good should be allowed to be
acted by all societies who wished to act it & that it would be selfish to confine it to one society.'
She also revealed that she had told the Cumann na nGaedheal that WBY 'would not mind any
Nationalist Society acting "Kathleen". . . . You gave it originally to Inginide & not to Fay. Would
you have taken it back? I hardly think so.'
⁴ Earlier this month MG had written (see p. 383) to tell WBY that she thought it 'best for me
to cease to be the vice president of the Theatre Co, I won't undertake any but National fights, &
the theatre Co does not seem inclined for such fights. I have no wish to injure the Co, so please
let me know how to gently withdraw without harming it—From all I can hear I think Synge's
play is horrid & I will have no responsibility for it—' WBY had evidently suggested some diplomatic reasons that might soften her withdrawal, but in her reply MG said she could not 'quite
write the letter of resignation you suggest. I have no intention of narrowing in the future my
activities any more than I have in the past—I don't think Cumann na Gaedhal N.T. Company
intends to confine itself to purely political plays, for instance it would accept joyfully plays like Dr
Hyde's or Deirdre or most of yours if you ever entrusted us with them . . .'

To George Roberts,[1] *25 September* [*1903*]

Coole Park, | Gort,
Sept 25.

My dear Roberts,

I return the circular.[2] Please show it to the company, and if they approve my modifications, send it to Sealy Bryers to print. It should be printed on good paper, I send you a model which please return to me. Ask Sealy Bryers to print it upon whatever sized paper will enable him to get the text into four pages. But ask him to keep to the sized type of the enclosed model and to let me have proofs.

I am adding at the end an advertisement of Samhain. The modifications I am anxious about are the additions of the Dublin Press opinions which I think are really important. To leave them out would play into the hands of our rivals. Let the company do what they like about the merely practical suggestions, the method of reserving seats &c.

Yrs sny
W B Yeats

[*In WBY's hand*]
I know nothing of what circlars cost & hope this wont cost too much. It looks bulky.

TLS Harvard.

---

[1] George Roberts (1873–1953), a native of Belfast, was at this time a commercial traveller. He had lately joined the INTS, and was shortly to appear as Dan Burke in *In the Shadow of the Glen*. He had succeeded Fred Ryan as Secretary of the Society and in this capacity arranged its publicity. He helped set up the Dublin publishing house of Maunsel and Co. in 1905, and early in the following year seceded from the Abbey Theatre.

[2] The folded four-page circular explained that the INTS had been formed 'to continue on a more permanent basis the Irish Literary Theatre': 'Its objects are to endeavour to create an Irish National Theatre; by producing plays written by Irish writers, on Irish subjects, and of such dramatic works of foreign authors as would tend to develop an interest in dramatic art. At present the work of the Society is done under great disadvantages, there being no hall in Dublin properly equipped for Dramatic Performances, but it is hoped it will be possible to secure such a hall in the near future; where performances can be more frequently given, and a centre created for the Dramatic Movement in Ireland.' It announced the plays for the coming season, and invited those interested in the Society's work to become Associates for a subscription of 10/- for the season. The second page printed favourable notices from eight Dublin papers, and the third and fourth gave extracts from the London press about the May 1903 visit.

To Maud Gonne, 25 September 1903

Mention in letter to Frank Fay, 25 September [1903], and in letter from
MG, 28 September [1903], (*G–YL*, 178).
Discussing the ownership of the wig used in productions of *Cathleen ni
Houlihan.*[1]

To Maire Quinn, 25 September 1903

Mention in following letter.
Discussing the whereabouts and possession of the wig used in *Cathleen ni
Houlihan.*

To F. J. Fay, 25 September [*1903*]

Coole Park, | Gort,
Sep 25.

My dear Fay, I have returned to Roberts the proposed circular but have
added to it a number of Dublin Press Opinions.[1] This will increase the
expense but we would be playing into the hands of our rivals if we quoted
only English papers. I have given practically the whole of Walkeley's article in Samhain, but I suppose you are right in wishing for it & the other
opinions in this circular—. I have also made a suggested emendation. That
the following sentence be added after the word performances at end of
circular. 'It being understood however that these seats can only be reserved
until five minutes before the curtain rises.'[2] The Stage Society has a rule of
this kind and it prevents large empty spaces, and discourages people from

---

[1] In March 1902 (*G–YL*, 151) MG had described the 'beautiful untidy grey wig' in which she
was to play Cathleen ni Houlihan, and in replying to this letter reminded WBY that he had subsequently given it into Fay's keeping. She asked that Fay should pass it on to Maire Quinn 'who
in my absence has charge of all the *very few* theatrical properties we have succeeded in getting
together for the Cumann na Gaedhal National Theatre Co—'

[1] The second page of the circular consisted of favourable press opinions from the *United Irishman*, the *Freeman's Journal*, the *Irish Times*, the *Daily Express*, the *Independent*, the *Leader*, the
Evening Telegraph, and the *Evening Mail*.

[2] This sentence was added, and the conclusion of the circular read: 'For the convenience of
those interested in the work of the Society it has been decided to admit Associates at the subscription of 10s. for the season (payable in advance), which will entitle them to one reserved seat
on the opening night of the five ensuing monthly performances (exclusive of the October performances). These seats, however, will be reserved only till five minutes before the curtain rises.' For
A. B. Walkley's *TLS* article on the INTS see p. 356.

coming in during the performance of the play. I suggest also that you consider the advisability of adding this further sentence. Ladies in the first five rows are requested not to wear hats, as owing to the floor being flat it makes it difficult for people in the back seats to see the stage.[3]

I am very sorry that you have put the officers in the advertisement in the United Irishman. Mrs MacBride has only remained thus far an officer of the society through a desire not to injure us. Her name appearing now as one of our supporters may result in attention being drawn to her resignation. Technically she is still of course our Vice President, and remains so until we receive her letter of resignation. We are therefore of course perfectly within our rights in using her name, but I think it is a mistake of tact. I suggest that next week you slightly change the advertisement leaving out all officers names and putting in the press opinion from the United Irishman which I have added to the circular.[4] I suggest further that instead of putting the words 'United Irishman' merely, as in the circular, you put 'Editorial from United Irishman of April 18, '02.' I think this will be an amusing way of turning the table on our opponents, who found the greater part of their objections to our Theatre on your own predominance in it.

I have had a letter from Miss Quinn asking me for a 'grey shaggy wig' which she left in my rooms, and is now she says in want of. This is of course Cathleen ni Houlihan's wig, and she wants it for the performance, though she doesn't say so.[5] I have replied telling all that I know of the subject, which is that I offered it to Mrs Mac Bride to bring over to Dublin, and that she didn't take it for some reason or other, but that finally either Mrs MacBride or some member of the company did take it so far as I can recollect, though I am not quite sure. I think somebody told me that the wig belonged to Mrs Mac Bride. If so it should be returned to her on her asking for it or to whoever she points out. I have written to her on the matter. Therefore whether you have or have not the wig, you had better get a new one, to have it in time—always supposing it is her property.

Before you send out the circular I want you to consider a project which I have been meaning for some time to write to you about. ⟨I dont suppose it makes any difference to the circular. It may make a difference as it may make it difficult for you to offer to reserve seats at the first five performances as one or two or more may be for a special purpose.⟩ I suggest that we give a special free performance of our most popular plays or at any rate

---

[3] This sentence was not added to the circular.

[4] The advertisements in the press were altered immediately, and MG's name dropped from the list of vice-presidents. A similar change was made to the programmes for the Molesworth Hall productions after the first night. MG's name did not appear in the circular.

[5] As WBY correctly divined, this request was a signal that Cumann na Gaedhal were insisting upon their right to perform *Cathleen ni Houlihan*, a right that MG pressed with much vigour in her letter of 25 Sept (see p. 431, n. 1).

of our most patriotic ones, and invite to this performance the members of the Dublin Working men's organization and also if it seems advisable to the society members of certain other clubs. I would charge no one for admission to these performances all seats would be by invitation. We might announce on the invitations that a plan would be laid before those present for the formation of a national Theatre, at very popular prices or a plan for a series of special performances at popular prices. One might use the word a People's Theatre in this case. We would then propose to issue blocks of tickets on the plan of the People's Theatre in Berlin.[6] The seats costing a few pence each, to workman's societies, but on the condition of these seats being sold in books of a certain number at a time. Miss Horniman probably knows the German system. In any case there is an article on it, which I daresay I could find with some little trouble. I am not proposing that any of the Theatre money should be spent on such a performance, for I think I can raise a special fund for the purpose. On the other hand it might be necessary for the Company to work up another play or two. The performance should take place on Sunday evening. And I think that ⟨our first three⟩ such performances would set us beyond all rivalry if we put on nothing above the heads of the working men and a good deal that was national. Probably, though you certainly know more about this than I do, "the King's Threshold", would be above their heads. You have not said what you think either of "Heads or Harps" or "Rising of the Moon", but I think one or other should be worked up for the first performance. I say this because I am afraid there will be some little commotion over Synge's morality, and that we had better not actually start with it among the working men. Should "the King's Threshold" seem to you above the heads of the audience, the Pot of Broth might take its place. I suppose three special Sunday evening performances, including the free one, will be as many as we could give during this winter. If the company feels that these 3 special performances would overtax its resources and leisure, I suggest that it may still be advisable to give a single free entertainment to the workingmen societies. It might be given about the twentieth of October and if we produced at it Cathleen, and another patriotic play, we would I think take the ground completely from under the feet of our rivals. I hope you

[6] This plan, which came to nothing, was probably inspired by the letter from MG of 9 and 25 Sept (see pp. 423, 431) which accused W. G. Fay of pandering to the Unionists and neglecting nationalist audiences: 'He openly boasted now that he had a better class of public . . . he didn't care for them & wouldn't consider them.' She had also alleged that 'Fay drove hard bargains about money when playing for any nationalist Society, while he played for *nothing* for the Unionists'. Die Freie Volksbühne of Berlin had been set up by Bruno Wille in 1890 for working people who could not afford commercial theatre prices. Admission was fixed at 50 pfennigs, and by 1903 the movement, which had spread to other German towns, had over 10,000 members. In 1919 WBY was to acknowledge that the Abbey had become 'A People's Theatre' but regretted this: 'its success has been to me a discouragement and a defeat' (*Expl*, 250).

understand this somewhat intricate letter. It is difficult to put things plain in a hurry. Let me know what you think of it as soon as possible. I value it for the moment chiefly as a very big advertisement.

If you have definitely decided the dates of your performance during the winter please let me know by return, and I will try and get them into Samhain, that the rival performance of Miss Quinn may not seem one of them. They should also be in the circular.

Yrs sny
W B Yeats

Your clothes are being made.

TLS NLI.

To George Roberts, 29 September [1903]

Coole Park | Gort, Co Galway.
Sept 29,

Dear Roberts,

I have no photograph of myself. If Irish Society wants the photograph, you had better refer them to Chancellor and let them pay the usual fee. They may if the[y] like photograph the frontispiece to my poems, Fisher Unwin's edition, and without asking leave of anybody.[1] The only difficulty is that half tone blocks dont photograph well. However they can decide this for themselves. My father has gone away and there is no chance of getting a sketch from him.

Now on a matter of considerable importance. I hope this is only a proof of the programme, for there is something in it that will lead to trouble if it is not changed. If you have not received Mrs MacBride's resignation by this time you will in a day or two. She sent me a copy of her letter of resignation a few days ago. Fay has known for some time that she is on the point of resigning, and only refrained from doing so that she might do it with the least embarassment to us. If her name is simply left out of the list of Vice Presidents, or if no officers are mentioned at all, her resignation may pass unnoticed. On the other hand, to publish her name as a Vice

---

[1] The Dublin weekly, *Irish Society*, wanted WBY's picture to illustrate the announcement of the INTS's autumn season in its issue of 3 Oct 1903. In fact, no picture was published then or in subsequent numbers. The frontispiece of *Poems* (1901) was JBY's pencil portrait, dated 28 Jan 1899. He had done a sketch of WBY on 3 June of this year, but until recently had been staying with Jack and Cottie.

President at this moment and thereby to gain positive support from it as against Miss Quinn's new company, is not only to invite a public statement from Miss Quinn or somebody else, but as I think to justify it. I want you therefore to bring this question before the proper authority in the Society and either to have the programme altered before any new programmes are issued or to have completely new programmes made. I asked Fay last week to see that Mrs Mac Bride's name did not again occur in the U.I. advertisement. I hope you will all agree with me that this also should be seen to. I suggest the leaving out of all officers names, in the avertisement, and the insertion of the U.I. notice from circular instead.[2]   ·

Now about the circular. Get a thousand printed by all means, and we will see about their distribution when I get to Dublin which will be next Saturday.

You might also get a few hundred copies of the Press Opinions printed on a separate sheet from the type used in the circular. This will make a leaflet which we can slip into circulars and programmes later on.

The Samhain advertisement might be as follows: SAMHAIN. An occasional Review edited by W. B. Yeats: containing Notes and an article on theatrical reform by the Editor, a play in English by J. M. Synge; a play in Irish by Dr Douglas Hyde, with translation by Lady Gregory. Price Sixpence. Sealy Bryers and Walker, Dublin. 1903.

Yrs sny
W B Yeats

TLS Harvard.

[2] MG had included a copy of her letter of resignation, addressed to 'Mr R[oberts]', in her letter of 25 Sept (see p. 431):

> I wish to resign my position as Vice-President of the N. T. Society.
> When I joined the Society I understood it was formed to carry on National & propagandist work by combating the influence of the English stage.
> I find it has considerably changed its character & ideals & while I shall always be interested and glad of its success, I can no longer take an active part in the direction & work.

Douglas Hyde, Maire Quinn, and Dudley Digges resigned at the same time, and, despite MG's desire to 'gently withdraw' (see p. 429, n. 4), these resignations did not pass unnoticed. The Dublin society paper, *Figaro*, headlined 'Maudie MacBride's Revolt' on 17 Oct, reporting (663) that she had withdrawn 'because she objected to the morality or religion of this play [i.e. *In the Shadow of the Glen*]. Her seccession [*sic*] was followed by that of Miss Quinn, the leading actress and a devoted admirer of Mrs. MacBride . . . and Mr. Digges. . . . Another, and much more probable reason is given for Mrs. MacBride's seccession [*sic*]—that Mr. Yeats and his colleagues were not willing to make the National Theatre subservient to the special political aim that is the one end of all Mrs. MacBride's efforts in Ireland. It is to be hoped that they will adhere to this position. Truth and beauty—a noble and sincere presentation of life should be the sold [*sic*] end of dramatic art.' MG gave her views on the nature of a National Theatre in the *United Irishman* of 24 Oct 1904.

To George Russell (AE), [late September 1903]

Mention in letter from AE, [*c.* 1 October 1903].
Asking about 'storms' in the INTS and the damage that the rival company might inflict on the Society.[1]

MBY.

To John Quinn, 2 October [1903]

Coole Park, | Gort,
Oct 2.

My dear Quinn,

I am setting out tomorrow for Dublin where I hope to see the performance of 'The King's Threshold' (Seanchan) next week. I will send you the new Samhain programme &c when I get to Dublin. I thank you very much for sending me the copies of the Hour Glass and Pot of Broth,[1] I will send you a copy of last year's Samhain with Cathleen, and other material for new volumes of Plays for an Irish Theatre in two or three days. I am being delayed by lack of a copy of The King's Threshold.

My only copy went to London for the copyright performance, and has not come back.[2]

Miss Quinn and Digges have revolted, and founded a company to play for Cumann na Gaedal. I dont think they will do us any harm. They were restless and having to play under Fay's direction, and were suspicious of our plays, which has not prevented them from stealing my Cathleen ny Houlihan, which unfortunately I never copyrighted. They try to persuade themselves that I wrote it for one of their societies, the Daughters of Erin, which I didn't. We have taken the lesson, and have made our first hole in your £50 to copyright two plays of Synge's.[3] Apart from this precaution, we are trying to work in the friendliest spirit with our rival. The Patriotic Societies were bound sooner or later to want a theatrical company of a directly propagandist nature. They will be able to get a certain number of

---

[1] AE replied reassuringly that he had 'heard nothing about storms and I do not think the rival company will do the Theatre Society the smallest harm'.

[1] They had been published in the *North American Review* and the *Gael* (NY) respectively.

[2] The American edition of *The Hour-Glass and Other Plays* was published by Macmillan in January 1904. *The King's Threshold* was entered in the Lord Chamberlain's register on 5 Oct 1903 (see p. 422), and Quinn had 100 copies of the play privately printed for American copyright in March 1904 (see p. 398, n. 2).

[3] See p. 422, n. 1.

plays which will serve their political purpose very well, without being sufficiently well written or sufficiently human to serve ours. I think our little
company is now perfectly united and satisfied. Those who remain have all
an artistic ideal, and put that first. I hear good accounts of the rehearsal
and the Irish Literary Society has invited the company to play Seanchan in
London at Christmas.[4] I will write and tell you how the plays go off. Lady
Gregory send[s] best remembrances.

Yr snly
W B Yeats

TLS NYPL, with envelope addressed to 120 Broadway, New York, postmark 'ORANMORE
OC 2 03'.

To Lady Augusta Gregory, [after 3 October 1903]

Nassau Hotel

My dear Lady Gregory
  I had hoped to have been able to send you the introduction before this,
but the typewriter could not make out the writing and now I am about to
dictate it. I will let you have it this post,[1] I dont quite like the sentence in
the middle of your dedictation, I think the phrase "until you find your real
home is here" too unqualified. It is impossible that more than the minority
of any body of men or generation of men could disentangle themselves
enough from circumstance to come over here. The impossibility of the
hope gives a slightly sentimental air to the dedictation. I think you should
rather say something like this "till many of you may have found that your
real home is here and until their children and ours say" etc. With this
change or some change like it I think the dedictation would be charming.[2]
We have good prospects here in the theatrical matters. I expect good audiences and possible rows after they are over. I am organising a body of
young men pledged to intellectual freedom and have asked them to come
to the Hotel on Sunday night. My Father [h]as written the most beautiful
and powerful essay suggested by Synge's play. It is to appear in the next

---

[4] See p. 427, n. 3.

[1] WBY was writing the Preface for AG's *Gods and Fighting Men*, published in February 1904.
[2] In her 'Dedication to the Members of the Irish Literary Society of New York', AG revised
the phrasing (vii) to read: 'A few of you have already come to see us, and we begin to hope that
one day the steamers across the Atlantic will not go out full, but come back full, until some of you
find your real home is here'.

"U. I.".[3] The costumes are extraordinary beautiful. The fame of them is going abroad and I think is helping us a good deal. I have met Captain Shaw Taylor,[4] two or three times in the street, but he tells me that he has to go to Belfast on politics and will miss the plays.

Yrs ever

W B Yeats

[In WBY's hand]
PS. Typing will not be done in time. Will finish tomorrow.

TLS Berg, with envelope addressed to Coole, postmark indecipherable.

To the Editor of the Irish Times, *8 October 1903*

SIR,—A writer in to-day's *Irish Times* quotes from my magazine "Samhain" as follows:—"I found some time ago that though it (the National Library) had two books on the genius of Flaubert it had refused on moral grounds to have any books written by him." Your reviewer then comments as follows:—"One does not know exactly what date 'some time ago' can mean, but as a matter of fact during the past four years five of Flaubert's masterpieces have been added to the catalogue." Your reviewer, who is in all else so sympathetic, then complains that I have "lightly aspersed" "The National Library."[1] Now some of those four or five masterpieces of Flaubert were added because of my protest, and the others, and one of these the most famous of all Flaubert's books, were only added some four months ago. Someone wrote in the suggestion book that every other national library in Europe had them, and at that the trustees surrendered. At this moment "the National Library" refuses to have any book written by Nietzsche, although it has a book upon his genius. Of course I agree with all that anyone has said about the serviceable work of this library. Its librarian is the most zealous man I know,[2] and even its Com-

---

[3] JBY's essay, 'Ireland out of the Dock', appeared in the *United Irishman* on 10 Oct 1903 (2). Inspired by Synge's *In the Shadow of the Glen*, which opened with WBY's play on 8 Oct, JBY wrote that he did not know 'whether Mr. Synge is as great as Shakespeare, but he has begun well. And I cannot conceive any events more important in Irish History for some time to come, than a few more plays by him. . . . Mr. Synge has the true Irish heart—he lives in Arran, speaks Irish, and knows the people. He is, besides, a man of insight and sincerity, that is to say, a man of genius. Such men are the salt of Ireland.'   [4] See p. 230.

[1] The notice of *Samhain* appeared in the *Irish Times* of 7 Oct (7). The reviewer quoted from WBY's essay, 'Moral and Immoral Plays' (*Expl*, 111–13), and went on to insist that 'The National Library is doing, under great difficulties, a splendid work, which should not be lightly aspersed, least of all by a poet engaged in founding a National Theatre'.

[2] Thomas William Lyster; see p. 121.

mittee of Selection is doing as well as the admirable moral characters of its members will permit.—

Yours, &c.,
W B Yeats

Printed letter, *Irish Times*, 8 Oct 1903 (6). *UP* II. 305.

To the Editor of the United Irishman,[1] *10 October 1903*

When we were all fighting about the selection of books for the New Irish Library some ten years ago we had to discuss the question, "What is National Poetry?" In those days a patriotic young man would have thought but poorly of himself if he did not believe that "The Spirit of the *Nation*"[2] was great lyric poetry, and a much finer kind of poetry than Shelley's "Ode to the West Wind," or Keats's "Ode to a Grecian Urn." When two or three of us denied this we were told that we had effeminate tastes or that we were putting Ireland in a bad light before her enemies. If one said that "The Spirit of the *Nation*" was but salutary rhetoric England might over-hear us and take up the cry. We said it, and who will say that Irish literature has not a greater name in the world to-day than it had ten years ago. One never serves one's cause by putting one's head into a bag.

To-day there is another question that we must make up our minds about, and an even more pressing one, "What is a National Theatre?" A man may write a book of lyrics if he have but a friend or two that will care for them, but he cannot write a good play if there are not audiences to listen to it. If we think that a national play must be as near as possible a page out of "The Spirit of the *Nation*" put into dramatic form, and mean to go on thinking it to the end, then we may be sure that this generation will not see the rise in Ireland of a theatre that will reflect the life of Ireland as the Scandinavian theatre reflects the Scandinavian life. The brazen head has an unexpected way of falling to pieces. We have a company of admirable and disinterested players, and the next few months will, in all likelihood, decide whether a great work for this country is to be accomplished. The poetry of Young Ireland, when it was an attempt to change or strengthen

---

[1] WBY's open letter to the *United Irishman* for the week ending 10 Oct was written to prepare the Dublin audience for the production of Synge's *In the Shadow of the Glen*. He reprinted the letter in *Samhain* and in *CW* IV, where he noted (120) that the suspicion that the *United Irishman* 'managed to arouse among the political clubs against Mr. Synge especially led a few years later to the organised attempt to drive *The Playboy of the Western World* from the stage'.

[2] *The Spirit of the Nation* (1845) was a popular anthology of national ballads and songs by the Young Irelanders who wrote for the *Nation*, the influential nationalist weekly founded in 1842 by Thomas Davis, Charles Gavan Duffy, and John Dillon.

opinion, was rhetoric; but it became poetry when patriotism was transformed into a personal emotion by the events of life, as in that lamentation
written by Doheny on his keeping among the hills.[3] Literature is always
personal, always one man's vision of the world, one man's experience, and
it can only be popular when men are ready to welcome the visions of others. A community that is opinion-ridden, even when those opinions are in
themselves noble, is likely to put its creative minds into some sort of a
prison. If creative minds preoccupy themselves with incidents from the
political history of Ireland, so much the better, but we must not enforce
them to select those incidents. If in the sincere working out of their plot,
they alight on a moral that is obviously and directly serviceable to the
National cause, so much the better, but we must not force that moral upon
them. I am a Nationalist, and certain of my intimate friends have made
Irish politics the business of their lives, and this made certain thoughts
habitual with me, and an accident made these thoughts take fire in such a
way that I could give them dramatic expression. I had a very vivid dream
one night, and I made Cathleen ni Houlihan out of this dream. But if some
external necessity had forced me to write nothing but drama, with an obviously patriotic intention, instead of letting my work shape itself under the
casual impulses of dreams and daily thoughts, I would have lost, in a short
time, the power to write movingly upon any theme. I could have roused
opinion; but I could not have touched the heart, for I would have been
busy at the oakum-picking that is not the less mere journalism for being in
dramatic form. Above all, we must not say that certain incidents which
have been a part of literature in all other lands are forbidden to us. It
may be our duty, as it has been the duty of many dramatic movements, to
bring new kinds of subjects into the theatre, but it cannot be our duty to
make the bounds of drama narrower. For instance, we are told that the
English theatre is immoral, because it is pre-occupied with the husband,
the wife and the lover. It is, perhaps, too exclusively pre-occupied with
that subject, and it is certain it has not shed any new light upon it for a
considerable time, but a subject that inspired Homer and about half the
great literature of the world will, one doubts not, be a necessity to our
National Theatre also. Literature is, to my mind, the great teaching
power of the world, the ultimate creator of all values, and it is this, not
only in the sacred books whose power everybody acknowledges, but by

---

[3] Michael Doheny (1805–63), a barrister and Young Irelander who wrote ballads for the
Nation, fled to America after the failure of the 1848 insurrection and there helped found the Fen-
ian Brotherhood, fought in the Civil War, and published *The Felon's Trade: History of the
Attempted Outbreak in Ireland* (1867). His poem, 'A Cuisle Gael Mo Chroidhe' ('Bright Pulse of
My Heart'), was written in the mountains after the collapse of the insurrection; WBY had
included it in *A Book of Irish Verse*, where he described it as 'one of the most moving ballads'.

every movement of imagination in song or story or drama that height of intensity and sincerity has made literature at all. Literature must take the responsibility of its power, and keep all its freedom: it must be like the spirit and like the wind that blows where it listeth,[4] it must claim its right to pierce through every crevice of human nature, and to describe the relation of the soul and the heart to the facts of life and of law, and to describe that relation as it is, not as we would have it be, and in so far as it fails to do this it fails to give us that foundation of understanding and charity for whose lack our moral sense can be but cruelty. It must be as incapable of telling a lie as nature, and it must sometimes say before all the virtues, "The greatest of these is charity."[5] Sometimes the patriot will have to falter and the wife to desert her home, and neither be followed by divine vengeance or man's judgment. At other moments it must be content to judge without remorse, compelled by nothing but its own capricious spirit that has yet its message from the foundation of the world. Aristophanes held up the people of Athens to ridicule, and even prouder of that spirit than of themselves, they invited the foreign ambassadors to the spectacle.

As far as I know I am only speaking for myself, but I would sooner our theatre failed through the indifference or hostility of our audiences than gained an immense popularity by any loss of freedom. I ask nothing that my masters have not asked for, but I ask all that they were given. I ask no help that would limit our freedom from either official or patriotic hands, though I am glad of the help of any who love the arts so dearly that they would not bring them into even honourable captivity. A good Nationalist is, I suppose, one who is ready to give up a great deal that he may preserve to his country whatever part of her possessions he is best fitted to guard, and that theatre where the capricious spirit that bloweth as it listeth, has for a moment found a dwelling-place, has good right to call itself a National Theatre.[6]

W B Yeats

Printed letter, *United Irishman*, 10 October 1903 (2). Republished with emendations and omissions in *Expl*, 114–18.

---

[4] John 3:8.   [5] 1 Cor. 13:13.

[6] MG responded to this letter in the *United Irishman* of 24 Oct 1903. In calling for a truly national theatre, she noted (2–3) that only Douglas Hyde had freed himself from English bondage: 'The best and truest writings of our greatest living poet, W. B. Yeats, are understood and appreciated by the people; the poems and essays they do not understand are those touched by foreign influence, from which Mr. Yeats has not altogether escaped, having lived long out of Ireland. . . . Mr. Yeats asks for freedom for the Theatre, freedom even from patriotic captivity. I would ask for freedom for it from one thing more deadly than all else—freedom from the insidious and destructive tyranny of foreign influence.'

To John Quinn, 14 October 1903

Nassau Hotel, | Dublin.
Oct. 14th.,/03.

My dear Quinn,

You will recognise the handwriting, Miss Horniman has come over for the performance of "The King's Threshold" & to fit the costumes which she has made. I send you "The King's Threshold" & a copy of "The Countess Kathleen" to go to the printers. I am also sending Bullen his copy for England. We have had a great success here. We have done far better than ever before & are giving an extra performance. Synge's play played beautifully, but has stirred up no end of a row by its morals. After the attacks which will come in the weekly papers[1] we expect a row on Saturday. I have been all the afternoon correcting "The King's Threshold" & will not catch the mail unless I post it now. I will have to send a few words of preface next mail.

Yrs snly
W B Yeats

Dict AEFH, signed WBY; NYPL; with envelope addressed to 120 Broadway, New York, postmark 'DUBLIN OC 14 03'.

---

[1] WBY's anticipations were fulfilled: *In the Shadow of the Glen* was attacked by most of the weekly papers, in particular by the *Leader*, *An Claidheamh Soluis*, and the *United Irishman*, which on 17 Oct (1) asserted that it was 'no more Irish than the Decameron. It is a staging of a corrupt version of that old-world libel on womankind—the "Widow of Ephesus," which was made current in Ireland by the hedge-schoolmaster. . . . Men and women in Ireland marry lacking love, and live mostly in a dull level of amity. Sometimes they do not—sometimes the woman lives in bitterness—sometimes she dies of a broken heart—but she does not go away with the Tramp. . . . Norah Burke is a Lie. It is not by staging a Lie we can serve Ireland or exalt Art.' JBY addressed these charges in a letter to the paper on 31 Oct (7), writing that the 'outcry against Mr. Synge's play seems to me largely dishonest; the real objection not being that it misrepresents Irishwomen, but that it is a very effective attack on loveless marriages—this most miserable institution so dear to our thrifty elders among the peasants and among their betters, by whom anything like impulse or passion is discredited, human nature coerced at every point and sincerity banished from the land. . . . My complaint of Mr. Synge's play is that it did not go far enough, since he did not make it quite clear that the wife will not return to the house into which she should never have entered, a view of the play I would earnestly commend to Mrs. MacBride, who, though a politician, is also a woman.' There was, however, no trouble in the theatre itself.

To the Editor of the Daily Express *(Dublin)*,[1]
[*15 October 1903*]

SIR—I have read in several papers that the Irish National Theatre Society "proposes to attempt," as one writer puts it, to give another performance of Mr. Synge's "Shadow of the Glen" on next Saturday evening.[2] I agree with those who say that to represent upon the stage an Irish woman as committing a sin is to insult the womanhood of Holy Ireland. Such plays ought not to be permitted upon the stage. But it is not only Ireland that is insulted. There are notorious plays which insult other nations, and good taste as well as our sympathy for morality and national spirit should make us protest in every instance. It is impossible to deny that the people of Egypt, now down-trodden under a foreign yoke, are insulted by the play of "Antony and Cleopatra." We all know that the heroine of a play is neces-sarily a typical woman; what insult could be greater than to represent the women of any nation by a heroine of many lovers who betrayed her coun-try. "Macbeth"[3] is an insult to the humanity of Scotland—think of the murder of Macduff's children! "Romeo and Juliet," a play which describes the children of Catholic Italy as disobeying and deceiving their parents, is as little deserving of tolerance. Why insult every learned and laborious German by representing him as selling his soul to the Devil in the play of "Faust"? But I have given enough instances. I now invite all those who are sensitive for the honour of all countries to meet me to-night upon O'Con-nell Bridge at 10.30. They will know me by my Gaelic League button and the pike which I shall carry in my right hand. We will then adjourn to a spot where the police will not disturb us until eleven.[4]—Yours sincerely

Robert Emmet MacGowan.

Printed letter, *Daily Express* (Dublin), 16 Oct 1903 (6).

[1] In her press-cutting book (NLI) AG identifies this letter as the work of WBY, and as having been written on 15 Oct 1903. It was published in the Dublin *Daily Express* (under the heading 'National Theatre and Irish Womanhood') on 16 Oct (6) and mistakenly dated 'Oct. 17th, 1903'. Jack Yeats sometimes used a similar pseudonym.

[2] This probably refers to a letter from A. MacGiolla an Chluig, published in the *Irish Daily Independent* on 14 Oct (6), regretting that 'those responsible for the Irish National Theatre Soci-ety have seen fit to propose to reproduce *In the Shadow of the Glen* on next Saturday night' and hoping 'that wiser counsels may prevail in the meantime'. The letter went on to assert that the play was an attack on 'the women of Ireland'.

[3] In an interview in the *Freeman's Journal* on 30 Jan 1907 (8), during the *The Playboy of the Western World* controversy, WBY again cited *Macbeth* to refute reductive political correctness and a too narrowly representative interpretation of art: 'Art, as a French writer has said, is "exaggera-tion apropos". Is Lady Macbeth a type of the Queens of Scotland, or Falstaff of the gentlemen of England?'

[4] Then the closing time in Dublin public houses.

To Lady Augusta Gregory, [*16 October 1903*]

Nassau [Hotel][1] | Du[blin]

My dear Lady Gregory . . . the letters. They sho . . . earlier but I forg . . .
hotel & thought . . . them somewhere e . . . send an Irish typ . . . for you.
I have h . . . severe cold in t . . . nothing but got . . . sent the MSS . . .
Horniman is be . . . company, seeing . . . a place with a . . . reherse in & go
. . . told Fay to do . . . them comfortab[le] . . . a hall to morrow with a view
to doing it up. Gogarty told me a plan for a play yesterday & repeated
some bits of good dialogue—I think he will do a good play yet.[2] The 'Independent' has woke up & attacked again with a note & a letter of a
threat[en]ing nature warning us not to perform Singe again.[3] I expect there

---

[1] Only a vertical fragment of the first page of this letter remains, the PS on the verso having
been torn away. Although fragmentary, it refers to the attempts by the Fays to find a more suitable theatre venue than the cramped Camden Street Hall (see p. 220). AEFH had come over to fit
her costumes for *The King's Threshold* (see p. 413).

[2] Gogarty's play has not survived. Because of his early classical training, he disapproved of the
folk plays being produced by the INTS, but WBY was to ask him to translate *Oedipus Rex* the
following year. The first of his plays to be produced at the Abbey, *Blight*, was not staged until
December 1917, followed by two further pieces in 1919. In the 'Scylla and Charydbis' episode of
Ulysses Buck Mulligan, based on Gogarty, announces that he has 'conceived a play for the mummers', the bawdy fragment *Everyman His Own Wife*.

[3] In an editorial on 8 Oct 1903, the *Irish Daily Independent and Nation* (4) made an attack on
the INTS and *In the Shadow of the Glen* that WBY would refer to for years. Of the Society's proposal to produce foreign masterpieces, the paper said 'we mislike the importation proposal
because of its dangers, though these could be obviated were those charged with the selections of
plays persons on whose taste or judgement reliance could be placed'. The editorial, after asserting
that 'Mr. Synge did not derive his inspiration from the Western isles', continued: 'We do not for
a moment think that all the members of the Irish National Theatre Society can be held account-
able for the eccentricities and extravagances of Mr. Yeats and his friends. But, once they are made
acquainted with what is being done in their name, we hold that those who ambition the uprise of
a dramatic art that shall be true, pure, and National, should make their voices heard against the
perversion of the Society's avowed aims by men who, however great their gifts, will never consent
to serve save on terms that never could or should be conceded.' The paper returned to the attack
on 13 Oct with a note (4) under the heading 'Gossip of the Day': 'The "Freeman" on Friday gave
prominence, with evident approval, to a long defence made of the National Theatre by Mr. W. B.
Yeats at the close of the performances in the so-called National Theatre. In justification of our
strictures, we quote two sentences of his brother [*sic*], Mr. J. B. Yeats, in the current number of
the "United Irishman". We apologise to our readers for quoting such stuff, but sometimes the
best cure for a disease is to cut open the cancer.' It then quoted from JBY's *United Irishman* article on Synge (see p. 438, n. 3) that it was better for Norah to leave her husband than endure 'the
foulness of her marriage', and that the 'lesson enforced' by the play was 'that rent contracts are
not the only ones that stand in need of revision, and that morality will often gain its ends by loosening the ligature'. 'Fancy national ideals and national journalism being elevated by lessons thus
inculcated!' the *Irish Daily Independent* exclaimed, and concluded by once again condemning the
'support of the "Freeman" for this kind of thing'. As the repeated (and forced) references to the
Freeman's Journal suggest, this second attack was prompted as much by inter-press and political
antagonism (the *Freeman's Journal* supported John Redmond and John Dillon, the leaders of the
Irish Party, whereas the *Irish Daily Independent* championed their bitter rival, Tim Healy; see

will be a row—as both 'UI' & 'Leader' will attack us tomorrow.[4] I think Russell is a little sad at seeing the Hermetic Society getting stage-struck ⟨but⟩ bit by bit[5]—above all at their going to America.

I am afraid you must have had a dreadful crossing.[6]

Yrs alway
W B Yeats

PS
[*The PS has been torn away*]

ALS Berg, with envelope marked 'Lady Gregory'.

To the Editor of the United Irishman, *17 October 1903*

I was very well content when I read an unmeasured attack in the *Independent and Nation* on the Irish National Theatre.[1] There had, as yet, been no performance, but the attack was confident, and it was evident that the writer's ears were full of rumours and whisperings. One knew that some such attack was inevitable, for every dramatic movement that brought any new power into literature arose among precisely these misunderstandings and animosities. The attack was not dangerous, like the attack on "The

p. 187, n. 2) as by the alleged moral turpitude of the INTS, but the following day the paper published the letter from A. MacGiolla an Chluig (see p. 443, n. 2), regretting that *In the Shadow of the Glen* was to be repeated, and hoping 'that wiser counsels may prevail in the meantime, and that those who have hitherto supported the ventures of the Society may not be rewarded for their forbearance during last week by having this production, of which most of the audience obviously disapproved, again put upon the stage'. After giving a tendentious resumé of the plot, the letter denounced the play's 'Zolaism', and—in an oblique but tasteless reference to the recent death of Emile Zola by asphyxiation—regretted that charcoal was 'not yet an article of common domestic use' in Ireland. The *Independent* was under the control of Healy's friend and ally, William Martin Murphy (1844–1919), the Catholic businessman and enemy of Parnell whom WBY was to describe in 'To a Shade' (*VP*, 292–3) as 'old foul mouth'.

[4] For the attacks in *United Irishman* on 17 Oct see previous letter. The *Leader*, as ever, did not disappoint WBY's expectations, and on 17 Oct its drama critic, 'Chanel', announced (124–5) that 'for its length' *In the Shadow of the Glen* was 'one of the nastiest little plays I have ever seen. . . . an evil compound of Ibsen and Boucicault. . . . grossly untrue to nature'. He discovered that the play was 'informed by a sort of negative idealism, which, by selecting the worst features of everything, arrives at forms much worse than anything actually existing in real life. That it should be put forward as a true picture of Irish existence and, worse still, as an embodiment of Irish reflections on life, is a species of misrepresentation that cannot be tolerated.'

[5] Among the members of the Hermetic Society who had joined the INTS were James Cousins, Thomas Keohler, Helen Laird, Harry Norman, George Roberts, and James Starkey.

[6] AG had left for London to visit her son, Robert, who had recently started an art course at the Slade. Strong winds had made the Irish sea crossing particularly rough that week.

[1] i.e. the editorial in the *Irish Daily Independent and Nation* of 8 Oct 1903 (see p. above, n. 3). The *Daily Nation* had led the attacks on the ILT production of *The Countess Cathleen* in May 1899.

Countess Kathleen" made by the same paper, but it was alike in its arguments, and there will be many more of the kind. The more open they are better. One cannot fight a battle in whispers. I need not enumerate, for I have done so twice already in THE UNITED IRISHMAN, tumults that have surrounded the birth of dramatic movements. Drama, the most immediately powerful form of literature, the most vivid image of life, finds itself opposed, as no other form of literature does, to those enemies of life, the chimeras of the Pulpit and the Press. When a country has not begun to care for literature, or has forgotten the taste for it, and most modern countries seem to pass through this stage, these chimeras are hatched in every basket. Certain generalisations are everywhere substituted for life. Instead of individual men and women and living virtues differing as one star differeth from another in glory, the public imagination is full of personified averages, partisan fictions, rules of life that would drill everybody into the one posture, habits that are like the pinafores of charity schoolchildren. The priest, trained to keep his mind on the strength of his Church and the weakness of his congregation, would have all mankind painted with a halo or with horns. Literature is nothing to him, he has to remember that Seaghan the Fool might take to drinking again if he knew that pleasant Falstaff was not sober, and that Paudeen might run after Red Sarah again if some strange chance put Plutarch's tale of Antony or Shakespeare's play into his hands, and he is in a hurry to shut out of the schools that Pandora's box, "The Golden Treasury." The newspaper he reads of a morning has not only the haloes and horns of the vestry, but it has crowns and fools' caps of its own. If other papers will not describe an eviction for fear of putting a landlord or a politician or a soldier in a bad light, his will not mention among the decorations at Maynooth the portrait of Ambush II., or quote in detail the statistics of illegitimacy in the country. Because fewer illegitimate children are born in Ireland than in England, its leading articles must be written as if none were ever born there at all. Life, which in its essence is always surprising, always taking some new shape, always individualising is nothing to it, it has to move men in squads, to keep them in uniform, with their faces to the right enemy, and enough hate in their hearts to make the muskets go off. It may know its business well, but its business is building and ours is shattering. We cannot linger very long in this great dim temple where the wooden images sit all round upon thrones, and where the worshippers kneel, not knowing whether they tremble because their gods are dead or because they fear they may be alive. In the idol house every god, every demon, every virtue, every vice, has been given its permanent form, its hundred hands, its elephant trunk, its monkey head. The man of letters looks at those kneeling worshippers who have given up life for a posture, whose nerves have dried up in the contemplation of lifeless wood. He swings his silver hammer and the keepers of the temple cry out, prophesying evil, but he must not mind their cries and their prophecies, but break the wooden necks in two and throw down the wooden bodies. Life will put living bodies in their place till new image brokers have set up their benches.

Whenever literature becomes powerful, the priest whose forerunner imagined St. Patrick driving his chariot-wheels over his own erring sister,[2] has to acknowledge, or to see others acknowledge, that there is no evil that men and women may not be driven into by their virtues all but as readily as by their vices, and the politician that it is not always clean hands that serve a country or foul hands that ruin it. He may even have to say at last, as an old man who had spent many years in prison to serve a good cause said to me, "There never was a cause so evil that it has not been served by good men for what seemed to them sufficient reasons."[3] And if the priest or the politician should say to the man of letters, "Into how dangerous a state of mind are you not bringing us?" the man of letters can but answer, "It is dangerous, indeed," and say, like my Seancan, "When did we promise safety?"[4]

Thought takes the same form age after age, and the things that people have said to me about this intellectual movement of ours have, I doubt not, been said in every country to every writer who was a disturber of the old life. A man said only yesterday that he had seen our plays, but would not go again because our players were Nationalists; others gave up their support of us because I had protested against the Queen's visit, and others because there were Unionists in the audience. We were disordering the discipline of the squads. When "The Countess Kathleen" was produced, the very girls in the shops complained to us that to describe an Irishwoman as selling her soul to the devil was to slander the country. The silver hammer had threatened, as it seems, one of those personifications of an average. Someone said to me a couple of weeks ago, "If you put on the stage

---

[2] In *The Tripartite Life of Patrick With Other Documents Relating to that Saint*, 2 vols, ed Whitley Stokes (1887) it is reported (234–5) that although St Patrick was particularly attached to his sister Lupait, whom he restored to health after a near fatal accident, he turned against her when he discovered that she had been unchaste: 'Patrick was enraged with his sister, namely, Lupait, for the sin of lust which she committed(?) so that she became pregnant. When Patrick came into the church from the east Lupait went to meet him, and she cast herself down on her knees before the chariot in the place where the cross stands in Both-Arcall. "The chariot over her!" saith Patrick. The chariot went over her thrice, for she still would come in front of it. Wherefore she there went to heaven at the Ferta, and she was afterwards buried by Patrick, and her requiem was sung.' *The Tripartite Life of Patrick* was written in Irish, probably in the 11th century, and is of uncertain authorship.

[3] i.e. John O'Leary; see *Aut*, 95.

[4] In *The King's Threshold* King Guaire argues (*VPl*, 306) that if he gives way to the poet Seanchan's demands 'I must offend / My courtiers and nobles till they, too, / Strike at the crown. What would you have of me?' Seanchan replies: 'When did the poets promise safety, King?'

any play about marriage that does not point its moral clearly, you will make it difficult for us to go on attacking the English theatre for its immorality." Again, we were disordering the squads, the muskets might not all point in the same direction.

Now that these opinions have found a leader and a voice in the *Independent and Nation*, it is easy at anyrate to explain how much one differs from them. I had spoken of the capricious power of the artist and compared it to the capricious movements of a wild animal, and the *Independent*, speaking quite logically from its point of view, tells me that these movements were only interesting when "under restraint." The writers of the Anglo-Irish movement, it says, "will never consent to serve except on terms that never could or should be conceded." I had spoken of the production of foreign masterpieces, but it considers that foreign masterpieces would be very dangerous. I had asked in *Samhain* for audiences sufficiently tolerant to enable the half-dozen minds who are likely to be the dramatic imagination of Ireland for this generation to put their own thought and their own characters into their work. That is to say, I had asked for the amount of freedom which every nation has given to its dramatic writers. But the newspaper hopes and believes that no "such tolerance will be extended to Mr. Yeats and his friends." With the cheers of our crowded Saturday audience in my mind, cheers that were given not more loudly for the landing of the French in "Cathleen ni Houlihan" than for the part of our programme that has been most attacked, I know that we will receive the tolerance I have asked for.

I have written these lines to explain our thoughts and intentions to many personal friends, who live too deep in the labour of politics to give the thought to these things that we have given, and because not only in our theatre, but in all matters of national life, we have need of a new discovery of life—of more precise thought, of a more perfect sincerity. I would see, in every branch of our National propaganda, young men who would have the sincerity and the precision of those Russian revolutionists that Kropotkin and Stepniak tell us of,[5] men who would never use an argument to convince others which would not convince themselves, who would not make a mob drunk with a passion they could not share, and who would

---

[5] Prince Pyotr Alexeievitch Kropotkin (1842–1921), Russian revolutionary, geographer, and social philosopher, was imprisoned in St Petersburg in 1874 for spreading the message of the Jura Federation. He escaped in 1876 and after expulsion from Switzerland and imprisonment in France, eventually settled near London, where his writings in English included *Memoirs of a Revolutionist* (1899). WBY met him 'once or twice' at William Morris' Sunday evening suppers at Kelmscott House (*Aut*, 140). Sergius Stepniak (1852–95), revolutionist and writer, fled Russia after participating in the assassination of the tsarist chief of police and eventually settled in London. He is best known for *The Career of a Nihilist; or, Andrei Kozhokhov* (1889). JBY did a portrait of him when he was a member of Calumet, the Bedford Park conversation club. The morning after one of their meetings in December 1895 he was accidentally killed by a locomotive.

above all seek for fine things for their own sake, and for precise knowledge for its own sake, and not for its momentary use. One can serve one's country alone out of the abundance of one's own heart, and it is labour enough to be certain that one is in the right, without having to be certain that one's thought is expedient also.[6]

These are some of the thoughts I put into "Where There is Nothing" or into "The King's Threshold," and it is natural they should be much in my mind just now.

W B Yeats

Printed letter, *United Irishman*, 17 October 1903 (2). Republished with emendations and omissions in *Expl*, 119–23.

To Allan Wade, 17 October 1903

NASSAU HOTEL, | 22, South Frederick Street, | D U B L I N .
17/10/03/

Dear Mr. Wade,

There is an American edition published by Mac.Millan in New York. I will not reprint the book in England but will split it into two. The dramatic part will come out with an addition in Vol. 3 in plays for an Irish Theatre (A. H. BULLAN). I will put the lyrical and narrative part into a book of verse to be published next year.[1]

Yrs sny
W B Yeats

[*In WBY's hand*]
Excuse typed letter, but I have to dictate for the sake of my eyes.

TLS Indiana.

[6] Ironically, WBY was criticized in this very issue of the *United Irishman* (2) for supporting Synge, for quoting English newspapers in *Samhain*, and for taking the Society to London the previous May. Griffith asserted that when the Society 'ceases to be national it will also cease to be artistic, for nationality is the breath of art'.

[1] WBY was unhappy with the American edition of *In the Seven Woods*, published by Macmillan in August 1903; see p. 397, n. 1. Moreover, he already had plans for a larger collection, containing *The Wind Among the Reeds*, although contractual difficulties with John Lane thwarted these. *On Baile's Strand* was published with *The King's Threshold* as vol. III of 'Plays for an Irish Theatre' in 1904, but WBY did not split the book into two, and his *Poems, 1899–1905* (1906) contains both drama and poems.

To Lady Augusta Gregory, 17 October 1903

Handed	}		Received	}	
		Dublin 11:50 pm			12:16 a[m]
in at	}		here at	}	

TO Lady Gregory 54 Gower St Ldn
Enthusiastic audience no trouble whatever[1]

Yeats

Telegram NLI, stamped 'Oct 18, '03 Strand'.

To an unidentified correspondent, 18 October 1903

Nassau Hotel, | Dublin.
Oct. 18th.,/03.

Dear Sir,

I arrived at the theatre rather late last night to find two red chairs in the middle of the front row. The company, who had been dressing or arranging the stage, knew nothing about them.

I would be very much obliged to know who put them there, & if they were there upon previous evenings. If not, why was the change made?[1]

Yrs sncly
W B Yeats

Dict AEFH, signed WBY; Harvard.

[1] See p. 442.

[1] W. G. Fay explained the reason for the change in *The Fays of the Abbey Theatre* (1935), pp. 141–2: 'We had a message from Dublin Castle that the Chief Secretary for Ireland . . . was bringing a party of six to the show, and would we kindly reserve seats? As the Molesworth Hall did not boast any special accommodation for distinguished visitors, I . . . got together a mixed lot to the required number, which I placed in the front row, quite pleased to think that we had done our best to show due courtesy. Next day, to my horror, I read in the Press that the chair I had allotted to the Chief Secretary was upholstered in RED!—"England's cruel red." What a scandal, what an outrage!' But given MG's complaints that the Fays were selling out to the Unionists (see p. 433, n. 5), the rivalry of the political Cumann na Gaedhal theatre company, and press hostility to the INTS over the production of *In the Shadow of the Glen*, WBY's consternation is understandable.

To P. D. Ellis,[1] [*21 October 1903*]

Dear Sir—I use words rather with a literary than with a philosophical precision. It would be difficult without collating the passages to give you a definition of 'imagination'—I probably use it in its older meaning of the image making power [*remainder of card in WBY's hand*] or image perceiving power.[2]

Yr sny
W B Yeats

APS Dict AG, signed WBY; Private. Addressed to Kirkwhelpington, Northumberland, and postmark 'OC 21 03'.

To the Editor of the United Irishman, *24 October 1903*

Much that has happened lately in Ireland has alarmed Irishmen of letters for the immediate future of the intellectual movement. They would sooner do their work in peace, writing out their speculations or telling the stories that come into their heads without being dragged into a battle, where the worst passions must of necessity be the most conspicuous for perhaps a long time. I have listened of late to a kind of thought, to which it is customary to give the name "obscurantism," among some who fought hard enough for intellectual freedom when we were all a few years younger. Extreme politics in Ireland were once the politics of intellectual freedom also, but now, under the influence of a violent contemporary paper, and under other influences more difficult to follow, even extreme politics seem about to unite themselves to hatred of ideas. The hatred of ideas has come whenever we are not ready to give almost every freedom to the imagination of highly-cultivated men, who have begun that experimental digging in the deep pit of themselves, which can alone produce great literature, and it has already brought the bad passions, when we accuse old friends and allies of changing their policy for the sake "of the servants of the English men who

[1] Philip Davenport Ellis, (*c.* 1880–1957), the son of the vicar of Kirkwhelpington, a small village above the River Wansbeck, 12 miles west of Morpeth, had graduated from Emmanuel College, Cambridge, in 1902 and was taking holy orders. He was shortly to be appointed a curate of Plumpstead, Kent, and went on to serve as incumbent in a number of parishes, mainly in the London area, including Turnham Green, close to WBY's early home in Bedford Park. His last appointment, from 1954 to 1956, was in Woburn Square, another area with strong Yeatsian associations.

[2] Since Ellis's letter is now lost, it is impossible to tell which passages he had brought to WBY's attention. Presumably he had been reading the recently published *IGE*, nearly all the essays in which are concerned with the imagination.

are among us," or when we pervert their work out of all recognition or split hairs to find a quarrel. It will save some misunderstandings in the future if I analyse this obscurantism.

1st. There is the hatred of ideas of the more ignorant sort of Gaelic propagandist, who would have nothing said or thought that is not in country Gaelic. One knows him without trouble. He writes the worst English, and would have us give up Plato and all the sages for a grammar. 2nd. There is the obscurantism of the more ignorant sort of priest, who, forgetful of the great traditions of his Church, would deny all ideas that might perplex a parish of farmers or artisans or half-educated shopkeepers. 3rd. There is the obscurantism of the politician and not always of the more ignorant sort, who would reject every idea which is not of immediate service to his cause. He lives constantly in that dim idol-house I described last week. He is more concerned with the honour and discipline of his squad than with the most beautiful or the most profound thought, and one has only right to complain when he troubles himself about art and poetry, or about the soul of man. One is under the shadow of his darkness when one refuses to use, even in the service of one's own cause, knowledge acquired by years of labour, when that knowledge is an Englishman's and is published in a London paper. Nor is one out of that shadow when one complains that someone has found a Cleopatra in the villages. Everyone knows who knows the country-places intimately, that Irish countrywoman do sometimes grow weary of their husbands and take a lover. I heard one very touching tale only this summer. Everyone who knows Irish music knows that "The Redhaired Man's Wife" is sung of an Irish woman,[1] and I do not think anybody could gather folk-tales along the Galway coast without coming on the ancient folk-tale (certainly in no way resembling the Widow of Ephesus as it is told by Pogius of Florence)[2] which Mr. Synge has softened in his play. These things are inconvenient one thinks when one is under that heavy shadow, for it is easier to go on believing that not only with us is virtue and Erin, but that the virtue has no bounds, for in that way our hands may

[1] 'The Red-Haired Man's Wife', a Gaelic ballad inspired by adulterous love for the eponymous heroine, was widely known throughout Ireland. Hyde gives two versions of it in *Love Songs of Connacht*, and Sigerson publishes it in *Bards of the Gael and Gall*; both editors comment on its popularity.

[2] Gian Francesco Poggio Bracciolini (1380–1459), the Florentine, published a fable about a lascivious widow in his version of Aesop, translated into English as the 'Fable . . . of the woman, and of the ypocryte' in *Aesop Fables in Englysshe With All His Lyfe* (1560). The widow invites a poor man to dinner and makes sexual advances to him. He resists for some time but seeing that 'he might not excuse him self, he said to the widow in this manner. My frinde sith that thou desirest to for to do so much & great an euil I take God to my witnes that thou arte causer of it, for I am not consenting to the faute or deede, but saying these wordes consented to hir will.' Arthur Griffith had maintained, and was to go on maintaining, that the plot of Synge's *In the Shadow of the Glen* derived from this story.

not grow slack in the fight. It will be safer to go on, one says, thinking about the Irish country people, as if they were "picturesque objects," "typical peasants," as the phrase is, in the foreground of a young lady's water-colour.

Now, I would suggest that we can live our national life without any of these kinds of ignorance. Men have served causes in other lands and gone to death and imprisonment for their cause without giving up the search for truth, the respect for every kind of beauty, for every kind of knowledge, which are a chief part of all lives that are lived, thoughtfully, highly, and finely. To me it seems that ideas, and beauty and knowledge are precisely those sacred things, an Ark of the Covenant as it were, that a nation must value even more than victory.[3]

W B Yeats

Printed letter, *United Irishman,* 24 October 1904 (2). *UP* II. 306–8.

To A. C. Benson,[1] 25 October [*1903*]

18 Woburn Buildings, | Euston Road, London.
Oct 25.

Dear Mr Benson,

A great many thanks for your book. I should have read it before this but that I am very busy with preparations for a visit to America, but I still [?hope] to find a little quiet time when I can enjoy it.

Yrs sny
W B Yeats

TLS Cambridge.

[3] In a note following this letter Griffith denied that WBY's account of an unfaithful Irish wife had any relevance: 'Had Mr. Yeats heard a score of such stories, it could not alter the fact which we all of us know—that Irishwomen are the most virtuous women in the world. A play which leads those who witness it to form a contrary conclusion can only be a lie and nothing more.' He repeated that the play was founded on the 'Widow of Ephesus', denied that he had impugned WBY's nationalism, but accused him of 'acting on a mistaken policy in connection with the Irish National Theatre. . . . His policy, if persisted in, will end in smash for the Theatre . . .'

[1] Arthur Christopher Benson (1862–1925), the essayist and biographer, was at this time an Eton housemaster. He had probably sent WBY his collection of supernatural tales, *The Hill of Trouble,* which had appeared in February of this year. The opportunity of editing the letters of Queen Victoria in the summer of 1903 released him from schoolmastering into free-lance writing, and in 1904 he was elected to a fellowship at Magdalene College, Cambridge.

To Edward Jenks,[1] 25 October [1903]

18 Woburn Buildings, | Euston Road,
Oct 25.

Dear Mr Jenks,

I send you a story of mine, thinking it might do for the Independent Review. I am not sure however if you take stories at all. If you do not, please let me have it back at once that I may place it elsewhere. It forms part of a book my sisters are now going to print, and which will probably be published soon after Christmas, so I must lose no time about it. Red Hanrahan is a character in my 'Secret Rose' and this is a new story about him.[2]

Yr sy
W B Yeats

TLS Private.

[1] After a brilliant academic career at Cambridge, Edward Jenks (1861–1939) taught Law in the universities of Melbourne and Liverpool, and had recently resigned as Reader in English Law at Oxford to become Principal and Director of Legal Studies of the Law Society. He was subsequently elected Professor of English Law and Dean of the Faculty of Laws at London University. *Parliamentary England*, one of his many distinguished books on Law, History, and Politics, had appeared in October of this year. He had been appointed editor of the *Independent Review*, an intellectual Liberal monthly, from its first number earlier this month, and his editorial council included G. Lowes Dickinson, C. F. G. Masterman, and G. M. Trevelyan. Very little creative work appeared in the magazine, which was mainly given over to articles on national and international politics, but it was issued by WBY's publisher, T. Fisher Unwin, who may have suggested that he should try it.

[2] 'Red Hanrahan', a new story, replaced 'The Book of the Great Dhoul and Hanrahan the Red' as the opening story in the Red Hanrahan group (previously published in *The Secret Rose*). Jenks did publish it in the *Independent Review* in December 1903, and it was reprinted in *Stories of Red Hanrahan*, issued by the Cuala Press on 16 May 1905.

To Alfred Noyes,[1] *25 October* [*1903*]

18 Woburn Buildings | Euston Road,
Oct 25

Dear Mr Noyes,

I have never written to thank you for the book you sent me through Mrs Emery.[2] It is full of beautiful things, some of which I have read again and again. I am dictating this, where I have not your book at hand, and cannot go as much into detail as I would like to, but I know I have read your 'imitation' from Theophile Gautier to quite a number of people, who have shared my liking for it. I believe I suggested it to Mrs Emery for the psaltery, if I have not done so I will do so. I have only just come back from Ireland, and go to America next week or would hope to make your personal acquaintance, but that is I hope only deferred for a while.

Yr sny
W B Yeats

TLS NLI. Wade, 412.

---

[1] Alfred Noyes (1880–1958), a popular and prolific poet, novelist, and biographer, became the first writer since Tennyson to live by his poetry. He is best known for his poem, 'The Highwayman', his epic, *Drake* (1906–8), his multi-volume depictions of the evolution of modern science, and his biography of Voltaire. From 1914 to 1923 he was a professor of modern literature at Princeton University. WBY did not retain admiration for him, and in a letter to Gogarty of 2 Feb 1922 (Bucknell) gave as one of his reasons for moving from Oxford that 'a woman today & in a quite respectable house recommended me to read Noyes . . .'.

[2] Noyes's first book of verse, *The Loom of Years* (*YL*, 1461), published in October 1902. Derivative to the point of pastiche from a number of other poets, its very obvious debt to WBY appears in 'Song of Hanrahan the Red' and 'In the Heart of the Woods'. The poem, 'Art', imitated from Théophile Gautier's celebrated 'Ars Victrix', was already familiar to WBY in Arthur Symons's version.

To John O'Leary,[1] *25 October 1903*

18 Woburn Buildings, | Euston Road,
Oct 25.

My dear O'Leary,

I go to America next week, and will be very much obliged for some introductions. You will remember that you kindly offered me them.[2] I had a debate against Father Maloney[3] last night at the Irish Literary Society. The subject was O'Connell. Father O'Connell [*for* Maloney] described O'Connell giving the laurel wreath to George IV, and said such a thing could never happen again now that Catholic and Gaelic Ireland had got the upper hand. I replied in my speech that it had happened again when Maynooth hung up the King's racing colours and the portrait of the King's racehorse which I called 'Ambush II out of Laurel Crown'. There was immense applause, and Father Maloney got very dark in the face and Mrs Emery saw some priests groping for their hats to go home she supposes.[4]

---

[1] John O'Leary (1830–1907; see I. 503), President of the Irish Republican Brotherhood, had been imprisoned and exiled for his part in the Fenian movement. On his return to Ireland in 1885 he exercised a profound influence on WBY's thinking about the relationship between literature and nationalism. He loaned WBY books from his extensive library of Anglo-Irish works, encouraged him to contribute to Irish periodicals, and organized the subscriptions for *The Wanderings of Oisin*. Of late years O'Leary's irascibility and his heavy drinking had made him something of a recluse. JBY wrote to WBY in May 1901 (MBY) that it was 'the awful dreariness of his life that makes the poor fellow take to evil courses' and the following year described O'Leary 'as he sits among his books sorting or thinking he is sorting his papers. It is the most affecting & moving thing I ever saw. Whatever he is doing he is as alert as if he was only beginning his life. You are conscious of his age & infirmities, *but he isn't*, he is far too busy. You are conscious of his lonely life deserted by every one or almost every one, but he isn't.' As President of the Irish Republican Brotherhood O'Leary had many contacts among Irish-Americans.

[2] O'Leary was true to his word; on receipt of this letter, on 26 Oct, he wrote (Private) to J. I. C. Clarke (and probably others) 'to introduce my friend William Yeats', describing him as 'undoubtedly a man of genius', and endorsing him as 'a very good Irishman, in every acceptation of the word'.

[3] The Revd Michael Moloney (1867–1905), born in Knocklong, Co. Limerick and now a priest at the Most Holy Trinity Church in Bermondsey, London, was an active worker for the Gaelic League, a member of the Irish Texts Society, and on the Committee of the ILS. He had arranged the first Irish Mass to be celebrated in London, and had attended the Killeeneen Feis in honour of Raftery in August 1902 (see p. 221, n. 2). This was not the only occasion upon which Father Moloney had been discommoded by an Irish writer. In *Aut* (404) WBY recalls that he ill-advisedly struck up a conversation with George Moore in a restaurant full of priests, and 'set out upon his favourite topic': ' "I have always considered it a proof of Greek purity that though they left the male form uncovered, they invariably draped the female". "Do you consider, Father Moloney," said Moore in a voice that rang through the whole room, "that the female form is inherently more indecent than the male?" Every priest turned a stern and horrified eye upon Father Moloney, who sat hunched up and quivering.'

[4] See p. 411. The debate followed Dr Arthur Houston's lecture, 'Daniel O'Connell', which, according to the *Pall Mall Gazette* of 26 Oct (7), retold 'many stories of the fifty stormy strenuous years in which O'Connell fought for Catholic emancipation, and not a few of the many famous sayings of the "Liberator" were quoted'. *New Ireland* (London), a weekly non-sectarian

However Barry O'Brien interrupted me, but it didn't matter, I had had my say. I think Arthur Griffith has behaved handsomely in the U.I.[5]

Yrs sny
W B Yeats

TLS NLI. Wade, 411–12.

To William Rothenstein, 25 October [*1903*]

18 Woburn Buildings, | Euston Road,
Oct 25.

Dear Rothenstein,

I hoped to have given you sittings this month, but I have to be off to America early next week, and have still all my lectures to prepare.[1] I will let you know when I come back, which will be some time towards the end of January.

Yrs sny
W B Yeats

TLS Harvard.

paper for Irishmen, reported on 31 Oct (14) that WBY 'said that he regarded Parnell as the Tragedian and O'Connell as the Comedian of Irish politics, and declared that Ireland was still suffering for having produced a comedian like O'Connell'. He was to persist in this view: see *Mem*, 212–13, *Expl*, 336, and 'Parnell's Funeral' (*VP*, 541–2). O'Leary, who was anti-clerical and who had once advised WBY (*Aut*, 209) that in Ireland 'a man must have upon his side the Church or the Fenians, and you will never have the Church', would have relished WBY's attack on Maynooth.

[5] In allowing WBY space to reply to the *United Irishman*'s attacks on *In the Shadow of the Glen*; see pp. 439–41 and 445–9.

[1] WBY first sat for Rothenstein in 1898, for a half-length lithograph portrait that was printed in his *Liber Juniorum* (1899). Rothenstein exhibited the portrait at the second exhibition of the Society of Twelve in 1905, but did no further drawings of WBY until 1914.

To Charles Elkin Mathews, 3 November [1903]

18 Woburn Buildings
Nov 3—

My dear Matthews,
I return Tables of the Law, corrected in pencil—The changes are chiefly in the second story. I also send a preface.

Yr sny
W B Yeats

[*Horizontally across top of page*]
Do not send Tables of the Law for review to any Irish paper—Please send my 6 copies to c/o Lady Gregory Coole Park Gort Co Galway.

W B Yeats

[*Enclosed with this letter*]

Preface—

These two stories were privately printed some years ago. I do not think I should have reprinted them had I not met a young man in Ireland the other day who liked them very much and nothing else at all that I have written.[1]

W B Yeats

Dict AG, signed WBY; Leeds.

---

[1] It was James Joyce's approval of the stories that moved WBY to bring out the 1904 edition of *The Tables of the Law and The Adoration of the Magi*, originally published in 1897. Joyce said they were 'work worthy of the great Russian masters'. Stanislaus Joyce recounts (*My Brother's Keeper*, 214) Joyce's chanting the passage from *The Tables of the Law* which ends with the words, 'Why do you fly from our torches that were made out of sweet wood, after it had perished from the world and come to us who made it of old times with our breath?' A note on the back flyleaf of WBY's copy of the book, possibly in WBY's hand, reads 'James Joyce in 1904' (see *YL*, 2428). There are minor differences of punctuation and diction between the two editions. Mathews told Watt in a letter of 2 Nov 1903 (Private) that WBY 'had promised me to make the necessary alterations before he left for America if I would get the file copy of the privately-printed ed^n. This was done, and he is to let me have it ready for press before he sails'.

To Lady Augusta Gregory, [*5 November 1903*]

R. M. S. "OCEANIC".[1]

My dear Friend: 9.45. AM

The one desirable acquaintance I have made, a young man in the mounted police of Alaska, who knows nobody & dressed for dinner, turns out to have had for mother a Galway Concannon. I told him of our friend & he is certain they are related. His people are however Concannons of Tuam & I have not told him that our young man was born in a thached house.[2] It might break our chief bond of sympathy & I hope to learn all about Alaska. We are in Queenstown harbour & Mrs Byrne & O Donovan will come aboard in about an hour.[3] It was perfectly smooth all night & still is. I wrote the enclosed for Maclaggan. If it is all right post it if not you might right [*for* write] a few words your self to say that I liked the banner & had not time to write before I left. I thought it better to show I was not quite at one with my sisters about the business as he may hear or have heard from them.

Yours always
W B Yeats

The young man from Alaska wants to argue the fiscal contraversy instead of telling me about the American Indians.[4]

ALS Berg, with envelope addressed to 54 Gower St, London, postmark 'QUEENSTOWN NO 5 03'.

---

[1] WBY sailed first class from Liverpool on the 17,273 ton *Oceanic* on 4 Nov for a planned six-week tour of the USA, organized by Quinn in association with the Irish Literary Society of New York. In the event, his lectures proved so popular that the tour was extended until 9 Mar 1904, in which time he lectured to more than 30 colleges as well as numerous Irish literary societies and other groups in the USA and Canada.

[2] AG's 'friend', Thomas Concannon (b. 1870), was a native of the Aran Islands. He had emigrated to the USA in 1878, studied in Boston and California, and travelled widely in Central America, before returning to Ireland in 1898. The following year he was present with AG and Hyde at the establishment of the Kiltartan branch of the Gaelic League, and in 1901 he became the League's national organizer. He translated a number of writers into Irish, including George Moore. His Alaskan kinsman is unidentified.

[3] Helen MacGregor Byrne (1869–1945), patroness of the arts, had visited Coole the previous summer with her husband, James F. Byrne (1857–1942), a leading New York corporation lawyer. He was a friend of John Quinn's, and founder of the 'Irish Industrial Society of America', which had invited Father Jeremiah O'Donovan (see p. 112) to lecture in the USA on behalf of the Irish Agricultural Organisation Society, accompanied by Father Finlay and Robert A. Anderson. O'Donovan lectured on the revival of Irish arts, and on the co-operative movement, but shortly after his return to Ireland he left both Loughrea and the priesthood.

[4] A lengthy international debate on Tariff Reform was in progress at this time, provoked in part by Joseph Chamberlain's advocacy that Britain should return to Protection, and Imperial Preference.

To Eric Maclagan, 5 November 1903

R. M. S. "OCEANIC".
Nov 5 1903

My dear Maclagan:

I have been meaning for some time to write to you about your banner which is in my care at present. I think it exactly right, solemn dignified and traditional. I wish I could make my sisters understand that this is precisely what all their work should be. My brother has been doing banners for them, which are I think too fanciful and modern. If the cathedral people had sense they would try them for protestant heresies.

I saw your introduction to *Jerusalem*, Archie Russell showed it to me and I thought it excellent.

Yours sincerely
W B Yeats

I am on my way to America where I lecture. I shall be back some time in February.

TS copy Indiana.

To Lady Augusta Gregory, [5 November 1903]

R. M. S. "OCEANIC".

My dear Lady Gregory

11. AM. No sign yet of the Queenstown passengers—the mails are late I hear people say. There are rows of boats along side with lace & shillalaghs and I see passenger proudly carrying an emmense shillalagh tied up in queer ribbons. The convent lace sellers are a special privilaged I see. They are on board. The others send up their goods in baskets tied to ropes. My friend who dressed for dinner & knew nobody has been talking all morning with a very pretty girl, their chairs are side by side away from the other chairs & when I turn a certain corner I see this—blue skirt & then beyond brown boots.

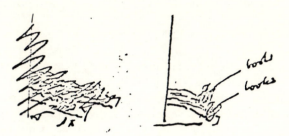

I shall post this on the chance of its getting off before New York—11 is supposed to be the hour for clearing box.

Yr ev
W B Yeats

I hear what sounds like the tender coming

ALS Berg, with envelope addressed to 54 Gower St, London, postmark 'QUEENSTOWN NO 6 03'.

To Lady Augusta Gregory, 9 November 1903

R. M. S. "OCEANIC".
Monday | 9.30

My dear Lady Gregory: The ship is perfectly steady & the sun is shining. We get in about noon to morrow. This is the first perfectly fine day except the day we left Queenstown. Yesterday it was blowing a gale & the ship was tossing greatly & from time to time covering her bows with spray. The day before there was a high wind but not so high & the day before that little wind but a heavy swell—that was my worst day. I have not been actually seasick but I have been uncomfortable enough. Father O Donovan & Anderson[1] held out pretty well & pretended to be quite happy until yesterday (our stormiest day) when both got very miserable: neither however will admit that the sea affected them. O Donovan says it was dyspepsia & he would have been as bad ashore & Anderson says it was all because of something he did for his sore throat. I have made one acquaintance I like. I have seen no more of the young man, whose mother was a Concannon. He

[1] Robert Andrew Anderson (1861–1942), one of the founders of the Co-operative Movement in 1890, served as Secretary of the Irish Agricultural Organisation Society from his appointment by Plunkett in 1895 to 1921. His book on the Co-operative Movement, *With Horace Plunkett in Ireland*, which appeared in 1935, gives an account (138–9) of this crossing and of the cauterising of his throat by the ship's doctor.

devotes every moment he is on deck to the pretty passenger. My new acquaintance is an accountant from Edinburgh (whose father was a great friend of Stevensons father & in one of Stevensons poems).[2] He has read 'Samhain' (I lent him a copy) & is coming to my lecture but is very much afraid I am going to talk politics. I notice that English people always are. I have had the enclosed note from Ryan I am sorry to say. It shows that Fay, who said not a word at the reading committee woke up again when he got us out of the way. I am very much inclined to beleive that he wants to get out of playing political plays. I shall have to wait until I get back, & then have a new general meeting & go to it myself. I am also half inclined to write to Fay & ask him straight out if he wants to drop political plays. I will tell him that if he does I wont call him "no nationalist" or anything of that kind for a differance in policy, but that I shall certainly differ from him on the point. It is very irritating & all the more because their readiness to play my other plays makes it hard to fight over "Heads or Harps".[3] I shall be able to make a better fight for "The Rising of the Moon". I have been reading Molière all day long, or nearly, & everyday. You should look through him again. Some of his more farcical comedy is pure "folk" in its way of seeing life. He is full too of stage tricks one could adapt to our kind of material. I have a three act satirical comedy in his manner floating vaguely in my head—I dare say the next book of plays I read may put it out & something else in.[4] Mrs Byrne met Hyde in Dublin. He was very much put out at the playing of his Trinity College play, in rehearsal. The principal man was he said very bad.[5] She had seen somebody who had been to the first performance but I did not get much from her as

[2] Although the *Oceanic*'s passenger list gives neither the address nor profession of first-class passengers, this was possibly Mowbray Douglas (d. 1928), an accountant of 22 Hill Street, Edinburgh, and perhaps a kinsman of David Douglas who had published the second edition of Thomas Stevenson's *Christianity confirmed by Jewish and Heathen Testimony* (Edinburgh, 1877), and who supported Robert Louis Stevenson's application for the chair of History at Edinburgh University in July 1881. Robert Louis Stevenson's father, Thomas Stevenson (1818–87), was a civil engineer and designer of lighthouses.

[3] WBY and Lady Gregory had collaborated on the writing of *Heads or Harps*, an unpublished and unproduced play; see p. 295, n. 2. On 4 Nov Fred Ryan had written to WBY (NLI) to tell him that a General Meeting of the INTS the previous evening had endorsed the Reading Committee's recommendation of *On Baile's Strand* and *Riders to the Sea*: 'The enclosed "The Local Situation" [*presumably an alternative title for* Heads or Harps] however the meeting decided to refer to you for further consideration. The general feeling seemed to be that it was too short and not enough substance in it. George Russell said if I sent it to you by Queenstown, you might have time on the voyage or in America to look over it.'

[4] WBY did not write a play inspired by Molière, but AG was to produce a number of successful translations, beginning with *The Doctor in Spite of Himself*, produced at the Abbey in April 1906.

[5] Cathal McGarvey, who was later to write a number of short comic plays, took the part of Mahaffy in *The Bursting of the Bubble* on 2 Nov. Although the Dublin press praised the acting on patriotic grounds, it was privately acknowledged to be amateurish.

the weather got rough & she went below & did not come up again until today.

12 O'clock.

I have just been talking to Mrs Byrne but not about the theatre. She has been saying how suspicious people are in Ireland & a question of mine drew from her the fact that some people have not liked my going out the same time as O Donovan (you will remember I thought that this must be so from Quinns vehemence). She says that O'Donovan himself was a little hurt that I did not tell him about it. He did not know it until he got your letter about the introductions. She thinks that somebody must have put it into his head or he would not have minded. There seems to ha[ve] been quite a little disturbance somewhere or other about my lectures—I dare say I shall hear all from Quinn. I[t] does not matter in any case—one cannot move in Ireland without somebody thinking one has done something or other from the worst motives. I suppose an unfriendly silence & a desire to upset co-operative plans is the present accusation. I dare say however that the whole thing is very trifling. I thought I had told O'Donovan all about the lectures. Mrs Byrne says that her husband is very anxious about Plunketts book.[6] She says it is most interesting but will make him many enemies especially in America. It has a chapter about Irish Americans seen too much from the point of view of the well to-do anglicized American. It comes out in about a month—in time to make things difficult for O'Donovan. Dr Bonn (that little German who was doing a book about Ireland) is back & says the Gaelic League is now becoming a most dangerous political

---

[6] Sir Horace Curzon Plunkett (see p. 183, n. 2), a Unionist MP from 1892 to 1900 and founder of the Irish Agriculture Organisation Society in 1894. His book, *Ireland in the New Century*, aimed (p. xii) at 'promoting a greater definiteness of aim and method' among the 'various progressive movements in Ireland', mainly by pointing out 'economically paralysing' defects in the Irish character: 'the lack of moral courage, initiative, independence and self-reliance'. It did not appear until February 1904, too late to embarrass O'Donovan on this trip, but it was savagely attacked (and misrepresented) in Ireland, largely because of its animadversions on Catholics. It also criticized Irish-Americans for allowing blind Anglophobia to sap their individuality and political acumen so that they lacked 'the capacity . . . to use their undoubted abilities in a large and foreseeing manner, and are becoming less and less powerful as a force in American politics'. Plunkett was an advocate of agricultural self-help and co-operation in the face of modern competition, and President Theodore Roosevelt, in his conservation and country life policy, adopted Plunkett's slogan, 'Better farming, better business, better living'.

[7] Moritz Julius Bonn (1873–1965), a professor of economics from Munich, was gathering material in Ireland for his *Modern Ireland and Her Agrarian Problem*, translated by T. W. Rolleston (1906). AG would have been interested in Bonn's change of views, for when she first met him in 1897 (diary, Berg) she described him as 'an odious little German . . . studying political economy & not seeing "what relation the Celtic movement had to it"'. Although he makes only passing reference to the Gaelic League in his book, Bonn was to suggest in his autobiography, *Wandering Scholar* (New York, 1948), that the Gaelic revival was embraced 'as a buttress to . . . claims for agrarian socialism. . . . Use of the Gaelic language opened up the way to primeval

organization.[7] He is constantly about with Plunkett. Mrs Byrne has heard nothing but praise of my sisters banners, Tom Kelly[8] & some one else I forget who seem to have been praising them.

3.30.

Still beautiful weather. Mrs Byrne knows no more about the Quinn & Digges plays except that Miss Butler[9] liked their opening show. The last paragraph in Ryans letter means that I told him to send account to Miss Horniman.

Yrs always
W B Yeats

ALS Berg, with envelope addressed to 54 Gower St, London, postmark 'DUBLIN & QUEENSTOWN PAQUETBOAT NO 18 03'.

To J. I. C. Clarke,[1] 13 November 1903

120 BROADWAY | New York,
Nov. 13, 1903.

Dear Sir:

I enclose a note of introduction from Mr. John O'Leary. I am looking forward with pleasure to a call upon you, at your convenience. A line to me, care of my friend, John Quinn, 120 Broadway, New York, or No. 1

Celtic institutions; their adoption would cut the country off from English domination and British civilization much more effectively than the most far-reaching constitutional reforms. . . . yet somewhere deep down in the bottom of my mind I sensed its unreality' (95–8).

[8] Thomas Hughes Kelly (1865–1933), son of the wealthy Irish-American banker Eugene Kelly (1804–84), was treasurer of the Irish Industrial League of America, and, as an enthusiastic vice-president of the Irish Literary Society of New York, had worked for the success of WBY's plays. Earlier this year he had endowed Padraic Colum with an annual subsidy so that he could devote himself to literature, and Colum dedicated his play *The Land* (1905) to him.

[9] Mary Ellen Lambert Butler, later Mrs Thomas O'Nolan (1872–1920), journalist and short-story writer, was a regular contributor to the *Irish Homestead* and edited a column 'Eire Og', for the *Weekly Independent*. Her popular collection of Irish stories, *A Bundle of Rushes*, appeared in 1901, and her one-act pastoral play, *Kithe*, was published in the *Weekly Independent* in May 1902. Although a cousin of Sir Edward Carson, she became a Daughter of Erin and a protégé of MG, and suggested the name of Sinn Fein to Griffith for his political movement.

[1] Joseph Ignatius Constantine Clarke (1846–1925), editor of the Sunday edition of the *New York Herald*, had been born near Dublin, and was a leader of the Irish Republican Brotherhood before escaping to Paris and the USA, where he became a journalist and later a playwright. WBY owned a copy of his *Robert Emmet: A Tragedy of Irish History* (1888); *YA4*, 281. He was a friend of John O'Leary's who had written to introduce him to WBY (see p. 456, n. 2). The two did meet (see below, p. 476), and on 17 Jan 1904 Clarke arranged for an article on WBY by Florence Brook to be published in the *Sunday Herald*.

West 87th Street, New York City, will find me at once.

I have a vivid recollection of the pleasure it gave me when I came upon—a good many years ago—and read ⟨with interest⟩ your play of *Robert Emmet*, which interested me greatly.

Sincerely yours,
W B Yeats

Mr. J. I. C. Clarke,
    c/o The New York Herald,
        New York City

TLS Private.

To John Devoy,[1] *13 November 1903*

13 November, 1903.

Dear Sir,

Before leaving London Dr. Ryan[2] gave me your name and suggested that I should call upon you when in your City. I have come over to lecture upon the intellectual movement in Ireland and kindred subjects and shall look forward with pleasure to meeting you.

Yours very truly
W B Yeats

Text from *Devoy* II. 350–1.

[1] John Devoy (1842–1928) had been a leading member of the Fenian Brotherhood before his arrest in 1866. After five years in prison he emigrated to the USA where he became an influential member of the Clan na Gael. He had supported Michael Davitt and Parnell, and was for many years the most influential of the Irish-American nationalists. He attended WBY's lecture on Robert Emmet on 28 Feb 1904.

[2] Dr Mark Ryan (1844–1940), a Fenian agent and London physician, was a close friend of John O'Leary, through whom WBY had met him in the late 1880s. A founder-member of the ILS and the Gaelic League, he was active in numerous Irish societies in London, and was a member of the Supreme Council of the Irish Republican Brotherhood. His autobiography, *Fenian Memories*, appeared in 1945.

To Cornelius Weygandt, 13 November 1903

120 BROADWAY | New York,
Nov.13, 1903.

My dear Mr. Weygandt:
I received your note of the 23d just before sailing. I am glad to know from my friend, John Quinn, that I am to lecture in Philadelphia at your University and I shall be very glad indeed to be your guest.[1] I shall have great pleasure in meeting both you and Mrs. Weygandt.

Sincerely yours
W B Yeats

Professor Cornelius Weygandt,
University of Pennsylvania,
Philadelphia, Pa.

P.S.—I understand I am to lecture at your university on November 23d and before the Contemporary Club on December 8th, and also will deliver two lectures at Bryn Mawr. Mr. Quinn will advise you definitely as to the dates and time of my arrival.

TLS Private, with envelope addressed to University of Pennsylvania, Philadelphia, postmark 'NEW YORK N. Y. NOV 13 1903'.

To Lady Augusta Gregory, [16 November 1903]

1 West 87 St, | New York, | USA

My dear Friend: I am now established at Quinns—I came here from the hotel last night.[1] Since I arrived I have been busy with a long stream of reporters. When I got out of the steamer I was beset by half a dozen at once & two of them had cameras.[2] I give my first lecture at Yale on Monday, I then lecture at some Irish Literary Society in New Market [*for* New Haven] & then back to New York & off again on Thursday. I give about 4

---

[1] For Cornelius Weygandt see p. 100. WBY lectured at the University of Pennsylvania on 'The Intellectual Revival' on 23 Nov.

[1] WBY had been staying at the Plaza Hotel, 59th St. and West Avenue, but had now moved in with Quinn at 1 West 87 St.

[2] WBY had been interviewed in the New York *Sun* and in the *New York Daily Tribune* of 15 Nov 1903; see p. 470, n. 1; 469.

lectures a week & I have already more than 30 to give to Universities.[3]
There will also if all goes well be big public lectures which will make much
more money. But even with the lectures I have already certain I will make
a good deal of money.[4] Everybody is very kind but I am refusing all but
the most important invitations as my chief anxiety is not to break down for
the work will be hard & dinner parties & the like would make it harder. I
have found the reporters much more fateguing than I have ever found lecturing. I had a long struggle with a woman reporter yesterday who wanted
to print & probably will a number of indiscreet remarks of mine. Here is
an example. "What do you think of Kipling?" "I shall say nothing what
ever about Kipling if you please. I will say nothing about any living poet. If
he would have the goodness to die I would have plenty to say. Good heavens have you written that down?"
"Yes it is the one Irish remark you have made."
"You will please rub it out again."
Thereon we had a struggle of ten minutes & inspite of her promise I
expect to see printed in large black letters "Yeats desires Kiplings death". I
have sent an urgent message demanding a proof. I had been painfully judicious for days, as the reporters had been Irish & asked about Ireland but
this woman asked about general literature & I was off my guard.[5] Burke
Cocran has called & a certain Judge who found 'Ideas of Good and Evil' in
a hotel in a southern state & was pleased by what I said of Morris.[6] He is

---

[3] WBY prepared four lectures for his tour, 'The Intellectual Revival in Ireland', first delivered
at Yale on 16 Nov; 'Heroic Literature of Ireland', first given to the New Haven Irish Literary
Society the following day; 'The Theatre and What it Might Be', and 'Poetry in the Old Time and
in the New'.

[4] WBY made a total of $3,230.40 for the seventeen-week tour.

[5] Evidently Marie Mattingly in the *Sun* (see p. 470), who reported that the mention of Kipling
'brought out an unexpected hesitancy in his manner. "Kipling? Oh, Kipling had a soul to sell, and
he sold it to the devil. . . . Undoubtedly Kipling is a man of great genius. He has done a work of
great beauty and a new kind. But latterly he has turned himself into a kind of imperialist journalist in prose and verse, and with all that I have no sympathy. Ten years ago Kipling mattered
greatly to men of letters—today he matters much to journalists. His might have been a very great
name indeed, but he has made what Dante calls 'the great refusal'—the refusal to be himself. It is
disappointing to discuss Mr. Kipling; let us talk about the theatre, America or Ireland"' (Sect.
III, p. 7).

[6] William Bourke Cockran (1854–1923), Co. Sligo-born lawyer, political orator, and later US
Congressman from New York, had called on WBY at the Plaza Hotel at 5 p.m. on 12 Nov. He
was to introduce WBY at his big public lecture at Carnegie Hall on 3 Jan 1904, where WBY
thanked him for contributing thousands of dollars to Sligo industries. Blunt had met 'Cochrane'
on 19 Feb 1903, 'having been introduced to me by John Redmond as the most prominent Irishman in America. I found him an intelligent, old-fashioned Irishman, and altogether worthy. . . .
He had seen George Wyndham in Ireland, and had talked to him, and was confident he meant
well with his Irish Land Bill' (II. 42–3).
  The judge was Martin Jerome Keogh (1855–1928), Irish-born Justice of the Appellate Division
of the New York Supreme Court, and one of Quinn's close friends. WBY was to spend Christmas
1903 with him. *IGE* contained WBY's essay on William Morris, 'The Happiest of the Poets'.

now starting on Morris. I lunch with him to-morrow & Quinn is I can see full of his sense of the judges importance, who is clearly a pillar in Quinns house of labour. I also go to lunch with Cocran, or to stay with him I forget which. I have also been sent visitors cards for three of the chief clubs.[7] I hear too that I am to lecture to the Pauline Fathers who say they dont mind my heretical theology.[8] I go to the pacific coast in January a five days journey & lecture in Father Yorkes town & stay with his worst enemy.[9]

Quinns rooms are charming. Jacks pictures & Russells & my fathers portrait of me pretty well cover the walls & look very well. My fathers portrait of me has a class [*for* glass] over it & seems to have been rubbed over with some kind of wax by the framer. It looks extremely well & has a richness of dark colour I never noticed in it before.[10]

I have just heard a very painful rumour. Major Mac Bride is said to be drinking. It is the last touch of tragedy if it is true. Mrs Mac Bride said in one [of] her last letters that he has been ill all summer.[11]

Yrs alway
W B Yeats

[7] On 14 Nov Quinn reported (NYPL) to James Phelan (see below) that the 'newspapers are already full of Yeats and he has been put up [*i.e. for visitor's membership*] at the University Club, the Metropolitan Club, the Century Club, and others . . .'

[8] Quinn had arranged for WBY to lecture on 'The Intellectual Revival' at St Paul Seminary in St Paul, Minnesota, on 21 Jan 1904.

[9] The Revd Peter Christopher Yorke (1864–1925), Catholic priest, editor, and author of religious books, was a cousin of John MacBride. Born in Galway, and educated at Maynooth, he emigrated to America in 1886, where he served as rector of St Peter's Church, San Francisco, from 1903 to 1913, and where his vigorous support for the San Francisco teamsters in their strike of 1901 led him into conflict with the mayor, James Phelan. In 1902 he founded the *Leader* (San Francisco), a weekly modelled on D. P. Moran's Dublin counterpart, and devoted to the cause of Irish nationalism and labour rights. He was President of the Gaelic League in California. Sean O'Casey dedicated his play, *The Drums of Father Ned*, to Yorke, 'who warned Irish-Ireland of fond delusions many years ago, and who told Dr McDonald, his friend that in the *Rerum Novarum*, the Church was offering the workers no more than platitudes'.

James Duval Phelan (1861–1930), former mayor of San Francisco (1897–1902), was WBY's host there and helped Quinn arrange the lectures in California. He served as US Senator from California, 1915–21. Quinn recalled the circumstances of his quarrel with Yorke in a letter to Hyde of 4 Feb 1906 (NLI): 'Phelan wasn't against the strikers and neither was he radically in favor of them, and Yorke got mad at him because Phelan wasn't on strike with the strikers. In short, Phelan apparently pleased neither party. He didn't please the rich, who refused to re-elect him, and he didn't please the poor, who refused to vote for him, and he didn't please Yorke, who had a large and copious vocabulary of abuse for him. Yeats stopped with Phelan while he was in San Francisco and this I think hurt him a little with "the masses" (or "them asses").'

[10] Quinn had purchased JBY's portrait of WBY for £20 in 1901 (see p. 120), and had collected it from Woburn Buildings during his trip to England and Ireland in July 1902.

[11] MacBride's drinking was to be one of the grounds advanced by MG for a legal separation in 1905. She had mentioned his illness in letters to WBY of 9 and 25 Sept, without specifying the cause.

PS. Burke Cocran has read Cuchullain & praised your style very ardently "lympid like a crystal" & so on. "A wonderful thing to put those stories into the popular mind" & so on.

[*On back of envelope*]
I was about to send papers but Richardson[12] says he is sending them. Have just got letter. Line in preface should be 'a high crested chief'. 'chiefs' & no 'a' is bad meater.[13] WBY

ALS Berg, with envelope addressed to 54 Gower St, London, postmark 'NEW YORK N.Y. NOV 16 1903; London postmark, 'NO 24 03'. Wade, 412–14.

John Quinn to Severance Johnson,[1] [*21 November 1903*]

120 Broadway
Saturday.

Severance Johnson Esq.
  c/o New York Tribune.

Dear Sir: Mr Yeats has asked me to thank you for the article in last Sunday's Tribune & for the good things you said of him.

[12] Stephen J. Richardson (1851–1922), was National President of the Gaelic League in America, Treasurer of the New York Irish Literature Society, and editor and publisher of the *Gael* (NY) from Oct 1901 to Dec 1904, when publication ceased.

[13] In his Preface to AG's *Gods and Fighting Men* WBY had quoted ll. 323–5 from Robert Browning's confessional monologue, 'Pauline' (1833). Describing the Fianna hunters as 'hardly so much individual men as portions of universal nature', he asks (p. xiii) if such hunters are not 'poetical' when encountered suddenly in verse, as in Browning's description of 'an old hunter / Talking with gods, or a high-crested chief / Sailing with troops of friends to Tenedos'. WBY was to use the reference again in his essay 'Bishop Berkeley', where he described it (*E & I*, 409) as one of 'my favourite quotations', in *A Vision (A)* (43), in *AV* (110), and in his late poem, 'Are You Content?' (*VP*, 604–5, ll. 22–3).

[1] F. Severance Johnson (b. 1874) was a New York journalist, whose unsigned interview with WBY, 'W. B. Yeats, Irish Poet', appeared in the *New York Daily Tribune* on 15 November 1903 (see p. 466, n. 2). Johnson met WBY in his room at the Plaza Hotel and described him (Part II, p. 7) as 'Gaunt of body, with a classical, finely chiselled face and a heavy shock of black hair, finely sprinkled with silver. . . . He listens to one in a dreamy sort of way, but as soon as he himself begins to speak he talks with a stress of voice and a play of expression which show his intensity.' Explaining that 'my work is to educate the Irish people with the Irish theatre', WBY launched into an account of the intellectual and political state of Ireland which led to the setting up of the ILT, the discovery of the Fays, their method of rehearsal and delivery, and the success of the company's trip to London, and 'became so enthusiastic over his subject that he had half climbed the chair on which he first rested his foot. He now sat on the brass bar of the bed, and was apparently entirely oblivious of any uncomfortableness. With his right hand he emphasized each sentence with a grace which showed him to be as much an actor as a playwright.'

    In the 1920s Johnson became a special investigator for the *Boston Advertiser*, testifying against racketeers charged with violating the Prohibition Law. His poems, *Voices of the Morning*, had appeared in 1896 and he was to publish a narrative poem, *The Dictator and the Devil*, in 1940.

He also asks me to say he will be very glad if you will return to him *in my care* the stage photograph he loaned you.[2] It is the only one he has with him here & he is very anxious to have it back. I hope you can conveniently attend to its return.

Very truly yours
John Quinn

MS copy NYPL.

John Quinn to Marie Mattingly,[1] [*21 November 1903*]

120 Broadway
Saturday

Miss M. Mattingly
    The Uptown Sun Office
    1393 Broadway, NY.

Dear Miss Mattingly:

Mr Yeats asks me to write you for the return of the stage photograph which he loaned you. It is the only one of the kind he has with him in this

Other publications include *Capitol jokes of the legislative session of 1901–19* (1919), *The Enemy Within* (1920), *When We Were Boys* (1930), a commentary on the New Deal, and *The Gold of Croesus* (1949), a drama in four acts.

[2] The photograph, which was reproduced with the interview, showed MG playing Cathleen ni Houlihan in the Dublin production of 1902. The caption read: 'A "Fly By Night" Play of Irish Peasant Life. / A scene from "Kathleen Ni Houlihan", written by William Butler Yeats, and produced at Irish villages by performers who work in the shops and factories of Dublin in the daytime.'

[1] Marie Mattingly (d. 1943), described by WBY as 'a nice little thing, with pretty eyes and all that' in the New York *World* of 22 Nov, was the daughter of Sarah Irwin (Mrs Cyprian P.) Mattingly (1852–1934), one of the leading feminists of the time. She was born in Kentucky, and turned to a precocious career in journalism when a riding accident thwarted her ambition of becoming a concert pianist. She joined the *Washington Post*, and at eighteen became the Washington bureau chief of the *Denver Post*. Moving to New York, she wrote first for the *World*, and was at this time on the staff of the *Sun*, to which she contributed a regular column, 'Men About Town'. Her marriage in June 1904 to William Brown Meloney (1852–1934), an editor of the *World*, temporarily interrupted her career, but she returned to work in 1913 and soon became one of the leading women journalists in the USA. In 1926 she joined the New York *Herald Tribune*, edited its Sunday magazine, and was appointed editorial director of the paper shortly before her death.

Her interview with WBY, 'A Poet's Views of the Drama', appeared in the New York *Sun* on 15 Nov 1903. She described him (Sect. III, 7) as a 'tall, slender young man of boyish manner, with a long, narrow face, sharp features, gray tinged, coarse black hair and deep set dark eyes', and he spoke of Irving ('that greatest genius of the present stage has done more than anybody else to kill poetic drama'); the need for simplified scenery; the decadence of the modern English stage; Ibsen ('a great intellect, a great temperament perfectly achieved. But since he has given up romances he has written about wornout people of a wornout age'); America ('has it in her to produce the very greatest kind of literature'); Shakespeare ('in reality he was always writing about Elizabeth in [*sic*]

Drawing of WBY denouncing the English stage, from the *San Francisco Examiner*,
31 January 1904

country & he is anxious to have it with him. I hope you can conveniently return it to him *in my care.*

The interview read very well. A writer remarked to me that "*it was too short.*"

Very truly yours
John Quinn

MS copy NYPL.

To Cornelius Weygandt, [22 November 1903]

120 Broadway.
Sunday

Dear Mr. Weygandt:

I have just arrived in New York an hour or two ago.[1] I believe Mr. Quinn wrote to you that I would not be back until today. I leave for Philadelphia tomorrow (Monday) at 10 or 11 o'c and will telegraph you (or Quinn will) at the University the time of my arrival.[2]

I accept with pleasure Dr Furness' invitation for Tuesday Evening.[3] I must return to New York Wednesday morning, as I have a lecture on Wednesday at the College of the City of New York.[4]

England'); and women's education ('I don't think a woman can be too highly educated, but her education should be as unlike that of a man as possible. . . . Art and civilization will come to an end when women are allowed to become masculine'). There was no stage photograph accompanying the interview.

[1] From Trinity College, Hartford, where he had lectured on 20 Nov.

[2] See p. 466. Weygandt's account of WBY's 23 Nov lecture, 'Mr. Yeats' Houston Hall Lecture', appeared in the University of Pennsylvania's *Alumni Register*, December 1903. His biographical sketch, 'The Life-Work of Mr. Yeats', was published there the following month.

[3] Dr Howard Horace Furness (1833–1912), Elizabethan scholar and editor of the *Variorum Edition* of Shakespeare, introduced WBY in Philadelphia as 'a poet whose winged words have been wafted to us through the pure ether of sympathy and admiration and have woven between us a bond of kinship firmer than that of the steel strands which "down in the sunless retreats of the ocean" binds this great Continent to his emerald home' (*Alumni Register* [see n. 1], 98–9).

[4] WBY lectured on 'The Intellectual Revival' at the City College of New York on the evening of 25 Nov.

I shall be glad if you will send tickets for my lecture tomorrow to Dr. Carroll, No 617 South 16*th* Street and also to Prof. Robt Ellis Thompson.[4] I am looking forward very much to seeing you.

Sincerely Yours
W B Yeats

Dict John Quinn, signed by Quinn for WBY; Private; with envelope addressed to University of Pennsylvania, Philadelphia, postmark 'NEW YORK NOV 22'.

To the Editor of the Evening Bulletin *(Philadelphia)*, *24 November 1903*

Sir: There is an alleged interview with me in yesterday's "Bulletin".[1] An interviewer who said he came from your paper did ask me certain questions, but he did not ask me about Mr. George Moore, or Mayworth [*for* Maynooth] or the things that are in this interview. I must deny that I have come here to collect money for the Irish National Theatre or for any other

---

[4] Dr William Carroll (1835–1926), a physician and descendant of Charles Carroll, one of the signatories of the American Declaration of Independence. As an influential member of the Irish Republican Brotherhood he had played a prominent part in gaining Clan na Gael support for Parnell in the late 1870s and had probably been recommended to WBY by John O'Leary or Mark Ryan both of whom knew him well. Robert Ellis Thompson (1844–1924), Irish-born teacher, editor, and scholar, was Principal of the Central High School, Philadelphia, from 1894 to 1921. Since 1884 he had been a staff member of the *Irish World*, which on 5 Dec was to praise WBY for his criticism of Kipling (see p. 467, n. 5). In 1901 he had organized a non-sectarian, non-political Celtic Association in Philadelphia, and presented WBY with a copy of its proceedings, *Celtic Association of Philadelphia, U.S.A. Contributions* (1904).

[1] In the offending interview, 'Irish Poet Comes Here To Lecture', which appeared in the *Evening Bulletin* on 23 Nov (1), WBY managed to disabuse the reporter of the *canard* that he had come to America 'to escape the surveillance of the English police who are constantly watching him', but not of the notion that his 'object . . . is to gain the financial support and the sympathy of Americans in the establishment of a national theatre in Ireland'. The comments on George Moore were plagiarized, with a few changes in punctuation, from Kate Carew's interview in the magazine section of the New York *World* of 22 Nov (3), in which WBY, asked whether it was true that George Moore had renounced Catholicism because the hierarchy had welcomed the King to Ireland, replied that

> 'the character of the ecclesiastical attentions to the King shocked us—simply shocked us! . . . when Maynooth was decorated with the King's racing colors and a picture of his horse, Ambrose II., we really did feel called upon to be shocked! Hence the extreme step taken by my friend, George Moore.'
> 'Had Mr. Moore been a devoted Catholic?'
> 'Oh, that is hardly the point', protested Mr. Yeats, with a demure effort to repress the curling of his lips. 'Probably nobody had known that he was a Catholic; but it was a question of principle with him.'

movement. I have come to tell Americans and American-Irish people about
our work, but our . . . [*last line illegible*].[2]

W B Yeats

Printed letter, *Evening Bulletin* (Philadelphia), 24 Nov 1903 (2).

To Lady Augusta Gregory, [27 November 1903]

1 West 87th Street | New York.

My dear Friend: I am well into my work now. I gave seven lectures last
week (one informal one for nothing except a paistboard box full of roses to
Quinns disgust), & two already this week.[1] Tomorrow I ⟨go to⟩ speak at
Boston.[2] I had a week of dinners & receptions last week. I felt quite well at
the end of it—better than is common with me indeed—however I must
have over worked my nervous power for my lecture here last Tuesday[3] was
not I think good. I seemed to please my audience but I felt all the time that
my words were quite dead. I had a slight difficulty in speaking—a nervous
difficulty with the muscles of my tongue or so it seemed—that kept me
from getting any fire into my work. However I was surrounded with
enthusiastic people at the end of it & Quinn was pleased—You would not
have liked it however for it really was very cold & heavy—I had no eloquence, nothing but beleif in my ideas. I think my measure of success
came from the ideas themselves which were new to the audience. I am fealing just a little anxious because of this lecture but am resting to day & have
resolved to see less people in future. Yesterday I had Brian (publisher of

---

[2] This letter did not appear in all editions of the Philadelphia *Evening Herald* of 24 Nov, and,
since it seems that no hard copy of this particular edition survives, the text is taken from an
imperfect microfilm version.

[1] In addition to those noted, WBY had lectured at Smith College (18 Nov, 'Heroic Literature'), Amherst (18 Nov, 'The Theatre'), Mount Holyoke (19 Nov, 'The Theatre'), and Trinity
College, Hartford (20 Nov, 'Heroic Literature').

[2] In Boston WBY lectured at Wellesley College (28 Nov, 'The Intellectual Revival', and 30
Nov, 'Heroic Literature') and at Harvard (1 Dec, 'Poetry').

[3] An error for Wednesday 25 Nov, when he had lectured at the City College of New York on
'The Intellectual Revival'; see p. 472, n. 3.

the new Irish Anthology)[4] the editor of the 'Critic' to interview me,[5] &
Krans who is writing a little book about my work & a dreadful dramatic
poet who stayed 3 hours & a half & told the plots of his plays.[6] He once
sent 300 copies of a book of poems which had not sold to the editor of the
Freemans Journal with £5 & a request to him to expend the money in circulating the book. He never heard of the book or the £5 since. It was five
years ago, & he is afraid to ask for an account as he does not want to draw
attention to the fact that his book had not sold. I saw Gaffney & he & some
other Irish people here brought me to see Archbishop Ireland, who is I
beleive to arrange a lecture for me.[7] Gaffney apologized for not hav[ing]
seen me before. He had called & missed me. He was sorry as you had
urged him so much to see me & so on. One would have thought you were
his closest friend. He complained that unprincipled persons had spread a
rumour that he had gone to Rome to secure a cardinals hat for Archbishop
Ireland. For some reason these people made him very angry. It was rather

---

[4] George James Bryan (1852–1915) was on the Editorial Board of the University Society,
which sponsored a number of series, especially of children's books. He was working with Charles
Welsh, managing editor of J. D. Morris & Co., Philadelphia, (and also a member of the University Society), to produce a 10-volume anthology of *Irish Literature*, edited by the Irish politician
and man-of-letters, Justin McCarthy. Bryan was eager to see WBY to explain the scope of the
book and to put right misunderstandings with Quinn. He had enlisted Quinn's support for the
project the previous spring, and Quinn had sketched out a plan of the book with WBY, AG, AE,
and Hyde on his trip to Ireland in August, as well as arranging for their participation in it. He
wired for Bryan (then visiting London) to meet him in Dublin and to go down to Coole, but
Bryan's failure to acknowledge the wire and invitation angered him, and his misgivings were
increased when he heard from Dublin that Bryan had disregarded his suggestions as to the content and scope of the anthology. On 21 Nov, therefore, he had written to tell him (NYPL) that
neither he nor WBY would have anything to do with him 'if the work . . . is to be anything like
what I am informed it is'. Bryan, replying immediately, insisted that the project had been misrepresented, and sent the final list of contents. This satisfied Quinn, who arranged for him to see
WBY at 12 noon on 26 Nov, writing on 23 Nov that 'you seem to be on the right track now. Mr.
Yeats will undoubtedly be glad to know . . . that the work is to be better than we anticipated.'
[5] Jeanette Leonard Gilder (1849–1916), journalist and critic, was editor of the *Critic*, which she
started in 1881 with her brother, Joseph B. Gilder (1858–1936).
[6] Horatio Sheafe Krans (1872–1952) received his Ph.D. from Columbia in 1903, the year he
published *Irish Life in Irish Fiction* (*YA4*, 285). His article, 'Mr. Yeats and the Irish Literary
Revival', which grew out of this interview, appeared in the *Outlook* on 2 Jan 1904. A copy of his
William Butler Yeats and the Irish Literary Revival (1904), inscribed 'To William Butler Yeats |
with the compliments | of the author | April 15 1904', is in WBY's library (*YL*, 1074), but in
December 1913 he described it to Carlos Linati (Pierpont Morgan) as 'an absurd little book'. The
'dreadful' dramatist was perhaps Augustus Thomas (1857–1934), a playwright and former St
Louis journalist, whom WBY met at this time.
[7] Thomas St John Gaffney (1864–1944) was an Irish immigrant, political author and activist
for the Republican party, and Secretary of the McKinley League. He strongly supported movements and societies on behalf of Irish nationalism. John Ireland (1838–1918), Archbishop of St
Paul, established thousands of Catholic colonies in Minnesota and played a major role in founding
the Catholic University in Washington DC. Archbishop Ireland and the Knights of Columbus
gave a dinner for WBY before his lecture on 'The Intellectual Revival' at St Paul Seminary on 21
Jan 1904.

an exasperating gathering—a supper, after my lecture, & the visit to the Archbishop—Roche of the Boston Pilot got very drunk on a horrid ⟨black⟩ looking American drink called 'black strap' & blasphemed at first excitedly & then dreamily,[8] Clarke (another Irish journalist & writer) recited a poem of his, a very bad poem with that line you know about 'The Irish Archangel', & everybody admired the poem.[9] I had a great audience at Philadelphia—numbers could not get in & there were people standing in the little dressing rooms at either side of the platform. I spoke only fairly well. I beleive however that a couple of weeks will make me a really good lecturer & that my lecture on the heroic literature will be the best. I think by the by it should have increased your sales here.[10] I am just going out to get lunch. This is the first day I have had to myself. In the afternoon I go to be phot[og]raphed for some paper & at 9 or 10 take the train for Boston. I sleap on the train—I give a lecture at 4 tomorrow & another next evening. I must stop now as I am going to revise my proofs of 'The Kings Threshold' at last

Yours always
W B Yeats

PS. I have just got your letter for which I thank you. I am very sorry that you are ill. Please write soon & tell me that you are well—I will be a little anxious.[11]

I have just been to a photographers for some paper. I think I did better than I thought the other night as Quinns messenger heard a professor say it was the best lecture he ever heard. The porter at the door says the audience was the largest for 27 years.

It is about 5.30. Quinn will be soon in. I have had a peaceful day.

ALS Berg, with envelope addressed to 54 Gower St, London, postmark 'NEW YORK N.Y. NOV 28 1903'.

[8] James Jeffrey Roche (1847–1908), was an Irish-born author, poet, and from 1890 to 1905 editor of the *Boston Pilot*, to which WBY had contributed from 1887–92. In 1904 Roosevelt appointed him Consul-General at Genoa. Blackstrap is a mixture of spirits, usually rum, and molasses.

[9] Joseph Clarke (see p. 464) had recited Roche's poem, 'The Fighting Race', inspired by the list of Irish casualties on the USS *Maine* in 1898 and including the line 'When Michael, the Irish Archangel, stands'.

[10] In this lecture WBY praised and quoted from AG's *Cuchulain of Muirthemne*.

[11] On 20 Nov (Berg) AG had written that 'some poison microbes had taken possession of me' but that she was 'better now'.

To G. W. Wickersham,[1] *3 December 1903*

⟨120 BROADWAY⟩
1 West 87th Street,
Dec. 3, 1903.

G. W. Wickersham, Esq.,
42 West 47th Street,
New York City.

My dear Sir:

I have been out of the City and have on my return for a few hours received your note of November 30th. Unfortunately I shall hardly be in town except for a few hours now and then between this and Christmas and so am unable to accept your kind invitation to dinner.[2]

I thank you for sending me the card of invitation to the Club, though I have not had the time to call there.[3]

Very truly yours
W B Yeats

TLS LC.

---

[1] George Woodward Wickersham (1858–1936), a lawyer with the New York firm of Strong and Cadwalader from 1887 to 1909, was to serve as US Attorney General in the Taft administration from 1909 to 1913, thereafter founding the firm of Cadwalader, Wickersham and Taft. He and his wife, Mildred Wendell (d. 1944), whom he had married in 1883, were generous hosts, and R. A. Anderson reports in *With Horace Plunkett in Ireland* (139) that he and O'Donovan received a dinner invitation from them while still on board ship: 'I thanked her for having singled us out for such hospitality. But the good lady rather startled me by saying, "Don't make any mistake. *You* haven't been singled out. This is only ordinary American politeness".'

[2] Wickersham had already made an earlier attempt to get WBY to dinner, but this was apparently squashed by Quinn, who wrote to James Byrne on 14 Nov (NYPL): 'Yeats told me of Mr. Wickersham's kind suggestion about a dinner at which he would have Mr. Gilder and some other literary men in New York. This it seems to me would be excellent if it were not for the fact that ... I am planning a dinner under the auspices of the Society about a week before the lecture here at which we will have Mr. Gilder, Mr. Stedman, Robert Bridges, Mr. Harland, Mr. Cockran, Judge Keogh and others, and have it more or less of a function and reported in the papers etc. ... I hope that you will agree that this is the better plan.' In the event neither dinner took place, although the Irish Literary Society of New York held a reception for WBY at the Metropolitan Club on 5 Mar, shortly before his departure.

[3] Wickersham was a member of the Century Club, which had put WBY up for visitor's membership; see p. 468, n. 7.

To Edith Craig, 6 December 1903

1 West 87th Street, | New York,
Dec. 6, 1903.

My dear Miss Craig:

Please forgive me for dictating this letter, but I am up to my ears in occupations and must get through my work as quickly as possible. I lectured last night, I lecture again tomorrow, and so on.[1] I have heard from Miss Smith and others about the collapse of the Masquers.[2] I was doubtful somewhere about midsummer when I thought we were not going to get subscribers, but I don't think that the Society should have been dropped, once that it got so much into the public eye and got so much money.[3] Such things should be left undone or done altogether. Personally it rids me of some inconvenience, as my time will be so much taken up with the theatrical movement in Dublin. I am sorry, however, that a plan of yours should have gone astray.

It is not, however, about this that I write to you, but to thank you for your support at the Stage Society, who are I am told now at last going to do "Where There is Nothing"[4] and to say that Lady Gregory will represent me in the matter of that play while I am away. Please consult her about anything that may arise in connection with it. I had hoped to make some changes, but I am afraid it will be impossible, for I cannot write in railway trains and I have no other place to write for the most of the time.

I have already given a great many lectures and shall give a great many more before I get back.

Yours sincerely
W B Yeats

[1] On 5 Dec WBY lectured on 'The Intellectual Revival' to the Long Island Historical Society, Brooklyn, under the auspices of the Brooklyn Italian Settlement, before travelling to Bryn Mawr College on 7 Dec to speak on 'Heroic Literature'.

[2] The Masquers had broken up on 12 Nov, and on the same day Murray had written to WBY: 'You will hear with mixed feelings that the Masquers Society is no more!' (*LWBY* I. 131). Pamela Colman Smith must have written at the same time in a letter now lost, and she repeated the message on 16 Dec (*LWBY* I. 132): '*The Masquers* is dead—at least for the present'.

[3] See p. 416, n. 2. Despite WBY's worries the subscriptions had proved sufficient, but in his letter (see n. 2) Murray had told him that everyone 'was for winding up and returning the subscriptions except Miss Craig, who contended that she could put a piece on the stage in a fortnight, and do it well. . . . We are returning subscriptions, and explaining that, though we had enough money and members to justify us in starting, we found other circumstances unfavourable and thought that the attempt at a "Theatre of Beauty" should be postponed, though we still keep our faith in it.'

[4] See pp. 262–3. Pamela Colman Smith had probably told him of its acceptance in her letter announcing the demise of the Masquers (see above, n. 2). *Where There Is Nothing* was produced by the Stage Society on 26–8 June 1904.

Miss Edith Craig,
    7 Smith Square,
        Westminster,
            London,
                England.

TLS Tenterden.

To Cornelius Weygandt, 6 December 1903

1 West 87th Street, | New York,
Dec. 6, 1903.

My dear Mr. Weygandt:

I have received your letter of the 3d and thank you for the newspaper clippings enclosed.

I did leave my muffler at Dr. Furness's house. If you could kindly drop him a note (I have not his address with me) asking him to send it to me at either Mr. Lippincott's house, 204 West Rittenhouse Square, or to the Contemporary Club, it will reach me all right.[1] I am sorry to give you so much trouble.

Yes, I have no doubt you are right; I think it would be best to change the subject of the lecture. I rather suggest to you my lecture on the Irish Heroic Literature instead of Poetry in the Old Time and in the New. I think this lecture follows better from the general lecture I gave in Philadelphia before, and if you like to ask me to read some of my own poetry I can do so more readily after the Heroic Literature than after the other.[2] I will modify my lecture on Heroic Literature and make it cover some of the ground of Poetry in the Old Time and in the New. My feeling about the subject you have yourself proposed is that it is rather general and a little like the lecture I have given in Philadelphia.

I enjoyed my stay so much with you.

Sincerely yours,
W B Yeats

[1] Joshua Bertram Lippincott (1857–1940), publisher, was at this time Vice-President of his father's firm, the J. B. Lippincott Company. On 8 Dec he hosted a dinner for WBY before his lecture on 'The Theatre' at the Contemporary Club.

[2] On 15 Dec WBY returned to Philadelphia to lecture on 'Irish Fairy and Folk Lore' for the Science and Art Club of Germantown at the home of Weygandt's father, Cornelius Nolen Weygandt (1832–1907).

Professor Cornelius Weygandt,
    University of Pennsylvania,
        Philadelphia, Pa.

TLS Private, with envelope addressed to University of Pennsylvania, Philadelphia, Pa., post-mark 'NEW YORK NY DEC 6 1903'.

To Samuel Burns Weston,[1] *6 December 1903*

1 West 87th Street, | New York,
Dec. 6, 1903.

S. Burns Weston, Esq.,
    Corresponding Secretary,
        Contemporary Club,
            1305 Arch Street,
                Philadelphia, Pa.

Dear Sir:

I have your letter of November 27th.

Unfortunately I have mislaid the two cards of invitation to the meeting of the Club Tuesday evening.

I shall be glad if you will send to my friend Dr. William Carroll of No. 617 South 16th Street a card of invitation for Tuesday night's lecture; also a card to Professor Robert Ellis Thompson at the Central High School, corner of Broad and Green Streets.[2]

I am glad that there will be a discussion following my lecture and that I am to be given an opportunity to close the discussion.

It is very kind of you to offer to entertain me at the University Club but I have already accepted an invitation to take dinner with Mr. Lippincott on Tuesday evening and hence cannot avail myself of your kindness.

Yours very truly,
Yours sny
W B Yeats

TLS Philadelphia.

[1] Samuel Burns Weston (1855–1936) was corresponding secretary of the Contemporary Club, director of the Philadelphia Society for Ethical Culture, and editor of the *International Journal of Ethics* from 1890 to 1914.
[2] See p. 473, n. 4.

To the Duchess of Sutherland, [7 December 1903]

⟨THE DEANERY, | BRYN MAWR, | PENNSYLVANIA.⟩
1 West 87 St, | New York, | U S A

My dear Duchess of Sutherland: I have been trying to write for you but I have been running from place to place giving lectures. At first I had my lectures to prepare, & then I found that the distraction of lecturing thoughts made it impossible to write in the very few moments I have. If I had not got your letter I would none the less have written to tell you this & that I will have some three days at the week end & some more days in a fortnight & that I will certainly send you something then. Indeed I have come down to this great girls college where I am to lecture to night, quite early that I may get a little time to start something for you.[1] I am sorry for all this delay but Mr Sharp will tell you that there never was a writer who wrote with so much difficulty. I am lecturing to practically all the American colleges of any importance on our Celtic literature. I hope to turn the thoughts of a good many here to my Irish & your highland things.[2]

'Where there is nothing' of which you ask has not be[en] acted but will be by the Stage Society next spring I think. It has too large a caste for my own company.

Yrs sny
W B Yeats

ALS UCLA.

To Lady Augusta Gregory, [8 December 1903]

THE DEANERY, | BRYN MAWR, | PENNSYLVANIA.
1 West 87 St | New York.

My dear Friend: You will see by the note-paper that I am on tour. This is the chief womans college of America, the one to which the richer classes send their girls. I have just given my second lecture.[1] I write to tell you of my success. At first I did not like my lectures at all. But last week I gave a lecture here which was I thought the best I have ever given. It was on the

---

[1] See pp. 421–2. WBY gave his first lecture at Bryn Mawr College on 3 Dec ('The Intellectual Revival'), and the second on 7 Dec ('Heroic Literature').

[2] The Duchess of Sutherland wrote on highland themes in the Glasgow *Celtic Monthly*, 'A Magazine for Highlanders', and had recently published a volume of seven love stories, *The Winds of the World* (1902). As the wife of a Scottish duke she took an interest in Scottish cultural affairs.

[1] See previous letter, n. 1.

"intellectual movement". Last night I lectured again on heroic poetry &
there was not standing room in the hall. Not only the girls were there but
a number of people from the neighbourhood. I could even see a few people
standing out in the passage. One of the professors told me that I was the
most 'vital influence' that had come near the college "for 15 years". What
has pleased me so much is getting this big audience by my own effort. It
has not meant much to me getting big audiences where I have never been
heard—like the big Philadelphia one. They are getting all our books here
now. Do you know I have not met a single woman here who puts 'tin tacks
in the soup'? & I find that the woman that does is recognized as an English
type. One teacher explained to me the difference in this way 'we prepare
the girls to live their lives but in England they are making them all teachers'.[2] The head of this college has a passion for statistics & the head of a
rival college declares that she once made a speach containing this sentence
'Fifty per-cent of my girls get married & sixty per cent have children'. It is
not known what she intended to say. She is a charming woman however &
the college buildings made under her management are some of them really
beautiful.[3]

I have written to Miss Craig about 'Where there is nothing' & given you
Authority. I doubt if I shall or can alter it till I get back. I wish you would
get Mrs Emery to write a note on the way to speak those poems in
'Kathleen-ni-Hoolihan' & please revise her style—she wont mind. I wish
too that Fay would give you the music Mrs MacBride used for the lines

[2] WBY expanded upon this observation in his essay, 'America and the Arts', published in the
Metropolitan Magazine of April 1905. Comparing college-educated women in America and England, he wrote (*UP* II. 340–1) that in America he 'never met that typical argumentative woman of
the English college, who was meant, it may be, to have a happy natural charm but has learned an
unhappy pose. Ever censorious, ever doing battle for the commonplace, her mind fashioned for
joy and triumph, is full of virulent peevish negation; one would as soon sit down to supper with a
host who dropped tin tacks into the soup tureen as converse with her; but these American women
are as charming, as well-educated in all necessary things, as if they had spent their youth in the
impulsive laborious ignorance of the studio.'
[3] Martha Carey Thomas (1857–1935), suffragist and controversial educationalist, was President
of Bryn Mawr from 1894 to 1922. She was famous for her 'slips', and this one is repeated in
Edith Finch's biography, *Carey Thomas of Bryn Mawr* (1947), which also tells (234–5) of WBY's
behaviour at a dinner party, attended by faculty members and local worthies, that she gave in his
honour: 'Warmed at first by the satisfaction of seeing a poet who looked and spoke the part, they
were amused, then bewildered, then affronted by this gravely dark and lanky young man who
talked with arrogant insistence about things beneath their contempt. Turn the conversation as his
hostess would, all through dinner and afterwards he persisted in discoursing to this wholly
uncomprehending audience on fairies and Celtic magic. The air grew chill with ironic disapproval
and then with flat boredom. By the evening's end Carey Thomas was exhausted, torn between
laughter and annoyance. To her reproachful question, "Why did you do it, Mr. Yeats?" he
replied only, "They needed to hear about fairies." He might have retaliated that she herself had
not started the dinner off happily, for when the guests were being served grape juice, the usual
beverage at Deanery dinners of that time, she had turned to Mr. Yeats on her right hand: "You,
Mr. Yeats," she had said in tones that rang in the ears of her other guests, "*you* may have claret."'

'They shall be remembered for ever'. That might go in too (as well as Mrs Emerys)—it was a tune heard by clairvoyance.[4] In fact all the music even the unrhymed verses would be a gain. There may be some delay with the poetical plays. I am trying to get 'The Kings Threshold' in the North American Review for January. If I can manage this both books can come out almost at once. If I cannot there will be delay.[5] I hear that somebody here is writing about 'Cuchullain'. He told a friend of Quinns that it was 'one of the great books of the world a book like Homer'.[6] I speak to night at a club in Philadelphia on The Theatre. The ground is covered with snow & where the roads have not been beaten bare with horses hoofs one is driven in sleighs with jingling bells.

I will stop now for I am trying to write a poem.[7]

Yours always
W B Yeats

I find that I am keeping very well—a little nervous feategue of the voice at times but very slight. At first I accepted invitations rather recklessly but now I am wiser & am keeping fresh.

[*On back of envelope*]
If necessary you could instead of getting Mrs Emery to make a note merely refer to the essay in 'Ideas of Good & Evil'. I dare say Bullen is talking nonsense about the scores he always talks some kind of petulent nonsense before one gets a book out.
W B Y.

ALS Berg, with envelope addressed to 54 Gower St, London, redirected to Coole; postmark 'BRYN MAWR DEC 8 1903'. London postmark 'DE 19 03'. Wade, 414–15.

[4] See p. 373, n. 5. AG had written to WBY on 20 Nov (Berg) that she had 'got the Cathleen chant from Mrs. Emery, & have written to F. Fay to try to get me the Pot of Broth music, if he does, I will give them to Bullen'. FF's music for the lyrics in *Cathleen ni Houlihan* was printed in Bullen's edition of 'Plays for an Irish Theatre', vol. II, but was apparently not in time for the earlier American edition, *The Hour-Glass and Other Plays* of January 1904. The scores for these and other lyrics were later published in *CW* III (1908).

[5] *The King's Threshold* did not appear in periodical form, and the publication of both books was delayed until March 1904.

[6] So echoing WBY's own pronouncement (*Expl*, 3) that *Cuchulain of Muirthemne* was 'the best book that has ever come out of Ireland: for the stories which it tells are a chief part of Ireland's gift to the imagination of the world'. In the 'Scylla and Charybdis' episode of *Ulysses* (I. 465) Buck Mulligan mimics 'the Yeats touch'

mopping, chanting with waving graceful arms:
—The most beautiful book that has come out of our country in my time. One thinks of Homer.

[7] 'Old Memory', sent to the Duchess of Sutherland *c.* 20 Dec. Quinn's inscription in a copy of *Poems: Second Series* (Indiana) reveals that WBY finished 'Old Memory' and 'Never Give All the Heart' 'in my place in New York'.

To George J. Bryan, [14] December 1903[1]

Dec. 15, 1903.

George J. Bryan, Esq.,
    Care The University Society,
        78 Fifth Ave., New York.

My dear Sir:
    I received your note in regard to the selection of my poems.[2] I think that
the selection had better be made by Mr. Russell.[3]

Yours very truly
[*No signature on carbon*]

TS copy NYPL.

To Mrs Helen MacGregor Byrne, [14] December 1903

Dec. 15, 1903.

Dear Mrs. Byrne:
    Mr. Quinn has read to me your note of December 4.[1] I was sorry that an
engagement at Brooklyn prevented me joining you at the Carnegie Hall

---

[1] This and the following letters were dictated at Quinn's office in the law firm of Alexander
and Colby at 120 Broadway, to James O'Neill, a stenographer employed by Quinn to type WBY's
letters and his Carnegie Hall speech. Although dated 'Dec. 15', they were evidently dictated on
14 Dec and typed the following day, after WBY's departure for Philadelphia. Quinn signed them
with an imitation of WBY's signature.

[2] Bryan wanted to discuss the selection from WBY's work for *Irish Literature* (see p. 475, n. 4),
and the use of material from his *Fairy and Folktales of the Irish Peasantry* (1888) and *Irish Fairy
Tales* (1892) for an article on Irish Folklore there.

[3] AE did, in fact, make the selection from WBY's work; see below, p. 493.

[1] See p. 459, n. 3. Mrs Byrne had evidently asked WBY and Quinn to join her on Sunday
evening, 6 Dec 1903, at the Carnegie Hall to hear the Revd T. A. Finlay and the Revd Jeremiah
O'Donovan speak on the aims of the Irish Agricultural Organisation Society under the auspices of
the Irish Industrial League. On that evening WBY was already engaged to attend a private dinner
party in Brooklyn, but Mrs Byrne, already nettled by the clash between WBY's and O'Donovan's
lecture tours (see p. 463), and by the embarrassingly sparse turn-out for the meeting, was not
mollified by this apology, and early in January 1904 Quinn heard that she 'thought that there is an
explanation coming from me for my failure to attend'. He gave the 'explanation' in a letter of
7 Jan (NYPL) to her husband: 'The fact is that Mr. Yeats had in a moment of thoughtlessness
promised to go to Brooklyn that night to "an informal little supper". We started for there at six
o'clock on the express promise that we would be able to get away at 8:30 and I intended to come
back to the meeting with him. The eating did not begin until nearly seven and when it was
over about eight people kept dropping in and it was impossible to get away . . . until after ten,
and it was eleven before we got over to New York. I didn't know that I was down as secretary
of the meeting or that I was expected to [?]return any resolution until . . . three weeks after the
meeting.'

meeting. I am still busy lecturing and leave for Philadelphia to-morrow and then go to Montreal, Canada, and on Saturday night I lecture in Brooklyn before the Twentieth Century Club. Later on I shall have more time and shall be glad to spend a quiet evening with yourself and Mr. Byrne as you have been so kind as to ask me. My public lecture is, I believe, at Carnegie Hall, Sunday evening, January 3.

Sincerely yours
[*No signature on carbon*]

TS copy NYPL.

To Charles M. Fitzgerald,[1] [14] December 1903

Dec. 15, 1903.

C. M. Fitzgerald, Esq.,
    123 West 48th Street,
        New York.

Dear Mr. Fitzgerald:

I must have come in just after you called this afternoon. I am very sorry indeed to have missed you, and hope I may see you in a few days. I go to Philadelphia to-morrow morning and then on to Canada and will not be back until late Saturday to lecture in Brooklyn on Saturday night. Could you come in here next Sunday afternoon any time between 3 and 5 o'clock? Mr. Quinn tells me that you know my old friend Frederick Gregg.[2] I have been looking forward to meet[ing] him here, but my time has been so fully occupied that I have not ventured to write to appoint a meeting. Tell him if you see him please that I hope to see him very shortly.

Sincerely yours
[*No signature on carbon*]

TS copy NYPL.

---

[1] Charles M. Fitzgerald (b. 1872), journalist and drama critic, was the son of Dr Charles Edward Fitzgerald, the celebrated Dublin oculist and friend of JBY (see p. 630). He had emigrated to the USA in 1895 and, after working as a reporter in Niagara Falls, moved to New York and subsequently became a drama critic.

[2] Frederick James Gregg (1864–1927) had been WBY's schoolfellow at the Dublin High School (see I. 7). He had emigrated to the USA in 1891 and worked as a journalist on the *New York Evening Sun*. He was a close friend of John Quinn, who nicknamed him 'El Greggo'.

To Emma B. Lewis,[1] [14] December 1903

Dec. 15, 1903.

Miss Emma B. Lewis,
    Corresponding Secretary,
        Twentieth Century Club,
            47 Pierrepont Street, Brooklyn.

Dear Madam:
I received your note of December 5, enclosing the invitations to my lecture for Saturday evening, 19th instant. Thanking you very much for sending them,

Yours very truly
[*No signature on carbon*]

TS copy NYPL.[2]

To James Mavor,[1] [14] December 1903

Dec. 15, 1903.

Professor James Mavor,
    University of Toronto,
        Toronto, Canada.

Dear Professor Mavor:
I shall be glad to meet you again when I lecture in Toronto, and accept with pleasure your invitation to stay with you while there. Mr. Quinn will notify you by letter or telegraph of the time of my arrival.

Yours very truly
[*No signature on carbon*]

TS copy NYPL.

[1] Emma Burnham Lewis (1853–1944), a charter member and former Secretary of Mrs Field's Literary Club and a long-time member of the Twentieth Century Club, was the daughter of Judge Alexander Newman Lewis (1818–95), a prominent Brooklyn Republican who had been appointed by President Lincoln to serve as Internal Revenue Collector in New York during the Civil War. She was active in the Grace Church of Brooklyn for over half a century and served on the advisory board of the Mission of Help of the Episcopal Church. As a member of the American Red Cross she took part in relief work during the First World War. WBY lectured to the Twentieth Century Club of Brooklyn on 19 Dec for his usual fee of $75.
[2] Through an oversight the stenographer retyped this letter verbatim on 16 Dec.

[1] As editor of the short-lived *Scottish Arts Review* in 1890, James Mavor (1854–1925), Scottish-born economist and statistician, had solicited contributions from WBY (see I. 215). He was

To Mrs Isabel Moore, [*14*] *December 1903*

120 BROADWAY
Dec. 15, 1903.

Mrs. Isabel Moore,
　The Judson,
　　53 Washington Square,
　　　New York City.

Dear Mrs. Moore:

Mr. Quinn has handed to me your article in "The Bookman".[1] Many thanks for your admirable and sympathetic notice. I am sorry not to have been able to have thanked you personally for the notice, but I am still exceedingly busy going from place to place on my lectures and will be so for some little time to come.

Sincerely yours
W B Yeats

TL, signed by John Quinn for WBY; Harvard.

appointed Professor of Political Economy in the University of Toronto in 1892, and remained in Canada for the rest of his life, producing important reports on relief of the poor, railway administration, and the Canadian Copyright Act. He had spent the summer of 1903 in the principal US cities conducting an enquiry into municipal administration in the USA. WBY stayed with him during his visit to Toronto from 13 to 14 Feb 1904, and was to meet him again during his tour of February 1914.

[1] See p. 387. Isabel Moore published her general survey of WBY's works, 'William Butler Yeats', in the *Bookman* (New York) of December 1903, together with the photograph by Elliott and Fry, London (see Plate 13).

To Charles E. Moyse,[1] *[14] December 1903*

Dec. 15, 1903.

Professor Charles E. Moyser,
 Vice Principal of McGill University,
  802 Sherbrooke Street,
   Montreal, Canada.

Dear Sir:

I received your note of December 8th and shall be very glad to be your guest during my stay in Montreal. I should like to take the day ride along the Hudson and Lake Champlain,[2] but fear that if I took the morning train on Thursday from New York I might be a little rushed for time upon my arrival in Montreal. I think, therefore, that I will take an evening train from New York on Wednesday. Mr. Quinn will telegraph you what train I will take and what time I shall arrive in Montreal. I hope that I can take an early Friday morning train back so that I can pass along the Lake Champlain and Hudson River country by daylight.

Yours very truly
[*No signature on carbon*]

TS copy NYPL.

[1] Charles Ebenezer Moyse (1852–1924) had been born in Devon and educated at London University before emigrating to Canada, where he became Headmaster of St Mary's College, and, in 1878, Molson Professor of English Literature at McGill University. Earlier this year he had been appointed Dean of the Faculty of Arts and Vice-Principal of McGill. His *The Dramatic Art of Shakespeare* had appeared in 1879 and *Poetry as a Fine Art* in 1883, and he was to publish volumes of verse in 1910 and 1911. WBY spoke on 'Heroic Literature' at Royal Victoria College, McGill University, on 17 Dec 1903. The Montreal *Daily Star* of 19 Dec reported that in 'thanking the lecturer for his delightful address, Dean Moyse referred to the part the Irish citizens had taken in bringing Mr. Yeats on'.

[2] Lake Champlain lies on the upper reaches of the Hudson River, and, situated between the Green Mountains and the Adirondacks, is an area of great natural beauty.

To George Haven Putnam,[1] *[14] December 1903*

Dec. 15, 1903.

George Haven Putnam, Esq.,
27 & 29 West 23rd Street,
New York City.

Dear Mr. Putnam:
I was very sorry not to be able to accept your kind invitation to lunch with you at the City Club.[2] I have been constantly lecturing and leave to-morrow for Philadelphia to lecture there and go from there to Canada. I shall have more time towards the end of the month, and shall hope to see some friends then.

Sincerely yours
[Signed for WBY by John Quinn]

TS copy NYPL.

To Robert Ellis Thompson,[1] *[14] December 1903*

Dec. 15, 1903.

Professor Robert Ellis Thompson,
Central High School,
Philadelphia, Pa.

Dear Professor Thompson:
I lecture to-morrow night in Germantown at the Science and Art Club, and I have a business appointment here in New York before starting

---

[1] George Haven Putnam (1844–1930) emigrated to America from London as a child and served in the Union Army during the Civil War. He became President of the New York publishing firm of G. P. Putnam, founded by his father, and played a leading role in the American Copyright League leading up to the Copyright Bill of 1891. His firm was to become AG's American publishers from 1912. He wrote a number of works on the book trade and, in 1909, a biography of Abraham Lincoln. His *Memories of a Publisher* appeared in 1915.

[2] The City Club was founded in late 1892 to educate the voters of New York, to improve the proficiency and integrity of City government, and to counter the practices of Tammany Hall and other forms of municipal corruption. Its committees kept watch over the various City and State executive bodies, and brought delinquent officials to account.

[1] See p. 473, n. 4.

to-morrow.[2] I go to Canada the day after to-morrow and will have to leave Philadelphia early to-morrow in order to catch the New York train, so I fear it is impossible for me to address your students. Please make my apologies to the members of your staff who were so kind as to ask me.

Sincerely yours
[*No signature on carbon*]

TS copy NYPL.

John Quinn to Henry L. Jayne,[1] 15 December 1903

Dec. 15, 1903.

Henry L. Jayne, Esq.,
    Treasurer,
        505 Chestnut Street,
            Philadelphia, Pa.

Dear Sir:
Mr. Yeats has asked me to acknowledge the receipt of your note of December 10th, enclosing him check for $75. for his lecture before the Contemporary Club. He regrets that it was impossible for you to attend his lecture.

Yours very truly
John Quinn

TS copy NYPL.

[2] Under Quinn's instructions, WBY left New York on 15 Dec by the 2.30 p.m. train from 23rd Street for his lecture in Germantown. He stayed overnight with Weygandt senior (see p. 479, n. 2), who wrote in his diary next morning (Private): 'I bade *Yeats* goodbye, with an invitation to come again. He has an engaging personality, high ideals, and at times an abstracted manner. He did not at all remember Mrs. C—, who sat next to him at the Lippincott dinner, and he told her so in my hearing! Rather mortifying to such a woman . . .'

[1] Henry LaBarre Jayne (1857–1920), a prominent lawyer in Philadelphia, was educated at the universities of Pennsylvania and Leipzig, and admitted to the bar of the Supreme Court in 1896. He took an active interest in the arts throughout his life, becoming a member of the Academy of Music, the Browning Society, the American Philosophical Society, and the National Institute of Social Sciences. He helped found the Drama League of Philadelphia and was treasurer of Plays and Players. He was also treasurer, and later president, of the Contemporary Club of Philadelphia, where WBY had spoken on 8 Dec (see p. 479).

John Quinn to Evert Jansen Wendell,[1] *15 December 1903*

Dec. 15, 1903.

Evart Jansen Wendell, Esq.,
    8 East 38th Street,
      New York City.

Dear Sir:

Mr. Yeats has asked me to reply to your note of November 24, from Cooperstown, N.Y.

Mr. Yeats will lecture on Sunday evening, January 3, on "The Intellectual Revival in Ireland". Hon. W. Bourke Cockran will preside and deliver a short introductory address. I write thinking you may be interested to go when he speaks in New York. He expects to make it quite an event.

Yours very truly
John Quinn

TS copy NYPL.

To Jeremiah O'Donovan, 16 December 1903

Dec. 16, 1903.

Rev. J. O'Donovan,
    Albermarle Hotel,
      Madison Square West, New York

My dear O'Donovan:

I wish very much that you could send me that little play "Heads or Harps".[1] I know that you are very busy, and I am sorry to trouble you about it, but I think if I had it I might be able to place it somewhere.

---

[1] Evert Jansen Wendell (1859–1917), a famous Harvard sprinter, was the younger brother of Barrett Wendell, the Harvard professor of English whom WBY had met in Boston on 1 Dec. He had successfully built up the family woollen commission firm, and was now devoting himself to athletic and philanthropic activities. He also took a lifelong interest in the theatre. He was a member of the Amateur Athletic Union and of the International Committee of the Olympic Games. WBY had taken a youthful interest in American track events, and as an enthusiastic runner at the Godolphin School, Hammersmith (*Aut*, 39), had 'followed the career of a certain professional runner. . . . described as "the bright particular star of American athletics"'.

[1] For *Heads or Harps* see pp. 295, n. 2; 462, n. 3; and 502, n. 9. WBY had presumably loaned O'Donovan the MS of the play while crossing on the *Oceanic*.

I am glad to hear from Quinn that your meeting at Newark, and also the one in New York, had been so successfully [*for* successful].[2]

I am still going the rounds hither but hope to see you presently.[3]

Very truly yours
[*Signed for WBY by John Quinn*]

TS copy NYPL.

To J. O'Neill Ryan,[1] 16 December 1903

Dec. 16, 1903.

Hon. O'Neill Ryan,
   St. Louis, Mo.

Dear Sir:

I received your note of Nov. 24th. I am to lecture in St. Louis on, I believe, January 6 and 7. One lecture is, I think, to be given before the Pedagogical Society.[2] I shall be glad to meet you in St. Louis.[3]

Yours very truly
[*Signed for WBY by John Quinn*]

TS copy NYPL.

---

[2] According to R. A. Anderson (*With Horace Plunkett in Ireland*, 143–4) neither occasion was in fact successful. The New York meeting, to endorse the efforts of the Irish Agricultural Organisation Society, had taken place at the Carnegie Hall on 6 Dec (see p. 484, n. 1) and was chaired by Justice Morgan O'Brien. O'Donovan spoke after the chief speaker, the Revd T. A. Finlay, who urged support for the Society which was, he claimed, helping to stem Irish emigration, but 'the audience was so sparse and scattered that it only made the vast hall appear more empty'. The Newark meeting, held on 11 Dec, had been ruined by Bourke Cockran, who was running for Congress, and who insisted on attending 'accompanied by two musical ladies. He spoke much . . . and his two fair friends wasted the time and patience of the meeting with their musical interludes. I was "snowed under", but Father Finlay managed to deliver a brief but effective speech.' The newspaper reports, which WBY would have read, were far more enthusiastic than Anderson's accounts would appear to warrant, but Cockran certainly got the lion's share of the coverage in the Newark press.

[3] On 3 Feb 1904 Quinn reported to Mrs Byrne that WBY had invited O'Donovan to lunch at the Plaza Hotel on New Year's Day 'in order to discuss the St. Louis project. Neither he nor I then knew that Father O'Donovan had sailed . . .'

[1] John O'Neill Ryan (1860–1939), the son of Irish immigrants, had practised law in his native St Louis since 1880, and was appointed a judge in the Circuit Court of the city from 1900–6, and again from 1929 to his death. He was to act as the first Dean of the St Louis University Institute of Law from 1908–15 and served on the boards of the Catholic Charities of St Louis and of the Catholic High School.

[2] WBY lectured to the St Louis Society of Pedagogy on 5 Jan 1904, and to the Wednesday Club on the following day.

[3] 'Meet Me In St. Louis, Louis' was the title of a popular song, written by Andrew Stirling with music by Kerry Mills. The song, inspired by the St Louis World Fair, was one of the hits of 1904.

To George Russell (AE), [*16*] *December 1903*

1 West 87th Street, | New York,
Dec. 18, 1903.

My dear Russell:

Bryan has written to me as to selection from my poems in his proposed Irish Anthology. He asks me whether I or you are to make the selection. Now I have a very great objection to making a selection from my own poems. I don't think an author should authoritatively take out certain poems and give them a sort of special imprimatur. Besides I have another objection. I don't want to be connected with the editorial side of Mr. Bryan's book; he is a more enthusiastic advertiser than I think becomes my dignity. So I think you had better make the selections as you are doing the introductory notice. At the same time, I think I must ask you to make it entirely from the last editions. I mean that I don't want any of the poems I have discarded to come into it. Rolleston did not please me over well by giving long extracts from what I think immature verse. With this reservation you can pick whatever you like from the garden.[1]

I am constantly lecturing and I think doing fairly well. I am just on my way to Canada,[2] and go to the Pacific Coast in January. I bring your work into the greater number of my lectures, and I notice from the number of people who ask me about you afterwards that you have a considerable following here. I am expecting every day a copy of your new book at the Dun

---

[1] See p. 484. WBY did not join the editorial and advisory board, which included Douglas Hyde and AG, but he was listed as one of the authors of 'Biographies and Literary Appreciations', which are identified in the index. WBY had already been irritated by AE's republication of his earlier work (see pp. 274, 276), but in spite of these instructions AE chose thirteen, mostly early, poems, five of which had appeared in Rolleston's *A Treasury of Irish Poetry* (1900), and the only recent poem was 'The Old Age of Queen Maeve' from *In the Seven Woods*. He also printed *Cathleen ni Houlihan* and prose selections from *The Celtic Twilight* and *IGE*. For his introductory notice (*Irish Literature* IX. 3651–4) he reprinted the article he had published in the *Reader* of August 1903 (see p. 387, n. 1).

[2] This letter was probably dictated on 16 Dec, as WBY lectured in Canada on 17 Dec; he presumably signed it and added the P. S. on his return the next day, after a twelve-hour train journey.

Emer press.[3] I suppose it cannot be delayed much longer. When you write
let me know how Colum's play has gone.[4]

> Faithfully yours,
> W B Yeats

[*In WBY's hand*]
I dont want to be connected with the editorial side of Bryan book because
as I have been lecturing here Quinn thinks he would probably make some
use of [my] name that might make me seem responsible for his sheme as a
whole. I think of writing to UI challenging Griffith to a discuss[ion]—in
the manner of Martyn & Redmond.[5]

TLS Indiana. Wade, 415–16.

To the Duchess of Sutherland, [c. 20 December 1903]

1 West 87 St | New York | U S A

My dear Duchess of Sutherland: I enclose that poem.[1] I could not make
myself do it, when I did get a couple of days free of lectures, partly
because I had a cold partly because the rymes would not come; but at last I
did it the other day when shut up in a railway carriage for twelve hours
coming from Canada.[2] I think that we poets would all write the most
admirable poetry if government would shut us up in American trains &
keep us ever on the road & give us nothing but American newspapers to
read. I think the little poem good but then ones last poem always does

---

[3] *The Nuts of Knowledge*, published by the Dun Emer Press on 1 Dec. In an undated reply to
this letter (MBY) AE told WBY: 'Your sister told me she sent you a copy of the Nuts of Knowledge a month ago, enclosed with Quinns copies. . . . I think it looks well.' The book reached
WBY on Christmas Day, and he inscribed one of Quinn's copies: 'AE is the Irish Swedenborg
but unlike Swedenborg all he sees is beautiful.'

[4] *Broken Soil*, produced by the INTS at the Molesworth Hall on 3 Dec. In his reply (see
above) AE said: 'Colum's play interested a great many people. It acted much better than I
thought it would. There were certain passages which were extraordinary moving and original and
which affected every one. I feel more & more convinced that the boy has a great faculty. It was
very well acted. Kelly did in it quite the best piece of acting I have seen by any member of the
company. He is wooden in poetic plays but very good in rural characters.'

[5] There was no formal discussion between WBY and Griffith, although they were to conduct a
series of increasingly acrimonious controversies over the relationship of nationalism to literature
in the pages of the *United Irishman*. Edward Martyn's challenge to John Redmond (see p. 230,
n. 1) has not come to light, but would probably have involved the Irish Party's lukewarm attitude
to the revival of the Irish language.

[1] 'Old Memory'; see p. 483, n. 7.
[2] See p. 488, n. 1; WBY had lectured in Montreal on 17 Dec.

seem good. Perhaps you will let me have a proof sheet. I shall be here until the first or second week of February. I am lecturing to colleges & beleive I am setting a good many people reading our Celtic books & it was for that I came here—& our Celtic books mean to me not in the end books but in the end a more passionate kind of life—a present revery 'calling up a new age, calling to mind the queens that were imagined long ago' as I say in the poem of a fair woman.[3]

Yrs sinly
W B Yeats

ALS Private.

To Susan Mary Yeats, 25 December 1903

1 West 87th Street, | New York,
December 25, 1903.

My dear Lilly:

I have just seen the "Nuts of Knowledge". Tell Lolly I think it perfectly charming. It is better than "The Seven Woods" and should, I think, advance the fame of the press. But there are moments when I think that the winged sword is a little large as well as a little vague in design. I am very uncertain about this, but I think, on the whole, I would have liked it smaller; small, perhaps, as a penny piece, and up in the top right hand corner. Probably, though, if I saw it small I would think it ought to be big.[1]

Please do not think I am responsible for those interviews about Drum Cliff and the rest.[2] The interviewer asks me a certain number of questions and then goes home and adds the rest from his imagination, and then another interviewer in another paper gets hold of what he has written and adds more imagination. I have been interviewed about places that I have never seen and have talked copiously about them. However, on the whole, I think I have been fortunate, as really nothing has been put into my

---

[3] ll. 3–5 of 'Old Memory', the poem he was enclosing, and addressed to MG: 'Your strength, that is so lofty and fierce and kind, / It might call up a new age, calling to mind / The queens that were imagined long ago . . .'.

[1] AE's circular device, 'The Sword of Light', 7 cm. in diameter on the first preliminary page, was also used in the Dun Emer edition of AE's *By Still Waters* (1906) and in the Cuala Press editions of *Some Passages from the Letters of A.E. to W. B. Yeats* (1936) and *Words for Music Perhaps* (1932).

[2] Perhaps a reference to an article by Katharine Lee Bates in the *Boston Evening Transcript* of 11 Nov (16), which described the fairy lore of the environs of Drumcliff. Miss Bates (1859–1929) was head of the English department at Wellesley College, and dined with WBY after his lecture there on 28 Nov. She was the author of the national hymn, 'America the Beautiful'.

mouth that mattered. I am keeping in very good health and enjoying the novelty of the thing very much. Unhappily, the letter you forwarded me from Aunt Grace[3] only reached me the day I arrived back here from Canada. I have not yet written to her, but will.

All you have told me about the theatre was very interesting. I heard, of course, also from Lady Gregory. Columb's success has overjoyed me. I was more nervous about that play than anything else, for my position would have been impossible if I had had to snuff out the work of young men belonging to the company. It would have always seemed that I did so from jealousy or some motive of that sort. Now, however, one can push on Columb and keep one's snuffers for the next. One man that we did snuff out, Cousins, has been avenging himself on Columb in the United Irishman.[4]

I have been sent a privately printed book by somebody here. It is not at all good. I think I will send it to Lolly as a bad example and tell her that I have seen the Ryecroft books. These were the books that Russell said had colored illustrations. They have, and nothing could be worse. The books are eccentric, restless and thoroughly decadent.[5]

I have given about twenty lectures—rather more than twenty, I think— and I have about twenty-four still to give. I speak in a big hall in New York on the 3d of January and go to the Pacific Coast the day after, five days' journey in railway trains. There, I am told, I shall find a delightful climate. I get back from there sometime about the beginning of February or end of January, and after one or two more lectures round about New York start for home, where I should arrive about the 20th of February.[6]

I have seen a great deal that is very charming here—charming people and charming houses. The houses that cultivated people live in here seem to me the best things of the kind that I have seen. I was in a beautiful

---

[3] JBY's sister, Grace Jane Yeats (1846–1935), who lived in Toronto.

[4] Cousins, writing as 'Spealadoir' in the *United Irishman* on 12 Dec, criticized *Broken Soil* (6) as too 'abstractedly emotional', as lacking 'sequential development', and reported that ' "Immature inadequacy" is the only phrase I can find which expresses the ultimate impression left on the mind when the final curtain has fallen'. The play was defended the following week by Oliver St John Gogarty, who accused Spealadoir of a 'piteous' lack of criteria in his critical judgements.

[5] Elbert Hubbard (1856–1915), an American disciple of William Morris, set up his private press, the Roycroft Shop, in East Aurora, New York, after a visit to Morris in 1892. They are justly described by Roderick Cave (*The Private Press* [1971], 155) as ' "articrafty" in the most vulgar and meretricious sense—poorly printed on rough, heavy paper, using ugly types with the nastiest of art nouveau decoration, and bound in the cheap soft suede known appropriately in the trade as "limp ooze" ', and Holbrook Jackson remarked that the Kelmscott Press 'found its nemesis in Elbert Hubbard's Roycroft books'.

[6] The *Gael* (NY) of January 1904 announced that WBY was scheduled to lecture to the ILS in London on 27 Feb 1904; in fact he stayed on in America until early March.

house belonging to a rich merchant a couple of days ago.[7] He lives about an hour's journey from New York, on the side of a wooded hill, and his house, which is in what they call here their "old colonial style", would have been a delight to Morris. Everything very sober and stately, rather bare. Comfort, but only such comfort as an alert spirit can enjoy. Nothing to suggest a soft, lounging life. The woman of the house is a very cultivated woman, and I suppose a great part of the taste is hers, but her husband has done his share, too, I think. He is a great hunter. He is constantly out in the woods and the mountains hunting moose and the like. There is something of his life in the decoration; something athletic, as it were. And I have seen a great many houses which have the same spirit though not in the same degree. Indeed, the thing that has surprised me in America has been the fine taste of the people, or, at any rate, of those I have met—and I have met a great number. I think the cultivated class is a good deal larger than it is in England. Certainly, it is more widely spread.

Well, I must stop now, for I am going to dictate a lecture.[8] I have found that, after giving a lecture seven or eight times, I begin to get tired of it, and I am going to try to make it vivid to myself again by dictating it and so getting it much more highly finished. After seven or eight times, one begins to remember sentences one used before, to speak by rote, and so one may as well finish highly. At first one has the joy of improvisation, and that gives one fire.

Yours affecly
W B Yeats

TLS MBY. Wade, 416–18.

[7] Hydewood Hall, situated on the side of a wooded hill in Plainfield, New Jersey, and one of the best examples of colonial architecture in the state, was the home of Francis DeLacey Hyde (d. 1911) and his wife, Carolyn Knowland Hyde (1869–1959). WBY had stayed overnight with the Hydes on 22 Dec, after his lecture on 'The Intellectual Revival' at the Park Club, Plainfield. Francis Hyde, the third son of Charles Hyde (1822–1901), a self-made businessman who had amassed a fortune in the Pennsylvania oilfields, was a banker and property owner; his wife, a social and civic leader in Plainfield, was prominent on several educational boards, and was the only woman on the planning commission for Greater New York. The Hydewood estate boasted one of the first privately owned golf courses in the USA.

[8] On 24 Dec Quinn had wired WBY: 'Stenographer unable to come this afternoon. Will come tonight eight and be with you all day tomorrow.' It is not known by what means Quinn persuaded a stenographer to spend Christmas Eve and Christmas Day taking dictation from WBY, but he notes in his list of expenses (NLI) that he paid T. J. Curtin $20 'for writing speech and letters'.

To James Huneker, [c. *28 December 1903*]

W. B. Yeats wrote to me in 1903 that John Quinn had told him I wrote the article in *The Sun* on the Irish movement in two hours; which was true.[1] Yeats adds: "That seems to me a wonderful feat, for it is precisely what journalism is not—detailed and philosophical and accurate. . . . Of course, my critic in *The Evening Post* was right in one sense in calling me decadent.[2] We are all decadent, our sins are the sins of our forefathers. But I am struggling against it, always trying to get the fire to the centre, not to the circumference.[3] I don't think this critic knew that Lionel Johnson, who

[1] James Gibbon Huneker (1860–1921), a friend of Quinn and an influential journalist and critic, had welcomed WBY to the USA in his column, 'The Week's Output of Plays', in the New York *Morning Sun* of 22 Nov 1903 (section III, p. 4), but WBY refers here to his much longer article, 'Mystic, Poet and Dramatist', published in the same paper on 27 Dec (section III, p. 4), which was a reply to charges of decadence brought against WBY's work by the New York *Evening Post*.

[2] Even before WBY's arrival in America, the New York *Independent* of 12 Nov 1903 (2691–2) had disapproved of his latest work and voiced a suspicion 'that the Irish revival is nothing, after all, but another form of decadence'. Although this article was unsigned, it may well have been by the literary editor, Paul Elmer More, who was in process of moving to the New York *Evening Post* where, on 12 Dec, he amplified these views under the initials 'P.E.M.' in his article, 'Two Poets Of The Irish Movement' (Book Section. p. 1). More (1864–1937), who had given up a career as a teacher of Sanskrit for literary journalism, was closer in his religious and literary sensibilities to T. S. Eliot (with whom he was later to correspond) than to WBY, whom he accused of failing to distinguish between exalted mysticism and loose reverie. He also detected 'a sense of failure and decay, rather than of mastery and growth' in WBY's successive works, and alleged that the 'real kinship of Mr. Yeats's present style is with that of Arthur Symons, himself a disciple of the French decadents; only one must add in justice that no taint of moral degeneration has appeared in the Irish writer—and that is much to concede to a decadent.' Nevertheless, an audit of the references to hair (twenty-three) in *The Wind Among the Reeds*, led him to the ominous conclusion that here was 'withal something troubling and unwholesome; one thinks of the less chaste descriptions of Arthur Symons or the morbid women of Aubrey Beardsley's pencil rather than of the strong ruddy heroines of old Irish story. The trait is significant of much.'
    Quinn wrote to Huneker on 15 Dec 1903 (NYPL), pointing out More's inaccuracies and complaining that it was 'absurd to argue that a man of the great vital influence of Yeats . . . is a decadent in any sense of that variously used word. . . . The danger of criticisms of this sort is that they will be copied by other men of affairs who also write, or attempt to write, criticism and do some damage to the reputation of one of the greatest of living poets. . .' Huneker took the hint, and in a wide-ranging article (see above, n. 1) set WBY in the context of the Irish literary revival, praised his work as combining 'Celtic melancholy, with an heroic quality rare since the legendary days and all welded into music, lyric, symphonic and dramatic', and attacked (without actually naming him) More's 'New England boiled dinner style of criticism', arguing that 'Decadence is . . . an aesthetic, not a moral mode; and in that sense Mr. Yeats belongs to the school of Decadence, as do all his contemporaries from Wagner, Tolstoy and Ibsen down to the latest minor poeticule. But to call his work decadent, meaning that it is false, artificial, morbid or immoral, is not to say the truth.'

[3] More's remarks were particularly disturbing to WBY in that he regarded himself as developing in precisely the opposite direction (see pp. 369–70), and he elaborated upon this idea in a series of brief essays, 'Discoveries', over the next few years: 'There are two ways before literature—upward into ever-growing subtlety . . . or downward, taking the soul with us until all is simplified and solidified again' (*E & I*, 266–7). He later elaborated this metaphor in his writings on the 'Condition of Fire' (see *Myth*, 356–7, 364–6).

is his type of classic health, never got up till dark or went to bed till daylight, wrote poems to absinthe, and died, poor man, of a fall he got when
intoxicated.[4] Of course, this isn't the same thing as literary decadence, but
I imagine it would have seemed so to him. I have a notion that everybody
has been decadent since Shakespeare, and the reason for it is partly a question of language—but that is too big a question for a letter."[5]

Printed extract from James Gibbons Huneker, *Steeplejack* (New York, 1921), II. 242–3.

To F. J. Fay, [29] December 1903

1 West 87th Street, | New York,
December 30, 1903.

My dear Fay:

It is very hard to find out the truth about the St. Louis project.[1] Since
writing to you I have got an opinion which is quite the reverse of
Thomas's. Major McCrystal,[2] who is a prominent Gaelic League propagandist here, thinks that our theatre would be a success in St Louis. All I
can say under the circumstances is that it would be well for you and your
brother to suspend your judgment until you hear further from me. I will

[4] In his article, More had contrasted WBY unfavourably with Lionel Johnson (see p. 240,
n. 2), in whom he found 'something of the classic saint. His intellect was trained in the learning
of Greece and Rome, and possessed the firmness and wholesome clearness that we associate with
the word classic. . . . From the wistfulness, I had almost said the sickliness, of Mr. Yeats who
seeks relief in wasteful revery, we pass to the sternly idealized sorrow of Lionel Johnson, well knit
with intellectual fibre.' Johnson had been WBY's closest London friend in the early 1890s and
introduced him to the ideas of Pater. Although a first-class Classical scholar at Winchester
College and Oxford, Johnson had the unorthodox life-style WBY mentions here, and which
he recounts in more detail in *Aut* (304–8), where he also recalls that the discovery in 1895 that
Johnson was drinking heavily 'was a great shock to me, and, I think, altered my general view of
the world'. After 1895 Johnson's problem grew rapidly worse, and he died on 29 Sept 1902 of a
ruptured blood vessel after a fall while trying to sit on a chair in the Green Dragon pub in Fleet
Street, an accident WBY recollects with grim irony in 'In Memory of Major Robert Gregory'
(*VP*, 324): 'much falling he / Brooded upon sanctity . . .'.
[5] WBY was to address the question of poetic language in the coming years, particularly in his
revision of *The Shadowy Waters* in the summer of 1905, and in 'Discoveries': 'In literature, partly
from the lack of that spoken word which knits us to normal man, we have lost in personality, in
our delight in the whole man . . .' (*E & I*, 266).
[1] The St Louis World Fair, billed as 'The Greatest of Exhibitions', ran from 30 Apr to 1 Dec
1904, and there had been some talk of the INTS performing there. Augustus Thomas (see p. 475,
n. 6) a playwright and former St Louis journalist, had, however, advised WBY that the literary
theatre could not compete with the more popular attractions of the World Fair.
[2] Major Edward T. McCrystal (1883–1913), a veteran of the Spanish–American war, was
National Director of the Ancient Order of Hibernians in America, and President of the New York
Gaelic Society.

send you all the information I can so that you will form your opinion with fairly full knowledge before you. I am going to talk the matter over with Byrne,[3] whose judgment in a matter of that kind would be excellent, and next Monday I go to St Louis itself and will write to you as soon as I can after getting there.

Miss Horniman has sent me some notices of the plays and I have seen the other papers. I know pretty well now how they have been received. I think that the reception of the plays has been the best we have yet had. I do not say this because it is more enthusiastic than the reception of our plays before, but I notice that we are now accepted as a matter of course as an established institution. I am inclined to think that the coldness of the United Irishman towards us is helping us in several quarters.

Two people here in America are about to write books on the intellectual movement in Ireland.[4] One of these books will I think be of considerable importance and influence the movement in Ireland.

I am very well content with my success here. I have given more than twenty lectures and shall give more than twenty further ones before I get back. I lunched with the President yesterday and found him extraordinarily well informed about our whole movement—indeed, one of the best read men I have met.[5] Today I was given a reception by the New York Press

---

[3] Quinn's friend, James F. Byrne, husband of WBY's co-passenger on the *Oceanic*; see p. 459. WBY also wanted to discuss the matter with Fr O'Donovan, but he had sailed for Ireland (see p. 492, n. 3).

[4] Both Horatio Krans (see p. 475) and Cornelius Weygandt were planning books on the literary movement. Although he published an article on 'The Irish Literary Revival' in the *Sewanee Review* for October 1904, Weygandt's *Irish Plays and Playwrights* did not appear until 1913. WBY was critical of Krans's *William Butler Yeats and the Irish Literary Revival* (1904), writing in Quinn's copy: 'Lack of proportion, inadequate as to Hyde: O'Grady: Lady Gregory . . . not true as to plays, all true in regards to some earlier poetry; not true as to many of his stories.'

[5] WBY was invited to lunch with President Theodore Roosevelt (1858–1919) in Washington on 28 Dec, and as Roosevelt's friend, Maurice Egan, explains (210–11) in *Recollections of a Happy Life* (1924)

> he was to come from New York to the Cosmos Club. He had not finally accepted; I waited for him until midnight. At last I received a telegram saying that he would be at the luncheon. It was too late then for President Roosevelt to make a circle to meet him. At the luncheon table, there were Mrs Roosevelt, Ethel, I think, and the smaller boys—all eager to hear about the fairies. Yeats was silent. He could not be induced to open his mouth until President Roosevelt turned to me and said:
> 'Following out our conversation the other day, about the balance of power in Europe, I believe as earnestly as you can possibly believe in helping to preserve at all risks the autonomy of the little peoples.'
> Yeats raised his head from the depths of his flowing necktie:
> 'Sure,' he said, 'you'll find the little people all over Ireland. Every old man that's raked the hay in the meadow has seen one of the little people. I have seen some of them myself.'
> Mr Roosevelt looked as if he had been struck suddenly by a thunderbolt. I had presence of mind enough to ask:
> 'What are the little people like?'

Club and spoke of the movement and the theatre and so on.[6] I am pretty confident that we are going to get a good many readers and sympathizers here. I have always felt that the effect we have made in England has been discounted because of a natural Irish suspicion of English opinion. If the intellectual movement makes, as I am convinced it will make, a large public for itself here,, that will help us greatly in Ireland. It is impossible to discount American opinion the way English opinion can be discounted. If it only turns out to be possible to get the company over and if they make a success here, that will be the greatest gain of all.

I think that you will find that the "Hour Glass" will really go better, or rather that it will be criticized more favourably, a little time hence.[7] My impression from the performance I saw in Dublin and from the performance I saw in London was that it held the audience throughout but that their afterthoughts were sometimes a little hostile. Some of them felt that because I had written it, it must of necessity contain some hidden heresy, while others, finding it impossible to believe that I really thought those things, supposed I had written it out of a mere archaistic emotion and that it was therefore a mere literary experiment.

I hope you will try and put off the performance of Balies Strand as long as you can, as I may not be able to be back by the 20th of February. I may be kept here a week or two later. My trip to the coast will take over twenty days and I find that I am getting new engagements here. For example, I have just heard that I am going to be invited to give four lectures in the Catholic University of Washington.[8]

I wish I could have seen you in the "Hour Glass". Judging by what I have heard your "Wise Man" was a beautiful performance.

Please tell Colm how delighted I am at his success and please set him to work at a new play if you can.

'They're not like the little insignificant English fairies', Yeats said contemptuously. 'They're over seven feet high; they're the old gods come back again!'

'My Heavens,' said Roosevelt *sotto voce*; the children were delighted evidently. But Yeats subsided into silence, in contemplation of the sweetness and strength of the Irish fairies.

Roosevelt, who was an honorary vice-president of the Irish Literary Society of New York, became an influential supporter of the Irish literary movement; in November 1911 he attended a performance of *The Playboy of the Western World* to quell Irish-American opposition to the play, and he published 'In the Eyes of our Friends: The Irish Theatre' in the *Outlook* of 16 Dec 1911.

[6] The reception at the New York Press Club took place on 29 Dec 1903 and was attended by a number of Irish-American politicians and academics, as well as journalists. WBY spoke at it and, according to the *Gaelic American* of 9 Jan 1904 (3), 'branched out into an address at once pathetic and stirring. . . . To make Irishmen good Irishmen, to create an Irish Ireland was the way to make Ireland happy, prosperous and free.'

[7] *The Hour-Glass* had been revived from 3 to 5 Dec (see p. 496).

[8] See p. 556.

I shall look at "Heads or Harps" and see if I can amend it anywhere.[9]

Sincerely yours
W B Yeats

TLS Private.

[9] See pp. 462, 491. Fay had persuaded the Reading Committee to turn down *Head or Harps*, and had evidently written to give WBY the reasons for his objections.

1904

To George P. Brett, 1 January 1904

1 West 87th Street, | New York,
January 1, 1904.

George P. Brett, Esq.,
66 Fifth Avenue,
New York City.

Dear Mr. Brett:

I am very sorry that I missed you in New York. I understand that a letter was sent to me or to Mr. Quinn making an appointment for the 18th, but neither I nor Mr. Quinn got that letter. When Mr. Quinn telephoned to make an appointment for last week, he heard that you were out of town, not to return until about January 10th. Now, I myself am going out of town on Monday, the 4th. I am lecturing in Chicago and St. Louis and a number of Western cities. I have nearly thirty lectures to deliver before I get back, going as far as the Pacific Coast. Meanwhile time is pressing.

I have arranged to bring out both the three prose plays which you are to publish here and another volume of two verse plays simultaneously.[1] The publisher is getting impatient for leave to publish, as the volumes are in print and the proofs corrected. One of the plays in the verse volume is "On Baile's Strand",[2] but the other, "The King's Threshold", has not been

---

[1] See p. 361, n. 3. Although Macmillans were to bring out an American edition of the prose plays on 9 Mar 1904, they declined the verse plays. Quinn had sent them the MS of *The King's Threshold* (see p. 483) on 10 Nov 1903 and urged them to publish it with *The Countess Cathleen*, but the reader found it not 'of equal merit with Mr. Yeats's preceding work', pointed out that *The Countess Cathleen* was already published, and concluded: 'Under the circumstances, I see no reason for your re-issuing the old work and for publishing the single new play. Mr Yeats seems to be making frantic efforts to interest the American public in himself, in advance of his lecture season here this winter.' *The King's Threshold* was finally published in a copyright edition by Quinn on 18 Mar 1904; Bullen's English edition appeared at the same time.

[2] Evidently an error for *The Countess Cathleen*; see below, pp. 511–12.

published here, and in order to secure my copyright I must publish it and do so at once.

Now, I made some time ago a proposal to you, through Mr. Quinn, that you should publish this new play and "The Countess Cathleen", an old play of mine, in one volume. I feel confident that if you could arrange this now you would have a sale, as my lectures must have drawn a great deal of attention to my work. People are constantly saying to me that they can't get my books; that they are asking at shops for them and they cannot be got. Can you, therefore, arrange at once to publish the book I have proposed? If so, I must ask you either to give me an agreement terminable at the end of so many years, five, let us say, or even six, or else to give me a better royalty than 10%. Mr. Unwin gives me a royalty of 17-½%, and I am getting 20% on a new book. Both you and I are looking into the future. You are probably taking my books rather with a view to their future sale than their present sale. But I also must look into the future. I am ready to take a small royalty, but I must have a terminable contract if I do. On the other hand, if you prefer to give me a somewhat larger royalty now, I am ready to make an interminable agreement.

I had hoped to see you to talk over all these things, and now I am in the difficulty that I must publish "The King's Threshold" at once with somebody. I have been approached by one or two other publishers, but I am very anxious not to scatter my works. They are scattered about badly enough in England now and I don't want to scatter them here, but still, unless I choose to lose the stage copyright as well as the book copyright of "The King's Threshold", I must publish it simultaneously with the English edition, and I cannot keep my English publisher waiting much longer. I think I should have 17% or 17-½%, but if you are ready to take the two books, that is to say, "The King's Threshold" and "The Countess Cathleen" in one volume and the other poems in another volume, I should be content with 15% on an interminable agreement.

There are some notes to the volume of poems, one long note to "The Countess Cathleen", which would be at the end of the first volume, and the notes of the other poems, and these Mr. Quinn understands about and could readily separate. In addition to that, for the volume containing "The King's Threshold" and "The Countess Cathleen" I would do a short preface on the theatre which I think would be of some interest. I could send this from Chicago or St. Louis if you care to take this up.

I am sorry to raise the matter in a hurry, but I have had rather an urgent letter from my publisher in London, and any time that I have been able to see you you have, unfortunately, been out of the office.

You will remember that Mr. Quinn told one of your men that there were to be three pages of music to be printed as an appendix to the volume of 3 shorter plays, the music to accompany the lyrics in the plays. Two pages of the proof have come and the third is expected daily. Mr. Quinn will send it on and advise you of the date of the English publication, I expect, in the course of the next week.[3]

Mr. Quinn is familiar with the details of this, and if you will write to him or send for him he will be glad to see you. Any letter to me will be forwarded by him, but my address for the next month will be somewhat uncertain.

I have been so busy lecturing in Canada, Boston, Philadelphia, Washington and so on that I have found it quite impossible to see you, but I hope to do so on my return from the Coast.

Very truly yours
W B Yeats
per pro

[*In John Quinn's hand*]
Dear Mr Brett,

Mr Yeats left so early Monday that this letter missed him. He told me on the way to the train to sign & send it to you. I shall be glad to stop in to see you some morning if you care to see me about these matters.

JQ

TL signed by John Quinn for WBY; NYPL.

To Lady Augusta Gregory, 2 January 1904

1 West 87th Street, | New York,
January 2, 1904.

My dear Lady Gregory:

On Monday I go to St. Louis, a long journey—a day and a half, I think, on the train. I speak there on Tuesday and Wednesday and after that have quite a number of lectures to deliver. I will hardly be back in New York for another three weeks.[1] I lecture to-night somewhere in the neighborhood of New York[2] and to-morrow night in Carnegie Hall, my big lecture, the most important of the whole lot. I wonder what kind of an audience I

---

[3] The delay in sending the music caused the American edition to be postponed several times. In the end Macmillans lost patience and issued the book without it.

[1] In fact WBY's tour of the Midwest, California, and Canada was extended to six weeks from 4 Jan to his return to New York on 14 Feb.

[2] WBY lectured at the Brooklyn Institute on the evening of 2 Jan.

will have, for the hall is too big?[3] It was the only one, however, Quinn could get. I have been down practising my oratorical passages in the empty hall that I may not be put out if there are some empty benches. I got one compliment. I had just finished my peroration when I heard the clapping of hands in a dark corner. It was the Irish caretaker. You remember my old organ peroration, the one I wound up the speech with at the Horace Plunkitt dinner? Well, there is a big organ on the platform at Carnegie Hall. I turn towards it meditatively and then, as if the thought suddenly struck me, speak that old peroration.[4] It was this piece of extemporizing that pleased the caretaker. I am working at this speech as I never worked at a speech before, and that is why I have to dictate this letter to you. I have already dictated the whole speech once; indeed, I have already dictated some parts of it several times, and I am now going to go through it all again. Then I shall go down to the Hall and speak the whole lecture in the empty place. This is necessary, because I have found out that the larger the audience the more formal, rhythmical, oratorical must one's delivery be. My ordinary conversational, happy-go-lucky, inspiration-of-the-moment kind of speaking gets all wrong when I get away from the small audiences I am accustomed to. Oratory does not exist, in any real sense, until one's got a crowd.

A great many thanks for your letter, which reached me this morning, and thanks, too, for the musical notes. But I wish you could send to me as soon as you get them a proof of your commentary upon them, for I shall want to put something of the kind into the American edition of the book.[5]

Do you know, I hope the company will not adopt Colm's suggestion and play The Hypolitus. It is altogether too soon for us to stray away from Irish subjects. Above all, it is too soon for us to put on any non-Irish work

<hr />

[3] Snow and sub-zero temperatures kept the audience down to a disappointing five to six hundred. In his lecture, 'The Intellectual Revival in Ireland' (*YA8*, 102–15), WBY traced the growing cultural self-awareness in Ireland from the Young Irelanders of the 1840s to the ILT, and argued that the conflict between Ireland and England was 'a war between two civilizations, two ideals of life'. His careful rehearsals evidently paid off, for Quinn told him on 7 Jan (NLI) that he had been 'perfectly audible throughout the whole large hall and the speech delighted everyone, Gaelic Leaguers and Catholics alike'.

[4] WBY had first used the analogy that 'nations are like the stops upon an organ' in an after-dinner speech at an annual conference of the Irish Co-operative Societies in Dublin on 3 Nov 1897, with Horace Plunkett presiding. He ended his Carnegie Hall lecture with the words: 'The nations of the world are like a great organ. And in that organ there are many pipes. . . . A little while ago . . . the great pipe that is the Empire of Spain was sounding, and its music was filling the world. And then that pipe fell silent. The Divine Hand moved to another stop on the organ, and the pipe that is the Empire of England began to sound and is still sounding. But it may be that it, too, will fall silent, and it is certain that at last the pipe that is Ireland will awake and that its music will be heard through the whole world!!!' (*YA8*, 115). WBY repeated this peroration on a number of occasions, most notably at the end of his Emmet lecture in New York on 28 Feb.

[5] The music for vols. II and III of 'Plays for an Irish Theatre'; see previous letter, n. 3.

of such importance as The Hypolitus. It would be playing into the hands of our enemies. On the other hand, if we get through this season keeping our audience with us and playing a considerable variety of good, new Irish work, we will be able to do as we like. If we are to play The Hypolitus, I want to be there before it comes on and to find out if I cannot get Ricketts, let us say, to stage it. Now that The Masquers has come to an end, I must see if I cannot get hold of that £170 Ricketts has for theatrical adventure. As soon as we feel strong enough to play non-Irish work, we should, I think, approach Ricketts and see if he will work for us.[6] This is really important, so do try and restrain them over The Hypolitus, if you agree with me. If we had a big Irish play—a three-act play in verse, let us say, or a really important play in prose—we might then start with that and The Hypolitus and announce that we intend to carry out our full policy, Irish work and foreign masterpieces. I should like, however, to play Shaw first.

Yes, there are plenty of newspaper accounts, and I know Quinn is saving some for you. There have not been many actual reports of lectures, however. The accounts are, for the most part, interviews and descriptive paragraphs.

I spoke a couple of nights ago at the Authors' Club. You know the kind of people who make up authors' clubs in England—placid, rather Philistine writers, who have more practical capacity than anything else. They strike me as just the same here, only their practical capacity is rather more frank; and there is less pretence about their literature. However, a certain professor, who, I am told, is a person of great eminence here, made a very self-complacent speech, in which he said that writers ought not to think of posterity but merely write what it gave them pleasure to write and for their own time. Of course, there is a half-truth in this, but he put it in such a way that it became a whole falsehood. I was asked to speak when he had finished and I took the other side altogether, and Quinn thinks got the better of him.[7] He was the only man there I didn't like, for he was the only man there who pretended to literature, which it was quite obvious he had not got. I spoke of style and the painful labor that all style is, and so on.

I have just re-read your letter, and if there is any great trouble in sending a proof of your note about the music do not bother. I can make a good note out of what you say in the letter and add a few words about the method of delivery.[8]

[6] See p. 478, n. 2. After disbandment, Murray handed the *Hippolytus* to William Archer, who produced it at the New Century Theatre later in the year. Ricketts gave the £150 (not £170) to Sturge Moore, who eventually used it to help establish the Literary Theatre Society Ltd. in December 1905.

[7] WBY spoke in reply to the unidentified professor at a reception held by the Authors' Club on 31 Dec.

[8] This letter is untraced, but on 25 Dec 1903 (Berg) AG complained of a persistent cough and told him that she was hard at work on her new play [*Kincora*].

I have had difficulty in seeing Macmillan's man here. That is why there is so much delay. When I am here, he is away. When he wants to see me, I am away. I have just written to him and placed the matter in Quinn's hands, as I shall now not be able to attend to it. Quinn is very anxious for me to secure the copyright of the Red Hanrahan Tales by running them through the Gael before my sister brings them out. How do you feel about this. It should not be an injury to my sisters and if one does not do it Mosher may very likely pirate the book, for I have a notion that the Red Hanrahan Tales will be about the most popular thing I have done in prose. If you think well of this idea, I can arrange with the Gael and you can let them have a copy of the manuscript.[9]

I am afraid it will be quite out of the question my getting to work on "Where There Is Nothing" while I am here. I have hardly a moment, running from place to place and answering necessary letters.[10] I am always, too, working at my lectures, changing them and bettering them, I hope. I find that if I do not keep making a continual effort I begin to get worse, for I lose the joy of improvisation and do not get finish to take its place. After all, I don't feel it would have been worth coming here unless I was to get full advantage out of the practice in speaking. And I can only get that advantage by working over and over my words. One does not want to speak as badly as a clergyman or a lawyer, and I have found to my surprise that, while they speak badly, they get too idle and easy. In a way, I think I spoke better years ago when I had to make more effort; and now I am making an effort again and hope to come back with a far better style.

Did I tell you my idea of challenging Griffith to debate with me in public our two policies—his that literature should be subordinate to nationalism and mine that it must have its own ideal? I think that a challenge to him would be quite amusing, for his own party sent out so many that he would be a little embarrassed to refuse. I would offer to debate it with him or any other person appointed by his societies. He will refuse, of course, but the tactical advantage will be mine. I shall wait and choose my moment but will let him have the challenge before I get back. In any case, I am

[9] None of the revised tales in *Stories of Red Hanrahan*, published by the Dun Emer Press in 1905, appeared in the *Gael*. 'Red Hanrahan' had already appeared in the *Independent Review* for December 1903. AG helped WBY rewrite several of the stories from *The Secret Rose*, and in June 1905 he wrote in Quinn's copy of the new volume (*Bibl*, 74) that they were 'but half mine now, & often her beautiful idiom is the better half'. Thomas B. Mosher (1852–1923), a Welsh-born editor and publisher now settled in Portland, Maine, pirated numerous authors, including WBY, for his series, 'The Bibelot' (1895–1915), and for private editions. As a member of the Boston Authors' Club Mosher attended WBY's lecture at Wellesley College on 30 Nov 1903, where they may have met.

[10] In her untraced letter (see above, n. 8), AG had evidently asked WBY about the changes he had said he was making in *Where There Is Nothing*.

rather inclined to give a lecture as soon as I get to Dublin and to discuss very frankly the future of our movements.

No, the North American is not going to print "The King's Threshold." It is too long for them to use in time not to delay Bullen even further.

I have so much work to do for this big lecture that I cannot write more now, but I will find time somewhere, in some railway train, probably, to write again and very soon.

W B Yeats

[*In John Quinn's hand*]

Dear Lady Gregory:

Yeats had to go away before this was writ[n] out & the stenographer did not get it to me till Saturday too late for the boat. He was an outside man (not from our office) and Yeats asked me to sign this in his name & explain it to you.

I send you Prof W[m] James letter: also one from Prof Robinson of Harvard & one from a Mrs Ford here—this last to show how I've tried to keep Yeats away from bores & tedious people. Mabie the man referred to in her letter is The Editor of the Outlook & I suggested that she get him to preside at Yeats lecture & he did & made a fine speech.[11]

I send you a copy of my letter to Yeats which will tell you about the Carnegie Hall Meeting. It was a bitter cold day & that, I am *now* sure, is the reason we did not have a larger crowd. His speech was magnificent! He has just telegraphed me from Indiana & I feel sure that he will get on all right. I sent you Saturday some papers & magazines with articles on him and his work. The clippings I will sort out and send to you. With my legal work & being with him & the writing about his lectures I have neglected everything else & so have not sooner written to you to wish you a happy New Year & to say that we are all looking forward to your new book eagerly. Your other two books are selling very well & Yeats's lectures will do all I hoped for them for you & Hyde & Russell & himself. In fact you are today quite the rage—Yeats refers to you in his lectures constantly. His lecture on Heroic literature is largely a song to your work.

This is written to catch the boat. I have many things to say but you are

---

[11] WBY met William James (see p. 140) at Harvard, and James's letter to Quinn is now in NYPL. F. N. Robinson (1871–1966), the celebrated Chaucerian and Celtic philologist, was WBY's host in Cambridge. He had attended the Pan Celtic Congress in Dublin in 1901. Mrs Simeon Ford, née Julia Ellsworth Shaw (1859–1950), was the wife of the wealthy New York hotelier and property developer Simeon Ford (1855–1933). She had arranged WBY's lecture to the New York Arts Club on 30 Dec 1903, presided over by Hamilton Wright Mabie (1846–1916), who had been associate editor of the *Outlook* since 1884, and who was gradually changing it from a religious to a literary periodical. He had written to Quinn on 7 Dec 1903, hoping to meet WBY (NYPL), and Quinn had arranged an invitation to the Press Club on 29 Dec (see pp. 500–1). WBY would have found him a critical ally since he championed the claims of romance against realism.

interested in his success (and that is assured) and in his health (& that is splendid). So the other things I'll write about later. Of course the work is hard but the "receptions" (especially if there is a dinner *before* the lecture) are the awful things! I think some people feel I'm the "dragon" but if I did not save him he'd be tired out completely long ago. His trip to Washn & meeting with the President was a pleasant experience.

A happy new year to you and yours!

Sincerely John Quinn

TL signed by John Quinn for WBY; Berg. Partly in Wade, 419–22.

To Susan Mary Yeats, 2 January 1904

1 West 87th Street, | New York,
January 2, 1904.

My dear Lilly:

Your letter has just reached me. On Monday I go to St. Louis, a day and a half in the railway train, I think, and give a number of lectures there. I will be away three weeks before I get back again to New York. I lecture tonight in the neighborhood of New York, and to-morrow I give the most important lecture of all in the big Carnegie Hall. A great place, which will be rather hard to speak in, if it is only partly filled, as is pretty certain. I could not get it at the time I wanted, and this is not a good time, for various reasons. Still, I expect to do fairly well. I have been down there practising, trying my eloquent passages in the big, empty hall. I got one compliment. I had just finished an elaborate passage, when I heard the clapping of hands in a dark corner. It was the Irish caretaker. The Lord Dudley portrait is a great piece of luck for our father, but he will have some trouble to keep off politics, I expect.[1] When you write again, if you do, you might tell me what the cottage scene Fay got made for Colm's play turned out like. Nobody has told me. What color did they make it and had it a solid look? I asked Fay to have it all painted a dull smoke color that it

---

[1] Hugh Lane had commissioned JBY to do a series of portraits of notable Irish figures, including the Unionist and Conservative Rt. Hon. William Humble Ward, Earl of Dudley (1867–1932), Lord Lieutenant of Ireland from 1902 to 1905. Jack Yeats had written to Quinn about the portrait in December 1903 (NYPL): 'It's rather feeble to have him in, I think, but I don't suppose the governor chooses who the portraits are to be of.'

might tell as a tolerably flat homogeneous mass behind the figures of the players.[2] When does Lolly expect to get through with Hyde's book?[3]

I have got a certain number of people to write for copies. I want to have some idea, too, as to when the Red Hanrahan Tales are likely to be printed.[4] I cannot write any more, for I have one or two more letters to do, and then my whole lecture to re-dictate. I cannot trust myself to extemporize before an immense audience. The larger an audience, the less conversational and the more formal rythmical and oratorical must one's manner be. Oratory hardly exists for a small audience. I trust, therefore, to the inspiration of the moment when speaking to a college, but I have to elaborate everything for a great audience.

Yrs affectly
W B Yeats

[In John Quinn's hand]
P.S. by JQ
I've been so busy that I have not writ*n* to you & your sister but I will this week. The lectures are a big success. He goes West tom*oro* to be gone a month going to the Pacific Coast. He is doing well & enjoying things, I think.

Kind regards to your Sister & Father. Sincerely

John Quinn

TLS MBY. Partly in Wade, 418–19.

To A. H. Bullen, 2 January 1904

1 West 87th Street, | New York,
January 2, 1904.

My dear Bullen:

I hope not to have to delay your two books much longer, but I know nothing definite yet.[1] This is my difficulty: I have as yet made no arrangement here about the time of publishing ⟨book containing⟩ the three prose plays. I have, however, had some trouble about "The King's Threshold." I

---

[2] SMY obliged, sending him a picture postcard of the scenery on 1 Feb 1904 (NLI), with the message 'This is a bad print but it will give you an idea of the scene'. The card arrived in New York on 13 Feb.

[3] The Dun Emer edition of Hyde's *The Love Songs of Connacht*, with a Preface by WBY, was published in July 1904.

[4] In an undated letter [1 Jan 1904; Berg] AG reported that ECY did not want the Red Hanrahan stories for two months.

[1] i.e. vols. II and III of 'Plays for an Irish Theatre'.

want Macmillans to publish it together with "The Countess Cathleen" and to bring out the rest of my poems that are not issued in America in another volume. I have tried two or three times to see Brett to talk over this, but when I have called or written he has been away and when he wrote to me I was away. I have now, however, written to him and made my proposal in writing and left the arrangements as to details to my friend John Quinn (120 Broadway, New York), who will most probably write to you. Should any difficulty arise with Brett, we will ourselves print an edition of "The King's Threshold" here and so secure the copyright.[2] There will, therefore, be but little further delay. I still think it important to bring out your two volumes simultaneously. They will come out at a rather good time, for the Irish National Theatre Society will perform in London in March or April. They will probably play "The King's Threshold" and certainly will play a number of my plays.[3] This will be about the biggest advertisement the books could get. I shall manage things here so that it can be out considerably before that date.

I am overwhelmed with work, lecturing several times a week. I start for St. Louis, a day and a half's journey in the railway train, on Monday, and speak to-night and to-morrow night here.

Sincerely yours
W B Yeats

[*In John Quinn's hand*]
P.S.

Mr Yeats had not received this letter before he started west and asked me to sign it & send it on to you. As soon as I hear from Mr. Brett of the Macmillan Co. I will write or cable you date of publication. The three prose plays are ready for printing—awaiting only the *music* copy. The Kings Threshold is the only thing to arrange for now & as to this Yeats has written to Brett.

Yours truly
John Quinn

TL signed by John Quinn for WBY; Texas.

[2] See pp. 503-4.
[3] The INTS played at the Royalty Theatre, London, on 26 Mar 1904, including *The King's Threshold* in their bill. Gwynn's circular announcing the performances is dated February 1904.

To William Bourke Cockran,[1] 4 January 1904

Mention in McGurrin, 230.

Expressing appreciation of 'the enchanting beauty of your introductory address'; and adding 'I shall not soon forget your extraordinary kindness'.

To Lady Augusta Gregory, [6 January 1904]

TERMINAL HOTEL, | EUROPEAN. | UNION STATION. | ST. LOUIS,

My dear Lady Gregory: ⟨I enclose typed letter which I forgot. The bit about Godgkin[1] is my chief reason for sending it⟩ I had a huge audience last night—an audience more than half of school teachers, a difficult audience, my first western audience. I think I shall find the western different from the others I have met. I expect I shall have to be more flamboyant before I move them. I had the sore throat last night & was there fore uncomfortable. This afternoon I speak on theatre & hope to be more myself.[2] I am in a horrid hotel—the train was five hours late so I had no choice—a hotel much like the Galway one except for the tumult & bustle.

---

[1] See p. 467. The *New York Times* (see p. 506, n. 3) reported that

W. Bourke Cockran presided, he and Mr. Yeats having come, as the latter explained, from the same town in the west of Ireland.

In introducing his fellow-countryman Mr. Cockran said he wished to present 'the last and the greatest of Irish poets'. 'The intellectual revival in Ireland', he added, 'had been due largely to the result of Mr. Yeats's labors'.

Mr. Yeats began his address by paying a compliment to Mr. Cockran, saying that the latter had given many thousands of dollars toward the establishment of different industries in the County Sligo, from which he came.

'No movement would have prospered in Ireland', declared the speaker, 'without the help of Irishmen in America'.

See also *YA8*, 102–3. In a letter to WBY of 7 Jan 1904 Quinn reported (NLI) that Cockran had told him on 5 Jan that 'no Irishman in his lifetime was your equal for oratory of the finest and best kind . . . that you seemed to be universally gifted'.

[1] Edwin Lawrence Godkin (1831–1902) was born in Wicklow and educated at Belfast, Oxford, and Harvard. He was the *London News* war correspondent in the Crimea before emigrating to the USA where he studied law and subsequently worked for the *New York Times*. In 1865 he founded and edited the *Nation* (NY), merging it in 1882 with the New York *Evening Post*. He wrote a number of books on history and politics, and was a close friend of Henry James, and of Quinn, who described him as 'a good Irishman but a Protestant', and who respected him for his honesty and religious tolerance. WBY evidently decided not to send the typed letter, which is untraced.

[2] On the evening of 5 Jan WBY lectured on 'Heroic Literature' to the St Louis Society of Pedagogy. The following day he spoke on the 'Theatre' to the Wednesday Club of St Louis, but a third lecture scheduled at the Contemporary Club was cancelled.

I have not yet seen the exhibition people, but will before I leave this.[3] John Devoy,[4] the fenian brought a deputation of Clan-na-Gael men to see me after my big New York lecture & he said I had "got at people here in America no Irish man had ever got at before". I am getting a great longing to be back, but shall go through with it to the end, that is go through some twenty more lectures. I should make between 400 & 500 pounds, my lectures are all to Colleges & Societies which means the best audiences possible for the spread of our thought. Please tell me when you think the London performances will come off—I should like to see them.

Yrs ev
W B Yeats

ALS Berg, with envelope addressed to Coole, redirected to the Nassau Hotel, Dublin, postmark 'ST. LOUIS, MO JAN 6 1904'.

John Quinn to Alice Boughton,[1] *7 January 1904*

Jan. 7, 1904.

Miss Alice Boughton,
   312 Madison Avenue,
     New York City.

Dear Miss Boughton:
   Thank you very much for the two solio prints and the two platinum.[2] Unfortunately there was no time to make the lithographs from them in time to be of any advantage for Mr. Yeats' lecture.

[3] In preparing the itinerary for WBY's Western trip, John Quinn, acting for T. P. Gill, asked him (NLI) to meet three men in St Louis to discuss Irish participation in the World Fair, scheduled to open there on 30 Apr 1904. These were Thomas E. Hanley, contractor for the Fair 'and the real business manager of the Irish concession', with whom WBY was to discuss 'all details of the Irish part and . . . the possibility of taking a company there'; James A. Reardon, 'chairman of the commission that first started the Irish Exhibition idea' and commissioner to Ireland; and Oscar Enders (1886–1926), the architect who was to design the buildings: 'Gill says it is most important for you to see him as to interior decorations for concert hall, dun, etc'. WBY was also to investigate plans for the archaeological, historical, and artistic exhibition, and arrangements for the 'publication of artistic and literary movements in Ireland'.

[4] See p. 465.

[1] Alice Boughton (1866–1943), the celebrated photographer, had been born in Brooklyn, and studied art in Paris. On her return to New York she took up photography and opened her own studio where she photographed many famous contemporaries. WBY may have visited her studio at 11 a.m. on 22 Dec 1903, when Quinn tried to make an appointment for him: 'one of the objects in making the appointment is to have a good photograph taken as early as possible, and developed to-day, if possible. I would say quite frankly to her that we want a lithograph made and that the photographs that have been made were not satisfactory' (NLI).

[2] 'Solio' was Eastman Kodak's brand name for a popular gelatin-emulsion chloride printing-out paper which came into use in 1892 and remained in production until the 1960s. For platinum prints, platinum salt was used instead of silver to give more permanence and better tone to the photograph.

Mr. Yeats received the three photographs which you sent him and was charmed with them, and asked me before he had to hurry away Monday on his Western trip to write and thank you for sending them.

I particularly like the one showing him reading the book. What would you charge me for a dozen of them and when could you have them for me?[3]

Yours very truly
John Quinn

TS copy NYPL.

John Quinn to J. Cassidy,[1] *7 January 1904*

Jan. 7, 1904.

Mr. J. Cassidy,
    Lyons,
        Wayne County, N. Y.

My dear Sir:

Mr. Yeats received your note written on New Year's day at Carnegie Hall Sunday night. His lecture was a splendid one, although on account of the bitter cold the attendance was not as large as expected. He was delighted to hear from you but was compelled to leave for the West early Monday morning before he had a chance to reply to your note and asked me to say to you that he would write you on his return.

Sincerely yours
John Quinn

TS copy NYPL.

[3] Although these prints were not ready in time, Quinn had used one of the earlier three photographs of WBY in the circular for the Carnegie Hall lecture. The photograph of WBY reading a book was to appear as an illustration for Florence Brook's article on WBY in the *New York Herald* on 17 Jan. For other appearances of Miss Boughton's portraits of WBY see p. 561, n. 1.

[1] John Cassidy (1863–1913) was born in Massachusetts but worked as a general contractor in the Lyons area of New York, living at various times in the nearby townships of Galen and Clyde, before moving sometime after 1910 to Syracuse, where he was in business with his son at the time of his death.

John Quinn to Julia Ellsworth Ford,[1] *7 January 1904*

Jan. 7, 1904.

Mrs. Simeon Ford,
  Milton Point,
    Rye, N. Y.

Dear Mrs. Ford:
  Mr. Yeats received your note enclosing the check and asked me to acknowledge the receipt of it. He had to leave early Monday morning after his lecture at Carnegie Hall for the West and had no time to answer his letters before he left. His lecture at your place was one of the best I have heard him deliver and he told me that he enjoyed his dinner with you and Mr. Ford very much.

Sincerely yours
John Quinn

TS copy NYPL.

To John Quinn, [*10 January 1904*]

Clapool Hotel | Indianapolis

My dear Quinn: There are two cancelled lectures—one St Louis lecture & the Bloomington lecture. The St Louis people seem distressed & Prof Chase[1] came here from Bloomington to explain so far as he is concerned. He had a lot of telegrams. In one you had wired the date had been fixed

---

[1] Mrs Ford (see p. 509, n. 11) had studied WBY's work at a New York literary class (see *JBYL*, 285) and had met him at Yale on 16 Nov 1903. Her article, 'The Neo-Celtic Poet—William Butler Yeats', written in collaboration with Kate V. Thompson, had recently appeared in *Poet-Lore* (Winter 1903). She had arranged for WBY to lecture on 'Poetry' at the New York Arts Club in 34th St. on 30 Dec 1903, an occasion recalled by Nina Wilcox Putnam in *Laughing Through* (New York, 1930): 'Mrs. Ford collected celebrities as some people collect postage stamps. . . . ugly, overburdened with art-jewelry, nervous and all-enveloping, [she] was a sort of intellectual mother. . . . And when William Butler Yeats . . . came to America, looking mildly and somewhat reproachfully at our country through a cloud of tangled black hair that was never tidy and the thick lenses of his spectacles, he came as a hero, for Mrs. Ford saw to it that this was so. Under her direction we all sat at his feet to hear his timid, shy utterances. These were so erudite and scholastic and impersonal as to seem like a half-hearted message from another world' (213–14).

[1] Lewis Nathaniel Chase (1873–1937), a recent graduate of Columbia University and author of *The English Heroic Play* (1903), was Assistant Professor of English at Indiana University from 1903 to 1907. He later published *Bernard Shaw in France* (1910) and *Poe and His Poetry* (1913). Quinn wired WBY on 12 Jan (NYPL) to say that he had rearranged the lecture at Indiana University, Bloomington, for 18 Jan.

on a certain day by a telegram from you. Now he displayed all his telegrams to show that telegram had never reached him. I told him I would write to you & explain. Such accidents are inevitable & one must take them cheerfully. Could I not take in Bloomington on my way back from S Fransico as 28th wont work. I have been very successful here I beleive & have just been entertained here at lunch by the principal Irishmen—I am in a charming hotel & am in the best of spirits. Whitcome Reilly[2] gave me a lunch yesterday & he told me that 10 per cent is the Universal Royalty here in America, he thinks publishers have some agreement on the subject. He seems to think that they also are accustomed to get books for good and all but says one should always have a clause to make a collected edition possible. I should say from this advice that I have been trying to get more than is possible from Macmillans.[3] By the by Prof Chase offered to get up a subztitute lecture at some small club for 25 dollars & expenses but I refused this as I think he knew I would. The good opinions of my Carnegie Hall lecture are a great pleasure[4] I was most anxious about it as I did not want to bring your promises for me to nothing. I spoke better than usual last night because of the good spirits the letter put me in. I am tired out after that long lunch party[5] & will go rest for a bit, to morrow I shall set out for Lafayette.[6]

Yrs always
W B Yeats

better look on cancelled lectures as spilt milk & say it does not matter & I have done well that it really does not.

ALS NYPL, with envelope addressed to 120 Broadway, New York, and postmark 'INDINAPOLIS. IND. JAN 11 1904'.

[2] James Whitcomb Riley (1853–1916), an American poet of Irish descent, wrote in dialect and was familiarly known as 'the Hoosier Poet'. On the evening of 9 Jan he presided when WBY lectured on 'The Theatre' to the Athenaeum Club at Butler University, Indianapolis. Joseph Smith, a member of the audience, recalled in the *Boston Herald* of 16 Oct 1911 (6) that at the end of the lecture WBY was presented with a four-foot harp of moss and roses:

He wondered how he could carry it around; he even marvelled how he could dispose of it. . . . Turning to James Whitcomb Riley . . . he said . . . 'You have been very kind to me Mr. Riley, and I'd like to give you this harp as some recognition of my appreciation.'
Jimmy backed up: 'With all these Irish admirers of yours looking at me? Never! I'd love to take the harp, but I want to preserve my hide.'
With a sigh, Yeats carried his harp to his hotel, but he lost it on the train the next day.

[3] See p. 504.
[4] On 7 Jan Quinn had written (see p. 513, n. 1) to tell WBY of the success of his Carnegie Hall speech.
[5] The Emmet Club of Indianapolis gave a banquet luncheon for WBY on 10 Jan, when he spoke on 'The Intellectual Revival'.
[6] WBY spoke at Purdue University, Lafayette, on 12 Jan on 'The Intellectual Revival', with Clarence A. Waldo (1852–1926), Professor of Mathematics, in charge of arrangements.

To John Quinn, [15 January 1904]

UNIVERSITY OF NOTRE DAME, | NOTRE DAME, IND.

My dear Quinn: I am here as you see. I had a great time at Chicago &
roused my audiences as well as I could have hoped.[1] At Perdue I had a
heavy audience who liked my verse—I spoke well.[2] Here I am afraid of the
audience—too many boys, who dont know what I am at. I spoke to them
on poetry in the old time & the new an hour ago & did not rouse them—it
was the worst of the four lectures for such an audience. At St Lewis I
spoke badly & had sympathetic audiences, God help me at the Girls College to night on the theatre. I suspect they have no general knowledge of
the things I assume knowledge of.[3] I like the priests here very much—huge
men full of vitality. I am in the best of spirits & health—But you will be
indignant at one thing. When I was at Chicago a pretty lady came & asked
me to go to a special performance of my 'Land of Hearts Desire' got up by
the girls at the College. I could not resist, but would not dine & meet the
faculty—I went for the play & said a few words after wards. I thought such
friendly students should be encouraged, even though the proffesors have
been shabby.[4] This reminds me that I think it would be a mistake to push
things to[o] far against those St Lewis people. Even if they paid up that
would be but small counterpoise to the trouble of having a knot of ene-

---

[1] On 13 Jan WBY lectured on 'The Intellectual Revival' to the Twentieth Century Club,
Chicago, at the home of Harriet Sanger Pullman (1842–1921), widow of George M. Pullman
(1831–97), industrialist and designer of the luxurious railway carriages which still bear his name.
The following morning he spoke on 'Poetry' to the Chicago Women's Club.

[2] The *Exponent* (Purdue) noted on 14 Jan (5) that WBY's 'manner and voice were very charming and befitting a man of his calling. He spoke at some length of the history and recent revival of
Irish literature and of the relations of Ireland to England and to the United States. He concluded
the lecture by reading some very satisfactory verses from his own works.'

[3] Quinn urged WBY to undertake a heavy programme at Notre Dame and its sister institution,
St Mary's College (until March 1903 St Mary's Academy), since, as he explained ('Western Itinerary', NLI), 'Notre Dame is more generous than any other Catholic college in taking two lectures, and I would like to have you lecture at the Academy, if possible.' WBY spoke at the
Washington Hall on 15 Jan on 'Poetry', and on the following afternoon talked informally to students from advanced English classes on poetry, Sligo, Innisfree, and Thoreau's writings. That
evening he again lectured in the Washington Hall, on 'The Intellectual Revival'.

[4] This performance, by the University of Chicago Dramatic Club, took place on the evening of
14 Jan. Quinn had instructed WBY to shun all invitations from the University of Chicago which
had, he thought, behaved underhandedly by trying to negotiate four lectures at a lower fee, without disclosing its intention to charge for admission (he had refused to allow WBY to lecture at
Columbia University for similar reasons). He was indeed 'indignant', and on 16 Jan, before this
letter could have reached him, fired off a telegram (NYPL): 'Hope newspaper account your visit
incorrect. They wanted lectures reduced rates and concealed fact intended to charge admissions.'
On 6 Feb he wrote (NYPL) that he had forgiven WBY 'only because it was a *pretty* girl that
invited you', but hoped the play 'was badly performed'. In a note in the Rapallo MS Book (NLI),
written after Quinn's death, WBY recalled this incident as an example of 'how irrascible he was'.

mies, to turn the friends I have made for the cause, it may be, into enemies also. I did well there though I did not deserve too for I spoke badly. I did best of all at Chicago & Indianapolis. I think my audiences here will be the most difficult I have had.

Yrs ev
W B Yeats

I must stop as I am off to the Womans College.

ALS NYPL.

To John Quinn, [16 January 1904]

Notre Dame.

My dear Quinn: I dont think it did any harm my going to the University.[1] I was asked by students & not by the faculty, though I confess that when I accepted I thought it was a womans College affiliated with University like that at Harvard. I knew nothing of the co-education system, however I think my going was all right. I refused to dine, & was invited & conducted entirely by students & I had not seen that play for ten years. I said to my self when students get up my play that absolves them from the action of the professors. I spoke well last night & am better content—last night it was St Mary College.[2] I am just off there again & then speak here—There is no great news from the other side except that a hint has been conveyed to Lady Gregory that the King would like to patronize our Theatre. The hint I need hardly say was not taken. I suppose this means another Royal visit in the offing—it means also that we are going up in the world. I hope you do not mind about the College. I was very sorry afterwards that I accepted as I thought you would think it unconsiderate considering all you have said about it. When one is in a whirl as I was in Chicago one has to do everything in a hurry. The parcel of under linnen has just come. Many thanks.

Yrs ever
W B Yeats

ALS NYPL, with envelope addressed to 120 Broadway, New York, USA, and postmark 'NOTRE DAME JAN 16 1904'.

[1] See previous letter; WBY had evidently just received Quinn's telegram of 16 Jan.
[2] An article in the *St. Mary's Chimes* of February 1904 reported that he lectured at the College on 'The Theatre' on 15 Jan, followed by 'Heroic Poetry' on 16th, and that his enthusiasm so 'kindled his audience' that 'the response of complete sympathy was awakened'.

To Lady Augusta Gregory, [*18 January 1904*]

THE CONGRESS HOTEL COMPANY. | THE AUDITORIUM, | THE ANNEX,
APARTMENT BUILDING. | CHICAGO.

My dear Lady Gregory: I am on my way to a place called Indiana University & have just come from Notre Dame a Catholic university & before that I spoke here where I made a big success & before that at an Engineering University[1] where I spoke my best & made a big failure—scientific students attentive & polite but like wet sand until I got to my poetry which they liked. I have been entirely delighted by the big merry priests of Notre Dame—all Irish & proud as lucifer of their success in getting Jews & nonconformists to come to their college,[2] & of the fact that they have no endowments. I did not succeed in my first lecture. I began of a sudden to think, while I was lecturing, that these Catholic students were so out of the world that my ideas must seem the thunder of a battle fought in some other star. The thought confused me & I spoke badly & so I asked if I might go to the literary classes & speak to the boys about poetry & read them some verses of my own. I did this both at Notre Dame & St Marys the girls college near, & delighted them all. I gave four lectures in one day & sat up late talking ghost stories with the Fathers at night. I said when I was going away 'I have made a great litter on the floor' & pointed to torn up papers & one fat old priest said with a voice full of sincerity 'I wish you were making it there for a month'. I think they were delighted to talk about Ireland & the faery—one priest, or rather a teaching brother told me that nothing could heal the touch of the fool except the touch of the queen & that she always wanted some thing in return sometimes a good looking young man to be her husband. He said the fool was ugly & deformed & always gave some deformaty of body or mind. I think these big priests would be fair teachers, but I cannot think they would be more than that. They belong to an easy going world that has passed away,—mores the pity perhaps—but certainly I have been astonished at one thing the general lack of religeous prejudice I find on all sides here. I liked the woman's college much less. The nun I saw most of, the teacher of literature, showed me her

---

[1] Purdue University, Indiana; see p. 517, n. 6 and p. 518, n. 2.

[2] This aspect of American academic life, so different from the sectarianism rife in Ireland, continued to impress WBY and in his first interview on his return to England he went out of his way to tell the *Daily Chronicle* reporter (18 Mar, p. 3) that 'one thing that amazed me in America is the entire lack of intolerance. While I was there I got papers from Ireland telling me of the difficulties at home over the Irish University question. Now, at the Catholic University of Notre Dame, in Indiana, where all the professors are priests, I found about 100 Nonconformists, and I was told that a Jew had just carried off the prize in Christian doctrine! This problem, as others, America has solved very efficiently.'

course of instruction,—no real grasp of ideas in it, & mere prettiness getting the foremost thought it seemed to me—Mrs Meynells essays among the books taught & the like.[3] But the radical defect was that the girls had obviously no real social life. I thought of the girls at the other colleges, with their abundant freedom, their pretty dressy look & heard sister Rita complain of their attention to such things. The boys too, though in a less degree struck me as less masterly in their life—but the priests were a delight—big children & all over six feet. A Sligo lad came to the train with me & was very sad at parting he has it seems known my poetry since he was in Sligo & knew it for a neighbours.[4] I put a picture of the college in this lecture [*for* letter]. I go to San Fransisco in a few days & am getting very tired of railway trains—Tomorrow I shall dine with Prof Sampson—do you remember him.[5] He is at Bloomington & after that S Pauls & more big priests. No—I cannot do those changes in Paul—I never have a moment—I find it hard enought to write a mere letter especially now that I am doing all in a rush & I seem to have lost some of the desire to change it.[6] They can do it as it is if they like though I had sooner get home first & think it out in quiet, much sooner. A Chicago woman asked if she might send Theatre 100 dollars & I gave her your address.

---

[3] Sister Mary Rita (Louise Heffernan; 1860–1910) had been appointed head of the English Department when St Mary's became a College in the previous year. In 1905 she published the first history of the College, *A Story of Fifty Years*, and a selection of her verse, *The Book of the Lily*, appeared in 1910. Alice Thompson Meynell (1847–1922), the English Catholic poet and essayist, was the wife of Wilfred Meynell (b. 1852), with whom she edited the *Weekly Register* (1881–95) and the monthly *Merry England* (1883–95). Her essays for these and other publications were collected in several volumes: *The Rhythm of Life* (1893), *The Colour of Life* (1896), and *The Children* (1897).

[4] Probably Patrick J. MacDonough, who had prepared a pamphlet on WBY to help the students of Notre Dame 'towards a better appreciation of our esteemed visitor'. His essay in this, 'The Poet of the Gael', shows an intimate knowledge of the countryside around Sligo, and so impressed Quinn that he paid for the pamphlet to be distributed among a number of newspaper editors. MacDonough was on the editorial board of the Notre Dame magazine, *Scholastic*, where his essay and poem from the pamphlet were reprinted on 15 Jan, and to which he contributed a further article on WBY on 23 Jan 1904.

[5] Martin Wright Sampson (1866–1930) was Professor of English at Indiana University from 1893 to 1906, editing *Milton's Lyric and Dramatic Poems* (1901) and *Plays of John Webster* (1904). He moved permanently to Cornell University in 1907. A frequent visitor to Europe, AG could have met him in London in 1896 or 1899, but probably made his acquaintance in 1901–2, either in London where, like her, he was working at the British Museum, or in Dublin, which he visited during this trip.

[6] In her letter of 1 Jan 1904 (see p. 511, n. 4) AG reported that ECY had told her that '"the Stage Society want to play Where there is Nothing, but that WB wants to rewrite the second act, and Miss Craig says they can't get an answer from Willie to know what change he wants and that she can not give an estimate of the cost of production till they hear what Willie wants altered". I think it would be spirited of you to attack that act.' WBY was subsequently to collaborate with AG in a radical revision of *Where There Is Nothing*, under a new title, *The Unicorn from the Stars*.

I will write again very soon. I am tired out. I have been up every morning very early & to day I had a long journey.

Yrs ev
W B Yeats

ALS Berg, with envelope addressed to Coole, postmark 'CHICAGO ILL. JAN 18 1904'. Wade, 422-4.

To John Quinn, [*18 January 1904*]

THE CONGRESS HOTEL COMPANY. | THE AUDITORIUM, | THE ANNEX,
APARTMENT BUILDING. | CHICAGO.
Monday

My dear Quinn: I am very tired & so I dare say this will be short. I did well at Notre Dame before I left. I was wretched the first time & partly because I felt that these young men were out of the battle & that my opinions could mean nothing to them. I wanted to give good measure so I asked if I might speak to them again, in class or when they liked, & read them some of my poems as they were the best I had. I made the same offer to the girls college, & my little talks to the litterary classes were a really great success, & delighted the boys especially, & that put me in good conceit with myself again. The Fathers were a delight, big merry Irish priests who told me fairy stories & listened to mine & drank punch with me on Friday night. They were quite happy talking of Ireland & when I came away a Sligo lad came to the train & parted very sadly. I go to Bloomington at 8.30 AM & get there at 3.42 PM.[1] I have about 60 or 70 dollars left & suppose I will want some more, will I not?, before St Fransisco.[2] My chief expense has been Railways & this hotel which does more for ones dignity than ones purse—its devilish expensive. I begin to dislike that man Stevenson who discovered railway trains.[3] I think it was a monotinous invention.

Yours alway
W B Yeats

ALS NYPL, with envelope addressed to 120 Broadway, New York, postmark 'CHICAGO. ILL. JAN 18 1904'.

---

[1] To give his rescheduled lecture on 'The Theatre' (see p. 516, n. 1).
[2] In a telegram of 18 Jan (NYPL), which had presumably just reached WBY, Quinn asked him to 'wire me how much money you now have'.
[3] George Stephenson (1781–1848), the English inventor and founder of railways.

John Quinn to Arthur Brisbane,[1] *18 January 1904*

Jan. 18, 1904

Arthur Brisbane, Esq.,
   c/o New York Evening Journal,
     Tribune Building,
      New York City.

My dear Mr. Brisbane:

Mr. Yeats wants me to thank you very much for your kindness in printing the notice of his lecture in the Evening Journal of January 2nd.[2] He wanted to write himself and thank you for this notice, but left early Monday morning, January 4th, after his lecture Sunday evening, January 3rd, for the West, and has been travelling and lecturing since. The lecture at Carnegie Hall was as a lecture a magnificent one, although the blizzard on Saturday night and the bitter cold on Sunday kept many indoors who doubtless would have been glad to attend the lecture if the weather had been better.

Our Society is going to give a dinner to Mr. Yeats upon his return,[3] and an invitation will be sent to you and I hope that you can make it convenient to come.

Sincerely yours,
John Quinn

TS copy NYPL.

---

[1] Arthur Brisbane (1864–1936), a leading New York journalist, made his name as the London correspondent of the *New York Sun* in 1886–7. In 1887 he was appointed managing editor of the newly established *Evening Sun*, and in 1890 moved to the editorship of the New York *World*. In 1897 he went to work for Randolph Hearst as editor of the New York *Evening Journal*, and soon became the most influential editorial writer in America, his work being syndicated not only in all the Hearst papers but in well over a thousand others.

[2] The 10 p.m. edition of the New York *Evening Sun* of 2 Jan 1904 had carried a prominent boxed notice of WBY's Carnegie Hall lecture across three columns at the head of page two. The notice, headlined 'Mr. Yeats' Lecture To-Morrow', and, illustrated with a photograph of WBY, read:

> Readers of the Evening Journal, those especially that are interested in the welfare of Ireland, are earnestly ADVISED to attend Mr. Yeats' lecture at Carnegie Hall to-morrow night.
>
> Mr. Yeats is the foremost poet of Ireland and of the English-speaking race.
>
> His work has benefited Ireland and encouraged the genius of the Irish. His work honors the Irish nation that has produced so many men of genius. All of those who can should hear him before his return to Ireland, which will not be long postponed.

[3] The dinner at the Metropolitan Club on 5 March; see p. 477, n. 2.

To Charles Welsh,[1] 18 January 1904

Jan. 18, 1904.

Mr. Charles Welsh,
  c/o University Society,
    78 Fifth Avenue,
      New York City.

Dear Sir:

In accordance with Mr. Yeats' directions, I acknowledge the receipt of yours of January 8th stating that you are preparing the article on fairy tales and the folk lore of Ireland for the forthcoming Library of Irish Literature and requesting his permission "to quote very liberally" from his prefaces to the two collections made by him some years ago.[2]

Mr. Bryan requested, as I understand it, Mr. Yeats' permission to print these articles in toto but Mr. Yeats declined to give the permission because they were early and somewhat immature work. Whether he would like to have them "quoted from very liberally" I cannot tell but I will lay the matter before him on his return. He is lecturing in the West now and I will call your letter to his attention when he returns about the 10th of February.

Yours very truly,
John Quinn

TS copy NYPL.

[1] Charles Welsh (1850–1914), was managing editor of the 10-volume compendium of *Irish Literature* (see p. 475). An active man of letters, Welsh had written a biography of Goldsmith's friend, John Newbery, and then devoted himself to producing multi-volume series and children's books. He was general editor of Heath's *Home and School Classics*, the 20-volume *The Young Folks' Library*, and the 4-volume *Famous Battles of the Nineteenth Century*. He worked on *Irish Literature* for over five years, aided by a team of copy- and sub-editors, as well as by a Selection Committee which included AG, Hyde, AE, Stephen Gwynn, Standish O'Grady, D. J. O'Donoghue, and F. N. Robinson of Harvard (see p. 509).

[2] See p. 484, n. 2. Welsh's article, 'Irish Fairy and Folk Tales' appeared in vol. III of *Irish Literature*, and he evidently wished to make use of WBY's Introductions to *Fairy and Folk Tales of the Irish Peasantry* (1888) and *Irish Fairy Tales* (1892). WBY apparently refused him permission to quote liberally and he used only two sentences from the Introduction to the former, although his classification of the Irish fairies (pp. xviii–xx) is taken almost verbatim, but without acknowledgement, from the same source.

To John Quinn, [*19 January 1904*]

Auditorium Annex | Chicago.
Tuesday

My dear Quinn: I spoke well last night & to attentive but not very large or demonstrative audience.[1] I begin to find that these half country audiences—Perdue & Bloomington—are less demonstrative than the big towns & I am therefore not dissapointed when they applaud less. I told Chase that it would be enough if he paid my ticket. He took my ticket back but I paid 2 dollars for sleaping car which he will remember I have no dou[b]t. I went back the same night I spoke. The extras were only meals & room at hotel & I did not like to seem grasping for sake of 4 or 5 dollars & besides I was not certain if I could charge food which I would have had to get any way. I dont like Prof Chase. He seems to me heavy, obviously a little mean—& I should think a little underbred. Perhaps he is only business like according to some local type—I can see there is a rather local type. I shall leave here for St Paul Wednesday night, travell all night & get there about 8 AM, the day I speak. I want a good nights rest to-night for I [?]have not had good sleap—journeys by night or early in the morning are hard on the nerves. I have just made out expenses—A return ticket (had I had the sense to get one) would have been

6. 7. 5 return
take from this
3. 7. 5 for ticket paid to Chicago by Chase
& you get
3. 0 0
add
2. 0 0 for sleaper car (people here say over charge of 50 but what I paid)
  &
1. . for Chair Car

Chase owes me ⟨7.50⟩ 6 dollars expenses
I confess had I known it was so little I would have charged for meals & hotel as I waited extra day but I told him I would not. I got mixed about price & thought it was 7 dollars each way & that 14 would be a heavy increase to price of lecture. I enclose a letter which explains itself—I have

[1] At Bloomington; see p. 516, n. 1.

acknowledged it & that is all. I am tired out that is why I write so badly. I shall take a bath & lie down for a bit.

Yrs ev
W B Yeats

ALS NYPL, with envelope addressed to 120 Broadway, New York, and postmark 'CHICAGO. ILL. JAN 19 1904'.

To Maud Gonne, [c. *19 January 1904*]

Mention in letter to AG, 21 January, and from MG, 12 February 1904. Discussing their differences over the relationship between nationalism and literature; and mentioning an article she has published in the *United Irish-man*.[1]

G–YL, 180–1.

To F. J. Fay, [*20 January 1904*]

1 West 87 St, | New York.

My dear Fay: I send the new Cuchullain dialogue. I think it is all you will want. The repetition on Cuchullain's entrance will fix it on the mind.[1] I write from Chicago though I give my New York address. I start for San Francisco in a couple of days & have just come from the Catholic College of Notre Dame where I gave four lectures—no, six but two were only little lectures on my own poetical doctrines to the literary classes at the college for men & the affiliated womans college. Tomorrow I speak at St Pauls another Catholic College—in Ireland neither Catholic nor protestant college would let me among its students I suspect—here I find a really wonderful large tolerant spirit. One Catholic Proffessor was told that I was a pagan & said 'There is a great deal that is very good about paganism' & now he has arranged for four lectures I believe,—& yet I think people are

[1] This was a 'somewhat vehement' reply to a letter from MG which apparently repeated many of the charges she had made in her *United Irishman* article of 24 Oct 1903 (see p. 441, n. 4), and which accused him of abandoning his nationalist views. On 12 Feb she described this as 'the letter you did not like', and assured him that she had not meant 'to say anything to pain you & I would be *very* VERY sorry if I thought there was any serious misunderstanding between us'.

[1] While in America WBY had substantially revised *On Baile's Strand* for a proposed spring production in Dublin and London, although this was subsequently postponed until the opening of the Abbey Theatre on 27 Dec 1904, and the new version was not printed until *Poems, 1899–1905* in 1906. He had probably sent Fay new dialogue for the Fool, just before Cuchulain's first entry (*VPl,* 475–6, ll. 184–99).

very pious here. Yet Catholics go without protest to the state schools in New England where the protestant Bible is read every day & there are a hundred Non-conformists & Jews in Notre Dame where all the teachers are priests. There are some intolerants but they seem to be fading out.

About Cuchullain. You have Lady Gregorys book I know. Remember however that epic & folk literature can ignore time as drama cannot—Helen never ages, Cuchullain never ages. I have to recognize that he does for he has a son who is old enough to fight him. I have also to make the refusal of the sons affection tragic by suggesting in Cuchullains character a shadow of something a little proud, barren & restless as if out of shere strength of heart or from accident he had put affection away. He lives among young men but has himself outlived the illusions of youth. He is probably about 40, not less than 35 or 36 & not more that 45 or 46, certainly not an old man, & one understands from his talk about women that he does not love like a young man. Probably his very strength of character made him put off illusions & dreams (that make young men a womans servant) & made him become quite early in life a deliberate lover, a man of pleasure who can never really surrender himself. He is a little hard, & leaves the people about him a little repelled—perhaps this young mans affection is what he had most need of. Without this thought the play had not had any deep tragedy. I write of him with difficulty for when one creates a character one does it out of instinct & may be wrong when one analyses the instinct afterwards. It is as though the character embodied itself. The less one reasons the more living the character.[2] I felt for instance that his boasting was necessary, & yet I did not reason it out. The touch of something hard, repellent yet alluring, self assertive yet self immolating is not all but it must be there. He is the fool—wandering passion, houseless & all but loveless. Concobar is reason that is blind because it can only reason because it is cold. Are they not the cold moon & the hot sun?

Now about scenery. I think you will find that the persons in Cuchullain will stand out clearly against the plain sacking. It is not necessary to do this by contrasting colour always—light & dark will do it. 'The Shadowy Waters' I thought an exception to rule & thought one should lose the persons in the general picture. I had a different feeling about [the] stage when I wrote it—I would not now do anything so remote, so impersonal. It is legitimate art however though a kind that has I should think by this time proved itself the worst sort possible for our theatre. The whole picture as it were moves togeather—sky & sea & cloud are as it were actors. It is almost religious, it [is] more a ritual than a human story. It is deliberately without

[2] Compare his comments on Gautier and Hamlet, p. 155.

human characters. 'Cuchullain' or 'The Kings Threshold' are the other side of the halfpenny. I do not think the greys kept the people in the latter from standing out though there were other deffects—too many colours & so on. Miss Horniman has to learn her work however & must have freedom to experiment. I think her 'Bailes Strand' will prove much better. I had told her that old stages permitted elaborate dress though not elaborate scenes & this combined with [the] fact of its being a Court misled her into overdoing colour & the like in certain parts.[3] Surely the people of heroic age wore trews? I have heard that bare leggs & kilts of the highlander come from the Romans, that the Celts had both kinds. Anyway Miss Horniman has Joyces 'Social Ireland' & was deep in it when I saw her.[4]

Yr ev
W B Yeats

ALS Private. Wade, 424–6.

To Lady Augusta Gregory, 21 January 1904

C. D. AND THOS. D. O'BRIEN, | ATTORNEYS AND COUNSELORS AT LAW,
212 GLOBE BUILDING, | ST. PAUL, MINN.
St. Paul, Minn.,[1] January 21st, 1904.

My dear Lady Gregory,—
I am dictating this in St. Paul where I am to lecture at a Catholic College; Archbishop Ireland is partly responsible for arranging the lecture for me.

[3] AEFH had made the costumes for the first production of *The King's Threshold* on 8 Oct 1903, and evidently supposed that designing would be her creative contribution to the Irish dramatic movement, for the following day she had written to WBY (NLI): 'I am so anxious to help effectually as best I may and it seems as if it were already ordained. . . . Do you realise that you have given me the right to call myself "artist"? How I thank you!' Others found her costumes over-elaborate and lacking in a sense of style and colour, and, despite a diplomatic letter from WBY, her efforts for *On Baile's Strand* were no better. Holloway records (*Abbey Theatre*, 49–50) that at the first rehearsal on 16 Dec 1904 some of the costumes 'were found to border on the grotesque or eccentric' and that this led to a public altercation between WBY and AEFH: 'Yeats likened some of the kings to "extinguishers", their robes were so long and sloped so from the shoulders. Father Christmas was another of his comparisons.'

[4] P. W. Joyce's *A Social History of Ancient Ireland* (1903) confirmed WBY's contention (II. 207): 'The ancient Irish wore a trousers. . . . The usual Irish name was *triubhas* . . . which is often correctly anglicised *trews*, and from which the modern word "trousers" is derived.' Patrick Weston Joyce (1827–1914), Irish scholar, folklorist, and historian, was President of the Royal Society of Antiquaries from 1906 to 1908.

[1] Christopher Dillon O'Brien (1848–1922), was born in Co. Galway and emigrated to the USA with his parents in 1856. He moved to St Paul in 1867, was admitted to the Minnesota bar in 1870, and as Mayor of St Paul from 1883 to 1885 led a reforming administration which enforced saloon and gambling laws. He was in partnership with his brother Thomas Dillon O'Brien

The stenographer I am dictating this to is in the office of an Irishman who has had something to do with my lecture. I find myself here (between lunch and lying down to rest a bit before lecturing) and snatch at a few minutes to write this to you.

I got rather a heavy cold a couple of days ago and have it clinging about me, and that is the only inconvenience I think that has come to me in all this traveling. Tomorrow I go to San Francisco then New York, then Toronto, then home. I am awaiting the news of the plays in Dublin with great impatience. It will reach me at San Francisco a good many days late.[2]

It does not matter a bit,—Mrs. Emery's note not going in that book of plays; indeed the note has disappointed me; it is too meager to mean anything; but I thought her notation was to go in as well as the Dublin notations.[3] I suppose Bullen objected, but it is a great mistake to humor him by giving in to him. However, it does not matter. I have sent off the proof sheets of "The King's Threshold" to Quinn and if he can't arrange an immediate edition with McMillan, who seems to be traveling about, we will bring it out ourselves in the way he did with "Where There is Nothing", so that Bullen will not have any further delay.[4]

I am full of curiosity to know what your "King Brian" will be like.[5] Remember that a play, even if it is in three acts, has to seem only one action—at any rate it is the better for seeming only one action. Your danger will be that having thought of Act I first your other acts will be episodes by themselves. When you write to me next let me know, if you know yourself, when the performances come on in London. I want to try to keep that as a fixed date in my head; that and the performance in Dublin. I hope to leave here about February 10th, but I may be delayed four or five days longer.

I have written a long letter to Fay as to the character of Cuchullain and I have sent him the new lines he wanted, the bits about Cuchullain being a

---

(1859–1935), who was born in La Pointe, Wisconsin, acted as a member of the Democratic national committee from 1896 to 1904, and was appointed associate justice of the Minnesota Supreme Court from 1909 to 1911. They were members of the Knights of Columbus which helped Archbishop Ireland (see p. 475, n. 7) arrange a dinner and the lecture at the St Paul Seminary on 'The Intellectual Revival'.

[2] The INTS produced WBY's *The Shadowy Waters* and Seamus MacManus's *The Townland of Tamney* at the Molesworth Hall from 14 to 16 Jan.

[3] See p. 506.

[4] See pp. 503–5. *The King's Threshold* was published privately by Quinn in a New York edition of 100 copies in March 1904. With the American copyright thus secured, the play was issued by A. H. Bullen in the same month as part of vol. III of 'Plays for an Irish Theatre'.

[5] AG's three-act historical play, *Kincora*, first produced at the Abbey Theatre on 25 Mar 1905, with Frank Fay playing King Brian, dramatizes the intrigues of Brian Boru's wife, Gormleigh, which culminated in the Battle of Clontarf. AG had great difficulty in constructing the play and subsequently radically revised it.

small dark man.[6] He is anxious about the scenery and I have written to Miss Horniman suggesting as delicately as I could that there ought not to be gorgeousness of costume.

I have had a letter from Paris[7] that rather irritates me. It speaks of my once having thought that our literature should be national but having given up that conviction. I replied on the first day of my cold and was somewhat vehement, and am now sorry that I was. One doesn't mind the misunderstandings of the indifferent world but one is hurt by the misunderstandings of friends.

This isn't much of a letter but the chance arose of dictating it in a hurry and I did not like to lose it.

Bye the bye I sent that poem to the Duchess of Sutherland. I would let you have a copy but the copy is in New York and I am some hundreds of miles away from it. I think it was a very good poem.[8] I made it when shut up in a railway train coming from Canada. I think a railroad train a good place to write when the journey is long enough. One will exhaust the scenery in the first two or three hours and the newspaper in the second two or three hours (even an American newspaper), and towards the end of the day one can hardly help oneself, but one has to begin to write. Indeed I think that if some benevolent government would only shut one up in the smoking car of a railway train and send one across the world one would really write two or three dozen lyrics in the year.
(Dict. W.B.Y.)

Yours alwy
W B Yeats

[*In WBY's hand*]
I have just heard from Quinn. Alas more lectures. I lecture in Canada on Feb 13th. That does not look like getting back as soon as I thought. I am very homesick so you may be certain I will hurry all I can. In spite of my cold & some hoarseness my lecture last night was a great success. A great audience too—300 turned away. Most of audience clerical students. Archbishop entertained me at dinner before lecture—the owner of the office where I dictated this is the son of a Galway landlord—Dillon O'Brien who

[6] See p. 526, n. 1. When the revised version came to be printed the fact that Cuchulain was a dark man was revealed in a stage direction rather than dialogue, and there was no mention of his stature.
[7] See p. 526. The letter seems to have upset him so much that he did not keep it.
[8] See pp. 494–5.

lived near the town (or near Athlone which sounds vague but it is what they told me) & had a house called 'Fairview'.[9] He sold out long ago.

TLS Berg, with envelope addressed to Coole, postmark 'SAINT PAUL, MINN. JAN 22 1904'. Wade, 426–8.

To Susan Mary Yeats, 21 January 1904

C. D. AND THOS. D. O'BRIEN, | ATTORNEYS AND COUNSELORS AT LAW,
212 GLOBE BUILDING, | ST. PAUL, MINN.
St. Paul, Minn., Jan. 21st, 1904.

My dear Lilly,—

I am writing from St. Paul where I am to lecture tonight, dictating this to a stenographer in the office of one of the people who have got up my lecture. I have been so busy running from place to place that I have not had time to write. I am just about beginning to think that when Stevenson invented the railway he invented something that is very tedious and very disagreeable. I have just about enough of it.

I had a charming time in Chicago where I was entertained by a certain woman's club, lectured to it and also lectured to another club—the Twentieth Century Club.[1] The lecture to this club was given in Mrs. Pullman's house, the widow of the man who made all the Pullman cars; and the house was decorated right through in the style of a Pullman car. One could see that the somewhat flamboyant woodwork of the cars was an expression of his enthusiasm. I have seen a great many charming places but I do not like the Pullman type.

I hear from Fay that Miss Quinn played "Kathleen" at Dundrum and

---

[9] Dillon O'Brien (1818–82) was born in Kilmore, Co. Roscommon and educated at Clongowes Woods College. He married Elizabeth Kelly in 1839, and they lived at Fairfield, Co. Galway before emigrating to the USA in 1856. He taught at Indian schools in Wisconsin from 1857 to 1863, and settled in St Paul in 1865, where he became the first editor of the Catholic weekly, *Northwest Chronicle*. He worked closely with Archbishop Ireland both in promoting Catholic, and especially Irish, colonization of Minnesota, and in establishing total abstinence societies. He died suddenly while conversing with the Archbishop on 12 Feb 1882.

[1] See p. 518, n. 1.

that you have seen it. Write and tell me what kind of a performance it was, addressing your letter care of John Quinn of course.[2]

I had a delightful time in the University of Notre Dame. I was entertained there by big Irish priests who told ghost stories and fairy stories. They ⟨are very proud—or rather they⟩ take it as a matter of course that they should have in their college a hundred jews and non-conformists. It is entirely a clerical college; all the teachers are priests. Imagine Irish non-conformists going to a clerical college! On the other hand in Pennsylvania I found Catholics going to school where the Bible was read. One Bible reader, who was a Catholic, had given one school nothing but the book of Proverbs for many years, as he thought that quite safe.

The man here who has most to do with getting up my lecture, at any rate the man I have communicated with about it, knows Jack's name very well and asked me a lot of questions about him. Of course he does not know his work but he sees all our propagandist weekly newspapers and so keeps posted on things.

I do not know that I have very much news else. One does not gather much in railway trains. I am growing a little tired of my own voice and shall be glad when I am on the high seas. I am keeping very well, however, not really feeling the fatigue of so much travel at all.

Yrs affecly
W B Yeats

(Dict. W.B.Y.)

TLS MBY, with envelope addressed to Gurteen Dhas, postmark 'ST PAUL, MINN. JAN 22 1904'.

---

[2] Dramatic performances were often staged in Evelyn Gleeson's garden at Dun Emer, in the village of Dundrum, Co. Dublin; on 22 Aug 1903 the INTS had produced AE's *Deirdre* there, and a Digges–Quinn production of *Cathleen ni Houlihan* was staged in mid-January 1904. SMY had not liked the latter, and replying on 2 Feb (NLI) told WBY that

> to begin with the platform was so small that they were all on top of each other—they acted it as nearly as possible like the Fay company, grouping & moving in just the same way, Digges was good.
>   Miss Quinn has not at all the right kind of appearence [*sic*] for the part, her impudent turned up nose appearing from among the gray [*sic*] hair was absurd & then she always acts as if she was wanting to fight you, her northern accent heightens this last feeling.

After the disputes over the rights of the play, and the ownership of the wig (see pp. 429, 431), WBY perhaps read this report with a certain satisfaction.

'This is Willy lecturing on Speaking to the Psaltery in the Wild and Woolly West'
(cartoon by Jack Yeats).

To John Quinn, [*24 January 1904*]

THE OVERLAND LIMITED | CHICAGO, SAN FRANCISCO, LOS ANGELES[1]

My dear Quinn: I am on my way as you will see by this rickety handwriting. We have left the snow behind us & are in the middle of mud coloured plains that I suspect are prairies. I shall be in good time. I saw that autograph man at Mineapolis & liked him & spent some hours with him.[2] He

---

[1] WBY was travelling in style. 'The Overland Limited', described in advertisements as 'perhaps the most finely equipped train in the world', took the direct route to California ('an important item in the winter'), running over the Chicago & North Western tracks from Chicago to Omaha, and those of the Union Pacific to Ogden, Utah, where it became the flagship of the Southern Pacific on its way to San Francisco and Los Angeles.

[2] James Carleton Young (1856–1918), capitalist, land speculator, and bibliophile, was among the leading proponents of colonization of the North West, and became the President or Vice-President of numerous estate, mortgage, and investment companies. He was also a member of the most prestigious book societies in America, Britain, and France, and built up a library containing autograph manuscripts and inscribed books by the most celebrated living writers. He was fond of inviting writers to his house in Minneapolis, and wrote to WBY soon after his arrival in America. A further letter came after WBY had left for the West, and Quinn forwarded it on 15 Jan (NYPL), remarking that 'Mr. Young evidently wants you to visit him. . . . I would not waste much time on Mr. James Carlton Young. At any rate, I would not spend a day there.'

drove me to the train & saved me a great deal of trouble. I did well at St Paul & they talk of another lecture. 300 people could not get in. I had a very bad cold & my voice almost gave out but I did well. I wish it could get out in Ireland that Archbishop Ireland gave me that dinner & got up lecture & also that I gave those *Notre D'Ame* lectures. It would help there. My St Paul audience was one of the easiest to stir that I have had—a great part of it priests to be. I got money etc all right & have bought a round ticket (a station so handwriting improves) coming back by same route (union pacific) it cost 111 dollars (a devil of a price) & 11 dollars more for sleaper. I have therefore 105 dollars (I had some over). (off again). It is a pleasure to see little towns flit by the windows, in which there are no factory chimneys and hardly a big house—leisurely looking places—but I wish I could see a hill. I think my least responsive audiences have been Bloomington & Perdue, & St Paul & Chicago & Brynmore my most responsive. I am beginning to understand how an actor feals. I have met several Sligo men—& will have one curious tale to tell you, a tale an old Sligo man told me.[3]

Yrs ev\
W B Yeats

I could get to Los-Angeles without extra expense as I find my ticket is good for there to[o]

ALS NYPL, with envelope addressed to 120 Broadway, New York, postmark 'OMAHA & OGDEN R.P.O. JAN 24 1904'.

To John Quinn, 27 January 1904

Mention in following letter.\
Telegram declining a proposed lecture on Emmet.

---

[3] Perhaps the account of the Fool's Touch (see p. 520), or the story WBY mentions (and perhaps mislocates) in *Reveries Over Childhood and Youth* (1914), where he recalls (*Aut*, 31) that 'ten years ago when I was in San Francisco, an old cripple came to see me who had left Sligo before her [*i.e. WBY's mother*] marriage; he came to tell me, he said, that my mother "had been the most beautiful girl in Sligo".'

To Lady Augusta Gregory, [28 January 1904]

San Fransisco.

Dear Lady Gregory: Yesterday Quinn wired asking me if I would accept an engagement for March 6 in New York to address Irish Societies on Emmet. They offer very good terms—about £40. I wired that I could not stay so long, play coming on in Dublin. I have just had another wire, urging again. I am about to answer. 'Subject difficult to me, outside my work, dislike political speaking. Will accept if you think very desirable. leave decision to you. Sooner spend few days with you in quiet'. I wish I had not [to] decide in a hurry. It means more than £40 for Quinn talks of 2 or 3 other lectures & am not sure that I should refuse but I hate the delay here.[1] I am getting tired out, not bodily, but am getting bored & homesick. The only thing to be said for this new lecture is that with Toronto on 14th & an inevitable few days with Quinn I could hardly get away before end of month. I shall be at least £70 the richer—but the boredom of another month here my heart at home all the while—& I have so much to tell you. I left St Paul last Friday, amid ice & snow—14 degrees below zero & the first thing I saw in the railway station when I got here was a notice to say that for 11 dollars return people could take their children to see "real ice & snow". Here there are palm trees & pepper trees & one walks about without a coat. The bay is beautiful, all is beautiful. I gave my first lecture here, at a university amid great trees, great ever greens, in a huge gym[n]asium to some 2000 people. I spoke on the theatre & did not do well because I was hoarse & a little deaf with a cold & I gave my second to about 2000 people, Irish mostly last night, & did well I think.[2] I hope Moore does not see the interview I send. I lunched with the interviewer & forgot it was an interview & so told about the Shelbourne.[3] O the weariness of another month here, it would be a little less weary if it were here in this tropical place but ice & snow & cold & wet

---

[1] As Quinn reported in a letter of 26 Jan (NYPL), he had just wired to say that John Devoy and Judge Daniel F. Cohalan (1865–1946) had constituted themselves as a committee to invite WBY to lecture on 6 Mar: 'Both very anxious you accept, guaranteeing two hundred dollars net. . . . I think well of proposition'. This wire evidently did not reach WBY until 27 Jan, and Quinn followed it up with two further telegrams on 28 Jan, the second presumably a response to the wire WBY was about to send. The lecture, which WBY finally arranged to give on 28 Feb, was to be a late centenary commemoration of the death of the Irish patriot, Robert Emmet (1778–1803), and at an honorarium substantially above WBY's standard fee of $75.

[2] At 4 p.m. on 27 Jan, the afternoon after his arrival, WBY lectured on 'The Theatre' in the Harmon Gymnasium at the University of California, Berkeley. That evening he spoke on 'The Intellectual Revival' for the League of the Cross, a Catholic temperance society, at the Alhambra Theatre, an occasion which also included a recital of Irish melodies and ballads, including WBY's 'Father Gilligan'.

& the weariness of ever new faces—but I am tired out to day. You will I suspect have to be my eyes at 'Bailes Strand'.[4]

Yr ev
W B Yeats

ALS Berg, with envelope addressed to Coole, postmark '?? JAN 28 1904'. Wade, 428–9.

To John Quinn, 28 January 1904

Mention in previous letter.
Telegram, expressing doubts about the proposed lecture on Emmet.

To Lady Augusta Gregory, [29 January 1904]

San Fransisco

Dear Lady Gregory: Have just written Quinn to cancel Emmett lecture—I was perfectly miserable when I agreed—for I knew he would accept for me—The depression I should have endured during coming weeks would not have been worth £70 & besides I have made several hundred & whats £70 now that I am fealing so rich. I am just setting out to a lecture & must stop[1] keep papers I send.

yr ev
W B Yeats

I shall spend few days with Quinn after 14th & then start home. He may want to go to sea shore for a few days with me.

ALS Berg, with envelope addressed to Coole, postmark 'SAN FRANCISCO. CAL. JAN 29 1904'. Wade, 429.

---

[3] Edward F. Cahill interviewed WBY at length in the *San Francisco Examiner* of 28 Jan 1904, in the course of which (3) WBY recounted 'George Moore's tragic experience when he came back to Dublin to live. Moore went to the Shelburne Hotel. In the course of his dinner he quarrelled with the waiter. That was perhaps natural and inevitable. Then he sent for the landlord and had a quarrel with him. But he was not yet satisfied and went downstairs to scold the cook. "Why should an Irish beefsteak taste like brown paper?" A butcher who was a good Gaelic Leaguer finally explained to him: "Mr. Moore, all the good meat goes to England." That was convincing. Moore went back to the Shelburne Hotel and apologized to the cook.'

[4] This was unnecessary since the production was postponed; see p. 526, n. 1.

[1] On the afternoon of 29 Jan WBY spoke on 'Heroic Literature' to an audience of 800 at Stanford University. That evening he lectured on 'The Intellectual Revival' at Santa Clara College, whose President, Robert Kenna SJ, was Phelan's uncle. He then toured the printing-presses of the *Daily Mercury* and spent the night in San Jose at the Vendome Hotel.

To John Quinn, [*30 January 1904*]

San Jose

Tel rec^d accept for Feb 28th—Yeates[1]

MS copy of telegram NYPL.

To John Quinn, [*30 January 1904*]

San Fransisco.

My dear Quinn: I have accepted Devoys offer, as 28 Feb will enable me to get back in time to see plays in Dublin before the London performances which come on at end of month.[1] Miss Horniman has written to me that she may have gone well on with her proposed purchase of hall to turn into theatre, before I return.[2] This makes London success of great importance. I felt therefore that I must be back in time to influence choice of plays & manner of presentation. Feb 28 gives me time. I am anxious about my speach for my mind is not full on politics, but with your advice I will get through with it however. I think I am begginning to get a little tired—I got pulled down by a cold—so better let me have no new lectures between my Devoy lecture & my return to New York. I can then give all my time to Emmett speach. I shall speak of Emmett & his time for a few minutes, I should think, & then go on to general national principles. Think of any thing you can to give me matter—national ideal better than race ideal alone, as can better take in new thought, importance of gaelic & race how-

---

[1] This telegram is now lost, but James Phelan reported to Quinn in a letter of 30 Jan (NYPL) that on 29 Jan he and WBY 'spent the night in San Jose, where I wired you this a.m.: "Tel rec^d accept for Feb 28th—Yeates". This is Emmett [*sic*] speech. He will take up Irish Nationality for his main theme at my suggestion—.' WBY's wire was in response to Quinn's telegram of 28 Jan (NYPL): 'As telegraphed previously Committee require telegraphic decision. Impossible await arrival letter. Audience friendly. Ample time preparation. Suggest making decision turn on feeling about lecture disregarding Dublin play.'

[1] See previous letter. WBY wanted to return in time to see the INTS productions of *On Baile's Strand* and Synge's *Riders to the Sea*, planned for late February 1904. Since he remained in America until early March, he missed Synge's play, which ran from 25 to 27 Feb, and *On Baile's Strand* was put off until December.

[2] AEFH had begun negotiations to acquire 99-year leases on the Hall of the Mechanics' Institute in Abbey Street, at an annual rent of £110, and on the old Dublin City Morgue, adjoining in Marlborough Street, at £60 a year, and was planning to spend £1,600 to convert them into the Abbey Theatre.

ever, & so on. I dont know whether I shall do well or ill—have no experience to guide me but glad of a new task.

Yr ev

W B Yeats

All here lovely—palm trees, pepper trees & clear starry nights

ALS NYPL, with envelope addressed to 120 Broadway, New York, postmark 'SAN FRANCISCO. CAL. JAN 31 1904'.

To Lady Augusta Gregory, [*30 January 1904*]

S. W. COR. OF | VALENCIA & SEVENTEENTH STS. | SAN FRANCISCO.[1]

My dear Lady Gregory: I have had an urgent letter from Quinn. The Irish Societies offer 250 dollars (£50) if I will give Emmett address & will change date to Feb 28.[2] I have accepted this not wanting to dissapoint Quinn. As I had made up my mind to spend a weak with him after I get back from Canada on the 15th or 16th this will cause but little delay. I shall have to speak I suppose some 15 minutes or so on Emmett & then 3 quarters of an hour on general doctrine. It will be hard to speak so long on a more or less political theme, but I shall try & serve the good causes— Hyde in chief. I send you Father Yorkes paper, he is a great Moranite & as he is also an enemy of my host a San Fransico rich man & ex Mayor I had rather expected attack.[3] He is supposed to attack everyone. It is very hot here—I have sat all afternoon without coat or waistcoat with the window wide open. Yesterday I spoke at two colleges among palm trees & there was an orange tree by the hotel where I slept.[4] Next week I shall be in Chicago, with the barometer below zero & then in Canada—colder still.

---

[1] Address and stationery of James D. Phelan, WBY's host.

[2] The lecture, 'Emmet the Apostle of Irish Liberty' (*UP* II. 310–27), delivered at the Academy of Music, was printed in full in John Devoy's newspaper, the *Gaelic American*, on 5 Mar 1904, with a report that '4000 people, the cream of the Irish race in New York and vicinity, were packed into the great hall, in spite of the fact that it had rained all day and that the weather was still threatening up to the time the doors were opened. The address . . . was a great intellectual treat that was fully appreciated by the audience and will long be remembered.'

[3] Yorke (see p. 468) had praised WBY in the San Francisco *Leader* of 30 Jan 1904 (1) as 'the most gifted of all the sons of Erin, [who] has charmed and captivated California. In one week he has done more for the Irish name and the Irish cause in the centres of culture than could be done in years. And he has inspired his own people with enthusiasm, with pride, with fresh courage.' Quinn had also expected Yorke to attack WBY, writing to Phelan on 14 Nov 1903 that he was 'the very type of man that Yeats infuriates and that Yeats rather delights in infuriating. York [*sic*] won't know enough about Yeats before he speaks to do him much damage and I am going to tell Yeats that he doesn't need to be afraid of wounding the voluble gentleman's tender susceptibilities.'

[4] See p. 536, n. 1.

Do not let them give Bailes Strand till I return. I shall leave by the first boat after the 28th.

Yrs ever

W B Yeats

I get emmense audiences here.

I hear that the O'Donovan, Father Finlay, Anderson, lecture tour was a failure & that Finlay at a dinner where there were some 14 or 15 people or so made a violent attack on me. I was neither dramatist, poet, or orator & so on. Finlay is a "Leader" sympathizer I beleive.[5]

ALS Berg, with envelope addressed to Coole, postmark 'SAN FRANCISCO. CAL. JAN 31 1904'. Wade, 429–30.

To Maud Gonne, [late January 1904]

Mention in letter from MG, 12 February [1904].
Discussing his attitude to nationalism and literature.[1]

G–YL, 180–1.

---

[5] The Irish Agricultural Organisation Society fund-raising deputation (see p. 459) had met with little success. In *With Horace Plunkett in Ireland*, R. A. Anderson recalled (141–7) that the self-made Irish-Americans treated them with cold politeness, and that Bourke Cockran sabotaged their efforts under the pretence of helping: 'Various meetings were arranged for us, but were poorly attended and without much result. . . . Our efforts had only resulted in cash to the tune of about £1500, mostly contributed by Plunkett's personal friends. . . . This expedition was a mistake and a failure. . . . America was dead sick of subscribing to Irish causes. The bulk of the Irish-American population might still be induced to subscribe to a political fund, but those to whom our humdrum policy would appeal were very few.' Quinn reported to Mrs Byrne on 3 Feb (see p. 492, n. 3), shortly after Finlay's attack (which took place at the end of December 1903), that one of the other diners told him: 'Your friend Yeats and his writings were very severely criticised the other evening at a dinner I attended—"roasted" was I think the word he used—by the "visitors from the other side"; Father Finlay was "particularly severe on him" . . .'. Quinn thought the attack 'in bad taste to say the very least', told WBY about it, and asked him 'whether Finlay had anything personal against him'. Quinn had evidently also written of it to AE, who replied *c.* 24 Jan 1904 (NYPL): 'Father Finlay hates Yeats and deservedly so, for if Yeats' ideas are accepted then Father Finlay's must disappear. . . . Father O'Donovan is different. He is one of the best fellows in the world.'

[1] The second of the three letters MG acknowledged on 12 Feb, and probably a more temperate rejoinder than his 'somewhat vehement' letter of *c.* 19 Jan (see p. 526), which he now regretted.

To John Quinn, [*1 February 1904*]

San Fransisco

My dear Quinn: Many thanks for your letter. I am getting over my cold & feal strong & ready for work again—yet let me have a few days to work out that Emmett speach—other lectures if they turn up. How long will it have to be? An hour I suppose & it will be no end of a job to speak an hour on Emmett & abstract nationality. I shall have to read his life & some life of Napolean.[1] I wish I knew where I could get particulars of the struggles of small European Nationalities—how they grew strong through language & historical movements. That Chicago interview you talk of must have been invented by some reporter. I never said Chicago was ugly nor have I spoken against America which would have been very ungracious of me, & ungrateful.[2] I enclose a letter from Fay (F). He seems despondent but he has always had these moods[3]—I send it because of what he says about America—about the St Lewis project. The show has been as I feared little of a success this time. Lady Gregory & my sister are enthusiastic about beautiful effect of 'The Shadowy Waters' scenery speach & so on, but as I warned the company such things cannot be popular.[4] MacManus play is rubbish & I was furious at its acceptance—it seems however to have

[1] In his lecture WBY described Emmet's meeting with Napoleon and Talleyrand (*UP* II. 316–17): 'He was then but twenty-four, and yet these men, the mightiest in Europe, listened to his plans and discussed with him the liberation of Ireland. . . . Emmet returned to Ireland to raise there a rebellion which was to strike at Dublin Castle when Napoleon struck at England.'

[2] The Chicago *Inter-Ocean* of 17 Jan 1904 (3) quoted WBY as saying that part of the population 'must always be fleeing and hiding from the hideousness of your cities. There is so little romance about American cities. . . . But I want to repeat that America is great, great even in its ugliness.'

[3] Frank Fay's letter is untraced, but on 18 Jan AG reported (Berg) that 'Fay was low at the lack of long plays', and the small audiences at the latest INTS performances would also have depressed him.

[4] *The Shadowy Waters*, now irreverently styled *The Watery Shadows* by Dublin wags, had perplexed and irritated the reviewers. The *Irish Times* of 15 Jan (8) asserted that the play 'is not, and in its present form can never be, a drama. It is too vague, too weak, too artificial, too much laboured. It lacks energy in writing, it lacks action, it lacks human interest. If we are to have an Irish drama by all means let us have it. But let us not deceive ourselves. No living drama ever yet was written on a bogus harp, a handful of white birds, some conies hiding in the last ridge of the barley, a ship controlled by a vague dreamer whose spell lies bound up in the harp which plays a thing that is not music . . .' The *Irish Daily Independent* of the same day found it (5) 'a most cryptic composition', containing a 'great deal of versified vapourings about love, sometimes in involved metaphor, but lacking in the smallest trace of passion. . . . The whole course of the piece is incoherent and unconvincing . . .' However, AG wrote on 14 Jan (Berg) that 'the Shadowy Waters was a most beautiful performance, the beautiful verse beautifully spoken, Dectora looking quite beautiful and the staging beautiful'.

amused people for the moment.[5] I am delighted at Fays desire for more vigerous drama—they [*for* their] tendency has been a little the other way—but all shows me I must hurry back after the Emmett speach. I must be there before the London programe is decided upon & before any new plays are put in rehersal.[6] Lady Gregory says Anthony MacDonell was there & enthusiastic & talking of performance before King & vexed at being told it could not be.[7] Miss Horniman writes saying that she is busy about buying Mechanics—I hope she gets it before Martyn.

I wrote in a despondent mood about my strength but I think I shall get through all write [*for* right]. What I thought fateague was merely the result of cold caught in that dreadful Chicago, St Paul weather—I have still a stuffed up ear.

I am very sorry that you are not well—the weather too I suppose. Here it is rather too hot—at least it is sometimes. Palm trees on all sides & even flowers.

[*Unsigned*]

ALS NYPL, with envelope addressed to 120 Broadway, New York, postmark 'SAN FRANSISCO. CAL. FEB 1 1904'.

[5] See p. 529, n. 2. Seumas MacManus (*c*. 1868–1960) was a prolific author of popular stories, verse, and plays. His brief marriage to the Irish poetess Anna Johnston ('Ethna Carbery') had been ended by her death in April 1902, and shortly afterwards he settled permanently in America. In 1911 AG was to dub him 'Shame-Us MacManus' for his virulent attacks on the *Playboy* during he Abbey players' first American tour. His autobiography, *The Rocky Road to Dublin*, appeared in New York in 1938. In his one-act comedy, *The Townland of Tamney*, three brothers tell tall stories to a wise man in contesting their right to the lands of Tamney. The play, which has genuine folklore roots, is slight but not without energy and verve; in tone and spirit it is, however, the very antithesis of *The Shadowy Waters*, and its production was marred by gagging and overplayed stage business. On 18 Jan AG had written (Berg) that the actors had 'left out about half the stories, put in the dialogue; even with that it was, Fay says, touch and go (very tedious), and then AE came to me and said "Now you see how wrong Willie was, it went splendidly!"'

[6] In her letter of 18 Jan AG had told WBY that the 'London performance is last Saturday in March. They are a little puzzled about plays, another farce is wanted and they are evidently not inclined either for Rising of the Moon or the Workhouse.'

[7] His hints (see p. 519) having fallen on deaf ears, MacDonnell, as AG reported to WBY (*70 Years*, 414), 'asked me straight out if a performance could be managed before the King, I said I thought not, but would consult Fay. I am rather vexed, he had hinted at the matter to your father privately and he had already proclaimed it to five of the company! Colum was sitting near, and I brought him into the conversation and he said presently he saw the eye of some important member of Cumann-na-Gael fixed on him in suspicion. Sir Anthony said he himself would be under suspicion if he were seen talking to two such rebels!' On 4 Feb JBY wrote (MBY) to tell WBY that he had suddenly become sought after by the Dublin Castle establishment: 'All these great people, Sir Anthony, his Excellency & the Wyndhams at once showed themselves ready to sit, BECAUSE as I knew at this time I was your father—As time went on I discovered that they had a very definite object in contemplation—nothing less than to capture you & the Irish National Theatre, & to induce the latter to play before the King when he arrives here next April—when it gradually leaked out that this was impossible—all interest in me subsided.'

To Maud Gonne, [early February 1904]

Mention in letter from MG, 12 February [1904].
A 'nice letter', reminding her that he had provided Hyde with the scenarios for many of his plays, and telling her that his American tour is a success.[1]

G–YL, 180–1.

To John Quinn, [4 February 1904]

GOLDEN EAGLE | HOTEL | SACRAMENTO, CAL.

My dear Quinn:
   Phelan gave me enclosed account at the last moment & as a mistake about tickets was giving him trouble & as I had had to collect a part myself I did not like to ask him to send it on. I send 600 dollars—I have kept back 50, as I have about 70 dollars left of what you sent but feared I might want more before I got back from Canada. I should have kept less than 50 but 600 dollars seemed a nice easily remembered sum to send.[1] All well but am a bit hoarse.

Yrs ev
W B Yeats

ALS NYPL, with envelope addressed to 120 Broadway, New York, stamped 'REGISTERED FEB 4 1904 SACRAMENTO, CAL'. With enclosure.

[1] MG had not replied to WBY's two earlier letters (see pp. 526, 539) because, as she explained on 12 Feb, she had been 'very ill for a couple of months before my baby was born, but did not write to any of my friends as I didn't want to make them anxious'. She added that she 'knew well that you gave the scenario to Dr Hyde for his plays & worked him up to write to them too', but that this merely showed the danger of cosmopolitanism and foreign models: 'You get a purely Irish conception of a play, & as you work it out, it becomes less & less Irish. . . . You give an Irish scenario to Hyde & he who has been but little out of Ireland is influenced to a much lesser degree than you by the foreign schools—will work it out in a way which makes it more Irish, & more in affinity with the thought of the nation . . .'

[1] Although this account is untraced, on 30 Jan (see p. 537, n. 1) James Phelan had given Quinn a full statement of WBY's Californian activities and earnings up to that date:

Yeates arrived in good form Wednesday morning early & I have him domiciled here. We went that p.m. to the University of Cal where he had a fine audience & was introduced by Prest B. J. Wheeler. Yeates was much interested in the amphitheater there—made of concrete after a Grecian model—seating 12000. He is taken with our climate which has been perfect for weeks—brilliant sunshine & clear skies. That Evening he lectured to a fine audience—about 1200—in this City—Subject "Intellectual Development in Ireland"—He was well received.
   He has had splendid advertising, I arranged for several interviews &c. Personally we all like him very much.

To Lady Augusta Gregory, [c. *5 February 1904*]

Mention in letter to AG, 8 February 1904.

To George P. Brett, [c. *7 February 1904*]

THE CONGRESS HOTEL COMPANY. | THE AUDITORIUM, | THE ANNEX, APARTMENT BUILDING. | CHICAGO.[1]

Dear M[r] Brett: I have been running from place to place & still see no likelihood of my being able to go into business details until I return to New York. I shall however get there by next week & we can then talk over matters. I have no doubt you have sold very few books of mine, but giving

Thursday he drove to the Ocean & dined with some friends of mine. Friday he went to Stanford for afternoon & St Clara College S.J. for Evening. I joined him at latter place where we dined. I made introductory address. . . . To night Sat[ur]day he has his 2[d] lecture here on "The Theater". Sunday we may visit Joaquin Miller out of town—Monday he may address a local college; Tuesday a girls college; Wednesday a Sacramento Club & from Sacramento he goes direct East on Thursday the 4[th].

He c[d] not have had a better reception & seems well pleased.

I do not know yet how his city lectures will pay. If he gets only the guarantee here it is $250. So it stands as follows:

Wed & Sat	S Francisco lectures (2)	250
Wed	U of California	75
Friday	U of Stanford	75
Friday	College of S Clara	75
Tuesday	" Sacred Heart (SJ)	50
Wednesday	Tuesday Club (Sacramento)	75
		$600

(Monday lecture doubtful—possibly in afternoon if they decide—). . . . He dines with me at Bohemian club Monday night. I have invited local literary people & some representative Irishmen to meet him—about 40 in all. We sh[d] have some good talking—I am now president of Club—Sorry you did not make this a "personally conducted" tour.

WBY earned a further $50 for a lecture at St Ignatius College, but kept back the $50 from the College of the Sacred Heart (which had been paid to him personally) for the expenses he mentions in this letter.

[1] WBY arrived in Chicago from Sacramento on 7 Feb to find a busy programme. Quinn wrote on 6 Feb (*LWBY* II. 136): 'I have given you enough to do at Chicago to provide you with a good excuse for declining invitations to the stock yards or to the university [*see p. 518*]. Chicago boasts of but two things, first the stock yards and second the university; but the stock yards always come first.' WBY lectured on 8 Feb at Hull-House, a social settlement modelled on Toynbee Hall, and founded in 1889 by Jane Addams, social reformer and co-winner of the Nobel Peace Prize in 1931. In *Twenty Years at Hull-House* (New York, 1910) she recalled (387, 394–5) that she had introduced drama 'not only as an agent of recreation and education, but as a vehicle of self-expression for the teeming young life all about us', and that this 'visit from the Irish poet Yeats inspired us to do our share towards freeing the stage from its slavery to expensive scene setting, and a forest of stiff conventional trees against a gilt sky still remains with us as a reminder of an attempt not wholly unsuccessful, in this direction'.

away the future because I am doing ⟨well⟩ badly at present seems to me poor logic & worse sense.

Yr sny
W B Yeats

ALS NYPL.

To H. M. Bland,[1] [c. 7 February 1904]

[Chicago]

Many thanks for your kind letter. It is a great pleasure to think that one's work is cared for so far from home. My players have tried "Shadowy Waters" on the stage during my absence, but, to judge of the arrogance of the newspapers, with little success.[2] It was never meant for more than a few score people, and it is a pleasure to think of one out of the few score reading it in beautiful California.

Printed letter, *Town and Country Journal* (USA), vol. 22, no. 3, September 1905 (102).

To Helen Scribner,[1] [7 February 1904]

THE CONGRESS HOTEL COMPANY. | THE AUDITORIUM, | THE ANNEX,
APARTMENT BUILDING. | CHICAGO.

Dear Mrs Scribner: I have just got here & found your kind invitation—no I never got your other letter. I thank the "Womens University Club of

---

[1] Henry Meade Bland (1863–1931), poet and Californian regional writer, was a professor of English at San Jose State Teachers College. He had been on the platform for WBY's lecture at Santa Clara College on 29 Jan (see p. 536, n. 1), and had evidently entertained him that evening. In 1905 he founded the Pacific Short Story Club, which made WBY an Honorary Member in 1907. As editor of its journal, the *Pacific Short Story Magazine*, and as a regular contributor to the San Francisco *Town and Country Journal*, he kept his Californian readers up to date with WBY's publications in numerous articles and reviews.

[2] See p. 540, n. 4.

[1] Helen Culbertson Annan Scribner (*c.* 1870–1949), a graduate of Bryn Mawr and Columbia, was Vice-President of the Women's University Club, made up of members from 37 specified universities, with the largest contingents from Vassar, Smith, Columbia and Wellesley. In January 1900 she married Arthur Hawley Scribner (1859–1932), who had become Vice-President of his father's publishing firm, Charles Scribner's Sons, upon its incorporation in 1903. Quinn had been in negotiation with Scribners about the American rights to WBY's work for some time, writing on 15 Dec 1903 (NLI) that he had 'practically arranged with the Scribners for the future publication of all your books; at any rate they were most favorably inclined'. On 6 Feb 1904 he told WBY that he had gone 'over all of your different books with them this morning and I think that

New York" very much. I cannot however say at this moment what my New York engagements are. I get back there about the 14th I think but I am sending your note to John Quinn (120 Broadway) the friend who has arranged things for me & he will know what afternoons I am free. I do not myself know even where I shall be more than a few days a head.

Yrs sny
W B Yeats

ALS Texas.

To an unidentified correspondent, 7 February [*1904*]

THE CONGRESS HOTEL COMPANY. | THE AUDITORIUM, | THE ANNEX,
APARTMENT BUILDING. | CHICAGO.
Feb 7

Dear Sir: very many thanks for your eloquent verses. It was charming of you to write them & I only wish I had thanked you sooner.

Yrs sny
W B Yeats

ALS Mills College.

To Agnes Tobin,[1] *7 February* [*1904*]

THE CONGRESS HOTEL COMPANY. | THE AUDITORIUM, | THE ANNEX,
APARTMENT BUILDING. | CHICAGO.
Feb 7

My dear Miss Tobin: I have just written many dull necessary letters to all kinds of unnecessary people & can now give myself the deep pleasure of telling you how I delight in your Petrarch. I have read it over & over. It is

by the time that you return they will be ready to make you a good offer. Much better than Brett . . .'. Mrs Scribner had been trying to arrange a lecture and reception for WBY since December and, although Quinn confessed himself 'somewhat against it', WBY spoke to the New York Women's Club on 2 Mar.

[1] Agnes Tobin (1864–1939), poet and translator, was the daughter of a prominent banker in San Francisco, where she met WBY. Her first book of Petrarch translations, *Love's Crucifix* (1902), was introduced by Alice Meynell, who had 'discovered' her in 1895. She spent much time in England, where she also befriended Arthur Symons and Joseph Conrad, who dedicated his *Under Western Eyes* (1911) 'To Agnes Tobin who brought to our door her genius for friendship from the uttermost shore of the west.' Writing of his visit to San Francisco in 'America and the Arts' (*UP* II. 338–42), WBY recalled that 'the enchantment of a still sea, of a winter that endured the violets, and of a lovely book of verses from Petrarch, sent me by a young writer . . . made me fancy that I found there a little of that pleasure in the Arts, which brings creative art and not scholarship, because it is delight in art itself'.

full of wise delight—a thing of tears & ecstacy—especially that long lyric at the end.[2] But surely you must have written much more that it is a discredit not to know of. Write & tell me if you have & I will get it when I am in London again. You have style, loftiness & your little book is the best thing I have found here. Surely you have sung some song of your own or has the difficulty that besets us moderns, when we begin to dramatise ourselves kept you silent? We have only ourselves, & social usage bids us hide our treasure—we should be banished to some island where there are no newspapers, & where one writes for a few friends. But whether it is to be translation or dramatization write on—do not take to story writing, as your countrywomen do but make more verses. I hope I shall see you in London before very long & I shall have read more of your work before that day however soon it is—for there is more I am certain.

Yrs sny
W B Yeats

My address in America is

c/o John Quinn
120 Broadway
New York

and in London is

18 Woburn Buildings
Upper Woburn Place

When there I am at home on Mondays after eight but better write.

MS copy Private. Partly in *Agnes Tobin: Letters, Translations, Poems with Some Account of Her Life* (San Francisco, 1958), p. 74.

[2] The final poem in *Love's Crucifix*, 'The Passing of Sleep', a free version of Petrarch's canzone 'Quando il soave mio fido conforto', begins 'When my most constant comforter and stay / To rest my tired heart which so long has bled . . .', and recounts a visit to the poet by the ghost of Laura.

To Susan Mary Yeats, [8 February 1904]

THE CONGRESS HOTEL COMPANY. | THE AUDITORIUM, | THE ANNEX,
APARTMENT BUILDING. | CHICAGO.

My dear Lilly: I have just got your letter about Dun Emer & sent it to
Lady Gregory for advice.[1] I can hardly say anything now—I have not time
to think or write—but I shall be home in March. The printing looks like a
good investment but I can only say about the embroidery that if I were a
rich man I would require the opinion of some man like Image or Lewis
Davis[2] or Ricketts or Whall as to the excellence of the design. If I can do
anything I will do it but how can I know until I return.

Yours
W B Yeats

I have to run off to get a railway ticket and there [are] all sorts of things
beside to do.

ALS MBY. Dated 'Feb 8 1904' in another hand.

To Lady Augusta Gregory, [8 February 1904]

THE CONGRESS HOTEL COMPANY. | THE AUDITORIUM, | THE ANNEX,
APARTMENT BUILDING. | CHICAGO.

My dear Lady Gregory: I received the enclosed from my sister Lilly to
day. It is a worry. I have replied very shortly saying that I have asked your
advice, & that I do not know if I can do anything, & must be back in Ireland first. I have said also that the printing looks like a good investment,
but that if I were a rich man I would require the opinion of some authority
like Ricketts or Image or Whall as to the quality of the embroidery design.

[1] Although SMY's letter does not survive, it evidently gave details of a financial crisis, the first
of many, at Dun Emer Industries, which she ran in partnership with ECY and Evelyn Gleeson.
ECY, who managed the printing side of the business, had taken possession of an Albion hand-
press (similar to that used by William Morris) on 24 Nov 1902, and had already had some success
with the publication of WBY's *In the Seven Woods* and AE's *The Nuts of Knowledge*, set in the
fourteen-point Caslon Old Face that distinguished Dun Emer and Cuala Press books. SMY
wanted WBY to invest some of his American money in the firm, and particularly in her risky
attempts to establish an embroidery business.
[2] Louis Davis (1861–1941), a designer and illustrator influenced by the Pre-Raphaelite school,
was a member of the Royal Watercolour Society. He lived outside London in Pinner, Middlesex.

I hope my letter was not too cold but I have written it again & again. I enclose a copy. I have forseen this moment all the while but it is anoying. If I give much it will go without effect (for it will not be enough) & if I give little I shall be blamed always. I dont know whether it is selfish of one, but my sisters have for so many years written me so many complaints (I have had two letters of the usual kind since I came here—money that was coming from Sligo but coming too slowly & too much to do with it) that I feal a little cross. Lolly is business like within certain limits & a strong soul but my father is a heavy weight—Lilly would probably take advice but for him. I can think of nothing but going to George Pollexfen & having everything looked into, in a spirit of sound business, if he will consent to invest. I could then give what ever you thought right. I am fealing rather tired & cross—the lecturing has tired me a little at last & I am longing to be back & I confess I do not like the thought that the first money I ever earned beyond the need of the moment will be expected to go to Dun Emer for I suppose that is what is expected, & do no good there. If Lolly were by her self how gladly I would give it. I feal loyalty to an idea very keenly & could sacrafice a great deal for a cause but family duties—just perhaps because they are rather thrust upon one—leave me colder than they should. I feal too that the family difficulty has got into a mess that needs stronger hands than mine—of course the whole dun Emer venture should have been thought out carefully at the start. I suppose I had best go to Sligo after the plays in London & do what I can with George. My sisters would be content I have no doubt with a few pounds at once & then chaos but that seems to me hopeless. There is one possibility that Miss Gleesons[1] "panic" may pass & that the letter is merely like others I have had—the depression of the moment.

I wrote you a letter in the train from California but cannot remember if I posted it.[2] I plan to start back at end of month & to go direct to London. If you write at once on getting this I will get letter before starting. Quinn wants me to wait for 2 more lectures on 6th & 8th but I will not.[3]

---

[1] Evelyn Gleeson (1855–1944), was born in Cheshire, the eldest daughter of an Irish doctor, and at the age of 15 moved with her family to Athlone. She studied painting in London and Paris, and was a committed suffragette. Her father had founded the Athlone Woollen Mills to stimulate local employment and she returned to Ireland in 1902 to establish the Morris-inspired Dun Emer Industries in Dundrum for the production of hand-woven carpets, tapestries, embroideries, and hand-printed books. She had a volatile temper, and relations between her and WBY's sisters were often strained. The partnership was to break up in 1908, when the name Dun Emer was surrendered to her, and ECY continued as the Cuala Press.

[2] Apparently not.

[3] In his letter of 6 Feb Quinn announced that he had arranged further lectures at Newark on 6 Mar and Dobbs Ferry on 8 Mar, and suggested that WBY 'could sail on Wednesday the 9th and reach Ireland by about the 17th. Wouldn't that be time enough?' WBY undertook both lectures.

I have just got three letters of yours all togeather—sent on from New York—California is too far off & so they waited.

Yours always
W B Yeats

ALS Berg, with envelope addressed to Coole, postmark 'CHICAGO. ILL. FEB 8 1904'. Wade, 430–1.

To John Quinn, [8–9 February 1904]

THE CONGRESS HOTEL COMPANY. | THE AUDITORIUM, | THE ANNEX, APARTMENT BUILDING. | CHICAGO.
Monday

My dear Quinn: I dont like waiting so late as you suggest.[1] If I remain a day or two after ⟨28th or⟩ 29th I had rather be quiet with you. My objections to delay are that plays come on in London at end of March—how soon I dont know but soon after 17th—I think—I shall however like to be there rather before, to talk over stage & so forth. There is of course a possibility too that I might want to go to Dublin.

(Tuesday) I had got this far when I stopped because being tired out (I had not slept well) I was afraid that fategue made me anxious to refuse. Now I am fresh again & feal just as decided. It might be all right but it might not. If I am not there they may neglect little things & then it is important that I see journalists etc. Our success this time is of supreme importance as we must start in Dublin on larger scale very shortly. If I stayed I should feal worried—I have also some affairs of my sisters to look to. I must feal that I have done all in my power for the plays—Many thanks for kind thought about second gripp & thank Miss Smith for tie. I have expressed trunk.[2]

Yrs ev
W B Yeats

[1] Quinn had followed up his letter of 6 Feb (see above, n. 3) with a telegram on 8 Feb (TS copy, NYPL): 'Paterson Irish Societies want lecture Sunday evening March sixth; can arrange another lecture for Monday seventh. You can sail on Oceanic Wednesday ninth arriving Queenstown sixteenth. Wire whether you can wait till ninth.'

[2] In his letter (see above, n. 3) Quinn, who could make a mother hen seem blasé, had given WBY elaborate instructions as to his laundry, and had sent him a small extra dress suitcase so that he would not be encumbered by his large trunk on short trips. Miss Ada Smith, daughter of the proprietress of a boarding-house where Quinn once lived, had made a new black tie for WBY when his became soiled. Miss Smith was Quinn's mistress at the time, and remained a long-time family friend, to whom Quinn willed $25,000 'as a token of my regard and esteem for her and of her kindness, and as a mark of appreciation of her kindness to me and to my family'.

what a lot of trouble I am giving you.

PS. I enclose a note which I found here. I said you knew my dates & would answer.[3]

ALS NYPL, with envelope addressed to 120 Broadway, New York, postmark 'CHICAGO. ILL. FEB 9 1904'.

To James Mavor,[1] [c. *16 February 1904*]

1 West 87th Street,
⟨120 BROADWAY⟩

Professor James Mavor,
    University of Toronto,
        Toronto, Canada.

Dear Mr. Mavor:

I have yours of the 14th. There was no need in the world for you to have got up to see me off. I enjoyed my evening at your house very much and was sorry I had to hurry away from Toronto so soon.

Sincerely yours,
W B Yeats

TLS Toronto.

To Charles Elkin Mathews, 19 February 1904

⟨120 BROADWAY⟩
1 West 87th Street,
Feby. 19, 1904.

My dear Mr. Mathews:

Before I left London I asked you to write a letter to A. P. Watt stating your recollection of the arrangement we made with John Lane about my book "The Wind Among the Reeds". His term of years was the same as yours and you have already written to Mr. A. P. Watt saying that you had the book for a period of five years. It is really important that you write at once to Watt and state the limit of Lane's term. John Lane has been selling

---

[3] i.e. to Helen Scribner; see pp. 544–5.

[1] See p. 486, n. 1.

my book very well over here and I have never had either an account from him or anything else. I cannot do anything, however, unless you write to A. P. Watt for me.[1]

I am returning to London in March and have had a very successful time over here.

The reason that I am anxious to get this Lane business settled is that I shall very likely be transferring my books out of his hands to another American house and may even be discussing the preliminaries before I leave here.

Sincerely yours,
W B Yeats

Mr. Elkin Mathews,
    Vigo Street,
        London, W.,
            England.

TLS Leeds, with envelope addressed to Vigo St., Regents St., London, postmark 'NEW YORK FEB 24 1904'.

To Lady Augusta Gregory, 26 February 1904

⟨120 BROADWAY⟩
1 West 87th Street,
Feby. 26/04.

My dear Lady Gregory:

I am dictating this letter, as it is my only possible way of writing this week. I am dreadfully busy over my Emmet lecture, which is a frightful nuisance. It is indeed, as you say, a sword dance and I must give to it every

---

[1] Mathews had in fact written to Watt about this matter on 2 Nov 1903 (Private), shortly after he had seen WBY. He told Watt that WBY wished to terminate his arrangement with Lane over the American edition of "The Wind Among the Reeds", enclosed a copy of the original contract with Lane, dated 4 Aug 1898, and a subsequent letter of 27 Jan 1902 from himself, endorsed by WBY (see pp. 151–2). He went on: 'Mr Yeats' impression is the same as mine, viz: his control over the American rights terminates with my English ones, viz: 13th April 1904. As new editions of "The Wind Among the Reeds" are required they are printed off from the plates in New York, the joint property of Mr Lane and myself. Mr Yeats desires my term only to be extended to 1907—in other words to lapse at the same time as "The Tables of the Law" and the last Edn of "Poems" published by Mr Fisher Unwin.' The 1898 agreement with Lane set out the arrangements for printing the book in New York, but did not mention a terminal date for the rights, and WBY's attempts to retrieve the book from Lane were to drag on for several years.

moment.[1] I had no idea until I started on it of how completely I have thought myself out of the whole stream of traditional Irish feeling on such subjects. I am just as strenuous a Nationalist as ever, but I have got to express these things all differently. I feel as if I wanted at least a fortnight to make the speech, and I shall have to speak for an hour. When I accepted I thought I should be able to make it a plea for Irish Ireland, but Quinn seems to think that I must touch all that rather lightly. He is so anxious for my glory that he has set me I am afraid an impossible task.

I shall leave here by the "Oceanic" on the 9th and should be in London by the 18th. I will wire on the 9th when actually starting. Robert has my keys, so I suppose somebody will have to meet me at the station. I am staying the extra week instead of going back on the 2d because I have been so busy that I have not been to see anybody socially here in New York and I have been promised to a few people.[2] I have also two lectures between the 2d and the 9th.[3]

⟨Sincerely yours,⟩

[*Remainder of letter in WBY's hand*]

Emmett lecture going better the *Clan na Gael* ask for Irish Ireland thoughts rather than politics.

A note from my sisters. The panic has quite died out & they say all is well.

Yr ev
W B Yeats

TLS Berg, with envelope addressed to Coole, redirected to Queen Ann Mansions, postmark 'NEW YORK FEB 27 04'. Wade, 432.

[1] On 16 Feb (Berg) AG had written that she would have been 'very sorry if you had refused the lecture—it seizes my imagination—it is your last pulpit & your last great opportunity for this visit. It is your business to put a flame in the heart of every young man who hears you, & a hammer in his hand with which to hammer the heads of the brazen image, & a brick in his other hand to help the building of the temple.'

[2] One of WBY's social meetings was with the American poet, Witter Bynner (1881–1968), who wrote to a friend on 4 Mar: 'This morning . . . I spent with the Irish poet W. B. Yeats who said apropos of having lectured in San Francisco that "he did not feel the usual fitness of his words while out there, since his temperament and utterances was [*sic*] tenderly attuned and adapted to the temperate zone"! These things are worth saving for a laugh, when I should have otherwise forgotten why.' *Selected Letters*, ed. James Kraft (1981), 6–7.

[3] WBY was given a dinner at the Metropolitan Club on the 5th, a reception by the Irish Literary Society on the 6th, and spoke at Newark on the 6th and Dobbs Ferry on the 8th (see p. 548, n. 3). Ernest Crosby, co-editor of the *Whim* (Newark, NJ), reported in the April issue (96) that at Newark WBY 'proved to be a fluent and suggestive speaker as well as poet. He is not one of the men who seem smaller than their work and there is something of the magician in his person as well as in his pen. He is doing a great work in Ireland, endeavoring to arouse the national consciousness of his people and to re-create and re-vivify their oldtime individuality.'

To [*? Patrick J. MacDonough*],[1] [*late February 1904*]

Mention in the Notre Dame *Scholastic*, 5 March 1904 (371).

WBY wrote 'I think I enjoyed my time at Notre Dame more than at any place I have stayed on my travels here'; sending greetings to the 'Very Rev. President Morrissey[2] and the Rev. Fathers' for their kindness; and gracefully acknowledging the courtesy shown him by the members of the Faculty and students.

To an unidentified publisher, [*late February 1904*]

Mention in Bertram Rota's Special List 14, Spring 1982, Item 90.

TLS from New York, returning a proof.[1]

To Agnes Tobin, 7 March 1904

1 West 87th Street
March 7, 1904

My dear Miss Tobin:

This is merely a few words to tell you that I cannot write to you about your poems until I get to the other side of the water. I have been overwhelmingly busy, as you can imagine, and I start next Wednesday. I have

---

[1] The *Scholastic* prefaced this letter, probably addressed to Patrick J. MacDonough, who had looked after WBY at Notre Dame (see p. 521, n. 4), with the remarks that 'Mr. William Butler Yeats, whose visit to our University was so thoroughly appreciated, has returned to New York after a very successful lecturing tour through the United States and Canada. He has awakened a lively interest in the Irish literary movement among kinsmen and strangers. Though busy preparing an address on Robert Emmet to be delivered before his departure for Ireland, he found time to write a letter appreciative of his reception at Notre Dame.' It went on to reprint 'The Ballad of Father Gilligan' (*VP*, 132–4) as verses embodying 'a tradition current in the west of Ireland, and while having the Irish priest for a subject, they well exemplify the spirit of any priest under equally trying circumstances. . . . Surely the author of those lines has his ear attuned to the Irish heart. Notre Dame cordially reciprocates the sentiments of Mr. Yeats and wishes him a safe return to the land of his love and hopes' (371–2).

[2] Andrew Morrissey (1860–1921) was born in Co. Kilkenny, where he received his primary education before emigrating with his family to America. He graduated from Notre Dame in 1878 and, after a period teaching mathematics in Wisconsin, returned there as Director of Studies in 1885. He was appointed President in 1893 and served until 1905. WBY stayed as his guest at Notre Dame on 15–16 Jan.

[1] Perhaps one set of revise proofs of *The Tables of the Law and The Adoration of the Magi*, to be published by Elkin Mathews in June (he returned further proofs on 2 Apr); or possibly the proof of 'Emmet the Apostle of Irish Liberty', delivered at the Academy of Music on 28 Feb, and published in the *Gaelic American* on 5 Mar.

had many lectures at the last moment, as well as many people to see and letters to write, and I want to give your poems more careful attention than I can at this moment. I do not like them as well as the translations, but I shall want leisure to define exactly what I do feel about them.[1]

Yes, we should dramatize our emotions. There is no other way of writing well, but we must always be certain that the emotion has in it ecstasy. What delights me in your translations is that they have in them not only the words which were taken from Petrarch, but in your own rhythm and vocabulary a certain ecstasy, a certain elevation. I find in a certain amount of American poetry strong emotion, rather than strong emotion touched by ecstasy.

But I will write more about this when I get to London. Perhaps when I re-read the poems in the more tranquil air of my own house, where I shall be doing nothing for quite a long time, they will impress me quite differently from the impression I have from them just now. The beauty of your translations, that is a certainty; and I hope that you will soon bring out that larger book from Petrarch which you talked of.

Yours sincerely,
W B Yeats

MS copy. *Agnes Tobin: Letters, Translations, Poems with Some Account of Her Life* (75).

To George P. Brett, 8 March 1904

No. 1 West 87th Street, | New York City,
March 8, 1904.

George P. Brett, Esq.,
c/o Macmillan & Co., Ltd.,
London, England.

Dear Mr. Brett:

I was sorry to have missed you upon my return from the West. I sail tomorrow (March 9th) and will endeavor to see you in London.[1] My

---

[1] In response to WBY's suggestion that she 'must have written much more' (see p. 546), Miss Tobin had on 13 Feb (MBY) sent him some 'intimate personal' poems and asked his opinion of them. She told him that she had difficulty in making her emotions come to terms with life, but that his reading from *Deirdre* had been a revelation to her. Her second volume of Petrarch translations, *The Flying Lesson*, appeared in 1905.

[1] WBY and Quinn had called at the Macmillan offices at noon on 1 Mar. Brett had left for England but at his suggestion they saw Herbert Williams, who reported to Brett that they had 'a long talk', and that 'Yeats has an eye on what he calls a collective edition of his works. He wants them all under control of one publisher. He evidently prefers that we should be that publisher. He thinks 10% rather low; but he is perfectly willing to waive all objections on that score. What

address is No. 18 Woburn Buildings, Euston Road, and I shall be glad if you will drop me a line there saying where and when I can see you.

I have spoken at over sixty-four colleges and literary societies in America. At my first lecture in San Francisco there were upwards of two thousand and at my last lecture in New York at the Academy of Music, Sunday, February 28th, the building was packed and it was estimated that there were between four thousand and four thousand five hundred people. Mr Quinn estimates that I have spoken to between twenty-five and thirty thousand people while I have been here. As I have spoken on literary themes alone it is impossible to believe that there is not an awakened interest in Irish Literature here and I believe that that interest will continue. I only learned yesterday that Mosher's second edition of my little play "The Land of Hearts Desire", each edition being 950 copies, has become exhausted, and that this has been done within the last few months.[2] I believe that ultimately I shall have a considerable market in this country and I am anxious, therefore, to make my arrangements with some forethought. To illustrate my point—If I give you permanent rights in my books I should have some assurance from you that you will continue to publish my forthcoming books, and also I should have an understanding regarding the publication of a collective edition when the proper time comes for that, otherwise I may find my books more scattered a few years from now than they are today. I regard this as a more important question than what percentage of royalty shall be paid to me.[3] Should it turn out that we cannot come to any understanding on these two points I shall be glad to discuss with you upon what terms you will release the three books which you have the rights of, if not now, at least at the time when the collective edition comes. A prominent publishing house made an advance to me regarding the taking over of all my books here and becoming my permanent publishers,[4] and the stumbling block in the way was your permanent rights in the three books. I prefer, if I can, to go on with you, but I think if I do there should be some arrangement made by which some provision should be made for the publication of a uniform edition at some time subject to my reasonable discretion as to the form of the edition, and also an agreement on your part to take my forthcoming books.

he really objects to is having all his books on an interminable contract, without any agreement that we are to publish all his books. If, at some future time, we were to refuse to publish one of his books, so that he was obliged to seek another publisher, a collective edition would be difficult if not impossible to arrange.'

[2] Mosher (see p. 508) published, with WBY's permission, the revised version of *The Land of Heart's Desire* in at least 12 editions from June 1903. In a letter of *c.* 30 June 1908 (Private) accompanying a copy of the 7th edition (1908), SMY reported that WBY 'seems to bear no grudge against Mosher & just remarked that he wished honest publishers had such good taste—the little book is certainly well turned out'.

[3] See p. 504.   [4] i.e. Scribners; see p. 544, n. 1.

The contracts covering my other books that are copyrighted and published in America will expire within a year or two. However, we can discuss the different aspects of these questions when I have the pleasure of meeting you.

Yours very truly
W B Yeats

TLS NYPL.

To Thomas Shahan,[1] *8 March 1904*

⟨120 BROADWAY⟩
1 West 87th Street,
March 8, 1904.

Dr. Thomas J. Shahan,
  Catholic University of Washington,
    Washington, D. C.

Dear Dr. Shahan:
  I am just setting out on my return to England. My steamer goes tomorrow at 12 o'clock, but I cannot leave without thanking you for your kindness and above all for those invaluable notes about symbols.[2] They will help to guide me through the British Museum immediately on my return, for such things excite me very greatly. It was a very great pleasure to speak at the Catholic University at Washington and to meet there the Rector, Dr.

---

[1] Thomas Joseph Shahan (1857–1932), Professor of Church History and Patrology at the Catholic University of America from 1891 to 1909, and fourth Rector from 1909 until his retirement in 1928. He was a Vice-President of the Irish Texts Society, editor of the *Catholic Bulletin*, and associate editor of the *Catholic Encyclopedia*. He had edited *Myth and Legend*, a compilation for young readers, in 1902.

[2] Shahan had introduced WBY's 21 Feb lecture, 'The Intellectual Movement', which, according to the *Catholic University Bulletin* of April 1904 (301), a large and appreciative audience found 'of absorbing interest because of the unique idea of accomplishing national independence, not by force of arms nor radical politics, but by the gradual weaning of Irishmen from English custom and the English tongue'. His 'notes about symbols' are untraced.

Healy, Dr. Egan,[3] and the other professors. You have surely a great university and I wish we had its like in Ireland.

Yours sincerely,
W B Yeats

TLS Catholic University.

To John Quinn, [18 March 1904]

18 Woburn Buildings | Euston Road.

My dear Quinn: I had a beautiful passage[1]—smoked cigarettes all the time & was quite comfortable. Strang the painter was on board to my great surprize & we discussed everything under heaven & got an idea for a little play from him & he will design costumes if I ever write the play, which I think of doing at once.[2] I have just seen Horace Plunkett at Lady Gregorys. ⟨The St. Lewis have behaved very badl⟩ Be rather careful about Riorden and all those people.[3] The picture show there has broken down through their refusal to pay insurance after getting a lot of artists to withdraw from the English section & declare themselves Irish. Everybody is most indignant & an attempt is being made to get up an exhibition in the Guild Hall as a compensation. Gills vagueness of mind is partly responsible. If it had been possible at this stage I beleive the whole Irish exhibit would have been withdrawn as a protest. I saw Brett to day & have I think got a good arrangement with him, but shall not be confident till it comes in writing. I am to have the right to withdraw *all* books, on a valuation, if

---

[3] The Rt. Revd Mgr. Dennis Joseph O'Connell (d. 1927), former head of the American College in Rome, served as Rector of the Catholic University until 1909, when he was consecrated auxiliary Bishop of San Francisco. In 1912 he was appointed to the See of Richmond, Virginia, which he held until his death. Patrick Joseph Healy (1871–1937), Irish-born clergyman and teacher, had been ordained in 1897 and joined the faculty of Church History at the Catholic University in 1903, later becoming Dean of the Faculty of Theology. Maurice Francis Egan (1852–1924), journalist, teacher, and diplomat, had edited the *Catholic Review* from 1879 to 1880, before moving to the editorial board of the New York *Freeman's Journal*. He was Professor of English at the University of Notre Dame from 1888 to 1895 and at the Catholic University of America from 1895 to 1907. Thereafter he became a US diplomat in Denmark. He was one of the associate editors of *Irish Literature*, which appeared in 1904, and his autobiography, *Recollections of a Happy Life*, contains anecdotes of WBY's American tour (see p. 500, n. 5).

[1] WBY had arrived in Liverpool on the *Oceanic* on 16 Mar.

[2] William Strang, RA (1859–1921), etcher and painter, frequently visited the USA and the Continent. A member of the Art Workers' Guild since 1895, he became Master in 1907. A drawing by him of WBY in the Fitzwilliam Museum, Cambridge, tentatively dated '*c.* 1903', may have been executed on this voyage, as may another, also dated 1903, in the National Gallery, Dublin. He and WBY never collaborated on a play.

[3] See p. 514. James A. Reardon was the St Louis World Fair Commissioner to Ireland.

they refuse a book of mine. They are on the other hand to "have the refusal" of all my books. Also after a sale of 5,000 copies I am to get 15 per cent. Brett will publish no new book of mine until Autumn when he will bring out a collected edition of all my verse—plays & lyrics. I am facing the world with great hopes & strength & I owe it all to you & I thank you & shall always be grateful.

I will write at length & tell you how the plays go after the 26th when they come on.

Yrs ev
W B Yeats

ALS NYPL, with envelope addressed to 1 West 87 St, New York, U.S.A., postmark 'LONDON MR 18 04'.

To A. H. Bullen, 22 March [*1904*]

18 Woburn Buildings, | Euston Road,
March 22

My dear Bullen,

I think you should send a copy of each book to Max Beerbohm.[1] I dont know his address, but I suppose Saturday Review would find him. You might just as well do this at once, as it may help towards a good notice of the plays on Saturday.

Please also send a copy of each of the two books to Mrs Shakespeare, 4 Pembridge Mansions, Bayswater West.[2]

I also want to send copies to Gordon Craig, but I haven't yet got his address.

Send a copy also of each book to Bernard Shaw, 10 Adelphi Terrace, Adelphi.

Yours sny
W B Yeats

[1] Vols. II and III of 'Plays for an Irish Theatre', published this month (see p. 511). Max Beerbohm (1872–1956) was drama critic of the *Saturday Review* from 1898 to 1910, and was sympathetic to the Irish National Theatre; see p. 562.

[2] Olivia Tucker Shakespear (OS; 1863–1938; see I. 511-12), novelist and joint author with FF of two Egyptian plays (see p. 121), met WBY in 1894, through her cousin, Lionel Johnson. During his love affair with her in 1895–6, WBY wrote 'He Bids His Beloved Be At Peace' and other poems to her, and she appears as 'Diana Vernon' (the heroine in Scott's *Rob Roy*) in *Mem.* Her daughter, Dorothy, married Ezra Pound in 1914, and her brother, Henry Tudor Tucker, married Mrs Edith Ellen Hyde-Lees, whose daughter George became WBY's wife in 1917. When OS died in October 1938, WBY recalled (Wade, 916) that for 'more than forty years she has been the centre of my life in London and during all that time we have never had a quarrel, sadness sometimes but never a difference'. OS lived at 4 Pembridge Mansions from 1900 to April 1905.

[*In WBY's hand*]
Beerbohm is 'press' charge other copies to me.
                                                                WBY.
[*In AG's hand*]
Craigs address 5 Pembroke Walk Kensington.

TLS Texas.

To D. J. O'Donoghue, 24 March [*1904*]

1[8] Woburn Buildings, | Euston Road,
March 24.

Dear O'Donoghue,
    I have unluckily nothing by me.[1] As you can well imagine one doesn't
write much in railway trains. I am afraid if you want something of mine
you will have to take it from one of the old volumes, with a note saying
that in consequence of my long visit to America I had not time to write
anything new for the collection. The only books of verse of mine that are
copyright in America are the Seven Woods, Wind among the reeds, and
the King's Threshold. If you made any selection from these books you
would have to communicate with the publishers which would cause you
delay. But I forgot, the King's Threshold itself is still in my hands in
America, and you may if you like take a short extract from it. But I think
lyric will be more suitable to your purposes. You had better take something from the book published by Fisher Unwin. I am sorry not to have

---

[1] O'Donoghue had asked WBY to contribute to an anthology to be entitled *Irish Voices, and
Miscellany of Living Writers*. An advertisement in the programme for the INTS London performances on 26 Mar 1904 announced it was to be 'Ready in Early May', and that 'the entire proceeds . . . by the liberality of the Irish Exhibit Company of St. Louis (Mo.) will be devoted to the
Clarence Mangan Memorial Fund, to the printing and editing of valuable Irish texts, etc., and
other Irish literary purposes'. A prospectus was issued, and in June 1904 the *Gael* (NY) revealed
that there were to be two editions, at $1.50 and $5 each (the latter a special edition of 500 numbered copies). On 2 July the *Academy* listed among the contributors WBY, AG, Lady Gilbert,
Stephen Gwynn, Stopford Brooke, and Jane Barlow, but the volume never appeared. The history
of the venture was given in the *Irish Book Lover* (June–July 1919, p. 101), after O'Donoghue's
death: 'in spite of the fact that preliminary "pars." had appeared in the literary papers early in
1904 . . . it got no further than the Introduction, list of contributors and a few photographs. It
was his intention to give a portrait, biographical note, and two or three specimens, some specially
contributed, of forty living Irish writers. It was to be produced in Dublin and sold at the St.
Louis Exhibition to raise funds for the Gaelic League and other objects. There was a representative American Committee formed but for some reasons . . . the project fell through.'

been able to do more for you, but I cannot turn aside now amidst the whirl of the plays here to write.

Yrs sinly
W B Yeats

TLS Kenyon.

To A. P. Watt, 24 March [1904]

18 WOBURN BUILDINGS, | EUSTON ROAD,
March 24.

DEAR MR. WATT,

I can say still as I said to you at the beginning that it is the greatest possible comfort to know that one's agreements can't be lost. I am not certain that I could at this moment find any agreement that came into my possession before you took up my affairs, and I am certain that it would take me several days before I did find it. Besides it is a great comfort to know that even if one's books are not making very much, at all events one's publisher is not making more than his fair share out of them.

You have saved me a great deal of worry and I thank you.[1]

Yours sincerely
W B YEATS

Text from *Letters Addressed to A.P. Watt* (1905) p. 171.

To Clement Shorter, 31 [March 1904]

Coole Park, | Gort, Co Galway.
Thursday 31st

My dear Shorter,

I left London on Tuesday night, and just before I left found a letter asking me to give your photographer a sitting. I wish very much I could have done so, but it was too late when I got the letter and I will not be back for about a fortnight, and then it would be too late. I had some good photo-

---

[1] WBY had again been asked to contribute to a book of testimonial letters on behalf of A.P. Watt and Sons (see p. 153), and his name was listed among those 'not printed in former editions' [139]. Most of the letters in this category were written in 1904. WBY's letter was republished in *Letters Addressed to A.P. Watt and his Sons 1883–1924* (1924) and *Letters Addressed to A.P. Watt and his Sons 1883–1929* (1929).

graphs taken in America, and could send you one of those if you cared for it.[1]

A good many of the critics complain that my King's Threshold lacks action, but one has to pay a price for everything.[2] If a play is to go naturally into verse one has to keep it in a world of vast sentiments quite incompatible with the hurried action and with the kind of characterisation one puts into a prose drama.[3] I tried to put the Hour Glass into verse but I found that even that far-away play was too hurried in its action. The interest of a poetical drama must always be a poetical interest, and if one doesn't care for poetry poetical drama is somebody else's game. It must be dramatic, but in its own way.

Yrs srly

W B Yeats

TLS Leeds.

To Elkin Mathews, 2 April [1904]

COOLE PARK, | GORT, | CO. GALWAY.

April 2

My dear Matthews—

I return the proof sheets[1] to you but I find there is a page lacking at the end—Please send it, & I will let you have it back at once—Enclosed is paper I should like for the cover—I will return the others tomorrow—

I find you have not returned Lady Gregorys copy of Tables of the Law,

---

[1] This was for inclusion in a series of photographs, 'Writers in Their Rooms', currently running in the *Tatler*. A picture of WBY in his study at Woburn Buildings (see Plate 10) appeared there on 29 June 1904 (523). Among the best of the many photographs of WBY in America were the 'Yale Yeats', taken at New Haven *c.* 17 Nov 1903; a portrait evidently captured while he was visiting the University of Pennsylvania and published in the *Alumni Register* of December 1903; and two by Alice Boughton, which appeared respectively in the *New York Herald* on 17 Jan 1904, and the *Gaelic American* on 5 Mar 1904.

[2] On 28 Mar 1904 the *Daily Telegraph* (11) remarked that WBY's 'muse moves uneasily through the unaccustomed atmosphere of the theatre—in plain words Mr. Yeats possesses little of that peculiar gift, "le don du théâtre". . . . "The King's Threshold", doubtless, would make excellent reading . . . but its dramatic qualities . . . are scarcely discernible.' E. A. Baughan wrote in the *Daily News* of the same day (4) that there was 'but one dramatic moment in the little play, and except for that moment the idea might have been better expressed in an ode'. On 29 Mar, in an otherwise sympathetic review in the *World* (551), William Archer noted that the 'incidents succeed one another in careful and logical gradation, but have no complexity of interrelation. They form a series, not a system. They exist in two dimensions, not in three . . .'

[3] Compare pp. 501, 527.

[1] See p. 553, n. 1.

which she allowed me to send you to print from—Please send it back to her at above address—[2]

Yrs snly

W B Yeats

Dict AG, signed WBY; Leeds.

To John Quinn, 2 April [1904]

Coole Park, | Gort,

April 2

My dear Quinn.

I am dictating this to Lady Gregory, having come to Coole for a couple of weeks. We are doing various bits of work for the Theatre &c.

The plays are [*for* have] been a great success in London as you will see from The World which Miss Horniman has sent you, and the Westminster which goes with this.[1] I have not spare copies of any of the others. Max Beerbohm and Walkleys articles have not yet come.[2] The audience was as enthusiastic as possible, but several dramatic critics write much as the Westminster critic about the King's Threshold, which they thought lacking in action. They have been so long unused to poetic drama that they do not understand its limitations. Synge has had an unqualified triumph, and so too has the company. I thought Colum's play a great bore, but it was probably newer to the critics and to the audience than we had foreseen. People thought it immature and sketchy but interesting. F. Fay acted wonderfully in it, an old fiddler. The theatre was crowded morning and evening, and the Literary Society has cleared eighty pounds after paying all rather heavy expenses. I got an extraordinary call at the end of the King's Threshold. I bowed from the box but they were not satisfied with that and I had to go

[2] AG's unmarked vellum-bound copy of the 1897 edition of *The Tables of the Law* is now at Emory. It seems to have been a back-up copy, not used by Mathews (see p. 458, n. 1).

[1] In his enthusiastic review in the *World* of 29 Mar (see p. 561, n. 2), William Archer praised *The King's Threshold* and asked, 'Is there no London manager with insight and originality enough to make up a bill in which this lovely poem and moving drama should find a fitting place? . . . Everyone of these plays was listened to with real pleasure, and all were heartily applauded. A more frank and authentic success the Irish company could not have desired.' 'E.F.S.' in the *Westminster Gazette* of 28 Mar (4) said that the plays exhibited 'a simplicity and directness that might also be called primitive, and may well be indicative of something like a new development of drama'. He also, however, mentioned the lack of action.

[2] In the *Saturday Review* for 9 Apr (455) Max Beerbohm described the production as 'one of the rare oases that are in the desert of our drama'. Walkley's *TLS* review of the performances on 1 Apr (102) was also favourable.

round, and I lost my way and was a long time about it, and the band tried
to strike up two or three times but was shouted down and when I at last
appeared I had to make a speech which was very well received.[3] We had an
extraordinarily distinguished audience morning and evening, Wyndham the
chief Secretary, Campbell Bannerman, and many others,[4] and I heard nothing but enthusiasm. All the players are as happy as babies, and I anticipate
no difficulty in the keeping of the company together for another year at
least. Bernard Shaw has started on a play for us.

Many thanks for your telegram about Brett. I am waiting for his written
statement from America. I shall certainly bind myself in no way until I get
it. I think his man in America has behaved very badly about the publication of the Hourglass.[5] I stupidly forgot to send you copies of the Hour
Glass and the Kings Threshold before I left London, but am writing for
them and will send them by next mail.

I find I annoy English people extremely by my praises of America, and
to continue the annoyance I am going to do a little essay of impressions for
some magazine.[6]

---

[3] Not everyone approved of the speech; Walkley (see above, n. 2) noted that the 'applause on
Saturday occasionally had the air of a *parti-pris*, of a "demonstration." Mr. Yeats, in his speech,
said it was easy to know when "our people" were in the house. Well, that is a pity. Mr. Yeats
could not resist the opportunity of airing a theory of acting which may be right or wrong (we happen to think it right), but which was certainly out of place. And he was altogether too cock-a-
hoop.' Archer (see above, n. 1) also criticized the speech, observing that during the calls for the
author 'someone was inspired to lower the fireproof curtain. It was a happy idea; but, alas! the
fireproof curtain was not poet-proof.' He also deplored the reference to 'our people' as unjust to
the London audiences who had consistently supported the Irish drama. WBY, who had been
much disappointed by the lack of Irish support during the previous London visit (see p. 363), had
perhaps intended to encourage the Irish attendance rather than disparage the English.

[4] For Wyndham see p. 192. Sir Henry Campbell-Bannerman (1836–1908), former Chief Secretary of Ireland (1884–5), had been leader of the Liberal Party since 1899. As Prime Minister
from 1905 to 1908, he unsuccessfully supported Home Rule for Ireland. The audience also
included the Earl and Countess of Aberdeen, Lady Marjorie Gordon, the Hon. Alice Spring Rice,
Sir James Mathew, Lady Margaret Sackville, W. L. Courtney, Henry James, J. M. Barrie, Stopford Brooke, Gordon Craig, Hugh Law, G. B. Shaw, Mrs Humphrey Ward, Katharine Tynan,
and FF.

[5] The American edition of *The Hour-Glass and Other Plays*, originally intended for publication
in January 1904 had been held up to await the music (see p. 505, n. 3). Quinn finally sent the corrected proof and music to the printers, Norwood Press, on 10 Mar only to discover that the book
had been published, uncorrected and with no music, the day before. He sent an angry letter to
Brett on 16 Mar (NYPL), blaming him for the blunders of his two subordinates, Herbert
Williams and L. L. Walton, citing errors on 21 pages and pointing out that it was 'nothing short
of an outrage to act in that arbitrary manner; that it was in utter violation of Mr. Yeats' rights and
that any court would at once grant an injunction against the publication and sale of a book issued
as this was, in violation of the author's wishes; that if Mr Yeats were here I should so advise him.'
He sent a copy of this letter to WBY.

[6] Blunt, who attended a dinner party with WBY on 10 May, recorded (II. 103): 'Yeats is just
back from America, where they have made a great fuss with him, and he takes himself very seriously in consequence'. WBY's 'America and the Arts' (see p. 482, n. 2) was not published until
April 1905, when it appeared in the *Metropolitan Magazine*.

I suppose Jack has heard of the break down of the Irish art section of the S. Louis Exhibition, and the really disgraceful carelessness with which Gill and Reardon have treated the whole matter. Lane was promised everything, and urged to take up the collection, and when the pictures were packed ready for starting, he was told without any apology that owing to the high rate of insurance and the difficulty of getting a fireproof building, that part of the scheme was to be dropped.[7] Lavery,[8] the two Shannons[9] and many other artists had declared themselves Irish and refused their pictures to the British Commission, and are now thrown over. Lane is doing his best to get the Guildhall for an Irish art exhibition,[10] but as there is not likely to be much sale there it is a pity if Jack has lost his chance of having his pictures out to his New York Exhibition.[11] I hear Reardon is now collecting worthless rubbish from Williams[12] and such rubbishy painters who will run a risk on chance of sale, and there is danger that he will puff this

[7] Sir Hugh Percy Lane (1875–1915), Lady Gregory's nephew, and a member of the Board of Governors of the Irish National Gallery, was an art-dealer and collector who in 1908 was to establish the Municipal Gallery of Modern Art in Dublin. He had organized an exhibition of Irish painters for St Louis, supported by T. P. Gill who, as Secretary of the Department of Agriculture and Technical Instruction (which was responsible for the administration of official art activities), had sponsored Reardon as Ireland's commissioner to the World Fair. Unfortunately, Lane's disregard of bureaucratic procedures led to a breakdown in communication, and at a late stage the Department decided that the insurance for the pictures, inflated because of forest fires that had destroyed other American cities, was too high. This led to the scheme's cancellation, much to Lane's anger, who, as AG reports in *Hugh Lane's Life and Achievement* (1921), retorted that they 'ought at least to have looked into the cost before they asked me to find the pictures' (47).

[8] John Lavery, RA (1856–1941), knighted 1918, a painter influenced in his early work by Whistler, became best known for his portraits of women, particularly of his beautiful second wife, Hazel, whom he married in 1910 and whose portrait decorated Irish bank notes from 1923 to 1977. WBY recalled 'Hazel Lavery living and dying, that tale / As though some ballad-singer had sung it all' in 'The Municipal Gallery Revisited' (*VP*, 602).

[9] Charles Haslewood Shannon (1863–1937), RA (who had an Irish grandfather); and Sir James Jebusa Shannon (1862–1923), a portrait painter who, born in America of Irish parents, moved to England to study art and became a founding member of the New English Art Club in 1885.

[10] 'An Exhibition of a Selection of Works by Irish Painters', organized by Lane after negotiations over the St Louis World Fair broke down, opened at the Guildhall Art Gallery, London, on 30 May 1904, in the presence of a large gathering which included WBY, AG, John O'Leary, and Wilfrid Blunt. In spite of WBY's misgivings, it proved a success, running until 23 July and attracting 80,000 paying visitors. Its 465 exhibits included works by C. H. Shannon, J. J. Shannon, Lavery, Orpen, Mark Fisher, Furse, Brabazon, Hone, JBY, and others. As soon as the exhibition was under way, Lane began making plans for a Dublin show, and AG wrote in her *Hugh Lane* (54) that he 'looked on the success of the Guildhall Exhibition as another step toward the fulfilment of his purpose, now very definite, of creating a modern picture gallery in Ireland'.

[11] Quinn arranged an exhibition of Jack Yeats's paintings at Clausen's Gallery in New York from 31 Mar to 16 Apr. Only twelve paintings sold, ten of them to Quinn, but Jack and Cottie stayed on as guests in Quinn's apartment for seven weeks, sailing home on 14 May.

[12] Alexander Williams (1843–1930), was born in Co. Monaghan, but lived in Dublin and on Achill Island off the Mayo coast. A largely self-taught painter in oils and water colours, he studied briefly at the art schools of the Royal Dublin Society and had been elected to the Royal Hibernian Academy in 1891. He specialized in Irish landscapes, lakes, and sea-coasts.

as a true National exhibition. If Reardon represents it as such he ought to be exposed in the Press.

I have had a letter from Reardon who now wants some of our players to go to S. Louis. He says that "Mr Kelly and Mr Quinn consider that the Land of Hearts desire was done better in New York than by the National Theatre Society in Dublin" (it was never done in Dublin). He evidently wants to form an American company of players, and to take some of our plays and players that he may get the advertisement out of our success here. I am glad to say the players have no disposition to go, though they blame Gill more than him about the break down of the picture scheme. Reardon is telling people that a dramatic committee has been formed with myself and Father Finlay upon it. I havnt joined that committee and wont.

I have been talking about the Gael to Lady Gregory and am inclined to agree with her that the time has not come for reconstruction of it such as I proposed to Richardson.[13] Our best writers are mortgaged to different papers over here just now. However I cant deal with this question at the end of a long letter. The Gael has been very helpful to us up to the present, and I would not like to lead Richardson into trouble and expense without being quite sure it would repay him.

Yrs snly
W B Yeats

[In AG's hand]

My greetings to you & your guests—If you send Jack back as well & in as good heart as you have sent back his brother you will be a wonderful man! WBY is full of happy energy & of bright recollections—AG

TLS NYPL, with envelope addressed to 1 West 87 St, New York, postmark 'GORT AP 2 04'.

To George Russell (AE), 4 April 1904

Mention in following letter, and in an undated letter from AE, [*c.* 6 April 1904; MBY]

Urging AE not to give his play *Deirdre* to the Company going to the St Louis Exhibition; asking if he should let them have any of his plays; and telling him that as he hopes to organize an INTS American tour he does not want the American public confused.

<hr>

[13] i.e. Stephen J. Richardson, editor of the New York *Gael*; see p. 469. Under his editorship the *Gael* had become a leading organ of the Irish Literary Revival, and he had evidently discussed with WBY the possibility of attracting contributions directly from rising Irish writers. He was to publish an enthusiastic review of Jack Yeats's Clauson exhibition (see above, n. 10) in the April number.

To George Roberts, 4 April [1904]

Coole Park, | Gort,
April 4.

My dear Roberts,[1]
I have received a letter from Reardon as follows.
April 2. 'My dear Mr Yeats,
I have engaged the Digges Company to go to S. Louis, and write to ask whether you will offer any objection to permit them to use your dramas. There are several of them they would like to play including Cathleen ni Houlihan; The Land of Hearts Desire; and Diarmuid and Grania. I am compelled to remain here until Friday next and trust to receive your reply before my departure'.
I have replied to this:
"Dear Mr Reardon,
I certainly object to the Digges Company performing Cathleen ni Houlihan, The Land of Hearts Desire, Diarmuid and Grania or any other play of which I am author or part author.
If my plays are acted by the Company you are getting together, and if that Company can claim Irish actors who have been connected with the National Theatre Company, it will be confused with that body in the public mind. I have lectured a great deal on theatrical matters in America, and incidentally on the work of the National Theatre, and I cannot permit another company, of whose merits I have had but little opportunity of judging, to seem to be the company of which I have spoken. I am sorry to have to refuse, but your request is quite impossible to grant."
I have also written to Russell saying that I count on his refusing permission to play Deirdre. I shall very probably be in Dublin next Saturday.

Yrs sinly
W B Yeats

TLS Harvard.

[1] George Roberts (see p. 430, n. 1), while continuing as a commercial traveller, had also been appointed Secretary of the INTS and from early December 1903 was given a salary of £1 a week. Among his duties were the preparation and production of posters and programmes, but according to a letter from AG of 15 Jan 1904 (Berg) the Company 'complain of Roberts as secretary, he doesn't acknowledge cheques, sent them tickets too late so that they only sold half as many as last time, etc.'

To W. G. Fay, [c. *4 April 1904*]

Mention in letter from George Russell (AE), *c.* 6 April 1904.
Asking the Company to discuss AE's gift of *Deirdre* to the St Louis Company.

MBY.

To George Russell (AE), [c. *5 April 1904*]

Mention in letter from AE, [? 6 April 1904].
Again complaining that AE, although a Vice President of the INTS, has given his play to the rival group going to St Louis, and saying that an American tour is the only way for the INTS to make money; telling him that Digges will be incompetent as stage manager, and will fill up the Company with musicians. Also criticizing Reardon's behaviour over the picture exhibition.

MBY.

To the Editor of the Freeman's Journal, *6 April 1904*

April 6th.

Sir—I see an announcement in your columns that my play, "Cathleen Ni Houlihan," is to be acted at St. Louis by a company of Irish players who are going there.[1] As the National Theatre Society, of which I am president, has decided not to go to America at present, I have not given leave for any play of mine to be taken there by any other company.—Yours sincerely,

W B Yeats

Printed letter, *Freeman's Journal,* 7 April 1904 (6). A version of this letter appeared in the Dublin *Evening Mail.*

---

[1] In announcing the engagement of the Digges company for the St Louis Exhibition, the *Freeman's Journal* of 5 Apr (4) had asserted that amongst 'the plays to be performed will be several of those produced by the Irish Literary Theatre, first among them being "Deirdre" and "Cathleen-ni-Houlihan"'.

To George Russell (AE), [c. *7 April 1904*]

Mention in letter from AE, Friday [? 8 April 1904].
Asking AE to find out whether George Moore has given the St Louis
Company the rights to *The Bending of the Bough* and his part of *Diarmuid
and Grania.*[1]

MBY.

To Lady Augusta Gregory, [*8 April 1904*]

Nassau Hotel

My dear Lady Gregory: I have seen Reardon he is depressed but says he is
under contract to Quinn, Digges, Kelly Etc.[1] He blames Gill, who told
him he could get the best of both companies. He says they may all have to
be sent back. I distrust him greatly however, & have sent him the enclosed
letter to keep him from misrepres[ent]ing our conversation. I am sorry to
say that our dear company has expelled Kelly by a practically unanimous
vote—Keller & Ryan alone objected—& Fay says if the men had forgiven
him, the women would'nt. He made no defence they say.[2] The next

---

[1] In his reply AE said he would see Moore the following night, 'but I asked him before about
the play and he said he would not allow any of them to go over. He wanted as a condition a stage
manager to be selected by himself I think, and since this was not permitted he would not let anything go. I don't believe they have got Diarmuid and Grania, and if they have, you can bring an
action against Moore and get more out of damages than you would probably get out of royalties.'

[1] When the INTS refused the invitation to perform at the World Fair, Dudley Digges and
Maire Quinn, who had resigned from the Society in 1903, offered their services to Reardon. They
were accompanied by Charles Caulfield (who had left the INTS in late 1902 because of the theological discussions arising out of *The Hour-Glass*), Elizabeth Young ('Violet Mervyn'), who played
the original Deirdre in George Coffey's garden in 1902 (see p. 149), and P. J. Kelly, who was still
a member of the Society, and who was consequently expelled at a specially convened meeting on
6 Apr. The American stage manager was Luke Martin, an Irish-American actor-manager whose
standard role was the comic Irishman in plays by Boucicault, Chauncey Olcott, and others. The
theatre was housed, appropriately, in a replica of Blarney Castle.

[2] In an undated indictment (Widener), sent to George Roberts as Secretary of the INTS,
W. G. Fay had made 'the following charges of conduct detrimental to the interests of the Society
against P. J. Kelly. That withough [*sic*] the consent of the committee he took part in a dramatic
performance in Gloucester St last winter & that he entered into an engagement to Act in St Louis
with the oposition [*sic*] company without consulting the society. In consequence of these two
breaches of the rules I wish a meeting to be called & propose that this member be immediately
expelled from the Society.' In his article 'Early Days of the Irish Theatre', in the *Dublin Magazine*, Jan–Mar 1950 (20), Padraic Colum recalled Fay's implacability when 'P. J. Kelly was haled
up for trial. . . . Willie Fay was stern and demanded his expulsion from the Society. P. J. Kelly
was drummed out. I remember his leaving through the door that went out into Camden Street
and seeing the tense faces of his colleagues, the unbending look of Willie Fay, and realizing that a
change had come in the spirit of the Society.'

"show" is to be a *converstatione* to Gwynn & 'Kings Threshold' & 'Shadowy Waters' are both to be played. It will be at end of month or early May.[3] Starkie takes Kellys place.[4] Russell wanted to play 'Forgail' but I have quenched that. They are not angry with Russell aparently.[5] He is as impeccable as ever.

I said I was sorry about Kelly but Fay says they must keep up the *morale* of the Theatre or soon nobody could be depended on—

Yrs ev

W B Yeats

ALS Berg, with envelope addressed to Coole, postmark 'DUBLIN AP 8 04'.

To James A. Reardon, 8 April 1904

Nassau Hotel, | Dublin.

April 8th.,/04.

Dear Mr Reardon,

Conversations lead to such confusion that I think that I had better repeat and amplify what seemed to me the essentials of our conversation last night. I should be ready to lend my plays & to recommend other writers for our theatre to lend their plays, either to a competent Irish Company (no actors *not* from this side being in it) or to a competent American Company (no actors from this side being in it).

Certain details would still have to be arranged, but not vital matters.

I cannot under any circumstances lend plays to a mixed company. You asked me last night if I would re-consider this if you made a great success. As it would be impossible for us on this side of the water to judge the merits of the performances, I must simply hold to the principle I have laid down, I cannot depart from it in any way. I am very sorry for your difficulties, but neither Mr Gill nor yourself should have counted on our support, without submitting to us the cast & the details of your scheme.

Yrs sinly

W B Yeats

Dict AEFH, signed WBY; Texas.

[3] The private production of *The King's Threshold* and *The Shadowy Waters* at a conversazione (probably of the National Literary Society) was not covered by the press, largely because it took place on 26 Apr 1904, when the papers were giving over their columns to King Edward's widely reported second visit to Dublin.

[4] James Sullivan Starkey (see p. 424) replaced P. J. Kelly as King Guaire in rehearsals for *The King's Threshold*.

[5] AE had permitted Digges and Quinn to play his *Deirdre* in St Louis, without seeking permission of the Society to do so.

To John Quinn, 8 April 1904

18, Woburn Buildings, | Euston Road, | L O N D O N.
8th April, 1904.

Dear Mr. Quinn,

Though I date my letter from London I am really in Dublin, where I shall be for a few days seeing about national theatre business. The big question of our place of performance has to be settled and Miss Horniman is over. We have rather an unpleasant business this week. Do you remember what I told you about Reardon. I told you how either he or Gill, or both together tricked Lane over the Exhibition. They dropped the project when all the pictures were together packed and about to start. The whole thing has been disgraceful, and the Freeman would have exposed the department over it but for Lady Gregory's respect for Plunkett, which made her restrain her nephew. Well, a few days ago I got a letter from Reardon saying that he had engaged the Digges Company, and asking me to give them my plays. At the same time or soon after I got a letter from somebody else telling me that Kelly (who has been expelled by our people because of it I am sorry to say), Miss Quinn, Digges and one other were going out to form part of a company made up principally of Americans and working under an American stage Manager. I saw at once that Reardon's object in going to the expense in bringing out four actors was to give his company the advertisement of association with our work here. These Dublin actors, only one of whom is much good, will lose any merits they have when mixed up with his professionals, and acting in a method foreign to them. I got a letter from the National Theatre people full of indignation. They consider that their plays would be spoiled. That people would consider that they were played in their method and that the market would be spoiled for the Company if it ever went out itself. They would not have minded if Reardon had got together an exclusively American Company. I wrote to Reardon saying that I would permit my plays to be performed either by an exclusively Dublin Company or by an exclusively American one, but that I would not give them to a mixed Company. We are all feeling very exaspirated for Gill and Reardon had no business putting the whole thing off to the last moment and then trying to rush us into a project altogether different from the one they had spoken to us about. Apart from my disbelief in the utility of a mixed company and my strong belief in its power to compromise us I have other grounds of suspicion. Reardon is talking of dancers and musicians and God knows what kind of music hall abomination this might be. Then I hear there are to be other plays besides the Irish plays and God knows what they will be like. Everything may be about to be managed in the most admirable way, but we could not give our plays without more information and more guarantee than Reardon is likely to give us in his last four days in Dublin, for he leaves to-night. His Company at present unless they pirate have got nothing Irish to play except "The heather field"[1] and "Deirdre" (which Russell gave them without understanding the situation) and possibly though this is very doubtful for I hear he has asked for a London stage Manager, George Moore's "Bending of the Bough". Reardon has given them contracts and so cannot get out of the hole he has put himself in. He has never read any of the plays he has got, and he will have a fine time running a Theatre for seven months with the three of them. Even if he does put on other plays a good part of the time. The danger is that he will try to pirate some of our work here, if he does so, please let me know, and I will make things merry for the department, who have guaranteed him. I am sorry to have to write you a letter so full of contentious things, but there is no help for it. I am very sorry that the Company has expelled Kelly, but there is a rule which obliges a member to give the Company notice for engaging himself elsewhere and Kelly had broken this before. Fay said to me if the men would have forgiven him nothing could have made the women do it. I hear he was sad and made no defence. He will probably be let back alright.

We had a most wonderful success in London. The Company has greatly improved all round and gave beautiful performances. They had about the most distinguished audience I have seen in a London Theatre. Wyndham was there morning and evening Campbell Bannerman in the morning and Lord Aberdeen morning and evening, and in the evening the beautiful Duchess of Southerland and all manner of notabilities besides. Every seat was taken morning and evening. And the "Times" taunts us with becoming fashionable.[2] "The King's Threshold" had an immense success with the audience but I don't think you will ever get the majority of the London Dramatic Critics in our time to care about verse. The whole Company is full of spirit and excitement. Mrs. Bernard Shaw has written to say that Bernard Shaw is working on a play for us,[3] and if I can get some longish play done we will start finely in the Autumn. I am trying to do a little

---

[1] Edward Martyn's *The Heather Field* had first been produced by the ILT on 9 May 1899.

[2] Walkley had warned in his *TLS* review (see p. 562, n. 2) that the 'chief danger to be apprehended for the Irish National Theatre Society is premature success. If, while still in their green unknowing youth, they become "the fashion" (and a glance at the Royalty audience last Saturday showed that they are in the fair way of it), if they allow the tender plant of their art to be 'forced' for the London market, it will be a real misfortune. Already they seem to have lost something of their *naiveté*, something of their first fine careless rapture.'

[3] Charlotte Shaw's untraced letter was optimistic. Shaw had sketched out a scenario, and made some notes on the characters, on 15 Mar 1904 (Texas), but he did not begin drafting *John Bull's Other Island* until 17 June 1904, and on 20 June wrote hyperbolically to WBY (Private): 'Not a word of the play yet on paper'.

article on "America" saying that it is so much more educated and culti-vated, than England.[4]

Remember me to all good friends about you in New York.

Yrs sinly
W B Yeats

TLS NYPL.

To George Russell (AE), 8 April 1904

Nassau Hotel, | Dublin.
April 8th.,/04.

My dear Russell,

I send you the enclosed offer from Miss Horniman.[1] You need do nothing about it except hold your tongue absolutely. We must not let the slightest rumour get out until we have secured our patent. I go to-morrow I hope to Anthony Mac Donald about it.[2]

Yours snly
W B Yeats

[*Enclosure in AEFH's hand*]

[H]1 Montagu Mansions, | Portman Square, | London. W.
April 1904.

To the President of the Irish National Theatre.
(Copy)
Dear Mr Yeats,

I have a great sympathy with the artistic and dramatic aims of the Irish National Theatre as publicly explained by you on various occasions. I am glad to be able to offer you my assistance in your endeavours to establish a permanent theatre in Dublin.

I am taking the hall of the Mechanics Institute in Abbey Street and an adjoining building in Marlborough Street which I propose to turn into a small theatre with a proper entrance hall, green-room, and dressing-rooms.

As the company will not require the hall constantly, I propose to arrange

---

[4] See p. 563, n. 6.

[1] AEFH's 'Offer of Theatre', addressed to WBY and sent to each vice-president and to the stage-manager of the Society, was published with the 'Society's Acceptance' in the 1904 *Samhain*.
[2] i.e. Sir Anthony MacDonnell, the permanent Under-Secretary for Ireland; see p. 350.

to let it for lectures and entertainments at a rental proportionate to its seating capacity.

The company can have the building rent free whenever they want it for rehearsals and performances except when it is let. The green-room I hope to arrange to be kept for their sole use. They must pay for their own electric light and gas as well as for the repair of damages done during their occupation. The building will be insured and any additions to the lighting for special occasions or plays must be permitted by the Insurance Co. formally in writing.

If any President, Vice-President or member of the company want the hall for a lecture, concert or entertainment, the rent must be paid to me as by an ordinary person. If a lecture be given on a dramatic or theatrical subject and the gross receipts go to the Irish National Theatre, then the President, Vice-President, or member of the company can have the hall for nothing. But it must be advertised clearly as being for the sole benefit of the Irish National Theatre pecuniarily as well as in aid of its artistic objects.

The prices of the seats can be raised of course, but not lowered, neither by the Irish National Theatre, nor by anyone who will hire the hall. This is to prevent cheap entertainments from being given which would lower the letting value of the hall. I hope to be able to arrange to number most of the seats and to sell the tickets beforehand with a small fee for booking.

The entrance to the more expensive seats will be from Marlborough Street where there will be a cloak room.

The situation being near to the tramway terminus, is convenient for people living in any part of Dublin.

I shall take every possible means to insure the safety and convenience of the public. I can only afford to make a very little theatre and it must be quite simple.

You all must do the rest to make a powerful and prosperous theatre with a high artistic ideal.

A copy of this letter will be sent to each Vice-President and another to the Stage Manager for the company.

Yours sincerely
A. E. F. Horniman.

Dict AEFH, signed WBY; Indiana.

To Douglas Hyde, 8 April 1904

Nassau Hotel, | Dublin.
April 8ᵗʰ.,/04.

My dear Hyde,

Miss Horniman is sending you the enclosed statement. There is nothing particular for you to do about [it] except to say nothing about it, this is most important. The Hall has an old theatrical patent & we have to have this looked into with the greatest secresy and dispatch.[1] If the other theatres got wind of it they would spend any amount of money to thwart us.

You will see at once the enormous importance of the whole movement, of a proper theatre. I have several things to write to you about, but they will wait. Lady Gregory wrote to you about Reardon or I did. We cannot be too careful in dealing with him, he is going to mix up his Irish Plays with American Music Hall performers, as far as I can make out.

Yours snly,
W B Yeats

Dict AEFH, signed WBY; Private.

To Elizabeth Young,[1] *[c. 8 April 1904]*

Nassau Hotel. | South Fredrick St.

Dear Miss Young:

As I know Dublin delights in fables I think it will be best for me to give you my opinion on our Theatrical dispute & some account of my proposed

---

[1] In 1786 the Irish Parliament passed 'An Act for Regulating the Stage in the City and County of Dublin', requiring theatres to secure a patent from the Crown. Such patents were valid for 21 years and expensive to take out and renew, but included a licence for selling alcoholic drinks, and entitled the patentee to request a military guard when necessary. The Hall of the Mechanics Institute was built in the mid-19th century on the site of the old Theatre Royal, which had opened in 1821, and the Hall secured a patent as the Princess Theatre. It was rebuilt following a severe fire, and reopened in 1874 as the New Princess Theatre of Varieties, but neglected to renew the patent. As the *Irish Daily Independent* reported on 15 Oct 1904: 'Up to a few years ago the management of this interesting old concern used to run it for the production of plays of the blood-curdling and hair-raising type. Then the question of the patent, or rather the want of it, arose, and this was put a stop to, and the place gradually drifted into the condition of a cheap variety show.'

[1] See p. 149, n. 7. Elizabeth Young was the sister of Ella Young and acted under the name of Violet Mervyn. Following this American tour she took small parts in London, and returned to Dublin in or shortly after 1910. She remained in Ireland for the rest of her life.

action. First of all none of us feal that we have any complaint what ever against you, or Miss Quinn or Digges, for accepting Reordans offer. I have however heard on what seems good authority that some of your people have considered the possibility of 'pirating' plays by myself & others. I know that you have had no sympathy with this proposal & therefore I write to you, ⟨&⟩ but you can show the letter to your associates. If nothing is done to confuse your company with the National Theatre Society & its work, & if no play is taken without the authors consent we will all have the strongest wishes for your success. Even on purely selfish grounds we could not wish otherwise for your failure would injure us later on when we go to America & your success would help us. The pirating of a play (the taking of work which is the moral but not the legal property of an author without his leave) would on the other hand force me to act if I could not get the Department to do so. I wrote this to my friend John Quinn of the Irish Literary Society of New York, who would probably represent me. It is lamintable to have to take such precautions against ones own fellow countrymen & countrywomen but I had only too good reason for doing so. If any act of Reordons or another confused your company with ours or its work I might also have to take some steps.

The reason I did not wish Russell to give you Dierdre was that he is closely connected with our work & is our vice-president. I held that his giving his play would confuse you & us in the public mind.

I do not wish this confusion because I know from Reordan that in all most all your plays you will be mixed up with American actors & that you will be under the authority of an American stage manager. I know this from myself. I wrote to him that I would deal with a competent Irish company or with a competent American one but not with a mixed company. I considered & consider that Reordan engaged you merely to have the advertisement he will obtain from the success of our Irish actors in London & from my lectures in America. I lectured on the stage in most of the great colleges & spoke much of our work.

I am sorry to trouble you with what is now an old story but it is generally better to put ones action on record. Please show this to your associates to whom I wish every success.

Yrs sny
W B Yeats

ALS Berg.

To George Russell (AE), [April 1904]

Nassau Hotel | South Fredrick.

My dear Russell: I have been thinking over the Moore project.[1] Please do nothing at present. When we start in Autumn in the Abbey Theatre we will make our next appeal to the public & that will be the time for adding new people. If Shaws play suits us we can add him for instance, Gilbert Murray too & so get a representative list on which Moore will be as a matter of course. At present we would gain nothing. Please forgive me for giving expression to some of my general exasperation (I have ♄ transiting ☽s phase) & making Dierdre the scape goat.[2] I was foolish enough to quote a phrase of Lady Gregorys ⟨about Deirdre⟩ which must have annoyed you but when you think of it try & remember that she like myself puts your best poetry above any spiritual poetry written in our time & your best prose among the loftiest of the world. I myself sometimes give unbridled expression to my dislikes moved perhaps by my knowledge of the strength of my likings & my loyalty to them. I am nothing but an artist & my life is in written words & they get the most of my loves & hates & so too I am reckless in mere speach that is not written. You are the other side of the penny for you are admirably careful in speach having set life before art, too much before it as I think for one who is, in spite of himself perhaps, an artist. It is the careless printed word that remains after ones death to marr many people it may be, while the careless spoken word troubles an ear or two at most. That is I think the root of all our differences.

I have just been reading some reviews of 'new songs'. Miss Gore Booths little poem about the roads is charming & delights my conscience & I like

---

[1] George Moore, who had left the ILT in October 1901, was scheming to join the INTS as a stage-manager (director), but his attack on W. G. Fay's stage-management in *Dana* in September 1904 was to put this out of the question.

[2] i.e. Saturn transiting the moon's phase, an influence which WBY thought particularly baleful. WBY had made AE's *Deirdre* a focus of his dispute with Reardon and Digges when, against his wishes, AE granted them permission to produce the play in St Louis. AE defended his right to dispose of the play outside Ireland and England and, when WBY continued to press the matter before the Society, resigned as vice-president. There had evidently been a sharp exchange between the two, for AE told WBY that in his letter of resignation he had 'simply explained my position with regard to *Deirdre* and St. Louis better perhaps than I did when I wrote hastily in the office and rather in an ill temper' (*Some Passages from the Letters of AE to W. B. Yeats* [1936], 49). AG had never thought highly of AE's *Deirdre* (see p. 149, n. 6), and WBY had evidently been undiplomatic enough to pass on some of her reservations. WBY was correct in identifying AE as instrumental in enabling the rival company to go to St Louis, for, writing to Judge Richard Campbell on 13 August 1935 (Colby), Dudley Digges recalled that it 'was AE who brought us the final word that we were to be taken to the St. Louis Fair. There had been great uncertainty about it & we were anxious to go. We were waiting in his room one night when he bounded in and said "It's alright you're going". Our fate and all that was wound up in it was linked in some way with AE . . .'

the poem about the wise dead under grass & the strong gone over sea but it leaves my conscience hungry. Some of the poems I will probably under-ate (though I am certain I would recognize a masterpeice come out of any temprement) because the dominant mood in many of them is one I have faught in my self & put down.[3] In my 'Land of Hearts Desire' & in some of my lyric verse of that time there is an exageration of sentiment & senti-mental beauty which I have come to think unmanly. The popularity of the 'Land of Hearts Desire' seems to me to come not from its merits but because of this weakness. I have been fighting the prevelent decadence for years, & have but just got it under foot in my own heart—it is sentament & sentimental sadness & a womanish introspection—my own early subjective verse at rare moments, & yours nearly always rises above sentiment to a union with a pure energy of the spirit but between this energy of the spirit, & the energy of the will out of which epic & dramatic poetry comes there is a region of brooding emotions full of fleshly waters & vapours which kill the spirit & the will, ecstasy & joy equally. Yet this region of shadows is full of false images of the spirit & of the body. I have come to feal towards it as O'Grady feals towards it some times & even a little as some of my own stupidest critics feal. As so often happens with a thing one has been tempted by & is still a little tempted by I am roused by it to a kind of fren-zied hatred which is quite out of my control. Beardsley exasperated some people in this way but he was never the form of decadence that tempted me & so I am not unjust to him[4] but I cannot probably be quite just to any poetry that speaks to me with the sweet insinuating feminine voice of the dwellers in the country of shadows & hollow images. I have dwelt there too long not to dread all that comes out of it. We possess nothing but the will & we must never let the children of vague desire breath upon it nor the waters of sentiment rust the terrible mirror of its blade.[5] I flee from some

[3] *New Songs*, published the previous month, was an anthology made by AE from the poems of Padraic Colum, Eva Gore-Booth, Thomas Keohler, Alice Milligan, Susan Mitchell, Seumas O'Sullivan, George Roberts, and Ella Young. Eva Gore-Booth's 'The Little Waves of Breffny' describes 'the little roads of Cloonagh', and Seumas O'Sullivan's 'The Twilight People' reads: 'Twilight people why will you still be crying / Crying and calling to me out of the trees? / For under the quiet grass the wise are lying / And all the strong ones are gone over the seas . . .'. WBY's criticism, although unwelcome, would not have been unexpected to AE, who had written defiantly to Quinn on 20 Jan 1904 (NYPL): 'The people Yeats used scornfully to call my canary birds will produce among them some fine literature yet'.

[4] In *Mem* (92) WBY wrote that he found in the consumptive artist Aubrey Beardsley (1872–98) 'that noble courage that seems to me at times, whether in man or woman, the greatest of human faculties. I saw it in all he said and did, in the clear logic of speech and in [the] clean swift line of his art. His disease presented continuously before his mind, as one of its symptoms, lascivious images, and he drew them in their horror, their fascination, and became the first satirist of the soul English art has produced.'

[5] Compare *The Shadowy Waters*, ll. 131–5 (*VP*, 228), and see 'To a Poet, who would have me Praise certain Bad Poets, Imitators of His and Mine' (*VP*, 262).

of this new verse you have gathered as from much verse of our day knowing that I flee that water & that breath.

Yrs ever

W B Yeats

When the spirit sinks back weary from its flight towards the final White-
ness it sinks into the dim shadow region more often than less aspiring spirits. I am angry when I see it, whether it is my spirit, or your spirit, as in
'Dierdre', or the spirit of some of these young poets of yours. Someday
you will become aware as I have become of an uncontrollable shrinking
from the shadows, for as I beleive a mysterious command [h]as gone out
against them in the invisible world of pure energies. Let us have no emotions, however abstract, in which their is not an athletic joy.

ALS Indiana. Partly in Wade, 433–5.

To Edward Garnett,[1] *12 April 1904*

Nassau Hotel, | Dublin.

April 12.ᵗʰ,/04.

My dear Garnett,

I hear that you are literary editor of the Speaker. Do you feel inclined to
do a good deed? I daresay that you will remember that we performed a
play called "Broken Soil" a couple of weeks ago at the Royalty. It was an
immature play but most of the critics found it interesting & all I think
found it original. It was by a young man called Patrick Colm, he is twenty-
three & very young for his age but very simple & charming. His father was
a farm-labourer & he has had to educate himself as far as serious matters
are concerned.[2] He has read a great deal, especially of dramatic literature &
is I think, though of course one can never be certain about such things, a
man of genius in the first dark gropings of his thought. Some here think he

---

[1] Edward Garnett (1868–1937), son of the Keeper of Printed Books at the British Museum,
had, as a gifted young publisher's reader, encouraged T. Fisher Unwin to publish WBY's *John
Sherman* (1891) and *The Countess Kathleen* (1892), and had tried to support WBY's scheme for a
new 'Library of Ireland' (see I. 329–36, 349–52). Now a reader for Duckworth & Co., Garnett was
an influential literary critic with a reputation for recognizing and encouraging talented writers,
including Joseph Conrad, W. H. Hudson, Ford Madox Ford, John Galsworthy, and D. H.
Lawrence. In a luke-warm review of AG's *Cuchulain of Muirthemne* in the *Academy* of 14 Feb
1903 he had described himself (157) as 'an old friend of Mr. Yeats and an admirer of his work'.

[2] See p. 169, n. 2; Colum had been working as a clerk in the Irish Railway Clearing House, in
Kildare Street, Dublin. His father, Patrick Colum, was not a farm labourer: he had been master of
the Longford workhouse and was now the station-master of Sandycove, a Dublin suburb, where
Colum grew up, and where he had attended the local National School.

will become our strongest dramatic talent over here, though his work is little more at present than full of promise. I have seen some very good reviews by him in which there was always thought & sometimes beautiful sentences. I want to get him some reviewing. He has only £60 a year & supports a brother & a sister on this. At the same time I think that it is probable that he ought to be in benevolent editorial hands for a little. Could you send him one or two books to review, Irish books if possible? If you let him sign I think that his name would be interesting to a few people. His address is—

[*No address given*]³

I am sorry that I have not seen more of you in these recent years, but I get more & more absorbed in the work here & seem to be less & less in London.

Yours sinly

W B Yeats

Dict AEFH, signed WBY; Texas. Partly in Wade, 432–3.

To Lady Augusta Gregory, [c. *13 April 1904*]

Mention in letter from AG, 'Thursday' [14 April 1904].¹
Evidently discussing the production of Martyn's play,² and who should speak the prologue to *The Shadowy Waters*.³

Berg.

---

³ Colum did not contribute any reviews to the *Speaker*—although whether this was owing to Garnett's indifference or because WBY forgot to include his address, is not known. He was in fact touring the country gathering material for future plays and poems, and was to live in Ranelagh, Dublin, on his return.

¹ AG replied: 'Your letter came today. Don't be stingy about writing, it is so great a pleasure to me to hear from you, and to know what is going on.'

² Edward Martyn's *An Enchanted Sea* was produced by the Players' Club under the auspices of the National Literary Society at the Antient Concert Rooms on 18–19 April.

³ AG had written to WBY in America on 14 Jan (see p. 540, n. 4) that at the first production of *The Shadowy Waters* the 'Prologue as said by Miss Layard [*sic*] was a mistake. She did not make the words distinct, but her brogue was very distinct, and she was in a dreadful costume, a sort of nondescript robe that made her enormous, and one of those mock jewel crowns on her head.' Joseph Holloway had also recorded on the same day (NLI) that Miss Laird 'spoke a prologue in very Yeatsian singsong chant but she pitched her voice so low that the meaning of the words she uttered escaped me'.

To John Quinn, 15 April 1904

18, Woburn Buildings, | Euston Road, | LONDON.

15th April, '04

My dear Quinn,

I write from Dublin though I put my London address I am over here attending rehearsals. The Company is reviving the "King's Threshold" again but only for a conversatione,[1] and I am taking the opportunity of going through it line by line with William Fay. I am improving it here and there, there is so much one can only write when one has the actors under one's eyes. I have re-written all the bit about the Mayor of Kinvara, and made a lively scene which works itself up into a tumult of voices which are suddenly silenced by the entrance of the Court. I make good use of the cripples in this scene. Now that this is redone the whole play will be full of energy. The Reardon dispute has been unpleasant. When he went away he and I were on personally good terms though I was feeling pretty exasperated, I felt, and feel, the greatest suspicion, but have no better reason for it than everybody's vagueness of mind about the project. I got an impression from Reardon that he would say one thing today and another thing tomorrow, Moore must have got the same impression for he, I am told has got it into his mind, that Reardon may pirate Dairmuid and Grania. He seems to have given him a manuscript in some early stage of their negotiations. Miss Quinn certainly had piratical intentions and avowed them, but they have been given up, so it looks as if we might live in peace. I am still, of course, afraid of the St. Louis people mixing up in the public mind their half Irish, half American Company, with Fay and his people, who are most anxious to go out in a couple of years. I don't think I told you in my last letter that Miss Horniman has leased for us an old hall or theatre and is doing it up. There is to be electric light, good dressing rooms, and a good stage. It will hold 6 or 7 hundred people, and could be made to hold a good many more.[2] There are some legal formalities to be gone through, before we can play in it, and I should be anxious till they are done with. Sir Anthony McDonnell will help us all he can. Our start in this theatre of our own will make no end of a stir for we will be the first national theatre they have got over here. In London they are always talking about the desirability of such a thing but we shall have done it. Bernard Shaw is at work on his play for us and we think of starting in the autumn with it. The advertisement we will get out of the new building should launch us well.

---

[1] See p. 569, n. 3.

[2] In fact the Abbey Theatre had 562 seats: 178 in the stalls, 198 in the balcony, and 186 in the pit.

The notices of our London show keep on coming in even now. Lady Gregory's "Rising of the Moon" goes into rehearsal almost at once. Now that I have got over the excitement of being home again, I miss our talks, and the stir of America very greatly. If I had not my work here that fine vivid ⟨country⟩ place would have an even greater fascination. It should be the next home of the Arts for they come out of the lands that are most alive. England is half dead, and that is why every Englishman is a poseur. He hasn't enough life in him to be a fountain of sincere thought and emotion, and so he says "I am an Englishmen" or "I am a Tory" or "I am a gentleman". And so one gets a country which one can describe by a beautiful mistake that occurred in Russels "Dierdre" the last time they played it. One of the characters said of the sons of Usna, "These are not heroes, but living phantoms". Which they were surely in the play (The words heroes and phantoms were transposed).[3]

Yours sincly
W B Yeats

TLS NYPL, with envelope addressed to 1 West 87th Street, New York, postmark 'DUBLIN AP 15 04'.

To Lady Augusta Gregory, [16 April 1904]

Nassau Hotel

My dear Lady Gregory: I cross over to London to night. I will miss Martyns play but I shall have to return here in a week as 'Shadowy Waters' & 'Kings Threshold' are to be played on the 26th (tuesday).[1] I am going over now entirely because I do not think it fair to leave Synge in London by himself. He should be meeting people. Please let me know when you think

[3] AE's *Deirdre* had been revived and presented at the Molesworth Hall with Synge's *Riders to the Sea* from 25 to 27 Feb 1904 while WBY was in America.

[1] i.e. *An Enchanted Sea*; see p. 148, n. 2. To Joseph Holloway (*Abbey Theatre*, 39–40), it 'proved a dreary, monotonous play full of daft ideas of the most improbable kind. Many a "back drawing-room theatre" would disown such crude acting as the Player's Club put into this piece of Martyn's; but I doubt very much if its fate would have been otherwise were the cast filled by first-class professionals. W. G. Fay put it on for rehearsal at the Irish National Theatre Society and finding it impossible, withdrew it after the second rehearsal.' For the private performances of *The King's Threshold* and *The Shadowy Waters* see p. 569, n. 3. AG, who was unable to attend any of these performances because she was nursing Robert Gregory through an illness at Coole, reported on 'Thursday' [21 Apr 1904; Berg] that Martyn had told her that 'although the play was well acted . . . An Enchanted Sea did not please the Audience'. AE had written to her by the same post that the play had 'fizzled out', and that the 4th Act 'was abominably acted, the actors did not know their parts & one of them could not get out of the room & the audience laughed at his efforts—I never felt sorrier for anyone than Martyn'.

to come to London & if you will be in Dublin on the 26th. I have got that comedy scene in 'Kings Threshold' very good now (the old version of play is to be played however) but have still further changes to make here & there. I have been going through the play line by line at rehearsal,[2] & will make it much stronger. I work the scene with the cripples up into a great racket all talking togeather—the cripples begging, the mayor saying he is mad, the servant saying he is not. In the might [*for* midst] of this the court enters & the stage is suddenly silent. I am very meloncholy going to London & you not there—do not delay long.

Miss Horniman, the architect[3] & myself were inspecting the theatre the other day when the present tenant (a Music Hall man who has it by the weak) came in, called us "Land Grabbers" & turned us out. The architect has however softened him so much that the plan is now partly made & looks very well. I saw the solicitors this morning & gave him the draft petition. That last sentence is the apple of Miss Hornimans eye. It is the only one that must not be changed it seems.[4] Our rivals start for St Lewis to morrow & are taking Cousins play & *Mʳ Duncans play.*[5] Moore gave them

[2] WBY's commitment was not to everyone's taste and Holloway (*Abbey Theatre*, 39) recorded that the 'great Yeats, by his interruptions every minute, proved himself an impossible man to rehearse before, and if I were Starkey [*who played the King*] I would have been inclined to tell him to go to the "old boy" more than once'.

[3] Joseph Holloway (1861–1944), inveterate theatre-goer and independent architect, was in charge of renovating the Mechanics' Institute. Selections from his valuable day-by-day journal of theatrical activities, 'Impressions of a Dublin Playgoer' (NLI), were published as *Joseph Holloway's Abbey Theatre* (Carbondale, 1967) and in three further volumes as *Joseph Holloway's Irish Theatre* (Dixon, Calif., 1968–70). Holloway records this incident in his entry for 11 Apr (*Abbey Theatre*, 38–9).

[4] AEFH had sent a copy of her draft petition for a theatre patent to AG for comment, and AG, as she told WBY on 14 Apr (see p. 579), had 'pointed out that her last paragraph repeated other sentences, & I would not say the new theatre will never interfere with the old ones for I hope it may do so'. Although the draft petition apparently no longer exists, it may have echoed the words of the 'Warrant for Letters Patent', reprinted as Appendix D of Peter Kavanagh's *The Story of the Abbey Theatre* (1950), 213–22, the first section of which (dealing with the motives and methods of AEFH as 'Memorialist') reads: 'And Memorialist prayed that a Patent under the Great Seal of Ireland . . . might be granted to Memorialist for a term of twenty-one years to enable Memorialist to establish and keep a well-regulated Theatre within the said City of Dublin and County of Dublin and therein at all lawful times publicly to act, represent or perform or cause to be acted represented or performed all Interludes, Tragedies, Comedies, Preludes, Operas, Burlettas, Plays, Farces, Pantomimes or any part or parts thereof and of what kind or nature whatsoever' (p. 215).

[5] Cousins's play was probably *The Sword of Dermot* (see p. 348, n. 3) in which Digges, Quinn, Kelly, and Caulfield had played the major roles. James Duncan's unpublished play, *A Gallant of Galway*, first performed at a National Literary Society 'original night' on 24 Mar 1902, is a comedy of manners set in the 18th century; the plot hinges on a romance between two children of feuding Galway families, and the abduction of the heroine by a fortune-seeking baronet. Duncan (d. *c.* 1938), who played the villain in the National Literary Society production, was a civil servant in charge of the Teachers' Pension Office in Dublin Castle, and the husband of Ellen Duncan (1850–1937), who in 1907 founded the United Arts Club, Dublin, and became the first curator of the Municipal Gallery of Modern Art, 1914–22.

nothing so heaven knows what they will act. I should think the American stage manager will condemn all they have. I am a little sorry for them.

Yours ev
W B Yeats

ALS Berg, with envelope addressed to Coole, postmark 'DUBLIN AP ? 04'.

To Charles Elkin Mathews, 17 April 1904

18 Woburn Buildings, | Euston Road,
April 17.ᵗʰ,/04.

My dear Matthews,

    I send you those four pages marked "for press". But on reading through the bits of Latin, I find what is probably a mis-print on page 21. Three lines from bottom of page the original edition has "decussa veste", your edition put "decussa vesta". Is this a misprint or a correction? I have no Latin Dictionary by me & my Latin is much too shaky to venture an opinion. It is probably a mis-print as I imagine that Lionel Johnson corrected the original proof. (He wrote the Latin.) See that it is correct. I mean that if your reader has changed it, look it up. If not please put "veste".[1]

Yrs snly
W B Yeats

Dict AEFH, signed WBY; Texas.

[1] Mathews corrected the phrase, which appeared as 'decussa veste Dei sidera' ('stars shaken out of the raiment of God'), in the 1904 edition of *The Tables of the Law and The Adoration of the Magi*. In Quinn's copy of the 1897 edition (*Bibl*, 43) WBY wrote: 'The portrait which is by my father, & the Latin which is by Lionel Johnson, are the only things which are worth anything in this little book. W. B. Yeats, Oct., 1901.'

To H. W. Nevinson, 19 April 1904

18 Woburn Buildings, | Euston Road,
April 19.ᵗʰ./04.

My dear Nevinson,

Are you free Saturday evening? And if so could you come in & meet Synge whose plays you saw, any time after eight.[1]

Yrs snly
W B Yeats

Dict AEFH, signed WBY; Southern Illinois.

To Lady Augusta Gregory, [21 April 1904]

18 Woburn Buil

My dear Lady Gregory

When do you come. Send me a wire when you are starting. I go to Dublin Monday night & think of going on from there to Stratford to see the Aeschulus which is on Friday or Saturday.[1] Or I may come here at the

---

[1] Nevinson replied on 20 Apr to say that he was unable to meet Synge on Saturday, 23 Apr, since he would be in Stratford to review Aeschylus' Oresteian Trilogy for the *Speaker*. WBY therefore decided to introduce Synge to Charles Ricketts, who noted (*SP*, 104) that he returned from dinner with 'Michael Field' to 'find Yeats, who spoke intelligently about Ireland and the Irish stage; he brought Synge, whom I liked greatly. He has a kindly, plain, yet attractive face, with human eyes and coarse hair. Synge's face reminds me of Gorki with a touch of Nietzsche. Later in life he may develop a resemblance to Balzac.'

[1] E. D. A. Morshead's abridged translation of Aeschylus' Oresteian Trilogy was produced by the Benson Company at the Stratford-upon-Avon Festival in late April (see previous letter, n. 1). WBY could have attended performances on 3 or 4 May, but probably went to the matinée on Saturday, 30 Apr. Recalling the production later this year, WBY, who was accompanied by AG, complained (*Expl*, 174–5) that he 'could not hear a word of the chorus, except in a few lines here and there which were spoken without musical setting. The chorus was not without dramatic, or rather operatic effect; but why should those singers have taken so much trouble to learn by heart so much of the greatest lyric poetry of Greece? "Twinkle, twinkle, little star", or any other memory of their childhood, would have served their turn. If it had been comic verse, the singing-master and the musician would have respected it, and the audience would have been able to hear.'

week end & go to Stratford for the last performance—I hope you will come
too. I write in a great hurry as I find I shall all but miss the post.

Yrs ever
W B Yeats

I miss you very much for Saturn is afflicting my moon[2] & I am in the
worst spirits & lonely.

ALS Berg, with envelope addressed to Coole, postmark 'LONDON AP 21 04'.

To A. H. Bullen, 24 April 1904

18 Woburn Buildings, | Euston Road.
April 24th.,/04.

My dear Bullen,
    Please send a copy of "The Hour Glass" & one of "The King's Thresh-
old" to
    Geo. Pollexfen Esq.
        Hotel Metropole,
            Charing Cross.
I want you to do this at once as if the books don't go to him to-morrow
morning, they may not reach him as he is shifting about.

Yr snly
W B Yeats

Dict AEFH, signed WBY; Texas.

[2] See p. 576, n. 2.

To John Quinn, 25 April 1904

18 Woburn Buildings, | Euston Road, | London.

April 25ᵗʰ.,/04.

My dear Quinn,

I am dictating this to Miss Horniman having tired my eyes [reading] Honneker's last book which he sent me.[1] I am going to Dublin to-night to see a performance of "The Shadowy Waters," got up for my benefit. It is being given at a conversazione at which "The King's Threshold" is also being performed. This is being done for Stephen Gwynn who was too ill to see it in London. Next month "The Foundations" and "The Rising of the Moon" are to be given, either with a short lecture by me, or with recitations by Mrs Emery to the Psaltery. My sisters have just started work on the Hanrahan Stories. They believe that they will work very quickly, so my not having heard anything from M'Clure becomes serious. He was to have let us know in a few days. Have you heard from him. If even the first two of them could appear in some magazine it would doubtless prevent piracy.[2] I have received what looks like a satisfactory agreement from Macmillan, who proposes to bring out a collected edition of my poems in the Autumn.[3] I am already re-writing "The King's Threshold" and there fore rejoice at the chance of getting my re-written play into print. I have made it much stronger dramatically. I think I told you in my last letter, that Miss Horniman had taken a little theatre for us & that it was being done up, electric light being put in & so forth. It will be quite a charming place. It had a theatrical patent years ago & Miss Horniman has applied for the revival of this patent. We will have no lack of good work for the Autumn. We will have Shaw's play & Synge's three-act play is a master-piece.[4] Bye-the-bye, what did I do about that cheque for £8-10 that I got from "The Independent Review", did I leave it behind me or did I by any possible chance, give it to you to be cashed? My mind is entirely a blank

---

[1] Huneker (see p. 498) would have sent a copy of *Overtones* (1904), a collection of essays on 19th-century writers and composers, of which the chapter on 'Nietzsche the Rhapsodist' might have been of particular interest to WBY. Quinn tried unsuccessfully to persuade Huneker to include a chapter on the Irish theatre in his study of modern dramatists, *Iconoclasts* (1905).

[2] Having failed to place them in the *Gael* (see p. 508, n. 9), Quinn had sold two stories, 'Hanrahan's Vision' and 'Hanrahan's Curse', to *McClure's Magazine* for $100 each, but only the former appeared there, in March 1905. Samuel Sidney McClure (1857–1949), an Irish-born American publisher, had founded *McClure's Magazine* in New York in 1893.

[3] WBY had agreed an 'interminable agreement' with Macmillans (see p. 504), which governed all his subsequent dealings with American publishers.

[4] Frank Fay organized a reading of Synge's three-act play, *The Well of the Saints*, at the Camden Street Theatre on 17 June. Holloway noted (*Abbey Theatre*, 40) that the members of the Society 'listened with breathless attention the while the reader read'.

upon the subject.[5] And how has Jack's Exhibition gone & the performance of "The Hour-Glass"?[6]

Yours sinly
W B Yeats

Dict AEFH, signed WBY; NYPL; with envelope addressed to 120 Broadway, New York, postmark 'LONDON. W AP 25 04'.

To Charles Elkin Mathews, 25 April 1904

18 Woburn Buildings, | Euston Road.
April 25.ᵗʰ,/04,

Dear Mr Matthews,

I send you the proof sheets of "Tables of the Law". I cannot remember if we ever had any formal agreement about it. You may have written to A. P. Watt. I believe my edition with you was not to interfere with my right to incorporate these stories with other stories of mine at some later time.[1]

Yrs sny
W B Yeats

Dict AEFH, signed WBY; Leeds. Marked by recipient 'see L. B. Ap 26 '04'.

[5] Quinn corrected WBY's absent-mindedness with studied patience in a letter of 14 May (NYPL): 'The London check for the article in *The Independent Review* (which as I recall it was six pounds), you will recall I called to your attention the morning you sailed and put it with one or two personal letters and put an elastic around the side and around the end marking the parcel like a London hot-cross bun, and called your attention to the fact that this check was there. You remarked that Lady Gregory would look after your things when you got there and that the check would be all right. If you don't find it among your papers after another search, I would suggest that you at once interview the editor of *The Review* and have him stop payment on the check. It is the only thing to do.'

[6] For Jack Yeats's New York exhibition see p. 564, n. 11. *The Hour-Glass* was produced at the Garrick Theatre on 7 Apr, 'one of a series of performances', as a sardonic review in the *New York Times* of 8 Apr noted (2), 'apparently arranged to display the talents of Miss Josephine Arthur'. Miss Arthur played the Angel, and the *Times*, while acknowledging that there was 'strangeness and fascination in the little play, as there is in everything of Mr. Yeats's', felt that 'its effect yesterday afternoon fell short of the absolute. The fault may have been with the angel, who was lacking in celestial presence, being a very mundane young person, whose hair waved as by tongs, and who stood in a very theatrical limelight. It is more probable, however, that the weakness was inherent in the play.' A programme of the performance is among the Quinn papers (NYPL).

[1] In a letter to Watt of 2 Nov 1903 (see p. 458, n. 1) Mathews had offered terms of '15% on published price counting 13/12—Agreement to hold good till the expiration of the term of the last edⁿ of the 'Poems' published by Fisher Unwin in 1901' [i.e. 1907].

To Lady Augusta Gregory, [26 April 1904]

Nassau Hotel | South Fredrick St

My dear Lady Gregory: I shall return to morrow (wednesday) night. I shall go to bed when I arrive (about eight) but shall be up & wanting a talk about 12 on Thursday. Will you come to me & lunch with me? If not please write to Woburn Build & tell me when I can go to you. It is 6.15 & post goes in a few minutes.

Yrs ev
W B Yeats

ALS Berg, with envelope addressed to 49 George St, Portman Square, London, postmark 'DUBLIN AP 26 04'.

To W. G. Fay, [early May 1904]

18 Woburn Buildings

My dear Fay.

Please send me details to answer enclosed. I see in Belfast News Letter of April 29th that 'Kathleen' & 'Dierdre' have been given by a society called 'The Belfast Branch of the Irish Literary Theatre Society'. It was probably a bad performance & the paper says in criticizing it "it is true that the Dublin branch of this society lately took London by storm & one [*for* won] golden opinions from critics so opposed as Walkley Beerbom & Archer". I did not give leave for Kathleen.[1] What would you think of putting notice in papers to say Kathleen is copyright by Theatre & that leave can be given on conditions? This would enable us to keep some control of title of societies etc & so prevent confusion.

Yours snly
W B Yeats

ALS Harvard. No enclosure.

[1] The two plays were produced by a small troupe of young amateur actors in the Ulster Hall, Belfast, on 28 and 29 Apr. The well-disposed notice in the *Belfast News Letter* (9) praised the audacity of their 'daring experiment', but its comments on the stiffness of the acting, although constructive, suggest that the performances left much to be desired. Its main criticism was levelled at the choice of plays, questioning whether *Deirdre* had sufficient popular appeal to be the main feature of the evening, but observing that *Cathleen ni Houlihan* 'contrasted wonderfully with "Deirdre". Mr. Yeats is a dramatic poet when he likes, A. E. is a poet who would like to be a dramatist.' WBY was particularly sensitive to questions of copyright at this time because of the dispute with the St Louis World Fair. A photograph of a scene from this performance of *Deirdre* appeared with an article by 'Ardrigh' in the *Gael* for June 1904 (236).

To Clement Shorter, [7 May 1904]

18 Woburn Buildings | Euston Road.

Will you be at home to morrow (Sunday) evening? Can you send me a wire.[1]

Yrs
W B Yeats

APS Berg, addressed to 16 Marlborough Place, Marlborough Road, postmark 'LONDON. W. MY 7 04'.

To Dermot Freyer,[1] 7 May [1904]

18 Woburn Buildings | Euston Road
May 7

Dear Mr. Freyer

I am engaged 21st. and 26th.[2]—but if you will give me two or three dates other than these, I think I shall be able to lecture to your club.

[1] WBY presumably wished to discuss Shorter's comments in the *Sphere* of 30 Apr 1904 (116) which accused him and AG of reducing the Irish literary movement to 'a matter of clique or cliques', and deplored their 'inclination to mutual admiration and log-rolling' since it did 'not serve the cause which they both honestly love'. He described WBY's praise of *Cuchulain of Muirthemne* as the greatest book to have come out of Ireland in his time as 'unmitigated nonsense', and pointed out that Eleanor Hull had been publishing Irish mythology 'before Lady Gregory came into the field as had also a number of other enthusiasts for Irish literature and folklore'. Shorter's outburst was apparently prompted by an interview with AG, 'Ireland in Letters', which had appeared in the March number of *Book Monthly*, but since he and WBY were friends, his article was perhaps written tongue-in-cheek, and may even have been engineered between them for its publicity value, since WBY was an old hand at managing such campaigns (see I. 296–300; 430–50). If it was a publicity stunt, it worked, for it attracted the attention of the *Freeman's Journal*, and a columnist in the *Daily News* of 29 Apr (4) suggested that even Shorter would 'agree that log-rolling is no worse than abuse', called attention to WBY's 'magnificent reception' in America, and pointed out that 'certain it is that Mr. Yeats is primarily responsible for the revival of interest in Irish literature, whether that interest is deserved or not. It is he who figures most prominently in the public eye, whose books are most widely read.'

[1] Dermot Johnston Freyer (1883–1970), poet and author of short stories, was the son of a Harley Street surgeon. He read chemistry and physiology at Trinity College, Cambridge, from 1901 to 1905, published his first book of verse, *Rhymes and Vanities*, in 1907, and the following year became one of the earliest members of T. E. Hulme's Poets' Club, contributing to its first publication, *For Christmas MDCCCCVIII*. His second collection of poems, *Sunlit Leaves*, appeared in 1909, followed by *In Lavender Covers* (1912), and *For Christmas and For Easter, Poems* (1915).

[2] WBY's engagement on 21 May is untraced, but on 26th he attended the opening performance of Gilbert Murray's translation of Euripides' *Hippolytus* at the Lyric Theatre, with FF leading the chorus.

I do not think there is any performance of Kathleen-ni-Houlihan coming on now—Some Irish players thought of doing it, but they have gone to S. Louis—What you tell me of your people is very interesting—I have never been at Cleggan, but have spent a good deal of time in South Galway.[3]

Yrs sinly

W B Yeats

Dict AG, signed WBY; Private; with envelope addressed to Trinity College, Cambridge, redirected to 57 Bridge Street, postmark 'LONDON N. MY 7 04'.

To the Editor of the Gael[1] *(New York), 7 May 1904*

London, May 7, 1904.

Dear Sir:—I see in an article in THE GAEL that the holders of the Irish Concession at St. Louis have named their theatre "The Irish National Theatre."

This choice of name is unfortunate, as a certain number of people will confuse it with the original Irish National Theatre, on which I spoke a good deal in my lectures in America. It has no connection with it.

The article states that certain of my plays are to be acted at St. Louis. This is not the case. In accordance with the wish of the Irish National Theatre Society, of which I am president, I, together with others of our playwriters, refused permission.

[3] Freyer's father, Sir Peter Freyer (d. 1921), came from Selerna, west Galway, near the village of Cleggan, and Freyer was later to buy Captain Boycott's family home in Keem, Achill.

[1] In an editorial comment immediately following this letter, the *Gael* came to the defence of the St Louis company:

> It is true the theatre in the Irish section at the St. Louis World's Fair has been named The Irish National Theatre, but we are assured it was so named because of the intention to present there a series of typical Irish plays truly National in spirit and sentiment, and not with any idea of trading on the fame of the original society in Ireland.
>
> The fact that a National Theatre Society has just been formed in Cork indicates that the word national is not considered the exclusive property of any organization, even in Ireland.
>
> We think what Mr. Yeats means to convey is that he does not wish his plays presented to the American public through the medium of the Irish actors now in St. Louis, and does not wish to see their art taken as the standard of art of the original company or society of which he is president.
>
> We sincerely hope Mr. Yeats will reconsider his refusal to permit his plays to be produced at the Fair, as we feel Mr. Myles J. Murphy, a thoroughly competent and experienced manager and director, can be safely intrusted with the arrangements of the cast, the staging of the plays, and their production in a manner that will leave nothing to be desired.

The society does not wish to be identified with any other body of play-ers. I hope America may have an opportunity of seeing their own fine and characteristic work within the next two or three years.

Yours faithfully
W B Yeats

Printed letter, the *Gael* (New York), June 1904 (234). *UP*, II. 329.

To W. G. Fay, 9 May [*1904*]

18 Woburn Buildings | Euston Road
May 9

My dear Fay—

I enclose you a letter which I have received from Quinn—[1]

You can read to the company such parts as you think relevant—I leave the matter entirely in the hands of the company and yourself—I see nothing in the letter to change my opinion. The only thing that makes me a little sorry is that I think Murphy is the man who staged my plays in America—I enclose a letter from him.[2] I dont send

[1] Quinn's letter has not survived, but evidently proposed that the Fays' Company should visit America in September and October. He had first mentioned this in a letter of 26 Jan 1904, telling WBY he had discussed it at dinner with Hanlon, who held the Irish concession at the St Louis World Fair, and with Kelly, Richardson, and Mrs Barker 'who took part in your plays'. Quinn, Richardson, and Mrs Barker had pledged their support: 'The only stumbling block is Kelly, who has some sort of a paper that Gill got up for him, but I think that things will work around so that the company can come over in September and October and then have two or three weeks in New York.'

[2] Myles J. Murphy, general manager of the Irish Industrial Exhibition and director of amuse-ments, was already dissatisfied with the Irish company's performance, and was sceptical about the suitability of AE's *Deirdre* for an audience described by T. W. Rolleston as 'an amazing crowd of Sioux Indians, Western cowboys, Parisian dancing ladies of questionable character, negroes, Moors, Arabs, and miscellaneous holiday makers of every nation tongue and colour'. He had added to the original repertoire a farce called *An Irishman's Stratagem*, given by a local company strengthened by Digges and Miss Quinn, and was now trying to negotiate with the INTS for bet-ter plays. He was apologetic about the misuse of the Society's name, explaining to Quinn on 7 June (NYPL) that he had banned all references to an Irish National Theatre, and adding that it was 'very hard to get a newspaper man to understand that we are not connected with the Dublin project without going into a complete dissertation on the subject of the Quinn and Digges seces-sion. The error in the letter in the newspaper arose from the fact that I described this play as being one written by Mr. George Russell, who was connected with the National Association in Dublin, and which has been played there, for I positively gave no information which would in the least identify this company or this theatre with that of the National Theatre of Dublin'. Murphy was a New York theatre manager and had helped stage WBY's plays for the Irish Literary Soci-ety, New York, in 1903 (see pp. 373, 389).

Kellys[3] letter, as Quinn marked it 'private'—The point of it is that he thinks the players going out will fail, but does not want the Irish Lit Society to help towards their fall—Please wire the decision, tomorrow if possible, as I must write to Quinn—

Yrs snly
W B Yeats

Dict AG, signed WBY; Harvard.

To Clement Shorter, [*10 May 1904*]

18 Woburn Buildings

My dear Shorter: I should have replied before but I have been waiting to hear from some body I had written to before I could know if I am free to morrow. I have not heard but may hear in the morning & so must keep myself free. I am sorry but perhaps you will be in ⟨next Saturday⟩ some other evening.

Yrs ev
W B Yeats

ALCS Berg, addressed to 16 Marlborough Place, Marlborough Road, postmark 'LONDON W MAY 11 1904'.

To the Editor of the Daily News, *11 May 1904*

Sir—I have just seen in your issue of May 4 a letter from my friend, Mr. Clement Shorter, objecting to my description of Lady Gregory's "Cuchulain of Muirthemne" as "the best book that has come out of Ireland in my time".[1]

I have come to agree with him: I withdraw that description; it is no longer true. Her "Gods and Fighting Men" is a better book, containing, as it does, an even greater amount of the heroic foundations of the race.

---

[3] See above, n. 1. Thomas Hughes Kelly (see p. 464, n. 8), Quinn's wealthy friend who promoted WBY's plays for the Irish Literary Society, New York, in June 1903, had an agreement with T. P. Gill about the Digges company and was unwilling to interfere with their enterprise on behalf of the Society.

[1] Shorter had replied to the *Daily News* columnist (see p. 589, n. 1) on 4 May in a letter which justified and amplified his remarks in the *Sphere*. He described WBY's hyperbolic praise of *Cuchulain of Muirthemne* as 'absurd' since it took no account of 'the many great writers, Burke, Goldsmith, Sheridan, and Sterne, and a hundred others of whom England and Ireland may be equally proud', or even of the fact that 'several of those very stories from the Irish language have been translated many times before they were given to us by Lady Gregory'.

All[2] is personal preference in the end, and Mr. Shorter, who is very modern in his interests, naturally prefers Swift, Burke, and Goldsmith, who hardly seem to me to have come out of Ireland at all.[3] I, on the other hand, having found but one thing in Ireland that has stirred me to the roots—a conception of the heroic life come down from the dawn of the world and not even yet utterly extinguished—would give all those great geniuses for the first book that has retold the old epic fragments in a style so full at once of dignity and simplicity and lyric ecstasy, that I can read them with entire delight. And what is it to the point that others have translated these stories into less admirable language? I read them, and they were the chief influence of my youth; but[4] I had to put them into better English as I read. How could one be interested in a hero who "ascended to the apex of an eminence" unless one had reminded oneself that he had but climbed a hill?—

Yours, etc.,
W B Yeats

Printed letter, *Daily News* (London), 11 May 1904 (4). *UP* II. 328.

To John Quinn, 11 May [1904]

18 Woburn Buildings
May 11

My dear Quinn—(re plays)

The moment I got your letter I wrote to Fay[1]—He has all your argument & all Murphys—I simply said that I thought the situation was not changed—I expected to hear from Fay today but I have not, but I got the

---

[2] An undated ALS draft of the rest of this letter (Berg) is substantially the same as the printed version, but has some variation of spelling and punctuation.

[3] Although WBY later came to regard the 18th-century Anglo-Irish writers as central to the Irish tradition, at this period he thought of them as alien influences and, probably with Shorter's remarks in mind, was to assert in *Samhain* later this year (*Expl*, 159) that 'Goldsmith and Sheridan and Burke had become so much a part of English life, were so greatly moulded by the movements that were moulding England, that, despite certain Irish elements that clung about them, we could not think of them as more important to us than any English writer of equal rank. Men told us that we should keep our hold of them, as it were, for they were a part of our glory; but we did not consider our glory very important.' Shorter had mentioned the translations of Eleanor Hull, but WBY had first read the Irish heroic legends in the *Transactions of the Ossianic Society*, in the editions of Standish Hayes O'Grady, and the histories of Standish James O'Grady. Standish Hayes O'Grady's *Silva Gadelica* is particularly weighted with Latinisms (see *E&I*, 512–13).

[4] The Berg draft reads: 'They were great scholars but as I read them . . .'.

[1] See pp. 591–2.

enclosed telegram. I feel the opinion of Fay & the Company must be final
with me, as their whole lives are in this business & must be in it to succeed—I am extremely sorry we had not you & Murphy to deal with on this
side—A straightforward & definite proposal such as that in Murphys letter
would have been dealt with in a much more amicable spirit, and something
probably arranged—The proposals, if they can be so called, made to the
Company in Dublin, did not inspire confidence—following as they did on
the scandalous dropping of the picture project. I enclose a copy of my final
letter to Reardon which I wrote after consultation with Fay[2]—I am very
sorry to cause all this inconvenience, & of course I myself would have been
very glad of the money etc but you see what the circumstances are. The
writing up of our company's name over the door hardly increases one's
confidence in the management—I am particularly sorry at inconveniencing
Murphy who is the Murphy I suppose I met in America—Fay was most
careful in talking to me not to put his objections on the grounds of antagonism to the Digges Company. Had he done so he would have been fully
justified for they would use every success they made to injure us at home.
There would have been no trouble about giving the plays to a purely
American Company—

Now as to money—You have not sent the duplicate cheque £513—so of
course I have done nothing with the one I have. As my total income since
I came back has been £2.13—I am in the somewhat amusing position of
not being able to settle up with my landlady, while feeling such a millionaire as to capital—Your management of my affairs has certainly been
[?]wonderful successful, you got a big price for those 2 little stories & I was
not counting on anything from the Hour Glass—[3]

I have been talking over investments with Lady Gregory—but we have
not come to a fixed conclusion—except that I should like to invest say
£400—I have not been able to explain very clearly your proposal as to
investment—as I know so little about such things. The case is this—I have
never had a penny to invest before. I shall not like to run any risk of losing
what may be my only capital for many years to come—I could not get a
safe investment here at over 4 p c. & that is very little on so small a sum—
I am inclined to rely entirely on your advice—What do you suggest?

The application for a patent for our new theatre, the Abbey Theatre
goes in in a few days—

[*Remainder of letter in WBY's hand*]

Synge's new play—his three act play of peasant life is a masterpeice, but

---

[2] Since WBY's letter of 8 Apr had gone astray (see p. 609), this was probably a copy of the letter to Reardon of the same date (see p. 569).

[3] See above p. 586. Quinn had sent WBY a cheque for $20 from Miss Arthur for her produc-
tion of *The Hour-Glass* (see pp. 586–7, n. 4).

I have not yet got ⟨Hydes⟩ Shaws.[4] I am about to set out on some long drama but am still vacilating about the subject. Lady Gregorys 'King Brian'[5] which she started a fresh a few weeks ago is going to turn out very well I think. I told you I think, that 'On Baile's Strand' has been postponed till we get our new big stage where we should be able to start in September. Our London success this year was far greater than last year.

Yr ev
W B Yeats

My regards to Miss Smith, Miss Coates, Mrs Brown & every body.[6]

Dict AG, signed WBY; NYPL; with envelope addressed in AG's hand to 120 Broadway, New York, and postmark 'LONDON W MAY 11 1904'. Stamped in New York 'MAY 19' and 'DUE 10 CENTS'.

To Dermot Freyer, 11 May [*1904*]

18 Woburn Buildings | Euston Road
May 11

Dear Mr. Freyer

I could lecture June 2nd. (Thursday) if that will suit you—I would arrive that afternoon[1]—My subject will be the Heroic Poetry of Ireland—

It will interest me to see Cambridge as I have never been there—

Yours snly
W B Yeats

Dict AG, signed WBY; Private; with envelope addressed to Trinity College, Cambridge, redirected to 57 Bridge St, postmark 'LONDON W. MY 11 04'.

---

[4] i.e. *The Well of the Saints* and *John Bull's Other Island.*

[5] The early title for AG's three-act historical drama *Kincora*, see p. 529.

[6] Dorothy Coates, who succeeded Ada Smith (see p. 549) as Quinn's mistress, was destined to be the cause of an estrangement between the two men from 1909 to 1914, when Quinn accused WBY of making overtures to her while she was on a European visit. WBY allegedly denied the charge: 'If it had been your wife, yes . . . but your mistress — never!' Mrs Brown was probably Quinn's housekeeper.

[1] It was as well that WBY arranged to lecture late in the day, for on the morning of 2 June he called on his Californian friend James Phelan (see p. 468, n. 9) who was unexpectedly in London. In early September 1904 Gogarty reported to G. K. A. Bell (*Many Lines*, 37–8) that Freyer was 'a Yeatsian. He took Yeats around Cambridge when Yeats appeared there to lecture. . . . He told me amusing things of Yeats at Cambridge.' WBY's lecture is untraced but was probably to the Hibernian Society.

To Annie Horniman, 11 May 1904

34 LOWER CAMDEN STREET, | DUBLIN:
11*th May*, 1904.

[COPY.]

DEAR MISS HORNIMAN,

We, the undersigned members of the Irish National Theatre Company, beg to thank you for the interest you have evinced in the work of the Society and for the aid you propose giving to our future work by securing a permanent Theatre in Abbey Street.

We undertake to abide by all the conditions laid down in your letter to the company, and to do our utmost to forward the objects of the Society.[1]

W. B. YEATS.

F. J. FAY.

WILLIAM G. FAY.

JAMES G. STARKEY.

Pᴘoinᴘιᴀ́ᴘ mᴀc Sιúᴃᴌᴀιᵹ (Frank
    Walker)

ADOLPHUS WRIGHT.[3]

mᴀ́ᴘᵹeᴛ ní ᵹᴀ́ᴘᴃᴀιᵹ (Miss Garvey).

VERA ESPOSITO.

DORA L. AINNESLEY.[4]

GEORGE ROBERTS,

ᴀn Cᴘᴀoιᴃín ᴀoιᴃín (Douglas Hyde).[5]

THOMAS G. KOEHLER.[2]

HARRY F. NORMAN

HELEN S. LAIRD.

GEORGE RUSSELL.

mᴀ́ιᴘe nιc Sιúᴃᴌᴀιᵹ (Miss
    Walker)

J. M. SYNGE.

SARA ALLGOOD.

FREDERICK RYAN.

pᴀ́oᴘᴀιᵹ mᴀcCuιᴌιm (Patrick Colm)

STEPHEN GWYNN.

A[U]GUSTA GREGORY.

Text from *Samhain* (1904), 54.

---

[1] This letter was the INTS's formal reply to AEFH's 'Offer of Theatre' (see pp. 572–3 and Appendix). On 29 July AEFH wrote to George Roberts from Bayreuth, thanking him for sending it on, and adding that the 'delay has not mattered at all. I am anxious that all the members, in the future as well as in the present, should quite understand our artistic aims. I am rather amused at the Irish lettering of some of the names & am much obliged to you for your translations.'

[2] Thomas Goodwin Keohler, later Keller (1874–1942), solicitor, poet and theosophist, had been a member of the Fays' group since 1901. His account of 'The Irish Theatre Movement' appeared in the Dublin *Sunday Independent* in January 1929.

[3] Udolphus ('Dossie') Wright (1887–1952) was introduced into the INTS in 1903 by W. G. Fay, with whom he worked as an electrician. He remained with the Company until his death, as electrician, stage manager, and bit-part actor.

[4] Dora L. Annesley was a Dublin music teacher, who was at this time associated with the INTS, although she seems never to have taken a part. She was to have played one of the Young Kings in *On Baile's Strand* but was dropped.

[5] 'An Craoibhin Aoibhin' (The Pleasant Little Branch) was Hyde's Gaelic pseudonym.

To David Parkhill, 18 May 1904

18, Woburn Buildings, | Euston Road,
May 18, 1904.

[*In WBY's hand*]
Copy of letter
to D Parkhill
of Belfast Society.

[*In TS*]
Dear Sir,
   Mrs. MacBride has sent me a letter of yours on the subject of Kathleen
ni Houlihan.[1] Both the Fay Company and Mrs. McBride were giving leave
for the performance of the play and as this led to a great deal of confusion,
partly through Mrs. McBride being so much out of the country I have had
to make a change. The Fay Company alone now arrange for the performances of my plays. They charge a small fee which is spent on the work of
the Society. All the Plays are copyright. As you performed Kathleen under
a misapprehension I have written to the Secretary asking him to charge you
nothing for your late performance of that play. I am interested in hearing of
your work which may go to very great importance. As it goes on you will
yourselves recognise that some supervision is necessary as to the performance of plays. They would be no use to you or to anyone else if they were
lowered in public estimation by such performances as that of a play of Dr.
Hyde's which I described in a late number of Samhain.[2] Judging by what I
have seen in the papers you have done well, and I am sure that as time goes
on you will find yourselves more and more in sympathy with us in our
endeavour to raise the standard of artistic work in our country.

Yours sny
W B Yeats

TS copy Harvard.

[1] See p. 588. David Parkhill, pseudonym 'Lewis Purcell', had helped Bulmer Hobson
(1883–1969) found an Ulster version of the ILT in 1903. In November 1903 WBY had refused
them permission to produce *Cathleen ni Houlihan*, but they appealed to MG who told them:
'Don't mind Willie. He wrote that play for me and gave it to me. It is mine and you can put it on
whenever you want to' (Sam H. Bell, *The Theatre in Ulster* [1972], 2). This they did, on 20 Nov
1903, but when they revived the production in late April 1904 WBY decided to remind them of
his rights. Irritated by his attitude, the company decided to commission its own plays and to
change its name to the Ulster Literary Theatre. Its first productions under this name took place
on 8 Dec 1904 and the company survived until 1934, producing over 50 new Ulster plays.
[2] In *Samhain* for 1903 (*Expl*, 99) WBY had described the performance of Hyde's *Cleamhnas* at
the Galway Feis as 'the worst I ever saw. I do not blame the acting, which was pleasant and natural, in spite of insufficient rehearsal, but the stage-management.'

To George Roberts, [*18 May 1904*]

18, Woburn Buildings,

My dear Roberts,

I have had a mass of correspondence sent me by Mrs Mac Bride concerning the Belfast people. I needn't trouble you with the details of it, but you will presently see a letter of mine in the paper.[1] I did not consider it necessary to submit the letter to the Society as it only concerned my own plays and an arrangement which you had already agreed upon. Kathleen is now in the hands of the Society again, I have withdrawn the permission to give leave for its performance from the President of the Daughters of Erin. I have written to this effect to a member of the Belfast Society, a letter from whom was sent on to me. I enclose copy of my letter ⟨I am not quite sure how far this correspondence is private and so I do not send copies.⟩ I want you to ask no fee for Kathleen ni Houlihan from the Belfast people. They performed it during the old state of things when Mrs. McBride had a right to give permission and gave it without charging anything to anybody who asked. We can charge a small fee for any future performances. What fee are you asking? I think it would be extremely wise to charge Cumann na Gael and the Gaelic League a quite nominal fee perhaps not more that 10/-. I mean, of course, when their performance does not directly interfere with performances of our own in which case we would refuse altogether. I think this is important and that the Society should pass some such resolution at once. I am not particular about the amount charged but I think that it should be half the ordinary rate, whatever that is. I am anxious for this in order to forestall any attack on us from the point of view that we are hostile to national societies. It is important that nobody should say we have decided upon charging a fee specially as a protection against national societies. In the case of the affiliation of a Society with us we might further reduce the fee or even abolish it in the case of all plays, this is a matter, however, for the consideration of the Society itself, affiliation or no affiliation we should, however, have the right to withhold permission in the case of any particular play. The great point for the moment is to be cautious and friendly in whatever we do for we want to have all these young men friendly to us and trusting us. You mention in your letter, or perhaps it was Fay mentions it in his that you were rehearsing again. I suggest that you do not definitely decide upon accepting any particular new play until we have a good many manuscripts and can consult together and arrange a programme for the winter as a whole. Another

---

[1] An unsigned letter to the *United Irishman* on 4 June; see pp. 603-4.

six weeks or so should bring us Bernard Shaw's play and Lady Gregory's three act play about King Brian should be ready in about the same time and I suppose Synge's play will be ready almost at once. In addition to these plays I have a play to suggest but cannot speak of it for two or three weeks.[2] I don't think we should definitely accept William Boyle's play[3] for instance, till we can consult together on the general programme. When we have a lot of plays before us we can pick out the best of them. We must make no mistakes this coming winter, for the whole future of the adventure may hang on the first months in the new theatre. Last winter we made serious mistakes, it may have been right to perform the Shadowy Waters, for instance, or Dierdre and I am sure it was right to perform Colms play. And 'the Townland of Tamney' seems to have amused some people but I am sure that having played anything so literary ⟨as⟩ any one of the first three of these plays we should have followed it by some lively play full of comedy or action. This is what I mean by considering our programme as a whole. I wish you would send me William Boyle's address. He shows a considerable capacity for dialogue and yet other parts of his play are very conventional. I want to have a talk with him about it. If I can get one or two obvious things into his head he will be quite a useful man.[4] You might show this letter to William Fay and the part that concerns the Company to the Company. If you could manage only formal business at the Annual Meeting I won't go over for it, but if matters of importance arise I shall have to do my best to go and it will be very inconvenient. I don't think we can decide anything very important wisely until we know when the new theatre will be ready, what plays we are getting and so forth. I think we should keep the number of vice-presidents very small for the present at any rate, but certainly it will be a well deserved compliment to add the names of Stephen Gwynn and Lady Gregory as you suggest. By the bye I

[2] This was his play *Deirdre*, which he began this summer but which was not produced until 1906.

[3] On 28 Apr William Boyle (1853–1923), playwright and excise officer, had submitted a three-act comedy, *The Building Fund*. It had come before the Reading Committee (Synge, Colum, and the Fays) on 6 May, when it was decided to submit it to AE and WBY for further consideration. It was eventually produced at the Abbey Theatre on 25 Apr 1905. Although WBY disliked Boyle's work, his three plays, including *The Eloquent Dempsey* and *The Mineral Workers*, both produced in 1906, were extremely popular at the Abbey. Boyle withdrew them after the *Playboy* riots in 1907, but he returned to the Theatre in 1912.

[4] Roberts evidently sent WBY the address (he was living in Grove Lane, Denmark Hill, London), for the two met at the ILS on 28 May, and Boyle reported to D. J. O'Donoghue (Hogan & Kilroy, II. 118–19) that WBY had been 'very complimentary of its general merits but says in his opinion the love business should be cut out of it in toto. . . . The fact seems to be the actor likes to give the public what it wants and the poets what *they* want the public to want. Honestly I must say from the point of truth . . . I believe Yeats is right. . . . Yeats was good enough to say that if I only stuck close to nature I could write little masterpieces, and if I make the little change he mentioned the play would be produced at once.'

think Lady Gregorys 'Kincora' is going on finely. I had some talk with Shaw about his play. That it will be amusing is certain, but whether it will be possible or not I don't know. It probably will for Mrs. Shaw is doing her best to keep him off dangerous subjects. We can't count absolutely on its suiting us, however. Tell Fay that I am afraid the expedition over here to play the Pot of Broth for that big theatrical charity will fall through.[5] Craig, impetuous as ever, had forgotten the payment of expenses of people coming from a distance was unusual for the organisers of the thing. They want somebody to give the money and I don't know who to ask as our own people have all seen the play. I will talk to Stephen Gwynn to night and let you know if anything comes of it.

Yr sny
W B Yeats

[*In WBY's hand*]
PS. Gwynn will I think do this summer a play with Emmett as one of the persons.[6] Miss Mcmanus & Shore have also one in 3 Acts.[7]

TLS Harvard.

[5] See p. 571, n. 3. A theatrical garden party in aid of the Actors Orphanage Fund was held in the Royal Botanical Garden, Regent's Park on 8 July 1904. The event, which was patronized by the Prince and Princess of Wales, included non-stop performances of orchestras, bands, melodrama, pastoral plays, and performing goats, as well as a cricket match between teams of actors and actresses, but not *The Pot of Broth.*

[6] WBY commented unfavourably on the play and rejected it for the Abbey Theatre in a letter to Gwynn of 30 July 1905. It was never performed or published, but Gwynn recast it as a historical novel which appeared as *Robert Emmet* in 1909.

[7] Charlotte Elizabeth ('Lily') MacManus (1853–1944), a prolific Irish historical novelist living in Killeaden, Kiltimagh, Co. Mayo, was a member of the National Literary Society, and had first seen WBY on 13 Apr 1898 at a '98 Banquet at the Holborn Restaurant. She contributed stories to the *Celtic Christmas* 1902–4 and a regular column entitled 'Seanchus' to the *Irish Emerald*, treating various aspects of Irish culture from a Gaelic League point of view. Before her conversion to Irish nationalism she had collaborated on a play with W. Teignmouth Shore (1866–1932), editor of the *Academy*, which, as she explains in her memoir, *White Light and Flame* (1929, p. 4), had started life as a short story: 'My hero was an Englishman, a trooper; the bad character a Fenian. I am thankful to say this story was never published. I sent it to Cassell & Co., whose reader, struck with the plot, wrote offering to write a play founded upon it in collaboration with me after the manuscript had been returned. This was Mr. Teignmouth Shore. I had an interview with him and the play was written. I am glad to say it came to nothing. A year later I burnt the manuscript.' Although none of her plays was staged at the Abbey Theatre, her *O'Donnell's Cross* was produced at the Rotunda in 1907 by the National Players. On 22 Mar 1904 Shore had played Father Hart in the Chelsea Mummers' production of *The Land of Heart's Desire* at 133 Queen's Gate, London.

To George Roberts, [c. *23 May 1904*]

18 Woburn Buildings | Euston Road.

My dear ⟨Griffith⟩ Roberts: I have been asked to say if I as a member of the reading Committee approve of Mr Colum's miracle play[1] being read to the company for their approval. I understand that certain corrections have been made, & that the miracle of the corn is now prepared for I certainly do approve. It should be a most admirable little play now that its one or two defects are put right & I shall look forward to it very much indeed. Colum always sees life dramatically and I think profoundly. Too many of our people seem content to but keep to the border of the wood, as though the depths were unholy.

I shall be over towards the end of June. Lady Gregory wanted Harringtons, not the Lord Mayors address,[2] she has however sent her letter to Fay to forward if he thinks fit.

I sent a copy of the letter of mine about the copyright of plays to the UI but they have not put it in. I am writing for an explination.

Yr sny

W B Yeats

It has just occurred to me the letter was probably excluded from UI through early printing because of holidays.[3]

ALS Harvard.

---

[1] Padraic Colum's one-act play, *The Miracle of the Corn,*—in which a miser's wife distributes his corn among her hungry neighbours, and then discovers that it has been miraculously restored—was published in the *United Irishman* on 9 Apr 1904. In spite of WBY's support and its recommendation by the Reading Committee, it was never performed by the INTS, but first produced (at the Abbey Theatre) on 22 May 1908 by Edward Martyn's Theatre of Ireland.

[2] The Rt. Hon. Timothy 'Tim' Charles Harrington (1851–1910), Parnellite, barrister, and MP for the Harbour Division of Dublin since 1885, had been Lord Mayor of Dublin 1901–2. The founder and editor of the *Kerry Sentinel*, he had been an architect of the Plan of Campaign in 1886, a Counsel for Parnell during the Parnell Commission of 1888–9, and was to become a member of the first Committee for the Municipal Gallery when the Corporation of Dublin passed a unanimous resolution in support of it in March 1905. Harrington had long been interested in the Irish drama, and in 1898 helped amend the law governing Dublin theatrical patents, so making the ILT possible. AG probably wanted to contact him to enlist his support in the Abbey Patent hearing, and was evidently successful for he appeared on behalf of the Theatre on 4 Aug, when, as the *Irish Times* reported on 5 Aug (3), he 'stated that he thought the Literary Society had done a great deal of good, but they were very much hampered by not having a proper place. It would not in any way interfere with the existing theatres.'

[3] The Whitsun bank holiday lasted from 21 to 23 May.

To Arthur Griffith, [c. *23 May 1904*]

Mention in previous letter.

To Gordon Bottomley, 1 June [*1904*]

18 Woburn Buildings | Euston Road
June 1

Dear Mr. Bottomley
  I shall be delighted to see you next Monday evening, any time after
8.^{00}—or the Monday after—you came too soon the other day—I was out.
My housekeeper merely knew that I had people coming & I suppose didnt
like to invite you on her own responsibility. Forgive my delay in answering—but I have had a great stream of letters—

Yrs snly
W B Yeats

Dict AG, signed WBY; Private.

To James D. Phelan, [*2 June 1904*]

⟨CARLTON HOTEL, | PALL MALL, | LONDON.⟩
18 Woburn Buildings | Upper Woburn Place.

My dear Phelan:[1] I am sorry to miss you. When can I find you in. I could
call any time to-morrow morning after (say) 11. I am engaged in the afternoon & evening. If I cannot see you to morrow can I call on Saturday
afternoon but that seems a devil of a time off.

Yr Snly
W B Yeats

I heard you were in London & have enquired at the Savoy & the Cecil.

ALS Private.

---

[1] See p. 595.

To Lady Augusta Gregory, [*2 June 1904*]

18 Woburn Buildings

My dear Lady Gregory: Phelan goes out of town to-morrow. He asks me if I can be at hotel at 1. He has to be in city all morning but will try & get back then. He is to telephone to hotel. If I see him I will not get to you for lunch. Let us meet at the box office of the lyric Theatre about 2.40 or 2.45. Do not take a ticket as I will try & change my 7/6 ticket for two 5/- seats.[1]

George Moore was at Symons' last night. He refused to shake hands & walked out of the room without a word. He had no time to think & was left to his natural impulses which are bad. Symons went to the door with him & thought that he seemed undecided. Mrs Symons was furious.[2]

I am off to see Granville Barker about cast.

Yrs ev

W B Yeats

I find I left ticket for play at George St. Please look for it & bring it with you. I hope it is not lost.

ALS Berg, with envelope addressed to 10 York St, Baker St,[3] marked 'EXPRESS', and postmark 'CENTRAL DISTRICT JU 2 04'. Partly in Wade, 435.

To the Editor of the United Irishman, *4 June 1904*

Mr. Yeats sends us the following:—

Some confusion has arisen about the right to perform my plays. Some societies wishing to act them have written to the Secretary of the Irish National Theatre Society, one has written to the Editor of a newspaper,

---

[1] WBY and Lady Gregory attended the last of a series of matinée performances of Gilbert Murray's translation of Euripides' *Hippolytus* which were given from 26 May to 3 June. The production was directed by Granville-Barker, who was also to direct WBY's *Where There Is Nothing* for the Stage Society later in the month. WBY had also been at the opening performance.

[2] WBY recounted this incident to Quinn in October of this year (*MNY*, 25–6), saying that when he held out his hand 'G. M. bolted straight for the door and went home although it was immediately after dinner'. WBY went on to say that Moore 'was a brute saved by intellect, that he had a magnificent mind, that his only emotions were all bad but that his mind when he had a chance to think before he acted saved him. That he had many good qualities and would do many kind things and especially if a thing appealed to his intellect or artistic conscience he was capable of great generosity and kindness . . .' (see p. 228, n. 2.)

[3] A temporary address: AG's seventh-floor flat was in Queen Anne Mansions in St James Park.

one or two have performed them without writing to anybody. It will spare me and others some correspondence if you will allow me to say that all my plays are copyright, but that the National Theatre Society can give leave for their performance when it seems advisable, and on payment of a small fee towards the work of the society.

[*Unsigned*]

Printed letter, *United Irishman*, 4 June 1904 (3). *UP* II. 329.

To Norman McKinnel,[1] *13 June* [*1904*]

18 Woburn Buildings | Euston Road
June 13

Dear Mr. McKinnel—

Please excuse my delay in answering—I have been very busy—'Where there is Nothing' has been licensed—I have made alterations in it since then—but have added nothing that the Censor could object to—[2]

There is no 'National Theatre Society' over here—It consists only of the actors & some play writers—all living in Ireland—But the Irish Literary Society, 20 Hanover Square, might be useful in distributing advertisements to its members I will ask the Sec. to find you a list—

We had circulars of the Irish plays distributed at the door of the Court Theatre at your matinees—by boy messengers, at a very small cost—I daresay it would be worth doing this at such matinees as 'Venice Preserved'.[3]

Lady Gregory (10 York St, Portman Square,) looked after this part of the business, & would help us in any way—but you have probably your own system of circularising—

Yrs sincerely
W B Yeats

Dict AG, signed WBY; Private.

[1] Norman McKinnel (1870–1932), an accomplished Scots actor and director, appeared frequently on the London stage from 1895 to 1929. He had played the Revd James Morell in Shaw's *Candida* at the Court Theatre from 26 April to 10 May 1904 and was to act there regularly until 1907. He had recently succeeded Aubrey Smith as Secretary of the Stage Society and was later to become Chairman of the Actors' Association.

[2] *Where There Is Nothing* and *The Hour-Glass* were read for licensing on 20 Oct 1902 (see p. 245, n. 6).

[3] Thomas Otway's *Venice Preserved* (1682) was produced by the Otway Society for three matinée performances at the Royalty Theatre, 13–16 June.

To H. Granville-Barker, [*14 June 1904*]

18 Woburn Buildings
Tuesday

My dear Barker

I and my friends will guarantee the £20 you asked for, if the Society loses by the performance & should you not be able to reduce the expenses—[1]

I heard last night that Miss Craig was to arrive in London today—Miss Pixie Smith had heard this—Would she not be of use to us?—

It would cause some delay to get the Committee of the Irish Literary Society together, but I may get them to take some tickets—

Let me know final decision at once—

Yr sny
W B Yeats

Dict AG, signed WBY; Private.

To Holbrook Jackson,[1] *16 June* [*1904*]

18 Woburn Buildings | London
June 16

Dear Sir—

I must refer you to my publisher Mr. T. Fisher Unwin with whom I leave such matters—I have personally no objection—I believe my publisher makes some small charge.

Yrs sinly
W B Yeats

Dict AG, signed WBY; UCLA.

[1] The production of *Where There Is Nothing* by the Stage Society had run into financial difficulties, but was in fact staged from 26 to 28 June. It attracted mixed notices, and the *Sketch* of 6 July 1904 (412), observing that the play 'acts better than it reads, yet a good deal of it acts very badly', reported that WBY made a short speech at the end of the performance to explain its moral: 'he stated he had noticed that the Irish were very rich in patron saints, but there was none for the spirit of Mischief. Apparently, we were asked to assume that Mischief is the patron saint of the play and moving spirit of the author; so one must explain the hero's vagaries by the idea that he is suffering from a mania for destruction . . . of conventional ideas concerning social life in the first three Acts, and religion during the other two.' The reviewer added that the 'desire to go out "on the road" seems to haunt modern Irish drama, and may be taken as a symbolical expression of a national dislike for conventional life'.

[1] Holbrook Jackson (1874–1948) was an editor, biographer, and author of *The Eighteen Nineties* (1913), where he describes WBY (184) as 'the fullest expression of the intellectual Celt—poet,

To the Treasurer of the Stage Society, 18 June 1904

TO THE HONORARY TREASURER,
THE STAGE SOCIETY.

Dear Sir,

In order that the production of "Where there is Nothing" may be rendered financially possible to your Society, I am willing to purchase Tickets for the Matinees on 27th. and 28th.[1] June to the amount of twenty pounds, and I authorise you to dispose of these Tickets on my behalf in the usual way. On receiving your statement of the proceeds of the Tickets so disposed of I shall remit you whatever amount may be required to bring the total sale up to twenty pounds.

Yours faithfully,
W B Yeats

TLS Private. Dated in another hand '18th June 1904'.

To F. J. Fay, [19 June 1904]

18 Woburn Buildings | Euston Road.

My dear Fay: I enclose the particulars you ask for, from todays Observer.[1] 'Where there is Nothing' is to be on Sunday—& matinees Monday & Tuesday. I shall be able to talk over several things if you come over.

Yrs sny
W B Yeats

ALS Private.

mystic and patriot—expressing himself in an imaginative propaganda which has affected the thoughts and won the appreciation of the English-speaking world'. Jackson was seeking permission to publish WBY's 'A Fairy Song' and 'The Lake Isle of Innisfree' in his anthology for children, *Everychild* (Leeds, 1905), compiled 'with the idea of appealing to the capacity for wonder and delight in the things of daily life, and the more real things of the imagination, which forms a large part of the temperament of children'.

[1] W. Hector Thomson had been Treasurer of the Stage Society since 1900.

[1] Fay was going to London to see *Where There Is Nothing* and, as an enthusiastic student of French drama, would have been excited by the *Observer*'s announcements that two of his favourite French actresses would be appearing in London during his visit, Madame Gabrielle Réju Réjane (1857–1920) at the Prince of Wales and Sarah Bernhardt (1845–1923) at Her Majesty's Theatre. He would also have been interested in the review (5) of Felix Riche's production of Romain Coolus's *Antoinette Sabrier* and Tristan Bernard's *Les Coteaux du Medoc* at the Avenue Theatre. While in London Fay took the opportunity of seeing his hero, Andre Antoine (see p. 341, n. 5), whom Madame Réjane had brought over to play Lafont to her Clotilde in Henri Becque's naturalist play, *La Parisienne* (1885). Recording his attendance at *Where There Is Nothing* on 27 July, Ricketts mentioned (*SP*, 109) that he 'met Fay the Irish actor, who had to return

To George Bernard Shaw, [c. *19 June 1904*]

Mention in letter from Shaw, 20 June 1904.
Asking Shaw if he is back in London, and how he is progressing with his play for the INTS.[1]

Private.

To George P. Brett, 21 June 1904

18, Woburn Buildings, | Euston Road, N. W
June 21, 1904.

Dear Mr. Brett,

I hope you will forgive my vacillating over the arrangements for my books.[1] In the matter that concerns one's arrangements for a lifetime one cannot make up one's mind in a hurry, especially when one is as unfamiliar with business as I am. I have come to the conclusion that it would be best for me to publish with you in the autumn a collected edition of my poems up to date without, however, signing any agreements in relation to the future. I would want you to publish this book on the terms proposed in the draft agreement. That is to say, 10% at once and 15% after the number of sales specified 5,000. It is obvious that it is so much against my interest to scatter my books that I shall in all likelihood send you my future books. This arrangement is simpler than the one proposed in the Agreement for one thing I don't think that the proposal that you surrender past books at a price settled by mutual agreement would amount to much. It would be too easy for us to fall out over the price. Nor do I think it advisable for me to

to Ireland that night not to miss his berth of thirty-five shillings a week. I spoke to him only for a few minutes outside the theatre about Réjane and Antoine.' On 30 June Fay told Maire Garvey (NLI) that he had been 'somewhat disappointed' by Antoine, and that he had not liked *Where There Is Nothing*, but that 'Lady Gregory and W. B. were kindness personified' and introduced him to Symons, Ricketts, Shannon, Edith Craig, Granville-Barker, and John Todhunter. He saw the exhibition of Irish paintings at the Guildhall (see p. 564, n. 10) 'in company with W. B. &— who do you think?—Mrs MacBride. She was grimly gracious. I was ditto' (see pp. 310, 428–9).

[1] In his reply Shaw said he was back, but that had not yet written a word of the play (see p. 571, n. 3). Under a sketch of his head with steam rising from its open lid, he wrote: 'Seething in the brain. I have been abroad for more than a month & letters & business have accumulated frightfully. When I have cleared these, the play will start.' In fact Shaw had begun to draft the play at Hindhead on 17 June (Texas), and finished the first version (provisionally entitled *Rule Britannia*) on 23 Aug. On 31 Aug he enquired (*BSCL* II. 452) whether the new theatre boasted modern machinery to manage awkward scene changes in the second and fourth acts, since 'as you will deal in fairy plays you may have indulged yourself with hydraulic bridges'.

[1] See pp. 504, 512, 554–8.

absolutely pledge all my future work as it would be pledged by Clause 11 of the Draft Agreement. I am in communication with John Lane thro A. P. Watt in order to get some work of mine out of his hands for purpose of this collected edition.[2] May I say in conclusion, or rather repeat that I see every likelihood of my going on sending you my books. I do not want to bind myself but apart from that I am quite satisfied with you as my publisher.

Yrs sny
W B Yeats

My address after this week will be
    C/o Lady Gregory
        Coole Park
            Gort, co. Galway
                Ireland.
I shall be there until the autumn.

TLS NYPL.

To S. C. Cockerell, [21 June 1904]

18 Woburn Buildings | Euston Road.

My dear Cockerell: Yes do make the enquiries for me. It is an affair of some importance, & I dont know Charles Rowley.[1]

Yrs ever
W B Yeats

ALCS Texas, addressed to 16 Cliffords Inn, Fleet St, London, postmark 'LONDON JU 21 04'.

---

[2] i.e. *The Wind Among the Reeds*; see pp. 550–1.

[1] Charles Rowley (1839–1933), Manchester civic leader, social reformer, and art critic, was Chairman of the Municipal School of Art and an intimate friend of William Morris, Walter Crane, Ford Madox Brown, the Rossettis, and other members of the Pre-Raphaelite Brotherhood, many of whose paintings he secured for the Manchester Art Gallery and Town Hall. WBY had recently attended an informal meeting to discuss Hugh Lane's winter exhibition of contemporary French paintings in Dublin, intended to form the nucleus of a Gallery of Modern Art, and probably wanted to consult such a successful entrepreneur in artistic matters about the best way of establishing provincial galleries.

To Douglas Hyde, [c. *22 June 1904*]

Mention in following letter.
Sending on a letter from Dr Charles Murray's relations.

To John Quinn, 22 June 1904

18, Woburn Buildings, | Euston Rd.
June 22, 1904.

My dear Quinn,

I got back from the Dead Letter Office a long letter which I wrote to you some months ago.[1] I addressed it to 20, Broadway by mistake. It is all ancient history now but I send it on to you to show that I have not forgotten you, because there may be some detail in it new to you. Everything has fallen out at St. Louis exactly as we foresaw except that Miss Quinn's talent for mak[ing] demonstrations has found an opportunity we did not foresee. The Dublin papers have got the story now and in the process of crossing the Atlantic it has enlarged itself into Digs [*for* Digges] knocking the piper down before an applauding audience.[2] I don't think that as things are at present that our theatre should make any statement, and I don't feel inclined to write to the papers unless the occasion arises for correcting some matter of fact. I shall act very much as Fay wants me to and I have

---

[1] Probably that of 8 Apr 1904 (see p. 594). Quinn's address was 120 Broadway.

[2] The members of the Irish company were affronted when Patrick Tuohy, a New York actor celebrated for his piping and for his caricature of the 'Bowery' Irishman, was included on the same programme as their production of *Deirdre*, and Digges boiled over when he heard Tuohy sing 'It Takes the Irish to Beat the Dutch'. He and Maire Quinn refused to perform their play and when he complained to the stage-manager, Luke Martin, there was a fracas during which, according to the report in the *Gaelic American* for 11 June (5), 'Martin grabbed him and jerked him aside. Digges claims that Martin assaulted him. Martin claims he simply brushed him aside. Digges quit the theatre forthwith. . . . The management ordered both to remain away from the Irish village and cancelled their contracts. The rest received two weeks notice.' Rolleston believed that Quinn and Digges, realizing they were about to be fired for incompetence, decided to go out with a bang, and on grounds which would have the savour of a nationalist demonstration. In this they were successful: their cause was espoused by Irish-American papers in New York and by the nationalist press in Dublin (see especially the *United Irishman* of 9 July 1904, p. 5), and, largely owing to the intervention of John MacBride, the row dragged on for a month.

not heard from him since sending the duplicates of Murphy's letter and the other letter.[3] It has obviously done us all a great injury. The lease is not yet signed for the theatre Miss Horniman is buying. All kinds of difficulties have arisen but I believe it is to be settled next week. I have seen the plans for alteration and they will make it a thoroughly comfortable and efficient little theatre. It has an excellent stage quite large enough for all our purposes. The Company has just begun to rehearse Synge's new play and are very delighted with it. It is in three acts and full of wild humour wavering over a deep pit of tragedy. A really astonishing play one of the masterpieces of our time as I think. We are to open with it but with all these delays can hardly hope to get started before the end of November. The Twisting of the Rope has been put into Highland Gaelic and played together with the Pot of Broth in English at a great Highland celebration at Oban.[4] This is probably the beginning of quite a new development of the Movement. They propose to do Catherine [*for* Cathleen] ni Houlihan next year and some play in Scottish Gaelic. I hope that in the long run our Company will be able to travel about to these various centres of Gaelic life. By the bye an amusing and rather irritating thing has happened. I got a letter from Dublin the other day directed to Mr. W. B. Yeats, Esq. It was rather ungrammatical and misspelt and told me that the brother of the writer a certain Dr. Charles Murray who died in California shortly after I lectured there left his money to Dr. Douglas Hyde and myself to be expended upon Gaelic propaganda. The writer of the letter, however, assures me that he was not in his right mind and in order to prove this says that when he made his will he had forgotten the fact that he had a brother and a sister who needed the money. I foresee that whatever happens I shall make a fine crop of enemies, either Dr. Charles Murray's Dublin relations or the Gaelic League. I have sent the letter on to Hyde and shall try and

[3] Quinn had sent WBY an account of two St Louis letters (NYPL) he had lately received, from Myles J. Murphy, director of amusements for the Irish Exhibition, and from T. W. Rolleston. Murphy's letter, of 7 June, apologized for the erroneous association of the Digges company with Yeats and the INTS (see p. 590, n. 1), while that from Rolleston, on 3 June, gave a full account of the Quinn–Digges row. In a further letter, dated 8 June, Rolleston commented: 'They will never get any good, either in acting or anything else, out of Miss Quinn, who is a perfect vixen . . .'.

[4] Alexander Carmichael, President of the Celtic Union, had arranged for the production of Hyde's and WBY's plays at the Mòd Dhuneideann, held in the Philosophical Institution, Edinburgh (not Oban), on 27 May. WBY probably confused the venue because he had read of the event in the *Oban Express*, which on 1 June (5) reported that Hyde's play, specially translated into Scottish Gaelic, had been performed for an audience with standing room only by 'ladies and gentlemen connected with the Gaelic classes'. The acting of *The Pot of Broth* was 'highly creditable and greatly enjoyed'.

leave as much responsibility with him as I can, for after all, the Gaelic Leaguers are his brooded chickens and not mine.[5]

We are busy rehearsing "Where There is Nothing". I think it is going to be quite well played.

Yrs sny
W B Yeats

[*In WBY's hand*]
write to me at
   Coole Park
      after this—Lady Gregory & I myself thank you for the International Quarterly[6]

TLS NYPL.

To W. Graham Robertson,[1] *22 June 1904*

18, Woburn Buildings, | Euston Road,
June 22, 1904.

Dear Mr. Robertson,
   Many thanks for your invitation. If I am in London I will certainly go to you on the 30th, but there is a chance that I may go to Ireland next week.

Yrs sny
W B Yeats

TLS Huntington, with envelope addressed to William G. Robertson, 23 Rutland Gate, S.W., postmark 'LONDON. W JU 22 04'.

[5] Dr Charles Hugh Murray, was born in Donegal, and had graduated from the College of Physicians and Surgeons, Edinburgh, in 1889. After practising in Scotland, he moved to Portrush, Co. Antrim, and joined the Anchor Line as ship's surgeon. In 1900 he was licensed as medical practitioner in California and had offices at 2119 Hyde St., San Francisco. Rumours circulating in Dublin about the amount of the bequest turned out to be greatly exaggerated.

[6] The final issue of the *International Quarterly* (Dec–Mar 1903–4) contained an article on 'The Symbolical Drama' by Emile Faguet (329–41). In seeking to define authentic 'dramatic symbolism', Faguet contrasted Ibsen with Maeterlinck, concluding that 'Ibsen is the only dramatic poet to write symbolic dramas'.

[1] Walford (whom WBY erroneously addresses as 'William') Graham Robertson (1866–1948) was an artist, illustrator, author, and leading collector of the paintings of William Blake. He added numerous reproductions of Blake's drawings to his 1-volume edition of Gilchrist's *Life of William Blake* (1907), and he later wrote the notes for *The Blake Collection of W. Graham Robertson*, ed. Kerrison Preston (1952). In *Time Was* (1931) he reminisces (18) about a meeting with WBY, who 'seemed to have a way with Ghosts and Spirits, and under his kindly sway they dropped many of their ill-bred tricks and showed (occasionally) quite ordinary intelligence'.

To Cornelius Weygandt, 22 June 1904

18, Woburn Buildings, | Euston Road,
June 22, 1904.

Dear Mr. Weygandt,

I have been a very long time about thanking you for the article. It was very good of you to write out those impressions of me in the midst of the woods and by the water that I love the best.[1] I am going there again at the end of next week and hope to begin another play in verse. A friend is buying for us a little theatre in Dublin so that our Company may have a house of its own, and we are going to start there with a really wonderful Peasant Comedy by J. M. Synge. I don't know whether you have seen Synge's work. He has only published one little play up to this and that not his best. He will publish a volume of three short plays in the autumn.[2] Please don't think we have anything to do with the Irish company that has gone to the St. Louis Exhibition. They are a little company partly made up by secessions from us & are rather more politicians than players. One or two of them were quite good when we had them but I doubt their being much good without the Fays to stage manage. We were all rather angry at their going to St. Louis as they have no plays which are even tolerable. We could have gone there but for one thing the work at home needed all our energies.

Yrs sinly
W B Yeats

TLS Private.

To an unidentified correspondent, 22 June 1904

18, Woburn Buildings, | Euston Rd.
June 22, 1904.

Dear Sir,

I am afraid I have left your note a very long time without an answer, but I have bad sight, and have to answer my letters through an amanuensis,

---

[1] Weygandt's 'With Mr. W. B. Yeats in the Woods of Coole' had appeared in *Lippincott's Magazine* for April 1904 (see p. 216, n. 1).

[2] *Riders to the Sea* had appeared in the 1903 *Samhain*, and Synge was now negotiating with Elkin Mathews to republish it in the Vigo Cabinet Series with *The Tinker's Wedding* and *In the Shadow of the Glen*. Mathews, however, decided that inclusion of *The Tinker's Wedding* would make the volume too large, and the play was not published until 1907.

and some times I let them accumulate for a long time and answer them in batches. In this way a letter gets sometimes forgotten. I think I have answered and I have not. I cannot make any arrangements for lectures at present as work connected with our Irish Dramatic Movement may make it necessary for me to be a great deal in Dublin during the coming autumn and winter.

Yrs sny
W B Yeats

TLS Washington.

To Prince Peter Alexeievitch Kropotkin, [c. 23 June 1904]

Mention in letter from Kropotkin, 5 July 1904.
Inviting Kropotkin to his 'Monday Evening' on 27 June, and telling him of the production of *Where There Is Nothing*.[1]

Anne Yeats.

To Violet Hunt, [27 June 1904]

18 Woburn Buildings | Euston Road | London.
Monday.

Dear Miss Violet Hunt: I shall come on Tuesday July 5th with pleasure. I hope you will excuse my delay in answering but I have been drowned in a sea of theatre business.

Yrs sny
W B Yeats

Excuse half sheet. I find I had taken a sheet with another letter on the back.

ALS Berg.

[1] WBY had based Paul Ruttledge, the hero of *Where There Is Nothing*, partly on the writings of Prince Kropotkin, the syndico-anarchist (see p. 448, n. 5), whom he had first met at William Morris's house and who was now living in Bromley, Kent. Kropotkin, described by George Bernard Shaw as 'amiable to the point of saintliness', and 'with his red full beard and loveable expression' resembling 'a shepherd from the Delectable Mountains', was a follower of Bakunin rather than Marx, and a *narodnik*, a believer in decentralization and the 'back to the people' movement. But, as he explained in his letter of 5 July, he was unable to attend WBY's Monday evening as he 'was going that same day to Brussels' to see his great friend and fellow-anarchist Jacques Elisée Reclus (1830–1905), who was dangerously ill. He added: 'I need not say how interested I am in your play. Are you going to publish it? It would be such a pleasure to *read* it but I hope it will be played soon once more.'

To Lady Augusta Gregory, [*1 July 1904*]

18 Woburn Buildings | Euston Road.

My dear Lady Gregory: I send a proof which my sister wants back by Monday. There is little news of any kind—I am just off to see the Maeterlinck with Sarah Bernhart & Mrs Pat in it—I go with Mrs Emery.[1]

Bullen wants to open a publishing house in Dublin with me as reader & perhaps Lolly in charge of the printing Etc. He seems to have quite definite plans.

Yr ev
W B Yeats

ALS Berg.

To John Quinn, [c. *6 July 1904*]

18 Woburn Buildings, | Euston Road. | London—

My dear Quinn,

I have owed you a letter for some time or rather I have forgotten a number of things out of my last letter which I should have said. I have, however, been very busy over the production of my play. I forgot to tell you that I wrote my article on American impressions and asked A. P. Watt to send it to Maclure. I sent it to Watt instead of direct to you as I thought it possible he might be able to arrange simultaneous American and English publication. I was delighted to get your letter about the production in America of my three plays.[1] You have certainly done wonders for me. I have thought out a new and perfectly simple scenario of "Where there is

---

[1] A special matinée performance of Maeterlinck's *Pelléas et Mélisande* was staged in French at the Vaudeville Theatre on 1 July, with Sarah Bernhardt as Pelléas and Mrs Patrick Campbell as Mélisande. The performance was reviewed in *The Times* on 2 July, which described (12) 'an audience for which the conventional epithet of "brilliant" seems miserably inadequate'. The success of the performance led to three more special performances on 18 and 19 July, also at the Vaudeville. The production altered WBY's view of the play, as Holloway recorded in his diary on 28 Apr 1905 (*Abbey Theatre*, 59): 'Mention of Maeterlinck's play of *Pelleas and Melisande* cropped up, and Mr. Yeats said he never understood its meaning clearly until he saw Mrs. Patrick Campbell and Madame Bernhardt enact the roles of the lovers as if they were a pair of little children. Mr. Martin Harvey as "Pelleas" did not convey that idea to his mind, hence his non-appreciation of the play when he saw Harvey in it. Harvey presented a real grown-up lover; there lay his fault.'

[1] As WBY reported in the 1904 *Samhain*, the American actress, Margaret Wycherly (1884–1956), had formed a company 'to take some of our plays on tour' and 'has begun with three one-act plays of mine, *Cathleen ni Houlihan*, *The Hour-Glass* and *The Land of Heart's Desire*. It announces on its circulars that it is following the methods of our Theatre' (*Expl*, 139).

nothing". I had always, you know, plans for re-writing it, but I was only able to get a perfectly convincing scenario after seeing the performance. On the stage the subject seemed to me extremely rich but I thought my construction the very devil. I have brought in too many things and one does not get any definite atmosphere. The play has had rather a curious reception, the theatre was packed for the three performances. This was to have been expected on Sunday night when the members of the Society ⟨almost⟩ filled the house as always but a considerable part of the Monday and Tuesday audiences were brought by the play itself. Quite a number of people, including Ada Rehan,[2] have said enthusiastic things about it, and on the Tuesday and Wednesday the play got an extremely good reception. On Sunday night it was spoilt by the actor who played Paul[3] losing nearly all his voice before the scene with the monks. I have however found myself in entire agreement with the dramatic critics, who are all more or less hostile. The tinker acts went magnificently, but the play seemed as a whole a patchwork not an organism. I believe, however, that I will be able to make a really powerful and beautiful play out of it now. I consented to the Stage Society production because it would enable me to find out what was wrong, and without going too much before the general public to make the experiment. I had rather a romantic and curious experience after the last performance. A certain Cou[n]tess Cromartie[4] was introduced to me by Lady Gregory on Tuesday at the theatre. She invited me to have tea with her after the performance the next day. My mind was full of other things and the words "Suffolk House" in the address suggested nothing particular to me.[5] I went there in my old blue coat and found myself to my

[2] The Limerick-born Ada Rehan (1860–1916) became one of America's leading actresses, making her first appearance in Newark in 1874. She played over 200 roles as a member of Augustin Daly's company from 1879 to 1899, and was extremely popular both in New York and London, but after his death her career declined, although she remained one of Shaw's favourite actresses. She did not appear on the stage after 1906.

[3] E. Lyall Swete; see p. 267, n. 4.

[4] Sibell Lilian, Countess of Cromartie (1878–1962), the niece of the Duchess of Sutherland (see p. 368), was an authoress whose works reflect her interest in the occult. In 1899 she had married Major Edward Walter Blunt-Mackenzie of Castle Leod, Strathpeffer, Ross-shire and in 1902 she became a member of the Celtic Association. Her first book, *The End of the Song*, a collection of twelve Highland tales, had just appeared (*YA4*, 282). She occasionally attended WBY's Monday Evenings, and he was her guest in Ross-shire in January 1906. On meeting her in April 1907 Nevinson described her (Bodleian) as 'a young witch . . . who looked very wicked & sorceress'. In an inscription in *Discoveries* (Stanford) WBY identifies her as the model for 'A Guitar Player' (*E & I*, 268–9).

[5] Probably because the correct name of the Duchess of Sutherland's residence was Stafford (now Lancaster) House. A magnificent town house facing Buckingham Palace from the eastern fringe of Green Park, it was a favourite gathering place for artists and literati and William Rothenstein recalled (*Men and Memories* II. 71) that the parties there 'were not only the most splendid, but the most delightful parties I ever went to. The Duchess, kind and considerate to everyone, was an admirable hostess. Her radiant beauty as she stood at the head of the great staircase to welcome her guests is fresh in my memory.'

amazement in what I believe has been described as the only palace in London. We were shown into the Countess of Cromartie's room at the end of a long corridor. At the other end of the corridor I could see beautifully dressed children flitting about. Presently the Duchess of Sutherland came in, a most beautiful person and said "There is a children's party at the other side of the house. You had better come and see it, it is a beautiful sight." We went with her and found ourselves presently in a great room where fifty or sixty children were dancing with long muslin scarves which they wound and unwound, the scarves as it were uniting them all together. A tall and really very handsome woman was standing amid a crowd of young beauties and the Duchess said to me suddenly, "May I present you to the Queen?" I had about five minutes conversation with her. She professed to admire my poetry but I was ⟨much⟩ too wise to ask her which poems. I have no doubt she had thought out before hand (and I have no doubt always does think out before-hand) some such gracious thing to say. The whole scene was very unexpected and curious and seemed to me not unlike a scene on the stage. I never saw so many beautiful people together. As I was going back to the Countess of Cromartie's room for tea we met the Queen again. I bowed but when she had gone by said to the Duchess "Should I have crossed myself?"[6] I have been waiting to see if the rumour reaches the United Irishmen, and in what form it gets to them. I am looking forward to seeing the effect of it on Mrs. Macbride. I shall tell her as soon as I can. She gave a very fiery Irish address here the other day. It was really very fine, I hear, quite self-restrained, for her, at least, and eloquent as ever.[7] I go to Lady Gregory's on Monday, and am going to start a play on Dierdre. It will be a long one-act play with choruses, rather like a Greek play.[8] It may possibly suit the woman who is taking the other plays in America. I have never written a part for a woman of any importance since

[6] Queen Alexandra (1844–1925) was godmother to a sister of the Duke of Sutherland. Ricketts wrote in his diary for 12 Nov 1904 (*SP*, 112): 'Yeats spoke of his interview with the Queen and made us laugh. Out of innocence he disregarded all the conventions and spoke to her in the Yeats way. She knew nothing, of course, of Yeats' disloyal manifestoes when royalty was in Ireland, knew his poems, and wished to hear when next he gave one of his plays.' The Countess of Cromartie gave a significantly different account to Ella Hepworth Dixon, who recalled it much later in *As I Knew Them* (1930), 192: 'Suddenly the door opened, and in walked, arm-in-arm, Queen Alexandra and the lovely Duchess of Sutherland. Presentations had to be made, but the Sovereign, being deaf, probably never heard the name of her "disloyal subject". The embarrassment of aunt and niece was great.'

[7] On 25 June MG lectured on 'The Shan Van Vocht' [i.e. 'The Poor Old Woman' a traditional personification of Ireland] to the Irish National Club in Holborn Town Hall, with John O'Leary in the chair. After the lecture Nevinson wrote admiringly in his diary (Bodleian): 'She was most lovely—more beautiful even than I remembered—the mops of loose tawny hair, the strong face and frank eyes, the sudden transformation of the smile. In black with open neck showing her splendid throat. Only ornament the Tara broach at the waist belt. So tall she is, her voice most beautiful. Read or rather recited her address on the Shan Van Vocht—in exquisite language.'

[8] See pp. 413, 619, n. 1.

I have had experience of the stage and I am going to try and do it in this play. Lady Gregory's Kinkora has turned out magnificently. It is one of the best constructed historical plays I know. Frank Fay has heard it and is delighted. They will probably start with it in Dublin, with that and Synge's play which is a really great play they should do finely. I hear that Russell is very sorry now he let his Dierdre go to St. Louis.[9]

Yr sny
W B Yeats

[*In WBY's hand*]
I send Walkleys' & Archers notices of that play & another.[10]

TLS NYPL; with envelope addressed to 120 Broadway, postmark indecipherable.

To John Quinn, 13 July [*1904*]

Coole Park, | Gort, Co Galway.
July 13

My dear Quinn,

Many thanks for all you are doing about Mrs Wycherly and the plays. I shall be quite satisfied with any arrangement you make. Thanks also for all the trouble you are taking about the Irish Library. You wrote advising me not to send my essay or to send it to you, that you might negociate with them. I had unfortunately sent it before I got your letter. They also asked for leave to give some selections. I said I would consent to any selections made by Russell,[1] but that if they took copyright work they would have to deal with my publishers. I did not keep a copy of the letter, but this is what

[9] In a letter of 11 June, giving details of the St Louis débâcle, Quinn had commented (NYPL) that it was 'exceedingly unfortunate that Russell consented to their performing Dierdre [*sic*]. That gave these *fakirs* a chance to pose as having one of the plays at least of the Irish National Theatre Society.'

[10] A. B. Walkley, who had earlier noticed the text of *Where There Is Nothing* (see pp. 391–2), reviewed the performance in *The Times* of 28 June, observing (11) that 'In the book it was a wandering, straggling thing; on the stage it still wanders and straggles, and sometimes to wearisome length; it still seems to take every opportunity of avoiding, instead of seeking, the dramatic moment; but, on the whole, it "comes together" into a single thing far better than the reading of it promised.' William Archer, who reviewed the play with Sarah Bernhardt's production of *Pelléas et Mélisande* in the *World* on 5 July, wrote (28–9) that he approached the performance with prejudice: '"It is a feeble hash-up of Ibsen and Tolstoy and Maeterlinck," I was told; and as I clearly recollected the Ibsenish opening and the Tolstoyan trial of the magistrates, I was not indisposed to accept that view.' By the end of the play, however, he allowed that he 'had only some three minutes of boredom to set off against three hours of rare and stimulating enjoyment'.

[1] See p. 493. Russell, one of several editors, selected the poems by WBY included in the 10-volume anthology *Irish Literature* (1904), while WBY himself contributed 'Modern Irish Poetry', a revised version of the introduction to his *A Book of Irish Verse* (1900).

it was, so far as I recollect. They have not my permission to take anything that Russell does not choose. My publishers frequently make a charge for copyright work, but I dont know what has happened in the present case.

The essay I sent was of course the essay on Irish poetry, the one I arranged for in New York.

I am not sure you will get this letter, as you talk of sailing on the 20th. A great many thanks for your invitation to Paris. I will tell you exactly how things are with me, and you can decide. We must manage to be together somewhere, but if you could manage to come here for even a few days, it would be better for us to have our talk out here. I have just started a new play (a play about Deirdre) and I would like to have it ready for the new Theatre. I have never settled properly to work until now since my return from America. If however it is our only chance of having our talk out, I will go to Paris. It would of course be very enjoyable. We should all like to know your plans as soon as possible.

Thank you for the list of names, I cant get the cards off by this mail I'm afraid, but will send them by next and perhaps if you are away your clerk can manage the business.[2]

The leases have at last been signed for our little Theatre. There have been endless delays, but the workmen are I think now started. I shall have to go to Dublin presently to give evidence about the Patent application. It is to be called the Abbey Theatre, and is being decorated and so forth quite admirably. Miss Horniman will try and get back part of her expenses by letting it, but we are to get it free. I accuse Lady Gregory of having had her head turned by the enthusiastic reception of *Kincora* by the Company.

I cannot say with what pleasure I look forward to seeing you.

Yrs sincely
W B Yeats

My dear Mr Quinn, I am adding these few lines to say how eagerly Robert and I as well as W.B.Y. are looking forward to your visit. I will, directly I hear your date of arrival, try to arrange with Craoibhin to come here. I do hope you wont hurry away as you did last year. We might make an expedition to the cliffs of Moher, a fine coast drive.[3]

Yours always sincerely
Augusta Gregory

TLS NYPL, with envelope addressed to 120 Broadway, New York, postmark 'ORANMORE JY 13 04'.

[2] Presumably those to be sent out with the complimentary copies of Quinn's private edition of *The King's Threshold*. The list of names is now lost.

[3] In the event, Quinn did not get away until mid-October, and then only for three weeks. After a brief visit to Paris and Chartres, he arrived in Dublin on 25 Oct where WBY and AG met him since he did not have time to go to Coole. He returned to London with WBY for a week at the beginning of November. For 'Craoibhin' see p. 596, n. 5.

To Charles Elkin Mathews, 17 [July 1904]

Coole Park, | Gort, Co Galway.
June 17.

My dear Matthews,

I heard the other day that you were hesitating about Synge's book. I wish you would let me know what you propose to do. Synge is staying here now, and I think it very important for him and for our dramatic movement to have the plays published early in the autumn.[1]

I would like to have a selection from Lionel Johnson's poems printed at the Dun Emer Press,[2] a book probably about the same size as the selections from A. E. I thought that the copyright belonged to the family, but I have just had a letter from his sister[3] saying it is yours. I enclose her letter, which please return to me. Do you think that such a book of selections (a very limited edition of course) would be injurious to the sale of the two books of his you have published?[4]

I should think it might help the sale. When I was discussing the project of the Dun Emer Press with Emery Walker, he said to me 'You can publish your new book with the Press without doing any injury to the subsequent ordinary edition. You will find that it advertises the ordinary edition'. I cannot of course however profess to speak with authority upon such a matter. It is for you to decide.

In writing to the family I mentioned a Royalty, but such arrangements ought to be made directly with the Press. I am merely literary adviser.

Yrs snly
W B Yeats

TLS Leeds, with envelope addressed in AG's hand to Vigo St, Regent St, London, postmark 'ORANMORE JY 17 04'. Marked in another hand 'LB 19/7/04 no letter enclosed'.

[1] Mathews had two of Synge's books under consideration: *The Aran Islands* and a book of plays. He replied to WBY on 19 July (TCD): 'I think I did hint to Mr Dermot Freyer that I was a bit doubtful about issuing the Aran book this year. . . . I find the Aran MS. very attractive but think it should come on later . . .' *The Aran Islands* did not appear until April 1907 when it was published jointly by Mathews and Maunsel, while publication of *In the Shadow of the Glen* and *Riders to the Sea*, as No. 24 in the Vigo Cabinet Series (see p. 612, n. 2), was delayed until May 1905. WBY compensated for this by printing *In the Shadow of the Glen* in *Samhain* in December 1904.
[2] See p. 240. Johnson's *Twenty-One Poems*, published in an edition of 220 copies on 21 Feb 1905, was the fourth book issued by the Dun Emer Press.
[3] Miss Isabella Johnson (1862–1955).
[4] WBY selected the contents of *Twenty-One Poems* from Johnson's two previous volumes, *Poems* (1895), and *Ireland, With Other Poems* (1897), both published by Elkin Mathews. It is significant that he took fifteen poems from the former, and only seven from the latter, which he thought too propagandist. In reviewing it in the *Bookman* of February 1898 (*UP* II. 90–1), he observed that the 'poems, which are not pure poetry . . . will, I think, have their uses in Catholic anthologies, and in those Irish papercovered books of more or less political poetry which are the only imaginative reading of so many young men in Ireland'.

To Charles Elkin Mathews, [*17 July 1904*]

COOLE PARK, | GORT, | CO. GALWAY.

Cannot find Miss Johnson's letter[1] but it was a very cordial assent so far as she was concerned. It told me that you had the copyright.

Yrs sinly
W B Yeats

APS Leeds, with envelope addressed to Vigo St, postmark 'ORANMORE JY 17 04'.

To Horace Plunkett,[1] [*July 1904*]

PLAYS PRODUCED BY THE IRISH LITERARY THEATRE AND BY THE IRISH NATIONAL THEATRE SOCIETY.

(1) Irish Literary Theatre.

"Heather field"   At the start of the movement in 1899 the Irish Literary Theatre performed in the Antient Concert Rooms the "Heather Field" by Mr. Edward Martyn. This play which has since been translated into German and revived in America, proved itself in performance an extremely powerful play. It describes the conflict between an idealist and his practical, sensible but narrow and bitter wife who drives him finally into madness. The scene of the play—like that of all the other plays produced by the movement—is laid in Ireland, and the plot could not have worked itself out in that way (there would have been little differences everywhere) had it been transacted in any other country.

"Countess Cathleen"   My own "Countess Cathleen" was played at the same time. I must leave you to speak of its merits or demerits. I may remind you that it describes the life of a woman who sells her soul that she may get enough money to keep the people from selling theirs, or from dying of starvation. The event proved that it had at least the merit in starting a

---

[1] See previous letter.

[1] This Memorandum was to brief Plunkett who on 4 Aug was to support AEFH's application for a Theatre Patent for the Abbey Theatre. The application was opposed by the other Dublin theatres.

discussion about intellectual things in a country that prefers to discuss anything else. These plays were performed in May.

"Maeve"

"Bending of the Bough"

In May the next year 1900 another play by Mr. Edward Martyn "Meave" was played in the Gaiety Theatre, and a play by Mr. George Moore called "The Bending of the Bough" and a little play called "The Last Feast of Fianna" by Miss Milligan. Mr. Martyn's play had again for its theme the conflict between an idealist and the world. This time, however, the idealist was a girl and the conflict was typified by her being made to waver between her devotion to certain apparitions of beauty which typify noble art and a rich match. In addition to the primary meaning of the allegory there was a secondary meaning. The girl was Ireland wavering between her religious ideal, her spiritual dreams and the material civilisation of England. The audience showed itself a very clever audience by very quickly understanding this. The remarkable thing in the play however was the character of Peg Inerny, the curious witch, who was beggar woman by day and a Queen of Fairy by night. She typified Ireland. "The Bending of the Bow" [*for* "Bough"] was a satire on the disunions of the Irish Party. It was witty and bitter and roused a good deal of enthusiasm. "The Last Feast of Fianna" not remarkable as a play, contains some beautiful verses. Its subject is taken from Irish heroic legends.

"Diarmuid and Grania"

In October 1901 Mr. Benson and his Company produced for the Irish Literary Theatre "Diarmuid and Grania" by George Moore and myself, and every night after this play, a Company of Gaelic Leaguers produced "The Twisting of the Rope" by Doctor Douglas Hyde. I need not say much about the long play. I will remind you, however, that the last half of the second act proved itself powerful and exciting upon the stage. Mrs. Patrick Campbell would have produced this play in London had not Moore and myself held out for a first performance in Dublin.

Dr. Hyde's little play was a very wonderful piece of folk art, something quite unique, something that reminded one of an old mystery by its simplicity, by its lack of any modern influence. Since then it has been played countless times in such places as Galway, as Ballaghaderecn, and the like and in the Highlands of Scotland[2]—where it has been translated in the Scottish gaelic. It has been the start of the now vigorous movement of Gaelic drama.

(2) *IRISH NATIONAL THEATRE SOCIETY.*

The performances of the Irish Literary Theatre were in every case carried out with English actors. It was obvious that this could only be a temporary expedient.

In 1902 we started afresh with a company of Irish actors. Mr. William Fay alone had had professional experience and he taught the others. Furthermore we gave up all idea of performing in the big Theatres. We desired to be free—and to be free we must begin on a very small scale and gradually draw our own public to us. This was especially necessary as we desired to make innovations not only in the nature of the play but in the nature of the acting. For a statement of our principles I refer you to the article called "The reform of the Theatre" in the last number of "Samhain" (which I send). We began to work in St. Teresa's Hall in the Spring of 1902 with "Deirdre" by A. E. and with "Cathleen ni Hoolihan" by myself. "Deirdre" is by a dear friend and a charming writer, but I do not consider it a good play. I need not discuss it, but the fact that we are able to perform it to a crowded house for three days, turning away large numbers of people, proved the interest which our project excited, and the readiness of the people to approach with sympathy a drama which lacked certainly all meretricious attractions. I feel that "Cathleen ni Hoolihan" may perhaps raise a difficulty. It has been a great success, I think I may say, it has been

"Cathleen ni
Houlihan"

---

[2] Ballaghaderreen is a country town near Hyde's home at Frenchpark in Co. Roscommon. For the 'Highland' production see p. 610.

revived several times in Dublin, as well as being played in Belfast and in various parts of the provinces. It has also been played in New York. And I have had two offers from managers of Syndicates to take it on tour. The "Freeman" reporter told me that he never saw an audience so excited as were its first audiences in Dublin. On the other hand it may be said that it is a political play of a propagandist kind. This I deny. I took a piece of human life, thoughts that men had felt, hopes they had died for, and I put this into what I believe to be sincere dramatic form. I have never written a play to advocate any kind of opinion and I think that such a play would be necessarily bad art, or at any rate a very humble kind of art. At the same time I feel that I have no right to exclude for myself or for others, any of the passionate material of drama.

In October 1902 the Irish National Theatre Society began its work for the Winter with, I think, six plays. I suppose I may say the most important of these were "The Foundation" by Mr. Frederick Ryan[3]—a very witty though rather rambling attack on municipal corruption of a slightly socialistic tinge, and my little farce "The Pot of Broth" and the revival of my "Cathleen ni Hoolihan". Our next performances were a month or so later in a little Hall in Camden Street, which we had taken for our work. Some of the plays already mentioned were revived, but the Hall proved to be too out of the way and too inconvenient. There were no dressing rooms for instance. The same plays were repeated that winter in the Rathmines Town Hall, but the unsuitableness of our own Hall and some disputes in our Company kept us from performing anything new until March 1903, when Lady Gregory's "Twenty Five"—a rather slight peasant little comedy, about a returned emigrant, who helps his old sweetheart out of a difficulty by insisting on losing money at cards to her husband, and my miracle

"The Foundation"

"The Pot of Broth"

"Twenty Five"

---

[3] i.e. *The Laying of the Foundations*, see p. 232.

"The Hour Glass"   play "The Hour Glass". For some commendation of "The Hour Glass" I refer you to pages 34 and 35 of the present number of "Samhain."[4]

"The Hour Glass" has been twice revived in America by different Companies, and I have at present an offer from a Syndicate to take it on tour through university towns. For fear however, that these facts may make you think that we are going to be a serious commercial rival to the existing theatres, I may say that hitherto the Americans have always pirated me.

In May 1903 we brought to London "The Fountain" [*for* "Foundations"], "The Hour Glass" "Cathleen ni Hoolihan" and "The Pot of Broth", and had, as you know, and as you will see in "Samhain" a great success.

"The King's Threshold"   Last Winter we started by producing "The King's Threshold" a play inversed [*for* in verse] by me—a hungry poet reducing a King to order by starving on his threshold. J. M. Synge's very wonderful "Shadow of the Glen" and my "Pot of Broth". During the winter we performed practically every month. I was away and have no record, but I think the plays came in something like this order "Broken Soil" by Column—Lady Gregory's "Twenty Five" re-written and improved. A bad play by MacManus[5] "Deirdre" over again. "The

"The riders to the   Shadowy Waters" by myself—"The riders to the
sea"   sea" by J. M. Synge.

About May we went to London and played in the Royalty Theatre, producing there Synge's two plays, Column's play and my "King's Threshold".

We have ready for our winter's work:—(1) "The well of the Saints" an Irish peasant play in three acts, by Synge, which I say in entire confidence is one of the most powerful plays done in English for

---

[4] WBY had had A. B. Walkley's laudatory *TLS* review of the first INTS London productions (see p. 356) reprinted in the 1903 *Samhain* (34–6). In his notice Walkley compared *The Hour-Glass* favourably with Sardou's *Dante*, and described its 'whole tone' as 'grave and subdued, its texture such stuff as dreams are made of. A little thing it may be, but it haunts the mind for days afterwards.' The play had been produced in New York by Josephine Arthur (see p. 587, n. 5), and by Margaret Wycherly (see p. 614).

[5] *The Townland of Tamney*; see pp. 540–1.

many years. (2) We have a long play on an Irish subject by George Bernard Shaw.[6] (3) We have a long heroic play on the subject of King Bryan by Lady Gregory.[7] This play which has Queen Gormley for its principal character, is the second part of an heroic trilogy, upon the events that led up to the back [*for* battle] of Clontarf. The one play which has been finished and which will find an evening is very powerfully constructed, and the characterization of Queen Gormley is very clever and very curious. She is made a type of an ungovernable heroic emotion.

Besides these plays we have a number of One–Act Plays:—

(1) "On Baile's Strand", a play in verse by myself and we will shortly have another play in verse by me on the subject of "Deirdre". We have also a little miracle play by Column[8] a fine one-act comedy by Hyde.[9] An amusing three–act play by a new writer. A one–act play by a new writer, and promises of other plays by competent writers— comedies for the most part.[10]

To use the old saying I could have made all this shorter if I had more time. I claim that leaving aside my own work, we have done a great deal for the intellect of this country in discovering and training into articulateness J. M. Synge, whom I believe to be a great writer, the beginning it may be

---

[6] *John Bull's Other Island*, not in fact produced at the Abbey until September 1916.

[7] *Kincora*, produced on 25 Mar 1905.

[8] *The Miracle of the Corn* (see p. 601), not finally produced by the INTS.

[9] The next play of Hyde's to be produced by the INTS was *The Poorhouse* (*Teach na mBocht*), written in collaboration with AG, but not staged at the Abbey until April 1907.

[10] The new three-act play was William Boyle's *The Building Fund*, produced on 25 Apr 1905. In the 1904 *Samhain* WBY announced (*Expl*, 138) that 'Mr. Tarpey, an Irishman' had promised 'a little play which I have not yet seen'. This was *Sigrid*, which had been passed for performance under unusual circumstances on 12 Mar 1904, while WBY was on his way back from America. According to the Reading Committee minutes (Widener), the play was accepted at a general meeting of the INTS on the recommendation of individual members of the Committee, some of whom had passed it 'on the grounds that we might be short of new plays for the next season'. In the event, no play by W. Kingsley Tarpey (1858–1911), barrister, playwright, and eldest son of Hugh T. Tarpey, sometime Lord Mayor of Dublin, was staged at the Abbey and, indeed, no one-act play by a new writer was performed there until W. M. Letts's *The Eyes of the Blind* in April 1907. Tarpey's comedy *Windmills* had been produced by the Stage Society on 16–17 June 1901, and AEFH's Gaiety Theatre, Manchester, was to produce his *The Amateur Socialist* in November 1908.

of a European figure. We have done well too in getting Bernard Shaw to apply his logical wit to an Irish subject. We have started too a great deal of dramatic interest throughout the country. Were it not for us, all these gaelic plays, which are being played perpetually, would never have existed. Lady Gregory's "Twenty Five" has for instance been expanded into three acts and played in Irish to a great crowd in New York.[11] I am told that about 500 people were unable to get admittance. We have caused a great deal of intellectual discussion, and we have done all this without playing to any party. We have pleased and affronted all in succession. We desire a permanent patent that we may go on fearlessly in future, and that we may be able to form a fund to pay actors and authors. We cannot do our work properly till we are free of amateurism till our people are able to give all their time and thought to their work. Here you have something which the Country is doing for itself, which it has carried to its present point, by sheer enthusiasm, by unpaid labour, without guarantors (the Irish Literary Theatre had some, we have none) without patronage, without the arts of the demagogue. Every rightful scheme of education thinks it more important to encourage what a country already has than to give it what it has not.

A thousand apologies for giving you so immense a document.

[*At top of document in WBY's hand*]
Written for use of Horace Plunkett Counsel Etc in Patent Enquiry 1904 re Abbey Theatre.

TS copy NLI.

[11] This was Andrew J. O'Boyle's *Ar Son Cáit, A Céad Grád* (For the Sake of Kate, His First Love), which had been produced at the Lyric Hall on 42nd St., New York, earlier this month by the Fuireann Drama Gaedealac under the auspices of the Philo-Celtic Society. Based on AG's *Twenty-Five*, the play was revived at the Mendelssohn Hall on 2–3 May 1905. WBY had evidently seen a notice in *An Claidheamh Soluis* of 18 June, which reported (7) that the 'hall was crowded to a point of discomfort and the stairway, even an hour after the curtain was raised, was thronged with ticket holders who could not get in'.

To Charles Ricketts, 26 July [*1904*]

Coole Park, | Gort, | Co Galway.
July 26.

My dear Ricketts,[1]

I have been a long time in writing to thank you for having sent me such admirable designs for the Black Jester.[2] I showed them to Frank Fay in Dublin, and he was delighted with them. And so soon as I can make some little progress with the poems I have in my mind for recitation, I will have the costume made. The Black jester is one of the characters in a play I am now writing, and for that too the design will serve. I should have written to you before, but my eyes have been unusually bad, even a very few lines have been enough to set them aching.

Some people dont like type written letters, but I hope you dont mind.

Lady Gregory has just read me a letter from Shannon, which has given her much pleasure.[3] Those strange tales, with that curious wildness of theirs which is their compensation for lacking classic measure, and their sense of fine life, of a life that was lifted everywhere into beauty, are the energies I think behind all our movement here. I notice that when anybody here writes a play, it always works out, whatever the ideas of the writer, into a cry for a more abundant and a more intense life. Synge and A. E. the poet are staying here, and though they have come to their task from the

---

[1] See p. 297.

[2] WBY wanted a minstrel in the guise of a Black Jester to open the Abbey Theatre and asked Ricketts to make costume designs. In 1937 he recalled (*E & I*, 529–30) that 'Charles Ricketts once designed for me a black jester costume for the singer, and both he and Craig helped with the panorama, but my audience was for comedy—for Synge, for Lady Gregory, for O'Casey—not for me. I was content, for I knew that comedy was the modern art.' In 'Literature and the Living Voice' (*Expl*, 216–17), written immediately after the Abbey opening but first published in the 1906 *Samhain*, he imagined 'a jester with black cocks-comb and black clothes. He has been in the faery hills; perhaps he is the terrible *Amadán-na-Breena* himself; or he has been so long in the world that he can tell of ancient battles.' In spite of this the Black Jester does not appear in *Deirdre*, which WBY began at Coole in July 1904, or in any of his plays. An unfinished draft prologue for the Black Jester, perhaps intended for *Deirdre*, is printed in *Druid Craft*, ed. M. J. Sidnell, E. P. Mayhew, and D. R. Clark (Dublin, 1972), 303–4; in it the Jester, an agent of the heroic imagination, defies the orders of the Realist stage-manager by conjuring up a world of symbolic absolutes.

[3] Shannon had written on 23 July (Berg) to thank AG for 'the noble gift of your books' and to 'tell you how much I like them. What has struck me most is the high order of civilization and sense of chivalry & dignity in human intercourse notably among the men. I also like the love of beauty and pleasure in dwelling on beautiful objects large pin brooches and cup-shaped caps—I think the Song of Finn in The Coming of Finn singularly beautiful. . . . I like the Dairmuid [*sic*] & Grania stories most and the sidelight they cast on Finn as an older man & of course the story of Deirdre.'

opposite side of the heavens they are both stirring the same pot, something of a witches cauldron I think.

Yrs sinly
W B Yeats

TLS BL. Wade, 436.

To Olivia Shakespear,[1] [*? 29 July 1904*]

at | COOLE PARK, | GORT, | CO. GALWAY.
Friday

My dear Mrs Shakespear: The novel is a delight.[2] I am only about two thirds through—I have got to Tonys discovery of his mothers drug taking—I cannot go quicker for my eyes are very bad indeed. It is much the best thing you have done. I know all the people intimately & I find all true & not the less charming & that is a rare thing. The meeting with the young man in the train is a very fine invention, very dramatic & yet convincing. At first I thought the Russian prince a little unreal & then I remembered that he was an image in the mind of a child, that he is a childs 'bad man' & he became excellent. I wonder at the skill with which you make one feal the passage of Time & at the same time make the change gradual like time itself. Tony grows up under our eyes—you do not seem to skip a year. You must have been a young man & gone to school in Babylon or Alexandria. Perhaps you played with a pegtop somewhere in the hanging gardens.

I will write when I have finished the book but that will be some days hence. I have got rather run down with a series of colds & can hardly use

---

[1] See p. 558, n. 2.
[2] OS's fifth novel, *The Devotees* (originally entitled *Tony*), was published in June 1904. Tony Atherton, first seen as a boy of six, and Marie, daughter of the sinister Russian, Prince Libanoff, are the 'devotees', the object of their devotion being Tony's beautiful, amorous, and finally indifferent mother. Tony is in fact the illegitimate son of his mother's aristocratic English lover, but when the lover is killed in a riding accident, she runs away with Prince Libanoff, for whom Tony entertains a jealous hatred. Although obsessed with her memory, Tony sees no more of her until he is a young man, by which time she has left Libanoff and taken to swanning about Europe with his daughter as her companion. Travelling to see her in Rome, he meets George Lascelles, a young man who confides that he is visiting a mistress who has become a drug addict. In Rome Tony realizes that this is his mother. Although Tony's displaced Oedipal jealousy makes Prince Libanoff appear an unpleasantly ominous man, this is not merely a childish fantasy, for another character remarks (118) 'of course he is a brute—most Russians are' and describes his hold over Tony's mother (119) as 'a kind of dreadful, unholy fascination—she was like a bird with a snake'.

my eyes at all. It is a passing inconvenience but anoying enough. Please write.

Yrs ever
W B Yeats

ALS MBY. Wade, 436–7.

To an unidentified correspondent, *30 July* [*1904*]

Coole Park, | Gort, Co Galway.
July 30

Dear Sir, I write very late in the day to thank you for your kind good wishes on June 13.[1] I am sorry to have been so long in answering them, but I have been very busy, and my eyes trouble me very much, so that I have to put off letter writing until I find someone to dictate to.

Yours sincly
W B Yeats

TLS Texas. Marked in another hand '1904'.

To Lady Augusta Gregory, *3 August 1904*

Nassau Hotel, | South Frederick Street, | DUBLIN
3rd August 1904.

My dear Lady Gregory
　　The really important things first—this day is so hot that I have been filled with alarm lest the lake may begin to fall again, and the boat be stranded high up on the bank and I be unable to try my new bate. I brought the boat up to a very shallow place the day I left. I have been running about all over the place collecting witnesses and have now quite a number.[1]

---

[1] WBY had celebrated his thirty-ninth birthday on 13 June 1904.

[1] WBY was gathering witnesses for the Abbey Theatre patent hearings on 4 Aug. Those examined in support of the application included AEFH, WBY, W. G. Fay, T. P. Gill, T. W. Rolleston, T. C. Harrington (see p. 601), Horace Plunkett and the Rt. Hon. William Frederick Bailey (1857–1917), lawyer and author, who had been appointed Irish Estates Commissioner under the Land Act of 1903. An influential supporter of the Abbey Theatre, he became a shareholder and member of the Financial Committee in 1911. AG dedicated her *New Irish Comedies* (1913) to Bailey as 'Counsellor, Peacemaker, Friend'. He edited collections of Gray and Coleridge and was well known for his *Ireland Since the Famine* (1902). He became a Privy Councillor in 1909 and later served as a Governor of the National Gallery of Ireland.

Horace Plunkett and Commissioner Bailey seem to be the most important. I lunched with Plunkett today. I spoke of your new Play and said how unlike a woman's work it was, so powerful and so on. He said "I don't wonder at it being powerful, she is the hardest woman I know to speak up to. I have been in a controversy with her and know." He evidently feels you had very much the best of it.[2] I don't think George Moore will be let down to rehearsal any more.[3] He has been abusing Fay's stage management, and is supposed to have got Gogarty to undertake an article for Danna on this subject.[4] He also seems to be making no secret of the fact that he wants to stage manage the Company himself. I am also amused to find that it was Russell who brought him down. This Russell never told me. I will wire tomorrow if there is anything definite about decision. In any case I will write full particulars. I shall probably return Saturday morning. I see FitzGerald[5] on Friday afternoon.

Yours snly
W B Yeats

TLS Berg.

[2] AG had admired Plunkett in the late 1890s but felt that he had become too Unionist of late years. She opposed his stand on the financial relations between Britain and Ireland, and his support for the Boer War. However, they remained friends and in May 1900 (diary, Berg) he urged her to join the committee of the Gort Convent Co-operative 'as he says his department will have to fight with them, & I will be someone reasonable to fight with!'

[3] Moore had been undermining rehearsals since the beginning of the year. On 6 Feb 1904 Frank Fay confessed to Maire Garvey (NLI) that 'George Moore's presence upset me. . . . when he is there I cannot help feeling the futility of our efforts', and on 13 July had told her 'We had a most depressing rehearsal. George Moore was there . . .'

[4] Oliver St. John Gogarty; see p. 576, n. 1. On 27 Aug Gogarty, whose first poems had appeared in *Dana*, wrote to G. K. A. Bell (*Many Lines*, 32): 'He [Moore] was awfully angry about my not wishing to put my name to an attack on the Irish National Theatre—a covert attack on Yeats with whom he now disagrees—and take the consequences in "Dana"'. *Dana*, 'A Magazine of Independent Thought' (1904–5), was founded by Frederick Ryan and John Eglinton. Moore's 'Stage Management in the Irish National Theatre' finally appeared in the September 1904 issue (150–2), under the tartly chosen pseudonym 'Paul Ruttledge', echoing his name of the hero of the disputed play *Where There Is Nothing* (see pp. 228 ff.). Moore focused his argument on 'Mr. Fay's method or want of method in presenting the play on the stage. The actors and actresses in a National Theatre play scramble about practically anyhow and they remind one very often of three little boys and a little girl reciting a story on a barn door.' Throughout the article he contrasted Fay's methods unfavourably with Antoine's, alleging that his productions tended to disintegrate, that the 'simplest stage tactics are unknown to him', that he 'does not know his A.B. and C. of stage management', and that the London successes depended merely upon novelty since the critics 'would have praised any little bushman who came over to London with a boomerang'. He concluded by suggesting that Fay should employ a stage manager. The article not only annoyed Fay and WBY, but also earned Moore the implacable enmity of AEFH, not apparently for his criticism of the acting, but, as Holloway later recorded in his diary (*Abbey Theatre* III. 230), because 'he wrote in *Dana* that "at last W. G. Fay had found an admirer in Miss Horniman," and she took it up that he meant that they were "carrying on," as the saying goes. . . . Probably Moore never meant anything of the kind. The lady had her own thoughts on the matter and loathes Moore ever since. Refusing to be introduced to him and all that sort of thing.'

[5] Dr Charles Edward Fitzgerald (1843–1916), a Dublin oculist with a surgery at 27 Upper

To Lady Augusta Gregory, 4 August 1904

Nassau Hotel, | South Frederick St. | DUBLIN
4/8/04.

My dear Lady Gregory:—

Final decision is postponed until Monday but the battle is won to all intents and purpose. There appears to be no difficulty about our getting a patent for the plays of the Society. The difficulty comes in from the proposal to let the Theatre to other players when it is not being used by the Society. The Solicitor General has referred the matter back to our Counsel to draft in consultation with the opposing Counsel—some limitation of patent which will prevent Miss Horniman from letting to commercial travelling Companies of the ordinary kind.[1] It looks as if it will be very difficult to find a definition. We have another consultation with Counsel tomorrow. I send you a paper with the report of proceeding. Miss Horniman gave her evidence first and was entirely admirable. She was complimented by the Solicitor General and is as proud as punch. Excitement always seems to give her the simplicity which she sometimes lacks. She was really most impressive. Plunkett and Comissioner Bailey did well for us, but I must say I was rather amused at their anxiety to show that they supported us— not out of love for the Arts but because of our use as anti-emigration agents and the like. I think I was a bad witness. Counsel did not examine me but asked me to make a statement. The result was having expected questions and feeling myself left to wander through an immense subject I said very little. I was disappointed at being hardly cross-examined at all by that time I got excited, and was thirsting for every body's blood. One Barrister in cross-examining T. P. Gill who came after me tried to prove that Ibsen & Maeterlinck were immoral writers. He asked was it not true that a play by Maeterlinck called "The Intruder" had raised an immense out cry

Merrion St. (see p. 485, n. 1), prescribed new glasses for WBY. He was an early admirer of JBY's paintings (see I. 139), and presented two of them, 'My Daughter' and 'The Bird Market', to Lane's Municipal Gallery of Modern Art in 1905. In *The Dublin of Yesterday* (1929) P. L. Dickinson describes him (31–2) as 'one of the best-known figures in the life of the Irish capital in the years about 1900. He was an oculist, but looked like a Parisian artist of the Du Maurier period. He invariably wore a black suit, with a wideawake hat with an enormous brim, and a long flowing bow-tie. He wore a pointed beard and walked rapidly with a light and swinging step. He was . . . to me a romantic figure of picturesque adventure in my young days.'

[1] The Solicitor-General for Ireland was J. H. Campbell, KC; AEFH's counsel was Herbert Wilson, instructed by her Dublin solicitors, Whitney and Moore, who represented the Abbey until the 1920s. The opposing counsel for the Gaiety, Royal, and Queen's Theatres were J. F. Moriarty KC, Denis Henry, KC, and Thomas Lopdell O'Shaughnessy, KC, who, as the *Irish Daily Independent* reported on 5 Aug 1904 (2), 'contended that there was no necessity for the theatre, and instanced the case of his clients, who were only able to make five or six percent'.

in London because of its immorality. Quite involuntarily I cried out "My God" and Edward Martyn burst into a loud fit of laughter. I suppose he must have meant "Mona Vanna". He also asked if the Irish National The- atre Society had not produced a play which was an attack on the institution of marriage. Somebody asked him what was the name of the play. He said it didn't matter and dropped the subject. He had evidently heard some vague rumours about "The Shadow of the Glen". The immense ignorance of these eminent Barristers was really rather surprising.[2]

I have just been down to see the work on the Abbey Theatre. It is all going on very quickly and the Company should be able to rehearse there in a month. The other day while digging up some old rubbish in the morgue which is being used for dressing rooms, they found human bones. The workmen thought they [had] lit on a murder at least but the Caretaker said, "Oh I remember we lost a body about 7 years ago. When the time for the inquest came it could'nt be found."

I forgot to say that Wm. Fay gave his evidence very well as one would expect. He had the worst task of us all for O'Shaughnesy—a brow beating cross-examiner of the usual kind[3]—fastened on to him. Fay however had his answer for everything. I suppose I will have to wait for Monday. I have a good many odds and ends of news.

I hear that some man of a fairly respectable class was taken up with a lot of tinkers somewhere in Munster, and that the Magistrate compared him to "Paul Rutledge". The next night one of the Tinkers seems to have said something to the others about their being in a book. The others resented this in some way and there was a fight which brought them all into Court again.[4] I am trying to get the papers.

Yrs snly
W B Yeats

TLS Berg. Wade, 437–8.

[2] The *Irish Times* of 5 Aug 1904 (3) reported the following exchange during J. F. Moriarty's questioning of Gill:

Do you know that Mr. Yeats produced a play at the Independent Theatre, London?
Mr. Yeats—Never.
Mr. Moriarty—Do you know that the *Times* newspaper in its critique characterised it as 'preaching the doctrine of revolt against marriage'?
Mr. Wilson, K. C. —What is the name of the play?
Mr. Moriarty, K. C. —Well, no matter now. (Laughter). To witness—You know nothing about it?
Mr. Day—You don't know the name of the play? (Laughter).

[3] In *The Dublin of Yesterday* Dickinson recalled that 'Tommy' O'Shaughnessy 'was notorious as having one of the worst tongues at the Bar, and was a terror in cross-examination' (35).

[4] A more circumstantial version of this story appeared in William Bulfin's travel book, *Rambles in Eirinn* (see p. 245, n. 5), 296–8. Touring near Abbeyshrule, Bulfin met a tinker, a relation of the Wards, who had fought a fellow tinker over the veracity of *Where There Is Nothing*: 'and the

To Olivia Shakespear, [8 August 1904]

Nassau Hotel | South Fredrick St | Dublin.
Monday.

My dear Mrs Shakespear: I am up in Dublin on theatrical business but shall be back in Galway by Wednesday. My eyes have been very bad or I had written before—(I have to get new glasses I find) to tell you again how the novel has delighted me. The end is entirely right much better than the end I suggested.[1] The book has a very curious charm—one has an effection for the people that keeps them long in the memory. Your Marie is a creation—her gambling is a very fine invention. In a wonderful way it makes one feal there are depths of fealing in her that life has hardly touched—it gives her the mysteriousness of all reality.[2] It is always bad when a writer makes you feal that he knows all that is in any of his people—we can only salute the soul & let it pass by, we cannot understand it. If we would understand too much it flies away in terror. The whole book has a beautiful wisdom & sanity & gentleness.

We have practically got our theatrical patent now—we have been opposed by the Theatres with the most absurd arguments. We have the first endowed theatre in Great Britain, & I am glad to say no lack of plays

day was goin' against me entirely, so it was, until Peggy, over there, came to me with the half of th' ass's hames. So when they parted us I had the best of it. And be the same token, as I was coming through Carrick last night they towld me that Ward himself went up before a lot of madgisthrates and denied the whole story about his girl and young Ledwitch, and said he never gave him lave or licence to make so free with his name, and that he knew nothin' at all about the pote, and never had any thruck with him whatsomever, and that it's damages he'd be claimin' if the story in any way intherfared with his girl gettin' a good match; and all the people that crowded the court to hear the thrial cheered, bedad.' (See pp. 648-9.)

[1] See p. 628. At the end of the novel Tony discovers that he is in love with Marie Libanoff and she accepts his proposal. His mother, however, makes it clear that if they marry she will leave them, and so great is her emotional hold that they postpone their wedding indefinitely to prevent this. The problem is finally solved when she makes a hasty marriage to the raffish and much younger George Lascelles, leaving them merely a short conventional note as a reward for their unstinted devotion. It is probable that OS or WBY had originally planned to let the mother die (at one point she seems close to death), but her sudden flight with a young cad is more in keeping with her selfish irresponsibility.

[2] Marie Libanoff, first seen as a wayward and imaginative child, grows into an enigmatic and eccentric young woman. In Tony's mother's view (143) she 'takes up the most foolish of poses. She does not like men. . . . She has seen a great deal of life, too young. It has sickened her. Why, I cannot tell you . . .' To Tony, however, she seems (144) 'to have lost everything, while possessing so much. . . . she gave the impression of being illimitably, horribly old. She was a stimulating companion, but her talk always left him with an after-taste of sadness.' Of small stature, she has (246) 'the air of an old miniature', and looks (235) 'as though she saw a number of things he didn't see'. Her one weakness, besides her devotion to Tony's mother, is a passion for gambling: 'it is not the *money*—it is the excitement, the feeling that you are at the mercy of chance, the uncertainty' (137).

but it will be hard work. I am tired out with the excitement the work of hunting out witnesses dictating statements for them & so on—Tomorrow at 3.30 in the afternoon I shall be fishing for pike & perch on Coole lake.

I shall await your reading me the new book[3] with expectation now that you are so fine a master.

Yr ev

W B Yeats

ALS MBY, with envelope addressed to 4 Pembridge Mansions, Dublin postmark torn away, but second postmark 'PADDINGTON AU 10 04'. Wade, 439.

To John Quinn, [*17 August 1904*]

at | COOLE PARK, | GORT, | CO. GALWAY.

My dear Quinn: many thanks for the 'Kings Threshold' looks the look. It is a beautiful edition.[1] Thanks too for the contracts about the plays. You have taken a great deal of trouble & their performances will be in every way a great help—they like every performance on the ordinary stage help to lift one out of the amateur in the public mind. The work on our little theatre goes on as quickly as possible but it will hardly be ready for us before December so we may have to give a couple of country shows to fill up the gap. Lady Gregorys Kinkora is finished now—a very fine play full of vigerous drama & beautiful language. So far we have nothing really bad accepted & are in good hope.

I cannot write more now as I am off to Galway Feis.[2] Lady Gregory asks me to give you her rem[em]brances.

Yr ev

W B Yeats

I am looking forward very much to seeing you.

[*In AG's hand*]

It was the greatest disappointment when I came back from a visit to the real Kincora on Sat evening to find your message![3] We had been making so

---

[3] OS's next and final novel, *Uncle Hilary*, did not appear until 1910.

[1] Quinn's handsome private edition of *The King's Threshold*, published in March 1904 (see p. 398, n. 2), was issued in grey paper boards, with the title stamped in gold on the spine and gilt top edges. The volume was enclosed in a grey cardboard slip case.

[2] The Great Connaught Feis and Industrial Exhibition was held in Galway from 16 to 19 August. Douglas Hyde and Edward Martyn were the adjudicators for the competitions in literature and music.

[3] Presumably Quinn's message that he would have to put off his trip until later; originally he had hoped to be in Ireland by 20 Aug (see p. 618, n. 3).

many plans. But we have still next month to look forward to. I shall be here all through September and hope you will come straight from Queenstown—We have got our theatre patent all right—I hope we may be worthy of it.

Yours always sinly
A Gregory

ALS NYPL, with envelope addressed to 120 Broadway, New York, postmark 'ORANMORE AU 17 04'.

To George Roberts, c. 18 August 1904

I suspect from this Bullen is giving up his project.[1]

WBY.

ANS NLI.

To John Millington Synge, 21 August [1904]

Coole Park, Gort, Co Galway,
August 21

Dear Mr. Synge,
   I was going to write to you, and Yeats says he has things to say, so he is dictating this.

---

[1] This note was written across the top of a letter from Bullen to WBY (NLI) addressed from 47, Great Russell Street, Bloomsbury, W. C. and dated 17 Aug 1904: 'I think Messrs. Roberts & Starkie had better leave me out of account for the present. If they produce good books in Dublin I might be of some service to them by buying editions for the English markets, but they may prefer to open accounts with the English booksellers. Publishing runs away with a lot of money, and they will need to be very wary. When I am in Dublin I should like to make their acquaintance; or if they are ever in London I should be glad to see them. Lately I have started a private printing establishment of my own and am printing a book in ten handsome superroyal octavo volumes. The venture causes me some anxiety.'
   As WBY reported to AG on 1 July (see p. 614), Bullen had contemplated opening a Dublin Office, and WBY evidently told him that George Roberts and James Starkey were planning an Irish publishing house to issue Starkey's slim volume of poems, *The Twilight People*, and later the texts of Abbey plays. Bullen, who had recently embarked on the ambitious ten-volume *Stratford Town Shakespeare* he mentions at the close of his letter, was unwilling to risk a Dublin venture, but he helped Roberts in November this year by taking 100 copies of *The Twilight People* off his hands, and by supplying him with the sheets of his English editions for the first four volumes of the 'Abbey Theatre Series'. He was also to advise Roberts and Joseph Hone (1882–1959) on the setting up of their Dublin-based publishing firm, Maunsel and Co., in the summer of 1905.

I saw your play rehearsed in Dublin, or rather I saw the first act several times. Of course it was imaginative and original from the very first, but at first I was inclined to think that it would lack climax gradual and growing interest. Then I forced myself to attend to the [impact] of the picture to the eye, the bell in the girls hand, the cloak, the withered faces of the old people, and I saw that these things made all the difference. It will be very curious beautiful and I think exciting.

One or two criticisms occurred to me. There is a place where you make the saint say that some one of the characters has a low voice or should have a low voice, and that this is a good thing in women. This suggests that he has been reading King Lear, where Cordelia's voice is described as low 'an excellent thing in woman'. I think this is a wrong association in the mind.[1] I do not object to another passage about the spells of smiths and women which suggests that he has been reading S. Patricks hymn.[2] He might naturally have done so. This point is not however very important. But I do think it of some importance that you should cross out a number of the Almighty Gods. I do not object to them on the ground that they are likely to shock people but because the phrase occurs so often that it may weary and irritate the ear. I remember the disastrous effect of the repetition of the word beauty in the last act of Edward Martyns *Maeve*.[3] I daresay the people do repeat the word very often, but unhappily the stage has its laws which are not those of life. Fay told me that you gave him leave to cross out what he will, but though he is very anxious to reduce the number of

---

[1] At the end of Act I of *The Well of the Saints* (*JMSCW* III. 101) the Saint admonishes the enraged Mary Doul 'not [to] be raising your voice, a bad thing in a woman'. He is not, like Lear (v, iii, 272–3), commending a low voice but criticizing a loud one, a fact that WBY seems to have misinterpreted. Since he habitually associated low voices in women with sexual attraction (see 'Adam's Curse', l. 17 and 'Hound Voice', ll. 8–9), WBY perhaps thought it inappropriate for a saint to notice such things. Synge, no doubt perplexed by this criticism, left the lines unaltered.

[2] In Act I of the play (*JMSCW* III. 91) the Saint advises the crowd 'to be saying a prayer for your own sakes against . . . the words of women and smiths'. In a letter of 12 Aug 1905 to Max Meyerfeld, his German translator, Synge explained (*JMSCL* I. 121) that 'this phrase is almost a quotation from an old hymn of Saint Patrick. In Irish folklore smiths were thought to be magicians, and more or less in league with the powers of darkness.' The hymn, 'St. Patrick's Breastplate', summons heavenly powers 'Against spells of women and smiths and wizards'.

[3] The name of God is invoked frequently in the play, and Synge does not seem to have acted upon WBY's advice, perhaps because he felt that one of the themes of the play—the opposition of Martin Doul's peasant theology with the Saint's orthodoxy—required such reiteration. 'Beauty' or 'beautiful' occur over twenty times in one short scene in Act II of Martyn's *Maeve*, first produced by the ILT on 19 Feb 1900—repetition which merely emphasized the unsatisfactory characterization of the heroine noted by Joseph Holloway (*Abbey Theatre*, 10): ' "Maeve's" cold inanimate manner and wistful far-away look and visionary talk only created laughter among a most kindly disposed audience. On occasion they could not refrain from irreverent mirth at the daft behaviour of this eminently unloveable young woman, and one old play-goer was heard to remark as he left the theatre that "They ought to have clapped that one into an asylum . . .".'

the God Almightys he does not like to do it himself. He wants you to do it.
We have not your MSS here, as Roberts wrote to ask for it.[4]

When I left Dublin Fay had made up his mind to play Kincora first if he
could get Tunney to take the part of Malachi. He was set against beginning
with your play but wavered between Kincora and a triple bill. He said he
would go and see Tunney himself. I haven't heard whether he has done
this or not, but I do hear that Kincora has been formally adopted and that
two new men neither of them Tunney have been added to the company.
One of them, a man called I think Butler has been pupil to Digges.[5] I dont
know where [*for* whether] they are any good. It was also formally decided
to play the Workhouse[6] in Irish, together with Kincora. Having heard that
neither of the Walkers[7] on whom the chief responsibility would have
rested have sufficiently correct Irish I have written against this proposal,
and suggested that Hyde who is willing, be asked to take a part. I have said
however that it would be better still if the play were done in English.

As Lady Gregory is typing this, you will understand my object in saying
that I have nothing but praise of Kincora in its present form. She has
greatly simplified and elevated the character of Brian, she has given his
character a touch of magnificence, in the renaissance sense of that word.
She has put in a number of really beautiful speeches here and there, a few
words in nearly every page, with the result that the play has lost its old
harsh wrangling tone, without losing strength, has a certian richness a kind
of soft shining. (If Mrs Lewis your present housekeeper[8] writes a play, I
am sure you will describe it like this, and leave the letter about).

I forgot to say that I think William Fay will be as fine as possible in your
play if I can judge by the first act. Frank Fay will be good as the saint. I
like the women rather less. Miss Allgood has some objectionable trick of

[4] As Secretary of the INTS Roberts had procured the MS for use at rehearsals. Apologizing to
Bullen on 14 Jan 1905 for the much corrected proofs of the first half of the play, Synge explained
(*JMSCL* I. 104) that 'the MS. was used by our company for rehearsing . . . and I find that the
prompter has written in a certain number of technical stage directions which could not be left in
the printed volume'.

[5] William James Tunney played minor roles in several amateur performances from 1897 to
1904, appearing in James Duncan's *A Gallant of Galway* (24 Mar 1902), AE's *Deirdre* (13 Apr
1903), Cousins's *The Sword of Dermot* (20 Apr 1903), and in the Players' Club production of
Martyn's *An Enchanted Sea* (18 Apr 1904). He did not appear in *Kincora*. M. Butler appeared
only once on the Abbey stage, in a small part in AG's *The White Cockade*, on 9 Dec 1905.

[6] WBY is probably thinking of Hyde's play *Teach na mBocht* (see p. 625). It was not produced
in Irish by the INTS, although it was staged on 31 Oct 1905 at the Cumman na Gael Samhain
Festival in the Molesworth Hall. AG's and Hyde's English version, *The Poorhouse*, was performed
at the Abbey in April 1907, and a year later AG presented a revised version, entitled *The Workhouse Ward*.

[7] Mary and Frank Walker were members of the INTS, acting under their Irish names, Maire
Nic Shiubhlaigh (see p. 172) and Prionsias MacSiubhlaigh.

[8] AG had misread Synge's latest letter (*JMSCL* I. 92) in which he had told her that he was
staying with 'Mrs Harris', at Mountain Stage, Glenbeigh, Co. Kerry.

voice, certain sounds that she gets wrong. I could not define it though I tried again and again. Miss Esposito is not without cleverness, but she does not seem to me to have a right ideal. One of our difficulties is that women of the class of Miss Garvey and Miss Walker have not sensitive bodies, they have a bad instrument to work with, but they have great simplicity of feeling, a readiness to accept high ideals, a certain capacity for noble feeling.[9] Women of our own class on the other hand have far more sensitive instruments are far more teachable in all that belongs to expression but they lack simplicity of feeling, their minds are too full of trivial ideals, and they seldom seem capable of really noble feeling. I have no real hopes of Miss Esposito, though she certainly works very hard, and has made the company believe in her. I wish very much you had Miss Walker for your heroine or Miss Garvey. I think at the same time that Miss Esposito's performance will be adequate, and that the fine acting of the Fays will secure your success.

We went in to Galway Feis one day, chiefly to see the Lost Saint, which was announced in the programme. It was taken off, O'Toole the workhouse Schoolmaster anti-emigration play put in its place,[10] and some ladies who came to ask for tickets to see Hydes play were told at the door that 'it was not good enough' and that 'a much better play' had been put in its stead. In consequence we would not stay. Robert had speacially come in to see that, Lady Gregory was indignant that this slight to the Craoibhin had been given in her own country, and W.B.Y. was so anxious to draw somebodys blood on the subject that it was thought safer to remove him. Miss Horniman is staying here now with a lady who acts as chorus.[11] The

---

[9] Sara Allgood (1883–1950), a student of Frank Fay, joined the company in 1903 and first appeared in Horse Show performances in August and in WBY's *The King's Threshold* in October of that year. She quickly became Maire Walker's rival as the Company's leading lady and stayed on until 1913, playing major roles. In 1914 she joined the Liverpool Repertory Theatre, but she returned to the Abbey in 1923 to play Juno Boyle (her favourite part) in O'Casey's *Juno and the Paycock*. She took up a film career in 1929, moved to Hollywood in 1940, and became a US citizen in 1945. She played Molly Byrne in the first production of *The Well of the Saints*. Vera Esposito, who took the part of Mary Doul under her stage-name 'Emma Vernon', was the daughter of the musician and composer Michele Esposito. Her first appearance for the Company was in Synge's *Riders to the Sea* in February of this year. She remained with the Company until 1905, when she moved to London, joining the Theatre of Ireland on her return in 1906. Maire Garvey, 'Maire Ni Gharbhaigh' (d. 1946), was one of the signatories of the letter accepting AEFH's original terms (see p. 596). She first appeared as an extra in *Riders to the Sea*, and thereafter played a variety of minor roles, including Delia Cahel in *Cathleen ni Houlihan* and Bride in *The Well of the Saints*.

[10] *The Lost Saint* by Douglas Hyde had been published in the 1902 *Samhain*; see p. 289, n. 2. *An Deoraidhe* (*The Exile*) by Labhrás O'Tuathail (John O'Toole), the schoolmaster at Aughrim School, Clifden, was put on with Hyde's *Teach na mBocht* (see above, n. 6) at the Galway Feis, and according to *An Claidheamh Soluis* of 27 Aug 1904 (7) 'combined genuine comedy with wholesome propagandism'.

[11] Probably Mary Price Owen (see p. 253), who was much with AEFH at this time.

theatre is not to open till December. We may have a performance in the country to tide over the time. We have done nothing about copyrighting as there is no hurry. Quinn cant come over till next month.

This is as far as W. B. Y. goes. He took the Horniman party out fishing yesterday, and they got ten, mixed pike and perch. I hope your asthma is better, yesterday was fine, and now we have drizzle again, and the hay is not yet saved.

Moore has written an article for Dana in which he says the one thing the company requires is a stage manager. He tried to induce Gogarty to sign it, but he backed out, and I fancy Moore has toned down the writing since then. But it wont make the Fays love him.

A Gregory
for W.B.Y.

TL signed AG; TCD. Saddlemyer, 57–62.

To William Archer, 23 August [*1904*]

Coole Park, | Gort, Co Galway.
August 23.

My dear Mr Archer,

I enclose a letter from Frank Fay who played the poet in the King's Threshold. The letter explains itself.[1] When I was in Dublin Edward Martyn told me that Moore was anxious to stage manage something, and that we should take him, as Martyn's own company had quarrelled with him, or at any rate objected to be stage managed by him any more.[2] I heard also th[at] he had been down to my own people, and abusing their stage management. I stayed a week in Dublin and was rather puzzled at a certain young man[3] who generally calls several times during the first two hours, not turning up for a whole week. Presently he did turn up, and I thought there was something strange about him. He was pre-occupied, he clearly had something on his mind. Presently it came out. Moore had written an article abusing William Fay's stage management, and had sent it to this young man to sign. I knew by the vehemence with which he declared that

---

[1] In seeking ammunition for his proposed refutation of Moore, Frank Fay had asked Archer for details of the first Norwegian production of *Ghosts*, which Archer had seen.

[2] Martyn was a vice-president of the National Players' Society (see p. 390, n. 3), but he also commissioned his company, The Players' Club, to produce his *An Enchanted Sea* on 18 Apr 1904.

[3] Oliver St. John Gogarty; see p. 630. Gogarty subsequently admitted to Bell (*Many Lines*, 39) that 'I edited the letter signed "Paul Routledge" which was written by George Moore & which he tried to father on me'.

he would do nothing of the kind that at some moment or other he was to have put his name to it. He told me he would write to Moore to say that it was no use Moore trying to disguise his authorship as every second man he met in the street seemed to know all about it. The next thing I heard was that the M. S. S. had somehow or other taken to wandering about Dublin. It was read by two members of the company, and now Frank Fay as you see is in a state of excitement. It you can answer his question without putting yourself to any trouble please do. The article is to appear in a little Dublin magazine called Dana, and Frank Fay thinks of answering it there.

Some time ago Fay asked me to try and get him a copy of the report which was made for Tree and read at the opening of his school of acting, or whatever he calls it. It dealt with the methods of teaching of the Conservatoire. Do you know has it ever been published? or if it is possible to get it.[4]

You will have seen in the papers that we have got a patent for our ne[w] theatre.[5] It will not however be ready to open till December. I hope some day you will make up your mind to face the sea, and will visit it.

I have to thank you once again for your generous praise of some very imperfect work of mine. The Press Cuttings sent me something the other day which had the marks of your hand in it.[6]

Yr sny
W B Yeats

TLS BL.

[4] Herbert Beerbohm Tree had opened his Academy of Dramatic Art at His Majesty's Theatre on 25 Apr 1904. Founded on principles similar to those of the Paris Conservatoire, the Academy offered instruction in elocution, fencing, dancing, deportment, pantomime, and rehearsal techniques. The *Stage* announced on 26 Apr (16) that Laurence Jerrold had prepared a special report on the constitution of the Conservatoire, and George Bancroft, Secretary of the Academy, read salient passages from this during the meeting. Copies of the report were distributed to members of the audience after the meeting, but there is no record of publication, and no copies have been traced.

[5] On 20 Aug, in the Library of Dublin Castle, the Solicitor General granted the INTS a 21-year patent, to be renewed after six years, for the Mechanics' Institute. As AEFH resided outside Ireland, AG was named patentee. The proceedings were reported in the Dublin *Daily Express* and in the *Irish Daily Independent* on 22 Aug. Holloway recorded the terms of the patent in his journal (*Abbey Theatre*, 42):

> The patent shall only empower the patentee to exhibit plays in the Irish or English language written by Irish writers on Irish subjects, or such dramatic works of foreign authors as would tend to interest the public in the higher works of dramatic art; all foregoing to be selected by the Irish National Theatre Society under the provision of Part 6 of its rules now existing and subject to the restrictions therein contained, a clause to be inserted against the assignment to any person or persons other than the trustee for Miss Horniman her executors or assignees, the patent to cease if the Irish National Theatre is dissolved. No enlargement of the theatre is to be made, so as to provide for a greater number of spectators than it is capable of holding at present. No excise license to be applied for or obtained.

[6] Evidently a belated acknowledgement of Archer's sympathetic review of *Where There Is Nothing* in the *World* of 5 July (see p. 617, n. 10).

To D. J. O'Donoghue, 23 August [1904]

Coole Park, | Gort, Co Galway.
August 23.

My dear O'DONO⟨U⟩GHUE,

I have just come across enclosed which I omitted to answer. I suppose it is to[o] late now, but if not, Chancello[r] has a negative and you might ask for a copy.

I have been looking out for your Irish Voices;[1] I wonder is it out yet.

Yrs sny
W B Yeats

TLS Southern Illinois.

To John Masefield, [c. 23 August 1904]

Mention in letter from Masefield, 24 August 1904.
A 'charming' letter inviting Masefield to come to Dublin for the first production of *Spreading the News*.

LWBY I. 143–5.

To F. J. Fay, 28 August [1904]

Coole Park | Gort, Co Galway.
August 28.

My dear Fay,

I send you Archer's letter.[1] You will see by it that you cant make very much out of that point in stage management. You can of course say that as Ibsen, who always gave the stage directions when he was certain, did not direct the actor to stand up, the stage management is free. I rather suggest however that you go very little into details of this kind, for your audience

---

[1] O'Donoghue probably wanted the photograph for *Irish Voices* (see p. 559), which was still projected in July 1904, and which was to have contained a picture of each of the contributors.

[1] In his reply of 26 Aug (NLI) Archer confessed that, although he had seen the first Norwegian production of *Ghosts*, it was 'so long ago that details of the performance have quite escaped me'. He went on to advise that, while Ibsen's stage directions should be followed, the director is at liberty to provide 'business at points where he does not prescribe anything in particular'.

will be interested in general principles they will not care three straws about Moore's competence. If I were you I would make your article an attack on realistic stage management. The position of attack is far stronger than the position of defence. Put Moore on the defensive and you will win. Be just to Antoine's genius, but show the defects of his movement. Art is art because it is not nature, and he tried to make it nature.[2] A realist, he cared nothing for poetry, which is founded on convention. He despised it and did something to drive it from the stage. He broke up convention, we have to re-create it. It would be quite easy for us to get a superficial finish by choosing for our stage manager somebody who understood the perfected though temporary art of Antoine and his school. To do this would be to become barren. We must grope our way towards a new yet ancient perfection. We can learn from nobody to recreate tradition and convention except from those who have preserved it. We have learned with devout humility from the players of Phedre,[3] and though our problem is not quite theirs it is like theirs but unlike Antoine's. We desire an extravagant, if you will unreal, rhetorical romantic art, allied in literature to the art on the one hand of Racine and [on] the other hand of Cervantes. We can no more learn from Antoine than a writer of verse or a writer of extravagant comedy could learn from a realistic novelist. Moore once said to an interviewer 'nobody will ever write a realistic novel again. We are all gone now, Zola is dead Huyssmans is in a monastery, and I am in Dublin.'[4] Moore knows that his kind of novel is obsolete, but because he is an amateur in plays and stage management, he does not understand that his kind of play and his kind of stage management is equally obsolete. Our movements are clumsy for we are children, but we are a devil of a long way farther from our coffins. If you care for this scheme, and I know of course that nobody can do more than suggest to another something that can awake that others imagination, you will know how to carry it out, filling it with little bits of learning from your knowledge of the history of the stage, making my vague principles definite knowledge. Moore says for instance that the effect of words depends upon the place they are spoken on from the stage. There is the whole business in a thimble. There is the stage management that came to its perfection with Antoine. It is the art of a theatre which knows noth-

---

[2] WBY's favourite quotation from Goethe, although Goethe never put it quite so succinctly. WBY perhaps derived it from his reflection that 'the Arts also produce much out of themselves, and . . . add much where Nature fails in perfection, in that they possess beauty in themselves' (*Maxims and Reflections of Goethe*, trans. Bailey Saunders, 1893).

[3] The Comédie Française, for whom Fay had a great admiration. WBY was perhaps thinking in particular of Sarah Bernhardt, whom Fay had described as 'one of the wonders of the world', whose 'greatest part' was Phèdre.

[4] In his letter to Bell of 27 Aug (see p. 630, n. 4), Gogarty wrote: 'Moore is a chameleon. . . . "Huysmans is in a monastery, Zola's dead and I'm in Dublin" is his little mot when he wishes to pity himself before an audience & joke at Dublin'.

ing of style, which knows nothing of magnificent words, nothing of the music of speech. Racine and Shakespeare wrote for a little stage where very little could be done with movement, but they were as we know careful to get a great range of expression out of the voice. Our art like theirs without despising movement must restore the voice to its importance for all our playwrights, Synge just as much as myself, get their finest effects out of style, out of the expressiveness of speech itself. Then too all Moore's ideas of stage management and the ideas of stage management of the people he believes in, De Lange[5] for instance, (I cannot judge of Antoine in this matter) seem to me to aim at keeping the stage in a state of quite superficial excitement. Drama for them consists in a tension of wills excited by commonplace impulses especially by those impulses that are the driving force of rather common natures. This is a very difficult thing to put, partly because I have not the necessary technical knowledge. Your brother understands for instance that in the first act of the Well of the Saints there must be long quiet periods, a suggestion of dreams, of indolence.[6] The same is true of Cathleen ni Houlihan. Moore wanted Cathleen to walk up and down all the time in front of the footlights. When I explained that this would not be true to the play, that she was as it were wandering in a dream, made restless as it were by the coming rebellion, but with no more fixed intention than a dreamer has, he wanted me to re-write the play.[7] Such emotions were impossible in drama; she must be Ireland calling up her friends, marshalling them to battle. The commonplace will, that is, the will of a successful business man, the business will, is the root of the whole thing. Indeed when I see the realistic play of our time even Ibsen and Sudermann, much more when I see the plays of their imitators, I find that blessed business will keeping the stage most of the time. What would such writers or their stage managers do with the mockery king of snow? Or with Lear upon his heath? They would succeed with them just insofar as they forgot all that had given them their fame, and groped for fragments of a tradition they had done their best to destroy. But why do we want their stage managers? The commercial theatre is full of them, and we have

---

[5] Hermann Nenmark, called Herman DeLange (1851–1929), a Dutch diamond cleaner and amateur actor, moved to England in 1879 to begin a career in the professional theatre, where his accent and appearance brought him numerous stock roles as the foreigner. He eventually became associated with the Independent Theatre, initially as an actor-manager and subsequently as a member of the board. The character Hermann Goetze in *Evelyn Innes* was modelled on DeLange, and Moore briefly describes an encounter with him in Chap. 3 of *A Communication to My Friends* (1933).

[6] Although Synge's *The Well of the Saints* was in rehearsal, it was not produced until 4 Feb 1905; on 27 Jan 1905 WBY wrote in his preface to Bullen's 1905 edition of the play (*E & I*, 304) that it was 'the preoccupation of his characters with their dream that gives his plays their emotional subtlety'.

[7] See p. 162.

founded our own theatre because we and certain people who agree with us, dislike it. The little fame we have won has come to us because we have had the courage to do this. I dont suppose there is anything in this letter that will be of help to you, but make any use of it you like. If you take any of the ideas you may either put them into your own words, or leave them in my words, and so make them part of your article, or you may quote them as from a letter written to you by one of the company. You may as well keep this letter, as I have taken some trouble to collect my ideas and express them clearly.

Lady Gregory I know has sent you Kincora; the chief amendment is in the part of King Brian. It is now I think a very fine part, perfectly coherent, and with great dignity. At first Gormleith seemed to run away with the play, but now the balance is struck even.

Yrs sny
W B Yeats

TLS Private. Wade, 439–42.

To A. H. Bullen, 29 August [1904]

Coole Park, | Gort, Co Galway.
August 29

My dear Bullen,

I have just found this among a heap of letters. Heaven knows when you sent it to me. Please answer it yourself. Do whatever is usual; but make some arrangement to secure the right of translation lapsing if the translation does not appear within a stated period.

You will remember that I made no arrangement for the publication of an American edition of the King's Threshold, owing to my arrangements with Macmillan being in a state of uncertainty. I had however to do something to keep the American stage rights as well as ordinary copyright, and with this object my friend John Quinn had a hundred copies printed privately. Some of these were given to friends in America who had been kind to me, and he has been trying to make the expenses of the edition by selling a few copies at I think a pound each. He has sent me a certain number of copies. Would you object to either he or I giving Elkin Matthews a few of these? No copy to be sold less than twenty shillings, and for as much more as he likes. The object is merely to pay the expenses of the edition, and I cant imagine that a few copies sold for a pound would interfere with the three and sixpenny sales. I have been working every day since I left London at my new play Deirdre. It has lyric choruses, and should I think be the most poetical of my plays. After that I shall do some lyrics and ballads. We have got our theatrical patent as you will have seen, and you should time your visit to Dublin so that you may come in for one of our shows.

Yrs sny
W B Yeats

TLS Texas.

To Frank Benson, [c. *4 September 1904*]

Mention in letter from Benson, 5 September 1904.
Asking Benson for the MS of *Diarmuid and Grania*;[1] telling him of the purchase of the Abbey Theatre, and thanking him for helping to make this possible.[2]

NLI.

To Charles Elkin Mathews, [*September 1904*]

COOLE PARK, | GORT, | CO. GALWAY.

My dear Matthews: I have just got the complete proofs of my selection from Lionel Johnson—A little book—22 poems. Have you the block of the old colophon by Image? Would there be any objection to our using it? Can you let me know by return as my sister wants to print at once.[1] Many thanks for your permission to select & at your very reasonable royalty.

Yrs sny
W B Yeats

ALS Texas.

[1] Benson replied from the Spa Theatre, Scarborough, that he could return the play in a week, but 'if six weeks will do, it would suit me better, as I shall then be nearer home'. WBY planned intermittently to revise the play, perhaps for Mrs Patrick Campbell, and, after the alarm over its possible production in St Louis (see p. 580), probably wanted to make sure that the MS should not fall into the wrong hands.
[2] Benson replied: 'I heartily congratulate you and Lady Gregory on the start you have made, the whole idea is splendid and I wish I could think that you owed me any thanks at all. My hearty congratulations to all concerned.'

[1] The Dun Emer edition of Johnson's *Twenty One Poems* (see p. 619) was finished on 31 Oct 1904 and published on 21 Feb 1905. A colophon by Selwyn Image (see p. 57), designed as a floral wreath, appeared at the end of Johnson's *Poems* (1895) but was not used in the Dun Emer edition.

To A. P. Watt, [mid-September 1904]

Mention in letter to Quinn, 28 September 1904.
Sending him correspondence with Bryan over *Irish Literature*; asking him for advice about it; and instructing him to write to Bryan.

To John Butler Yeats, [mid-September 1904]

Mention in letter from JBY, 22 September 1904.

MBY.

To A. E. F. Horniman, 20 September [1904]

Coole Park | Gort, Co Galway.
Sept 20.

My dear Miss Horniman,

Do what seems to you right about the stained glass windows, but I dont think the arms of the four provinces is quite the best possible idea.[1] I think armorial bearings of that kind on a stained glass window in a public building, rather cheapen the effect. One has seen them on restaurant windows so often. They will be quite safe however. I dont think that the four symbols would have made any trouble.[2] Russell and myself happen to attach certain private meanings to them, but to the majority of Irish people they are simply patriotic properties, and properties much more closely connected with the country than the coats of arms which were made by the

[1] One of the first commissions of The Tower of Glass (An Túr Gloine), founded in 1903 by Edward Martyn and Sarah Purser (see p. 57, n. 3), was for the stained glass for the vestibule of the Abbey Theatre. The work was executed by Sarah Purser and her apprentice, and a colour reproduction appears in Michael O'hAodha, *Pictures at the Abbey* (Dublin, 1983), 10. AEFH, who was paying for the work, and who had already heard that her motives in fitting out the Theatre were being impugned in Dublin, was insistent that the designs should not be open to misinterpretation, as she made clear to Sarah Purser in a letter of 21 Sept (NLI): 'To put it brutally—I won't give myself away by either Church, Mystic, Free Mason, Heroic, Irish, English, or Patriotic symbolism of any sort whatsoever.' For this reason, as she explained to Purser in a letter of 19 Sept (NLI), she favoured the heraldic shields of the provinces of Ireland: 'This is to be a public building & I have already had to take public ignorance into account. My poor "Crusaders" were accused of carrying a Union Jack, so I am very determined to be extremely cautious.' It was finally agreed not to add any further designs to the trees already decided upon, and, Maire Nic Shiubhlaigh recalled two 'stained-glass windows, fashioned in the image of a tree in leaf, on either side of the Marlborough Street entrance'.

[2] The four symbols WBY used for his Celtic Mysteries (see p. 78) were the four sacred talismans of Irish myth—the Cauldron of the Dagda, the Spear of Lugh, the Sword of Light, and the Stone of Scone or Lia Fail.

Norman invader. The moon pierced with arrows is of course a more definit[el]y mystical thing.[3] I suggest to you an alternative to the talismans which will cause the least possible alteration on Sarah Pursur's design, and be quite without mysticism. I think you will find she will prefer it to the armorial bearings, which will probably make it necessary to change the shape of her medallions, as well as filling them with details, too minute and complicated for the simple lines of the nut tree. It would also go better with the nut tree itself than even the talismans. Let us have the shield-signs of four chief heroes of Ireland, and their names on scrolls underneath. The mermaid for Conochar, the hound for Cuchulain, and on the other window the rising sun for Finn, and either the Broom for Osgar, or Conan's briar—(Conan may be emblematical of satiric drama). I am sure Sarah Purser will like this better than armorial bearings, an alternative that I had already discussed with her. She objects to it on the ground of its being like a restaurant. After all can we do more than make suggestions to the artist. Must not the final decision be always the artists?

By the bye I haven't yet found out whether those crusaders had or had not the Union Jack. If they had not, I dont see why you made any change. There is no point in objection to symbols as such, and after all the Union Jack is not a symbol in our sense of the word. It is a coat of arms and a very ugly one. So far as I can make out, the banners flown by the crusaders were, if they were anything, the banner of Scotland which has no party significance.

I hear that Cumann-na-Gael wants the theatre for nothing in October. It had been suggested this is the reason U. I. has been so friendly lately. In this case the theatre would be opened with Mrs Mac Bride's own play.[4] I hope they will write and ask you for it.

Yrs always
W B Yeats

TLS NLI.

---

[3] In her letter of 19 Sept (see n. 1) AEFH asked Purser if she knew 'the meaning of the phrase "to shoot the Moon"? Perhaps Mr Yeats and I would be the only people who would understand this—"the forces of the Path of Sagittarius entering the Sephira Jesod". To the ordinary person it would mean—"a midnight bolt to avoid paying rent". As the rent must be paid before the light is turned on, a symbol of what I intend to prevent would be quite out of place.' A vision of a naked woman shooting at a star was among WBY's most powerful occult experiences (see *Aut*, 371–5, 576–9, and *Mem*, 100–1) and he had recently used the design on the cover of the revised edition of *The Celtic Twilight* (1902). As AEFH says, 'to shoot the moon' was Victorian slang for a midnight flit by tenants to avoid paying rent.

[4] MG's one-act play, *Dawn*, a patriotic melodrama with strong echoes of *Cathleen ni Houlihan* and Colum's *The Saxon Shilling*, was published in the *United Irishman* on 29 Oct 1904 and in the *Gaelic American* on 5 Nov 1904, but there is no record of its performance. The play is included in *Lost Plays of the Irish Renaissance*, ed. Robert Hogan and James Kilroy (Dixon, Calif., 1970).

To William Archer, 25 September 1904

Coole Park, | Gort, Co. Galway
25th September 1904

My Dear Archer,

I have had so many letters to write that I have not written to thank you. The information you sent was altogether to the point. Fay however has decided not to answer Moore. Thank you also very much for the copy of "An Enemy of the People." I am very much interested in a letter of Ibsen's in the preface.[1] I may probably quote it in "Samhain." The situation here in Ireland is precisely what it was in Norway according to his letter.[2] Here too we have all to fight against the plebeianising of life through party politics. Our Theatre flourishes like a blade of grass between big stones which have all high-sounding names. You were wrong in supposing that our National Theatre ever gave an Ibsen play. Martyn has a little company which he pays and this company has done so, but merely, I think, "A Doll's House" and "Hedda Gabler".[3] The point about the stage management of "Ghosts" was merely an academic one.

I hear that a band of tinkers are even more angry than the London critics about "Where there is Nothing." A bystander on a Connaught road discovered that one of them was called Charlie Ward, and taunted him with having let his daughter marry an omadhaun like Paul. A free fight started in which I believe other bystanders joined, and they were all had up before the magistrate, and the account of it all is in the county newspaper. I find also, from one of the Dublin papers, that Charlie Ward, of whose existence

---

[1] In the introduction to his edition of Ibsen's *An Enemy of the People*, trans. Eleanor Marx Aveling (1901), Archer quotes (vi) Ibsen's letter of 3 Jan 1882 to George Brandes: 'When I think how slow and heavy and dull the general intelligence is at home, when I notice the low standard by which everything is judged, a deep despondency comes over me, and it often seems to me that I might just as well end my literary activity at once. They really do not need poetry at home; they get along so well with the *Parliamentary News* and the *Lutheran Weekly*. . . . I feel, too, most painfully affected by the crudity, the plebian element, in all our public discussion. The very praiseworthy attempt to make of our people a democratic community has inadvertently gone a good way towards making us a plebian community. Distinction of soul seems to be on the decline at home.'

[2] WBY did not quote the letter in *Samhain*, but he did (*Expl*, 160–1) draw parallels between the Norwegian and Irish cultural situations: 'In the small nations which have to struggle for their national life, one finds that almost every creator . . . sets all his stories in his own country. I do not recollect that Björnson ever wrote of any land but Norway, and Ibsen, though he lived in exile for many years, driven out by his countrymen, as he believed, carried the little seaboard towns of Norway everywhere in his imagination. So far as we can be certain of anything, we may be certain that Ireland with her long National struggle, her old literature, her unbounded folk-imagination, will, in so far as her literature is National at all, be more like Norway than England or France.'

[3] For Martyn's productions of *A Doll's House* see p. 390. His company, The Players' Club, had produced *Hedda Gabler* in the Antient Concert Rooms on 21 Apr 1904.

I never heard, threatens to take an action against me if the play keeps his
daughter from making a good match. I am afraid, from this, he has not
read the play, as Sibby was not his daughter.[4]

I do not know when we open here, or even what we shall open with. We
have a great deal in rehearsal and the theatre should be ready soon.

Yr sincerely

W B Yeats

TLS BL.

To John Quinn, 28 September [1904]

Coole Park | Gort, Co Galway.

Sept 28.

My dear Quinn,

It has been the greatest disappointment to me and to everyone in this
house, your having had to give up coming.[1] We hoped against hope, and
made all our plans for you, trying to think there was no uncertainty in our
voices, till your last letter came. You were right in supposing that I delayed
in answering about Bryan,[2] hoping to see you. When your arrival became
doubtful however, I sent the correspondence to A. P. Watt. My reason for
doing this was that he would know far better than I could what I was entitled to. In order that I might have the benefit of his advice without asking
him to consider a complicated matter for nothing, I asked him to write to
Bryan, in which case he would have taken his percentage. I enclose his
answer. You will see that he says that Bryan should have the permission of
all the publishers who have books of mine in America, even if those books
are not copyright. The only book of mine which is not in some publishers

---

[4] See p. 632. WBY had read the account by 'Che Buono' (William Bulfin) in the *United Irishman* of 24 Sept 1904 (2–3) which quoted one of the black-eyed antagonists as reporting that Charlie Ward had been taken to court for letting his asses trespass on a field of oats, but in defending
himself with 'a wondherful great flow of speech' complained of Yeats's 'libel'. Asked what part of
WBY's play he objected to he replied: ' "To the whole of it, sir. I disown it all, body and bones,"
says he, "its all wrong, lock, stock and barrel. Neither that pote, nor nobody else who isn't a tinker knows our saycrets," says he, "and never will." ' Ward reportedly added 'that it's damages
he'd be claimin' if the story in anyway intherfared with his girl gettin' a good match'.

Charlie Ward is the leader of the tinkers in *Where There Is Nothing*. Sibby (Sabina Silver) is a
member of his band, but her father has died just before the play begins; in the course of the play
she 'marries' the hero Paul Ruttledge without benefit of clergy, by jumping over the tinker's budget. An omadhaun (Irish: amadán) is a fool or a clodhopper.

[1] See p. 618, n. 3; Quinn's trip to Ireland was delayed until 25 Oct.
[2] The editor with Bigelow, Smith & Co., publishers of the 10-volume *Irish Literature* (1904);
see p. 475, n. 4.

hands or other in America is a book called 'Poems' published by Fisher
Unwin. My agreements with Brett are not definitely settled, if they were it
would be in his hands. ⟨It may be too late for Brett⟩ I conclude that Bryan
has done this already except in the case of the last book. Now about the
question of payment. I certainly understood either from correspondence
with Mr Bryan or conversation with him, that his book is not to be piracy
under any circumstances. I did not mean by this merely that he was to take
no work legally protected in America. It is not necessary to guard against
that kind of thing. I understood him to mean that he would take no work
the taking of which interfered with the moral property of the writer. This
is a confused phrase, but you will understand. I should not have objected
to his taking a few poems, as many say as Rolleston took for his Anthology,
but sixty pages of my work is quite another story.[3] Get out of him whatever you think you can. Dont be too hard on him, for I feel I have come
back leaving pleasant recollections behind me, and I dont want to spoil
them. Bryan did write to me some nine months ago asking if A. E. might
make a selection from my verse. I said he might but I meant half a dozen
poems, and even then left the question of payment open. I say this in case
he revives that letter.

I enclose a letter from Fisher Unwin about Bryan's book, from which
you see he is alarmed at Bryan's anthology which he calls piracy. I feel
rather shabby in getting payment for myself, as my original intention was
to have prevented him from pirating my friends and neighbours.

We are all very much excited over our theatre, there is a window or
rather two windows in the entrance hall made by Sarah Purser. They are a
representation in stained glass of the Nuts of Knowledge. And I have just
got from Miss Monsell who is staying here a very charming picture of
Queen Maeve with a big wolfhound to go on the programme. We think of
it for a poster later on.[4]

It is still uncertain what we are to open with. It lies between Lady Gregory's Kincora, Synge's Well of the Saints, and my Baile's Strand. The
company want Kincora, but we are afraid that the part of Gormleith, a
very big passionate part, overtakes Miss Walker's somewhat narrow range
of emotions. Both Lady Gregory and I are going to Dublin in a few days
finally to decide about it.[5]

[3] In addition to his essay on 'Modern Irish Poetry' in vol. III, 54 pages of WBY's poetry,
drama, and prose were printed in vol. IX.

[4] See p. 335, n. 1. Elinor Mary Monsell (1878–1954), artist and illustrator, designed the woodcut of Queen Maeve and the Irish wolfhound which became the crest of the Abbey Theatre, used
on stationery, programmes, and posters.

[5] The Abbey Theatre opened on 27 Dec with WBY's *On Baile's Strand*, followed by *Cathleen
ni Houlihan* and AG's *Spreading the News*.

I have been working for weeks upon weeks at my Deirdre. It goes very slowly and gives me a great deal of trouble, but it is going to be the best of all my plays. I have just today finished my first chorus. Here it is. It accompanies the first entrance of Deirdre.

FIRST MUSICIAN
Why is it Queen Edain said
If I do but climb the stair
In the tower overhead
When the winds are calling there
Or the gannets calling out
In waste places of the sky
There's so much to think about
That I cry, that I cry.

SECOND MUSICIAN
But her good man answered her:
'Love would be a thing of naught,
Had not all his limbs astir
Born out of immoderate thought.
Were he anything by half,
Were his measures running dry,
Wherefore, if we may not laugh,
We must cry, we must cry.'
(Deirdre and Naisi enter)

ALL THE MUSICIANS TOGETHER
But is Edain worth a song
Now the hunt begins anew?
Praise the beautiful and strong;
Praise the redness of the yew;
Praise the blossoming apple-stem,
Yet would silence have been wise
What is all our speech to them,
That have one another's eyes?[6]
(The last three lines they say turning away.)

F. Fay has been here, and is in great enthusiasm over my Deirdre, so I think Russells Deirdre will fade away. My Deirdre at any rate is not

---

[6] These verses were to become the Musicians' songs in WBY's play *Deirdre* (see *VPl*, 352–3). The first two appeared as 'Queen Edaine' in *McClure's Magazine* of September 1905, and all three were subsequently published as 'The Praise of Deirdre' in *Shanachie*, 1 (1906), where they were described as 'a chorus from an unfinished play called "The House of Usnach"'.

melancholy but full of a sort of tragic exultation. Lady Gregory has done a little play called 'Spreading the News' and it is (she begins to protest already) a very joyful little masterpiece, though it is the anatomy of a melancholy man. She seems to me to have suddenly found herself in drama, and I foresee that the Pot of Broth will fade before its popularity.

Yr ever
W B Yeats

[*In WBY's hand*]
I cant find Unwins letter but he said that he supposed Bryans book was the 'usual piracy'.
[*TS resumes*]

Dear Mr Quinn, I cant say how sorry we were to find your coming was definitely put off. We had so many plans for it and so many things to talk of. Philosophers would say it will be all the more joy when you do come, but we have too much of the child in us not to think a hope deferred is the same as lost. I sent your letter on to Hyde. I doubt his going to America yet a while.[7] Yeats talked a good deal to him about it, he said he wouldn't go unless the necessities of the League drove him there. He did not want to encourage it to expect help from America instead of helping itself. He thought that its poverty had been one of its spurs to activity or some such thing. Whether there was any of Mrs Hyde's objection to his going away hidden behind this, he doesnt know. Of course a talk with you might have set his imagination on fire and got him out, but I doubt his going unless that happens. [*In AG's hand*] Many thanks for the photograph, I am very glad to have it—I wish the dogs were having a run here—yours always snl

A Gregory

TLS NYPL.

To Florence Farr, [c. 28 September 1904]

. . . there is an account of it in the county paper. 'The United Irishman'[1] has interviewed the tinker who threatens me with a libel action if the play keeps his daughter from making a good match. He says indignantly he'd never let her marry a man like Paul with no right way of supporting her.

---

[7] Douglas Hyde's visit to the USA took place from November 1905 to June 1906, in the course of which he collected over $64,000 for the Gaelic League.

[1] See p. 632, n. 4.

I had a charming dream of you last night.

Yrs ev
W B Yeats
P.T.O.

    First Musician.[2]
'Why is it?' Queen Edaine said
'If I do but climb the stair
In the tower over head
When the winds are calling there
Or the gannets calling out
In waste places of the sky
Theres so much to think about
That I cry, that I cry.'
    Second Musician.
But her good man answered her
'Love would be a thing of naught
Had not all his limbs a stir
Born out of immoderate thought;
Were he anything by half;
Were his measures running dry.
Lovers, if they may not laugh,
Have to cry, have to cry.'
    All togeather on seeing Dierdre enter
But is Edaine worth a song
Now the hunt begins anew.
Praise the beautiful and strong,
Praise the redness of the yew,
Praise the blossoming apple stem
      (*in a softer voice & turning away*)
But our silence had been wise.
What is all our praise to them
That have one anothers eyes.

A frag MBY.

---

[2] Compare previous letter, p. 651. WBY told FF on 4 Nov 1906 that the 'first musician was written for you—I always saw your face as I wrote very curiously your face even more than your voice and built the character out of that'. He also inscribed these songs on the endpapers of AG's copy of *Poems* (1901) now at Emory.

To George Roberts, 29 September [1904]

Coole Park | Gort, Co Galway.
Sept 29

My dear Roberts,

I sent you THE CAUSEWAY by Frank Fay.[1] It has no merits of any kind and would bore an audience to death. This is not my opinion for the committee, for I will give the Committee my opinion when it meets. Now that we are starting afresh on a larger scale and now above all that our whole position depends upon the legality of our actions, we must be very careful to act constitutionally. Seven separate opinions are not the opinions of a committee. A Committee is a deliberative body, and must meet. I think it is quite right for every member of the committee to read whatever play is under discussion, but the voting should only take place at the proper meeting. We must decide upon a quorum and absent members can give their opinion in writing. We shall have to decide whether we can permit people to vote who are not present. The present arrangement might lead us into trouble at any moment. If a member who objected to any decision were to raise the question of the legality of the acceptance of a play accepted under the old arrangement, and if that objection came before the chairman at any of our meetings, I cannot see how that chairman could do otherwise than rule against the acceptance. Certainly I should so rule. If the play had been performed, we would have given an illegal performance and the theatres could attack us for going beyond our patent. Of course it is wildly unlikely that anything of this kind would happen, but less evils would happen. I have had a long experience of societies, and I have never known a society that was lax about its rules without getting into trouble sooner or later. Things go well enough at first, but as soon as differences of opinion arise, and become at all heated, there is endless confusion and suspicion if the habit of legality has not been acquired. Apart from all this, the present method of selection by seven individual opinions is unfair to the best opinions. When men meet and discuss, the men who know most about it convince the others. If on the other hand anyone has an objection which is merely frivolous it is talked out and he gives it up. Suppose for instance that I have received a play for my opinion and I hear through some acci-

---

[1] The play was neither published nor produced, but it was evidently not by Fay, since the manuscript, now in NLI, records it as the work of an anonymous lady. The INTS Reading Committee, comprising AE, F. J. Fay and W. G. Fay had considered the play on 14 Sept and decided (NLI) that it 'would not be done as it stands, some alter[ations] proposed & if made the play to be reconsidered'.

dent that William Fay and Synge are against it, but do not know their reasons, how am I to give my opinion? William Fay may for instance know that the Company are entirely incapable of performing it. Synge may have discovered that it is let us say a mere imitation of some French play; or he may have reasons which would convince me it was bad dramatically the moment I heard them. We do not require many Committee meetings; meetings at stated intervals when we are pretty well together will do. In any case if say a fortnight's notice is given one would either attend or write at length what one had to say. Minutes also should be kept as to the work of the selection Committee, and these should be signed by the chairman in the usual way. The issues are now far too important not to take the usual precautions. Remember that if the society were to split and the governing authorities were not able to carry a certain percentage of the members with them, our patent would lapse. Please show this letter to all who it may concern.[2]

I shall be in town very shortly, and we can hold a committee meeting then. Please let me know, as soon as you are sure, when they will be

---

[2] A meeting of the INTS Reading Committee, held on 26 Oct and attended by WBY (in the Chair), Synge, the Fays, and Colum, acted upon these suggestions, and, as the Minutes (NLI) record, carried through far-reaching changes to the Committee.

Mr Yeats proposed that the following bylaws for the working of this committee be adopted:—
That a quorum of 4 members be necessary at each meeting.
A chairman to be elected at each meeting & to have a casting vote. A definite date to be fixed for each meeting, the secretary to ascertain from the members when a meeting could be held & fourteen days notice to be sent. In cases where members cannot attend proxy voting to be allowed, the letters containing the opinion of absent members to be read before the votes of those present is taken.
That there be three forms for acceptance of plays viz:—
    Absolute acceptance
    Provisionally accepted
    The plays in this last class may be reconsidered & performed if at any time new plays are required & no more suitable work is forthcoming.
Reading Committee when accepting plays should arrange with authors what rights society are to have over plays & that complete copyright for Ireland should be asked for for a period of 5 years & a notification of any performance elsewhere will be expected by the Society.
                                                                                        Passed unanimously
Proposed by Mr Yeats that a special general meeting be summoned—at a date to be arranged later—to alter rule regarding acceptance of plays as follows:—
    'That the decision upon all the grounds of the reading committee as to the acceptance or rejection of a play be final'
and
    'That any member shall be exempt from playing on conscientious grounds in any play accepted.'
Decided that above may be put before society at a general meeting called for the purpose.

rehearsing in the new theatre.[3] When we meet we will consider whether some bye laws are not necessary—

Yrs sny

W B Yeats

TLS Harvard.

To James Sullivan Starkey, [1 October 1904]

at | COOLE PARK, | GORT, | CO. GALWAY.

My dear Starkie: send me the verses by all means. I shall go through them with pleasure & tell you what I think.[1]

I hear the 'Hermetic Society' thinks of becoming a theosophical society. I hope Russell will keep his independence. He is so mixed up with the whole movement in Ireland that it will be a pity if he gives our enemies a chance to rake up old theosophical scandals against him—charges against H P Blavatsky which are no integral part of his battle. I shall write to him about this but I think that you should all weigh the matter. Is it well to give a ready stone into your enemies hands at the very outset of a movement which may bring us into conflict with public opinion on grounds, which are definitely our grounds.[2]

---

[3] The first day of rehearsal in the Abbey Theatre was on 31 Oct when Holloway (*Abbey Theatre*, 44) found AG and Quinn 'seated on the half-finished front pit seat, and W. B. Yeats wandering excitedly about among the planks and rubbish in momentary danger of coming a-cropper'.

[1] Emboldened by the reception of his verse in *New Songs* (see p. 577), Starkey was now planning a slim volume of poetry, and was eager for WBY's advice. The book, *The Twilight People*, appeared in 1905, and, as the title suggests, owed much to WBY's earlier but now discarded style.

[2] The power struggle in the Theosophical Society, following Madame Blavatsky's death in 1891, had resulted in a schism between the American branch, led by William Quan Judge (1851–96), and that based in Adyar under the guidance of Annie Besant (1847–1933) and Col. H. S. Olcott (1832–1907); see I. 408. Alone among the European lodges, the Dublin Society had supported Judge, but after his death quickly dissociated itself from his successor, Mrs Katherine Tingley, and in 1898 AE resigned from the Theosophical Society and founded the Hermetic Society. This Society was now proposing to join the Adyar Theosophists and on 20 Oct 1904 Col. Olcott chartered a second Dublin Lodge, whose members included Russell, his wife, Starkey, W. G. Fay, Mr and Mrs Powis Hoult, Mrs Greene, Mrs Charles Kelly, John Quigley, and H. F. Norman (Secretary). WBY, who had always disliked the limpness of Theosophical attitudes, clearly felt that such an affiliation was retrograde, and especially inopportune at a time when Catholic bigotry was finding a strident voice in periodicals like the *Leader*. The Dublin group seceded from Adyar in 1909 when Annie Besant succeeded Olcott as President, but continued as an independent Hermetic Society until 1933 when AE left Ireland. Madame Blavatsky, founder of the Theosophical Society, had acquired notoriety in 1885 when, accused of faking occult phenomena, she was investigated by Richard Hodgson of the Society for Psychical Research who described her as 'one of the most accomplished, ingenious, and interesting impostors in history'. WBY, who knew her in London, had read Hodgson's report and 'awaited with impatience the explanation that never came' (*Mem*, 24).

My "Dierdre" goes on slowly, but prosperously.[3] It will be my best play—my Dierdre is a very confident serene person.

Yr ev
W B Yeats

ALS Texas, with envelope addressed to Irish National Theatre Society, 34 Lower Camden St, Dublin, postmark 'ORANMORE OC 1 04'.

To James Joyce, 2 October [1904]

Coole Park, | Gort, Co Galway
Oct 2

My dear Joyce,

I cannot send you your plays[1] today, as it is Sunday, and the post wont take parcels. I shall send them tomorrow, but have not quite finished them. I gave them to a friend who is a German scholar to read some time ago, and she saw, what indeed you know yourself, that you are not a very good German scholar. I have been meaning however myself to go over them, and have just got into them. I think however it is very unlikely that we can make any use of them for the theatre. I have already a translation of a Sudermann play made by a friend who seems anxious to do anything of that kind.[2] You see at present we have absolutely no fund out of which we can pay for work of any kind. We are given a theatre but we shall have to make out of our performances every penny of our working capital. Later on of course we hope to be able to pay. Nor do I think it very likely we could attempt German work at present. We must get the ear of our public with Irish work. I am very sorry I cannot help you with money. I did my best to get you work as you know, but that is all I can do for you.

Yours snly
W B Yeats

TLS Yale.

[3] *Deirdre* was published by A. H. Bullen in 1907 as vol. v of 'Plays for an Irish Theatre'.

[1] Joyce had sent WBY his translations of Hauptmann's *Before Dawn* (*Vor Sonnenaufgang*, 1889) and *Michael Kramer* (1900) for possible production at the Abbey Theatre. WBY had discussed the plays with AG, who told George Roberts on 22 Sept (Widener) that WBY would 'return Mr. Joyce's translations in a day or two', and who speaks in *70 Years* (393) of her renewed use of German while writing *Cuchulain of Muirthemne* and *Gods and Fighting Men*.

[2] i.e. Alice Spencer; see p. 289, n. 3. AG's translation of Hermann Sudermann's *Teja* (1896) was first produced on 19 Mar 1908 at the Abbey Theatre.

To Maud Gonne, [*early October 1904*]

Mention in following letter.

To George Russell (AE), [*early October 1904*]

COOLE PARK, | GORT, | CO. GALWAY.

My dear Russell: please send on the enclosed—her letter only gives me a country address in France & I suppose her to be now in Paris.[1] I liked your pamphlet well enough—except that the Leader *does* hate thought of other peoples. I dont like the long letter however.[2] If the Leader was to be answered it should, as I think have been on a quite impersonal ground. Neither your character nor the character of any of us need defence. We should not discuss such things with any but our equals. Of course you make points—but why should you make them. Had you attacked the paper, not fearing to fall into a passion, though surely a polite one, because of its abusiveness, & its hate for all ideas not part of its own very narrow programe it would have been Quixotic & probably useless but at least you would have written a fine essay, & to use Blakes phrase, turned your enemy into ornament.[3] I wish you would return, (probably in *Dana* would

[1] WBY's letter, evidently to MG, is untraced.

[2] Following the journalistic attacks on Horace Plunkett's *Ireland in the New Century* for its allegedly anti-Catholic bias (see p. 463, n. 6), AE published an article, 'Physical Force in Literature', in the September number of *Dana* (129–33), denouncing the 'thoughtless savagery' and blind bigotry of the Irish press, and calling for humanity, tolerance, and independent thought. Although he did not mention the *Leader* by name, it was clearly one of his main targets and in a coat-trailing rejoinder there on 10 Sept (37–9) its editor, D. P. Moran (see p. 6), describing AE as an 'eminently business-like and skilfully advertised minor poet', challenged him to 'join issue with us on the Bigotry . . . question and we will give him space'. AE took up the gauntlet on 17 Sept (52), and asked permission to reprint Moran's article with his own in a pamphlet, *Controversy in Ireland*, published *c.* 23 Sept 1904. The *Leader* returned to the attack on 24 Sept through 'Imaal' (John O'Toole), one of its regular columnists, who rejected AE's arguments and complained (76) of an 'air of moral superiority about this gentleman which is simply unendurable, just as there is an equally intolerable air of superiority in mind and culture about his set'. Answering this in the 'long letter' of 1 Oct (88–90), which WBY did not like, AE oscillated unhappily between patronising hauteur and lame concessiveness, maintaining on the one hand that 'my friends . . . would no more think of replying to you than a member of the aristocracy would dream of noticing some petty scandal invented of him in a society paper read by housemaids', but confessing on the other that the accusation of his being smugly superior 'did touch me a little. I probably deserved that.' Printing the letter under the heading 'A Minor Poet in Eruption', Moran gibed at the 'pretty exhibition he makes of himself. . . . Biddy Moriarty has her arms akimbo and is giving forth.' The controversy continued in the paper until 15 Oct.

[3] In 'Public Address' from *The Note-Book* (*c.* 1810) Blake wrote (Bentley, 1045): 'I wonder who can say, "Speak no Ill of the dead" when it is asserted in the Bible that the name of the Wicked shall Rot. It is Deistical Virtue, I suppose, but as I have none of this I will pour Aqua fortis on the Name of the Wicked & turn it into an Ornament & an Example to be Avoided by Some & Imitated by Others if they Please.'

be best), to this question of abusiveness.[4] If you write on it & do not bring in that other question of thought (which will seem to the Irish papers to mean atheistic thought) you may have a great effect. I dare say however you might have a difficulty in leaving out what is so near your heart, & wish there was some one—this is hardly work for you—who would review the Irish papers from time to time constantly on this one point. I wish that 'Dana' would say every month 'such & such a paper has called M^r so & so such & such'—& do this exaustively. I had a plan once for a thermometer of abuse—rows of adjectives & nouns like this to be published at stated intervals—a weather chart

Irish Times.   Freeman.   Leader.   United Irishman.

a prize to be given at the end of the year for the most copious. Lady Gregorys little play 'Spreading the News' is I think a delight. It has a fine part for Fay—a meloncholy man, the image of George Pollexfen.[5]

Yr ev
W B Yeats

ALS Harvard.

[4] AE did not publish any more articles on the Irish press in *Dana*, but he returned to the subject of 'abusiveness' in the *Leader* on 15 Oct.

[5] The lugubrious Bartley Fallon, upon whom misfortunes pitch 'like a flock of crows on seed potatoes'.

To George Bernard Shaw, 5 October [1904]

Coole Park | Gort, Co Galway
Oct 5

My dear Shaw,

I have been very long about thanking you for the play.[1] I waited until I could give you Fay's opinion and Synge's. I sent the play to Synge the moment I had read it, and he went off to Belmullet, and neither wrote nor sent an address until yesterday. He sent the play back however through a member of the company he met on the way to Belmullet, and I sent it to William Fay, from whom I have heard this morning. I enclose his letter. Synge who is always rather languid in his letter writing tells me very little, except that he will tell me a great deal when we meet next week at rehearsal.[2] Now as to my own opinion.

I was disappointed by the first act and a half. The stage Irishman who wasn't an Irishman was very amusing,[3] but then I said to myself 'What the devil did Shaw mean by all this Union of Hearts-like conversation? What do we care here in this country, which despite the Act of Union is still an island, about the English Liberal party and the Tariff, and the difference between English and Irish character, or whatever else it was all about.[4]

[1] Shaw told WBY on 31 Aug that he hoped to have a prompt copy of the play ready by 10 Sept (*BSCL* II. 452), and, since he sent the MS to the typist on 7 Sept, WBY presumably received it on or shortly after that date. As Shaw explained in his 'Preface for Politicians', *'John Bull's Other Island* was written in 1904 at the request of Mr. William Butler Yeats, as a patriotic contribution to the repertory. Like most people who have asked me to write plays, Mr. Yeats got rather more than he bargained for. The play was at that time beyond the resources of the new Abbey Theatre. . . . There was another reason for changing the destination of *John Bull's Other Island*. It is uncongenial to the whole spirit of the neo-Gaelic movement, which is bent on creating a new Ireland after its own ideal, whereas my play is a very uncompromising presentment of the real old Ireland' (p. v). The play reverses the clichéd opposition of stage Irishman and hard-headed Englishman, when the supposedly sensible English civil engineer, Thomas Broadbent, sentimentalises over Irish stereotypes on a trip to develop the village of Rosscullen into a holiday resort, while his Irish partner, Larry Doyle, looks on with shrewd and despairing realism.
[2] Synge's letter does not survive. On 17 Sept he had visited Mayo for the first time, going by boat from Sligo to Belmullet, a small seaport on the western coast.
[3] In planning his journey, Broadbent is deceived into taking Tim Haffigan, a drunken sponger, playing up to the stage-Irish image, as an authentic Irishman, and is wheedled out of large amounts of whisky and a banknote. He subsequently learns that Haffigan was born in Glasgow.
[4] This is disingenuous since much writing of the Irish literary revival, including WBY's own prose, and Martyn's and Moore's plays for the ILT, had been concerned with Anglicization and with differentiating the supposed qualities of the Irish and English mind. But WBY no doubt found Shaw's association of the 'spirit of the neo-Gaelic movement' (see n. 1) with Broadbent's English sentimentality 'uncongenial', and a number of Doyle's deflating observations unpalatable: 'When people talk about the Celtic race, I feel as if I could burn down London. That sort of rot does more harm than ten Coercion Acts. . . . An Irishman. . . . cant be intelligently political: he dreams of what the Shan Van Vocht said in ninetyeight. If you want to interest him in Ireland youve got to call the unfortunate island Kathleen ni Hoolihan and pretend she's a little old

Being raw people, I said, we do care about human nature in action, and that he's not giving us.' Then my interest began to awake, That young woman who persuaded that Englishman, full of the impulsiveness that comes from a good banking account, that he was drunk on nothing more serious than poteen, was altogether a delight. The motor car too, the choosing the member of Parliament, and so on right to the end, often exciting and mostly to the point. I thought in reading the first act that you had forgotten Ireland, but I found in the other acts that it is the only subject on which you are entirely serious. In fact you are so serious that sometimes your seriousness leaps upon the stage, knocks the characters over, and insists on having all the conversation to himself. However the inevitable cutting (the play is as you say immensely too long)[5] is certain to send your seriousness back to the front row of the stalls. You have said things in this play which are entirely true about Ireland, things which nobody has ever said before, and these are the very things that are most part of the action. It astonishes me that you should have been so long in London and yet have remembered so much. To some extent this play is unlike anything you have done before. Hitherto you have taken your situations from melodrama, and called up logic to make them ridiculous. Your process here seems to be quite different, you are taking your situations more from life, you are for the first time trying to get the atmosphere of a place, you have for the first time a geographical conscience. (for instance you have not made the landlords the winning side, as you did the Servians in the first version of Arms and the Man).[6]

woman. It saves thinking. It saves working. It saves everything except imagination . . .' In the first act Broadbent, a strong supporter of the Liberal Party and Free Trade, expostulates against the iniquities of tariffs.

[5] Shaw was worried by the length of the play, and had confided to Granville Barker on 27 Sept: 'The cutting will be awful. All the tissue seems to me to be vital: I cant get the blue pencil in without cutting an artery. However, it's got to be done.' (*Bernard Shaw's Letters to Granville Barker*, ed. C. B. Purdom [1956], p. 37). In fact, the only substantial cut in the play was made in Act I, and is quoted by Daniel Leary in *Bulletin of the New York Public Library* (November, 1970), pp. 598–606.

[6] See I. 384, 386. FF's production of *Arms and the Man* at the Avenue Theatre opened on 21 Apr 1894, with WBY's *The Land of Heart's Desire* as curtain-raiser, and was first published in *Plays, Pleasant and Unpleasant* (1898). Situated in a small Bulgarian town during the Serbo-Bulgarian War of 1885, it amusingly questions and subverts received ideas about heroism and military prowess. In an interview in *To-day*, 28 Apr 1894, Shaw explained that, his 'historical information being rather confused', Sidney Webb had suggested 'that the Servo-Bulgarian was what I wanted. I then read the account of the war in the *Annual Register*, with a modern railway map of the Balkan Peninsula before me, and filled in my blanks, making all the action take place in Servia, in the house of a Servian family. I then read the play to . . . the Admiral who commanded the Bulgarian Fleet during the war, who happens to reside in London just now. He made me change the scene from Servia to Bulgaria, the characters from Servians to Bulgarians, and gave me descriptions of Bulgarian life and ideas, which enabled me to fit my play exactly with local colour and character.' In *John Bull's Other Island* the bankrupt landlord, Nick Lestrange, is treated with sympathy.

Synge who is as good an opinion as I know, thinks that "it will hold a Dublin audience, and at times move them if even tolerably played." He thinks however that you should cut the Grasshopper, and a scene which I cannot recall, but which he describes as "The Handy Andy like scene about carrying the goose"[7] and some of the Englishman's talk about Free Trade, Tariffs &c. I asked him to make suggestions about cuts, as I thought that our knowledge of local interests here might be valuable to you. I shall myself have one or two suggestions on details to make, but they can stand over. I have no doubt you will cut in your own way, but you may as well hear them. I had a theory when I was a boy that a play should be very long, and contain a great deal about everything, put in quite without respect to times and occasions, and that every man who played it should take the slice that suited him. I cannot say I hold that theory now, but there is something in it, the two parts of Goethe's Faust for instance, and the use all sorts of people make of them. To my surprise I must say, I do not consider the play dangerous. There may be a phrase, but I cannot think of one at this moment. Here again, you show your wonderful knowledge of the country. You have laughed at the things that are ripe for laughter, and not where the ear is still green.[8] I dont mean to say that there wont be indignation about one thing or another, and a great deal of talk about it all, but I mean that we can play it, and survive to play something else. You will see by Fay's letter that he is nervous about being able to cast it. I imagine the Englishman will give us most difficulty, but it will all be difficult.

I shall be in Dublin next week, and will talk the whole matter over with the company. It would be a help if you could let me know your own feeling about cuts. I will then have the play in my hands again and can go into detail.

Yours sny
W B Yeats

[7] At the beginning of Act II Peter Keegan, a spoilt priest, conducts an ironic conversation with a grasshopper on the state of Ireland. This is followed by a scene in which an over-encumbered servant, Patsy Farrell, drops the luggage and provisions, including a goose, he is delivering. In an attempt to pick everything up he offers to carry the goose by the neck in his mouth. Shaw retained both incidents. The eponymous hero of Samuel Lover's novel *Handy Andy* (1842) is a broadly drawn version of the stage Irishman.

[8] In a lecture, 'Modern Ireland', delivered on his American tour of 1932, WBY said that Shaw had 'displayed in the character of the spoilt priest Ireland as it appears to the Irish novelists and dramatists of today, and summed up what might be their final thought. Four years [ago], while ill in Italy, and not sure I would know active life again, I wrote in my diary the events of life and art that had most [moved] me, and I numbered the moralizing of the spoilt priest' (*Massachusetts Review* [Winter, 1964], pp. 267–8).

[*With enclosure*]

56 High

Dear Mr Yeates

I have read through Shaw's play I think it is a wonderful piece of work. But as to our using it I would like a longer time to consider it for I only read it yesterday. It is full of fine things but the difficulty of getting a cáste for it would be considerable. I dont know how he expects to get a show of it in London for with the exception of the Englishman & his valet the rest would have to be Irish born & bred to get the hang of what he wants.

In sending you stage directions for Kathleen & Pot, they can be gummed into the book edition and contain all that I know they want. Photos to follow. About what you wrote Roberts re Reading Committee I agree but dont see how it can be done with you in London, Russell & Synge different parts of the country as it generally happens when a play comes in.[9]

WGF

TLS BL. W. G. Fay's letter card is addressed to Coole, postmark 'Dublin OC 4 04'.

To Phillip Bayard Veiller, [c. *12 October 1904*]

Mention in following letter.

To John Quinn, [*12 October 1904*]

at | COOLE PARK, | GORT, | CO. GALWAY.

My dear Quinn: I dont think I ever thanked you for 'Child Christopher'[1] which was such a delight to me during the hardest part of my travels—my days in the worst end of St Lewis. I shall read it all through again presently. You have been so infinitely kind about so many things that I fear I sometimes forget to thank you for the individual things. I have had to send the letter for 'Veiller' about the plays C/o of you as the address in his

---

[9] See pp. 654–5.

[1] Quinn had probably sent WBY a copy of J. B. Mosher's American edition of William Morris's *Child Christopher and Goldilind the Fair* (Portland, 1900) reprinted from the 2-volume Kelmscott Press edition of 1895. For WBY's experience of the 'worst end' of St Louis see p. 513.

letter seems to be a passing one.² I wish you could see the delightful comedy 'Spreading the news' Lady Gregory has just finished. It is a little thing, but perfect, one of the best I ever read. Fay is delighted. Shaws play has come, & is a very unequal work but some of it very amusing. It is greatly too long & there is a deal of irrelevant conversations which he is to cut out but it has throughout a curious new & I think true view of Ireland to-day—It is not so dangerous as I feared. It has a little dissapointed me but if we can play it should enliven things a good deal.

The post is going out.

Yr ev
W B Yeats

PS. I have written to Veiller to day & suggested his doing 'Pot of Broth' making the woman in it quite young as when we play it.

ALS NYPL.

To A. H. Bullen, 30 October [1904]

18 Woburn Buildings | Euston Road
Oct 30

My dear Bullen
The Income Tax people are trying to make me pay Income Tax on £500 a year—They refuse to accept my word & I have to go to an enquiry before them next Thursday—& to bring accounts.¹ I am sorry to give you so much trouble, but I shall be greatly obliged if you will write me a letter stating roughly what you have paid me during the three years ending April 1904. I am crossing over to London Tuesday night—

Yr ev
W B Yeats

Dict AG, signed WBY; Texas.

² The American playwright Bayard Veiller (1869–1943) was the husband and manager of Margaret Wycherley (see p. 614, n. 1), and had been in negotiations with Quinn since July to arrange her tour of WBY's plays. In a letter of 5 Aug (MBY) Quinn had promised him that, while in Dublin, he would procure 'the prompt copies of the plays . . . and also any photographs or drawings already made and will also get the music used in the songs of Cathleen-ni-Houlihan. . . . I will . . . get from Mr. Yeats and Mr. Fay their suggestions in regard to the staging of the plays.' Since his trip to Ireland had been postponed, he had presumably asked WBY to supply this information direct. WBY's letter to Veiller is now lost but Miss Wycherley did not include *The Pot of Broth* in her programme.

¹ The Income Tax Inspectors refused to believe that a man so much in the public eye could earn so little, and had estimated the tax they thought payable on his supposed income. He evidently managed to convince the Enquiry that his figures were correct.

To Charles Elkin Mathews, 30 October 1904

18 Woburn Buildings, | Euston Road.
Oct 30, 1904

My dear Mathews: The income tax people have assessed my income at a preposterous sum & I have to appear before them next Thursday morning. I will be greatly obliged if you will write me a letter stating roughly what you have paid me during the three years up to April 1904.

Printed extract, listed in Kirgo's catalogue, New Haven, March 1952, Item 395, with an envelope and enclosing a pencilled note from AG, ordering a copy of *The Tables of the Law*.

To James Sullivan Starkey, [30 October 1904]

Nassau Hotel
Sunday

My dear Starkie—

I have your M. S. for you but I would like to have a talk with you about it[1]—Could you come in about eleven tomorrow morning? Or if not, please leave word what time would suit you.

Yrs sny
W B Yeats

Dict AG, signed WBY; TCD; with envelope addressed to 28 Dawson Chambers, Dawson St., postmark 'DUBLIN OC 30 04'.

To Lady Augusta Gregory, 7 November 1904

18 Woburn Buildings | Euston Rd.
7th November 1904.

My dear Lady Gregory,

Jack is to design scenery for Synge's play, some tree wings, a cottage, and two big chairs. I went out to Ricketts on Friday evening[1] and he

---

[1] Of *The Twilight People*; see p. 656, n. 1.

[1] In *SP* (111) Ricketts records that on 4 Nov 1904 'Yeats and American, Pissarro [*i.e. Lucien Pissarro (1893–1944), an artist and eldest son of Camille Pissarro*] and Lady [*a mistranscription for 'young'*] Gregory and friend in evening'.

offered to do scenery for a play, we must think what we must set him at. I
will discuss this with you when we meet. He said when we wanted him we
should say how much money we could spend and so forth. He is full of
fine ideas. If Robert wants advice about Kincora he will give it him. Robert
came out on Friday evening, we met him there; he came on from Miss
Horniman's. I have seen Shaw's play; it acts very much better than one
could have forseen, but is immensely long.[2] It begins at 2.30 and ends at 6.
I don't really like it. It is fundimentally ugly and shapeless, but certainly
keeps everybody amused.[3] O'Donovan and Quinn and Mrs Emery are dining with me to-night. I have also asked Symons and Mrs Symons to dine
on Tuesday or Wednesday to meet Quinn. I haven't been able to do much
for O'Donovan, as Masefield is in Manchester and Nevenson is on his way
up the Congo to study the slave trade.[4] I brought Quinn out to Mrs Emery
on Sunday to hear her speak to the Psaltery. Quin[n] wants to get a photograph of George Meredith and Holery [*for* Hollyer] won't sell it to him
without permission from the family. Quin[n] wants you to send him a note
of introduction to young Meredith.[5] He is staying at the Carlton Hotel[6]
and would like to have the note if you could send it, by Wednesday morning. I went to a performance at "His Majestys". Tree has turned the tem-

[2] *John Bull's Other Island* was first produced by the Vedrenne–Barker management at the
Court Theatre in a series of six matinées from 1 to 11 Nov.

[3] At a command performance of the play in 1906, Edward VII laughed so much that he broke
his chair.

[4] Gerald O'Donovan, formerly Father Jeremiah O'Donovan of Loughrea (see p. 112), had left
the priesthood in September of this year, moving first to Dublin, and then to London where,
armed with a letter from George Moore, he was seeking journalistic work. Masefield had begun
writing the daily 'Miscellany' column in the *Manchester Guardian* in October. Nevinson, who
wrote for the *Daily Chronicle*, had left not for the Congo but for the Portuguese colony of Angola
to investigate the slave trade, returning in August 1905 to present his findings in *A Modern Slavery* (1906).

[5] Frederick Hollyer's photograph of the novelist George Meredith, taken in 1887, attracted
considerable fame, but copies could only be obtained through personal contact since Meredith, as
he explained to a correspondent on 12 Oct 1904 (*LGM* III. 1508), had 'laid an interdict on the sale
of Hollyer's photograph, and cannot raise it without doing injustice to others making the request'.
In 1907 (*LGM* III. 1588) he revealed that he had imposed the ban because 'otherwise it might
soon be in the shop-windows'. Hollyer had photographed WBY for W. E. Henley in 1890, and
another Hollyer photograph appears in Michael MacLiammoir and Eavan Boland, *W. B. Yeats
and His World* (1971), 23. William Maxse Meredith (1865–1937) was George Meredith's son by
his second wife, Marie Vulliamy. Quinn, a great admirer of Meredith, had an extensive collection
of his first editions, but does not seem to have obtained the photograph he wanted.

[6] WBY apparently lodged at the Carleton Hotel on the eve of Quinn's departure for America
and, as he told Shannon and Ricketts on 12 Nov 1904 (BL): 'in the evening, a note had been
delivered to his room, but as it was addressed to the singer, Jean de Reszke, he sent it away. During the night, on hearing soft knocking, he turned on the light and opened the door in the belief
that it was his friend Shine [*for* Quinn] getting him up early. In came a lady in a bright rose-
coloured dressing gown. "Oh, I beg your pardon" and she laughed and fled. Ricketts admired the
lady's laugh and rather wished she had kissed Yeats on each cheek "on each side the forelock".'

pest into a very common and vulgar pantomime, the verse is very badly spoken too. The whole thing is the worst that even Tree has done.[7]

Yrs sny

W B Yeats

PS. I shall go back very soon—as soon probably as Quinn goes. There is nothing to do here & nothing coming on that I can wait for.

TLS Berg, with envelope addressed to the Nassau Hotel, South Fredrick St, Dublin, and redirected to 49 George Street, Portman Square, London; postmark 'LONDON S.W. NO 7 04'. Wade, 442–3.

To F. J. Fay, 7 November 1904

18 Woburn Buildings, | Euston Rd.

7th November 1904.

My dear Fay,

I have made arrangements about the designs and Miss Horniman will have told you the result of my conversation with her. It would be a great mistake for us to use anything in connection with our show in which there is not the mark of an individual intellect. I feel very strongly that even the slightest use of the stereotype patterns of the commercial scene painter would be injurious. It would be a great loss of emphasis. I feel this even more strongly than when I left Dublin owing to the effect upon me of Tree's production of "*The Tempest*"—unspeakable in its vulgarity. I suggested to Miss Horniman that she should herself arrange the details of the two drawing-room scenes which she proposes. One she says is to be for concert purposes and has to be thought out in relation to the architecture and colour of the Theatre itself the other which she thinks may be painted on the back of this is to be an ordinary room. This is the scene which concerns us, and if she arranges it, it will have the look of an ordinary drawing-room not of a stage drawing-room. Remember I object to the stage drawing-room, more because it is a stereotyped form than because it [is] necessarily bad in itself. It generally is, but that is another story. The real difficulty comes in with the open air scenes. I have seen both Charles

---

[7] *The Tempest* played at His Majesty's Theatre from 14 Sept 1904 to 19 Jan 1905, with Tree in the role of Caliban. Hesketh Pearson described the production as 'a presentation so gorgeous that several critics raised the lament that poetry was being sacrificed to pomp. The opening scene showed a complete ship rocking in a realistic sea, the breakers roaring, the waves splashing over the deck, the wind tearing the sails. The pantomimic scenes towards the end were Shakespeare's, and the producer did his best to make them effective. Those who disliked stage illusion need not go to the theatre, said Tree: "The bookworm has always his book"' (*Beerbohm Tree* [1956], 132). Such sumptuousness ran counter to WBY's views on stage scenery.

Ricketts and my brother about these. Charles Ricketts would have designed them if I had asked him but I thought it better to reserve him for something later on. I have however told his ideas to Jack who had already come to practically the same conclusions. Jack promises to send you by next Thursday designs for six tree wings as well as a cottage design. The cottage design will probably be very much what you would have made yourself but there will be certain little inventions as to characteristic objects on the wall and so forth. The departure from type will come in the tree wings. I never saw tree wings that were not vulgar and we may have to experiment a bit. Jack will recognise the fact that he is working on a flat surface exactly as a potter recognises that he is decorating a round surface. He will no more disguise the flatness of the surface than a sculptor the marble upon which he works. Jack will mass colour and form and treat the whole thing decoratively. Later on he will send designs for Synge's play. The preliminary experiments for these tree wings will help him; should it happen, which is very unlikely, that these wings prove unsuitable for ordinary letting purposes, then we should get others, but the commercial article should be kept out of our plays. Even if an artist's work prove to be less effective than the ordinary stage scene to ordinary eyes, it will soon grow even to ordinary eyes much more effective, as the artist learns his business, and from the first it will show an individual mind. Jack will also send to me two designs for great chairs and these I will get made either here in London or over in Dublin.

I saw Bernard Shaw's play. It is amusing but immensely too long. I don't know what to say about it. Quin[n] thinks we should do it if we could do it adequately but to do that we should need two Englishmen.

Yours snly
W B Yeats

TLS Private.

To John Quinn, 7 November 1904

18 Woburn Buildings | Euston Rd.
7th Nov. 1904.

My dear Quinn,

As you know my sisters have a private press in Dublin. They are bringing out limited editions of certain Irish books. They have an edition of The Hanrahan Stories printed and ready for binding. They had hoped to be able to publish them at Christmas, but McClure writes to me to say that he hopes to have the stories published in his magazine by March or April. I want you to find out from him if you see him whether he would object to my sister's edition coming out in December or during the holidays.[1] If he has the slightest objection she will keep it back. Please either write or cable me as soon as you have seen McClure. I also send you a couple of lyrics,[2] as McClure writes that he is anxious for some more of my verse—at least that is my recollection of his letter or may be I got it from you. You will recognise that one of them is a chorus out [of] my new play "Deirdre".

Soon after my return from America I wrote a short article of about 18,000 words of "Impressions of America". I took some pains with it and think it a good article. I sent it to A. P. Watt, my agent here. There has been some unaccountable delay and I have only just heard that the "Fortnightly Review" has taken it on this side.[3] I told Watt to send it to McClure but I don't suppose he has done so. I will write to him about it at once, and he will doubtless write to McClure about it direct.

Yours snly
W B Yeats

TLS NYPL.

To Henry D. Davray,[1] *13 November 1904*

18 Woburn Buildings, | Euston Road, | London.
Nov. 13^(th)./04.

My dear Davary,
    I cannot find your letter but I suppose that the "Mercure de France" will find you.

---

[1] This letter, written while Quinn was still in London, seems intended as a memorandum for his return to New York. One of the stories, 'Red Hanrahan's Vision' (later 'Hanrahan's Vision'), appeared in *McClure's Magazine* for March 1905 (see p. 586, n. 2). The Dun Emer Press delayed publication of *Stories of Red Hanrahan* until May 1905.
[2] 'Queen Edaine', which appeared in *McClure's Magazine* in September 1905, followed by 'Never Give All the Heart' in December 1905.
[3] See p. 563. Published as 'America and the Arts' in the *Metropolitan Magazine* of April 1905. It did not appear in the *Fortnightly Review*.

[1] Henry D. Davray (1873–1944), editor, translator, critic, and journalist, played a valuable role for 50 years in establishing literary contacts between England and France. As an editor of *Le Mercure de France*, he had since 1898 been responsible for the 'Lettres Anglaises' section, which reviewed English books and periodicals. He translated works by Gosse, Meredith, Wells, Bennett, Kipling, Conrad, and Fiona Macleod among others, including WBY's 'The Sad Shepherd' and 'The Untiring Ones' (*L'Hermitage*, July 1896) and 'Rosa Alchemica' (*Le Mercure de France*, October 1898). WBY had met him in Paris in January 1897 and February 1899, and was to see him there again in April 1911 and August 1917. Davray moved to London after the First World War, and co-edited the *Anglo-French Review* from 1918 to 1921. He translated no more of WBY's stories after 1898.

As far as I am concerned you are quite welcome to translate those stories. The business side will have to be arranged with my publisher A. H. Bullen 47 Great Russell Street, London. W. C. Let him make what arrangement he likes, so long as he does not bother me about it. Please tell him this. Perhaps you might send him this letter. I am very sorry that I left your letter so long unanswered, but I am in a whirl of work; our new Irish Theatre opens some time in December.

I hope that I shall meet you again some of these days.

I always look back with great pleasure to our many meetings in Paris, perhaps some day you may come to Ireland & I may be able to introduce you to our young men of letters.

Yrs sncly
W B Yeats

Dict AEFH, signed WBY; Claremont.

To F. J. Fay, 13 November 1904

18 Woburn Buildings, | Euston Road, | London.
Nov 13th./04.

My dear Fay,

I don't understand the point about Cuchulain's exclamation, I don't remember where he sinks on the bench,[1] but I'll be over in Dublin in the middle of the week & we can discuss it then. I can't get your proofs I'm sorry to say, for there is no new edition coming for the present.[2] I can however get you bound copies of the play to cut up if you like. I should have thought that everyone knew by this time that Moore's return to the theatre is out of the question. If there were not other reasons, and there are very sufficient ones, it is enough that he represents a rival tradition of the stage & would upset your brothers plans at every turn. He is very jealous of the success of the theatre & has been laying pipe to get into it, for

---

[1] Fay's letter has not survived, but evidently asked for guidance in the production of *On Baile's Strand*, then in rehearsal. Towards the end of the play, the Blind Man reveals to Cuchulain that the young champion he has just killed is his own son. Although there is no stage direction to indicate that he sinks down at this point, he must do so since the Blind Man feels the bench shaking with his emotion (*VPl*, 525).

[2] *On Baile's Strand*, which originally appeared in *In the Seven Woods*, had last been published in March 1904 with *The King's Threshold* as vol. III of 'Plays for an Irish Theatre'. A Dublin edition, published by Maunsel & Co., appeared in 1905.

months past. He made up with me the other day.[3] I also had my object,
(keep it to yourself) I want to get Dermot & Grania into my hands & think
I see my way to an arrangement which will leave him free to do what he
likes with it in England for a certain time; I to reshape it for you—it would
make a fine verse play.

Lift the horn if it is effective,[4] God knows what the old Irish did.

Yrs sny

W B Yeats

Dict AEFH, signed WBY; Private. Wade, 443.

To Charles Shannon, [*13 November 1904*]

18 Woburn Buildings | Euston Road.

Sunday

My dear Shannon: I was very sorry the question of my portrait arose last
night. When I said 'I think Quinn will be one of your buyers' I had in
mind a possible large purchase of lithographs he spoke of. Lady Gregory
did not know of this & did know that he had said something about a portrait. She did not know that Quinns offer was quite inadequate & that I
had meant to say nothing about it. I shall however ask you to do a lithograph or something of that kind for the collected edition of my writings if
it comes off & if Bullen will pay you properly (which I am sure he will).
You are the one man I would like to be drawn by.[1]

[3] See p. 228, n. 2. A public demonstration of this *rapprochement* occurred on 8 Dec when WBY
proposed the vote of thanks at Moore's lecture, 'Personal Reminiscences of Modern Painters', at
the Royal Hibernian Academy. As Holloway reported (*Abbey Theatre*, 48): 'Mr. Yeats in opening
his remarks said that, "Mr. Moore and I are sometimes great friends and sometimes great enemies", and I may say myself I was astonished to see them on the same platform, because I
thought they were at daggers drawn.'

[4] Perhaps a drinking scene, later omitted, following the arrival of the younger kings at
Conchubar's meeting, but probably the episode in which Cuchulain, immediately after killing his
son, drinks from an ale-horn he has taken from the Fool (*VPl*, 518).

[1] See p. 564, n. 9. Ricketts and Shannon had gone to AG's on the previous evening to discuss
scenery with her and WBY. Shannon did paint an oil portrait of WBY for Quinn in January 1908
and at a reduced fee, for WBY wrote to him on 7 Jan 1908 (NYPL): 'I have arranged about the
Shannon portrait and for the price you said—£100. Please keep it to yourself that he is getting no
more than this, for his ordinary price is, I understand, £300.' The portrait was reproduced in
CW, III, and now hangs in the Houghton Library, Harvard University.

I am very much obliged to Ricketts for all the trouble he has taken about the scenery.

Yr ever
W B Yeats

[*On verso page*]
⟨You see tha⟩

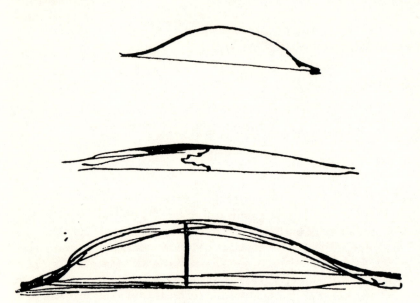

I find there are stage properties on this page.

ALS Private.

To Louis Esson,[1] *15 November 1904*

18 Woburn Buildings, | Euston Road, | London.
Nov. 15th.,/04.

Dear Mr Esson,

I have left your letter for a very long time without an answer. I have never been quite so busy as I have been this Summer & Autumn. You ask

---

[1] Louis Esson (1879–1943), an Australian journalist and playwright, helped Leon Brodzky found the Australian Theatre Society in Melbourne in 1904. Modelled on the INTS, the

if I can recommend you Irish plays, especially plays of my own, which suit your Melbourne Stage Society. You had better get a copy of Vol II of "Plays for an Irish Theatre" (A. Bullen) it is called "The Hour Glass" etc. It contains three little prose plays which have all been done in New York, two by the Society there that you think of. These plays are quite easy to produce & are popular with our people. My other plays are in verse which is necessarily difficult with the exception of Where there is Nothing, a rather wild business that wants a good deal of re-writing. If you could get a few actors capable of play[ing] Irish peasants decently, you will find J. M. Synge's "Shadow of the Glen" (it will be in this year's Samhain) or Lady Gregorys "Spreading of the News" (which will be published some time during the Winter with other plays of hers)[2] as good as anything you could get. They are both very humerous. Synge has done a three-act play which will I think make a sensation, but we shall not be performing or publishing it, until after Xmas & it may be too long for you at the start.

     We don't yet know when we open in Dublin in December. Coming on to the time you might write to—Miss Horniman, [H]1 Montagu Mansions, Portman Square, London, she will give you particulars.[3] Should you desire to produce any of the plays I have named, please write to the author or authors formally asking permission. It will do if you address them—Abbey Theatre, Dublin.

Yrs sny
W B Yeats

Dict AEFH, signed WBY; Private.

Melbourne Society did not long survive Brodzky's departure for America, but Esson persevered to become a significant force in the development of Australian drama, and WBY's influence was apparently crucial in this process. This was Esson's first trip to Europe and, as he recalled in the *Australian Quarterly* (June 1939), 55–64, WBY had met him in late March 'at Lady Gregory's drawing-room for a talk about literature and drama', and had urged him to give up cosmopolitan ambitions and return to Australian themes: 'Yeats's first words were, "keep within your own borders"—words coming from such an authority at such an impressionable time I have never forgotten. . . . Yeats was an extraordinarily eloquent speaker and in my inner soul I felt that he was right. To my objection that we had no traditions, he made the reply that it was no disadvantage that we had no conventionally romantic past to draw on, and that it should be our aim to conquer the outlying provinces and bring them within the kingdom of Art.' He advised Esson to establish a national theatre on the lines of the INTS, beginning with one-act rural comedies which consolidated a country's traditions, rather than dramas of ideas which tended to divide and shatter them. Esson had attended the London productions of *Riders to the Sea* and *Broken Soil* on 26 Mar, and AG's reception for the Company at the Criterion Restaurant on the same day. He was to visit WBY again in Oxford in January 1921.

  [2] Fifty copies of *Spreading the News* were printed by John Quinn on 10 Dec 1904 for private distribution, and WBY printed the play in *Samhain* in the same month. It subsequently appeared with *The Rising of the Moon* and *The Poorhouse* as vol. IX of the 'Abbey Theatre Series' (Dublin, 1906).

  [3] Esson went to Dublin in late December for the opening of the Abbey Theatre and attended all the performances, as well as seeing *The Well of the Saints* in rehearsal. On 1 Jan 1905 he again met WBY at AE's house.

To John Millington Synge, 15 November 1904

18 Woburn Buildings, | Euston Road, | London.
Nov. 15.th./04.

Dear Synge,

I enclose you Bullen's letter.[1] I had mislaid it or I would have sent it before.

Of course I do not know how my brother's designing will turn out,[2] it won't make any difference to you, as if his design is not quite right, I shall get young Gregory to work over it. He is enthusiastic about decorative scenery & Ricketts has told him that some great painter or other, advised a favourite pupil to make scenery. I am nearly wild over the difficulties of getting a new tree-wing however. If I can get a morning in the British Museum Print Room over the Japanese prints, I may find out something. I am delighted about your new play,[3] that is the best thing that could have happened to us. I know that you will be an upholder of my musical theories ere long, they follow logically from certain principles which we have all accepted. One must have a complete asthetisism when one is dealing with a synthetic art like that of the stage.

Yrs ev
W B Yeats

Dict AEFH, signed WBY; TCD; with enclosure and envelope addressed to 15 Maxwell Road, Rathgar, Dublin, postmark 'LONDON NO [??] 04'. Saddlemyer, 66–7.

[1] WBY enclosed a letter from Bullen, dated 9 Nov (TCD), offering 'to publish Mr. Synge's play on your recommendation & pay him a royalty of 15% of the published price', and also suggesting that Jack Yeats might illustrate the book. Bullen issued *The Well of the Saints*, unillustrated but with an introduction by WBY, as vol. IV of 'Plays for an Irish Theatre' in January 1905, and the sheets for this edition were published separately in Dublin the following month as vol. I of the 'Abbey Theatre Series'.

[2] i.e. for the Abbey plays, including *The Well of the Saints* (see p. 643). The play was finally designed by neither Jack Yeats nor Robert Gregory but by Pamela Colman Smith and Edith Craig.

[3] i.e. *The Playboy of the Western World*, not produced until January 1907. Synge had sketched out three acts in September 1904 under the title *The Murderer (A Farce)*.

To the Countess Con Markiewicz, [? 19 November 1904]

Nassau Hotel
Saturday

My dear Countess Markievicz: If Sunday morning at 12 will suit you I will come with pleasure & stay to lunch. Very many Thanks.[1]

Yrs sny
W B Yeats

I wrote you a note from Theatre last night but it was only posted to day.

ALS Harvard.

To Lady Augusta Gregory, [22 November 1904]

Nassau Hotel.

My dear Lady Gregory: I saw Madam Macrovitch (Con Gore Booth)'s work yesterday.[1] It is not good enough. However there is plenty of time yet. Jacks design should come to-morrow.

Yr ev
W B Yeats

I cannot write more because of eyes.

ALS Berg, with envelope addressed to 49 George St, Portman Square, London, postmark 'DUBLIN NO 22 04'.

To Lady Augusta Gregory, 24 November 1904

Abbey Theatre, | D U B L I N.
24th Nov. 1904.

My dear Lady Gregory,

I am afraid the postponement is inevitable. I have had a letter from Miss Horniman who seems to think that the delay is to suit your convenience. It

---

[1] See p. 198, n. 2. The Markiewiczs were living in a substantial early Victorian villa in Frankfort Avenue in the well-to-do Dublin suburb of Rathgar. WBY wanted to see her paintings to discover if she was good enough to design scenery for the Abbey Theatre.

[1] As Constance Gore-Booth, Madam Markiewicz had studied painting at the Slade and in Paris in the 1890s. She and her husband were now active in Dublin artistic circles, and held annual exhibitions with AE and others from 1904 to 1911. They became leading lights in the Arts Club, and in 1908 established the Independent Dramatic Company.

is not, but we could modify the new date by a day or two. The delay is caused by the fact that the stage will hardly be finished in time to let us have sufficient dress rehearsals. Also Sarah Pursur says she can't have the stained glass window ready for the first week in December. They were to have been finished by her contract in the middle of this month. I daresay we could be ready for the middle of December, though I am not even sure about this, but we are afraid to perform in Advent.[1] I cannot give an opinion about dates as it depends on local knowledge. I asked Synge last night to make a cut in Jack Smith's speech that we might find out how much he could speak while struggling in the hands of the crowd. He can hardly speak more than about 3 or 4 lines. I am afraid that you will have to cut altogether that speech beginning "Isn't Bartley Fallon the boastful man". It checks the speed of the play, we will try it again however to see if the shortening of the other speech makes it possible. Let us have your shortening up of Jack Smith's speech as soon as possible.[2] On Bailie's Strand is the best play I have written. It goes magnificiently, and the end is particularly impressive. When I got here I found that Frank Fay seemed to have a curious incapacity to understand the part. He could do nothing with it and was in despair. It now promises to be his finest part. I think I shall be able to arrange the scenery for spreading of the news alright. I am waiting on Jack's designs for Synge's play, as it may be possible to use some bits of scenery which will afterwards come in useful for Synge. They should come to-day or to-morrow. Failing this I shall get Pixie Smith who alone seems to understand what I want to make a design,[3] I am extremely anxious now that I am here and for the moment at any rate Master of the situation to get designs of a decorative kind, which will set a standard and come in serviceable for different sorts of plays. Don't be in any anxiety about the wings for your play. I shall get everything made under my own eyes, but the moment I am gone the old business will begin again. Robert's wing will be very good for a remote play like the "Shadowy Waters" but it is too far from realism to go with comedy or with any ordinary play.[4] I am very glad

---

[1] The period of Advent falls in the four weeks before Christmas, and is a time of restraint and spiritual exercise for Catholics.

[2] In AG's *Spreading the News* a series of misunderstandings convince people at a country fair that Jack Smith has been murdered by Bartley Fallon so that the latter can run away to America with Smith's wife. On his reappearance at the end of the play, Smith is convinced that Fallon has made up the story of his death in order to elope with his wife, and has to be restrained by the crowd from attacking him. He does not, however, use the words 'Isn't Bartley Fallon the boastful man', and AG evidently pruned the scene.

[3] See p. 674; Pamela Colman Smith designed the scenery for the first production of Synge's *The Well of the Saints* in February 1905.

[4] Robert Gregory's designs for a stage wing were used for the production of AG's *Kincora* in March 1905. The annotated back of the design is reproduced in Liam Miller, *The Noble Drama of W. B. Yeats* (Dublin, 1977), 122.

to have it. I have found out that the exact thing I want is the sort of tree one finds in Japanese prints. If Robert could find time to look up some prints and to make me a wing of this sort in the next three or four days I would be very glad. I may probably use it in your play, certainly, in fact if suitable, if not it will come in for something else. We are in great need of different types of design. The wings are 16 ft. high and 6 ft. wide at their greatest width. They must never be very narrow. "Spreading the News" is going magnificently.

There is great and ever growing indignation over the 6d. seats,[5] I hear from Mrs. MacBride that the Clubs say I am lost in [?*for* to] Nationalism. They had all got to look upon the Hall as their property.

Yrs ev
W B Yeats

[*On back of envelope*]
theatre book came. I sent it on papered up as it was to Council. WBY—

TLS Berg, with envelope addressed to Coole, postmark 'DUBLIN NO 24 04'. Wade, 444–5.

To Lady Augusta Gregory, [26 November 1904]

Abbey Theatre
Saturday

My dear Lady Gregory: There is room at the Nassau & I can see that nobody has had the sitting room since you left as your things are all there. I am very glad you are coming over—there are many things I want you for. It is a long business getting the scenery right—I have a fairly good scene from Jack but too slap dash here & there. Your play will be all right—nothing but bare walls with plenty of notices

[5] At AEFH's insistence seats at the Abbey Theatre were priced at 3/-, 2/-, and 1/-, whereas the cheapest seats in the commercial Dublin theatres were sixpence. Nor could any other company which hired the theatre lower these charges. These higher prices were fixed, as AEFH had explained in her letter offering the Theatre (see p. 573), 'to prevent cheap entertainments from being given, which would lower the letting value of the hall', but they caused great discontent and much adverse comment among the audience and in the press. As WBY suggests, the discontent was exacerbated by the memory that this was the old 'Mechanics Institute'—'the meeting place of the Nationalist artisans of Dublin' where, as the *United Irishman* had recalled on 13 Aug of this year (5), 'they debated Irish questions, listened to lectures on Irish subjects, held Irish concerts and entertainments, and as far as possible then kept themselves steeped in an Irish atmosphere'. Nevertheless, AEFH resisted pressure to reduce the cheapest seats to sixpence until October 1906.

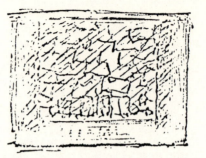

Miss Horniman has got some more from the country. Synge is writing music for Kathleen-ni-Hoolihan & Miss Walker is very fine in the part.[1] I am very impatient for your coming—I feal lost without you.

Yr ever
W B Yeats

ALS Berg, with envelope addressed to 49 George St, Portman Square, London, postmark 'DUBLIN NO 27 04'.

To Lady Augusta Gregory, [4 December 1904]

⟨18 Woburn Buildings | Euston Road | Londo⟩
Nassau Hotel | Dublin.

My dear Lady Gregory: I send you the posters, after looking at them in artificial light we have come to the conclusion that Miss Monsolls own choice is the right one.[1] It shows the drawing best as the blue becomes dark enough to obscure the outline at night. Ask her not to let Cahills put their name on it.[2] I send her letter which I opened as you said I might. The design should go at top of page leaving about a half inch margin. Fay would like 500 of the posters & to have these words printed under neath.

[1] *Cathleen ni Houlihan* was revived as the third play for the opening night of the Abbey Theatre. WBY had already printed the traditional airs for the three songs in vol. II of 'Plays for an Irish Theatre'; Synge's music was not published. Holloway (*Abbey Theatre*, 50–1) thought the play 'exquisitely enacted, and all present were thrilled by the weird beauty and intense pathos of Miss Maire nic Shiubhlaigh's embodiment of "Cathleen". . . . Of all the "Cathleens" I have seen, this was the truest embodiment. The sorrows of centuries were on her brow and in her eye, and her words pierced the heart with grief at her woe!'

[1] See p. 650. The woodcut of Maeve and the wolfhound was printed in black on a light brown background. A proof of the design is among AG's papers at the Berg.

[2] A. and E. Cahill were Dublin printers.

Irish National Theatre Society
at the Abbey Theatre in
Abbey St.

No space need be left for anything else as we will post another bill by its side. It would be better if 'The' could be put before 'Irish' in the first line. We all think the poster beautiful.

I am very sorry about Robert.[3] You must have found it a shock to find he had two nurses. My father says he was constantly ill when he first began going to art schools at night. He used to get dreadful colds. Miss Horniman talks of coming over next Wednesday so unless you arrange well you may have her with you.

Yours alway
W B Yeats

I am well again.
[*On back of envelope*]
I have no other envelope & no blotting paper.

ALS Berg, with envelope addressed to 18 Woburn Buildings, Euston Road, London, postmark 'DUBLIN DE 4 04'.

To Lady Augusta Gregory, [*4 December 1904*]

My Dear Lady Gregory,
    In writing to you to-day, I forgot to enclose Miss Monsell's letter which I now do. I went round to Moore's on Saturday and he told me that he had asked Mrs. Craigie if she would object to my being arbitrator in the dispute between them.[1] From quarrelling with him over "Where there is

---

[3] Robert Gregory was in his first term at the Slade School of Art, having come down from Oxford the previous year. He was suffering from an attack of influenza, which AG caught from him.

[1] See p. 671. Mrs Pearl Teresa Craigie, 'John Oliver Hobbes' (see p. 208), first collaborated with Moore at the beginning of their intermittent (and apparently chaste) relationship in 1894, when they published 'The Fool's Hour' in *The Yellow Book*. They also wrote *Journeys End in Lovers' Meeting* (1894), but she published this under her name with no reference to Moore. A resumption of their courtship led to their stormy co-authorship of a play entitled *The Peacock's Feathers*, about which Moore wrote to Edouard Dujardin on 4 Feb 1905: 'My play is finished and I am in mortal enmity with "the lady", who has collaborated with the manager in an arrangement of the piece. I will see neither rehearsal nor production, but I mean to howl in the papers like a wolf—a she-wolf I should say, from whom her whelps have been stolen' (*Letters from George Moore to Ed. Dujardin 1886–1922* [New York, 1929], 56). The relationship finally terminated, he told Dujardin (Joseph Hone, *The Life of George Moore*, [1936], 254), when 'I was walking in the Green Park . . . and I saw her in front of me. I was blind with rage and I ran up behind her and

Nothing" to arbitrating in his quarrel with somebody else is an unexpected leap. He has also lent me his play and asked me to tell him whether it is good enough to go on fighting on. If his version is not good, he thinks he had better give in. I am at present hoping that I shall like the second act. In the first act a George Moore, who has joined the literary movement in Malvern and is trying to write in dialect instead of Irish reads out his love letters with all details as to who the lady is, and where she lives, to a large audience after a dinner party. I went round to remonstrate, and I find by a curious coincidence that Mrs. Craigie had also objected to this incident. I found a way out for him and he is very grateful, or says he is.

Please tell me how Robert is going on.

Yours ever
W B Yeats

TLS Berg. Wade, 445–6.

To Hugh Lane, [5 December 1904]

Nassau Hotel,

Dear Lane,

I hear from Madam Marcovitch—how the devil do you spell that name—that some academician or other wants to make you responsible for George Moore's letter in to-day's Express.[1] You had nothing whatever to do with it. You will remember it was Sir Thomas Drew[2] himself who told me the facts. You were standing by at the time, I told them to George Moore but if I hadn't it would not have made any difference for he would certainly hear them from somebody else. Every second man one meets knows all about it. I know my Dublin sufficiently well that the tale will grow till it becomes a monstrous fable of s[ome] kind in the course of a few

---

kicked her.' After her death Moore rewrote the play twice and published it under his name alone, first as *Edith Cooper* in 1913 (the year it was first produced by the Stage Society), and in 1920 as *The Coming of Gabrielle*.

[1] George Moore's letter of 5 Dec to the *Daily Express* (4) objected to the enforced closing of Hugh Lane's Loan Exhibition of Modern Art. The Exhibition (see p. 608, n. 1) had opened at the Royal Hibernian Academy on 21 Nov, but the academicians had a long-standing contract to let the galleries to the Decorators' Guild of Great Britain for their Triennial Exhibition in January 1905. In his letter Moore alleged that it was 'a matter of public notoriety that these arrangements might have been altered but for the fear of many of the Academicians that an Exhibition containing so many famous works may overshadow their own Spring Exhibition'.

[2] Sir Thomas Drew (1838–1910), the Irish architect, was President of the Royal Hibernian Academy from 1900 until his death.

days. At present to judge by my conversation with Sir Thomas Drew, it is in a truthful stage. You may show this letter to anybody you like.

Yours snly
W B Yeats

P.S. I know from my conversation with Moore that you had never even spoken to him about the matter.

TLS NLI.

To the Editor of the Daily Express *(Dublin)*, *6 December 1904*

December 6th, 1904.

SIR—I see by Mr. Catterson Smith's letter in to-day's "Express" that he did not know of Mr. Hugh Lane's Exhibition project until the Academy received Mr. Lane's formal application on September the 7th.[1] His letter implies that had he been aware of the project he would have done his best to keep the Academy at Mr. Lane's disposal for the winter. One is glad to know this, but Mr. Smith will find it easier to understand Mr. George Moore's point of view if I run over certain facts and dates. It was at an informal meeting at the end of June, or in early July—it was the week before the death of Watts[2]—and at this meeting it was decided that Mr. Lane should issue a circular and ask Sir Thomas Drew[3] to sign it, as representing the Hibernian Academy. This circular, of which I have a copy, was signed and issued a few days later, and in the week that followed a great part of Mr. Lane's work was done. Had Mr. Lane known that he could only have the Academy for a little more than a month, instead of the

---

[1] See previous letter. Stephen Catterson Smith (1849–1912), portrait painter and Secretary of the Royal Hibernian Academy, replied on 6 Dec (5) to refute George Moore's suggestion that the academicians were closing down Lane's exhibition for fear of its overshadowing their own show. He went on to point out that the Decorators' Guild had booked the rooms many months before Lane, that it had been made perfectly clear to Lane that he must vacate the premises by 7 Jan 1905, that the Academy was legally bound to its agreement with the Decorators' Guild, that it had abandoned its own Winter Exhibition to accommodate Lane, and that it had received no formal request from Lane for an extension of time. Although it seemed that Lane's disregard of legal niceties was once again going to thwart his plans (see p. 564, n. 7), he managed to have the Exhibition moved to the Round Gallery of the National Museum of Ireland in Kildare Street after 7 Jan.

[2] George Frederick Watts (1817–1904), the English artist, had died on 1 July 1904. Lane was to mount a Watts Exhibition at the Royal Hibernian Academy in January 1906, and WBY gave an appreciation of him in his lecture 'The Ideal of Art' (*UP* II. 343–5).

[3] See p. 608.

whole winter, I doubt if he would have undertaken the great expense and labour of gathering together the finest collection of modern French painting which has been seen out of Paris. He certainly believed that he had the whole winter before him. He sent in his formal application at the request of Sir Thomas Drew, merely to regularise, as he believed, an understanding arrived at with Sir Thomas Drew and other Academicians when the circular was issued. I believe that even after September the 7th, however, possibly even as late as last week, the paper-hangers could have been persuaded to forego their contract if the Academy had approached them. The attempt should, at any rate, have been made. It is certain, if Mr. Catterson Smith's letter represents the general feeling of the Academicians, that they would have supported him had Sir Thomas Drew acted on his own responsibility. Perhaps it is not still too late. The Lord Mayor would probably be willing to give the paper-hangers the use of the Round Room at the Mansion House.

I myself am for the first time beginning to feel that I understand French Art a little. I go almost every day to the Exhibition, and I know of others who will think the closing of this great Exhibition a personal misfortune.

Yours truly
W B Yeats

Printed letter, *Daily Express* (Dublin), 7 December 1904 (5). *UP* I. 330–1.

To Mrs William Allingham,[1] *7 December 1904*

Nassau Hotel, | Sth. Frederick Street, | D U B L I N.
Dec. 7. '04.

Dear Madam,

I would very much like, if you would give me permission to make a small selection from your husband's poetry for publication by the Dun Emer Press.[2] These book which are printed by my sister in a very beauti-

[1] Helen Allingham, née Patterson (1848–1926), was educated at the Royal Academy Schools and worked as a black and white artist for the *Graphic* and *Cornhill*. Best known as a water-colour painter of rural scenes and for her studies of children, she exhibited at the Royal Academy and was from 1890 a Member of the Royal Watercolour Society. Ruskin wrote admiringly of her work in *The Art of England* (1883). She had married the Irish poet William Allingham (1824–89) in August 1874.

[2] WBY's admiration for William Allingham had increased throughout the 1890s (see I. 394). He had already made a selection of his poems for Alfred Henry Miles's *The Poets and Poetry of the Century* (1892), and in the introduction to *A Book of Irish Verse* (p. xx) placed him 'among those minor immortals who have put their souls into little songs to humble the proud'. WBY's edition, *Sixteen Poems* by William Allingham, was published by the Dun Emer Press on 27 Nov 1905 in an edition of 200 copies.

ful old type, have had considerable success. The edition is of course very small 250 or 300 copies but we could pay you a small royalty. It would be quite a small book let us say 25 poems and could not in any case interfere with the sale of the ordinary editions. Books by A. E., by Lionel Johnston, by Douglas Hyde and by myself have already been printed and a book by Lady Gregory will follow the selection from your husband's poems should you give me permission. We are anxious to bring out in this series representative Irish books. I have the greatest posible admiration for Mr. Allingham's poetry. I am sometimes inclined to believe that he was my own master in Irish verse, starting me in the way I have gone whether for good or evil. I believe that I shall be able to make a little volume of his work which will be a great joy to a great many people.

Yrs snly
W B Yeats

TLS Illinois. Wade, 446.

To Hugh Lane, [c. 12 December 1904]

Nassau Hotel.

My dear Lane,

I find a postscript in Lady Gregory's letter which I had over-looked. "If you give my letter to a paper, you might get them to print off some copies on decent paper that I may send it about".[1]

I don't know whether The Freeman's Journal can or will do this.

I leave the matter in your hands. Lady Gregory's phrase about the last paragraph in her letter is "I would as soon leave out the last paragraph but thought it might be necessary. Perhaps the sum I am ready to spend would be better".[2]

---

[1] AG had written a long letter to the press as part of her contribution to the proposed Gallery of Modern Art in Dublin, and WBY and Lane passed this onto the *Freeman's Journal*, where it appeared under the heading 'A Stone in the Building' on 13 Dec 1904 (8). Taking as her text the Prophet Nehemiah's words 'Let us build up the wall of Jerusalem that we be no more a reproach', she urged her readers to contribute to the purchase of the loan pictures, the possession of which would 'be an advance in the dignity of our country in its place among nations, a worthy building-stone laid upon its walls'. She went on to give the names of those to whom subscriptions could be sent, and added in a concluding paragraph: 'That I may not seem to ask others to help while I myself do nothing, I may say that I have offered to buy a small picture in the collection and to present it to the Gallery, in memory of a friend'.

[2] This letter was not, apparently, reprinted on superior paper, but a further letter of appeal, to the *Irish Times* on 5 Jan 1905, signed by AG, WBY, AE and Douglas Hyde, among others, was re-issued as a circular entitled 'A Modern Art Gallery for Dublin'.

She is very anxious that either you or I should see a proof of the letter.

Yrs sry

W B Yeats

Dict AEFH, signed WBY; Southern Illinois.

To Clement Shorter, 12 December 1904

Nassau Hotel, | Dublin.

Dec. 12th.,/04.

My dear Shorter, I am dictating this.

I daresay that you know that Hugh Lane is trying to get up a permanent gallery of modern art in Dublin. He has had three exhibitions and bought a number of pictures with this object, spending upon them a good many thousands of pounds of his own money & now he is appealing to rich Irish people to buy the Forbes collection of pictures which he has on exhibition here in Dublin.[1] It seems to be very generally agreed that the exhibition now going on here under his management is the largest collection of modern French masterpieces ever gathered together outside Paris. Lane has committees of all kinds at work trying to raise the money. Meanwhile somebody has drawn his attention to the fact that Dr Sigerson proposed just such a gallery years ago,[2] suggesting that the building now full of stuffed birds & beasts at the other side of the square from our National Gallery, should be used for the purpose. I thought because of this and because the collection itself is so extraordinary fine, that you might give us a lift in the Tatler or the Sphere.[3] If we can get enough thousands here in Ireland to make a decent show of ourselves, we think of appealing to America & any notice the Tatler or the Sphere might give us, would help

[1] Lane described the exhibition in the official Catalogue as 'Pictures given to the City of Dublin to form the Nucleus of a Gallery of Modern Art . . . and Pictures lent by the Executors of the late J. Staats-Forbes and Others'. James Staats-Forbes, a railway chairman who had died on 5 Apr 1904 at the age of 81, was a noted art patron and collector, particularly of modern French and continental artists. The *Burlington Magazine* of April 1904 (159) described him as 'one of the most far-seeing and enlightened connoisseurs of modern painting, as well as one of the truest and most intelligent lovers of art in England'.

[2] George Sigerson was Shorter's father-in-law, and WBY must have hoped that this would encourage him to lend his support to the scheme.

[3] Shorter obliged; the *Sphere* of 28 Jan 1905 reproduced pictures by Rothenstein, Puvis de Chavannes, Corot, Fisher, and Manet under the headline 'A Remarkable Collection of Modern Pictures Which may Remain Permanently in Dublin'. It went on to explain (121) that a 'remarkable collection of pictures is being exhibited at the Royal Hibernian Academy, Dublin, of which these are specimens. A movement has been started to keep the collection in Dublin. A sum of between £30,000 and £40,000 is required, of which several thousands have already been collected in Ireland. An appeal is now issued to the larger public.'

us over the water. When this idea got into Lane's head, he sent a very urgent person to me to write & ask Shorter "to get out a supplement to the Sphere or Tatler with reproductions of the pictures, nothing would help us so much as that". I wonder at my audacity at sending you this request even in inverted commas, but I am ashamed not to do whatever Lane asks me when I recollect that he himself has spent all he practically possesses on the project. I have no doubt a much less imposing notice would be very serviceable. The Hibernian Academy is giving a lot of trouble, one of them is anonymously attacking the exhibition in the papers[4] & the President has written to Lord Drogh[e]da[5] who had joined the committee & promised £100, urging him to resign because there are such rebellious people on that committee, as Edward Martyn & myself.

Indeed the political question is giving a lot of trouble.

I have got my first press notices from America concerning, I am glad to say, the success of a company in Boston who have started touring about with Kathleen ni Houlihan, The Hour-Glass & "The Pot of Broth".[6]

I should have said that what I imagine Lane wants you to do, is to notice the excellence of the pictures & their importance. ⟨He does not expect you to help⟩ The raising of the money is naturally the business of us Irish people. Both the Freeman & the Irish Times have opened subscription lists. It is pretty certain that even if Lane fails in getting the whole sum, which is likely, he will get enough to buy some of the pictures.[7] Some people are giving pictures as a memorial to dead friends.

Yrs sinly

W B Yeats

P.S. We open on Dec. 27ᵗʰ in the Abbey Theatre. Rehearsals are going very well & we expect a success.

Dict AEFH, signed WBY; Berg.

---

[4] The anonymous academician signed himself 'Viator' and was thought to be Count Plunkett.

[5] William M. Ponsonby, 9th Earl of Drogheda (1846–1908), chaired a committee of thirty-three, including WBY, Edward Martyn, the Earl of Mayo, Sir Thomas Drew, Col. Sir W. Hutcheson Poe, C. B. and T. Harrington, the artist Dermod O'Brien (Treasurer), and Hugh Lane (Secretary). He ignored Sir Thomas Drew's letter, and remained on the committee.

[6] See p. 614. The plays, the third of which was in fact *The Land of Heart's Desire*, not *The Pot of Broth*, opened in Boston on 26 Nov 1904 and played there for seven weeks at various theatres. Bayard Veiller (see p. 664, n. 2) describes their enthusiastic reception in his autobiography, *The Fun I've Had* (1941).

[7] This happened. In January 1905 the executors of the Staats-Forbes estate agreed to divide the collection, and permitted Lane's committee to make a smaller selection of 160 paintings (out of the original 4,000) for £20,000 rather than £220,000. A subscriber's circular issued at that time listed the revised selections and prices, and announced that the pictures would be on view in the Round Gallery of the Museum, Kildare Street, until the end of March.

To Lady Augusta Gregory, [mid-December 1904]

Mention in letter to AG of [22 Dec 1904] and in a letter from AG of 'Tuesday' [20 Dec 1904; Berg].
AG wrote: 'Many thanks for yr letters only you didnt send the one you wrote at the hotel & forgot—please let me have it'.

Henry D. Davray, 13 December 1904

Nassau Hotel, | Dublin.
Dec. 13th.,/04.

My dear Davoray,
  Certainly I will let you have any books of mine that you want. But please let me have a list, either of those you have or those you have not. No—I did not see the article in the "Revue de Paris".[1] If you would tell me the number, probably I could get it. I would like to send a poem to Dr F. T. Marrinetti,[2] but the worst of it is, that I have been so busy writing poetical dramas, for my little theatre here in Dublin, that I have only done two lyrics in the last year. One of these appeared in a book got up for a charity by the Duchess of Sutherland[3] & I have sent the other to somebody & for the life of me, I cannot recollect who.[4] I shall know when I get a proof. I suppose a poem that had already appeared in America, let us say, would not do. I am afraid that I have let your letter lie unanswered for a great many days, but the approaching first night of the Abbey Theatre has plunged me into that busy idleness in which one seems to be doing everything under the sun except answering letters. Some day you must come to Ireland & when you come, you will I hope find my little company of National players prospering in the fine new house a friend has made for them. We open on the 27th with two one act plays of mine, one of them

[1] Henry Potez's two-part essay, 'W. B. Yeats et la renaissance poétique en Irlande', appeared in *La Revue de Paris* on 1 and 15 Aug 1904.
[2] Filippo Tommaso Marinetti (1876–1944), Italian poet, author, and journalist, had spent his youth in Paris and began writing in French, but had recently established the Milan-based poetry review, *Poesia*, and was looking for contributors. Its issue for winter 1906–7 (2: 9–12), 12, published WBY's 'A Dirge over Deirdre e Naisi'. In 1909 Marinetti became the bombastic founder and leader of Futurism, a movement which, dedicated to the destruction of tradition and worship of the machine, had no appeal for WBY. Marinetti did not have a doctorate, and WBY may have misread 'Sr' as 'Dr'.
[3] 'Old Memory' in *Wayfarer's Love*; see pp. 494–5.
[4] Evidently 'Never Give All The Heart', finished on 6 Mar 1904 (Texas) and recently sent through Quinn to Witter Bynner, editor of *McClure's Magazine*, where it appeared in December 1905.

new to the stage "On Baile's Strand" a play in verse which you may know, the other "Kathleen ni Houlihan" a prose play about Ireland. We play with these a very brilliant little comedy of Lady Gregory's.

Yr snry
W B Yeats

Dict AEFH, signed WBY; Private.

To Lady Augusta Gregory, [*17 December 1904*]

Nassau Hotel | Dublin.
Saturday

My dear Friend: I am very sorry to hear that you have been so ill—you take care of everybody but your self.[1] I wish I had enough eyesight to help you, as you have helped me, by reading or writing for you while you are getting better. Get Robert to write to tell me how you are without leaving me too long without knowing.

I am wanted here at rehearsal. We had our first dress rehearsal last night— 'The Bailes Strand' costumes are not very good, I am sorry to say, & I am trying to get little changes made here & there[2] & we have done nothing yet with the lighting. We have another too-night. My father has sketched Synge for you—he came to Theatre last night—& F Fay as Cuchullain for *Samhain*. Both are very fine.[3]

I have heard from Shorter.[4] He had already decided when he got my letter to have a number of reproductions of the pictures & says he will do all he can.

Masefield comes over to write up the Theatre & the pictures.[5]

[1] AG was suffering from an attack of influenza which was to prevent her attendance at the opening of the Abbey Theatre.

[2] See p. 528. Joseph Holloway attended the dress rehearsals on 16 Dec and recorded (*Abbey Theatre*, 49–50) that 'many of the costumes, especially those of the old kings and the long, streaky hair worn by them, were found to border on the grotesque or eccentric, and at the conclusion of the play the entire company was recalled on the stage, and an exciting and amusing exchange of difference of opinion took place between author Yeats and designer Miss Horniman. . . . Candidly I thought some of the costumes trying, though all of them were exceedingly rich in material and archaeologically correct. "Hang archaeology!" said the great W. B. Yeats. "It's effect we want on the stage!" And that settled it!'

[3] Holloway also noted (50) that during the dress rehearsal 'Mr. J. B. Yeats sketched J. M. Synge in the dressing room. He sketched on the corner of a table, and Synge rested against the back of a chair. They chatted freely as the sketch progressed'. The drawing 'Frank Fay as Cuchullain' appeared in *Samhain* (1904), as did the portrait of Synge.

[4] See pp. 684–5.

[5] Masefield's unsigned articles, 'The Irish National Theatre', ran in the *Manchester Guardian* from 28 Dec 1904 to 4 Jan 1905 and gave an enthusiastic account of the opening performances of the Abbey Theatre.

I am so sorry that you are ill, & I hope you will rest a long time before you think of working again. I must go now to Fay at theatre to see about the actors shoes.

Yr ev
W B Yeats

ALS Berg, with envelope addressed to Coole, postmark 'DUBLIN DE 19 04'.

To Lady Augusta Gregory, [*22 December 1904*]

Nassau Hotel. | Dublin

My dear Friend: I am afraid I have put all in that old letter into letters since. You should not let Marian bother you. I had hoped the shooting party had been put off. You should send Marian to manage by herself & the shooters to the sea shore to fire at sand-pipers. You should not think of doing anything until you are quite well.[1]

Griffith has made a retraction in the U I—so that matter is settled.[2] Masefield (and alas Mrs Masefield) come to the Nassau on the 27th. There has been a little passage of arms between my father & Catterson Smith in

---

[1] In a letter dated 'Tuesday' [20 Dec 1904; Berg] AG thanked him for his recent letters, but added that 'you didnt send the one you wrote at the hotel & forgot—please let me have it'. She also told him that this was 'the first time I have been able to write—I dont know what to say— fever & headache have gone, but I am dreadfully weak & cough a gt deal & food will not always stay down & neuralgia comes & settles in the eyes—But no doubt I am on the mend, & only want patience—I was sure you cd not come & it is best for I dont know when I can leave my room. . . . We have the house full for shooting Monday to Friday—next week.' Marian M'Guinness had been AG's housekeeper since 1893, and was pensioned following a stroke in 1927. In *Me and Nu* (Gerrards Cross, 1970) Anne Gregory describes 'all 18 stone of her' and recalls that she had a 'really violent temper'. In her will AG left her £20 a year for life.

[2] In a short paragraph on the 'squalid . . . if not unamusing' dispute between Lane and the Academicians, the *United Irishman* of 17 Dec three times drew attention to the fact that Lane was a professional picture-dealer. The following week (24 Dec, p. 1) Griffith announced that he had been 'assured the inference which might be drawn from a fact we referred to last week—that Mr. Hugh Lane is a professional picture-dealer, would do Mr. Lane injustice . . . Mr. Lane, we are assured, has gathered the present collection solely with the object of advancing art in Ireland, and his efforts in that direction, instead of benefiting, have involved him in heavy pecuniary loss. We have been invited to verify the assurance by examining his accounts. It is quite unnecessary. The word of a gentleman is sufficient in such a matter.' This apology was the result of WBY's direct intervention, for on 7 Feb 1908 he told Quinn (NYPL) that his 'first serious quarrel with Arthur Griffith was when I went down to the Office and told him what I thought of his conduct in hinting at a preposterous scandal against Hugh Lane in his paper'.

the Irish Times[3]—I will send papers—& Sir Walter Armstrong[4] is to value the pictures in answer to an anonimous person—beleived to be Count Plunkett—who has written to the Irish Times to say they are not worth 3.000—so the Armstrong difficulty is finished.

I will send a poster to day—the corrected posters only came yesterday, there was a misprint in the first lot—& a programe cover if I can get one. I am confident of a fairly good start with the plays—the stars are quiet & fairly favourable—no rows I think. It is hard to judge about impersonal things but all seems favourable.

I have put Synges portrait into *Samhain* also.[5]

Rest all you can, & lock Marian out. I wish I could be at Coole but there are endless things to do.

Yr ev
W B Yeats

ALS Berg, with envelope addressed to Coole, postmark 'DUBLIN DE 22 04'.

[3] Catterson Smith (see p. 681) had complained in the *Irish Times* of 20 Dec (8) that the Circular for the Gallery of Modern Art misleadingly requested that subscriptions be sent to the Secretary of the Royal Hibernian Academy—the post that he held. Insisting that the Royal Hibernian Academy had 'absolutely no concern with the project', he asked the editor to announce that 'communications on the subject should not be so addressed'. The next day JBY wrote (6) as a member of the Academy, censuring Catterson Smith's letter and attitude: 'Quite apart from the policy of such letters as affecting our position in public esteem, it is besides quite futile. We have lent our galleries to Mr. Hugh Lane, and for so long as it is lent we cannot deprive him of the address. If you lend a man a house you lend him also the halldoor and the letter-box.'

[4] Sir Walter Armstrong (1850–1918), art critic and editor, was Director of the National Gallery of Ireland from 1892 to 1914. On 22 Dec with Count Plunkett presiding, he lectured at the Royal Hibernian Academy on 'Pictures and Picture Galleries', when he gave his prestigious support to the new gallery. Next to the report of this lecture, on 23 Dec, the *Irish Times* published a letter from Dermod O'Brien (8) announcing that 'the director of our National Gallery (Sir Walter Armstrong) considers the sum required for these Forbes' pictures as very reasonable, and has kindly offered to make a careful valuation for the use and assistance of the committee in view of the executors allowing a further revision to be made'. Armstrong was apparently responding to a letter, published in the *Irish Times* on 21 Dec and signed 'Viator', which asserted that 'there is not one picture of first-rate importance', and that the whole collection would not fetch £3,000 if sold at auction. It is not known whether 'Viator', who described himself as 'having a long experience of modern pictures and prices', was Count Plunkett, but WBY's disgust when he was appointed Curator of the National Museum in 1907 in preference to Hugh Lane is registered in his poem 'An Appointment' (*VP*, 317–18). In the present case, however, he may have confused the name, for 'Viator' might well have been Lieutenant-Colonel George Tindall Plunkett (1842–1922), Director of the Science and Arts Institutions in Dublin since 1895, who was an enemy of Lane's, and who had already seriously embarrassed him by throwing doubt on the authenticity of a Corot presented to his collection by the King.

[5] See p. 687.

To George P. Brett, 25 December 1904

Nassau Hotel, | Dublin.
Dec. 25.ᵗʰ./04.

Dear Mr Brett,

    Many thanks for the cheque for £28-8-6.[1] I have not written to you about the collected edition because I have been entirely busy altering for stage purposes, two of the plays that are to go into it. I want them to appear there in their final acting form & I can only get a play into its final shape at rehearsal.

Yrs snly
W B Yeats

P.S. I will send you "Samhain" a publication I issue here in connection with my theatrical work.

Dict AEFH, signed WBY; NYPL.

To Lady Augusta Gregory, 27 December 1904

Handed ⎱	Nassau St Dublin at 10.28	Received ⎱	10.50
in at ⎰		here at ⎰	

TO Lady Gregory Coole Park Gort Co Galway[1]
Your play immense success. all plays successfully packed house[2]

Yeats

Telegram Berg, stamped 'GORT AM 6 DE 28 04', with envelope addressed to Coole.

---

[1] Presumably royalties for the American edition of *In the Seven Woods*; see p. 361, n. 3.

[1] AG replied on 28 Dec (Berg): 'So many thanks for telegram. I have seen paper & like to feel all have gone well especially our Kathleen.'

[2] Joseph Holloway (*Abbey Theatre*, 51) corroborated WBY's view of the success of AG's play: 'A merry, homely, little farce by Lady Gregory, *Spreading the News*, caught on at once. . . . Miss Allgood was admirably real. . . . and as the dialogue was capitally true to life the effect was most amusing. . . . All three plays were completely successful, and the audience dispersed delighted; and the opening night of the Abbey Theatre must be written down a great big success.' The *Freeman's Journal* also agreed that 'The Messrs. Fay had another triumph in the roles assigned to them by Lady Gregory, while Miss Allgood's "Mrs. Fallon" was to the village manner born . . .'

To Lady Augusta Gregory, [*29 December 1904*]

THE IRISH NATIONAL THEATRE SOCIETY, | ABBEY THEATRE, | DUBLIN,

My dear Lady Gregory: I could not write earlier to day because an interviewer came & was with me till after the post hour.[1] Russell will see Dowden on Sunday & ask him to sign circular.[2] I suggest that you delay it until you get all the signatures. Russell will sign & of course I will. We had a very poor house so far as the reserved seats were concerned last night but a good pit. I have come round to see what sort the house is to night—people are just arriving—& then I go to my fathers lecture where I speak.[3] Fay never acted as last night—there was great applause. Macgrath has become a wild enthusiast for plays & players.[4] Masefield has returned to Manchester. I want to rewrite 'Bailes Strand'. I can make a great play out of it by rewriting a good deal up to the young mans entrance—from that to the end I cannot better it. You will want to condense a bit in the first half of your play also—your crisis too is excellent. The scenery is being much admired.

---

[1] 'The National Theatre Society—A Chat with Mr. W. B. Yeats', an interview with WBY by 'R. M.', appeared in the Dublin *Evening Mail* on 31 Dec 1904 (4) and was reprinted in the Dublin *Daily Express* on 2 Jan 1905. WBY showed the interviewer over the Theatre, and in the course of 'a long and interesting conversation' told him that the Company hoped to play one week in every month if circumstances permitted. He announced that AG's *Kincora*, and Synge's *The Well of the Saints* would be produced in the new year, and that his own *Deirdre*, 'with choruses somewhat in the Greek manner, and . . . stage managed by Mr. Charles Ricketts—may be ready for production in the early spring'. WBY also revealed that they intended to produce an English version of a Molière play, and Sophocles' *Oedipus the King*, although this was 'banned in England', and presented the 'greatest difficulty in the management of the chorus'.

[2] Dowden's name does not appear in the Circular, 'A Modern Art Gallery for Dublin', which was being prepared for the press.

[3] The *Freeman's Journal* of 30 Dec (7) reported JBY's Royal Hibernian Academy lecture on 'The Art Instinct'. The Chairman, Robert Elliott, spoke afterwards 'strongly in favour of establishing a modern art gallery in Dublin'. In seconding this resolution WBY reopened the controversy between JBY and Elliott (see p. 349, n. 7):

> Mr. W. B. Yeats . . . said Millet's "Angelus" had been described as merely painting a vertical line on a horizontal plane. If that was so, a lamp-post on a street pavement would be a great painting.
> The Chairman—It is easier to discover the defects in one than in the other.
> Mr. Yeats said that might be so, but he did not think the idea of the sound of distant bells could be as well conveyed in the one picture as in the other (laughter). Put Sargent, or Shannon, or Michael Angelo to paint a lamp-post—one of the new ones put up by the Corporation—they would not be raised to any powerful emotions with their minds full of irrelevant religion and irrelevant poetry. He would suggest to the modern artist the motto, 'Who wants to know the truth'. (loud laughter)
> Chairman—Do you mean by the absence of truth deception?
> Mr. Yeats—I mean too great a respect for outer appearance, and a greater respect for inner reality.

[4] John McGrath (see p. 69, n. 2), was now a journalist on the *Freeman's Journal*, and evidently reviewed the opening performances of the Abbey Theatre, writing on 28 Dec (5–6) that 'If last night's promise is fulfilled, the new theatre has a long and prosperous career before it'.

There was a strange scene last night. After the plays were over Roberts took off his coat to fight young Walker, because Walker had not put a mattress on the bed in 'The Shadow of the Glen' & his bones were sore from the bare boards.[5] Fay imposed order in great stile & to day there is peace.

Everybody tells me that the danger of influenza is in the getting well so be very careful. Do not do any work.

Yrs alway
W B Yeats

I am looking forward to Saturday.[6]

ALS Berg, with envelope addressed to Coole, postmark 'DUBLIN DE 30 04'.

---

[5] George Roberts played the part of Dan Burke in the revival of Synge's play, which followed *On Baile's Strand* from 28 Dec to 3 Jan. Dan Burke spends the greater part of the play feigning death on a bed. Frank Walker (Prionsias Mac Siubhlaigh) took the part of Michael Dara.

[6] AG came up to Dublin on Saturday, 31 Dec, to see in the New Year with WBY.

BIOGRAPHICAL AND HISTORICAL
APPENDIX

THE ABBEY THEATRE was constructed out of the Mechanics' Institute, which had enjoyed a chequered career as a theatre and place of entertainment in the nineteenth century. If the first necessity for an Irish dramatic movement had been plays, and the second a company of Irish actors to play them, it quickly became clear that the third requirement was a fixed base. From its very outset the ILT (q.v.) had had difficulties with Dublin's antiquated Patent Laws, which restricted theatrical licences, and in 1898 the Dublin commercial theatres made a concerted attempt to stifle other performances in the City. Although the ILT overcame these difficulties, it never had the resources to find a permanent home, and when the Fays (q.v.) proclaimed their company the Irish National Theatre Society in 1902, they were obliged to rehearse in the Dublin mountains, and even thought of converting a 'tin tab', a Nonconformist chapel constructed of corrugated iron. Instead they took a hall in Camden Street, but this proved to be wholly inadequate for performances and most of their subsequent productions were staged at the Molesworth Hall.

As early as April 1902 AEFH (q.v.) had dropped hints that she might buy WBY a theatre, and in 1903 she conducted a number of experiments with Tarot cards to guide her in the matter. WBY's speech at that autumn's productions, in which he said that the company should perform foreign drama as well as Irish plays, strengthened her resolve, and an unexpected rise in shares she held in the Hudson Bay Company made the scheme feasible. On 1 January 1904, while WBY was in America, she wrote to George Roberts hinting at the purchase of a theatre and also told William Fay of these hopes after the January productions.

No practical steps were taken until WBY's return, but in early April 1904 AEFH sent her letter, 'Offer of a Theatre', to the members of the Company. In this she announced that she was 'taking the Hall of the Mechanic's Institute in Abbey Street, and an adjoining building in Marlborough Street', which she proposed 'to turn into a small Theatre, with a proper Entrance Hall, Green-room, and Dressing-rooms'. She reserved the right to let the Theatre when the Company was on tour or resting, but agreed to pay the rent, rates, and taxes on it. Because of the anticipated opposition of the commercial theatres, the offer was kept secret while WBY looked into the legal aspects of the purchase and Patent, but she immediately employed the Dublin architect and indefatigable theatre-goer, Joseph Holloway, to help her with the conversion. Although their visit to the building the following day was not a success—they were chased out as 'land-grabbers' by the manager—they soon gained access, and by 15 April Holloway had sketched out a rough plan of the new Theatre.

The objections to the granting of a Patent, lodged by the other Dublin theatre managers, were heard on 4 August 1904 and overruled, although the Patent, formally granted on 20 August, stated that it would lapse if the INTS was dissolved, that the Theatre could not be enlarged to accommodate an audience larger than its existing capacity, and that it could only play Irish drama and such foreign works 'as would tend to interest the public in the higher forms of dramatic art'. AEFH and Holloway corresponded frequently thereafter on details of the reconstruction, an exchange which makes clear that AEFH, inspired by her knowledge of German municipal theatres (she sent him a plan of Wagner's

Bayreuth Theatre as a model), had very definite ideas on what she wanted, and was prepared to spend whatever she could afford to get it. W. G. Fay was employed to oversee the installation of the technical and electrical fittings, and the final cost of the renovation was nearly £3,000, plus leasing costs of £170 per annum.

The first rehearsal in the new Theatre, attended by WBY, AG (q.v.), and John Quinn (q.v.), was called on 31 October, and WBY was particularly concerned to commission appropriate stage designs for the first performances. The opening, originally arranged for early December, had to be postponed as neither the stage nor the stained-glass was finished in time, but finally took place on 27 December when *On Baile's Strand*, *Spreading the News*, and *Cathleen ni Houlihan* were presented before a distinguished audience which included WBY, AEFH, Synge, AE, Martyn, Gwynn, JBY, Hugh Lane, and John Masefield, although AG was prevented by illness from attending.

Nearly all the materials used in the renovation were Irish, although the lighting was the latest German design. Situated on the corner of Lower Abbey Street and Marlborough Street, the main entrance was from Marlborough Street, the central one being sheltered by a verandah. The large carpeted hall boasted stained-glass windows designed by Sarah Purser and portraits of AEFH, William Fay, Frank Fay, and Maire Nic Shiubhlaigh, painted by JBY, while the green-room was decorated with portraits of Douglas Hyde and AE, also by JBY, as well as a painting of WBY by Madame Troncy. A carpeted stairway led down from the hall to the stalls, which seated 178 people, behind which was the pit, seating 186. Both stalls and pit were arranged so that every seat had a perfect view of the stage. A balcony, accommodating 198 people and also inclined to give every seat a clear view, extended round the interior, but there was no gallery. The seats were upholstered in scarlet leather, and divided by polished brass work. The auditorium was illuminated by a large electric light in the centre of the ceiling, and by fourteen triple lamps, also electric, distributed round the theatre. The walls were painted in colours which harmonized with the rest of the appointments, and large medallions of the city arms, the Irish harp, and other national devices adorned the walls. Room for a small orchestra was afforded by removing the front row of stalls. The acting area was only about 20 feet by 15, but the converted Morgue provided dressing-rooms and space for the expanding wardrobe. There was no licensed bar, but a buffet sold tea and coffee during the intervals.

The cheapest seat was 1s., twice the amount charged at other Dublin theatres, because, as AEFH explained in her original letter, she wished 'to prevent cheap entertainments from being given, which would lower the letting value of the Hall', but this caused great indignation among the audience and in the press—especially since the old Mechanics' Institute had been the meeting place of the Nationalist artisans of Dublin. The seat prices were finally lowered in October 1906.

The INTS henceforward used the Abbey Theatre as its base, mounting spring and autumn seasons, and AEFH continued to spend money on it. By September 1905 she announced that it had cost her over £4,000, and that

November she purchased a house in Abbey Street and built another green-room in the yard at a cost of £1,250 and an annual rent of £70. In July 1907 she bought an annexe and later that year paid for the stables behind the Theatre to be converted into a rehearsal room. By December 1910, as she was relinquishing her interest, she estimated that she had spent £10,350 on the Abbey Theatre.

PADRAIC COLUM (1881–1972) was born in Longford where his father was in charge of the workhouse. He moved to Dublin as a boy, on his father's appointment as station master in the suburb of Sandycove. After leaving school, Colum became a clerk in the Irish Railway Clearing House, and began to contribute poems and short plays to Irish newspapers and periodicals. He joined the INTS (q.v.) and first became acquainted with WBY in the autumn of 1902. William Fay (q.v.) controversially turned down his one-act play *The Saxon Shilling* early in 1903, although it was performed by the Inghinidhe na hEireann in May, and in December that year he scored a success with the INTS production of *Broken Soil*, subsequently revised as *The Fiddler's House*. An allowance from the Irish-American millionaire Thomas F. Kelly enabled him to give up his job and spend three years travelling in the Irish countryside and writing. In April 1905 AG (q.v.) invited him to Coole with WBY so that he could finish a new play, and this, as *The Land*, received an enthusiastic reception when it was produced at the Abbey in June. Unhappily this marked the end of his collaboration with the Abbey: he was distressed by the reorganization of the Company that autumn and, in spite of strenuous efforts by WBY and AG, seceded with others to form the Theatre of Ireland in 1906. The breach seemed to deepen when his father was arrested and fined for demonstrating against *The Playboy of the Western World* in January 1907, but in June Colum agreed to allow the Abbey Company to revive *The Land* and gradually resumed friendly relations with WBY. In the same year he published *The Fiddler's House* (which had been produced by the Theatre of Ireland in March), a collection of short plays, *Studies*, and a book of poems, *The Wild Earth*. In 1910 the Abbey produced his last substantial Irish play, *Thomas Muskerry*. He helped found the monthly *Irish Review* in 1911 and became its sole editor from 1912 to 1913. In 1912 he married Mary Maguire, and in the same year published his sociological travelogue, *My Irish Year*.

He and his wife taught for a time in Patrick Pearse's Gaelic schools, St Enda's and St Ita's, but in 1914 they emigrated to America where, apart from occasional trips to Ireland and a period in France from 1930 to 1933, they remained for the rest of their lives, supporting themselves with part-time university teaching and freelance literary work. Colum became a successful writer of children's stories, specializing in rendering myths in simple narrative form, and in 1923 the Hawaiian Legislature commissioned him to prepare a collection of the Islands' legends for use in local schools. He also reviewed widely, and wrote biographies of Arthur Griffith (q.v.) and James Joyce (q.v.), whom he had known in Dublin and Paris. After his wife's death in 1957 he spent more time in Ireland, and continued writing and publishing until his death.

Although his regard for Colum's work was always qualified, WBY encouraged his early poetic and dramatic efforts, seeing in him the one dramatist from the

Fays' Company who might contribute significantly to the Irish dramatic move-ment. While pleased with the success of *Broken Soil*, in which an old fiddler chooses between the satisfying uncertainties of the open road and the drab sufficiencies of settled life, WBY found it 'a great bore' in performance. He called *The Land*, which dramatizes the agrarian struggle and the problem of emi-gration, 'a really fine work', although he found the heroine's character 'very unsatisfactory', and thought Colum created 'the main elements of his art more out of the critical capacity than out of the emotional or imaginative'. For WBY Colum's success was not only desirable on artistic grounds—the performance of his work could be used to block that of inferior writers such as James Cousins—but also politically valuable, for, as a Catholic who identified directly with the country people, his plays could be cited as evidence against those who claimed that the Abbey Theatre was dominated by Anglo-Irish Protestants. In reforming the INTS in the autumn of 1905 WBY regarded Colum as one of the four writ-ers whose interests were most involved in the Abbey (himself, AG, and Synge being the others); yet, like others, he found Colum 'impressionable' and sus-pected that his love of popularity would make him an uncertain ally. He there-fore opposed suggestions that Colum should be made a director in the new Abbey Company. After Colum's return to the Abbey WBY got him to render English medieval Miracle Plays in Anglo-Irish dialect, and, although they saw little of each other after the Colums settled in America, entertained a growing admiration for his literary criticism.

EDWARD GORDON CRAIG (1872–1966), the illegitimate son of the actress Ellen Terry and the architect, critic, and stage designer Edward William God-win, made his acting début at the Court Theatre, London, at the age of 6. After school at Bradfield College and university in Heidelberg, he went on the stage, acting in England and America before joining his mother in Henry Irving's com-pany at the Lyceum in 1889. During the next eight years he played a variety of minor and leading roles at the Lyceum, where WBY saw him in 1897. By May that year his acting career seemed assured when, at extremely short notice and to resounding acclaim, he took over the role of Hamlet in a Ben Greet production, but a few months later, increasingly frustrated by the limitations of realistic stage management, he suddenly quit acting. He began drawing for newspapers and magazines and developed his skill at woodcuts, an art that became a major medium for his stage designs. In 1898 he founded and edited *The Page*, which published his striking designs and engravings until it folded in 1901.

In 1900 Craig collaborated with the composer, Martin Shaw, on a short pro-duction of Purcell's *Dido and Aeneas* for the Purcell Operatic Society at Hamp-stead. Here he experimented with innovative stage techniques, removing the footlights and lighting his symbolic scenes from above and from the sides, and harmonizing music, lighting, colour, and movement. When the production was revived with Purcell's *A Masque of Love* the following year, WBY immediately recognized the possibilities of Craig's scenery and lighting for his own plays. Following a revival of *A Masque of Love* and a new production of Handel's *Acis and Galatea* in 1902, he wrote warmly of Craig's experiments and hoped that they might collaborate. Craig expressed interest in producing WBY's plays, and WBY attended his production of Laurence Housman's *Bethlehem* and two acts of Roze's *Sword and Song* at the end of the year.

In April 1903 Craig joined forces with his mother and sister, Edith Craig, a costume designer, to mount a production of Ibsen's *The Vikings*, which WBY saw, but their plan to form a new company based on Craig's stage management collapsed in June as debts mounted and their second production, *Much Ado About Nothing*, was taken off after a few performances. Craig was elected to the Society of Twelve for his designs and engravings, but he was now determined to establish a School for the Art of the Theatre in London. While trying unsuccessfully to raise public and private support for this, he wrote and designed a series of masques for production by the Masquers Society (q.v.), but when the Masquers collapsed at the end of the year his prospects for establishing a new theatrical art collapsed with it. Following an exploratory trip to Germany to meet Otto Brahm of the Lessing Theatre, Craig received an invitation to stage a production of Thomas Otway's *Venice Preserved* there. Thus in August 1904, with nothing to hold him in England, he left London for Berlin.

Craig left behind his wife, Elena Meo, with whom he had eloped during the production of *Acis and Galatea*, and she was soon displaced by Isadora Duncan, the dancer, who inspired his designs for movement. Craig's work thrived in Germany, and his book on *The Art of the Theatre* (1905) was first published there. Max Reinhardt and his assistants visited Craig's studio to seek ideas for the Deutsches Theatre, and Craig visited Vienna, Florence, and St Petersburg to discover new European locations for his productions. Finding the English stage uncongenial after the death of Irving in 1905, he turned more intently to writing about his ideas, publishing *The Artists of the Theatre of the Future* and *The Actor and the Uber-Marionette* in 1907. In 1908 he launched his periodical, *The Mask*, which served intermittently as a vehicle for his theatrical theories and designs until 1929. Later that year he moved to Florence and took a workshop-studio at the Arena Goldoni. Seemingly settled at last, he asked WBY to contribute an essay, 'The Tragic Theatre' (1910), to *The Mask*, and also to join his circle in Florence.

In 1910 Craig visited Stanislavsky at the Moscow Arts Theatre, where he agreed to mount his great production of *Hamlet*, for which he developed a model stage and a series of folding 'screens'. The same height as the proscenium, these screens could be opened or closed by the stage designer to suggest various effects, and arranged to alter the size of the proscenium opening and to create a desired sense of space. Craig had explained this new technique to WBY on a visit to London in late December 1909, and provided him with a model stage and free rights in a set of screens for the Abbey. In January 1911 they were used for productions of Lady Gregory's *The Deliverers* and WBY's *The Hour-Glass*, which was rewritten especially for them. New productions of *The Land of Heart's Desire* and *The Countess Cathleen* followed, and Craig's designs for the plays were published in WBY's *Plays for an Irish Theatre*. When Craig returned to London in July 1911 to arrange for exhibitions of his model stage, screens, and designs, WBY was on the committee that arranged a public banquet in recognition of his achievements. In his testimonial, WBY stated that 'a great age was an age that employed its men of genius, and a poor age one that could not do so. This age found it difficult to employ men of genius like Mr. Craig.' In October he asked Craig to undertake the production of his work, and in November the two tried unsuccessfully to set up a special company financed by the impresario George Tyler.

Following the success of his *Hamlet* production in Moscow in January 1912, Craig, now an acknowledged leader of the theatre in Europe, redoubled his efforts to found a School for the Art of the Theatre. He worked with the Society of the Theatre on plans to open a School in London, and also carried on extensive discussions with WBY and the English actress Letitia Darragh to found 'The London Repertory Company'. In March 1913 WBY gave two enthusiastic lectures on Craig during an exhibition of his work in Dublin, but plans for the London enterprise were shelved shortly afterwards when Lord Howard de Walden offered Craig a year's financial support, and he returned to Florence to prepare his School in the Arena Goldoni, an open-air theatre with work-rooms and offices. By the summer of 1914 he had constructed five large model theatres in wood for projected performances, but when war was declared his funding dried up, the premises were requisitioned, and he broke up the models.

During the war Craig studied theatre history, wrote puppet plays, published *The Marionette* (1918), and revived *The Mask*, which was interrupted from 1915 to 1918, and again from March 1919 to 1923. Though he continued to hold exhibitions of his work in major European cities, and to publish his designs for the plays of Shakespeare, Ibsen, and other dramatists, he staged his last major production, Ibsen's *The Pretenders*, in 1926.

In October 1934 Craig and WBY met for the last time when they attended the Convegno Volta in Rome. On numerous occasions since 1901—in essays, lectures, and on public platforms—the two had acknowledged their collaboration and mutual inspiration. Before and after the war WBY lectured frequently on 'The Theatre of Beauty', in which he underscored the significance of Craig's art for the modern stage, and what he learned from Craig was eventually applied to his adaptations of Japanese Noh drama. As Craig had written in *The Mask*, 'I have myself acted as a most willing aid in the interpretation of the drama of WBY and it has been one of the special happinesses of my life to have been connected with his poetic dramas in Dublin . . . but only as a servant . . . seeing him as a "brother art".' For his part WBY described Craig to Miss Darragh as 'a great genius', although one with 'a difficult temperament'. Craig continued to write about the theatre for the remainder of his long life, including biographies of Henry Irving and Ellen Terry. His autobiography, *Index to the Story of My Days*, appeared in 1957.

FRANK JOHN FAY (1870–1931), actor, producer, and elocution teacher, and WILLIAM GEORGE FAY (1872–1947), were born in Dublin, the sons of a minor civil servant, and both were educated at Belvedere College. After leaving school Frank became secretary to the director of a firm of accountants, but had a consuming passion for the drama. Besides patronizing performances in Dublin, he accumulated a library of second-hand plays, handbooks, and histories of the theatre, and his enthusiasm awakened the interest of his brother. They began to produce amateur plays in Dublin as 'The Ormond Drama Company', named after the road in which they lived, and performed for temperance societies in church halls and at the Coffee Palace in Townsend Street. Frank enhanced his light voice by studying elocution and voice-production, further improving his technique at Maud Randford's Dublin Acting School, which his brother also attended after failing the Civil Service Examination. While Frank remained in his Dublin office, Willie became advance agent for Maud Randford and her husband, J. W. Lacy, in a fit-up company touring the Irish provinces. He also took small parts and made his first appearance on the professional stage at the Queen's Theatre, Dublin. When the Lacy Company broke up in 1891 he toured in Ireland and England, gaining theatrical experience with a series of actor-managers, including J. W. Whitbread, R. B. Lewis, H. E. Bailey, and Lloyd's Mexican Circus. Extensive travelling with the latter brought him into contact with the different accents and habits of provincial Ireland, knowledge that he was to turn to good effect in his acting for the Abbey Theatre.

In 1899 he took a job in Dublin as an electrician, but kept up his theatrical interests by joining his brother in the Ormond Dramatic Society in the evening, playing a mixture of short melodramas, comedies, and farces. He also formed the W. G. Fay Comedy Combination, and with Frank regularly saw visiting English and French companies. They also kept up with the latest developments in European drama through William Archer's articles in the *Morning Leader*, and were particularly inspired by what Archer wrote of Antoine's *Théâtre Libre*. In 1899 Frank Fay began writing theatre reviews for the newly established *United Irishman*; he welcomed the ILT (q.v.), but he followed Griffith (q.v.) in urging WBY to widen the appeal of the plays, and insisted above all that Irish drama could only be performed by Irish actors. He first came to WBY's notice through a review of *The Land of Heart's Desire* in June 1901, and the two began a correspondence on theatrical matters. The Fays had already come into association with MG's Daughters of Erin, through Willie's direction of Fr. Dinneen's *An Tobar Draoidheacta* in 1900, and they strengthened the relationship in August 1901 by contributing to the production of Alice Milligan's *The Deliverance of Red Hugh* and P. T. MacGinley's *Eilis agus an Bhean Déirce*. WBY saw these performances, and 'came away with my head on fire', Frank's acting having revealed the potential for Irish drama of Irish accents and modulations. Later that autumn Willie introduced himself to George Moore and assisted him with the production of Hyde's *Casadh an tSugain*, which formed part of the final ILT season.

In 1901, with the three-year ILT experiment at an end, the Fays obtained AE's permission to produce his *Deirdre*, and AE prevailed upon WBY to give them *Cathleen ni Houlihan*. The resources of the Ormond Society were inadequate for these performances and so Fay took actors and actresses from the Hermetic Society, the Daughters of Erin, and elsewhere, to form the expanded W. G. Fay's Irish National Dramatic Society. Frank threw himself into the work of rehearsals with what James Cousins was later to recall as 'appalling earnestness', insisting that every speech and detail be gone over again and again until it was right. This paid dividends: the performances in April 1902 were a success with audiences and critics alike, while WBY praised the gravity and simplicity of the acting and picked out Fay's Conchubar for particular commendation. This triumph persuaded the Fays to establish the Irish National Theatre Society (q.v.), with WBY as President and AE, Hyde, and MG as Vice-Presidents. The Society leased Camden Hall, but this proved too small and inconvenient as a theatre, and in 1903 they used the Molesworth Hall. A high point for the Society was its visit to London in May 1903, where it gained golden opinions and wide press coverage, so raising the morale of the company and greatly enhancing its reputation in Dublin. Over the next six years Frank Fay took leading parts in most of the major INTS productions, scoring his greatest successes in WBY's poetic tragedies, most notably with his interpretation of Seanchan in *The King's Threshold* and Cuchulain in *On Baile's Strand*.

When AEFH (q.v.) bought the Mechanics' Institute to convert into the Abbey Theatre (q.v.), Willie gave up his job as an electrician to oversee the reconstruction, and the year and a half following the opening of the Abbey, when he was full-time manager of the Company, were the happiest in his relations with WBY. They conferred on details of productions and discussed emendations of texts and the casting of plays. It was Willie Fay who began the initial discussions with AE about restructuring the INTS in 1905, although the scheme as finally agreed involved a diminution of his executive power. At first this did not signify, since the secession of most of the Company in late 1905 made him and his brother of even greater importance to the continuity of the Theatre, but the length and difficulties of a British tour in 1906 showed up inadequacies in acting and production, and led to bouts of ill-discipline off stage which shocked AEFH and worried WBY. But Willie Fay's greatest mistake was to blaze out (although under considerable provocation) at AEFH, whose financial control of the Abbey had been increased by the 1905 changes, and who henceforward regarded him with dislike and suspicion. She decided that she could no longer do business through him, and insisted that a controlling manager should be appointed, an initiative that greatly undermined his power by making the actors and staff of the Abbey responsible to another authority. In a misguided attempt to shore up his influence he grew more dictatorial and there was constant friction between him, the Company, and the Directors. Things would probably have come to a head earlier had not the controversy over *The Playboy of the Western World* in 1907 obliged the Company to close ranks, but a final split could not be long delayed, and, after an autumn of mounting irritations, this finally occurred in January 1908.

During the restructuring of the INTS in 1905 WBY had been particularly eager to find money for Frank Fay, thinking him essential to the success of poetic work at the Abbey, and convinced that he would never find satisfying work outside the Irish Theatre. At first he thought of appointing him Secretary of the new Limited Company, but in February 1906 he asked him to take classes in voice production and verse-speaking, telling him that he was 'the most beautiful verse speaker I know'. Later that year, however, he was to qualify his praise, observing that while Fay was 'a born teacher of elocution up to a point', his pupils came from him without passion or expression in voice or gesture. But Frank Fay, alone of the Company, supported the Directors in touring *The Playboy of the Western World* in Britain in 1907.

Although not directly involved in Willie's argument with the Company and the Directors, he felt that he should resign in solidarity with him. He accompanied his brother and sister-in-law (the actress Brigid O'Dempsey, whom Willie had married in 1906) to London, and soon afterwards to New York, where the impresario Frohman arranged for them to produce *The Pot of Broth*. Controversy dogged them, for WBY heard that they were using the INTS and Abbey names in unauthorized ways, and withdrew permission for them to produce any more of his plays. They took *The Pot of Broth* and William Boyle's *The Building Fund* to Chicago, and on their return to London the three appeared as the witches in William Poel's production of *Macbeth*, this being the last time they appeared on the same stage. In the following years Frank toured in Britain with various companies, and had a spell at the Birmingham Repertory Company. In 1918 he moved back to Dublin, and spent the rest of his life teaching elocution and producing plays for amateur societies. Although there was occasional talk of his returning to the Abbey, these plans never materialized.

Meanwhile Willie Fay remained in England, taking parts in productions by William Poel, Granville Barker, and Sir Herbert Tree. He had a success as Thaddeus Golligher in Charles Hawtrey's production of George Birmingham's *General John Regan* in 1913, and became Chairman of the Actors' Association the following year. During the latter years of the First World War he helped produce plays for military camps and in 1920 began what turned out to be a three-year appointment at the Nottingham Repertory Theatre, followed by a similar engagement at the Birmingham Repertory Theatre in 1926. Thereafter he had a series of theatrical jobs: producing, taking small parts, teaching acting, and doing some film work.

Unlike his brother, who was an energetic, outgoing man of action, Frank Fay tended to moroseness, self-doubt, and caution. Although he had considerable knowledge of stage history and of acting styles, he always deferred to his brother's more practical experience of the theatre, and remained in his shadow. He trained the Irish players in what he understood to be the French acting tradition, and in his reviews for the *United Irishman* he enthused over Coquelin, Rejane, and Bernhardt on their visits to Dublin, while disparaging most of the English companies (especially Benson's) for their lack of training, and their reliance on 'business', spectacle, and tricks instead of on vocal modulation and articulation. He repeated with approval Coquelin's opinion that articulation was 'at once the ABC and the highest point of art', and his own acting and tuition was based upon this view. Nevertheless, he was constantly dissatisfied with his own performances, hypersensitive to criticism, and doubtful about the ability of the Company. He even advised against the 1903 trip to London, which did so much to establish the reputation and confidence of the INTS, and spent the voyage to England pacing the deck in extreme agitation. His uncertainties and self-doubts issued in virulent eruptions of temper which caused friction in the

Company. Both his qualities and his limitations meant that he suffered even more than his brother through his departure from the Abbey Theatre: less versatile than Willie, he found few parts on the British commercial stage to suit his gifts in verse-speaking, while his lack of vocal power was a handicap in large theatres. His major achievement lay in the past: through his study of the drama, his observation of different acting styles, his dedication and perpetual hard work, he had managed to give a troupe of Irish amateurs a distinctive style of acting that became famous on both sides of the Atlantic.

While Frank Fay's forte was verse drama and tragedy, Willie excelled as comedian, character actor (especially in dialect work), and producer. Yet, although outgoing and extrovert, he had the unhappy gift of rubbing people the wrong way, and WBY developed a deep-seated antipathy towards him that increased after the summer of 1906 and which made relations between them increasingly strained. Willie Fay had started with a small group of amateurs and within a few years found himself at the centre of an important theatrical movement, which put unforeseen administrative, artistic, and psychological pressures on him. At the same time he saw his authority in the Company appropriated by the Directors and undermined by business managers brought in from England. He was finally put into a position where he felt that resignation was his only course. He shared many of his brother's views on acting and articulation, but was more flexible than him, and managed to make the transition from the Abbey to the British commercial stage more successfully. Nevertheless, as with his brother, his lasting achievement was his contribution to the Irish dramatic movement.

LADY ISABELLA AUGUSTA GREGORY (1852–1932), the seventh daughter of Dudley Persse of Roxborough, Co. Galway, was by birth a member of the landed Irish Protestant Ascendancy. A plain but intelligent girl, she was neglected by her fundamentalist mother in favour of her prettier sisters, and she seems to have resigned herself from an early age to a life of quiet family service, nursing an invalid brother and helping to look after the house and estate. All this changed in 1879 when she met Sir William Gregory, some thirty-five years her senior, a former Governor of Ceylon (Sri Lanka), and owner of Coole Park, whom she married in 1880.

Marriage opened a new world; she travelled in Europe and took an active part in London social and political life. Her only child, Robert, was born in May 1881, and in October she and Gregory left for Egypt where she met Wilfrid Scawen Blunt. Under Blunt's influence she took up the cause of Arabi Bey, the Egyptian nationalist leader, and her pamphlet, *Arabi and his Household*, was published in 1882, the year in which she began a brief affair with Blunt. Over the next years the Gregorys divided their time between Coole, London, and foreign tours, which included a visit to India from 1885 to 1886. In January 1892 her sequence, 'A Woman's Sonnets', inspired by her affair with Blunt, was published anonymously in Blunt's Kelmscott edition of *Love Lyrics and Songs of Proteus*. In March of the same year Sir William Gregory died; she sold their London house and returned to Ireland where she devoted herself to paying off the debts on Coole incurred by her husband's early gambling excesses. The following year she published anonymously *A Phantom's Pilgrimage, or Home Ruin*, a pamphlet which envisaged the catastrophic economic and social consequences of independence to Ireland.

In 1894 she took an apartment in London, where she was to retain a *pied-à-terre* for ten years. She met WBY for the first time early that summer, when she recorded in her diary that he looked 'every inch a poet, though I think his prose "Celtic Twilight" is the best thing he has done'. Later that year she published her edition of Sir William Gregory's autobiography. The friendship with WBY that had not sparked in 1894 prospered when they met again at Edward Martyn's house in August 1896, and Yeats's long visit to Coole the following summer (the first of twenty summer visits) cemented it. During this stay they began planning a Celtic theatre, a project that was to result in the Irish Literary Theatre (q.v.) and the Abbey Theatre (q.v.). In the winter and spring of 1898 she saw a great deal of WBY in London, and her edition of *Mr. Gregory's Letter-Box 1813–35* appeared in March. WBY had encouraged her to collect folklore and in May she visited the Aran Islands for that purpose; she was also helping to drum up guarantors for the ILT, which gave its first productions in May 1899. Increasingly concerned with cultural nationalism, she edited *Ideals in Ireland* (1901), a collection of essays dedicated to this cause, and in the summer began to collaborate with WBY on his plays in dialect, and to plan and translate plays in Gaelic with Douglas Hyde.

She also found her own voice as a dramatist, having made a false start with *Colman and Guaire* in 1900, and wrote *The Jackdaw* (1901) and *Twenty-Five* (1901). She had already started work on a version of the Ulster cycle of Irish myths, which appeared to critical acclaim in 1902 as *Cuchulain of Muirthemne*. In August 1902 she met John Quinn (q.v.) for the first time, and in October of that year assisted WBY and Douglas Hyde in the hasty writing of *Where There Is Nothing* to forestall the use of the theme by George Moore. In March 1903 she published her collection of folklore and translations, *Poets and Dreamers*, and in the same month a revised version of her *Twenty-Five* was produced by the INTS (q.v.) at the Molesworth Hall. Her sequel to *Cuchulain of Muirthemne*, *Gods and Fighting Men*, which retold the exploits of Finn MacCool, appeared in January 1904, and in August the Patent for the Abbey Theatre was granted in her name.

The Theatre opened on 27 December, with her *Spreading the News* on the bill, but she was unable to attend because of ill-health. In March of the following year her first historical play, *Kincora*, was produced, followed by another, *The White Cockade*, in December. Much of the first part of 1906 was taken up with trying to make peace with the players who had recently seceded from the Abbey Company, and she persuaded WBY not to sue Maire Walker for breach of contract. In April the first of her versions of Molière, *The Doctor in Spite of Himself*, was produced, and this was followed by well over thirty further plays and adaptations. As well as keeping up a constant supply of drama, she was also deeply involved in the day-to-day running of the Theatre, especially after the resignation of the Fays (q.v.).

In May 1907 she took WBY to Italy with her son Robert, and that September Robert married Margaret Parry. In late January 1909 she was seriously ill from what was apparently a cerebral haemorrhage, and WBY feared that she was about to die. She recovered to aid him in his successful fight with Dublin Castle over the production of Shaw's *The Shewing-Up of Blanco Posnet* in August. Her relations with AEFH (q.v.) were already strained, and they stretched to breaking point after the Abbey remained open on the day after King Edward's death in May 1910, although she had advised closing through courtesy. The remainder of the year and much of the following one were taken up with an appeal for funds to purchase the Abbey and to replace AEFH's subsidy, and with an arbitration dispute with AEFH.

In late September 1911 she followed the Abbey Company to America on its first tour, and took charge of it after WBY's return to Ireland. Hostility to the Company over its production of Synge's plays, which had been whipped up by Irish-American papers, culminated in theatre riots in Philadelphia, and the arrest of the Company. AG stood up to her adversaries and brought the tour to a successful close. While in America she had given numerous lectures and also begun an affair with Quinn. She returned to Ireland in March 1912, shortly before the publication of her two-volume *Irish Folk-History Plays* was published in New York. In December she left with the Abbey Company for a second, less troubled, tour of America, which lasted until late April 1913. In November of that year she published *Our Irish Theatre*, an account of the Irish dramatic movement to date. From January to April 1913 she accompanied the third Abbey tour to the USA. In May her nephew, Hugh Lane, was drowned when the *Lusitania* was torpedoed. After the discovery of an unwitnessed codicil to his will, leaving a collection of Impressionist paintings to Dublin, she began what was to be an unsuccessful lifelong crusade to have the pictures given to the Municipal Gallery there. In October she set out for her last tour of North America, and her son Robert enlisted in the Connaught Rangers. She gave WBY practical help with his purchase of Thoor Ballylee in 1917, and later in the year emotional support during the troubled period leading up to his marriage, even interceding with his prospective mother-in-law on his behalf.

On 23 January 1918 she received the telegram at Coole informing her that her son, who had transferred to the Royal Flying Corps, had been shot down and killed over northern Italy, and she travelled to Galway to break the news to his wife. In 1919 she played the title role in *Cathleen ni Houlihan* at the Abbey Theatre, and in March directed a production of Shaw's *John Bull's Other Island*. *Visions and Beliefs in the West of Ireland*, the large folklore collection that she and WBY had been working on since 1901, finally appeared in April 1920, and in October she contributed the first of a series of anonymous articles in the *Nation*, 'A Week in Ireland', which revealed to British readers the excesses of the Black and Tans in the Coole area. In 1921 her biography of her nephew, *Sir Hugh Lane's Life and Achievement*, was published. The war in Ireland touched her more nearly in May of that year when her daughter-in-law was the only one to escape an IRA ambush; and in April 1924 when her family house, Roxborough, was burned out by Republicans.

In 1923 she had her first operation for breast cancer, followed by another in 1926. In April 1927 Margaret Gregory sold Coole to the Forestry Commission, but AG was able to lease it for the period of her life. In 1928 she was involved in the controversy over the rejection of O'Casey's *The Silver Tassie*, and her attempts at conciliation could not prevent his temporary withdrawal from the Abbey Theatre. Her health continued to decline, and in 1931 WBY moved almost permanently to Coole to keep her company. On 23 May 1932 she died while WBY was temporarily away in Dublin.

WBY and AG were drawn to each other by psychological, social, artistic, and political needs. The sex and age difference suggest that psychologically the friendship owed something to a mother–son relationship, and Susan Yeats's maternal shortcomings may have rendered her eldest child particularly susceptible to such an involvement. The social differences point to a hostess–protégé relationship, in which the worldly-wise lady from the big house takes up a gauche, unhappy, but talented young man, and helps to bring him out and shape his career. Certainly Lady Gregory played this role, especially in the early days, and it was one that WBY found congenial. There is also the patron–artist relationship, in which Coole became a modern Penshurst or Urbino, where Lady Gregory presided over a gathering of geniuses. The benefits of such a rural salon to WBY were incalculable, and are gratefully celebrated in his poetry. The arrangement also appealed to his sense of tradition since it allowed him to adopt the position of an Ancient Irish *file* at the board of his Lord, a position that not only suited his notion of decorum but also touched a more instinctive response: 'I think I was meant not for a master but for a servant . . . and so it is that all images of service are dear to me.'

The relationship was two-way: if Lady Gregory conferred a quasi-maternal affection, WBY returned a quasi-filial regard and admiration; if she as hostess could introduce him to influential and useful members of the British and Irish establishments, he could bring her into artistic and literary circles that would otherwise have been closed to her; and if she as patron provided a salon and financial support for his art, he, after some initial reservations, encouraged and promoted her own ventures into literature and drama. Their literary and cultural interests were moreover complementary and mutually useful: she could help him to folklore and provide him with appropriate dialect when necessary, while he gave her advice on dramaturgy and helped her to shape her plays and other writings.

It is also evident that the relationship found its sources at a far deeper level than that of merely hostess and protégé. WBY's subconscious understood this, and in February 1909, shocked by the discovery that she was in danger of death, his wandering mind imagined that it was his mother who was ill: 'Then I remember that my mother died years ago and that more than kin was at stake. She had been to me mother, friend, sister and brother.' He told Mario Rossi shortly after her death that she was one 'who has been to me for nearly forty years my strength and my conscience'.

While the relationship had a profound influence on both their lives, it changed his more than hers. Had she not met him her life would have been far less rich but its basic contours would have remained unchanged. Yet, if WBY's friendship did not alter the direction of her life, he gave it focus. His encouragement of her writing, although slow at first, became a constant and necessary reassurance, and not infrequently tipped into overpraise.

It is harder to envisage what would have become of WBY had they not met. There would have been more hack journalism to make ends meet and so less time for poetry. He would have attempted to have his plays staged, but the brief histories of the Masquers (q.v.) and the Theatre of Ireland suggest that productions would have been fitful and unsatisfactory. Although Lady Gregory overstates her part in the Abbey Theatre, her presence was crucial to WBY for administrative as well as artistic reasons. Her applied tact prevented the Irish dramatic movement from disintegrating at several points of crisis. And without the constant resources of his own theatre WBY would not only have been a different playwright, he would also have been a very different poet.

But the practical assistance that she rendered WBY went beyond the provision of money, board, and administrative and secretarial help. Coole not only offered him space and time to write, it also surrounded him with the tangible symbols of a tradition and quality of life that seemed a microcosm of the cultural unity he wished to establish at a national level. In the troubles of its unfolding contemporary history he saw played out the problems and contradictions of his own cultural and political attitudes. His experience of Coole helped him to define those attitudes more confidently, and at the same time taught him how unlikely they were to be implemented in a twentieth-century world. Without Coole as both a refuge and an example, this discovery might have led to isolation and despair, but AG and her house saved him from this desolation, and from the extremism it might have provoked, by providing him with a haven in which he could recuperate his imaginative energies and distance himself from the exhausting and potentially corroding squabbles of public life. As he wrote to Dorothy Wellesley in May 1936: 'I long for quiet; long ago I used to find it at Coole. It was part of the genius of that house. Lady Gregory never rebelled like other Irish women I have known who consumed themselves & their friends; in spite of Scripture she put the new wine into the old bottles.'

ARTHUR GRIFFITH (1871–1922), journalist and politician, was born in Dublin, the son of a printer. From his adolescence he and his great friend and hero, William Rooney, concerned themselves with Irish politics and culture, and became the driving forces in a number of small nationalist clubs, notably the Leinster Literary Society and the more important Celtic Society. Both were deeply influenced by the writings of Thomas Davis, and ardent supporters of Parnell. At the age of 15 Griffith was apprenticed as a printer to Underwoods, a Protestant firm which produced a great deal of Masonic material, and where he may have acquired his almost superstitious dread of the influence of Masonry. There was a slump in Irish printing in the mid-1890s, and in 1896 he joined John MacBride in the Transvaal. It was here that he had his first experience of editing a newspaper—a short-lived undertaking since it was an English-language journal and he insisted on taking a pro-Boer line.

In 1899 Griffith returned to Dublin and with Rooney immediately founded the weekly *United Irishman*, the name of which, echoing John Mitchell's earlier journal, proclaimed its radical nationalism. The new paper was woefully underfunded and much of it was written by the two editors under various pseudonyms. As a sometime member of the IRB and an admirer of Wolfe Tone, Mitchell, and the Fenians, Griffith never entirely discounted the prospect of armed rebellion against British rule, but he did not think it a possibility in the foreseeable future, and his paper devoted itself to a policy of fostering Irish self-dependence in culture, education, and above all, economics, and to mordantly attacking all those it felt were subverting these national duties.

These aims were central to a new loose-knit political movement, 'Cumann na nGaedheal', which he founded in the autumn of 1900, and to which he gave greater ideological coherence over the coming years with the adoption of the 'Hungarian Policy' and Friedrich List's economic theories. In *The Resurrection of Hungary* (1904) Griffith made parallels between the relationship of Ireland to Britain and that of Hungary to Austria, urging that the Augsleich of 1867, by which Austria conceded an independent parliament to Hungary and made the two countries separate entities linked by allegiance to the Emperor, should be the model for Anglo-Irish relations, and citing the Irish Parliament of 1782 as a precedent for this. Although Griffith's reading of constitutional history considerably simplified the complexities, his description of the success of Francis Deak's policy of non-co-operation with Austrian rule, and of the Magyarization of Hungary, had an important influence on subsequent Irish history. The German economist Freidrich List had argued in his *National System of Political Economy* (1841-4) for the necessity of tariffs in building up national industries and Griffith enthusiastically adopted his protectionist views, maintaining that an agricultural country could never acquire prestige and power in the modern world, and insisting that real independence for Ireland must involve economic as well as political separation.

Griffith outlined his policy, to which Maire Butler gave the name 'Sinn Fein', at the First Annual Convention of the National Council in November 1905. He also called for a Council of Three Hundred who would form an Irish Assembly and whose decrees would be carried out by the county councils and other locally elected bodies. Although the organization was strengthened by the amalgamation of the Dungannon Clubs and Cumann na nGaedheal with the National Council in 1908, Sinn Fein remained a minority movement and at the North Leitrim election of 1907 its candidate had been decisively beaten. The revival of the Irish Parliamentary Party, the promise of Home Rule, and chronic financial difficulties put Sinn Fein into decline after 1908. Although Griffith did not take part in the Easter 1916 Rising, the event was mistakenly identified with his party by the British authorities and he was interned until February 1917. Sinn Fein made sweeping gains at the general election of 1919 and immediately put into practice Griffith's policy of abstention from Westminster and the creation of an independent legislature in Dublin. This led to hostilities between Irish and British forces and in December 1920 he was once again imprisoned, but after his release the following year he became the leader of the delegation which negotiated the

Anglo-Irish Treaty. Although Griffith did not think the Treaty an ideal solution, he believed that it was honourable, and the best that could be achieved for Ireland. After the victory of the pro-Treaty candidates in the election of June 1922, he became the Head of the new Irish Free State and prosecuted the Civil War against de Valera and the republicans, but died suddenly from a cerebral haemorrhage in August 1922.

Although Griffith and WBY were on amicable terms in the early years of the century they held divergent views on the relationship of art to nationality and it was inevitable that they would eventually quarrel. Griffith remained a disciple of Thomas Davis, and regarded literature as pre-eminently a vehicle for education and for unambiguously raising national consciousness. He found WBY's later style too mystical to be effectively national, and too far above the people's heads to be popular. He also thought this true of the ILT (q.v.), and while the *United Irishman* welcomed the initiative, it regretted the absence of robust melodrama. The production of the nationalistic *Cathleen ni Houlihan* helped to allay his doubts about WBY, but the performance of Synge's plays, which he bitterly resented as 'anti-Irish', brought their fundamental disagreements to a head. From 1905 the *United Irishman* and its successor, *Sinn Fein*, were constantly sniping at the Abbey, and Griffith developed a personal antipathy towards WBY. For WBY Griffith came to represent intellect without the sanctity of culture, and therefore prey to envy, revenge and jealousy, and it was of Griffith he was mainly thinking when he described those who attacked *The Playboy of the Western World* as eunuchs staring upon Don Juan's 'sinewy thigh' (*VP*, 294). Nevertheless, during his internment in 1918 he and Desmond Fitzgerald prevailed upon the governor of Gloucester Gaol to give the Irish prisoners a special dinner in celebration of WBY's birthday, on which occasion Griffith proclaimed WBY the greatest poet to have come out of Ireland.

ANNIE ELIZABETH FREDERICKA HORNIMAN (1860–1937) was born in London, the daughter of a wealthy tea-merchant. Educated at home, her childhood was strict as well as lonely, but although her parents forbade visits to the theatre, a German governess took her secretly to a performance of *The Merchant of Venice* at the Crystal Palace in 1874, and she fell immediately under the spell of the stage. She built her own model theatre, and her governess told her of the central role played by municipal theatres in German towns.

From 1882 to 1886 she studied art at the Slade School under Alphonse Legros, and although the experience taught her that she was no artist, it also brought her into the world, gained her the nickname 'Tabbie' (she was thought to look like a cat), and introduced her to Moina Bergson, the sister of the philosopher, who was to be her confidante for the next ten years. In 1884 she made her first trip to the Wagner festival in Bayreuth, and was to return every year but one until 1914. Her regard for Wagner's music increased an already warm admiration for Germany, and she spent extended periods in her favourite city, Munich, where she saw her first Ibsen play, *An Enemy of the People*, in 1889, and *Hedda Gabler* (and Ibsen himself) the following year.

Early in 1888 Moina Bergson introduced her to MacGregor Mathers (see I.

497–9), who was founding the magical society, the Golden Dawn (GD; see I. 486–8), and after two years of hesitation she joined the Order in January 1890. It was here that she met WBY, who was the next initiate after her, and FF who became a member that July. Moina Bergson married Mathers in June 1890, and it seems that AEFH came to depend upon them both for emotional support during a series of nervous crises. She found Mathers a post at her father's private museum in South London, as well as making him a regular financial allowance. He, in return, furthered her occult career: in 1892 she became Sub-Praemonstratrix in the Isis–Uranus Temple; later that year Mathers (who was now living in Paris) sent her to settle disputes in the Bradford Temple; and in January 1894 she consecrated Mathers's new Ahathoor Temple in Paris.

Her grandfather died in 1893, leaving her a substantial legacy, and with this she secretly funded FF's season at the Avenue Theatre, which saw productions by Todhunter and Shaw, and the first performance of WBY's *The Land of Heart's Desire*. Although the venture was a financial failure, it gave her an admiration for WBY's plays and a taste for theatrical patronage that was to result in the Abbey and Gaiety Theatres.

Her worries about Mathers's heavy drinking and his incursions into Jacobite politics made relations between them increasingly difficult, and in July 1896 she cut off her allowance to him, and resigned the office of Sub-Praemonstratrix. That November Moina Mathers sent a desperate letter, begging for funds, but AEFH remained obdurate, and on 3 December an enraged Mathers expelled her from the GD. This peremptory action alarmed a number of the other members, and F. L. Gardner organized a petition (although WBY was not apparently approached) asking Mathers to reconsider his action. This he refused to do, explaining that she had been expelled on orders from the Secret Chiefs, but in October 1899, with rebellion brewing in the London Temple, he offered her a conditional reconciliation. Characteristically she refused, telling him that she was waiting for an apology from the Chiefs. The London revolt broke out in March 1900, Mathers's authority was overthrown, and on 21 April a General Meeting of the Second Order of the GD appointed AEFH Scribe (Secretary). She immediately mounted a vigorous campaign against irregularities that had been allowed to flourish in her absence, especially the formation of secret groups. Her aggressive crusade caused dissension, and this came to a head at a contentious meeting on 1 February 1901, when AEFH and WBY, her only supporter, were outvoted and her honesty impugned. She continued to denounce the Groups and demanded a 'Banishing Ceremony' against them as well as a public hearing presided over by three judges, chosen by herself. Although the new Chiefs of the Order permitted her a Banishing Ceremony, they refused a public hearing, and she—now apparently regarding herself as the Senior Adept and therefore the real Chief—resigned from the GD in February 1903.

The energies thus set free she now devoted to the Irish Theatre. She had been drawn into the movement through acting as WBY's amanuensis, and now she designed and made the costumes for the first production of *The King's Threshold*. Both she and WBY evidently hoped that this might be her artistic contribution to the theatre, but the designs were so unsatisfactory that she did not continue with the work after this. As early as April 1902 she had given hints that she might be prepared to buy and subsidize an Irish theatre, and she consulted the tarot cards on this topic in 1903. She finally made up her mind to do so after WBY's speech at the first production of *The King's Threshold* in which he outlined his plans and stressed that the INTS should perform foreign masterpieces as well as native Irish plays. She began negotiations for the lease on the Mechanics Institute early in 1904, while WBY was lecturing in America, and by April arrangements were complete, although the acquisition of a Patent for the new theatre took until August. The conversion of the Hall into the Abbey Theatre was done on a generous scale and the work lasted until December. In 1905 she increased her subsidy to allow the INTS to reconstitute itself as a limited company, guaranteed the actors' salaries, and made a separate fund available for the Company's tours. A little later she agreed to underwrite the publication costs of WBY's eight-volume *Collected Works*, which finally appeared in 1908.

Although AEFH refused to take shares in the reconstituted theatre company, and assured WBY that she would hold only a watching brief in it, she found a non-interventionist role too much for her. She helped organize the British tours of late 1905 and 1906 but during the latter fell out with William Fay (q.v.), and began to doubt his abilities. The appointment of a business manager failed to check her growing impatience with the Abbey; by the summer of 1907 she had decided to invest money in a Manchester Repertory Theatre, and in August informed WBY that she would do nothing more for Dublin when her Patent lapsed in 1910. Her English Company mounted its first production at the Midland Hotel Theatre in the autumn of 1907, and in November that year she acquired the Gaiety Theatre, which opened the following year.

From 1908 AEFH's relations with Dublin became increasingly difficult: she wrote a libellous letter to the National Players after mistaking them for the Theatre of Ireland, found fault with the Abbey Theatre's accounts, and criticized the acting and selection of plays. WBY suspected that she was looking for a pretext to withdraw her subsidy before its official expiry date, and this opportunity presented itself in May 1910 when the Abbey remained open on the day following the death of Edward VII. Although this was an accident, due to the late delivery of a telegram, AEFH insisted on construing it as a political act and refused to pay the last instalment of the subsidy. The dispute dragged on into 1911 when the editor and journalist, C. P. Scott, who had agreed to arbitrate, found in favour of the Directors.

Nor were her relations with her Manchester Theatre altogether smooth. In October 1911 her first manager, Ben Iden Payne, resigned and was succeeded by Lewis Casson, whom she found less satisfactory. In February and March of the following year she joined the Company on a tour of Canada, and that summer they scored their greatest success with the production of Stanley Houghton's controversial *Hindle Wakes*. A second tour to Canada and the USA in the spring of 1915 met with an indifferent reception and there were no more excursions to North America. In October 1913 she attacked Casson over his innovatory production of *Julius Caesar* and he resigned. The receipts of the Gaiety had begun to drop and the war made the situation more critical. The actors' contracts were not renewed in June 1917, and henceforward the Gaiety became a receiving theatre. Although AEFH hoped that peace might mend matters, this was not to be, and when a public appeal for funds in 1920 failed she sold the Theatre to a cinema company. After disposing of the Gaiety she travelled widely, especially in Germany and Spain. Public recognition for her services to the theatre came in 1932, when she was made a Companion of Honour.

AEFH had many unusual qualities. The daughter of conventional Victorian parents, she nevertheless showed an independent and energetic spirit. She was an early, although never militant, suffragist, made solitary cycling tours through Europe, and kept an informed interest in the arts. Yet while capable of many private and public generosities (in the first six months of 1906 alone she gave nearly half of her annual income to the Abbey), she was burdened with a nervous instability that made her difficult to work with. As Shaw put it: 'she was one of those good women who do things, but are incorrigibly cantankerous'. She quarrelled with every member of her family, alienated most of her fellow mystics in the GD, antagonized a great number of Irish writers and actors, and regularly fell out with those she employed at the Gaiety.

Although she helped establish an Irish national theatre, she was antipathetic towards Irish national aspirations, and had little time for the peasant work or verse drama upon which the Abbey's reputation chiefly rested. Her ideal was the German municipal theatre which drew upon the international repertoire. Her interest in the Irish drama centred on WBY—a trump card that he played at various times, for without the Abbey building and her financial backing he could not have gained the pre-eminence he enjoyed in the dramatic movement. Ironically, however, the very success of the enterprise drew him from her: it enhanced his international reputation, brought him even closer to AG (q.v.), and made AEFH feel that, although she footed the bills, she had been relegated to the sidelines. Frustrated at being an artist *manqué* in a creative group, and faced with a nation she did not understand, plays of which she did not approve, and, in AG's case, a landed ambience of which she was suspicious, she played up to the role of middle-aged, middle-class, suburban, dissenting English spinster with an unstable mixture of defiance and self-pity.

As the Abbey Theatre deviated increasingly from the aims that she and WBY had proposed for it she became disillusioned, but her criticisms, though often justified, were too carping to be constructive. She made attempts to woo WBY from Ireland, and when he refused grew yet more shrill. After her dispute with the Directors, and the announcement of Scott's award, WBY wrote a generous and conciliatory letter, declining to accept the last instalment of the subsidy if she thought the decision unfair, but was rewarded with a 'violent telegram': 'You have shewn me that I do not matter in your eyes the money is paid supermen cannot associate with slaves may time reawaken your sense of honour then you may find your friend again but repentance must come first.'

Communication of a kind continued since the Abbey Company hired the Gaiety Theatre on tours to Manchester, but when in 1912 she claimed the right to censor their intended programmes, this arrangement ceased. Thereafter she kept in touch with the Dublin theatre through correspondence with Joseph

Holloway, revealing to him that she had spent £10,350 on the Abbey, not including the losses made on the Company's British tours. It was not until a quarter of a century later that she again wrote to WBY. He responded immediately, addressing her as 'My Old and Dear Friend', and in March 1937, shortly before her death, had tea with her, reporting that she was 'little changed except for infirmity. Much talk of old times . . .'.

THE IRISH DRAMATIC MOVEMENT, which reached a decisive point in December 1904 with the opening of the Abbey Theatre, began as an initiative by WBY, AG (q.v.), and Edward Martyn. The idea was first discussed on a visit to Duras House in Co. Clare during a rainy afternoon in the summer of 1897, but WBY had been planning an Irish Theatre long before this, and had hoped in 1892 that the National Literary Society would establish a travelling company. This did not happen, and the first of his plays to be produced, *The Land of Heart's Desire*, was not performed until 1894, and then in a London theatre. In early 1897 he was eager to have *The Shadowy Waters* staged, and was planning with FF a small theatre in a London suburb. Edward Martyn also wanted plays produced and was in inconclusive negotiations with London managers.

That a casual conversation turned into a permanent institution was due to the energy, prestige, and wealth of those involved. AG and WBY immediately set about raising financial guarantees and issued a 'Statement', setting out their intentions for what they then envisaged as a 'Celtic' Theatre. They hoped to mount their first season in 1898, in connection with the annual Feis, but when WBY and Martyn went to Dublin at the beginning of November 1897 to make arrangements they found unexpected difficulties: the 1898 Feis was to be held in Belfast, the regular Dublin theatres were already booked, and the Patent Laws made it difficult to perform in unlicensed halls. After much frustration they successfully lobbied Irish MPs to amend the Patent Laws, and by December 1898 were able to hire the Antient Concert Rooms for the following May on behalf of the 'Irish Literary Theatre' (ILT), a name thought to be less 'dangerous' than 'Celtic Theatre'.

The plays were cast in London, mainly with English actors, and rehearsals took place there under the direction of George Moore and FF. Things seemed to be going well when, at the end of March 1899, Edward Martyn, upon whose financial guarantee the project depended, had sudden qualms about the orthodoxy of *The Countess Cathleen*, and divines on both sides of the Irish Sea had to be consulted before he was reassured. A few days later Frank Hugh O'Donnell, an Irish politician and journalist with whom WBY had quarrelled on political and personal grounds, issued *Souls for Gold!*, a pamphlet denouncing the play as anti-Irish and irreligious, charges which were endorsed by Cardinal Logue. Despite this, a further attack by O'Donnell, and barracking by certain sections of the audience, the first ILT season, which took place from 8 to 10 May 1899 with productions of *The Countess Cathleen* and Martyn's *The Heather Field*, was a palpable success.

That summer AG and WBY asked the guarantors to renew their pledges, and began preparations for the second season. In the autumn WBY and George

Moore began collaboration on *Diarmuid and Grania*, and also worked together on revising Martyn's loose-knit political satire, *The Tale of a Town*, as *The Bending of the Bough*. The second season of the ILT took place on 19 and 20 February 1900, with productions of Martyn's *Maeve*, Alice Milligan's *The Last Feast of the Fianna*, and *The Bending of the Bough* now credited to George Moore alone.

The revision of *The Tale of a Town* had disaffected Martyn, and his guarantee for the third and final season was put in doubt; at the same time, problems of collaboration made the writing of *Diarmuid and Grania* far slower than anticipated, while plans for parallel London and Dublin productions caused administrative difficulties. It was finally decided that the Benson Company, a leading English troupe, should present the play in October 1901 on the same bill as Hyde's *Casadh an tSugain*, played by Irish-speaking amateurs.

These productions brought the three-year ILT experiment to a conclusion and, reviewing the possibilities of continuing the dramatic movement in that autumn's *Samhain*, WBY supposed that the choice lay between a small stock company, taught by well-trained English actors, which would divide its time between Dublin, the Irish provinces, and Britain, or a purely touring company, perhaps based on the Fays (q.v.), which would build up an Irish theatre from the grass roots. Although inclined to the former, WBY refused to commit himself, shrinking from the administrative chores it would involve. Yet he also saw that if he wanted a national theatre he 'must get it now, when the work of the Literary Theatre is in people's minds', and he set up a committee to explore the idea. He also knew that the most pressing need was for Irish actors; he had seen the Fays' production of Alice Milligan's costume drama, *The Deliverance of Red Hugh*, in August 1901, and had come away with his 'head on fire', whereas the Benson Company's inability to sustain authentic Irish accents in *Diarmuid and Grania* was grating to the ear and offensive to Irish *amour propre*. The audience's demonstrative preference for *Casadh an tSugain* (directed by W. G. Fay) proved to WBY that there was a public for native drama played by Irish actors.

From his letters to AG in late 1901 it is clear that the Fays were already a part of WBY's plans for a possible continuation of the ILT, although he doubted their ability to perform his more demanding roles, and waited to see how arrangements with Martyn and Moore developed. Frank Fay had long been wooing WBY with the idea of an Irish company through his regular drama column in the *United Irishman*, and the two had begun a correspondence after his article on the American productions of *The Land of Heart's Desire*. In late December 1901 James Cousins brought the Fays to meet AE, part of whose play, *Deirdre*, had appeared in *The Celtic Christmas*, 'on the chance of collaboration'. AE agreed to finish the play and let them put it into rehearsal, and he also urged WBY to give them *Cathleen ni Houlihan* for the same bill. WBY did not assent at once, but when by late January 1902 it had become obvious that Martyn was unwilling to go on funding the ILT, and that there was no chance of a London production of *Cathleen ni Houlihan*, he handed it over to the Fays, the more contentedly in that MG wished to play the title role.

Since the Fays' dramatic society had neither the acting nor the financial resources to mount the productions unaided, it enlisted the help of the women's political society, Inghinidhe na hEireann (Daughters of Erin), for whom Fay had produced the Milligan plays, and of AE's group of Hermetists. The success of the productions in early April 1902 surpassed all expectations, and on the strength of this the Fays decided to reconstitute the now enlarged Ormond Drama Company as an Irish National Theatre. Shortly afterwards Arthur Griffith (q.v.) recruited the Fays' help in arranging an autumn 'Samhain' Festival at which plays in Irish and English would be performed under the auspices of the nationalist groups comprising Cumann na nGaedheal. In correspondence with Frank Fay, WBY had hinted that money might be found for a permanent theatre, but in the meantime the Company met in a cramped hall behind a shop in High Street, hired for a few nights a week, and in the summer of 1902 they rehearsed in the Dublin Mountains.

In late July 1902 WBY sent the Fays *The Hour-Glass* and *The Pot of Broth*, and on 8 August 1902 the Company found a fixed abode, taking a small hall in Camden Street for twelve months at a rent of 10s. a week. This turned out to be far from perfect—its total area (formed by roofing over a yard at the back of a grocery shop) was only 20 feet by 40, it could seat no more than 200, and was situated on a noisy thoroughfare, with a stage less than nine feet deep and lacking any dressing-rooms. In the end it was only used for one set of performances, although it continued to serve as a rehearsal room, scenery dock, and workshop.

Having found a home, the 'Irish National Dramatic Society', as it was briefly known, began to organize itself. It was formally constituted on 9 August 1902 with W. G. Fay, Frank Fay, Dudley Digges, P. J. Kelly, Maire Walker, Maire T. Quinn, Helen Laird, Fred Ryan, James Starkey, and George Roberts as founding members. At this first General Meeting they appointed WBY as President (after AE had declined); AE, MG, and Hyde as Vice-Presidents (Edward Martyn, also proposed as Vice-President, declined the office); and Frederick Ryan as Secretary. The same meeting elected James Cousins, Frank Walker, Thomas Keohler, H. Norman, Synge (q.v.), Colum (q.v.), and Sarah Allgood as members, and AG, Stephen Gwynn, Mary Garvey, Udolphus Wright, and Vera Exposito were admitted at a subsequent meeting.

The first public performances of the new Society took place at the Antient Concert Rooms from 27 October to 1 November, as part of the Cumann na nGaedheal Festival. These productions received less attention than those of the previous April but the *United Irishman* maintained that they had 'laid the foundations of the National Theatre', while the £60 profits provided the Camden Street Hall with a stage, curtains, and seating, and from 4 to 6 December 1902 the INTS gave its first and last performances there to small but appreciative audiences, playing Ryan's *The Laying of the Foundations*, WBY's *The Pot of Broth*, MacGinley's farce in Irish, *Eilis agus an Bhean Déirce*, and Cousins's *The Racing Lug*.

In late December there was a quarrel between WBY and Willie Fay over the proposed production of James Cousins's farce, *Sold*. The play was dropped after WBY threatened to resign, and replaced with Colum's *Saxon Shilling*, but this, too, caused controversy when MG accused Fay of trying to suppress it on political grounds. These disagreements fomented a rebellion in the Society, and showed the need for clear rules, especially with regard to the selection of plays.

Early in 1903 the Society, prompted by a letter from MG, and under the guidance of AE, set about drafting these, registering itself under the Friendly Societies Act as a co-operative venture, not under the Companies Act as a commercial undertaking. The new rules, amended by WBY, were approved at a General Meeting on 15 February 1903, and stated that the objects of the Society were to 'create an Irish National Theatre, to act and produce plays in Irish or English, written by Irish writers or on Irish subjects, and seeking dramatic works of foreign authors as would tend to educate and interest the public of this country in the higher aspects of dramatic art'. The membership was defined as:

(i) The seven signatories to these rules and hereafter those whom they may admit at the first General Meeting of the Society.

(ii) After the first General Meeting of the Society those who have been elected by 6 of members present at a meeting called for that purpose.

(iii) President, Vice-Presidents and Secretary, all *ex officio* members.

(iv) Associate members who pay 10s. per annum expenses.

(v) A member may be expelled by a vote of ⅔ of the members at a Special General Meeting upon the charge, in writing, of conduct detrimental to the Society, communicated one fortnight before the meeting is summoned.

It was also decided that plays proposed for production should be vetted by the officers before being put into rehearsal, but that no one member should have the right of veto. This was found to be impracticable, and on 2 June 1903 AE proposed as a substitution that:

A Reading Committee of five members shall be elected who shall first consider all plays proposed for performance by the Society. No play shall be performed until it has been considered and recommended by the Committee. The power of final acceptance or rejection of any play thus recommended shall rest with the members of the Society, to whom such plays shall be read at meetings summoned for the purpose when a three-quarters majority of those present shall decide. The author shall not be allowed to be present when the vote is taken.

This motion passed unanimously, and a reading committee comprising WBY, AE, Colum, and the Fays was set up at once.

On 14 March 1903 the INTS played *Twenty-Five* and *The Hour-Glass* to a capacity house of nearly 500 at the Molesworth Hall, and WBY lectured on 'The Reform of the Theatre' in the interval. The Society was making its way financially, but only just, and on WBY's hint John Quinn (q.v.) sent £50 towards making it secure. In April 1903 the Company undertook its first tour to the west of Ireland, playing in Galway and Loughrea with a repertoire that included WBY's *Cathleen ni Houlihan* and *The Pot of Broth*, AE's *Deirdre*, and MacGinley's *Eilis agus an Bhean Déirce*. Allegiance to the Society was still by no means uniform, and a number of the actors, particularly Digges, Kelly, and Maire Quinn, took roles with other companies. On 26 April 1903, therefore, a general meeting adopted the rule that members of the Society must seek permission before taking part in any other performance.

The event that did most to establish the INTS as a significant cultural force took place on 2 May 1903. This was the triumphant visit to London, arranged by Stephen Gwynn, as Secretary of the Irish Literary Society, London, which also guaranteed £50 for expenses. The Society produced five plays at a matinée and an evening performance at the Queen's Gate Hall, South Kensington: *The Laying of the Foundations*, *The Hour-Glass*, *Cathleen ni Houlihan*, *The Pot of Broth*, and AG's *Twenty-Five*. WBY reported to AG (who was in Italy) that he 'never saw a more enthusiastic audience', and this metropolitan success greatly enhanced the Company's reputation in Dublin.

The increasing prominence of Synge's work caused the first major rupture in the Society when in late September 1903 MG, Digges, and Maire Quinn resigned over the proposed production of *In the Shadow of the Glen*, and started a rival group, the short-lived Cumann na nGaedheal Theatre Company, which produced five plays at the Molesworth Hall in late October. WBY welcomed the founding of a political theatre, as hiving off the propagandist elements in the INTS, but was less happy when they appropriated his *Cathleen ni Houlihan*; in future care was taken to copyright all INTS plays and to chase up those who produced them without permission.

From 8 to 10 October 1903 the INTS presented *The King's Threshold*, *In the Shadow of the Glen*, and *The Countess Cathleen*. WBY made a curtain speech after the opening performances, and, stung by an attack in the Dublin press, advocated the production of foreign masterpieces as well as native drama. This had an important consequence, for it finally persuaded AEFH (q.v.) to purchase and subsidize a permanent Dublin theatre. While WBY was away in America the Society continued to consolidate its position with further productions at the Molesworth Hall: in early December it mounted *The Hour-Glass*, *The Pot of Broth*, and Colum's *Broken Soil*, and from 14 to 16 January 1904 *The Shadowy Waters*, Seamus MacManus's *The Townland of Tamney*, and a revival of AG's *Twenty-Five*. After these performances AEFH told W. G. Fay that if her shares in the Hudson Bay Company rose she would buy the Company a theatre. They did, and on Fay's advice and with the help of the architect Joseph Holloway, she acquired and refitted the disused Mechanics' Institute.

The INTS paid a second visit to London on 26 March 1904, this time to the Royalty, a West End theatre. It presented five plays in matinée and evening performances: *The King's Threshold*, *The Pot of Broth*, *In the Shadow of the Glen*, *Broken Soil*, and *Riders to the Sea*, which had first been produced in Dublin on 25 February. The visit was successful and profitable, although the Company's acting came under more critical scrutiny, and a number of reviewers deplored WBY's 'altogether too cock-a-hoop' speech in the interval.

Further stages in the professionalization of the Company were marked in April 1904 when a special meeting expelled P. J. Kelly for joining players performing at the St Louis Exhibition, and when, later that month, AEFH wrote formally to WBY offering a rent-free theatre to the INTS. AEFH had to apply for a patent for the new theatre, and despite opposition from the Dublin commercial theatres, this was permitted: on 20 August 1904, in the Library of Dublin Castle, the Solicitor-General granted the INTS a 21-year patent for the Mechanics' Institute, to be renewed after six years. As AEFH resided outside Ireland, AG was named patentee. The INTS could produce only 'plays in the Irish or English language written by Irish writers on Irish subjects, or such dramatic works of foreign authors as would tend to interest the public in the higher works of dramatic art'.

The first day of rehearsal in the Abbey Theatre was on 31 October and was attended by WBY, AG, and Quinn. But the Theatre was not ready as quickly as hoped and the first productions had to be postponed until after Christmas, opening at last, on 27 December 1904, with *On Baile's Strand*, *Spreading the News*, and *Cathleen ni Houlihan*. WBY, Synge, AE, Martyn, Gwynn, JBY, and Hugh Lane were all present, although AG was kept in Galway by influenza. The Theatre had 562 seats: 178 in the stalls, 198 in the balcony, and 186 in the pit. WBY delivered a speech after *On Baile's Strand*, and Frank Fay's Cuchulain and Maire Nic Shiubhlaigh's Cathleen ni Houlihan received enthusiastic reviews.

The Irish National Theatre Society was the product of a confluence of several distinct tributaries: the ILT, which provided it with dramatists and an audience drawn mainly from the Ascendancy classes; the Fays' amateur Ormond Dramatic Society, which supplied native actors and working- or lower-middle-class dramatists with a more obvious political commitment; the Inghinidhe na hEireann, a source of actresses with advanced nationalist views; and AE's socialistic Hermetists. It soon became clear that this confluence was not to flow serenely; conflicts blew up through clashes of temperament, and because of political, religious, and social differences. These disputes were both public and internal. The Dublin press attacked the Society's artistic policy on political, religious, and moral grounds, while internal pressures increased as a loose-knit, small-scale undertaking grew into a major institution. Despite the pretensions expressed in its title, the 'Irish National Theatre' was initially little different from a host of ephemeral dramatic societies that flourished briefly in Dublin. What distinguished it was its access to WBY's and Synge's plays, the support it derived from the socially and financially superior ILT, the Fays' dedication to the arts of the theatre, and AEFH's generous financial backing, gained through WBY's influence. These factors rapidly transformed an easy-going, democratic conglomeration, which mounted occasional performances, into a legally registered society which set itself consistent artistic standards and regular productions. This involved the framing and enforcement of rules, and a level of self-discipline and organization that some of the original members found increasingly authoritative and irksome, especially as power was seen to be concentrating in the hands of WBY and AG. Three of the ten founding members and two of the three original Vice-Presidents had already left the Society by the opening of the Abbey Theatre, and within the next eighteen months the rest, with the exception of the Fays, were also to secede. This high rate of attrition was justified by the continuing success of the Abbey: the companies formed by those who left were artistically and technically far less accomplished, and none survived long. Despite a series of managerial and financial crises, the Abbey maintained its national and international reputation, and much of the credit for this was due to WBY's and AG's unremitting artistic and administrative commitment to it.

JAMES AUGUSTINE JOYCE (1882–1941), novelist, playwright, and poet, was born in Dublin. He was the eldest child and in his early years the family was relatively well-off. In September 1888 he was sent as a boarder to Clongowes Wood College, the leading Jesuit school in Ireland. The increasing family (eventually there were four boys and six girls), together with his father's profligacy in financial matters, began to strain resources, and at the end of 1892 Joyce was withdrawn from Clongowes. At the beginning of 1892 the family had moved from Bray to a less imposing house in Blackrock, and they descended to even more humble quarters in North Dublin in 1893. A chance meeting between his father and Joyce's ex-headmaster at Clongowes led to his being given a free place as a day boy at another Jesuit school, Belvedere College. In February 1894 he accompanied his father on a visit to Cork to dispose of the remaining family property, all the money raised going to pay off moneylenders.

Joyce enjoyed a distinguished academic career at Belvedere, winning a series of examination prizes, but his schooldays were disturbed by sexual and religious perturbations and, before he left, he had positively decided not to become a priest. In 1889 he enrolled at University College, then part of the Royal University of Ireland, where he developed an enthusiasm for modern drama, particularly that of Ibsen. Early in 1900 he read a controversial paper, 'Drama and Life', to a College society, and in April of the same year the *Fortnightly Review*, one of the leading British literary periodicals, published his article on Ibsen's *When We Dead Awaken*, for which he was rewarded with a letter of thanks from Ibsen himself. In the summer he wrote a play, *A Brilliant Career*, strongly influenced by Ibsen but never published; he had already begun to write poems in the manner of the 1890s.

Joyce graduated in the summer of 1902 and decided to train as a doctor at the St Cecilia Medical School in Dublin. He made the acquaintance of most of the leading Irish writers, including WBY, AE, and AG (q.v.), all of whom tried to help his literary ambitions. In the autumn of 1902 he decided to pursue his medical studies in France and set out for Paris at the beginning of December. This first visit lasted only two weeks, but he returned there in the middle of January 1903 and, abandoning thoughts of a medical career, settled down to writing reviews and reading Aristotle. In April 1903 he went back to Ireland to be near his dying mother (she died of cancer in August), and he remained in Dublin until October 1904, living a life of mild dissipation, mainly in the company of Oliver St John Gogarty. It was at this time that he wrote the first version of *A Portrait of the Artist as a Young Man*, but it was turned down by *Dana*, the Irish monthly for which it was intended, and he immediately began to rewrite it in a much expanded version, entitled *Stephen Hero*. In June 1904 he met and fell in love with a servant girl from Galway, Nora Barnacle, and in October eloped with her to the Continent. He taught English at the Berlitz School in Pola where he continued writing *Stephen Hero* and finished a number of stories that were to be included in *Dubliners*. In March 1905 the Joyces moved to Trieste where they were to remain for ten years and where, in July, their son, Giorgio, was born. Although his attempts to have *Dubliners* published were frustrated (the book did not appear until 1914), his volume of poetry, *Chamber Music*, was issued in 1907. While in hospital with rheumatic fever in the summer of that year he decided to rewrite *Stephen Hero* as what was to become *A Portrait of the Artist*.

In 1912 Joyce paid his last visit to Ireland, where he was badly treated by his prospective publisher, George Roberts. His affairs began to look up in January 1914 when Ezra Pound—to whom WBY had introduced him—arranged for *A Portrait of the Artist* to be published serially in the *Egoist*. Encouraged by this success, he began to work on his play, *Exiles*, and upon his most ambitious work to date, *Ulysses*, which he had been planning since 1907. After the entry of Italy into the First World War in 1915 the family moved to Zürich, and the following year he published *A Portrait of the Artist* in book form and was awarded (partly through the influence of WBY) a grant of £100 from the Civil List. In 1920 the Joyces left Zürich for Paris, and *Ulysses* was published there in 1922, although because of its supposed pornographic episodes it was banned from the USA (until 1933) and from Britain (until 1936). For seventeen years after the publication of *Ulysses*, Joyce worked at his most revolutionary novel, *Finnegans Wake*, sections of which appeared in the late 1920s and 1930s. The book finally appeared in 1939, just before the outbreak of the Second World War obliged him to move back to Zürich, where he died of a perforated ulcer at the age of 59.

WBY and Joyce can be seen as complementary aspects of the Irish literary consciousness: WBY with an emphasis on tragedy, poetry, the sovereignty of language, the heroic, and the aristocratic; Joyce concerned with comedy, prose, the subversiveness of language, the anti-heroic, and the democratic. Despite these differences, WBY recognized Joyce's genius, without perhaps ever fully understanding or appreciating it (he confessed in 1923 that he had not been able to finish *Ulysses*), while Joyce, after an initial impatience with WBY, developed a respect for him and an admiration for his poetry. In 1899 Joyce applauded *The Countess Cathleen* against the hisses of fellow-students, and refused to sign their petition condemning it. Although he retained an admiration for the play—he quotes lines from it in both *A Portrait* and *Ulysses*—he could not as a dedicated Ibsenite approve of the direction the Irish theatre movement was taking, and in 1901 he published 'The Day of the Rabblement', which attacked the ILT's reactionary nationalism, and reproved WBY's 'treacherous instinct of adaptability'.

The two men did not meet until the late summer of 1902 when Joyce read out his 'Epiphanies' and WBY tried to explain why he went to tradition and the folk for his themes. Unimpressed, Joyce replied that he was not talking like a poet but like a man of letters, and concluded the interview with the retort 'I have met you too late. You are too old.' In spite of this rebuff, WBY went out of his way to help Joyce find literary work, encouraged him to write a play for the INTS (q.v.), but was unable to produce his translations of two Hauptmann plays at the Abbey Theatre. Joyce, discontented with Dublin, mocked WBY in 'The Holy Office' as 'him who hies him to appease / His giddy dames' frivolities'; in 1906 he described him as one of the 'blacklegs of literature', and the following year said that he did not understand the Irish people. Thereafter his opinion improved; the two had friendly reunions in London in 1909 and 1912, and Joyce not only wrote a favourable review of the Abbey for a Triestine newspaper, but helped an Italian friend translate *The Countess Cathleen*.

Joyce's play, *Exiles*, proved to be a disappointment when WBY read it in 1917, and he refused to produce it at the Abbey because it was 'too far from the folk drama' to which the Company was used, but he was deeply impressed by the early episodes of *Ulysses* as they appeared in the *Little Review* the following year, writing to Quinn that Joyce had 'surpassed in intensity any novelist of our time'. He made a more sustained attempt at the novel on its publication in 1922, finding in it a 'cruel playful mind like a great soft tiger cat'. WBY invited Joyce to come and stay with him in Dublin, but Joyce declined, as he did an invitation to the Tailteann Games in August 1924. It was on this occasion that WBY declared *Ulysses*, then banned in Britain and the USA, and almost impossible to obtain in Ireland, 'indubitably a work of genius'. The two met again in 1930, when Joyce gave him an account of his progress on *Finnegans Wake*, and in 1932 WBY made strenuous efforts to persuade him to join the Irish Academy of Letters, but Joyce, while acknowledging that it was 'now thirty years since you first held out to me your helping hand', politely refused to become a member. He sent a telegram of congratulations to WBY on his seventieth birthday, and a wreath and tribute to his grave in 1939.

In spite of the many differences in aesthetic outlook and temperament between them, Joyce retained a lifelong admiration for WBY's poetry, much of which he had by heart. This astonished his avant-garde Parisian friends, and he recalled in 1935 reciting WBY to them for two hours: 'everybody congratulated me on my extraordinary memory, my clear diction and my charming voice. Someone added: What a pity he is such a fool!'

THE LONDON THEATRE SOCIETIES which flourished after the 1880s were ultimately a consequence of the Theatre Licensing Act of 1737, which gave the Lord Chamberlain's office legal control over the stage and effectively stifled serious drama in England. Although originally political in intention, by the nineteenth century this censorship had become moralistic, and playwrights looking for success tailored their plays to conform to its narrow prejudices. This led to an expansion of popular forms and to the prominence of the actor-manager and the scene designer over the dramatist. The late-century dramatic revival in Scandinavia, France, and Germany was welcomed in England by George Bernard Shaw, William Archer, and other critics, but many of the works of Ibsen, Strindberg, Maeterlinck, Zola, and Hauptmann were banned from public performance by the Censor. The only possibility of fostering literary drama was through private societies, which successively worked for theatrical reform and pioneered the 'theatre of ideas' and the 'theatre of beauty'.

J. T. Grein, the Dutch-born dramatic critic, used the proceeds from a production of English plays in Amsterdam in 1890 to form the Independent Theatre Society in London, which he modelled on Antoine's *Théâtre Libre* in Paris. The Society achieved instant notoriety with its opening production of Ibsen's *Ghosts* in March 1891, but weathered this outcry and persisted in its aim 'to give special performances of plays which have a LITERARY and ARTISTIC, rather than a commercial value'. Grein continued legally to defy the Censor, and staged translations of Ibsen, Strindberg, and Zola, as well as new plays by Shaw, George Moore, John Todhunter, and other friends of WBY, who approved of the Society's aims but not its penchant for realistic and naturalistic drama. Grein's

business interests led him to resign as active director of the Society in 1895, and
the Society came to an end in December 1898, but by this time it had mounted
twenty-two productions, and its members went on to organize and inspire other
drama societies that continued the struggle for freedom from the commercial
theatre and stage censorship.

William Archer, the drama critic, translator of Ibsen, and proponent of a
national theatre, kept the dramatic movement alive by founding the New Century Theatre Society with a production of Ibsen's *John Gabriel Borkman* on 3
May 1897. However, the Society turned down more productions than it produced (including Edward Martyn's *The Heather Field*, eventually produced at
the opening of the ILT (q.v.)), and in 1899 the New Century was effectively
absorbed by the Incorporated Stage Society.

The Stage Society was announced in a circular letter of 8 July 1899 by a
Committee comprising Frederick Whelan, Charles Charrington, Janet Achurch,
Grant Richards, Walter Crane, and William Sharp. At its inauguration on 19
July it agreed to meet monthly, to give at least six performances a year, and to
include 'high comedy' as well as serious works by English and Continental
authors. Shaw, whose wife was on the reading and advisory committee,
described the Stage Society as 'a sort of Sunday night Independent Theatre'.
Sunday evenings were chosen for its meetings and performances so that professional actors could participate in its productions, and because Sunday was the
only day on which theatres could be leased for single performances. The initial
production, Shaw's *You Never Can Tell* on 26 November 1899, was followed by
a season of single performances in various London theatres of plays by Ibsen,
Maeterlinck, Fiona MacLeod, Hauptmann, and Shaw. In July 1900 it was
decided to give two performances of each play and to increase the maximum
subscription to 500 members and 100 associates. With this strong membership
and its access to extraordinary talent, the Society staged, beyond the reach of the
Censor, 'plays such as would be included in the repertory of any of the chief
repertory theatres of the continent, but which under the prevailing conditions of
the English stage had no opportunity of production in England'. In November
1902 Edith Craig, a member of the reading committee, proposed a production of
Where There Is Nothing for January 1903 and, although the production was postponed, this new association was to advance WBY's theatrical prospects in
London.

At the beginning of 1897 WBY had planned with FF to hire or build a little
theatre in a London suburb to produce romantic drama, believing that there
would be a reaction after the realism of Ibsen. Nothing came of this, but late in
1900 he came into contact with the Literary Theatre Club, recently founded in
the suburb of Limpsfield by W. A. Pye, his daughters Sybil and Ethel,
T. Sturge Moore, and Laurence Binyon. Dismayed by the plans of Edward
Martyn and George Moore to turn the ILT into a stock company under the
realistic stage management of F. R. Benson, the English actor-manager, WBY
saw the Literary Theatre Club as the nucleus of a romantic theatre in London
should his Irish theatre fail. The Club was formally established on 30 July 1901
with a copyright reading of Sturge Moore's *Aphrodite Against Artemis* at the

Dalston Theatre by new members who included Charles Ricketts, May Morris, and FF. Though the Club discussed several plays, including *The Cenci*, *Prometheus Bound*, and *Hippolytus*, WBY was determined that they should learn the arts that would enable them to produce his own *The Countess Cathleen* and *The Shadowy Waters*. Sturge Moore and FF began to train members in verse-speaking, and Gwendolyn Bishop was cast as the Countess Cathleen, but the Club lacked the resources to go forward with a production. However, Ricketts, greatly impressed with *The Countess Cathleen* after his first reading, offered to use the proceeds of his Vale Press edition of Marlowe's *Faustus* to have the play staged for them by Gordon Craig. But WBY's new association with Edith Craig had convinced him that the aims of the Club would be better served if it expanded into a more highly organized and professionally experienced group. Describing this enlarged society to Gilbert Murray as 'a new sort of Stage Society' but one which would have 'little dealing with the problem plays', he proposed that it be known as the 'Theatre of Beauty'.

The Theatre of Beauty held its organizational meeting on 28 March 1903 at Edith Craig's costumery in Covent Garden, with Walter Crane in the chair. One of the first items of business was to change the name, which Gilbert Murray and others thought 'preposterous'. The members also rejected WBY's second choice, 'The Order of the Rose', in favour of Crane's less occult suggestion, the Masquers Society, reserving WBY's idea of theatrical beauty for its aim rather than its name: 'The object of the Society is to give performances of plays, masques, ballets, and ceremonies; and to produce only those works which convey a sentiment of beauty. One of its chief endeavours will be to bring the stage back again to that beauty of appropriate simplicity in the presentation of a play which will liberate the attention of an audience for the words of a writer and the movements of an actor.' The Masquers were to hold their meetings on Sundays and to be managed by a Committee that included Crane, WBY, Sturge Moore, Arthur Symons, Edith Craig, Edith Wheeler, Pamela Colman Smith, and later Gilbert Murray. In its first prospectus, the Society declared its intention to give eight performances during the season and included a list of plays from which a first choice would be made: Marlow's *Faustus*; Congreve's *The Way of the World*; Ford's *The Broken Heart*; Gilbert Murray's translation of Euripides' *Hippolytus*; Sir Richard Jebb's translation of Sophocles' *Oedipus Tyrannus*; Alfred de Musset's *Fantasio*; Villiers de l'Isle Adam's *La Revolte*; Ibsen's *Peer Gynt*; Maeterlinck's *Les Aveugles*; Purcell's *Masque of Love*; and a ballet by Rameau. Future productions would include plays and masques by WBY, d'Annunzio, Bridges, Gordon Craig, Douglas Hyde, Laurence Irving, and others.

By July 1903 the Masquers had decided to give WBY's new play, *The King's Threshold*, for their opening performance, to be followed by Murray's translation of *Hippolytus*. WBY began writing a masque (now lost) and drafted his 'Opening Ceremony for the Masquers'. Enthusiasm was high, but was to be thwarted by the disappointing response to an appeal for subscriptions, since most of the potential subscribers were already members of the Stage Society, which also held its meetings on Sundays when trains were bad and restaurants were shut. Furthermore, the Masquers could not agree on a starting date owing to the previous commitments of its members, while Ricketts's Vale Press *Faustus* had brought only £150 of the projected £600. Murray, all too aware of their limited resources and competition with the Stage Society, urged WBY, whose tour of America was impending, to dissolve the Society. WBY was indecisive, but Edith Craig, fighting disbandment to the end, tried to strengthen the management by placing the experienced Acton Bond on the Committee.

As soon as WBY sailed for America in November, Acton Bond moved that the Society should remain inactive until its members were available for work. Murray, burdened by his sense of responsibility to subscribers, went further; overcoming Edith Craig's resistance, he wound up the Society, writing to WBY on 12 November that they were 'returning subscriptions, and explaining that, though we had enough money and members to justify us in starting, we found other circumstances unfavourable and thought that the attempt at a "Theatre of Beauty" should be postponed, though we still keep our faith in it'.

Edith Craig, still determined that WBY's plays should be seen in London, insisted that the Stage Society should revive its plan to stage *Where There Is Nothing*, and this was done under the direction of Harley Granville-Barker on 26–8 June 1904. AEFH (q.v.), an original member of the Stage Society, had meanwhile given her financial support to the establishment of the Abbey Theatre (q.v.) in Dublin, thereby obviating WBY's desire to establish a society for romantic drama in London.

Shortly after the Masquers disbanded, Ricketts gave his £150 to Sturge Moore, who held the money for two years in the hope of putting together a new theatre project. Finally, in December 1905, W. A. Pye, Sturge Moore, Binyon, Ricketts, Charles Shannon, Gwendolyn Bishop, and FF revived the Literary Theatre Club as the Literary Theatre Society, Ltd., which FF described to Murray as 'a Theatre of Poetry'. It opened on 1 April 1906 with a performance of Sturge Moore's *Aphrodite Against Artemis* at King's Hall, Covent Garden, returning in June for two performances of Oscar Wilde's *Salome* and *A Florentine Tragedy*. Already there were proposals that the Society should merge with the Stage Society, but, as Sturge Moore explained to W. A. Pye, they decided to hold off, maintaining their identity and moving slowly by way of experiment towards eventual amalgamation. The final experiments of the Society took place at Terry's Theatre on 23 March 1907 with productions of Harley Granville-Barker's *A Miracle* and Q. J. Ryan's translation of Aeschylus' *The Persians*. Soon thereafter the Literary Theatre Society merged with the Stage Society, and on 12 May 1908 a disillusioned Sturge Moore wrote to Pye that he was giving up any idea of success with the theatre, 'as poetic drama is not yet enjoyed in England'.

The persevering Stage Society survived in part because it embraced other modes of literary drama, besides the poetic. WBY was deeply indebted to the Stage Society for dramatic experiments employed at the Abbey Theatre, and for several years the two theatre groups worked amicably and sympathetically toward similar goals. When Shaw's *The Shewing-Up of Blanco Posnet* was banned in 1909, WBY gladly produced it at the Abbey, where the English Censor had no jurisdiction. The Stage Society then invited the Abbey Players to give a private performance of the play in London that December, when it reciprocated with performances of WBY's *Cathleen ni Houlihan* and AG's *The Workhouse Ward*. For thirty more years, until it expired in 1939, the Stage Society worked to create an audience for literary drama, to bring an end to censorship, and to keep alive the movement for a national repertory theatre. Though the English National Theatre was eventually established at the Old Vic in 1962, stage censorship was not finally abolished until 1968. The National Theatre, free at last to perform a repertoire of English and foreign classics to large public audiences, was the heir of the London theatre societies, 1890–1939.

THE PSALTERY, and WBY's experiments with it from 1901 to 1912, were the most visible of his continuous attempts to reunite poetry and music. His earliest images of the poet were Homeric and bardic, and the testimony of family and friends confirms that he chanted his poems all his life. When WBY was 18, JBY told Edward Dowden that his 'bad metres arise very much from his composing in a loud voice manipulating of course the quantities to his taste', and Katharine Tynan described how, when staying with the Yeatses, she 'used to be awakened in the night by a steady, monotonous sound rising and falling. It was Willie chanting poetry to himself.' But it was not until he heard the deep incantatory voice of FF in an 1890 production of John Todhunter's *A Sicilian Idyll* that WBY was seriously moved to revive the ancient art of minstrelsy; later, describing these performances as 'a discovery that was to influence my life', he recalled that her delivery gave the verse 'a nobility, a passionate austerity that made it akin for certain moments to the great poetry of the world'.

For the next twenty-two years WBY and FF collaborated in efforts to return musical speech to lyrical, narrative, and dramatic verse. Their belief in the magical quality of speech was heightened at the outset by their membership of the Golden Dawn, and they gradually transformed other elements of ceremonial magic into dramatic methods. Their first verse-speaking experiments resulted in 1894 in the 'dreamy and strange' chanting of FF's niece Dorothy Paget as the fairy child in *The Land of Heart's Desire*. The failure of their subsequent plans to open a suburban theatre for romantic drama in London temporarily halted their momentum but not their enthusiasm for chanting, and when the ILT (q.v.) opened in Dublin in May 1899 with a production of WBY's *The Countess Cathleen*, FF as the bard Aleel chanted the two lyrics 'Impetuous Heart' and 'Who will Go Drive with Fergus Now'. WBY had forewarned the audience in *Beltaine* that the lyrics 'are not sung, but spoken, or rather chanted, to music, as the old poems were probably chanted by bards and rhapsodists'. He went on to explain that while modern delivery often submerged the rhythm, emphasis, and even intelligibility of words in the rhythms and emphases of the music, a 'lyric which is spoken or chanted to music should . . . reveal its meaning, and its rhythm so become indissoluble in the memory'.

Though the reviews praised the strange beauty of FF's delivery, George Moore and others were severely critical of WBY's insistence on applying the chanting to dramatic verse, a criticism that he would hear repeatedly in coming years. Though his experiments were often mocked on the grounds that he was tone deaf, he declared that this condition kept him free from modern tonal music and closer to the ancient music of the bards.

After numerous experiments with technique and notation, WBY and FF presented their 'new art' to a London audience for the first time on 16 February 1901. With the aid of a harp and a piano to sound the notes and indicate the changes of pitch, FF and Anna Mather chanted poems and WBY explained the method in a lecture entitled 'New Methods of Speaking Verse'. Still unhappy with their performances and with their attempts at musical notation, they shortly afterwards enlisted the help of the musician Arnold Dolmetsch, and by October 1901 he had perfected the notation and constructed a psaltery to accompany the chanting. This lyre-shaped instrument had twenty-six alternating strings of fine steel and twisted brass arranged an octave apart so that the octave could be played with one finger. The instrument covered all the chromatic intervals within the range of the speaking voice, and Dolmetsch taught them to regulate their speech by ordinary musical notes. To publicize the new art and their forthcoming public recitals, WBY wrote his essay 'Speaking to the Psaltery', in which he declared his intention henceforth 'to write all my longer poems for the stage, and all my shorter ones for the psaltery'. Not only did he think that chanting was ideally expressive, but also that it would make poetry available to a wider audience by rescuing it from the written page, since the spoken word would 'appeal to the workers who had no leisure to read, and the illiterate, who are not the less spiritually educated'. At a packed recital at Clifford's Inn on 10 June 1902, he felt confident enough to announce the recovery of the lost art of 'regulated declamation' as demonstrated by FF and Dorothy Paget, who aptly chanted his new poem, 'The Players Ask for a Blessing on the Psalteries and on Themselves'. That autumn WBY and FF repeated this lecture-demonstration at the Samhain festival in Dublin.

In 1903 the two presented over a score of lectures to London societies, as well as venturing a well-received performance in Manchester, and when WBY went on his first American tour in 1903 he tried (although with little success in the absence of FF) to explain the new art in various cities. After his return in 1904, the prospect of the Abbey Theatre intensified his desire to convert the somewhat sceptical members of the INTS (q.v.) to chanting and the use of the psaltery, and he wrote 'Literature and the Living Voice' shortly after its opening, in which he envisaged a double role for the theatre—to train not only actors but also reciters who would carry lyrical and narrative verse to the provinces of Ireland. With WBY absorbed by the Abbey, FF became the chorus leader for productions of Gilbert Murray's translations of Euripides' plays, controversially instructing the chorus in speaking to the psaltery. In July 1905 she staged a production of *The Shadowy Waters*, chanting WBY's verse to the psaltery for an international congress of the Theosophical Society.

In 1906 WBY and FF took their lecture-demonstration on a provincial tour that included Liverpool, Leeds, Edinburgh, Aberdeen, and Dundee. The following year they planned to tour America, but when John Quinn advised against this, on grounds that their travelling together would cause scandal, FF went alone. The *Playboy* riots in 1907 and the departure of the Fays (q.v.) from the

Abbey (q.v.) in 1908 dimmed WBY's hopes that his Theatre would help create a new aural culture in Ireland, and in revising the text of 'Literature and the Living Voice' the following year he noted that the essay told 'of things we have never had the time to begin. We still dream of them.'

In 1908 FF's illustrated lecture on chanting to the Poets' Club sparked the first stage of the Imagist Movement—by provoking her friend T. E. Hulme into writing his seminal 'Lecture on Modern Poetry'. Hulme, urging the displacement of an aural by a visual paradigm, asserted that the character of poetry 'has changed from the ancient art of chanting to the modern impressionist, but the mechanism of verse has remained the same. It can't go on doing so.' The two friends soon seceded from the Poets' Club and gathered the first grouping of Imagists at the Tour d'Eiffel restaurant on 25 March 1909. In that month FF published *The Music of Speech*, dedicated to WBY and Dolmetsch, and intended as a defence of chanting against the criticism of the Imagists, as well as a testimonial to the place of WBY's auditory poetics in the newly emerging mainstream of modern poetry. In April she introduced Ezra Pound to the new group, and in May WBY invited him to Woburn Buildings to hear her chant to the psaltery. Pound became interested in their techniques, and on 10 December 1908 WBY wrote to AG that 'this queer creature Ezra Pound, who has become really a great authority on the troubadours, has I think got closer to the right sort of music for poetry than Mrs. Emery—it is more definitely music with strongly marked time and yet it is effective speech'. The following week WBY, in the company of FF and the psaltery, dined with the Imagist group and, as Ernest Rhys recalled, held forth at length on this new art of bringing poetry and music together. The insistence of WBY, FF, Pound, and a growing number of allies that poetry was first and foremost an aural, not a visual, art finally persuaded the Imagists, and the second volume of *Some Imagist Poets* (1916) conceded that poetry 'is a spoken and not a written art'.

On 16 February 1911, the tenth anniversary of their first recital, WBY and FF gave their final lecture-demonstration together at the Little Theatre, London, in a programme entitled 'Ireland and the Arts of Speech'. Although Rabindranath Tagore's arrival in London with accounts of the minstrel culture in Bengal reaffirmed for WBY the possibility of establishing a similar culture in Ireland, these hopes were cut short by FF's sudden decision to emigrate to Ceylon (Sri Lanka). She gave her final performance of chanting at the Clavier Hall on 18 July 1912, after which she presented WBY with her psaltery.

'I gave up the fight', WBY later wrote, recalling the psaltery years and FF's departure. This surrender was only temporary. He now 'began writing little dance plays, founded upon a Japanese model . . . thinking that some group of students might . . . gradually elaborate a technique that would respect literature and music alike', and in the mid-1930s, seeing Margot Ruddock as a successor to FF, hoped to make her 'a noble speaker of verse—a singer and sayer'. In September 1935 he told Dorothy Wellesley that he intended 'to make another attempt to unite literature and music', and during the next two years, as he wrote ballads and 'words for music', he published two volumes of *Broadsides*, containing illustrated poems set to music, and began a series of BBC broadcasts in which he and others chanted his poems. Before failing health forced him to abandon the broadcasts, he summed up his lifetime's ambition in 'An Introduction For My Plays' (1937): 'I wanted all my poetry to be spoken on a stage or sung and, because I did not understand my own instincts, gave half a dozen wrong or secondary reasons; but a month ago I understood my reasons. I have spent my life in clearing out of poetry every phrase written for the eye, and bringing all back to syntax that is for ear alone.'

JOHN QUINN (1870–1924) was born in Ohio, the eldest son of Irish immigrants. He developed an early interest in book-collecting and politics, and ran a successful campaign for a local congressman, Charles Foster, while still in his teens. He entered the University of Michigan in 1888 to study Law, but at the end of his first year moved to Washington as Foster's private secretary, and transferred to Georgetown University, where he graduated in 1893. In 1895 he took a second Law degree at Harvard, subsequently becoming a law clerk in New York, where he specialized in financial law, and read widely in literature, history, philosophy, and theology. In 1900 he was appointed junior partner in the firm of Alexander and Colby, and the following year contacted JBY and later WBY about purchasing pictures.

He made his first trip to Europe in 1902, visiting London and Dublin, where he met WBY, AG (q.v.), and other leading Irish writers, before going to stay at Coole. On his return to America he set about copyrighting *Where There Is Nothing*, the first of many legal and publishing chores he was to undertake for WBY, AG, and Synge (q.v.). He also sent WBY copies of Nietzsche's works. He spent considerable energy setting up an Irish Literary Society in New York, but when WBY was appointed a vice-president it ran into clerical opposition, and, although it produced plays by WBY in June 1903, soon faded away. In August Quinn paid his second visit to Europe, spending most of his time in Ireland where he became patron of the Dun Emer Industries and went on a walking tour with Jack Yeats. He suggested an American tour to WBY, and on his return to New York set about organizing the programme in meticulous detail. WBY stayed in Quinn's apartment soon after his arrival in America in November 1903, and Quinn ensured maximum publicity while protecting him from overexposure. The tour was a great success and WBY earned well over $3,000. Shortly after WBY's departure for Europe Quinn arranged an exhibition for Jack Yeats at the Clausen Gallery, and acted as host to Jack and Cottie Yeats for seven weeks.

Pressure of work caused by his business success delayed his next European trip until October 1904, when he once again spent most of his time in Dublin. He returned to London with WBY who introduced him to a number of literary figures, including Symons, Ricketts, and Shannon. Back in New York he became caught up in a long struggle for control of the Equitable Life Assurance Society, the successful outcome of which he regarded as the crucial event in his career. Early in 1905 he was drawn into MG's divorce proceedings, and hired detectives to trail MacBride. He did not visit Europe that year, but arranged an American tour for Douglas Hyde which lasted from November to July 1906; ECY also visited Quinn in the summer of 1906. In August he resigned from Alexander and Colby to set up his own firm. Despite the extra work that this involved, and his involvement in the Democratic Party and Tammany Hall, Quinn organized a tour for FF, and, having dissuaded WBY from accompanying her for fear of scandal, seems to have had an affair with her himself. He strongly supported Synge (with whom he identified) during the controversy over *The Playboy of the Western World* early in 1907, and in December entertained SMY and JBY on their trip to New York—an entertainment which lasted for the rest of JBY's life, for he refused to return to Ireland.

In 1908 Quinn was assiduous in pursuing the Fays (q.v.) over their use of the Abbey Theatre name in the USA, and for royalties due on the plays of WBY they had performed there. He bought most of the portraits for WBY's *Collected Works*, and this indicated a shift in allegiance away from literature to painting. He was also growing tired of what he now saw as Irish sponging, and the death of Synge, after the bitter attacks on him in the Irish press, intensified this feeling. On his next trip to Europe, in July 1909, he spent most of his time in London, seeing Symons, and meeting Augustus John, who did a portrait of him. Although he went to Dublin, he had no time to go to Coole, and spent time buying pictures and discussing art with Sarah Purser, AE, Hone, and Jack Yeats. He also had a serious quarrel with WBY whom he accused of trying to seduce his mistress, Dorothy Coates, and the two men did not communicate for five years.

On his return to New York in September 1909 Quinn announced that he would no longer purchase books but collect paintings, and, to a lesser extent, literary manuscripts. In December he became the formal patron of Augustus John, but from 1911 grew increasingly interested in French artists. That year he had an affair with AG when she came to the USA on an Abbey tour, and he assisted her in her battles over the hostile reception of Synge's *The Playboy of the Western World*, a controversy which aggravated his impatience with the Irish and Irish-Americans. Although estranged from WBY, he continued to meet JBY frequently and commissioned a self-portrait from him. In 1913 he helped organize and contributed to the Armory Show which did much to alert America to new developments in European art.

During WBY's American tour of 1914, Dorothy Coates, now ill with consumption, urged Quinn to make peace with him, and on 9 February he wrote a letter offering reconciliation. WBY eagerly accepted the olive branch, and spent a good deal of the latter part of the tour with Quinn, who organized a large farewell dinner for him in New York. After WBY's departure, Quinn wrote offering to buy WBY's manuscripts on an annual basis, and WBY was to use this arrangement to defray JBY's New York expenses. AG again stayed with Quinn on her American tour of 1915, and he insisted that she return to Ireland on a neutral American ship; later that year he tried unsuccessfully to persuade Hugh Lane not to sail home on the ill-fated *Lusitania*.

At the end of 1917 Quinn became ill with stomach cramps, and in January 1918 this was diagnosed as cancer. Surgery the following month successfully stayed the disease, and he returned to work in April. He had been a long-term patron of Conrad, and was now helping Eliot and Joyce, as well as subsidizing

The Little Review at Pound's request. He met Jeanne Robert Foster, who was to become his last mistress, when they both visited JBY during a severe attack of influenza in November 1918, and later that year Quinn engaged in the most important case of his career, the Botany Mills Case. In February 1920 WBY introduced his new wife to Quinn on an American tour, and Quinn wrote to Conrad that WBY 'great artist that he is, he is as much a boy as he ever was, and one of the most delightful companions I have ever known'.

Quinn bought the manuscript of *Ulysses* and in July 1921 met Joyce with Pound in Paris. On this visit he bought a great number of French pictures and managed at last to meet the artist Gwen John, with whom he had been in correspondence for many years. In 1921 WBY asked him to be his son Michael's godfather. Quinn took an active interest in the Irish question, which had erupted into violence after the First World War, adopting a moderate nationalist position, advocating dominion status, and contributing a large sum to float Plunkett's *Irish Statesman*.

On his return from Europe in 1921 he found himself in the middle of a financial scandal: his partners had sold off the stock of a bankrupt company without due advertisement and the firm was being sued for over £1,000,000. Although he successfully, if somewhat dubiously, recouped the losses through insurance claims, the tension aggravated his bad health, and in January 1922 he experienced what he described as 'complete nervous collapse, hypertension and blood-pressure and insomnia and nerves'. Nevertheless, in February he attended JBY on his death-bed and looked after the funeral arrangements. Later that year WBY dedicated *The Trembling of the Veil* to him.

Quinn contributed to Pound's 'Bel Esprit' scheme to release Eliot from Lloyds Bank, and Eliot made him his American agent for *The Waste Land*, with excellent results, for Quinn arranged advantageous terms both with Boni and Liveright and the *Dial*. To thank him, Eliot sent him the uncut manuscript of the poem, which remained among his papers and was finally published in 1971. To make funds and room available for his new acquisitions of French paintings he decided to dispose of his English works and late in 1922 shipped 6½ tons of art to London for sale. In 1923 Conrad visited America without telling him, and rebuffed all his efforts to meet him, a snub which upset Quinn deeply. Perhaps because of this he suddenly decided in the spring of 1923 to sell two-thirds of his vast library, and the sale at the Anderson Galleries took place the following year. In September 1923 he paid his last visit to Europe in connection with a libel case and in Paris he again met Joyce and Pound, as well as Ford Madox Ford (whose *transatlantic review* he helped to fund) and Brancusi and Satie.

Quinn was now increasingly ill and in pain, and in June his doctor told him that he was unlikely to recover. Although he fought against the illness, telling Mrs Foster that 'when I get out of this I'm going to live. I've never lived', he died on 28 July 1924.

Shortly after his death WBY recalled him in an unpublished note as 'a friend of many years, to whom I could seldom speak, whose swiftly dictated letters, for all their forcible generalization, told me little. I remember his generosity, his audacity, his irascibility. . . . good Heavens how irascible he was. . . . Without anything of Roosevelt's creative gift he had something of his temperament, and though associated in public life with the Democratic [Party], was drawn to his side by sympathy. . . . [He] shared with Roosevelt the charm of those whose passions compel and illuminate their decisions. Such men are difficult, touchy, and I think always important. It is not possible to forget John Quinn.' Quinn not only helped WBY, and the other Yeatses, financially, he also helped to liberate him intellectually, by pressing him to read Nietzsche at a time when WBY was particularly susceptible to Nietzschean ideas, and by arranging the first American tour of 1903-4, which not only earned WBY money but expanded his outlook and confidence at a time when the squabbles in Dublin seemed likely to sap his energies. The generosity with which Quinn treated the Yeatses he also extended to other artists: Conrad, Pound, Joyce, Eliot, AE, Plunkett, and James Stephens being but a few of the many writers he helped. Nor were his benefactions always on the grand scale: in 1918 he paid JBY's $100 bill for false teeth, and later put up $500 so that children at a French convent could have jam on their bread.

Quinn said he hated vagueness in law as much as sloppiness in art, and it was his desire for precision that attracted him to modern art. He had little expert or technical knowledge of painting, but he collected according to his own developing predilections, relying for more expensive purchases upon professional advice. His taste was excellent, and his collection contained fine examples of most of the modern European masters, as well as many American painters of distinction.

But there was, as WBY and everyone else noted, the 'irascible' side to his character. A self-made man of powerful intelligence, he dedicated himself to efficiency and drove himself, and others, remorselessly. At times this appeared as opinionated bullying, and his racial prejudice was particularly virulent and unpleasant. He was notorious in New York for having fired five law partners in one year, and, as a perfectionist, found it almost impossible to delegate responsibility. Nor did he confine his high-handedness to his chosen profession: despite his own verbosity and flaccid style he tried to correct Richard Curle's book on Conrad (Curle described him as 'peremptory' and 'didactic'), Sherwood Anderson's prose, and T. S. Eliot's punctuation. Nevertheless, without Quinn the history of modern literature would not only have been different, it would have been poorer.

JOHN MILLINGTON SYNGE (1871–1909), playwright and poet, was born in Dublin. His father, a lawyer, died the year following his birth, and he was brought up by his forceful and strongly evangelical mother. Suffering from chronic ill-health, he was educated mainly by private tutors. He developed a keen interest in natural history, but his discovery of Darwin at the age of 14 caused him to question his family's religious orthodoxies and his spiritual crisis was deepened by his reading of the Positivists and Materialists. He began studying the violin in 1887, and from 1889 to 1892 he not only attended Trinity College, Dublin, but also studied at the Royal Irish Academy of Music, where he won scholarships in counterpoint and harmony.

He decided to become a professional musician and in 1893 went to Coblenz to study German, moving to Würtzburg in January 1894 for tuition in the piano and violin. On his return to Dublin he took courses in Irish at Trinity College, and, finding himself torn between music and literature, began to write poetry. In January 1895 he enrolled as a student at the Sorbonne, and for the next seven years spent much of the winter in Paris, reading widely in contemporary literature and philosophy. In 1895 and 1896 he proposed to Cherrie Matheson, and her refusal on religious grounds (she was a member of the Plymouth Brethren) caused him great emotional and intellectual anguish which he later registered in his first play, *When the Moon has Set*. The turbid spiritual and psychological crises of this period are articulated in his veiled autobiographical fragments, *Vita Vecchia* (1895–7) and *Étude Morbide* (1899). He was also physically unfit, and in 1897 underwent an operation to remove a swollen neck gland—a sign of the onset of Hodgkin's disease which was ultimately to prove fatal.

In December 1896 he met WBY and MG in Paris. WBY advised him to abandon his attempts to become a decadent poet (since Arthur Symons was doing it better), and to make use of his knowledge of Irish by going to the Aran Islands for his themes. He joined MG's Parisian Young Ireland Society, but resigned when he found that it advocated a revolutionary and semi-military programme. In May 1898 he took up WBY's suggestion and visited the Aran Islands; henceforward he was to find his subject-matter in rural Ireland. Between 1898 and 1902 he spent part of each summer on Aran, and recorded his experiences in *The Aran Islands*, which he described as his 'first serious piece of work' but which, although finished in 1901, and despite WBY's vigorous advocacy, was not published until 1907.

In the summer of 1902 he wrote two one-act plays, *Riders to the Sea* and *In the Shadow of the Glen*, and drafted his two-act comedy, *The Tinker's Wedding*. WBY's enthusiasm for these plays encouraged Synge to throw in his lot with the INTS (q.v.); in March 1903 he gave up his apartment in Paris, and returned to Ireland. The furore raised by the Fays' (q.v.) production of *In the Shadow of the Glen* in October 1903 made him suspect to many Irish nationalists and anticipated later disturbances over his plays, but *Riders to the Sea*, first performed in February 1904, was well received—although some in the audience were so horrified at the sight of a corpse on the stage that they left while the performance was in progress.

Since Synge now lived permanently in Dublin, whereas WBY was often in London and AG (q.v.) at Coole, he began to play an active part in the day-to-day running of the INTS, liaising with the Fays, taking rehearsals, and sitting on the Reading Committee. His *The Well of the Saints* was produced at the Abbey (q.v.) in February 1905. After the reorganization of the Company in the autumn of 1905, Synge joined WBY and AG as one of the three Directors of the Abbey, and, much to their consternation, fell in love with one of the actresses, Maire O'Neill. He accompanied the Abbey tour of Britain in 1906 and earned AEFH's (q.v.) wrath by sympathizing with the players in her quarrel with them. In January 1907 long-held Dublin suspicions of Synge erupted in a riot during the production of his three-act comedy *The Playboy of the Western*

World, but WBY, AG, and AEFH supported him throughout the trouble. His illness now began to take a stronger hold. He had embarked upon his final play, *Deirdre of the Sorrows*, but had not polished it to his satisfaction before his death in April 1909, and it was first performed posthumously in 1910.

Although Synge had been studying Irish long before their meeting, WBY's advice that he should go to the Aran Islands, and his subsequent encouragement of his work, was of crucial importance. WBY was 'delighted' with his first Irish plays, and returned to London in April 1904 specifically to introduce Synge to literary life there. WBY at once hailed *The Well of the Saints* as a masterpiece, never wavered in his support and admiration of *The Playboy*, and went to great pains to get Synge's works properly published after his death. His insistence that Synge was a major talent earned him the scorn of contemporary Dublin, but he never ceased to broadcast the fact and repeated it in eloquent essays after his death.

Yet, oddly, the two men do not appear to have been close. Complaining of loneliness in Dublin in 1908, WBY described Synge as 'always faint & far off', and while Synge was an efficient and conscientious Director of the Abbey as far as his health would permit, both WBY and AG were to complain of his lack of urgency in several crises, and his lack of authority on tours. In fact Synge was closer in temperament to Jack Yeats than to WBY: like Jack he had an ability to get on with ordinary people without WBY's aloofness or AG's patronizing air. This made him more tolerant and more understanding of the Fays and of the attitudes of the Company, and, as essays like 'A Landlord's Garden in County Wicklow' show, more sensitive to the ambivalences of the Anglo-Irish position.

If WBY helped and supported Synge, Synge was an important catalyst in WBY's career. He had a gift for vivid if heightened idiomatic dialogue that WBY could not rival, and his language and plots were grounded in his experience of the energies, including the sexual energies, of the people of the west of Ireland. For WBY, who was tiring of the disembodied Celtic Twilight, this was a revelation, as was the work of François Villon to whom Synge introduced him, and accelerated his movement towards a more dramatic and earthy poetry. He saw the key to Synge's drama as 'the dream of the impossible life', but understood how much more compelling that dream was when it issued not out of strained transcendental longings but as a compensation for the harshness, frustrations, and desires of everyday life. WBY recognized that Synge possessed qualities he had been extolling from his earliest writing: personality, energy, and the command of a vivid language, based on demotic speech yet capable of reaching lyrical and tragic heights. As such he regarded Synge as a vital example and antidote to a modern Ireland which he thought had succumbed to abstraction, didacticism, and utility.

INDEX OF RECIPIENTS

INDEX

Galway, 110; sends MG his article, 'Magic', 113; broaches possibility of an Irish National Theatre, 116; urges Bernard Shaw to attend 1901 ILT productions, 117; questions the point of providing literary drama to philistine Dublin audiences, 118; hopes ILT will continue 'a wise disturber of the peace', and opposes Moore's proposal of clerical censorship, 118–9; 'literature is the principal voice of the conscience', 119, 132; on George Moore's lack of experience of public life, 120; on Finn and the Feanna, 120, 127, 133, 141; on Bjornson's *Beyond Human Power*, 120–1, 122–3; plans lecture to pay for psaltery, 121; sees FF's and OS's *The Beloved of Hathor*; on Mrs Pat Campbell's acting, 122; essence of genius is precision, 122; seeks to write work 'where passion and thought are one', 122; on decadence of London stage, 123; on Fiona Macleod's work, 123–5; his work must be hard and clear because he writes for a fierce nation, 125; much of his work by the critical not creative faculty, 125; working on Cuchulain at British Museum, 126, 142; sees Mrs Pat Campbell about *Diarmuid and Grania*, 126; suggests Fay should produce *Cathleen ni Houlihan* to establish permanent Irish company, 126; limitations of Fays' company, 126; rewriting *On Baile's Strand*, 126; suggests Martyn should employ Craig as scene–designer, 128; discusses scenario for *The Marriage*, 128–9; refuses to have O'Brien Butler living at Woburn Buildings, 130; reads MS of Synge's *The Aran Islands*, 130; Binyon at his Monday Evening, 130; on censorship, 132–4; conscience made powerful by religion but regulated by literature, 134; literature deals with problems of soul and character, 134; asks to attend Mrs Patrick Campbell's rehearsals, 135; arranges for John Murray to publish AG's *Cuchulain of Muirthemne*, 135–6; guest at Johnson Club, 137; writes 'The Folly of Being Comforted' and essays for *The Celtic Twilight*, 138; Watt agrees that he abandon *The Speckled Bird* for a book of essays 138; Watt arranges terms for new versions of *The Celtic Twilight* and *The Secret Rose*, 138–9; Dolmetsch pronounces the chanting 'perfect in theory', 139; writes his first letter to John Quinn, 140; on William James, 140; to write Preface for *Cuchulain of Muirthemne*,

145; evokes himself into a nerveless state, 145; meets Sandford and Eugenie Strong, 146; preparing new *Celtic Twilight* for press, 146, working on magical rites, 147; to edit selections from Edmund Spenser, 148; Masefield calls, 148; finishes *The Celtic Twilight*, 148; spends weekend with William Gibson, 150; FF chants to new notation at WBY's Monday Evening, 150; visits Watt, Bullen, the British Museum, and ILS committee meeting, 150; reads biography of Girolamo Cardano, 150; agrees to Fays' producing *Cathleen ni Houlihan* with AE's *Deirdre*, 151; negotiates over John Lane's contractual rights in *The Wind Among the Reeds*, 151, 550–1; occupied with his 'mystics', 153; sends 'Speaking to the Psaltery' to the *Monthly Review*, 153; Violet Hunt, Lady Margaret Sackville, and Stephen Gwynn at his Monday Evening to hear FF chant, 155–6; reads Gautier's *Mademoiselle de Maupin*, 155; 'Nothing has life except the incomplete', 155; meets Joseph Nunan, 156; lectures to mystics, 157; meets William Stirling, architect and cabbalist, 157; excited by Craig's designs for Purcell Society's productions, 159; Symons reads WBY his essay 'The New Art of the Stage', 159–60; attends Elizabethan Stage Society's production of *Everyman*, 160; introduces Symons to Craig, 160; dines with Nevinson and FF, 160; reading Nevinson's *The Plea of Pan*, 161; helps with proofs of *Cuchulain of Muirthemne*, 161, 166; thinks of taking small parts on the London stage, 161; complains to AG about bowdlerizing in *Cuchulain of Muirthemne*, 163–6; Dolmetsch enthusiastic about chanting experiments, 166; goes to Dublin, 166; reads proofs of *Cuchulain of Muirthemne* to MG, 166; attends Fays' triumphant production of AE's *Deirdre and Cathleen ni Houlihan* at St Teresa's Hall, 166–7, 168; thinks of revising *Cathleen ni Houlihan*, 167; dictates new second act of *Diarmuid and Grania* to Moore, 167; meets Standish James O'Grady, 168; Moore helps him simplify *On Baile's Strand*, 168; sends 'Speaking to the Psaltery' to the *Monthly Review*, 169; Colum reads him an early version of *Broken Soil*, 169; amends an MS story by JBY, 170; praises the acting of the Fays' company, 171–2, 177–6; arranges reviews and reviewers of *Cuchulain of Muirthemne*, 174; irritated by

ADDENDA

The following letters came to light too late for inclusion in the main body of the text. They should appear respectively on pages 138, 314, 323, 354, 424.

To Clement Shorter, 16 December [1901]

18 Woburn Buildings | Euston Road.
Dec 16.

My dear Shorter: Yes Masefield thinks the price (£2) all right for those poems; but he would like to publish the Xmas one at Xmas.[1]

Yours snly
W B Yeats

His address is
15 Coram St
WC.[2]

ALS Berg.

To A. P. Watt, 9 February 1903

18 Woburn Buildings | Euston Road.
Feb. 9th,/03

Dear Mr Watt,
I accept Mr Bullen's proposal as stated in your letter of the 6th of Feb. There will be two volumes 'Where there is Nothing' being Vol. I of 'Plays for an Irish Theatre' & 'Shorter Plays' being Vol. II of 'Plays for an Irish

---

[1] Shorter published three of Masefield's poems in The *Tatler*. The 'Xmas one' was 'Christmas Eve, 1901' (later 'Christmas Eve at Sea'), published on 25 Dec 1901 (558), followed by 'Off Cape St. Vincent' (later 'A Ballad of Cape St. Vincent'), published on 5 Feb 1902 (264), and 'The Fever Ship' (later 'Fever Ship') published on 26 Feb 1902 (392). All were republished under their new titles in *Salt Water Ballads* in November 1902.
[2] Masefield had moved from Walthamstow to 8 Barton Street, Westminster, in the early summer, and in late autumn from there to 15 Coram Street, off the Euston Road and only a few minutes walk from Woburn Buildings.

Theatre'. The second volume may be as much as two or three months later than the first.[1]

Yr ever
W B. Yeats

Dict AEFH, signed WBY; Private.

To Hilaire Belloc,[1] 11 March [1903]

18 Woburn Buildings | Euston Road.
March 11.

Dear Mr Belloc
I can lecture for you on May 7th if you like[2]—I am going to Ireland tomorrow & my address after next Monday will be
    Coole Park
      Gort
        Co Galway—

Yr snly
W B Yeats

Dict AG, signed WBY; Boston College.

---

[1] See pp. 297, 299. Bullen had written to Watt on 29 Jan (Private), telling him that WBY had handed him *Where There Is Nothing* 'and I have had a specimen page, which he approves, set up at the Chiswick Press. He seems to think that these plays are likely to find a large public, and I need hardly say that I should be very glad if he were to prove a true prophet.' He proposed to print a thousand copies in the first instance, and to pay a royalty of 15% on the published price of 3s 6d, rising to 20% after the first thousand, and to 25% after 2,500. He added that he had already given WBY a five guineas advance, but confessed that he was 'very doubtful whether this prose play will have any success . . . the first thing is that I should get a proper text of the play. I understand that he wishes to make large alterations (and certainly there is room for plenty of revision). Naturally I do not want a big bill for printing corrections.' Watt's untraced letter of 6 Feb evidently told WBY of these financial proposals, which were incorporated in an Agreement drawn up on 11 Feb 1903. By this Bullen undertook to publish the play by 30 Apr 1903.

[1] Hilaire Belloc (1870–1953), essayist, historian, novelist and poet, was born in France of a French father and English mother. He was educated in England, and became a prolific essayist and propagandist for Catholicism. His friend G. K. Chesterton illustrated a number of his novels.

[2] No report of this lecture has been traced.

To Gordon Craig, [c. 1 May 1903]

Mention in letter from Craig, [*c.* 2 May 1903]
Congratulating Craig on his production of *The Vikings at Helgeland*, and
apparently discussing the amount the Stage Society would be prepared to
put up for their production of *Where There Is Nothing*.[1]

NLI.

To A. P. Watt, 14 September [1903]

COOLE PARK, | GORT. | CO. GALWAY

Sept 14

Dear Mr Watt: I am very sorry to have left the enclosed among a heap of
unanswered letters so long. My correspondence this summer has got much
out of hand. In your letter of July 24 you make a suggestion about terms
for 'Ideas of Good & Evil'. I of course approve but am afraid I never wrote
to say so.[1] I shall see you about a couple of books shortly.

Yrs ever

W B Yeats

ALS Private

---

[1] See pp. 252–3. In his reply Craig thanked WBY for 'your letter about the Vikings', and
went on to discuss the production of *Where There Is Nothing*: 'I hear feeble sums
mentioned for doing your play with. Better to wait & have the thing done *well* than to let it be
spoiled. I believe Granville Barkers play cost the Society £200. Your play could be done for that
I dare say, but—Yours Gordon Craig'.

[1] In his letter of 24 July 1903 A. P. Watt had pointed out that there was no formal agreement
covering WBY's arrangement with Bullen for the publication of *Ideas of Good and Evil*, which
had appeared earlier that year, and of which a second edition was proposed. He added that he had
discussed the matter with Bullen, who agreed to pay 'a royalty of 15% on the nominal selling
price of all copies which he may sell up to the number of 1,000 and a royalty of 17½% of the
nominal selling price on all copies sold over and above the first 1,000. On sales of the book in
America he is willing to pay a royalty of 20% of the actual price he receives for the copies he
sends out.' Bullen had already paid WBY an advance of £56. 5s 6d, as well as paying Oldmeadow
the ten guineas for use of the Introduction to *A Book of Images* (see p. 380).
    Watt lost no time in drawing up a formal agreement on receipt of WBY's letter. This reiterated
the terms proposed in Watt's letter to WBY, but made no mention of the ten guineas Bullen had
paid to Oldmeadow. It also stipulated that Bullen should do his best to dispose of copies, or an
edition, in America at the royalty of 20% already suggested.